INTERNATIONAL LAW REPORTS

Volume 165

Volumes published under the title:

ANNUAL DIGEST AND REPORTS OF PUBLIC INTERNATIONAL LAW CASES

Vol. 1 (1919-22) } Edited by Sir John Fischer Williams, KC,
Vol. 2 (1923-24) } and H. Lauterpacht, LLD

Vol. 3 (1925-26) } Edited by Arnold D. McNair, CBE, LLD,
Vol. 4 (1927-28) } and H. Lauterpacht, LLD

Vol. 5 (1929-30)
Vol. 6 (1931-32)
Vol. 7 (1933-34)
Vol. 8 (1935-37)
Vol. 9 (1938-40)
Vol. 10 (1941-42)
Vol. 11 (1919-42)   } Edited by H. Lauterpacht, QC, LLD, FBA
Vol. 12 (1943-45)
Vol. 13 (1946)
Vol. 14 (1947)
Vol. 15 (1948)
Vol. 16 (1949)

Volumes published under the title:

INTERNATIONAL LAW REPORTS

Vol. 17 (1950)
Vol. 18 (1951)
Vol. 19 (1952)
Vol. 20 (1953)   } Edited by Sir Hersch Lauterpacht, QC, LLD, FBA
Vol. 21 (1954)
Vol. 22 (1955)
Vol. 23 (1956)

Vol. 24 (1957)   Edited by Sir Hersch Lauterpacht, QC, LLD, FBA, and E. Lauterpacht

Vol. 25 (1958-I) } Edited by E. Lauterpacht, QC
Vol. 26 (1958-II)

Vols. 27-68 *and* Consolidated Tables and Index to Vols. 1-35 *and* 36-45
    Edited by E. Lauterpacht, QC
Vols. 69-150 *and* Consolidated Index and Consolidated Tables of Cases
    and Treaties to Vols. 1-80, Vols. 81-100
    and Vols. 1-125
    Edited by Sir Elihu Lauterpacht, CBE, QC,
    and Sir Christopher Greenwood, CMG, QC
Vols. 151-65   Edited by Sir Elihu Lauterpacht, CBE, QC, LLD,
    Sir Christopher Greenwood, CMG, QC,
    and K. L. Lee

Lauterpacht Centre for International Law
University of Cambridge

INTERNATIONAL LAW REPORTS

VOLUME 165

Edited by

SIR ELIHU LAUTERPACHT, CBE, QC, LLD
Honorary Professor of International Law, University of Cambridge
Bencher of Gray's Inn

SIR CHRISTOPHER GREENWOOD, CMG, QC
Judge of the International Court of Justice
Bencher of Middle Temple

and

KAREN LEE
Fellow of the Lauterpacht Centre for International Law, University of Cambridge
Vice-Mistress and Fellow of Girton College, Cambridge

GROTIUS PUBLICATIONS
CAMBRIDGE UNIVERSITY PRESS

CAMBRIDGE
UNIVERSITY PRESS

University Printing House, Cambridge CB2 8BS, United Kingdom

Cambridge University Press is part of the University of Cambridge.

It furthers the University's mission by disseminating knowledge in the pursuit of education, learning and research at the highest international levels of excellence.

www.cambridge.org
Information on this title: www.cambridge.org/9781107059108

© Cambridge University Press 2016

This publication is in copyright. Subject to statutory exception and to the provisions of relevant collective licensing agreements, no reproduction of any part may take place without the written permission of Cambridge University Press.

First published 2016

Printed in the United Kingdom by TJ International Ltd. Padstow Cornwall

A catalogue record for this publication is available from the British Library

ISBN 978-1-107-05910-8 Hardback

Cambridge University Press has no responsibility for the persistence or accuracy of URLs for external or third-party internet websites referred to in this publication, and does not guarantee that any content on such websites is, or will remain, accurate or appropriate.

CONTENTS

	Page
Preface	vii
Editorial Note	ix
Table of Cases (alphabetical)	xiii
Table of Cases (according to courts and countries)	xv
Digest (main headings)	xvii
Digest of Cases Reported in Volume 165	xix
Table of Treaties	xxxiii
Reports of Cases	1
Index	677
Consolidated Tables of Cases Volumes 126-165	713

PREFACE

The present volume contains the 2012 judgment of the Inter-American Court of Human Rights in *Artavia Murillo* v. *Costa Rica*. International jurisprudence is further reflected in decisions from the Court of Justice of the European Union (*Firma Brita GmbH* v. *Hauptzollamt Hamburg-Hafen*), the European Court of Human Rights (*Paksas* v. *Lithuania*, *Hutchinson* v. *United Kingdom* and *Misick* v. *United Kingdom*) and the United Nations Human Rights Committee (*Paksas* v. *Lithuania*, *Paadar* v. *Finland*, *Horvath* v. *Australia* and *Ory* v. *France*). The volume also contains national decisions from the courts of England (*Corner House Research*, *EM (Lebanon)*, *Misick*, *Yukos (No 2)*, *Khan* and *Iraqi Civilians*).

The Editors are particularly grateful to Ms Ellie Fogarty, who summarized the cases from the Court of Justice of the European Union, the United Nations Human Rights Committee and England, and has thus made an enormous contribution to this volume. They also wish to thank Dr Marina Brilman for selecting and summarizing *Artavia Murillo*, Professor Gerald L. Neuman for selecting the cases from the United Nations Human Rights Committee and supplying the text of the Views for reproduction in these *Reports*, and Sir Michael Wood for supplying the text of the English decisions in *Misick*. Ms Maria Netchaeva, the ILR Editorial Assistant, prepared the Tables of Cases and Digest, as well as the Consolidated Tables of Cases, and provided invaluable assistance. Miss Maureen MacGlashan, CMG, compiled the Table of Treaties and the Index, Mrs Diane Ilott checked the copy and Mrs Jenny Macgregor read the proofs. Ms Karen Lee wrote the summaries of the cases from the European Court of Human Rights and saw the volume through the press.

The Editors also wish to thank the Inter-American Court of Human Rights, the Court of Justice of the European Union and the European Court of Human Rights for kindly permitting these *Reports* to use the electronic files posted on their official websites. The judgments from England published in this volume carry Parliamentary copyright and contain Parliamentary information licensed under the Open Parliament Licence v3.0, or Crown copyright, and contain public sector information licensed under the Open Government Licence v3.0; the electronic files were sourced from the UK Parliament website where possible and also from the British and Irish Legal Information Institute website.

Finally, our thanks go to all the others who have worked to complete this volume, particularly our publishers, Cambridge University Press, and typesetters, SPi Technologies India Pvt Ltd, and their staff.

E. LAUTERPACHT

Lauterpacht Centre
  for International Law,
  University of Cambridge

C. J. GREENWOOD

The Peace Palace,
The Hague

K. L. LEE

Lauterpacht Centre
  for International Law,
  University of Cambridge

November 2015

EDITORIAL NOTE

The *International Law Reports* endeavour to provide within a single series of volumes comprehensive access in English to judicial materials bearing on public international law. On certain topics it is not always easy to draw a clear line between cases which are essentially ones of public international law interest and those which are primarily applications of special domestic rules. For example, in relation to extradition, the *Reports* will include cases which bear on the exception of "political offences" or the rule of double criminality, but will restrict the number of cases dealing with purely procedural aspects of extradition. Similarly, while the general rules relating to the admission and exclusion of aliens, especially of refugees, are of international legal interest, cases on the procedure of admission usually are not. In such borderline areas, and sometimes also where there is a series of domestic decisions all dealing with a single point in essentially the same manner, only one illustrative decision will be printed and references to the remainder will be given in an accompanying note.

DECISIONS OF INTERNATIONAL TRIBUNALS
The *Reports* seek to include so far as possible the available decisions of every international tribunal, e.g. the International Court of Justice, or ad hoc arbitrations between States. There are, however, some jurisdictions to which full coverage cannot be given, either because of the large number of decisions (e.g. the Administrative Tribunal of the United Nations) or because not all the decisions bear on questions of public international law (e.g. the Court of Justice of the European Union). In these instances, those decisions are selected which appear to have the greatest long-term value.

Human rights cases. The number of decisions on questions of international protection of human rights has increased considerably in recent years and it is now impossible for the *Reports* to cover them all. As far as decisions of international jurisdictions are concerned, the *Reports* will continue to publish decisions of the European Court of Human Rights and of the Inter-American Court of Human Rights, as well as "views" of the United Nations Human Rights Committee. Decisions of national courts on the application of conventions on human rights will not be published unless they deal with a major point of substantive human rights law or a matter of wider interest to public international lawyers such as the relationship of international law and national law, the extent of the right of derogation or the principles of the interpretation of treaties.

International arbitrations. The *Reports* of course include arbitral awards rendered in cases between States which involve an application of public international law. Beyond this, however, the selection of arbitral decisions is more open to debate. As these *Reports* are principally concerned with matters of public international law, they will not include purely private law commercial arbitrations even if they are international in the sense that they arise between parties of different nationality and even if one of them is a State. (For reports of a number of such awards, see *Yearbook Commercial Arbitration* (ed. Albert Jan van den Berg, under the auspices of the International Council for Commercial Arbitration).) But where there is a sufficient point of contact with public international law then the relevant parts of the award will be reported. Examples of such points of contact are cases in which the character of a State as a party has some relevance (e.g. State immunity, stabilization clauses, *force majeure*) or where there is a choice of law problem involving discussion of international law or general principles of law as possible applicable laws. The same criteria will determine the selection of decisions of national courts regarding the enforcement of arbitral awards.

Decisions of National Tribunals

A systematic effort is made to collect from all national jurisdictions those judicial decisions which have some bearing on international law.

Editorial Treatment of Materials

The basic policy of the Editors is, so far as possible, to present the material in its original form. It is no part of the editorial function to impose on the decisions printed in these volumes a uniformity of approach or style which they do not possess. Editorial intervention is limited to the introduction of the summary and of the bold-letter rubric at the head of each case. This is followed by the full text of the original decision or of its translation. Normally, the only passages which will be omitted are those which contain either statements of fact having no bearing on the points of international law involved in the case or discussion of matters of domestic law unrelated to the points of international legal interest. The omission of material is usually indicated either by a series of dots or by the insertion of a sentence in square brackets noting the passages which have been left out.

PRESENTATION OF MATERIALS
The material in the volume has been typeset for this volume. The source of all such material is indicated by the reference to the "Report" in square brackets at the end of the case. The language of the original decision is also mentioned there. The bold figures in square brackets in the body of the text in non-English cases indicate the pagination of the original report.

NOTES
Footnotes. Footnotes enclosed in square brackets are editorial insertions. All other footnotes are part of the original report.

Other notes. References to cases deemed not to be sufficiently substantial to warrant reporting will occasionally be found in editorial notes either at the end of a report of a case on a similar point or under an independent heading.

DIGEST OF CASES
With effect from Volume 75 the decisions contained in the *Reports* are no longer arranged according to the traditional classification scheme. Instead a Digest of Cases is published at the beginning of each volume. The main headings of the Digest are arranged alphabetically. Under each heading brief details are given of those cases reported in that volume which contain points covered by that heading. Each entry in the Digest gives the name of the case concerned and the page reference, the name of the tribunal which gave the decision and an indication of the main points raised in the case which relate to that particular heading of the Digest. Where a case raises points which concern several different areas of international law, entries relating to that case will appear under each of the relevant headings in the Digest. A list of the main headings used in the Digest is set out at p. xvii.

CONSOLIDATED INDEX AND TABLES
A Consolidated Index and a Consolidated Tables of Cases and Treaties for volumes 1-80 were published in two volumes in 1990 and 1991. A further volume containing the Consolidated Index and Consolidated Tables of Cases and Treaties for volumes 81-100 was published in 1996. A Consolidated Index, a Consolidated Tables of Cases and a Consolidated Table of Treaties for volumes 1-125 were published in 2004. Volume 165 contains Consolidated Tables of Cases for volumes 126-165.

TABLE OF CASES REPORTED
ALPHABETICAL

(Cases which are reported only in a note are distinguished from cases which are reported in full by the insertion of the word "note" in parentheses after the page number of the report.)

Artavia Murillo and Others ("*In vitro* fertilization") v. Costa Rica 1

Brita GmbH v. Hauptzollamt Hamburg-Hafen (Case C-386/08) 188

Corner House Research Case 402

EM (Lebanon) v. Secretary of State for the Home Department (AF (a Child) and Others intervening) 485

Firma Brita GmbH v. Hauptzollamt Hamburg-Hafen (Case C-386/08) 188

Horvath v. Australia (Communication No 1885/2009) 354

Hutchinson v. United Kingdom (Application No 57592/08) 235

Iraqi Civilians v. Ministry of Defence 660, 676 (note)

Khan Case 622

Misick v. United Kingdom (Application No 10781/10) 544
Misick Case 515, 544

Ory v. France (Communication No 1960/2010) 384

Paadar and Others v. Finland (Communication No 2102/2011) 330
Paksas v. Lithuania (Application No 34932/04) 252
Paksas v. Lithuania (Communication No 2155/2012) 303

R (Corner House Research and Another) v. Director of the Serious Fraud Office (JUSTICE intervening) 402
R (Khan) v. Secretary of State for Foreign and Commonwealth Affairs 622
R (Misick) v. Secretary of State for Foreign and Commonwealth Affairs 515

Yukos Capital SARL v. OJSC Rosneft Oil Company (No 2) 554

TABLE OF CASES REPORTED
ARRANGED ACCORDING TO COURTS AND
TRIBUNALS (INTERNATIONAL CASES) AND
COUNTRIES (MUNICIPAL CASES)

(Cases which are reported only in a note are distinguished from cases which are reported in full by the insertion of the word "note" in parentheses after the page number of the report.)

I. DECISIONS OF INTERNATIONAL TRIBUNALS

Court of Justice of the European Union

2010
Firma Brita GmbH v. Hauptzollamt Hamburg-Hafen (Case C-386/08) 188

European Court of Human Rights

2011
Paksas v. Lithuania (Application No 34932/04) 252

2012
Misick v. United Kingdom (Application No 10781/10) 544

2015
Hutchinson v. United Kingdom (Application No 57592/08) 235

Inter-American Court of Human Rights

2012
Artavia Murillo and Others ("*In vitro fertilization*") v. Costa Rica 1

United Nations Human Rights Committee

2014
Horvath v. Australia (Communication No 1885/2009) 354
Ory v. France (Communication No 1960/2010) 384
Paadar and Others v. Finland (Communication No 2102/2011) 330
Paksas v. Lithuania (Communication No 2155/2012) 303

II. DECISIONS OF MUNICIPAL COURTS

United Kingdom, England

2008
EM (Lebanon) v. Secretary of State for the Home Department (AF (a Child) and Others intervening) 485
Regina (Corner House Research and Another) v. Director of the Serious Fraud Office (JUSTICE intervening) 402, 409, 457

2009
Regina (Misick) v. Secretary of State for Foreign and Commonwealth Affairs 515, 519, 533

2012
Regina (Khan) v. Secretary of State for Foreign and Commonwealth Affairs 622, 627
Yukos Capital SARL v. OJSC Rosneft Oil Company (No 2) 554

2014
Iraqi Civilians v. Ministry of Defence 660
Regina (Khan) v. Secretary of State for Foreign and Commonwealth Affairs 622, 643

DIGEST OF CASES
List of Main Headings

(Those headings for which there are entries in the present volume are printed in italics. For a guide to the Digest, see the Editorial Note at p. xi.)

Air	*International Tribunals*
Aliens	*Jurisdiction*
Arbitration	Lakes and Landlocked Seas
Canals	Nationality
Claims	Recognition
Comity	*Relationship of International Law and Municipal Law*
Conciliation	
Consular Relations	Reprisals and Countermeasures
Damages	Rivers
Diplomatic Relations	Sea
Economics, Trade and Finance	Sources of International Law
Environment	Space
Expropriation	*State Immunity*
Extradition	State Responsibility
General Principles of International Law	State Succession
Governments	States
Human Rights	*Territory*
International Court of Justice	Terrorism
International Criminal Law	*Treaties*
International Organizations	*War and Armed Conflict*

DIGEST OF CASES REPORTED IN VOLUME 165

Page

Claims

Jurisdiction — Law of the forum — Whether governing assessment of damages — Procedural and substantive law — State responsibility — Occupation of Iraq — Unlawful detention — Ill-treatment — Claims in tort — Human rights — Damages — Aggravated damages — Private International Law (Miscellaneous Provisions) Act 1995 — England, High Court, Queen's Bench Division

Iraqi Civilians v. *Ministry of Defence*   660

Comity

Act of State doctrine — Judicial acts of foreign State acting within its territory — Whether lawful — Whether subject to adjudication by English courts — Relevance of cogent evidence and argument — Role of proper respect — England, Court of Appeal

Yukos Capital SARL v. *OJSC Rosneft Oil Company (No 2)*   554

Damages

Reparations — Monetary and other — Costa Rica to take appropriate measures to annul prohibition of IVF — Costa Rica to regulate implementation of IVF — Costa Rica to include IVF in infertility treatments offered by health-care services — Article 63(1) of American Convention on Human Rights, 1969 — Inter-American Court of Human Rights

Artavia Murillo and Others ("In vitro fertilization") v. *Costa Rica*   1

Governments

Separation of executive and courts — Independent prosecutors — Exercise of statutory powers and discretion — Independent decision-making — Taking relevant considerations into account — Effect of opinions and advice of others on independence of decisions — Shawcross exercises — Threats — Impact of threats on independent decision-making — The rule of law — Whether decision of Director of Serious Fraud Office to

Governments (*cont.*)

discontinue investigation lawful — Criminal Justice Act 1987 — England, High Court, Queen's Bench Division (Administrative Court) and House of Lords

> *Regina (Corner House Research and Another)* v. *Director of the Serious Fraud Office (JUSTICE intervening)*   402

United Kingdom Government — United States Government — Conduct and responsibilities of United Kingdom Agency, General Communications Headquarters — United States Central Intelligence Agency — UK Agency under responsibility of Secretary of State — Claimant requesting clarification of UK policies and practices concerning provision of locational intelligence to US agents for potential use in drone attacks — UK policy to "neither confirm nor deny" matters where disclosure could compromise national interests — Claimant seeking permission to apply for judicial review of Secretary of State's "decision" to provide intelligence for use in drone strikes concerns — England, High Court, Queen's Bench Division (Administrative Court) and Court of Appeal

> *Regina (Khan)* v. *Secretary of State for Foreign and Commonwealth Affairs*   622

Human Rights

Asylum — European Convention on Human Rights, 1950 — Article 8 — Right to respect for private and family life — "Flagrant breach" of Article 8 right being so fundamental as to amount to nullification or destruction of very essence of right — "Flagrant breach" not distinct from "complete denial" and "nullification" — Article 8 rights of all persons affected by decisions to be taken into account — Article 14 — Prohibition of discrimination — Discrimination on grounds of sex — Whether aliens can claim entitlement under Convention to remain in Contracting State to escape discriminatory or arbitrary system in country of origin in exceptional circumstances — Right of States to control entry, residence and expulsion of aliens — Best interests of the child — England, House of Lords

> *EM (Lebanon)* v. *Secretary of State for the Home Department (AF (a Child) and Others intervening)*   485

Elections — Electoral rights — Right to vote — Right to stand in parliamentary elections — Applicant's complaints under Article 3 of Protocol No 1 to European Convention on Human Rights, 1950 — Whether admissible — Whether complaint under Article 3 of

DIGEST OF CASES xxi

Protocol No 1 admissible in so far as it concerned applicant's removal from office or his ineligibility to stand for election as President of Lithuania — Whether complaint under Article 3 of Protocol No 1 admissible in so far as it concerned applicant's inability to stand for election to Seimas — Whether Article 3 of Protocol No 1 applicable to election of members of Seimas — Whether failure to exhaust domestic remedies — Whether compliant with six-month time limit — Whether Article 17 of European Convention applicable — Examination on merits — Importance of Article 3 of Protocol No 1 in Convention system — Fundamental principle of effective democracy — Right to vote — Right to stand for election — Whether absolute rights — Margin of appreciation of States — Whether restrictions on electoral rights impairing essence of right or its effectiveness — Whether restrictions pursuing legitimate aim — Whether proportionate — Whether Lithuania violating Article 3 of Protocol No 1 on account of applicant's inability to stand for election to Seimas — European Court of Human Rights (Grand Chamber)

Paksas v. *Lithuania* 252

Elections — Right to free elections — Right to stand as candidate — Former President barred from standing for office because of impeachment — Admissibility of author's communication to Human Rights Committee — Examination of claim under another procedure of international investigation or settlement — European Court of Human Rights — Council of Ministers — Whether author's claims incompatible *ratione materiae* with International Covenant on Civil and Political Rights, 1966 — Consideration of merits — Entitlement to a fair and public hearing by a competent, independent and impartial tribunal established by law in determination of any criminal charges or of rights or obligations in a suit at law — Protection against finding of criminal liability for any act or omission not constituting a criminal offence when committed — Right to take part in the conduct of public affairs — European Convention on Human Rights, 1950, Article 3 of Protocol No 1 — International Covenant on Civil and Political Rights, Articles 14, 15 and 25 — United Nations Human Rights Committee

Paksas v. *Lithuania* 303

Equality of all persons before courts and tribunals — Right to fair and public hearing by a competent, independent and impartial tribunal established by law — All persons equal before the law and entitled without discrimination to the equal protection of the

Human Rights (*cont.*)

law — Right of minorities to enjoy their own culture — International Covenant on Civil and Political Rights, 1966, Articles 14, 26 and 27 — Remedy for violation — United Nations Human Rights Committee

Paadar and Others v. *Finland*   330

Fair hearing — Applicant's complaints under Articles 6 and 7 of European Convention on Human Rights, 1950 and Article 4 of Protocol No 7 — Whether admissible — Whether Article 6(1) of European Convention applicable in either its civil or criminal aspect to Lithuanian Constitutional Court proceedings in issue — Whether this part of application compatible *ratione materiae* with Convention provisions — European Court of Human Rights (Grand Chamber)

Paksas v. *Lithuania*   252

Liberty of movement — Equality before the law — Right to freedom from discrimination — Right to effective remedy — International Covenant on Civil and Political Rights, 1966, Articles 12 and 26 — Admissibility of author's communication to Human Rights Committee — Case previously submitted to European Court of Human Rights — Whether European Court had considered claim on the merits — Remedy for violation — United Nations Human Rights Committee

Ory v. *France*   384

Obligation to respect rights — Article 1(1) of American Convention on Human Rights, 1969 — Principle of non-discrimination — Whether to analyse violation under Article 24 of American Convention on Human Rights — Whether interference with treaty-based rights — Whether interference proportionate — Whether interference having indirect discriminatory effects — Disability — Gender — Financial situation — Whether Costa Rica violating Article 1(1) in relation to Articles 11(2) and 17(2) of American Convention on Human Rights — Inter-American Court of Human Rights

Artavia Murillo and Others ("In vitro fertilization")
v. *Costa Rica*   1

Prohibition of torture and cruel, inhuman or degrading treatment — Applicant receiving life sentence — Applicant given whole life order by Secretary of State — Whether whole

DIGEST OF CASES xxiii

life order violating Article 3 of European Convention on Human Rights, 1950 — Need for review mechanism in respect of whole life sentences — General principles — Whether life sentence irreducible as matter of law and practice — Whether prospect of release and possibility of review of sentence — Whether review mechanism available to applicant sufficient to comply with requirements of Article 3 of European Convention — European Court of Human Rights (Fourth Section)

Hutchinson v. United Kingdom 235

Prohibition of torture and cruel, inhuman or degrading treatment or punishment — Freedom from arbitrary arrest and detention — Persons deprived of liberty to be treated with humanity and respect for inherent dignity of the person — Freedom from arbitrary interference with privacy, family and home — No implied right of the State to engage in any activity aimed at destruction of rights and freedoms — Admissibility of author's communication to Human Rights Committee — Consideration of merits — Right to effective remedy — International Covenant on Civil and Political Rights, 1966, Articles 2, 7, 9, 10 and 17 — Remedy for violation — United Nations Human Rights Committee

Horvath v. Australia 354

Remedy — Applicant's complaint under Article 13 of European Convention on Human Rights, 1950, taken in conjunction with Article 3 of Protocol No 1 — Whether admissible — Whether Article 13 of European Convention requiring provision of a remedy allowing constitutional precedent with statutory force to be challenged — Damage — Just satisfaction — Article 41 of European Convention — European Court of Human Rights (Grand Chamber)

Paksas v. Lithuania 252

Right to liberty and security — Individuals detained by British troops in Iraq — British troops part of Multinational Force under United Nations Security Council Resolutions — Whether rights of individuals under European Convention on Human Rights, 1950 breached — Whether obligations under United Nations Security Council Resolutions overriding rights under European Convention — United Nations Charter, 1945, Article 103 — Human Rights Act 1998 — England, High Court, Queen's Bench Division

Iraqi Civilians v. Ministry of Defence 660

Human Rights (*cont.*)

Right to life — Right to humane treatment — Right to personal liberty — Right to privacy — Rights of the family — Obligation to respect rights — American Convention on Human Rights, 1969 — Costa Rica party to Convention — Human rights violations — Judgment of Constitutional Chamber of Supreme Court of Justice — Unconstitutional Executive Decree regulating IVF — Prohibition of IVF in Costa Rica — Whether Costa Rica violating Articles 4(1), 5(1), 7(1), 11(2), 17(2) and 24 in relation to Articles 1(1) and 2 of American Convention on Human Rights — Inter-American Court of Human Rights

Artavia Murillo and Others ("In vitro fertilization") v. *Costa Rica*   1

Right to privacy and rights of the family — Articles 11(2) and 17(2) of American Convention on Human Rights, 1969 — Scope of these rights — Whether right to private life including reproductive autonomy and access to reproductive health services — Whether these rights extending to right to enjoy benefits of scientific progress — Whether Costa Rica violating Articles 11(2) and 17(2) in relation to Article 1(1) of American Convention on Human Rights — Inter-American Court of Human Rights

Artavia Murillo and Others ("In vitro fertilization") v. *Costa Rica*   1

Right to respect for private life — Participation in political activities — Whether applicant's removal from elected office affecting aspects of his private life — Whether Article 8 of European Convention on Human Rights, 1950 applicable — Territorial scope of application of Convention — Overseas territories — Admissibility of application — European Court of Human Rights (Fourth Section)

Misick v. *United Kingdom*   544

Right to self-determination — Whether right to self-determination a free-standing principle in Turks and Caicos Islands — Whether State's undertaking to hold free elections including commitment not to amend decisions of electorate unless compelling grounds for democratic order — Due process — Right to a fair hearing by an independent and impartial court established by law — Right to a fair trial — Trial by jury — Whether a fair hearing conditional on trial by jury — England, High Court, Queen's Bench Division (Administrative Court) and Court of Appeal

Regina (Misick) v. *Secretary of State for Foreign and Commonwealth Affairs*   515

International Criminal Law

Terrorism — Counter-terrorism measures — Drone strikes — Locational intelligence sharing — Defence of combatant immunity — Relevance — Principal and secondary criminal liability — Whether UK Agency employees might be guilty of assisting or encouraging crime under English law or ancillary to war crime and/or crime against humanity — Serious Crime Act 2007 — International Criminal Court Act 2001 concerns — England, High Court, Queen's Bench Division (Administrative Court) and Court of Appeal

Regina (Khan) v. Secretary of State for Foreign and Commonwealth Affairs   622

International Tribunals

Inter-American Court of Human Rights — Preliminary objections by Costa Rica — Exhaustion of domestic remedies — Article 46 of American Convention on Human Rights, 1969 — Time-barred petitions by victims — Interpretation of six-month requirement — Article 46(1)(b) of American Convention on Human Rights — Supervening facts — Competence of Court — Judgment on Preliminary Objections, Merits, Reparations and Costs — Inter-American Court of Human Rights

Artavia Murillo and Others ("In vitro fertilization") v. Costa Rica   1

Jurisdiction

Justiciability — Agency of United Kingdom providing locational intelligence to United States authorities for use in drone strikes — UK Agency under responsibility of Secretary of State — Claimant seeking declaration that UK Agency employees might be guilty of assisting or encouraging crime under English law or ancillary to war crime and/or crime against humanity — Whether claimant effectively seeking advisory opinion — Whether issues justiciable — Whether declaratory relief entailing condemnation of United States activities — Whether United Kingdom sitting in judgment on acts of a foreign State — Whether any exceptional circumstances concerns — England, High Court, Queen's Bench Division (Administrative Court) and Court of Appeal

Regina (Khan) v. Secretary of State for Foreign and Commonwealth Affairs   622

Relationship of International Law and Municipal Law

Act of State doctrine — Whether courts of one State barred from sitting in judgment on acts of a foreign State — Whether doctrine applicable to foreign court decisions — England, Court of Appeal

    Yukos Capital SARL v. *OJSC Rosneft Oil Company (No 2)*   554

Treaties — European Community — Court of Justice of the European Communities — Referral of questions to the Court of Justice — Obligations of Member States of European Community under the EC–Israel Association Agreement and EC–PLO Association Agreement — Court of Justice of the European Union (Fourth Chamber)

    Firma Brita GmbH v. *Hauptzollamt Hamburg-Hafen*   188

Treaties — European Convention on Human Rights, 1950 — Article 8 — Sharia law — Family law — Custody of children — Lebanese automatic entitlement of father or male paternal relative to custody of children from age seven — England, House of Lords

    EM (Lebanon) v. *Secretary of State for the Home Department (AF (a Child) and Others intervening)*   485

Treaties — European Convention on Human Rights, 1950 — Protocol No 1 to European Convention, 1952 — West Indies Act 1962 — Constitution of Turks and Caicos Islands 2006 — Orders in Council — Turks and Caicos Islands Constitution (Interim Amendment) Order 2009 — England, High Court, Queen's Bench Division (Administrative Court) and Court of Appeal

    Regina (Misick) v. *Secretary of State for Foreign and Commonwealth Affairs*   515

Treaties — Interpretation — Scope — Article 3 of European Convention on Human Rights, 1950 prohibiting torture and inhuman or degrading treatment or punishment — Whether whole life order violating Article 3 of European Convention — State choosing its criminal justice system — Sentence review and release arrangements — Requirement of compatibility with Convention principles — Whether life sentence compatible with Article 3 of European Convention — Whether life sentence irreducible as matter of law and practice — Whether prospect of release and possibility of review of sentence — Human dignity — Aim of imprisonment — Rehabilitation — European penal policy — International law — Article 10(3) of International

Covenant on Civil and Political Rights, 1966 — Human Rights Committee's General Comment on Article 10 — Need for review mechanism in respect of whole life sentences — General principles — Whether review mechanism available to applicant sufficient to comply with requirements of Article 3 of European Convention — Strasbourg jurisprudence — English jurisprudence — Interpretation of domestic legislation — Whether European Court of Human Rights to accept national court's interpretation of domestic law — Whether Secretary of State's discretionary power to release under domestic law complying with requirements of Article 3 of European Convention — European Court of Human Rights (Fourth Section)

Hutchinson v. *United Kingdom*   235

Treaties — Interpretation and application — Convention on Combating Bribery of Foreign Public Officials in International Business Transactions, 1997 — Article 5 — Relevance — Organization for Economic Cooperation and Development — OECD Working Group on Bribery in International Business Transactions — Whether municipal courts to desist from interpretation of unincorporated international instruments — Value of uniform interpretation of international instruments — Whether municipal courts can consider unincorporated international instruments considered by decision-makers when assessing legality of decisions — Criminal Justice Act 1987 — Serious Fraud Office — Investigations and prosecutions — Anti-terrorism, Crime and Security Act 2001 — England, High Court, Queen's Bench Division (Administrative Court) and House of Lords

Regina (Corner House Research and Another) v. *Director of the Serious Fraud Office (JUSTICE intervening)*   402

Treaties — United Nations Charter, 1945, Article 103 — European Convention on Human Rights, 1950, Article 5 — United Nations Security Council Resolution 1483 — United Nations Security Council Resolution 1511 — Coalition Provisional Authority — Coalition Provisional Authority Regulation 1 — Legal effect of Security Council Resolutions — Whether defendant having duty to detain individuals for security reasons — Whether any duty overriding defendant's obligations under Article 5 of European Convention — Human Rights Act 1998, Schedule 1 — England, High Court, Queen's Bench Division

Iraqi Civilians v. *Ministry of Defence*   660

State Immunity

Act of State doctrine — Limitations on act of State doctrine — Russian courts setting aside Russian arbitral awards — Whether due to interference by Russian State — Whether judicial acts of State for purposes of act of State doctrine — Judicial standards and duty of courts to adhere to rule of law — Issue estoppel — Dutch court setting aside Russian arbitral awards — Relevance — Differing meanings and standards of "public order" across States — Whether arbitral awards enforceable in England — England, Court of Appeal

Yukos Capital SARL v. *OJSC Rosneft Oil Company (No 2)*   554

Territory

Occupied territory — Territorial scope of treaty — West Bank and Gaza Strip — EC–Israel Association Agreement — Preferential customs treatment for goods originating in Israel imported into the European Community — Whether applicable to goods originating in the occupied territories — Court of Justice of the European Union (Fourth Chamber)

Firma Brita GmbH v. *Hauptzollamt Hamburg-Hafen*   188

Overseas territories — Governance — Turks and Caicos Islands — Right to self-determination — Judicial review — Whether Orders for peace, order and good government generally beyond scrutiny by courts — England, High Court, Queen's Bench Division (Administrative Court) and Court of Appeal

Regina (Misick) v. *Secretary of State for Foreign and Commonwealth Affairs*   515

Treaties

Application and interpretation — European Community–Israel Association Agreement — Protocol 4 to the EC–Israel Association Agreement — Territorial scope — Free movement of goods — Customs duties — Originating product — Exporting State best placed to verify place of origin — Certification of place of origin — Verification of place of origin — Whether importing States bound by exporting States' verification — Preferential treatment — Refusal of preferential treatment in absence of adequate verification — Customs Cooperation Committee — Whether importing States bound to refer disputes to Customs Cooperation Committee — Association Council — Israeli customs authorities' failure to certify products originating in occupied territories as having originated in Israel — Products originating in occupied territories not qualifying for preferential treatment under EC–Israel Association Agreement — Court of Justice of the European Union (Fourth Chamber)

Firma Brita GmbH v. *Hauptzollamt Hamburg-Hafen*   188

Application and interpretation — European Community–Palestine Liberation Organization Association Agreement — Territorial scope — West Bank and Gaza Strip — Originating product — Preferential treatment only applicable to products originating in the occupied territories under the EC–PLO Association Agreement and where certified by Palestinian customs authorities — Treaties not binding third parties without their consent — Vienna Convention on the Law of Treaties, 1969, Article 34 — Court of Justice of the European Union (Fourth Chamber)

Firma Brita GmbH v. *Hauptzollamt Hamburg-Hafen*   188

European Convention on Human Rights, 1950 — Article 6 — Right to a fair trial — Protocol No 1 to European Convention, 1952 — Article 3 — Right to free elections — Article 4 — Withdrawal from Article 3 — England, High Court, Queen's Bench Division (Administrative Court) and Court of Appeal

Regina (Misick) v. *Secretary of State for Foreign and Commonwealth Affairs*   515

Interpretation — Articles 31(2), 31(3) and 31(4) of Vienna Convention on the Law of Treaties, 1969 — Right to life — Article 4(1) of American Convention on Human Rights, 1969 — Ordinary meaning of terms — Use of scientific literature — Systematic and historical interpretation — *Travaux préparatoires* of human rights treaties — Evolutive interpretation — Object and purpose — Interpretation of "human being", "person", "in general", "moment of conception" — Whether embryo having a right to life under Article 4(1) of American Convention on Human Rights — Inter-American Court of Human Rights

Artavia Murillo and Others ("In vitro fertilization") v. *Costa Rica*   1

Interpretation — Convention on Combating Bribery of Foreign Public Officials in International Business Transactions, 1997 — Article 5 — Relevance — Investigation and prosecution of bribery of foreign public officials — Applicable rules and principles of

Treaties (*cont.*)

Contracting Parties — Parties not to be influenced by considerations of national economic interest, potential effect on relations with other States or identity of natural or legal persons involved — National security — Intersection of national security and relations with other States — European Convention on Human Rights, 1950 — Article 2 — Right to life — Vienna Convention on the Law of Treaties, 1969 — Article 31 — Interpretation of treaties in good faith in light of object and purpose — England, High Court, Queen's Bench Division (Administrative Court) and House of Lords

Regina (Corner House Research and Another) v. *Director of the Serious Fraud Office (JUSTICE intervening)*   402

Interpretation — European Convention on Human Rights, 1950, Article 3 — Prohibition of torture and inhuman or degrading treatment or punishment — Whether applicant's whole life order compatible with Article 3 of European Convention — Whether life sentence irreducible as matter of law or practice — Whether prospect of release and possibility of review of sentence — Whether review mechanism available to applicant sufficient to comply with requirements of Article 3 of European Convention — European Court of Human Rights (Fourth Section)

Hutchinson v. *United Kingdom*   235

War and Armed Conflict

Belligerent occupation — West Bank and Gaza Strip — Status — Whether Israeli territory — EC–Israel Association Agreement — Preferential customs treatment for goods originating in Israel imported into the European Community — Whether applicable to goods originating in the occupied territories — Court of Justice of the European Union (Fourth Chamber)

Firma Brita GmbH v. *Hauptzollamt Hamburg-Hafen*   188

Drone strikes in Pakistan killing civilians — United Kingdom providing locational intelligence to United States for potential use in drone strikes — Claimant seeking judicial review of decision to provide intelligence — National security concerns — England, High Court, Queen's Bench Division (Administrative Court) and Court of Appeal

Regina (Khan) v. *Secretary of State for Foreign and Commonwealth Affairs*   622

Occupation — Iraq — Detention of Iraqi civilians during occupation — Whether unlawful — Whether contrary to Article 5 of European Convention on Human Rights, 1950 — Whether duty to detain Iraqi civilians under United Nations Security Council Resolutions — Whether duty overriding obligation under Article 5 of European Convention — England, High Court, Queen's Bench Division

Iraqi Civilians v. *Ministry of Defence*   660

TABLE OF TREATIES

This table contains a list, in chronological order according to the date of signature, of the treaties referred to in the decisions printed in the present volume. It has not been possible to draw a helpful distinction between treaties judicially considered and treaties which are merely cited.

In the case of bilateral treaties, the names of the parties are given in alphabetical order and references to the texts of treaties have been supplied, including wherever possible at least one reference to a text in the English language unless these are known to be included in the Flare Index to Treaties available at http://ials.sas.ac.uk/treatyindex.htm. Multilateral treaties, all included in the Flare Index, are referred to by the name by which they are believed commonly to be known.

1945
June 26   Charter of the United Nations
           Chapter XI
               Art. 73(a) 541-3
               Art. 73(b) 541-3

1950
Nov. 4   European Convention for the Protection of Human Rights and Fundamental Freedoms: Convention entries subsequent to 1 November 1998 are at 1998, Nov. 1 European Convention for the Protection of Human Rights and Fundamental Freedoms (1950) as amended by Protocol 11, effective as of 1 November 1998
           First Protocol (20 March 1952)
               Art. 1 561
               Art. 3 .... 284-302, 527-8
               Art. 4 .... 527-8, 535
           Seventh Protocol (22 November 1984)
               Art. 4(1) 274-7

1959
May 20   European Convention on Mutual Assistance in Criminal Matters
               Art. 2 481

1963
Sept. 12   EEC–Turkey Association Agreement 203-4, 207

1966

Dec. 16　International Covenant on Civil and Political Rights (ICCPR)
　　　　　Art. 1 527
　　　　　Art. 1(3) 541-3
　　　　　Art. 2 .... 361-2, 364-8, 374-5
　　　　　Art. 2(2) 378-9
　　　　　Art. 2(3) 361-2, 376-7, 378-80, 381-2
　　　　　Art. 2(3)(a) 328, 380-2, 400
　　　　　Art. 2(3)(c) 379
　　　　　Art. 6 .... 44, 99-100
　　　　　Art. 7 .... 362-3, 368-9, 373, 380, 381-2
　　　　　Art. 9 380
　　　　　Art. 9(1) 363, 369, 373-4
　　　　　Art. 9(5) 363
　　　　　Art. 10 369-70
　　　　　Art. 10(1) 363, 379
　　　　　Art. 10(3) 245-6
　　　　　Art. 12 .... 373-4, 375
　　　　　Art. 12(1) 387, 389-92, 398-9
　　　　　Art. 12(3) 391-5, 398-9
　　　　　Art. 14 .... 310-23, 325, 342-5
　　　　　Art. 14(1) 340, 346-9
　　　　　Art. 15 .... 310-23, 325
　　　　　Art. 17 .... 363, 370, 374, 380
　　　　　Art. 25 .... 310-23, 328-9, 536-7, 542-3
　　　　　Art. 25(b) 323-4, 326-8
　　　　　Art. 25(c) 323-4, 326-8
　　　　　Art. 26 .... 341-5, 349-51, 387, 389-93,
　　　　　　　　　　　　　　　　　　　　　　　　　　　　　　　　　　　　　　396-7, 400-1
　　　　　Art. 27 .... 340-51, 341-2

Dec. 16　International Covenant on Civil and Political Rights, Optional Protocol (First)
　　　　　Art. 1 324-5
　　　　　Art. 4 325
　　　　　Art. 5(1) 326, 348, 377, 398
　　　　　Art. 5(2) 324
　　　　　Art. 5(2)(a) 323-4, 346-8, 376, 397
　　　　　Art. 5(2)(b) 391, 397-8
　　　　　Art. 5(4) 328, 351

Dec. 16　International Covenant on Economic, Social and Cultural Rights (ICESCR)
　　　　　Art. 1 527
　　　　　Art. 15(1)(b) 72

1969

May 23   Vienna Convention on the Law of Treaties (VCLT)
    Art. 1 .... 218, 226
    Art. 2(1)(a) 161-2
    Art. 3(b) 218, 226
    Art. 31 218
    Art. 31(1) 176-9, 446
    Art. 31(2) 179-81
    Art. 31(3) 183-4
    Art. 31(3)(b) 446-7
    Art. 31(4) 176, 179
    Arts. 31-3 165-72
    Art. 32 446-7
    Art. 34 218
    Art. 39 161-2

Nov. 22   American Convention on Human Rights (ACHR)
    Art. 1 44
    Art. 1(1) 15-16, 65-6, 124-33
    Art. 1(2) 81-9
    Art. 2 .... 15-16, 66, 141-3
    Art. 4(1) 42-5, 66, 73-137, 157-87
    Art. 4(5) 182
    Art. 5(1) 65-72, 137-8
    Art. 7 .... 66-72, 137-8
    Art. 7(1) 65
    Art. 11(2) 15-16, 65-72, 124-33, 137-8
    Art. 17 .... 65, 124-33
    Art. 17(2) 15-16, 65, 68-9
    Art. 24 .... 15-16, 65, 124-6
    Art. 29 .... 106-7, 183-4
    Art. 46(1)(a) 23-4
    Art. 46(1)(b) 27-9
    Art. 46(2) 23-4
    Art. 50 14-15
    Art. 62(3) 30, 161-2
    Art. 63(1) 138-55
    Art. 66(2) 161-2
    Art. 76(1) 161-2
    Protocol in the Area of Economic, Social and Cultural Rights (17 November 1988) (San Salvador Protocol)
        Art. 14(1)(b) 72
        Art. 15(3)(a) 98
        Art. 18 .... 127, 182

1972
Dec. 19   Cyprus–EEC, Association Agreement 215-16
          Additional Protocol (1977) 215-16

1979
Dec. 18   Convention on the Elimination of All Forms of Discrimination
          Against Women (CEDAW) 100-1
          Art. 16(1)(d) 495
          Art. 16(1)(e) 69

1981
June 26   African Charter on Human and Peoples' Rights (ACHPR)
          Art. 4 106

1989
Nov. 20   Convention on the Rights of the Child (CRC)
          Art. 1 101-2
          Art. 6(1) 101-2

1994
Jan. 6   UK–US, Treaty on Mutual Legal Assistance in Criminal Matters
          Art. 3(1) 445

1995
Sept. 28 Israel–Palestine, Interim Agreement 199-201
          Preamble 199-200
          Art. I(1) 200
          Art. IX(5)(b)(1) 200
          Art. X 200
          Art. XI(2)(c) 201, 214-15
          Annex III
            Art. IV 201
          Annex V 214-15
            Art. VIII(11) 214-15
            Art. IX 201
            Art. IX(6) 214-15

Nov. 20   EC–Israel, Association Agreement
          Preamble 195
          Art. 6(1) 219, 227
          Art. 7 195-6
          Art. 8 .... 195-6, 219
          Art. 67 196
          Art. 68 208

Art. 75(1) 196, 208, 210, 219, 232-3
Art. 79(2) 196
Art. 83 .... 196-8, 208-9, 210-16, 219, 225-9
Protocol 4
  Art. 2(2)(a) 196
  Art. 2(2)(b) 196, 219
  Art. 5(2)(a) 205, 219
  Art. 6 205
  Art. 17 229
  Art. 17(1)(a) 196-7, 205, 219-20
  Art. 17(1)(b) 219-20
  Art. 18(1) 205
  Art. 18(6) 205
  Art. 22(1)(a) 220, 228
  Art. 23 220
  Art. 23(1) 228
  Art. 32 .... 197, 203-5, 206-9, 216-17, 220-1,
                                        224-5, 230-2
  Art. 32(1) 197, 205
  Art. 32(2) 203, 205, 224-5
  Art. 32(3) 197, 205
  Art. 32(5) 205
  Art. 32(6) 197, 202, 205, 231-4
  Art. 33 .... 197, 203-4, 209-10, 221, 224-5, 232-3
  Art. 39 .... 221, 232-3

1997

Apr. 4   Convention for the Protection of Human Rights and Dignity of the Human Being with regard to the Application of Biology and Medicine (Oviedo Convention)
        Art. 18 108

Nov. 24   EC–PLO, Association Agreement
        Art. 1(2) 199, 213-14, 221-3
        Art. 2(2)(a) 199
        Art. 2(2)(b) 199
        Art. 3 .... 221-2, 227
        Art. 5 .... 199, 222, 227
        Art. 6 .... 199, 222, 227
        Art. 73 .... 199, 222, 225-9
        Protocol 3
          Art. 2(2) 222
          Art. 4 199
          Art. 15(1) 222-3, 229

	Art. 16(1) 223
	Art. 16(4) 214, 223
	Art. 20(1) 222-3
	Art. 20(1)(a) 223, 228
	Art. 21 223
	Art. 21(1) 223
	Art. 23(1) 228
	Art. 67 199
Dec. 17	OECD Convention on Combating Bribery of Foreign Public Officials in International Business Transactions 417, 458
	Art. 1 444
	Art. 5 .... 415, 421-3, 439-54, 461, 468-9, 475-7, 478-84
	Art. 12 .... 452, 476, 482

1998

Nov. 1   European Convention for the Protection of Human Rights and Fundamental Freedoms (1950) as amended by Protocol 11, effective as of 1 November 1998 (ECHR)

Art. 1 296-7
Art. 2 .... 69-70, 426, 466, 468-9, 492-5
Art. 2(1) 102-5
Art. 3 .... 238-51, 491-5
Art. 5 666-72
Art. 6 .... 522-3, 526, 540-1, 561
Art. 6(1) 274-7
Art. 6(2) 274-7
Art. 6(3) 274-7
Art. 7 274-7
Art. 8 .... 482, 489-514, 545-53
Art. 9 .... 493-4, 496
Art. 13 274-7
Art. 14 .... 482, 489-514
Art. 18 561
Art. 27(2) 258
Art. 27(3) 258
Art. 29(3) 258
Art. 30 258
Art. 34 .... 247, 257
Art. 35(3) 274-7
Art. 35(3)(a) 244, 552-3
Art. 35(4) 552-3
Art. 41 295-8

Art. 45(2) 249-50, 298
Art. 46 296-7
Art. 46(2) 323-4

1999
Aug. 6   Inter-American Convention on the Elimination of all Forms of Discrimination against Persons with Disabilities (ICEFDPD) 127

2003
July 11   Protocol to the African Charter on Human and Peoples' Rights on the Rights of Women in Africa (Maputo Protocol) 106

2006
Dec. 13   Convention on the Rights of Persons with Disabilities (CRPD)
Preamble 127
Art. 25(1) 126-7

2007
Dec. 13   Treaty of Lisbon on the Functioning of the European Union (TFEU)
Part V The Union's External Action, Title V International Agreements
Art. 217 226
Art. 218 .... 203-4, 226
Part VI Institutional Financial Provisions, Title I Institutional Provisions, Chapter 1 The Institutions, Section 5 The Court of Justice of the European Union
Art. 267 226
Art. 267(b) 203-4
Art. 272 203-4

Human rights — Right to life — Right to humane treatment — Right to personal liberty — Right to privacy — Rights of the family — Obligation to respect rights — American Convention on Human Rights, 1969 — Costa Rica party to Convention — Human rights violations — Judgment of Constitutional Chamber of Supreme Court of Justice — Unconstitutional Executive Decree regulating IVF — Prohibition of IVF in Costa Rica — Whether Costa Rica violating Articles 4(1), 5(1), 7(1), 11(2), 17(2) and 24 in relation to Articles 1(1) and 2 of American Convention on Human Rights

Human rights — Right to privacy and rights of the family — Articles 11(2) and 17(2) of American Convention on Human Rights — Scope of these rights — Whether right to private life including reproductive autonomy and access to reproductive health services — Whether these rights extending to right to enjoy benefits of scientific progress — Whether Costa Rica violating Articles 11(2) and 17(2) in relation to Article 1(1) of American Convention on Human Rights

Human rights — Obligation to respect rights — Article 1(1) of American Convention on Human Rights — Principle of non-discrimination — Whether to analyse violation under Article 24 of American Convention on Human Rights — Whether interference with treaty-based rights — Whether interference proportionate — Whether interference having indirect discriminatory effects — Disability — Gender — Financial situation — Whether Costa Rica violating Article 1(1) in relation to Articles 11(2) and 17(2) of American Convention on Human Rights

Treaties — Interpretation — Articles 31(2), 31(3) and 31(4) of Vienna Convention on the Law of Treaties, 1969 — Right to life — Article 4(1) of American Convention on Human Rights, 1969 — Ordinary meaning of terms — Use of scientific literature — Systematic and historical interpretation — *Travaux préparatoires* of human rights treaties — Evolutive interpretation — Object and purpose — Interpretation of "human being", "person", "in general", "moment of conception" — Whether embryo having a right to life under Article 4(1) of American Convention on Human Rights

International tribunals — Inter-American Court of Human Rights — Preliminary objections by Costa Rica — Exhaustion of domestic remedies — Article 46 of American Convention on Human Rights — Time-barred petitions by victims — Interpretation of six-month requirement — Article 46(1)(b) of American Convention on Human Rights — Supervening facts — Competence of Court — Judgment on Preliminary Objections, Merits, Reparations and Costs

Damages — Reparations — Monetary and other — Costa Rica to take appropriate measures to annul prohibition of IVF — Costa Rica to regulate implementation of IVF — Costa Rica to include IVF in infertility treatments offered by health-care services — Article 63(1) of American Convention on Human Rights

ARTAVIA MURILLO AND OTHERS
("*IN VITRO FERTILIZATION*") *v.* COSTA RICA[1]

Inter-American Court of Human Rights

Preliminary Objections, Merits, Reparations and Costs
28 *November* 2012

(García-Sayán, *President*; Franco, Macaulay,
Abreu Blondet, Pérez Pérez and Vio Grossi, *Judges*)[2]

SUMMARY:[3] *The facts*:—The technique of *in vitro* fertilization ("IVF") for married couples was authorized and regulated in Costa Rica by Executive Decree No 24029-S of 3 February 1995 ("the Executive Decree").[4] From 1995 to 2000, IVF was practised by a private entity and resulted in fifteen births. The IVF technique was declared unconstitutional by the Constitutional Chamber of the Costa Rican Supreme Court of Justice ("the Constitutional Chamber") on 15 March 2000. In its judgment,[5] the Constitutional Chamber annulled the Executive Decree, finding that the regulation of the right to life

---

[1] The names of the parties' representatives can be found at paras. 4-5 and 8-9 of the judgment.
 On 31 March 2014, the Court issued an Order on a Request for Provisional Measures, which is not reported in the *International Law Reports*, but can be found at www.corteidh.or.cr.
[2] Judge Ventura Robles, a Costa Rican national, did not participate in the deliberation of the judgment, pursuant to Article 19(1) of the Court's Rules of Procedure which provides that: "[i]n the cases referred to in Article 44 of the Convention, a Judge who is a national of the respondent State shall not be able to participate in the hearing and deliberation of the case".
[3] Prepared by Dr M. Brilman.
[4] For the text of the relevant provisions of the Executive Decree, see paras. 68-9 of the judgment.
[5] For the text of relevant parts of Judgment No 2000-02306 of the Constitutional Chamber, see paras. 72-6 of the judgment.

and dignity by the executive branch was incompatible with constitutional law and that IVF violated that law, as well as Article 4 of the American Convention on Human Rights, 1969 ("the American Convention"),[6] since Article 4 protected the right to life from the moment of conception.

In May 2008, one applicant, who claimed to be a victim of the decision, filed an action on unconstitutionality against the Constitutional Chamber's judgment, which was rejected. She subsequently filed a judicial complaint against the Costa Rican Social Security Institute. The Superior Court of Accounts for Contentious Administrative and Civil Proceedings concluded that IVF was not prohibited in Costa Rica if it did not entail the problems indicated by the Constitutional Chamber. The Costa Rican Social Security Institute appealed this judgment and, in May 2009, the First Chamber of the Supreme Court of Justice annulled the judgment.

On 19 January 2001, an initial petition had been submitted to the Inter-American Commission on Human Rights ("the Commission"), which issued its Report on Merits No 85/10 on 14 July 2010, making a number of recommendations to Costa Rica. That same year, in an attempt to comply with those recommendations, a bill was submitted to the Costa Rican Legislative Assembly to regulate IVF based on the protection of all human rights from the moment of fertilization. The bill was not approved.

In July 2011, the Commission submitted to the Inter-American Court of Human Rights ("the Court") a case against Costa Rica.[7] The Commission requested the Court to decide whether Costa Rica had violated the rights contained in Articles 11(2) (right to privacy), 17(2) (rights of the family) and 24 (right to equal protection) in relation to Articles 1(1) (obligation to respect rights) and 2 (domestic legal remedies) of the American Convention[8] to the detriment of Ms Artavia and the other alleged victims[9] as a consequence of the alleged general prohibition on IVF that had been in effect since 2000, following the Constitutional Chamber's judgment. The Commission also requested that Costa Rica inter alia lift the ban on IVF in the country through the corresponding legal procedures and pay reparations for pecuniary and non-pecuniary damage.

Preliminary Objections

Costa Rica filed three preliminary objections: (i) that domestic remedies had not been exhausted; (ii) that the petition presented by two alleged victims was

---

[6] Article 4(1) of the American Convention provided: "Every person has the right to have his life respected. This right shall be protected by law and, in general, from the moment of conception. No one shall be arbitrarily deprived of his life."

[7] Costa Rica became a State Party to the American Convention on 8 April 1970 and recognized the competence of the Court on 2 July 1980.

[8] The victims' representatives alleged a violation by Costa Rica of the same rights. One of these representatives, in addition, alleged a violation of the rights contained in Articles 4(1) (right to life), 5(1) (right to humane treatment) and 7 (right to personal liberty) of the American Convention.

[9] For the names of the other alleged victims, see para. 3 of the judgment.

time-barred; and (iii) that the Court lacked competence to consider supervening facts that occurred after the submission of the case by the Commission.

Held (unanimously):—Costa Rica's three preliminary objections were dismissed.

(1) Regarding the exhaustion of domestic remedies, Costa Rica submitted one brief at the proper procedural moment for filing this objection, prior to the issue of the admissibility report by the Commission. That brief referred to the possibility for the victims to file an application for *amparo*. The State's argument that the Constitutional Chamber's judgment did not imply a prohibition of IVF pertained to the merits of the case. If victims had filed an application for *amparo*, the same Constitutional Chamber that issued the judgment on IVF would have had to decide it. Therefore, it was unreasonable to require the victims to continue exhausting such applications. This remedy was not appropriate to protect the legal situation harmed by the judgment and, consequently, could not be considered a domestic remedy that had to be exhausted (paras. 24-7).

(2) Regarding the time-barred petition by two victims, the specific circumstances of this case required an interpretation of the six-month requirement established in Article 46(1)(b) of the American Convention.[10] Infertility generated different reactions, so that it was not possible to place the burden on victims to make a decision to lodge a petition within a specific time frame. Also, (a) the Constitutional Chamber's judgment continued to be in force, (b) victims did not have to be aware of their infertility at the time it was rendered, and (c) the petition was lodged during the year in which it was learned that this judgment would prevent access to IVF (paras. 35-6).

(3) Regarding the alleged lack of competence to consider supervening facts, the analysis of the factual framework corresponded to the merits of the case (para. 40).

Merits

Held (by five votes to one, Judge Vio Grossi dissenting):—Costa Rica had violated Articles 5(1), 7, 11(2) and 17(2) in relation to Article 1(1) of the American Convention, to the detriment of eighteen victims.[11]

(1) Article 11 of the American Convention required the State to protect individuals against arbitrary actions of State institutions that affected private and family life. The concept of private life encompassed the right to personal autonomy and the decision whether or not to become a parent. This right was related to: (i) reproductive autonomy; and (ii) access to reproductive health services. The Court had interpreted Article 7 of the American Convention

---

[10] For the text of Article 46(1)(b) of the American Convention, see para. 32 of the judgment.
[11] For the operative paragraphs of the judgment, see para. 381.

broadly, so that every person had the right to organize, in keeping with the law, his individual and social life according to his own choices and beliefs. Article 17 of the American Convention recognized the central role of the family and family life in a person's existence and society in general. This was such a basic right of the American Convention that it could not be waived even in extreme circumstances (paras. 141-6 and 149).

(2) The right to enjoy the benefits of scientific progress was contemplated in the Inter-American context in Article XIII of the American Declaration of the Rights and Duties of Man, 1948, and Article 14(1)(b) of the Protocol of San Salvador, 1988. In keeping with Article 29(b) of the American Convention, the scope of the rights to private life, reproductive autonomy and to found a family encompassed the right to benefit from scientific progress and its applications. The latter included the right to have access to the best healthcare services in assisted reproduction techniques and, consequently, the prohibition of disproportionate and unnecessary restrictions, *de jure* or *de facto*, to exercise reproductive decisions (para. 150).

(3) The Court, in the context of the right to personal integrity, had analysed situations that caused particular distress and anxiety to the individual, as well as serious impacts of the lack of medical care or problems of accessibility to certain health procedures. States were responsible for regulating and overseeing the provision of health services to ensure effective protection of the rights to life and personal integrity (paras. 147-8).

(4) IVF had not been practised in Costa Rica since the Constitutional Chamber's judgment. Since that judgment conditioned the possibility of applying IVF on ensuring there was no embryonic loss whatsoever, in practice the judgment entailed a prohibition of IVF since compliance was impossible. The judgment led to the interruption of the medical treatment of some of the victims, while others were forced to travel to other countries for access to IVF. This constituted an interference with the private and family lives of the victims. This interference existed owing both to the prohibitive effect resulting from the Constitutional Chamber's judgment and the impact that it had on the victims in this case (paras. 157-62).

(5) The interference with the victims' rights was partly based by the Constitutional Chamber on its interpretation of Article 4(1) of the American Convention, according to which the absolute protection of the "right to life" of the embryo was compulsory within the framework of the inviolability of life from conception. The Court was the ultimate interpreter of the American Convention. The scope of Articles 1(2) and 4(1) of the American Convention[12] in relation to the terms "person", "human being", "conception" and "in general" had to be interpreted by reference to the ordinary meaning of terms, systematic and historical interpretation, evolutive interpretation, most favourable interpretation, and object and purpose of the treaty (paras. 171-3).

---

[12] For the text of these Articles, see paras. 174-5 of the judgment.

(6) With regard to the ordinary meaning of "conception" and "human being", the scope of these terms was assessed based on scientific literature.[13] The former, in the sense of Article 4(1), occurred at the moment when the embryo became implanted in the uterus so that, before this event, Article 4 of the American Convention was not applicable. From the words "in general" could be concluded that the protection of the right to life under this provision was not absolute and exceptions to the general rule were admissible (paras. 174-90).

(7) Regarding systematic and historical interpretation, the interpretation of a treaty should take into account not only the agreements and instruments formally related to it, but also its context (Article 31(2) and (3) of the Vienna Convention on the Law of Treaties, 1969) ("the Vienna Convention"): international human rights law. The Court analysed the Inter-American,[14] universal,[15] European[16] and African systems[17] with regard to the right to life of the embryo. Also, Article 31(4) of the Vienna Convention was relevant for determining the interpretation of Article 4(1) of the American Convention, which was directly related to the meaning intended by the States Parties to the American Convention (paras. 191-244).

(8) Regarding the evolutive interpretation, it was consistent with the general rules of interpretation established in Article 29 of the American Convention, as well as Article 31(3) of the Vienna Convention that authorized the use of means such as agreements or practice or relevant rules of international law. The Court had granted special relevance to comparative law, using domestic norms or the case law of domestic courts. In this case, evolutive interpretation was particularly relevant bearing in mind that IVF was a procedure that did not exist when the authors of the American Convention adopted the content of Article 4(1). The Court considered (i) the pertinent developments in international and comparative law concerning the specific legal status of the embryo, and (ii) the regulations and practice of comparative law in relation to IVF.[18] In the context of the practice of most States Parties, the American Convention allowed IVF to be performed. This practice by States was related to the way in which they interpreted the scope of

---

[13] For the Court's discussion of the various positions, see paras. 180-5 of the judgment, with references to scientific literature in the corresponding footnotes.

[14] For reference to the *travaux préparatoires* of the American Declaration of the Rights and Duties of Man, 1948, see paras. 194-200 of the judgment. For reference to the *travaux préparatoires* of the American Convention on Human Rights, 1969, see paras. 201-19.

[15] For reference to the universal human rights system, see paras. 224-33 of the judgment, *inter alia* on the *travaux préparatoires* of the Universal Declaration of Human Rights, 1948, International Covenant on Civil and Political Rights, 1966, and Convention on the Rights of the Child, 1989.

[16] For reference to the European human rights system, see paras. 234-42 of the judgment.

[17] For reference to the African human rights system, see para. 243 of the judgment, on the *travaux préparatoires* of the African Charter on Human and Peoples' Rights, 1981.

[18] The Court concluded, based on the expert opinions presented by the parties at the public hearing, that Costa Rica was the only country in the region that prohibited and did not practise IVF. See paras. 254-5 of the judgment for references to IVF regulations and practice in the comparative law of countries in the region.

Article 4 of the American Convention and was associated with the principle of gradual and incremental, rather than absolute, protection of prenatal life (paras. 245-56).

(9) The object and purpose of Article 4(1) of the American Convention was that the right to life should not be understood as an absolute right, the alleged protection of which could justify the total negation of other rights. The object and purpose of the expression "in general" was to allow an adequate balance between competing rights and interests (paras. 257-63).

(10) The different methods of interpretation led to similar results according to which the embryo could not be understood as a person for the purposes of Article 4(1) of the American Convention (para. 264).

(11) A right could be restricted by States provided that interference was not abusive or arbitrary. It had to be established by law, pursue a legitimate aim and comply with the requirements of suitability, necessity and proportionality. The absolute right to life of the embryo as grounds for the restriction of the rights involved was not supported by the American Convention (paras. 272-84).

(12) Since the effects of the Constitutional Court's judgment were related to the protection of the right to private and family life, and the right to found a family, and not to the application or interpretation of a specific domestic law that regulated IVF, the Court analysed the alleged violation of the right to equality and non-discrimination not under Article 24, but in light of Article 1(1) of the American Convention, in relation to Articles 11(2) and 17 thereof. The interference with the victims' rights had indirect discriminatory effects because it had a disproportionate impact owing to their situation of disability, gender stereotypes and, for some of the victims, financial situation (paras. 285-304).

(13) A weighing up of the severity of the limitation of the rights involved in this case as compared to the importance of the protection of the embryo affirmed that the effects on rights to personal integrity, personal liberty, private life, intimacy, reproductive autonomy, access to reproductive health services and to found a family were severe and entailed a violation of these rights. It involved an arbitrary and excessive interference in private and family life that made this interference disproportionate (paras. 314-16).

(14) Taking into account these conclusions and the considerations concerning Article 4(1) of the American Convention, the Court did not consider it pertinent to rule on the State's argument that it had a margin of appreciation to establish prohibitions such as the one established by the Constitutional Chamber (para. 316).

Reparations and Costs

Held (by five votes to one, Judge Vio Grossi dissenting):—The judgment was, in and of itself, a form of reparation.

(1) Costa Rica had to adopt, as soon as possible, appropriate measures to annul the prohibition to practise IVF and provide information on the measures adopted within six months (para. 336).

(2) Costa Rica had to regulate, as soon as possible, the aspects it considered necessary for the implementation of IVF, taking into account the principles established in the judgment, and establish systems of inspection and quality control of the institutions and professionals qualified to perform IVF. It had to provide information every year on the gradual implementation of these systems (para. 337).

(3) Costa Rica had to include the availability of IVF within the infertility treatments and programmes offered by its health-care services, in accordance with the obligation to respect and guarantee the principle of non-discrimination, and provide information every six months on the measures adopted to make these services available gradually to those who required them (para. 338).

(4) Costa Rica had to provide the victims with psychological treatment, free of charge and immediately, for up to four years, through its specialized health-care institutions (para. 326).

(5) Costa Rica had to publish the judgment and its summary in the Official Gazette, a newspaper and an official website of the judiciary (para. 329).

(6) Costa Rica had to implement permanent education and training programmes and courses on human rights, reproductive rights and non-discrimination for judicial officials in all areas and at all echelons of the judiciary (para. 341).

(7) Costa Rica had to pay the sum of US $5,000, established in equity, as compensation for pecuniary damage to eight victims who travelled abroad to obtain access to IVF, and US $20,000 to each victim, established in equity, as compensation for non-pecuniary damage, as well as US $10,000, US $2,000 and US $3,000 to the respective representatives of the victims for reimbursement of costs and expenses (paras. 355 and 363).

(8) Costa Rica had to submit a report on compliance measures within one year from notification of the judgment. The Court was to oversee compliance. The case would be concluded once Costa Rica had fully carried out the provisions in the judgment (paras. 377 and 379).

Concurring Opinion of Judge García-Sayán, joined by Judge Abreu Blondet:
(1) To justify the absolute prohibition of IVF through the alleged "right to life" was a twofold contradiction. First, indicating that IVF resulted in embryonic loss failed to take into account that such loss also occurred in natural pregnancies and other reproduction techniques. Second, the prohibition on IVF resulted, paradoxically, in an impediment to life by obstructing the right of men and women to have children (para. 2).

(2) The disability consisting in infertility required special treatment. State policies should be inclusive rather than exclusive. The ban on IVF had a disproportionate effect to the detriment of infertile couples whose only possibility of procreation was access to IVF and who did not have the required financial resources. The fact that the State refused them the right to use this scientific

method, owing to the ban established in March 2000, seriously harmed the rights of those affected by the disease of infertility (paras. 5, 7 and 11).

(3) The Court's interpretation and the available scientific evidence led inter alia to the conclusion that it could not be determined that Article 4(1) of the American Convention sought to confer the status of "person" on the embryo (para. 9).

(4) The reparations were established not only directly with regard to the persons declared victims. They also established measures addressed at society as a whole, such as those concerning non-repetition. The essence of these measures was that the State had not only to cease creating discriminatory regulations and practices but also to annul the prohibition and gradually facilitate the use of IVF to those who needed and wanted it (paras. 10-11).

(5) This judgment not only established which Articles of the American Convention had been violated and the corresponding reparations. It also made a fundamental contribution to life, as expressed by the more than 5 million people who today enjoyed life because their parents used this type of method to counter infertility, and who would not have existed otherwise (para. 12).

Dissenting Opinion of Judge Vio Grossi: (1) The Court had to interpret and apply the American Convention, instead of assuming the role of the Commission or the lawmaking function. The latter belonged to the States, which had the exclusive power to modify the American Convention (paras. 1-2).

(2) It was more logical for the judgment to address this case, primarily, as a possible violation of Article 4(1) of the American Convention. One of the victim's representatives alleged such a violation and the Constitutional Chamber's judgment was explicitly based on Article 4(1). The judgment ended up minimizing and subordinating the right to life to the other referred rights. It did not refer in its operative paragraphs to Article 4(1) of the American Convention and made no reference to whether it was unnecessary to refer to this Article, or whether the State was responsible for the alleged violation or was blameless (paras. 3-14 and 106).

(3) At the Specialized Inter-American Conference on Human Rights, where the American Convention was approved, the elimination of the sentence "and, in general, from the moment of conception" was proposed by three countries so that abortion would not be forbidden. However, the majority of States rejected this proposal. Thus the American Convention decided to leave no doubt that Article 4(1) protected life, irrespective of its stage of development (paras. 35-9).

(4) This judgment departed from recent case law and would severely limit its scope, suggesting inter alia that the case law regarding the right to life was only applicable to extrajudicial executions and enforced disappearances and not to the case under review (paras. 57-60).[19]

---

[19] Referring specifically to para. 172 of the judgment and the omission by the Court of the phrase contained in its case law that: "[o]wing (to the) fundamental nature (of the right to life), restrictive approaches to it are inadmissible".

(5) Regarding the application of Article 4(1) to this case, it was not appropriate to have recourse to medical science for valuing or understanding the meaning and scope of Article 4(1) of the American Convention. It was not what medical science understood by "conception" that mattered, but what the parties to the American Convention intended by the term, which was its ordinary dictionary meaning. The scientific definition of a term was relevant inasmuch as it had been integrated into law, or when the law submitted itself to science, neither of which had occurred in this case (paras. 61-8).

(6) The judgment acknowledged that there were several scientific positions on "when life begins" and the understanding of "conception". However, the judgment sided with only one: that conception was produced at the moment of the embryo's implantation in the woman's uterus. The judgment did not analyse the other positions, particularly the one that considered that human life began with the fusion of spermatozoid and egg, which it simply dismissed (para. 69).

(7) When the American Convention was signed in 1969, it was not possible to know that "conception" and "fertilization" were two distinct phenomena. Hence, it was impossible to share the understanding that "the definition of 'conception' accepted by the authors of the American Convention has changed".[20] Some medical scientists could have changed their views, but the definition of the term enshrined by the Convention's framers remained unchanged (paras. 70-4).

(8) International treaties and judgments of international and European courts, as well as provisions of domestic law of Member States to the American Convention, were not applicable to this case. Some did not bind Member States nor consider the situation of the unborn or the conceived, in order to allow, or not to prohibit, abortion. None contained such a provision as Article 4(1) of the American Convention, a particularity of the Inter-American system on human rights. The judgment omitted a rule of general legal interpretation found in international law and the Law of Treaties, which provided that "specialized law prevails over general law". Article 4(1) of the American Convention was part of the body of international laws which, although they could not be qualified as Latin American, regional or particular international law, were particular to the Member States to the American Convention. Hence, this provision could not be interpreted by means of other general international law norms or human rights systems that did not include this provision, otherwise those systems would prevail over the American Convention, eventually modifying it in practice (paras. 75-83).

(9) Some parts of this judgment led to the conclusion that not only embryos before implantation, but also unborn or conceived children, had no inherent "right to have [their] life respected".[21] Their right would be dependent not only on respect for the pregnant woman's life, but also on her will to respect the rights of her child. Such an approach was contradictory to the letter and spirit of Article 4(1) of the American Convention, which evidently related to matters such as the juridical regime of abortion (paras. 84-98).

---

[20] Referring to para. 179 of the judgment.
[21] Referring specifically to para. 222 of the judgment.

(10) Assisted reproduction was only practised in eleven of the twenty-four Member States to the American Convention, many of which forbade some IVF-related procedures. The natural conclusion was not that "the Convention allows IVF to be performed",[22] but that the majority of Member States abstained from referring to it, probably because they understood this technique not, per se, to be regulated by international law. This, together with the judgment making Article 4(1) of the American Convention inapplicable to the embryo, at least until the moment of implantation in the woman's uterus, could make the majority of Member States understand that IVF regulation was within their internal, domestic or exclusive jurisdiction (paras. 99-106).

(11) Nevertheless, the Court had to decide the relevant issue. This did not, however, exempt States from fulfilling their duty to exercise their normative function as they deemed best. If they failed to do so, there was the risk that the Court would not only decide these issues, which required a more political pronouncement, but also assume this normative function. This would distort the Court's jurisdictional function, affecting the performance of the whole Inter-American system of human rights (paras. 107-10).

The opinions of the judges commence at pp. 157 and 161. The following is the text of the judgment of the Court:

TABLE OF CONTENTS

I. Introduction of the Case and Purpose of the Dispute	14
II. Proceedings Before the Court	16
III. Preliminary Objections	21
A) Failure to exhaust domestic remedies	21
B) Time-barred petition filed by Karen Espinoza and Héctor Jiménez Acuña	26
C) Lack of competence of the Court to hear "new facts not included" in the "facts of the application"	29
IV. Jurisdiction	30
V. Evidence	30
A) Documentary, testimonial and expert evidence	31
B) Admission of the evidence	32
B.1) Admission of documentary evidence	32
B.2) Admission of the statements of the presumed victims, and of the testimonial and expert evidence	34

---

[22] Referring specifically to para. 256 of the judgment.

VI. Facts 37
   A) Assisted reproduction and *in vitro* fertilization techniques 37
   B) The Executive Decree 40
   C) Judgment of the Constitutional Chamber of March 15, 2000 41
   D) Remedies filed by Ileana Henchoz and Karen Espinoza 45
   E) Draft legislation 48
   F) Specific situation of the presumed victims 49
      F.1) Grettel Artavia Murillo and Miguel Mejías Carballo 49
      F.2) Ileana Henchoz and Miguel Yamuni 50
      F.3) Oriéster Rojas and Julieta González 53
      F.4) Víctor Sanabria León and Claudia Carro Maklouf 54
      F.5) Giovanni Vega and Joaquinita Arroyo 55
      F.6) Karen Espinoza and Héctor Jiménez 56
      F.7) Carlos Eduardo de Jesús Vargas Solórzano and María del Socorro Calderón Porras 57
      F.8) Enrique Acuña Cartín and Ana Cristina Castillo León 58
      F.9) Andrea Bianchi Bruna and Germán Moreno Valencia 59
VII. Prior Consideration on the Purpose of the Instant Case 60
VIII. Right to Private and Family Life and Right to Personal Integrity in relation to Personal Autonomy, Sexual and Reproductive Health, the Right to Enjoy the Benefits of Scientific and Technological Progress and the Principle of Non-Discrimination 64
   A) Scope of the rights to personal integrity, personal liberty, and private and family life in this case 65
   B) Effects of the absolute prohibition of IVF 73
   C) Interpretation of Article 4(1) of the Convention as relevant in this case 77
      C.1) Interpretation in accordance with the ordinary meaning of the terms 82
      C.2) Systematic and historical interpretation 89

C.2.a) Inter-American human rights
system 90
C.2.b) Universal human rights system 98
C.2.c) European human rights system 102
C.2.d) African human rights system 106
C.2.e) Conclusion concerning systematic
interpretation 106
C.3). Evolutive interpretation 106
C.3.a) The legal status of the embryo 108
C.3.b) IVF regulations and practice in
comparative law 110
C.4) The principle of the most favorable
interpretation, and the object and
purpose of the treaty 113
C.5) Conclusion on the interpretation
of Article 4(1) 115
D) Proportionality of the prohibition 116
D.1) Severity of the limitation of the rights
involved in this case 121
D.2) Severity of the interference as a result of
indirect discrimination owing to the
disproportionate impact in relation to
disability, gender and financial situation 124
D.2.a) Indirect discrimination in relation
to the condition of disability 126
D.2.b) Indirect discrimination in relation
to gender 129
D2.c) Indirect discrimination in relation
to financial situation 132
D.3) Dispute regarding the alleged
embryonic loss 133
D.4) Conclusion regarding the assessment
of the severity of the interference in
relation to the impact on the intended
purpose 137
E) Final conclusion on the merits of the case 137
IX. Reparations 138
A) Injured party 139
B) Measures of rehabilitation and satisfaction,
and guarantees of non-repetition 140
B.1) Measures of psychological rehabilitation 140

B.2) Measures of satisfaction: publication
of the Judgment   141
B.3) Guarantees of non-repetition   141
   B.3.1) State measures that do not prevent
         the practice of IVF   141
   B.3.2) Campaign on the rights of persons
         with reproductive disabilities   143
   B.3.3) Other measures requested   144
C) Compensation for pecuniary and non-pecuniary
   damage   145
   C.1) Pecuniary damage   145
   C.2) Non-pecuniary damage   149
D) Costs and expenses   152
E) Method of compliance with the payments
   ordered   154
X. Operative Paragraphs   155

Concurring opinion of Judge Diego García-Sayán   157

Dissenting opinion of Judge Eduardo Vio Grossi   161

I. INTRODUCTION OF THE CASE AND PURPOSE OF THE DISPUTE

1. On July 29, 2011, the Inter-American Commission on Human Rights (hereinafter the "Inter-American Commission" or "the Commission") submitted a brief to the jurisdiction of the Inter-American Court (hereinafter "brief submitting the case"), under the provisions of Articles 51 and 61 of the Convention, against the State of Costa Rica (hereinafter "the State" or "Costa Rica") in relation to case 12,361. The initial petition was submitted to the Commission on January 19, 2001, by Gerardo Trejos Salas. On March 11, 2004, the Inter-American Commission approved Admissibility Report No 25/04.[1]

---

[1] In this Report the Inter-American Commission declared admissible the petition regarding the alleged violation of Articles 11, 17 and 24 of the American Convention, in relation to Articles 1(1) and 2 thereof. *Cf.* Admissibility Report No 25/04, Case 12,361, *Ana Victoria Sánchez Villalobos et al.*, Costa Rica, March 11, 2004 (file of attachments to the pleadings and motions brief of the representative Gerardo Trejos, tome I, annex 2, folios 3900 to 3914). In this report, the Commission declared that the "complaint was inadmissible with regard to the firms *Costa Rica Ultrasonografía SA* and *Instituto Costarricense de Fertilidad.*"

On July 14, 2010, the Commission approved Report on Merits No 85/10,[2] under the terms of Article 50 of the American Convention (hereinafter also "the merits report" or "Report No 85/10"), in which it made a number of recommendations to the State. Having granted the State three extensions to allow it to comply with the said recommendations, the Commission decided to submit the case to the Court. The Commission designated Rodrigo Escobar Gil, Commissioner, and Santiago A. Canton, then Executive Secretary, as delegates and appointed Elizabeth Abi-Mershed, Deputy Executive Secretary, and the lawyers Silvia Serrano Guzmán, Isabel Madariaga, Fiorella Melzi and Rosa Velorio as legal advisers.

2. The Commission indicated that this case concerned alleged human rights violations resulting from the presumed general prohibition of the practice of *in vitro* fertilization (hereinafter "IVF"), which had been in effect in Costa Rica since 2000, following a ruling of the Constitutional Chamber of the Costa Rican Supreme Court of Justice (hereinafter "Constitutional Chamber"). Among other aspects, the Commission alleged that this absolute prohibition constituted arbitrary interference in the right to private life and the right to found a family. It further alleged that the prohibition violated the right to equality of the victims, inasmuch as the State had denied them access to a treatment that would have enabled them to overcome their disadvantage with regard to the possibility of having biological children. It also argued that this ban had a disproportionate impact on women.

3. The Commission asked the Court to declare the international responsibility of the Costa Rican State for the violation of Articles 11(2), 17(2) and 24 of the American Convention, in relation to Articles 1(1) and 2 of this instrument, to the detriment of Grettel Artavia Murillo, Miguel Mejías Carballo, Andrea Bianchi Bruno, Germán Alberto Moreno Valencia, Ana Cristina Castillo León, Enrique Acuña Cartín, Ileana Henchoz Bolaños, Miguel Antonio Yamuni Zeledón, Claudia María Carro Maklouf, Víctor Hugo Sanabria León, Karen Espinoza Vindas, Héctor Jiménez Acuña, María del Socorro Calderón P., Joaquina Arroyo Fonseca, Giovanni Antonio Vega, Carlos E. Vargas Solórzano, Julieta González Ledezma and Oriéster Rojas Carranza.

---

[2] Merits Report No 85/10, Case No 12,361, *Grettel Artavia Murillo et al. v. Costa Rica*, July 14, 2010 (merits file, folios 7 to 37).

II. PROCEEDINGS BEFORE THE COURT

4. On August 29 and September 14, 2011, Boris Molina Acevedo forwarded to the Court the powers of attorney to represent 12 of the presumed victims.[3]

5. On August 31, 2011, Gerardo Trejos Salas forwarded to the Court the powers of attorney to represent six of the presumed victims.[4]

6. The submission of the case was notified to the State and to the representatives on October 18, 2011. In view of the fact that the representatives of the presumed victims did not reach agreement on the appointment of a common intervener, the President of the Court, in application of Article 25(2) of the Court's Rules of Procedure, ordered the appointment of Mr Molina Acevedo and Mr Trejos Salas as common interveners with autonomous participation.

7. On December 19, 2011, the common interveners submitted to the Court their respective briefs with pleadings, motions and evidence (hereinafter "pleadings and motions brief"), under Article 40 of the Court's Rules of Procedure. The common interveners agreed, in general terms, with the arguments of the Commission. Representative Molina alleged the violation of Articles 17(2), 11(2) and 24 of the American Convention, in relation to Articles 1(1) and 2 thereof, to the detriment of the presumed victims that he represents. Representative Trejos Salas alleged the violation of Articles 4(1), 5(1), 7, 11(2), 17(2) and 24 of the Convention, in relation to Articles 1(1) and 2 thereof, to the detriment of the presumed victims he represents.

8. On April 30, 2012, Costa Rica submitted to the Court its brief with preliminary objections, in answer to the brief submitting the case, and with observations on the pleadings and motions brief (hereinafter "answering brief"). In this brief, the State filed two preliminary objections and denied that any human rights had been violated in the instant case. The State appointed Ana Lorena Brenes Esquivel, Attorney General, as its Agent and Magda Inés Rojas Chaves, Deputy Attorney General, as co-agent.

9. On May 8, 2012, Huberth May Cantillano advised that the presumed victims represented by Gerardo Trejos had appointed him as

---

[3] Presumed victims: Ileana Henchoz Bolaños, Joaquinita Arroyo Fonseca, Julieta González Ledezma, Karen Espinoza Vindas, Enrique Acuña Cartín, Carlos E. Vargas Solórzano, Miguel Antonio Yamuni Zeledón, Giovanni Antonio Vega Cordero, Oriéster Rojas Carranza, Héctor Jiménez Acuña, Víctor Hugo Sanabria León and María del Socorro Calderón Porras.

[4] Presumed victims: Germán Alberto Moreno Valencia, Miguel Gerardo Mejías Carballo, Grettel Artavia Murillo, Ana Cristina Castillo León, Claudia Carro Maklouf and Andrea Bianchi Bruna.

their new representative owing to the death of Mr Trejos. He presented the respective powers of attorney.

10. On June 21 and 22, 2012, respectively, the Inter-American Commission and the common interveners submitted their observations on the preliminary objections filed by the State (*supra* para. 8).

11. In an Order of August 6, 2012,[5] the President of the Court required that the statements of two deponents for informative purposes, four presumed victims and seven expert witnesses be received by affidavit, and these were duly presented on August 24, 2012. In the Order the President also summoned the parties to a public hearing (*infra* para. 12).

12. The public hearing took place on September 5 and 6, 2012, during the ninety-sixth regular session of the Court held at its seat.[6] During the hearing, the statements of two presumed victims and four expert witnesses were received, together with the final oral observations and arguments of the Inter-American Commission, the representatives and the State, respectively. During this hearing, the Court required the parties and the Commission to submit certain helpful documentation and evidence.

13. In addition, the Court received 46 *amicus curiae* briefs submitted by: (1) Mónica Arango Olaya, Regional Director for Latin America and the Caribbean of the Center for Reproductive Rights, and María Alejandra Cárdenas Cerón, the Center's Legal Adviser; (2) Marcela Leandro Ulloa of the Group in Favor of IVF; (3) Filomena Gallo, Nicolò Paoletti and Claudia Sartori, representatives of the Association "*Luca Coscioni per la libertà di ricerca scientifica y del Partito Radicale Nonviolento Transnazionale e Transpartito*"; (4) Natalia Lopez Moratalla, President of the Spanish Association of Bioethics and Medical Ethics; (5) Lilian Sepúlveda, Mónica Arango, Rebecca J. Cook and

---

[5] *Cf. Case of Artavia et al.* (*In vitro fertilization*) v. *Costa Rica*. Order of the President of the Inter-American Court of Human Rights of August 6, 2012. Available at: www.corteidh.or.cr/docs/asuntos/artavia_06_08_12.pdf.

[6] The following persons appeared at the hearing: (a) for the Inter-American Commission: Tracy Robinson, Commissioner, Emilio Álvarez-Icaza, Executive Secretary, Elizabeth Abi-Mershed, Deputy Executive Secretary, and Silvia Serrano Guzmán, Legal Adviser; (b) for the representative Huberth May Cantillano: Huberth May Cantillano, representative of the presumed victims, and Antonio Trejos Mazariegos, lawyer; (c) for the representative Boris Molina Acevedo: Boris Molina Acevedo, representative of the presumed victims, William Vega Murillo, lawyer, Alicia Neuburger, Maria Lorna Ballestero Muñóz, Alejandro Villalobos Castro, Alejandra Cárdenas Cerón, Carlos Valerio Monge, Boris Molina Mathiew, Mauricio Hernández Pacheco and Ángela Rebeca Martínez Ortiz; and (d) for the State of Costa Rica: Ana Lorena Brenes Esquivel, Attorney General, Agent of the State of Costa Rica, Magda Inés Rojas Chaves, Agent of the State of Costa Rica, and Alonso Ernesto Moya, Silvia Patiño Cruz, Ana Gabriela Richmond Solís, Grettel Rodríguez Fernández and Jorge Oviedo Álvarez, officials of the Attorney General's Office.

Bernard M. Dickens;[7] (6) Equal Rights Trust and the Human Rights Clinic of the University of Texas Law School;[8] (7) International Human Rights Clinic of Santa Clara University Law School;[9] (8) Viviana Bohórquez Monsalve, Beatriz Galli, Alma Beltrán y Puga, Álvaro Herrero, Gastón Chillier, Lourdes Bascary and Agustina Ramón Michel;[10] (9) Ricardo Tapia, Rodolfo Vásquez and Pedro Morales;[11] (10) Alejandro Leal Esquivel, Coordinator of the Department of Genetics and Biotechnology of the School of Biology of the *Universidad de Costa Rica*; (11) Rita Gabriela Cháves Casanova, Member of the Legislative Assembly of Costa Rica; (12) Alexandra Loría Beeche; (13) Claudio Grossman, Dean of the American University Washington College of Law, and Macarena Sáez Torres, Director of the Impact Litigation Project of the American University Washington College of Law; (14) John O'Brien, President of Catholics for Choice, and Sara Morello, Executive Vice President of that organization; (15) Carlos Polo Samaniego, Director of the Latin American Office of the Population Research Institute; (16) Reynaldo Bustamante Alarcón, President of the *Instituto Solidaridad y Derechos Humanos*; (17) Hernán Collado Martínez; (18) Carmen Muñoz Quesada, Rita Maxera Herrera, Cristian Gómez, Seidy Salas and Ivania Solano;[12] (19) Enrique Pedro Haba, Professor at the Universidad de Costa Rica; (20) *Organización de Litigio Estratégico de Derechos Humanos* (Litiga OLE);[13] (21) Susie

---

[7] Lilian Sepúlveda is the Director of the Center for Reproductive Rights; Mónica Arango Olaya is the Regional Director for Latin America and the Caribbean of the Center. Rebecca J. Cook and Bernard M. Dickens are co-Directors of the International Reproductive and Sexual Health Law Programme of the Faculty of Law of the University of Toronto.

[8] The brief was signed by Ariel E. Dulitzky, Professor of the University of Texas Law School and Director of the School's Human Rights Clinic.

[9] The brief was submitted by Francisco J. Rivera Juaristi, Director and Supervising Attorney of the International Human Rights Clinic of Santa Clara University Law School; Britton Schwartz, Supervising Attorney of the Clinic; and Amanda Snyder, Bernadette Valdellon and Sophia Areias, interns at said clinic.

[10] Viviana Bohórquez Monsalve, member of the *Mesa por la Vida y la Salud de las Mujeres*; Beatriz Galli, member of IPAS; Alma Beltrán y Puga, Legal Coordinator of the *Grupo de Información de Reproducción Elegida* (GIRA); Álvaro Herrero, Executive Director of the *Asociación por los Derechos Civiles*; Gastón Chillier, Executive Director of the Center for Legal and Social Studies (CELS); Lourdes Bascary, member of the Center for Legal and Social Studies; and Agustina Ramón Michel, intern attached to the Health Area of CEDES.

[11] Ricardo Tapia is the President of the *Colegio de Bioética AC* (Mexico). Rodolfo Vásquez is the Vice President of this group and Pedro Morales is its Executive Secretary.

[12] Carmen Muñoz Quesada is a Deputy of the Legislative Assembly of Costa Rica. Rita Maxera Herrera and Ivania Solano are both lawyers. Cristian Gómez is a member of the Costa Rican Demographic Association. Seidy Salas is a member of the *Colectiva por el Derecho a Decidir*.

[13] The brief was submitted by Graciela Rodríguez Manzo, Director General of Litiga OLE; Geraldina Gónzalez de la Vega, Collaborator of Litiga OLE; Adriana Muro Polo, Lawyer at Litiga OLE; Marisol Aguilar Contreras, Lawyer at Litiga OLE.

Talbot, Lawyer of the Center for the Legal Protection of Human Rights (INTERIGHTS) and Helen Duffy, Head Counsel of INTERIGHTS; (22) Andrea Acosta Gamboa; (23) Andrea Parra, Natalia Acevedo Guerrero, Matías González Gil and Sebastián Rodríguez Alarcón;[14] (24) Leah Hoctor, Legal Adviser of the International Commission of Jurists; (25) Margarita Salas Guzmán, President, and Larissa Arroyo Navarrete, Lawyer, of the *Colectiva por el Derecho a Decidir*; (26) Fabio Varela, Marcelo Ernesto Ferreyra, Rosa Posa, Bruna Andrade Irineu and Mario Pecheny;[15] (27) María del Pilar Vásquez Calva, Coordinator of *Enlace Gubernamental Vida y Familia AC*, Mexico; (28) Latin American Network for Assisted Reproduction, and Ian Cooke, Emeritus Professor of the University of Sheffield; (29) Priscilla Smith, Senior Fellow of the Program for the Study of Reproductive Justice of the Information Society Project (ISP) of the University of Yale, and Genevieve E. Scott, Visiting Professor of the ISP; (30) Latin American Network for Assisted Reproduction, and Santiago Munné, President of Reprogenetics; (31) *Centro de Estudios de Derecho, Justicia y Sociedad* (DEJUSTICIA);[16] (32) José Tomás Guevara Calderón; (33) Carlos Santamaría Quesada, Head of the Molecular Diagnosis Division of the Clinical Laboratory of the *Hospital Nacional de Niños*; (34) Cesare P. R. Romano, Law Professor and Joseph W. Ford Fellow at Loyola Law School, Los Angeles;[17] (35)

---

[14] Andrea Parra, Director of the Action Program for Equality and Social Inclusion (PAIIS) of the Law Faculty of the *Universidad de los Andes*, Colombia, and Natalia Acevedo Guerrero, Matías González Gil and Sebastián Rodríguez Alarcón, students attached to PAIIS.

[15] Caio Fabio Varela, Human Rights Defender; Marcelo Ernesto Ferreyra, in representation of Heartland Alliance, the *Coalização de Lésbicas, Gays, Bissexuais, Transgêneros, Transexuais, Travesti e Intersexuais (LGBTTTI) na América Latina e no Caribe* and of the *Campanha por uma Convencao Interamericana de Direitos Sexuais e Direitos Reprodutivos*; Rosa Posa, in representation of AKAHATA; Bruna Andrade Irineu and Mario Pecheny.

[16] The brief was submitted by Rodrigo Uprimny Yepes, Director of the *Centro de Estudios de Derecho, Justicia y Sociedad* (DEJUSTICIA), and Diana Esther Guzmán, Paola Molano, Annika Dalén and Paula Rangel Garzón, Researchers at DEJUSTICIA.

[17] The brief was submitted by the Clinic in collaboration with 11 human rights and international law academics and professionals who also signed the *amicus curiae*: Roger S. Clark, Law Professor, Rutgers School of Law, Camden, New Jersey; Lindsey Raub Kantawee, Associate at Clifford Chance, law firm; Yvonne Donders, Professor of International Human Rights and Cultural Diversity and Executive Director of the Amsterdam Center for International Law of the Faculty of Law of the University of Amsterdam; Ellen Hey, Professor of International Public Law of the Faculty of Law of the Erasmus University Rotterdam; Jessica M. Almqvist, Lecturer on International Public Law of the *Universidad Autónoma de Madrid*, Faculty of Law; Freya Baetens, Assistant Professor of Public International Law of the Grotius Centre for International Legal Studies of the Faculty of Law of Leiden University; Konstantinos D. Magliveras, Associate Professor of the Department of Mediterranean Studies of the University of the Aegean, Unit of Rhodes; Belén Olmos Giupponi, Associate Professor of International Law of the *Universidad Rey Juan Carlos* of Madrid; Miguel Ángel Ramiro

the Ombudsman's Office;[18] (36) Hernán Gullco and Martín Hevia, professors of the Law School of the Universidad Torcuatto Di Tella; (37) Alejandra Huerta Zepeda, professor of the Biomedical Research Institute (IIB) of the *Universidad Nacional Autónoma de México*, and José María Soberanes Diez, professor of the *Universidad Panamericana*, Mexico; (38) *Asociación de Médicos por los Derechos Humanos* (AMEDEH);[19] (39) Latin American Federation of Obstetrics and Gynecology;[20] (40) Carlo Casini, Antonio G. Spagnolo, Marina Casini, Joseph Meaney, Nikolas T. Nikas and Rafael Santa María D'Angelo;[21] (41) Rafael Nieto Navia, Jane Adolphe, Richard Stitch and Ligia M. de Jesus;[22] (42) Hugo Martin Calienes Bedoya, Patricia Campos Olázabal, Rosa de Jesús Sánchez Barragán, Sergio Castro Guerrero and Antero Enrique Yacarini Martínez;[23] (43) Julian Domingo Zarzosa; (44) Kharla Zúñiga Vallejos of the Berit Family Institute of Lima; (45) Guadalupe Valdez Santos, President of the *Asociación Civil Promujer y Derechos Humanos*, and (46) Piero A. Tozzi, Stefano Gennarini, William L. Saunders and Álvaro Paúl.[24]

14. On September 26 and 28, 2012, Hany Fahmy, of the Human Rights Centre of the University of Peace of the United Nations, and

Avilés, Professor of Legal Philosophy of the *Universidad Carlos III* of Madrid, Director of the Master's Program in Fundamental Rights and Co-Director of the Master's Program in Human Rights and Democratization of the *Universidad Externado* of Colombia; Margherita Salvadori, Associate Professor of the Faculty of Law of the University of Turin, and Jaume Saura, Professor of International Law of the *Universidad de Barcelona* and President of the Human Rights Institute of Catalonia.

[18] The brief was submitted by the Costa Rican Ombudsman's Office. The brief was signed by Ofelia Taitelbaum Yoselewich, Ombudsman of Costa Rica.

[19] The brief was submitted by the *Asociación de Médicos por los Derechos Humanos* (AMEDEH). It was signed by Carlos María Parellada Cuadrado, President, and Juan Pablo Zaldaña Figueroa, Vice President of the association.

[20] The brief was submitted by the Latin American Federation of Obstetrics and Gynecology. The note was signed by Ivonne Díaz Yamal, Luis Távara Orozco, Executive Director, and Pio Iván Gómez Sánchez, Coordinator of the Federation's Committee on Sexual and Reproductive Rights.

[21] Carlo Casini, Magistrate, Member of the European Parliament for the Italian Pro-Life Movement and President of the Constitutional Affairs Committee of the European Parliament; Antonio G. Spagnolo, Director of the Bioethics Institute of the Sacred Heart Catholic University of Rome; Marina Casini, adjunct professor of Bioethics at the Bioethics Institute of the Sacred Heart Catholic University of Rome; Joseph Meaney, Director of the International Coordination at Human Life International; Nikolas T. Nikas, President and General Counsel of the Bioethics Defense Fund (BD); and Rafael Santa María D'Angelo, Lawyer, President of *Crece Familia* (CRECEFAM).

[22] Rafael Nieto Navia, Professor at the *Universidad Javeriana* in Bogotá; Jane Adolphe, Professor, Ave Maria School of Law; Richard Stitch, Professor, Valparaiso School of Law; and Ligia M. de Jesus, Professor, Ave Maria School of Law.

[23] Hugo Calienes Bedoya, Rector and Director of the Bioethics Institute of the *Universidad Católica Santo Toribio de Mogravejo* (USAT), Peru; Patricia Campos Olázabal, Dean of the Faculty of Medicine of USAT; and Rosa de Jesús Sánchez Barragán, Sergio Castro Guerrero and Antero Enrique Yacarini Martínez, members of the USAT Bioethics Institute.

[24] Piero A. Tozzi of the Alliance Defense Fund; Stefano Gennarini of the Center for Legal Studies at C-Fam; William L. Saunders of Americans United for Life; and Álvaro Paúl.

Olga Cristina Redondo Alvarado, psychoanalyst, respectively, forwarded *amicus curiae* briefs. Given that the public hearing took place on September 5 and 6, 2012, and, consequently, the time frame for submitting *amicus curiae* briefs expired on September 21, 2012, on the instructions of the President of the Court, the foregoing were advised that said briefs could not be considered by the Court or included in the case file.

15. The Court observes that the *amicus curiae* briefs filed by Equal Rights Trust and the Human Rights Clinic of the University of Texas, INTERIGHTS, and jointly by Caio Varela, Marcelo Ferreyra, Rosa Posa, Bruna Andrade and Mario Pecheny were presented within the time frame established in Article 44 of the Rules of Procedure, but in a language that is not the official language of the instant case. Subsequently, the translations into Spanish were forwarded 5, 7 and 34 days, respectively, after the time frame had expired. Based on the provisions of Article 28(1) of its Rules of Procedure, the Court considers that, since the Spanish version of two of these *amici curiae* was presented within the 21-day period provided for to accompany the originals or all the annexes, these briefs are admissible. However, as the Spanish version of the brief of Caio Fabio Varela and others was presented with a delay of 34 days, it was declared inadmissible.

16. On October 4, 5 and 6, 2012, the representatives and the State forwarded their final written arguments and the Inter-American Commission presented its final written observations in this case, respectively. These briefs were forwarded to the parties, who were given until October 17, 2012, to submit any observations they deemed pertinent regarding the information provided in response to the Court's questions. Observations were forwarded by representative Molina. The Inter-American Commission stated that it had no observations to make. Representative May and the State did not submit observations.

III. PRELIMINARY OBJECTIONS

17. The State submitted three "preliminary objections": failure to exhaust domestic remedies, the fact that the petition presented by Karen Espinoza and Héctor Jiménez was time-barred, and the Inter-American Court's lack of competence to hear supervening facts after the submission of the petition.

A) *Failure to exhaust domestic remedies*

18. The State argued that it had not "waive[d] the filing" of objections. It indicated that the Constitutional Chamber had "declared

unconstitutional a certain type of *in vitro* fertilization" and explained that "if the technique advances to the point where it permits it to be performed without the loss of embryos, it can be used." Consequently, the State indicated that "the petitioners could apply both to the constitutional jurisdiction and to the contentious administrative jurisdiction, so that the possibility that the health services could treat their infertility could be discussed," including the possibility of "a particular *in vitro* fertilization technique ... under the hypotheses provided by the Constitutional Chamber." The State indicated that, in the constitutional jurisdiction, "the existence of the ruling" did not "prevent the Constitutional Chamber from reviewing the matter by means of an action of unconstitutionality" given that the Law of Constitutional Jurisdiction states that the rulings of the said Chamber "are not binding for the Chamber itself, [which] could review the matter once again." It added that "the existence of a decision by the Constitutional Chamber does not preclude a ruling on the part of the Chamber itself," either "by means of a constitutional appeal or through the contentious administrative courts." Furthermore, the presumed victims "could have requested that the administrative authorities, respecting the decision of the Constitutional Chamber, provide a remedy for their condition of infertility" or "create a new regulation" on IVF, "in line with the parameters established by the ruling of the Constitutional Court." "If the administrative authorities refused to provide the required attention," it would have been appropriate to file an application for *amparo*. However, "none of the couples filed" this appeal.

19. The State further argued that "faced with the refusal of the administrative authorities, the presumed victims could have initiated a contentious administrative proceeding"; however, none of them did so before beginning the proceedings before the Commission. It added that the domestic remedies were "efficient" and that "proof of this is that one of the presumed victims turned to the contentious administrative court, after the petition had been filed before the Commission."

20. The Commission pointed out that, in the proceedings prior to the admissibility report, the State merely limited itself to "suggesting the possibility that the [alleged] victims could file an application for *amparo*." It indicated that the State "did not specify the legal basis for that possibility nor did it explain how, through such an appeal, it was possible to eliminate the effects of an abstract ruling of unconstitutionality ... regulated as not being subject to appeal." It pointed out that the State "did not provide the required evidence to explain the reasons why the remedy of *amparo* could be effective."

21. Representative May stated that, in the proceedings before the Commission, "the State indicated that it expressly waived the privilege of filing preliminary objections," a waiver that "once filed is irrevocable and irreversible." He argued that the appropriate domestic remedy "must be suited to the purpose"; in other words, it must satisfy the claims and interests at stake, and since the fundamental objective of the victims is the annulment of the judgment of the Constitutional Chamber and the reinstatement of IVF, "there is no remedy within the domestic jurisdiction that would make it possible to achieve this objective." Representative Molina indicated that the State "had not proved the effectiveness of the remedies mentioned." Furthermore, he emphasized that "the decision of the Constitutional Chamber is a judgment against which there is no remedy whatsoever and its effects are *erga omnes*." He argued that the appeal filed by Ileana Henchoz was rejected.

Considerations of the Court

22. Article 46(1)(a) of the American Convention establishes that, when determining the admissibility of a petition or communication submitted to the Inter-American Commission under Articles 44 or 45 of the Convention, the domestic remedies must have been pursued and exhausted, according to the generally accepted principles of international law.[25] The Court recalls that the rule of prior exhaustion of domestic remedies is designed for the benefit of the State, since it seeks to exempt it from the need to respond before an international body for acts attributed to it before having had the opportunity to resolve them through its own remedies.[26] This not only means that such remedies must formally exist, but also that they must be adequate and effective, as contemplated in the provisions of Article 46(2) of the Convention.[27]

23. Furthermore, this Court has consistently held that an objection to the exercise of the Court's jurisdiction based on the alleged failure to exhaust domestic remedies should be presented at the proper procedural stage,[28] that is, during the admissibility proceeding before the

---

[25] *Cf. Case of Velásquez Rodríguez* v. *Honduras. Preliminary objections.* Judgment of June 26, 1987. Series C No 1, para. 85, and *Case of Furlan and family* v. *Argentina. Preliminary objections, merits, reparations and costs.* Judgment of August 31, 2012. Series C No 246, para. 23.
[26] *Cf. Case of Velásquez Rodríguez* v. *Honduras. Merits.* Judgment of July 29, 1988. Series C No 4, para. 61, and *Case of Furlan and family* v. *Argentina*, para. 23.
[27] *Cf. Case of Velásquez Rodríguez* v. *Honduras. Merits*, para. 63, and *Case of Furlan and family* v. *Argentina*, para. 23.
[28] *Case of Velásquez Rodríguez* v. *Honduras, Preliminary objections*, para. 88, and *Case of Furlan and family* v. *Argentina*, para. 24.

Commission.[29] In alleging the failure to exhaust domestic remedies, the State must indicate, at the proper procedural moment, which remedies must be exhausted and their effectiveness. In this regard, the Court reiterates that it is not the duty of the Court or the Commission to identify *ex officio* the domestic remedies that have not been exhausted. The Court emphasizes that it is not up to the international organs to correct the imprecision in the State's arguments.[30]

24. The Court observes that the first point to be determined in relation to this objection is the type of arguments submitted by the State prior to the issue of the admissibility report; in other words, at the proper procedural moment for filing this objection. In this regard, the State only submitted one brief in relation to this matter, on January 23, 2004, in which it indicated that one of the victims "could have filed an application for *amparo*."[31] The brief in which the State analyzed the possible effectiveness of the contentious administrative jurisdiction to decide this case was submitted in 2008,[32] four years after the admissibility report was issued. Consequently, the Court considers that the arguments presented regarding the need to exhaust contentious administrative proceedings or bring an action for the failure to regulate the IVF procedure in keeping with the parameters established by the Constitutional Chamber are time-barred and therefore the analysis will focus on the arguments concerning the remedy of *amparo*.

25. With regard to the exhaustion of the remedy of *amparo*, the State raised two different arguments. First, with regard to the scope that the State attributed to the decision adopted by the Constitutional Chamber in this case, the State considered that this decision did not imply a prohibition of IVF but rather of a means of practicing this procedure. Thus, it claimed that the victims had other possibilities to address their infertility and, if appropriate, to use the application for *amparo* if these alternatives were denied. The Court considers that this is a matter of merits which will be decided opportunely when determining whether the Constitutional Chamber's decision constituted a limitation of the rights of the presumed victims (*infra* paras. 160 and 161).

---

[29] *Cf. Case of Velásquez Rodríguez* v. *Honduras, Preliminary objections*, para. 88, and *Case of Furlan and family* v. *Argentina*, para. 24.
[30] *Cf. Case of Reverón Trujillo*, para. 23, and *Case of Furlan and family* v. *Argentina*, para. 25. See also: ECHR, *Case of Bozano* v. *France*, Judgment of 18 December 1986, para. 46.
[31] Brief No 03-AM-03 presented to the Inter-American Commission on January 23, 2004, by the Minister of Foreign Affairs of Costa Rica (file of attachments to the merits report, volume III, folios 1056 and 1058).
[32] Brief No DJO-486-08 of November 17, 2008 (file of annexes to the merits report, volume V, folio 2276).

In this regard, the Court has stated that preliminary objections are acts that seek to prevent the analysis of the merits of a disputed matter by contesting the admissibility of a case or the competence of the Court to hear a specific case or any of its aspects, due either to the person, matter, time or place, provided that these objections are of a preliminary nature.[33] Since this first claim by the State cannot be examined without previously analyzing the merits of the case, it cannot be examined by means of this preliminary objection.[34]

26. Second, the State argued that an application for *amparo* could have provided the Constitutional Chamber with a fresh opportunity to assess the possible violation of rights in the instant case. In this regard, the Court observes that it is an uncontested fact that a final and binding decision from the highest court of Costa Rica on constitutional matters exists declaring that the practice of *in vitro* fertilization, as regulated at the time, was unconstitutional. As will be analyzed below in more detail (*infra* para. 135), the purpose of this case is to determine whether this decision by the Constitutional Chamber entailed the State's international responsibility. Consequently, the matter of exhaustion of remedies is related to the remedies existing against the ruling of unconstitutionality. In this regard, the Court observes that in conformity with Article 11 of the Law of Constitutional Jurisdiction of Costa Rica, judgments, decisions or rulings of the Constitutional Chamber cannot be appealed.[35] In addition, in Costa Rica the control of constitutionality is concentrated,[36] so that this Chamber hears all applications for *amparo* filed in the country.

27. Based on the foregoing, the Court considers that filing an application for *amparo* was not appropriate to remedy the situation of the presumed victims, because the highest court in the constitutional

---

[33] *Cf. Case of Las Palmeras* v. *Colombia. Preliminary objections.* Judgment of February 4, 2000. Series C No 67, para. 34, and *Case of Vélez Restrepo and family* v. *Colombia. Preliminary objection, merits, reparations and costs.* Judgment of September 3, 2012. Series C No 248, para. 30.

[34] Similarly, *cf. Case of Castañeda Gutman* v. *Mexico. Preliminary objections, merits, reparations and costs.* Judgment of August 6, 2008. Series C No 184, para. 39, and *Case of Vélez Restrepo and family* v. *Colombia. Preliminary objection, merits, reparations and costs.* Judgment of September 3, 2012. Series C No 248, para. 30.

[35] Law of the Constitutional Jurisdiction, Law No 7135 of October 11, 1989. Article 4 of this law establishes that "the constitutional jurisdiction is exercised by the Constitutional Chamber of the Supreme Court of Justice." The second section of Article 11 establishes that "There shall be no remedy against the judgments, decisions or rulings of the constitutional jurisdiction." *Cf.* file of the annexes to the report on merits, volume I, annex 1, folios 42 and 44.

[36] Article 2 of the Law of the Constitutional Jurisdiction (Law 7135 of October 11, 1989) establishes a concentrated constitutional control exercised by the Constitutional Chamber of the Supreme Court of Justice, making it the only body with competence to decide on the remedy of *amparo* and the constitutionality of laws of any nature.

jurisdiction had issued its final decision with regard to the main legal problems that had to be resolved in this case concerning the scope of the protection of prenatal life (*infra* para. 162). Since the Constitutional Chamber hears all applications for *amparo* filed in Costa Rica, if the victims had filed an application for *amparo*, this same Chamber would have had to decide it. Furthermore, the presumed victims sought to receive the IVF treatment under the regulation contained in the Executive Decree. In view of the declaration of the unconstitutionality of the decree as a whole, the possibility of obtaining access to IVF under the conditions established by the Constitutional Chamber was substantially different from the interests and claims of the presumed victims. Consequently, in the specific circumstances of this case, the Court considers it unreasonable to require the presumed victims to continue exhausting applications for *amparo* if the highest judicial instance on constitutional matters had already ruled on the specific aspects contested by the presumed victims. Thus, the function of this remedy of domestic law was not appropriate to protect the legal situation harmed and, consequently, could not be considered a domestic remedy that had to be exhausted.[37]

28. Based on the foregoing, the Court rejects the preliminary objection filed by the State.

B) *Time-barred petition filed by Karen Espinoza and Héctor Jiménez Acuña*

29. The State argued that the Inter-American Commission had indicated that the petition filed by Karen Espinoza and Héctor Jiménez was "time-barred, because it had been submitted outside the six-month period established by Article 46(1)(b) of the American Convention." It indicated that these presumed victims "cannot be included in the petition of January 19, 2001, given that, at that time, they were unaware of their condition" of infertility, because Ms Espinoza found out about her infertility in July 2002. It argued that "if it is considered that the brief of October 2, 2003, introduces for the first time" the complaint by these presumed victims, "it is clear that, from the time that she learned of her condition—July 2002—to October 2003, considerably more than six months elapsed," which is the term established by the Convention to file a complaint. It added that "the problem with this petition was the Commission's delay in analyzing the admissibility of the request presented, a process that lasted approximately three years (from January 2001 to

---

[37] Similarly, *cf. Case of Herrera Ulloa* v. *Costa Rica. Preliminary objections, merits, reparations and costs.* Judgment of July 2, 2004. Series C No 107, para. 85.

March 2004); this is why the petitioners were included who, in [their] own words, could not have been included in the original petition because they had not even been declared infertile at that time." The State indicated that in another admissibility report, "the Commission itself had noted that, in order to determine the time frame for presenting the petition in [IVF] cases, the date on which the person was declared infertile must be taken into account." It added that the alleged victim "was diagnosed with infertility in 2002, and the IVF technique was suggested in 2004, which results in the paradox that when she was presented before this Court as a presumed victim, she had not even thought of IVF as an applicable technique." Consequently, when they were included as petitioners in these proceedings "the six-month term had already expired; hence their petition should be considered time-barred."

30. The Commission indicated that "the vast majority of the arguments submitted by the State ... were not presented before the Commission" and they "differ substantially from the arguments submitted by the State at the admissibility stage," which is precisely the stage at which the Commission "decides on this requirement [of six months] in light of the information provided by the parties." It indicated that "the fact that the petitioner omits a specific requirement when presenting the initial complaint, and that this requirement is subsequently rectified, does not mean that the presentation of the complaint is time-barred."

31. Representative Molina Acevedo indicated that "whether or not a couple were aware of their infertility when the judgment of the Constitutional Court was issued does not close the door for any person, to date, to be limited by the six months established in the American Convention." Nevertheless, he argued that, in this case, "what determines the condition to be an alleged victim is not whether these persons were being treated by certain doctors in 2001, but whether they were aware of their possible and later confirmed infertility" and that, in addition, the only way they could procreate was through IVF. Lastly, the representative indicated that "hostility existed regarding the condition of those who might be on the confidential list of presumed victims in this case."

Considerations of the Court

32. Article 46(1)(b) of the Convention indicates the following:

Admission by the Commission of a petition or communication lodged in accordance with Articles 44 or 45 shall be subject to the following requirements: ...

b. that the petition or communication is lodged within a period of six months from the date on which the party alleging violation of his rights *was notified* of the final judgment; ([Emphasis] added)

33. In the instant case, the initial petition was filed on January 19, 2001. At that time the then legal representative of the victims had not made a specific and individual determination of the presumed victims. The inclusion of Ms Espinoza and Mr Jiménez occurred in a brief presented on October 10, 2003. In the proceedings before the Court it was reported that Ms Espinoza found out about her infertility in July 2002.[38]

34. On January 16, 2004, the State submitted a brief asking the Commission to declare the inadmissibility of the petition with regard to Ms Espinoza due to the "time-barred" nature of her claim, "because it was filed more than six months after the presumed victim of the violated rights had been notified of the decision" of the Constitutional Chamber.[39]

35. The Court considers that the specific circumstances of this case require an interpretation of the six-month requirement established in Article 46(1)(b). The Court takes into account that the phenomenon of infertility generates different reactions that cannot be associated with a strict rule on the courses of action that a person should necessarily take. A couple may take months or years to decide whether to use a specific technique of assisted reproduction or other alternatives. Thus, the criterion of the time when the alleged victim learns of his or her infertility is a limited criterion in the circumstances of this case, where it is not possible to place the burden on the victims to make the decision to lodge a petition before the inter-American system within a specific time frame. Similarly, the European Court has indicated that the "six-month rule is autonomous and must be construed and applied according to the facts of each individual case, so as to ensure the effective exercise of the right to individual petition."[40]

36. Therefore, the Court considers that in this case there are no elements to cause it to diverge from the admissibility decision adopted by the Inter-American Commission, given that: (a) the judgment delivered by the highest instance of the constitutional jurisdiction continues to be in force; (b) the victims did not have to be aware of

---

[38] Epicrisis (medical diagnosis) of Karen Espinoza Vindas (file of annexes to the pleadings and motions brief of Boris Molina, annex XIV, folio 5477).
[39] Brief No 03-AM-03 of January 16, 2004.
[40] *Cf.* ECHR, *Sabri Günes* v. *Turkey*, Grand Chamber, judgment of June 29, 2012; *Büyükdağ* v. *Turkey* (dec.), No 28340/95, judgment of April 6, 2000; *Fernández-Molina González and 369 Others* v. *Spain* (dec.), No 64359/01, judgment of October 8, 2002; and *Zakrzewska* v. *Poland*, No 49927/06, para. 55, judgment of December 16, 2008.

their infertility at the time this judgment was issued; and (c) the petition was lodged during the year after it was learned that this judgment would prevent access to IVF.

37. Based on the foregoing, the Court rejects the preliminary objection filed by the State.

C) Lack of competence of the Court to hear "new facts not included" in the "facts of the application"

38. The State argued that "both representatives included in their briefs with pleadings the State's responsibility for exposing the situation of the presumed victims to the media, owing to the media coverage during the proceedings before both the Commission and this Court." Similarly, the State argued that "none of the facts denounced by the representatives [in this regard] is included in the facts alleged by the Commission, and it cannot be considered that they are derived from the main or supervening facts." Therefore, it asked the Court "to declare inadmissible the petitions of the presumed victims related to facts not included by the Commission in the application it submitted."

39. Representative Molina indicated that "since the facts contested by the State are supervening facts and have a direct causal relationship to the fact that gave rise to the human rights violations in this case, it is fully in keeping with the proceedings" that "they have been presented" for the Court's consideration. Representative May argued that these are not "new facts," "they are situations all of which fall within the factual scenario of the prohibition" of IVF; in other words, they are "all conducts, personal situations, experiences, decisions and actions, and events that occurred in the life of the victims owing to the prohibition." He added that the corresponding decision should be made when deciding the merits of the case.

Considerations of the Court

40. As indicated, preliminary objections are acts that seek to prevent the analysis of the merits of a disputed matter by contesting the admissibility of a case or the competence of the Court to hear a specific case or any of its aspects, due to either the person, matter, time, or place, provided that these objections are of a preliminary nature.[41] If

---

[41] *Cf. Case of Las Palmeras* v. *Colombia. Preliminary objections*, para. 34, and *Case of González Medina and family members* v. *Dominican Republic. Preliminary objections, merits, reparations and costs.* Judgment of February 27, 2012. Series C No 240, para. 39.

the objections cannot be reviewed without entering into a prior analysis of the merits of the case, they cannot be analyzed by a preliminary objection.[42] In the instant case, the Court considers that it is not appropriate to rule in a preliminary manner on the factual framework of the case, because this analysis corresponds to the merits of the case (*infra* para. 133). However, the arguments presented by the State when filing the preliminary objection will be taken into consideration when establishing the facts that this Court finds proved and determining whether the State is internationally responsible for the alleged violations of the treaty-based rights, as well as when establishing the types of damage that could eventually arise to the detriment of the presumed victims. Based on the foregoing, the Court rejects the preliminary objection filed by the State.

IV. JURISDICTION

41. The Inter-American Court has jurisdiction to hear this case under Article 62(3) of the Convention, because Costa Rica has been a State Party to the American Convention since April 8, 1970, and accepted the binding jurisdiction of the Court on July 2, 1980.

V. EVIDENCE

42. Based on the provisions of Articles 46, 47, 50, 51 and 57 of its Rules of Procedure, and on its case law regarding evidence and the assessment thereof,[43] the Court will examine and assess the documentary evidence submitted by the Commission and by the parties at the different procedural stages, the statements of the presumed victims and witnesses and the expert opinions provided by affidavit and at the public hearing before the Court, as well as the helpful evidence requested by the Court (*supra* para. 11). To this end, the Court will abide by the principles of sound judgment, within the applicable legal framework.[44]

---

[42] *Cf. Case of Castañeda Gutman* v. *Mexico. Preliminary objections, merits, reparations and costs*, para. 39, and *Case of González Medina and family members* v. *Dominican Republic. Preliminary objections, merits, reparations and costs*, para. 39.

[43] *Cf. Case of the "White Van" (Paniagua Morales et al.)* v. *Guatemala. Merits.* Judgment of March 8, 1998. Series C No 37, paras. 69 to 76, and *Case of the Kichwa Indigenous People of Sarayaku* v. *Ecuador. Merits and reparations.* Judgment of June 27, 2012. Series C No 245, para. 31.

[44] *Cf. Case of the "White Van" (Paniagua Morales et al.)* v. *Guatemala*, para. 76, and *Case of the Kichwa Indigenous People of Sarayaku* v. *Ecuador*, para. 31.

A) Documentary, testimonial and expert evidence

43. The Court received diverse documents offered as evidence by the Inter-American Commission, the representatives and the State, together with their main briefs. The Court also received affidavits provided by the deponents: Gerardo Escalante Lopez and Delia Ribas Valdés; the presumed victims: Andrea Regina Bianchi Bruna, Ana Cristina Castillo León, Claudia María Carro Maklouf and Víctor Hugo Sanabria León; and from the expert witnesses: Andrea Mesén Fainardi, Antonio Marlasca López, Alicia Neuburger, Maureen Condic, Martha Garza and Paul Hunt. As to the evidence provided at the public hearing, the Court heard the testimony of the presumed victims Miguel Mejías and Ileana Henchoz, and of the expert witnesses Fernando Zegers-Hochschild, Anthony Caruso, Paola Bergallo and Marco Gerardo Monroy Cabra.[45]

44. Representative Molina informed the Court that he had filed an application for *amparo* "against the physicians treating four of the [presumed] victims, because [these physicians had] allege[d], in two of these cases, that the former wives of [his] clients had expressly forbidden" them to provide representative Molina with "a copy of the medical records that led to the infertility consultations." In this regard, the representative indicated that this situation left him "at a clear disadvantage" and, for that reason, he had resorted to "domestic legal channels to try to gain access to the information required in order to submit it as evidence" before the Court. The representative indicated that his application had been denied. He stated that this was "a clear procedural violation and breach of the good faith that should prevail in any litigation, because it had harmed the 'body of evidence,' in the understanding that, for the purposes of these proceedings, the medical records contain important information that, although it can be substituted with other types of evidence, cannot be concealed if one of the parties has had access to it, because they are obliged to share it."

45. The representative requested "additional time" to refer to "and, as part of the brief with pleadings, motions and evidence, make any observation on the evidence presented by Ana Cristina Castillo León and Claudia Carro Maklouf, former wives of Enrique Acuña Cartín and Víctor Hugo Sanabria León," inasmuch as, "if they had furnished the relevant medical records," they would be using this evidence in

---

[45] The purpose of all these statements is established in the Order of the President of the Court of August 6, 2012. Available at: www.corteidh.or.cr/docs/asuntos/artavia_06_08_12.pdf. In a communication of August 9, 2012, the Commission withdrew the statement of Florencia Luna.

clear violation of the principle of "community of evidence" and "of good faith in litigation." The representative asked the Court "to consider the possibility of requesting the State, through the appropriate channels, to require Drs Gerardo Escalante López and Delia María Ribas Valdéz" to "hand over a copy of the medical records of the said individuals and of María del Socorro Calderón Porras and Carlos Vargas Solórzano, to whom for no reason, as of this date, a copy of the medical file was provided." Accordingly, the President took note of these requests and indicated that, if the Court determined that this evidence would be required in order to decide on aspects concerning the purpose of this case, it would be requested at the appropriate time. The Court considers that the said information is not essential to decide this case.

B) Admission of the evidence

B.1) Admission of documentary evidence

46. In this case, as in others, the Court grants probative value to those documents that were forwarded at the appropriate time by the parties and the Commission, and that were not disputed or challenged, and the authenticity of which was not questioned.[46] The documents requested by the Court as helpful evidence (*supra* para. 11) are incorporated into the body of evidence, in application of the provisions of Article 58 of the Rules of Procedure.

47. The Court decides to admit those documents that are complete or that, at least, allow the source and publication date to be verified, and will assess them taking into account the body of evidence, the arguments of the State, and the rules of sound judicial discretion.[47]

48. Also, regarding certain documents referred to by the parties and the Commission by means of their electronic links, the Court has established that if a party provides at least the direct electronic link to the document cited as evidence, and it is possible to access this document, legal certainty and procedural balance will not be affected, because it can be located immediately by the Court and the other parties.[48] In this case, the other parties and the Commission did not

---

[46] *Cf. Case of Velásquez Rodríguez v. Honduras. Merits*, para. 140, and *Case of the Kichwa Indigenous People of Sarayaku v. Ecuador*, para. 35.

[47] *Cf. Case of Velásquez Rodríguez v. Honduras. Merits*, para. 146, and *Case of the Kichwa Indigenous People of Sarayaku v. Ecuador*, para. 36.

[48] *Cf. Case of Escué Zapata v. Colombia. Merits, reparations and costs.* Judgment of July 4, 2007. Series C No 165, para. 26, and *Case of the Kichwa Indigenous People of Sarayaku v. Ecuador*, para. 37.

oppose or submit observations on the content and authenticity of such documents.

49. Furthermore, considering that the representatives submitted, with their final written arguments, vouchers for litigation expenses related to this case, the Court will only consider those that refer to requests for costs and expenses incurred in relation to the proceedings before this Court, after the date on which the pleadings and motions brief was filed.

50. The State asked the Court to reject "the psychological reports provided" by representative Molina "to prove the supposed damage caused by the State." It indicated that the said reports do not analyze "the supposed impact of the prohibition" of IVF on the presumed victims, "but merely indicate the effects on their condition of infertility," which "is not the result of any act or omission of the State." It added that the reports "appear to mention the effects" that IVF ha[s] "had on the women, which far from recommending the technique, reveals the serious effects suffered by the women who submit to this procedure," which "cannot be attributed to the State, and nor can compensation be claimed on this basis." Lastly, it indicated that "the psychological reports appear to reveal the opinion of the presumed victims and not the objective opinion of the psychologists." Similarly, the State asked the Court to reject the "psychological reports issued by Dr Andrea Meses Fernardi, in the cases of Ana Cristina Castillo León and Claudia María Carro Maklouf," which were presented by representative May, because they merely "analyze the impact that infertility has had on the supposed victims."

51. The State also asked the Court to reject the "financial files" of the presumed victims that were presented by representative Molina and that include "bank statements" and "certifications of earnings" based on which "compensation is sought from the State." The State argued that the said documentation "does not reveal in any way the expenses that the supposed victims say they have incurred and, to the contrary, contain[s] mere numbers without any identification that has a relationship" to the proceedings. It added that "no explanation is provided regarding the significance of the banking and earnings information for the settlement" of the case.

52. Regarding these observations of the State concerning the documentary evidence, the Court understands that they do not contest its admissibility, but rather are designed to question its probative value. Consequently, there is no problem as regards the admissibility of this evidence and it will be assessed together with the rest of the body of

evidence, taking into account the State's observations and in keeping with the rules of sound judicial discretion.

B.2) Admission of the statements of the presumed victims, and of the testimonial and expert evidence

53. With regard to the statements of the presumed victims and the witnesses and the expert opinions provided at the public hearing and by affidavit, the Court considers these pertinent only insofar as they relate to the purpose defined by the President of the Court in the Order requiring them (*supra* para. 11). These statements will be assessed in the relevant chapter, together with the entire body of evidence, taking into account the observations made by the parties.[49]

54. According to this Court's case law, the statements made by the presumed victims cannot be assessed separately, but only as part of the entire body of evidence in the proceedings, because they are useful insofar as they can provide more information on the alleged violations and their consequences.[50] Accordingly, the Court admits these statements (*supra* para. 11) and will assess them based on the criteria indicated.

55. In addition, in relation to the affidavits, the State requested that the Court declare inadmissible the statements of Paul Hunt, Antonio Marlasca, Gerardo Escalante and Delia Ribas. Likewise, it made observations on the substance of some of the statements.

56. On the matter of admissibility, the State indicated that the statements of Antonio Marlasca and Paul Hunt omitted any reference to the questions posed by the State, which affects the obligation of procedural cooperation, the principle of good faith, the adversarial principle and the right to defense. The Court reiterates that the fact that the Rules of Procedure permit the parties to submit written questions to the deponents offered by the opposing party and, if applicable, by the Commission, imposes the corresponding obligation of the party that offered the testimony to coordinate and take the necessary steps to forward the questions to the deponents, and that the respective answers are provided. In certain circumstances, failure to answer several questions may be incompatible with the obligation of

---

[49] *Cf. Case of Loayza Tamayo* v. *Peru. Merits*. Judgment of September 17, 1997. Series C No 33, para. 43, and *Case of the Kichwa Indigenous People of Sarayaku* v. *Ecuador*, para. 43.

[50] *Cf. Case of Loayza Tamayo* v. *Peru. Merits*, para. 43, and *Case of Díaz Peña* v. *Venezuela. Preliminary objection, merits, reparations and costs*. Judgment of June 26, 2012. Series C No 244, para. 27.

procedural cooperation and with the principle of good faith that governs international proceedings.[51] Nevertheless, the Court considers that failure to provide answers to the questions of the opposing party does not affect the admissibility of a statement and is an aspect which, depending on the extent of a deponent's silence, could eventually affect the probative value that an expert opinion might have, and should be assessed when considering the merits of the case.

57. The State argued that "the failure to present" the Spanish translation of Paul Hunt's statement within the established time frame "breaches the obligation of procedural cooperation and good faith that should govern international proceedings." The State pointed out that it had "complied with [the requirement] to submit two translations within the same time frame granted [to] the Commission, which clearly implied a reduction in the time for preparing the report," which "places it in a position of procedural inequality, since it also reduced the time ... granted ... to present the respective comments." In this regard, the Court observes that the English version of the report was submitted within the established time frame and that there was a delay of seven days in submitting the Spanish version. The Court takes into account that, in the proceedings before the Commission, the parties submitted various elements of information and evidence in English without providing a translation, which did not merit an objection from the parties and, furthermore, shows that, during the proceedings, steps were taken to ensure a proper procedural balance between the parties. Likewise, in the proceedings before the Court various time limits have been granted to the Commission and to the parties to forward translations into Spanish of some documents that were presented in English. Based on the foregoing, the Court concludes that the lack of a timely translation of the said statement did not create a disproportionate burden for the State or the representatives that could justify its inadmissibility.

58. The State asked the Court to reject the expert opinion of Antonio Marlasca, because "he should have appeared before a notary public," "and not as occurred in this case where it is clear from the document submitted that no such appearance took place, since the notary public affirms that he merely transcribed the report provided previously." In this regard, the Court has indicated that, in relation to the reception and assessment of evidence, the proceedings before it are not subject to the same formalities as the domestic judicial proceedings,

---

[51] *Case of Díaz Peña* v. *Venezuela*, para. 33, and *Case of Uzcátegui et al.* v. *Venezuela. Merits and reparations*. Judgment of September 3, 2012. Series C No 249, para. 29.

and that the incorporation of certain elements into the body of evidence must be made paying particular attention to the circumstances of the specific case.[52] Furthermore, on other occasions, the Court has admitted sworn statements that were not made before notary public, when legal certainty and the procedural balance between the parties[53] are not affected, and this is respected and guaranteed in this case.

59. The State contested the admissibility of the statements of Gerardo Escalante and Delia Ribas, and the opinion of Alicia Neuburger, because they presumably refer to matters that were not contemplated within the purpose of their statements. The Court reiterates that it will only take into account the statements provided by affidavit to the extent that these are in keeping with the purpose established in the Order issued by the President.

60. As to the substantial issues, the State indicated the following: (i) Paul Hunt "omits the analysis of the balance of interests that is essential in order to determine the existence of a disproportionate impact"; (ii) the expert opinion of Alicia Neuburger "is not useful evidence to prove the causal relationship between the alleged violations of rights" and "the damage supposedly suffered by the presumed victims," and "is based on a series of facts that have not been proved in these proceedings"; (iii) "Mr Marlasca fails in his attempt to draw a distinction that could be considered rational or objective between a human life and a human person"; (iv) "the statement [of Andrea Mesen] is so general that it makes it impossible to try to justify, much less prove, an alleged non-pecuniary damage to the presumed victims"; (v) Gerardo Escalante "limits the nature and content of his statement to the way in which IVF was practiced in Costa Rica at the time when he practiced it, so that he cannot make assessments or render opinions on the *in vitro* fertilization technique in general, or on its international regulation," and (vi) with regard to Delia Ribas: "she continually refers to the term 'pre-embryo,' using it as a basis to justify the treatment received by the embryo from its conception (or fertilization) until the moments before it is transferred to the mother's womb . . . and, therefore, it is not acceptable that she tries to justify its manipulation by hiding behind that concept, because it is scientifically proved that a full and complete organism exists at this initial stage." The State also argued that "it is not correct . . . to justify

---

[52] *Case of the Serrano Cruz Sisters* v. *El Salvador. Merits, reparations and costs*. Judgment of March 1, 2005. Series C No 120, para. 33.

[53] *Cf. Case of the Miguel Castro Castro Prison*, para. 189; *Case of Servellón García et al.*, para. 46; and *Case of Claude Reyes et al*. Judgment of September 19, 2006. Series C No 151, para. 51.

the practice of the IVF technique as a treatment for a disease that improves the health of the 'patients'"; "in her document, she advocates the practice of cryopreservation—or the freezing of the embryos—which is incompatible with the right to life and to human dignity"; "she does not answer the second question that was opportunely asked."

61. Regarding these observations made by the State regarding the expert opinions, the Court understands that these do not contest their admissibility, but rather are designed to question their probative value. The Court will consider the content of these expert opinions to the extent that they serve the purpose for which they were required (*supra* para. 11). Based on the foregoing, the Court admits the said expert opinions and will assess them together with the rest of the body of evidence, bearing in mind the State's observations and in accordance with the rules of sound judicial discretion.

VI. FACTS

A) Assisted reproduction and in vitro *fertilization techniques*

62. Infertility can be defined as "the failure to achieve a clinical pregnancy after 12 months or more of regular unprotected sexual intercourse."[54] The most common causes of infertility are, *inter alia*, damage to the Fallopian tubes, pelvic infections, male factors (for example, low sperm count), endometriosis, immunological factors or diminished ovarian reserve.[55] It is estimated that the incidence of infertility extends to approximately 10% of women [of] reproductive age.[56]

63. Assisted reproductive techniques or procedures are a group of different medical treatments used to help infertile individuals and couples achieve pregnancy; they include "the manipulation of both ovocytes and spermatozoids, or embryos ... for the establishment of

---

[54] *Cf.* Written summary of the expert opinion provided by Fernando Zegers-Hochschild at the public hearing before the Court (merits report, volume VI, folio 2818); Affidavit prepared by expert witness Garza (merits report, volume V, folio 2558); Opinion provided by expert witness Caruzo before the Inter-American Court during the public hearing held in this case and Statement by deponent Ribas (merits report, volume V, folio 2241).

[55] *Cf.* Written summary of the expert opinion provided by Fernando Zegers-Hochschild at the public hearing before the Court (merits report, volume VI, folio 2828). As expert witness Zegers-Hochschild explained, according to the World Health Organization, infertility is a disease of the reproductive system (merits report, volume VI, folio 2818).

[56] *Cf.* Written summary of the expert opinion provided by Fernando Zegers-Hochschild at the public hearing before the Court (merits report, volume VI, folio 2820).

a pregnancy."[57] The techniques include *in vitro* fertilization, embryo transfer, gamete intratubal transfer, zygote intratubal transfer, intratubal embryo transfer, cryopreservation of ovocytes and embryos, oocyte donation and embryo donation and surrogate motherhood.[58] Assisted reproduction techniques do not include assisted or artificial insemination.[59]

64. For its part, *in vitro* fertilization is "a procedure in which a woman's eggs are removed from her ovaries, and are then fertilized with spermatozoids in a laboratory procedure; once this is completed, the fertilized egg (embryo) is re-implanted in the woman's uterus."[60] This technique is used when infertility is caused by the absence or blockage of the woman's Fallopian tubes; in other words, when an egg cannot pass through the Fallopian tubes to be fertilized and subsequently implanted in the uterus,[61] or in cases of male infertility,[62] and also in cases where the cause of infertility is unknown. The stages followed during IVF are:[63] (i) ovulation induction; (ii) retrieval (aspiration) of eggs from the ovaries; (iii) insemination of eggs with spermatozoids; (iv) monitoring of the embryo fertilization and incubation process, and (v) embryo transfer to the mother's uterus.

65. There are five stages in embryonic development in IVF and they last a total of five days. First, mature ovules are selected and fertilized, which leads to the development of the zygote. In the first 26 hours of development, the zygote divides into two cells, which subsequently divide into four cells on day 2 and, finally, these divide again to form

---

[57] Written summary of the expert opinion provided by Fernando Zegers-Hochschild at the public hearing before the Court (merits report, volume VI, folio 2821).

[58] *Cf.* Written summary of the expert opinion provided by Fernando Zegers-Hochschild at the public hearing before the Court (merits report, volume VI, folio 2820).

[59] *Cf.* Written summary of the expert opinion provided by Fernando Zegers-Hochschild at the public hearing before the Court (merits report, volume VI, folio 2820).

[60] Affidavit prepared by expert witness Garza (merits report, volume V, folio 2559).

[61] In this regard, expert witness Zegers-Hochschild indicated that "fertilization cannot occur if there is no Fallopian tube; embryonic development cannot occur, if the spermatozoids deposited in the vagina are not capable of reaching the [Fallopian] tube, just as there is no fertilization if the spermatozoids reach it but are not capable of fertilizing." Statement of expert witness Zegers-Hochschild at the public hearing held in this case. Also, Written summary of the expert opinion provided by Anthony Caruso at the public hearing before the Court (merits report, volume VI, folio 2937.210), and testimony of deponent Ribas (merits report, volume V, folio 2243).

[62] *Cf.* Written summary of the expert opinion provided by Anthony Caruso at the public hearing before the Court (merits report, volume VI, folio 2937.214).

[63] *Cf.* Written summary of the expert opinion provided by Fernando Zegers-Hochschild at the public hearing before the Court (merits report, volume VI, folios 2825 to 2830); Affidavit prepared by expert witness Garza (merits report, volume V, folio 2559); and Statement by deponent Ribas (merits report, volume V, folios 2245 to 2248).

eight cells on day 3. On day 4, the embryo reaches the morula stage, and on day 4 and day 5, the blastocyst stage. The embryos can remain in culture for up to five days before being transferred to a woman's uterus.[64] Consequently, the embryo can be transferred from day 2 until the evening of day 5. The decision on when to transfer the embryo is taken based on the morphological and dynamic nature of the cellular division.[65] The embryo can be transferred directly to the uterus or to the Fallopian tubes. It is possible to know if a woman has become pregnant 12 days after embryo transfer based on the marker hormones present in the woman.[66]

66. The first birth of a baby resulting from *in vitro* fertilization occurred in England in 1978.[67] In Latin America, the first baby born through *in vitro* fertilization and embryo transfer was reported in Argentina in 1984.[68] Since the birth of the first person as a result of Assisted Reproductive Techniques (hereinafter "ART") was reported, "five million people in the world have been born thanks to the advances in this technology."[69] Furthermore, "each year, millions of ART procedures are performed. It is estimated that, in 2008, 1.6 million treatments resulted in the birth of 400,000 individuals between 2008 and September 2009" globally.[70] In Latin America, "it is estimated that from 1990 to 2010, 150,000 individuals were born," according to the Latin American Register of Assisted Reproduction.[71]

67. Based on the evidence in the case file, Costa Rica is the only State in the world that expressly prohibits IVF.[72]

---

[64] *Cf.* Written summary of the expert opinion provided by Fernando Zegers-Hochschild at the public hearing before the Court (merits report, volume VI, folios 2828 and 2829).
[65] *Cf.* Written summary of the expert opinion provided by Fernando Zegers-Hochschild at the public hearing before the Court (merits report, volume VI, folios 2828 and 2829).
[66] *Cf.* Written summary of the expert opinion provided by Fernando Zegers-Hochschild at the public hearing before the Court (merits report, volume VI, folios 2828 and 2829).
[67] *Cf.* Written summary of the expert opinion provided by Fernando Zegers-Hochschild at the public hearing before the Court (merits report, volume VI, folio 2821) and Statement by deponent Ribas (merits report, volume V, folio 2242).
[68] *Cf.* Written summary of the expert opinion provided by Fernando Zegers-Hochschild at the public hearing before the Court (merits report, volume VI, folio 2822).
[69] *Cf.* Written summary of the expert opinion provided by Fernando Zegers-Hochschild at the public hearing before the Court (merits report, volume VI, folios 2821 and 2822).
[70] *Cf.* Written summary of the expert opinion provided by Fernando Zegers-Hochschild at the public hearing before the Court (merits report, volume VI, folios 2821 and 2822).
[71] *Cf.* Written summary of the expert opinion provided by Fernando Zegers-Hochschild at the public hearing before the Court (merits report, volume VI, folios 2821 and 2822).
[72] The expert witness Zegers-Hochschild explained that "ART are used worldwide. This includes all the countries of Europe, Oceania, Asia and the Middle East, as well as the countries that have this

B) The Executive Decree

68. In Costa Rica, Executive Decree No 24029-S of February 3, 1995, issued by the Ministry of Health, authorized the technique of *in vitro* fertilization for married couples and regulated its practice. Article 1 of the Executive Decree regulated the practice of assisted reproduction techniques between married couples, and established rules for their practice.[73] Article 2 defined assisted reproduction techniques as "all those artificial techniques in which the union of the egg and the spermatozoid is achieved by a method of direct manipulation of the reproductive cells in the laboratory."[74]

69. The provisions of Decree Law No 24029-S that specifically regulated the technique of IVF at issue in the action of unconstitutionality were as follows:[75]

Article 9. In cases of *in vitro* fertilization, the fertilization of more than six of the patient's eggs in each treatment cycle is strictly prohibited.

Article 10. All the eggs fertilized in a treatment cycle shall be transferred to the patient's uterine cavity; discarding or eliminating embryos, or preserving them to be transferred during subsequent cycles of the same patient or of other patients, is strictly prohibited.

Article 11. Manipulation of the embryo's genetic code, as well as any form of experimentation on the embryo, is strictly prohibited.

Article 12. The trade in homologous or heterologous reproductive cells— eggs and spermatozoids—to be used for treating patients by means of assisted reproduction techniques is strictly prohibited.

Article 13. Failure to comply with the provisions established herein shall give the Ministry of Health the authority to cancel the health services operating permit and the accreditation of the establishment in which the violation was committed; the matter is to be immediately referred to the Public Prosecutor's Office and to the respective Professional Association, for the appropriate sanctions to be established.

---

kind of technology in Africa. In the Americas, ART are practiced in every country that has this kind of technology, with the exception of Costa Rica. Hence, it is reasonable to conclude that Costa Rica is the only country in the world that [prohibits] ART." *Cf.* Written summary of the expert opinion provided by Fernando Zegers-Hochschild at the public hearing before the Court (merits report, volume VI, folio 2821).

[73] Judgment No 2000-02306 of March 15, 2000, delivered by the Constitutional Chamber of the Supreme Court of Justice, File No 95-001734-007-CO (file of attachments to the report, volume I, folio 85).

[74] Judgment No 2000-02306 of March 15, 2000, delivered by the Constitutional Chamber of the Supreme Court of Justice, File No 95-001734-007-CO (file of attachments to the report, volume I, folio 85).

[75] Judgment No 2000-02306 of March 15, 2000, delivered by the Constitutional Chamber of the Supreme Court of Justice, File No 95-001734-007-CO (file of attachments to the report, volume I, folios 85 and 86).

70. *In vitro* fertilization was practiced in Costa Rica from 1995 to 2000[76] by the private entity *Instituto Costarricense de Infertilidad*.[77] During that period, 15 Costa Rican babies were born.[78] The technique was declared unconstitutional by the Constitutional Chamber in Judgment No 2000-02306 of March 15, 2000.

C) Judgment of the Constitutional Chamber of March 15, 2000

71. In accordance with Article 75 of the Law on Constitutional Jurisdiction,[79] any citizen may file an action of unconstitutionality against a norm "when, owing to the nature of the matter, there is no direct individual injury, or when it relates to the defense of diffuse interests or those that relate to the community as a whole." Based on this article, on April 7, 1995, Hermes Navarro del Valle filed an action of unconstitutionality against the Executive Decree that regulated IVF in Costa Rica, using different arguments relating to the violation of the right to life.[80] The petitioner requested that: (i) the Decree be declared unconstitutional because it violated the right to life; (ii) the practice of *in vitro* fertilization be declared unconstitutional; and (iii) "the public authorities be instructed to monitor medical practice closely, to ensure that such acts do not recur." The arguments put forward in the action for unconstitutionality included the following: (i) "in general, the percentage of malformations was greater than that recorded for natural fertilization"; (ii) "the generalized practice [of IVF] violates human life

---

[76] "On October 14, 1995, the first child resulting from *in vitro* fertilization was born." *Cf.* Statement by deponent Escalante (merits file, volume V, folio 2388). See also newspaper articles in *La Nación* of October 15, 1995, entitled "*Nació Esteban*" and "*Esteban, alianza fecunda*" (merits file, volume I, folio 587.40).

[77] *Cf.* Statement by deponent Ribas: "In Costa Rica, our group started *in vitro* fertilization in September 1994 ... Our results for 1994 to 1996 were published in the *Acta Medica Costarricense* ... As we were the only center in the country, we decided to submit our efforts to the scrutiny of the *Red Latinoamericana de Reproducción Asistida* [Latin American Assisted Reproduction Network], which we had been members of since its creation until the decision that prohibited the technique" (merits report, volume V, folios 2242 and 2248).

[78] Deponent Escalante stated that "[f]rom September 1994 to March 2000, 121 couples were treated with 149 complete cycles of *in vitro* fertilization; [of these,] 15 full-term pregnancies that resulted in the birth of a child were achieved" (merits report, volume V, folio 2392).

[79] Article 75 stipulates that "[i]n order to file an action of unconstitutionality, there must be a matter pending a decision by the courts, including for *habeas corpus* or *amparo*, or in the proceedings to exhaust the administrative jurisdiction, in which this unconstitutionality is cited as a reasonable means of protecting the right or interest that is considered harmed. This previous case pending a decision shall not be necessary when, owing to the nature of the matter, there is no individual and direct harm, or in the case of the defense of diffuse interests or those that relate to the collectivity as a whole."

[80] Action on unconstitutionality filed on April 7, 1995 (file of annexes to the answering brief, volume VII, folios 10455, 10456, 10458, 10464, 10465 and 10466).

[and] owing to the private and isolated characteristics ... in which this insemination takes place, any regulation would be difficult for the State to implement and monitor"; (iii) "human life begins from the moment of fertilization; therefore, following conception, any elimination or destruction—whether voluntary or arising from the negligence of the doctor or the inaccuracy of the technique used—would result in a clear violation of the right to life contained" in the Costa Rican Constitution; (iv) reference was made to the Inter-American Convention on Human Rights, the International Covenant on Civil and Political Rights and the Convention on the Rights of the Child; (v) it was argued that "the business of *in vitro* fertilization [is] a business, ... it does not provide a cure for ... a disease, and [is] not an emergency treatment to save a life"; and (vi) "the elimination of the product of conception, in other words, children, discarding them, produces the same violation as eliminating them deliberately owing to the lack of technique in the procedure, attempting to play some kind of 'Russian roulette' with the six children introduced into the mother."

72. On March 15, 2000, the Constitutional Chamber of the Supreme Court delivered a judgment,[81] whereby it declared "the admissibility of the action [and] annulled Executive Decree No 24029-S due to unconstitutionality."[82] The reasons given by the Constitutional Chamber to support its decision were, first, the "violation of the legal principle" whereby "only through a formal law issued by the Legislature, according to the procedure established in the Constitution for the enactment of laws, is it possible to regulate and, if appropriate, restrict fundamental rights and freedoms." Based on the foregoing, the Chamber concluded that the Executive Decree regulated the "right to life and dignity of the human being," and therefore "[t]he regulation of these rights by the Executive Branch [was] incompatible with Constitutional law."

73. In addition, when considering that Article 4(1) of the American Convention was applicable, the Constitutional Chamber stated the following:

The question of when human life begins is of transcendental importance in the matter under discussion here, since it is necessary to determine the

---

[81] Judgment No 2000-02306 of March 15, 2000, delivered by the Constitutional Chamber of the Supreme Court of Justice, File No 95-001734-007-CO (file of annexes to the report, volume I, folios 76 to 96).

[82] Judgment No 2000-02306 of March 15, 2000, delivered by the Constitutional Chamber of the Supreme Court of Justice, Case file No 95-001734-007-CO (file of annexes to the merits report, volume I, folio 95).

moment from which the human being is subject to protection under our legal system. There are different views among specialists. Some consider that human embryos are entities at a stage of development where they have nothing more than a simple potential for life ... They point out that prior to its attachment, the pre-embryo is composed of undifferentiated cells, and that cellular differentiation does not occur until after it has attached to the lining of the uterus and after the appearance of the primitive cell line—the first outline of the nervous system; from that moment the organ systems and the organs are formed ... Others, on the contrary, maintain that every human being has a unique beginning that occurs at the very moment of fertilization. They define the embryo as the original form of a being, or as the earliest form of a being, and consider that the term pre-embryo does not exist, since prior to the embryo, at the preceding stage, there is a spermatozoid and an egg. *When the spermatozoid fertilizes the egg that entity becomes a zygote and therefore an embryo. The most important feature of this cell is that everything that will allow it to evolve into an individual is already in place; all the necessary and sufficient information to determine the characteristics of a new human being appear to come together in the union of the twenty-three chromosomes of the spermatozoid and the twenty-three chromosomes of the ovocyte* ... In describing the segmentation of the cells that occurs *immediately after fertilization,* this view holds that at the three-cell stage a minuscule human being exists and from that stage every individual is unique, rigorously different from any other. *In short, as soon as conception occurs, a person is a person and we are in the presence of a living being, with the right to be protected by the legal system.*[83] ([Emphasis] added)

74. The Constitutional Chamber also determined that the practice of IVF "clearly jeopardizes the life and dignity of the human being."[84] In its reasoning, the Constitutional Chamber indicated that: (i) "[h]uman beings have the right not to be deprived of their life or to suffer unlawful attacks by the State or by private individuals, but not only this: public authorities and civil society must help them defend themselves from the dangers to their life"; (ii) "once conceived, a person is a person, and we are dealing with a living being, with the right to be protected by the law"; and (iii) "since the right [to life] is declared for everyone, with no exception, it must be protected for both the individual who has been born, and also for the unborn child."[85]

---

[83] Judgment No 2000-02306 of March 15, 2000, delivered by the Constitutional Chamber of the Supreme Court of Justice, Case file No 95-001734-007-CO (file of annexes to the merits report, volume I, folios 88 and 89).
[84] Judgment No 2000-02306 of March 15, 2000, delivered by the Constitutional Chamber of the Supreme Court of Justice, Case file No 95-001734-007-CO (file of annexes to the merits report, volume I, folio 94).
[85] Judgment No 2000-02306 of March 15, 2000, delivered by the Constitutional Chamber of the Supreme Court of Justice, Case file No 95-001734-007-CO (file of annexes to the merits report, volume I, folios 88 and 90).

75. In addition, the Constitutional Chamber stated that "[i]nternational law ... establishes strong guiding principles regarding the issue of human life,"[86] citing Article I of the American Declaration, Article 3 of the Universal Declaration of Human Rights, Article 6 of the International Covenant on Civil and Political Rights, and Article 4 of the American Convention. Regarding Article 4 of the Convention, the Chamber considered that "[t]his international instrument takes a decisive step, given that it protects the right [to life] from the moment of conception[; in addition,] it emphatically prohibits imposing capital punishment on pregnant women, which constitutes direct protection and, therefore, full recognition of the legal and real personality of the unborn child and its rights."[87] The Chamber also referred to Article 6 of the Convention on the Rights of the Child. In this regard, it concluded that "[t]he norms cited impose the obligation to protect the embryo from the abuse that it could be subject to in a laboratory and, especially, the most severe of all, the one that can eliminate its existence."[88]

76. Lastly, the Chamber concluded:

The human embryo is a person from the time of conception; hence it cannot be treated as an object for investigation purposes, be submitted to selection processes, kept frozen and, the most essential point for the Chamber, it is not constitutionally legitimate to expose it to a disproportionate risk of death ... The main objection of the Chamber is that the application of the technique entails a high loss of embryos, which cannot be justified by the fact that it is intended to create a human being, providing a child to a couple who would otherwise be unable to have one. The key aspect is that the embryos whose life is first sought and then violated are human beings, and constitutional law does not allow any distinction among them. The argument that in natural circumstances there are embryos that are not implanted, or that even if they are implanted they do not develop until birth, is not admissible either, simply because the application of [IVF] entails a conscious and voluntary manipulation of the female and male reproductive cells in order to produce a new human life, which leads to a situation where it is known in advance that the human life, in a considerable percentage of the cases, has no possibility to continue. As the Chamber has been able to verify, the application of the

---

[86] Judgment No 2000-02306 of March 15, 2000, delivered by the Constitutional Chamber of the Supreme Court of Justice, Case file No 95-001734-007-CO (file of annexes to the merits report, volume I, folio 90).

[87] Judgment No 2000-02306 of March 15, 2000, delivered by the Constitutional Chamber of the Supreme Court of Justice, Case file No 95-001734-007-CO (file of annexes to the merits report, volume I, folio 91).

[88] Judgment No 2000-02306 of March 15, 2000, delivered by the Constitutional Chamber of the Supreme Court of Justice, Case file No 95-001734-007-CO (file of annexes to the merits report, volume I, folio 92).

technique of *in vitro* fertilization and embryo transfer, as it is currently performed, jeopardizes human life. This Court knows that advances in science and biotechnology are so dramatic that the technique could be improved so that the reservations included herein disappear. However, *the conditions in which it is currently applied lead to the conclusion that any elimination or destruction of embryos—whether voluntary or derived from the negligence of the person executing the technique or its inaccuracy—violates the right to life, hence the technique is not in keeping with constitutional law and, consequently, the regulation under consideration is unconstitutional as it violates Article 21 of the Constitution and Article 4 of the American Convention on Human Rights. Since the technique violates the right to life, it shall be expressly placed on record that its application cannot be authorized even based on a norm with legal status, at least while its scientific development remains at the current state and entails conscious damage to human life.*[89] ([Emphasis] added)

77. Justices Arguedas Ramírez and Calzada Miranda presented a joint dissenting opinion on the judgment.[90] In this opinion, the justices considered that IVF "is not incompatible with the right to life or human dignity; on the contrary, it constitutes a scientific instrument and technique created to assist humanity, given that infertility ... must be regarded as a genuine disease."[91] They also indicated that "assisted reproduction techniques ... are offered as a way to exercise the legitimate right to human reproduction which, even though it is not expressly recognized in [the] Constitution, is derived from the right to freedom and to self-determination, the right to privacy and family life, and the freedom to found a family."[92]

D) Remedies filed by Ileana Henchoz and Karen Espinoza

78. On May 30, 2008, Ms Henchoz filed an action on unconstitutionality against the judgment of the Constitutional Chamber of March 15, 2000, which was rejected summarily.[93] In its decision, the Chamber considered that its case law was binding "*erga omnes* except for

---

[89] Judgment No 2000-02306 of March 15, 2000, delivered by the Constitutional Chamber of the Supreme Court of Justice, Case file No 95-001734-007-CO (file of annexes to the merits report, volume I, folios 94 and 95).
[90] Dissenting opinion of March 15, 2000, of Justices Arguedas Ramírez and Calzada Miranda (file of annexes to the answering brief, volume VII, folios 10994 to 10996).
[91] Dissenting opinion of March 15, 2000, of Justices Arguedas Ramírez and Calzada Miranda (file of annexes to the answering brief, volume IX, folio 10994).
[92] Dissenting opinion of March 15, 2000, of Justices Arguedas Ramírez and Calzada Miranda (file of annexes to the answering brief, volume IX, folio 10994).
[93] *Cf.* Decision No 2008009578. Action of unconstitutionality filed by Ileana Henchoz Bolaños of June 11, 2008 (file of annexes to the pleadings and motions brief, volume V, annex XXVIII, folio 5842).

itself, so that the opinion provided in it can be amended when this is justified or for reasons of public order."[94]

79. Subsequently, Ms Henchoz filed a judicial complaint against the Costa Rican Social Security Institute with the purpose that she be allowed to undergo IVF. The Institute argued that it was not possible to practice this procedure owing to the judgment of March 15, 2000.[95] In a judgment of October 14, 2008, the Superior Court of Accounts for Contentious Administrative and Civil Proceedings concluded that IVF as an assisted reproduction mechanism was not prohibited in Costa Rica while it did not entail the problems indicated by the Constitutional Chamber, "especially because the actual evolution of this medical procedure makes it possible to fertilize a single egg during the female reproductive cycle for its subsequent transfer to the mother's uterus."[96]

80. The Superior Court of Accounts for Contentious Administrative and Civil Proceedings ordered the Costa Rican Social Security Institute to make a diagnosis and perform the corresponding medical tests in order to determine the feasibility of practicing assisted reproduction methods, including IVF, on Ms Henchoz.[97] In addition, it indicated that this procedure should be performed respecting the guidelines established by the Constitutional Chamber, based on the current development of the technique, "so that it [was] not permitted to fertilize more than one ovule in each of the patient's reproductive cycles for transfer, or to fertilize two or more ovules in the same reproductive cycle and much less to select one embryo among several, and destroy, discard, freeze or experiment on any of them."[98]

---

[94] Judgment of the Constitutional Chamber 2005-10602 of August 16, 2005 (file of annexes to the pleadings and motions brief, volume V, annex XXVIII, folio 5842).

[95] Judgment No 835-2008 delivered by the Fifth Section of the Court of Accounts for Contentious Administrative and Civil Proceedings in the case brought by Ileana Henchoz Bolaños seeking a declaratory judgment against the Costa Rican Social Security Institute, Case file No 08-00178-1027-CA of October 14, 2008 (file of annexes to the pleadings and motions brief, volume V, annex XXVIII, folios 5845 to 5872).

[96] Judgment No 835-2008 delivered by the Fifth Section of the Court of Accounts for Contentious Administrative and Civil Proceedings in the case brought by Ileana Henchoz Bolaños seeking a declaratory judgment against the Costa Rican Social Security Institute, Case file No 08-00178-1027-CA of October 14, 2008 (file of annexes to the pleadings and motions brief, volume V, annex XXVIII, folio 5859).

[97] Judgment No 835-2008 delivered by the Fifth Section of the Court of Accounts for Contentious Administrative and Civil Proceedings in the case brought by Ileana Henchoz Bolaños seeking a declaratory judgment against the Costa Rican Social Security Institute, File No 08-00178-1027-CA of October 14, 2008 (file of annexes to the pleadings and motions brief, volume V, annex XXVIII, folio 5871).

[98] Judgment No 835-2008 issued by the Fifth Section of the Administrative Court in the declaratory proceeding filed by Ileana Henchoz Bolaños against the Costa Rican Social Security

81. The Costa Rican Social Security Institute appealed the judgment delivered by the Superior Court and, on May 7, 2009, the justices of the First Chamber of the Supreme Court of Justice annulled the said ruling and declared the action unfounded.[99] The First Chamber indicated that "it has been proved ... that the technique of *in vitro* fertilization would not be advisable for the plaintiff based on her age, because at 48 years old she has already lost her reproductive capacity with her own ovules, which makes an assisted pregnancy extraordinarily improbable and remote," in addition to the fact that the plaintiff, "after the contested judgment, stated through the different media that she would not subject herself to *in vitro* fertilization owing to her age."[100]

82. Furthermore, on January 6, 2005, the Ombudsman's Office issued note No 00117-2005-DHR, based on a complaint filed by Ms Espinoza, indicating that, following an appointment with a hospital of the Costa Rican Social Security Institute, the hospital had denied her the possibility of a fertility treatment, arguing the absence of the relevant programs,[101] and had not provided her with a medicine called Menotropin, which the patient had been given on other occasions.[102] In the said note, the Ombudsman's Office issued a series of recommendations, including:

[The establishment of] a special program for the treatment of infertility and sterility of all couples and women experiencing this situation, who wish to exercise their right to maternity and paternity, and do not have the financial resources to opt for private medical service, attention and treatment.[103]

83. The Ombudsman's Office also recommended improving the provision of services and medical attention in those areas in which medical treatment and monitoring is required, such as infertility and,

---

Institute, File No 08-00178-1027-CA of October 14, 2008 (file of annexes to the pleadings and motions brief, volume V, annex XXVIII, folio 5872).

[99] First Chamber of the Supreme Court of Justice, Judgment of May 7, 2009, Case file 08-000178-1027-CA, Decision 000465-F-S1-2009 (file of annexes to the pleadings and motions brief, volume V, annex XXVIII, folios 5873 to 5879).

[100] First Chamber of the Supreme Court of Justice, Judgment of May 7, 2009, Case file 08-000178-1027-CA, Decision 000465-F-S1-2009, forwarded by the State with the communication of January 22, 2010 (file of annexes to the pleadings and motions brief, volume V, annex XXVIII, folios 5873 to 5879).

[101] *Cf.* Note No 00117-2005-DHR of the Ombudsman's Office of January 6, 2005 (file of annexes to the pleadings and motions brief, volume IV, annex XV, folios 5556 to 5562).

[102] *Cf.* Doctor's prescription for Menotropin (file of annexes to the pleadings and motions brief, volume IV, annex XV, folio 5520).

[103] *Cf.* Note No 00117-2005-DHR of the Ombudsman's Office of January 6, 2005 (file of annexes to the pleadings and motions brief, volume IV, annex XV, folio 5561).

lastly, the establishment of clear guidelines with regard to health care medicines.[104]

E) *Draft legislation*

84. The Court observes that, in the context of an attempt to comply with the recommendations made by the Inter-American Commission (*supra* para. 1), a bill was submitted to the Legislative Assembly in 2010 to try and regulate IVF.[105] Among other elements, the bill was based on the protection of all human rights from the moment of fertilization[106] and established that IVF could only be practiced "if all eggs fertilized during a treatment cycle are transferred to the woman who produced them."[107] Furthermore, it prohibited "the reduction or destruction of embryos."[108] In addition, the bill established that "whoever, when applying the [IVF] technique, destroys or reduces or in any other way causes the death of one or more embryos, shall be punished with one to six years' imprisonment."[109] The Court observes that the bill was not approved.[110] For its part, the Pan-American Health Organization (PAHO) criticized the bill and emphasized the "risks of multiple pregnancies that may occur when all the eggs fertilized in a treatment cycle are transferred to the woman who produced them, which also increases the risk of spontaneous abortions, obstetric complications, premature births and neonatal morbidity."[111] The PAHO indicated that the "transfer to a woman of all embryos produced in each treatment cycle, including the defective ones, may endanger the woman's right to life, and

---

[104] *Cf.* Note No 00117-2005-DHR of the Ombudsman's Office of January 6, 2005 (file of annexes to the pleadings and motions brief, volume IV, annex XV, folio 5561).
[105] *Cf.* Bill on *in vitro* fertilization and embryo transfer, File 17,900, October 22, 2010 (file of annexes to the answering brief, volume IX, folios 11055 to 11068).
[106] *Cf.* Article 6 of the bill on *in vitro* fertilization and embryo transfer, File 17,900, October 22, 2010 (file of annexes to the answering brief, volume IX, folios 11055 to 11068).
[107] *Cf.* Article 8 of the bill on *in vitro* fertilization and embryo transfer, File 17,900, October 22, 2010 (file of annexes to the answering brief, volume IX, folio 11064).
[108] *Cf.* Article 8 of the bill on *in vitro* fertilization and embryo transfer, File 17,900, October 22, 2010 (file of annexes to the answering brief, volume IX, folio 11064).
[109] *Cf.* Article 19 of the bill on *in vitro* fertilization and embryo transfer, File 17,900, October 22, 2010 (file of annexes to the answering brief, volume IX, folios 11055 to 11068).
[110] *Cf.* The State's answer to the application (answering brief file, volume III, folio 1007).
[111] Pan-American Health Organization, Technical opinion of the Pan-American Health Organization/World Health Organization (PAHO/WHO) regarding the content of the Costa Rican bill on *in vitro* fertilization and embryo transfer in the context of the human right to health (file of annexes to the merits report, volume II, folio 835).

even cause a therapeutic abortion which, in turn, negatively affects the enjoyment of the right to health and other related human rights that have been agreed on by PAHO member States."[112]

F) Specific situation of the presumed victims

F.1) Grettel Artavia Murillo and Miguel Mejías Carballo

85. Grettel Artavia Murillo and Miguel Mejías Carballo were married on December 13, 1993.[113] A work-related accident in 1985 when he was 19 years of age had left Mr Mejías permanently paraplegic;[114] the couple therefore decided to seek medical help.

86. Their doctor diagnosed that the couple would be unable to procreate naturally; thus, it was impossible to achieve a pregnancy without medical assistance. Accordingly, they underwent eight artificial insemination treatments.[115] To cover the cost of the inseminations, the couple applied for loans and mortgages; they mortgaged their home and sold some of their belongings.[116] However, the artificial inseminations were unsuccessful.[117]

87. In February 2000, their doctor informed the couple that their last alternative to treat their infertility would be to undergo IVF. One month later, on March 15, 2000, the Constitutional Chamber of Costa Rica delivered the judgment that banned this practice in the

---

[112] Pan-American Health Organization, Technical opinion of the Pan-American Health Organization/World Health Organization (PAHO/WHO) regarding the content of the Costa Rican bill on *in vitro* fertilization and embryo transfer in the context of the human right to health, folio 835.

[113] *Cf.* Certification of the Civil Registry of December 14, 2011 (file of annexes to the pleadings and motions brief, volume I, folio 4074).

[114] Mr Mejías indicated that "an embankment beside the construction buried [him] and when they were able to extract [him, he] was completely paraplegic (T10 to T12), and was told that he would never be able to walk again, because he had suffered a spinal cord injury." Testimony of Miguel Mejías Carballo at the public hearing held in this case.

[115] Brief of Ms Artavia and Mr Mejías of December 19, 2011 (file of annexes to the pleadings and motions briefs, volume I, folio 4075).

[116] In this regard, Ms Artavia indicated that "in order to meet the expenses, [her] former husband had to take out loans and mortgages which he has still not been able to pay off completely." Brief of Ms Artavia and Mr Mejías of December 19, 2011 (file of annexes to the pleadings and motions brief, volume I, folio 4075). Furthermore, Mr Mejías declared that he "had already mortgaged [his] house, had spent all [his] savings so that [they] could undergo *in vitro* fertilization in Costa Rica." Statement by Miguel Mejías Carballo at the public hearing held in this case.

[117] Brief of Ms Artavia and Mr Mejías of December 19, 2011 (file of annexes to the pleadings and motions brief, volume I, folio 4075). Similarly, Mr Mejías indicated that they had undergone all the inseminations, but "they were unsuccessful because there was a problem with [his wife's] uterus." Statement by Miguel Mejías Carballo at the public hearing held in this case.

country.[118] The couple did not have the financial resources to travel abroad to undergo the treatment.[119]

88. The couple divorced on March 10, 2001, and one of the reasons was the impossibility of having biological children.[120]

F.2) Ileana Henchoz and Miguel Yamuni

89. Miguel Antonio Yamuni Zeledón and Ileana Henchoz Bolaños were married on February 22, 1992.[121] Their family unit included a daughter from Ms Henchoz's first marriage.[122]

90. In 1994 they decided to have children. Starting in 1994 the couple underwent 16 artificial insemination treatments, which were unsuccessful.[123] In 1999, after undergoing three more artificial inseminations with another doctor, as well as other tests, they received the diagnosis that the only way they could have children was by IVF.[124] To this end, the couple underwent a series of laboratory tests.[125] Following this, their doctor indicated that "there was a suboptimal male factor, and an intracytoplasmic sperm injection procedure was performed without results."[126]

---

[118] Mr Mejías stated that, when his wife was operated on to resolve the problem she had with her uterus, and when "she was well enough to undergo the technique of *in vitro* fertilization, and [they] were happy and content, that was when it was banned and, to date, they have been unable to." Statement by Miguel Mejías Carballo at the public hearing held in this case.

[119] On this point, Ms Artavia indicated that, since the time the practice of IVF was banned, they had become desperate and frustrated "owing to the impossibility of going abroad to undergo ... this technique because of the lack of funds." Brief of Ms Artavia and Mr Mejías of December 19, 2011 (file of annexes to the pleadings and motions brief, volume I, folio 4076). Similarly, statement by Miguel Mejías Carballo during the public hearing held in this case.

[120] Brief of Ms Artavia and Mr Mejías of December 19, 2011 (file of annexes to the pleadings and motions brief, volume I, folio 4077) and Divorce certificate of March 10, 2011 (file of the State's annexes, volume VIII, folios 10269 to 10285).

[121] *Cf.* Certification of the Civil Registry of December 6, 2011 (file of annexes to the pleadings and motions brief, volume V, annex XXIX, folio 5902).

[122] Statement by Ileana Henchoz Bolaños at the public hearing in this case.

[123] In this regard, Ms Henchoz Bolaños indicated that "a doctor recommended [that they] undergo artificial insemination; [they] underwent approximately 15 or 16 artificial inseminations, but saw no results, which was very difficult because this went on for a long time." Statement by Ms Ileana Henchoz Bolaños at the public hearing held in the instant case.

[124] Affidavit of Ileana Henchoz Bolaños of December 13, 2011 (file of annexes to the pleadings and motions brief, volume V, annex XXIX, folio 5885) and Affidavit of Miguel Antonio Yamuni Zeledón of December 13, 2011 (file of annexes to the pleadings and motions brief, volume V, annex XXIX, folio 5881).

[125] *Cf.* Certifications from the *Laboratorio Clínico "La California"* of hematology, urine tests, "anti-sperm antibody test," hysterosalpingography, transvaginal ultrasound of June 1999 (file of annexes to the pleadings and motions brief, volume V, annex XXVII, folios 5700 to 5703).

[126] Written statement of Dr Gerardo Escalante Lopez of August 29, 2011 (file of annexes to the pleadings and motions brief, volume V, annex XXVII, folio 5827).

91. In 1999, Ms Henchoz underwent several procedures and medical tests; for example a myomectomy in which a fibroid was removed.[127] Her doctor stated that "in November that year, an unsuccessful insemination was performed."[128] On January 7, 2000, Ms Henchoz was prescribed ovarian stimulation medication.[129] On February 15, Ms Henchoz had two hormone laboratory tests and an ultrasound.[130]

92. On March 10, 2000, the judgment of the Constitutional Chamber was handed down; accordingly, the couple decided to travel to Spain to continue the treatment.[131] Prior to the trip, in April that year, they had several tests and were prescribed medication.[132]

93. The couple were in Spain from April 18 to 28, 2000.[133] On April 21 they underwent the necessary procedures and laboratory tests.[134] On April 23, two embryos were implanted in Ms Henchoz.[135] The cost of the treatment in Spain was 463,000 pesetas.[136]

---

[127] *Cf.* Certification of the *Centro Médico de Diagnostico por Ultrasonido "La California"* of vaginal and transvaginal ultrasounds of August and November 1999 (file of annexes to the pleadings and motions brief, volume V, annex XXVII, folios 5708, 5730 to 5733); certifications of the *Laboratorio Clínico "La California"* of hormone tests of November 23 and 25, 1999 (file of annexes to the pleadings and motions brief, volume V, annex XXVII, folios 5738, 5739 and 5742), and certification of the myomectomy of September 9, 1999 (file of annexes to the pleadings and motions brief, volume V, annex XXVII, folios 5789 and 5790).

[128] *Cf.* Written statement of Dr Gerardo Escalante Lopez of August 29, 2011 (file of annexes to the pleadings and motions brief, volume V, annex XXVII, folio 5827).

[129] *Cf.* Prescription by Dr Escalante for Ms Henchoz Bolaños of five ovary stimulation medicines of January 1, 2000 (file of annexes to the pleadings and motions brief, volume V, annex XXVII, folios 5744 and 5745).

[130] *Cf.* Certifications from *Laboratorio Clínico "La California"* for a transvaginal ultrasound and hormone tests of February 15, 2000 (file of annexes to the pleadings and motions brief, volume V, annex XXVII, folios 5748 to 5750).

[131] Affidavit of Miguel Antonio Yamuni Zeledón of December 13, 2011 (file of annexes to the pleadings and motions brief, volume V, annex XXIX, folio 5881). Similarly, Ms Henchoz Bolaños indicated that, since the only way they could have children was by undergoing IVF, "the only solution was to go abroad, because Costa Rica had just banned it. [Their] right to have children was curtailed in 2000." Affidavit of Ileana Henchoz Bolaños of December 13, 2011 (file of annexes to the pleadings and motions brief, volume V, annex XXIX, folio 5885).

[132] *Cf.* Certification of the *Laboratorio Clínico "La California"* of hormone tests and transvaginal ultrasounds of April 2000 (file of annexes to the pleadings and motions brief, volume V, annex XXVII, folio 5753 and 5756 to 5762), and hormone stimulation prescription from her doctor of April 10, 2000 (file of annexes to the pleadings and motions brief, volume V, annex XXVII, folio 5754).

[133] *Cf.* Certification of the Ministry of the Interior and Police of the exit on April 17, 2000, and entry on April 28, 2000, of Miguel Antonio Yamuni Zeledón and Ileana Henchoz Bolaños (file of annexes to the pleadings and motions brief, volume V, annex XXVII, folios 5764 and 5767); Invoice of the Hotel Renasa in Valencia dated April 24, 2000; Invoice for IVF of the *Instituto Valenciano de Infertilidad* (file of annexes to the pleadings and motions brief, volume V, annex XXVII, folio 5781).

[134] *Cf.* Certification of procedures and laboratory exams of April 21, 2000 (file of annexes to the pleadings and motions brief, volume V, annex XXVII, folios 5775 and 5776).

[135] *Cf.* Certification of embryo transfer (file of annexes to the pleadings and motions brief, volume V, annex XXVII, folio 5773).

[136] *Cf.* Invoice for treatment dated April 28, 2000 (file of annexes to the pleadings and motions brief, volume V, annex XXVII, folio 5781).

94. On May 2, 5, 8, 15 and 16, 2000, Ms Henchoz had seven hormonal tests in order to monitor her pregnancy.[137] The doctor indicated that "an IVF procedure was performed at the *Instituto Valenciano de Infertilidad* (IVI), Valencia, Spain, and a biochemical pregnancy was achieved but it disappeared in a few days. Biochemical abortion."[138]

95. The couple decided to travel to Colombia. Consequently, several medical tests were performed on Ms Henchoz for the first stage of IVF.[139] Mr Yamuni and Ms Henchoz flew to Colombia on November 25, 2000.[140] The IVF in Colombia took place between November 25 and December 3, 2000.[141] On December 5, 13, 14 and 22, 2000, Ms Henchoz underwent five hormone tests to monitor a possible pregnancy,[142] and two ultrasounds on December 19 and 27.[143] This new attempt was unsuccessful.[144] On April 27, 2001, the couple were given a cytogenetic report on the human genetics section, which indicated that there had been two abortions.[145]

---

[137] *Cf.* Certification from *Laboratorio Clínico "La California"* of hormone tests on May 2, 5, 8 and 15, 2000 (file of annexes to the pleadings and motions brief, volume V, annex XXVII, folios 5782 to 5787).

[138] *Cf.* Written statement of Dr Gerardo Escalante Lopez of August 29, 2011 (file of annexes to the pleadings and motions brief, volume V, annex XXVII, folio 5827).

[139] *Cf.* Certifications from *Laboratorio Clínico "La California"* for transvaginal ultrasounds from November 13, 20 and 23, 2000 (file of annexes to the pleadings and motions brief, volume V, annex XXVII, folios 5791 to 5794 and 5799 to 5802). Certification from *Laboratorio Clínico "La California"* for hormone test on November 15, 2000 (file of annexes to the pleadings and motions brief, volume V, annex XXVII, folio 5792).

[140] *Cf.* Certification of the Ministry of the Interior and Police of the exit on November 25, 2000, and entry on December 2, 2000, of Miguel Antonio Yamuni Zeledón and Ileana Henchoz Bolaños (file of annexes to the pleadings and motions brief, volume V, annex XXVII, folios 5764 and 5767).

[141] *Cf.* Certification of IVF from the "Conceptum" Laboratory of Bogotá, Colombia, of December 2000 (file of annexes to the pleadings and motions brief, volume V, annex XXVII, folio 5804).

[142] *Cf.* Certifications from *Laboratorio Clínico "La California"* for hormone tests on December 5, 13, 14 and 22, 2000 (file of annexes to the pleadings and motions brief, volume V, annex XXVII, folios 5805 to 5807 and 5810).

[143] *Cf.* Certifications from *Laboratorio Clínico "La California"* for transvaginal ultrasounds of December 19, 2000 (file of annexes to the pleadings and motions brief, volume V, annex XXVII, folios 5808 to 5809 and 5813 to 5814).

[144] Written statement of Dr Gerardo Escalante Lopez of August 29, 2011 (file of annexes to the pleadings and motions brief, volume V, annex XXVII, folio 5827). Similarly, Ms Henchoz Bolaños indicated that they "went to Colombia, and it was the same anguish, same lack of sleep, the same crystal box on the plane. [They] came back here and well, the baby did not happen." Statement of Ileana Henchoz Bolaños during the public hearing held in the instant case.

[145] *Cf.* Report of cytogenetic laboratory results, human genetics section, INISA, *Universidad de Costa Rica*, dated April 27, 2000 (file of annexes to the pleadings and motions brief, volume V, annex XXIX, folios 5817 and 5818).

F.3) Oriéster Rojas and Julieta González

96. Oriéster Rojas and Julieta González were married on July 20, 1996.[146] Several months later and in view of the absence of a pregnancy for Ms González, Mr Rojas started a treatment with the Costa Rican Social Security Institute. Between 1997 and 1999, Mr Rojas had an operation and various medical tests.[147]

97. On February 6, 2001, Ms González initiated the first stage to prepare for IVF, and was issued with two prescriptions for the medicines known as Puregon and Lupron,[148] so as to be able to undergo IVF in Panama. On March 3, 5, 9 and 12, 2001, Ms González started the ovulation induction cycle, one of the required prior steps, in order to subsequently travel to Panama for the IVF.[149]

98. Mr Rojas and Ms González were in Panama from March 13 to 20, 2001, in order to undergo the IVF procedure.[150] The IVF procedure was performed with intracytoplasmic sperm injection (ICSI) due to the severe male factor.[151] After this procedure they were prescribed several medicines.[152]

99. Upon returning from Panama Ms González again underwent hormone tests, which determined that there was no pregnancy.[153]

100. On January 23, 2002, Ms González and Mr. Rojas began a direct adoption procedure,[154] which was authorized.[155]

---

[146] Cf. Marriage certificate of Oriéster Rojas and Julieta González (file of annexes to the pleadings and motions brief, volume VIII, folio 10247).

[147] Cf. Medical records of Oriéster Rojas at the Costa Rican Social Security Institute's Hospital Mexico, medical examinations, reports, certifications and prescriptions of August, October and December 1997, May and July 1999 (file of annexes to the pleadings and motions brief, volume II, folios 4224 to 4234, 4256, 4257 and 4258).

[148] Cf. Medical records of Julieta González Rojas at the Costa Rican Social Security Institute's Hospital Mexico (file of annexes to the pleadings and motions brief, volume II, folios 4263 and 4264).

[149] Cf. Medical records of Julieta González, medical examinations and ultrasounds of March 3, 5, 9 and 12, 2001 (file of annexes to the pleadings and motions brief, volume II, folios 4270 to 4281).

[150] Cf. Receipts from Hotel Roma for March 13 to 16, 2001 (file of annexes to the pleadings and motions brief, volume II, folios 4283 to 4285).

[151] Cf. Certification by the treating physician that "[Julieta González] underwent ICSI in Panama, where she had to stay for three more days before returning to the country." Certification of June 8, 2001 (file of annexes to the pleadings and motions brief, volume II, folio 4300).

[152] Cf. Prescriptions issued by the treating physician (file of annexes to the pleadings and motions brief, volume II, folios 4286, 4289 and 4290); prescriptions issued by Clínica Hospital San Fernando (file of annexes to the pleadings and motions brief, volume II, folios 4288 and 4290), and receipts from several pharmacies, March 2001 (file of annexes to the pleadings and motions brief, volume II, folios 4287 and 4293).

[153] Cf. Medical records of Julieta González, medical examination of March 30, 2001 (file of annexes to the pleadings and motions brief, volume II, folio 4299).

[154] Cf. Adoption file of Oriéster Rojas and Julieta González, Notification of start of the adoption procedure (file of annexes to the pleadings and motions brief, volume II, folio 4302).

[155] Cf. Judgment No 318, File No 02-000029-0673-FA-3 authorizing the adoption (file of annexes to the pleadings and motions brief, volume II, folios 4498 to 4501).

F.4) Víctor Sanabria León and Claudia Carro Maklouf

101. Claudia Carro Maklouf and Víctor Sanabria were married on April 16, 1999. Ms Carro had three children from her first marriage, while Mr Sanabria had no children from his first marriage.[156] Before their marriage, the couple had both been to the doctor and, on September 21, 1998, Mr Sanabria was diagnosed with "hypomotility sperm" and "elevated seminal viscosity,"[157] associated with male infertility, a pathology that, if not corrected, would result in a low probability of obtaining a natural pregnancy.[158]

102. Meanwhile, Ms Carro, following a series of medical tests that included a hysterosalpingogram, was diagnosed with tubal damage; hence it was recommended that they undergo IVF.[159] In October 1998 she underwent surgery to repair the possible tubal damage. In December 1999, Ms Carro underwent the first IVF attempt, which was unsuccessful. In early 2000, Ms Carro had another operation.[160]

103. Owing to the Constitutional Chamber's judgment, the couple went to Spain to undergo IVF at the *Instituto Valenciano de Infertilidad* (hereinafter "IVI") in Madrid.[161]

104. The couple traveled to Spain in October 2001.[162] On October 22, 2001, the IVI issued an invoice for 413,000 Spanish pesetas, for "professional services to the patient."[163] The IVF performed in Spain was not successful, thus there was no pregnancy.[164]

105. The couple initiated an adoption procedure on December 10, 2002, and they were given the temporary guardianship of a

---

[156] *Cf.* Affidavit of Claudia María Carro Maklouf, "Life story."
[157] *Cf.* Medical certification from Dr Gerardo Escalante López dated August 12, 2011 (file of annexes to the pleadings and motions brief, volume II, folio 4700).
[158] *Cf.* Medical certification from Dr Gerardo Escalante López dated November 14, 2011 (file of annexes to the pleadings and motions brief, volume II, folio 4702).
[159] *Cf.* Medical certification from Dr Gerardo Escalante López dated August 29, 2011: "... with a history of infertility owing to posterior bilateral tubal impermeability after two caesarean sections during her first marriage" (file of annexes to the pleadings and motions brief, volume I, folio 4119).
[160] *Cf.* Medical certification from Dr Gerardo Escalante López dated August 29, 2011 (file of annexes to the pleadings and motions brief, volume I, folio 4119).
[161] To this end, she had to take daily doses of Lupron subcutaneously. *Cf.* Medical certification of Dr Gerardo Escalante López of October 1, 2001 (file of annexes to the pleadings and motions brief, volume II, folio 4688).
[162] *Cf.* Voucher for purchase of plane ticket dated September 20, 2001 (file of annexes to the pleadings and motions brief, volume II, folio 4695).
[163] *Cf.* Invoice for 413,000 Spanish pesetas issued by the IVI on October 22, 2001, in the name of Carro Maklouf, Claudia (file of annexes to the pleadings and motions brief, volume II, folio 4690).
[164] *Cf.* Psychiatric expert appraisal: "[t]wo embryos are implanted and the result is negative" (file of annexes to the pleadings and motions brief, volume I, folio 4127).

girl child.[165] Ms Carro and Mr Sanabria separated in November 2003, and were divorced on January 27, 2005.[166] On December 1, 2006, Mr Sanabria adopted a girl child on an individual basis[167] and, in April 2009, Ms Carro adopted a boy child on an individual basis.[168]

F.5) Giovanni Vega and Joaquinita Arroyo

106. Joaquinita Arroyo and Giovanni Vega were married on December 8, 1989.[169]

107. Around October 1990, since she had not become pregnant, Ms Vega began a medical treatment that entailed several tests.[170] Following this treatment, 12 artificial inseminations were performed.[171] Mr Vega also underwent several medical tests.[172]

108. The couple went to another doctor, and another series of artificial insemination procedures were performed. On some occasions, two inseminations were performed in a single cycle.[173]

---

[165] *Cf.* Adoption file, authorization by the National Child Welfare Agency, Adoptions Office, for the delivery of the child to Víctor Hugo Sanabria León and Claudia María Carro Maklouf on May 19, 2003 (file of annexes to the pleadings and motions brief, volume III, folio 4776).

[166] *Cf.* Civil Registry Office, Divorce certificate dated December 16, 2011 (file of annexes to the pleadings and motions brief, volume I, folio 4118).

[167] *Cf.* Judicial decision approving the request for individual adoption filed by Víctor Hugo Sanabria Leon dated December 1, 2006 (file of annexes to the pleadings and motions brief, volume III, folios 4928 to 4932).

[168] *Cf.* Psychiatric expert appraisal: "In 2009 [Claudia María Carro Maklouf] adopt[ed] her son" (file of annexes to the pleadings and motions brief, volume I, folio 4128).

[169] *Cf.* Certification of the Civil Registry of March 22, 2012 (file of annexes to the pleadings and motions brief, volume VIII, folio 10251).

[170] "In February 1991, the medical evaluations began to determine why [she] was not becoming pregnant, [her] ovulation was monitored for several cycles and [she] received treatments to stimulate ovulation." Affidavit of Joaquinita Arroyo Fonseca (file of annexes to the pleadings and motions brief, volume IV, annex XI, folio 5266). *Cf.* Certification of anovulation from *Clínica Ultrasonido Paseo Colon SA* dated October 15, 1991, and prescription for progesterone: 1 ml, and Omifin for five days (file of annexes to the pleadings and motions brief, volume III, annex X, folio 4990).

[171] Affidavit of Joaquinita Arroyo Fonseca (file of annexes to the pleadings and motions brief, volume III, annex X, folios 5266 and 5267). *Cf.* Certifications from *Clínica Ultrasonido Paseo Colon SA* of ultrasounds for follicular monitoring of March 24 and 27, and September 7, 1992 (file of annexes to the pleadings and motions brief, volume III, annex X, folios 4991, 4993, 4994 and 5267).

[172] *Cf.* Certification from *Laboratorio Clínico Doctor Valenciano*, UCR, of an ultrasound for follicular monitoring of April 23, 1992 (file of annexes to the pleadings and motions brief, volume III, annex X, folio 4992). Certification from *Laboratorio Clínico Doctor Valenciano*, UCR, for a spermogram dated March 29, 1995 (file of annexes to the pleadings and motions brief, volume III, annex X, folio 5003).

[173] In this regard Joaquinita Arroyo indicated that they "began the testing protocol that included fresh procedures to monitor ovulation, ultrasounds, a radiological study of the uterine cavity and

109. On October 25, 2000, Ms Arroyo underwent a laparoscopy in order to determine the reasons for her inability to conceive a child.[174] On October 13, 2001, her doctor classified the case as "unknown cause" and referred the couple to the Barraquer Clinic in Colombia, in order to undergo IVF.[175]

110. The couple programmed a trip to Colombia around October 25, 2001;[176] but this trip to Colombia, where the second phase of IVF would be carried out, was not made. Once again, the couple decided to begin preparing for IVF to be performed in Colombia; however, on March 7, 2002, Ms Arroyo was diagnosed with "intramural fibroids."[177] On April 4, 2002, she had a uterine myomectomy.[178] On April 15 a biopsy was carried out.[179]

111. In 2003, the couple adopted a child. In 2006, Ms Arroyo became pregnant and gave birth to a daughter on June 25, 2007.[180]

F.6) Karen Espinoza and Héctor Jiménez

112. Ms Espinoza and Mr Jiménez were married on February 10, 2001. Towards the end of 2001, the couple sought medical treatment, in order to obtain a pregnancy. During this treatment they underwent several tests.[181] On July 23, 2002, Ms Espinoza had a laparoscopy

---

Fallopian tubes." Affidavit of Joaquinita Arroyo Fonseca (file of annexes to the pleadings and motions brief, volume IV, annex XI, folio 5268), and Certifications from the *Centro Médico de Diagnostico por Ultrasonido "La California"* of vaginal ultrasounds of April 18, May 14 and September 5, 1996, and October 28 and 29, 1997 (file of annexes to the pleadings and motions brief, volume III, annex X, folios 5010, 5011, 5014, 5016 and 5017).

[174] *Cf.* Certification of diagnosis laparoscopy from the Costa Rican Social Security Institute's Hospital Mexico (file of annexes to the pleadings and motions brief, volume III, annex X, folios 5044 to 5046).

[175] *Cf.* Report of the treating physician referring the case to the specialist at the Barraquer Clinic in Bogotá, Colombia, dated October 13, 2001 (file of annexes to the pleadings and motions brief, volume III, annex X, folio 5050).

[176] Affidavit of Joaquinita Arroyo Fonseca (file of annexes to the pleadings and motions brief, volume IV, annex X, folio 5271).

[177] *Cf.* Certification from *Centro Médico de Diagnostico por Ultrasonido "La California"* for a transvaginal ultrasound on March 7, 2002 (file of annexes to the pleadings and motions brief, volume III, annex X, folio 5051).

[178] *Cf.* Certification from the *Asociación Hospital Clínica Católica de la Purisima Concepción* of uterine myomectomy of April 4, 2002 (file of annexes to the pleadings and motions brief, volume III, annex X, folios 5053 to 5082).

[179] *Cf.* Certification from *Laboratorio "Itopat" SA* of April 15, 2002 (file of annexes to the pleadings and motions brief, volume III, annex X, folio 5084).

[180] *Cf.* Birth certification of Sofia Alejandra Vega Arroyo from the Civil Registry dated December 6, 2011 (file of annexes to the pleadings and motions brief, volume IV, annex XI, folio 5316).

[181] *Cf.* Certifications of gynecological ultrasound, mammography, hysterosalpingography, spermogram and blood tests carried out in 2002 (file of annexes to the pleadings and motions brief, volume IV, annex XIV, folios 5462 to 5486).

owing to a diagnosis of endometriosis, seven-year primary infertility and tubal impermeability.[182]

113. Between August 2002 and 2004 the couple continued undergoing medical examinations[183] and laboratory tests.[184] In 2004, Ms Espinoza underwent three artificial inseminations and one laparoscopy, which determined "the presence of pelvic endometriosis and anatomic anomaly due to a primary tubal infertility factor" in the patient and, consequently, "the doctor recommended moving on to the assisted reproduction technique [IVF] as a conception method for her and her husband."[185]

114. On January 24, 2006, Ms Espinoza underwent an exploratory laparotomy due to infertility and pelvic pain.[186] In 2006, her doctor issued a second opinion about resorting to IVF. Consequently, the first phase of IVF was performed twice in Costa Rica in order to go to Colombia. However, there was no ovarian response;[187] therefore they did not continue with the following stage of IVF.

115. On October 26, 2007, the couple had a daughter by natural pregnancy.[188]

F.7) Carlos Eduardo de Jesús Vargas Solórzano and María del Socorro Calderón Porras

116. María del Socorro Calderón had two children from her first marriage. She began to live with Mr Vargas in 1989 and they were married in 1995.[189]

---

[182] *Cf.* Brief of the treating physician (file of annexes to the pleadings and motions brief, volume IV, annex XIV, folio 5512).

[183] *Cf.* Certifications of transvaginal ultrasounds and hormone tests, among other tests, carried out in 2002 (file of annexes to the pleadings and motions brief, volume IV, annex XIV, folios 5487 to 5499).

[184] *Cf.* Certifications of laboratory tests of March 16, 19, 20, 22 and 24, 2004 (file of annexes to the pleadings and motions brief, volume IV, annex XIV, folios 5503 to 5509).

[185] *Cf.* Brief of the treating physician (file of annexes to the pleadings and motions brief, volume IV, annex XIV, folio 5512).

[186] In this regard, Ms Karen Espinoza indicated that "in 2004, it was determined that [she] ha[d] cysts of a considerable size, and at Hospital Mexico [she] had an operation with a possible risk of hysterectomy." Affidavit of Karen Espinoza Vindas (file of annexes to the pleadings and motions brief, volume IV, annex XVI, folio 5567).

[187] Affidavit of Karen Espinoza Vindas (file of annexes to the pleadings and motions brief, volume IV, annex XVI, folio 5567).

[188] *Cf.* Birth certificate from the Civil Registry of December 6, 2011 (file of annexes to the pleadings and motions brief, volume IV, annex XVI, folio 5572).

[189] *Cf.* Affidavit of María del Socorro Calderón Porras of December 11, 2011 (file of annexes to the pleadings and motions brief, volume IV, folio 5616) and marriage certificate from the Civil

117. In 1994, a doctor told Ms Calderón that another doctor had cut her Fallopian tubes.[190] Subsequently, ovarian cysts were discovered and she had an operation. Then, Mr Vargas was diagnosed with varicocele, which called for various tests based on which it was determined that the only option that the couple had to conceive would be by IVF.[191]

118. Following the judgment of the Constitutional Chamber of March 15, 2000, the doctor explained the need to use medication and to travel abroad to carry out the second phase of IVF.[192] The couple decided to adopt a child, but they were not awarded custody of a child.[193]

F.8) Enrique Acuña Cartín and Ana Cristina Castillo León

119. Enrique Acuña Cartín and Ana Cristina Castillo León were married on September 27, 1988.[194] After four years of marriage they started to seek a pregnancy. While undergoing tests, Mr Acuña was diagnosed with varicocele in 1997, and it was found that the low spermatozoid count would make natural conception impossible; it was therefore suggested that they resort to IVF.[195]

120. Meanwhile, Ms Castillo went to several doctors and she was diagnosed with endometriosis and retroverted uterus. It was also determined that Ms Castillo suffered from "third degree prolapse of the uterus" and endometriosis in the Fallopian tubes. She therefore underwent surgery to correct the "prolapse" and inspect her Fallopian tubes. She also underwent hormone treatment to suspend her menstrual period for over a year.[196]

Registry dated December 6, 2011 (file of annexes to the pleadings and motions brief, volume IV, folio 5631).

[190] *Cf.* Affidavit of María del Socorro Calderón Porras of December 11, 2011 (file of annexes to the pleadings and motions brief, volume IV, folio 5616).

[191] He underwent a varicocelectomy, which improved the condition of his spermazoids by 60%, but without achieving normal parameters. Owing to both the irreversible tubal factor in the patient, and her spouse's male factor, the only option for this couple to conceive would be by *in vitro* fertilization. *Cf.* Attestation of the treating physician dated November 16, 2011 (file of annexes to the pleadings and motions brief, volume IV, folio 5614).

[192] *Cf.* Medical certification of Dr Ribas of November 16, 2011 (file of annexes to the pleadings and motions brief, volume IV, folio 5613).

[193] *Cf.* Affidavit of María del Socorro Calderón Porras of December 11, 2011 (file of annexes to the pleadings and motions brief, volume IV, folio 5618).

[194] *Cf.* Marriage certification from the Civil Registry dated December 6, 2011 (file of annexes to the pleadings and motions brief, volume IV, folio 5678).

[195] *Cf.* Affidavit of Enrique Francisco Acuña Cartín of December 7, 2011 (file of annexes to the pleadings and motions brief, volume IV, folio 5671), and attestation of the treating physician of October 27, 2011 (file of annexes to the pleadings and motions brief, volume I, folio 4080).

[196] *Cf.* Testimony of Ana Cristina Castillo León (file of annexes to the pleadings and motions brief, volume I, folio 4102).

121. Subsequently, the couple underwent 11 artificial inseminations.[197] In March 2000, Ms Castillo was following a medical protocol to control the problems diagnosed and awaiting the result of the latest insemination and, if the results were not positive, the next step would be to undergo the first IVF.[198]

122. Finally, Mr Acuña and Ms Castillo were divorced on March 21, 2007.[199]

F.9) Andrea Bianchi Bruna and Germán Moreno Valencia

123. Andrea Bianchi Bruna and Germán Moreno Valencia were married on June 15, 1996.[200]

124. After three years of marriage and since they were unable to achieve a pregnancy, the couple sought medical treatment. During the treatment Ms Bianchi underwent several medical tests, including a hysterosalpingogram, which revealed that she suffered from endometriosis.[201] Accordingly, Ms Bianchi underwent a first operation, an exploratory laparoscopy,[202] which revealed total obstruction of her Fallopian tubes. The doctor therefore indicated that there was no possibility of a pregnancy, because this involved using the passage through the Fallopian tubes.[203]

125. During 2000 the couple underwent three artificial inseminations without success. Following the March 15 judgment of the Constitutional Chamber, the couple were advised that their only option to achieve a pregnancy would be to travel to another country to do so and, in June 2001, it was recommended that they leave for Colombia immediately owing to the unexpected development of follicles in the ovary. The couple traveled to Bogotá, Colombia, to begin the tests. After several medical evaluations, IVF was performed;

---

[197] *Cf.* Affidavit of Enrique Francisco Acuña Cartín of December 7, 2011 (file of annexes to the pleadings and motions brief, volume IV, folio 5673).
[198] *Cf.* Testimony of Ana Cristina Castillo León (file of annexes to the pleadings and motions brief, volume I, folio 4103).
[199] *Cf.* Divorce certificate from the Civil Registry dated March 21, 2007 (file of annexes to the pleadings and motions brief, volume I, folio 4079).
[200] *Cf.* Marriage certificate from the Civil Registry dated December 19, 2011 (file of annexes to the pleadings and motions brief, volume I, folio 4107).
[201] *Cf.* Expansion of the expert deposition of Dr Delia Ribas (file of annexes to the pleadings and motions brief, volume I, folio 2374).
[202] *Cf.* Expansion of the expert deposition of Dr Delia Ribas (file of annexes to the pleadings and motions brief, volume V, folio 2374).
[203] *Cf.* Testimony of Andrea Bianchi Bruna and Germán Moreno Valencia of December 2011 (file of annexes to the pleadings and motions brief, volume I, folio 4112).

however, the procedure was unsuccessful.[204] In December 2001, the couple returned to Colombia, where a second IVF was performed.[205] On December 17, 2001, the pregnancy test was positive. Ms Bianchi gave birth to twins on July 11, 2002.[206]

VII. PRIOR CONSIDERATION ON THE PURPOSE OF THE INSTANT CASE

Arguments of the Commission and the parties

126. Representative Molina argued that, in this case, "the State of Costa Rica has, for over 11 years, maintained a consistent and ongoing policy of banning [IVF] and any other method of assisted reproduction, and this has permeated not only the acts and omissions of all branches of the State, but has extend[ed] to encouraging among civil society the repudiation of persons who suffer from this type of reproductive disability."[207] He also argued that, "after the ruling, the victims suffered social stigmatization that undermined their honor and social reputation." In this regard, he argued that "[t]he disclosure in the media of the ban on IVF, and the way that infertility was characterized by some persons[,] stigmatized the [presumed] victims and their family and violated their right to privacy. [In addition,] in their campaign against IVF, some of the media emitted offensive and denigrating messages against the plaintiffs in general, affecting their mental health." He added that the presumed "victims of the case were judged by civil society based on the lack of information on the subject; [thus] value judgments were constantly made in the different media with a broad range of defamatory terms, aimed at denigrating the struggle undertaken by these couples."

---

[204] *Cf.* Testimony of Andrea Bianchi Bruna and Germán Moreno Valencia of December 2011 (file of annexes to the pleadings and motions brief, volume I, folios 4113 to 4116).

[205] *Cf.* Testimony of Andrea Bianchi Bruna and Germán Moreno Valencia of December 2011; "By December we had saved enough for the second attempt . . ." (file of annexes to the pleadings and motions brief, volume I, folio 4116).

[206] *Cf.* Testimony of Andrea Bianchi Bruna and Germán Moreno Valencia of December 2011 (file of annexes to the pleadings and motions brief, volume I, folio 4116).

[207] In this regard, he added that the alleged "State policy [was] demonstrated by several and continuous acts and omissions of the State," for example: (i) "[t]he Constitutional Chamber's prohibition of the practice of . . . IVF"; (ii) "the Chamber's prohibition that the Legislature perform its function [of] legislating on the matter"; (iii) "the inactivity of the Legislature and the Executive regarding assisted reproduction methods"; (iv) "a complaint before the Ombudsman's Office"; (v) "an administrative proceeding"; and (vi) "an action on unconstitutionality against the Chamber's decision."

127. With regard to the public exposure of the presumed victims, representative May argued that "... the pain and suffering derived from the public exposure of the private life of the victims to society and the media persists, because it is clear that, ultimately, this is a fundamental and decisive consequence of the Constitutional Chamber's judgment."

128. Regarding the arguments of the representatives, the State presented a preliminary objection (*supra* para. 40) that these facts were not included in the brief submitting the case presented by the Commission, and were not supervening facts. It also argued that IVF "not only does not resolve the health problems of infertile persons, mainly women, but also increases the risks to their health[, inasmuch as] women can suffer from the syndrome of ovarian hyperstimulation, which in some cases can cause electrolyte imbalance, hepatic dysfunction and thrombotic phenomena that can be fatal. Other complications include bleeding, infection and adnexal torsion, which can put the mother's life at risk."[208] Furthermore, the State argued that "the psychological effects of IVF on women and on couples are well documented."[209] In addition, the State argued potential damage to the children conceived with the assistance of IVF and "abnormal syndromes."[210] The State asserted that "another problem associated with IVF technique and ovarian hyperstimulation is the generation of multiple births [which] are common in this practice," and which imply "a danger to the health of women."[211]

129. Regarding the cryoconservation of embryos, the State argued that "to achieve adequate conservation ... cryoprotectors are used;

---

[208] It assured that "[t]he mortality rate in pregnancies using [IVF] is higher than the rate of maternal mortality in the general population, [because it can] cause complications during birth and preeclampsia, as well as an increase in the risk of endometrial cancer and ovarian tumors."

[209] It indicated that, "the psychological problems reported in patients that undergo [IVF] include, above all, depression, anxiety, unresolved mourning; in addition to problems for the couple, in both their sexual relationship and life style."

[210] It argued that "in children conceived with the assistance of the [IVF] technique the risk is 2 times higher for heart septum defects, 2.4 times higher for harelip, with or without cleft palate, 4.5 times higher for esophageal atresia, 3.7 times higher for anal atresia, 9.8 times higher for gastrointestinal anomalies, and 1.54 times higher for musculoskeletal defects, in relation to children conceived naturally. In addition, ... it is more frequent to find abnormal syndromes." Furthermore, it indicated that "other studies ... show that [IVF] could be related to an alteration of the epigenetic changes in the gametes [IVF], thus affecting overall patterns of methylation and genetic regulation, and these changes could affect genetic expression in the long-term."

[211] It argued that "if multiple pregnancies are compared to single pregnancies, twins and triplets are, respectively, four and eight times more prone to perinatal death and have a higher risk of presenting disabilities in the long term." It indicated that an alternative for multiple births ... is a practice named "embryo reduction," a technique "intended to cause the selective death of the embryos already implanted," considering it a type of "provoked abortion" and thus subject to criminal sanctions.

these are chemical agents that ... exercise a certain degree of toxicity on the embryos depending on their concentration and the time that they are exposed." At the same time, "freezing and unfreezing embryos can cause alterations to their morphologic characteristics and the survival rate of blastocysts, which could translate into lower implantation rates." Lastly, the State indicated that "[IVF] entails a number of dilemmas and legal problems that are equally profound and complex to resolve." In this regard, it mentioned the following issues: (i) "there is no consensus ... regarding the legal status of frozen embryos, and on the regulation and duration of their conservation and purpose. Specifically, these situations are problematic when the parents ... separate or divorce"; (ii) "the separation of the parents who have frozen their embryos can lead to the problem of forced paternity ... if one of the parents demands the implantation of the embryo in spite of the separation or divorce," and (iii) "[IVF] poses a far-reaching problem with regard to the regulation of paternity," in particular the problem of "the paternity rights of the husband of the woman who under[went] a heterogeneous [IVF]—with genetic material from a man other than her husband or partner," given that "one of the essential factors to determine paternity is the determination of the genetic material."[212]

Considerations of the Court

130. The Inter-American Commission focused the purpose of this case on the effects of the judgment delivered by the Constitutional Chamber. However, the parties have presented arguments concerning the following issues, which exceed the analysis made in the Constitutional Chamber's judgment, namely: (i) a presumed "context" alleged by representative Molina; (ii) the alleged interference of the media and society in the private life of the presumed victims; and (iii) general arguments about the problems that IVF could represent. In order to determine the purpose of this case, the

---

[212] The State added that (iv) another area "where there is no consensus is the area of the maternity rights of the ovule donor or surrogate mother—an assumption that would have to be considered in the event that the sterile woman lacks a uterus"; (v) regarding "posthumous conception," meaning "when the woman requests the implanting of the frozen embryos of her husband or partner who is deceased ... conception occurs after the death of the bearer of the genetic material" and this "poses an unresolved question ... the inheritance rights of a child born from this conception," and (vi) "the regulation of the liability regime for clinics and doctors who practice [IVF] is particularly sensitive in cases where genetic material has been confused and embryos that are not her own have been implanted in a woman."

Court will establish whether these disputes fall within the framework of the case.

131. First, the Court has established that the factual framework of the proceedings before the Court consists of the facts included in the merits report submitted to the Court's consideration.[213] Consequently, it is not admissible for the parties to argue new facts that differ from the contents of this report, without prejudice to describing those that explain, clarify or reject the facts that it mentions and that were submitted to the Court's consideration.[214] The exceptions to this principle are facts categorized as supervening, provided that they are related to the facts of the proceedings. In addition, the presumed victims and their representatives can invoke the violation of rights other than those included in the merits report, provided they abide by the facts contained in the said document, because the presumed victims are the holders of all the rights recognized in the Convention.[215] In summary, it corresponds to the Court to decide in each case on the admissibility of arguments related to the factual framework in order to safeguard the procedural equality of the parties.[216]

132. The Court notes that the Commission did not allege the context mentioned by representative Molina. However, the facts used by the representative to allege this context were described by the Inter-American Commission in its merits report. In this regard, the Court considers that the representative did not provide sufficient information or arguments to allow it to be considered that this case falls within the framework of "a State policy" against IVF and "any other method of assisted reproduction" in Costa Rica. Therefore, the Court considers that this case is not related to the alleged "State policy" presented by representative Molina. Notwithstanding the above, it will take into account the facts described by the representative when analyzing the merits.

---

[213] *Cf. Case of the Five Pensioners* v. *Peru. Merits, reparations and costs.* Judgment of February 28, 2003. Series C No 98, para. 153, and *Case of Vélez Restrepo and family* v. *Colombia*, para. 47.

[214] *Cf. Case of the Five Pensioners* v. *Peru. Merits, reparations and costs.* Judgment of February 28, 2003. Series C No 98, para. 153, and *Case of the Río Negro Massacres* v. *Guatemala. Preliminary objection, merits, reparations and costs.* Judgment of September 4, 2012. Series C No 250, para. 52.

[215] *Cf. Case of the Five Pensioners* v. *Peru. Merits, reparations and costs*, para. 153, and *Case of the Río Negro Massacres* v. *Guatemala. Preliminary objection, merits, reparations and costs.* Judgment of September 4, 2012. Series C No 250, para. 52.

[216] *Cf. Case of the Mapiripán Massacre* v. *Colombia. Merits, reparations and costs.* Judgment of September 15, 2005. Series C No 134, para. 58, and *Case of Vélez Restrepo and family* v. *Colombia*, para. 47.

133. In relation to the violations alleged by the two representatives on the interference of the media and society in the private life of the presumed victims, regarding which the State filed a preliminary objection (*supra* para. 40), the Court observes that the facts that support this argument were not included in the merits report issued by the Commission; therefore, they will not be considered part of the factual framework of the case.

134. Lastly, the Court underscores that the State presented general arguments related to the presumed effects or problems that IVF could cause in relation to: (i) potential risks that the practice could have for women; (ii) alleged psychological effects on couples who seek this treatment; (iii) presumed genetic risks to the embryos and the children born as a result of the treatment; (iv) the alleged risk of multiple births; (v) the supposed problems resulting from cryoconservation of embryos; and (vi) the possible legal problems and dilemmas that could arise from the application of the technique.

135. In this regard, the Court considers that although the State produced evidence and arguments regarding the above, in order to analyze their merits, the Court will only take into account the evidence and allegations related to the arguments explicitly used in the reasoning of the Constitutional Chamber's judgment. Thus, and based on the subsidiary nature of the inter-American system,[217] the Court is not competent to decide disputes that were not taken into account by the Constitutional Chamber to support the judgment that declared Executive Decree No 24029-S unconstitutional.

VIII. RIGHT TO PRIVATE AND FAMILY LIFE AND RIGHT TO PERSONAL INTEGRITY IN RELATION TO PERSONAL AUTONOMY, SEXUAL AND REPRODUCTIVE HEALTH, THE RIGHT TO ENJOY THE BENEFITS OF SCIENTIFIC AND TECHNOLOGICAL PROGRESS AND THE PRINCIPLE OF NON-DISCRIMINATION

136. In this chapter, the Court will determine, first, the scope of the rights to privacy and to family life, and their relationship with other treaty-based rights, as relevant to settling the dispute (A). Next, it will

---

[217] *Cf. Case of Acevedo Jaramillo et al. v. Peru. Interpretation of the Judgment on preliminary objections, merits, reparations and costs.* Judgment of November 24, 2006. Series C No 157, para. 66, and *Case of Cabrera García and Montiel Flores v. Mexico. Preliminary objection, merits, reparations and costs.* Judgment of November 26, 2010. Series C No 220, para. 16.

analyze the effects of the ban on IVF (B). Then, it will interpret Article 4(1) of the American Convention as relevant to this case (C). Finally, it will decide the alleged violation of the treaty-based rights of the presumed victims in light of a determination of proportionality (D).

A) Scope of the rights to personal integrity,[218] personal liberty,[219] and private and family life[220] in this case

Arguments of the Commission and allegations of the parties

137. The Commission observed that "the decision ... to have biological children ... belongs to the most intimate sphere of private and family life, [and ...] the way in which couples arrive at this decision is part of a person's autonomy and identity, both as an individual and as a partner." It indicated that "living together and the possibility of procreating is part of the right to found a family." It considered that "[t]he use of IVF to combat infertility is also closely related to the enjoyment of the benefits of scientific progress."

138. Representative Molina argued that "the couple's decision on whether or not to have children occurs in the private sphere," and described the infertility of the presumed victims as a "disability owing to which they have been discriminated against as regards having a family."

139. Representative May argued that the regulation [of IVF] should "develop and facilitate the content of the rights to health, access to scientific progress, respect for privacy and autonomy in the family sphere, the right to found a family and the full exercise of the reproductive rights of the individual."

140. The State argued that "the possibility of procreating by means of *in vitro* fertilization techniques ... is not a right recognized in the context of personal liberty," and that "[e]ven though the right to found a family includes the possibility of procreating, the State should not permit this possibility at any cost." Furthermore, it argued that

---

[218] The pertinent part of Article 5 of the American Convention (Right to Humane Treatment) indicates: "1. Every person has the right to have his physical, mental, and moral integrity respected ..."
[219] The pertinent part of Article 7 of the American Convention (Right to Personal Liberty) indicates: "1. Every person has the right to personal liberty and security."
[220] The pertinent part of Article 11 of the American Convention (Right to Privacy) states: "... 2. No one may be the object of arbitrary or abusive interference with his private life, his family, his home, or his correspondence, or of unlawful attacks on his honor or reputation ..."
The pertinent part of Article 17 of the American Convention (Rights of the Family), indicates: "1. The family is the natural and fundamental group unit of society and is entitled to protection by society and the state. 2. The right of men and women of marriageable age to marry and to raise a family shall be recognized, if they meet the conditions required by domestic laws, insofar as such conditions do not affect the principle of nondiscrimination established in this Convention."

"[h]uman life and dignity does not need to prove its nature in the face of the demands of scientific or medical progress."

Considerations of the Court

141. As indicated previously (*supra* para. 3), the Commission considered that the prohibition of IVF violated Articles 11(2), 17(2) and 24, in relation to Article 1(1) of the American Convention, to the detriment of the presumed victims. The common interveners added the presumed violation of Articles 4(1), 5(1) and 7 of the Convention, in relation to Articles 1(1) and 2 thereof. The State rejected the violation of all these rights. In this regard, the Court observes that a dispute exists between the parties regarding the rights that were allegedly violated in this case. The Court will now proceed to interpret the American Convention in order to determine the scope of the rights to personal integrity and to private and family life, as relevant to decide the dispute.

142. Article 11 of the American Convention requires the State to protect individuals against the arbitrary actions of State institutions that affect private and family life. It prohibits any arbitrary or abusive interference with the private life of the individual, indicating different spheres of this, such as the private life of the family. Thus, the Court has held that the private sphere is characterized by being exempt from and immune to abusive or arbitrary interference or attacks by third parties or by public authorities.[221] In addition, this Court has interpreted Article 7 of the American Convention broadly when indicating that it includes a concept of liberty in a broad sense as the ability to do and not do all that is lawfully permitted. In other words, every person has the right to organize, in keeping with the law, his or her individual and social life according to his or her own choices and beliefs. Liberty, thus defined, is a basic human right, inherent in the attributes of the person, that is evident throughout the American Convention.[222] The Court has also underscored the concept of liberty and the possibility of all human beings to self-determination and to choose freely the options and circumstances that give meaning to their life, according to their own choices and beliefs.[223]

---

[221] *Cf. Case of the Ituango Massacres* v. *Colombia. Preliminary objection, merits, reparations and costs.* Judgment of July 1, 2006. Series C No 148, para. 194, and *Case of Atala Riffo and daughters* v. *Chile. Merits, reparations and costs.* Judgment of February 24, 2012. Series C No 239, para. 161.
[222] *Cf. Case of Chaparro Álvarez and Lapo Íñiguez* v. *Ecuador. Preliminary objections, merits, reparations and costs.* Judgment of November 21, 2007. Series C No 170, para. 52.
[223] *Cf. Case of Atala Riffo and daughters* v. *Chile*, para. 136. Mutatis mutandis, *Case of Chaparro Álvarez and Lapo Íñiguez* v. *Ecuador. Preliminary objections, merits, reparations and costs.* Judgment of November 21, 2007. Series C No 170, para. 52.

143. The scope of the protection of the right to private life has been interpreted in broad terms by the international human rights courts, when indicating that this goes beyond the right to privacy.[224] The protection of private life encompasses a series of factors associated with the dignity of the individual, including, for example, the ability to develop his or her own personality and aspirations, to determine his or her own identity and to define his or her own personal relationships. The concept of private life encompasses aspects of physical and social identity, including the right to personal autonomy, personal development and the right to establish and develop relationships with other human beings and with the outside world.[225] The effective exercise of the right to private life is decisive for the possibility of exercising personal autonomy on the future course of relevant events for a person's quality of life.[226] Private life includes the way in which the individual views himself and how he decides to project this view towards others,[227] and is an essential condition for the free development of the personality. Furthermore, the Court has indicated that motherhood is an essential part of the free development of a woman's personality.[228] Based on the foregoing, the Court considers that the decision of whether or not to become a parent is part of the right to private life and includes, in this case, the decision of whether or not to become a mother or father in the genetic or biological sense.[229]

---

[224] *Cf. Case of Atala Riffo and daughters* v. *Chile*, para. 135.
[225] *Cf. Case of Rosendo Cantú et al.* v. *Mexico. Preliminary objection, merits, reparations and costs.* Judgment of August 31, 2010. Series C No 216, para. 119, and *Case of Atala Riffo and daughters* v. *Chile*, para. 162. See also: ECHR, *Case of Dudgeon* v. *United Kingdom* (No 7525/76), Judgment of October 22, 1981, para. 41; *Case of X and Y* v. *Netherlands* (No 8978/80), Judgment of March 26, 1985, para. 22; *Case of Niemietz* v. *Germany* (No 13710/88), Judgment of December 16, 1992, para. 29; *Case of Peck* v. *United Kingdom* (No 44647/98), Judgment of January 28, 2003. Final, April 28, 2003, para. 57; *Case of Pretty* v. *United Kingdom* (No 2346/02), Judgment of April 29, 2002. Final, July 29, 2002, para. 61. ("The concept of [']private life['] is a broad term not susceptible to exhaustive definition. It covers the physical and psychological integrity of a person ... It can sometimes embrace aspects of an individual's physical and social identity ... Article 8 also protects a right to personal development, and the right to establish and develop relationships with other human beings and the outside world ... Although no previous case has established as such any right to self-determination as being contained in Article 8 of the Convention, the Court considers that the notion of personal autonomy is an important principle underlying the interpretation of its guarantees.")
[226] *Cf.* ECHR, *Case of RR* v. *Poland* (No 27617/04), Judgment of May 26, 2011, para. 197.
[227] *Cf. Case of Rosendo Cantú et al.* v. *Mexico*, para. 119, and *Case of Atala Riffo and daughters* v. *Chile*, para. 162. See also: ECHR, *Case of Niemietz* v. *Germany* (No 13710/88), Judgment of December 16, 1992, para. 29, and *Case of Peck* v. *United Kingdom* (No 44647/98), Judgment of January 28, 2003. Final, April 28, 2003, para. 57.
[228] *Cf. Case of Gelman* v. *Uruguay. Merits and reparations.* Judgment of February 24, 2011. Series C No 221, para. 97.
[229] Similarly, *cf.* ECHR, *Case of Evans* v. *United Kingdom* (No 6339/05), Judgment of April 10, 2007, paras. 71 and 72, where the ECHR indicated that "'private life' ... incorporates the right to

144. The Court considers that this case addresses a particular combination of different aspects of private life that are related to the right to found a family, the right to physical and mental integrity and, specifically, the reproductive rights of the individual.

145. First, the Court emphasizes that, unlike the European Convention on Human Rights, which only protects the right to family life under Article 8 of this instrument, the American Convention contains two articles that protect family life in a complementary manner.[230] In this regard, the Court reiterates that Article 11(2) of the American Convention is closely related to the right recognized in Article 17 of this instrument.[231] Article 17 of the American Convention recognizes the central role of the family and family life in a person's existence and in society in general. The Court has already indicated that the family's right to protection entails, among other obligations, facilitating, in the broadest possible terms, the development and strength of the family unit.[232] This is such a basic right of the American Convention that it cannot be waived even in extreme circumstances.[233] Article 17(2) of the American Convention protects the right to found a family, which is also comprehensively protected in different international human rights instruments.[234] For its part, the United Nations Human Rights

---

respect for both the decisions to become and not to become a parent" and, regarding the regulation of the practice of IVF, clarified that "the right to respect for the decision to become a parent in the genetic sense, also falls within the scope of Article 8." In the *Case of Dickson v. United Kingdom* (No 44362/04), Judgment of December 4, 2007, para. 66, the Court indicated, with regard to the technique of assisted reproduction, that "Article 8 is applicable to the applicants' complaints in that the refusal of artificial insemination facilities concerned their private and family lives which notions incorporate the right to respect for their decision to become genetic parents." In the *Case of SH and others v. Austria* (No 57813/00), Judgment of November 3, 2011, para. 82, the Court referred explicitly to the right of access to assisted reproduction techniques, such as IVF, indicating that "the right of a couple to conceive a child and to make use of medically assisted procreation for that purpose is also protected by Article 8, as such a choice is an expression of private and family life." See also ECHR, *Case of P and S v. Poland* (No 57375/08), Judgment of October 30, 2012, para. 96, where the ECHR indicated that, "[w]hile the Court has held that Article 8 cannot be interpreted as conferring a right to abortion, it has found that the prohibition of abortion when sought for reasons of health and/or well-being falls within the scope of the right to respect for one's private life and accordingly of Article 8."

[230] *Cf. Case of Atala Riffo and daughters v. Chile*, para. 175.
[231] *Cf. Case of Atala Riffo and daughters v. Chile*, para. 169.
[232] *Cf. Case of Gelman v. Uruguay. Merits and reparations*. Judgment of February 24, 2011. Series C No 221, para. 125, and *Case of Atala Riffo and daughters v. Chile*, para. 169. See also, *Juridical Status and Human Rights of the Child*. Advisory Opinion OC-17/02 of August 28, 2002. Series A No 17, para. 66.
[233] Article 27(2) of the American Convention establishes: "[t]he foregoing provision does not authorize any suspension of the following articles: ... 17 (Rights of the Family)."
[234] Paragraph 1 of Article 16 of the Universal Declaration of Human Rights establishes the right of men and women to marry and to found a family, and paragraph 3 establishes that "the family is the natural and fundamental group unit of society and is entitled to protection by society and the State."

Committee has indicated that the possibility of procreating is part of the right to found a family.[235]

146. Second, the right to private life is related to: (i) reproductive autonomy, and (ii) access to reproductive health services, which includes the right to have access to the medical technology necessary to exercise this right. The right to reproductive autonomy is also recognized in Article 16(e) of the Convention for the Elimination of All Forms of Discrimination against Women, according to which women enjoy the right "to decide freely and responsibly on the number and spacing of their children and to have access to the information, education and means that enable them to exercise these rights." This right is violated when the means by which a woman can exercise the right to control her fertility are restricted.[236] Thus, the protection of private life includes respect for the decisions both to become a mother or a father, and a couple's decision to become genetic parents.

147. Third, the Court emphasizes that, in the context of the right to personal integrity, it has analyzed some of the situations that cause particular distress and anxiety to the individual,[237] as well as some serious impacts of the lack of medical care or problems of accessibility to certain health procedures.[238] In the European sphere, case law has defined the relationship between the right to private life and the protection of physical and mental integrity. The European Court of Human Rights has indicated that, although the European Convention on Human Rights does not guarantee the right to a specific level of medical care as such, the right to private life includes a person's physical and mental integrity, and that the State also has the positive obligation to ensure this right to its citizens.[239] Consequently, the rights to private

---

Likewise, Article 23(2) of the International Covenant on Civil and Political Rights recognizes the right of men and women of marriageable age to marry and to found a family.

[235] *Cf.* Human Rights Committee, Compilation of general comments and general recommendations adopted by Human Rights Treaty Bodies, General Comment No 19: Article 23 (The Family) adopted at the thirty-ninth session, UN Doc. HRI/GEN/1/Rev.7 (1990), para. 5 ("The right to found a family implies, in principle, the possibility to procreate and live together").

[236] Committee on the Elimination of Discrimination against Women, General Recommendation No 24 (Women and Health), February 2, 1999, paras. 21 and 31(b).

[237] *Cf. Case of the Yean and Bosico Girls* v. *Dominican Republic.* Judgment of September 8, 2005. Series C No 130, paras. 205 and 206, and *Case of Furlan and family* v. *Argentina,* para. 250.

[238] *Cf. Case of Vélez Loor* v. *Panama. Preliminary objections, merits, reparations and costs.* Judgment of November 23, 2010. Series C No 218, para. 220, and *Case of Díaz Peña* v. *Venezuela,* para. 137.

[239] *Cf.* ECHR, *Case of Glass* v. *United Kingdom* (No 61827/00), Judgment of March 9, 2004, paras. 74 to 83; *Case of Yardımcı* v. *Turkey* (No 25266/05), Judgment of January 5, 2010. Final, June 28, 2010, paras. 55 and 56, and *Case of P and S* v. *Poland* (No 57375/08), Judgment of October 30,

life and to personal integrity are also directly and immediately linked to health care. The lack of legal safeguards that take reproductive health into consideration can result in a serious impairment of the right to reproductive autonomy and freedom. Therefore, there is a connection between personal autonomy, reproductive freedom, and physical and mental integrity.

148. The Court has indicated that States are responsible for regulating and overseeing the provision of health services to ensure effective protection of the rights to life and personal integrity.[240] Health is a state of complete physical, mental and social well-being, not merely the absence of disease or infirmity.[241] In relation to the right to personal integrity it is important to highlight that, according to the Committee on Economic, Social and Cultural Rights, "reproductive health means that women and men have the freedom to decide if and when to reproduce, and the right to be informed and to have access to safe, effective, affordable and acceptable methods of family planning of their choice, as well as the right of access to appropriate health care services."[242] The Programme of Action of the International Conference on Population and Development, held in Cairo in 1994, and the Declaration and Platform for Action of the Fourth World Conference on Women, held in Beijing in 1995, also contain definitions of reproductive health and of women's health. According to the International Conference on Population and Development (1994), "[r]eproductive rights embrace certain human rights that are already recognized in national laws, international human rights documents and other relevant UN consensus documents. These rights rest on the recognition of the basic right of all couples and individuals to decide freely and responsibly the number, spacing and timing of their

---

2012, para. 96. In this last case, the European Court of Human Rights declared that States have "a positive obligation to secure to their citizens the right to effective respect for their physical and psychological integrity [which] may involve the adoption of measures including the provision of an effective and accessible means of protecting the right to respect for private life"; see also ECHR, *Case of McGinley and Egan v. United Kingdom* (No 10/1997/794/995-996), Judgment of June 9, 1998, para. 101.

[240] *Cf. Case of Ximenes Lopes v. Brazil*, Judgment of July 4, 2006. Series C No 149, para. 99, and *Case of Albán Cornejo et al. v. Ecuador. Merits, reparations and costs*. Judgment of November 22, 2007. Series C No 171, para. 121.

[241] The Constitution of the World Health Organization was adopted by the International Health Conference held in New York from June 19 to July 22, 1946, signed on July 22, 1946, by the representatives of 61 States, and entered into force on April 7, 1948; www.who.int/governance/eb/who_constitution_sp.pdf.

[242] Committee on Economic, Social and Cultural Rights, General Comment No 14 (2000), The right to the highest attainable standard of health (Article 12 of the International Covenant on Civil and Political Rights), E/C.12/2000/4, August 11, 2000, para. 14, footnote 12.

children and to have the information and means to do so, and the right to attain the highest standard of sexual and reproductive health."[243] Moreover, adopting a broad and integrated concept of sexual and reproductive health, it stated that:

Reproductive health is a state of complete physical, mental and social well-being, and not merely the absence of disease or infirmity—in all matters relating to the reproductive system and to its functions and processes. Consequently, reproductive health implies that people are able to have a satisfying and safe sex life, that they are able to reproduce and that they have the freedom to decide if, when and how often to do so. Implicit in this is the right of men and women to be informed and to have access to safe, effective, affordable and acceptable methods of family planning of their choice, as well as other methods of their choice for regulation of fertility, which are not against the law, and the right of access to health-care services that will enable women to go safely through pregnancy and childbirth.[244]

149. Furthermore, according to the Conference's Programme of Action, "*in vitro* fertilization techniques should be provided in accordance with ethical guidelines and appropriate medical standards."[245] In the Declaration of the Fourth World Conference on Women (1995), the States agreed to "guarantee equal access to and equal treatment of men and women in . . . health care and promote sexual and reproductive health."[246] The Platform for Action, approved jointly with the Declaration, defined reproductive health care as the "constellation of methods, techniques and services that contribute to reproductive health and well-being by preventing and solving reproductive health problems."[247] According to the Pan-American Health Organization (PAHO), sexual and reproductive health "implies that people are able to have a satisfying

---

[243] *Cf.* Programme of Action of the International Conference on Population and Development, Cairo, 1994, para. 7.3; UN A/CONF.171/13/Rev.1 (1995).
[244] *Cf.* Programme of Action of the International Conference on Population and Development, Cairo, 1994, para. 7.2; UN A/CONF.171/13/Rev.1 (1995).
[245] *Cf.* Programme of Action of the International Conference on Population and Development, Cairo, 1994, para. 7.17; UN A/CONF.171/13/Rev.1 (1995).
[246] *Cf.* Declaration of the Fourth World Conference on Women, Beijing, 1995, para. 30; www.un.org/womenwatch/daw/beijing/pdf/BDPfA%20S.pdf.
[247] *Cf.* Platform for Action of the Fourth World Conference on Women, Beijing, para. 94, which also indicates that "[r]eproductive health therefore implies that people are able to have a satisfying and safe sex life and that they have the capability to reproduce and the freedom to decide if, when and how often to do so. Implicit in this last condition are the rights of men and women to be informed and to have access to safe, effective, affordable and acceptable methods of family planning of their choice, as well as other methods of their choice for regulation of fertility which are not against the law, and the right of access to appropriate health-care services that will enable women to go safely through pregnancy and childbirth and provide couples with the best chance of having a healthy infant"; www.un.org/womenwatch/daw/beijing/pdf/BDPfA%20S.pdf.

and safe sex life, that they are able to reproduce and that they have the freedom to decide if, when and how often to do so."[248] The right to reproductive health entails the rights of men and women to be informed and to have free choice of and access to methods to regulate fertility, that are safe, effective, easily accessible and acceptable.

150. Finally, the right to private life and reproductive freedom is related to the right to have access to the medical technology necessary to exercise that right. The right to enjoy the benefits of scientific progress has been internationally recognized[249] and, in the inter-American context, it is contemplated in Article XIII of the American Declaration[250] and in Article 14(1)(b) of the Protocol of San Salvador. It is worth mentioning that the General Assembly of the United Nations, in its declaration on this right, described its connection to the satisfaction of the material and spiritual needs of all sectors of the population.[251] Therefore, and in keeping with Article 29(b) of the American Convention, the scope of the rights to private life, reproductive autonomy and to found a family, derived from Articles 11(2) and 17(2) of the Convention, extends to the right of everyone to benefit from scientific progress and its applications. The right to have access to scientific progress in order to exercise reproductive autonomy and the possibility to found a family gives rise to the right to have access to the best health care services in assisted reproduction techniques, and, consequently, the prohibition of disproportionate and unnecessary restrictions, *de iure* or *de facto*, to exercise the reproductive decisions that correspond to each individual.

151. In this case, the State considered that the said rights could be exercised in different ways, under the assumption that IVF was not prohibited absolutely. This aspect has been contested by the other parties. Accordingly, the Court will proceed to determine whether there was a restriction of the rights mentioned and will then examine the justification given by the State to support this restriction.

---

[248] Pan-American Health Organization, *Health in the Americas 2007*, Volume I—Regional, Washington DC, 2007, p. 151, cited in the affidavit prepared by expert witness Paul Hunt.
[249] Article 15(b) of the International Covenant on Economic, Social and Cultural Rights establishes that "the States Parties to the present Covenant recognize the right of everyone: ... (b) to enjoy the benefits of scientific progress and its applications."
[250] Article XIII of the American Declaration establishes that: "Every person has the right ... to participate in the benefits that result from intellectual progress, especially scientific discoveries."
[251] *Cf.* United Nations, Declaration on the Use of Scientific and Technological Progress in the Interests of Peace and for the Benefit of Mankind, proclaimed by General Assembly resolution 3384 (XXX), of November 10, 1975, para. 3.

B) *Effects of the absolute prohibition of IVF*

Arguments of the Commission and allegations of the parties

152. The Commission described the result of the Constitutional Chamber's decision as a "prohibition" of IVF of an "absolute" nature, which constitutes "a restriction of the right to found a family according to the decision of the couple." The Commission also argued that, "inasmuch as [IVF] is a means to realize a decision protected by the American Convention, the prohibition of access to the technique necessarily constitutes an interference or restriction to the exercise of the treaty-based rights."

153. Representative Molina characterized the result of the Constitutional Chamber's judgment as an "absolute" and "continued prohibition" of IVF, because "it not only resulted in interference or an abusive and arbitrary invasion of the autonomy and privacy of the [presumed] victims in the case, but also constituted an absolute annulment of the right to decide to have biological children."

154. Representative May argued that "[t]he prohibition of [IVF] perpetuates a situation of physical inability to enjoy bodily health fully, which can be rectified by modern science" and, therefore, "it is also a form of physical abuse against sterile couples because it limits their possibility of overcoming their condition of disease or infirmity." He added that "[t]he prohibition of the practice [of IVF ...] is a real restriction of the full exercise of the natural functions of women and men."

155. The State argued that the ruling of the Constitutional Chamber did not result in a "prohibition" of IVF as such, because the judgment "did not annul definitively the possibility of practicing *in vitro* fertilization in Costa Rica, [but] only banned a specific technique that had existed since 1995, regulated by the Executive Decree." It added that "fertilization methods that endanger" "the right to life from the moment of conception cannot be practiced"; but, "when the State considers that a certain technique is compatible with those parameters, it may permit and regulate it." The State argued that "it should be considered a disputed fact that the presumed victims truly formed part of a waiting list to undergo the procedure" of IVF "in 2000 when the prohibition was announced"; particularly because "many of the couples were not diagnosed with infertility until a long time after the proceedings before the Commission had started and others were still undergoing insemination procedures at that time."

156. Furthermore, the State argued that the judgment "does not prohibit IVF in general, but refers exclusively to the technique that was

used at that time, in which it is known that, in a considerable percentage of the cases, human life had no possibility of continuing." Regarding the possibility of practicing IVF nowadays, the State indicated that "[t]o date science does not offer an *in vitro* technique that is compatible with the right to life protected in Costa Rica; proof of this is that, when the report of the Inter-American Commission on Human Rights was issued, an attempt was made to regulate the matter and a bill was submitted to the Legislative Assembly of Costa Rica that regulated this technique, but also protected the right to life from conception, as this has been understood in Costa Rica. In this regard, the bill prohibited the freezing of embryos and required all the fertilized eggs to be implanted without the possibility of making a selection." It added that this is why "any technique that is attempted in Costa Rica, protecting life from conception, would be medically non-viable at present, 12 years after the judgment of the Constitutional Chamber."

Considerations of the Court

157. The Court notes that the Constitutional Chamber declared unconstitutional and annulled the Executive Decree that authorized the practice of IVF (*supra* para. 72). Both the two representatives and the Inter-American Commission have described the decision as an "absolute prohibition" that does not allow this technique to be applied for any reason, while the State has argued that it was a "relative prohibition," inasmuch as the practice of IVF could be regulated when the technique was able to comply with the requirements established by the Constitutional Chamber in its judgment; in other words when, in the words of the State, IVF does not endanger "the right to life from the moment of conception."

158. In this regard, the Court observes that the Constitutional Chamber's judgment included a concept of absolute protection of the life of the embryo, because it stated that "since the right is declared in favor of everyone, without exception—any exception or limitation destroys the very content of the right—it must be protected for those who are born and also for the unborn."[252] Despite the foregoing, the Constitutional Chamber indicated that "advances in science and biotechnology are so rapid that the technique could be improved in such a

---

[252] Judgment No 2000-02306 of March 15, 2000, delivered by the Constitutional Chamber of the Supreme Court of Justice, Case file No 95-001734-007-CO (file of annexes to the merits report, volume I, folio 90).

way that the concerns that have been indicated disappear";[253] thus the Chamber stated that "it should be expressly recorded that, not even by norm of legal rank, is it possible to authorize legally [the] application of [IVF], at least, ... while its scientific development remains at its current stage and entails the conscious damage to human life."[254]

159. The Court notes that the Constitutional Chamber considered that, if the IVF technique could be applied respecting the concept of absolute protection of the life of the embryo, it could be practiced in the country. However, the Court considers that, although the Constitutional Chamber's judgment accepted the practice of IVF in the country under certain conditions, the fact is that 12 years after the judgment was delivered, this technique is not practiced in Costa Rica (*supra* para. 67). Therefore, the Court considers that the "suspended status" established in the judgment has not produced any real practical effects to date. Consequently, without proceeding to define it as an "absolute" or "relative" prohibition, it is possible to conclude that the Constitutional Chamber's decision resulted in the undisputed fact that IVF is not practiced in Costa Rican territory and that, therefore, couples wishing to use this technique cannot do so in this country. In addition, since the Constitutional Chamber conditioned the possibility of applying the technique to ensuring that there was no embryonic loss whatsoever, in practice, this entails a prohibition of IVF, because the evidence in the case file indicates that, to date, there is no option for practicing IVF without some possibility of embryonic loss.[255] In other words, it would be impossible to comply with the condition imposed by the Chamber.

160. Although the practical effect has been mentioned above, the Court considers that the restriction or interference caused to the presumed victims by the Constitutional Chamber's decision could not be foreseen adequately. In this regard, the Court recalls that a norm or mandate is foreseeable, if it is worded with sufficient precision to allow a person to regulate his conduct based on it.[256] In this regard,

---

[253] Judgment No 2000-02306 of March 15, 2000, delivered by the Constitutional Chamber of the Supreme Court of Justice, Case file No 95-001734-007-CO (file of annexes to the merits report, volume I, folio 95).

[254] Judgment No 2000-02306 of March 15, 2000, delivered by the Constitutional Chamber of the Supreme Court of Justice, Case file No 95-001734-007-CO (file of annexes to the merits report, volume I, folio 95).

[255] *Cf.* Opinion of expert witness Zegers-Hochschild (merits report, volume VI, folio 2848) and of expert witness Garza (merits report, volume VI, folio 2576).

[256] *Cf. Case of López Mendoza* v. *Venezuela. Merits, reparations and costs.* Judgment of September 1, 2011. Series C No 233, para. 199; see also ECHR, *Case of Landvreugd* v. *Netherlands* (No 37331/97), Judgment of June 4, 2002. Final, September 4, 2002, para. 59 ("[T]he Court reiterates that a rule

the Court observes that the judgment was not sufficiently clear, from the outset, in establishing whether or not the practice of IVF was proscribed in the country, and this is revealed by the discussion that has arisen between the parties as to whether the ban is absolute or relative (*supra* paras. 152 to 156) or by the judgment of the Superior Court of Accounts for Contentious Administrative and Civil Proceedings of October 14, 2008, which stated that it was possible to perform IVF in the country if "a single egg was fertilized for its subsequent transfer to the mother's uterus."[257]

161. Thus the judgment of the Constitutional Chamber implied that IVF would no longer be practiced in Costa Rica. In addition, the judgment led to the interruption of the medical treatment that some of the presumed victims in this case had begun, while others were forced to travel to other countries to be able to have access to IVF. These facts constitute an interference with the private and family life of the presumed victims, who had to modify or change their possibilities of having access to IVF, which involved a decision of the couples regarding the methods or practices that they wished to try in order to have biological children. The said judgment meant that the couples had to change their course of action with respect to a decision that they had already taken: to try to have children by means of IVF. The Court clarifies that, in this case, the interference is not related to the fact that the families could or could not have children since, even if they could have had access to the IVF technique, it is not possible to determine whether that objective could have been achieved; thus, the interference is circumscribed to the possibility of taking an autonomous decision on the type of treatments they wished to try to exercise their sexual and reproductive rights. Notwithstanding the foregoing, the Court observes that some of the presumed victims indicated that one of the reasons that influenced the breakup of the marriage bond was related to the impact of the prohibition of IVF on their possibility of having children.[258]

---

is 'foreseeable' if it is formulated with sufficient precision to enable any individual—if need be with appropriate advice—to regulate his conduct").

[257] Judgment No 835-2008 delivered by the Fifth Section of the Court of Accounts for Contentious Administrative and Civil Proceedings in the case brought by Ileana Henchoz Bolaños seeking a declaratory judgment against the Costa Rican Social Security Institute, Case file No 08-00178-1027-CA of October 14, 2008 (file of annexes to the pleadings and motions brief, volume V, annex XXVIII, folio 5859).

[258] *Cf.* Written statement by Grettel Artavia Murillo (file of annexes to the pleadings and motions brief, volume I, folio 4077) ("I wish to place on record that the State, through one of its Branches, curtailed my right to be a mother and, consequently, led to the failure of my marriage owing to the depression that both my former husband and I suffered because of [the] ban [on IVF], with the result

162. Having verified that interference existed, owing both to the prohibitive effect resulting from the Constitutional Chamber's judgment caused in general, and to the impact it had on the presumed victims in this case, the Court considers it necessary to proceed to examine whether this interference or restriction was justified. Before assessing the proportionality in that regard, the Court considers it pertinent to examine in detail the main argument developed by the Constitutional Chamber: that the American Convention makes the absolute protection of the "right to life" of the embryo compulsory and, consequently, makes it obligatory to prohibit IVF because it entails the loss of embryos.

C) Interpretation of Article 4(1) of the Convention as relevant in this case

Arguments of the Commission and allegations of the parties

163. The Commission indicated that "Article 4(1) of the Convention can be interpreted to mean that a State is granted the power to regulate the protection of life from the moment of conception, but is not necessarily a mandate to grant this protection." It argued that this article "does not establish an absolute or categorical right in relation to the prenatal stages of life" and that "an international and comparative recognition [exists] of the concept of gradual and incremental protection of life at the prenatal stage." The Commission added that "the interpretation of Article 4(1) of the Convention indicates that the exercise of a right conceived by this international instrument is not exempt from scrutiny [by the Court] when it interferes with the exercise of other rights established therein, such as, in this case, the rights to private life, family life, autonomy and to found a family."

164. Representative Molina argued that "conception ... is not a clear-cut concept," and that "the Chamber's decision adhered to a specific philosophical tendency as regards [its] definition, ... disregarding the protection required by the reproductive disability to procreate."

that we decided to end our marriage, leaving an even bigger wound, and with incalculable moral damage") and affidavit prepared by Ana Cristina Castillo León (merits report, volume V, folio 2224) ("Although it is true that a marriage may break up or be worn down for many reasons, eight years of constant hormonal treatments, visits to doctors, laboratories, pharmacies, constant financial disbursements, the exposure of our most intimate life to be judged by society, tension between ourselves because we could not resolve the problem of having children; definitively, this takes a toll on the relationship of a couple. That was my case. The great disappointment, the frustration of seeing the constitutional rights to found a family curtailed, and not having the financial resources to go to another country to seek IVF were a heavy burden for my marriage. The marriage bond ceded, divorce was imminent").

He added that "the phrase 'in general' ... presupposes the existence of sufficient exceptions to ensure that other rights are not left unprotected" and that "an interpretation is required with regard to the right to life that permits and does not restrict absolutely the safeguard of the treaty-based rights."

165. Representative May argued that the right to life "is not absolute or unrestricted" and "is subject to exceptions and conditions." He indicated that "the case law of the international human rights bodies ... has never affirmed that the unborn child deserves absolute, unrestricted and unconditional protection from the moment of conception or implantation" and "nor have the Constitutional Courts made this assertion." He noted that although "[d]omestic law can grant a broader protection, ... this expanded protection cannot eliminate the enjoyment and exercise of rights." He argued that the definitions in several dictionaries indicate that the "moment of fertilization is a distinct process to that of conception or implantation." In addition, he argued that any legal protection of life as of the moment of "conception" must arise as of the implantation of the embryo in the mother's uterus, "because prior to successful and healthy implantation in the maternal uterus, there is no possibility of creating a new being." He stated that "[p]ostulating fertilization as the creation of a new human being is arbitrary and incorrect" and "undervalues the role of the mother during development in the uterus." In addition, he argued that "live birth determines the existence of the human being and the recognition of his or her legal personality," so that the unborn child "is not the holder of an unlimited and unconditional right to life," and "[t]he unborn child is a legally protected interest, but not a person."

166. Representative May argued that "Article 4(1) [of the American Convention does not] contemplate ... the embryo within its content or *ratio legis*" and that international human rights treaties do not contain "an explicit indication from which it can be inferred that an embryo or a pre-embryo constitutes human life, and even less that it is a human person or a human being." He added that the "position of the margin of appreciation" was unsustainable because it would make the "substantive content of human rights depend on the State's interpretation." Representative May argued that "[n]o international text (except Article 4(1) [of the Convention]) protects the right to life from the moment or process of conception or implantation," while the "other international instruments only refer to a right that protects the life of the individual who has been born alive, and not the unborn child."

167. The State alleged that "scientific evidence ... reveals that human life begins with conception, or what is the same, with

fertilization," which occurs when "the membranes of the cells of the spermatozoid and the egg merge." It considered that "[s]cientifically, the zygote and the adult are equivalent, [because they are] complete human organisms at different stages of the human life cycle." It added that the zygote "is not simply a human cell ... but a new human being," that "contains all the instructions necessary to build the human body, and that immediately begins a complex sequence of events that establishes the molecular conditions for the continuous process of embryonic development" and that "by means of successive divisions and differentiation will form each of the cells present in the embryo, fetus, newborn, child and adult." In addition, it asserted that "if the human embryo is ... a human being, in accordance with the definition contained in Article 1(2) [of the Convention], the human embryo is a person."

168. With regard to the teleological interpretation, the State argued that "although, in 1968, when the American Convention was being drafted there was no certainty as to when conception occurred, and [IVF] did not exist, it is clear that the provision requires States to protect human life from its earliest embryonic stage," because "the intention of most of the States of the inter-American system was always to protect human life from [the] moment of conception," so that the "terms 'conception' and 'fertilization' should be treated as synonyms." It argued that the process of approving the American Convention "clearly reveals that it is not true that the intention of the States was not the protection of life as of conception, because that was indeed the objective pursued in approving the provision, contrary to what occurred many years previously when the American Declaration was issued." It alleged that the interpretation of the word 'conception' cannot be made by referring to the *Diccionario de la Real Academia de la Lengua Española*, because that is not "the reference work normally used to understand scientific terms," nor has "the definition of conception been updated in line with scientific advances since 1947," and an "interpretation of this nature has a restrictive nature, which is not permitted under Article 29(1) of the Convention." In addition, it argued that "the phrase 'in general' was only included for exceptional cases, such as legitimate defense, the risk of death of the mother, or involuntary abortion."

169. As for other international human rights instruments, the State indicated that the Universal Declaration of Human Rights "protects the human being from the moment of its individualization, which can be determined from the moment when the spermatozoid and the egg unite" and that the "International Covenant on Civil and Political Rights ...

recognizes the life of the embryo separately from that of its mother." It added that the "absolute right to life has been accepted ... even by the Human Rights Committee," and that the Convention on the Rights of the Child protects "the child even before birth." Regarding this last treaty, it argued that "the States agreed that the concept [of child] should be sufficiently broad to enable countries that chose to provide protection to children from before birth to be parties to the international instrument without having to amend their respective laws"; it therefore argued that "a margin of appreciation [exists] to grant the status of child to unborn children," as the relevant Costa Rican law does.

170. Finally, the State alleged that "the doctrine of moral consensus as a factor in the margin of appreciation ... has established that, in order to restrict it, the consensus must be clear and evident." In this regard, it argued that: (i) "there is no consensus regarding the legal status of the embryo"; (ii) "there is no consensus on the beginning of human life, [therefore] a margin of appreciation should also be granted concerning the regulation of the technique" of IVF; and (iii) it is not valid to argue that, "since, through legislative omission, the practice of IVF is permitted in other States, Costa Rica has lost its margin of appreciation." It considered that "[t]he doctrine of the margin of appreciation has been comprehensively developed by the European Court of Human Rights" and that, in the case law of the Inter-American Court, there are precedents that "contemplate the State's possibility of regulating certain matters according to its discretion."

Considerations of the Court

171. The Court has indicated that the purpose of this case focuses on establishing whether the Constitutional Chamber's judgment resulted in a disproportionate restriction of the rights of the presumed victims (*supra* para. 135). The decision of the Constitutional Chamber considered that the American Convention required the prohibition of IVF, as regulated in the Executive Decree (*supra* para. 76). To this end, the Constitutional Chamber interpreted Article 4(1) of the Convention based on the understanding that the Convention requires the absolute protection of the embryo (*supra* para. 75). For its part, the State has offered complementary arguments to defend the interpretation made by the Chamber. In this regard, the Court has analyzed this case with great thoroughness, taking into account that the highest court of Costa Rica has intervened and that, in its judgment, it made an interpretation of Article 4 of the American Convention. However, this Court is the ultimate interpreter of the Convention, so that it finds it relevant to

make the relevant clarification with regard to the scope of this right. Consequently, the Court will analyze whether the interpretation of the Convention that substantiated the interferences that occurred (*supra* para. 75) is admissible in light of this treaty, bearing in mind the pertinent sources of international law.

172. To date, the Court's case law has not ruled on the disputes that have arisen in this case with regard to the right to life. In cases of extrajudicial executions, enforced disappearances and deaths that can be attributed to the failure of the States to adopt measures, the Court has indicated that the right to life is a fundamental human right, the full enjoyment of which is a prerequisite for the enjoyment of all other human rights.[259] Based on this fundamental role assigned to it in the Convention, States have an obligation to create the conditions to ensure that no violations of that right occur. The Court has also indicated that the right to life presupposes that no one may be arbitrarily deprived of his life (negative obligation) and that the States must adopt all appropriate measures to protect and preserve the right to life (positive obligation) of all those who are subject to their jurisdiction.[260] This includes adopting the necessary measures to create an adequate regulatory framework that deters any threat to the right to life and safeguards the right to have access to conditions that ensure a decent life.

173. In the instant case, the Constitutional Chamber considered that these and other aspects of the right to life require the absolute protection of the embryo within the framework of the inviolability of life from conception (*supra* para. 76). To determine whether an obligation of absolute protection exists in those terms, the Court proceeds to analyze the scope of Articles 1(2) and 4(1) of the American Convention in relation to the terms "person," "human being," "conception" and "in general." The Court reiterates its case law according to which a provision of the Convention must be interpreted in good faith, according to the ordinary meaning to be given to the terms of the treaty and their context, and bearing in mind the object and purpose of the American Convention, which is the effective protection of the human person,[261] as well as by an evolutive interpretation of

---

[259] *Cf. Case of the "Street Children" (Villagrán Morales et al.).* Judgment of November 19, 1999. Series C No 63, para. 144, and *Case of the Xákmok Kásek Indigenous Community v. Paraguay. Merits, reparations and costs.* Judgment of August 24, 2010. Series C No 214, para. 186.

[260] *Cf. Case of the Pueblo Bello Massacre v. Colombia. Merits, reparations and costs.* Judgment of January 31, 2006. Series C No 140, para. 120, and *Case of Massacres of El Mozote and nearby places v. El Salvador. Merits, reparations and costs.* Judgment of October 25, 2012. Series C No 252, para. 145.

[261] *Mutatis mutandis, Case of González et al. ("Cotton field") v. Mexico. Preliminary objection, merits, reparations and costs.* Judgment of November 16, 2009. Series C No 205, para. 244.

international instruments for the protection of human rights.[262] Within this framework, the Court will now make an interpretation that is: (i) in accordance with the ordinary meaning of the terms; (ii) systematic and historic; (iii) evolutive; and (iv) of the object and purpose of the treaty.

C.1) Interpretation in accordance with the ordinary meaning of the terms

174. Article 1 of the American Convention establishes:

1. The States Parties to this Convention undertake to respect the rights and freedoms recognized herein and to ensure to all persons subject to their jurisdiction the free and full exercise of those rights and freedoms, without any discrimination for reasons of race, color, sex, language, religion, political or other opinion, national or social origin, economic status, birth, or any other social condition.

2. *For the purposes of this Convention, "person" means every human being.* ([Emphasis] added)

175. Article 4(1) of the American Convention states:

Every person has the right to have his life respected. This right shall be protected by law and, in general, from the moment of conception. No one shall be arbitrarily deprived of his life.

176. In this case the Court observes that the concept of "person" is a legal term that is analyzed in many of the domestic legal systems of the States Parties. However, for the purposes of the interpretation of Article 4(1), the definition of person stems from the mentions made in the treaty with regard to "conception" and to "human being," terms whose scope should be assessed based on the scientific literature.

177. The Court notes that the Constitutional Court chose one of the scientific positions on this issue to define as of when it was considered that life began (*supra* para. 73). On this basis, the Constitutional Court understood that conception would be the moment when the egg is fertilized and assumed that, as of that moment, a person existed who held the right to life (*supra* para. 73).

178. In this regard, in the instant case, the parties also forwarded as evidence a series of scientific articles and expert opinions that will be used in the following paragraphs to determine the scope of the literal

---

[262] *Cf. Case of Ivcher Bronstein* v. *Peru. Competence.* Judgment of September 24, 1999. Series C No 54, para. 38, and *Case of González et al.* ("*Cotton field*") v. *Mexico. Preliminary objection, merits, reparations and costs.* Judgment of November 16, 2009. Series C No 205, para. 33.

interpretation of the terms "conception," "person" and "human being." In addition, the Court will refer to the literal meaning of the expression "in general" in Article 4(1) of the Convention.

179. The Court underlines that the evidence in the case file shows that IVF has transformed the discussion on how the phenomenon of "conception" is understood. Indeed, IVF has revealed that some time may elapse between the fusion of the egg and the spermatozoid and implantation. Therefore, the definition of "conception" accepted by the authors of the American Convention has changed. Prior to IVF, the possibility of fertilization occurring outside a woman's body was not contemplated scientifically.[263]

180. The Court observes that in the current scientific context there are two different interpretations of the term "conception." One school of thought understands "conception" as the moment of union, or fertilization of the egg by the spermatozoid. Fertilization results in the creation of a new cell: the zygote. Certain scientific evidence considers the zygote as a human organism that contains the necessary instructions for the development of the embryo.[264] Another school of thought understands "conception" as the moment when the fertilized egg is implanted in the uterus.[265] The implantation of the fertilized egg in the mother's uterus allows the new cell, the zygote, to connect with the mother's circulatory system, providing it with access to all the hormones and other elements necessary for the embryo's development.[266]

---

[263] In this regard, expert witness Zegers-Hochschild indicated that, "in 1969, no one imagined that it would be possible to create human life outside a woman's body. It was 10 years later that the birth of the first baby using ART was announced." Written summary of the expert opinion provided by Fernando Zegers-Hochschild at the public hearing before the Court (merits report, volume VI, folio 2846).

[264] *Cf. inter alia*, the following scientific articles provided by the State: Tanya Lobo Prada, *Inicio de la vida* (file of annexes to the answering brief, volume I, folios 6653 to 6656); Maureen L. Condic, "Preimplantation Stages of Human Development: The Biological and Moral Status of Early Embryos," in: *Is This Cell a Human Being?*, Springer-Verlag Berlin, 2011 (file of annexes to the answering brief, volume I, folios 6576 to 6594); Maureen L. Condic, "When Does Human Life Begin? A Scientific Perspective," in: *The Westchester Institute for Ethics and the Human Person*, Vol. 1, No 1, 2008 (file of annexes to the answering brief, volume I, folios 6621 to 6648); Jerome Lejeune, "*El Origen de la Vida Humana,*" in: *Diario ABC*, Madrid, 1983 (file of annexes to the answering brief, volume I, folio 6652), and Natalia Lopez Moratalla and María J. Iraburu Elizalde, *Los primeros quince días de una vida humana*, Ediciones Universidad de Navarra, 2004 (file of annexes to the answering brief, volume VI, folios 9415 to 9503).

[265] Written summary of the expert opinion provided by Fernando Zegers-Hochschild at the public hearing before the Court (merits report, volume VI, folio 2846).

[266] *Cf. inter alia*, the following scientific articles provided by the State: Tanya Lobo Prada, *Inicio de la vida* (file of annexes to the answering brief, volume I, folios 6653 to 6656); Maureen L. Condic, "Preimplantation Stages of Human Development: The Biological and Moral Status of Early Embryos," in: *Is This Cell a Human Being?*, Springer-Verlag Berlin, 2011 (file of annexes to the answering brief, volume I, folios 6576 to 6594); Maureen L. Condic, "When Does Human Life Begin? A Scientific

181. For his part, expert witness Zegers-Hochschild indicated that when the American Convention was signed in 1969, the *Real Academia de la Lengua Española* defined "conception" as "the action and effect of conceiving,"[267] "to conceive" as "for the female to become pregnant," and "to fertilize"[268] as "to unite the male and female reproductive elements, to create a new being."[269] The Court observes that the current dictionary of the *Real Academia de la Lengua Española* maintains almost completely the definitions of these words.[270] Furthermore, the expert witness indicated that:

A woman has conceived when the embryo has been implanted in her uterus ... The word conception makes explicit reference to pregnancy or gestation, [which] begins with the implantation of the embryo, ... since *conception or gestation is an event of the woman, not of the embryo*. There is only evidence of the presence of an embryo when it is joined to the woman at a cellular level and the chemical signals of this event can be identified in the woman's fluids. This signal corresponds to a hormone called chorionic gonadotropin and *the earliest that it can be detected is seven days after fertilization, with the embryo already implanted in the endometrium*.[271] ([Emphasis] added)

Perspective," in: *The Westchester Institute for Ethics and the Human Person*, Vol. 1, No 1, 2008 (file of annexes to the answering brief, volume I, folios 6621 to 6648); Jerome Lejeune, "*El Origen de la Vida Humana*," in: *Diario ABC*, Madrid, 1983 (file of annexes to the answering brief, volume I, folio 6652), and Natalia Lopez Moratalla and María J. Iraburu Elizalde, *Los primeros quince días de una vida humana*, Ediciones Universidad de Navarra, 2004 (file of annexes to the answering brief, volume VI, folios 9415 to 9503).

[267] *Cf. Diccionario de la Real Academia de la Lengua Española*, 1956 edition. Available at: http:// ntlle.rae.es/ntlle/SrvltGUIMenuNtlle?cmd=Lema&sec=1.0.0.0.0. (last visited November 28, 2012).

[268] *Cf. Diccionario de la Real Academia de la Lengua Española*, 1956 edition. Available at: http:// ntlle.rae.es/ntlle/SrvltGUIMenuNtlle?cmd=Lema&sec=1.1.0.0.0. (last visited November 28, 2012).

[269] *Cf. Diccionario de la Real Academia de la Lengua Española*, 1956 edition. Available at: http:// ntlle.rae.es/ntlle/SrvltGUIMenuNtlle?cmd=Lema&sec=1.2.0.0.0. (last visited November 28, 2012). Similarly, expert witness Bergallo stated that the *Diccionario de la Real Academia*, "in its 19th edition, which was in force at the time the Convention was drafted, defined 'conception' including the fact of the fertilization and the protection of the implanted embryo." Opinion of expert witness Paola Bergallo before the Court during the public hearing held in this case.

[270] In this regard, the current edition of the *Diccionario de la Real Academia de la Lengua Española* defines "conception" as "action and effect of to conceive." The expression is defined in its third acceptance as "said of a female: 'to become pregnant'"; and the expression "to fertilize" is defined as "to unite the male and female reproductive cell in order to create a new being." Available at: http:// lema.rae.es/drae/?val=concepci%C3%B3n; http://lema.rae.es/drae/?val=concebir, and http://lema.rae .es/drae/?val=fecundar (last visited November 28, 2012).

[271] Written summary of the expert opinion provided by Fernando Zegers-Hochschild at the public hearing before the Court (merits report, volume VI, folio 2846). Furthermore, expert witness Zegers-Hochschild stated that "[i]f the intention had been to define the right to protection as of the moment of fertilization, this word would have been used, which is defined perfectly in the dictionary." Written summary of the expert opinion provided by Fernando Zegers-Hochschild at the public hearing before the Court (merits report, volume VI, folio 2846).

182. Furthermore, according to expert witness Monroy Cabra, the term conception is "a medical-scientific term that has been interpreted to mean that it takes place [at the moment of] the fusion of the egg and the spermatozoid."[272] In similar terms, expert witness Condic considered that "human life begins with the fusion of spermatozoid and egg, an observable 'moment of conception.'"[273]

183. However, in addition to these two possible hypotheses on the moment at which "conception" should be understood to occur, the parties have presented a different thesis regarding the moment when it is believed that the embryo reaches a sufficient degree of maturity to be considered a "human being." Some hold the view that life begins with fertilization, recognizing the zygote as the first corporal manifestation of the continuing process of human development,[274] while others consider that the starting point for the development of the embryo, and subsequently of its human life, is its implantation in the uterus where it has the capacity to add its genetic potential to the mother's potential.[275] Moreover, others emphasize that life begins when the nervous system develops.[276]

184. The Court observes that, while some articles consider that the embryo is a human being,[277] others stress that fertilization occurs in one minute but that the embryo is formed seven days later, for which

---

[272] *Cf.* Statement by expert witness Monroy Cabra before the Inter-American Court during the public hearing held in this case.

[273] Affidavit prepared by expert witness Condic (merits report, volume V, folio 2592).

[274] *Cf.* in this regard, *inter alia*: Tanya Lobo Prada, *Inicio de la vida* (file of annexes to the answering brief, volume I, folios 6653 to 6656), and Maureen L. Condic, "Preimplantation Stages of Human Development: The Biological and Moral Status of Early Embryos," in: *Is This Cell a Human Being?*, Springer-Verlag Berlin, 2011 (file of annexes to the answering brief, volume I, folios 6576 to 6594).

[275] *Cf.* Written summary of the expert opinion provided by Fernando Zegers-Hochschild at the public hearing before the Court (merits report, volume VI, folio 2846).

[276] In this regard, expert witness Condic indicated that "a number of alternative definitions have been offered as to when human life starts, including syngamy (approximately 24 hours after the fusion of the spermatozoid and egg); implantation (approximately five days after the fusion of the spermatozoid and egg); formation of the primitive streak (approximately 14 days after the fusion of the spermatozoid and egg), and the beginning of the neural function." Affidavit prepared by expert witness Condic (merits report, volume V, folio 2589).

[277] *Cf. inter alia* the following scientific articles provided by the State: Tanya Lobo Prada, *Inicio de la vida* (file of annexes to the answering brief, volume I, folios 6653 to 6656); Maureen L. Condic, "Preimplantation Stages of Human Development: The Biological and Moral Status of Early Embryos," in: *Is This Cell a Human Being?*, Springer-Verlag Berlin, 2011 (file of annexes to the answering brief, volume I, folios 6576 to 6594); Maureen L. Condic, "When Does Human Life Begin? A Scientific Perspective," in: *The Westchester Institute for Ethics and the Human Person*, Vol. 1, No 1, 2008 (file of annexes to the answering brief, volume I, folios 6621 to 6648); Jerome Lejeune, "*El Origen de la Vida Humana*," in: *Diario ABC*, Madrid, 1983 (file of annexes to the answering brief, volume I, folio 6652), and Natalia Lopez Moratalla and María J. Iraburu Elizalde, *Los primeros quince días de una vida humana*, Ediciones Universidad de Navarra, 2004 (file of annexes to the answering brief, volume VI, folios 9415 to 9503).

reason they refer to the concept of a "pre-embryo."[278] Some articles associate the concept of pre-embryo with the first 14 days because, after this, it is known whether there is one child or more.[279] Expert witnesses Condic and Caruzo, and some scientific literature, reject these ideas associated with the notion of pre-embryo.[280]

185. Regarding the dispute as to when human life begins, the Court considers that this is a question that has been assessed in different ways from a biological, medical, ethical, moral, philosophical and religious perspective, and it concurs with domestic and international courts[281] that there is no one agreed definition of the

---

[278] Deponent Escalante affirmed that "[f]rom the moment of fertilization—in other words, penetration of the egg by the spermatozoid—and during the following 14 days, the fertilized egg consists of a growing cell group, with identical cells, where there are no specialized tissues or organs. During this period (pre-embryonic) there is no individuality given that one of eight cells can divide itself into two of four and if both are implanted, identical twins would be born and, similarly, in the opposite sense, the fusion of two of four cells in one of eight, would result in the birth of only one baby." Statement of deponent Escalante (merits file, volume V, folio 2441).

[279] In this regard, deponent Escalante stated that "prior to day 14 in the formation of the human species there is no individuality... Therefore, a patient who has, for example, two embryos in an IVF laboratory in preparation for their transfer two or three days later, still has 'children in progress'; she is not pregnant." Statement of deponent Escalante (merits report, volume V, folio 2386).

[280] In this regard, expert witness Caruso stated that he "did not know what a 'pre-embryo' was." The term was first used by a frog biologist, Clifford Grobstein, in 1979. He believed that, since identical twins can occur 14 days after fertilization, before this, "only one 'genetic individual' is present, not a developing individual; and, therefore, an embryo or 'person' was not present. Moreover, the terms 'pre-embryo' and individuality have been discredited by almost all human biologists and rejected by the Terminology Committee of the American Association of Anatomists for inclusion in the Embryological Terminology. These terms are not used in any official work on human embryology or in the Carnegie Stages of human embryonic development." Written summary of the expert opinion provided by Anthony Caruso at the public hearing before the Court (merits report, volume VI, folio 2937.216). In addition, expert witness Condic indicated that "[s]ome people have tried to refer to an embryo prior to syngamy (or prior to the implantation or the formation of the primitive streak) as a 'pre-embryo,' but this is not a legitimate scientific term." Affidavit prepared by expert witness Condic (merits report, volume V, folio 2590).

[281] With regard to decisions of constitutional courts: the United States Supreme Court, *Case of Roe v. Wade*, 410 US 115, 157 (1973) ("We need not resolve the difficult question of when life begins. If those trained in the respective disciplines of medicine, philosophy and theology are unable to arrive at any consensus, the judiciary... is not in a position to speculate as to the answer"); the [High] Court of the United Kingdom, *Case of Smeaton v. Secretary of State for Health*, [2002] EWHC 610 (Admin), Opinion of Justice Munby, paras. 54 and 60 ("It is no part of my function, as I conceive it, to determine the point at which life begins... Thus, even biology and medicine cannot tell us precisely when it is that 'life' really starts"); the Supreme Court of Ireland, *Case of Roche v. Roche & Ors*, Judgment of December 15, 2009, [2009] IESC 82, Opinion of Judge Murray CJ ("In my opinion, it is not for a court of law, faced with the most divergent, although most learned views, in the said disciplines available to it, to rule on the truth of the precise moment at which human life begins"); Opinion of Judge Denham J: para. 46 ("This is not the appropriate arena for attempting to define 'life', 'the beginning of life', 'the timing of ensoulment', 'potential life', 'the unique human life', when life begins, or other imponderables relating to the concept of life. This is not the forum for deciding principles of science, theology or ethics. This is a court of law which has been asked to interpret the Constitution and to make a legal decision on the interpretation of an article of the Constitution");

beginning of life.[282] Nevertheless, it is clear to the Court that some opinions view a fertilized egg as a complete human life. Some of these opinions may be associated with concepts that confer certain metaphysical attributes on embryos. Such concepts cannot justify preference being given to a certain type of scientific literature when interpreting the scope of the right to life established in the American Convention, because this would imply imposing specific types of beliefs on others who do not share them.

186. Despite the foregoing, the Court considers that it is appropriate to define how to interpret the term "conception" in relation to the American Convention. In this regard, the Court underscores that the scientific evidence agrees in making a difference between two complementary and essential moments of embryonic development: fertilization and implantation. The Court observes that it is only after completion of the second moment that the cycle is concluded, and that conception can be understood to have occurred. Taking into account the scientific evidence presented by the parties in this case, the Court notes that, even though, once the egg has been fertilized, this gives rise to a different cell with sufficient genetic information for the potential development of a "human being," the fact is that if this embryo is not implanted in a woman's body its possibilities of development are nil. If an embryo never manages to implant itself in the

---

Constitutional Court of Colombia, Judgment C-355 of 2006 ("This Court considers that determining the exact moment at which human life begins is a problem that has been dealt with in different ways, not only from different perspectives such as those of genetics, medicine, religion or morals, but also based on the different criteria expressed by each of the respective experts, whose assessment does not correspond to the Constitutional Court in this decision"); ECHR, *Case of Vo* v. *France* (No 53924/00), GC, Judgment of 8 July 2004, para. 84 ("The Oviedo Convention on Human Rights and Biomedicine ... is careful not to give a definition of the term 'everyone,' and its explanatory report indicates that, in the absence of a unanimous agreement on the definition, the member States decided to allow domestic law to provide clarification for the purposes of the application of that Convention ... The same is true of the Additional Protocol on the Prohibition of Cloning Human Beings and the Additional Protocol on Biomedical Research, which do not define the concept of 'human being'").

[282] *Cf.* Maureen L. Condic, "Pre-implantation Stages of Human Development: The Biological and Moral Status of Early Embryos" (file of annexes to the answer to the application, volume III, folios 6580 to 6594). In particular, she indicates that "[c]urrently, there is little consensus among scientists, philosophers, ethicists, and theologians regarding when human life begins. While many assert that life begins at 'the moment of conception,' precisely when this moment occurs has not been rigorously defined. Indeed, the legislative bodies of different countries have defined the 'moment' of conception quite differently. For example, Canada defines a human embryo as 'a human organism during the first 56 days of its development following fertilization or creation,' a definition that is very similar to the one proposed in the United States of America. Recent statements by bioethicists, politicians, and scientists have suggested that human life commences even later, at the eight-cell stage (approximately 3 days post-fertilization) (for example, Peters 2006); at the implantation of the embryo in the uterus (5-6 days post-fertilization: Agar (2007), Hatch (2002)), or at formation of the primitive streak (2 weeks post-fertilization)."

uterus, it could not develop, because it would not receive the necessary nutrients, nor would it be in a suitable environment for its development (*supra* para. 180).

187. Thus, the Court considers that the term "conception" cannot be understood as a moment or process exclusive of a woman's body, given that an embryo has no chance of survival if implantation does not occur. Proof of this is that it is only possible to establish whether or not pregnancy has occurred once the fertilized egg has been implanted in the uterus, when the hormone known as "chorionic gonadotropin" is produced, which can only be detected in a woman who has an embryo implanted in her.[283] Prior to this, it is impossible to determine whether the union between the egg and a spermatozoid occurred within the body or whether this union was lost prior to implantation. In addition, it has already been pointed out that when Article 4 of the American Convention was drafted the dictionary of the *Real Academia* differentiated between the moment of fertilization and the moment of conception, understanding conception as implantation (*supra* para. 181). When drafting the relevant provisions in the American Convention, the moment of fertilization was not mentioned.

188. Furthermore, with regard to the expression "in general," the *Diccionario de la Real Academia Española* states that this means "in common, generally" or "without specifying or individualizing anything."[284] According to the structure of the second phrase of Article 4(1) of the Convention, the term "in general" is related to the expression "from the moment of conception." The literal interpretation indicates that the expression relates to anticipating possible exceptions to a particular rule. The other methods of interpretation would suggest the meaning of a provision that contemplates exceptions.

189. Taking the above into account, the Court understands the word "conception" from the moment at which implantation occurs, and therefore considers that, before this event, Article 4 of the American Convention cannot be applied. In addition, the term "in general" infers exceptions to a rule, but the interpretation in keeping with the ordinary meaning does not allow the scope of those exceptions to be specified.

190. However, taking into consideration that Article 4(1) is a matter that is the subject of the discussion in this case and also in the context

---

[283] *Cf.* Written summary of the expert opinion provided by Fernando Zegers-Hochschild at the public hearing before the Court (merits report, volume VI, folio 2846).
[284] *Cf. Diccionario de la Real Academia de la Lengua Española*. Available at: http://lema.rae.es/drae/?val=en%20general (last visited November 28, 2012).

of the deliberations of the Constitutional Chamber, the Court finds it appropriate to interpret this article using the following methods of interpretation, namely the systematic and historical, and the evolutionary and teleological interpretation.

C.2) Systematic and historical interpretation

191. The Court emphasizes that, according to the systematic argument, norms should be interpreted as part of a whole, the meaning and scope of which must be defined based on the legal system to which they belong.[285] Thus, the Court has considered that "the interpretation of a treaty should take into account not only the agreements and instruments formally related to it (Article 31(2) of the Vienna Convention), but also its context (Article 31(3))";[286] in other words, international human rights law.

192. In this case, the Constitutional Chamber and the State based their arguments on an interpretation of the Universal Declaration of Human Rights, the International Covenant on Civil and Political Rights (hereinafter "ICCPR"), the Convention on the Rights of the Child, and the 1959 Declaration on the Rights of the Child. In particular, the State affirmed that treaties other than the American Convention require the absolute protection of prenatal life. The Court will proceed to examine this argument based on a general assessment of the provisions established by the protection systems in relation to the protection of the right to life. Accordingly, it will analyze: (i) the inter-American system; (ii) the universal system; (iii) the European system; and (iv) the African system.

193. Moreover, according to Article 32 of the Vienna Convention, "the supplementary means of interpretation, especially the preparatory work of the treaty, can be used in order to confirm the meaning resulting from that interpretation or when it leaves an ambiguous or obscure meaning, or leads to a result which is manifestly absurd or unreasonable."[287] This means that they are usually used only in a subsidiary manner,[288] after the methods of interpretation set out in Article 31 of the Vienna Convention have been used, in order to

---

[285] *Cf. Case of González et al. ("Cotton field") v. Mexico. Preliminary objection, merits, reparations and costs.* Judgment of November 16, 2009. Series C No 205, para. 43.

[286] *Cf. The Right to Information on Consular Assistance in the Framework of the Guarantees of the Due Process of Law.* Advisory Opinion OC-16/99 of October 1, 1999. Series A No 16, para. 113, and *Case of the "Street Children" (Villagrán Morales et al.) v. Guatemala. Reparations and costs.* Judgment of May 26, 2001. Series C No 192.

[287] *Cf. Restrictions to the Death Penalty (Arts. 4.2 and 4.4 American Convention on Human Rights).* Advisory Opinion OC-3/83 of September 8, 1983. Series A No 3, para. 49.

[288] *Cf. Case of González et al. ("Cotton field") v. Mexico. Preliminary objection, merits, reparations and costs.* Judgment of November 16, 2009. Series C No 205, para. 68.

confirm the meaning that was found or to establish whether ambiguity remains in the interpretation or whether the application is absurd or unreasonable. However, in the present case, the Court considers that Article 31(4) of the Vienna Convention, which provides that a special meaning shall be given to a term if it is established that the parties so intended, is relevant for determining the interpretation of Article 4(1) of the American Convention. Therefore, the interpretation of the text of Article 4(1) of the Convention is directly related to meaning intended by the States Parties to the Convention.

C.2.a) Inter-American human rights system

i) Preparatory work of the American Declaration of the Rights and Duties of Man

194. Pursuant to Resolution XL of the 1945 Inter-American Conference on Problems of War and Peace, the Inter-American Juridical Committee drew up a draft Declaration of the Rights and Duties of Man to be considered by the Ninth International Conference of American States in 1948.[289] This text was analyzed during the Conference in conjunction with the preliminary text of the International Declaration on Human Rights prepared by the United Nations in December 1947.[290]

195. Article I of the draft declaration submitted by the Juridical Committee stated the following with regard to the right to life:

Every person has the right to life. This right extends to the right to life from the moment of conception; to the right to life of incurables, imbeciles and the insane. Capital punishment may only be applied in cases in which it has been prescribed by pre-existing law for crimes of exceptional gravity.[291]

196. Subsequently, a working group was created,[292] which submitted a new preliminary text to the Sixth Committee entitled American Declaration of the Fundamental Rights and Duties of Man,[293] the new Article 1 of which reads:

Every human being has the right to life, liberty, and the security and integrity of his person.[294]

---

[289] *Cf.* Inter-American Juridical Committee, Reports and Recommendations, Official Documents, 1945-7, Rio de Janeiro, 1960.
[290] *Cf.* Inter-American Commission on Human Rights, *Baby Boy* v. *United States*, Case 2141, Report No 23/81, OEA/Ser.L/V/II.54, doc. 9 rev. 1 (1981), para. 19(a).
[291] *Cf. IX Conferencia Internacional Americana—Actas y Documentos, Vol. V,* p. 449.
[292] *Cf. IX Conferencia Internacional Americana—Actas y Documentos, Vol. V,* pp. 474 and 475.
[293] *Cf. IX Conferencia Internacional Americana—Actas y Documentos, Vol. V,* pp. 476 and 478.
[294] *Cf. IX Conferencia Internacional Americana—Actas y Documentos, Vol. V,* p. 479.

197. In its report to the Sixth Committee, the working group explained this new article and other changes introduced as a compromise to resolve the problems raised by the delegations of Argentina, Brazil, Cuba, Mexico, Peru, Uruguay, the United States of America and Venezuela, mainly as a result of the conflict existing between the laws of those States and the draft prepared by the Juridical Committee,[295] because the definition of the scope of the right to life in the Juridical Committee's draft was incompatible with the laws on capital punishment and abortion in most American States.[296]

198. On April 22, 1948, the Sixth Committee approved Article I of the Declaration with a slight change in the wording of the Spanish text.[297] The definitive text of the Declaration was approved at the seventh plenary session of the Conference on April 30, 1948.[298] The only difference in the final version was the elimination of the word "integrity."[299] The final version that was approved stated:

Every human being has the right to life, liberty and the security of his person.[300]

199. The Court observes that, in their domestic law, several countries, including Argentina, Brazil, Costa Rica, Cuba, Ecuador, Mexico, Nicaragua, Paraguay, Peru, Uruguay and Venezuela, established exceptions to the criminalization of abortion in cases of danger to a woman's life, grave danger to a woman's health, eugenic abortions, or rape.[301]

200. Taking into account this background information leading up to the American Declaration, the Court considers that the preparatory work does not provide a clear answer to the matter in dispute.

ii) Preparatory work of the American Convention on Human Rights

201. During the Fifth Meeting of Consultation of Ministers of Foreign Affairs of the OAS, held in 1959, the decision was taken to facilitate the

---

[295] *Cf.* Inter-American Commission on Human Rights, *Baby Boy* v. *United States*, Case 2141, Report No 23/81, OEA/Ser.L/V/II.54, doc. 9 rev. 1 (1981), para. 19(d) (citing *IX Conferencia Internacional Americana—Actas y Documentos, Vol. V*, pp. 474-84, 513-14).
[296] *Cf.* Inter-American Commission on Human Rights, *Baby Boy* v. *United States*, Case 2141, Report No 23/81, OEA/Ser.L/V/II.54, doc. 9 rev. 1 (1981), para. 19(e).
[297] *Cf. IX Conferencia Internacional Americana—Actas y Documentos, Vol. V*, p. 578. The final text was: "Every human being has the right to life, liberty and the safety and integrity of his person."
[298] *Cf. IX Conferencia Internacional Americana—Actas y Documentos, Vol. V*, pp. 231, 234 and 236.
[299] *Cf. IX Conferencia Internacional Americana—Actas y Documentos, Vol. V*, p. 248.
[300] *Cf. IX Conferencia Internacional Americana—Actas y Documentos, Vol. V*, pp. 231, 234 and 236.
[301] *Cf.* Luis Jiménez de Asúa, *Códigos Penales Iberoamericanos*, Vols. I, II, cited in Inter-American Commission on Human Rights, *Case of Baby Boy* v. *United States of America*. Decision No 23/81, Case 2141 (1981), para. 19(f).

preparation of a human rights convention, and the Inter-American Council of Jurists was entrusted with the preparation of the respective draft document.[302] The Inter-American Council of Jurists drew up this draft[303] to be considered at the Ninth International American Conference to be held in 1960. The Inter-American Council took into account the experiences of the European human rights system with regard to the European Convention on Human Rights, and the United Nations universal human rights system. Regarding the right to life, the following wording was included in Article 2 of the draft convention:

Every person has the right to have his life respected. The right to life is inherent in the human being. This right shall be protected by law from the moment of conception. No one may be deprived of life arbitrarily.[304]

202. This wording, without the phrase "in general" which was incorporated later, was proposed in the three drafts on which the American Convention was based.[305]

203. Subsequently, the 1965 Second Special Conference of Inter-American States commissioned the OAS Council to update and complete the "draft human rights convention" prepared by the Inter-American Council of Jurists in 1959, taking into account the draft conventions presented by the Governments of Chile and Uruguay and obtaining the opinion of the Inter-American Commission on Human Rights.[306]

---

[302] *Cf. Anuario Interamericano de Derechos Humanos* 1968, OAS, Washington DC, 1973, p. 97.
[303] Approved on September 8, 1959, by Resolution No XX of the Inter-American Council of Jurists.
[304] *Cf.* draft human rights convention, approved by the fourth meeting of the Inter-American Council of Jurists, Final Proceedings, Santiago de Chile, September 1959, Doc. CIJ-43, in: *Anuario Interamericano de Derechos Humanos* 1968, OAS, Washington DC, 1973, p. 236.
[305] *Cf.* the draft human rights convention, approved by the fourth meeting of the Inter-American Council of Jurists, Santiago, Chile, September 1959; the draft human rights convention presented by the Government of Chile at the Second Inter-American Special Conference, Rio de Janeiro, 1965, doc. 35, and the draft human rights convention presented by the Government of Uruguay at the Second Inter-American Special Conference, Rio de Janeiro, 1965, doc. 49. *Cf. Anuario Interamericano de Derechos Humanos* 1968, OAS, Washington DC, 1973, pp. 236, 280 and 298.
[306] It also commissioned the OAS Council to ensure that the revised draft was submitted to the Governments so that they could make any observations and amendments they considered pertinent and to convene an Inter-American Specialized Conference to consider the draft and the observations, and to approve the Convention. The OAS Council asked the Inter-American Commission for its opinion and the latter issued an opinion on the matter that it forwarded to the OAS Council on November 4, 1996 (Part I) and on April 10, 1967 (Part II). *Cf.* "Opinion prepared by the Inter-American Commission on Human Rights on the draft Convention on Human Rights approved by the Inter-American Council of Jurists (Civil and political rights), Part I," OEA/Ser.L/V/II.15/doc.26, and "Opinion prepared by the Inter-American Commission on Human Rights on the draft Convention on Human Rights approved by the Inter-American Council of Jurists Part II," OEA/Ser.L/V/II.16/doc.8, in: *Anuario Interamericano de Derechos Humanos* 1968, OAS, Washington DC, 1973, pp. 320 ff. and 334 ff. In addition, by a resolution of June 7, 1967, the OAS Council consulted the Governments of

204. In order to accommodate the different opinions concerning the wording "from the moment of conception" that had been voiced since the Ninth International Conference of American States held in Bogotá in 1948 owing to the legislation of the American States that permitted abortion, the Inter-American Commission on Human Rights redrafted Article 2 (Right to Life) to introduce the words "in general" immediately before the phrase "from the moment of conception."[307] This compromise was the origin of the new text of Article 2(1) that indicated:

Every person has the right to have his life respected. This right shall be protected by law, in general, from the moment of conception.[308]

205. This proposal was reviewed by the Commission's rapporteur, who reiterated his dissenting opinion and proposed the elimination of the entire phrase, "in general, from the moment of conception," in order to avoid any possible conflict with paragraph 1 of Article 6 of the International Covenant on Civil and Political Rights, which establishes this right in a general way only.[309] However, the Commission considered that "on principle, it was essential to establish the protection of the right to life as recommended by the Council of the Organization of American States in its Opinion (Part I)."[310] It was accordingly decided to keep the proposed text of Article 2(1) without change.

206. At the Inter-American Specialized Conference on Human Rights, held from November 7 to 22, 1969, which approved the American Convention, the delegations of the Dominican Republic and Brazil introduced separate amendments to delete the phrase "in general, from the moment of conception."[311]

---

the Member States on the possibility of the coexistence of the conventions signed within the United Nations and an inter-American convention on human rights. Subsequently, the Council commissioned the Inter-American Commission on Human Rights to draft a revised and complete text for a draft Convention. *Cf.* Inter-American Specialized Conference on Human Rights, San José, Costa Rica, November 7 to 22, 1969, Proceedings and documents, General Secretariat, OAS, Washington DC, OEA/Ser.K/XVI/1.2.

[307] *Cf.* "Opinion prepared by the Inter-American Commission on Human Rights on the draft Convention on Human Rights approved by the Inter-American Council of Jurists (Civil and political rights), Part I," OEA/Ser.L/V/II.15/doc.26, in: *Anuario Interamericano de Derechos Humanos* 1968, OAS, Washington DC, 1973, p. 320.

[308] *Anuario Interamericano de Derechos Humanos* 1968, OAS, Washington DC, 1973, p. 321.
[309] *Anuario Interamericano de Derechos Humanos* 1968, OAS, Washington DC, 1973, p. 98.
[310] *Anuario Interamericano de Derechos Humanos* 1968, OAS, Washington DC, 1973, p. 98.
[311] *Cf.* "Observations and comments on the draft convention for the protection of human rights presented by the Government of the Dominican Republic, June 20, 1969," and "Observations and amendments to the draft inter-American convention for the protection of human rights presented by the Government of Brazil, November 10, 1969," in: Inter-American Specialized Conference on

207. Regarding the text of the right to life (Article 3), the delegation of the Dominican Republic considered that "it would enhance the universal concepts of human rights if the inter-American text was the same as the one adopted by the United Nations in article 6(1) of the Covenant."[312]

208. The Brazilian delegation justified its proposal to delete the phrase by considering that "[t]his final phrase is vague and, thus, would not be effective to prevent the States Parties to the future convention including in their domestic law the most diverse cases of abortion."[313] It argued that "[t]he said phrase could ... raise doubts that would impede not only the acceptance of this article, but also its application, if the actual wording is retained,"[314] concluding that "thus, it would be better to eliminate the phrase 'in general, from the moment of conception,' because this is a matter that should be left to the legislation of each country."[315]

209. The United States delegation, supporting Brazil's position, suggested that "this text should be harmonized with article 6, paragraph 1, of the United Nations Covenant on Civil and Political Rights."[316]

210. The delegation of Ecuador proposed the deletion of the words "in general"[317] and the Venezuelan delegate considered that "regarding the right to life from the moment of the conception of the human being, no concessions can be made,"[318] considering "inacceptable a convention that did not establish this principle."[319]

211. Finally, by majority vote, the Conference adopted the text of the draft submitted by the Inter-American Commission on Human

Human Rights, San José, Costa Rica, November 7 to 22, 1969, *Proceedings and Documents*, General Secretariat, OAS, Washington DC, OEA/Ser.K/XVI/1.2, pp. 50 ff., and 121 ff.

[312] *Cf.* "Observations and comments on the draft convention for the protection of human rights presented by the Government of the Dominican Republic, June 20, 1969", p. 57.

[313] *Cf.* "Observations and amendments to the draft inter-American convention for the protection of human rights presented by the Government of Brazil, November 10, 1969," in: Inter-American Specialized Conference on Human Rights, San José, Costa Rica, November 7 to 22, 1969, *Proceedings and Documents*, p. 121.

[314] *Cf.* "Observations and amendments to the draft inter-American convention for the protection of human rights presented by the Government of Brazil, November 10, 1969," p. 121.

[315] *Cf.* "Observations and amendments to the draft inter-American convention for the protection of human rights presented by the Government of Brazil, November 10, 1969," p. 121.

[316] *Cf.* Inter-American Specialized Conference on Human Rights, San José, Costa Rica, November 7 to 22, 1969, *Proceedings and Documents*, p. 160.

[317] *Cf.* Inter-American Specialized Conference on Human Rights, San José, Costa Rica, November 7 to 22, 1969, *Proceedings and Documents*, p. 160.

[318] *Cf.* Inter-American Specialized Conference on Human Rights, San José, Costa Rica, November 7 to 22, 1969, *Proceedings and Documents*, p. 160.

[319] *Cf.* Inter-American Specialized Conference on Human Rights, San José, Costa Rica, November 7 to 22, 1969, *Proceedings and Documents*, p. 160.

Rights,[320] which became the present text of Article 4(1) of the American Convention.

212. When ratifying the Convention, only Mexico made an interpretative declaration, clarifying that "regarding paragraph 1 of Article 4, [it] considers that the expression 'in general' ... does not constitute an obligation to adopt or to maintain in force legislation that protects life 'from the moment of conception,' because this matter pertains to the domain reserved to the States."[321]

213. Since the Costa Rican State defines the embryo as "human being" and "person," the Court will now review briefly the preparatory work concerning these expressions. Article 1 of the draft human rights convention, approved by the Fourth Meeting of the Inter-American Council of Jurists,[322] established that:

The States parties to this Convention undertake to respect the rights and freedoms recognized herein and to ensure to all persons who are in their territory and who are subject to their jurisdiction the free and full exercise of those rights and freedoms.[323]

214. Meanwhile, Article 2(1) established that:

The right to life is inherent in the human being. This right shall be protected by law from the moment of conception.[324]

215. The wording of Article 1 of the draft human rights convention submitted by the Government of Uruguay[325] was identical to the draft prepared by the Inter-American Council of Jurists,[326] while Article 2(1) indicated:

Every human being has the right to have his life respected. This right shall be protected by law from the moment of conception. No one can be deprived of life arbitrarily.[327]

---

[320] *Cf.* Inter-American Specialized Conference on Human Rights, San José, Costa Rica, November 7 to 22, 1969, *Proceedings and Documents*, pp. 161 and 481.
[321] *Cf.* Interpretative Declaration by Mexico. Available at: www.oas.org/es/cidh/mandato/Basicos/convratif.asp (last visited November 28, 2012).
[322] *Cf.* draft human rights convention, approved by the fourth meeting of the Inter-American Council of Jurists, Final proceedings, Santiago de Chile, September 1959, Doc. CIJ-43, in: *Anuario Interamericano de Derechos Humanos* 1968, OAS, Washington DC, 1973, p. 236.
[323] *Anuario Interamericano de Derechos Humanos* 1968, OAS, Washington DC, 1973, p. 236.
[324] *Anuario Interamericano de Derechos Humanos* 1968, OAS, Washington DC, 1973, p. 236.
[325] Draft human rights convention, presented by the Government of Uruguay, Second Special Inter-American Conference, Rio de Janeiro, 1965, doc. 49, in: *Anuario Interamericano de Derechos Humanos* 1968, OAS, Washington DC, 1973, p. 298.
[326] *Cf. Anuario Interamericano de Derechos Humanos* 1968, OAS, Washington DC, 1973, p. 236.
[327] *Anuario Interamericano de Derechos Humanos* 1968, OAS, Washington DC, 1973, p. 236.

216. In the "Opinion of the Inter-American Commission on Human Rights on the draft Convention on Human Rights approved by the Inter-American Council of Jurists (Civil and Political Rights), Part I," and the "Text of the amendments suggested by the Inter-American Commission on Human Rights to the draft Convention on Human Rights prepared by the Inter-American Council of Jurists,"[328] the Commission suggested, with regard to Article 1 of the draft of the Inter-American Council of Jurists, "in the interests of greater brevity and technical precision of the wording" the substitution of the expression "human beings" by "persons."[329] However, at the same time, it maintained the expression "human being" in Article 2(1), proposing the following wording that included the phrase "in general":

Every person has the right to have his life respected. This right shall be protected by law, in general, from the moment of conception.[330]

217. Finally, Article 1 of the draft Inter-American Convention on Protection of Human Rights established:

1. The contracting States undertake to respect the rights and freedoms recognized herein and to ensure to all persons within their territory and subject to their jurisdiction the free and full exercise of those rights and freedoms ...
2. "Person" for the intents and purposes of this Convention, means every human being ...

218. In addition, Article 3(1) indicated:

Every person has the right to have his life respected. This right shall be protected by law, in general, from the moment of conception. No one shall be arbitrarily deprived of his life.

219. The Court observes that during the preparatory work the words "person" and "human being" were used without the intention of making a distinction between the two terms. Article 1(2) of the Convention specifies that the two terms must be understood as synonyms.[331]

---

[328] Text of the amendments suggested by the Inter-American Commission on Human Rights to the draft human rights convention prepared by the Inter-American Council of Jurists, Annex to the document, OEA/Ser.L/V/II.16, doc. 18, in: *Anuario Interamericano de Derechos Humanos* 1968, OAS, Washington DC, 1973, pp. 356 ff.
[329] *Cf. Anuario Interamericano de Derechos Humanos* 1968, OAS, Washington DC, 1973, p. 318.
[330] *Anuario Interamericano de Derechos Humanos* 1968, OAS, Washington DC, 1973, pp. 320 and 356.
[331] Article 1(2) has been analyzed by the Court in cases in which the violation of rights has been alleged to the detriment of legal persons, and the Court has rejected this, because they have not been recognized as holders of the rights established in the American Convention. *Cf. Case of Cantos* v. *Argentina. Preliminary objections.* Judgment of September 7, 2001. Series C No 85, para. 29, and *Case of Perozo et al.* v. *Venezuela. Preliminary objections, merits, reparations and costs.* Judgment of January 28,

220. The Court also observes that the Inter-American Commission on Human Rights, in the case of *Baby Boy* v. *United States of America*,[332] rejected the petitioners' request to declare that two judgments of the United States Supreme Court of Justice[333] that legalized unrestricted abortion before fetal viability violated the American Declaration of the Rights and Duties of Man. Regarding the interpretation of Article I of the American Declaration, the Commission rejected the argument of the petitioners according to which "Article I of the Declaration has incorporated the notion that the right to life exists from the moment of conception,"[334] considering that, when approving the American Declaration, the Ninth American International Conference had "discussed this matter and decided not to adopt wording that would have clearly established this principle."[335] Regarding the interpretation of the American Convention, the Inter-American Commission indicated that the protection of the right to life was not absolute.[336] It considered that "[t]he addition of the phrase 'in general, from the moment of conception' did not mean that those who drafted the Convention had the intention of modifying the concept of the right to life established in Bogotá, when the American Declaration was approved. The legal implications of the phrase 'in general, from the moment of conception' are substantially different from those of the shorter phrase 'from the moment of conception,' which appeared repeatedly in the petitioners' document."[337]

221. The Court concludes that the preparatory work indicates that the proposals to eliminate the phrase "and, in general, from the moment of conception," did not prosper, and neither did the proposal of the delegations that merely requested the elimination of the words "in general."

2009. Series C No 195, para. 398. However, in these cases, the Court did not develop significant arguments on the meaning of Article 1(2) in the context of the disputes in this case.

[332] *Cf.* Inter-American Commission on Human Rights, *Baby Boy* v. *United States*, Case 2141, Report No 23/81, OEA/Ser.L/V/II.54, doc. 9 rev. 1 (1981).

[333] *Cf.* United States Supreme Court of Justice, *Cases of Roe* v. *Wade*, 410 US 113, and *Doe* v. *Bolton*, 410 US 179.

[334] *Cf.* Inter-American Commission on Human Rights, *Baby Boy* v. *United States*, Case 2141, Report No 23/81, OEA/Ser.L/V/II.54, doc. 9 rev. 1 (1981), para. 19(h).

[335] *Cf.* Inter-American Commission on Human Rights, *Baby Boy* v. *United States*, Case 2141, Report No 23/81, OEA/Ser.L/V/II.54, doc. 9 rev. 1 (1981), para. 19(h).

[336] *Cf.* Inter-American Commission on Human Rights, *Baby Boy* v. *United States*, Case 2141, Report No 23/81, OEA/Ser.L/V/II.54, doc. 9 rev. 1 (1981), para. 25.

[337] *Cf.* Inter-American Commission on Human Rights, *Baby Boy* v. *United States*, Case 2141, Report No 23/81, OEA/Ser.L/V/II.54, doc. 9 rev. 1 (1981), para. 30.

iii) Systematic interpretation of the American Convention and the American Declaration

222. The expression "every person" is used in numerous articles of the American Convention[338] and the American Declaration.[339] When analyzing these articles, it is not feasible to maintain that an embryo is the holder of and exercises the rights established in each of these articles. Also, taking into account, as indicated previously, that conception can only take place within a woman's body (*supra* paras. 186 and 187), it can be concluded with regard to Article 4(1) of the Convention, that the direct subject of protection is fundamentally the pregnant woman, because the protection of the unborn child is implemented essentially through the protection of the woman, as revealed by Article 15(3)(a) of the Protocol of San Salvador, which obliges the States Parties "to provide special care and assistance to mothers during a reasonable period before and after childbirth," and Article VII of the American Declaration, which establishes the right of all women, during pregnancy, to special protection, care and aid.

223. Consequently, the Court concludes that the historic and systematic interpretation of precedents that exists in the inter-American system confirms that it is not admissible to grant the status of person to the embryo.

C.2.b) Universal human rights system

i) Universal Declaration of Human Rights

224. Regarding the State's argument that "the Universal Declaration of Human Rights ... protects the human being from ... the moment of the fusion of the egg and the spermatozoid," the Court considers that, according to the preparatory work of this instrument, the word "born" was used precisely to exclude the unborn child from the rights recognized in the Declaration.[340] The authors expressly rejected the idea of eliminating that word, so that the resulting text expresses with full intention that the rights set forth in the Declaration are "inherent from the moment of birth."[341] Therefore, the expression

---

[338] *Cf.* in this regard, Articles 1(1), 3, 4(6), 5(1), 5(2), 7(1), 7(4), 7(5), 7(6), 8(1), 8(2), 10, 11(1), 11(3), 12(1), 13(1), 14(1), 16, 18, 20(1), 20(2), 21(1), 22(1), 22(2), 22(7), 24, 25(1) and 25(2) of the American Convention.
[339] *Cf.* in this regard Articles II, III, IV, V, VI, VIII, IX, X, XI, XII, XIII, XIV, XV, XVI, XVII, XVIII, XIX, XX, XXI, XXII, XXIII, XXIV, XXVI and XXVII of the American Declaration.
[340] E/CN.4/SR/35 (1947).
[341] E/CN.4/SR/35 (1947).

"human being" used in the Universal Declaration of Human Rights has not been understood to include the unborn child.

ii) International Covenant on Civil and Political Rights

225. Regarding the State's argument that the "International Covenant on Civil and Political Rights ... recognizes the life of the embryo independently from that of its mother," the Court observes that, during the second session of the Commission on Human Rights, held from December 2 to 17, 1947, Lebanon proposed the protection of the right to life from the moment of conception.[342] In view of the resistance to the wording "from the moment of conception" in light of the admissibility of abortion in many States, Lebanon suggested the wording "at any stage of human development."[343] This wording, which was initially accepted,[344] was subsequently eliminated.[345] A proposal made by the United Kingdom to regulate the issue of abortion in a separate article was initially considered,[346] but then was also discarded.[347] During the sixth session of the Commission on Human Rights from March 27 to May 19, 1950, a new attempt made by Lebanon to protect human life from the moment of conception failed.[348] In the deliberations of the Third Committee of the General Assembly from November 13 to 26, 1957, a group of five States (Belgium, Brazil, El Salvador, Mexico and Morocco) proposed an amendment to Article 6(1) in the following terms: "from the moment of conception, this right [to life] shall be protected by law."[349] However, this proposal was rejected by 31 votes against, 20 votes in favor and 17 abstentions.[350] Thus, the preparatory work for Article 6(1) of the ICCPR reveals that the States did not seek to treat the unborn child as a person and grant it the same level of protection as those who are born.

226. The Human Rights Committee did not comment on the right to life of the unborn child in either General Comment No 6 (Right to Life)[351] or General Comment No 17 (Rights of the Child).[352] On the

---

[342] *Cf.* UN Doc. E/CN.4/386 and 398.
[343] *Cf.* UN Doc. E/CN.4/AC.3/SR.2, para. 2f (1947).
[344] *Cf.* UN Doc. E/CN.4/AC.3/SR.2, para. 2f (1947).
[345] *Cf.* UN Doc. E/CN.4/AC.3/SR.9, para. 3 (1947).
[346] *Cf.* UN Doc. E/CN.4/AC.3/SR.9, para. 3 (1947).
[347] *Cf.* UN Doc. E/CN.4/SR.35, para. 12 (1947).
[348] *Cf.* UN Doc. E/CN.4/SR.149, para. 16 (1950).
[349] *Cf.* UN Doc. A/C.3/L.654.
[350] *Cf.* UN Doc. A/C.3/SR.820, para. 9 (1957).
[351] *Cf.* Committee on Human Rights, General Comment No 6, Right to Life (Article 6), UN Doc. HRI/GEN/1/Rev.7 at 143 (1982).
[352] *Cf.* Committee on Human Rights, General Comment No 17, Rights of the Child (Article 24).

contrary, in its concluding observations on the reports of the States, the Human Rights Committee has indicated that the right to life of the mother is violated when laws that restrict access to abortion force women to resort to unsafe abortion, exposing them to death.[353] These decisions allow the Court to state that an absolute protection of the prenatal life or the life of the embryo cannot be inferred from the ICCPR.

iii) Convention on the Elimination of All Forms of Discrimination against Women

227. The reports of the Committee on the Elimination of Discrimination against Women (hereinafter also "CEDAW") makes it clear that the fundamental principles of equality and non-discrimination require that precedence be given to protecting the rights of pregnant women over the interest of protecting the life in formation. In the case of *LC* v. *Peru*, the Committee found the State responsible for violating the rights of a girl who was denied a crucial surgical operation, based on the excuse that she was pregnant, giving priority to the fetus over the mother's health. In view of the fact that the continuation of the pregnancy represented a grave danger for the young woman's physical and mental health, the Committee concluded that denying her a therapeutic abortion and postponing the operation constituted

---

[353] For example, the Human Rights Committee has issued the following Concluding Observations in this regard: Argentina, para. 14, UN Doc. CCPR/CO/70/ARG (2000); Bolivia, para. 22, UN Doc. CCPR/C/79/Add.74 (1997); Costa Rica, para. 11, UN Doc. CCPR/C/79/Ad.107 (1999); Chile, para. 15, UN Doc. CCPR/C/79/Add.104 (1999); El Salvador, para. 14, UN Doc. CCPR/CO/78/SLV (2003); Ecuador, para. 11, UN Doc. CCPR/C/79/Add.92 (1998); The Gambia, para. 17, UN Doc. CCPR/CO/75/GMB (2004); Guatemala, para. 19, UN Doc. CCPR/CO/72/GTM (2001); Honduras, para. 8, UN Doc. CCPR/C/HND/CO/1 (2006); Kenya, para. 14, UN Doc. CCPR/CO/83/KEN (2005); Kuwait, para. 9, CCPR/CO/69/KWT (2000); Lesotho, para. 11, UN Doc. CCPR/C/79/Add.106 (1999); Mauritius, para. 9, UN Doc. CCPR/CO/83/MUS (2005); Morocco, para. 29, UN Doc. CCPR/CO/82/MAR (2004); Paraguay, para. 10, UN Doc. CCPR/C/PRY/CO/2 (2006); Peru, para. 15, UN Doc. CCPR/C/79/Ad.72 (1996); Peru, para. 20, UN Doc. CCPR/CO/70/PER (2000); Poland, para. 8, UN Doc. CCPR/CO/82/POL (2004); Republic of Tanzania, para. 15, UN Doc. CCPR/C/79/Ad.97 (1998); Trinidad and Tobago, para. 18, UN Doc. CCPR/CO/70/TTO (2000); Venezuela, para. 19, UN Doc. CCPR/CO/71/VEN (2001), and Vietnam, para. 15, UN Doc. CCPR/CO/75/VNM (2002). Also, in the *Case of KL* v. *Peru*, the Human Rights Committee determined that, by having refused a therapeutic abortion to a woman, even though the continuation of the pregnancy placed her life and mental health in grave danger, the State had violated her right not to be subjected to cruel, inhuman or degrading treatment. *Case of KL* v. *Peru*, HRC, Communication No 1153/2003, Doc. UN CCPR/C/85/D/1153/2003 (2005). This interpretation was ratified in the *Case of LMR* v. *Argentina*, where the Committee observed that refusing legal abortion in a case of rape caused the victim physical and mental suffering, so that her right to privacy and not to be subjected to torture or to cruel, inhuman or degrading treatment was violated. *Case of LMR* v. *Argentina*, HRC, Communication No 1608/2007, Doc. UN CCPR/C/101/D/1608/2007 (2011).

gender-based discrimination and a violation of her right to health and non-discrimination.[354]

228. The Committee also expressed its concern over the potential of anti-abortion laws to jeopardize women's rights to life and health.[355] The Committee has established that the total ban on abortion, as well as its criminalization under certain circumstances, violates the provisions of the Convention.[356]

iv) Convention on the Rights of the Child

229. The State argued that the embryo should be considered a "child" and, consequently, that there is a special obligation to protect it. The Court will proceed to analyze whether this interpretation has a basis in the international *corpus juris* on the protection of children.

230. According to Article 6(1) of the Convention on the Rights of the Child, "States Parties recognize that every child has the inherent right to life." The term "child" is defined in Article 1 of the Convention as "every human being below the age of eighteen years, unless under the laws applicable to the child majority is attained earlier." The Preamble to the Convention states that "the child, by reason of his physical and mental immaturity, needs special safeguards and care, including appropriate legal protection, before as well as after birth."[357]

231. Articles 1 and 6(1) of the Convention on the Rights of the Child do not refer explicitly to protection of the unborn child. The Preamble refers to the need to provide "special safeguards and care ... before ... birth." However, the preparatory work shows that this phrase was not intended to extend the provisions of the Convention, particularly the right to life, to the unborn child. In fact, the preparatory work indicates that this phrase did not intend to extend to the unborn child the provisions of the Convention, especially the right to life. Indeed, although the preamble of the revised draft of a convention

---

[354] *Case of LC v. Peru*, CEDAW, Communication No 22/2009, para. 8.15, UN Doc. CEDAW/c/50/D/22/2009 (2011).
[355] *Cf.* CEDAW, Concluding comments on: Belize, para. 56, Doc. UN A/54/38/Rev. 1, GAOR, fifty-fourth session, Supl. No 38 (1999); Chile, para. 228, Doc. UN A/54/38/Rev. 1, GAOR, fifty-fourth session, Supl. No 38 (1999); Colombia, para. 393, Doc. UN A/54/38/Rev. 1, GAOR, fifty-fourth session, Supl. No 38 (1999); Dominican Republic, para. 337, Doc. UN A/53/38/Rev.1, GAOR, fifty-third session, Supl. No 38 (1998); Paraguay, para. 131, Doc. UN A/51/38, GAOR fifty-first session, Supl. No 38 (1996).
[356] *Cf.* CEDAW, Concluding comments: Chile, para. 228, Doc. UN CEDAW/A/54/38/Rev.1 (1999), and CEDAW Committee, Concluding comments: Nepal, para. 147, Doc. UN CEDAW/A/54/38/Rev.1 (1999).
[357] *Cf.* Convention on the Rights of the Child, para. 9 of the Preamble.

on the rights of the child presented by Poland made no mention of prenatal life,[358] the Vatican requested that the expression "before and after birth" be included in the preamble,[359] which prompted conflicting opinions among the States. As a compromise, the delegations agreed to use an expression taken from the 1959 Declaration on the Rights of the Child.[360]

232. Faced with the difficulty of finding a definition of "child" in Article 1 of the draft convention, the reference to birth as the beginning of childhood was eliminated.[361] Subsequently, during the deliberations, the Philippines requested the inclusion of the expression "both before and after birth" in the preamble,[362] which was opposed by several States.[363] As a compromise, it was agreed to include this reference in the preamble, but the preparatory work made it clear that the preamble would not determine the interpretation of Article 1 of the Convention.[364]

233. The Committee on the Rights of the Child has not issued any comments from which the existence of a right to prenatal life can be inferred.

C.2.c) European human rights system

234. Article 2(1) of the European Convention on Human Rights states that "[e]veryone's right to life shall be protected by law."[365] The authors of the Convention based their wording on the Universal Declaration of Human Rights, owing to its "moral authority and technical value."[366]

235. The former European Commission of Human Rights and the European Court of Human Rights (hereinafter "the ECHR") have

---

[358] *Cf.* UN Doc. E/CN.4/1349 (1979).
[359] *Cf.* UN Doc. E/CN.4/1408, para. 91 (1980).
[360] *Cf.* UN Doc. E/CN.4/1408, paras. 95 and 96 (1980) ("Recognizing that, as indicated in the Declaration of the Rights of the Child adopted in 1959, the child due to the needs of his physical and mental development requires . . . legal protection in conditions of freedom, dignity and security").
[361] *Cf.* UN Doc. E/CN.4/1408, para. 97 (1980).
[362] *Cf.* UN Doc. E/CN.4/1989/48, para. 34 (1989).
[363] *Cf.* UN Doc. E/CN.4/1989/48, para. 36 (1989).
[364] UN Doc. E/CN.4/1989/48, paras. 39, 41 and 43 (1989) ("In adopting this preambular paragraph, the Working Group does not intend to prejudice the interpretation of Article 1 or any other provision of the Convention by State Parties").
[365] European Convention for the Protection of Human Rights and Fundamental Freedoms, Art. 2(1), approved on November 4, 1950, 213 STNU 222, ST Eur. No 5 (in force as of 3 September 1953). ("The Committee considered that it was preferable . . . as by reason of the moral authority and technical value of the document in question, to make use, as far as possible, of the definitions set out in the 'Universal Declaration of Human Rights.'")
[366] Committee on Legal and Administrative Questions Report, Section 1, Para. 6, September 5, 1949, in Collected Edition of the Preparatory Work, Vol. 1 (1975), p. 194.

ruled on the non-absolute scope of the protection of prenatal life in the context of cases of abortion and medical treatments related to *in vitro* fertilization.

236. In the 1980 *Case of Paton* v. *United Kingdom*, concerning the alleged violation of Article 2 of the European Convention to the detriment of the unborn child owing to an abortion carried out at the request of the mother in accordance with domestic law, the European Commission of Human Rights held that the wording of the Convention "tends to support the view that [Article 2] does not include the unborn child."[367] It added that recognizing an absolute right to prenatal life would be "contrary to the object and purpose of the Convention."[368] It indicated that "[t]he 'life' of the foetus is intimately connected with, and cannot be regarded in isolation from, the life of the pregnant woman. If Article 2 were held to cover the foetus and its protection under this Article were, in the absence of any express limitation, seen as absolute, an abortion would have to be considered as prohibited even where the continuance of the pregnancy would involve a serious risk to the life of the pregnant woman. This would mean that the 'unborn life' of the foetus would be regarded as being of a higher value than the life of the pregnant woman."[369] The Commission confirmed this position in the cases of *RH* v. *Norway* (1992) and *Boso* v. *Italy* (2002), concerning the presumed violation of the right to life to the detriment of the unborn child owing to State laws that permitted abortion.[370]

237. In the *Case of Vo* v. *France*, in which the petitioner had to undergo a therapeutic abortion due to the danger to her health as a result of inadequate medical treatments, the European Court stated that:

---

[367] *Case of Paton* v. *United Kingdom*, Application No 8416/79, European Commission of Human Rights, Dec. & Rep. 244 (1980), para. 9. (Thus both the general usage of the term 'everyone' ('toute personne') of the Convention (para. 7 above) and the context in which this term is employed in Article 2 (para. 8 above) tend to support the view that it does not include the unborn.)

[368] Case of *Paton* v. *United Kingdom*, Application No 8416/79, European Commission of Human Rights, Dec. & Rep. 244 (1980), para. 20. (The Commission finds that such an interpretation would be contrary to the object and purpose of the Convention.)

[369] *Case of Paton* v. *United Kingdom*, Application No 8416/79, European Commission of Human Rights, Dec. & Rep. 244 (1980), para. 19. ("The 'life' of the foetus is intimately connected with, and cannot be regarded in isolation from, the life of the pregnant woman. If Article 2 were held to cover the foetus and its protection under this Article were, in the absence of any express limitation, seen as absolute, an abortion would have to be considered as prohibited even where the continuance of the pregnancy would involve a serious risk to the life of the pregnant woman. This would mean that the 'unborn life' of the foetus would be regarded as being of a higher value than the life of the pregnant woman.")

[370] *Cf. RH* v. *Norway*, Decision on Admissibility, Application No 17004/90, 73. European Commission of Human Rights, Dec. & Rep. 155 (1992), *Boso* v. *Italy*, Application No 50490/99, European Commission of Human Rights (2002).

Unlike Article 4 of the American Convention on Human Rights, which provides that the right to life must be protected "in general, from the moment of conception," Article 2 of the Convention is silent as to the temporal limitations of the right to life and, in particular, does not define "everyone" ... whose "life" is protected by the Convention. The Court has yet to determine the issue of the "beginning" of "everyone's right to life" within the meaning of this provision and whether the unborn child has such a right ...

The issue of when the right to life begins comes within the margin of appreciation which the Court generally considers that States should enjoy in this sphere, notwithstanding an evolutive interpretation of the Convention, a "living instrument which must be interpreted in the light of present-day conditions" ... The reasons for that conclusion are, firstly, that the issue of such protection has not been resolved within the majority of the Contracting States themselves, in France in particular, where it is the subject of debate ... and, secondly, that there is no European consensus on the scientific and legal definition of the beginning of life ...

At European level, the Court observes that there is no consensus on the nature and status of the embryo and/or fetus ... although they are beginning to receive some protection in the light of scientific progress and the potential consequences of research into genetic engineering, medically assisted procreation or embryo experimentation. *At best, it may be regarded as common ground between States that the embryo/fetus belongs to the human race. The potentiality of that being and its capacity to become a person—enjoying protection under the civil law, moreover, in many States, such as France, in the context of inheritance and gifts, and also in the United Kingdom ...—require protection in the name of human dignity, without making it a "person" with the "right to life"* for the purposes of Article 2 ...

It is neither desirable, nor even possible as matters stand, to answer in the abstract the question of whether the unborn child is a person for the purposes of Article 2 of the Convention ...[371] ([Emphasis] added)

238. In the case *A, B and C v. Ireland*,[372] the European Court reiterated that:

The question of when the right to life begins came within the States' margin of appreciation because there was no European consensus on the scientific and legal definition of the beginning of life, so that it was impossible to answer the question whether the unborn was a person to be protected for the purposes of Article 2. Since the rights claimed on behalf of the fetus and those of the mother are inextricably interconnected ... the margin of appreciation accorded to a State's protection of the unborn necessarily translates into a

---

[371] ECHR, *Case of Vo v. France* (No 53924/00), GC, Judgment of July 8, 2004, paras. 75, 82, 84 and 85.
[372] ECHR, *Case of A, B and C v. Ireland* (No 25579/05), Judgment of December 16, 2010, para. 237.

margin of appreciation for that State as to how it balances the conflicting rights of the mother.

239. However, the ECHR made it clear that "this margin of appreciation is not unlimited" and that "the Court must supervise whether the interference constitutes a proportionate balancing of the competing interests involved ... A prohibition of abortion to protect unborn life is not therefore automatically justified under the Convention on the basis of unqualified deference to the protection of pre-natal life or on the basis that the expectant mother's right to respect for her private life is of a lesser stature."[373]

240. Regarding cases relating to the practice of *in vitro* fertilization, in the case of *Evans* v. *United Kingdom*, the ECHR had to rule on the presumed violation of the right to life of preserved embryos because domestic law required their destruction after the partner of the applicant had withdrawn his consent for their implantation. The Grand Chamber of the ECHR reiterated its case law established in the case of *Vo* v. *France*, stating that:

In the absence of any European consensus on the scientific and legal definition of the beginning of life, the issue of when the right to life begins comes within the margin of appreciation which the Court generally considers that States should enjoy in this sphere. Under English law, as was made clear by the domestic courts in the present applicant's case ... an embryo does not have independent rights or interests and cannot claim—or have claimed on its behalf—a right to life under Article 2.[374]

241. The Grand Chamber of the ECHR confirmed the decision regarding the non-violation of the right to life, recognized in Article 2, when indicating that "the embryos created by the applicant and [her partner] do not have a right to life within the meaning of Article 2 of the Convention, and that there has not, therefore, been a violation of that provision."[375]

242. In the *Cases of SH* v. *Austria*[376] and *Costa and Pavan* v. *Italy*,[377] which related respectively, to the regulation of IVF with respect to egg and spermatozoid donation by third parties, and pre-implantation genetic diagnosis, the ECHR did not even refer to an alleged violation of a specific right of the embryos.

---

[373] ECHR, *Case of A, B and C* v. *Ireland* (No 25579/05), Judgment of December 16, 2010, para. 238.
[374] ECHR, *Case of Evans* v. *United Kingdom* (No 6339/05), Judgment of April 10, 2007, para. 54.
[375] ECHR, *Case of Evans* v. *United Kingdom* (No 6339/05), Judgment of April 10, 2007, para. 56.
[376] *Cf.* ECHR, *Case of SH et al.* v. *Austria* (No 57813/00), Judgment of November 3, 2011.
[377] *Cf.* ECHR, *Case of Costa and Pavan* v. *Italy* (No 54270/10), Judgment of August 28, 2012.

C.2.d) African human rights system

243. Article 4 of the African Charter on Human and Peoples' Rights establishes that "[h]uman beings are inviolable. Every human being shall be entitled to respect for his life and for the integrity of his person."[378] The authors of the Charter expressly ruled out the use of terminology that would protect the right to life from the moment of conception.[379] The Protocol to the African Charter on Human and Peoples' Rights on the Rights of Women in Africa (Protocol of Maputo) does not refer to the beginning of life, and establishes that the States must take all appropriate measures to "protect the reproductive rights of women by authorizing medical abortion in cases of sexual assault, rape, incest and where the continued pregnancy endangers the mental and physical health of the mother or the life of the mother or the fetus."[380]

C.2.e) Conclusion concerning systematic interpretation

244. The Court concludes that the Constitutional Chamber based its decision on Article 4 of the American Convention, Article 3 of the Universal Declaration, Article 6 of the International Covenant on Civil and Political Rights, the Convention on the Rights of the Child and the 1959 Declaration on the Rights of the Child. However, it is not possible to use any of these articles or treaties to substantiate that the embryo can be considered a person in the terms of Article 4 of the Convention. Similarly, it is not possible to reach this conclusion from the preparatory work or from the systematic interpretation of the rights recognized in the American Convention or in the American Declaration.

C.3) Evolutive interpretation

245. This Court has indicated on other occasions[381] that human rights treaties are living instruments, whose interpretation must keep abreast of the passage of time and current living conditions. This

---

[378] African Charter on Human and Peoples' Rights, approved on June 27, 1981, Art. 4, Doc. OAU CAB/LEG/67/3 Rev. 5, 21 ILM 58 (1982) (in force since October 21, 1986).
[379] Proposal for an African charter on human and peoples' rights, Art. 17, Doc. OAU CAB/LEG/ 67/1 (1979) (where the wording of Art. 4(1) of the American Convention on Human Rights is adopted, replacing "moment of conception" [with] "moment of birth"—"This right shall be protected by law and, in general, from the moment of his birth").
[380] Protocol to the African Charter on Human and Peoples' Rights on the Rights of Women in Africa, adopted by the second ordinary session of the Assembly of the African Union, on July 11, 2003, Art. 14.2.c.
[381] *Cf. The Right to Information on Consular Assistance in the Framework of the Guarantees of the Due Process of Law.* Advisory Opinion OC-15/97 of November 14, 1997. Series A No 15, para. 114, and *Case of Atala Riffo and daughters v. Chile*, para. 83.

evolving interpretation is consistent with the general rules of interpretation established in Article 29 of the American Convention, as well as in the Vienna Convention on the Law of Treaties.[382] In making an evolutive interpretation, the Court has granted special relevance to comparative law, and has therefore used domestic norms[383] or the case law of domestic courts[384] when analyzing specific disputes in contentious cases. For its part, the European Court[385] has used comparative law as a mechanism to identify the subsequent practice of States; in other words, to determine the context of a particular treaty. In addition, for the purposes of interpretation, Article 31(3) of the Vienna Convention authorizes the use of means such as agreements or practice[386] or relevant rules of international law[387] that States have mentioned in relation to the treaty, which is related to an evolutive view of the interpretation of the treaty.

246. In the instant case, the evolutive interpretation is particularly relevant, bearing in mind that IVF is a procedure that did not exist when the authors of the Convention adopted the content of Article 4(1) of the Convention (*supra* para. 179). Therefore, the Court will analyze two issues in the context of the evolutive interpretation: (i) the pertinent developments in international and comparative law concerning the specific legal status of the embryo, and (ii) the regulations and practice of comparative law in relation to IVF.

---

[382] *Cf. The Right to Information on Consular Assistance in the Framework of the Guarantees of the Due Process of Law*, para. 113, and *Case of Atala Riffo and daughters* v. *Chile*, para. 83.

[383] In its analysis in the *Case of Kawas Fernández* v. *Honduras*, the Court took into account that: it can be seen that a considerable number of States Parties to the American Convention have adopted constitutional provisions that expressly recognize the right to a healthy environment.

[384] In the cases of *Heliodoro Portugal* v. *Panama* and *Tiu Tojín* v. *Guatemala*, the Court took into account the judgments of the domestic courts of Bolivia, Colombia, Mexico, Panama, Peru and Venezuela on the inapplicability of the statute of limitations for permanent crimes such as enforced disappearance. In addition, in the case of *Anzualdo Castro* v. *Peru*, the Court used rulings of constitutional courts of the countries of the Americas to support its definition of the concept of enforced disappearance. Other examples are the *Case of Atala Riffo and daughters* v. *Chile* and the *Case of the Kichwa Indigenous People of Sarayaku* v. *Ecuador*.

[385] For example, in the *Case of TV Vest AS & Rogaland Pensioners Party* v. *Norway*, the European Court took into account a document of the European Platform of Regulatory Authorities which compared 31 countries in the region to determine which of them permitted either paid or unpaid political advertising and in which countries such publicity was free. Likewise, in the case of *Hirst* v. *United Kingdom*, the Court took into account the "Law and practice in the Contracting States" in order to determine which countries suspended the right to vote of a person convicted of a crime, for which purpose it surveyed the legislation of 48 European countries.

[386] *Cf.* ECHR, *Case of Rasmussen* v. *Denmark* (No 8777/79), Judgment of November 28, 1984, para. 41; *Case of Inze* v. *Austria* (No 8695/79) Judgment of October 28, 1987, para. 42, and *Case of Toth* v. *Austria* (No 11894/85), Judgment of November 25, 1991, para. 77.

[387] *Cf.* ECHR, *Case of Golder* v. *United Kingdom* (No 4451/70), Judgment of December 12, 1975, para. 35.

C.3.a) The legal status of the embryo

247. It has been noted that, in the *Case of Vo* v. *France*, the European Court of Human Rights indicated that the potentiality of the embryo and its capacity to become a person requires a protection in the name of human dignity, without making it a "person" with the "right to life" (*supra* para. 237).

248. For its part, Article 18 of the Oviedo Convention for the Protection of Human Rights and Dignity of the Human Being with regard to the Application of Biology and Medicine (hereinafter "the Oviedo Convention"), adopted within the framework of the European Union,[388] establishes the following:

> *Article 18. Research on embryos* in vitro:
>
> 1. Where the law allows research on embryos *in vitro*, it shall ensure adequate protection of the embryo.
> 2. The creation of human embryos for research purposes is prohibited.

249. Consequently, this treaty does not prohibit IVF, but rather the creation of embryos for research purposes. Regarding the status of the embryo in this Convention, the ECHR has indicated that:

> The Oviedo Convention on Human Rights and Biomedicine ... is careful not to give a definition of the term "everyone," and its explanatory report indicates that, in the absence of unanimous agreement on the definition, the member States decided to allow domestic law to provide clarification for the purposes of the application of that Convention ... The same is true of the Additional Protocol on the Prohibition of Cloning Human Beings and the Additional Protocol on Biomedical Research, which do not define the concept of "human being."[389]

250. For its part, the Court of Justice of the European Union[390] in the *Case of Oliver Brüstle* v. *Greenpeace eV*[391] indicated that the purpose

---

[388] The Oviedo Convention establishes that States Parties "shall protect the dignity and identity of all human beings and guarantee everyone, without discrimination, respect for their integrity and other rights and fundamental freedoms with regard to the application of biology and medicine" and adds that "[e]ach Party shall take in its internal law the necessary measures to give effect to the provisions of this Convention." The Oviedo Convention was adopted on April 4, 1997, in Oviedo, Asturias, and entered into force on December 1, 1999. It was ratified by 29 Member States of the Council of Europe, with six reservations.

[389] ECHR, *Case of Vo* v. *France* (No 53924/00), GC, Judgment of July 8, 2004, para. 84.

[390] The Court of Justice of the European Union is an institution of the European Union (EU) entrusted with the jurisdictional powers or judicial authority in the Union. Its mission is to interpret and apply the law of the European Union and it is characterized by its structure and composition and its supranational authority and functioning. Its seat is in Luxembourg.

[391] *Cf.* European Court of Justice, Grand Chamber, Judgment of October 18, 2011, Case C-34/10, *Oliver Brüstle* v. *Greenpeace eV*.

of Directive 98/44/CE of the European Parliament and of the Council, of July 6, 1998, on the legal protection of biotechnological inventions, was "not to regulate the use of human embryos in the context of scientific research, [and that it was] limited to the patentability of biotechnological inventions."[392] However, it clarified that "although the purpose of scientific research must be distinguished from industrial or commercial purposes, the use of human embryos for research, which constitutes the reason for the application for a patent, cannot be separated from the patent itself and the rights attaching to it."[393] Consequently "the exclusion from patentability concerning the use of human embryos for industrial or commercial purposes in Article 6(2)(c) of the Directive also covers use for purposes of scientific research, only use for therapeutic or diagnostic purposes which is applied to the human embryo and is useful to it being patentable."[394] In this decision the European Court of Justice reaffirmed the exclusion of the patentability of human embryos, understood in a broad sense,[395] for ethical and moral reasons,[396] when it is associated with industrial or commercial purposes. However, neither the Directive, nor the judgment state that human embryos should be considered as "persons" or that they have a subjective right to life.

251. Furthermore, in the *Case of SH et al. v. Austria*, the ECHR considered permissible the ban on practicing IVF with eggs and spermatozoids donated by third parties, emphasizing that:

---

[392] European Court of Justice, Grand Chamber, Judgment of October 18, 2011, Case C-34/10, *Oliver Brüstle* v. *Greenpeace eV*, para. 40.
[393] European Court of Justice, Grand Chamber, Judgment of October 18, 2011, Case C-34/10, *Oliver Brüstle* v. *Greenpeace eV*, para. 43.
[394] European Court of Justice, Grand Chamber, Judgment of October 18, 2011, Case C-34/10, *Oliver Brüstle* v. *Greenpeace eV*, para. 46.
[395] *Cf.* European Court of Justice, Grand Chamber, Judgment of October 18, 2011, Case C-34/10, *Oliver Brüstle* v. *Greenpeace eV*, para. 38 ("any human ovum after fertilization, any non-fertilized human ovum into which the cell nucleus from a mature human cell has been transplanted and any non-fertilized human ovum whose cell division and further development have been stimulated by parthenogenesis constitute a 'human embryo' within the meaning of Article 6(2)(c) of the Directive." Article 6 of the Directive states: "1. Inventions shall be considered unpatentable where their commercial exploitation is contrary to public order or morality; however, exploitation shall not be deemed to be so contrary merely because it is prohibited by law or regulation. 2. On the basis of paragraph 1, the following, in particular, shall be considered unpatentable: . . . (c) uses of human embryos for industrial or commercial purposes").
[396] *Cf.* European Court of Justice, Grand Chamber, Judgment of October 18, 2011, Case C-34/10, *Oliver Brüstle* v. *Greenpeace eV*, para. 6, stating that the "preamble to the Directive states the following: '. . . whereas public order and morality correspond in particular to the ethical and moral principles recognized in a Member State, respect for which is particularly important in the field of biotechnology, in view of the potential scope of inventions in this field and their inherent relationship to living matter; whereas such ethical and moral principles supplement the standard legal examinations under patent Law, regardless of the technical field of the invention.'"

The Austrian legislature has not completely ruled out artificial procreation ... The legislature tried to reconcile the wish to make medically assisted procreation available and the existing unease among large sections of society as to the role and possibilities of modern reproductive medicine, which raises issues of a morally and ethically sensitive nature.[397]

252. Also, in the *Case of Costa and Pavan* v. *Italy*, the ECHR, in its prior considerations on European law relevant for the analysis of the case, emphasized that in "the case of *Roche* v. *Roche and others* ([2009] IESC 82 (2009)), the Irish Supreme Court established that the concept of the unborn child did not apply to embryos created through *in vitro* insemination, which accordingly did not benefit from the protection provided for in article 40.3.3 of the Irish Constitution recognizing the right to life of the unborn child. In that case the applicant, who had already had a child following *in vitro* fertilization, had applied to the Supreme Court for leave to have implanted three other embryos created by the same fertilization process, despite the lack of consent of her former partner from whom she had separated in the meantime."[398]

253. Accordingly, the Court observes that the regulatory trends in international law do not lead to the conclusion that the embryo should be treated in the same way as a person, or that it has a right to life.

C.3.b) IVF regulations and practice in comparative law

254. Based on the expert opinions presented by the parties at the public hearing, it was established that Costa Rica is the only country in the region that prohibits and, therefore, does not practice IVF (*supra* para. 67).

---

[397] *Cf.* ECHR, *Case of SH et al.* v. *Austria* (No 57813/00), Judgment of November 3, 2011, para. 104.

[398] ECHR, *Case of Costa and Pavan* v. *Italy* (No 54270/10), Judgment of August 28, 2012, para. 33 ("33. The Court also observes that in the case of *Roche* v. *Roche and others* ([2009] IESC 82 (2009)), the Irish Supreme Court established that the concept of the unborn child did not apply to embryos created through *in vitro* insemination, which accordingly did not benefit from the protection provided for in article 40.3.3 of the Irish Constitution recognizing the right to life of the unborn child. In that case the applicant, who had already had a child following *in vitro* fertilization, had applied to the Supreme Court for leave to have implanted three other embryos created by the same fertilization process, despite the lack of consent of her former partner from whom she had separated in the meantime"). The Court takes note that on November 28, 2012, the Italian Government filed a request for review of this case before the Grand Chamber of the European Court of Human Rights, "because the original application was filed directly before the European Court of Human Rights without previously having exhausted ... all the domestic remedies and without, of necessity, taking into consideration the margin of appreciation that each State has in the adoption of its own legislation." Available at: www.governo.it/Presidenza/Comunicati/dettaglio.asp?d=69911 (last visited November 28, 2012).

255. Nevertheless, from the evidence provided by the parties to the case file, the Court observes that, although IVF is performed in many countries,[399] this does not necessarily mean that it is regulated by law. In this regard, the Court notes that the comparative legislation on assisted reproduction techniques submitted by the parties (Brazil, Chile, Colombia, Guatemala, Mexico, Peru and Uruguay) reveals that there are norms that regulate some practices in this area. The Court notes that, for example: (i) human cloning is prohibited in Chile[400] and Peru;[401] (ii) the laws of Brazil,[402] Chile[403] and Peru[404] prohibit the use of assisted reproductive techniques for purposes other than human procreation; (iii) Brazil stipulates that the ideal number of eggs and pre-embryos to be transferred may be no more than four, to avoid increasing the risk of multiple births,[405] and prohibits the use of procedures "aimed at embryonic reduction"[406] and the commercial-

---

[399] The 2009 Report of the *Registro Latinoamericano de Reproducción Asistida* (RLA) indicated that, during this period, "135 centers from 11 countries reported. The majority of the centers that reported are in Brazil and Mexico, and the majority of the cycles were carried out in Brazil and Argentina." *Cf.* Written summary of the expert opinion provided by Fernando Zegers-Hochschild at the public hearing before the Court (merits report, volume VI, folio 2825).
[400] *Cf.* Law 20,120 of 2006, Ministry of Health of Chile, Article 5 (file of attachments to the answering brief, volume IV, annex 2, folios 8424 to 8426).
[401] *Cf.* General Health Law of Peru No 26,842 of July 15, 1997, Article 7 (file of attachments to the answering brief, volume IV, annex 2, folio 8357).
[402] *Cf.* Decision of the Federal Medical Board No 1358 of 1992, General Principle No 5 (file of attachments to the merits report, volume I, annex 18, folios 425 to 428).
[403] *Cf.* Bill on Assisted Human Reproduction, Article 1 (file of attachments to the answering brief, volume IV, annex 2, folios 8437 to 8443).
[404] *Cf.* General Health Law of Peru No 26,842 of July 15, 1997, Article 7 (file of attachments to the answering brief, volume IV, annex 2, folio 8357).
[405] *Cf.* Decision No 1358 of 1992 of the Federal Medical Board, General Principle No 6 (file of attachments to the merits report, volume I, annex 18, folios 425 to 428). Regarding embryo transfer, expert witness Garza explained that "the guidelines issued by the American Society of Reproductive Medicine (ASRM) in 1999 recommend that no more than two embryos be transferred to the women who have the greatest probability of becoming pregnant and no more than five to patients with a lower probability of pregnancy. In 2006, in an effort to reduce even more the occurrence of high-order multiple pregnancy, ASRM and the Society for Assisted Reproduction Technologies (SART) developed guidelines to help ART programs and patients determine the appropriate number of cleavage stage (usually 2 or 3 days after fertilization) embryos or blastocysts (usually 5 or 6 days after fertilization) to transfer. These guidelines recommend that: women under the age of 35, who have a greater probability of becoming pregnant, should be encouraged to consider single-embryo transfer; women aged from 35 to 37 who have a favorable prognosis should not receive more than two embryos; women aged from 38 to 40 who have a favorable prognosis should not receive more than three cleavage-stage embryos or no more than two blastocysts. Women aged 40, and those with less probability of becoming pregnant, can have more embryos transferred." Affidavit prepared by expert witness Garza (merits report, volume V, folios 2566 and 2567).
[406] General Principle No 7, Decision of the Federal Medical Board No 1358 of 1992 (file of attachments to the merits report, volume I, annex 18, folios 425 to 428).

ization of biological material is a crime;[407] and (iv) there are different types of regulations on cryopreservation. For example, Chile prohibits the freezing of embryos for deferred transfer,[408] while Brazil[409] and Colombia[410] allow the cryopreservation of embryos, spermatozoids and eggs. In addition, some countries, such as Argentina,[411] Chile[412] and Uruguay,[413] are trying to take measures so that assisted reproduction treatments will be covered by State health care programs and policies.

256. The Court considers that, even though there are few specific legal regulations on IVF, most of the States of the region allow IVF to be practiced within their territory. This means that, in the context of the practice of most States Parties to the Convention, it has been interpreted that the Convention allows IVF to be performed. The Court considers that this practice by the States is related to the way in which they interpret the scope of Article 4 of the Convention, because none of the said States has considered that the protection of the embryo should be so great that it does not permit assisted

---

[407] Article 5 of Law No 11,105, of March 24, 2005, Brazil (merits file, volume I, annex 20, folios 249 to 262).

[408] *Cf.* Regulations applicable to *in vitro* fertilization and embryonic transfer, No 1072 of June 28, 1985, Santiago, Ministry of Health, Republic of Chile (file of attachments to the answering brief, volume IV, annex 2, folios 8456 to 8459). Article 8 establishes that: "the Institution and the respective team of experts must keep and provide to the authorities of the Ministry of Health complete and reliable information on: (a) place or site where IVF and ET are performed; (b) the institution that sponsors and is responsible for the IVF and ET program, clearly defining the program's objectives and procedures; (c) the experts and professionals who perform and assist with the IVF and ET procedures, their training and suitability; (d) work protocols in which the details of IVF and ET procedures are recorded, indicating the number of eggs obtained, fertilized or implanted. In this regard, the protocols must establish that all normal fertilized eggs must be transferred to the mother and prohibit the freezing of embryos for deferred transfer, much less for research purposes."

[409] *Cf.* Decision of the Federal Medical Board No 1358 of 1992 (file of attachments to the merits report, volume I, annex 18, folios 425 to 428).

[410] *Cf.* Decree No 1546 of 1998, President of the Republic of Colombia, Article 48 (file of attachments to the answering brief, volume IV, annex 2, folios 8277 to 8303).

[411] Bill approved by the Chamber of Deputies on June 28, 2012, establishing that social welfare agencies, pre-paid medicine entities and the public health system must include as obligatory services full and interdisciplinary coverage of the procedures that the World Health Organization defines as "Assisted Human Reproduction." Text of the six articles available [in Spanish] at: www1.hcdn.gov.ar/proyxml/expediente.asp?fundamentos= si&numexp=0492-D-2010.

[412] Expert witness Zegers-Hochschild stated that, even though Chile "has not formally discussed the coverage of infertility treatments at the legislative level; nevertheless, the Government has allocated special financial resources to the National Health Fund to cover ART treatments to a growing number of women with limited means." Written summary of the expert opinion provided by Fernando Zegers-Hochschild at the public hearing before the Court (merits report, volume VI, folio 2824).

[413] *Cf.* Bill on "Assisted reproduction techniques" approved by the Chamber of Representatives on October 9, 2012, and currently being examined by the Senate's Public Health Committee. Available at: www0.parlamento.gub.uy/indexdb/Distribuidos/ListarDistribuido.asp?URL=/distribuidos/contenido/camara/D20120417-0218-0997.htm&TIPO=CON (last visited November 28, 2012).

reproduction techniques and, in particular, IVF. Thus, this generalized practice[414] is associated with the principle of gradual and incremental—rather than absolute—protection of prenatal life and with the conclusion that the embryo cannot be understood as a person.

C.4) The principle of the most favorable interpretation, and the object and purpose of the treaty

257. In a teleological interpretation, the purpose of the norms involved is examined and, to this end, it is pertinent to analyze the object and purpose of the treaty itself and, if relevant, the purposes of the regional protection system. Thus, there is a direct relationship between the systematic and the teleological interpretations.[415]

258. The precedents examined so far allow it to be inferred that the purpose of Article 4(1) of the Convention is to safeguard the right to life, without this entailing the denial of other rights protected by the Convention. Thus, the object and purpose of the expression "in general" is to permit, should a conflict between rights arise, the possibility of invoking exceptions to the protection of the right to life from the moment of conception. In other words, the object and purpose of Article 4(1) of the Convention is that the right to life should not be understood as an absolute right, the alleged protection of which can justify the total negation of other rights.

259. Consequently, it is not admissible that the State argue that its constitutional norms grant a greater protection to the right to life and, therefore, proceed to give this right absolute prevalence. To the contrary, this approach denies the existence of rights that may be the object of disproportionate restrictions owing to the defense of the absolute protection of the right to life, which would be contrary to the protection of human rights, an aspect that constitutes the object and purpose of the treaty. In other words, in application of the principle of the most favorable interpretation, the alleged "broadest protection" in the domestic sphere cannot allow or justify the suppression of the enjoyment and exercise of the rights and freedoms recognized in the Convention or limit them to a greater extent that the Convention establishes.

---

[414] Article 31.3(b) of the Vienna Convention establishes that: "[t]here shall be taken into account, together with the context: any subsequent practice in the application of the treaty which establishes the agreement of the parties regarding its interpretation."
[415] *Case of González et al. ("Cotton field") v. Mexico. Preliminary objection, merits, reparations and costs.* Judgment of November 16, 2009. Series C No 205, para. 59.

260. In this regard, the Court considers that other judgments in comparative constitutional law endeavor to find an adequate balance between possible competing rights and, consequently, constitute a relevant reference to interpret the scope of the expression "in general, from the moment of conception" contained in Article 4(1). The Court will now refer to some examples of case law in which a legitimate interest in protecting prenatal life is recognized, but where this interest is differentiated from entitlement of the right to life, stressing that any intent to protect the former interest must be harmonized with the fundamental rights of other individuals, especially the mother.

261. In the European sphere, for example, the German Constitutional Court, stressing the State's general obligation to protect the unborn child, has established that "[t]he protection of life, ... is not so absolute to the extent that, without any exception, it enjoys prevalence over all the other rights,"[416] and that "[t]he fundamental rights of women ... subsist in the face of the right to life of the *nasciturus* and, consequently, must be protected."[417] Moreover, according to the Constitutional Court of Spain, "[t]he protection that the Constitution provides to the *nasciturus* ... does not mean that the said protection must be of an absolute nature."[418]

262. In the Americas, the United States Supreme Court has indicated that "[i]t is reasonable and logical for a State, at certain times, to protect other interests ... such as, for example, those of the potential human life," which should be weighed with the personal intimacy of the woman—which cannot be understood as an absolute right—and "other circumstances and values."[419] Furthermore, according to the Constitutional Court of Colombia, "[a]lthough it corresponds to Congress to adopt appropriate measures to comply with the obligation to protect life, ... this does not mean that all the measures that it takes to this end are justified, because, despite its constitutional relevance, life does not have the nature of an absolute value or right and must be weighed with the other constitutional values, principles and rights."[420] The Argentine Supreme Court of Justice has indicated that no mandate is derived from either the American Declaration or the American Convention under which the scope of the criminal norms that permit

---

[416] BVerfG, Judgment BVerfGE 88, 203, May 28, 1993, 2 BvF 2/90 and 4, 5/92, para. D.I.2.b.
[417] BVerfG, Judgment BVerfGE 88, 203, May 28, 1993, 2 BvF 2/90 and 4, 5/92, para. D.I.2.c.aa.
[418] Constitutional Court of Spain, Judgment on action on unconstitutionality 53/1985, April 11, 1985, paras. 8 and 12.
[419] United States Supreme Court, *Case of Roe* v. *Wade*, 410 US 115, 157 (1973).
[420] Constitutional Court of Colombia, Judgment C-355 of 2006, VI.5.

abortion in certain circumstances must be interpreted restrictively, "because the wording of the pertinent provisions of these instruments was expressly delimited so that the invalidity of a supposed abortion [such as the one established in the Argentine Penal Code] could not be derived from them."[421] Similarly, the Supreme Court of Justice of Mexico has declared that, based on the fact that life is a necessary condition for the existence of other rights, it cannot be validly concluded that life should be considered more valuable than any of those other rights.[422]

263. Consequently, the Court concludes that the object and purpose of the expression "in general" in Article 4(1) of the Convention is to allow, as appropriate, an adequate balance between competing rights and interests. In the case that the Court is examining, it is sufficient to indicate that the said object and purpose implies that the absolute protection of the embryo cannot be alleged, annulling other rights.

C.5) Conclusion on the interpretation of Article 4(1)

264. The Court has used different methods of interpretation that have led to similar results according to which the embryo cannot be understood to be a person for the purposes of Article 4(1) of the American Convention. In addition, after analyzing the available scientific data, the Court has concluded that "conception" in the sense of Article 4(1) occurs at the moment when the embryo becomes implanted in the uterus, which explains why, before this event, Article 4 of the Convention would not be applicable. Moreover, it can be concluded from the words "in general" that the protection of the right to life under this provision is not absolute, but rather gradual and incremental according to its development, since it is not an absolute and unconditional obligation, but entails understanding that exceptions to the general rule are admissible.

---

[421] Supreme Court of Justice of Argentina, "F., A.L. ref/ self-realization measure," Judgment of March 13, 2012, F. 259. XLVI, considering paragraph 10.

[422] *Cf.* Judgment of the Supreme Court of Justice of the Nation of August 28, 2008, action on unconstitutionality 146/2007 and joindered action 147/2007. In particular, the judgment indicated that: "In other words, we can accept as true that unless one is alive, one is unable to exercise any right; but, we cannot infer from this that the right to life enjoys pre-eminence in the face of any other right. To accept a similar argument would force us to accept also, for example, that the right to food is more important than the right to life, because the former is a condition for the latter." For its part, the Federal Supreme Court of Brazil has indicated that "in order for an embryo—*in vitro*—to be recognized the full right to life, it would be necessary to recognize the right to a uterus; a view that is not established in the Constitution." Federal Supreme Court. Action on unconstitutionality No 3510 of May 29, 2008, p. 5.

D) Proportionality of the prohibition

Arguments of the Commission and allegations of the parties

265. The Commission indicated that the requirements of legality, necessity and suitability had been met. However, the Commission considered that, when analyzing suitability, the scientific evidence "that the assisted reproduction technique of [IVF] imposes a risk of embryo loss [... that] is comparable to the natural reproduction process" "may be relevant." Regarding the need for the measure, the Commission indicated that "there were less restrictive ways to accomplish the State's objective and to reconcile the interests at stake; for example, by some other form of regulation that could produce results that more closely resembled the natural process of conception, such as a regulation that reduced the number of eggs fertilized." Lastly, it argued that "sufficient elements" exist to conclude that: (i) "the rights affected, ... are particularly relevant for the identity of a person and his or her autonomy"; (ii) "the protection of life in the comparative constitutional and international sphere is usually subject to degrees of protect[ion] that are applied incrementally"; (iii) "the severe nature of the impact on the rights involved" should be considered, because "[t]he effect was equivalent to an annulment of the exercise of their rights"; (iv) "it is feasible to consider that, in practice, the ban on [IVF] does not contribute to a significant protection of the life of the embryos, if it is compared to the high frequency [of embryonic loss] in the natural conception process"; and (v) it is important to mention "the consistency and coherence of the State's action in relation to the embryo," because there are "practices that are currently allowed in Costa Rica [... that] entail a risk of fertilization of the said eggs, of embryonic loss, and of multiple pregnancies." The Commission observed that the ban on IVF "had two effects that fall within the scope of the right to equality: (i) it prevented the [presumed] victims from overcoming their situation of disadvantage by benefitting from scientific progress, in particular, from a medical treatment, and (ii) it had a specific and disproportionate impact on women."

266. Representative Molina concurred with the Commission and added, with regard to the legality of the measure, that the Constitutional Chamber "exceeded its authority, limiting the Legislature's exercise of its primordial function." In addition, he argued that "the ambiguity" in the way the Constitutional Chamber formulated the prohibition "g[ave] rise to uncertainty and open[ed] the way to arbitrariness by the authorities." He added that the purpose of the judgment was "the absolute protection [of the] right to life of human

embryos," and therefore considered it a "supposed legitimate purpose." However, he refuted the suitability of the measure, considering the judgment "a discriminatory" and "arbitrary measure" that "failed to weigh or gauge the different convention-based rights." Furthermore, he argued that "[t]he State chose the most harmful measure of all; the measure that completely annulled the only possibility that the couples had to achieve their private decision to become biological parents."

267. Representative Molina argued that realization of the right to life does not justify the presumed restriction of the rights of the family, to honor and dignity, and to equality before the law. He characterized the presumed victims' infertility as a "disability for which they had been discriminated against as regards having a family." He also argued that "no benefits were obtained from the measure, while the maximum harm was caused by the prohibition, [so that] it cannot be said that the ban on IVF is a proportionate measure." In addition, he argued that "the Constitutional Chamber's decision ... resulted in discrimination owing to reproductive incapacity," considering that the "judgment establishes a clear differentiation between ... couples ... who are able to conceive naturally and ... couples who can only do so by using assisted reproduction methods," and that "[t]he discrimination made by the Chamber is evident not only in the judgment as such, but also in its effects on the individuals and couples who sought to conceive using assisted reproduction methods." Lastly, he considered the judgment was a "form of discrimination based on their financial possibilities."

268. Representative May argued that "[i]nfertility is a disease, a disability, and, consequently, an inability of the human being to fertilize or to conceive; in sum, an inability to procreate." He argued that, even though "the absolute ban" on the practice of IVF "could appear to be neutral," "it does not have the same effect on each individual, [but ...] has a disproportionate impact on those who are infertile, denying them the opportunity to overcome their physical condition and to conceive biologically."

269. The State alleged that the Commission "has not questioned the legality of the measure adopted by the Constitutional Court" and "has accepted that the restriction ... constitutes a limitation established by law and under the legal system." It argued that "the purpose sought by the Costa Rican State when prohibiting [IVF] is legitimate, because it was intended to protect the right to life of the embryos." It asserted that "the legitimacy of the purpose depends on how the word 'conception' is defined, because if it is equated to the word 'fertilization,' the measure adopted by the State when prohibiting [IVF] would be

suitable." Regarding the need for the measure, it argued that "the Commission bases its arguments on a false premise, which is to indicate that, in this case, the Costa Rican State could have adopted a less restrictive measure." In this regard, it argued that "it has been shown that in the actual state of science, there is no evidence that [IVF] offers guarantees of protection of life to the unborn child fertilized *in vitro.*"

270. Regarding the proportionality of the measure, the State argued that "when weighing the harm that the restrictive measure causes to the holder of the freedom, and the benefit that the collectivity obtains from it by protecting society's most fundamental value, which is the right to life, the State must necessarily incline the balance in favor of the latter." It indicated that the "problems associated with *in vitro* fertilization are the high death rate of the human embryos that are transferred to the uterine cavity by artificial means." It cited some phenomena "to explain some of the problems that may be involved in the high inefficiency of IVF": (i) the state of development of the ovules used: "the induction of multi-ovulation, which is usually carried out in order to practice IVF, is carried out using gonadotropins, but the state of development of the ovules obtained by this procedure is often inadequate"; (ii) "since the procedure of the selection of normal and mature spermatozoids that occurs naturally does not occur in [IVF], conception occurs with defective spermatozoids in many cases"; (iii) "the percentage of embryos whose development ceases between the stages of zygote and blastocyst is higher when their development is generated *in vitro* rather than *in vivo* ... The embryo that is generated has a better intrinsic viability than the one created *in vitro*; in other words, the embryos created in the laboratory are less healthy"; and (iv) "it has been demonstrated that the embryo sends signals to prepare the endometrium for the implantation, which could provide a partial explanation why the rate of implantation is so low in the case of IVF, since the pre-implanted embryo is not present in the woman's body." Thus the State argued that "[t]he only solution is to prohibit the technique, because this is the only way to guarantee the life of the embryo as of fertilization" and that, therefore, "it could not be obliged to weigh the rights involved differently in this case, because there is no way to do so." In addition, the State asserted that "the Constitutional Chamber's judgment ... is not omissive as regards weighing the factors involved, [because] it considered that the constitutional prohibition of the *in vitro* technique was necessary to protect the right to life of the embryo." It added that "[t]he fact that, in Costa Rica, the Constitutional Chamber has endorsed the existence of therapeutic abortion ... is not contrary to the prohibition of" IVF, because, in that case, "the

weighing up process must be made between the right to life of the mother and the right to life of the embryo."

271. Finally, regarding the alleged indirect discrimination, the State indicated that "[i]nfertility is a natural condition that is not induced by the State." In addition, it argued that "there is no consensus that infertility is, *per se*, a disease" or that it can "be considered a disability." In this regard, the State argued that "[a]ssisted conception is different from the treatment of an illness"; IVF does not "cure" infertility, because "it does not constitute a treatment to change the situation that causes a couple or an individual to be infertile, but constitutes a means to substitute the natural fertilization process." In addition, it argued that the prohibition of IVF "is not designed to establish discrimination against those who are unable to have children naturally, and especially against women," because the prohibition "was addressed at everyone irrespective of their condition: single, married, women or men, fertile or infertile." Consequently, it argued the ban on IVF has not had a "special intensity" in relation to women, thus it does not discriminate indirectly, because "it does not originate only from problems suffered by women."

Considerations of the Court

272. The Court has indicated that the decision to have biological children using assisted reproduction techniques forms part of the sphere of the right to personal integrity and to private and family life. In addition, the way in which this decision is arrived at is part of the autonomy and identity of a person, in both the individual dimension and as part of a couple. The Court will now analyze the State's interference in relation to the exercise of these rights.

273. In this regard, in its case law, the Court has established that a right may be restricted by the States provided that the interferences are not abusive or arbitrary; consequently, they must be substantively and formally established by law,[423] pursue a legitimate aim, and comply with the requirements of suitability, necessity and proportionality.[424] In the instant case, the Court has underlined that the "absolute right to life of the embryo" as grounds for the restriction of the rights involved,

---

[423] *Cf. The Word "Laws" in Article 30 of the American Convention on Human Rights*. Advisory Opinion OC-6/86 of May 9, 1986. Series A No 6, paras. 35 and 37.
[424] *Cf. Case of Tristán Donoso v. Panama. Preliminary objection, merits, reparations and costs.* Judgment of January 27, 2009. Series C No 193, para. 56, and *Case of Atala Riffo and daughters v. Chile*, para. 164.

is not supported by the American Convention (*supra* para. 264); thus, it is not necessary to make a detailed analysis of each of these requirements, or to assess the disputes regarding the declaration of unconstitutionality in the formal sense based on the presumed violation of the principle of legal reserve. Despite the foregoing, the Court considers it appropriate to indicate the way in which the sacrifice of the rights involved in this case was excessive in comparison to the benefits referred to with the protection of the embryo.[425]

274. To this end, the restriction would have to protect prenatal life significantly, without annulling the rights to private life and to found a family. In order to weigh these factors the Court must analyze: (i) the level of harm to one of the rights at stake, determining whether the level of this harm was serious, intermediate or moderate; (ii) the importance of ensuring the contrary right; and (iii) whether ensuring the latter justifies restricting the former.[426]

275. The European Court of Human Rights has indicated that the possible conflict between the right to private life, which includes the rights to autonomy and to the free development of the persona, and "the possibility that, in certain circumstances, safeguards may be extended to the unborn child [must be] determined by weighing various ... rights or freedoms claimed by a mother and a father involved in a relationship with one another or *vis-à-vis* the foetus."[427] This Court has stated that "undue deference for the protection of prenatal life or on the basis that the right of the future mother to respect for her private life is of a lower rank, does not constitute a reasonable and proportionate weighing up of competing rights and interests."[428] Also, in the case of *Costa and Pavan* v. *Italy*, the European Court considered that the absolute prohibition of pre-implantation diagnosis was not proportionate, owing to the inconsistent domestic legislation concerning reproductive rights that, while prohibiting the pre-implantation diagnosis, permitted the termination of the pregnancy if the fetus subsequently revealed symptoms of a grave illness detectable by pre-implantation diagnosis.[429]

---

[425] *Case of Kimel* v. *Argentina, Merits, reparations and costs*. Judgment of May 2, 2008. Series C No 177, para. 83, and *Case of Chaparro Álvarez and Lapo Íñiguez*, para. 93.
[426] *Case of Kimel* v. *Argentina*, para. 84.
[427] *Cf.* ECHR, *Case of Vo* v. *France* (No 53924/00), Judgment of July 8, 2004, para. 80; *Case of RR* v. *Poland* (No 27617/04), Judgment of May 26, 2011, para. 181.
[428] *Cf.* ECHR, *Case of A, B and C* v. *Ireland* (No 25579/05), Grand Chamber Judgment of December 16, 2010, para. 238.
[429] *Cf.* ECHR, *Case of Costa and Pavan* v. *Italy* (No 54270/10), Judgment of August 28, 2012, para. 71.

276. The Court will weigh up the factors analyzing: (i) the severity of the interference that took place in the rights to private and family life and the other rights involved in the instant case. In addition, this severity is analyzed based on the disproportionate impact in relation to: (ii) disability, (iii) gender, and (iv) socio-economic situation. Lastly, the Court will analyze (v) the dispute on the alleged embryonic loss.

D.1) Severity of the limitation of the rights involved in this case

277. As previously indicated (*supra* para. 144), the scope of the right to private and family life bears a close relationship to personal autonomy and reproductive rights. The Constitutional Chamber's judgment had the effect of interfering in the exercise of these rights of the presumed victims, because the couples had to change their course of action in relation to a decision to try and have children using IVF. Indeed, the Court considers that one of the direct interferences in private life is related to the fact that the Constitutional Chamber's decision prevented the couples from deciding whether or not they wished to submit to this treatment to have children in Costa Rica. The interference was even more evident when it is considered that IVF, in most cases, is the technique that individuals or couples resort to after having tried other treatments to overcome infertility (for example, Mr Vega and Ms Arroyo underwent 21 artificial inseminations) or, in other circumstances, it is the only option the person has in order to be able to have biological children, as in the case of Mr Mejías Carballo and Ms Calderón Porras (*supra* paras. 85 and 117).

278. The Court has indicated that the interference in this case is not related to the fact of not being able to have children (*supra* para. 161). It will now analyze the degree of severity of the harm to the right to private life and to found a family, and to the right to personal integrity, taking into account the impact of the prohibition of IVF on the intimacy, autonomy, mental health and reproductive rights of those concerned.

279. First, the prohibition of IVF had an impact on the intimacy of the individuals, because, in some cases, one of the indirect effects of the prohibition was that, since it was not possible to practice this technique in Costa Rica, the procedures undergone in order to obtain medical treatment abroad required revealing aspects that were part of private life. In this regard, Ms Bianchi indicated that:

For the couple, for us—as husband and wife—taking out this amount of money as quickly as possible signified great financial stress; because here time is also very important, since one already has a diagnosis ... and one does not know how much time it will take to collect this amount; especially if it will have to be collected several times; this kind of stress that a couple has to endure—many couples separate owing to normal financial stress. The lack of privacy is tremendous because, in the workplace, all my employers had to realize that I was submitting to this treatment because I was constantly asking for leave; at the same time I told myself that I had to resign just before I had to travel because no one was going to give me leave to travel at 24 hours' notice. The monitoring continued until 24 hours before I travelled. Afterwards I had to travel with 24 hours' notice to Colombia and then I continued the procedure for five days and then I had to return to Costa Rica and 10 days later do a pregnancy test and then monitor the pregnancy. This meant that everyone knew ... One's intimacy is totally violated; everyone not only knows that, even if it is the woman who is infertile, everyone assumes that the couple is also infertile or that they have not been capable of procreating. He found that very difficult; also having to support me constantly in things that he really doesn't understand ... I was subject to social and family stress because my family was suddenly divided.[430]

280. Thus, Ms Henchoz Bolaños explained similar additional problems that it can be inferred would not have arisen if she had been able to access IVF in her own country. She indicated that, regarding her trip to Europe to undergo IVF, "the day [they] arrived [they] had to look for a hotel, [they] had to look for the clinic, the doctor; [they] had never been to Europe before, ... it is a totally strange place; [she] did not have [her] family, [her] loved ones; [they] were alone; [she] felt like an exile. [They] arrived, [they] found the doctor, but a doctor that did not know [them], who did not know who [they] were."[431]

281. Second, regarding the harm to personal autonomy and the life project of the couples, the Court observes that IVF is usually used as a last resort to overcome serious reproductive difficulties. Its ban had a greater impact on the life plans of the couples whose only option to procreate was IVF, as in the case of Mr Mejías and Ms Calderón Porras. In this context, Ms Arroyo Fonseca, who had attempted several inseminations and who subsequently was able to have children, indicated that, at the time, she "was unable to overcome [her] infertility problems with an assisted reproduction technique that [at that time] would have allowed [her] to have more children."[432]

---

[430] Statement made by Bianchi Bruna during the hearing held before the Inter-American Commission on October 28, 2008.
[431] Statement made by Ileana Henchoz during the public hearing held in this case.
[432] Affidavit of Joaquinita Arroyo Fonseca (file of annexes to the pleadings and motions brief, volume IV, annex XI, folio 5266).

282. Third, the psychological integrity of the individual is harmed by denying him or her the possibility of acceding to a procedure that makes it possible to exercise the desired reproductive freedom. In this regard, one of the victims stated that, following the prohibition, he and his partner, "became extremely depressed; she cried all the time, she shut herself up in her room and refused to come out; she continually reminded [him] of the desire to have [their] own child, of the names [they] had chosen ... [They] also underwent unpleasant experiences; for example, [they] stopped going to church because each Sunday it was painful to go to mass and to hear the priest refer to those who wanted [IVF] as people who killed children and that God rejected and abominated those children ... [They] did not go back to any church and [they] felt abandoned by God himself."[433]

283. Meanwhile, Ms Carro Maklouf stated that she "felt indescribable interference in [her] private life" and stressed that her other children "also wanted to have a baby brother or sister, because they were adults, and the matter had become a family project; they also suffered with [her] all the pain caused by the Constitutional Chamber's decision."[434] For her part, Andrea Bianchi Bruna explained that when IVF, as her "final option, ... had been banned, [... she] felt a whirlwind of pain and incredulity in [her] mind." Ms Artavia Murillo testified that the State's decision "led to the failure of [her] marriage owing to the depressions that both [her] former husband and [she] suffered because of this ban [on *in vitro* fertilization], so [they] decided it was better to end the relationship, leaving an even greater wound, and with incalculable moral damage."[435]

284. Thus, for the said reasons, the couples suffered a severe interference in relation to their decision-making concerning the methods or practices they wished to attempt in order to procreate a biological child. However, differentiated impacts also existed in relation to the situation of disability, gender and financial situation, aspects related to the factors alleged by the parties regarding possible indirect indiscrimination in the instant case.

---

[433] Affidavit (file of annexes to the pleadings and motions brief, volume IV, annex XXI, folio 5620).
[434] *Cf.* Affidavit of Claudia María Carro Maklouf, "Life story" (file of annexes to the pleadings and motions brief, volume I, folio 4140).
[435] Brief of Ms Artavia and Mr Mejías of December 19, 2011 (file of annexes to the pleadings and motions brief, volume I, folio 4077).

D.2) Severity of the interference as a result of indirect discrimination owing to the disproportionate impact in relation to disability, gender and financial situation

285. The Inter-American Court has indicated repeatedly that the American Convention does not prohibit all differentiation in treatment. The Court has signaled the difference between "differentiation" and "discrimination,"[436] so that the former are differences that are compatible with the American Convention because they are reasonable and objective, while the latter constitute arbitrary differences that result in harm to human rights. In the instant case, the effects of the ruling on unconstitutionality are related to the protection of the right to private and family life, and the right to found a family, and not to the application or interpretation of a specific domestic law that regulates IVF. Consequently, the Court will not analyze the presumed violation of the right to equality and non-discrimination under Article 24,[437] but rather in light of Article 1(1)[438] of the Convention in relation to Articles 11(2) and 17 thereof.[439]

286. The Court has indicated that the principle of the peremptory right to equal and effective protection of the law and non-

---

[436] Regarding the concept of "discrimination," although neither the American Convention nor the International Covenant on Civil and Political Rights includes a definition of this term, the Commission, the Court and the United Nations Human Rights Committee have taken as a basis the definitions contained in the International Convention on the Elimination of All Forms of Racial Discrimination and in the International Convention on the Elimination of All Forms of Discrimination against Women in order to maintain that discrimination constitutes "any distinction, exclusion, restriction or preference which is based on any ground such as race, colour, sex, language, religion, political or other opinion, national or social origin, property, birth or other status, and which has the purpose or effect of nullifying or impairing the recognition, enjoyment or exercise by all persons, on an equal footing, of all rights and freedoms"; *cf.* United Nations, Human Rights Committee, General Comment No 18, Non-discrimination, November 10, 1989, CCPR/C/37, para. 7; IACourtHR, *Juridical Status and Rights of Undocumented Migrants*. Advisory Opinion OC-18/03 of September 17, 2003. Series A No 18, para. 92.

[437] Article 24 of the Convention (Right to Equal Protection) stipulates that: "All persons are equal before the law. Consequently, they are entitled, without discrimination, to equal protection of the law."

[438] Article 1(1) of the American Convention (Obligation to Respect Rights) establishes that: "The States Parties to this Convention undertake to respect the rights and freedoms recognized herein and to ensure to all persons subject to their jurisdiction the free and full exercise of those rights and freedoms, without any discrimination for reasons of race, color, sex, language, religion, political or other opinion, national or social origin, economic status, birth, or any other social condition."

[439] The Court has indicated that if a State discriminates in the respect or guarantee of a convention-based right, it would violate Article 1(1) and the substantive right in question. If, to the contrary, the discrimination refers to an unequal protection under domestic law, it would violate Article 24. *Cf. Case of Apitz Barbera et al.* ("First Administrative Law Court") v. Venezuela. Preliminary objection, merits, reparations and costs. Judgment of August 5, 2008. Series C No 182, para. 209, and *Case of the Xákmok Kásek Indigenous Community* v. Paraguay, para. 272.

discrimination means that the States must abstain from producing discriminatory regulations or those with discriminatory effects on the different groups of the population when exercising their rights.[440] The Human Rights Committee,[441] the Committee on the Elimination of Racial Discrimination,[442] the Committee on the Elimination of Discrimination against Women,[443] and the Committee on Economic, Social and Cultural Rights[444] have all recognized the concept of indirect discrimination. This concept implies that a law or practice that appears to be neutral has particularly negative repercussions on a person or group with specific characteristics.[445] It is possible that whoever established this law or practice was unaware of these practical consequences and, in that case, the intention to discriminate is not essential, and an inversion of the burden of proof is in order. In this regard, the Committee on the Rights of Persons with Disabilities has indicated that "a law that is applied impartially may have a discriminatory effect if it does not take into consideration the particular circumstances of the persons to which it is applied."[446] For its part, the European Court of Human Rights has also developed the concept of indirect discrimination establishing that, when a general policy or measure has an effect that is disproportionately prejudicial to a particular group, this may be considered discriminatory even if it was not specifically addressed [to] that group.[447]

287. The Court considers that the concept of disproportionate impact is related to that of indirect discrimination, and will therefore

---

[440] *Cf. Case of the Yean and Bosico Girls* v. *Dominican Republic*, para. 141, and *Juridical Status and Rights of Undocumented Migrants*. Advisory Opinion OC-18/03, para. 88.

[441] *Cf.* Human Rights Committee, Communication No 993/2001, *Althammer* v. *Austria*, August 8, 2003, para. 10.2 ("that a violation of article 26 [equality before the law] can also result from the discriminatory effect of a rule or measure that is neutral at face value and without intent to discriminate"). Human Rights Committee, General Comment No 18, Non-discrimination.

[442] *Cf.* Committee on the Elimination of Racial Discrimination, Communication No 31/2003, *LR et al.* v. *Slovakia*, March 7, 2005, para. 10.4.4.

[443] *Cf.* Committee on the Elimination of Discrimination against Women, General Recommendation No 25 on temporary special measures (2004), note 1 ("Indirect discrimination against women may occur when laws, policies and programmes are based on seemingly gender-neutral criteria which in their actual effect have a detrimental impact on women").

[444] *Cf.* Committee on Economic, Social and Cultural Rights, General Comment No 20, Non-discrimination in economic, social and cultural rights (Art. 2, para. 2 of the International Covenant on Economic, Social and Cultural Rights), July 2, 2009.

[445] *Case of Nadege Dorzema et al.* v. *Dominican Republic. Merits, reparations and costs*. Judgment of October 24, 2012. Series C No 251, para. 234.

[446] *Cf.* Committee on the Rights of Persons with Disabilities, Communication No 3/2011, *Case of HM* v. *Sweden*, CRPD/C/7/D/3/2011, April 19, 2012, para. 8.3.

[447] ECHR, *Case of Hoogendijk* v. *Netherlands*, No 58641/00, First Section, 2005; ECHR, Grand Chamber, *DH et al.* v. *Czech Republic*, No 57325/00, November 13, 2007, para. 175, and ECHR, *Case of Hugh Jordan* v. *United Kingdom*, No 24746/94, May 4, 2001, para. 154.

analyze whether there was a disproportionate impact in relation to disability, gender and financial situation.

D.2.a) Indirect discrimination in relation to the condition of disability

288. The Court takes note that the World Health Organization (hereinafter "WHO") has defined infertility as "a disease of the reproductive system defined by the failure to achieve a clinical pregnancy after 12 months or more of regular unprotected sexual intercourse" (*supra* para. 62). According to expert witness Zegers-Hochschild, "infertility is a disease that has numerous effects on the physical and psychological health of the individual, as well as social consequences, which include unstable marriages, anxiety, depression, social isolation and loss of social status, loss of gender identity, ostracism and abuse ... [I]t results in anguish, depression and isolation and weakens the family ties." Expert witness Garza testified that "[i]t is more exact to consider infertility as a symptom of an underlying disease. The diseases that cause infertility have a two-fold effect ... preventing fertility from functioning, but also causing, in both the short- and the long-term, health problems for men and women." Similarly, the World Medical Association has recognized that assisted conception "differs from the treatment of illness in that the inability to become a parent without medical intervention is not always regarded as an illness. While it may have profound psychosocial, and thus medical, consequences, it is not in itself life limiting. It is, however, a significant cause of major psychological illness and its treatment is clearly medical."[448]

289. The right of persons with disabilities to have access to the necessary techniques to resolve reproductive health problems can be inferred from Article 25 of the Convention on the Rights of Persons with Disabilities (hereinafter "CRPD").[449] While expert witness Caruso considered that infertility can only be referred to as a disability under certain conditions and presumptions and, thus, only in

---

[448] The World Medical Association, Statement on Assisted Reproductive Technologies, adopted by the WMA General Assembly, Pilanesberg, South Africa, October 2006. Available at: www.wma.net/e/policy/r3.htm, para. 6. Statement cited in the Inter-American Commission's merits report (merits report, volume I, footnote 36) and in the answering brief (merits report, volume III, folio 1086).

[449] Article 25(1) establishes: "Health: States Parties recognize that persons with disabilities have the right to the enjoyment of the highest attainable standard of health without discrimination on the basis of disability. States Parties shall take all appropriate measures to ensure access for persons with disabilities to health services that are gender-sensitive, including health-related rehabilitation. In particular, States Parties shall: (a) Provide persons with disabilities with the same range, quality and standard of free or affordable health care and programmes as provided to other persons, including in the area of sexual and reproductive health and population-based public health programmes."

determined cases,[450] expert witness Paul Hunt observed that "involuntary infertility is a disability,"[451] considering that:

The Preamble to the Convention on the Rights of Persons with Disabilities, to which Costa Rica is a party, recognizes that "disability is an evolving concept and that disability results from the interaction between persons with impairments and attitudinal and environmental barriers that hinder their full and effective participation in society on an equal basis with others." According to the WHO biopsychosocial model on disability, this entails one or more of the three levels of difficulty in human functions: a physical-psychological impairment; a limitation of activity owing to an impairment (activity limitation), and a participation restriction owing to an activity limitation. According to the WHO International Classification of Functioning, Disability and Health, impairments are problems in body functions; activity limitations are difficulties an individual may have in executing activities, and participation restrictions are problems an individual may experience in involvement in life situations.[452]

290. Article 18 of the Additional Protocol to the American Convention in the Area of Economic, Social and Cultural Rights ("Protocol of San Salvador") states that "[e]veryone affected by a diminution of his physical or mental capacities is entitled to receive special attention designed to help him achieve the greatest possible development of his personality." The Inter-American Convention for the Elimination of All Forms of Discrimination against Persons with Disabilities (hereinafter "ICEFDPD") defines the term "disability" as "a physical, mental or sensory impairment, whether permanent or temporary, that limits the capacity to perform one or more essential activities of daily life, and which can be caused or aggravated by the economic and social environment." For its part, the CRPD establishes that "persons with disabilities include those who have long-term physical, mental, intellectual or sensory impairments which in interaction with various barriers may hinder their full and effective participation in society on an equal basis with others." The disability results from the interaction between an individual's functional limitations and the barriers that exist in the environment that prevent the full exercise of his rights and freedoms.[453]

---

[450] Opinion provide by expert witness Anthony Caruso at the public hearing held in this case.
[451] Affidavit provided by expert witness Paul Hunt (merits report, volume VI, folio 2650).
[452] Affidavit of expert witness Paul Hunt, folio 2650.
[453] The Preamble of the CRPD recognizes "that disability is an evolving concept and that disability results from the interaction between persons with impairments and attitudinal and environmental barriers that hinders their full and effective participation in society on an equal basis with others."

291. The above-mentioned Conventions take into account the social model in their approach to disabilities, which means that the disability is not defined exclusively by the presence of a physical, mental, intellectual or sensorial impairment, but that it is interrelated to the barriers or limitations that exist in society for the individual to be able to exercise his rights effectively.[454] The types of limits or barriers that are commonly encountered in society by individuals with functional diversity include those that are attitudinal[455] or socio-economic.[456]

292. Anyone in a situation of vulnerability is subject to special protection owing to the special duties that the State must comply with in order to satisfy the general obligation to respect and guarantee human rights. The Court recalls that it is not sufficient that the States abstain from violating rights; rather it is essential that they adopt positive measures, to be determined based on the specific needs for protection of the subject of law, either owing to his personal condition or to the specific situation in which he finds himself,[457] such as with a disability.[458] In this regard, States are obliged to facilitate the inclusion of persons with disabilities by means of equality of conditions, opportunities and participation in all spheres of society,[459] in order to guarantee that the said limitations are dismantled. Thus, the States must promote social inclusion practices and adopt measures of positive differentiation to remove the said barriers.[460]

---

[454] *Case of Furlan and family* v. *Argentina*, para. 133.
[455] *Case of Furlan and family* v. *Argentina*, para. 133. *Cf.* UN General Assembly, ONU, Standard rules on the equalization of opportunities for persons with disabilities, GA/RES/48/96, March 4, 1994, forty-eighth session, para. 3 ("In the disability field, however, there are also many specific circumstances that have influenced the living conditions of persons with disabilities. Ignorance, neglect, superstition and fear are social factors that throughout the history of disability have isolated persons with disabilities and delayed their development").
[456] *Cf. Case of Ximenes Lopes* v. *Brazil. Merits, reparations and costs.* Judgment of July 4, 2006. Series C No 149, para. 104, and *Case of Furlan and family* v. *Argentina*, para. 133. *Cf. also* Article III.2 of the Inter-American Convention for the Elimination of All Forms of Discrimination against Persons with Disabilities, and Committee on Economic, Social and Cultural Rights, General Comment No 5, Persons with Disabilities, UN Doc. E/C.12/1994/13 (1994), September 12, 1994, para. 9.
[457] *Cf. Case of the "Mapiripán Massacre"* v. *Colombia. Merits, reparations and costs.* Judgment of September 15, 2005. Series C No 134, paras. 111 and 113, and *Case of the Kichwa Indigenous People of Sarayaku* v. *Ecuador*, para. 244.
[458] *Cf. Case of Ximenes Lopes* v. *Brazil*, para. 103, and *Case of Furlan and family* v. *Argentina*, para. 134.
[459] *Cf. Case of Furlan and family* v. *Argentina*, para. 134. *Cf.* Article 5 of the Standard rules on the equalization of opportunities for persons with disabilities.
[460] *Cf. Case of Furlan and family* v. *Argentina*, para. 134, and Committee on Economic, Social and Cultural Rights, General Comment No 5, para. 13.

293. Based on these considerations and taking into account the definition developed by the WHO according to which infertility is a disease of the reproductive system (*supra* para. 288), the Court considers that infertility is a functional limitation recognized as a disease and that persons with infertility in Costa Rica, faced with the barriers created by the Constitutional Chamber's decision, should consider that they are protected by the rights of persons with disabilities, which include the right to have access to the necessary techniques to resolve reproductive health problems. This condition requires special attention in order [to have] reproductive autonomy.

D.2.b) Indirect discrimination in relation to gender
294. The Court considers that the ban on IVF can affect both men and women and may have differentiated disproportionate impacts owing to the existence of stereotypes and prejudices in society.
295. Regarding the situation of infertile women, expert witness Hunt explained that "in many societies infertility is attributed mainly and disproportionately to women owing to the persisting gender stereotype that defines a woman as the basic creator of the family." Citing the conclusions of research by the WHO Department of Reproductive Health and Research (RHR), he indicated that:

Responsibility for infertility is usually shared by the couple ... However, for biological and social reasons, the blame for infertility is not shared equally. In most societies, the psychological and social burden of fertility is borne especially by women. A woman's situation is frequently identified with her fertility, and the absence of children may be seen as a social disgrace or cause for divorce. The suffering of the infertile woman can be very real.[461]

296. The Court observes that the WHO has indicated that, while the role and status of women in society should not be defined solely by their reproductive capacity, femininity is often defined by motherhood. In these situations, "the personal suffering of the infertile woman is exacerbated and can lead to unstable marriage, domestic violence, stigmatization and even ostracism."[462] According to data from the Pan-American Health Organization, there is a gender gap with regard to sexual and reproductive health, because ailments related to sexual

---

[461] Affidavit provided by expert witness Paul Hunt (merits report, volume VI, folio 2206).
[462] Preamble, *Current Practices and Controversies in Assisted Reproduction: Report of the meeting on "Medical, Ethical and Social Aspects of Assisted Reproduction,"* Geneva: WHO (2002) XV-XVII to XV [*sic*]. Cited in the affidavit provided by expert witness Paul Hunt (merits report, volume VI, folio 2206).

and reproductive health affect around 20% of women and 14% of men.[463]

297. The Committee on the Elimination of Discrimination against Women has indicated that, when a decision to postpone "[s]urgery due to pregnancy is influenced by the stereotype that protection of the fetus should prevail over the health of the mother," this is discriminatory.[464] The Court considers that the instant case reveals a similar situation of the influence of stereotypes, in which the Constitutional Chamber gave absolute prevalence to the protection of the fertilized eggs without considering the situation of disability of some of the women.

298. Meanwhile, expert witness Neuburger explained that "[t]he gender identity model is socially defined and molded by the culture; its subsequent naturalization responds to socio-economic, political, cultural and historic determinants. According to these determinants, women are raised and socialized to be wives and mothers, to take care of and attend to the intimate world of affections. The ideal for women, even nowadays, is embodied in sacrifice and dedication, and the culmination of these values is represented by motherhood and the ability to give birth ... A woman's fertility is still considered by much of society to be something natural that admits no doubts. When a woman has fertility problems or is unable to become pregnant, the reaction of society tends to be skepticism, disgrace and, at times, even ill-treatment ... The impact of infertility in women is usually greater than in men because ... motherhood has been assigned to women as an essential part of their gender identity, transformed into their destiny. The burden of their self-blame increased exponentially when the ban on IVF arose ... The pressure of the family and society constitute[s] an additional burden that increases the self-blame."[465]

299. In addition, although infertility can affect both men and women, the use of assisted reproduction technologies is especially related to a woman's body. Even though the ban on IVF is not expressly addressed at women, and thus appears neutral, it has a disproportionately negative impact on women.

300. In this regard, the Court underlines that the initial IVF procedure (induction of ovulation) was interrupted for some of the

---

[463] *Cf.* Pan-American Health Organization (PAHO), "Chapter 2: Health Conditions and Trends" in *Health in the Americas 2007*, Volume I—Regional, Washington, 2007. Cited in the affidavit provided by expert witness Paul Hunt (merits report, volume VI).

[464] Committee on the Elimination of Discrimination against Women, *Case of LC v. Peru*, Communication No 22/2009, para. 8.15, Doc. UN CEDAW/c/50/D/22/2009 (2011).

[465] Affidavit provided by expert witness Alicia Neuburger (merits report, volume V, folios 2519 and 2520).

couples: for example, the couples consisting of Ms Artavia Murillo and Mr Mejías Carballo (*supra* para. 87), Mr Yamuni and Ms Henchoz (*supra* para. 92), Ms Arroyo and Mr Vega (*supra* para. 108), Mr Vargas and Ms Calderón (*supra* para. 118) and Mr Acuña and Ms Castillo (*supra* para. 121). This type of interruption in the continuity of a treatment has a differentiated impact on women because interventions, such as ovary induction and other interventions destined to achieve the family project associated with IVF, were being performed on their bodies. Moreover, women may resort to IVF without the need for a partner. The Court concurs with CEDAW when it has emphasized that it is necessary to consider "the health rights of women from the perspective of women's needs and interests in view of the distinctive features and factors that differentiate women from men, namely: (a) biological factors ... such as ... their reproductive function."[466]

301. For his part, regarding the situation of infertile men, Mr Mejías Carballo declared that he "is fearful of forming part of a couple again." He added that "it was very hard following [the ban on IVF]; they began to have problems when it was like a requirement wanting to have a child, and the years passed, birthdays came and went, Mother's Day, Father's Day, Christmas, when all [his] siblings and nephews and nieces gave presents to their children, and ... another Mother's Day, and yet another one, and [he] still did not have a child; in other words, all this troubles one morally."[467] Meanwhile, Mr Vargas stated that "for years [he] felt diminished, [he] did not feel like a man, and thought that [his] inability to conceive a child was unmanly. Thus, [he] punished [him]self in the silence of [his] own thoughts, in the pain of swallowing thousands of tears so nobody could see [him] cry."[468] For his part, Mr Sanabria León explained that he received "the message of impossibility and, together with this, [he] felt disabled, [his] perception of [him]self was negatively affected and [he] became angry with and resentful of his body; [he] rejected [him]self; in brief, [his] self-image was severely diminished."[469] Expert witness Neuburger explained that "fertile disability causes men to feel a strong sense of impotence and, consequently, a questioning of their gender identity.

---

[466] *Cf.* Committee on the Elimination of Discrimination against Women, General Recommendation No 24, para. 12.
[467] *Cf.* Statement made by Mr Mejías Carballo at the public hearing held in this case.
[468] *Cf.* Affidavit of Giovanni Vargas (file of annexes to the pleadings and motions briefs, volume IV, folio 5281).
[469] Affidavit of Víctor Sanabria León (file of annexes to the pleadings and motions brief, volume II, folio 4937).

Concealing their fertile dysfunction socially is the usual defensive strategy because they fear being laughed at or questioned by other men."[470]

302. The Court emphasizes that these gender stereotypes are incompatible with international human rights law and measures must be taken to eliminate them. The Court is not validating these stereotypes and only recognizes them and defines them in order to describe the disproportionate impact of the interference caused by the Constitutional Chamber's judgment.

D.2.c) Indirect discrimination in relation to financial situation

303. Finally, the ban on IVF had a disproportionate impact on the infertile couples who did not have the financial resources to undergo IVF abroad.[471] The case file shows that Grettel Artavia Murillo, Miguel Mejías Carballo, Oriéster Rojas, Julieta González, Ana Cristina Castillo León, Enrique Acuña, Giovanni Vega, Joaquinita Arroyo, Carlos Eduardo de Jesús Vargas Solórzano and María del Socorro Calderón Porras did not have the financial resources to undergo IVF treatment abroad.[472]

304. In his testimony during the public hearing before this Court, Mr Mejías Carballo declared that he and his former wife felt "very sad ... because they could not travel to another country because they did not have the resources; and they could not do it here in Costa Rica because it had been banned."[473] In her affidavit, Grettel Artavia Murillo indicated that she and her former partner, Miguel Mejías, felt "totally desperate and tremendously frustrated, and [their] relationship began to have many problems on seeing the hopes of becoming parents curtailed, together with the impossibility of going abroad to undergo this practice owing to a lack of resources, which effectively resulted in a lessening of their individual usefulness and, thus, a net loss of [their] social well-being."[474] Ana Cristina Castillo León explained that they

---

[470] Affidavit provided by expert witness Alicia Neuburger (merits report, volume V, folios 2519 and 2520).

[471] *Cf.* Article 1(1) of the American Convention ("The States Parties to this Convention undertake to respect the rights and freedoms recognized herein and to ensure to all persons subject to their jurisdiction the free and full exercise of those rights and freedoms, without any discrimination for reasons of ... economic status").

[472] *Cf.* Affidavit of Oriéster Rojas (file of annexes to the pleadings and motions brief, volume II, folio 4516).

[473] Likewise, Mr Mejías declared that he wanted to go abroad to undergo the treatment but he "did not have the money and had already spen[t] a great deal and [he] subsist[ed] on a State pension, and everyone knows that State pensions are not sufficient to cover an expense like that; therefore [they] could not go." *Cf.* Statement made by Mr Mejías Carballo at the public hearing held in this case.

[474] *Cf.* Affidavit of Grettel Artavia Murillo (file of annexes to the pleadings and motions brief, volume I, folio 4077).

"did not have the necessary financial resources to go abroad to obtain" IVF.[475] Furthermore Mr Vargas stated that "the only alternative was to consider traveling to Spain or Colombia to undergo IVF; however, the corresponding costs had tripled for [them], and [they] simply felt defeated, discriminated against and punished by a court that had curtailed the possibility of having access to a medical treatment that was permitted in every other country in the world."[476]

D.3) *Dispute regarding the alleged embryonic loss*

305. As indicated previously (*supra* para. 76), the Constitutional Chamber justified the prohibition of IVF based on the "high loss of embryos," their "disproportionate risk of death," and the inadmissibility of comparing the loss of embryos in a natural pregnancy with the loss in IVF. The State considered that "to date, the [IVF] technique entails discarding, by act or omission, embryos that, otherwise, could come to term." The Constitutional Chamber indicated that:

The argument that, under natural circumstances, there are also embryos that do not become implanted or even if they achieve implantation do not develop up until birth ... is irreceivable, simply due to the fact that the application of [IVF] entails a conscious and voluntary manipulation of male and female reproductive cells in order to obtain a new human life, during which a situation is promoted in which it is known in advance that human life has no possibility of continuing in a significant percentage of cases.[477]

306. In this regard, the Court observes that the Decree that the Chamber declared unconstitutional included measures of protection for the embryo, because it established the number of eggs that could be fertilized. In addition, it prohibited "discarding or eliminating embryos, or preserving them for transfer in subsequent cycles of the same patient or other patients." In this regard, there were measures to ensure that a "disproportionate risk" for the life expectation of the embryos was not created. In addition, according to the said decree, the only possibility of loss of viable embryos was if they failed to become

---

[475] *Cf.* Testimony of Ana Cristina Castillo León (file of annexes to the pleadings and motions brief, volume I, folio 4102).
[476] *Cf.* Affidavit of Giovanni Vargas (file of annexes to the pleadings and motions briefs, volume IV, folio 5280).
[477] Judgment No 2000-02306 of March 15, 2000, delivered by the Constitutional Chamber of the Supreme Court of Justice, Case file No 95-001734-007-CO (file of annexes to the merits report, volume I, folio 85).

implanted in the woman's uterus once the embryonic transfer had taken place.

307. The Court finds it necessary to examine this aspect further based on the evidence provided in these proceedings in relation to the similarities and differences concerning the loss of embryos in both natural pregnancies and in IVF.

308. The Constitutional Chamber based the prohibition of IVF on the difference in the loss of embryos transferred by IVF and embryonic loss in a natural pregnancy, considering that when applying IVF there was a "conscious [and] voluntary manipulation" of the embryos. The Court observes that a scientific debate exists about the rates of embryonic loss in the natural process and in assisted reproduction. In the proceedings before the Court, different medical positions have been presented concerning the cause of embryonic loss in both the application of IVF and in natural pregnancy, as well as the percentage of losses in both cases. Expert witness Zegers-Hochschild indicated that "[t]he scientific information that has been produced indicates that the embryonic death that occurs in IVF procedures does not occur as a direct result of the technique, [but rather] it occurs as part of the process expressed by our nature,"[478] and that "[i]n women with healthy eggs, the possibility of conceiving from an embryo generated *in vitro* is no different from one generated spontaneously."[479] For her part, expert witness Garza stated that "embryo mortality is around 30% in natural circumstances and, for IVF, it is calculated that embryonic loss is around 90%." However, she clarified that "it is difficult to estimate the exact embryonic mortality in natural circumstances, because some losses cannot be detected in early pregnancy." Expert witness Caruso stated that "the percentage of losses is much higher" in IVF than "in natural conception."[480]

309. It is not incumbent on the Court to determine which scientific theory should prevail on this issue; nor must it make a thorough analysis of which expert witness is right on these matters that are outside the Court's expertise. For the Court, it is sufficient to verify that the evidence in the case file is consistent in indicating that there is embryonic loss in both a natural pregnancy and in the context of IVF. In addition, both expert witness Zegers-Hochschild and expert witness

---

[478] Written summary of the expert opinion provided by Fernando Zegers-Hochschild at the public hearing before the Court (merits report, volume VI, folio 2835).

[479] Written summary of the expert opinion provided by Fernando Zegers-Hochschild at the public hearing before the Court (merits report, volume VI, folio 2839).

[480] Affidavit prepared by expert witness Garza.

Caruso indicated that it is difficult to measure embryonic loss in natural pregnancies compared to the measurement of losses in IVF, and this places limits on the implications that it has been attempted to give to some of the statistics submitted to the Court.[481]

310. Bearing in mind that embryonic loss occurs in both natural pregnancies and when IVF is applied, the argument of the existence of conscious and voluntary manipulation of cells in the context of IVF can only be understood in relation to the argument developed by the Constitutional Chamber concerning the absolute protection of the right to life of the embryo, which has been invalidated in preceding sections of this Judgment (*supra* para. 264). To the contrary, the Court observes that expert witness Zegers-Hochschild emphasized that "[t]he process that generates human life includes embryonic death as part of a natural and necessary process. Of every 10 embryos spontaneously generated in the human species, no more than 2 to 3 are able to survive natural selection and be born as a person. The remaining 7 or 8 embryos die in the female genital tract, generally without the parents' knowledge."[482]

---

[481] During the public hearing, the Commission questioned expert witness Caruso on this point, indicating that in both IVF and in the natural conception process there is embryonic loss, and stressing that the difference would be that, in IVF, it is possible to measure those losses. The Commission inquired whether the difference would therefore be that, in IVF, it was simply possible to measure these losses. Expert witness Caruso answered that "In IVF you can say to a certain extent; you can answer that question somewhat. The difference, as I've said before, is that there is a very big difference between the environment of the natural process in the Fallopian tube and the dish with a medium in an incubator at 95 degrees and 5% CO_2 in an IVF lab. So yes, you are going to see in IVF you can quantify the loss of the embryos that you have. Number one, you cannot extrapolate that back to compare it to natural pregnancy laws. And two: there may be reasons beyond nature that those embryos are lost." *Cf.* Opinion provided by expert witness Anthony Caruso at the public hearing held in this case.

[482] Opinion provided by expert witness Zegers-Hochschild at the public hearing held in this case. He explained that "[t]he results of ART vary significantly according to the age of the woman and the number of embryos transferred and, in some cases, to the severity of the condition that gave rise to the disease ... The proportion of chromosomally abnormal eggs is very high in the human species. This means that a large percentage of fertilized eggs do not advance in embryonic development and a high proportion of transferred embryos do not implant and do not result in a pregnancy ... The analysis of these data reveals that ... the technique of IVF or [intracytoplasmic sperm injection] ICSI does not generate embryos of a lesser biological value than those generated spontaneously in a woman's body, [and] that embryonic death as part of a medical treatment does not occur as a direct result of the technique, but as the result of the poor quality of the oocyte and embryo that are natural to both women and men. In women with healthy eggs, the possibility of conceiving from one embryo generated *in vitro* is no different from one generated spontaneously. In itself, the IVF/ICSI does not affect the possibility of implantation and conception. Hence, the lower rates of pregnancy in women with IVF are not due to the interference of the technique; but rather they are mainly the result of the underlying disease that determines a lower reproductive performance ... The process that creates human life includes embryonic death as part of a natural and necessary process. Of every 10 embryos generated spontaneously in the human species, no more than 2 to 3 are able to survive natural selection

311. Bearing in mind the above, the Court finds it disproportionate to aspire to an absolute protection of the embryo in relation to a risk that is common and even inherent in processes where the IVF technique has not been used. The Court shares the opinion of expert witness Zegers-Hochschild that "[f]rom a biomedical perspective, it is essential to differentiate the meaning of *protecting* the right to life from the meaning of *ensuring* the right to life of cellular structures that are regulated by mathematics and biology, which transcend any social or legal regulation. The institutions responsible for [assisted reproduction techniques] should provide the cellular structures (gametes and embryos) with the optimum conditions offered by medical and scientific knowledge so that potentiality of being a person can be expressed at birth..." The Court reiterates that, precisely, one of the purposes of IVF is to contribute to the creation of life (*supra* para. 66).

312. The Court also observes that Costa Rica permits artificial insemination techniques even though the use of such techniques does not guarantee that each egg will result in a pregnancy, thus entailing the possible loss of embryos. The decision to become pregnant, even by natural fertilization, may also be preceded by a conscious act that takes measures to increase the probability of the egg being fertilized. According to the State's final arguments:

Artificial insemination is one of the treatments offered by the Costa Rican Social Security Institute. At times, as a result of hormone treatment and as an individual response, patients may present greater stimulation of the ovaries than expected; consequently, when this follicle production is 6 or more in both ovaries, the cycle is annulled.[483]

313. In brief, embryonic loss exists in both natural pregnancy and in techniques such as artificial insemination. The Court observes that scientific debate exists about the differences between the type of embryonic losses that occur in these processes and their reasons. But the analysis made above allows the Court to conclude that, taking into account the embryonic losses that occur in a natural pregnancy and in other reproduction techniques permitted in Costa Rica, the protection of the embryo sought by banning IVF has a very limited and moderate scope.

---

and be born as a person. The remaining 7 or 8 embryos die in the female genital tract, generally without the parent's knowledge. The question that must be answered is whether the ART, such as IVF or ICSI, contribute to the death of embryos because they have been fertilized outside a woman's body and then transferred to her. The answer to this question is that neither IVF [n]or ICSI affect the possibility of survival of embryos and, evidently, do not kill them."

[483] The State's final written arguments (merits report, volume XI, folio 5314).

D.4) Conclusion regarding the assessment of the severity of the interference in relation to the impact on the intended purpose

314. A weighing up of the severity of the limitation of the rights involved in this case as compared to the importance of the protection of the embryo allows it to be affirmed that the effects on the rights to personal integrity, personal liberty, private life, intimacy, reproductive autonomy, access to reproductive health services, and to found a family [are] severe and entail a violation of these rights because, in practice, they are annulled for those persons whose only possible treatment for infertility is IVF. In addition, the interference had a differentiated impact on the victims owing to their situation of disability, gender stereotypes and, for some of the victims, to their financial situation.

315. In contrast, the impact on the protection of prenatal life is very slight, because the risk of embryonic loss is present both in IVF and in natural pregnancy. The Court underlines that the embryo, prior to implantation, is not covered by the terms of Article 4 of the Convention, and recalls the principle of the gradual and incremental protection of prenatal life (*supra* para. 264).

316. Therefore, the Court concludes that the Constitutional Chamber based itself on an absolute protection of the embryo that, by failing to weigh up or take into account the other competing rights, involved an arbitrary and excessive interference in private and family life that makes this interference disproportionate. Moreover, the interference had discriminatory effects. In addition, taking into account these conclusions about the assessment and the considerations concerning Article 4(1) of the Convention (*supra* para. 264), the Court does not consider it pertinent to rule on the State's argument that it has a margin of appreciation to establish prohibitions such as the one established by the Constitutional Chamber.

E) Final conclusion on the merits of the case

317. Based on all the considerations in this chapter, the Court declares the violation of Articles 5(1), 7, 11(2) and 17(2), in relation to Article 1(1) of the American Convention, to the detriment of Grettel Artavia Murillo, Miguel Mejías Carballo, Andrea Bianchi Bruno, Germán Alberto Moreno Valencia, Ana Cristina Castillo León, Enrique Acuña Cartín, Ileana Henchoz Bolaños, Miguel Antonio Yamuni Zeledón, Claudia María Carro Maklouf, Víctor Hugo Sanabria León, Karen Espinoza Vindas, Héctor Jiménez Acuña, María del Socorro Calderón P., Joaquinita Arroyo Fonseca, Giovanni Antonio Vega,

Carlos E. Vargas Solórzano, Julieta González Ledezma and Oriéster Rojas Carranza.

IX. REPARATIONS

(APPLICATION OF ARTICLE 63(1) OF THE AMERICAN CONVENTION)

318. Based on the provisions of Article 63(1) of the American Convention,[484] the Court has indicated that every violation of an international obligation which causes damage entails the obligation to provide adequate reparation[485] and that this provision reflects a customary law that is one of the fundamental principles of contemporary international law on State responsibility.[486]

319. The reparation of the damage caused by the violation of an international obligation requires, whenever possible, full restitution (*restitutio in integrum*), which consists of the re-establishment of the previous situation. If this is not feasible, as in most cases of human rights violations, the Court will determine measures to guarantee the rights infringed and to repair the consequences of the violations.[487] Consequently, the Court has considered the need to award different measures of reparation in order to redress the damage comprehensively, so that, in addition to pecuniary compensation, measures of restitution and satisfaction and guarantees of non-repetition have special relevance for the damage caused.[488]

320. The Court has established that reparations must have a causal nexus to the facts of the case, the violations declared, the damage proved, and the measures requested to repair the respective damage.

---

[484] Article 63(1) of the American Convention establishes that "[i]f the Court finds that there has been a violation of a right or freedom protected by this Convention, the Court shall rule that the injured party be ensured the enjoyment of his right or freedom that was violated. It shall also rule, if appropriate, that the consequences of the measure or situation that constituted the breach of such right or freedom be remedied and that fair compensation be paid to the injured party."

[485] *Cf. Case of Velásquez Rodríguez* v. *Honduras. Reparations and costs.* Judgment of July 21, 1989. Series C No 7, para. 25, and *Case of Nadege Dorzema et al.* v. *Dominican Republic*, para. 238.

[486] *Cf. Case of Velásquez Rodríguez* v. *Honduras. Reparations and costs*, para. 25, and *Case of Nadege Dorzema et al.* v. *Dominican Republic*, para. 238.

[487] *Cf. Case of Velásquez Rodríguez* v. *Honduras. Reparations and costs*, para. 25, and *Case of the Río Negro Massacres* v. *Guatemala. Preliminary objection, merits, reparations and costs.* Judgment of September 4, 2012. Series C No 250, para. 245.

[488] *Cf. Case of Velásquez Rodríguez* v. *Honduras. Reparations and costs*, para. 25, and *Case of the Río Negro Massacres* v. *Guatemala*, para. 248.

Therefore, the Court must observe that these requirements have been met in order to rule appropriately and in keeping with the law.[489]

321. Based on the considerations on the merits and the violations of the American Convention declared in the preceding chapter, the Court will now analyze the claims, arguments and recommendations presented by the Commission and the claims of the representatives, as well as the arguments of the State, in light of the criteria established in the Court's case law regarding the nature and scope of the obligation to make reparation,[490] in order to establish measures designed to redress the damage caused to the victims.

A) Injured party

322. The Court reiterates that, under Article 63(1) of the Convention, those persons who have been declared victims of the violation of a right recognized in the Convention are considered the injured party. Therefore, this Court considers as "injured party": Grettel Artavia Murillo, Miguel Mejías Carballo, Andrea Bianchi Bruno, Germán Alberto Moreno Valencia, Ana Cristina Castillo León, Enrique Acuña Cartín, Ileana Henchoz Bolaños, Miguel Antonio Yamuni Zeledón, Claudia María Carro Maklouf, Víctor Hugo Sanabria León, Karen Espinoza Vindas, Héctor Jiménez Acuña, María del Socorro Calderón P., Joaquinita Arroyo Fonseca, Giovanni Antonio Vega, Carlos E. Vargas Solórzano, Julieta González Ledezma and Oriéster Rojas Carranza, who, as victims of the violations declared in Chapter VII, will be considered beneficiaries of the reparations ordered by the Court.

323. The Court will determine measures that seek to repair the pecuniary and non-pecuniary damage, and will establish measures of public scope or repercussion.[491] International case law, and specifically that of the Court, has repeatedly established that the judgment constitutes *per se* a form of reparation.[492] However, considering the circumstances of the case *sub judice*, and based on the effects on the victims, as well as the intangible and non-pecuniary consequences of the violations

---

[489] *Cf. Case of Ticona Estrada* v. *Bolivia. Merits, reparations and costs.* Judgment of November 27, 2008. Series C No 191, para. 110, and *Case of the Massacres of El Mozote and nearby places* v. *El Salvador. Merits, reparations and costs.* Judgment of October 25, 2012. Series C No 252.

[490] *Cf. Case of Velásquez Rodríguez* v. *Honduras. Reparations and costs,* para. 25, and *Case of the Río Negro Massacres* v. *Guatemala,* para. 246.

[491] *Cf. Case of the "Street Children" (Villagrán Morales et al.)* v. *Guatemala. Reparations and costs.* Judgment of May 26, 2001. Series C No 77, para. 84, and *Case of Vélez Restrepo and family* v. *Colombia,* para. 259.

[492] *Cf. Case of Neira Alegría et al.* v. *Peru. Reparations and costs.* Judgment of September 19, 1996. Series C No 29, para. 56, and *Case of Vélez Restrepo and family* v. *Colombia,* para. 259.

of the Convention declared to their detriment, the Court finds it pertinent to establish measures of rehabilitation and satisfaction, and guarantees of non-repetition.

B) *Measures of rehabilitation and satisfaction, and guarantees of non-repetition*

B.1) *Measures of psychological rehabilitation*

Arguments of the parties

324. Representative Molina asked the Court to "order the State to provide psychological and/or psychiatric treatment to the victims who so wish, with trained professionals for the specific damage to their life project."

325. The State argued that this measure "should be rejected, given that ... the Costa Rican social security system already provides the service of psychological and psychiatric support and treatment to patients who have fertility problems."

Considerations of the Court

326. The Court has indicated that this case is not related to a presumed right to have children or a right to have access to IVF. To the contrary, the case has focused on the impact of a disproportionate interference in decisions regarding private and family life, and the other rights involved, and the impact that this interference had on mental integrity. Consequently, the Court finds, as it has in other cases,[493] that it is necessary to establish a measure of reparation that provides adequate attention to the psychological problems suffered by the victims, addressing their specific needs, provided they have requested this. The Court observes different problems suffered by the victims owing to the arbitrary interference in access to an assisted reproduction technique. Therefore, having verified the violations and the damage suffered by the victims in this case, the Court establishes the State's obligation to provide them with the psychological treatment they require, free of charge and immediately, for up to four years. In particular, the psychological treatment must be provided by State institutions and personnel specialized in attending victims of events such as those that occurred in this case. When providing this treatment, the specific circumstances and needs of each victim should also be

---

[493] *Cf. Case of Barrios Altos* v. *Peru. Reparations and costs.* Judgment of November 30, 2001. Series C No 87, paras. 42 and 45, and *Case of the Río Negro Massacres* v. *Guatemala*, para. 287.

considered, so that they are provided with family and individual treatment, as agreed with each of them, after an individual assessment.[494] The treatments must include the provision of medicines and, if appropriate, transportation and other expenses that are directly related and strictly necessary.

B.2) Measures of satisfaction: publication of the Judgment

Arguments of the parties

327. Representative Molina requested "the publication of the pertinent parts of the judgment in a newspaper with widespread national circulation, in its printed version, and the full text of the judgment online, as well as the summary," and "that the State create a summary of the judgment in simple terms, approved by the Court, so that the general public may understand what this case entailed, and that this version also be published in a national newspaper."

328. Representative May asked the Court to "declare that the State must publish, once, within six months of notification of this Judgment, the operative paragraphs of this Judgment in the Official Gazette and in two other newspapers with widespread circulation."

Considerations of the Court

329. The Court orders that the State publish, within six months of notification of this Judgment: (a) the official summary of this Judgment prepared by the Court, once, in the Official Gazette; (b) the official summary of this Judgment prepared by the Court, once, in a newspaper with widespread national circulation; and (c) the full text of the Judgment, available for one year on an official website of the Judiciary.

B.3) Guarantees of non-repetition

B.3.1) State measures that do not prevent the practice of IVF

Arguments of the Commission and claims of the parties

330. The Commission recommended that the State "lift the ban on *in vitro* fertilization in the country through the corresponding legal procedures" and "ensure that, once the ban is lifted, the regulation of the practice of *in vitro* fertilization is compatible with the State's

---

[494] Cf. *Case of the 19 Tradesmen* v. *Colombia. Merits, reparations and costs.* Judgment of July 5, 2004. Series C No 109, para. 278, and *Case of the Barrios Family* v. *Venezuela. Merits, reparations and costs.* Judgment of November 24, 2011. Series C No 237, para. 329.

obligation with regard to the rights recognized in Articles 11(2), 17(2) and 24, [in order that] couples that need and want the treatment have access to the technique of *in vitro* fertilization so that the treatment can serve its purpose."

331. Representative Molina asked the Court to order the State to approve "a formal and substantive law that weighed the rights to life and the rights [violated] in this case." In this regard, he proposed the "prohibition to discard embryos arbitrarily and to sell them; to allow the implanting of no more than three embryos to avoid multiple pregnancies, and to allow the freezing of eggs and not of embryos, as a measure of embryo protection." He stressed "the importance of permitting the law to adjust to the new methods of assisted reproduction that science discovers in a way that maintains a balance between rights." He asked the Court to "order the State to regulate and to establish all necessary mechanisms to offer the population existing and future assisted reproduction methods in order to assist couples with infertility problems."

332. Representative May asked that the State "adopt all legal, administrative or other measures to be able to provide full access progressively to IVF treatment within the social security system to sterile or infertile persons who are contributors of the Costa Rican Social Security Institute, incorporating the technological advances available nowadays in countries with more experience, which permit not only better statistical results of success with this treatment, but also increased safety for the patients who undergo the procedure."

333. The State argued that "the Costa Rican Social Security Institute has a complete program of attention for those who have infertility problems, and the only procedure not offered at this time is [IVF]."

Considerations of the Court

334. The Court recalls that the State must prevent the recurrence of human rights violations such as those that have occurred and, therefore, adopt all necessary legal, administrative and other measures to prevent similar events from occurring in the future, in compliance with its obligation of prevention and to guarantee the fundamental rights recognized by the American Convention.[495]

335. In particular, and in accordance with Article 2 of the Convention, the State has the obligation to adopt the necessary measures to ensure the enjoyment of the rights and freedoms recognized in the

---

[495] *Cf. Case of Velásquez Rodríguez. Merits*, para. 166, and *Case of the Kichwa Indigenous People of Sarayaku v. Ecuador*, para. 221.

Convention.[496] In other words, States have not only the positive obligation to adopt the necessary legislative measures to ensure the enjoyment of the rights established in the Convention, but must also avoid enacting those laws that prevent the free exercise of these rights, and avoid the elimination or amendment of laws that protect them.[497]

336. First, and taking into account the considerations in this Judgment, the pertinent State authorities must take the appropriate measures to ensure that the prohibition of the practice of IVF is annulled as rapidly as possible so that those who wish to use this assisted reproduction technique may do so without encountering any impediments to the exercise of the rights that this Judgment has found to have been violated (*supra* para. 317). The State must provide information on the measures taken in this regard within six months.

337. Second, the State must, as soon as possible, regulate those aspects it considers necessary for the implementation of IVF, taking into account the principles established in this Judgment. In addition, the State must establish systems for the inspection and quality control of the qualified professionals and institutions that perform this type of assisted reproduction technique. The State must provide information every year on the gradual implementation of these systems.

338. Third, in the context of the considerations made in this Judgment (*supra* paras. 285 to 303), the Costa Rica Social Security Institute must make IVF available within its health care infertility treatments and programs, in accordance with the obligation to respect and guarantee the principle of non-discrimination. The State must provide information every six months on the measures adopted in order to make these services available gradually to those who require them and on the plans that it draws up to this end.

B.3.2) Campaign on the rights of persons with reproductive disabilities

Claims of the parties

339. Representative Molina asked the Court to "order the implementation of a national information campaign on the rights of persons with reproductive disabilities."

340. The State argued that "it already has mechanisms to create awareness on reproductive health" and "that the determination of the contents of campaigns on reproductive health corresponds to the

---

[496] *Cf. Case of Gangaram Panday* v. *Suriname. Preliminary objections.* Judgment of December 4, 1991. Series C No 12, para. 50, and *Case of Furlan and family* v. *Argentina*, para. 300.

[497] *Cf. Case of Gangaram Panday* v. *Suriname. Preliminary objections*, para. 50, and *Case of Furlan and family* v. *Argentina*, para. 300.

States, which are responsible for determining the use given to the health system's scarce financial resources."

Considerations of the Court

341. The Court observes that the State did not specify the existing mechanisms to raise awareness on reproductive health.[498] Therefore, it orders the State to implement permanent education and training programs and courses on human rights, reproductive rights and non-discrimination for judicial employees in all areas and at all echelons of the Judiciary.[499] These programs and training courses should make special mention of this Judgment and the different precedents in the *corpus iuris* of human rights relating to reproductive rights and the principle of non-discrimination.

B.3.3) Other measures requested

Claims of the parties

342. Representative May asked the Court to "ask the Permanent Council of the Organization of American States to request the Inter-American Juridical Committee ... to draft, within a reasonable time, an international norm on the embryo, bearing in mind the need to establish certain limits or the exclusion of human embryos from all commercial agreements." He also asked that "the Constitutional Chamber of the Supreme Court of Justice [carry out] a public act in order to apologize to the victims for the violation of their human rights and for the pain and suffering caused to them, acknowledging publicly that, because of its judgment, this judicial organ thwarted the life project of the victims." He also asked the Court to "declare that the Costa Rican Social Security Institute ... should establish a specialized IVF clinic named after Gerardo Trejos Salas."

343. The State argued that "there is no norm that grants the Inter-American Court competence to request the Juridical Committee to advise it or to draft normative documents; therefore, the request is irreceivable."

Considerations of the Court

344. Regarding the other measures of reparation requested, the Court considers that the delivery of this Judgment and the reparations

---

[498] The State merely mentioned the existence of a "Workshop on monitoring the MDG in Latin America" (merits report, volume III, folio 1253).
[499] Similarly *cf. Case of Atala Riffo and daughters* v. *Chile*, para. 271.

ordered in this chapter are sufficient and adequate to remedy the violations suffered by the victims, and does not find it necessary to order the said measures.[500]

C) *Compensation for pecuniary and non-pecuniary damage*

C.1) *Pecuniary damage*

Arguments of the Commission and claims of the parties

345. The Commission asked the Court to order the State to "make full reparation to the victims of the instant case, for both the pecuniary and the non-pecuniary aspects."

346. Representative Molina indicated that consequential damage has been demonstrated "with evidence such as, although not limited to, medical prescriptions, invoices, epicrises, and medical reports." He pointed out that "the collection of evidence from all the victims permits an overall reconstruction of the expenses arising from the medical procedure that is the purpose of this claim." He requested the "payment of all expenses incurred by the victims in their attempts to found a family with biological children, which, since it was not offered by the State as a health service, meant that they had to resort to private medicine and, in general, incur expenditure for items such as medical consultations, laboratory tests, ultrasounds and x-rays, the purchase of medicines, transportation, trips abroad and meals, payment of the costs of artificial insemination procedures, *in vitro* fertilization, and ICSI [intracytoplasmic sperm injection]." For pecuniary damage, he requested: (i) for María del Socorro Calderón and Carlos Vargas, the sum of US $4,821.69 each; (ii) for Enrique Acuña Cartín, the sum of US $9,677.04; (iii) for Ileana Henchoz and Miguel Yamuni, the sum of $17,516.29 each; (iv) for Julieta González and Oriéster Rojas, the sum of US $9,661.07 each; (v) for Karen Espinoza and Hector Jiménez, the sum of US $5,015.52 each; (vi) for Víctor Sanabria León, the sum of US $19,287.59, and (vii) for Joaquinita Arroyo and Giovanni Vega the sum of $7,188.08 each.

347. Representative May requested "payment of compensation for pecuniary and non-pecuniary damage." In particular, he asked for the following payments: (i) for Grettel Artavia Murillo, the sum of US

---

[500] *Cf. Case of Radilla Pacheco* v. *Mexico. Preliminary objections, merits, reparations and costs.* Judgment of November 23, 2009. Series C No 209, para. 359, and *Case of Vélez Restrepo and family* v. *Colombia*, para. 287.

$830,000; (ii) for Miguel Mejías Carballo, the sum of US $740,000; (iii) for Claudia María Carro Maklouf, the sum of US $700,000; (iv) for Andrea Bianchi Bruna, the sum of US $210,000; (v) for Germán Alberto Moreno Valencia, the sum of US $120,000; and (vi) for Ana Cristina Castillo León, the sum of US $1,500,000. He argued that the Court "has defined the concept of pecuniary damage, including within it the costs and expenses incurred by the parties during all the proceedings and based on the causes for responsibility that can be attributed to the State." He indicated that "all of the expenditure and disbursements made by the victims that are found to be proved either with documents or determined reasonably based on the events and circumstances proved in this case" should be recognized. He also indicated that "all the expenditure incurred by the couples in relation to the medical attention they received during the procedures to verify and determine their infertility should be recognized, because a medical diagnosis would not have been possible without these investments." In addition, he stated that "the travel and other related expenses incurred by those victims who had to go abroad in order to undergo this technique should be compensated, because in the absence of the prohibition the technique would have been available to them free of charge under the social security system."

348. The State "analyzed the claims presented based on the specific situation of each claimant couple" and concluded that the requests for pecuniary damage should be rejected for the following reasons: (i) the expenses incurred by the couples "relating [to the] infertility treatment, [are] the same as those they would have incurred even if the decree regulating [IVF] had not been annulled"; therefore "they have no causal relationship to the violations allegedly attributed to the State"; (ii) the medical expenses prior to the declaration of unconstitutionality cannot be attributed to the State or considered for the purposes of the requested compensation; (iii) "the violations attributed to the Costa Rican State have no effect on the presumed victims' employment"; (iv) the couples that had biological children do not qualify as infertile couples and therefore "it cannot be considered that the State limited the only possibility they ha[d] to become biological parents by declaring the decree that regulated [IVF] unconstitutional, since it is clear that they were able to have a biological child without undergoing [the said] procedure"; and (v) representative May's arguments did not provide "a clear and accurate determination of the reasons why it [was] alleged that the State produced pecuniary or non-pecuniary damage."

Considerations of the Court

349. In its case law, the Court has developed the concept of pecuniary damage, and has established that it supposes "the loss or detriment to the victims' incomes, the expenses incurred owing to the facts and the pecuniary consequences having a causal nexus to the facts of the case."[501]

350. Based on the arguments presented by the parties, the Court considers it necessary to determine the criteria that it will take into account in order to establish the amounts for pecuniary damage. First, the Court emphasizes that the violations declared above are related to the impediment to exercise a series of rights autonomously (*supra* para. 317), and not for being able or unable to have biological children; consequently, the State's argument that the couples that could have children should not be compensated is not receivable. Second, the Court takes into account that the IVF technique was not a procedure covered by the Costa Rican Social Security Institute (*supra* para. 70); thus the couples would have had to incur the above-mentioned medical expenses irrespective of the Constitutional Chamber's judgment. Consequently, the Court finds that there is no causal nexus between all the expenses mentioned above (*supra* paras. 346 and 347) and the violations declared in this Judgment. Bearing in mind the foregoing, the Court concludes that the expenses that have a causal nexus to the violations in this case are only those resulting from the Constitutional Chamber's decisions; mainly those expenses incurred by the couples that had to travel abroad to undergo the treatment.

351. In the instant case, the Court observes that representative Molina provided documentary evidence[502] for the couples consisting of Ileana Henchoz and Miguel Yamuni, Julieta González and Oriéster Rojas, and Víctor Sanabria León and Claudia Carro Maklouf,[503] who traveled abroad to undergo this technique. For his part, representative

---

[501] *Cf. Case of Bámaca Velásquez* v. *Guatemala. Reparations and costs.* Judgment of February 22, 2002. Series C No 91, para. 43, and *Case of Nadege Dorzema et al.* v. *Dominican Republic*, para. 281.

[502] There is an invoice from Hotel "Renasa" (file of annexes to the pleadings and motions briefs, volume V, annex XXVII, folio 5772) where they were in Valencia dated April 24, 2000, with the hotel expenses from April 18, 2000, to April 24, 2000, for a total of 640.33 euros. There are the receipts for the four days that they were in the Hotel Roma in Panama paying US $33 for the four nights (file of annexes to the pleadings and motions briefs, volume II, annex I, folios 4283 to 4285). The other is an Iberia ticket (file of annexes to the pleadings and motions briefs, volume II, annex V, folio 4695) in the name of Víctor Sanabria, between San José and Madrid for a total of US $681.58. Also, the representative submitted several tables in which he had calculated in colones and dollars different expenses that he associated with the pecuniary damage (merits report, volume II, folios 587.24 to 587.39).

[503] It is worth noting that Ms Carro was represented by representative May, but representative Molina presented evidence in her favor.

May did not present specific evidence with regard to Andrea Bianchi Bruna and Germán Alberto Moreno, who traveled abroad twice to undergo the treatment.

352. In this regard, the Court recalls that the criterion of equity has been used in this Court's case law to quantify non-pecuniary damage[504] and pecuniary damage,[505] and to establish loss of earnings.[506] However, the use of this criterion does not imply that the Court can act discretionally when establishing the compensatory amounts.[507] The parties must clearly specify the evidence of the harm they suffered, as well as the relationship of the specific pecuniary claim to the facts of the case and the alleged violations.[508]

353. In this particular case, representative May did not specify the amounts for pecuniary and non-pecuniary damage, thus the type of damage for which he requested compensation is unclear. Furthermore, he did not indicate the causal nexus between the violations declared in this case and the amounts requested for the victims; therefore it is not possible to determine the exact amount of the expenses incurred by Ms Bianchi and Mr Moreno.

354. For his part, representative Molina presented different types of documentary evidence on these expenses. However, the Court could not make an exact calculation of the amount owed, taking into account that the documentation presented, which corresponds to different dates, is in different currencies such as pesetas, Colombian pesos, and balboas. Even though he submitted information on the equivalent of these amounts in colones and dollars, he failed to explain clearly the type of exchange rate used. In this regard, it is not the Court's task to calculate the value of the dollar at the date of each invoice or documentary proof. However, the Court can presume that during these trips disbursements were made for airfares and daily expenses.

355. Therefore, the Court establishes, based on the equity principle, the sum of US $5,000.00 (five thousand United States dollars) in favor of each of the following persons: Ileana Henchoz, Miguel Yamuni, Julieta González, Oriéster Rojas, Víctor Sanabria León, Claudia Carro

---

[504] *Cf. Case of Velásquez Rodríguez* v. *Honduras. Reparations and costs.* Judgment of July 21, 1989. Series C No 7, para. 27, and *Case of the Barrios Family* v. *Venezuela,* para. 378.
[505] *Cf. Case of Neira Alegría et al.* v. *Peru. Reparations and costs.* Judgment of September 19, 1996. Series C No 29, para. 50, and *Case of the Barrios Family* v. *Venezuela,* para. 373.
[506] *Cf. Case of Neira Alegría et al.* v. *Peru. Reparations and costs.* Judgment of September 19, 1996. Series C No 29, para. 50, and *Case of the Barrios Family* v. *Venezuela,* para. 373.
[507] *Cf. Case of Aloeboetoe et al.* v. *Suriname. Reparations and costs.* Judgment of September 10, 1993. Series C No 15, para. 87.
[508] *Cf. Case of Furlan and family* v. *Argentina,* para. 313.

Maklouf, Andrea Bianchi Bruna and Germán Alberto Moreno, victims of this case who had to travel abroad to obtain access to IVF.

C.2) Non-pecuniary damage

Arguments of the Commission and claims of the parties

356. The Commission asked the Court to order the State "to make full reparation to the victims of the present case, to include both the pecuniary and the non-pecuniary aspects."

357. Representative Molina argued that the State "created a situation of lack of protection for these persons to the point of affecting them in their most intimate personal sphere, and re-victimizing them by not responding to their reproductive disability." He also argued that "in this case, it is essential to consider the damage to their life project as part of the non-pecuniary damage because, after all, these couples were seeking to found their family with biological children, and this road map they had prepared for their life was curtailed by the State's arbitrariness and inactivity." Therefore, he argued that "[i]n the case of the victims of the instant case, it is evident that the State's acts and omissions that prejudiced them impeded the achievement of their highest hopes."

358. In this regard, representative Molina argued that the non-pecuniary damage could be calculated by three methods, namely: (i) "monthly temporary income"; (ii) "psychological loss of earnings"; and (iii) "equity and justice." Regarding "monthly temporary income" he argued that it was possible to estimate the non-pecuniary damages in the sum of US $3,500 per month for the men, and US $4,500 for the women, calculated from the date on which IVF was prohibited and until the date of its eventual authorization, which, "following the Court's parameters to make the calculation based on simple interest and the LIBOR rate at the beginning of each year," would result in "a sum of US $654,435.84 for each woman, and US $466,651.98 for each man [... which] would mean that they could turn around their 'life project' and prepare to enjoy, with a monthly temporary income, their old age in better financial conditions." Regarding the "psychological loss of earnings," he argued that this was not "about the person who stopped working or who died and, consequently, this capital has to be replaced; but rather about a person who continues working or whose work is not remunerated; . . . this would be the case for a housewife or student who, without working in exchange for a salary, can also be the victim of damage and who is not, because of this condition, left unprotected as a beneficiary of compensation. Thus, we classify this

kind of damage as non-pecuniary, because its causal nexus arises from a psychological or affective harm, more than direct harm to their salary."[509] Regarding the criterion of "equity and justice," he asked that "significant financial compensation be established in favor of the victims." He concluded that "a sum no less than US $800,000 ... should be established in favor of each victim in these proceedings, as a way of establishing a true balance between the arbitrariness of the State and the intense, prolonged, and now perpetual, suffering of the victims."

359. Representative May argued that "the Constitutional Chamber's decision ... produced a loss of opportunity that is included in the principle of full reparation," because "the victims' real and genuine possibility of becoming parents, founding a family, and being able to enjoy the right to equality in relation to the rest of the community disappeared with the prohibition, while before the prohibition (the harmful event), the victims had a real and genuine possibility of having biological children." The sums requested for non-pecuniary damage are those presented for pecuniary damage (*supra* para. 346).

360. With regard to the presumed non-pecuniary damage, the State argued the lack of a causal nexus between this and the judgment of the Constitutional Chamber, considering that: (i) "[i]n none of the cases ... had it contributed, by act or omission, to the infertility of the persons who appear as victims"; (ii) that "the suffering that the couples might feel because they were unable to procreate children ... is related to their natural condition of being unable to have children, and not to the prohibition indicated by the Constitutional Chamber"; and (iii) that "there would have to be absolute certainty that the use of *in vitro* fertilization techniques ... would have resulted in the birth of a child or, at least, that there was a high level of probability of this," when "the evidence provided by the State allows it to be established that the probability that a child would be born following the practice of the *in vitro* fertilization technique is very low, both nowadays and at the time the Constitutional Chamber's decision was issued." In addition, it considered that "Joaquinita Arroyo and ... Giovanni Vega and ...

---

[509] Representative Molina requested as "psychological loss of earnings": (i) for María del Socorro Calderón Porras the sum of US $180,847.05; (ii) for Carlos Eduardo Vargas Solórzano the sum of US $201,213.61; (iii) for Julieta González Ledezma the sum of US $187,787.01; (iv) for Oriéster Rojas Carranza the sum of US $485,114.98; (v) for Joaquinita Arroyo Fonseca the sum of US $771,489.23; (vi) for Giovanni Antonio Vega the sum of US $1,814,061.98; (vii) for Ileana Henchoz Bolaños the sum of US $1,013,454.54; (viii) for Miguel Antonio Yamuni Zeledón the sum of US $1,259,961.59; (ix) for Karen Espinoza Vindas the sum of US $752,620.35; (x) for Héctor Jiménez Acuña the sum of US $590,306.84; (xi) for Víctor Hugo Sanabria León the sum of US $1,862,581.64; and (xii) for Enrique Acuña Cartín the sum of US $1,268,470.28 (merits report, volume II, folio 587.35).

Karen Espinoza and Héctor Jiménez ... had children conceived naturally, so that it is clear that they were not infertile," and that "in the case of Grettel Artavia Murillo ... she also had a child who was born on July 27, 2011." Lastly, the State denied the existence of a "causal nexus between the violations of which the State is accused and the work-related difficulties that some of the individuals supposedly experienced."

Considerations of the Court
361. In its case law, the Court has developed the concept of non-pecuniary damage and has established that "it can comprise both the suffering and afflictions caused to the direct victims and to those close to them, the impairment of values that [are] very significant to the individual, as well as alterations, of a non-pecuniary nature, to the living conditions of the victims or their family."[510] Since it is not possible to assign a precise monetary value to non-pecuniary damage, it can only be compensated for purposes of the victim's full reparation, by the payment of a sum of money or the delivery of goods or services with a measurable financial value that the Court determines in reasonable application of sound judicial discretion and based on equity.[511]

362. Furthermore, the Court reiterates the reparatory nature of the compensation, the nature and amount of which depend on the damage caused, and, therefore, should not signify either the enrichment or the impoverishment of the victims or their heirs.[512]

363. In the instant case, the Court recalls that the damage does not depend on whether or not the couples were able to have children (*supra* para. 350), but corresponds to the disproportionate impact on their lives of the inability to exercise their rights autonomously (*supra* para. 317). As revealed in Chapter VII, the feelings of anguish, anxiety, uncertainty and frustration, and the effects on the possibility of deciding their own, autonomous and independent life project, have been verified in these proceedings. Based on the suffering caused to the victims, as well as the changes in their living conditions and the other consequences of a non-pecuniary nature that they experienced, the

---

[510] *Cf. Case of the "Street Children" (Villagrán Morales et al.)* v. *Guatemala. Reparations and costs.* Judgment of May 26, 2001. Series C No 77, para. 84, and *Case of Nadege Dorzema et al.* v. *Dominican Republic*, para. 284.
[511] *Cf. Case of Palamara Iribarne* v. *Chile. Merits, reparations and costs.* Judgment of November 22, 2005. Series C No 135, para. 244, and *Case of the Yean and Bosico Girls* v. *Dominican Republic*, para. 223.
[512] *Cf. Case of the "White Van" (Paniagua Morales et al.)* v. *Guatemala. Reparations and costs.* Judgment of May 25, 2001. Series C No 76, para. 79, and *Case of Bayarri* v. *Argentina. Preliminary objection, merits, reparations and costs.* Judgment of October 30, 2008. Series C No 187, para. 161.

Court finds it pertinent to establish, in equity, the sum of US $20,000.00 (twenty thousand United States dollars) for each victim as compensation for non-pecuniary damage.

D) Costs and expenses

Claims of the parties

364. Representative Molina asked the Court to order the State to reimburse the expenses incurred for the proceedings before the Court corresponding to US $60,000.00, because he "had to litigate it up until the judgment was delivered and taking into consideration also that the proceedings before the Inter-American Court are very complex, and even presume that experts on matters such as health, assisted reproduction, and psychologists must be consulted." Additionally, he requested US $10,926.43 for "the cost of expert evidence, the notary and expenses resulting from the preparation of briefs."

365. In his pleadings and motions brief, representative Trejos asked the Court to order the State to reimburse the costs and expenses he had incurred. In total, he asked the Court to establish, in equity, the sum of US $45,000.00 for "representing the victims" and for "the measures taken at the domestic and the international level since 2001 in order to obtain justice for all of the victims as *de facto* representative of all of the petitioners in this case before Costa Rica's judicial and administrative authorities and before the Inter-American Commission, as well as of the couples represented ... before the Inter-American Court." In his final arguments, representative May repeated the requests made by representative Trejos and asked that the Court include "invoices for supervening procedural expenses."

366. The State indicated that "the State cannot agree to the sum that is being requested, because the amounts are unreasonable, and even some of the amounts claimed are in excess of the non-pecuniary damage claimed for some of the presumed victims."

Considerations of the Court

367. As the Court has indicated on previous occasions, costs and expenses are included in the concept of reparation established in Article 63(1) of the American Convention.[513]

---

[513] *Cf. Case of Garrido and Baigorria* v. *Argentina. Reparations and costs.* Judgment of August 27, 1998. Series C No 39, para. 79, and *Case of Nadege Dorzema et al.* v. *Dominican Republic*, para. 290.

368. The Court has stated that the claims of the victims or their representatives for costs and expenses, and the evidence that supports them, must be presented to the Court at the first procedural moment granted them, in other words in the pleadings and motions brief, notwithstanding the possibility of updating the said claims subsequently, in keeping with the new costs and expenses incurred during the proceedings before this Court.[514]

369. Regarding the reimbursement of costs and expenses, it corresponds to the Court to evaluate their scope prudently; they include the expenses generated before the authorities of the domestic jurisdiction, as well as those arising during the proceedings before the inter-American system, taking into account the circumstances of the specific case and the nature of the international jurisdiction for the protection of human rights. This assessment may be made based on the equity principle and taking into account the expenses indicated by the parties, provided that the *quantum* is reasonable.[515] Moreover, the Court reiterates that it is not enough to submit evidentiary documents, but rather the parties must also provide arguments relating the evidence to the fact it is considered to represent and, since this relates to alleged financial disbursements, the items and their justification must be established clearly.[516]

370. In the instant case, the Court observes that representative Trejos, who represented the victims during the proceedings before the Commission (*supra* paras. 1 and 8), died before these contentious proceedings were completed. Nevertheless, in his pleadings and motions brief, he was able to describe his claims for costs and expenses.

371. Furthermore, the Court observes that representative Trejos presented expense vouchers for US $1,376.96.[517] With his final arguments, representative May provided invoices corresponding to five affidavits for a total of US $2,500.00 dollars, without indicating why

---

[514] *Cf. Case of Chaparro Álvarez and Lapo Íñiguez* v. *Ecuador*, para. 275, and *Case of Nadege Dorzema et al.* v. *Dominican Republic*, para. 292.
[515] *Cf. Case of Garrido and Baigorria* v. *Argentina. Reparations and costs.* Judgment of August 27, 1998. Series C No 39, para. 82; *Case of the Río Negro Massacres* v. *Guatemala. Preliminary objection, merits, reparations and costs.* Judgment of September 4, 2012. Series C No 250, para. 314.
[516] *Cf. Case of Chaparro Álvarez and Lapo Íñiguez* v. *Ecuador. Preliminary objections, merits, reparations and costs.* Judgment of November 21, 2007. Series C No 170, para. 277, and *Case of Vélez Restrepo and family* v. *Colombia*, para. 307.
[517] In his pleadings and motions brief, representative Trejos presented as expenses during the proceedings: (i) the invoice for the purchase of a plane ticket in the name of Andrea Bianchi (US $439.72); (ii) the invoice for the purchase of a plane ticket in the name of Gerardo Trejos Salas (US $468.62); and (iii) the invoice for the purchase of a plane ticket in the name of Gloria Mazariegos (US $468.62), totaling US $1,376.96 (file of annexes to the pleadings and motions brief, volume I, folios 4071 and 4072).

the cost of each notarial service had been calculated at US $500.00. In addition, in his final arguments, representative May requested the same amount that representative Trejos had asked for in his pleadings and motions brief, without clarifying whether these were two autonomous requests, or else, which part of the latter request corresponded to fees for Mr Trejos and which part to fees for Mr May. For his part, representative Molina provided expense vouchers for the sum of US $9,243.00, which corresponds mostly to the partial calculation of some professional services.[518]

372. The Court observes that the case file does not contain any supporting evidence to justify the sums that the representatives are requesting for professional fees and services. Indeed, the amounts requested for fees were not accompanied by specific proof of their reasonableness and scope.[519]

373. Therefore, the Court establishes, in equity, the sum of US $10,000.00 (ten thousand United States dollars) for costs and expenses in favor of representative Gerardo Trejos, which must be paid directly to his heirs, in keeping with the applicable domestic law. Furthermore, the Court establishes, in equity, the sum of US $2,000.00 (two thousand United States dollars) for costs and expenses in favor of representative May, and the sum of US $3,000 (three thousand United States dollars) for costs and expenses in favor of representative Molina.

E) *Method of compliance with the payments ordered*

374. The State must make the payments of the compensation for pecuniary and non-pecuniary damage and reimbursement of costs and expenses established in this Judgment directly to the persons indicated herein, within one year of notification of this Judgment, in the terms of the following paragraphs. If the beneficiaries are deceased or die before they receive the respective compensation, this shall be delivered directly to their heirs, in accordance with the applicable domestic law.

---

[518] In his pleadings and motions brief, representative Boris Molina Acevedo presented as expenses during the proceedings: (i) invoice for professional services issued to María Lorna Ballestero Muñóz for US $6,000.00; (ii) receipt of payment for professional services to Gabriela Darsié and Enrique Madrigal for US $1,375; (iii) receipt for payment of professional services for advice and assistance provided by William Vega for US $1,600; and (iv) [receipt] for photocopies and administrative expenses [for] 131,850 colones (file of annexes to the pleadings and motions brief, volume VI, folios 6537 and 6364).
[519] *Cf. Case of Chitay Nech et al. v. Guatemala. Preliminary objections, merits, reparations and costs.* Judgment of May 25, 2010. Series C No 212, para. 287.

375. The State must comply with the pecuniary obligations by payment in United States dollars or the equivalent in local currency, using the exchange rate in effect on the New York Stock Exchange, United States of America, on the day before the payment.

376. If, for causes that can be attributed to the beneficiaries of the compensation or their heirs, it is not possible to pay the amounts established within the indicated time frames, the State must deposit the said amounts in their favor in an account or certificate of deposit in a solvent Costa Rican financial institution, in United States dollars, and in the most favorable financial conditions allowed by law and banking practices. If, after 10 years, the sum allocated has not been claimed, the amounts must be returned to the State, with the interest accrued.

377. The amounts allocated in this Judgment as compensation for pecuniary and non-pecuniary damage, and as reimbursement of costs and expenses, must be delivered to the persons and organizations indicated in full, in keeping with the provisions of this Judgment, without any reductions arising from eventual taxes or charges, within one year of notification of this Judgment.

378. If the State falls into arrears, it must pay interest on the amount owed, corresponding to the bank interest on arrears in Costa Rica.

379. In accordance with its consistent practice, the Court reserves the authority inherent in its attributes and also derived from Article 65 of the American Convention to monitor full compliance with this Judgment. The case will be closed when the State has complied fully with the provisions of this Judgment.

380. The State must provide the Court with a report on the measures adopted to comply with this Judgment within six months and one year of its notification.

X. OPERATIVE PARAGRAPHS

381. Therefore,
THE COURT
DECIDES,
unanimously,

1. To reject the preliminary objections filed by the State, in the terms of paragraphs 17 to 40 of this Judgment.

DECLARES,
By five votes to one, that:

1. The State is responsible for the violation of Articles 5(1), 7, 11(2) and 17(2) in relation to Article 1(1) of the American Convention, to the detriment of Grettel Artavia Murillo, Miguel Mejías Carballo, Andrea Bianchi Bruno, Germán Alberto Moreno Valencia, Ana Cristina Castillo León, Enrique Acuña Cartín, Ileana Henchoz Bolaños, Miguel Antonio Yamuni Zeledón, Claudia María Carro Maklouf, Víctor Hugo Sanabria León, Karen Espinoza Vindas, Héctor Jiménez Acuña, María del Socorro Calderón P., Joaquinita Arroyo Fonseca, Giovanni Antonio Vega, Carlos E. Vargas Solórzano, Julieta González Ledezma and Oriéster Rojas Carranza, in the terms of paragraphs 136 to 317 of this Judgment.

AND ESTABLISHES

By five votes to one, that:

1. This Judgment constitutes *per se* a form of reparation.
2. The State must adopt, as soon as possible, appropriate measures to annul the prohibition to practice IVF, so that those persons who wish to use this assisted reproduction technique can do so without any impediment to the exercise of the rights that were declared violated in this Judgment. The State must provide information on the measures adopted in this regard, in accordance with paragraph 336 of this Judgment.
3. The State must regulate, as soon as possible, the aspects that it considers necessary for the implementation of IVF, taking into account the principles established in this Judgment, and must establish systems of inspection and quality control of the institutions and professional[s] qualified [to] perform this type of assisted reproduction technique. The State must provide information every year on the gradual implementation of these systems, in accordance with paragraph 337 of this Judgment.
4. The State must include the availability of IVF within the infertility treatments and programs offered by its health care services, in keeping with the obligation of guarantee in relation to the principle of non-discrimination. The State must provide information every six months on the measures adopted to make these services available gradually to those who require them and on the plans made to this end, in accordance with paragraph 338 of this Judgment.
5. The State must provide the victims with psychological treatment, free of charge and immediately, for up to four years, through the State's specialized health care institutions, as established in paragraph 326 of this Judgment.

6. The State must make the publications indicated in paragraph 329 of this Judgment, within six months of its notification.
7. The State must implement permanent education and training programs and courses on human rights, reproductive rights and non-discrimination for judicial officials in all areas and at all echelons of the Judiciary, as established in paragraph 341 of this Judgment.
8. The State must pay the amounts established in paragraphs 355 and 363 of this Judgment, as compensation for pecuniary and non-pecuniary damage, and for reimbursement of costs and expenses, in the terms of paragraph 373 of this Judgment.
9. The State must submit to the Court a general report on the measures adopted to comply with this Judgment within one year of its notification.
10. The Court will monitor full compliance with this Judgment, in exercise of its authority and in compliance with its obligations under the American Convention on Human Rights, and will consider this case concluded when the State has complied fully with the measures ordered herein.

CONCURRING OPINION OF JUDGE DIEGO GARCÍA-SAYÁN

1. This Judgment is a very clear and important decision of the Court that enhances the right to personal integrity, to private and family life, and to the principle of non-discrimination. All of them were seriously harmed by the facts that gave rise to this litigation. By establishing which rights had been violated and the corresponding reparations, the Court addressed the Judgment, essentially, as an affirmation of life.

2. Justifying the absolute prohibition of *in vitro* fertilization (IVF) by the alleged "right to life" is a twofold contradiction. First, because indicating that IVF would result in "embryonic loss" fails to take into account that, as it has been proved in the instant case, embryonic loss also occurs in natural pregnancies and in other reproduction techniques. Second, because the prohibition, allegedly based on the right to life, resulted, paradoxically, in an impediment to life by obstructing the right of men and women to have children. Thus, an unwarranted obstacle to life was established, which will continue until the measures of reparation ordered by the Court in this Judgment have been fully implemented.

3. Since reproductive self-determination is closely related to the rights to privacy and to personal integrity (paras. 146 and 147), the absolute prohibition of IVF decreed by the Costa Rican Constitutional

Chamber on March 15, 2000, harmed these rights, resulting in a serious impact on the victims.

4. This was increased by the discriminatory impact of the ban. As the Court recalled, States must not introduce regulations that have a discriminatory impact on different groups of the population when exercising their rights (para. 286). The Court established that the ban had a discriminatory impact on the victims in relation to crucial aspects such as their situation of disability or their financial situation (para. 284).

5. It is clear, as proved during these proceedings, that the disability consisting in infertility requires special treatment and that State policies should be inclusive rather than exclusive; also, that the ban had a disproportionate effect to the detriment of infertile couples with less income because, in order to undergo IVF treatment, they had to travel abroad.

6. Men and women who are infertile suffer from a disease, as the Court recalled in this Judgment (para. 288), bearing in mind that the World Health Organization (WHO) has established that infertility is "a disease of the reproductive system defined by the failure to achieve a clinical pregnancy after 12 months or more of regular unprotected sexual intercourse."[1]

7. Taking this into consideration, the fact that the State refused them the right to use this scientific method, owing to the ban established in March 2000, seriously harmed the rights of those affected by this disease.

8. Furthermore, to the extent that the State has based many of its arguments on a certain interpretation of Article 4(1) of the American Convention on Human Rights, in this Judgment, the Court has proceeded to interpret this article for the effects of this case. And it has done so, as required by international law, in accordance with the ordinary meaning given to the terms, as well as with a systematic and historical interpretation and one that corresponds to the object and purpose of the treaty, using as supplementary means of interpretation the preparatory work of this article of the Convention.

9. The Court's interpretation and the available scientific evidence led, among other consequences, to the conclusion that it cannot be determined that Article 4(1) seeks to confer the status of "person" on the embryo, emphasizing that "... the regulatory trends in

---

[1] *Cf.* Written summary of the expert opinion provided by Fernando Zegers-Hochschild at the public hearing before the Court (merits file, volume VI, folio 2828). As expert witness Zegers-Hochschild explained, according to the World Health Organization (WHO) infertility is a disease of the reproductive system (merits file, volume VI, folio 2818).

international law do not lead to the conclusion that the embryo should be treated in the same way as a person . . ." (para. 253).

10. The reparations have been established not only directly with regard to the persons declared victims. They also establish measures addressed at society as a whole, such as those concerning non-repetition, and specific guidelines to create the appropriate conditions to ensure compliance with the State's duty to comply with the obligations set out in the Judgment with regard to personal integrity, private and family life, and the principle of non-discrimination.

11. The essence of the measures of reparation is, therefore, that the State must not only cease creating discriminatory regulations and practices, but that it must also annul the prohibition and gradually facilitate the use of this reproduction technique to those who need and want it. In this regard, the Court basically establishes, *inter alia*, three precise lines of action designed to constitute guarantees of non-repetition and to ensure that the conduct of the State is in keeping with its international obligations:

(a) The first is that the State must "take the appropriate measures to ensure that the prohibition of the practice of IVF is annulled as rapidly as possible so that those who wish to use this assisted reproduction technique may do so without encountering any impediments" (para. 336). Thus, the State must adopt promptly the necessary measures, within its own institutional framework, to ensure that the prohibition is annulled;
(b) The second is that the State must "regulate those aspects it considers necessary for the implementation of IVF" (para. 337), which refers to regulations to be drafted and implemented by the State to ensure that this technique is used correctly by qualified institutions and professionals;
(c) The establishment, in the third measure, that social security must gradually include IVF "within its health care infertility treatments and programs, in accordance with the obligation to respect and guarantee the principle of non-discrimination" (para. 338) is designed to ensure that the said technique is included gradually in the programs to treat infertility that are already offered. This does not mean that a disproportionate percentage of social security's institutional and budgetary resources should be devoted to this purpose, to the detriment of other programs and priorities, but is intended to ensure that this service is made available progressively.

It should be emphasized that this order of the Court is clearly and directly related to the principle of non-discrimination. Thus, it cannot be understood as an order that leads to situations of inequality. Consequently, regarding the said gradualness, it should be stressed that the Committee on Economic, Social and Cultural Rights[2] has indicated that the "precise nature" of the available health services and programs "will vary depending on numerous factors, including the State party's developmental level." This Committee has also indicated that one of the components of accessibility without discrimination to health services is related to "economic accessibility (affordability)," so that health facilities, goods and services must be affordable for all. The Committee has added that the payment for health care services "has to be based on the principle of equity, ensuring that these services, whether privately or publicly provided, are affordable for all, including socially disadvantaged groups. Equity demands that poorer households should not be disproportionately burdened with health expenses as compared to richer households."[3] These considerations allow me to stress the causal nexus of the order issued by the Court in relation to the particular situation of persons whose only possibility of procreation is access to IVF and who do not have the financial resources to access this type of assisted reproduction technique.

In addition, as revealed by the answer to the submission of the case and the final arguments of the State of Costa Rica, the State has medical programs and services that offer different treatments for infertility problems, including assisted reproduction techniques. The State advised that the only method excluded from the public programs to treat reproductive health problems has been IVF, owing to the ruling of the Constitutional Chamber. Thus, it is possible to relate the exclusion of IVF to the arguments developed in the judicial decision analyzed in this Judgment, and it is not evident that it was economic or budgetary considerations that justified the said exclusion. In addition, it was not proved that a situation existed, such as that of other States, in which the inexistence or insufficiency of resources to subsidize part of the access to assisted reproduction techniques has been alleged. Thus the State must continue making gradual progress to guarantee, without discrimination, access to the adequate and necessary treatments to deal with different forms of infertility.

---

[2] Committee on Economic, Social and Cultural Rights, General Comment 14 (2000): The right to the highest attainable standard of health (Article 12 of the International Covenant on Economic, Social and Cultural Rights), E/C.12/2000/4, August 11, 2000, para. 12.a.

[3] Committee on Economic, Social and Cultural Rights, General Comment 14 (2000): The right to the highest attainable standard of health (Article 12 of the International Covenant on Economic, Social and Cultural Rights), E/C.12/2000/4, August 11, 2000, para. 12.b.iii.

In this regard, I would stress that the Court's mandate is not addressed at modifying any type of prioritization at the domestic level, in the understanding that access to assisted reproduction techniques had already been incorporated into the comprehensive care provided by the State. The Court, as is its consistent practice, leaves in the hands of the local authorities the series of decisions on the nature and scope of the measures required to guarantee, progressively, whatever is pertinent in relation to the series of techniques associated with the different methods of IVF and, to this end, the authorities must implement the specific and necessary regulations.

12. Bearing in mind that the main fact that gave rise to this litigation was the prohibition of an assisted reproduction technique—IVF—in Costa Rica, this Judgment not only establishes which articles of the Convention have been violated and the corresponding reparations. In essence and based on its content, it makes a fundamental contribution to life as expressed by the more than 5 million people who today enjoy life because their parents used this type of method to counter infertility, and who would not exist if it had not been for this method.

DISSENTING OPINION OF JUDGE EDUARDO VIO GROSSI

Introduction

[1] This dissenting opinion[1] is issued with the utmost respect and consideration towards the Inter-American Court of Human Rights (hereinafter "the Court") and, certainly, to all of its members. The arguments that will be presented are, of course, limited solely and exclusively to what was addressed in the above judgment (hereinafter "the Judgment").[2] This opinion refers, particularly, to Article 4(1) of

---

[1] [Paragraph numbers have been editorially inserted in this opinion.] Art. 66(2) of the Convention: "If the judgment does not represent in whole or in part the unanimous opinion of the judges, any judge shall be entitled to have his dissenting or separate opinion attached to the judgment"; and Art. 24 (3) of the Statute of the Court: "The decisions, judgments and opinions of the Court shall be delivered in public session, and the parties shall be given written notification thereof. In addition, the decisions, judgments and opinions shall be published, along with judges' individual votes and opinions and with such other data or background information that the Court may deem appropriate." In this particular, see also *Declaration of Complaints*, presented to the Court on August 17, 2011, *regarding* part of the conjoint Concurring Opinion issued in relation to the Court's orders "Provisional Measures Regarding Colombia. Case of Gutiérrez Soler," June 30, 2011, "Provisional Measure Regarding the United Mexican States, Case of Rosendo Catú *et al.*," July 1, 2011, and "Provisional Measures Regarding the Republic of Honduras, Case of Kawas Fernández *v.* Honduras," July 5, 2011.

[2] Art. 65(2) of the Rules of the Court: "Any Judge who has taken part in the consideration of a case is entitled to append a separate reasoned opinion to the judgment, concurring or dissenting. These opinions shall be submitted within a time limit to be fixed by the Presidency so that the other Judges

the American Convention on Human Rights (hereinafter "the Convention"), because the author of this opinion considers that the analysis of this article was a determining factor in the outcome of all other issues of this case.

[2] The commentaries made in dissenting opinion are, certainly, based on the law and not on the author's wishes. This opinion also bears in mind that the Court must interpret and apply the Convention,[3] instead of assuming the role of the Inter-American Commission on Human Rights[4] or the lawmaking function. The latter belongs to the States, which have the exclusive power to modify the Convention.[5] Finally—and especially—, this dissenting opinion notes that the Court must determine the States' will, expressed in the Convention and in subsequent agreements and practices, so as to require from them what they really agreed to.[6]

[3] The reasoning of this dissenting opinion has two main prongs. The first is an analysis of Article 4(1), due to the fact that the violation of this provision is the ultimate issue of this case. The second refers to the way this Judgment made a shift in the Court's case law referring to this article.

I. Article 4(1) of the Convention

[4] In turn, the analysis of Article 4(1) of the Convention raises three issues. The first refers to the Judgment's perspective when addressing this case. The second regards the interpretation of this article. The third concerns the Court's case law on this issue.

---

may take cognizance thereof before notice of the judgment is served. Said opinions shall only refer to the issues covered in the judgment."

[3] Art. 62(3) of the Convention: "The jurisdiction of the Court shall comprise all cases concerning the interpretation and application of the provisions of this Convention that are submitted to it, provided that the States Parties to the case recognize or have recognized such jurisdiction, whether by special declaration pursuant to the preceding paragraphs, or by a special agreement."

[4] First sentence of Art. 4(1) of the Convention: "The main function of the Commission shall be to promote respect for and defense of human rights."

[5] Art. 76(1) of the Convention: "Proposals to amend this Convention may be submitted to the General Assembly for the action it deems appropriate by any State Party directly, and by the Commission or the Court through the Secretary General"; and Art. 39 of the Vienna Convention: "*General rule regarding the amendment of treaties.* A treaty may be amended by agreement between the parties. The rules laid down in Part II apply to such an agreement except insofar as the treaty may otherwise provide."

[6] Art. 2(1)(a) of the Vienna Convention on the Law of Treaties (hereinafter Vienna Convention): "*Use of terms.* 1. For the purposes of the present Convention: (a) "treaty" means an international agreement concluded between States in written form and governed by international law, whether embodied in a single instrument or in two or more related instruments and whatever its particular designation."

A. Perspective used for deciding this case

[5] There is no doubt that the Judgment's perspective when addressing this case will influence its outcome. This is why it is necessary, first and foremost, to refer to this perspective.

[6] In this regard, the Judgment states that it will, as the first issue on the merits of this case,

> determine the scope of the rights to personal integrity and to private and family life, as relevant to decide the dispute.[7]

[7] Then, it states that

> the purpose of this case focuses on establishing whether the Constitutional Chamber's judgment resulted in a disproportionate restriction of the rights of the presumed victims.[8]

[8] The Judgment is obviously referring to the Decision of March 15, 2000, of the Constitutional Chamber of the Supreme Court of Justice of the Republic of Costa Rica (hereinafter "the Decision"). The Decision declared unconstitutional the Executive Decree No 24029-S of February 3, 1995, regulating *in vitro* fertilization, because it infringed Article 4(1) of the Convention ("Right to Life").

[9] In this regard, the Judgment states that "[h]aving verified that interference existed, owing both to the prohibitive effect resulting from the Constitutional Chamber's judgment caused in general, and to the impact it had on the presumed victims in this case, the Court considers it necessary to proceed to examine whether this interference or restriction was justified." Hence, it "considers it pertinent to examine in detail the main argument developed by the Constitutional Chamber: that the American Convention makes the absolute protection of the 'right to life' of the embryo compulsory and, consequently, makes it obligatory to prohibit IVF because it entails the loss of embryos", stating also that it will "analyze whether the interpretation of the Convention that substantiated the interferences that occurred ... is admissible in light of this treaty, bearing in mind the pertinent sources of international law."[9]

[10] Now, it is true that the Inter-American Commission on Human Rights (hereinafter "the Commission") and the victims' representatives (hereinafter "the Representatives") alleged that the aforementioned Decision violated the following articles of the Convention:

---

[7] Para. 141 of the Judgment. Hereinafter, the expressions "para." or "paras." shall be understood as making reference to the Judgment.

[8] Para. 171.

[9] Para. 162 [note of the translator: and 171].

11(2) ("Right to Privacy"), 17(2) ("Rights of the Family") and 24 ("Right to Equal Protection"), in conjunction with Articles 1(1) ("Obligation to Respect Rights") and 2 ("Domestic Legal Effects"). Nevertheless, it is also true that one of the Representatives also alleged the violation of Articles 4(1) ("Right to Life"), 5(1) ("Right to Humane Treatment") and 7 ("Right to Personal Liberty").[10] In addition, the aforementioned Decision is explicitly based on Article 4(1).

[11] Hence, the issue at stake should not have been addressed in the way the Court did, but from the opposite perspective.

[12] In fact, considering the applicable customary law,[11] this case should determine whether, in light of the Convention,[12] the aforementioned Decision[13] is internationally licit or not.[14] This requires, first and foremost, contrasting this act of the State with Article 4(1), with the international obligation that the very State adduced as its justification. Only once this issue is elucidated will it be possible to address the conformity of the Decision with Articles 5(1), 11(2), 17(2) and 24.

[13] Thus, it was more logical for the Judgment to understand and address this case, primarily, as a possible violation of Article 4(1), rather than dealing with it the way it did.

[14] By acting as it did, the Judgment not only follows the procedural and argumentative rationales that were legitimately suggested by

---

[10] Para. 7.
[11] Contained in the Draft Articles on Responsibility of States for Internationally Wrongful Acts, prepared by the International Law Commission of the UN, adopted by Resolution approved by the General Assembly [based on the Report of the Sixth Committee (A/56/589 and Corr. 1)] 56/83. Responsibility of States for internationally wrongful acts, 85th plenary meeting, December 12, 2001, *Official Records of the General Assembly, Fifty-sixth Session, Supplement No 10* and corrigendum (A/56/10 and Corr. 1 and 2). 2 *ibid.* (hereinafter "Draft on the State's International Responsibility").
[12] Art. 62(3) of the Convention, already referred to.
[13] Art. 4 of the Draft on the State's International Responsibility: "*Conduct of organs of a State*. 1. The conduct of any State organ shall be considered an act of that State under international law, whether the organ exercises legislative, executive, judicial or any other functions, whatever position it holds in the organization of the State, and whatever its character as an organ of the central Government or of a territorial unit of the State. 2. An organ includes any person or entity which has that status in accordance with the internal law of the State."
[14] Articles of the Draft on the State's International Responsibility: "*Article 1. Responsibility of a State for its internationally wrongful acts*. Every internationally wrongful act of a State entails the international responsibility of that State"; "*Article 2. Elements of an internationally wrongful act of a State*. There is an internationally wrongful act of a State when conduct consisting of an action or omission: (a) is attributable to the State under international law; and (b) constitutes a breach of an international obligation of the State"; and "*Article 3. Characterization of an act of a State as internationally wrongful*. The characterization of an act of a State as internationally wrongful is governed by international law. Such characterization is not affected by the characterization of the same act as lawful by internal law."

the Commission and the Representatives in light of their own interests and procedural roles. It also ends up, in practice, minimizing and subordinating the "right to life" to the other previously referred rights. The perspective chosen by the Judgment has, in conclusion, the paramount practical effect of privileging these rights over the "right to life."

B. *Interpretation of Article 4(1)*

[15] As it was asserted, and in contrast to the path followed by the Judgment, the main issue raised in this case was the determination of whether the State, when issuing the relevant Decision, incurred an international responsibility[15] for violating Article 4(1) of the Convention, which provides:

Every person has the right to have his life respected. This right shall be protected by law and, in general, from the moment of conception. No one shall be arbitrarily deprived of his life.

[16] The interpretation of a provision of the Convention consists in elucidating the will of the Member States to the Convention, as it was expressed in this treaty. This must be done in accordance with the rules of the Vienna Convention on the Law of Treaties (hereinafter "the Vienna Convention"), which contains both the treaty-based and customary rules on this matter. Due to their importance for this case, it is necessary to quote them.

[17] Article 31 of the Vienna Convention provides:

General rule of interpretation

1. A treaty shall be interpreted in good faith in accordance with the ordinary meaning to be given to the terms of the treaty in their context and in the light of its object and purpose.

2. The context for the purpose of the interpretation of a treaty shall comprise, in addition to the text, including its preamble and annexes:

(a) any agreement relating to the treaty which was made between all the parties in connection with the conclusion of the treaty;

---

[15] Art. 12 of the Draft on the State's International Responsibility: "*Existence of a breach of an international obligation.* There is a breach of an international obligation by a State when an act of that State is not in conformity with what is required of it by that obligation, regardless of its origin or character."

(b) any instrument which was made by one or more parties in connection with the conclusion of the treaty and accepted by the other parties as an instrument related to the treaty.

3. There shall be taken into account, together with the context:

(a) any subsequent agreement between the parties regarding the interpretation of the treaty or the application of its provisions;
(b) any subsequent practice in the application of the treaty which establishes the agreement of the parties regarding its interpretation;
(c) any relevant rules of international law applicable in the relations between the parties.

4. A special meaning shall be given to a term if it is established that the parties so intended.

[18] Article 32 of the same Convention provides:

Supplementary means of interpretation

Recourse may be had to supplementary means of interpretation, including the preparatory work of the treaty and the circumstances of its conclusion, in order to confirm the meaning resulting from the application of article 31, or to determine the meaning when the interpretation according to article 31:

(a) leaves the meaning ambiguous or obscure; or
(b) leads to a result which is manifestly absurd or unreasonable.

[19] Now, in order to be able to interpret the aforementioned Article 4(1), it seems necessary to refer to the basic issues that are raised by this case, this is: the rights holder, the protection of this right, and the arbitrary deprivation of it.

1. Holder of this right

[20] After considering Article 31(1) of the Vienna Convention, it is evident that the aforementioned Article 4(1) enshrines a right consisting in that the holder's "life [is] respected." That is the "object and purpose" of the said provision, the actual purpose for its establishment, not to be voided of meaning.

[21] Accordingly, this provision presupposes that the holder of this right—whose life must be respected—exists.

[22] In addition, this provision is clear when stating that the rights holder is "every person," which means that this article makes no distinction whatsoever among the holders of said right. In fact, this is in full accord with the Convention's previous assertion that States undertake to respect and ensure rights

to all persons subject to their jurisdiction ... without any discrimination ...[16]

[23] And, by virtue of the "special meaning" rule of treaty interpretation, established in Article 31(4) of the Vienna Convention, the interpreter must follow what is provided in Article 1(2) of the Convention when interpreting the word "person." The latter article provides:

For the purposes of this Convention, "person" means every human being.

[24] As a conclusion, even though it may seem to be a truism, it can be asserted that Article 4(1) of the Convention recognizes or enshrines the right of "every person" or "human being," without any discrimination, to the respect of "his"—already existing—life. This means that the previously quoted provision, every sentence of it—as also all of the Convention—, refers exclusively to the "person" or "human being." They refer to his or her rights, not to other interests or to other beings.

2. Legal protection of the right

[25] Article 4(1) provides in its second sentence and following a period, that "this right [that is, that of "every person ... to have his life respected"] shall be protected by law and, in general, from the moment of conception." This sentence demands the interpretation of three expressions: first, what is understood as "law"; secondly, the meaning of "and, in general"; and thirdly, the term "conception."

a. "Law"

[26] When prescribing that the aforementioned right "shall be protected by law," the Convention imposed on the State the obligation to enact juridical norms to that effect. This obligation is also established, in more general and broad terms, in the previously quoted Article 2 of the Convention.[17]

[27] It must be understood that the Convention uses the word "law" in its broad sense. That is, as a juridical norm, be it constitutional, legal or regulatory, enacted by the competent State body for

---

[16] Art. 1(1) of the Convention: "The States Parties to this Convention undertake to respect the rights and freedoms recognized herein and to ensure to all persons subject to their jurisdiction the free and full exercise of those rights and freedoms, without any discrimination for reasons of race, color, sex, language, religion, political or other opinion, national or social origin, economic status, birth, or any other social condition."

[17] Art. 2 of the Convention: "Where the exercise of any of the rights or freedoms referred to in Article 1 is not already ensured by legislative or other provisions, the States Parties undertake to adopt, in accordance with their constitutional processes and the provisions of this Convention, such legislative or other measures as may be necessary to give effect to those rights or freedoms."

regulating, in a general and mandatory fashion, the conduct or activity of all of a country's population.[18]

[28] It must be also borne in mind that Article 4(1)'s stipulation that the right of "every person ... to have his life respected" must be "protected by law" does not mean that the Court cannot assess this law's compliance with international law, whether this law is internationally licit, especially in light of the Convention.

[29] As a commentary related solely to the case at hand, it must be highlighted that Article 21 of the 1949 Political Constitution of the State already provided that "human life is inviolable." It must also be considered that the Decision that gave rise to this case concluded explicitly that "the contested regulation (Executive Decree No 24029-S of February 3, 1995, issued by the Health Ministry) is unconstitutional due to its violation of Article 21 of the Political Constitution and of Article 4 of the Inter-American Convention on Human Rights".[19] Hence, it could be understood that, by doing this, the State was fulfilling Article 4(1)'s instruction of protecting by law the right of "every person ... to have his life respected."

b. "And, in general"

[30] As to the meaning and scope of Article 4(1)'s expression "and, in general," it should be borne in mind that the Convention gives no "special meaning" to these terms, so they must be interpreted according to their "ordinary meaning."[20]

[31] Among the definitions of the ordinary meaning of the term "general"—which are the same as those existing when agreeing on the Convention—are: "common, frequent, usual" and "common to all the individuals that constitute a whole, or to many objects, even if they are of a different nature." Among the meanings of the expression "in general" are those of "commonly, generally," and "without specifying or identifying anything in particular."

[32] In order to better understand these terms, it may be useful to consider their antonyms in the way they were understood by the time of the Convention[21]—which is the same as their current understanding. These antonyms are the terms "particular," which means "belonging exclusively to something, or belonging to it especially,"

---

[18] *The Word "Laws" in Article 30 of the American Convention on Human Rights.* Advisory Opinion OC-6/86, May 9, 1986. Series A No 6.
[19] Para. 76.
[20] Art. 31(1) of the Vienna Convention.
[21] *Ibid.*

"special, extraordinary, or rarely seen," "singular or individual, as opposed to universal or general"; "singular," whose definitions are "sole (unique in its kind)," "extraordinary, rare or excellent"; and "unusual," meaning "not usual, infrequent."

[33] The rule regarding the "context" of the terms[22] must be also taken into account. Hence, it should be added that when the article links the expressions "and, in general" with the obligation to "pro[tect] by law" the right of "every person ... to have his life respected," this provision is stating that this protection must be provided "from the moment of conception" of the relevant "person."

[34] In turn, the rule of the "object and purpose" of a treaty must be used for interpreting the expression "and, in general." The object and purpose of the Convention is to require States to respect human rights and to ensure their free and full exercise.[23] In turn, the object and purpose of Article 4(1) is the respect of life. Hence, the expression "and, in general" must have an *effet utile* to this end, so that it contributes effectively to this object and purpose, not providing an exception to it or, *a fortiori*, a negation of the right to life.

[35] In this regard, it must be noted that three countries proposed at the Specialized Inter-American Conference on Human Rights—where the Convention was approved—the elimination of the sentence "and, in general, from the moment of conception," so that abortion would not be forbidden. However, the majority of States participating in said Conference rejected this proposal, incorporating the aforementioned sentence in the Convention.[24] In other words, there was an evident intention of leaving no doubt as to the broad protection that the law must give to the right of every person to have his or her life respected, a protection that must be provided even when the person has been conceived or has not yet been born.

[36] Consequently, the aforementioned sentence was established in order to allow States to grant the unborn the legal protection that must be given to the right of "every person ... to have his life respected" "from the moment of conception." In other words, such protection must be "common" to those who are born and to the unborn. Consequently, no distinction can be made in this respect among them, "even if they are of a different nature," because they "constitute a whole." There is human life in both the born and the unborn. Both are a human being, a person.

---

[22] Art. 32(1) of the Vienna Convention.
[23] Art. 1(1) of the Convention, previously quoted.
[24] Paras. 203 to 205.

[37] The legally protected good in Article 4(1) is, then and ultimately, the right to life of "every person." This is why the Convention decided to leave no doubt as to the fact that Article 4(1) protects life, irrespective of its stage of development.

[38] In this regard, the expression "in general" constitutes a reference to the way the law may protect the unborn. Needless to say, this protection could be different to that which is granted to the person who is already born.

[39] Consequently, the expression "and, in general" makes no reference to an exception, to an exclusion. Quite the opposite, this expression is inclusive. It makes applicable the obligation, to protect the right to life of every person by law, from the moment of conception.

c. "Conception"

[40] Because of the aforementioned, in order to understand the relevant provision of Article 4(1), it is essential to elucidate the sense and scope of the term "conception," included in this article. It is from that moment that the State must protect by law the right "to have ... life respected." In other words, the sense of this provision is clear, it states that this right exists "from the moment of conception."

[41] The file and other background material show that, when signing the Convention, there was no determination as to what should be understood by "conception." This has not been specified afterwards either. On the other hand, the Convention gave no "special meaning" to this term.[25] It neither made a reference to the understanding of this concept according to medical science. Hence, the applicable rule in this case is, without any doubt, that of the "ordinary meaning" of the term.[26] In particular, the meaning must be the one existing by the time of adopting the Convention in 1969.

[42] According to the 1956 version of the Spanish Dictionary of the *Real Academia Española*[27]—applicable back then—, the term "conception" was understood as the "action and effect of conceiving"; "to conceive" was read as "for the female to become pregnant"; that of "pregnant" meant "the woman or the female of any species that has conceived, and has the fetus or creature in its womb"; that of "to make pregnant" as "to impregnate"; that of "impregnate" as "to make the female conceive"; and that of "fertilization" as "the union of the masculine and feminine reproductive elements, originating a new being."

---

[25] Art. 31(4) of the Vienna Convention.
[26] *Ibid.*
[27] 18th edition.

[43] And almost at the same time of adopting the Convention, that is, in the 1970 version of the aforementioned dictionary,[28] the term "to make pregnant" was understood as "to impregnate, to fertilize, to make a woman conceive." The current dictionary also gives this definition.[29]

[44] The foregoing means that it was understood—and it still is—that the being, in this case the human, originates with "the union of the masculine and feminine reproductive elements." When this happens, it is recognized that this "creature" is inside the woman's "womb." Hence, it was understood that the terms *fertilization* and *to make the woman conceive* were synonyms.

[45] Therefore, the term "conception," used by Article 4(1) of the Convention, should be legally understood—notwithstanding any other consideration—as the fertilization of the egg by the spermatozoid. This, nothing else, was agreed when adopting the Convention in 1969. This is still the legal understanding of this term. Furthermore, an important part of medical science—if not the majority—[30] shares this understanding.[31] This does not mean that medical science must be disregarded, but that its teachings must be considered only insofar as they are incorporated in the law.

[46] In this regard, due attention must be paid also to the fact that, according to the rules of treaty interpretation, there are no other agreements or treaties among the States parties to the Convention enshrining a different concept.[32] Member States have neither made subsequent agreements nor adopted practices in the application of the Convention that may indicate an alteration of this concept.[33] On the other hand, there is no applicable customary rule that may go against the aforementioned interpretation. Finally, it cannot be asserted that domestic legislations of these States have created a general principle of law enshrining a meaning diverse to the aforementioned.[34]

[47] Furthermore, it is evident and clear that Article 4(1) refers to the "conception" of "every person" whose right to life must be protected by law. This is in perfect agreement with the *context of terms*,[35] because this article, as the Convention,[36] refers only to the object "every person." It does not refer to a different entity, object or reality.

---

[28] 19th edition.
[29] 22nd edition.
[30] Notes 266 to 284 of the Judgment.
[31] Paras. 79 ff.
[32] Art. 31(2) of the Convention.
[33] Art. 31(3)(a) and (b) of the Vienna Convention.
[34] Art. 31(3)(c) of the Vienna Convention.
[35] Art. 31(3) of the Vienna Convention.
[36] Art. 1(1) of the Convention, previously quoted.

[48] Hence, if the aforementioned provision would have sought to grant or extend this protection—that must be given by law to the right of every person to have his or her life respected—to an entity, object or reality other than the person, it would have stated it clearly. It could have utilized a sentence or paragraph in the aforementioned Article 4(1), or it could have enshrined a different article. It could have even stated it in a different treaty. However, none of this happened. Thus, the relevant article and the Convention refer solely and exclusively to the "person," to the "human being."

[49] To sum up, the Convention considers that there is life in a person from the moment when he or she is conceived; in other words, that someone is a "person" or a "human being" from the "moment of conception," which happens when the egg is fertilized by the spermatozoid. The Convention provides that from this moment there is a "right to have ['every person's'] life respected". As a result, there is an obligation to protect this right.

[50] A different interpretation of Article 4(1) would deprive the phrase "from the moment of conception" of its ordinary and obvious meaning. A different interpretation would end up assigning no object to this phrase, even though it is strikingly clear that it refers to the "conception" of "every person."

d. Arbitrary deprivation of this right

[51] Finally, when the previously referred provision establishes that no one shall be arbitrarily deprived of his or her life, it is implicitly stating that the right of "every person ... to have his life respected" is not absolute, that it allows a restriction, as long as it is not arbitrary. This means that, according to what was understood as arbitrariness when the Convention was drafted—and what is still understood as such—, the restriction cannot be an "act or behavior against justice, reason or the law; based solely on the will or the whim."[37]

[52] The file of this case shows that this element has not been discussed during these proceedings.

C. *The Court's case law*

[53] The Court's case law has, in a steady and consistent fashion, made a precise description of the nature of the right of "every

---

[37] 18th and 22nd editions.

person ... to have his life respected." The Court has done so in the following terms:

The right to life is a fundamental human right, and the exercise of this right is essential for the exercise of all other human rights. If it is not respected, all rights lack meaning. Owing to the fundamental nature of the right to life, restrictive approaches to it are inadmissible,[38]

and that

States have the obligation to guarantee the creation of the necessary conditions to ensure that violations of this inalienable right do not occur.[39]

This has been the steady and consistent case law of the Court in this particular matter. It has been asserted in more than twelve cases.[40] It has even been reaffirmed twice this year.[41]

[54] Now, as a consequence of the paramount importance that the Court's case law attaches to the right to life regulated in Article 4(1) of the Convention, two principles must be applied to this right with a stronger emphasis: on the one hand, the guiding principle of the Law of Treaties, the principle of "good faith,"[42] which implies the understanding that agreements are made for their actual application; on the other hand, the principle *pro homine* or *pro persona*, enshrined in the Convention,[43] according to which the rules of human rights must be interpreted in the most favorable terms for the rights holders.

---

[38] *Case of the "Street Children" (Villagrán-Morales et al.* v. *Guatemala)*, Judgment of November 19, 1999. Series C No 63, para. 144.

[39] *Case of the Barrios Family* v. *Venezuela, Merits, Reparations and Costs*, Judgment of November 24, 2011. Series C No 237, para. 48.

[40] *Case of Myrna Mack-Chang* v. *Guatemala*, Judgment of November 25, 2003, Series C No 101, para. 152; *Case of Juan Humberto-Sánchez*, Judgment of June 7, 2003, Series C No 99, para. 110; *Case of 19 Tradesmen*, Judgment of July 5, 2004, Series C No 109, paras. 152 and 153; *Case of the Pueblo Bello Massacre*, Judgment of January 31, 2006, Series C No 140; *Case of Sawhoyamaxa Indigenous Community*, Judgment of March 29, 2006, Series C No 146, para. 150; *Case of Baldeón-García*, Judgment of April 6, 2006, Series C No 147, para. 82; *Case of the Massacres of Ituango*, Judgment of July 1, 2006, Series C No 148, para. 128; *Case of Ximenes-Lopes*, Judgment of July 4, 2006, Series C No 149, para. 124; *Case of Montero-Aranguren et al.* (Detention Center of Catia), Judgment of July 5, 2006, Series C No 150, para. 63; and *Case of Albán-Cornejo et al.*, Judgment of November 22, 2007, Series C No 171, para. 117.

[41] *Cases of Castillo-González et al.* v. *Venezuela* and *Massacres of El Mozote and Neighboring Locations* v. *El Salvador*, both judgments were issued in October, 2012.

[42] Art. 31(1) of the Vienna Convention.

[43] Art. 29 of the Convention: "*Restrictions Regarding Interpretation*. No provision of this Convention shall be interpreted as: a. permitting any State Party, group, or person to suppress the enjoyment or exercise of the rights and freedoms recognized in this Convention or to restrict them to a greater extent than is provided for herein; b. restricting the enjoyment or exercise of any right or

[55] In addition, the case law of the Court has used the expressions "children"[44] and "baby"[45] for referring to the unborn.

[56] In this regard, and as a comment related specifically to the case at hand, it is noteworthy that the year before the State's Decision of March 15, 2000, this is, in 1999, the important judgment of the "Street Children" was issued—giving rise to the aforementioned case law.[46] Hence, when the State's Decision was rendered, basing itself explicitly on Article 4(1) of the Convention,[47] it must be understood that it was taking into account the interpretation made in "Street Children." In other words, it should be presumed that the Decision complied with what is now called "conventionality control,"[48] and applied it.

II. Shift in the Court's case law

[57] This Judgment brings up an important change, breaking away from the recent case law in three different ways. First, by limiting the scope of what had already been defined by the Court's case law; secondly, regarding the application of Article 4(1) to this case; and third, in as much as it leaves many questions unanswered.

A. Limiting the scope of the Court's case law

[58] This judgment seems to restrict the Court's—up to now—consistent and uniform case law on the matter. This time around, the Court omits the phrase "[o]wing (to the) fundamental nature (of the right to life), restrictive approaches to it are inadmissible."

[59] Although this has happened in previous decisions, the Judgment's omission of this phrase becomes particularly relevant, because two preliminary annotations precede the reiteration of all other ideas

---

freedom recognized by virtue of the laws of any State Party or by virtue of another convention to which one of the said states is a party; c. precluding other rights or guarantees that are inherent in the human personality or derived from representative democracy as a form of government; or d. excluding or limiting the effect that the American Declaration of the Rights and Duties of Man and other international acts of the same nature may have."

[44] *Case of the Miguel Castro Castro Prison* v. *Peru, Merits, Reparations and Costs*, Judgment of November 25, 2006, para. 292.

[45] *Case of the Gómez-Paquiyauri Brothers* v. *Peru, Merits, Reparations and Costs*, Judgment of July 8, 2004, para. 67(x).

[46] *Case of the "Street Children" (Villagrán-Morales et al.* v. *Guatemala)*, Judgment of November 19, 1999, Series C No 63, para. 144.

[47] Para. 76.

[48] *Case of Cabrera-García and Montiel-Flores* v. *Mexico, Preliminary Objections, Merits, Reparations and Costs.* Judgment of November 26, 2010. Series C No 220, para. 225.

regarding the right to life. The first annotation points out that "[t]o date, the Court's case law has not ruled on the disputes that have arisen in this case," and the second asserts that, "[i]n cases of extrajudicial executions, enforced disappearances and deaths that can be attributed to the failure of the States to adopt measures, the Court has indicated that the right to life is a fundamental human right, the full enjoyment of which is a prerequisite for the enjoyment of all other human rights."[49]

[60] With these two annotations the Judgment would suggest that the Court's case law in reference to the right to life is only applicable to "extrajudicial executions, enforced disappearances and deaths that can be attributed to the failure of the States to adopt measures." Therefore, the right to life would not be applicable to the case under review because it applies to a different set of facts. Hence, the Judgment would be severely limiting the scope of what has already been set by the Court's case law on this matter.

B. *Inapplicability of Article 4(1) to the case under study*

[61] The Judgment's aforementioned statements are the basis for its following assertions:

"that 'conception' in the sense of Article 4(1) occurs at the moment when the embryo becomes implanted in the uterus, which explains why, before this event, Article 4 of the Convention would not be applicable";[50]
"it is not admissible to grant the status of person to the embryo";[51] and
"the embryo cannot be understood to be a person for the purposes of Article 4(1) of the American Convention."[52]

It is evident that the Judgment represents a very significant shift in the Court's case law.

[62] In order to find a basis for this change, the Judgment resorts to the interpretation of the terms "conception" and "in general." This, because the Court considers that "for the purposes of the interpretation of Article 4(1), the definition of person stems from the mentions made in the treaty with regard to 'conception' and to 'human being'."[53]

---

[49] Para. 172.
[50] Para. 264.
[51] Para. 223.
[52] Art. 264.
[53] Para. 176.

When doing so, the Court resorts to Articles 31 and 32 of the Vienna Convention, which provide for the interpretation according to the ordinary meaning of terms, the systematic and historical interpretation, and the evolutive interpretation.

1. Method in accordance with the ordinary meaning of terms

[63] This is one of the issues where this vote differs from the Judgment, because the majority uses as a starting point that the "scope" of the Convention terms "conception" and "human being," "should be assessed based on the scientific literature."[54]

[64] The Convention gave these terms no "special meaning" whereby the "intention of the parties" to the Convention is expressed.[55] Neither did it submit itself to the definition of medical science. The Judgment fails to note that because of this, the interpreter must abide by the "ordinary meaning" attributed to the aforementioned terms. The most natural and obvious meaning of them is that of the dictionary, which, as pointed out, understands conception as the union of the egg and the spermatozoid.

[65] It is not appropriate, then, to have recourse to medical science for valuing or understanding the meaning and scope of the terms in reference. It is not what medical science understands for "conception" that matters, but what the Parties to the Convention intended by the term, which is the ordinary meaning of the term "conception" (found in the dictionary). Besides, a significant part —if not the majority—[56] of the medical science[57] agrees with the ordinary meaning of the term "conception." The scientific definition of a term is relevant in as much as it has been integrated into law, or when the law submits itself to science, neither of which occur in the case at hand.

[66] In this regard, it is imperative to underline that the Judgment states that "some opinions [that] view a fertilized egg as a complete human life," "may be associated with concepts that confer certain metaphysical attributes on embryos. Such concepts cannot justify preference being given to a certain type of scientific literature when interpreting the scope of the right to life established in the American Convention, because this would imply imposing specific types of beliefs on others who do not share them."[58]

---

[54] Ibid.
[55] Art. 31(4) of the Vienna Convention.
[56] Notes 265 to 284 of the Judgment.
[57] Paras. 182 to 184.
[58] Para. 185.

[67] The latter assertion is correct, but the position adopted by the Judgment on this matter is not in agreement with it. The Judgment reproaches that the State's Decision opted for "one of the scientific positions on this issue to define as of when it was considered that life began" and that "understood that conception would be the moment when the egg is fertilized and assumed that, as of that moment, a person existed who held the right to life."[59] However, while asserting this, the Judgment adopts the opposite view, that which makes a difference between "two complementary and essential moments of embryonic development: fertilization and implantation," and holds that "only after completion of the second moment that the cycle is concluded, and that conception can be understood to have occurred."[60]

[68] In order to reach this conclusion the Judgment resorts to two reasons. One is of a scientific nature, "an embryo has no chance of survival if implantation does not occur."[61] The other is that "when Article 4 of the American Convention was drafted the dictionary of the *Real Academia* differentiated between the moment of fertilization and the moment of conception, understanding conception as implantation," and, thus, "[w]hen drafting the relevant provisions in the American Convention, the moment of fertilization was not mentioned."[62]

[69] As to the first argument, the Judgment acknowledges that there are several scientific positions on the matter of "when life begins"[63] and of the understanding of "conception."[64] In spite of this, the Judgment sides with only one of them: that conception is produced at the moment of the embryo's implantation in the woman's uterus. The Judgment does not analyze the other positions, particularly the one that considers that "human life begins with the fusion of spermatozoid and egg, an observable 'moment of conception'."[65] This Judgment simply dismisses this position.

[70] The Judgment's position seems to reveal some inconsistencies with other of its assertions. On the one hand, with the statement that "[t]he first birth of a baby resulting from *in vitro* fertilization occurred in England in 1978," and that "[i]n Latin America, the first baby born through *in vitro* fertilization and embryo transfer was reported in

---

[59] Para. 177.
[60] Para. 186.
[61] Para. 187.
[62] Para. 187.
[63] Para. 177.
[64] Paras. 180 to 185.
[65] Para. 182.

Argentina in 1984."⁶⁶ On the other hand, with the statement that "the definition of 'conception' accepted by the authors of the American Convention has changed" because "[p]rior to IVF, the possibility of fertilization occurring outside a woman's body was not contemplated scientifically."

[71] Indeed, these statements show that, when the Convention was signed—in 1969—, it was not possible to know that "conception" and "fertilization" were two absolutely differentiated and distinct phenomena. Hence, it is impossible to share the understanding that "the definition of 'conception' accepted by the authors of the American Convention has changed." It may well be the case that some medical scientists have changed their views, but the definition of the term enshrined by the Convention framers remains unchanged.

[72] Now, it is appropriate to refer to the second argument in which the Judgment bases its position, this is, that the Dictionary of the time, 1969, "differentiated between the moment of fertilization and the moment of conception, understanding conception as implantation." This dissenting opinion has already pointed out (*supra*) that this assertion is not, strictly speaking, accurate. It is not apparent that the 1959 Dictionary considered the terms "to conceive" and "to fertilize" as antagonistic or different. Furthermore, the 1970 edition of the Dictionary, issued a year after the subscription of this Convention, defines "to conceive" as "for the female to become pregnant," and the term "to make pregnant" as "to impregnate, to fertilize, to make a woman conceive." These definitions remain in the present edition of the Dictionary.

[73] Finally, and still in relation to the interpretation method of the ordinary meaning of terms, the Judgment asserts that "The literal interpretation indicates that the expression [in general] relates to anticipating possible exceptions to a particular rule."⁶⁷ It then concludes that "the term 'in general' infers exceptions to a rule."⁶⁸

[74] However, this dissenting vote has pointed out (*supra*) that the Dictionary's understanding of the expression "in general" has nothing to do with the establishment of exceptions. If the Convention [had] wanted to establish an exception, instead of providing "in general, from the moment of conception," it would have stated, for instance: "and, exceptionally, from the moment of conception." The Convention did

---

⁶⁶ Para. 66.
⁶⁷ Para. 188.
⁶⁸ Para. 189.

not do this, precisely, for providing that the law's protection of the right of "every person [to have] his life respected" *will be* granted always and in every case or circumstance—although perhaps in a somewhat different fashion—from the moment of conception.

2. *Systematic and historical interpretation*

[75] The Judgment also refers to the historical and systematic methods of interpretation. When doing so, it mentions Article 31 of the Vienna Convention, particularly its third paragraph. It does so in order to "'take into account not only the agreements and instruments formally related to it (Article 31(2) of the Vienna Convention), but also its context (Article 31(3))'; in other words, international human rights law."[69] Likewise, and under the same heading, the Judgment states that it will utilize the supplementary means of interpretation of Article 32 of the Vienna Convention [and,] "for determining the interpretation of Article 4(1) of the American Convention," it is relevant to consider "Article 31(4) of the Vienna Convention, which provides that a special meaning shall be given to a term if it is established that the parties so intended."[70]

a. Rule of the special meaning given to terms

[76] From a methodological standpoint, it is impossible to agree on the foregoing, because the reference to Article 31(4) of the Vienna Convention is out of context. This norm is the final or last among the rules that constitute what is known as the *general rule of interpretation*. Within them, Article 31(4) is the rule of the *special meaning of terms*, which is an exception to the norm of the *ordinary meaning of terms*. Hence, this rule is not part of the norms that constitute the *supplementary means of interpretation*, provided for in Article 32, the subsequent article of the Vienna Convention.

[77] In other words, according to Article 31(4), the "special meaning [of a term] that the parties so intended" must be stated in one of the following ways: either in the agreements, instruments and practices referred to in Article 31, paragraphs 2 and 3 (which are distinguishable because they are intimately connected with the relevant treaty or because they refer to an agreement about its interpretation); or in a rule of international law that is applicable to the relations between the Member States.

[69] Para. 191.
[70] Para. 193.

b. Rule of the context and of the progressive or evolutive development

[78] Now, following the State's allegations, the Judgment refers to the Universal Declaration of Human Rights,[71] the International Covenant on Civil and Political Rights,[72] the Convention on the Elimination of All Forms of Discrimination against Women,[73] and the Convention on the Rights of the Child.[74] It also refers to the provisions of the Universal,[75] European[76] and African human rights systems,[77] and also to the case law of the European Court of Human Rights[78] and of seven domestic constitutional courts.[79] The Judgment refers to all of them within the framework of the systematic and historical interpretation, even though it should have done so, in some cases, in application of the *rule of the context* (established in Article 31(2) of the Vienna Convention), and in other cases, in application of the rule of *progressive development of law* (provided for in Article 31(3) of the same convention).

[79] These agreements and instruments, however, lack the relevant features for being considered as instruments or agreements made as a consequence of or in connection with the Convention. Hence, they cannot be used as a means for interpreting the Convention. They neither refer, strictly speaking, to subsequent practice, to the way [in which] States parties to the Convention apply this treaty, [t]hereby showing their agreement regarding the Convention's interpretation. As to the rules of international law applicable in the relations between the State parties, it is evident that they do not fulfill Article 31(4) of the Vienna Convention's requirement of being "relevant" to the case.

[80] Even more so, the provisions of the previously referred treaties, the statements of the aforementioned judgments of international and European courts, and the provisions of domestic law of Member States to the Convention—all of which were quoted for interpreting the latter—can be neither considered a kind of customary law nor a general principle of law. They are not international custom because they are not precedents, that is, acts that are repeated constantly and uniformly with the understanding of being required by law. They are not general

---

[71] Para. 224.
[72] Para. 225.
[73] Paras. 227 and 228.
[74] Paras. 229 to 233.
[75] Para. 226.
[76] Para. 234.
[77] Para. 243.
[78] Paras. 236 to 242.
[79] Paras. 252, 261 and 262.

principles of law, either because they cannot be inferred or deduced logically from the international legal structure, or because they are not enough as for being considered common to the great majority of the States parties to the Convention.

[81] Nevertheless, what is even more important is that these agreements or instruments are not applicable to this case, not only because some of them do not bind the Member States to the Convention, but also because they clearly do not consider the situation of the unborn or the conceived, so as to allow or not to prohibit abortion.[80]

c. Rule regarding the prevalence of specialized law over general law

[82] It is due to this reality that none of these instruments contain a provision like Article 4(1) of the Convention, a particularity of the Inter-American system on human rights. The Judgment does not take this into account when interpreting this article. It, hence, omits a rule of general legal interpretation, found in international law and in the Law of Treaties, which provides that "specialized law prevails over general law."

[83] Article 4(1) is part of the body of international laws which—although it cannot be qualified as Latin American, regional or particular international law—are particular to the Member States to the Convention. Hence, this provision cannot be interpreted through the use of other general norms of international law or other human rights systems that do not include this provision. This would make the latter prevail over the American Convention, eventually modifying it in practice.

d. Incapacity

[84] Taking the above into account, this opinion does not share the Judgment's conclusion when making a systematic interpretation of the Convention and the American Declaration of the Rights and Duties of Man, when it indicates that "it is not feasible to maintain that an embryo is the holder of and exercises the rights established in each" of the articles of these texts. This is so, because the Judgment leaves out any consideration of the existing concepts of absolute and relative legal incapacity of persons. These concepts exist in different jurisdictions, and they may limit or preempt the exercise of these people's rights, without taking away their legal recognition as persons.

---

[80] Paras. 226, 227, 235, 236, 237 and 249.

[85] Even greater dissent needs to be expressed in the Judgment's statement that:

taking into account, as indicated previously, that conception can only take place within a woman's body (*supra* ...), it can be concluded with regard to Article 4(1) of the Convention, that the direct subject of protection is fundamentally the pregnant woman, because the protection of the unborn child is implemented essentially through the protection of the woman.[81]

[86] And this vote cannot agree with the affirmation in this paragraph because of its understanding of conception as a phenomenon that "can only take place within a woman's body," which is correct, but is based on a statement in another paragraph that "conception or gestation is an event of the woman, not of the embryo." This would lead to the conclusion that conception is an issue affecting the pregnant woman only.

[87] Second, this statement cannot be agreed with because, if the intent had been to protect the unborn's "right to have his life respected" through protection of the pregnant woman, the Convention would have specifically stated so, which was not the case.

[88] Third, this opinion dissents [from] the Judgment's assertion, given that Article 4(1) as written is sufficient to protect the pregnant woman and, consequently, the unborn. This protection is also found in Article 4(5) of the Convention, which prohibits the application of the death penalty on a pregnant woman. Reference to this protection can also be found in the San Salvador Protocol and the American Declaration of the Rights and Duties of Man, cited by the Judgment.[82] In all these instruments the pregnant woman is seen as subject of human rights rather than an object or instrument thereof.

[89] Finally, the author of this dissenting opinion disagrees with the findings of the cited paragraph because it leads to the conclusion that not only the embryos before implantation, but also unborn or conceived children, have no inherent "right to have [their] life respected." Their right would be dependent, not only on the respect for the pregnant woman's life, but also on her will to respect the rights of her child. Such an approach is contradictory to the letter and spirit of Article 4(1) of the Convention, which evidently relate to matters such as the juridical regime of abortion.

---

[81] Para. 222.
[82] *Ibid.*

3. Method of evolutive interpretation

[90] When interpreting Article 4(1) of the Convention, the Judgment also resorts to the method of evolutive interpretation of treaties. It states that "treaties are living instruments, whose interpretation must keep abreast of the passage of time and current living conditions," and that this interpretation "is consistent with the general rules of interpretation established in Article 29 of the American Convention, as well as in the Vienna Convention on the Law of Treaties."[83]

[91] And, effectively, it is so. Article 29 of the Convention[84] states that no provision of this Convention shall be interpreted as suppressing, excluding or limiting (the latter beyond the boundaries of the Convention), either the enjoyment of rights established in it or in laws of the Member States, or that are inherent to the human being or which derive from the democratic representative system of government, or the effects of the American Declaration of the Rights and Duties of Man, and other international instruments of this nature. In addition, Article 31(3) of the Vienna Convention provides for evolutive interpretation of treaties, basing it on any agreement or subsequent practice between Member States regarding the interpretation of a treaty, or where there is a clear agreement of States in this particular regard, and on any relevant rules of international law applicable in the relations between the parties.

[92] Nevertheless, the background material provided by the Judgment does not fulfill the requirements established in Article 29 of the Convention. In essence, they only seek to limit what is prescribed in Article 4(1) of the Convention to such an extent that it becomes inapplicable to this case and is stripped of its content and *effet utile* as to the phrase "in general, from the moment of conception."

[93] Regarding Article 31(3), some of the background material[s] referred to in order to determine the status of the embryo are judgments of other judicial bodies, and consequently are unrelated to agreements and practices of States parties to the Convention and to rules of international [law that are] applicable. Other background material referring to the laws of States parties to the Convention is insufficient, as it shall be illustrated below. It only demonstrates that assisted reproduction (of which *in vitro* fertilization is only one among several techniques) is used in eleven out of twenty-four Member States. It also shows that, among these countries, three prohibit this technique "for purposes other than human procreation"; one of them "prohibits

---

[83] Para. 245.
[84] Previously quoted.

the freezing of embryos for deferred transfer"; another "prohibits the use of procedures 'aimed at embryonic reduction'"; that the same State establishes that "the ideal number of eggs and pre-embryos to be transferred may be no more than four, to avoid increasing the risk of multiple births"; and where "the commercialization of biological material is a crime"; and that the said State and another allow "the cryopreservation of embryos, spermatozoids and eggs."[85]

[94] Therefore, the Judgment's conclusion that "[t]his means that, in the context of the practice of most States Parties to the Convention, it has been interpreted that the Convention allows IVF to be performed"[86] is inconsistent. This is so, not only because there is no such majority, but also because no evidence has been presented that demonstrates that the eleven States that allow assisted reproduction have done so based on their application or consideration of Article 4(1) of the Convention.

4. *The principle of the most favorable interpretation and the object and purpose of the treaty*

[95] The Judgment resorts to the *rule of the object and purpose of the treaty* for proving that the right to life from conception is not absolute. In this regard, it asserts that "the object and purpose of Article 4(1) of the Convention is that the right to life should not be understood as an absolute right, the alleged protection of which can justify the total negation of other rights."[87]

[96] It is impossible to be more in disagreement with this assertion. Interpreted in good faith and in accordance with the terms of the treaty in their context, the object and purpose of Article 4(1) cannot be other than to effectively protect by law the right of "every person . . . to have his life respected . . . and, in general, from the moment of conception." This means, to effectively protect the right of every person, including the conceived or the unborn.

[97] In addition, the Judgment further contradicts itself in this regard. While the Judgment first stated that Article 4(1) of the Convention was not applicable to this particular case, it now refers to it in order to assert that there must be an "adequate balance" between the clashing rights and interests.[88] It is puzzling how this balance could be reached if the Judgment has previously stated that "the embryo cannot

---

[85] Para. 255.
[86] Para. 256.
[87] Para. 258.
[88] Para. 260.

be understood to be a person for the purposes of Article 4(1) of the American Convention."[89] This means that it would have no right to "have his life protected," which is why there would be no rights to balance, harmonize or to make compatible.

[98] Finally, in order to justify its assertions, the Judgment resorts again to decisions, either absolutely foreign to the Convention Member States, or pertaining to only three of them. These grounds are not enough for reaching the attained conclusion.

C. Unanswered questions

[99] The Judgment states that, due to the fact that an "'absolute right to life of the embryo' as grounds for the restriction of [other] rights ... is not supported by the American Convention," "it is not necessary to make a detailed analysis of each of these requirements" required for restricting a right, this means, that "interferences are not abusive or arbitrary," which are "substantively and formally established by law," that pursue "a legitimate aim" and that meet "requirements of suitability, necessity and proportionality."[90]

[100] In spite of this, the Judgment keeps on with this analysis in order "to indicate the way in which the sacrifice of the rights involved in this case was excessive in comparison to the benefits referred to with the protection of the embryo."[91] By doing this, the Judgment contradicts itself, because it does not confront this sacrifice with a right (which, according to the Judgment, does not apply to this case), but with the prohibition of the technique of *in vitro* fertilization. If the Judgment would have confronted this sacrifice with a right, it would have harmonized the rights at stake.

[101] Obviously, the result of the confrontation made by the Judgment cannot be different than the one that was reached.[92] This is so because— we repeat—there was no confrontation between rights, but between some rights and a technique.

[102] However, even in this case, the background material can only be used for reaching very partial conclusions regarding the technique of *in vitro* fertilization. As it has been said, assisted reproduction—of which *in vitro* fertilization is only one method—is not practiced in the majority of Member States to the Convention. It is practiced only

---

[89] Art. 264.
[90] Para. 273.
[91] Para. 273.
[92] Paras. 277 ff.

in eleven of the twenty-four Member States, many of which forbid some proceedings related to this technique.

[103] The natural conclusion to these facts is not that "the Convention allows IVF to be performed,"[93] but that the majority of Member States have abstained from referring to it, probably because they have understood that this technique is not, *per se*, regulated by international law. This, together with the fact that the Judgment makes Article 4(1) inapplicable to the embryo—at least until the moment of implantation in the woman's uterus—may make the majority of Member States understand that the regulation of this technique is within their internal, domestic or exclusive jurisdiction.[94]

[104] This is the only reasoning that can explain why other State Parties of the Convention have prohibited certain techniques of assisted fertilization which are very similar to those which the Constitutional Chamber of the Supreme Court of the State had in mind when issuing the Decision that originated this case. This is so, even though these prohibitions could, at some point, be perceived as infringing some of the rights that the Court considers were violated by the State.

[105] The ultimate reason why the aforementioned Chamber of the Supreme Court declared the Decree unconstitutional and contrary to Article 4(1) of the Convention is because the embryo "cannot be treated as an object for investigation purposes, be submitted to selection processes, kept frozen and, the most essential point for the Chamber, it is not constitutionally legitimate to expose it to a disproportionate risk of death."[95] These reasons were also suggested by three Member States when forbidding assisted fertilization "for purposes other than human procreation"; by one of them when establishing that "the commercialization of biological material is a crime"; and by another of them when prohibiting "the freezing of embryos for deferred transfer." Nevertheless, one of the previously referred States and another one allow "the cryopreservation of embryos, spermatozoids and eggs."[96]

[106] Finally, it must be pointed out that the Judgment makes no reference in its operative paragraphs to Article 4(1). This may happen because the Judgment dismisses the allegation regarding this article.

---

[93] Para. 256.
[94] This concept was developed by the Permanent Court of International Justice in its advisory opinion *Nationality Decrees Issued in Tunis and Morocco* (February 7, 1923). In this opinion the Permanent Court concluded that the term domestic jurisdiction referred to issues that are not, in principle, regulated by international law, that is, matters where the State can take sovereign decisions. This may be the case, even though they may be closely related to the interests of more than one State.
[95] Para. 76.
[96] Para. 255.

Nevertheless, the Court makes no reference—as it has previously done—to whether it is unnecessary to refer to this article, or to whether the State is responsible for the alleged violation or is, on the contrary, blameless.

Final considerations

[107] When this dissenting opinion stated the reason why it disagreed with the Judgment, it tried to underline the importance of this case, where what is at stake is nothing less than the understanding of the "right to life" and of when does life begin.

[108] Strictly speaking, when a juridical provision on this issue is drafted, many legitimate material sources of international law come into play; not only juridical notions, but also philosophical, moral, ethical, religious, ideological, scientific and others. Once the juridical provision is in force, however, it can only be interpreted in accordance with the formal sources of international law.

[109] The Court has limits when exercising its interpretive function. This cannot be denied. Other jurisdictional bodies have already highlighted the difficulty—and even the inappropriateness—of deciding an issue which is within the realm (although not exclusively) of medical science, an issue regarding which there is still no consensus, even in this particular field.[97]

[110] Nevertheless, in spite of these difficulties, the Court has had to fulfill its duty and decide the issue that was brought forth. This, however, does not exempt the States from fulfilling their own duty, which in this case is to exercise their normative function in the way they deem best. If they fail to do so, there is the risk that—as somewhat happens in this case—the Court may not only decide on these issues, which require a more political pronouncement, but may also be obliged to assume this normative function. This would distort the Court's jurisdictional function, affecting thus the performance of the whole Inter-American system of human rights.

[Report: Inter-Am. Ct HR (Series C) No 257(2012)]

---

[97] Para. 185 and note 283.

Relationship of international law and municipal law — Treaties — Application and interpretation — European Community–Israel Association Agreement — Protocol 4 to the EC–Israel Association Agreement — Territorial scope — Free movement of goods — Customs duties — Originating product — Exporting State best placed to verify place of origin — Certification of place of origin — Verification of place of origin — Whether importing States bound by exporting States' verification — Preferential treatment — Refusal of preferential treatment in absence of adequate verification — Customs Cooperation Committee — Whether importing States bound to refer disputes to Customs Cooperation Committee — Association Council — Israeli customs authorities' failure to certify products originating in occupied territories as having originated in Israel — Products originating in occupied territories not qualifying for preferential treatment under EC–Israel Association Agreement

Treaties — Application and interpretation — European Community–Palestine Liberation Organization Association Agreement — Territorial scope — West Bank and Gaza Strip — Originating product — Preferential treatment only applicable to products originating in the occupied territories under the EC–PLO Association Agreement and where certified by Palestinian customs authorities — Treaties not binding third parties without their consent — Vienna Convention on the Law of Treaties, 1969, Article 34

Territory — Occupied territory — Territorial scope of treaty — West Bank and Gaza Strip — EC–Israel Association Agreement — Preferential customs treatment for goods originating in Israel imported into the European Community — Whether applicable to goods originating in the occupied territories

War and armed conflict — Belligerent occupation — West Bank and Gaza Strip — Status — Whether Israeli territory — EC–Israel Association Agreement — Preferential customs treatment for goods originating in Israel imported into the European Community — Whether applicable to goods originating in the occupied territories

Relationship of international and municipal law — Treaties — European Community — Court of Justice of the European Communities — Referral of questions to the Court of Justice — Obligations of Member States of European Community under the

EC–Israel Association Agreement and EC–PLO Association Agreement — The law of the European Union

FIRMA BRITA GMBH v. HAUPTZOLLAMT HAMBURG-HAFEN[1]

(Case C-386/08)

Court of Justice of the European Union (Fourth Chamber)
25 February 2010

(Lenaerts, *President of the Third Chamber, acting for the President of the Fourth Chamber*; Silva de Lapuerta, Juhász, Malenovský (*Rapporteur*) and von Danwitz, *Judges*; Bot, *Advocate General*)

SUMMARY:[2] *The facts*:—Following the Euro-Mediterranean Ministerial Conference of November 1995, the European Community ("EC") and Member States entered into two Agreements with Israel and the Palestine Liberation Organization ("PLO") to strengthen economic links. The EC–PLO Association Agreement and EC–Israel Association Agreement entered into force in July 1997 and June 2000 respectively.

Article 7 of the EC–Israel Association Agreement provided that the Agreement applied to products "originating in" the Community and the State of Israel. Article 83 likewise confined the territorial scope of the Agreement to the State of Israel. Under Article 8, where the origin of a product was certified with a EUR.1 certificate (issued under Article 16 of Protocol 4 to the Agreement), customs duties were not to apply. In cases of doubt as to a product's origin, under Article 32 of Protocol 4, an importing State could seek verification from an exporting State; if no verification or no sufficient verification was provided within ten months, the importing State was to refuse preferential treatment to the relevant product. Article 33 of Protocol 4 provided that, where a product origin dispute could not be resolved, it "shall" be submitted to the Customs Cooperation Committee.

As relevant, the EC–PLO Association Agreement was materially equivalent to the EC–Israel Association Agreement. Article 6 of the EC–PLO Association Agreement provided that "[i]mports into the Community of products originating in the West Bank and Gaza Strip shall be allowed free of customs duties . . .".

Between February and June 2002, Brita ("the plaintiff") applied for goods supplied by the company Soda-Club Ltd, based in Mishor Adumin in the West Bank, to be given preferential treatment under the EC–Israel

---

[1] Observations to the Court were submitted on behalf of Brita GmbH by D. Ehle, Rechtsanwalt, and on behalf of the European Commission by C. Tufvesson, F. Hoffmeister and L. Bouyon, acting as Agents.
[2] Prepared by Ms E. Fogarty.

Association Agreement, noting that the Israeli customs authorities had certified Soda-Club's invoices. The German customs authorities requested Israel's verification of the products' origin. Israel replied that it had confirmed that the goods had originated in an area under Israeli customs' responsibility. Considering that verification insufficient, the German customs authorities sought confirmation as to whether the products had originated in the Israeli-occupied settlements in the territories occupied by Israel following the 1967 Arab–Israel armed conflict. Israel did not reply and the Hauptzollamt Hamburg-Hafen (Principal Customs Office, Hamburg; "the defendant") refused preferential treatment, charging the plaintiff EUR 19,155.46 in customs duties. The plaintiff brought proceedings before the Hamburg Finanzgericht (Finance Court) for the decision to be annulled.

The Finanzgericht referred several questions to the Court of Justice for a preliminary ruling. In particular, it sought the Court's opinion on whether, under the EC–Israel Association Agreement, the German customs authorities were bound by the results of a verification request and had to bring any dispute between them and the Israeli customs authorities before the Customs Cooperation Committee; and whether either the EC–Israel Association Agreement or EC–PLO Association Agreement could be applied without distinction with respect to goods which had originated in the occupied territories.

Opinion of the Advocate General

Held:—(1) Article 32 of Protocol 4 to the EC–Israel Association Agreement was an administrative cooperative mechanism based on mutual trust between States Parties' customs authorities, mutual recognition of the documents issued by those authorities, and the presumption that an exporting State's customs authorities were best placed to verify the origin of relevant products. However, mutual recognition was not absolute. In certain cases, an importing State's customs authorities would not be bound by the result of an exporting State's verification (where the exporting State's authorities were not in a position duly to carry out an origin verification, for example). Article 32 expressly provided for an importing State's refusal of preferential treatment where verification was not forthcoming within ten months, or did not contain sufficient information to determine the origin of a product (paras. 76-9 and 82-3).

(2) The presumption that the exporting State was best placed to verify a product's origin did not apply in the present case, as the origin of the relevant products in the West Bank was not disputed. Instead, the main proceedings were to ascertain whether the point of origin fell within the scope of the EC–Israel Association Agreement. The German authorities were therefore not bound by the result of the Israeli verification carried out under Article 32. Neither were they bound to refer the dispute to the Customs Cooperation Committee, which was mandated to consider disputes concerning origin verification under Article 32 rather than the interpretation of the scope of the Agreement. The correct procedure under the Agreement was that provided for under Article 75, whereby a State "may" refer a dispute relating to the

application of the Agreement to the Association Council (paras. 86-91, 94-6, 98-102 and 104).

(3) The referring court had been wrong to consider that it did not matter whether preferential treatment was provided to products originating in the West Bank under the EC–Israel Association Agreement or the EC–PLO Association Agreement. The EC–Israel Association Agreement provided that it "shall apply to the territory of the State of Israel", which, under the Plan for the Partition of Palestine of 1948, excluded the West Bank and Gaza Strip. Conversely, the EC–PLO Association Agreement had been executed for the EC to assist in developing the flow of trade to and from the West Bank and Gaza Strip, where the Palestinian Authority had competent customs authorities. Preferential treatment could therefore only be given to goods originating in the West Bank or Gaza Strip under the EC–PLO Association Agreement, and only then where the goods were certified by the relevant Palestinian authorities. Goods certified by Israeli customs authorities as being of Israeli origin, but proven to have originated in the occupied territories, were not entitled to preferential treatment under either the EC–Israel Association Agreement or the EC–PLO Association Agreement (paras. 105-12, 120, 123, 126-31 and 138-9).

(4) The Court should reply as follows: (a) the customs authorities of an importing State were not bound by the result of a verification carried out by the customs authorities of an exporting State where the dispute related to the territorial scope of the relevant Agreement; (b) the German authorities were not under an obligation to submit the dispute to the Customs Cooperation Committee; and (c) goods certified by the Israeli customs authorities as being of Israeli origin, but which proved to have originated in the West Bank or Gaza Strip, were not entitled to preferential treatment under either the EC–Israel Association Agreement or the EC–PLO Association Agreement (para. 140).

Judgment of the Court of Justice

Held:—Customs authorities of importing States could refuse to grant preferential treatment under the EC–Israel Association Agreement to goods originating in the West Bank. Where goods originated in the West Bank, an importing State could not make an elective determination as to which Agreement applied for the purposes of preferential treatment.

(1) Under Articles 1 and 3 of the Vienna Convention on the Law of Treaties, 1969, that Convention applied to treaties between States as well as to treaties between States and other subjects of international law. Under Article 31, a treaty was to be interpreted in good faith in light of its object and purpose, and Article 34 provided that a treaty did not create either obligations or rights for a third State without its consent (paras. 3-6 and 40-4).

(2) The referring court's questions were principally concerned with the territorial scope of the EC–Israel Association Agreement. Article 83 of that

Agreement provided that it applied to "the territory of the State of Israel", while Article 73 of the EC–PLO Association Agreement provided that it applied to the "territories of the West Bank and the Gaza Strip". Both Agreements provided that the customs authorities of the relevant exporting State or territory had exclusive competence to issue certificates concerning products' origin within their territorial jurisdiction. To interpret Article 83 of the EC–Israel Association Agreement as meaning that Israeli customs authorities enjoyed competence with respect to products that originated in the West Bank would therefore be tantamount to imposing on the Palestinian customs authorities an obligation to refrain from exercising the competence conferred upon them under the EC–PLO Association Agreement. This would create an obligation for a third party without its consent, contrary to the general principle of international law, *pacta tertiis nec nocent nec prosunt*, as consolidated under Article 34 of the Vienna Convention (paras. 37 and 47-52).

(3) Article 83 of the EC–Israel Association Agreement excluded products originating in the West Bank from the territorial scope of that Agreement, and therefore from preferential treatment under that Agreement. The German customs authorities were consequently entitled to refuse to grant preferential treatment to products in that situation (paras. 53-4 and 58).

(4) It was not possible to adopt the referring court's suggested approach of granting preferential treatment to products originating in the West Bank regardless of which Agreement applied simply because both Agreements provided for such treatment. That approach effectively denied the principle that, in general, the origin of a product had to be proven by the competent customs authority's issue of a valid certificate in order to be entitled to preferential treatment. Certificates were only valid where they were issued by the authority that had competence over the area in which the relevant products originated (paras. 55-8).

(5) Article 32 of the EC–Israel Association Agreement provided that, whenever the customs authorities of an importing State had reasonable doubts as to the authenticity of a certificate or the origin of a product, verification could be requested from the exporting State, which was usually best placed to verify origin. However, such a mechanism could only function if the customs authorities of the importing State accepted the determinations of the exporting State's authorities. In a system of mutual recognition, the customs authorities of an importing State could not unilaterally declare a certificate or invoice invalid where it had been properly approved by the customs authorities of an exporting State. Nevertheless, under Article 32(6) of Protocol 4 to the EC–Israel Association Agreement, an importing State was to refuse preferential treatment where an exporting State's response to a request for verification did not contain sufficient information to allow the true origin of a product to be determined, and was subsequently not bound by an exporting State's assertion in those circumstances (paras. 60-5 and 73-4).

(6) The Israeli customs authorities had made no response to the German authorities' request for further verification and their earlier information was

necessarily insufficient for the purposes of Article 32(6). Israel's assertion that the products at issue qualified for preferential treatment under the EC–Israel Association Agreement was therefore not binding on Germany. As the Customs Cooperation Committee was an administrative body entrusted with performing technical tasks in the customs field only, it was not competent to settle disputes concerning questions of law such as the interpretation of the EC–Israel Association Agreement, and Germany was therefore not bound to refer the present dispute to the Committee. States "may", however, refer such questions to the Association Council (paras. 66-9).

(7) Importing States could refuse to grant preferential treatment under the EC–Israel Association Agreement to products that originated in the West Bank. Member States could not make an elective determination as to whether to apply the EC–Israel Association Agreement or EC–PLO Association Agreement to products that originated in the West Bank (para. 74).

The text of the judgment of the Court commences at p. 217. The following is the text of the Opinion of Advocate General Bot:

OPINION OF ADVOCATE GENERAL BOT[1]

1. This reference for a preliminary ruling concerns the interpretation of the Euro-Mediterranean Agreement establishing an association between the European Communities and their Member States, of the one part, and the State of Israel, of the other part,[2] and of the Euro-Mediterranean Interim Association Agreement on trade and cooperation between the European Community, of the one part, and the Palestine Liberation Organization (PLO) for the benefit of the Palestinian Authority of the West Bank and the Gaza Strip, of the other part.[3]

2. It arises from the fact that the company Brita GmbH[4] has contested the customs duties imposed on it by the German authorities for importing drink-makers for sparkling water manufactured in the West Bank for which the Israeli customs authorities issued a movement certificate attesting to the Israeli origin of those products.

3. The Finanzgericht (Finance Court), Hamburg (Germany), asks the Court whether, under the EC–Israel Agreement, the German customs authorities are bound by the result of the subsequent verification of origin of those products carried out by the Israeli customs authorities.

---

[1] [Delivered on 29 October 2009.] Original language: French.
[2] OJ 2000 L 147, p. 3, the "EC–Israel Agreement".
[3] OJ 1997 L 187, p. 3, the "EC–PLO Agreement".
[4] "Brita".

4. The national court also seeks to ascertain whether the German customs authorities were required to bring the dispute between them and the Israeli customs authorities before the Customs Cooperation Committee established by that agreement.

5. Finally, the Court is asked to rule on whether the EC–Israel Agreement or the EC–PLO Agreement can be applied without distinction to goods certified as being of Israeli origin but which prove to originate in the occupied territories, more specifically the West Bank.

6. In this Opinion, I shall propose that the Court rule that, in so far as the dispute between the customs authorities of the States parties to the EC–Israel Agreement relates to the extent of the territorial scope of that agreement, the customs authorities of the importing State are not bound by the result of the subsequent verification carried out by the customs authorities of the exporting State.

7. Next, I shall ask the Court to declare that the German customs authorities were not under an obligation to submit the dispute between them and the Israeli customs authorities to the Customs Cooperation Committee.

8. Finally, I shall set out the reasons why I take the view that goods certified by the Israeli customs authorities as being of Israeli origin but which prove to originate in the occupied territories, more specifically the West Bank, are not entitled either to the preferential treatment under the EC–Israel Agreement or to that under the EC–PLO Agreement.

I. LEGAL FRAMEWORK

A. *Community law*

9. The Euro-Mediterranean Ministerial Conference held in Barcelona on 27 and 28 November 1995 provided an opportunity to give specific expression to the policies already defined by previous European Councils, namely to establish a partnership with the countries of the Mediterranean basin. Twelve non-Member States were involved at that time. These were the People's Democratic Republic of Algeria, the Republic of Cyprus, the Arab Republic of Egypt, the State of Israel, the Hashemite Kingdom of Jordan, the Lebanese Republic, the Republic of Malta, the Kingdom of Morocco, the Syrian Arab Republic, the Republic of Tunisia, the Republic of Turkey and the Palestinian Authority.

10. This new partnership comprises three chapters. The "political and security" chapter seeks to establish a common area of peace and

stability. The second chapter, the "economic and financial" chapter, is intended to facilitate the creation of an area of shared prosperity. Finally, the "social, cultural and human" chapter is aimed at developing human resources and promoting understanding between cultures and exchanges between civil societies.

11. Bilateral agreements were then concluded between the European Community and the Member States, of the one part, and the Mediterranean countries, of the other part. Those agreements follow a single format comprising the aforementioned three chapters together with a protocol of agreement relating to the definition of the concept of "originating products" and methods of administrative cooperation, which have to do in particular with the method for the issue and subsequent verification of certificates attesting to the origin of products.

12. Accordingly, the Community and the Member States signed the EC–Israel Agreement on 20 November 1995, and the EC–PLO Agreement on 24 February 1997, in Brussels.

13. Those agreements were approved, respectively, by Decision 2000/384/EC, ECSC of the Council and the Commission of 19 April 2000[5] and Council Decision 97/430/EC of 2 June 1997.[6]

1. The EC–Israel Agreement

14. The EC–Israel Agreement entered into force on 1 June 2000. The preamble to that agreement provides that "the Community, its Member States and Israel wish to strengthen [the existing traditional links between them] and to establish lasting relations based on reciprocity and partnership and promote a further integration of Israel's economy into the European economy".

15. The preamble to the EC–Israel Agreement also states that the parties have concluded that agreement in the light of "the importance [which they] attach to the principle of economic freedom and to the principles of the United Nations Charter, particularly the observance of human rights and democracy, which form the very basis of the Association".

16. Under Article 7 of that agreement, the provisions of the EC–Israel Agreement are to apply to products originating in the Community and in Israel. Article 8 of the Agreement provides that "customs duties on imports and exports, and any charges having equivalent

---

[5] OJ 2000 L 147, p. 1.
[6] OJ 1997 L 187, p. 1.

effect, shall be prohibited between the Community and Israel. This shall also apply to customs duties of a fiscal nature."

17. Article 67 of the EC–Israel Agreement provides for the establishment of an Association Council responsible for examining any major issues arising within the framework of the Agreement and any other bilateral or international issues of mutual interest.

18. Under Article 75(1) of the agreement, each of the parties may refer to the Association Council any dispute relating to the application or [interpretation] of the EC–Israel Agreement.

19. Article 79(2) of that agreement also states that a party is entitled to take appropriate measures if it considers that the other party has failed to fulfil an obligation under that agreement, provided that, before so doing, it supplies the Association Council with all relevant information required for a thorough examination of the situation with a view to seeking a solution acceptable to the parties.

20. The territorial scope of the EC–Israel Agreement is defined in Article 83 of that agreement. Under that article, the agreement is to apply to the territories in which the Treaties establishing the European Community and the European Coal and Steel Community are applied and under the conditions laid down in those Treaties and to the territory of the State of Israel.

21. Under Article 2(2)(a) and (b) of Protocol 4 to that agreement, concerning the definition of "originating products" and methods of administrative cooperation, products originating in Israel are defined as products wholly obtained in Israel within the meaning of Article 4 of that protocol[7] and products obtained in Israel which contain materials not wholly obtained there, provided that the said materials have undergone sufficient working or processing in Israel within the meaning of Article 5 of that protocol.

22. Protocol 4 to the EC–Israel Agreement also lays down the rules relating to proof of origin of products. Thus, Article 17(1)(a) of that protocol provides that originating products within the meaning of that protocol are to benefit from the EC–Israel Agreement upon submission of a EUR.1 certificate for the movement of goods.[8] Under Article 18(1) of Protocol 4 to the EC–Israel Agreement, that certificate is to be issued by the customs authorities of the exporting State on

---

[7] Article 4 lists the products considered as wholly obtained in the Community or in Israel. These include mineral products extracted from their soil or from their seabed, vegetable products harvested there or live animals born and raised there.

[8] "EUR.1 certificate".

application having been made in writing by the exporter or, under the exporter's responsibility, by his authorised representative.

23. Article 32 of that protocol establishes administrative cooperation between the State of Israel and the Member State concerned. Accordingly, where the customs authorities of the importing State have doubts as to the origin of products, they may request subsequent verification of the EUR.1 certificates. In such circumstances, the former authorities are to return the certificates concerned to the customs authorities of the exporting State and give the reasons of substance or form for an inquiry.

24. Article 32(3) of that protocol provides that verification is to be carried out by the customs authorities of the exporting State. Article 32(6) of Protocol 4 to the EC–Israel Agreement states that, "[i]f in cases of reasonable doubt there is no reply within ten months or if the reply does not contain sufficient information to determine the authenticity of the document in question or the real origin of the products, the requesting customs authorities shall, except in the case of force majeure or in exceptional circumstances, refuse entitlement to the preferences".

25. Finally, the first paragraph of Article 33 of that protocol provides that, "where disputes arise in relation to the verification procedures of Article 32 which cannot be settled between the customs authorities requesting a verification and the customs authorities responsible for carrying out this verification or where they raise a question as to the interpretation of this Protocol, they shall be submitted to the Customs Cooperation Committee".

26. The question of the rule governing origin and the extent of the territorial scope of the EC–Israel Agreement has been the subject of a dispute between the Community and the State of Israel for many years. The Community takes the view that products originating in the occupied territories of the West Bank and the Gaza Strip are not entitled to the preferential regime established by the EC–Israel Agreement, while the State of Israel takes the view that this is not the case.

27. As long ago as 1997, the Commission of the European Communities, in a notice to importers,[9] expressed its doubts about the validity of EUR.1 certificates submitted on importation into the Community of orange juice from Israel and complained of inadequate administrative cooperation between the State of Israel and the Community. According to the Commission, those doubts were capable of calling in question the validity of those certificates.

---

[9] Notice to importers—Importations from Israel into the Community, 8 November 1997 (OJ 1997 C 388, p. 13).

28. On 12 May 1998, the Commission, in a communication to the Council and the European Parliament,[10] reported on the difficulties encountered in implementing Protocol 4 to the EC–Israel Agreement, which was applicable pending ratification of the agreement itself by the Community.

29. In that communication, it stated that two obstacles to the correct implementation of that agreement remained. Those obstacles concerned exports to the Community of goods certified as originating in Israel but actually produced in the occupied territories.

30. Furthermore, at the second meeting of the EU–Israel Association Council,[11] the Commission had bemoaned the continuing differences of interpretation in relation to the territorial scope of the [EC–Israel] Agreement. It had also stated that it was legally bound to guarantee the implementation of that agreement and to protect the European Union's own resources.[12] Accordingly, the Commission had announced the publication of a new notice.[13]

31. In that notice, the Commission informed importers that "arising from the results of the verification procedures carried out, it is now confirmed that Israel issues proofs of origin for products coming from places brought under Israeli administration since 1967, which, according to the Community, are not entitled to benefit from preferential treatment under the [EC–Israel Agreement]". It goes on to say that "Community operators presenting documentary evidence of origin with a view to securing preferential treatment for products originating from Israeli settlements in the West Bank, Gaza Strip, East Jerusalem and the Golan Heights are informed that they must take all the necessary precautions and that putting the goods in free circulation may give rise to a customs debt."

2. *The EC–PLO Agreement*

32. The EC–PLO Agreement entered into force on 1 July 1997. The preamble to the agreement states that the parties have concluded the agreement in the light of "the importance which the parties attach to the principles of the United Nations Charter, particularly the observance of human rights, democratic principles and political and

---

[10] Implementation of the interim agreement on trade and trade-related matters between the European Community and Israel [SEC(1998) 695 final].
[11] See the draft minutes of the second meeting of the EU–Israel Association Council of 20 November 2001 (available on the website of the Council of the European Union).
[12] Page 4.
[13] Notice to importers—Imports from Israel into the Community, of 23 November 2001 (OJ 2001 C 328, p. 6).

economic freedoms which form the very basis of their relations". The agreement was also concluded in the light of "the difference in economic and social development existing between the parties and the need to intensify existing efforts to promote economic and social development in the West Bank and the Gaza Strip".

33. Under Article 1(2) of the EC–PLO Agreement, the objectives of the agreement are, in particular, to contribute to the economic and social development of the West Bank and the Gaza Strip and to encourage regional cooperation with a view to the consolidation of peaceful coexistence and economic and political stability.

34. Article 5 of that agreement provides that "[n]o new customs duty on imports, or any other charge having equivalent effect, shall be introduced on trade between the Community and the West Bank and Gaza Strip". Article 6 of the agreement goes on to state that "[i]mports into the Community of products originating in the West Bank and the Gaza Strip shall be allowed free of customs duties and of any other charge having equivalent effect and free of quantitative restrictions and of any other measure having equivalent effect".

35. The concept of "originating products" is defined in Protocol 3 to the EC–PLO Agreement concerning the definition of the concept of "originating products" and methods of administrative cooperation. Article 2(2)(a) and (b) of that protocol defines as products originating in the West Bank and Gaza Strip products wholly obtained in the West Bank and Gaza Strip[14] and those obtained there and incorporating materials which have not been wholly obtained there, provided that such materials have undergone sufficient working or processing in the West Bank and Gaza Strip.

36. In the event of a dispute between the parties relating to the interpretation or application of the EC–PLO Agreement, Article 67 of that agreement provides that either party may refer the dispute to the Joint Committee for settlement.

37. Finally, Article 73 of the agreement states that it is to apply to the territories of the West Bank and the Gaza Strip.

B. The Israeli–Palestinian Interim Agreement

38. The Madrid Process, started in 1991, seeks to establish lasting peace in the Middle East. As part of that process, the State of Israel and

---

[14] Article 4 of Protocol 3 to the EC–PLO Agreement defines as products wholly obtained in the West Bank and Gaza Strip, inter alia, mineral products extracted from their soil or from their seabed, vegetable products harvested there and products from live animals raised there.

the PLO, on 28 September 1995 in Washington, signed the Israeli–Palestinian Interim Agreement on the West Bank and the Gaza Strip.[15] That agreement, which, according to its preamble, replaces the Agreement on the Gaza Strip and the Jericho Area,[16] the Agreement on Preparatory Transfer of Powers and Responsibilities[17] and the Protocol on Further Transfer of Powers and Responsibilities,[18] has the objective, inter alia, of "establish[ing] [an] elected Council ... and [an] elected Ra'ees (Head) of the Executive Authority for the Palestinian people in the West Bank and the Gaza Strip ... leading to a permanent settlement based on [United Nations] Security Council Resolutions 242 and 338".[19]

39. The preamble also states that the elections of the elected Council and of the Ra'ees of the Executive Authority will constitute "a significant interim preparatory step toward the realisation of the legitimate rights of the Palestinian people and their just requirements and will provide a democratic basis for the establishment of Palestinian institutions".

40. In order to achieve that objective, the Israeli–Palestinian Agreement provides that the State of Israel is to transfer the powers and responsibilities of the Israeli military government and civil administration to the elected Council and that it is to continue to exercise the powers and responsibilities which have not been transferred.[20]

41. Following the first phase of redeployment,[21] three areas were established, Areas A, B and C. Since the products at issue in the main proceedings come from a territory in Area C, I shall focus exclusively on that area.

42. In that area, the State of Israel retains exclusive competence in matters of security.

43. Under Article IX(5)(b)(1) of the Israeli–Palestinian Agreement, the PLO may conduct negotiations and sign economic agreements with States or international organisations.

---

[15] The "Israeli–Palestinian Agreement".
[16] Agreement signed at Cairo in May 1994.
[17] Agreement signed at Erez on 29 August 1994.
[18] Protocol signed at Cairo on 27 August 1995.
[19] See the preamble to the Israeli–Palestinian Agreement.
[20] See Article I(1) of the Agreement.
[21] Article X of the Agreement provides that "the first phase of the Israeli military forces redeployment will cover populated areas in the West Bank—cities, towns, villages, refugee camps and hamlets—as set out in Annex I [of the Israeli–Palestinian Agreement], and will be completed ... 22 days before the day of the elections", the elections for the elected Council having taken place on 20 January 1996 [see the websites of the European Institute for Research on Mediterranean and Euro-Arab Cooperation (www.medea.be) and the United Nations (www.un.org)].

44. Furthermore, Article XI(2)(c) of that agreement provides that "[i]n Area C, during the first phase of redeployment, Israel will transfer to the Council civil powers and responsibilities not relating to territory, as set out in Annex III".

45. Article IV of Annex III to that agreement makes special provisions for the territories in Area C.

46. It thus states that, in relation to those territories, in the first phase of redeployment, powers and responsibilities relating to the fields listed in Appendix I will be transferred to and assumed by the elected Council in accordance with the provisions of that appendix.

47. Article 6 of that appendix provides that commerce and industry are among the spheres transferred to the elected Council. It states that the sphere of commerce and industry includes, inter alia, import and export. The economic aspects of that sphere are contained in Annex V to the Israeli–Palestinian Agreement.

48. Article IX (concerning industry) (6) of that annex states that Palestinians will have the right to export their industrial produce to external markets without restrictions, on the basis of certificates of origin issued by the Palestinian Authority.

II. FACTS AND DISPUTE IN THE MAIN PROCEEDINGS

49. Brita is a company established in Germany. It imports drinkmakers for sparkling water including accessories and syrups manufactured by the company Soda-Club Ltd,[22] based in Mishor Adumin in the West Bank, to the east of Jerusalem.

50. Under the Israeli–Palestinian Agreement, that territory, which was occupied by the State of Israel in 1967, is among the territories in Area C.

51. Between February and June 2002, Brita applied for release into free circulation of the goods supplied by Soda-Club. To that end, it filed 62 customs declarations stating that the State of Israel was the country of origin for those goods. The invoices produced by Soda-Club also stated that the products at issue in the main proceedings originated in Israel.

52. The German customs office, provisionally, allowed Brita's application and granted the preferential tariff to those products, in accordance with the EC–Israel Agreement. At the same time, it requested subsequent verification of the proof of origin of the products.

---

[22] "Soda-Club".

53. That request was made following a ministerial order of 6 December 2001 stating that requests for subsequent verification must be made in relation to all preferential certificates issued in Israel where there was good reason to suspect that the deliveries of goods concerned might be from Israeli-occupied settlements in the West Bank, the Gaza Strip, East Jerusalem or the Golan Heights.

54. The request for subsequent verification was forwarded to the Israeli customs authorities. In reply, the latter told the German customs authorities that "[the] verification [which they had carried out had] proven that the goods in question originate in an area that is under Israeli Customs responsibility. As such, they are originating products pursuant to the Israel–EU ... Agreement and are entitled to preferential treatment under that agreement."

55. Taking the view that the information provided by the Israeli customs authorities was insufficient within the meaning of Article 32(6) of Protocol 4 to the EC–Israel Agreement, the German customs authorities, by letter of 6 February 2003, again asked the Israeli customs authorities to indicate, by way of supplementary information, whether the goods referred to in the preferential certificates had been manufactured in Israeli-occupied settlements in the West Bank, the Gaza Strip, East Jerusalem or the Golan Heights.

56. The Israeli customs authorities failed to reply to that request. Consequently, by notice of 25 September 2003 addressed to Brita, the Hauptzollamt (Principal Customs Office), Hamburg-Hafen, refused to grant entitlement to preferential treatment on the ground that it could not be established conclusively that the imported goods fall within the scope of the EC–Israel Agreement.

57. Post-clearance recovery of customs duties in the amount of EUR 19,155.46 was therefore sought. Brita brought an appeal against that recovery before the Hauptzollamt, Hamburg-Hafen. That appeal was dismissed by decision of 21 June 2006 as being unfounded.

58. On 10 July 2006, Brita brought an action before the referring court. Being uncertain as to how to interpret the EC–Israel Agreement, that court stayed its proceedings and referred a number of questions to the Court of Justice for a preliminary ruling.

III. THE QUESTIONS REFERRED

59. The following questions are put to the Court:

(1) Should the importer of goods which originate in the West Bank be granted the preferential treatment requested in any event in light of the fact

that preferential treatment is provided under two agreements which come under consideration in the present case—namely the [EC–Israel Agreement] and the [EC–PLO Agreement]—for goods originating in the territory of the State of Israel or in the West Bank, even if only a formal certificate of origin from Israel is submitted?

If Question 1 is to be answered in the negative:

(2) Is the customs authority of a Member State bound under the [EC–Israel Agreement], vis-à-vis an importer who is requesting preferential treatment for goods which have been imported into Community territory, by a proof-of-origin certificate issued by the Israeli authority—and the verification procedure under Article 32 of Protocol 4 to the [EC–Israel Agreement] has not been opened—as long as the customs authority has no doubt as to the originating status of the goods other than that as to whether the goods originate in an area which is merely under Israeli control—that is, pursuant to the terms of the [Israeli–Palestinian Agreement]—and as long as no dispute-settlement procedure was carried out pursuant to Article 4 to the [EC–Israel Agreement]?

If Question 2 is to be answered in the negative:

(3) May the customs authority of the country of importation refuse automatically to grant preferential treatment for the following reason alone, namely that, pursuant to its request for verification under Article 32(2) of Protocol 4 to the [EC–Israel Agreement], it was confirmed by the Israeli authorities (only) that the goods were manufactured in an area which is subject to Israeli customs jurisdiction and that they were for that reason of Israeli origin, and where the subsequent request by the customs authority of the country of importation for further specification by the Israeli authorities remained unanswered, in particular without the actual origin of the goods having to be taken into account?

If Question 3 is to be answered in the negative:

(4) May the customs authorities refuse automatically to grant preferential treatment under the [EC–Israel] Agreement in the case where—as has become clear in the meantime—the goods originate in the West Bank, or should preferential treatment also be granted under the [EC–Israel Agreement] for goods originating in that area, in any event as long as no dispute-settlement procedure has been carried out under Article 33 of Protocol 4 to the [EC–Israel Agreement] concerning the interpretation of the expression "territory of the State of Israel" used in the [EC–Israel Agreement]?

IV. ANALYSIS

60. First of all, with regard to the Court's jurisdiction to interpret the association agreements at issue in this case, I wish to point out that, on the subject of the Agreement establishing an association between the

European Economic Community and Turkey,[23] the Court held in *Demirel*[24] that an agreement concluded by the Council under Articles 228 and 238 of the EC Treaty,[25] is, as far as the Community is concerned, an act of one of the institutions of the Community within the meaning of Article 177, first paragraph, subparagraph (b), of the EC Treaty,[26] that the provisions of such an agreement form an integral part of the Community legal system, and that, within the framework of that system, the Court has jurisdiction to give preliminary rulings concerning the interpretation of such an agreement.[27]

61. In my view, the questions referred can be dealt with as follows.

62. By its second and third questions, the referring court asks whether, under Article 32 of Protocol 4 to the EC–Israel Agreement, the customs authorities of the importing State are bound by the result of the subsequent verification of proof of origin carried out by the customs authorities of the exporting State.

63. It also seeks to ascertain whether, in order to settle the dispute between them and the customs authorities of the exporting State, the customs authorities of the importing State were required, under Article 33 of that protocol, to submit the dispute to the Customs Cooperation Committee before taking measures unilaterally.

64. Finally, by the first and fourth questions, the Court is asked to give a ruling on whether goods certified by the Israeli customs authorities as originating in Israel and produced in the occupied territory of the West Bank are entitled without distinction either to the preferential treatment under the EC–Israel Agreement or to that established by the EC–PLO Agreement.

A. *Whether the customs authorities of the importing State are bound by the result of the subsequent verification carried out by the customs authorities of the exporting State*

65. First of all, I think it is worth reminding ourselves of the relevant provisions of the EC–Israel Agreement concerning verification of a product's origin.

---

[23] Agreement signed at Ankara on 12 September 1963 by the Republic of Turkey, of the one part, and by the Member States of the EEC and the Community, of the other part. That agreement was concluded, adopted and confirmed on behalf of the Community by Council Decision 64/732/EEC of 23 December 1963 (OJ 1977 L 361, p. 29).
[24] Case 12/86 [1987] ECR 3719.
[25] Article 228 of the EC Treaty (now, after amendment, Article 300 EC) and Article 238 of the EC Treaty (now Article 310 EC).
[26] Now Article 234, first paragraph, subparagraph (b), EC.
[27] See *Demirel*, paragraph 7. See also Case C-162/96 *Racke* [1998] ECR I-3655, paragraph 41.

66. In order to be entitled to preferential treatment, the exporter must, under Article 17 of Protocol 4 to the EC–Israel Agreement, submit a EUR.1 certificate. That certificate is issued by the customs authorities of the exporting State, who must take any steps necessary to verify the originating status of the product and the fulfilment of all the other requirements laid down by that protocol.[28]

67. That certificate is then submitted to the customs authorities of the State into which the product is imported. If those authorities have reasonable doubt as to the authenticity of the EUR.1 certificate, the originating status of the product concerned or the fulfilment of the other requirements laid down by that protocol, a subsequent verification of that certificate is carried out.[29]

68. The customs authorities of the importing State then return the certificate to the customs authorities of the exporting State and explain, where appropriate, the reasons of substance or form for an inquiry. The latter authorities carry out the verification and must inform their counterparts within ten months at the latest of the result of that verification. They must indicate whether the documents are authentic, whether the product concerned can be considered as an originating product and whether it fulfils the other requirements of that protocol.[30]

69. If in cases of reasonable doubt there is no reply within ten months or if the reply from the customs authorities of the exporting State does not contain sufficient information to determine the authenticity of the certificate concerned or the real origin of the product, the customs authorities of the importing State must refuse entitlement to preferential treatment.[31]

70. The administrative cooperation provided for in Article 32 of Protocol 4 to the EC–Israel Agreement was therefore introduced for the purposes of verifying the accuracy of information relating to the origin of a product. Subsequent verification may, for example, serve to ensure that the value of an item not originating in the State of Israel which is a constituent element of the final product for which a EUR.1 certificate has been issued does not exceed 10% of the ex-works price of that product[32] or to establish the processing operations which the product may have undergone.[33]

---

[28] Article 18(1) and (6) of Protocol 4 to the EC–Israel Agreement.
[29] Article 32(1) of that protocol.
[30] See Article 32(2), (3) and (5) of that protocol.
[31] See Article 32(6) of Protocol 4 to the EC–Israel Agreement.
[32] See Article 5(2)(a) of that protocol.
[33] See Article 6 of that protocol.

71. It is appropriate now to ask whether, in the case at issue, the result of the subsequent verification carried out by the customs authorities of the exporting State is binding on the customs authorities of the importing State.

72. The Court has already had occasion to answer this question in the context of other agreements between the Community and third States.

73. In *Les Rapides Savoyards and Others*,[34] concerning the interpretation of the Free-trade Agreement between the European Economic Community and the Swiss Confederation,[35] which contains a protocol similar to that in the EC–Israel Agreement, the Court held that "the determination of the origin of goods ... is based on a division of powers between the customs authorities of the parties to the free-trade agreement inasmuch as origin is established by the authorities of the exporting country and the proper working of that system is monitored jointly by the authorities concerned on both sides".[36]

74. The Court goes on to say that that mechanism can function only if the customs authorities of the importing State accept the determinations legally made by the customs authorities of the exporting State.[37]

75. More recently, the Court held that "the customs authorities of the State of import may not unilaterally declare invalid a EUR.1 certificate duly issued by the customs authorities of the State of export. Likewise, in cases of subsequent verification, the same authorities are bound by the results of such verification."[38]

76. The administrative cooperation mechanism established generally by an association agreement, and in particular by Article 32 of Protocol 4 to the EC–Israel Agreement, is therefore based on mutual trust between the customs authorities of the States parties to the agreement and on mutual recognition of the documents which they issue.

77. However, such mutual recognition is not absolute. The Court has accepted in certain cases that the customs authorities of the importing State are not bound by the result of the subsequent verification carried out by the customs authorities of the exporting State.

---

[34] Case 218/83 [1984] ECR 3105.
[35] Agreement signed at Brussels on 22 July 1972, "concluded, adopted and confirmed" on behalf of the Community by Council Regulation (EEC) No 2840/72 of 19 December 1972 (OJ English Special Edition 1972(I), p. 190).
[36] See *Les Rapides Savoyards and Others*, paragraph 26.
[37] Ibid., paragraph 27.
[38] See Joined Cases C-23/04 to C-25/04 *Sfakianakis* [2006] ECR I-1265, paragraph 49.

78. The Court has thus recognised that, in specific circumstances where the customs authorities of the exporting State are not in a position duly to carry out the subsequent verification envisaged by the protocol in question, the customs authorities of the importing State may themselves check the authenticity and accuracy of the EUR.1 certificate by taking account of other evidence as to the origin of the goods.[39]

79. The Court has also held that, when there is reasonable doubt as to the origin of the goods and there is no reply from the customs authorities of the exporting State within ten months of the date of the verification request or if the reply given by those authorities does not contain sufficient information to enable the origin to be determined, the certificates which they have issued may be revoked by the customs authorities of the importing State.[40]

80. Furthermore, where the preferential system is established not by an international agreement binding the Community to a non-Member State on the basis of reciprocal obligations but by a unilateral Community measure, the customs authorities of the exporting State do not have the power to bind the Community and its Member States in their interpretation of Community rules. In those circumstances, the findings reached by the Commission in relation to the origin of goods in the course of a mission of enquiry must take precedence over those of the customs authorities of the exporting non-Member State.[41]

81. The Court has also held, with regard to the Agreement establishing an association between the European Economic Community and Turkey,[42] that the customs authorities of the importing State retain the right to take action for post-clearance recovery on the basis of the results of checks carried out by the Commission after the import transactions, without being obliged to have recourse to the mechanism for settling disputes provided for by that agreement.[43]

82. It is therefore only in the event of a failure to act on the part of the customs authorities of the exporting State or in the case of an independent Community measure that the customs authorities of the importing State do not have an obligation to recognise the decisions taken by the former authorities.

---

[39] Case C-12/92 *Huygen and Others* [1993] ECR I-6381, paragraph 27.
[40] *Sfakianakis*, paragraph 38.
[41] See Joined Cases C-153/94 and C-204/94 *Faroe Seafood and Others* [1996] ECR I-2465, paragraphs 24 and 25.
[42] See footnote 23 of this Opinion.
[43] See Case C-251/00 *Ilumitrónica* [2002] ECR I-10433, paragraph 74.

83. This is explained by the fact that there is a presumption that the customs authorities of the exporting State are in the best position to verify directly the facts which determine the origin of the product.[44]

84. The customs authorities of the importing State are therefore, in principle, bound by the result of the subsequent verification carried out by the customs authorities of the exporting State.

85. It is my view, however, that the circumstances of this case are different from those which the Court has hitherto had occasion to hear and determine.

86. The main proceedings are not concerned with verifying the accuracy of information relating to the product origin that creates entitlement to preferential treatment, since the origin is known and is not contested. They are in fact concerned with ascertaining whether that origin falls within the scope of the EC–Israel Agreement.

87. As I have already said,[45] the dispute between the customs authorities of the importing State and those of the exporting State was raised as long ago as the second meeting of the EU–Israel Association Council of 20 November 2001. I would point out that, under Article 75 of the EC–Israel Agreement, the Association Council is competent to hear disputes relating to the application or interpretation of the Agreement.

88. At that meeting, the Commission, as member of the Association Council,[46] mentioned the dispute relating to the rules of origin and the consequent difficulty of applying the EC–Israel Agreement and announced that it would take measures accordingly. The Commission bemoaned the ongoing differences of interpretation in relation to the territorial scope of that agreement and announced that it would therefore publish a new notice to importers in the *Official Journal of the European Union* clarifying and replacing the 1997 notice.

89. To date, the dispute between the Community and the State of Israel has still not been resolved.

90. The referring court is now faced with this issue in a dispute between a German company which imports products originating in the occupied territories and the German customs authorities. It has therefore now turned to the Court for a resolution of that issue.

91. The dispute between the Community and the State of Israel has, after all, been going on for many years, thus depriving economic

---

[44] See *Les Rapides Savoyards and Others*, paragraph 26.
[45] Points 26 to 31 of this Opinion.
[46] See Article 68 of the EC–Israel Agreement.

operators of any legal certainty as to whether or not the EC–Israel Agreement applies to products originating in the occupied territories.

92. Furthermore, allowing the customs authorities of one of the parties to that agreement, or their courts, to interpret unilaterally whether that agreement applies to products originating in the occupied territories would without any doubt lead to the non-uniform application of the EC–Israel Agreement, which, it should be recalled, forms an integral part of the Community legal order.

93. Specifically, the effect of so doing would be that products from the occupied territories would benefit from the preferential treatment established by the EC–Israel Agreement when exported to one Member State but those same products would not be granted such preferential treatment when exported to another Member State.

94. Consequently, I take the view that the presumption that exists with respect to verification of the accuracy of the facts by the customs authorities of the exporting State cannot apply in circumstances such as those in the main proceedings, since, in this case, none of the parties to the EC–Israel Agreement is in the best position to give a unilateral interpretation of the scope of that agreement.

95. I do not therefore see how the German customs authorities could be bound by the result of the subsequent verification carried out by the Israeli customs authorities.

96. In the light of all the foregoing considerations, I take the view that, since the dispute between the customs authorities of the States parties to the EC–Israel Agreement relates not to a question of fact but to the extent of the territorial scope of that agreement, the customs authorities of the importing State are not bound by the result of the subsequent verification carried out by the customs authorities of the exporting State as part of the verification procedure provided for in Article 32 of Protocol 4 to that agreement.

B. *The obligation to refer the matter to the Customs Cooperation Committee*

97. By its second question, the referring court asks whether the German customs authorities were required, before adopting their decision to seek post-clearance recovery of customs duties, to refer the matter to the Customs Cooperation Committee in accordance with the first paragraph of Article 33 of Protocol 4 to the EC–Israel Agreement, which provides that, where disputes arise in relation to the subsequent verification procedures or they raise a question as to the interpretation of that protocol, they are to be submitted to the Customs Cooperation Committee.

98. The issue is, in reality, whether the German customs authorities were entitled to adopt a measure unilaterally, namely the post-clearance recovery of customs duties, without first referring the matter to the Customs Cooperation Council.

99. I do not think that the procedure established by the first paragraph of Article 33 of the Protocol is the appropriate framework for resolving a conflict relating to the scope of the EC–Israel Agreement.

100. That procedure is intended for cases where a dispute arises following a subsequent verification under Article 32 of Protocol 4 to that agreement, the purpose of such verification being to check the accuracy of the information relating to the origin of a product.[47]

101. In my view, however, the dispute between the customs authorities of the importing State and the customs authorities of the exporting State does not relate to the facts determining the origin of the products at issue in the main proceedings but to the interpretation of the scope of that agreement.

102. I am of the opinion that the procedure to be followed in the event of a dispute such as that in the main proceedings, and, indeed, the procedure which *was* followed, is that provided for in Article 75(1) of the EC–Israel Agreement.

103. That provision states that "[e]ach of the parties may refer to the Association Council any dispute relating to the application or interpretation of this Agreement". I would point out that the Association Council is responsible, under Article 67 of that agreement, for examining any major issues arising within the framework of that agreement and any other bilateral or international issues of mutual interest.

104. Consequently, in the light of the foregoing, I take the view that the German customs authorities were not under an obligation to submit the dispute between them and the Israeli customs authorities to the Customs Cooperation Committee.

C. *The possibility of making an elective determination as to classification*

105. By its first and fourth questions, the referring court essentially wishes to ascertain whether goods certified as being of Israeli origin but which prove to originate in the occupied territories, more specifically the West Bank, are entitled without distinction either to the

---

[47] See point 70 of this Opinion.

preferential treatment under the EC–Israel Agreement or to that under the EC–PLO Agreement.

106. The referring court is of the opinion that it does not ultimately matter which customs authorities are competent to issue a EUR.1 certificate and that products originating in the occupied territories should be granted preferential treatment in any event since both the EC–Israel Agreement and the EC–PLO Agreement provide for such preferential treatment.

107. I do not share that view.

108. I would point out, first of all, that Article 83 of the EC–Israel Agreement provides that "[it] shall apply . . . to the territory of the State of Israel".

109. The borders of the State of Israel were defined by the Plan for the Partition of Palestine, drawn up by UNSCOP[48] and approved on 29 November 1947 by United Nations General Assembly Resolution 181. On 14 May 1948, the Head of the Provisional Government of the State of Israel proclaimed the birth of that State on the basis of the borders which had been defined by the Plan for the Partition of Palestine.[49]

110. Furthermore, the preamble to the EC–Israel Agreement reads as follows:

Considering the importance which the Parties attach to the principle of economic freedom and to the principles of the United Nations Charter, particularly the observance of human rights and democracy, which form the very basis of the Association.

111. Under United Nations Security Council Resolution 242 of 22 November 1967, referred to in the preamble to the EC–PLO Agreement, Israeli troops were asked to withdraw from the occupied territories, to terminate all claims or states of belligerency and to respect the sovereignty, territorial integrity and political independence of every State in the area. The United Nations Security Council sought the application of that resolution in another resolution, namely Resolution 338 of 22 October 1973.

112. In the light of the foregoing, the Court cannot but conclude, in my view, that the territories of the West Bank and the Gaza Strip do not form part of the territory of the State of Israel.

---

[48] United Nations Special Committee On Palestine. Made up of 11 States, this committee, which was set up by the United Nations General Assembly in 1947, was entrusted with the task of finding a solution to the conflict in Palestine, in particular by drawing up a partition plan.

[49] See the websites of the United Nations (www.un.org) and the Ministry of Foreign Affairs of the State of Israel (www.mfa.gov.il).

113. I would add that, following written question P-2747/00 by Mr Lipietz, European Parliament,[50] relating to the territorial scope of the EC–Israel Agreement, the Council stated that "[r]egarding the territorial scope of [that agreement], Article 83 applies only to the territory of the State of Israel [and that] [t]he term Israel covers the territorial waters, which surround Israel, and under certain conditions also some sea-vessels. No further definition is contained in the [EC–Israel] agreement. The [Community] considers that [that] agreement applies solely to the territory of the State of Israel within its internationally recognised waters in accordance with the relevant United Nations Security Council resolutions."[51]

114. Furthermore, under Article XI(1) of the Israeli–Palestinian Agreement, the State of Israel and the PLO both view the West Bank and the Gaza Strip as a single territorial unit.

115. In the light of the foregoing, it seems difficult to maintain that a product originating in the West Bank and, more generally, in the occupied territories, is entitled to preferential treatment under the EC–Israel Agreement.

116. It is true that the tension which exists in the relations between the State of Israel and the PLO should not penalise the producers of those territories and preclude their entitlement to preferential treatment.

117. The solution envisaged by the referring court, pragmatic as it is, is nonetheless not satisfactory in my view, for the following reasons.

118. First of all, the Court has held that the system of generalised preferences is based on the principle of the unilateral grant by the Community of tariff advantages in favour of products originating in certain developing countries with the aim of facilitating the flow of trade with those countries. The benefit of that preferential system is thus linked to the origin of the goods and the verification of that origin is therefore a necessary element of that system.[52]

119. The certificate issued by the customs authorities of the exporting State must therefore be capable of certifying unambiguously that the product in question does indeed come from a given State so that the preferential treatment relating to that State can be applied to that product.

120. It is not therefore acceptable, in my view, for the preferential treatment under the EC–Israel Agreement to be applied to a product originating in the West Bank.

---

[50] OJ 2001 C 113 E, p. 163.
[51] Paragraph 2 of the Council's reply.
[52] See to this effect Case 827/79 *Acampora* [1980] ECR 3731, paragraph 5.

121. Moreover, it appears to me that the reason the Community, years after the conclusion of the EC–Israel Agreement and after the annexation of the occupied territories in 1967, took the trouble to conclude the EC–PLO Agreement with a view to granting a tariff preference to products originating in the West Bank and the Gaza Strip was that it considered that those products were not entitled to such a preference under the EC–Israel Agreement.

122. Indeed, it is clear from a note drafted by the Council's "Mashreq/Maghreb" Working Party setting out the Union's position ahead of the fifth meeting of the EU–Israel Association Council that, pursuant to a technical agreement negotiated between the State of Israel and the Commission, the Israeli customs authorities are required to indicate the place of production on all certificates of origin issued in Israel for products entitled to preferential treatment which are exported to the Union. The purpose of this is to draw a distinction between goods originating in Israel, which are entitled to preferential treatment under the EC–Israel Agreement, and those from the settlement areas, which are not so entitled.[53]

123. It is also clear that, by concluding the EC–PLO Agreement, the Community sought to develop the flow of trade from and to the West Bank and the Gaza Strip. Indeed, it follows from Article 1 of that agreement that its objective is, inter alia, to contribute to the social and economic development of the West Bank and Gaza Strip and to encourage regional cooperation with a view to the consolidation of peaceful coexistence and economic and political stability.

124. In its communication of 12 May 1998,[54] the Commission points out that the purpose of introducing preferential treatment for the territories of the West Bank and the Gaza Strip was to rectify an anomaly, namely that the States neighbouring those territories already enjoyed such treatment but the territories of the West Bank and the Gaza Strip did not.[55]

125. In 2007, the West Bank and the Gaza Strip ranked only 168th in the classification of the Union's imports trade partners.[56] The EC–PLO Agreement is specifically intended to stimulate trade between those territories and the Union. To accept that products originating in those territories are entitled to preferential treatment under the

---

[53] See the Council's note of 3 December 2004 (15638/04, paragraph 40).
[54] See footnote 10 to this Opinion.
[55] Page 9 of the communication.
[56] See the Commission's website (http://trade.ec.europa.eu/doclib/docs/2006/september/tradoc_113382.pdf).

EC–Israel Agreement and are thus regarded as products of Israeli origin would have the consequence of divesting the EC–PLO Agreement of some of its effectiveness.

126. Finally, Brita considers that the Palestinian customs authorities were in any event unable to issue EUR.1 certificates for products from the West Bank. It is true that, taking into account the situation in the occupied territories, it may seem difficult for exporters in those territories to get those certificates issued by the customs authorities in the West Bank and the Gaza Strip. It might therefore be acceptable, as the referring court appears to maintain, for the Israeli customs authorities to issue those certificates and for the exporters of products originating in those territories to benefit from the preferential treatment established by the EC–PLO Agreement.

127. However, under Article 16(4) of Protocol 3 to the EC–PLO Agreement, responsibility for issuing EUR.1 certificates lies with the customs authorities of the West Bank and the Gaza Strip.

128. Moreover, it is clear from Annex V to the Israeli–Palestinian Agreement, relating to economic relations between the two parties, that the Palestinian authorities are not divested of all powers and responsibilities concerning commerce and the customs sphere.[57]

129. Indeed, under Articles VIII(11) and IX(6) of that annex, Palestinians must be able to export their agricultural and industrial produce without restriction, on the basis of certificates of origin *issued by the Palestinian authorities*.[58]

130. There are indeed, therefore, competent authorities responsible for issuing EUR.1 certificates for products originating in the West Bank and the Gaza Strip. In fact, it would seem that economic operators can request those certificates from the Palestinian Chamber of Commerce.[59]

131. In my view, therefore, in order to benefit from the preferential treatment established by the EC–PLO Agreement, EUR.1 certificates proving the origin of products must be issued only by the Palestinian customs authorities. It would not be consistent for the preferential treatment established by that agreement to be applied to a product

---

[57] See Article 3 of that annex.
[58] My emphasis. It is worth pointing out that these articles are applicable to the territories in Area C, pursuant to Article XI(2)(c) of the Israeli–Palestinian Agreement, which refers to Annex III to that agreement. Under Article 6 of Appendix I to that annex, the economic aspects of the sphere of commerce and industry relating to the territories in Area C are dealt with in Annex V to the Israeli–Palestinian Agreement.
[59] See paragraph 17 of the Commission's observations.

for which a EUR.1 certificate has been issued by authorities other than the Palestinian authorities.

132. Moreover, that analysis is confirmed, in my opinion, by *Anastasiou and Others*,[60] in which the Court was called upon to hear a case which I consider to be comparable to that in the main proceedings.

133. In the former case, concerning the Agreement of 19 December 1972 establishing an association between the European Economic Community and the Republic of Cyprus[61] and containing a mechanism for the proof of origin of goods similar to the mechanisms established by the EC–Israel Agreement and the EC–PLO Agreement, the Court was asked to rule on whether, on the one hand, the EEC–Cyprus Agreement precluded the customs authorities of the importing State from accepting EUR.1 certificates issued by authorities other than the customs authorities of the Republic of Cyprus or, conversely, required them to do so, and, on the other hand, whether the position would be different if certain circumstances connected with the special situation of the Republic of Cyprus were taken as established.

134. The situation was as follows. Producers and exporters of citrus fruits established in the northern part of Cyprus exported their products to the United Kingdom. The EUR.1 certificates attached to those products were issued by authorities other than those of the Republic of Cyprus.

135. The Court held that, "[w]hile the de facto partition of the territory of Cyprus, as a result of the intervention of the Turkish armed forces in 1974, into a zone where the authorities of the Republic of Cyprus continue fully to exercise their powers and a zone where they cannot in fact do so raises problems that are difficult to resolve in connection with the application of the [EEC–Cyprus] Agreement to the whole of Cyprus, that does not warrant a departure from the clear, precise and unconditional provisions of the 1977 Protocol [concerning the definition of the concept of 'originating products' and methods of administrative cooperation[62]]".[63]

136. The Court went on to say that "[a]cceptance of certificates by the customs authorities of the importing State reflects their total confidence in the system of checking the origin of products as implemented by the competent authorities of the exporting State. It also

---

[60] Case C-432/92 [1994] ECR I-3087.
[61] Agreement annexed to Council Regulation (EEC) No 1246/73 of 14 May 1973 (OJ 1973 L 133, p. 1, the "EEC–Cyprus Agreement").
[62] Protocol annexed to the Protocol to the EEC–Cyprus Agreement, itself annexed to Council Regulation (EC) No 2907/77 of 20 December 1977 (OJ 1977 L 339, p. 1).
[63] See *Anastasiou and Others*, paragraph 37.

shows that the importing State is in no doubt that subsequent verification, consultation and settlement of any disputes in respect of the origin of products or the existence of fraud will be carried out efficiently with the cooperation of the authorities concerned."[64]

137. According to the Court, such cooperation is "excluded with the authorities of an entity such as that established in the northern part of Cyprus, which is recognised neither by the Community nor by the Member States; the only Cypriot State they recognise is the Republic of Cyprus".[65] It also considers that the "acceptance of certificates [of origin] not issued by the Republic of Cyprus would constitute, in the absence of any possibility of checks or cooperation, a denial of the very object and purpose of the system established by the 1977 Protocol".[66]

138. It is therefore clear, in the light of the Court's analysis in *Anastasiou and Others*, that certificates issued by authorities other than those designated by name in an association agreement cannot be accepted as valid. While it is true that difficult situations in territories such as those of the northern part of Cyprus or the West Bank and the Gaza Strip might argue in favour of a solution such as that proposed by the referring court, I nonetheless take the view that choosing this course of action would ultimately have the effect of negating the efforts made to set up a system of administrative cooperation between the customs authorities of the Member States and those of the West Bank and the Gaza Strip and to encourage trade with those territories.

139. Consequently, in the light of all of the foregoing, it is my view that goods certified by the Israeli customs authorities as being of Israeli origin but which prove to originate in the occupied territories, more specifically the West Bank, are not entitled either to the preferential treatment under the EC–Israel Agreement or to that established by the EC–PLO Agreement.

V. CONCLUSION

140. In the light of the foregoing, I propose that the Court should reply as follows to the Finanzgericht Hamburg:

(1) The customs authorities of the importing State are not bound by the result of the subsequent verification carried out by the customs

---

[64] Ibid., paragraph 39.
[65] Ibid., paragraph 40.
[66] Ibid., paragraph 41.

authorities of the exporting State as part of the verification procedure provided for in Article 32 of Protocol 4 to the Euro-Mediterranean Agreement establishing an association between the European Communities and their Member States, of the one part, and the State of Israel, of the other part, where the dispute existing between the customs authorities of the States parties to that agreement relates to the extent of the territorial scope of that agreement.

(2) Furthermore, the German customs authorities were not under an obligation to submit the dispute between them and the Israeli customs authorities to the Customs Cooperation Committee.

(3) Goods certified by the Israeli customs authorities as being of Israeli origin but which prove to originate in the occupied territories, more specifically the West Bank and the Gaza Strip, are not entitled either to the preferential treatment under the Euro-Mediterranean Agreement establishing an association between the European Communities and their Member States, of the one part, and the State of Israel, of the other part, or to that established by the Euro-Mediterranean Interim Association Agreement on trade and cooperation between the European Community, of the one part, and the Palestine Liberation Organization (PLO) for the benefit of the Palestinian Authority of the West Bank and the Gaza Strip, of the other hand.

[The following is the text of the judgment of the Court:]

JUDGMENT OF THE COURT (FOURTH CHAMBER)

1. This reference for a preliminary ruling concerns the interpretation of the Euro-Mediterranean Agreement establishing an association between the European Communities and their Member States, of the one part, and the State of Israel, of the other part, signed in Brussels on 20 November 1995 (OJ 2000 L 147, p. 3; "the EC–Israel Association Agreement"), account being taken of the Euro-Mediterranean Interim Association Agreement on trade and cooperation between the European Community, of the one part, and the Palestine Liberation Organization (PLO) for the benefit of the Palestinian Authority of the West Bank and the Gaza Strip, of the other part, signed in Brussels on 24 February 1997 (OJ 1997 L 187, p. 3; "the EC–PLO Association Agreement").

2. The reference has been made in the context of a customs dispute between Brita GmbH ("Brita"), a company incorporated under German law, and the Hauptzollamt Hamburg-Hafen (the main customs office of the port of Hamburg) concerning the refusal of the

Hauptzollamt to grant Brita preferential treatment with regard to the importation of products manufactured in the West Bank.

LEGAL CONTEXT

The Vienna Convention

3. Under Article 1 of the Vienna Convention on the Law of Treaties of 23 May 1969 (*United Nations Treaty Series*, vol. 1155, p. 331; "the Vienna Convention"), which is entitled "Scope of the present Convention", the Vienna Convention applies to treaties between States.

4. Article 3 of the Vienna Convention, which is entitled "International agreements not within the scope of the present Convention", provides:

The fact that the present Convention does not apply to international agreements concluded between States and other subjects of international law or between such other subjects of international law, or to international agreements not in written form, shall not affect:

...

(b) the application to [such agreements] of any of the rules set forth in the present Convention to which they would be subject under international law independently of the Convention;

...

5. Under Article 31 of the Vienna Convention, which is entitled "General rule of interpretation":

1. A treaty shall be interpreted in good faith in accordance with the ordinary meaning to be given to the terms of the treaty in their context and in the light of its object and purpose.
2. ... for the purpose of the interpretation of a treaty, ...
3. ... there shall be taken into account, together with the context:
   ...
   (c) any relevant rules of international law applicable in the relations between the parties.
   ...

6. Article 34 of the Vienna Convention, which is entitled "General rule regarding third States", provides:

A treaty does not create either obligations or rights for a third State without its consent.

The EC–Israel Association Agreement

7. The EC–Israel Association Agreement, approved by Decision 2000/384/EC, ECSC of the Council and the Commission of 19 April 2000 (OJ 2000 L 147, p. 1), entered into force on 1 June 2000.

8. In Title II of the EC–Israel Association Agreement, which concerns the free movement of goods, Article 6(1) provides:

The free trade area between the Community and Israel shall be reinforced according to the modalities set out in this Agreement and in conformity with the provisions of the General Agreement on Tariffs and Trade of 1994 and of other multilateral agreements on trade in goods annexed to the Agreement establishing the World Trade Organization (WTO) . . .

9. Under Article 8 of the EC–Israel Association Agreement, with regard to industrial products as defined in that agreement and subject to the exceptions provided for, "customs duties on imports and exports, and any charges having equivalent effect, shall be prohibited between the Community and Israel . . .".

10. Article 75(1) of the EC–Israel Association Agreement provides:

Each of the Parties may refer to the Association Council any dispute relating to the application or interpretation of this Agreement.

11. The territorial scope of the EC–Israel Association Agreement is defined as follows in Article 83 thereof:

This Agreement shall apply, on the one hand, to the territories in which the Treaties establishing the European Community and the European Coal and Steel Community are applied and under the conditions laid down in those Treaties and, on the other hand, to the territory of the State of Israel.

12. Protocol 4 to the EC–Israel Association Agreement ("the EC–Israel Protocol") lays down the rules relating to the definition of "originating products", as well as methods of administrative cooperation.

13. In accordance with point (2) of Article 2 of the EC–Israel Protocol, products wholly obtained in Israel, within the meaning of Article 4 of that protocol, are to be treated as originating in Israel, as are products obtained in Israel which contain materials not wholly obtained there, provided that those materials have undergone sufficient working or processing in Israel, within the meaning of Article 5 of the EC–Israel Protocol.

14. Article 17(1) of the EC–Israel Protocol states:

Originating products within the meaning of this Protocol shall, on importation into one of the Parties, benefit from the Agreement upon submission of either:

(a) a movement certificate EUR.1 ...
(b) in the cases specified in Article 22(1), a declaration, ... given by the exporter on an invoice, a delivery note or any other commercial document which describes the products concerned in sufficient detail to enable them to be identified ["the invoice declaration"].

15. Under paragraph (1)(a) of Article 22 of the EC–Israel Protocol, which is entitled "Conditions for making out an invoice declaration", the invoice declaration referred to in Article 17(1)(b) of the protocol may be made out by an approved exporter within the meaning of Article 23 of that protocol.

16. Under Article 23 of the EC–Israel Protocol, the customs authorities of the exporting State may authorise any exporter (an "approved exporter") who makes frequent shipments of products under the EC–Israel Association Agreement, and who offers to the satisfaction of the customs authorities all guarantees necessary to verify the originating status of those products as well as the fulfilment of the other requirements of the EC–Israel Protocol, to make out invoice declarations. Such a declaration is proof that the products concerned possess the appropriate originating status and thus allows the importer to benefit from the preferential treatment provided for under the agreement.

17. Article 32 of the EC–Israel Protocol governs, in the following terms, the procedure for verifying proof of origin:

1. Subsequent verification of movement certificates EUR.1 and of invoice declarations shall be carried out at random or whenever the customs authorities of the importing State have reasonable doubt as to the authenticity of such documents, the originating status of the products concerned or the fulfilment of the other requirements of this Protocol.

2. For the purposes of implementing the provisions of paragraph 1, the customs authorities of the importing [State] shall return the movement certificate EUR.1, and the invoice, if it has been submitted, or the invoice declaration, or a copy of these documents, to the customs authorities of the exporting country giving, where appropriate, the reasons of substance or form for an inquiry.

They shall forward, in support of the request for subsequent verification, any documents and information that have been obtained suggesting that the information given on the movement certificate EUR.1 or the invoice declaration is incorrect.

3. The verification shall be carried out by the customs authorities of the exporting [State]. For this purpose, they shall have the right to call for any evidence and to carry out any inspection of the exporter's accounts or any other check which they consider appropriate.

4. ...

5. The customs authorities requesting the verification shall be informed of the results of this verification within a maximum period of 10 months. These results must indicate clearly whether the documents are authentic and whether the products concerned can be considered as originating products and fulfil the other requirements of this Protocol.

...

6. If in cases of reasonable doubt there is no reply within 10 months or if the reply does not contain sufficient information to determine the authenticity of the document in question or the real origin of the products, the requesting customs authorities shall, except in the case of *force majeure* or in exceptional circumstances, refuse entitlement to the preferences.

18. On the subject of dispute settlement, Article 33 of the EC–Israel Protocol provides:

Where disputes arise in relation to the verification procedures of Article 32 which cannot be settled between the customs authorities requesting a verification and the customs authorities responsible for carrying out this verification or where they raise a question as to the interpretation of this Protocol, they shall be submitted to the Customs Cooperation Committee.

...

19. Under Article 39 of the EC–Israel Protocol, which is entitled "Customs Cooperation Committee":

1. A Customs Cooperation Committee shall be set up, charged with carrying out administrative cooperation with a view to the correct and uniform application of this Protocol and with carrying out any other task in the customs field which may be entrusted to it.

2. The Committee shall be composed, on the one hand, of experts of the Member States and of officials of the department of the Commission of the European Communities who are responsible for customs questions and, on the other hand, of experts nominated by Israel.

EC–PLO Association Agreement

20. The EC–PLO Association Agreement, approved by Council Decision 97/430/EC of 2 June 1997 (OJ 1997 L 187, p. 1), entered into force on 1 July 1997.

21. Article 3 of the EC–PLO Association Agreement states:

The Community and the Palestinian Authority shall establish progressively a free trade area ... in conformity with the provisions of the General Agreement on Tariffs and Trade of 1994 and of the other multilateral agreements on trade in goods annexed to the agreement establishing the World Trade Organization (WTO) . . .

22. Articles 5 and 6 of the EC–PLO Association Agreement provide:

Article 5

No new customs duty on imports, or any other charge having equivalent effect, shall be introduced on trade between the Community and the West Bank and the Gaza Strip.

Article 6

Imports into the Community of products originating in the West Bank and the Gaza Strip shall be allowed free of customs duties and of any other charge having equivalent effect and free of quantitative restrictions and of any other measure having equivalent effect.

23. As regards the territorial scope of the EC–PLO Association Agreement, Article 73 provides:

This Agreement shall apply, on the one hand, to the territories in which the Treaty establishing the European Community is applied and under the conditions laid down in that Treaty and, on the other hand, to the territory of the West Bank and the Gaza Strip.

24. Protocol 3 appended to the EC–PLO Association Agreement ("the EC–PLO Protocol") lays down the rules concerning the definition of "originating products", as well as methods of administrative cooperation.

25. Under Article 2(2) of the EC–PLO Protocol, products wholly obtained in the West Bank and the Gaza Strip are to be treated as products originating in the West Bank and the Gaza Strip, as are products obtained in the West Bank and Gaza Strip incorporating materials which have not been wholly obtained there, provided that such materials have undergone sufficient working or processing in the West Bank and Gaza Strip.

26. Article 15(1) of the EC–PLO Protocol provides that, on importation into the Community, products originating in the West Bank and the Gaza Strip are to benefit from the EC–PLO Association Agreement upon submission of either a movement certificate EUR.1 or—in the situations listed in Article 20(1) of the protocol—a declaration made out by the exporter on an invoice, or on a delivery note, or on any other commercial document, which describes the products concerned in

sufficient detail to enable them to be identified. That declaration is referred to as an "invoice declaration".

27. Article 16(1) of the EC–PLO Protocol provides that the movement certificate EUR.1 is to be issued by the customs authorities of the exporting State. Under Article 16(4), such a certificate is to be issued by the customs authorities of the West Bank and Gaza Strip if the products concerned can be considered to be products originating in the West Bank and Gaza Strip and if they fulfil the other requirements laid down in the protocol.

28. Under paragraph (1)(a) of Article 20 of the EC–PLO Protocol, which concerns the conditions for making out an invoice declaration, such a declaration may be made out by an approved exporter within the meaning of Article 21 of the protocol. Under Article 20(2) of the EC–PLO Protocol, an invoice declaration may be made out if the products concerned can be considered to be products originating in the Community, the West Bank and Gaza Strip and if they fulfil the other requirements laid down in that protocol.

29. Paragraph 1 of Article 21 of the EC–PLO Protocol, which concerns approved exporters, provides that the customs authorities of the exporting State may grant authority to make out invoice declarations to any exporter who makes frequent shipments of products under the EC–PLO Association Agreement and who offers to the satisfaction of the customs authorities all guarantees necessary to verify the originating status of the products as well as the fulfilment of the other requirements laid down in the protocol.

THE DISPUTE IN THE MAIN PROCEEDINGS AND THE QUESTIONS REFERRED FOR A PRELIMINARY RULING

30. Brita, the applicant in the main proceedings, is established in Germany. It imports drink-makers for sparkling water, as well as accessories and syrups, all produced by an Israeli supplier, Soda-Club Ltd, at a manufacturing site at Mishor Adumin in the West Bank, to the east of Jerusalem. Soda-Club Ltd is an approved exporter within the meaning of Article 23 of the EC–Israel Protocol.

31. During the first six months of 2002, Brita applied for some imported goods to be released for free circulation, filing more than 60 customs declarations in total. It stated that the country of origin for those goods was "Israel" and sought the application of the preferential tariff provided for under the EC–Israel Association Agreement on the

basis of invoice declarations made out by the supplier confirming that the products concerned originated in Israel.

32. The German customs authorities provisionally granted the preferential tariff applied for, but commenced the procedure for subsequent verification. On being questioned by the German customs authorities, the Israeli customs authorities replied that "[o]ur verification has proven that the goods in question originate in an area that is under Israeli Customs responsibility. As such, they are originating products pursuant to the [EC–Israel] Association Agreement and are entitled to preferential treatment under that agreement."

33. By letter of 6 February 2003, the German customs authorities asked the Israeli customs authorities to indicate, by way of supplementary information, whether the goods in question had been manufactured in Israeli-occupied settlements in the West Bank, the Gaza Strip, East Jerusalem or the Golan Heights. That letter remained unanswered.

34. By decision of 25 September 2003, the German Customs authorities therefore refused the preferential treatment that had been granted previously, on the ground that it could not be established conclusively that the imported goods fell within the scope of the EC–Israel Association Agreement. Consequently, a decision was taken to seek post-clearance recovery of customs duties amounting to a total of EUR 19,155.46.

35. The objection filed by Brita was dismissed, whereupon it brought an action before the Finanzgericht Hamburg (Finance Court, Hamburg) for annulment of that decision. The Finanzgericht Hamburg takes the view that the outcome of the dispute depends on the interpretation of the EC–Israel Association Agreement, the EC–Israel Protocol and the EC–PLO Association Agreement.

36. In those circumstances, the Finanzgericht Hamburg decided to stay proceedings and to refer the following questions to the Court for a preliminary ruling:

(1) Should the importer of goods which originate in the West Bank be granted the preferential treatment requested in any event in light of the fact that preferential treatment is provided under two agreements which come under consideration in the present case—namely the [EC–Israel Association Agreement] and the [EC–PLO Association Agreement]—for goods originating in the territory of the State of Israel or in the West Bank, even if only a formal certificate of origin from Israel is submitted?

If Question 1 is to be answered in the negative:

(2) Is the customs authority of a Member State bound under the EC–Israel Association Agreement, vis-à-vis an importer who is requesting preferential treatment for goods which have been imported into Community territory, by a proof-of-origin certificate issued by the Israeli authority—and the verification procedure under Article 32 of the [EC–Israel] Protocol has not been opened—as long as the customs authority of that Member State has no doubt as to the originating status of the goods other than that as to whether the goods originate in an area which is merely under Israeli control—that is, pursuant to the terms of the Israeli–Palestinian Interim Agreement of 1995—and as long as no dispute-settlement procedure was carried out pursuant to Article 33 of the [EC–Israel] Protocol?

If Question 2 is to be answered in the negative:

(3) May the customs authority of the country of importation refuse automatically to grant preferential treatment for the following reason alone, namely that, pursuant to its request for verification under Article 32(2) of the [EC–Israel] Protocol, it was confirmed by the Israeli authorities (only) that the goods were manufactured in an area which is subject to Israeli customs jurisdiction and that they were for that reason of Israeli origin, and where the subsequent request by the customs authority of the country of importation for further specification by the Israeli authorities remained unanswered, in particular without the actual origin of the goods having to be taken into account?

If Question 3 is to be answered in the negative:

(4) May the customs authorities [of the importing Member State] refuse automatically to grant preferential treatment under the EC–Israel Association Agreement in the case where—as has become clear in the meantime—the goods originate in the West Bank, or should preferential treatment also be granted under the [EC–Israel Agreement] for goods originating in that area, in any event as long as no dispute-settlement procedure has been carried out under Article 33 of the [EC–Israel] Protocol concerning the interpretation of the expression "territory of the State of Israel" used in that agreement?

THE QUESTIONS REFERRED FOR A PRELIMINARY RULING

Questions 1 and 4

37. By Questions 1 and 4, which it is appropriate to examine together, the referring court asks, essentially, whether the customs

authorities of the importing Member State may refuse to grant the preferential treatment provided for under the EC–Israel Association Agreement where the goods at issue originate in the West Bank.

38. By way of a preliminary point, it should be noted that the answer to Questions 1 and 4 closely depends on the interpretation to be given to Article 83 of the EC–Israel Association Agreement, which defines the territorial scope of that agreement.

39. In this respect, it should be recalled that an agreement concluded by the Council of the European Union with a non-Member State in accordance with Articles 217 TFEU and 218 TFEU, constitutes, as far as the European Union is concerned, an act of one of the institutions of the Union, within the meaning of point (b) of the first paragraph of Article 267 TFEU; that, from the moment it enters into force, the provisions of such an agreement form an integral part of the legal order of the European Union; and that, within the framework of that legal order, the Court has jurisdiction to give preliminary rulings concerning the interpretation of such an agreement (see, to that effect, Case 12/86 *Demirel* [1987] ECR 3719, paragraph 7, and Case C-162/96 *Racke* [1998] ECR I-3655, paragraph 41). In addition, having been concluded by two subjects of public international law, the EC–Israel Association Agreement is governed by international law and, more specifically, as regards its interpretation, by the international law of treaties.

40. The international law of treaties was consolidated, essentially, in the Vienna Convention. Under Article 1 thereof, the Vienna Convention applies to treaties between States. However, under Article 3(b) of the Vienna Convention, the fact that the Vienna Convention does not apply to international agreements concluded between States and other subjects of international law is not to affect the application to them of any of the rules set forth in that convention to which they would be subject under international law independently of the convention.

41. It follows that the rules laid down in the Vienna Convention apply to an agreement concluded between a State and an international organisation, such as the EC–Israel Association Agreement, in so far as the rules are an expression of general international customary law. Consequently, the EC–Israel Association Agreement must be interpreted in accordance with those rules.

42. In addition, the Court has held that, even though the Vienna Convention does not bind either the Community or all its Member States, a series of provisions in that convention reflect the rules of customary international law which, as such, are binding upon the Community institutions and form part of the Community legal order (see, to that effect, *Racke*, paragraphs 24, 45 and 46; see, also, as regards

the reference to the Vienna Convention for the purposes of the interpretation of association agreements concluded by the European Communities, Case C-416/96 *El-Yassini* [1999] ECR I-1209, paragraph 47, and Case C-268/99 *Jany and Others* [2001] ECR I-8615, paragraph 35 and the case-law cited).

43. Pursuant to Article 31 of the Vienna Convention, a treaty is to be interpreted in good faith in accordance with the ordinary meaning to be given to the terms of the treaty in their context and in the light of its object and purpose. In that respect, account is to be taken, together with the context, of any relevant rules of international law applicable in the relations between the parties.

44. Among the relevant rules that may be relied on in the context of the relations between the parties to the EC–Israel Association Agreement is the general international law principle of the relative effect of treaties, according to which treaties do not impose any obligations, or confer any rights, on third States ("*pacta tertiis nec nocent nec prosunt*"). That principle of general international law finds particular expression in Article 34 of the Vienna Convention, under which a treaty does not create either obligations or rights for a third State without its consent.

45. It follows from those preliminary considerations that Article 83 of the EC–Israel Association Agreement, which defines the territorial scope of that agreement, must be interpreted in a manner that is consistent with the principle "*pacta tertiis nec nocent nec prosunt*".

46. In this respect, it is common ground that the European Communities concluded two Euro-Mediterranean Association Agreements, first with the State of Israel and then with the PLO for the benefit of the Palestinian Authority of the West Bank and the Gaza Strip.

47. Each of those two association agreements has its own territorial scope. Under Article 83 thereof, the EC–Israel Association Agreement applies to the "territory of the State of Israel". Under Article 73 thereof, the EC–PLO Association Agreement applies to the "territories of the West Bank and the Gaza Strip".

48. That being so, those two association agreements pursue an identical objective—referred to in Article 6(1) of the EC–Israel Association Agreement and Article 3 of the EC–PLO Association Agreement, respectively—which is to establish and/or reinforce a free trade area between the parties. They also have the same immediate purpose—defined, for industrial products, in Article 8 of the EC–Israel Association Agreement and in Articles 5 and 6 of the EC–PLO Association Agreement, respectively—which is to abolish customs duties, quantitative restrictions and other measures having equivalent effect in relation to trade between the parties to each of those agreements.

49. As regards methods of administrative cooperation, in the case, first, of the EC–Israel Association Agreement, it emerges from Articles 22(1)(a) and 23(1) of the EC–Israel Protocol that the invoice declaration needed in order to be allowed preferential treatment for exports is to be made out by an exporter who has been approved by the "customs authorities of the exporting [State]".

50. Secondly, in the case of the EC–PLO Association Agreement, it emerges from Articles 20(1)(a) and 21(1) of the EC–PLO Protocol that the invoice declaration needed in order to be allowed preferential treatment for exports is to be made out by an exporter approved by the "customs authorities of the exporting [State]". In addition, Article 16(4) of the EC–PLO Protocol implies that, if the products concerned can be regarded as products originating in the West Bank or the Gaza Strip, the "customs authorities of ... the West Bank and Gaza Strip" have sole competence to issue a movement certificate EUR.1.

51. It follows from the foregoing that the "customs authorities of the exporting [State]", within the meaning of the two protocols mentioned above, have exclusive competence—within their territorial jurisdiction—to issue movement certificates EUR.1 or to approve exporters based in the territory under their administration.

52. Accordingly, to interpret Article 83 of the EC–Israel Association Agreement as meaning that the Israeli customs authorities enjoy competence in respect of products originating in the West Bank would be tantamount to imposing on the Palestinian customs authorities an obligation to refrain from exercising the competence conferred upon them by virtue of the abovementioned provisions of the EC–PLO Protocol. Such an interpretation, the effect of which would be to create an obligation for a third party without its consent, would thus be contrary to the principle of general international law, "*pacta tertiis nec nocent nec prosunt*", as consolidated in Article 34 of the Vienna Convention.

53. It follows that Article 83 of the EC–Israel Association Agreement must be interpreted as meaning that products originating in the West Bank do not fall within the territorial scope of that agreement and do not therefore qualify for preferential treatment under that agreement.

54. In those circumstances, the German customs authorities could refuse to grant, in respect of the goods at issue, preferential treatment as provided for under the EC–Israel Association Agreement, on the ground that those goods originated in the West Bank.

55. For the purposes, still, of Question 1, the referring court asks, essentially, whether the customs authorities of the importing State may

grant preferential treatment when such treatment is provided for under both the agreements to be taken into account—namely, the EC–Israel Association Agreement and the EC–PLO Association Agreement—and it is not contested that the goods at issue originate in the West Bank and only a formal certificate of Israeli origin has been submitted. The referring court asks, more specifically, to what extent it is possible to accept that the customs authorities are free to choose between two substantively equivalent possibilities ("to make an elective determination"), leaving open the questions of which of the two agreements applies and of whether proof of origin falls to be issued by the Israeli authorities or by the Palestinian authorities.

56. To allow elective determination simply because both the agreements at issue provide for preferential treatment and because the place of origin of the goods is established by evidence other than that envisaged under the association agreement that is actually applicable would be tantamount to denying, generally, that, in order to be entitled to the preferential treatment, it is necessary to provide valid proof of origin issued by the competent authority of the exporting State.

57. It is clear, both from Article 17 of the EC–Israel Protocol and from Article 15 of the EC–PLO Protocol, that proof of origin must be produced in respect of products originating in the territories of the contracting parties if they are to qualify for the preferential treatment. That requirement of valid proof of origin issued by the competent authority cannot be considered to be a mere formality that may be overlooked as long as the place of origin is established by means of other evidence. In this respect, the Court has already held that the validity of certificates issued by authorities other than those designated by name in the relevant association agreement cannot be accepted (see, to that effect, Case C-432/92 *Anastasiou and Others* [1994] ECR I-3087, paragraphs 37 to 41).

58. In the light of the above considerations, the answer to Questions 1 and 4 is that the customs authorities of the importing Member State may refuse to grant the preferential treatment provided for under the EC–Israel Association Agreement where the goods concerned originate in the West Bank. Furthermore, the customs authorities of the importing Member State may not make an elective determination, leaving open the questions of which of the agreements to be taken into account—namely, the EC–Israel Association Agreement and the EC–PLO Association Agreement—applies in the circumstances of the case and of whether proof of origin falls to be issued by the Israeli authorities or by the Palestinian authorities.

Questions 2 and 3

59. By Questions 2 and 3, which it is appropriate to examine together, the referring court asks, essentially, whether, for the purposes of the procedure laid down in Article 32 of the EC–Israel Protocol, the customs authorities of the importing State are bound by the proof of origin that is submitted and by the reply given by the customs authorities of the exporting State. The referring court also asks whether, in order to settle a dispute that has arisen in relation to the verification of invoice declarations, the customs authorities of the importing State must, pursuant to Article 33 of the protocol, submit that dispute to the Customs Cooperation Committee before adopting measures unilaterally.

The question whether the customs authorities of the importing State are bound by the reply given by the customs authorities of the exporting State

60. It is clear from Article 32 of the EC–Israel Protocol that the subsequent verification of invoice declarations is carried out whenever the customs authorities of the importing State have reasonable doubt as to the authenticity of such documents or the originating status of the products concerned. The verification is carried out by the customs authorities of the exporting State. The customs authorities requesting the verification are to be informed of the results of that verification within a maximum period of ten months. Those results must indicate clearly whether the invoice declarations are authentic and whether the products concerned can be considered to be originating products. If, in cases of reasonable doubt, there is no reply within ten months or if the reply does not contain sufficient information to enable the authenticity of the invoice declarations or the real origin of the products to be determined, the customs authorities of the importing State are to refuse to grant the preferential treatment.

61. In a similar legal context, the Court has held that it follows from such provisions that the determination of the origin of goods is based on a division of powers between the customs authorities of the parties to the free-trade agreement concerned, inasmuch as origin is established by the authorities of the exporting State. That system is justified by the fact that the authorities of the exporting State are those best placed to verify directly the facts which determine origin (see, to that effect, Case 218/83 *Les Rapides Savoyards and Others* [1984] ECR 3105, paragraph 26).

62. However, a mechanism of that kind can function only if the customs authorities of the importing State accept the determinations legally made by the authorities of the exporting State (see, to that effect, *Les Rapides Savoyards and Others*, paragraph 27, and Joined Cases C-23/04 to C-25/04 *Sfakianakis* [2006] ECR I-1265, paragraph 23).

63. It follows that, in the context of that system of mutual recognition, the customs authorities of the importing State may not unilaterally declare invalid an invoice declaration made out by an exporter who has been properly approved by the customs authorities of the exporting State. Likewise, in cases of subsequent verification, the customs authorities of the importing State are generally bound by the results of such verification (see, to that effect, *Sfakianakis*, paragraph 49).

64. Nevertheless, in the case before the referring court, the subsequent verification pursuant to Article 32 of the EC–Israel Protocol did not concern the question whether the imported products were wholly obtained in a certain location or whether they had undergone sufficient working and processing there for them to be considered to be products originating in that location, in accordance with the EC–Israel Protocol. The aim of the subsequent verification was to establish the precise place of manufacture of the imported products, for the purposes of determining whether those products fell within the territorial scope of the EC–Israel Association Agreement. The European Union takes the view that products obtained in locations which have been placed under Israeli administration since 1967 do not qualify for the preferential treatment provided for under that agreement.

65. In accordance with Article 32(6) of the EC–Israel Protocol, if the reply given by the customs authorities of the exporting State does not contain sufficient information to enable the real origin of the products to be determined, the requesting customs authorities are to refuse to grant preferential treatment in respect of those products.

66. As it is, it is apparent from the circumstances of the case before the referring court that, in the context of the subsequent verification, the Israeli customs authorities gave no reply to the letters which the German customs authorities had sent in order to check whether the products at issue had been manufactured in Israeli-occupied settlements in the West Bank, the Gaza Strip, East Jerusalem or the Golan Heights. The letter of 6 February 2003 from the German customs authorities even remained unanswered.

67. In circumstances such as those, it must be held that a reply such as that given by the customs authorities of the exporting State does not contain sufficient information, for the purposes of Article 32(6) of the

EC–Israel Protocol, to enable the real origin of the products to be determined, which means that, in a context such as this, the assertion made by those authorities that the products at issue qualify for preferential treatment under the EC–Israel Association Agreement is not binding upon the customs authorities of the importing Member State.

The obligation to bring the matter before the Customs Cooperation Committee

68. The first paragraph of Article 33 of the EC–Israel Protocol provides that, where disputes arise in relation to the verification procedures under Article 32 of the protocol or where they raise a question as to the interpretation of that protocol, they are to be submitted to the Customs Cooperation Committee.

69. Under Article 39 of the EC–Israel Protocol, the Customs Cooperation Committee is an administrative body composed of customs experts and officials from the Commission, the Member States and the State of Israel. Within the framework of that protocol, it is to be entrusted with the performance of any technical task in the customs field. Consequently, it cannot be regarded as having competence to settle disputes concerning questions of law such as those relating to the interpretation of the EC–Israel Association Agreement itself. On the other hand, such disputes may, in accordance with Article 75(1) of the EC–Israel Association Agreement, be submitted to the Association Council.

70. In a case such as that before the referring court, the reply given by the customs authorities of the exporting State in the context of the subsequent verification procedure provided for in Article 32 of the EC–Israel Protocol cannot be considered to be at the origin of a dispute between the contracting parties concerning the interpretation of that protocol. First, that reply fails to provide the information requested. Secondly, even though, in the case before the referring court, a dispute arose at the time of the subsequent verification procedure requested by the customs authorities of the importing State, that dispute does not concern the interpretation of the EC–Israel Protocol, but the determination of the territorial scope of the EC–Israel Association Agreement.

71. It follows that, in circumstances such as those in the case before the referring court, each of the contracting parties has the right to bring before the Association Council a question concerning the interpretation of the territorial scope of the EC–Israel Association Agreement. By contrast, there is no obligation to bring the matter before the

Customs Cooperation Committee since that question of interpretation does not fall within its sphere of competence.

72. In any event, even if it might have been conceivable, had there been a dispute concerning the interpretation of the Association Agreement as such, to bring the matter before the Association Council, it should be recalled that, as the Court has already held, the fact that the dispute was not referred to the Association Committee, an emanation of the Association Council, cannot be used as justification for derogating from the system of cooperation and respect for the areas of competence as allocated under the Association Agreement (see, by analogy, *Sfakianakis*, paragraph 52).

73. In the light of all of the foregoing, the answer to Questions 2 and 3 is that, for the purposes of the procedure laid down in Article 32 of the EC–Israel Protocol, the customs authorities of the importing State are not bound by the proof of origin submitted or by the reply given by the customs authorities of the exporting State where that reply does not contain sufficient information, for the purposes of Article 32(6) of the EC–Israel Protocol, to enable the real origin of the products to be determined. Furthermore, the customs authorities of the importing State are not obliged to refer to the Customs Cooperation Committee set up under Article 39 of that protocol a dispute concerning the territorial scope of the EC–Israel Association Agreement.

COSTS

74. Since these proceedings are, for the parties to the main proceedings, a step in the action pending before the national court, the decision on costs is a matter for that court. Costs incurred in submitting observations to the Court, other than the costs of those parties, are not recoverable.

On those grounds, the Court (Fourth Chamber) hereby rules:

1. The customs authorities of the importing Member State may refuse to grant the preferential treatment provided for under the Euro-Mediterranean Agreement establishing an association between the European Communities and their Member States, of the one part, and the State of Israel, of the other part, signed in Brussels on 20 November 1995, where the goods concerned originate in the West Bank. Furthermore, the customs authorities of the importing Member State may not make an elective determination, leaving open the questions of which of the agreements to be taken into

account—namely, the Euro-Mediterranean Agreement establishing an association between the European Communities and their Member States, of the one part, and the State of Israel, of the other part, and the Euro-Mediterranean Interim Association Agreement on trade and cooperation between the European Community, of the one part, and the Palestine Liberation Organization (PLO) for the benefit of the Palestinian Authority of the West Bank and the Gaza Strip, of the other part, signed in Brussels on 24 February 1997—applies in the circumstances of the case and of whether proof of origin falls to be issued by the Israeli authorities or by the Palestinian authorities.

2. For the purposes of the procedure laid down in Article 32 of Protocol No 4 appended to the Euro-Mediterranean Agreement establishing an association between the European Communities and their Member States, of the one part, and the State of Israel, of the other part, the customs authorities of the importing State are not bound by the proof of origin submitted or by the reply given by the customs authorities of the exporting State where that reply does not contain sufficient information, for the purposes of Article 32(6) of that protocol, to enable the real origin of the products to be determined. Furthermore, the customs authorities of the importing State are not obliged to refer to the Customs Cooperation Committee set up under Article 39 of that protocol a dispute concerning the territorial scope of that agreement.

[Report: [2010] ECR I-1289]

Human rights — Prohibition of torture and cruel, inhuman or degrading treatment — Applicant receiving life sentence — Applicant given whole life order by Secretary of State — Whether whole life order violating Article 3 of European Convention on Human Rights, 1950 — Need for review mechanism in respect of whole life sentences — General principles — Whether life sentence irreducible as matter of law and practice — Whether prospect of release and possibility of review of sentence — Whether review mechanism available to applicant sufficient to comply with requirements of Article 3 of European Convention

Treaties — Interpretation — European Convention on Human Rights, 1950, Article 3 — Prohibition of torture and inhuman or degrading treatment or punishment — Whether applicant's whole life order compatible with Article 3 of European Convention — Whether life sentence irreducible as matter of law or practice — Whether prospect of release and possibility of review of sentence — Whether review mechanism available to applicant sufficient to comply with requirements of Article 3 of European Convention

Relationship of international law and municipal law — Treaties — Interpretation — Scope — Article 3 of European Convention on Human Rights, 1950 prohibiting torture and inhuman or degrading treatment or punishment — Whether whole life order violating Article 3 of European Convention — State choosing its criminal justice system — Sentence review and release arrangements — Requirement of compatibility with Convention principles — Whether life sentence compatible with Article 3 of European Convention — Whether life sentence irreducible as matter of law and practice — Whether prospect of release and possibility of review of sentence — Human dignity — Aim of imprisonment — Rehabilitation — European penal policy — International law — Article 10(3) of International Covenant on Civil and Political Rights, 1966 — Human Rights Committee's General Comment on Article 10 — Need for review mechanism in respect of whole life sentences — General principles — Whether review mechanism available to applicant sufficient to comply with requirements of Article 3 of European Convention — Strasbourg jurisprudence — English jurisprudence — Interpretation of domestic legislation — Whether European Court of Human Rights to accept national court's interpretation of domestic law — Whether Secretary of

State's discretionary power to release under domestic law complying with requirements of Article 3 of European Convention

HUTCHINSON v. UNITED KINGDOM[1]

(Application No 57592/08)

European Court of Human Rights (Fourth Section)
3 February 2015

(Raimondi, *President*; Nicolaou, Bianku, Tsotsoria, Kalaydjieva, Mahoney and Wojtyczek, *Judges*)

SUMMARY:[2] *The facts*:—The applicant, Mr Hutchinson, was a British national who had been convicted of aggravated burglary, rape and murder in the United Kingdom. He was sentenced to life imprisonment, and given a whole life order by the Secretary of State. Following the entry into force of the Criminal Justice Act ("the 2003 Act"), the applicant applied to the High Court for a review of his minimum term of imprisonment; the Secretary of State's decision to give a whole life order was confirmed. The applicant's appeal was dismissed by the Court of Appeal.

The applicant lodged an application against the United Kingdom alleging that his whole life order violated Article 3 of the European Convention on Human Rights, 1950 ("the Convention").[3] He argued that his case was indistinguishable from *Vinter*,[4] which had considered relevant domestic case law, and that the international consensus was that the review of whole life orders required a judicial rather than governmental ministerial decision. The United Kingdom Government maintained that *Newell*,[5] which held that the whole life order was reducible under domestic law and thus compatible with Article 3 of the Convention, was the binding and authoritative statement of English law.

The Court declared, by a majority, that the complaint was admissible; it was neither manifestly ill-founded nor inadmissible on any other grounds.

---

[1] The names of the parties' representatives appear at para. 2 of the judgment. On 1 June 2015, the case was referred to the Grand Chamber at the applicant's request.
[2] Prepared by Ms Karen Lee, Co-Editor.
[3] Article 3 of the Convention provided: "No one shall be subjected to torture or to inhuman or degrading treatment or punishment."
[4] *Vinter* v. *United Kingdom* (judgment of 9 July 2013 of the Grand Chamber of the European Court of Human Rights), 156 ILR 115.
[5] *Re Attorney General's Reference No 69 of 2013*; *Regina* v. *McLoughlin*; *Regina* v. *Newell* (judgment of English Court of Appeal of 18 February 2014), 158 ILR 746.

Held (by six votes to one):—There had been no violation of Article 3 of the Convention.

(1) A State could choose its criminal justice system, including sentence review and release arrangements, provided that the system did not contravene Convention principles. While the imposition of a life sentence on adult offenders for serious crimes was not itself prohibited, it might raise an issue under Article 3 of the Convention if it was irreducible as a matter of law or practice (paras. 18-19).

(2) There had to be both a prospect of release and a possibility of review for a life sentence to remain compatible with Article 3 of the Convention. Domestic authorities could then assess progress towards rehabilitation and whether continued detention was justified on legitimate penological grounds. Human dignity was central to the Convention system. The emphasis in European penal policy, and in international law, as expressed inter alia in Article 10(3) of the International Covenant on Civil and Political Rights, 1966 and the General Comment on that Article, was now on the rehabilitative aim of imprisonment, even for life prisoners (para. 19).

(3) While it was not the Court's task to prescribe the form or timing of review, comparative and international law materials showed clear support for a mechanism guaranteeing a review no later than twenty-five years after the imposition of a life sentence, with periodic reviews thereafter (para. 20).

(4) Where domestic law did not provide any mechanism or possibility of review of a whole life sentence, incompatibility with Article 3 of the Convention arose at the moment of its imposition rather than at a later stage of incarceration. A whole life prisoner was entitled to know, at the outset of his sentence, what he had to do to be considered for release and under what conditions, including when a review could take place or be sought (para. 20).

(5) A life sentence that could be served in full was not irreducible. There was no Article 3 issue when a life prisoner had the right under domestic law to be considered for release but this was refused, for example, because of a continued danger to society (para. 21).

(6) In *Newell* the national court had expressly responded to the concerns detailed by the Grand Chamber in *Vinter*. Domestic law did therefore provide to an offender sentenced to a whole life order hope and the possibility of release in exceptional circumstances which meant that punishment was no longer justified (paras. 22-3).

(7) It was for the national authorities, notably the courts, to resolve problems of interpretation of domestic legislation. In the United Kingdom, as in other Convention States, the progressive development of the law through judicial interpretation was a well-entrenched and necessary part of legal tradition (para. 24).

(8) The Court had to accept the national court's interpretation of domestic law; the national court had set out an unequivocal statement of the legal position after the Court had questioned the clarity of domestic law (para. 25).

(9) The Secretary of State's discretionary power to release under domestic law, exercised in the manner delineated in the relevant domestic case law,[6] was sufficient to comply with the requirements of Article 3 of the Convention (paras. 25-6).

Dissenting Opinion of Judge Kalaydjieva: (1) The admissibility of the applicant's complaints might be questionable in so far as they concerned the availability of *de jure* and *de facto* possibilities for release; it was unclear whether the applicant had applied to the Secretary of State for early release (paras. 1-2).

(2) The relevant issue was whether in 2008 the applicant was entitled to know, at the outset of his sentence, what he must do to be considered for release and under what conditions, including when a review of his sentence would take place or could be sought, as required by the principles established in *Vinter*, which were uncontested (paras. 3-6).

The following is the text of the judgment of the Court:

PROCEDURE

1. The case originated in an application (No 57592/08) against the United Kingdom of Great Britain and Northern Ireland lodged with the Court under Article 34 of the Convention for the Protection of Human Rights and Fundamental Freedoms ("the Convention") by a British national, Mr Arthur Hutchinson ("the applicant"), on 10 November 2008.

2. The applicant was represented by Mr J. Turner, a lawyer practising in North Shields with Kyles Legal Practice, assisted by Mr J. Bennathan QC and Ms K. Thorne, counsel. The United Kingdom Government ("the Government") were represented by their Agent, Ms M. Addis, Foreign and Commonwealth Office.

3. The applicant alleged, in particular, that his whole life sentence gave rise to a violation of Article 3 of the Convention.

4. On 10 July 2013, the complaint under Article 3 was communicated to the Government and the remainder of the application was declared inadmissible.

THE FACTS

I. The circumstances of the case

5. The applicant was born in 1941 and is detained in Her Majesty's Prison Durham.

---

[6] *Regina v. Bieber* (156 ILR 402), *Regina v. Oakes* (156 ILR 423 (note)) and *Re Attorney General's Reference No 69 of 2013*; *Regina v. McLoughlin*; *Regina v. Newell* (158 ILR 746).

6. In October 1983, the applicant broke into a family home, stabbed to death a man, his wife and their adult son and repeatedly raped their 18-year-old daughter, having first dragged her past her father's body. He was arrested several weeks later and charged with the offences. At trial he pleaded not guilty, denying the killings and claiming that the sex had been consensual. On 14 September 1984, at Sheffield Crown Court, he was convicted of aggravated burglary, rape and three counts of murder.

7. The trial judge sentenced the applicant to a term of life imprisonment and recommended a minimum tariff of 18 years to the Secretary of State for the Home Office. When asked to give his opinion again on 12 January 1988, the judge wrote that "for the requirements of retribution and general deterrence this is genuinely a life case". On 15 January 1988, the Lord Chief Justice recommended that the period should be set at a whole life term, stating that "I do not think that this man should ever be released, quite apart from the risk which would be involved." On 16 December 1994, the Secretary of State informed the applicant that he had decided to impose a whole life term.

8. Following the entry into force of the Criminal Justice Act 2003, the applicant applied to the High Court for a review of his minimum term of imprisonment. On 16 May 2008, Tugendhat J handed down judgment in the applicant's case ([2008] EWHC 860 (QB)), finding that there was no reason for deviating from the Secretary of State's decision. The seriousness of the offences alone was such that the starting point was a whole life order. In addition, there were a number of very serious aggravating factors. Tugendhat J made express reference to an impact statement from the surviving victim, which described "sadistic as well as sexual conduct". There were no mitigating factors. On 6 October 2008, the Court of Appeal dismissed the applicant's appeal.

II. Relevant domestic law and practice

9. The domestic law and practice relating to the procedure for setting a whole life order under the Criminal Justice Act 2003 is set out in paragraphs 12-13 and 35-41 of the Court's judgment in *Vinter and Others* v. *United Kingdom* [GC], Nos 66069/09, 130/10 and 3896/10, 9 July 2013.

10. As regards the discretion of the Secretary of State for Justice to release a prisoner sentenced to a whole life order, section 30(1) of the Crime (Sentences) Act 1997 ("section 30") provides that he may at any time release a life prisoner on licence if he is satisfied that exceptional circumstances exist which justify the prisoner's release on

compassionate grounds. The criteria for the exercise of that discretion are set out in chapter 12 of the Indeterminate Sentence Manual ("the Lifer Manual"), issued by the Secretary of State as Prison Service Order 4700 in April 2010.

Chapter 12 of the Lifer Manual, where relevant, provides:

The criteria for compassionate release on medical grounds for all indeterminate sentence prisoners (ISP) are as follows:

- the prisoner is suffering from a terminal illness and death is likely to occur very shortly *(although there are no set time limits, 3 months may be considered to be an appropriate period for an application to be made to Public Protection Casework Section [PPCS])*, or the ISP (Indeterminate Sentenced Prisoner) is bedridden or similarly incapacitated, for example, those paralysed or suffering from a severe stroke;

and

- the risk of re-offending (particularly of a sexual or violent nature) is minimal;

and

- further imprisonment would reduce the prisoner's life expectancy;

and

- there are adequate arrangements for the prisoner's care and treatment outside prison;

and

- early release will bring some significant benefit to the prisoner or his/her family.

[[Emphasis] in the original.]

11. Under section 6 of the Human Rights Act 1998 the Secretary of State, as a public authority, is bound to act compatibly with the scheduled Convention rights, including Article 3. Under section 3 of the Human Rights Act, legislation is to be interpreted so far as it is possible to do so compatibly with the Convention.

12. A summary of the existing domestic case-law relating to the compatibility of the whole life order scheme with Article 3 of the Convention, notably the Court of Appeal's judgments in *R* v. *Bieber* and *R* v. *Oakes and Others* and the House of Lords judgment in *R (Wellington)* v. *Secretary of State for the Home Department*, was set out in *Vinter and Others*, cited above, §§ 47-58.

13. The Grand Chamber delivered its judgment in *Vinter and Others* on 9 July 2013. For reasons discussed in more detail below, it held that there had been a violation of Article 3 in relation to the whole life orders imposed on the applicants because, given the lack of clarity in domestic law concerning the existence of an Article 3-compliant review mechanism, it appeared that the sentences were irreducible. Following the *Vinter and Others* judgment, a special composition of the Court of Appeal was constituted, including the Lord Chief Justice of England and Wales, the President of the Queen's Bench Division, the Vice-President of the Court of Appeal Criminal Division, one other Lord Justice of Appeal and a senior High Court judge, to consider three appeals by defendants on whom whole life orders had been imposed and a reference by the Attorney General in a case where it was contended that the trial judge had been mistaken in his view that the judgment in *Vinter* precluded the imposition of a whole life order. The Court of Appeal's judgment in this case, *R v. Newell; R v. McLoughlin* [2014] EWCA Crim 188 was delivered on 18 February 2014. On the question whether whole life orders were reducible and thus compliant with Article 3, the Court of Appeal held:

25. The questions therefore arise as to whether the provisions of s. 30 provide such a regime compatible with Article 3 as interpreted by the Grand Chamber and on the assumption that, discharging our duty under s. 2 of the Human Rights Act to take into account the decision of the Strasbourg Court, we should adopt that interpretation.

26. Lord Phillips CJ in giving the judgment of this court in *R v. Bieber* concluded that the regime was compatible and a whole life order was reducible, because of the power of the Secretary of State under s. 30 of the 1997 Act. He said at paragraph 48:

At present it is the practice of the Secretary of State to use this power sparingly, in circumstances where, for instance, a prisoner is suffering from a terminal illness or is bedridden or similarly incapacitated. If, however, the position is reached where the continued imprisonment of a prisoner is held to amount to inhuman or degrading treatment, we can see no reason why, having particular regard to the requirement to comply with the Convention, the Secretary of State should not use his statutory power to release the prisoner.

In *R v. Oakes*, this was reaffirmed in the judgment of this court—see paragraph 15.

27. The Grand Chamber, whilst accepting that the interpretation of s. 30 of the 1997 Act as set out in *R v. Bieber* would in principle be consistent with the decision in *Kafkaris*, was concerned that the law might be insufficiently certain. It added at paragraphs 126-7:

The fact remains that, despite the Court of Appeal's judgment in *Bieber*, the Secretary of State has not altered the terms of his explicitly stated and restrictive policy on when he will exercise his s. 30 power. Notwithstanding the reading given to s. 30 by the Court of Appeal, the Prison Service Order remains in force and provides that release will only be ordered in certain exhaustively listed, and not merely illustrative, circumstances, …

These are highly restrictive conditions. Even assuming that they could be met by a prisoner serving a whole life order, the Court considers that the Chamber was correct to doubt whether compassionate release for the terminally ill or physically incapacitated could really be considered release at all, if all it meant was that a prisoner died at home or in a hospice rather than behind prison walls. Indeed, in the Court's view, compassionate release of this kind was not what was meant by a "prospect of release" in *Kafkaris*, cited above. As such, the terms of the Order in themselves would be inconsistent with *Kafkaris* and would not therefore be sufficient for the purposes of Article 3.

28. The Grand Chamber therefore concluded that s. 30 did not, because of the lack of certainty, provide an appropriate and adequate avenue of redress in the event an offender sought to show that his continued imprisonment was not justified. It concluded at paragraph 129:

At the present time, it is unclear whether, in considering such an application for release under s. 30 by a whole life prisoner, the Secretary of State would apply his existing, restrictive policy, as set out in the Prison Service Order, or would go beyond the apparently exhaustive terms of that Order by applying the Article 3 test set out in *Bieber*. Of course, any ministerial refusal to release would be amenable to judicial review and it could well be that, in the course of such proceedings, the legal position would come to be clarified, for example by the withdrawal and replacement of the Prison Service Order by the Secretary of State or its quashing by the courts. However, such possibilities are not sufficient to remedy the lack of clarity that exists at present as to the state of the applicable domestic law governing possible exceptional release of whole life prisoners.

29. We disagree. In our view, the domestic law of England and Wales is clear as to "possible exceptional release of whole life prisoners". As is set out in *R* v. *Bieber* the Secretary of State is bound to exercise his power under s. 30 of the 1997 Act in a manner compatible with principles of domestic administrative law and with Article 3.

30. As we understand the Grand Chamber's view, it might have been thought that the fact that policy set out in the Lifer Manual has not been revised is of real consequence. However, as a matter of law, it is, in our view, of no consequence. It is important, therefore, that we make clear what the law of England and Wales is.

31. First, the power of review under the section arises if there are exceptional circumstances. The offender subject to the whole life order is therefore required to demonstrate to the Secretary of State that although the whole life

order was just punishment at the time the order was made, exceptional circumstances have since arisen. It is not necessary to specify what such circumstances are or specify criteria; the term "exceptional circumstances" is of itself sufficiently certain.

32. Second, the Secretary of State must then consider whether such exceptional circumstances justify the release on compassionate grounds. The policy set out in the Lifer Manual is highly restrictive and purports to circumscribe the matters which will be considered by the Secretary of State. The Manual cannot restrict the duty of the Secretary of State to consider all circumstances relevant to release on compassionate grounds. He cannot fetter his discretion by taking into account only the matters set out in the Lifer Manual. In the passages in *Hindley* to which we have referred at paragraph 7 the duty of the Secretary of State was made clear; similarly the provisions of s. 30 of the 1997 Act require the Secretary of State to take into account all exceptional circumstances relevant to the release of the prisoner on compassionate grounds.

33. Third, the term "compassionate grounds" must be read, as the court made clear in *R* v. *Bieber*, in a manner compatible with Article 3. They are not restricted to what is set out in the Lifer Manual. It is a term with a wide meaning that can be elucidated, as is the way the common law develops, on a case by case basis.

34. Fourth, the decision of the Secretary of State must be reasoned by reference to the circumstances of each case and is subject to scrutiny by way of judicial review.

35. In our judgment the law of England and Wales therefore does provide to an offender "hope" or the "possibility" of release in exceptional circumstances which render the just punishment originally imposed no longer justifiable.

36. It is entirely consistent with the rule of law that such requests are considered on an individual basis against the criteria that circumstances have exceptionally changed so as to render the original punishment which was justifiable no longer justifiable. We find it difficult to specify in advance what such circumstances might be, given that the heinous nature of the original crime justly required punishment by imprisonment for life. But circumstances can and do change in exceptional cases. The interpretation of s. 30 we have set out provides for that possibility and hence gives to each such prisoner the possibility of exceptional release.

Conclusion

37. Judges should therefore continue to apply the statutory scheme in the [Criminal Justice Act] 2003 and in exceptional cases, likely to be rare, impose whole life orders in accordance with Schedule 21. Although we were told by [counsel for the Secretary of State] that it might be many years before the applications might be made under s. 30 and the three applicants in *Vinter* (Vinter, Bamber and Moore) did not seek to contend that there were no longer penological grounds for their continued detention, we would observe that we would not discount the possibility of such applications arising very much sooner. They will be determined in accordance with the legal principles we have set out.

THE LAW

I. Alleged violation of Article 3 of the Convention

14. The applicant complained that his whole life order violated Article 3 of the Convention, which reads as follows:

No one shall be subjected to torture or to inhuman or degrading treatment or punishment.

A. Admissibility

15. The Court notes that this complaint is not manifestly ill-founded within the meaning of Article 35 § 3(a) of the Convention. It further notes that it is not inadmissible on any other grounds. It must therefore be declared admissible.

B. Merits

1. The parties' arguments

16. The applicant submitted that his case was indistinguishable from *Vinter and Others*, cited above. The clarification offered by the Court of Appeal in *R v. Newell; R v. McLoughlin* was in substance identical to that set out in the earlier Court of Appeal judgments in *R v. Bieber* and *R v. Oakes*, which were considered by the Grand Chamber in *Vinter and Others* before it came to a finding of violation. Moreover, the applicant argued that the Convention was a living instrument and that there was a rapidly developing international consensus that the review of whole life orders required a judicial or quasi-judicial decision, rather than the decision of a Government Minister. The views expressed by the Secretary of State for Justice on the subject of whole life orders demonstrated that there was no realistic prospect of a fair, balanced and certain system under political control, and judicial review was no remedy for this, since it provided a review of process and not of substance. The reviewing court could examine whether the Secretary of State's decision was taken on improper grounds or was so unreasonable that no reasonable politician could have made it, but it was not open to the court to impose its own solution. In conclusion, in the applicant's submission, a mechanism "pieced together" from an executive discretion, a statutory provision limited to compassionate grounds and supervised at a distance by judicial review was too uncertain, lacked clarity and offered too vague a hope of release to pass the standard set out in *Vinter and Others*.

17. Prior to the delivery of the Court of Appeal's judgment in *R v. Newell; R v. McLoughlin*, the Government recognised that the principles set out by the Grand Chamber in *Vinter and Others* (cited above) "would appear on their face to apply to this case" and that they did not, therefore, consider themselves in a position to submit observations on the merits. However, after the delivery of the Court of Appeal's judgment the Government indicated that they wished to submit observations. They underlined that the judgment in *R v. Newell; R v. McLoughlin* was now the binding and authoritative statement of the law in England and Wales. In that judgment the Court of Appeal set out the operation of domestic law, finding that the Secretary of State's power to release under section 30 of the 2003 Act functioned in precisely the way which the Grand Chamber held was in principle sufficient to render a whole life order reducible and this was compatible with Article 3 of the Convention. The Court of Appeal was uniquely well placed to determine this issue and its judgment had put to rest any suggestion that domestic law was in any relevant respect unclear.

2. *The Court's assessment*

a. General principles relating to the need for a review mechanism in respect of whole life sentences

18. It is well established in the Court's case-law that a State's choice of a specific criminal justice system, including sentence review and release arrangements, is in principle outside the scope of the supervision the Court carries out at the European level, provided that the system does not contravene the principles set forth in the Convention. Contracting States must remain free to impose life sentences on adult offenders for especially serious crimes such as murder: the imposition of such a sentence on an adult offender is not in itself prohibited by or incompatible with Article 3 or any other Article of the Convention. This is particularly so when such a sentence is not mandatory but is imposed by an independent judge after he or she has considered all of the mitigating and aggravating factors which are present in any given case (see *Vinter and Others*, cited above, §§ 104-6).

19. However, if the life sentence is as a matter of law or practice irreducible, this may raise an issue under Article 3 (see *Kafkaris v. Cyprus* [GC], No 21906/04, § 97, ECHR 2008). In *Vinter and Others*, cited above, the Grand Chamber reviewed in detail the relevant considerations flowing from the Court's case-law and from recent comparative and international-law trends in respect of life sentences (ibid., §§ 104-18; see also *Öcalan v. Turkey (No 2)*, Nos 24069/03, 197/04,

6201/06 and 10464/07, §§ 193-8, 18 March 2014; *László Magyar* v. *Hungary*, No 73593/10, §§ 46-53, 20 May 2014; *Harakchiev and Tolumov* v. *Bulgaria*, Nos 15018/11 and 61199/12, §§ 245-6, ECHR 2014 (extracts)). On that basis, because a prisoner could not be detained unless there were legitimate penological grounds for incarceration, it held that a life sentence could remain compatible with Article 3 of the Convention only if there was both a prospect of release and a possibility of review (ibid., §§ 109-10). The Court noted in particular that the balance between the justifications for incarceration, such as punishment, deterrence, public protection and rehabilitation, could shift in the course of the sentence and it was only by carrying out a review of the justification for continued detention at an appropriate point in the sentence that those factors or shifts could properly be evaluated. If a prisoner was incarcerated without any prospect of release and without the possibility of having his life sentence reviewed, there was the risk that he could never atone for his offence and that whatever he did in prison, however exceptional his progress towards rehabilitation, his punishment would remain fixed (ibid., §§ 111-12). The Court therefore held that it would be incompatible with human dignity—which lay at the very essence of the Convention system—forcefully to deprive a person of his freedom without striving towards his rehabilitation and providing him with the chance someday to regain that freedom (ibid., § 113). It went on to note that there was now clear support in European and international law for the principle that all prisoners, including those serving life sentences, be offered the possibility of rehabilitation and the prospect of release if that rehabilitation was achieved (ibid., § 114). While punishment remained one of the aims of imprisonment, the emphasis in European penal policy, as expressed in Rules 6, 102.1 and 103.8 of the European Prison Rules, Resolution 76(2) and Recommendations 2003(23) and 2003(22) of the Committee of Ministers, statements by the Committee for the Prevention of Torture, and the practice of a number of Contracting States, and in international law, as expressed, *inter alia*, in Article 10 § 3 of the International Covenant on Civil and Political Rights and the General Comment on that Article, was now on the rehabilitative aim of imprisonment, even in the case of life prisoners (ibid., §§ 115-18).

20. Based on that analysis, the Grand Chamber established the following propositions in relation to life sentences:

(a) In the context of a life sentence, Article 3 of the Convention must be interpreted as requiring reducibility of the sentence, in the sense of a review which allows the domestic authorities to consider whether any changes in the life prisoner are so significant, and such progress towards rehabilitation has been made in the course of the sentence, as to mean that continued detention can no longer be justified on legitimate penological grounds (ibid., § 119);

(b) Having regard to the margin of appreciation which must be accorded to Contracting States in the matters of criminal justice and sentencing, it is not the Court's task to prescribe the form— executive or judicial—which that review should take, or to determine when that review should take place. However, the comparative and international law materials show clear support for the institution of a dedicated mechanism guaranteeing a review no later than twenty-five years after the imposition of a life sentence, with further periodic reviews thereafter (ibid., § 120);

(c) Where domestic law does not provide for the possibility of such a review, a whole life sentence will not comply with Article 3 (ibid., § 121);

(d) Although the requisite review is a prospective event necessarily subsequent to the passing of the sentence, a whole life prisoner should not be obliged to wait and serve an indeterminate number of years of his sentence before he can raise the complaint that the legal conditions attaching to his sentence fail to comply with the requirements of Article 3 in this regard, since this would be contrary both to legal certainty and to the general principles on victim status within the meaning of that term in Article 34 of the Convention. Furthermore, in cases where the sentence, on imposition, is irreducible under domestic law, it would be capricious to expect the prisoner to work towards his own rehabilitation without knowing whether, at an unspecified, future date, a mechanism might be introduced which would allow him, on the basis of that rehabilitation, to be considered for release. A whole life prisoner is entitled to know, at the outset of his sentence, what he must do to be considered for release and under what conditions, including when a review of his sentence will take place or may be sought. Consequently, where domestic law does not provide any mechanism or possibility for review of a whole life sentence, the incompatibility with Article 3 of the Convention on this ground already arises at the moment of the imposition of the whole life sentence and not at a later stage of incarceration (ibid., § 122).

21. It must be emphasised, however, that the fact that in practice a life sentence may be served in full does not make it irreducible. No Article 3 issue could arise if a life prisoner had the right under domestic law to be

considered for release but this was refused, for example, on the ground that he or she continued to pose a danger to society (ibid., § 108).

b. Whether the review mechanism available to the applicant is sufficient to comply with the requirements of Article 3

22. The dispute between the parties in the present case centres on whether the Secretary of State's discretion to release a whole life prisoner under section 30 of the 2003 Act (see paragraph 10 above) is sufficient to make the whole life sentence imposed on the applicant legally and effectively reducible. In *Vinter and Others*, cited above, the Court held that, if section 30 were to be interpreted, in the light of section 6(1) of the Human Rights Act, as imposing a duty on the Secretary of State to exercise his power of release if it could be shown that the prisoner's continued detention was no longer justified on penological grounds, as the Court of Appeal had held it should be in *R* v. *Bieber* and *R* v. *Oakes* (see paragraph 12 above), this would, in principle, be consistent with the requirements of Article 3 of the Convention (ibid., § 125). However, the Court considered that there was a lack of clarity in the law (ibid., §§ 125 and 126). In particular, it held that the fact that, despite the two Court of Appeal judgments, the Secretary of State had not amended chapter 12 of the Lifer Manual (see paragraph 10 above), which provided that release would be ordered only if the prisoner were terminally ill or physically incapacitated, gave rise to uncertainty as to whether the section 30 power would be exercised in a manner compliant with Article 3. In addition, the fact that the Lifer Manual had not been amended meant that prisoners subject to whole life orders derived from it only a partial picture of the exceptional conditions capable of leading to the exercise of the Secretary of State's power under section 30 (ibid., § 128).

23. However, subsequent to the Court's consideration of section 30 in *Vinter and Others* (cited above) the Court of Appeal delivered a judgment in which it expressly responded to the concerns detailed in *Vinter and Others* (*R* v. *Newell*; *R* v. *McLoughlin*: see paragraph 13 above). In *R* v. *Newell*; *R* v. *McLoughlin* the Court of Appeal held that it was of no consequence that the Lifer Manual had not been revised, since it was clearly established in domestic law that the Secretary of State was bound to exercise his power under section 30 in a manner compatible with Article 3. If an offender subject to a whole life order could establish that "exceptional circumstances" had arisen subsequent to the imposition of the sentence, the Secretary of State had to consider whether such exceptional circumstances justified release on compassionate grounds. Regardless of the policy set out in the Lifer Manual,

the Secretary of State had to consider all the relevant circumstances, in a manner compatible with Article 3. Any decision by the Secretary of State would have to be reasoned by reference to the circumstances of each case and would be subject to judicial review, which would serve to elucidate the meaning of the terms "exceptional circumstances" and "compassionate grounds", as was the usual process under the common law. In the judgment of the Court of Appeal, domestic law therefore did provide to an offender sentenced to a whole life order hope and the possibility of release in the event of exceptional circumstances which meant that the punishment was no longer justified.

24. The Court recalls that it is primarily for the national authorities, notably the courts, to resolve problems of interpretation of domestic legislation (see, amongst many other authorities, *Vučković and Others* v. *Serbia* [GC], No 17153/11, § 80, 25 March 2014; *Söderman* v. *Sweden* [GC], No 5786/08, § 102, ECHR 2013; and *Waite and Kennedy* v. *Germany* [GC], No 26083/94, § 54, ECHR 1999-I). Moreover, the Court recalls that in the United Kingdom, as in the other Convention States, the progressive development of the law through judicial interpretation is a well-entrenched and necessary part of legal tradition (see, *mutatis mutandis*, *CR* v. *United Kingdom*, 22 November 1995, § 34, Series A No 335-C).

25. In the circumstances of this case where, following the Grand Chamber's judgment in which it expressed doubts about the clarity of domestic law, the national court has specifically addressed those doubts and set out an unequivocal statement of the legal position, the Court must accept the national court's interpretation of domestic law (see, *mutatis mutandis*, *Cooper* v. *United Kingdom* [GC], No 48843/99, § 125, ECHR 2003-XII). Further, as the Grand Chamber observed in *Vinter and Others*, the power to release under section 30 of the 2003 Act, exercised in the manner delineated in the Court of Appeal's judgments in *Bieber* and *Oakes*, and now *R* v. *Newell; R* v. *McLoughlin*, is sufficient to comply with the requirements of Article 3 (and compare, also, the review mechanisms accepted by the Court to be Article 3-compliant in *Kafkaris*, cited above, §§ 100-5 [and] *Harakchiev and Tolumov*, cited above, §§ 257-61).

26. In conclusion, there has been no violation of Article 3 in the present case.

For these reasons, the Court

1. *Declares* by a majority, the complaint concerning Article 3 of the Convention admissible;

2. *Holds* by six votes to one that there has been no violation of Article 3 of the Convention.

In accordance with Article 45 § 2 of the Convention and Rule 74 § 2 of the Rules of Court, the separate opinion of Judge Kalaydjieva is annexed to this judgment.

DISSENTING OPINION OF JUDGE KALAYDJIEVA[7]

[1] I voted against the conclusion of the majority that the applicant's complaints are admissible in so far as they concern the compatibility of whole life sentences as such with Article 3 of the Convention. To the extent that these complaints concern the availability of *de jure* and *de facto* possibilities for release, their admissibility might be questionable in so far as it is unclear whether the applicant ever availed himself of the opportunity to apply to the Secretary of State for Justice in order to test the manner in which the latter would exercise his power to assess whether any exceptional circumstances justified the applicant's release. The applicant was entitled to do so at any time after 16 May 2008, when Tugendhat J found it "right that the applicant should remain in prison for the rest of his life by way of punishment" and ordered "that the early release provisions are not to apply to [him]".

[2] It should be noted that Mr Hutchinson's application (No 57592/08) was registered (one and two years respectively) earlier than those in the cases of *Vinter and Others* (Nos 66069/09, 130/10 and 3896/10) which were examined by the Grand Chamber of this Court in 2013. To the extent that the majority in the present case considered the applicant's complaints admissible and identical to the ones in *Vinter*, I find no reasons to disagree with the observation of the respondent Government of 14 January 2014 that "the principles of the judgment of the Grand Chamber in this case appear on their face to apply to this case" as well.

[3] The reasoning of the majority in the present case is based on the premise that the Grand Chamber erred in its understanding of the domestic law as expressed in the case of *Vinter and Others* in 2013, and also on the fact that, since "it is primarily for the national authorities, notably the courts, to resolve problems of interpretation of domestic legislation" (see paragraph 24 of the judgment), they were prepared to accept that the correct interpretation of the domestic law was provided in the post-*Vinter* judgment delivered by the special composition of the

[7 Paragraph numbers have been editorially inserted in this opinion.]

Court of Appeal on 18 February 2014 in the case of *R* v. *Newell; R* v. *McLoughlin* [2014] EWCA Crim 188. In that judgment, the Court of Appeal disagreed with the Grand Chamber's views on the clarity and certainty of the domestic law as first set out in *R* v. *Bieber* [2009], and reaffirmed that this interpretation was sufficiently clear and certain. Assuming that this is so, I fail to see the bearing of this progressive development of the law on the applicant's situation a year earlier, in 2008, when his complaints were submitted to the Court, or at the time of their examination by the Court in 2015.

[4] Unlike in the unanimous judgment of the same Section in the case of *Harakchiev and Tolumov* v. *Bulgaria* (Nos 15018/11 and 61199/12, ECHR 2014), the majority in the present case failed to express any view as to whether, how and at what point the interpretation of the domestic law established in *Bieber* [2009] and *R* v. *Newell; R* v. *McLoughlin* [2014] changed, ceased to apply or made the applicant's situation more compatible with the principles laid down by the Grand Chamber in examining the situation of the applicants in *Vinter*.

[5] The issue in the case of Mr Hutchinson is not whether the Court (see paragraph 25) "must accept the national court's interpretation of the domestic law" as clarified in the process of "progressive development of the law through [the] judicial interpretation" (paragraph 24) provided by the Court of Appeal after *Vinter* as being the correct one, but whether or not in 2008 the applicant was in fact "entitled to know, at the outset of his sentence, what he must do to be considered for release and under what conditions, including when a review of his sentence will take place or may be sought" as required by the principles established in *Vinter* (§ 122). These principles were not in themselves contested either by the 2014 judgment of the Court of Appeal or by the representative of the respondent Government in the present case.

[6] I do not deem myself competent to determine whether the Court of Appeal expressed an *ex tunc* trust or an *ex nunc* hope that, even though to date the Secretary of State for Justice has not amended the content of the Lifers Manual after *Vinter*, he was, is and always will be "bound to exercise his power ... in a manner compatible with Article 3" (see paragraph 23). I have no doubt that the Grand Chamber was informed as to the scope of his discretion and the manner of its exercise in reaching their conclusions in *Vinter*. In this regard, and in so far as the Court of Appeal's part in the admirable post-*Vinter* judicial dialogue said "Repent!", I wonder whom it meant?

[Reports: 38 BHRC 67; (2015) 61 EHRR 13]

Human rights — Elections — Electoral rights — Right to vote — Right to stand in parliamentary elections — Applicant's complaints under Article 3 of Protocol No 1 to European Convention on Human Rights, 1950 — Whether admissible — Whether complaint under Article 3 of Protocol No 1 admissible in so far as it concerned applicant's removal from office or his ineligibility to stand for election as President of Lithuania — Whether complaint under Article 3 of Protocol No 1 admissible in so far as it concerned applicant's inability to stand for election to Seimas — Whether Article 3 of Protocol No 1 applicable to election of members of Seimas — Whether failure to exhaust domestic remedies — Whether compliant with six-month time limit — Whether Article 17 of European Convention applicable — Examination on merits — Importance of Article 3 of Protocol No 1 in Convention system — Fundamental principle of effective democracy — Right to vote — Right to stand for election — Whether absolute rights — Margin of appreciation of States — Whether restrictions on electoral rights impairing essence of right or its effectiveness — Whether restrictions pursuing legitimate aim — Whether proportionate — Whether Lithuania violating Article 3 of Protocol No 1 on account of applicant's inability to stand for election to Seimas

Human rights — Fair hearing — Applicant's complaints under Articles 6 and 7 of European Convention on Human Rights, 1950 and Article 4 of Protocol No 7 — Whether admissible — Whether Article 6(1) of European Convention applicable in either its civil or criminal aspect to Lithuanian Constitutional Court proceedings in issue — Whether this part of application compatible *ratione materiae* with Convention provisions

Human rights — Remedy — Applicant's complaint under Article 13 of European Convention on Human Rights, 1950, taken in conjunction with Article 3 of Protocol No 1 — Whether admissible — Whether Article 13 of European Convention requiring provision of a remedy allowing constitutional precedent with statutory force to be challenged — Damage — Just satisfaction — Article 41 of European Convention

PAKSAS v. LITHUANIA[1]

(Application No 34932/04)

European Court of Human Rights (Grand Chamber). 6 *January* 2011

(Costa, *President*; Rozakis, Bratza, Lorenzen, Tulkens, Casadevall, Cabral Barreto, Garlicki, Spielmann, Jaeger, Myjer, Jebens, Björgvinsson, Popović and Tsotsoria, *Judges*; Baka, *Judge ad hoc*)

SUMMARY:[2] *The facts*:—The applicant, Mr Paksas, was a Member of the European Parliament who had been elected President of the Republic of Lithuania on 5 January 2003. He took office on 26 February 2003 following his inauguration, at which he took an oath to be loyal to the Republic and the Constitution of Lithuania, to fulfil the duties of his office conscientiously and to be equally just to all in accordance with Article 82 of the Constitution.[3]

On 11 April 2003, the applicant issued Decree No 40 ("the Decree") granting Lithuanian citizenship "by way of exception" to a Russian businessman, JB, who had received from a previous President a medal for services to Lithuania of which he had subsequently been divested. The Lithuanian Parliament ("the Seimas") requested that the Constitutional Court determine the lawfulness of the Decree and also instituted impeachment proceedings against the applicant. On 30 December 2003, the Constitutional Court held that the Decree did not comply with the Constitution or with the Citizenship Act. On 31 March 2004, the Constitutional Court found that the applicant had committed gross violations of the Constitution and breached his constitutional oath. On 6 April 2004, the Seimas removed the applicant from office as President for gross violations of the Constitution as established by the Constitutional Court.

On 4 May 2004, the Seimas amended the Presidential Elections Act[4] so as to prevent the election to the Presidency of a person who had been removed from parliamentary or other office by the Seimas in impeachment proceedings if less than five years had elapsed since his removal. Wishing to stand for the presidential election called for 13 June 2004, the applicant challenged the refusal to register his candidacy following the statutory amendment. Following a request by the Seimas to review the constitutionality of the amendment, the Constitutional Court held on 25 May 2004 that such a disqualification was compatible with the Constitution although the time limit was not. The Court held that a person who had been removed from the office of President for a

---

[1] The names of the parties' representatives appear at paras. 2 and 8 of the judgment. For related proceedings, see 165 ILR 303.
[2] Prepared by Ms Karen Lee, Co-Editor.
[3] For the text of Article 82 of the Constitution, see para. 54 of the judgment.
[4] For the text of the amendment to the Presidential Elections Act, see para. 31 of the judgment.

gross violation of the Constitution or a breach of the oath could never again be elected President, a Member of the Seimas or hold an office for which it was necessary to take an oath in accordance with the Constitution.[5] On 15 July 2004, the Seimas amended the Seimas Elections Act so that any official removed from office following impeachment proceedings was disqualified from being a Member of Parliament.

The applicant lodged an application, later supplemented, against Lithuania, alleging violations of Articles 6(1),[6] (2) and (3) and 7 of the European Convention on Human Rights, 1950 ("the Convention") and Article 4 of Protocol No 7.[7] He complained that he had not received a fair hearing with respect to the Constitutional Court proceedings concerning the Decree and the merits of the impeachment charges against him. He also alleged a violation of Article 3 of Protocol No 1,[8] claiming that permanent disqualification from elected office was contrary to the essence of free elections and disproportionate. In addition, he claimed that Lithuania had violated Article 13 of the Convention,[9] taken in conjunction with Article 3 of Protocol No 1, since no effective remedy was available in respect of the Constitutional Court's ruling of 25 May 2004. The Lithuanian Government contested the applicant's submissions, pleading a failure to exhaust domestic remedies with regard to his complaint under Article 3 of Protocol No 1. The Court decided to examine the admissibility and merits of the application at the same time.

Held (by fourteen votes to three):—There had been a violation of Article 3 of Protocol No 1 on account of the applicant's inability to stand for election to the Seimas.

(1) (unanimously) The complaints under Articles 6 and 7 of the Convention and Article 4 of Protocol No 7 were inadmissible. This part of the application was therefore incompatible *ratione materiae* with Convention provisions and had to be rejected.

(a) Article 6(1) of the Convention was not applicable in either its civil or its criminal aspect to the Constitutional Court proceedings in issue. Neither of the two sets of proceedings concerned the determination of the applicant's

---

[5] The Constitutional Court held that a person who had been removed from the office of President for a gross violation of the Constitution or a breach of the oath could never again be elected President, a member of the Seimas or hold an office for which it was necessary to take an oath in accordance with the Constitution. For excerpts of this Constitutional Court judgment, see para. 34 of the judgment.

[6] Article 6(1) of the Convention provided: "In the determination of his civil rights and obligations or of any criminal charge against him, everyone is entitled to a fair ... hearing ... by an independent and impartial tribunal established by law ..."

[7] For the text of Articles 6 and 7 of the Convention and Article 4 of Protocol No 7, see para. 63 of the judgment.

[8] Article 3 of Protocol No 1 provided: "The High Contracting Parties undertake to hold free elections at reasonable intervals by secret ballot, under conditions which will ensure the free expression of the opinion of the people in the choice of the legislature."

[9] For the text of Article 13 of the Convention, see para. 113 of the judgment.

civil rights or obligations. Neither did they concern a criminal charge as there had been no imposition of a sanction against the applicant. Although the second set of proceedings before the Constitutional Court formed a stage of the impeachment proceedings instituted by the Seimas, removal from office and disqualification from standing for election involved the head of State's constitutional liability and thus lay outside the criminal sphere. In any event, the decision to remove the President from office was taken by Parliament rather than the Constitutional Court (paras. 63-7).

(b) Since it followed that the applicant was not "charged with a criminal offence" within the meaning of Article 6(2) of the Convention in those proceedings, or "convicted" or "tried or punished ... in criminal proceedings" within the meaning of Article 4(1) of Protocol No 7, and that the proceedings did not result in his being held "guilty of a criminal offence" or receiving a "penalty" within the meaning of Article 7 of the Convention, those provisions also did not apply (paras. 68-9).

(2) (unanimously) The complaint under Article 3 of Protocol No 1 in so far as it concerned the applicant's removal from office or his ineligibility to stand for election as President of Lithuania was inadmissible. Since Article 3 of Protocol No 1 applied only to the election of the "legislature", this part of the application was incompatible *ratione materiae* with Convention provisions and had to be rejected (paras. 71-2).

(3) (by a majority) The complaint under Article 3 of Protocol No 1 in so far as it concerned the applicant's inability to stand for election to the Seimas was admissible.

(a) Given Lithuania's constitutional structure, Article 3 of Protocol No 1 was applicable to the election of Members of the Seimas (the "legislature") (paras. 71-2).

(b) There had been no failure to exhaust domestic remedies since the Lithuanian Government had not shown that a domestic remedy satisfying the requirements of Article 35(1) of the Convention was available to the applicant. Remedies had to be effective and accessible; only remedies that related to the breaches alleged, and which were available and sufficient, had to be exhausted. An appeal against a refusal to register the applicant as a candidate for election to the Seimas would have failed given that the Constitutional Court's ruling of 25 May 2004 prohibiting such an election was final according to Article 107 of the Lithuanian Constitution and that the Constitutional Court was bound by its own precedents (paras. 73-8).

(c) Since the applicant was complaining of this ruling, which gave rise to a continuing state of affairs for which there was no remedy, it was not out of time with respect to the six-month time limit (paras. 79-84).

(d) Article 17 of the Convention, which was applicable only in exceptional cases and was designed to prevent groups from exploiting the Convention principles in pursuit of totalitarian aims, could not apply as the applicant was seeking to regain full enjoyment of a Convention right secured to everyone and there was no indication that he was seeking to pursue totalitarian aims (paras. 85-9).

(e) The complex issues of fact and law required examination on the merits. This part of the application was not manifestly ill-founded within the meaning of Article 35(3)(a) of the Convention and no other ground for inadmissibility had been established (para. 90).

(4) (by fourteen votes to three) There had been a violation of Article 3 of Protocol No 1 on account of the applicant's inability to stand for election to the Seimas.

(a) Article 3 of Protocol No 1, which was of prime importance in the Convention system as it enshrined a fundamental principle of an effective democracy, implied the subjective rights to vote and to stand for election. Although important, those rights were not absolute. The margin of appreciation was wide given the different ways of running electoral systems and moulding democracies, and differences in historical development, cultural diversity and political thought within Europe (para. 96).

(b) Any electoral legislation or system had to be assessed in light of a country's political evolution. Contracting States could establish their own criteria for eligibility to stand for election. While the margin was wide, it was not all-embracing. The Court determined compliance with Article 3 of Protocol No 1 in the last resort. Restrictions could not impair the essence of the right or its effectiveness. They had to pursue a legitimate aim, which had to be compatible with the principle of the rule of law and the general objectives of the Convention, and employ means that were not disproportionate. Restrictions could not thwart "the free expression of the opinion of the people in the choice of the legislature" (para. 96).

(c) There had been an interference with the applicant's right to stand for election since he could not run as a parliamentary candidate following the Constitutional Court's ruling of 25 May 2004 and Act of 15 July 2004. The interference was lawful; the principle that a person removed from office as President following impeachment proceedings was no longer entitled to stand for election to the Seimas was clear from that ruling and Act, which were lawful. Since the prohibition imposed on the applicant was intended to preserve the democratic order, it constituted a legitimate aim for the purposes of Article 3 of Protocol No 1 (paras. 97-100).

(d) Article 3 of Protocol No 1 did not exclude the possibility of imposing restrictions on the electoral rights of a person, such as the applicant, who had seriously abused a public position or whose conduct had threatened to undermine the rule of law or democratic foundations. However, the applicant's permanent and irreversible disqualification from standing for election as a result of a general provision did not constitute a proportionate response to the requirements of preserving the democratic order. Free expression of the opinion of the people in the choice of legislature had to be ensured in all cases. The restriction was not subject to any time limit and there was no possibility of review. That the restriction was disproportionate was reinforced by the rapid amendment to the Seimas Elections Act, which barred anyone removed from office following impeachment proceedings from becoming a Member of Parliament (paras. 101-12).

(5) (unanimously) The complaint under Article 13 of the Convention, taken in conjunction with Article 3 of Protocol No 1, was inadmissible. This part of the application was manifestly ill-founded. Although the applicant's claim was arguable, Article 13 could not require the provision of a remedy allowing a constitutional precedent with statutory force to be challenged. The applicant's disqualification derived from the application of the rule laid down by the Constitutional Court rather than from an individual decision against him (paras. 113-15).

(6) (unanimously) The finding of a violation constituted in itself sufficient just satisfaction for the non-pecuniary damage sustained by the applicant. The remainder of the claim for just satisfaction was dismissed (paras. 116-22).

Partly Dissenting Opinion of Judge Costa joined by Judges Tsotsoria and Baka: The case was both political and unusual since impeachment proceedings were rare in Europe. While the majority was correct to dismiss several complaints as incompatible *ratione materiae* with the Convention and its Protocols, it was wrong to hold that the complaint under Article 3 of Protocol No 1 in so far as it concerned the applicant's inability to stand for election to the Seimas was admissible and well-founded. Although no judicial remedy was available, the application was out of time. The majority's continuing situation argument was artificial; time limits were to be taken seriously. Had the complaint been submitted in time, it was probably ill-founded. The State should have been allowed to exercise its wide discretion; the allegations against the applicant were serious and the case was complex (paras. 1-12).

The following is the text of the judgment of the Court:

PROCEDURE

1. The case originated in an application (No 34932/04) against the Republic of Lithuania lodged with the Court under Article 34 of the Convention for the Protection of Human Rights and Fundamental Freedoms ("the Convention") by a Lithuanian national, Mr Rolandas Paksas ("the applicant"), on 27 September 2004.

2. The applicant was represented by Mr E. Salpius, a lawyer practising in Salzburg, Mr V. Sviderskis, a lawyer practising in Vilnius, Mr F. Matscher, professor of law at the University of Salzburg, and Mr S. Tomas, researcher at the University of Paris-Sorbonne. The Lithuanian Government ("the Government") were represented by their Agent, Ms E. Baltutytė.

3. The application was allocated to the former Third Section of the Court and subsequently to the Second Section (Rule 52 § 1 of the Rules of Court).

4. Danutė Jočienė, the judge elected in respect of Lithuania, withdrew from the case (Rule 28). The Government accordingly appointed András Baka, the judge elected in respect of Hungary, to sit in her place (Article 27 § 2 of the Convention and Rule 29 § 1).

5. On 1 December 2009 a Chamber of the Second Section, composed of the following judges: Françoise Tulkens, Ireneu Cabral Barreto, Vladimiro Zagrebelsky, Dragoljub Popović, Nona Tsotsoria, Işıl Karakaş and András Baka, and also of Sally Dollé, Section Registrar, relinquished jurisdiction in favour of the Grand Chamber, neither of the parties having objected to relinquishment (Article 30 of the Convention and Rule 72).

6. The composition of the Grand Chamber was determined in accordance with Article 27 §§ 2 and 3 of the Convention and Rule 24.

7. The applicant and the Government each filed written observations on the merits.

8. A hearing took place in public in the Human Rights Building, Strasbourg, on 28 April 2010 (Rule 59 § 3).

There appeared before the Court:

(a) *for the Government*

Ms E. BALTUTYTĖ, *Agent*,
Ms K. BUBNYTĖ-MONVYDIENĖ, Head of the Division of Representation at the European Court of Human Rights, *Counsel*,
Mr E. SMITH, Professor, University of Oslo,
Mr D. ZALIMAS, Head of the International and European Union Law Institute, Faculty of Law, Vilnius University, *Advisers*;

(b) *for the applicant*

Mr E. SALPIUS, *Counsel*.

The Court heard addresses by Ms Baltutytė, Mr Smith and Mr Salpius. The applicant was also present at the hearing.

The Court decided to examine the merits of the application at the same time as its admissibility (Article 29 § 3 of the Convention and Rule 54A).

THE FACTS

I. The circumstances of the case

9. The applicant was born in 1956 and lives in Vilnius. He is currently a member of the European Parliament.

10. On 5 January 2003 the applicant was elected President of the Republic of Lithuania. He took office on 26 February 2003, following his inauguration. On that occasion, in accordance with Article 82 of the Constitution, he took an oath to be loyal to the Republic of Lithuania and the Constitution, to fulfil the duties of his office conscientiously, and to be equally just to all.

11. On 11 April 2003 the applicant issued Decree No 40, countersigned by the Minister of the Interior, granting Lithuanian citizenship "by way of exception" (*išimties tvarka*) to a Russian businessman, JB, who had been awarded the Medal of Darius and Girėnas in 2001 by the applicant's predecessor, Valdas Adamkus, for services to Lithuania (he was subsequently divested of the medal following the events outlined below).

A. Proceedings concerning the lawfulness of Presidential Decree No 40

12. On 6 November 2003 the Seimas (the Lithuanian Parliament) requested the Constitutional Court to determine whether Presidential Decree No 40 was in compliance with the Constitution and the Citizenship Act. The Seimas submitted that the procedure of granting citizenship by way of exception appeared to have been applied inappropriately in this case. In particular, it asserted that JB had no special merit warranting his exceptional treatment and that the applicant had in fact granted him citizenship as a reward for his substantial assistance by financial and other means to the applicant's election campaign.

13. On 10 November 2003 the Constitutional Court accepted the request for consideration as Case No 40/03. On 10 December 2003 it held a public hearing and examined witnesses.

14. On 12 December 2003 an article was published in a Lithuanian daily newspaper, *Respublika*, reporting that the President of the Constitutional Court had been seen in a coffee bar with the Deputy Speaker of the Seimas, who had been closely involved in the inquiry into the applicant's activities. The newspaper implied that during this informal meeting the two officials had discussed the proceedings taking place in the Constitutional Court, thus casting a shadow of suspicion over that court's objectivity. The two men had subsequently said that they often met professionally and socially, and denied discussing the merits of the case.

15. Referring to the above-mentioned newspaper article, the applicant's lawyers challenged the President of the Constitutional Court for bias, seeking his removal from the examination of Case No 40/03. Their challenge was dismissed on the ground that the mere fact that

the two officials had met informally did not constitute a basis for the withdrawal of a judge from proceedings before the Constitutional Court.

16. On 30 December 2003 the Constitutional Court gave its ruling in Case No 40/03, finding that Decree No 40 was not in compliance with Article 29 § 1, Article 82 § 1 and Article 84 § 21 of the Constitution, the constitutional principle of the rule of law and section 16(1) of the Citizenship Act.

17. On the last point, the Constitutional Court observed that citizenship could be granted by way of exception only to persons who had never been Lithuanian citizens. It noted in that connection that JB, a Russian citizen by birth from a Soviet military family, had acquired Lithuanian citizenship under the Citizenship Act of 3 November 1989, by which citizenship could be granted, *inter alia*, to persons who on that date had had their permanent residence and permanent place of work or source of income in Lithuania. In 1994 the Constitutional Court had ruled that "soldiers of the Soviet Union who previously served in the Soviet occupying military forces unlawfully stationed in the territory of Lithuania [could] not be regarded as permanently residing and working in Lithuania". On 4 November 1999 the Citizenship Commission (established in 1998 under section 4 of the 1995 Implementing Act for the Citizenship Act) had found that JB's status was unlawful, since he had served in the Soviet armed forces. It had nevertheless recommended that his status be regularised in accordance with the above-mentioned section 4, by which exceptions could be made for persons who had acquired citizenship in good faith before 31 December 1993 on that unlawful ground. On 11 November 1999 the Migration Department of the Ministry of the Interior had followed that recommendation. However, in 2000 JB had applied for Russian citizenship, which he had been granted in June 2002; on 18 March 2003 he had been issued with a Russian passport, thereby losing his Lithuanian citizenship. The Constitutional Court observed that the applicant had signed Decree No 40 on 11 April 2003 even though the Migration Department of the Ministry of the Interior had reminded him the day before that JB had previously lost his Lithuanian citizenship.

18. The Constitutional Court held that, as a result, Decree No 40 was also in breach of Article 84 § 21 of the Constitution—which provides that the President is to grant citizenship in accordance with the procedure established by law—and the constitutional principle of the rule of law.

19. The Constitutional Court went on to note that, although the Lithuanian authorities had already made an exception in his favour by regularising his status in 1999, JB had acquired Russian citizenship in 2000. This showed that "citizenship of the Republic of Lithuania was of less value to [JB] than citizenship of the Russian Federation". The Constitutional Court further noted that the Director of the State Security Department had informed the applicant, prior to 11 April 2003, that an investigation was being carried out into JB's activities as director of an aviation company and, on 17 March 2003, that JB had threatened to disseminate information discrediting the applicant if the latter failed to keep his promise to appoint him as an adviser. In the Constitutional Court's view, the applicant had knowingly ignored these circumstances, although they were of crucial importance in deciding whether or not to grant citizenship to JB by way of exception. Having regard also to the fact that JB had made a significant financial contribution to the applicant's election campaign, it concluded that the decision to grant him citizenship had been "determined not by any merit rendering [JB] worthy of becoming a citizen of the Republic of Lithuania, but by his significant assistance by financial and other means to [the applicant's] election campaign in 2002". Thus, "the granting of citizenship to [JB] by way of exception was nothing but a reward by the President of the Republic R. Paksas to [JB] for the aforesaid support"; consequently, in issuing Decree No 40, the President had heeded "neither the Constitution ... nor the law, nor the interests of the people and the State, but purely his own interests". The court therefore concluded that the applicant had "afforded [JB] exceptional treatment and knowingly disregarded the fundamental principles enshrined in Article 29 § 1 and Article 82 § 1 of the Constitution respectively, whereby all persons are equal before State institutions or officials, and the President of the Republic must be equally just to all".

20. In a public speech on 31 December 2003, and again in his New Year speech, the applicant declared that "politics [had] taken precedence over the law" in the Constitutional Court's ruling. In reply, on 5 January 2004 the Constitutional Court issued a public statement emphasising its independence and noting, *inter alia*, that the applicant had attempted to undermine its authority.

B. Impeachment proceedings

21. On 18 December 2003, eighty-six members of the Seimas submitted a proposal to initiate impeachment proceedings against the applicant. On 23 December 2003 the Seimas set up a special

commission to investigate the reasonableness and seriousness of certain allegations about the applicant's conduct, in order to determine whether such proceedings should indeed be initiated.

22. On 19 February 2004 the special investigation commission concluded that some of the charges levelled against the applicant were founded and serious. Accordingly, it recommended that the Seimas institute impeachment proceedings. The State Security Department had apparently provided the commission with transcripts of secretly taped telephone conversations involving the applicant. The applicant's lawyers were not given access to the transcripts by the Department or by the commission, because it had decided not to rely on them.

23. Also on 19 February 2004 the Seimas decided to follow the special investigation commission's recommendation and requested the Constitutional Court to determine whether the specific acts of the applicant cited by the commission had breached the Constitution. The impeachment charges submitted to the Constitutional Court included the following allegations in particular, involving purely private interests to the detriment of those of the nation, thus discrediting the institution of the presidency:

– that the applicant had undertaken to perform a number of actions in JB's favour in exchange for financial and other forms of support during his election campaign, and had later acted under JB's influence;
– that, as a reward for this support, the applicant had unlawfully granted Lithuanian citizenship to JB;
– that he had disclosed a State secret by informing JB that the secret services were investigating his activities, notably by telephone tapping; and
– that he had exercised undue pressure on the management decisions of a private company in order to secure pecuniary advantages for certain people close to him.

24. On 1 March 2004 the Constitutional Court accepted the request for consideration as Case No 14/04.

25. The applicant's lawyers sought the removal of the President of the Constitutional Court and all its members on grounds of bias, arguing that they had in effect already determined the case in the previous ruling of 30 December 2003 in Case No 40/03. The challenge was dismissed.

26. In a declaration of 25 March 2004 the Seimas unsuccessfully proposed that the applicant tender his resignation in order to avoid

protracted impeachment proceedings. The declaration alleged that his actions had become increasingly unpredictable and represented a danger to the State, its citizens and the prestige of the presidency.

27. On 31 March 2004 the Constitutional Court concluded that the applicant had committed gross violations of the Constitution and a breach of his constitutional oath on account of the following acts:

- unlawfully granting citizenship to JB by Decree No 40 as a reward for the latter's financial and other forms of support, in breach of section 16(1) of the Citizenship Act and Article 29 § 1, Article 82 § 1 and Article 84 § 21 of the Constitution;
- knowingly hinting to JB, in breach of sections 3(7), 9(2) and 14(1) of the Official Secrets Act and Article 77 § 2 and Article 82 § 1 of the Constitution, that the law-enforcement institutions were investigating him and tapping his telephone conversations; and
- exploiting his official status to influence decisions by the Žemaitijos keliai company concerning the transfer of shares with a view to defending the property interests of certain private individuals close to him, in breach of section 3 of the Adjustment of Private and Public Interests in the Public Service Act and Article 29 § 1, Article 77 § 2 and Article 82 § 1 of the Constitution.

28. The applicant sought clarification of these conclusions under section 61 of the Constitutional Court Act, but his request was refused by the Constitutional Court on 6 April 2004 on procedural grounds.

29. On 6 April 2004 the Seimas decided to remove the applicant from the office of President on account of the gross violations of the Constitution found by the Constitutional Court. Its decision was taken by eighty-six votes to seventeen for the first breach, eighty-six votes to eighteen for the second and eighty-nine votes to fourteen for the third.

C. Disqualification from elected office

30. The applicant wished to stand as a candidate in the presidential election called for 13 June 2004. On 22 April 2004 the Central Electoral Committee (CEC) found that there was nothing to prevent him from standing. By 7 May 2004 the applicant had gathered the required number of signatures in support of his candidacy, and submitted them to the CEC with a view to his registration as a candidate.

31. However, on 4 May 2004 the Seimas amended the Presidential Elections Act by inserting the following provision:

A person who has been removed from parliamentary or other office by the Seimas in impeachment proceedings may not be elected President of the Republic if less than five years have elapsed since his removal from office.

32. Following this amendment, the CEC refused to register the applicant as a candidate in the forthcoming election. The applicant lodged a complaint with the Supreme Administrative Court on 10 May 2004, arguing in particular that that decision thwarted the legitimate expectations of his supporters and ran counter to the principles of the rule of law and the prohibition of retrospective legislation.

33. On an unspecified date, a number of members of the Seimas requested the Constitutional Court to review the constitutionality of the amendment to the Presidential Elections Act, arguing that barring a person who had been removed from office from running for election as President was in itself in breach of the Constitution. The request was registered as Case No 24/04.

34. The Constitutional Court held on 25 May 2004 that disqualifying a person who had been removed from office from standing in presidential elections was compatible with the Constitution, but that subjecting such a restriction to a time-limit was unconstitutional. The court held, *inter alia*:

... The Constitutional Court has held that a breach of the oath is, at the same time, a gross violation of the Constitution, while a gross violation of the Constitution is, at the same time, a breach of the oath to the nation (Constitutional Court ruling of 30 December 2003; Constitutional Court conclusion of 31 March 2004) ...

A gross violation of the Constitution or a breach of the oath undermines trust in the institution of the presidency and in State authority as a whole ... Removal from office of a president who has grossly violated the Constitution or breached the oath is one of the ways of protecting the State for the common good of society, as provided for in the Constitution.

It needs to be stressed that, under the Constitution, a person in respect of whom the Seimas—following a finding by the Constitutional Court that he, as President, has committed a gross violation of the Constitution and breached the oath—has applied the constitutional sanction, namely removal from office, may not evade constitutional liability through fresh presidential elections, a referendum or any other means ...

The Constitution does not provide that, after a certain time has elapsed, a president whose actions have been recognised by the Constitutional Court as having grossly violated the Constitution, and who has been found to have breached the oath and has been removed from office by the Seimas [on that account] ... may [subsequently] be treated as though he had not breached the oath or committed a gross violation of the Constitution ... [A person] ... who has been removed from office by the Seimas, the body representing the people, will always remain someone who has breached his oath to the nation and grossly violated the Constitution, and who has been dismissed as President for those reasons ...

[A person removed from the office of President] may never again ... give an oath to the nation, as there would always exist a reasonable doubt ... as to its reliability ...

Impeachment is a form of public and democratic scrutiny of those holding public office, a measure of self-protection for the community, a ... defence against high-ranking officials who disregard the Constitution and laws ...

Where a person has been removed from the office of President ... for a gross violation of the Constitution or a breach of the oath ... he may never again be elected President of the Republic [or] a member of the Seimas; [he] may never hold office as ... a member of the Government, [or] the National Audit Officer, that is, [he] may not hold an office provided for in the Constitution for which it is necessary to take an oath in accordance with the Constitution ...

35. On 28 May 2004 the Supreme Administrative Court dismissed the applicant's complaint against the decision of the CEC, referring, *inter alia*, to the Constitutional Court's ruling of 25 May 2004. It noted in particular:

... It appears from the reasoning of the Constitutional Court that ... the applicant has forfeited the right to be elected President with effect from 6 April 2004. Therefore, he ... cannot take part in the election announced on 15 April 2004 ...

Until it was amended on 4 May 2004, the Presidential Elections Act did not specify the [residual] rights of a person who had forfeited the right to be elected President.

Article 6 § 1 of the Constitution provides that the Constitution is directly applicable ... [I]t follows that, from the moment ... the applicant submitted his candidacy for the election, his situation was governed by the Constitution, which, as the Constitutional Court has found, bars [a person removed from the office of President] from standing in presidential elections. In these circumstances ... there has been no breach of the principle of the prohibition of retrospective legislation ...

36. On 15 July 2004 the Seimas passed an amendment to the Seimas Elections Act, to the effect that any official who had been removed from office following impeachment proceedings was disqualified from being a Member of Parliament.

D. *Criminal proceedings against the applicant*

37. In autumn 2004 the Prosecutor General discontinued the investigation into allegations that while in office, the applicant had

abused his authority in relation to a private company (Article 228 of the Criminal Code).

38. On an unspecified date the applicant was charged with disclosing information classified as a State secret (Article 125 § 1 of the Criminal Code). On 25 October 2004 the Vilnius Regional Court acquitted him for lack of evidence. On 1 March 2005 the Court of Appeal reversed that decision, finding the applicant guilty. It held, however, that owing to new circumstances, namely the applicant's removal from office as President and disqualification from elected office, it was reasonable to discharge him from criminal liability and to discontinue the criminal proceedings. On 13 December 2005 the Supreme Court quashed the Court of Appeal's judgment, upholding the acquittal delivered by the Vilnius Regional Court.

E. Criminal proceedings against JB

39. On account of his threat to disseminate information discrediting the applicant if he failed to keep his promise to appoint him as an adviser (see paragraph 19 above), JB was convicted of having, for his own benefit and "by means of mental coercion, required a civil servant or person in a position of public authority to carry out or refrain from certain actions" (Article 287 § 1 of the Criminal Code). He was fined 10,000 Lithuanian litai, equivalent to approximately 2,900 euros (judgments of the Vilnius City 1st District Court of 22 November 2004, the Vilnius Regional Court of 6 April 2005, and the Supreme Court of 18 October 2005).

II. Relevant domestic law and practice

A. Competence of the Constitutional Court

40. The Constitutional Court has jurisdiction to review the constitutionality and lawfulness of the acts of the President (Articles 102, 105 and 106 of the Constitution). Acts of the President cease to have legal effect if the Constitutional Court rules that they are in breach of the Constitution (Article 107 of the Constitution).

41. Decisions of the Constitutional Court have statutory force and are final (Article 107 of the Constitution). The power of the Constitutional Court to declare a legal act unconstitutional may not be circumvented by the subsequent adoption of a similar legal act (section 72 of the Constitutional Court Act).

42. In addition, the Constitutional Court may be called upon to determine whether certain acts of a president against whom impeachment proceedings have been instituted are in breach of the Constitution (Article 105 of the Constitution). No appeal lies against the court's conclusions (section 83(2) of the Constitutional Court Act). However, the final decision on the sustainability of allegations giving rise to impeachment proceedings is taken by the Seimas on the basis of the Constitutional Court's conclusions (Article 107 § 3 of the Constitution; see also below).

43. Article 104 of the Constitution provides that, in discharging their duties, the judges of the Constitutional Court act independently of any other State institution, person or organisation, and are guided only by the Constitution.

44. Section 48 of the Constitutional Court Act provides that a judge of the Constitutional Court may withdraw or be removed from a case if he or she, *inter alia*, is a relative of one of the parties to the case or has publicly declared how it should be decided.

B. Impeachment proceedings

45. Article 86 of the Constitution provides that the President of Lithuania is immune from any criminal liability while in office. However, under Article 74 of the Constitution, he or she may be removed from office following impeachment proceedings, *inter alia* for a gross violation of the Constitution or a breach of the constitutional oath. The decision is taken by the Seimas (Article 107 § 3 of the Constitution).

46. In accordance with Articles 227 and 228 of the Statute of the Seimas, impeachment is a parliamentary procedure aimed at determining the constitutional liability of the highest-ranking officials, such as the President of the Republic or Members of Parliament, for acts carried out while in office which undermine the authorities' credibility. Impeachment proceedings may be initiated by a quarter of the members of the Seimas where such an official is alleged to have committed a gross violation of the Constitution and/or a breach of the constitutional oath and/or is suspected of committing a criminal offence (Articles 229 and 230 of the Statute of the Seimas). They are to be conducted in accordance with the rules of criminal procedure (Article 246 § 3 of the Statute of the Seimas).

47. Having received a petition for impeachment, the Seimas sets up a special investigation commission, which sits in private (Article 238 of

the Statute of the Seimas) and hears evidence from the parties to the procedure, witnesses and experts, in accordance with the rules of criminal procedure (Article 239 of the Statute of the Seimas). It reports its findings to the Seimas as to whether there are grounds to institute impeachment proceedings (Article 241 of the Statute of the Seimas). If the Seimas—sitting in public—considers that such grounds exist, it passes a resolution to initiate the proceedings, requesting the Constitutional Court to determine whether the acts of the person indicated in the impeachment charges are in breach of the Constitution (Article 240 of the Statute of the Seimas and Article 106 of the Constitution). On the basis of the Constitutional Court's conclusions (Article 105 of the Constitution), the Seimas conducts an inquiry (likewise observing the basic rules of criminal procedure) and ultimately decides whether the person against whom the proceedings have been brought should be removed from office for a gross violation of the Constitution, on the basis of the available evidence and testimony (Articles 246 to 258 and 260 of the Statute of the Seimas; Article 74 and Article 107 § 3 of the Constitution).

48. In its ruling of 31 March 2004, in which it set out its conclusions in Case No 14/04 (see paragraph 27 above), the Constitutional Court provided the following clarifications:

... The provision of Article 107 § 2 of the Constitution whereby decisions of the Constitutional Court on issues within its competence are final and not subject to appeal also means that when deciding whether or not to remove the President from office, the Seimas may not reject, change or question the Constitutional Court's conclusion that specific acts of the President are (or are not) in breach of the Constitution. No such powers are assigned to the Seimas by the Constitution. [Such a] conclusion ... is binding on the Seimas in so far as the Constitution does not empower it to decide whether the Constitutional Court's conclusions are well-founded and lawful; only the [Constitutional] Court can establish that the actions of the President are (or are not) in breach of the Constitution.

Under Article 74 of the Constitution, only the Seimas may remove the President from office for a gross violation of the Constitution.

Thus, the Constitution assigns the Seimas and the Constitutional Court different functions in impeachment proceedings, and confers on them the respective powers necessary to discharge those functions: the Constitutional Court decides whether specific acts of the President are in breach of the Constitution and submits its conclusions to the Seimas (Article 105 § 3, point (4), of the Constitution), whereas the Seimas, in the event that the President has committed a gross violation of the Constitution, decides whether or not to remove him from office (Article 74 of the Constitution) ... Under Article 107 § 3 of the Constitution, the Seimas is empowered to decide whether to remove the President from office, but not to determine whether his acts are in breach of the Constitution.

It should be noted that this constitutional provision whereby only the Constitutional Court is empowered to decide (through its conclusions on the matter) whether specific acts of the President are in breach of the Constitution represents a further guarantee for the President that his constitutional liability will not be incurred unreasonably. Thus, if the Constitutional Court reaches the conclusion that the President's acts are not in breach of the Constitution, the Seimas may not remove him from office for a gross violation of the Constitution ...

49. In addition to possible constitutional liability, a person removed from public office may incur ordinary liability (*teisinė atsakomybė*).

50. According to the Constitutional Court's ruling of 11 May 1999 on the compliance of Article 259 of the Statute of the Seimas of the Republic of Lithuania with the Lithuanian Constitution, "the constitutional sanction applied in the context of impeachment proceedings is of an irreversible nature". In the same ruling the Constitutional Court also stated that fair-trial principles applied in impeachment proceedings, meaning that the persons charged "must have the right to be heard and a legally guaranteed opportunity to defend their rights".

C. *Election of the President and of members of the Seimas*

51. Article 56 of the Constitution provides:

Any citizen of the Republic of Lithuania who is not bound by an oath or pledge to a foreign State, and who, on the date of the election, is at least twenty-five years of age and permanently resident in Lithuania, may be elected as a member of the Seimas.

Persons who have not completed a sentence imposed by a court, and persons declared legally incapable by a court, may not be elected as members of the Seimas.

52. As mentioned above, on 4 May 2004 the Seimas amended the Presidential Elections Act by inserting the following provision:

A person who has been removed from parliamentary or other office by the Seimas in impeachment proceedings may not be elected President of the Republic if less than five years have elapsed since his removal from office.

Following the Constitutional Court's ruling of 25 May 2004 (see paragraph 34 above), the Seimas passed an amendment to the Seimas Elections Act, to the effect that any official who had been removed from office following impeachment proceedings was disqualified from being a Member of Parliament.

53. The Constitution further provides:

Article 59

... Newly elected members of the Seimas shall acquire all the rights of a representative of the nation only after taking an oath before the Seimas to be loyal to the Republic of Lithuania.

Members of the Seimas who do not take the oath according to the procedure established by law, or who take a conditional oath, shall forfeit their parliamentary office ...

Article 78

Any person who is a Lithuanian citizen by birth, who has lived in Lithuania for at least the three years preceding the election, is at least 40 years old on the date of the election and is eligible for election as a member of the Seimas may be elected President of the Republic.

The President of the Republic shall be elected by the citizens of the Republic of Lithuania for a five-year term by universal, equal and direct suffrage by secret ballot.

The same person may not be elected President of the Republic for more than two consecutive terms.

Article 79

Any citizen of the Republic of Lithuania who satisfies the conditions set forth in the first paragraph of Article 78 and has collected the signatures of no fewer than 20,000 voters shall be registered as a candidate for the office of President.

There shall be no limit on the number of candidates for the office of President.

54. Article 82 of the Constitution provides:

The newly elected President of the Republic shall take office ... after swearing an oath to the nation in Vilnius, in the presence of the representatives of the people, namely the members of the Seimas, to be loyal to the Republic of Lithuania and the Constitution, to fulfil the duties of his office conscientiously, and to be equally just to all.

A person re-elected President of the Republic shall also take the oath.

The record of the oath taken by the President of the Republic shall be signed by him and by the President of the Constitutional Court or, in the latter's absence, by another judge of the Constitutional Court.

55. Pursuant to section 3 of the Presidential Office Act, the newly elected President takes the following oath:

I (name and surname)
Swear to the nation to be loyal to the Republic of Lithuania and the Constitution, to observe and enforce the law, and to protect the integrity of Lithuanian territory;
I swear to fulfil conscientiously the duties of [presidential] office, and to be equally just to all;
I swear to strengthen the independence of Lithuania, to the best of my ability, and to serve my homeland, democracy and the welfare of the people of Lithuania . . .

D. Other provisions

56. Article 29 of the Constitution provides that "[a]ll persons shall be equal before the law, the courts, and other State institutions and officials". Article 84 § 21 of the Constitution states that the President "shall grant citizenship of the Republic of Lithuania in accordance with the procedure established by law".

57. Section 16(1) of the Citizenship Act provides that the President may grant Lithuanian citizenship by way of exception—that is, without applying the usual eligibility requirements—to foreign citizens of special merit rendering them worthy of becoming a citizen of the Republic of Lithuania.

58. Articles 68 and 71 of the Constitution read as follows:

Article 68

The right to initiate legislation in the Seimas shall be vested in members of the Seimas, the President of the Republic and the Government.

Citizens of the Republic of Lithuania shall also have the right to initiate legislation. A Bill may be brought before the Seimas by 50,000 citizens with the right to vote, and the Seimas must consider it.

Article 71

Within ten days of receiving a law passed by the Seimas, the President of the Republic shall either sign and officially promulgate the law, or shall send it back to the Seimas, with reasoned observations, for reconsideration.

If a law passed by the Seimas is not sent back or signed by the President within the prescribed period, the law shall enter into force after it has been signed and officially promulgated by the Speaker of the Seimas.

The President of the Republic must, within five days, sign and officially promulgate any laws or other instruments adopted by referendum.

If such a law is not signed and promulgated by the President within the prescribed period, the law shall enter into force after it has been signed and officially promulgated by the Speaker of the Seimas.

III. Guidelines on Elections adopted by the Venice Commission

59. The relevant passages of the Guidelines on Elections adopted by the European Commission for Democracy through Law ("the Venice Commission") at its 51st session (5-6 July 2002) read as follows:

I. *Principles of Europe's electoral heritage*
The five principles underlying Europe's electoral heritage are *universal, equal, free, secret and direct suffrage.* Furthermore, elections must be held at regular intervals.

1. *Universal suffrage*

1.1. *Rule and exceptions*
Universal suffrage means in principle that all human beings have the right to vote and to stand for election. This right may, however, and indeed should, be subject to certain conditions:
  a. Age ...
  b. Nationality ...
  c. Residence ...
  d. Deprivation of the right to vote and to be elected:
     i. provision may be made for depriving individuals of their right to vote and to be elected, but only subject to the following cumulative conditions:
     ii. it must be provided for by law;
     iii. the proportionality principle must be observed; conditions for depriving individuals of the right to stand for election may be less strict than for disenfranchising them;
     iv. the deprivation must be based on mental incapacity or a criminal conviction for a serious offence;
     v. furthermore, the withdrawal of political rights or finding of mental incapacity may only be imposed by express decision of a court of law ...

The Explanatory Report, adopted by the Venice Commission at its 52nd session (18-19 October 2002), reads as follows (footnote omitted):

... provision may be made for *clauses suspending political rights.* Such clauses must, however, comply with the usual conditions under which fundamental rights may be restricted; in other words, they must:

– be provided for by law;
– observe the principle of proportionality;
– be based on mental incapacity or a criminal conviction for a serious offence.

Furthermore, the withdrawal of political rights may only be imposed by express decision of a court of law. However, in the event of withdrawal on grounds of mental incapacity, such express decision may concern the incapacity and entail *ipso jure* deprivation of civic rights.

The conditions for depriving individuals of the right to stand for election may be less strict than for disenfranchising them, as the holding of a public office is at stake and it may be legitimate to debar persons whose activities in such an office would violate a greater public interest ...

IV. Law and practice regarding impeachment in the member States of the Council of Europe

60. The term "impeachment" denotes a formal indictment procedure whereby the legislature may remove from office a head of State, a senior official or a judge for breaching the law or the Constitution. The purpose of impeachment is in principle to allow the institution of criminal proceedings in the courts against the person concerned, but in practice it does not necessarily produce such an outcome.

61. The legal systems of the majority of the Council of Europe's member States with a republican system make specific provision for the impeachment of the head of State (Albania, Austria, Azerbaijan, Bulgaria, Croatia, Czech Republic, France, Georgia, Germany, Greece, Hungary, Ireland, Italy, Lithuania, Moldova, Montenegro, Poland, Romania, Russian Federation, Serbia, Slovakia, Slovenia, "the former Yugoslav Republic of Macedonia", Turkey and Ukraine). Impeachment proceedings may be instituted on the following grounds (for Lithuania, see paragraph 46 above): breach of the Constitution or undermining of the constitutional order (Austria, Bulgaria, Croatia, Georgia, Germany, Greece, Hungary, Moldova, Romania, Slovakia, Slovenia, "the former Yugoslav Republic of Macedonia"); high treason (Bulgaria, Cyprus, Czech Republic, Finland, France, Greece, Italy, Romania, Russian Federation); breach of the law (Germany, Hungary); an ordinary or serious criminal offence (Finland, Russian Federation); or immoral conduct (Ireland).

62. In most of these republics, impeachment proceedings have no direct effects on the electoral and other political rights of a head of State who is removed from office. However, in Austria, if the Federal President is removed from office following impeachment proceedings, the Constitutional Court may order the temporary forfeiture of "political rights" if there are particularly aggravating circumstances. Similarly, in Poland the special court with competence in such matters may, in addition to removing the President from office, temporarily deprive him or her of certain political rights (general disqualification from standing for election for a period of up to ten years, prohibition from occupying certain positions for a similar period and revocation of

orders and other honorary titles). In Slovakia and the Czech Republic, a person removed from presidential office as a result of impeachment proceedings permanently forfeits the right to stand for election as President but may be a candidate in any other elections; in the Russian Federation he or she is barred only from standing in the presidential elections called as a result of his or her removal from office.

THE LAW

I. Alleged violation of Article 6 §§ 1, 2 and 3 of the Convention, Article 7 of the Convention and Article 4 of Protocol No 7

63. The applicant alleged a violation of his right to a fair hearing in connection with the two sets of proceedings in the Constitutional Court, concerning Decree No 40 and the merits of the impeachment charges against him. He submitted that because of collusion between the court's President and the member of the Seimas who had initiated the proceedings against him, the Constitutional Court could not be considered an independent and impartial tribunal, and noted that that court had subsequently issued a public response to his accusations of bias on its part; in a supplement to his application, dated 30 November 2006, he added that the Constitutional Court's endorsement of the conclusions of the declaration of 25 March 2004 by the Seimas showed that it had been put under considerable pressure by Parliament as a result of such collusion. He further submitted that he had been unable to defend himself effectively and that, in the impeachment proceedings, his lawyers had not had access to certain classified documents which the special investigation commission had examined and the Constitutional Court had exceeded its powers by making findings as to the facts and the issue of "guilt". He relied on Article 6 §§ 1 and 3(b) of the Convention, which provides:

1. In the determination of his civil rights and obligations or of any criminal charge against him, everyone is entitled to a fair ... hearing ... by an independent and impartial tribunal established by law.

...

3. Everyone charged with a criminal offence has the following minimum rights:

...

(b) to have adequate time and facilities for the preparation of his defence;

...

Furthermore, in another supplement to his application, dated 30 September 2005, the applicant submitted that by justifying his permanent disqualification from elected office on the ground that there would always be reasonable doubt as to the reliability of any constitutional oath sworn by him in future, the Constitutional Court's ruling of 25 May 2004 had established a presumption of guilt, in breach of Article 6 § 2 of the Convention. In the supplement of 30 November 2006 to his application, he added that the declaration of 25 March 2004 by the Seimas had breached the same provision, which provides:

Everyone charged with a criminal offence shall be presumed innocent until proved guilty according to law.

In addition, in the supplement of 30 September 2005 to his application the applicant complained that the sanction imposed on him as a result of the impeachment proceedings, namely removal from office and a lifelong ban on standing for election, was more severe than the penalties envisaged by the criminal law for equivalent offences, adding that lifelong disqualification from elected office was not provided for by law and was, to say the least, "bizarre". On that account he alleged a violation of Article 7 of the Convention, which provides:

1. No one shall be held guilty of any criminal offence on account of any act or omission which did not constitute a criminal offence under national or international law at the time when it was committed. Nor shall a heavier penalty be imposed than the one that was applicable at the time the criminal offence was committed.

2. This Article shall not prejudice the trial and punishment of any person for any act or omission which, at the time when it was committed, was criminal according to the general principles of law recognised by civilised nations.

Lastly, the applicant submitted that the institution of impeachment proceedings followed by criminal proceedings in his case amounted to trying him twice for the same offence. He relied on Article 4 § 1 of Protocol No 7, which provides:

No one shall be liable to be tried or punished again in criminal proceedings under the jurisdiction of the same State for an offence for which he has already been finally acquitted or convicted in accordance with the law and penal procedure of that State.

64. The Court must determine at the outset whether the provisions relied on by the applicant are applicable in the instant case.

65. With regard to Article 6 § 1 of the Convention, the Court reiterates that the fact that proceedings have taken place before a constitutional court does not suffice to remove them from the ambit

of that provision. It must therefore be ascertained whether the proceedings before the Constitutional Court in the instant case did or did not relate to the "determination" of the applicant's "civil rights and obligations" or of a "criminal charge" against him (see *Pierre-Bloch* v. *France*, 21 October 1997, § 48, *Reports of Judgments and Decisions* 1997-VI).

66. The first set of proceedings concerned the review of the compliance with the Constitution and the Citizenship Act of a decree issued by the applicant by virtue of his presidential powers, granting Lithuanian citizenship to JB "by way of exception". The purpose of the second set of proceedings was to determine whether, in discharging his duties as President, the applicant had committed gross violations of the Constitution or breached his constitutional oath. It is therefore clear that the proceedings in question did not concern the determination of the applicant's civil rights or obligations.

For the Court to conclude that they likewise did not concern a "criminal charge", it is sufficient for it to find that they did not involve the imposition of a sanction by the Constitutional Court against the applicant. Admittedly, it notes in this connection that the second set of proceedings formed a stage of the impeachment proceedings instituted by the Seimas, the purpose of which was to determine whether or not the applicant should remain in office as President and be eligible to stand for election. However, in any event, in the context of impeachment proceedings against the President of Lithuania for a gross violation of the Constitution or a breach of the presidential oath, the measures of removal from office and (consequent) disqualification from standing for election involve the head of State's constitutional liability, so that, by virtue of their purpose, they lie outside the "criminal" sphere. Furthermore, and above all, the decision to remove the President from office is taken not by the Constitutional Court but by Parliament.

67. The Court thus concludes that Article 6 § 1 of the Convention is not applicable in either its civil or its criminal aspect to the Constitutional Court proceedings in issue.

68. It also follows from the foregoing that the applicant was not "charged with a criminal offence" within the meaning of Article 6 § 2 of the Convention in those proceedings, or "convicted" or "tried or punished ... in criminal proceedings" within the meaning of Article 4 § 1 of Protocol No 7, and that the proceedings did not result in his being held "guilty of a criminal offence" or receiving a "penalty" within the meaning of Article 7 of the Convention. Those provisions likewise do not apply in the present case.

69. It follows that this part of the application is incompatible *ratione materiae* with the provisions of the Convention within the meaning of Article 35 § 3 and must be rejected pursuant to Article 35 § 4.

II. Alleged violation of Article 3 of Protocol No 1

70. In the supplement of 30 September 2005 to his application the applicant complained of his lifelong disqualification from elected office, arguing that permanently denying him the opportunity to stand for election although he was a politician enjoying considerable popular support was contrary to the very essence of free elections and was a wholly disproportionate measure. In the supplement of 30 November 2006 to his application he further submitted that the amendment of electoral law passed following his removal from office had been arbitrary and designed to bar him from holding any public office in future. He relied on Article 3 of Protocol No 1, which provides:

The High Contracting Parties undertake to hold free elections at reasonable intervals by secret ballot, under conditions which will ensure the free expression of the opinion of the people in the choice of the legislature.

A. Admissibility

1. Applicability of Article 3 of Protocol No 1

71. The Court reiterates that Article 3 of Protocol No 1 applies only to the election of the "legislature".

72. Regard being had to the constitutional structure of Lithuania, it is not in doubt that Article 3 of Protocol No 1 is applicable to the election of members of the Seimas. The reverse is true, however, as regards the election of the President of Lithuania. It follows that, in so far as the applicant complained about his removal from office or disqualification from standing for the presidency, this part of the application is incompatible *ratione materiae* with the provisions of the Convention within the meaning of Article 35 § 3 and must be rejected pursuant to Article 35 § 4.

2. Exhaustion of domestic remedies

73. The Government submitted that parliamentary elections had been held in 2004 and 2008 and that the applicant had not expressed the wish to be a candidate in them. Had his candidacy been refused, it would have been open to him to apply to the administrative courts, which could then have requested the Constitutional Court to review

the constitutionality of the Seimas Elections Act as amended on 15 July 2004. The Government further noted that, as President of Lithuania, the applicant could have applied to the Constitutional Court, under section 61 of the Constitutional Court Act, for an interpretation of its ruling of 11 May 1999, in which it had held that the constitutional sanction imposed in the context of impeachment proceedings was "of an irreversible nature", and asked it to clarify whether this meant lifelong disqualification from standing for election. He would then have had the option of resigning in order to avoid that outcome. In short, the Government argued, this part of the application should be declared inadmissible for failure to exhaust domestic remedies.

74. The applicant submitted in reply that since the Constitutional Court had very clearly ruled on 25 May 2004 that lifelong disqualification from standing for election was a consequence of removal from presidential office, it was certain not only that his registration as a candidate in the 2004 and 2008 parliamentary elections would have been refused but also that any subsequent remedies would have had no prospects of success. He added that an application to the Constitutional Court under section 61 of the Constitutional Court Act for an interpretation of the ruling of 11 May 1999 would have been ineffective, seeing that the meaning of the phrase "of an irreversible nature" was not open to doubt. Lastly, the argument that he would have avoided the impeachment proceedings if he had resigned did not, in his view, call for a response.

75. The Court reiterates that the purpose of Article 35 § 1 is to afford the Contracting States the opportunity of preventing or putting right the violations alleged against them before those allegations are submitted to it. Thus, the complaint to be submitted to the Court must first have been made to the appropriate national courts, at least in substance, in accordance with the formal requirements of domestic law and within the prescribed time-limits. Nevertheless, the only remedies that must be exhausted are those that are effective and capable of redressing the alleged violation (see, among many other authorities, *Remli* v. *France*, 23 April 1996, § 33, *Reports* 1996-II). More specifically, the only remedies which Article 35 § 1 of the Convention requires to be exhausted are those that relate to the breaches alleged and at the same time are available and sufficient; the existence of such remedies must be sufficiently certain not only in theory but also in practice, failing which they will lack the requisite accessibility and effectiveness (see, for example, *Selmouni* v. *France* [GC], No 25803/94, § 75, ECHR 1999-V). It falls to the respondent State, if it pleads non-exhaustion of domestic remedies, to establish that these various

conditions are satisfied (see, among other authorities, *Johnston and Others* v. *Ireland*, 18 December 1986, § 45, Series A No 112, and *Selmouni, loc. cit.*).

76. In the instant case the Court observes that in its ruling of 25 May 2004 the Constitutional Court held that a person who had been removed from the office of President for a gross violation of the Constitution or a breach of the oath could never again be elected President of the Republic or a member of the Seimas or hold an office for which it was necessary to take an oath in accordance with the Constitution. It follows from Article 107 of the Lithuanian Constitution that decisions of the Constitutional Court have statutory force and are final. Furthermore, as the Government pointed out in their written observations, the Constitutional Court itself is bound by its own precedents. An appeal against a refusal to register the applicant as a candidate for election to the Seimas would therefore have been bound to fail. Indeed, the Supreme Administrative Court's decision of 28 May 2004 provides an illustration of this point, since it attached decisive weight to the Constitutional Court's conclusions of 25 May 2004 in dismissing the applicant's complaint against the refusal of the Central Electoral Committee to register him as a candidate in the 2004 presidential election.

77. The Court also takes note of the Government's argument that the applicant could have made a prior request to the Constitutional Court for clarification of whether removal from office entailed lifelong disqualification from standing for election and that, if that position were confirmed, he could have resigned before the vote on whether to remove him from office. Such a request could not, however, have prompted an examination of the applicant's particular situation for the purposes of Article 3 of Protocol No 1. It would also have required him to resign voluntarily as President and thereby to accept such a restrictive condition that the remedy in question could not in any event be regarded as "accessible". It cannot therefore be classified as a domestic remedy that had to be used for the purposes of Article 35 § 1 of the Convention.

78. It follows from the foregoing that the Government have not shown that a domestic remedy satisfying the requirements of Article 35 § 1 of the Convention was available to the applicant.

3. Compliance with the six-month time-limit

79. The Government submitted that the applicant had raised his complaint under Article 3 of Protocol No 1 for the first time in a supplement to his application dated 30 September 2005, more than six

months after the final domestic decision (the Constitutional Court's ruling of 25 May 2004). They accordingly contended that this part of the application was out of time and, as such, inadmissible.

80. The applicant submitted in reply, in particular, that he had already raised the complaint under Article 3 of Protocol No 1 in substance in his application; as a result, his submissions of 30 September 2005 had simply expanded on an argument he had already submitted to the Court within the six-month period prescribed by Article 35 § 1 of the Convention. He pointed out in that connection that in the *Ringeisen* v. *Austria* judgment (16 July 1971, § 90, Series A No 13) the Court had accepted that initial applications could be followed by "additional documents", the purpose of which was "to fill the gaps or clarify obscure points".

81. The Court observes, as the Government did, that the applicant did not raise this complaint in his application, even in substance. He mentioned it for the first time in his supplement of 30 September 2005 to the application, more than six months after the Constitutional Court's ruling of 25 May 2004 to the effect that a person removed from office as President for a gross violation of the Constitution or a breach of the constitutional oath could never again be elected as a member of the Seimas—among other positions (see paragraph 34 above)—and the Act of 15 July 2004 amending the Seimas Elections Act accordingly.

82. However, regard should be had to the particular features of the present case. The Court notes in this connection that, in so far as the right under Article 3 of Protocol No 1 to stand in parliamentary elections is in issue here, the applicant's complaint concerns general provisions which did not give rise in his case to an individual measure of implementation subject to an appeal that could have led to a "final decision" marking the start of the six-month period provided for in Article 35 § 1 of the Convention. Admittedly, it might at first sight have appeared conceivable for the applicant to attempt to register as a candidate in parliamentary elections after his removal from office and, once his registration was refused, to apply to the administrative courts on the basis of Article 3 of Protocol No 1. However, as noted above, in view of the Constitutional Court's ruling of 25 May 2004, such a remedy would have been ineffective in the present case, and an applicant cannot be required to avail himself of a remedy lacking effectiveness (see paragraph 76 above).

83. It therefore appears that the applicant's complaint does not concern an act occurring at a given point in time or even the enduring effects of such an act, but rather the Constitutional Court's ruling of

25 May 2004 that a person removed from office as President for a gross violation of the Constitution or a breach of the constitutional oath can never again be elected as a member of the Seimas (among other positions), and the Act of 15 July 2004 amending the Seimas Elections Act accordingly. He is therefore complaining of provisions giving rise to a continuing state of affairs, against which no domestic remedy is in fact available to him. However, as the European Commission of Human Rights noted in the *De Becker* v. *Belgium* decision (9 June 1958, No 214/56, Yearbook 2), the existence of the six-month period specified in Article 35 § 1 of the Convention is justified by the wish of the High Contracting Parties to prevent past judgments being constantly called into question. Although this represents a "legitimate concern for order, stability and peace", it cannot be allowed to stand in the way of the consideration of a permanent state of affairs which is not a thing of the past but still continues without any domestic remedy being available to the applicant; since there is no justification for the application of the rule, there can be no question of his being debarred by lapse of time. The Commission added that accordingly, "when [it] receives an application concerning a legal provision which gives rise to a permanent state of affairs for which there is no domestic remedy, the problem of the six months period specified in Article 26 [of the Convention (current Article 35 § 1)] can arise only after this state of affairs has ceased to exist; ... in the circumstances, it is exactly as though the alleged violation was being repeated daily, thus preventing the running of the six months period". The Court itself has subsequently applied this principle. Thus, it has considered the merits of a number of applications which concerned statutory provisions that had not given rise to individual decisions against the applicants but had produced a permanent state of affairs, and which had been lodged more than six months after the entry into force of the provisions in question (see, for example, *Hirst* v. *United Kingdom (No 2)* [GC], No 74025/01, ECHR 2005-IX, and *Sejdić and Finci* v. *Bosnia and Herzegovina* [GC], Nos 27996/06 and 34836/06, ECHR 2009-VI).

84. In the instant case no domestic remedy is available to the applicant and the state of affairs complained of has clearly not ceased. It cannot therefore be maintained that this part of the application is out of time.

4. Application of Article 17 of the Convention

85. The Government submitted that it would be contrary to the general principles set forth in the Court's case-law concerning protection of democracy for the applicant to be able to stand in parliamentary

elections after having breached his constitutional oath. They added that his real aim was to be re-elected President in the election called for 13 June 2004, and not to become a member of the Seimas. In their submission, the applicant was seeking to use the Convention machinery to gain political revenge and regain the highest State office.

86. The applicant asserted in reply that his aim was to obtain a judgment from the Court which would have the effect of allowing him to stand in parliamentary or presidential elections, and that such an aim could not constitute an abuse of rights for the purposes of Article 17 of the Convention.

87. The Court reiterates, firstly, that "the purpose of Article 17, in so far as it refers to groups or to individuals, is to make it impossible for them to derive from the Convention a right to engage in any activity or perform any act aimed at destroying any of the rights and freedoms set forth in the Convention; ... therefore, no person may be able to take advantage of the provisions of the Convention to perform acts aimed at destroying the aforesaid rights and freedoms ..." (see *Lawless* v. *Ireland*, 1 July 1961, § 7, pp. 45-6, Series A No 3).

Since the general purpose of Article 17 is, in other words, to prevent individuals or groups with totalitarian aims from exploiting in their own interests the principles enunciated in the Convention (see *WP and Others* v. *Poland* (dec.), No 42264/98, ECHR 2004-VII, and *Norwood* v. *United Kingdom*, No 23131/03, ECHR 2004-XI), this Article is applicable only on an exceptional basis and in extreme cases, as indeed is illustrated by the Court's case-law.

88. The Court has held, in particular, that a "remark directed against the Convention's underlying values" is removed from the protection of Article 10 by Article 17 (see *Lehideux and Isorni* v. *France*, 23 September 1998, § 53, *Reports* 1998-VII, and *Garaudy* v. *France* (dec.), No 65831/01, ECHR 2003-IX). Thus, in *Garaudy* (ibid.), which concerned, in particular, the conviction for denial of crimes against humanity of the author of a book that systematically denied such crimes perpetrated by the Nazis against the Jewish community, the Court found the applicant's Article 10 complaint incompatible *ratione materiae* with the provisions of the Convention. It based that conclusion on the observation that the main content and general tenor of the applicant's book, and thus its aim, were markedly revisionist and therefore ran counter to the fundamental values of the Convention and of democracy, namely justice and peace, and inferred from that observation that he had attempted to deflect Article 10 from its real purpose by using his right to freedom of expression for ends which were contrary to the text and spirit of the Convention (see also *Witzsch* v.

Germany (dec.), No 4785/03, 13 December 2005). The Court reached the same conclusion in, for example, *Norwood* ((dec.), cited above) and *Pavel Ivanov* v. *Russia* ((dec.), No 35222/04, 20 February 2007), which concerned the use of freedom of expression for Islamophobic and anti-Semitic purposes respectively. In *Orban and Others* v. *France* (No 20985/05, § 35, 15 January 2005) it noted that statements pursuing the unequivocal aim of justifying war crimes such as torture or summary executions likewise amounted to deflecting Article 10 from its real purpose. In the same vein, the Court has held that Article 17 of the Convention prevented the founders of an association whose memorandum of association had anti-Semitic connotations from relying on the right to freedom of association under Article 11 of the Convention to challenge its prohibition, noting in particular that the applicants were essentially seeking to employ that Article as a basis under the Convention for a right to engage in activities contrary to the text and spirit of the Convention (see *WP and Others*, cited above).

89. In the present case there is no indication that the applicant was pursuing an aim of that nature. He relied legitimately on Article 3 of Protocol No 1 to challenge his disqualification from elected office, seeking to obtain a judgment from the Court whose execution at domestic level would have the likely effect of allowing him to stand in parliamentary elections. In other words, he is seeking to regain the full enjoyment of a right which the Convention in principle secures to everyone, and of which he claims to have been wrongly deprived by the Lithuanian authorities, the Government's allegation that the applicant's real aim is to be re-elected President of Lithuania being immaterial in this context. Article 17 of the Convention cannot therefore apply.

5. Conclusion

90. In so far as the applicant's complaint concerns his removal from office or his disqualification from standing for election as President of Lithuania, this part of the application must be rejected pursuant to Article 35 § 4 of the Convention.

In so far as it concerns his inability to stand for election to the Seimas, it raises complex issues of fact and law which can only be resolved after examination on the merits. It follows that this part of the application is not manifestly ill-founded within the meaning of Article 35 § 3(a) of the Convention. No other ground for declaring it inadmissible has been established. Within these limits, the application must therefore be declared admissible.

B. *Merits*

1. *The parties' submissions*

(a) The Government

91. The Government noted in the first place that the principle that a person removed from office as President for a gross violation of the Constitution or a breach of the constitutional oath could not stand in presidential or parliamentary elections resulted from an interpretation of the Constitution by the Constitutional Court. However, it was not a new judge-made rule applied for the first time by the Constitutional Court in the applicant's case, but an "implicit" provision of the Constitution which that court had simply confirmed. The Government pointed out that rulings of the Constitutional Court were final and binding on everyone, including the court itself, and that, like the actual text of the Constitution, "implicit" constitutional provisions could be amended only by changing the Constitution. They also emphasised that the conclusions reached by the Constitutional Court in the present case had not been unforeseeable, in particular given that, in a ruling of 11 [May] 1999 (see paragraph 50 above), that court had stressed that the constitutional sanction resulting from removal from office was irreversible; its ruling of 25 May 2004 had thus been consistent with its previous case-law.

92. The Government further noted that the restriction in question, which applied only to the passive aspect of the right protected by Article 3 of Protocol No 1, was not directed at the applicant personally but at a category of individuals to which he indisputably belonged.

They added that the purpose of the restriction was to prevent persons who had committed a gross violation of the Constitution or breached the constitutional oath from holding an office for which it was necessary to take an oath in accordance with the Constitution; it therefore pursued the legitimate aim not only of preserving the democratic order but also of "protecting national security".

In the Government's submission, taking into account what was at stake, the restriction could not be regarded as disproportionate. In that connection they emphasised that such conduct on the part of the highest authorities—especially the head of State—undermined people's trust in State institutions and posed a serious and imminent threat to democracy and the constitutional order. Furthermore, relying on *Ždanoka* v. *Latvia* [GC] (No 58278/00, §§ 100 and 103, ECHR 2006-IV), they highlighted the wide margin of appreciation afforded to States in this sphere and also, referring to the concept of a "democracy capable of defending itself", the need to take account of the evolution of the political context in which the measure in issue had been taken; features unacceptable in the context of one country's system could be justified in another system. On that point, they stressed that Lithuania had been a democracy only between 1918 and 1940 and after 1990; accordingly, it did not have a long-standing democratic tradition, society had not completely rid itself of the "remnants of the totalitarian occupying regime"—including corruption and a lack of public trust in State institutions—and there were numerous examples of inappropriate and unethical conduct in politics. Lithuania's political, historical, cultural and constitutional situation therefore justified the measure in question, even though it might appear excessive in a well-established democracy. That position was all the more compelling in this instance since the head of State was the institution to which the nation had entrusted the duties of protecting and defending the constitutional order and democracy. Lastly, the lack of a European consensus in this area served to confirm that in deciding that persons dismissed following impeachment proceedings should be permanently disqualified from elected office, Lithuania remained within its margin of appreciation.

93. In addition, relying on *Ždanoka* (cited above, §§ 112-14), the Government emphasised that the categories of persons affected by the prohibition imposed on the applicant were clearly and precisely defined and that the applicable rules afforded the highest possible degree of individualisation and guarantees against arbitrariness. They noted in that connection that two institutions were involved in impeachment proceedings, namely the Seimas and the Constitutional Court; only the former could initiate them, and only the latter could rule on whether there had been a violation of the Constitution or a breach of the constitutional oath. Only if the Constitutional Court had established such a violation could the Seimas remove the person concerned from office (and, moreover, this required a three-fifths majority of all members of the Seimas). They also pointed out that impeachment proceedings were judicial in nature, that the rules of criminal procedure applied, that in such proceedings the Seimas was presided over not by one of its members but by a member of the Supreme Court, and that the decision included reasons and was taken following an objective public investigation into the circumstances of the case. In the instant case, moreover, the applicant had had the opportunity to escape "full" constitutional liability by resigning after the Constitutional Court's opinion of 31 March 2004; he would thereby have avoided being removed from office and the resulting disqualification from standing for election.

(b) The applicant

94. In the applicant's submission, the Constitutional Court's finding that removal from office for a gross violation of the Constitution or a breach of the constitutional oath was irreversible—to such an extent that it could not even be challenged in a popular vote—was excessive. This was particularly true in his case since, although the charges forming the basis for his removal from office were criminal in nature, they had either not given rise to a criminal prosecution after his immunity had been lifted or they had resulted in his acquittal. He was therefore subject to a permanent sanction based on a questionable decision by a court that appeared biased, on account of acts constituting criminal offences in respect of which he had either been acquitted or not prosecuted.

95. The applicant—who likewise referred to the principles set forth by the Court in *Ždanoka* (cited above)—submitted that even assuming that the aim pursued had been legitimate, it was unacceptable for it to have been attained in his case through violations of the Constitution resulting, for example, from retrospective application of the law and denial of a fair trial.

He further contended that the restriction of his right under Article 3 of Protocol No 1 was disproportionate in that it was not subject to a time-limit. Noting in that connection that in the *Ždanoka* case the Chamber (judgment of 17 June 2004) had found a violation of that Article for that reason, he argued that since the authoritative nature of the Constitutional Court's rulings meant that his disqualification was permanent, a finding along similar lines was all the more compelling in his case. Although he nonetheless conceded that the European Commission of Human Rights had reached the opposite conclusion in several cases, he pointed out that all those cases had concerned persons found guilty of particularly serious offences such as war crimes or acts of high treason, whereas he had not been convicted of any criminal offence on account of the acts forming the basis of his disqualification from standing for election.

Furthermore, in justifying the lack of a time-limit for the disqualification from elected office of a person who had breached his constitutional oath as President by saying that there would always be a doubt as to the reliability of any new oath he would have to take in the event of his subsequent election, the Constitutional Court had lent that measure a preventive purpose which, rather than justifying it, made it even more disproportionate. In the applicant's submission, this amounted to a "presumption of guilt".

2. *The Court's assessment*

(a) General principles

96. The Court refers to the general principles concerning Article 3 of Protocol No 1, as set out in the following judgments in particular: *Mathieu-Mohin and Clerfayt* v. *Belgium* (2 March 1987, §§ 46-54, Series A No 113); *Hirst* (cited above, §§ 56-62), *Ždanoka* (cited above, §§ 102-15); *Ādamsons* v. *Latvia* (No 3669/03, § 111, ECHR 2008-...); and *Tănase* v. *Moldova* [GC] (No 7/08, §§ 154-62, ECHR 2010-III).

It follows from the foregoing that Article 3 of Protocol No 1, which enshrines a fundamental principle of an effective political democracy and is accordingly of prime importance in the Convention system, implies the subjective rights to vote and to stand for election (see *Mathieu-Mohin and Clerfayt*, cited above, §§ 47-51; *Hirst*, cited above, §§ 57-8; *Ždanoka*, cited above, §§ 102-3; and *Tănase*, cited above, §§ 154-5).

Although those rights are important, they are not absolute. There is room for "implied limitations", and Contracting States must be given a margin of appreciation in this sphere (see *Mathieu-Mohin and Clerfayt*, cited above, § 52; *Hirst*, cited above, § 60; and *Ždanoka*, cited above, § 103). The margin in this area is wide, seeing that there are numerous ways of organising and running electoral systems and a wealth of differences, *inter alia*, in historical development, cultural diversity and political thought within Europe, which it is for each Contracting State to mould into its own democratic vision (see *Hirst*, cited above, § 61, and *Ždanoka*, *loc. cit.*).

Thus, for the purposes of applying Article 3 of Protocol No 1, any electoral legislation or electoral system must be assessed in the light of the political evolution of the country concerned; features that would be unacceptable in the context of one system may accordingly be justified in the context of another, at least so long as the chosen system provides for conditions which will ensure the "free expression of the opinion of the people in the choice of the legislature" (see *Mathieu-Mohin and Clerfayt*, cited above, § 54; *Ždanoka*, cited above, §§ 106 and 115; and *Tănase*, cited above, § 157).

In particular, the Contracting States enjoy considerable latitude in establishing criteria governing eligibility to stand for election, and in general, they may impose stricter requirements in that context than in the context of eligibility to vote (see *Ždanoka*, cited above, § 115; *Ādamsons*, cited above, § 111; and *Tănase*, cited above, § 156).

However, while the margin of appreciation is wide, it is not allembracing. It is for the Court to determine in the last resort whether the requirements of Article 3 of Protocol No 1 have been complied with. It has to satisfy itself that the restrictions imposed do not curtail the right in question to such an extent as to impair its very essence and deprive it of its effectiveness; that they pursue a legitimate aim; and that the means employed are not disproportionate. In particular, such restrictions must not thwart "the free expression of the opinion of the people in the choice of the legislature" (see *Mathieu-Mohin and Clerfayt*, cited above, § 52; *Hirst*, cited above, § 62; *Ždanoka*, cited above, § 104; and *Tănase*, cited above, §§ 157 and 161).

(b) Application of these principles in the present case

97. In the most recent Grand Chamber case concerning Article 3 of Protocol No 1 the Court examined whether there had been interference with the applicant's rights under that Article, adding that such interference would constitute a violation unless it met the requirements of lawfulness, pursued a legitimate aim and was proportionate; it then sought to ascertain whether those conditions were satisfied (see *Tănase*, cited above, §§ 162 and 163-80).

98. Proceeding in the same manner in the instant case, the Court notes at the outset that the applicant, as a former President of Lithuania removed from office following impeachment proceedings, belongs to a category of persons directly affected by the rule set forth in the Constitutional Court's ruling of 25 May 2004 and the Act of 15 July 2004. Since he has thereby been deprived of any possibility of running as a parliamentary candidate, he is entitled to claim that there has been interference with the exercise of his right to stand for election.

99. As to whether the interference was lawful, the Court observes that the principle that a person removed from office as President following impeachment proceedings is no longer entitled to stand for election to the Seimas is clear from the Constitutional Court's ruling of 25 May 2004 and the Act of 15 July 2004.

The Court notes that the applicant complained that this rule had been applied with retrospective effect. It reiterates, however, that under Article 3 of Protocol No 1 it is only required to examine the applicant's inability to stand for election to the Seimas. In any event, in so far as the rule in question entails ineligibility for parliamentary office, it was not applied retrospectively in the applicant's case. In fact, the first parliamentary elections in which he was barred from standing were held in October 2004, long after the above-mentioned ruling and legislative enactment.

100. As to the aim pursued, given that Article 3 of Protocol No 1 does not contain a list of "legitimate aims" capable of justifying restrictions on the exercise of the rights it guarantees and does not refer to those enumerated in Articles 8 to 11 of the Convention, the Contracting States are free to rely on an aim not mentioned in those Articles, provided that it is compatible with the principle of the rule of law and the general objectives of the Convention (see, for example, *Ždanoka*, cited above, § 115).

The Court accepts that this is the position in the present case. The prohibition imposed on the applicant is the consequence of his removal from office following impeachment proceedings, the purpose of which, according to the Statute of the Seimas, is to determine the constitutional liability of the highest-ranking State officials for acts carried out while in office which undermine the authorities' credibility. The measure thus forms part, according to the reasons given in the Constitutional Court's ruling of 24 May 2004, of a self-protection mechanism for democracy through "public and democratic scrutiny" of those holding public office, and pursues the aim of excluding from the legislature any senior officials who, in particular, have committed gross violations of the Constitution or breached their constitutional oath. As the Government submitted, the measure is thus intended to preserve the democratic order, which constitutes a legitimate aim for the purposes of Article 3 of Protocol No 1 (see, for example, *Ždanoka*, cited above, § 118).

101. In assessing the proportionality of the interference, it should above all be emphasised that Article 3 of Protocol No 1 does not exclude the possibility of imposing restrictions on the electoral rights of a person who has, for example, seriously abused a public position or whose conduct has threatened to undermine the rule of law or democratic foundations (see, for example, *Ždanoka*, cited above, § 110). The present case concerns circumstances of this kind. In the context of impeachment proceedings, the Constitutional Court held that by having, while in office as President, unlawfully and for his own personal ends granted Lithuanian citizenship to JB, disclosed a State secret to the latter by informing him that he was under investigation by the secret services, and exploited his own status to exert undue influence on a private company for the benefit of close acquaintances, the applicant had committed a gross violation of the Constitution and breached his constitutional oath. On the basis of that finding, the Seimas removed the applicant from office, his inability to serve as a Member of Parliament being a consequence of that decision.

102. Furthermore, as the Court observed above, the categories of persons affected by the disqualification are very clearly defined in law, and as a former President removed from office following impeachment proceedings for a gross violation of the Constitution or a breach of the constitutional oath, there is no doubt whatsoever that the applicant belongs to that group. Indeed, that has never been in dispute. There is therefore a clear link between the applicant's disqualification from elected office and his conduct and situation. As a result, the fact that his disqualification was not based on a specific court decision following a review of its proportionality in the individual circumstances of his case is not decisive (see, for example, *Hirst*, cited above, § 71; *Ždanoka*, cited above, §§ 113-14, 115(d) and 128; and *Ādamsons*, cited above, §§ 124-5), especially since the finding that he had committed a violation of the Constitution and breached his constitutional oath was made by the Constitutional Court, which offers the guarantees of a judicial body.

More broadly, the Court observes that in the context of impeachment proceedings, following which a senior State official may be removed from office and barred from standing for election, domestic law provides for a number of safeguards protecting the persons concerned from arbitrary treatment. Firstly, it appears from the case-law of the Constitutional Court and the Statute of the Seimas that the rules of criminal procedure and fair-trial principles apply in impeachment proceedings (see paragraphs 46 and 50 above). In addition, while the decision to initiate such proceedings on account of a gross violation of the Constitution or a breach of the constitutional oath and the final decision to remove a senior official from office are the prerogative of a political body, namely the Seimas, it is the task of a judicial body, namely the Constitutional Court, to rule on whether there has been a violation of the Constitution; if the court finds no such violation, the Seimas cannot remove the official from office. Furthermore, when sitting in impeachment proceedings the Seimas is presided over not by one of its members but by a judge of the Supreme Court, and it cannot remove a person from office other than by a three-fifths majority of its members in a reasoned decision. Lastly, in the specific circumstances of the present case the Court observes that the applicant, assisted by counsel, gave evidence to the Seimas and the Constitutional Court at public hearings.

103. Be that as it may, the Court, while not wishing either to underplay the seriousness of the applicant's alleged conduct in relation to his constitutional obligations or to question the principle of his removal from office as President, notes the extent of the consequences

of his removal for the exercise of his rights under Article 3 of Protocol No 1; as positive constitutional law currently stands, he is permanently and irreversibly deprived of the opportunity to stand for election to Parliament. This appears all the more severe since removal from office has the effect of barring the applicant not only from being a Member of Parliament but also from holding any other office for which it is necessary to take an oath in accordance with the Constitution (see paragraph 34 above).

104. Admittedly, the Government contended that in assessing proportionality in the present case, regard should be had to the evolution of the local political context in which the principle of disqualification from elected office was applied. The Court does not disagree. It takes note in this connection of the Government's argument that, in a recent democracy such as (according to the Government) Lithuania, it is not unreasonable that the State should consider it necessary to reinforce the scrutiny carried out by the electorate through strict legal principles, such as the one in issue here, namely permanent and irreversible disqualification from standing in parliamentary elections. Nevertheless, the decision to bar a senior official who has proved unfit for office from ever being a Member of Parliament in future is above all a matter for voters, who have the opportunity to choose at the polls whether to renew their trust in the person concerned. Indeed, this is apparent from the wording of Article 3 of Protocol No 1, which refers to "the free expression of the opinion of the people in the choice of the legislature".

Still, as the Government suggested, the particular responsibilities of the President of Lithuania should not be overlooked. An "institution" in himself and the "personification" of the State, the President carries the burden of being expected to set an example, and his place in the Lithuanian institutional system is far from merely symbolic. In particular, he enjoys significant prerogatives in the legislative process since he has the right to initiate legislation (Article 68 of the Constitution) and the possibility, when a law is submitted to him for signature and promulgation, of sending it back to the Seimas for reconsideration (Article 71 of the Constitution). In the Court's view, it is understandable that a State should consider a gross violation of the Constitution or a breach of the constitutional oath to be a particularly serious matter requiring firm action when committed by a person holding that office.

105. However, that is not sufficient to persuade the Court that the applicant's permanent and irreversible disqualification from standing for election as a result of a general provision constitutes a proportionate response to the requirements of preserving the democratic order. It

reaffirms in this connection that the "free expression of the opinion of the people in the choice of the legislature" must be ensured in all cases.

106. The Court notes, firstly, that Lithuania's position in this area constitutes an exception in Europe. Indeed, in the majority of the Council of Europe's member States with a republican system where impeachment proceedings may be brought against the head of State, impeachment has no direct effects on the electoral rights of the person concerned. In the other States in this category, there is either no direct effect on the exercise of the right to stand in parliamentary elections, or the permissible restrictions require a specific judicial decision and are subject to a time-limit (see paragraph 62 above).

107. The Court further observes that the circumstances of the present case differ greatly from those of the *Ždanoka* case, to which the Government referred. The central issue in that case was a statutory provision barring persons who, like the applicant, had "actively participated after 13 January 1991" in the Communist Party of Latvia (CPL) from standing in parliamentary elections. The provision had been enacted by Parliament on account of the fact that, shortly after the Declaration of Independence of 4 May 1990, the party in question had been involved in organising and conducting attempted coups in January and August 1991 against the newly formed democratic regime. After observing in particular that, in the historical and political context in which the impugned measure had been taken, it had been reasonable for the legislature to presume that the leading figures of the CPL held an anti-democratic stance, the Court concluded that there had been no violation of Article 3 of Protocol No 1. It held in particular that while such a measure could not be accepted in the context, for example, of a country with a long-established framework of democratic institutions, it might be considered acceptable in Latvia in view of the historical and political context which had led to its adoption, and given the threat to the new democratic order posed by the resurgence of ideas which, if allowed to gain ground, might appear capable of restoring a totalitarian regime (see *Ždanoka*, cited above, §§ 132-6; see also *Ādamsons*, cited above, § 113). However, besides the obvious contextual differences between that case and the present one, the Court, without wishing to underplay the seriousness of the applicant's alleged conduct in relation to his constitutional obligations, observes that the importance of his disqualification for the preservation of the democratic order in Lithuania is not comparable.

108. The Court also notes that, in finding no violation in the *Ždanoka* case, it attached considerable weight to the fact that, firstly, the Latvian Parliament periodically reviewed the provision in issue and,

secondly, the Constitutional Court had observed that a time-limit should be set on the restriction. It further concluded that the Latvian Parliament should keep the restriction under constant review, with a view to bringing it to an early end, and added that such a conclusion was all the more justified in view of the greater stability which Latvia now enjoyed, *inter alia* by reason of its full European integration, indicating that any failure by the Latvian legislature to take active steps to that end might result in a different finding by the Court (see *Ždanoka*, *loc. cit.*).

109. Thus, in assessing the proportionality of such a general measure restricting the exercise of the rights guaranteed by Article 3 of Protocol No 1, decisive weight should be attached to the existence of a time-limit and the possibility of reviewing the measure in question. The need for such a possibility is, moreover, linked to the fact that, as the Government noted, the assessment of this issue must have regard to the historical and political context in the State concerned; since this context will undoubtedly evolve, not least in terms of the perceptions which voters may have of the circumstances that led to the introduction of such a general restriction, the initial justification for the restriction may subside with the passing of time.

110. In the present case, not only is the restriction in issue not subject to any time-limit, but the rule on which it is based is set in constitutional stone. The applicant's disqualification from standing from election accordingly carries a connotation of immutability that is hard to reconcile with Article 3 of Protocol No 1. This is a further notable difference between the present case and the *Ždanoka* case cited above.

111. The Court observes, lastly, that although it is worded in general terms and is intended to apply in exactly the same manner to anyone whose situation corresponds to clearly defined criteria, the provision in question results from a rule-making process strongly influenced by the particular circumstances.

In this connection it notes in particular that the second paragraph of Article 56 of the Constitution, which specifies the persons who cannot be elected as members of the Seimas, makes no reference to persons who have been removed from office following impeachment proceedings. When the Seimas decided to remove the applicant from office as President (on 6 April 2004), no legal provision stated that he was to be barred from standing for election as a result. Accordingly, when he informed the Central Electoral Committee of his intention to stand in the presidential election called for 13 June 2004 following his removal from office, the committee initially found (on 22 April 2004) that there was nothing to prevent him from doing so. The Seimas then introduced an amendment to the Presidential Elections Act to the effect that anyone who had been removed from office following impeachment proceedings could not be elected President until a period of five years had elapsed, as a result of which the committee ultimately refused to register the applicant as a candidate. Further to an action brought by members of the Seimas, the Constitutional Court held (on 25 May 2004) that such disqualification was compatible with the Constitution but that subjecting it to a time-limit was unconstitutional, adding that it applied to any office for which it was necessary to take an oath in accordance with the Constitution. The Seimas subsequently (on 15 July 2004) introduced an amendment to the Seimas Elections Act to the effect that anyone who had been removed from office following impeachment proceedings was ineligible to be a Member of Parliament.

The striking rapidity of the legislative process reinforces the impression that it was at least triggered by the specific desire to bar the applicant from standing in the presidential election called as a result of his removal from office. That, admittedly, is not a decisive factor for the purposes of Article 3 of Protocol No 1, which applies only to the election of the legislature. However, the Court considers that it constitutes an additional indication of the disproportionate nature of the restriction of the applicant's rights under that Article (see, *mutatis mutandis*, *Tănase*, cited above, § 179).

112. Having regard to all the above factors, especially the permanent and irreversible nature of the applicant's disqualification from holding parliamentary office, the Court finds this restriction disproportionate and thus concludes that there has been a violation of Article 3 of Protocol No 1.

III. *Alleged violation of Article 13 of the Convention taken in conjunction with Article 3 of Protocol No 1*

113. The applicant complained that he had not had an effective remedy available in respect of the Constitutional Court's ruling of 25 May 2004. He relied on Article 13 of the Convention taken in conjunction with Article 3 of Protocol No 1. Article 13 provides:

Everyone whose rights and freedoms as set forth in [the] Convention are violated shall have an effective remedy before a national authority notwithstanding that the violation has been committed by persons acting in an official capacity.

114. Having regard to its finding of a violation of Article 3 of Protocol No 1, the Court considers that the applicant had an "arguable claim" calling in principle for the application of Article 13 of the Convention.

However, it reiterates that the absence of remedies against decisions of a constitutional court will not normally raise an issue under this Article (see for example, *Wendenburg and Others* v. *Germany* (dec.), No 71630/01, ECHR 2003-II).

It further observes that in the instant case the applicant's complaint concerns his inability to challenge the rule laid down by the Constitutional Court in its decision on an action for review of constitutionality, to the effect that a person removed from office as President for a gross violation of the Constitution or a breach of the constitutional oath is no longer entitled to hold office as a Member of Parliament, among other positions. However, Article 13 of the Convention, which does not go so far as to guarantee a remedy allowing a Contracting State's laws as such to be challenged before a national authority on the ground of being contrary to the Convention (see, for example, *James and Others* v. *United Kingdom*, 21 February 1986, § 85, Series A No 98; *Christine Goodwin* v. *United Kingdom* [GC], No 28957/95, § 113, ECHR 2002-VI; *Roche* v. *United Kingdom* [GC], No 32555/96, § 137, ECHR 2005-X; and *Tsonyo Tsonev* v. *Bulgaria*, No 33726/03, § 47, 1 October 2009), likewise cannot require the provision of a remedy allowing a constitutional precedent with statutory force to be challenged. In the present case the complaint raised by the applicant under Article 13 falls foul of this principle, seeing that his disqualification does not derive from an individual decision against him but from the application of the above-mentioned rule (see, *mutatis mutandis*, *Tsonyo Tsonev*, cited above, § 48).

115. It follows that this part of the application is manifestly ill-founded and as such must be rejected as inadmissible pursuant to Article 35 §§ 3(a) and 4 of the Convention.

IV. Application of Article 41 of the Convention

116. Article 41 of the Convention provides:

If the Court finds that there has been a violation of the Convention or the Protocols thereto, and if the internal law of the High Contracting Party concerned allows only partial reparation to be made, the Court shall, if necessary, afford just satisfaction to the injured party.

A. Damage

117. The applicant sought 50,000 euros (EUR) in compensation for the non-pecuniary damage caused by the fact that he was deprived for life of the right to stand for election and by the extensive media coverage of the proceedings against him.

In respect of pecuniary damage, he sought an amount corresponding to forty-seven months' salary as President, making a total of EUR 183,912.88. He submitted in that connection that his monthly salary had been EUR 3,913.04 and that he had been removed from office after thirteen months of the five-year term for which he had been elected. He also sought reimbursement of his "final pension". He noted that under Lithuanian law, former presidents were entitled to a lifetime pension amounting to 50% of their salary; since the average life expectancy in Lithuania was seventy-seven years and he would have been fifty-three at the end of his term of office, he assessed the loss sustained on that account at EUR 586,956.

118. The Government contended that the claim for pecuniary damage was unfounded, unsubstantiated and excessive. They further argued that there was no causal link between the pecuniary damage referred to by the applicant and the alleged violation of Article 3 of Protocol No 1 and that he had not substantiated his claims under that head either.

119. The Court would point out that its finding of a violation of Article 3 of Protocol No 1 does not relate to the manner in which the impeachment proceedings against the applicant were conducted or to his removal from office as President, but solely to his permanent and irreversible disqualification from standing for election to Parliament. It thus concludes that there is no causal link between the alleged pecuniary damage and the violation of the Convention it has found and dismisses the applicant's claims under this head. In addition, while finding that the applicant is, on the other hand, entitled to claim that he has suffered non-pecuniary damage, it considers, having regard to the particular circumstances of the case, that such damage is sufficiently compensated by its finding of a violation of Article 3 of Protocol No 1.

That apart, the Court also reiterates that by virtue of Article 46 of the Convention, the Contracting Parties have undertaken to abide by the final judgments of the Court in any case to which they are parties. Furthermore, it follows from the Convention, and from Article 1 in particular, that in ratifying the Convention the Contracting States undertake to ensure that their domestic legislation is compatible with it. This means, *inter alia*, that a judgment in which the Court finds a breach of the Convention or its Protocols imposes on the respondent State an obligation to determine, subject to supervision by the Committee of Ministers, the general and/or, if appropriate, individual measures to be taken in its domestic legal order to put an end to the violation found by the Court and make all feasible reparation for its consequences, in such a way as to restore as far as possible the situation existing before the breach (see, for example, *Assanidze* v. *Georgia* [GC], No 71503/01, § 198, ECHR 2004-II, and *Verein gegen Tierfabriken Schweiz (VgT)* v. *Switzerland (No 2)* [GC], No 32772/02, § 85, ECHR 2009-IV).

B. *Costs and expenses*

120. The applicant also sought reimbursement of the costs of his representation before the Seimas and the Constitutional Court (EUR 35,000) and before the Court (EUR 39,000), and of the expenses incurred by him and his lawyer in travelling to Strasbourg for the Grand Chamber hearing (estimated at EUR 2,500).

121. The Government argued that the applicant had not produced any evidence in support of those claims. They further contended that he had omitted to show that the (unreasonable) amount claimed for the costs incurred in the domestic proceedings had been necessary to prevent the alleged breach of Article 3 of Protocol No 1. In addition, they argued that the claims relating to the proceedings before the Court were excessive.

122. The Court observes that the proceedings before the Constitutional Court and the Seimas were not intended to "prevent or redress" the violation of the Convention which it has found (see, for example, *Zimmermann and Steiner* v. *Switzerland*, 13 July 1983, § 36, Series A No 66; *Lallement* v. *France*, No 46044/99, § 34, 11 April 2002; and *Frérot* v. *France*, No 70204/01, § 77, 12 June 2007), since the violation results solely from the applicant's inability to stand for election to Parliament. The applicant is therefore not entitled to claim reimbursement of the costs and expenses relating to those proceedings.

With regard to those incurred in the proceedings before the Court, including in connection with the hearing on 28 April 2010, the Court reiterates that an award can be made in respect of costs and expenses only in so far as they have been actually and necessarily incurred by the applicant and are reasonable as to quantum; furthermore, Rule 60 §§ 2 and 3 of the Rules of Court requires the applicant to submit itemised particulars of all claims, together with any relevant supporting documents, failing which the Court may reject the claims in whole or in part (see, for example, *Frérot, loc. cit.*). In the present case, seeing that the applicant did not produce any documents in support of his claims, the Court decides to dismiss them in their entirety.

For these reasons, the Court

1. *Declares* unanimously the complaints under Articles 6 and 7 of the Convention and Article 4 of Protocol No 7 inadmissible;
2. *Declares* unanimously the complaint under Article 3 of Protocol No 1 in so far as it concerns the applicant's removal from office or his ineligibility to stand for election as President of Lithuania inadmissible;
3. *Declares* by a majority the complaint under Article 3 of Protocol No 1 in so far as it concerns the applicant's inability to stand for election to the Seimas admissible;
4. *Declares* unanimously the complaint under Article 13 of the Convention, taken in conjunction with Article 3 of Protocol No 1 inadmissible;
5. *Holds* by fourteen votes to three that there has been a violation of Article 3 of Protocol No 1 on account of the applicant's inability to stand for election to the Seimas;
6. *Holds* unanimously that the finding of a violation constitutes in itself sufficient just satisfaction for the non-pecuniary damage sustained by the applicant;
7. *Dismisses* unanimously the remainder of the applicant's claim for just satisfaction.

In accordance with Article 45 § 2 of the Convention and Rule 74 § 2 of the Rules of Court, the partly dissenting opinion of Judge Costa joined by Judges Tsotsoria and Baka is annexed to this judgment.

PARTLY DISSENTING OPINION OF JUDGE COSTA JOINED BY JUDGES TSOTSORIA AND BAKA

(Translation)

1. I disagree with the opinion of the majority of the Grand Chamber as expressed in the above judgment. My dissent is only partial but concerns two issues I consider important. I shall begin with some general observations.

2. The case is a political one. The applicant, Mr Rolandas Paksas, was elected President of the Republic of Lithuania by direct universal suffrage and held office as head of State from 26 February 2003 to 6 April 2004. On the latter date, the Lithuanian Parliament (the Seimas) removed him from office as President for gross violations of the Constitution as established by the Constitutional Court. The case is not only political but is also unusual because impeachment proceedings are rarely instituted in Europe and elsewhere in the world and are hardly ever carried through to completion; for example, Richard Nixon, the thirty-seventh President of the United States, resigned in August 1974 to avoid impeachment, which had become likely as a result of the Watergate scandal. More recently, in 2004 the South Korean Parliament impeached the country's President but the impeachment proceedings were declared void by the Constitutional Court two months later.

This conception of impeachment as both exceptional in nature and normally deterrent in effect has a very long history. In their work *Droit constitutionnel* (PUF, Thémis, Paris, 2004, p. 47), Professors Vlad Constantinesco and Stéphane Pierré-Caps point out that in 1742 the British Prime Minister Robert Walpole and his ministers resigned under threat of impeachment, as did Lord North and his ministers in 1782; of course, this British institution, dating back to the fourteenth century, inspired the United States, which nevertheless had (and still has) a presidential rather than parliamentary system.

3. The majority, rightly in my opinion, dismissed several complaints as incompatible *ratione materiae* with the Convention and its Protocols. In particular, they applied the well-known case-law deriving from *Pierre-Bloch* v. *France* (21 October 1997, *Reports of Judgments and Decisions* 1997-VI) in declaring Article 6 § 1 inapplicable to Constitutional Court proceedings; and they held that Article 3 of Protocol No 1, concerning the right to free elections—which the case-law of the European Commission and Court of Human Rights has extended to the right to vote and to stand in elections (as, indeed, seems to follow from the State's obligation to ensure "the free expression of the opinion of the people in the choice of the legislature")—applies only to the election of the "legislature": accordingly, it does not apply to the President's removal from office, or to eligibility to stand for election as President (or indeed to referendums, an issue not arising here).

4. Finding that the applicant's disqualification from standing for election to the Seimas thus fell within the scope of Article 3 of Protocol No 1, the majority went on to hold that this complaint was admissible and well-founded. I am unable to agree on either point.

5. Firstly, the judgment considers that both the admissibility criteria set forth in Article 35 § 1 of the Convention were satisfied. It takes the view that the applicant exhausted domestic remedies or did not have any available (which amounts to the same thing), and that his complaint was not lodged outside the six-month time-limit. These two findings are of unequal accuracy and to my mind are contradictory.

6. Following impeachment proceedings as provided for by the Constitution, the Seimas removed Mr Paksas from office on 6 April 2004. Fresh *presidential* elections were called for 13 June. The applicant applied to be registered as a candidate, but his candidacy was refused on 10 May by the Central Electoral Committee and on 28 May the Supreme Administrative Court dismissed his complaint against that decision. All this is mentioned as a reminder of the context, since the complaints concerning the applicant's removal from office and the presidential election are inadmissible *ratione materiae*.

As to the applicant's eligibility to stand for election *to the Seimas*, it was ruled out by an Act passed by the Seimas on 15 July 2004, further to the Constitutional Court's ruling of 25 May 2004 to the effect that a person who had been removed from office as head of State for a gross violation of the Constitution, such as Mr Paksas, could never again be (re-)elected as President or even as a member of the Seimas. As far as the latter disqualification is concerned, the decision forming the basis of the alleged violation of Article 3 of Protocol No 1 is either the Constitutional Court's ruling on the disqualification, or at the very latest the Act implementing that ruling and giving it statutory effect.

7. I can accept that the applicant did not have an effective remedy in respect of any of those measures. The Constitutional Court's ruling is final by virtue of Article 107 of the Constitution (see paragraphs 41 and 76 of our judgment). Moreover, any remedy used in an attempt to have the Act of 15 July 2004 declared unconstitutional would logically have been bound to fail, since the Constitutional Court would have no plausible reason to find fault with a legislative provision enacted by way of implementing its own ruling. Accordingly, I do not contest the conclusion reached by the majority in paragraph 78 of the judgment, while having some reservations as to the underlying reasoning, although it is unnecessary for me to express them.

8. On the other hand, I cannot accept in all legal conscience the finding that the application is not out of time, at least in respect of the only admissible complaint. Since no judicial (or other) remedy was available, the final domestic decision was, at the latest and at best from the applicant's perspective, the Act of 15 July 2004. That date constitutes the starting-point, the *dies a quo*, for the six-month period. Being

unable to apply to any national court, Mr Paksas would not have breached the principle of subsidiarity by applying to the European Court of Human Rights; quite the contrary. In paragraph 81, however, the judgment observes, as the Government did, that in his application (lodged on 23 September 2004, within the time-limit) the applicant did not raise, even in substance, the complaint concerning his ineligibility to stand for election *to the Seimas*. Although the applicant—who, moreover, was well informed and represented by qualified lawyers—could and should have done so, he did not raise that complaint until 30 September 2005, one year later, in a supplement to his application.

9. To counter this unassailable argument that this complaint is out of time, the majority resort to the notion of a *continuing situation*. In my view, the assistance thus offered to an applicant who has displayed a manifest lack of diligence is ingenious but artificial, and in any event I must say that I am not convinced. Admittedly, the provisions prescribing or governing Mr Paksas's inability to stand for election have a *permanent* effect. But that is the case with most instantaneous acts; they rarely have a *temporary* effect. When Article 2 (still in force) of the Civil Code of 30 Ventôse Year XII (21 March 1804) states that "the law provides only for the future; it has no retrospective effect", the words "for the future" mean "on a permanent basis", unless, of course, a subsequent law repeals or amends the initial law (*lex posterior derogat priori*).

Whether the disqualification from elected office is permanent or subject to a time-limit—an issue which may have a bearing on its compatibility with the substantive right guaranteed by Article 3 of Protocol No 1—this has nothing to do with the concepts of an instantaneous act or a continuing situation. Otherwise, nearly all legal measures would give rise to situations that could be described as such, and the six-month rule would scarcely ever be applicable.

10. The criterion of a time-limit is to be taken seriously. It does not reflect empty formalism. Time-limits for appealing exist for all national courts; they are generally shorter than the six-month period laid down in the Convention, which takes into account the difficulties for certain applicants (surely not the case for Mr Paksas) to obtain information about the Convention and to institute proceedings in Strasbourg. Time-limits for appealing pursue several legitimate aims, among them the proper administration of justice and, even more importantly, legal certainty and stability. In the case-law this admissibility criterion has been construed without excessive rigidity, but it must be applied rigorously. Rigidity and rigorousness are not synonymous, and any slackness would in my view be dangerous, not least for the future of

the European human-rights protection system. As to the notion of a continuing situation, it does not stem from the text of the Convention but is a judge-made construct that has developed in a quite different environment from the present case, for example in cases of disappearances. According it too much significance in the case-law would likewise be dangerous in my opinion, for while a sometimes legitimate exception to a rule explicitly laid down in the Convention may mitigate the effects of the rule, it should not render it nugatory; the case-law may interpret the text of the Convention, but should not take its place.

11. I therefore have no hesitation in finding that the complaint was out of time. I could leave it at that. Just to make things clear, however, I wish to add, not without some doubt, that if the complaint had been submitted in time, I would probably have concluded that it was ill-founded.

12. The judgment as a whole appears moderate and balanced, if I may express an opinion. It finds only a "narrow" violation. The conviction of the majority is that lifelong disqualification from standing for election is excessive and thus unacceptable. This view is all the more understandable because the penalty is severe (although in politics, nothing is ever final, not even electoral legislation; but one should not speculate on this point). And the case-law generally takes a strict approach to prohibitions of this type, as in the case of permanent exclusion orders against foreign nationals (see *Mehemi* v. *France*, 25 September 1997, *Reports* 1997-VI). However, the allegations against the applicant were not trivial either, and it was the national Parliament which, following a ruling by a high-level court, removed him from office and passed the impugned Act. In such a specific and delicate field as electoral law, and in a case involving the complex relations between the different public authorities, subject to the ultimate scrutiny of the electorate, and thus the sovereign people, I would advocate restraint; the State has a wide discretion, and therefore it seems to me that the legitimate European supervision in this case should be restricted or limited. For that reason, I would probably have voted against point 5 of the operative provisions even if the facts could have led me to vote in favour of point 3; it seems more honest for me to say so.

[Report: (2014) 59 EHRR 30]

Human rights — Elections — Right to free elections — Right to stand as candidate — Former President barred from standing for office because of impeachment — Admissibility of author's communication to Human Rights Committee — Examination of claim under another procedure of international investigation or settlement — European Court of Human Rights — Council of Ministers — Whether author's claims incompatible *ratione materiae* with International Covenant on Civil and Political Rights, 1966 — Consideration of merits — Entitlement to a fair and public hearing by a competent, independent and impartial tribunal established by law in determination of any criminal charges or of rights or obligations in a suit at law — Protection against finding of criminal liability for any act or omission not constituting a criminal offence when committed — Right to take part in the conduct of public affairs — European Convention on Human Rights, 1950, Article 3 of Protocol No 1 — International Covenant on Civil and Political Rights, Articles 14, 15 and 25 — United Nations Human Rights Committee

PAKSAS v. LITHUANIA[1]

(Communication No 2155/2012)

United Nations Human Rights Committee.[2] 25 March 2014

SUMMARY:[3] *The facts*:—The author, Mr Paksas, was a Lithuanian national who had been elected President of the Republic of Lithuania on 5 January 2003. A special commission was established by the Lithuanian Parliament ("the Seimas") to investigate serious allegations made against the author regarding his conduct during his first year as President. Finding some of those allegations to be founded, it recommended impeachment proceedings against him. At the request of the Seimas, the Constitutional Court examined the alleged offences. On 31 March 2004, the Constitutional Court ruled that the

---

[1] The author was represented by counsel, Mr Stanislovas Tomas. For related proceedings, see 165 ILR 252.
[2] The members of the Committee who participated in the examination of this communication were Mr Yadh Ben Achour (Tunisia), Mr Lazhari Bouzid (Algeria), Ms Christine Chanet (France), Mr Cornelis Flinterman (the Netherlands), Mr Yuji Iwasawa (Japan), Mr Walter Kälin (Switzerland), Ms Zonke Zanele Majodina (South Africa), Mr Gerald L. Neuman (United States of America), Sir Nigel Rodley (United Kingdom), Mr Víctor Manuel Rodríguez Rescia (Costa Rica), Mr Fabián Omar Salvioli (Argentina), Ms Anja Seibert-Fohr (Germany), Mr Yuval Shany (Israel), Mr Konstantine Vardzelashvili (Georgia), Ms Margo Waterval (Suriname) and Mr Andrei Paul Zlătescu (Romania).
[3] Prepared by Ms E. Fogarty.

author had grossly breached the Constitution and his constitutional oath by granting citizenship by exception to a Russian businessman, Mr Borisov, who had made substantial financial contributions to the author's election campaign; by informing Mr Borisov that law enforcement institutions were investigating him; and by abusing his office to influence decisions of a private company in order to protect the property interests of persons close to him. On 6 April 2004, the Seimas voted in favour of impeachment. Criminal investigations into the author's alleged abuse of office were commenced, though discontinued in October 2004, and he was acquitted of informing Mr Borisov of investigations into him in December 2005.

The Central Electoral Committee found no legal ground to prevent the author from standing in a presidential election called for 13 June 2004. On 4 May 2004, the Seimas amended the Presidential Elections Act, precluding persons who had been removed from office in impeachment proceedings from running for President within five years of removal. On 25 May 2004, the Constitutional Court declared that disqualification from standing for election as President was constitutional, and that the disqualification applied to all public office positions requiring a constitutional oath, including the positions of President, prime minister, minister, judge and state controller. It held, however, that the time limit was not constitutional, and that the spirit of the Constitution prohibited an impeached person from relevant public office positions for life. The Seimas subsequently amended the Elections Act accordingly, and in 2008 made a similar amendment to the Law on Local Self-Government, disqualifying impeached persons from running in local elections.

On 27 September 2004, the author lodged a claim against Lithuania's permanent disqualification of him from public office with the European Court of Human Rights ("ECtHR"). The ECtHR ruled on 6 January 2011 (165 ILR 252) that the author's permanent and irreversible disqualification from holding parliamentary office was disproportionate and violated Article 3 of Protocol No 1[4] to the European Convention on Human Rights, 1950 ("the European Convention"). The claims concerning other public offices were declared incompatible *ratione materiae* with the European Convention. The Lithuanian Government subsequently sought to amend the offending legislation; however, the amendments were deemed unconstitutional in September 2012.

On 24 June 2011, the author submitted his communication to the Committee, claiming that the legal proceedings against him and his disqualification from holding public office violated Articles 14(1) and (2),[5]

---

[4] Article 3 of Protocol No 1 to the Convention provided: "*Right to free elections*: The High Contracting Parties undertake to hold free elections at reasonable intervals by secret ballot, under conditions which will ensure the free expression of the opinion of the people in the choice of the legislature."

[5] Article 14 of the Covenant provided: "(1) All persons shall be equal before the courts and tribunals. In the determination of any criminal charge against him, or of his rights and obligations in a

15⁶ and 25(a), (b) and (c)⁷ of the International Covenant on Civil and Political Rights, 1966 ("the Covenant"). In particular, he submitted that the permanent disqualification from public offices had been applied to him retrospectively and with a presumption of his guilt, and that the Constitutional Court's determination that the proposed amendments to bring relevant legislation into line with the ECtHR's judgment were unconstitutional constituted a refusal to execute that judgment. He further submitted that the Constitutional Court had been biased and subject to pressure from the Seimas, and that the impeachment proceedings were effectively a criminal trial undertaken without the procedural guarantees provided for in Articles 14 and 15 of the Covenant. The State Party contested the admissibility and the merits of the claim.

Held:—The State Party had violated the author's rights under Article 25(b) and (c) of the Covenant. The author's claims under Articles 14 and 15 of the Covenant were inadmissible.

(1) The author's claims under Articles 14 and 15 of the Covenant were incompatible *ratione materiae* with the provisions of the Covenant. Article 14 guaranteed a right to a fair trial and a public hearing by a competent, independent and impartial tribunal in cases determining criminal charges or the rights and obligations of individuals in a suit at law. Article 15 of the Covenant protected persons from being held guilty of any criminal offence on account of any act or omission that did not constitute a criminal offence at the time it was committed. Contrary to the author's claim that the impeachment proceedings had been of a criminal nature, the President was immune from criminal liability under the Lithuanian Constitution, and the proceedings did not result in the author being charged with or found guilty of a "criminal offence". Nor were those proceedings to determine the rights and obligations in a suit at law. Instead, impeachment proceedings were measures against persons in their capacity as figures subordinated to a high degree of

---

suit at law, everyone shall be entitled to a fair and public hearing by a competent, independent and impartial tribunal established by law ... (2) Everyone charged with a criminal offence shall have the right to be presumed innocent until proved guilty according to law."

⁶ Article 15 of the Covenant provided: "(1) No one shall be held guilty of any criminal offence on account of any act or omission which did not constitute a criminal offence, under national or international law, at the time when it was committed. Nor shall a heavier penalty be imposed than the one that was applicable at the time when the criminal offence was committed. If, subsequent to the commission of the offence, provision is made by law for the imposition of a lighter penalty, the offender shall benefit thereby. (2) Nothing in this article shall prejudice the trial and punishment of any person for any act or omission which, at the time when it was committed, was criminal according to the general principles of law recognized by the community of nations."

⁷ Article 25 of the Covenant provided: "Every citizen shall have the right and the opportunity, without any of the distinctions mentioned in Article 2 and without unreasonable restrictions: (a) To take part in the conduct of public affairs, directly or through freely chosen representatives; (b) To vote and to be elected at genuine periodic elections which shall be by universal and equal suffrage and shall be held by secret ballot, guaranteeing the free expression of the will of the electors; (c) To have access, on general terms of equality, to public service in his country."

administrative or parliamentary control. In this case, the Seimas had initiated the proceedings as a parliamentary procedure, independent of the criminal procedures also being followed against the author. The author's claims with respect to Articles 14 and 15 of the Covenant were thus inadmissible under Article 3 of the Optional Protocol to the Covenant (paras. 7.7-7.8).

(2) The author made several claims under Article 25 of the Covenant concerning his disqualification from holding the office of President, from holding parliamentary office, from running in local elections and from holding judicial office. His claim with respect to his permanent disqualification from holding a parliamentary office was inadmissible. The ECtHR had already examined that claim and determined that the author's permanent and irreversible disqualification violated his right to stand in parliamentary elections. In accordance with Article 46(2) of the European Convention, the Council of Ministers was responsible for supervising the execution of that final judgment, and that claim was therefore being actively examined under another procedure of international investigation or settlement. However, the ECtHR had declared the author's claims with respect to offices other than parliamentary offices inadmissible, and the rights protected by Article 25(b) and (c) of the Covenant had no equivalent in the European Convention. The author's claims with respect to other public offices were not being examined under another procedure of international investigation or settlement; there was no obstacle to the admissibility of those claims under Article 5(2)(a) of the Optional Protocol to the Covenant (paras. 7.2-7.3).

(3) The author's claim with respect to disqualification from local elections had not been sufficiently substantiated for the purpose of admissibility. Likewise, his claims with respect to disqualification from office as a judge or state controller were insufficiently substantiated, as the author did not, in any event, satisfy the primary precondition for such roles of having a legal education. That claim was also inadmissible (paras. 7.4-7.5).

(4) The author's claim that the permanent disqualification from candidacy for the office of President and from appointment as prime minister or a minister amounted to a violation of Article 25 of the Covenant was admissible. It was not being considered under another procedure of international investigation or settlement, and domestic remedies had been exhausted. Article 25 protected the rights of all citizens to take part in the conduct of public affairs, to vote and to be elected, and to have access to public service. The exercise of those rights could not be suspended or excluded except on grounds established by laws that were objective and reasonable, and that incorporated fair procedures. On the date that the Seimas decided to remove the author from the office of President, no legal provision existed expressly stating that he could be barred from standing for election as a result. By way of immediate subsequent amendments to the Presidential Elections Act, the Seimas introduced a five-year disqualification of persons in the author's position from candidacy for President, which resulted in the Central Electoral Committee's refusal to register the author as a candidate for the June

2004 presidential election. Upon the Constitutional Court's determination that the disqualification was constitutional and should apply to all public offices requiring a constitutional oath, but permanently, the Seimas immediately amended the Elections Act to create a lifelong disqualification. The relevant amendments were highly linked in time and substance to the impeachment proceedings initiated against the author and lacked the necessary foreseeability and objectivity required, amounting to an unreasonable restriction of the author's rights under Article 25(b) and (c) of the Covenant (paras. 7.9-9).

(5) Under Article 2(3)(a) of the Covenant, the State Party was obliged to provide the author with an effective remedy, including revision of the lifelong prohibition of his candidacy in presidential elections, and of his taking office as a prime minister or minister. The State Party was also to take steps to avoid similar violations in the future, and was to provide the Committee, within 180 days, with information about the measures taken to give effect to its Views, which it was requested to publish and disseminate widely (paras. 10-11).

Individual opinion by Mr Neuman (partly dissenting): (1) The narrowness of the Committee's holding had to be stressed in light of the unusual manner in which the author's permanent disqualification from standing for certain offices was enacted. The decision was not to be misunderstood as calling into question permanent disqualification of impeached office-holders for future elections based on well-established ground rules (para. 2).

(2) The author's permanent ineligibility to stand for the office of President did not violate Article 25 of the Covenant. Impeachment was an extraordinary means for protecting the democratic political process against an otherwise irremovable president who abused the powers of office. Impeachments were both rare and difficult, and it was reasonable and foreseeable that a president who was removed by impeachment would be ineligible to run for election to that office again (paras. 3-4).

(3) Permanent ineligibility after impeachment was not a disproportionate consequence of abuse of office. If presidents who had successfully completed one or more terms could be permanently ineligible for re-election for the sake of ensuring a healthy and competitive political system, presidents who had been removed for abuse of office could surely also be permanently barred (para. 5).

The following is the text of the Views of the Committee:

1. The author of the communication is Rolandas Paksas. He claims that Lithuania[1] has violated his rights under articles 14 (paras. 1 and 2), 15 and 25(a), (b) and (c) of the International Covenant on Civil and Political Rights. Mr Paksas is represented by Stanislovas Tomas.

---

[1] The Optional Protocol entered into force for the State party on 20 February 1992, without reservation.

THE FACTS AS SUBMITTED BY THE AUTHOR

2.1 The author was elected President of the Republic of Lithuania on 5 January 2003 in direct and democratic elections. On 11 April 2003, the author issued Decree No 40, countersigned by the Minister of the Interior, granting Lithuanian citizenship by way of exception for service to Lithuania, to a Russian businessman, Jurij Borisov—who had been awarded the Medal of Darius and Girėnas for service to Lithuania for his efforts to glorify the name of Lithuania in the world and for assisting Lithuania in its integration into the world community of States, by the author's predecessor, Valdas Adamkus, via Presidential Decree No 1373 (2001).

2.2 On 6 November 2003, the Lithuanian Parliament (Seimas) requested the Constitutional Court to advise whether Presidential Decree No 40 was in compliance with the Constitution and with the Citizenship Act. The Seimas submitted that the procedure of granting citizenship on an exceptional basis appeared to have been applied inappropriately, considering that Mr Borisov had no special merit warranting exceptional treatment for him, and that the author had granted him citizenship as a reward for his substantial financial assistance to his election campaign.

2.3 The author submits that on 8 December 2003, the main impeachment initiator, Gintaras Steponavicius, Vice-President of the Seimas, met with Egidijus Kūris, President of the Constitutional Court, and that they discussed the granting of citizenship to Mr Borisov. On 18 December 2003, 86 members of the Seimas submitted a proposal to initiate impeachment proceedings against the author. On 23 December 2003, the Seimas set up a special commission to investigate the allegations about the author's conduct. On 19 February 2004, the special investigation commission concluded that some of the charges made against the author were founded and serious, and it recommended that the Seimas institute impeachment proceedings. On the same day, the Seimas requested the Constitutional Court to determine whether the specific acts of the author cited by the commission had breached the Constitution.

2.4 On 31 March 2004, the Constitutional Court adopted Ruling No 14/04 declaring a gross breach of the Constitution and of the author's constitutional oath on three points:

(a) Unlawfully granting citizenship to Mr Borisov by Decree No 40 as a reward for his financial support;
(b) Informing Mr Borisov that the law enforcement institutions were investigating him and tapping his telephone conversations; and

(c) Exploiting his official status to influence decisions of the private company Žemaitijos keliai Ltd concerning the transfer of shares, with a view to defending the property interests of certain private individuals close to him.

2.5 On 6 April 2004, the Seimas voted in favour of the impeachment. The author wished to stand as a candidate in the presidential election called for 13 June 2004. On 22 April 2004, the Central Electoral Committee found that there was no legal ground to prevent him from standing. However, on 4 May 2004, Parliament amended the Presidential Elections Act by inserting the following provision: "A person who has been removed from parliamentary or other office by the Seimas in impeachment proceedings may not be elected President of the Republic if fewer than five years have elapsed since his removal from office." Following this amendment, the Central Electoral Committee refused to register the author as a candidate. The issue was forwarded to the Constitutional Court.

2.6 On 25 May 2004, the Constitutional Court held (in Ruling No 24/04) that disqualifying a person from standing for election was compatible with the Constitution, but that subjecting such a disqualification to a time limit was unconstitutional. The Court further pointed [out] that the spirit of the Constitution prohibits the author from standing for presidential or parliamentary elections and from being a prime minister, minister, judge or state controller, for life. On 15 September 2008, Parliament amended the Law on Local Self-Government. The author considers that this amendment prohibits him, as an impeached president, from standing for local election.

2.7 On 21 October 2004, the Prosecutor General discontinued the criminal investigation into allegations that the author had abused his office as President in order to influence decisions made by the Žemaitijos keliai company concerning the transfer of its shares in violation of article 228 of the Criminal Code.

2.8 On 13 December 2005, the Lithuanian Supreme Court acquitted the author of the charge of informing Mr Borisov that the law enforcement institutions were investigating him and tapping his telephone conversations.

2.9 On 27 September 2004, the author lodged an application against Lithuania with the European Court of Human Rights. In its judgment of 6 January 2011,[2] the European Court held that Lithuania

---

[2] See European Court of Human Rights Judgment 34932/04, *Paksas* v. *Lithuania*, 6 January 2011.

had violated article 3 of Protocol No 1 of the European Convention for the Protection of Human Rights and Fundamental Freedoms, and considered that the author's disqualification from holding parliamentary office was disproportionate because of its permanent and irreversible nature. The remainder of the author's complaint was declared incompatible *ratione materiae* with the Convention. Following the European Court's judgment, the Government formed a working group to make proposals for carrying it out. On 31 May 2011, the working group submitted its conclusions, stating that it was necessary to remove the irreversible and permanent nature of the disqualification for persons removed from office following impeachment proceedings for committing a gross violation of the Constitution and breaching the constitutional oath. The proposed constitutional amendments were approved by the Government on 6 June 2011, but the Constitutional Court held them to be unconstitutional on 5 September 2012.

THE COMPLAINT

3.1 The author claims a violation of articles 14 (paras. 1 and 2), 15 and 25(a), (b) and (c) of the International Covenant on Civil and Political Rights.

3.2 The author considers that his complaint must be held admissible because: (a) he submitted it on 24 June 2011 and therefore did not delay in addressing the Committee after Judgment 34932/04 of the European Court of Human Rights, issued on 6 January 2011; and (b) the right to stand for presidential elections is not covered *ratione materiae* by the European Convention for the Protection of Human Rights and Fundamental Freedoms, and was therefore not examined by the European Court.[3]

3.3 With regard to the exhaustion of domestic remedies, the author refers to the amendment of the Law on Local Self-Government adopted on 15 September 2008 introducing a prohibition on an impeached president standing for local elections. According to the author, domestic litigation on this point would relate to general legislation and would not serve his purpose.

3.4 The author refers to Ruling No 24/04, in which the Constitutional Court gave its interpretation that it shall be prohibited to organize a referendum to determine whether the author violated the Constitution and whether the lifelong prohibition on standing for

---

[3] Ibid., para. 72.

election must be revoked, which he claims was in violation of article 25(a) of the Covenant. The author states that this breach was mentioned in his application to the European Court of Human Rights, but was not examined.

3.5 On the merits, the author considers that the lifelong prohibition on standing for presidential and local elections was not established by law, is not objective, is not reasonable, and is disproportionate, therefore violating his rights under article 25(a) and (b) of the Covenant. In this respect, the author makes reference to the Committee's jurisprudence in *Dissanayake* v. *Sri Lanka*, where the Committee recognized that a seven-year prohibition on standing in elections following a breach of the Constitution was disproportionate.[4]

3.6 The author argues that there was no fair trial, and that the requirement of procedural fairness as set out in article 25(c) was violated, including through the meeting held on 8 December 2003 between the Vice-President of the Seimas and the President of the Constitutional Court, where they discussed the granting of citizenship to Mr Borisov. On 16 March 2004, the author's lawyers submitted a motion for the removal of Justice Kūris on account of this meeting, but it was denied. The author therefore considers that the right to objective impartiality as developed in the jurisprudence of the Committee[5] was breached by the Constitutional Court.

3.7 The author also argues that the Constitutional Court was biased in two respects. Firstly, on 5 January 2004, the Constitutional Court made a comment on the author's New Year speech. Secondly, on 16 March 2004, the President of the Constitutional Court commented during the hearings that the motion for removal of the judges made by the author could be dismissed without consideration.[6]

3.8 The author considers that the Seimas exercised continuous pressure on the courts. For example, on 25 March 2004, it issued a "Declaration on the actions of President Rolandas Paksas", stating that the finding of the author's guilt by the Constitutional Court was "just a matter of time" and that "having regard to the fact that the impeachment proceedings would last for quite a long period, [the Seimas] proposes to Rolandas Paksas, President of the Republic, to resign".

---

[4] See communication No 1373/2005, *Dissanayake* v. *Sri Lanka*, Views adopted on 22 July 2008, para. 8.5.

[5] See communication No 1015/2001, *Perterer* v. *Austria*, Views adopted on 20 July 2004, para. 10.4.

[6] "The motion for removal might be denied together [with the request for leave to present video evidence], but such a question must be decided in the Deliberation Room. However until now you have not presented the reasons for removal."

According to the author, the Seimas was sure of the outcome of the ongoing impeachment proceedings, thereby breaching article 14, paragraph 2, of the Covenant.

3.9 The author argues that Constitutional Court Ruling No 24/04 states that the lifelong prohibition on his standing for election and being appointed to offices requiring a constitutional oath is based on a presumption of guilt that is contrary to article 14, paragraph 2, of the Covenant, and was applied to him retrospectively in breach of article 15 of the Covenant.

3.10 The author states that the lifelong prohibition on holding the office of Prime Minister or Minister was introduced, for the first time, with Ruling No 24/04 of the Constitutional Court on 25 May 2004 which was implemented after the acts of the author but before the end of the impeachment proceedings. The Seimas amended the Parliamentary Elections Act and the Presidential Elections Act accordingly.

3.11 The author considers that the principle of objectivity was violated because of the breach of basic procedural fairness, and because of the discrimination he suffered as compared to political opponents. The author reiterates the arguments developed with regard to the alleged violation of article 14 of the Covenant, arguing that neither of the two previous presidents were subjected to lifelong restrictions, despite granting citizenship on an exceptional basis, "for merits", in "much more controversial" cases. Referring to the Committee's jurisprudence,[7] the author considers that the sanction imposed on him is disproportionate and violates article 25 of the Covenant.

3.12 In a further submission dated 9 June 2012, the author argues that the Committee should examine the prohibition on the organizing of a referendum on the question of whether the author had violated the Constitution following Constitutional Court Ruling No 24/04, and on the question of whether the lifelong prohibition on standing for election must be revoked. The author also considers that, while the issue of the right to a fair trial was held inadmissible by the European Court of Human Rights, it should be considered admissible by the Committee in compliance with its jurisprudence.[8]

---

[7] The author refers to communication No 1373/2005, *Dissanayake* v. *Sri Lanka*, op. cit.; communication No 1134/2002, *Fongum Gorji-Dinka* v. *Cameroon*, Views adopted on 17 March 2005; and communication No 1392/2005, *Lukyanchik* v. *Belarus*, Views adopted on 21 October 2009, para. 8.5.

[8] The author refers to communication No 1774/2008, *Boyer* v. *Canada*, decision on inadmissibility adopted on 27 March 2009, para. 4.2; communication No 1015/2001, *Perterer* v. *Austria*, op. cit., para. 9.2; and communication No 1454/2006, *Lederbauer* v. *Austria*, Views adopted on 13 July 2007, para. 7.2.

3.13 In this regard, the author considers that the impeachment proceedings were of a criminal nature, as they were initiated following alleged criminal offences. The author also observes that according to article 246 of the Seimas Rules of Procedure, which were in force from February 1999 to November 2004, the impeachment proceedings had to comply with the "principles and fundamental rules of criminal proceedings". The author further considers that the impeachment proceedings before the Constitutional Court are a suit at law, since a group of members of the Parliament officially made an accusation against him before the Constitutional Court, and since the recognition of the breach unavoidably led to his removal from office. The author therefore argues that articles 14 and 15 are applicable.

3.14 The author argues that the Constitutional Court usurped the will of the people, removing their right to vote for the author and thereby threatening democracy. The author further observes that the Constitution does not include any *expressis verbis* ban on being re-elected after an impeachment.

3.15 The author considers that the Constitutional Court's ruling of 5 September 2012 amounts to a refusal to execute the judgment of the European Court, which required the re-establishment of the author's right to stand in parliamentary elections and violates article 25 of the Covenant.

3.16 The author therefore seeks recognition of violations of articles 14 (paras. 1 and 2), 15 and 25 of the Covenant, and the re-establishment of his right to stand for presidential, parliamentary and local elections and to hold offices that require a constitutional oath.

STATE PARTY'S OBSERVATIONS ON ADMISSIBILITY AND ON THE MERITS

4.1 In its notes verbales dated 21 September 2012 and 5 December 2012, the State party submitted its observations. The State party considers that the communication must be declared inadmissible and without merit insofar as the author's allegations are incompatible with the provisions of the Covenant and are unsubstantiated.

4.2 The State party considers that the impeachment proceedings are a form of constitutional liability and cannot be equated to disciplinary proceedings against civil servants or to criminal charges.[9] The purpose of the impeachment case instituted against the author was to determine

---

[9] See communication No 1015/2001, *Perterer* v. *Austria*, op. cit., para. 9.2.

whether he had committed gross violations of the Constitution and whether his constitutional oath had been breached. The State party considers that the impeachment proceedings did not concern the determination of the author's rights and obligations in a suit at law; instead, they involve the head of State's constitutional liability and therefore lie outside the criminal sphere.

4.3 The State party also considers that the author is incorrect in arguing that the gross violations of the Constitution for which he was removed from office should have been proved in a criminal court. This interpretation perverts the provisions of the Constitution on impeachment, as not all the grounds of the impeachment are related to the commission of a criminal act. According to the Constitution, criminal prosecution cannot be instituted against the President of the Republic as long as he is in office (article 86 of the Constitution).

4.4 The State party argues that even after the Constitutional Court concluded that the author had breached his oath and had violated the Constitution, he still had the possibility of resigning from office in order to avoid full constitutional liability. The specific restriction at issue is applicable only in cases where the Seimas removes a person from office by not less than a three-fifths majority vote following a relevant conclusion of the Constitutional Court. The State party argues that the author did not avail himself of the said opportunity to resign from office. It considers that a final decision by Parliament is the grounds for applying a constitutional sanction, and that article 14 of the Covenant is not applicable to proceedings before Parliament.

4.5 The State party further considers that the acquittal of the author on 13 December 2005 for disclosure of classified information cannot change the conclusion of the Constitutional Court that the author grossly violated the Constitution.[10] The impeachment procedure does not involve the determination of any criminal charge or of rights and obligations in a suit at law within the meaning of article 14 of the Covenant. This part of the communication should therefore be declared inadmissible *ratione materiae* under article 3 of the Optional Protocol.[11]

4.6 Should the Committee consider otherwise, the State party argues that the author's allegations concerning alleged violations of article 14, paragraphs 1 and 2, of the Covenant are unsubstantiated. In that regard, the State party considers that the author's

---

[10] Constitutional Court's conclusion of 31 March 2004.
[11] Communication No 1419/2005, *De Lorenzo* v. *Italy*, decision on inadmissibility adopted on 24 July 2007.

communication seeks the re-examination of the legality of the constitutional sanction imposed on him, and refers to the jurisprudence of the Committee, under which: "it is in principle for the courts of States parties to evaluate the facts and evidence, unless the evaluation of the facts and evidence was manifestly arbitrary or amounted to a denial of justice"[12]. The State party considers that this is clearly not the case in regard to the complaints made by the author. The State party recalls that Lithuanian law provides for a number of safeguards to protect persons implicated in impeachment proceedings from arbitrary treatment, as the rules of criminal procedure and fair trial principles apply to impeachment proceedings. While the decision[s] to initiate such proceedings and to apply a sanction are the prerogative of the Seimas, a political body, it is the task of a judicial body, the Constitutional Court, to rule on whether there has been a violation of the Constitution. If the Court finds no such violation, the Seimas cannot remove the official from office. Furthermore, when conducting impeachment proceedings, the Seimas is presided over by a judge of the Supreme Court, and it cannot remove a person from office other than by a three-fifths majority of its members in a reasoned decision. Lastly, the author was assisted by numerous counsels, and was able to provide his evidence during public hearings.[13]

4.7 The State party considers that the author has not submitted any reasoned arguments on the alleged arbitrariness and unfairness of the proceedings. Regarding the alleged bias of the Constitutional Court in its public statement of 5 January 2004 issued in reaction to the author's speech of 31 December 2003, the State party considers that the Court clearly refrained from engaging in any political polemics.

4.8 As regards the alleged bias resulting from the meeting between the President of the Constitutional Court and the Vice-President of the Seimas, the State party considers that these allegations are unsubstantiated, as the impeachment proceedings had not been initiated at that time. The State party considers that the Committee's jurisprudence in *Dissanayake* v. *Sri Lanka*[14] cannot be applied to the author's case because the restrictions referred to were not linked to the author's arbitrary conviction and sentence. Additionally, the State party considers that the gravity of the author's unconstitutional conduct cannot be compared to that of Mr Dissanayake, who was convicted for

---

[12] Communications No 1329/2004 and No 1330/2004, *Pérez Munuera and Hernández Mateo* v. *Spain*, decision on inadmissibility adopted on 25 July 2005.
[13] See judgment of the Grand Chamber, 6 January 2011, Application No 34932/04, § 102.
[14] Op. cit.

contempt of court. The State party considers that the present case also differs from the Committee's case of *Bandaranayake* v. *Sri Lanka*,[15] since the restriction imposed on the author's rights was the result of his removal under the constitutional impeachment proceedings (and not following criminal liability), without any kind of arbitrariness.

4.9 As regards the author's complaint under article 14, paragraph 2, of the Covenant, for alleged violation of the presumption of innocence, the State party considers that the author is perverting Lithuanian law by equating the impeachment proceedings with criminal or disciplinary law issues.

4.10 The State party further considers that when blaming the Seimas for breaching the presumption of his innocence, the author did not mention that the declaration that suggested his resignation from presidential office was made following his invitation to Mr Borisov to become his public adviser on 24 March 2004, and following the declaration that the author made on television the next day to apologize for that invitation, which he qualified as a "fatal mistake". The State party considers that the declaration of the Seimas responded to the vulnerability of the President, as reflected in the conviction of Mr Borisov for the use of psychological abuse against him. The State party therefore considers that the author's allegations concerning violation of article 14 of the Covenant are unsubstantiated.

4.11 As to the alleged violation of article 15 of the Covenant for the alleged arbitrary and retrospective application of a constitutional sanction, the State party refers to the Committee's jurisprudence under which article 15, paragraph 1, prohibits the retroactive application of laws only in relation to criminal law matters.[16] The measures of removal from office and (consequent) disqualification from standing for election involve the Head of State's constitutional liability and lie outside the "criminal" sphere.

4.12 Should the Committee consider otherwise, the State party maintains that the author's allegations concerning violations of article 15 of the Covenant are unsubstantiated and without merit. The constitutional sanction was not applied retrospectively, as it entered into force on the day on which the author was removed from office by the Seimas, and procedural safeguards were respected. Furthermore, the State party argues that the restriction adopted was not unforeseeable: in its ruling of 25 May 2004, the Constitutional Court further developed

---

[15] Communication No 1376/2005, *Bandaranayake* v. *Sri Lanka*, Views adopted on 24 July 2008.
[16] Communication No 1994/2010, *IS* v. *Belarus*, decision on inadmissibility adopted on 25 March 2011.

the concept of the irreversible nature of a constitutional sanction resulting from impeachment, already known since the ruling of the Constitutional Court of 11 May 1999. If the author had doubts as to the consequences of the constitutional liability, he could have requested the interpretation and revision of this ruling to the Constitutional Court under articles 60 and 61 of the Law on the Constitutional Court.

4.13 New amendments to the Law on Seimas Elections and to the Law on Presidential Elections were adopted in May and July 2004 respectively, with the aim of specifying the constitutional provisions and lessening the sanctions applicable following impeachment proceedings. The Constitutional Court declared those provisions unconstitutional. The State party considers that this decision was not unforeseeable for the author, and concludes that the alleged violation of article 15 of the Covenant should be held to be unsubstantiated and without merit.

4.14 As regards the alleged violation of article 25 of the Covenant, the State party considers that the scope and content of the constitutional sanction is clearly, precisely and narrowly defined, as the prohibition exclusively relates to passive presidential and parliamentary election rights, and positions requiring a constitutional oath. The right to vote and to participate in the conduct of public affairs is not restricted, as demonstrated by the author's political activities after his removal from presidential office.

4.15 As to the alleged violation of the author's right to initiate a referendum, the State party argues that the impeachment procedure is clearly regulated. The removal of a person or the revocation of his/her mandate and the imposition of subsequent constitutional sanctions cannot be decided by way of referendum. The State party considers that the complaint by the author on this matter is incompatible *ratione materiae* with the provisions of the Covenant: the author could have initiated a referendum for amendment of the respective constitutional provisions under article 9 § 3 of the Constitution. The State party therefore considers that the author's complaint under article 25(b) of the Covenant is inadmissible and without merit.

4.16 The State party further argues that the author has never been prevented from standing for municipal elections. He was listed as the first candidate of his political party for the Municipality of Vilnius City at the municipal elections of February 2007, and he was a member of Vilnius City Council from March 2007 to June 2009. The State party also argues that the amendments introduced in 2008, to article 22 of the Law on Local Self-Government, do not affect the author's rights insofar as the oath introduced for new members of the Self-Government Council is different from the constitutional oath. The author's claim under article 25 of the Covenant concerning his inability to stand for municipal elections is therefore without merit.

4.17 As regards the author's inability to stand for parliamentary elections, the State party considers that the author does not refer to any particular elections where he would have been prevented from exercising his right to do so. The State party considers that, in compliance with the jurisprudence of the Committee,[17] the author cannot claim to be a victim within the meaning of article 1 of the Optional Protocol.

4.18 Should the Committee consider otherwise, the State party argues that the author failed to exhaust domestic remedies with regard to his inability to stand for parliamentary elections. If the author had expressed his intention to become a member of the Seimas in October 2004 and October 2008 and the Supreme Electoral Commission had refused to register him as a candidate, he could have applied to the administrative courts for alleged interference with his right to do so. The Committee is therefore precluded from considering this part of the communication pursuant to article 5, paragraph 2(b), of the Optional Protocol. The State party argues that this position is supported by the recent reforms adopted by the Government following the judgment of the European Court of Human Rights.

4.19 The State party further considers that the newness of the democratic regime in Lithuania justifies the maintaining of the existing constitutional sanction, even though it might appear excessive in a well-established democracy. Only eight years have elapsed since the author's removal from presidential office. The restriction on standing for election can still be regarded as reasonable and proportional to the constitutional offences that he committed. Constitutional amendments were proposed and approved by the Government on 6 June 2011 and transmitted to the Seimas. It was decided to make relevant changes to the Law on Seimas Elections, and relevant constitutional amendments will be introduced in the very near future.

4.20 In respect of the alleged violation of article 25(b) of the Covenant regarding the restriction on standing for the presidential elections, the State party refers to the jurisprudence of the Committee under which the exercise of the right to vote and to be elected may not be suspended or excluded except on objective and reasonable grounds

---

[17] Communication No 1038/2001, *Dáithí Ó Colchúin* v. *Ireland*, decision on inadmissibility adopted on 28 March 2003.

that are established by law[18] and are compatible with the purpose of the law.[19] The State party reiterates that no criminal liability was applied to the author, and that only his passive right to stand for the presidential elections was restricted. Although of an irreversible nature, the constitutional restrictions are proportionate to the aim pursued and to the gravity of the related breaches. The State party concludes that the author has failed sufficiently to substantiate his claim under article 25(b), which should therefore be held inadmissible under article 2 of the Optional Protocol.

4.21 As to the reasonableness of the constitutional restriction on standing in presidential elections, the State party reiterates that its aim is to prevent any person who has grossly violated the Constitution and breached his/her constitutional oath from holding the office provided for in the Constitution. The constitutional restriction relates to the same office from which the author was removed. Given that the aim of the impeachment procedure is to protect and strengthen the democratic constitutional order and national security, the restriction must be considered as reasonable. Similar restrictions of a permanent nature exist in the legislation of other democratic States (such as the United States of America, the Czech Republic, Slovakia and Poland).

4.22 The State party further emphasizes that the constitutional restriction on standing in presidential elections only applies to categories of persons that are clearly defined in law, and there is no doubt that, as former President of the Republic, the author belongs to that group. The constitutional restriction could therefore not be described as discriminatory. The State party further recalls that since the restoration of the independence of Lithuania, seven similar procedures have been initiated in respect of other serving presidents. The restriction at issue is precisely worded; it applies in the same way to anyone and it is objective.[20]

4.23 The State party highlights the particular responsibilities of the President of the Republic of Lithuania, who is expected to set an example. It argues that the author still does not acknowledge the gravity and seriousness of the breaches that he committed, and concludes that the author expects the European Court of Human Rights and the Human Rights Committee to justify the gross violations that he

---

[18] General comment No 25 (1996) on the right to participate in public affairs, voting rights and the right of equal access to public service, para. 4; and communication No 1134/2002, *Fongum Gorji-Dinka* v. *Cameroon*, op. cit.
[19] Communication No 500/1992, *Joszef Debreczeny* v. *Netherlands*, Views adopted on 3 April 1995.
[20] General comment No 25, op. cit., para. 4.

consciously carried out. It considers that the restriction imposed is proportionate with the seriousness of the acts, and is neither discriminatory nor arbitrary.

4.24 As regards the alleged violation of article 25 of the Covenant regarding the author's inability to become a judge, state controller, prime minister or minister, the State party considers that the author has not provided any arguments or evidence. It reiterates the arguments presented as to the inapplicability of article 14 of the Covenant *ratione materiae* and considers that the present communication has nothing to do with the right not to be arbitrarily dismissed from public service.[21] The State party also submits that the author's claims relating to his inability to become a judge or a state controller are merely hypothetical, because he does not meet the specific eligibility requirements for any of those offices. It therefore considers that the author has no actual grievance to claim under article 25 of the Covenant and that his claim is inadmissible under articles 1 and 2 of the Optional Protocol. As to the author's complaint regarding his inability to become a prime minister or minister, the State party considers that the author does not demonstrate that he actually intended to stand for those positions and was prevented from doing so. Accordingly, he cannot claim to be a "victim" within the meaning of article 1 of the Optional Protocol.

AUTHOR'S COMMENTS ON THE STATE PARTY'S SUBMISSIONS

5.1 On 30 November 2012 and 22 December 2012, the author provided comments on the State party's submissions. The author specifies that he never talked about the possibility of appointing Mr Borisov as public adviser to the President, but only as a "voluntary (unpaid) adviser", and that the appointment never actually took place.

5.2 With regard to the argument of the State party that the author did not intend to stand for presidential elections or to become a minister during the last eight years, the author considers that his intention to stand for presidential elections or to become a minister would have been rejected in compliance with the very clear ruling of the Constitutional Court of 25 March 2004. Additionally, while the political party led by the author became part of the government

---

[21] The State party refers to communication No 1376/2005, *Bandaranayake* v. *Sri Lanka*, Views adopted on 24 July 2008.

coalition after the parliamentary elections of October 2012, the author could not become a minister since the lifelong prohibition was still in force.

5.3 The author maintains that the impeachment proceedings that were applied to his case were criminal, as the sanctions imposed were both deterrent and punitive. He therefore considers that articles 14 and 15 of the Covenant apply, and that the State party failed to present any substantial counterargument in that regard.

5.4 With regard to violation of article 14, paragraph 1, of the Covenant, the author considers that the State party was biased when it tried to justify the Constitutional Court's statement of 5 January 2004, by maintaining that the Constitutional Court had "refrained from political polemics", whereas the Court had actually participated in the related "political polemics" through its statements.

5.5 The author also argues that the State party presents false facts when trying to defend itself, with regard to the meeting between the President of the Constitutional Court and the Vice-President of the Seimas, and he considers that the pressure by the Seimas was not on the ordinary courts but on the Constitutional Court.

5.6 The author considers that the lifelong prohibition on standing for election and on being a minister was justified only by a presumption of guilt, in breach of article 14, paragraph 2, of the Covenant. In addition, he considers that the Seimas declaration of 25 March 2004 was made in breach of the presumption of innocence, prior to the Constitutional Court ruling of 31 March 2004. He argues that by voting to approve the declaration, the Seimas intended to punish the author for his political opinion.

5.7 Considering the State party's statement that he could have addressed the Constitutional Court for an interpretation of the sanction while in office, the author comments that he did not do so because the prohibition did not exist at that time. By introducing the sanction in question, the State party breached article 15 of the Covenant. Additionally, the author considers that article 15 was breached by the "conviction" by the Constitutional Court, whereas he was acquitted by the Supreme Court regarding the alleged disclosure of a State secret, whereas the alleged abuse of office resulting in influencing the decisions of the private company Žemaitijos keliai was discontinued, and whereas the investigation into the alleged buying of citizenship by Mr Borisov was never started. The author considers that his "conviction" results from an obvious error of assessment and constitutes a denial of justice, representing a breach by the Constitutional Court of the principle of *nulla poena sine lege*.

5.8 The author further argues that the State party violated article 25(b) of the Covenant through the ruling of the Constitutional Court of 5 September 2012, which declared as unconstitutional the March 2012 amendment to the Law on Seimas Elections. The author considers that this decision amounts to a refusal to execute the European Court judgment requiring the re-establishment of the right to stand for parliamentary elections retrospectively.

5.9 With regard to his right to become a minister, state controller or judge, the author argues that he has sufficient university background to become a state controller and that he may acquire the necessary qualification to become a judge.

5.10 Finally, the author considers that "elections" obviously cannot declare a person innocent, and that the State party's statement to the effect is an attempt to mislead the Committee. The author nevertheless considers that both "elections" and "referendums" may lead to an amendment to the Constitution and that the Constitutional Court prohibited referendums to avoid such an amendment.

STATE PARTY'S ADDITIONAL OBSERVATIONS

6.1 In its submission dated 15 March 2013, the State party made additional comments in which it maintained its position that the author's complaints regarding the alleged violations of articles 14 (paras. 1 and 2), 15 and 23(a), (b) and (c) are incompatible with the Covenant and are unsubstantiated.

6.2 The State party reiterates that the aim and purpose of the impeachment proceedings is to protect the State community and that these proceedings are therefore different from criminal proceedings.

6.3 The State party argues that it did not suggest to the author to apply to the Constitutional Court for the setting of a constitutional sanction, but for a revision of the irreversible nature of the constitutional sanction under review.

6.4 The State party considers that the author's statements regarding the alleged influence of the Seimas on the Constitutional Court are grounded in his personal beliefs, as in its decision of 31 March 2004, the Constitutional Court did not refer to the invitation made by the author to Mr Borisov, nor to the declaration made by the Seimas suggesting that the author resign from office.

6.5 The State party recalls that the special investigation commission concluded that the charges brought against the author were grounds for instituting impeachment proceedings in the Seimas. It emphasizes that the allegation that the author had unlawfully granted Lithuanian citizenship to Mr Borisov was only one of the grounds for the impeachment.

6.6 With regard to the author's assertion that the text of the Constitution did not include an *expressis verbis* ban on re-election after impeachment, the State party argues that the official constitutional doctrine is part of the Constitution. The author's statement that the judgment of the European Court of Human Rights of 6 January 2011 required the re-establishment of his right to stand for parliamentary elections retrospectively is misleading and incorrect. The Constitutional Court clearly recognized the duty to remove the incompatibility of the provisions of article 3 of Protocol No 1 of the Convention with the Constitution, and possible constitutional amendments are under review. Finally, the State party emphasizes that the Constitutional Court did not prohibit a referendum in order to prevent amendment of the restriction at issue. The statement of the Court in its ruling of 25 May 2004 is related exclusively to the finality and non-disputability of its conclusion in respect of a concrete person against whom impeachment procedures had been initiated. It does not mean that the constitutional legal regulation governing the impeachment procedure and its consequences may not be changed by way of referendum or ordinary legislative procedure.

ISSUES AND PROCEEDINGS BEFORE THE COMMITTEE

Consideration of admissibility

7.1 Before considering any claim contained in a communication, the Human Rights Committee must decide, in accordance with rule 93 of its rules of procedure, whether the communication is admissible under the Optional Protocol to the Covenant.

7.2 The Committee has to ascertain, in accordance with article 5, paragraph 2(a), of the Optional Protocol, whether the same matter is being examined under another procedure of international investigation or settlement. The Committee notes that the European Court of Human Rights on 6 January 2011 (application No 34932/04) decided that the author's permanent and irreversible disqualification from holding parliamentary office violated his right to stand in parliamentary elections. The author challenges the Constitutional Court's subsequent ruling of 5 September 2012 as a refusal to execute the judgment of the European Court. The Committee notes that, according to article 46, paragraph 2, of the European Convention for the Protection of Human

Rights and Fundamental Freedoms, the execution of final judgments of the European Court of Human Rights is supervised by the Committee of Ministers of the Council of Ministers, and considers that this matter is currently being actively examined under another procedure of international investigation or settlement. Accordingly, the Committee considers that the part of the communication which relates to the author's lifelong disqualification from parliamentary office is inadmissible under article 5, paragraph 2(a), of the Optional Protocol, in the present circumstances.

7.3 The Committee notes, however, that the remainder of the author's claims to the European Court of Human Rights, which related to his disqualification from office other than Parliament, was declared incompatible *ratione materiae* with the European Convention. The Committee recalls that the concept of "the same matter" has to be understood as including the same author, the same facts and the same substantive rights. The Committee notes that article 25, paragraphs (b) and (c), have no equivalent in the European Convention and its Protocols as regards access to public office other than the legislature, and therefore concludes that the communication does not concern the same matter in the sense of article 5, paragraph 2(a), of the Optional Protocol. The Committee also recalls that when adhering to the Optional Protocol, Lithuania did not enter a reservation to article 5, paragraph 2(a). Accordingly, the Committee concludes that it is not prevented under article 5, paragraph 2(a), from considering these claims.

7.4 As regards the alleged prohibition on standing in local elections as a result of the amendments to the Law on Local Self-Government adopted on 15 September 2008, the Committee notes the argument of the State party according to which the amendments do not affect the author's right to stand in local elections, since the oath introduced for new members of the Self-Government Council is different from the constitutional oath that the author is prevented from taking. The Committee considers that the author has not sufficiently substantiated his claims with regard to local elections and declares this claim inadmissible in accordance with article 2 of the Optional Protocol.

7.5 As regards the disqualification from serving as a judge or a state controller, the Committee notes the State party's argument that the author is not affected by this disqualification because he does not satisfy the specific prerequisites for these offices. The Committee notes that the author has not obtained a legal education and has not shown that he has taken any concrete steps to obtain such an education in the future. The Committee concludes that the author has not shown that he could be considered a victim of a violation of the Covenant with regard to the disqualification from these offices. This part of the communication is declared inadmissible in accordance with article 1 of the Optional Protocol.

7.6 The Committee notes the author's argument according to which the impeachment proceedings under review were linked to the alleged criminal offences and were therefore of a criminal nature. The Committee also notes that the author claims a violation of article 14, paragraphs 1 and 2, of the Covenant, resulting from an alleged collusion between the President of the Constitutional Court and the member of the Seimas who had initiated the proceedings against him, and from the pressure exercised on the Constitutional Court. The Committee notes that, under the Lithuanian Constitution, the President is immune from criminal liability but can be removed from office and held constitutionally liable through impeachment proceedings,[22] and that the Seimas is the only authority mandated to decide whether the person against whom the proceedings were initiated should be removed from office.[23]

7.7 The Committee recalls that the right to a fair and public hearing by a competent, independent and impartial tribunal is guaranteed in cases regarding the determination of criminal charges against individuals or of their rights and obligations in a suit at law. It further recalls that there is no determination of rights and obligations in a suit at law where the persons concerned are confronted with measures taken against them in their capacity as persons subordinated to a high degree of administrative or parliamentary control,[24] such as the impeachment procedure. In the case under review, the impeachment procedure was initiated by the Seimas as a parliamentary procedure, independently of the criminal procedures being followed against the author.

7.8 Similarly, the outcome of the impeachment proceedings was not to charge the author with a "criminal offence" and to hold him "guilty of a criminal offence" within the meaning of article 15 of the Covenant. Accordingly, the author's claims under articles 14 and 15 of the Covenant are incompatible *ratione materiae* with the provisions of the Covenant and are inadmissible under article 3 of the Optional Protocol.

---

[22] Articles 74 and 86 of the Constitution.
[23] Articles 246 to 258 and 260 of the Statute of the Seimas, and articles 74 and 107 § 3 of the Constitution.
[24] See general comment No 32 (2007) on the right to equality before courts and tribunals and to a fair trial, para. 17; and communication No 1015/2001, *Perterer v. Austria*, op. cit., para. 9.2 (disciplinary dismissal).

7.9 As regards the alleged violation of article 25, concerning the impeachment procedure and the restrictions adopted, the Committee notes the argument of the State party according to which the author could have applied to the Constitutional Court for an interpretation of its ruling of 11 May 1999, holding that the constitutional sanction imposed in the context of impeachment proceedings was "of an irreversible nature". The Committee also notes the position of the State party that the author could have resigned in order to avoid the impeachment procedure and its outcome. The Committee further notes the argument of the author according to which an application to the Constitutional Court would have been ineffective, as there was no doubt as to the meaning of the phrase "of an irreversible nature", and that under article 107 of the Lithuanian Constitution, the decisions of the Constitutional Court have statutory force and are final. In this respect, the Committee shares the analysis of the European Court of Human Rights according to which a prior request to the Constitutional Court for clarification of whether removal from office entailed lifelong restrictions "could not ... have prompted an examination of the author's particular situation ... It would also have required him to resign voluntarily as President and thereby to accept such a restrictive condition that the remedy in question could not in any event be regarded as 'accessible'." The Committee therefore considers that the author has exhausted all available domestic remedies with regard to the alleged violations of article 25, and that these claims are admissible. The Committee therefore proceeds to a consideration of the merits.

Consideration of the merits

8.1 The Human Rights Committee has considered the communication in the light of all the information made available to it by the parties, as provided for under article 5, paragraph 1, of the Optional Protocol.

8.2 Regarding the author's claims under article 25 of the Covenant, the issue before the Committee is whether the lifelong disqualifications adopted against him from being a candidate in presidential elections, or being a prime minister or a minister, amount to a violation of the Covenant.

8.3 The Committee recalls that article 25 of the Covenant recognizes and protects the right of every citizen to take part in the conduct of public affairs, the right to vote and to be elected, and the right to have access to public service. Whatever form of constitution or government is in force, the exercise of these rights by citizens may not be suspended or excluded except on grounds which are established by laws that are objective and reasonable, and that incorporate fair procedures.[25]

8.4 The Committee notes the State party's argument that the constitutional sanction restricting the author's rights is proportionate to the gravity of his unconstitutional conduct. It also notes the author's argument that the lifelong disqualifications adopted against him were not established by law, not objective and not reasonable, and are disproportionate. In this regard, the Committee notes the statements made by the Constitutional Court on 5 January 2004 and on 16 March 2004, insinuating the responsibility of the author prior to the outcome of the proceedings under review. The Committee also notes that on 6 April 2004, when the Seimas decided to remove the author from his office of President, no legal provision expressly stated that he could be barred from standing for election as a result. Accordingly, on 22 April 2004, the Central Electoral Committee authorized the author to stand in the June 2004 presidential election. However, on 4 May 2004, the Seimas introduced an amendment to the Presidential Elections Act stating that anyone who had been removed from office following impeachment proceedings was prevented from standing in presidential elections for a period of five years after those proceedings. Following that amendment, the Central Electoral Committee refused to register the author as a candidate. On 25 May 2004, the Constitutional Court held that such a disqualification was compatible with the Constitution, but that subjecting it to a time-limit was unconstitutional, adding that it applied to any office for which it was necessary to take a constitutional oath. On 15 July 2004, the Seimas adopted an amendment to the Elections Act, through which anyone removed from office following impeachment proceedings became ineligible as a Member of Parliament, and could not stand for the offices of President, Prime Minister, Minister, Judge or State Controller. In view of the foregoing, the Committee considers that the lifelong disqualifications on being a candidate in presidential elections, or on being a prime minister or minister, were imposed on the author following a rule-making process that was highly linked in time and substance to the impeachment proceedings initiated against him. Under the specific circumstances of the instant case, the Committee therefore considers that the lifelong disqualifications imposed on the author lacked the necessary foreseeability and objectivity and thus amount to an unreasonable restriction

---

[25] See general comment No 25, op. cit., paras. 3, 4 and 16.

under article 25(b) and (c) of the Covenant, and that the author's rights under these provisions have been violated.

9. The Human Rights Committee, acting under article 5, paragraph 4, of the Optional Protocol to the International Covenant on Civil and Political Rights, is of the view that the State party has violated the author's rights under article 25(b) and (c) of the International Covenant on Civil and Political Rights.

10. In accordance with article 2, paragraph 3(a), of the Covenant, the State party is under an obligation to provide the author with an effective remedy, including through revision of the lifelong prohibition of the author's right to be a candidate in presidential elections or to be a prime minister or minister, in light of the State party's obligations under the Covenant. Additionally, the State party is under the obligation to take steps to avoid similar violations in the future.

11. Bearing in mind that, by becoming a party to the Optional Protocol, the State party has recognized the competence of the Committee to determine whether there has been a violation of the Covenant and that, pursuant to article 2 of the Covenant, the State party has undertaken to ensure to all individuals within its territory or subject to its jurisdiction the rights recognized in the Covenant and to provide an effective and enforceable remedy when it has been determined that a violation has occurred, the Committee wishes to receive from the State party, within 180 days, information about the measures taken to give effect to the Committee's Views. The State party is also requested to publish the present Views and disseminate them broadly in the official languages of the State party.

APPENDIX

INDIVIDUAL OPINION BY COMMITTEE MEMBER
MR GERALD L. NEUMAN (PARTIALLY DISSENTING)

[1] I fully agree with the Committee's rulings on admissibility. In particular, it is important for the proper performance of the Committee's functions that litigants who have already prevailed in the European Court of Human Rights not be permitted to bring the same issue as a communication under the Optional Protocol merely to seek a second opinion.[26]

---

[26] [Paragraph numbers have been editorially inserted in this opinion.] Cf. communication No 712/1996, *Smirnova* v. *Russian Federation*, Views adopted on 5 July 2004, paras. 9.3 and 9.4 (finding

[2] Regarding the merits, I would stress the narrowness of the Committee's holding, which results from the unusual manner in which the author's permanent disqualification from standing for certain offices was enacted. The decision should not be misunderstood as calling into question permanent disqualification of impeached office-holders for future elections based on well-established ground rules. A wide variety of States, for example, provide expressly in their constitutions for ineligibility after impeachment as an authorized or mandatory consequence.[27]

[3] Even though the holding is narrow, I disagree with the Committee's conclusion in paragraph 8.4 of its Views that, under the circumstances, the author's permanent ineligibility to stand again for election to the particular office of President violates article 25 of the Covenant.

[4] Impeachment is an extraordinary means for protecting the democratic political process against an otherwise unremovable president who abuses the powers of the office. Impeachments are rare and difficult. An impeachment is not merely a vote of no confidence that contemplates renewed elections to test the president's popular support. It is both reasonable and foreseeable that a president removed by impeachment could be ineligible ever to stand again for election to that sensitive office.

[5] Permanent ineligibility after impeachment is also not a disproportionate consequence for abuse of the office. This Committee has observed that permanent disqualification of citizens who have been convicted of crimes from participating in the political process as voters may violate article 25.[28] Stricter requirements for candidates who seek to exercise great power over others can still be reasonable and proportionate under article 25. If presidents who have successfully completed one or more terms can be permanently ineligible for re-election for the sake of ensuring a healthy and competitive political system, then surely presidents who have been removed for abusing their office can also be permanently barred.

[Report: UN Doc. CCPR/C/110/D/2155/2012]

---

that the author was no longer a "victim" with regard to an issue on which she had prevailed in the European Court of Human Rights.
[27] See, for example, the constitutions of Angola (art. 65(3)); Argentina (sec. 60); Bangladesh (art. 48(4)); Colombia (art. 175(2)); Madagascar (art. 132); Philippines (art. XI, sec. 3); Slovakia (art. 107); South Africa (art. 89(2)); Timor-Leste (sec. 79); United States of America (art. I, sec. 3).
[28] General comment No 25, op. cit., para. 14.

Human rights — Equality of all persons before courts and tribunals — Right to fair and public hearing by a competent, independent and impartial tribunal established by law — All persons equal before the law and entitled without discrimination to the equal protection of the law — Right of minorities to enjoy their own culture — International Covenant on Civil and Political Rights, 1966, Articles 14, 26 and 27 — Remedy for violation — United Nations Human Rights Committee

PAADAR AND OTHERS v. FINLAND[1]

(Communication No 2102/2011)

United Nations Human Rights Committee.[2] 26 March 2014

SUMMARY:[3] *The facts:*—The authors, all Finnish nationals, were full-time traditional reindeer herders, and, with the exception of Mr Kari Alatorvinen, indigenous Sami people. They were members of the Ivalo Reindeer Herding Cooperative ("the Cooperative"), which comprised herders from the village of Ivalo and from the authors' village of Nellim. The larger Ivalo group used more modern herding methods, while the smaller, almost exclusively Sami Nellim group used traditional herding methods constitutive of the Sami culture, in particular, free-grazing on wild pastures.

Under Section 21 of the Reindeer Husbandry Act 1990 ("the Act"), every ten years, the Ministry of Agriculture and Forestry determined the maximum number of live reindeer a cooperative could have on its territory. Under Section 22 of the Act, if a cooperative's total number of reindeer exceeded the set limit, the cooperative had to adopt and execute a plan to reduce the total number to within the limit over the course of the following herding year.

At the material dates for the current communication, the Cooperative was permitted up to 6,000 reindeer. The authors submitted that, for several years

---

[1] The authors were Kalevi Paadar, Eero Paadar, Taimi Jetremoff, Hannu Paadar, Marko Paadar, Petri Paadar, Veijo Paadar, Kari Alatorvinen, Paula Alatorvinen, Johanna Alatorvinen, Jennika Alatorvinen, Joonas Alatorvinen and Juuli Alatorvinen. The authors were represented by counsel, Ms Johanna Ojala.
[2] The members of the Committee who participated in the examination of this communication were Mr Yadh Ben Achour (Tunisia), Mr Lazhari Bouzid (Algeria), Ms Christine Chanet (France), Mr Ahmad Amin Fathalla (Egypt), Mr Cornelis Flinterman (the Netherlands), Mr Yuji Iwasawa (Japan), Mr Walter Kälin (Switzerland), Ms Zonke Zanele Majodina (South Africa), Mr Gerald L. Neuman (United States of America), Sir Nigel Rodley (United Kingdom), Mr Víctor Manuel Rodríguez Rescia (Costa Rica), Mr Fabián Omar Salvioli (Argentina), Ms Anja Seibert-Fohr (Germany), Mr Yuval Shany (Israel), Ms Margo Waterval (Suriname) and Mr Andrei Paul Zlătescu (Romania).
[3] Prepared by Ms E. Fogarty.

prior to their communication, the Cooperative had used a slaughter plan to control reindeer numbers that had led to the Nellim group's reindeer numbers decreasing dramatically in comparison to the Ivalo group's. Under that plan, the number of reindeer to be slaughtered was determined based on the number of adult reindeer each herder held at the end of the herding year. Although newborn calves were not counted for that purpose, they could be slaughtered to reduce a herder's total number to within the set limit, sparing the adult reindeer. The authors submitted that, due to the Nellim group's traditional methods of free-grazing, which carried greater risks of natural attrition than the Ivalo group's modern methods, far more Nellim calves than Ivalo calves died each year. The result was that the Nellim group often did not have sufficient numbers of new calves to meet its slaughter quota and had to slaughter its mature reindeer, creating a perpetual reduction of adult reindeer and thus calves that could be slaughtered the following year in place of adult reindeer. Under applicable law, once a herder had lost all of his reindeer, he was unable to buy new reindeer, with the effect that the authors were facing the end of their reindeer husbandry.

In October 2007, the number of reindeer to be slaughtered by each Cooperative herder exceeded the number of adult reindeer owned by most of the Nellim herders. The authors complained to the Rovaniemi Administrative Court that the indiscriminate application of the Cooperative's slaughter plan to all the Cooperative members had a discriminatory and disproportionate impact on the Nellim group, and prevented them from practising their livelihood and culture. The complaint was dismissed on the basis that the slaughter plan was lawful and treated all Cooperative members equally regardless of ethnicity. The authors appealed to the Supreme Administrative Court, which upheld the Administrative Court's decision.

On 22 March 2011, the authors submitted their communication to the Human Rights Committee, claiming that the forced slaughter of their reindeer and the Supreme Administrative Court's dismissal of their appeal violated their rights under Articles 26,[4] 27[5] and 14[6] of the International Covenant on Civil and

---

[4] Article 26 of the Covenant provided: "All persons are equal before the law and are entitled without any discrimination to the equal protection of the law. In this respect, the law shall prohibit any discrimination and guarantee to all persons equal and effective protection against discrimination on any ground such as race, colour, sex, language, religion, political or other opinion, national or social origin, property, birth or other status."

[5] Article 27 of the Covenant provided: "In those States in which ethnic, religious or linguistic minorities exist, persons belonging to such minorities shall not be denied the right, in community with the other members of their group, to enjoy their own culture, to profess and practise their own religion, or to use their own language."

[6] Article 14(1) of the Covenant provided: "All persons shall be equal before the courts and tribunals. In the determination of any criminal charge against him, or of his rights and obligations in a suit at law, everyone shall be entitled to a fair and public hearing by a competent, independent and impartial tribunal established by law. The Press and the public may be excluded from all or part of a trial for reasons of morals, public order (*ordre public*) or national security in a democratic society, or when the interest of the private lives of the parties so requires, or to the extent strictly necessary in the opinion of the court in special circumstances where publicity would prejudice the interests of justice;

Political Rights, 1966 ("the Covenant"). They argued that the Supreme Administrative Court had dismissed their appeal without weighing the legal claims and facts of the case, and that the slaughter of their reindeer was discriminatory and violated their rights to enjoy their own indigenous culture in community with other Sami. The State Party contested the merits of the claim.

Held:—The State Party had not violated the authors' rights under Articles 14, 26 or 27 of the Covenant.

(1) With respect to the Article 14 claim, the materials submitted did not suggest that the courts had acted arbitrarily in evaluating the facts and evidence of the case, or that there had been any procedural flaw amounting to denial of justice. The acts complained of did not constitute a violation of the authors' rights under Article 14 of the Covenant (para. 7.2).

(2) In relation to the Article 26 and 27 claims, the Supreme Administrative Court's judgment indicated that some Sami members of the Cooperative had fulfilled their slaughter quotas, indicating that the slaughter plan did not result in unequal treatment between Sami and non-Sami members of the Cooperative. The judgment also showed that there were very different opinions concerning reindeer herding methods (para. 7.4).

(3) It was not disputed that the authors were members of a minority within the meaning of Article 27 of the Covenant and had the right to enjoy their own culture, of which reindeer husbandry was an essential element. Under Article 27, members of minorities were not to be denied the right to enjoy their culture, and measures whose impact amounted to a denial of that right would not be compatible with the obligations under Article 27. Although the rights protected under Article 27 were individual rights, they depended on the ability of the individual members of a minority group to maintain their common culture, language or religion. In certain circumstances it could be necessary for States Parties to take positive measures to protect the identity of a minority and the rights of its members to enjoy and develop their culture in community with other members (para. 7.6).

(4) The materials submitted by the authors did not contain figures to demonstrate that the Nellim group's calf losses were higher than those of the Ivalo group, and thus that the Cooperative's slaughter plan adversely and disproportionately affected them. Some figures were provided for 2010/11, but not for 2007/08 or earlier years. Neither did the materials submitted demonstrate how the reduction of the Nellim group's reindeer had progressed prior to 2007; how this compared with the Ivalo group; nor how, in concrete terms, the authors had reached a point where all their reindeer had to be slaughtered. In the absence of supporting information, it was not possible to conclude on the facts that the impact of the slaughter plan amounted to a denial of the authors' rights under Articles 26 and 27 of the Covenant (paras. 7.7-8).

---

but any judgment rendered in a criminal case or in a suit at law shall be made public except where the interest of juvenile persons otherwise requires or the proceedings concern matrimonial disputes or the guardianship of children."

Individual opinion by Mr Kälin, Mr Rodríguez Rescia, Ms Seibert-Fohr and Mr Shany (dissenting): (1) On the facts the State Party had violated the authors' rights under Article 27 of the Covenant (paras. 1 and 3).

(2) It was undisputed that the Cooperative had decided that the authors were to slaughter all their reindeer, and that this decision flowed from the cooperative system established by the State under the Act. Reindeer husbandry was an essential element of the authors' culture, and thus was protected under Article 27 of the Covenant (paras. 1-2).

(3) In the past the Committee had inquired whether interference by a State Party in husbandry was so substantial that the State Party had failed properly to protect individuals' rights to enjoy their culture. In the present case, the slaughter of all the authors' reindeer constituted a particularly grave interference with their rights under the Covenant, as it would deprive them of their ability to enjoy their traditional culture. Although the interference did not result from a direct State order, but rather from a Cooperative decision, a State Party was obliged under Article 27 of the Covenant not only to refrain from taking measures that amounted to a denial of the right of members of a minority to enjoy their culture, but also to take positive measures of protection against the acts of others within the State Party (paras. 2-3).

(4) It was reasonable and consistent with Article 27 of the Covenant for the State Party to allow herding cooperatives to impose slaughter quotas on their members in order to restrict the number of reindeer for economic and ecological reasons, and to secure the preservation and well-being of the Sami minority. However, in cases of apparent conflict between the legislation, which seemed to protect the rights of minorities as a whole, and its application to a single member of that minority, the Committee had previously considered that restrictions upon the rights of the individual members had to be shown to have a reasonable and objective justification in the particular circumstances and to be necessary for the continued viability and welfare of the minority as a whole. The State Party had not demonstrated that the slaughter of all the authors' reindeer was necessary to achieve its goal, that the objective could not have been achieved in another manner, or that attaining that objective justified the substantial impact on the authors' rights (para. 3).

The following is the text of the Views of the Committee:

1.1 The authors of the communication are Kalevi Paadar, Eero Paadar and his family (his wife Taimi Jetremoff and his three minor children Hannu, Marko and Petri Paadar), Veijo Paadar, and Kari Alatorvinen and his family (his wife Paula Alatorvinen, and his four children, Johanna, born on 13 December 1986; Jennika, born on 22 June 1988; Joonas, born on 21 March 1991; and Juuli Alatorvinen, born on 13 March 2001). All of them except Kari Alatorvinen are indigenous Sami. Mr Alatorvinen's wife and children are also Sami.

The authors allege a violation by Finland of article 14, paragraph 1; article 26; and article 27 read alone and in conjunction with article 1, of the Covenant. The authors are represented. The Optional Protocol entered into force for the State party on 23 March 1976.

1.2 On 23 September 2011, the Committee, acting through its Special Rapporteur on new communications and interim measures, requested the State party to refrain from any further forced slaughtering of the authors' reindeer while their case was under consideration by the Committee. On 23 March 2012, the State party indicated that it had complied with that request.

THE FACTS AS SUBMITTED BY THE AUTHORS

2.1 The authors are full-time reindeer herders. They live in the village of Nellim and belong to the Ivalo Reindeer Herding Cooperative ("the Cooperative"), which is divided into two herding groups, one in the north around the village of Nellim and one in the south around the village of Ivalo. The Nellim herding group and Nellim village form a distinct Sami community within the broader area of the Cooperative. The Nellim herding group is made up almost exclusively of Sami and retains traditional methods of herding that are constitutive of the Sami culture. The four authors and their families are the only remaining families whose income is based primarily on reindeer herding. The remaining herders in the Nellim group own smaller numbers of reindeer and do not earn their primary income from herding.

2.2 Reindeer herding is made difficult in the Nellim area by the winter conditions and different pastures, as compared to those of the Ivalo group. In addition to dissimilarities with regard to pastures, predators and snow conditions, the reindeer husbandry of the two groups differs in that the authors' reindeer herding is based solely on the utilization of natural pastures. Whereas the Ivalo group provides its reindeer with significant amounts of feed, the authors give hay to their reindeer in winter only to guide them, and to make them move to pastures of lichen and stay there. Reindeer feeding is not a part of Sami herding, which is based on free pasturage.

2.3 The Cooperative is a public law entity. It is not a private association established freely by its members; nor is it a traditional and voluntary reindeer herding unit established by the indigenous Sami people who used to herd reindeer in natural communities, such as a family or a village. The cooperative system was imposed through legislation in the 1930s and is currently regulated by the Reindeer Husbandry Act ("the Act"), which came into force in 1990.

2.4 The majority of the Cooperative's herders belong to the Ivalo group. The Nellim group has fewer reindeer and is in the minority as far as decision-making is concerned. The Nellim group has unsuccessfully tried to separate itself from the Cooperative to form its own. According to the authors, disagreements within the Cooperative are the result of State interference in Sami reindeer herding via the creation of artificially large units to administer reindeer herding, instead of leaving it to the Sami themselves to determine the kind of natural communities that are the most suitable for their herding. Traditional Sami reindeer husbandry is based on small herding groups comprised of natural communities that have their own traditional pastures.

2.5 Under section 21 of the Act, the Ministry of Agriculture and Forestry determines, for periods of ten years at a time, the maximum number of live reindeer that a cooperative may keep on its territory and the maximum number of such reindeer that a shareholder of a cooperative may own. When determining the maximum number of live reindeer that a cooperative may keep, the Ministry must ensure that the number of reindeer grazing on the cooperative's territory during the winter season does not exceed the sustainable production capacity of the cooperative's winter pasture.

2.6 Under section 22(1) of the Act, if the number of live reindeer of a cooperative or a reindeer owner exceeds the maximum number referred to in section 21, the cooperative must, in the course of the following herding year, decide on reducing the number of reindeer to the maximum allowable number. Under section 22(2), on special grounds, a cooperative may decide that the number of reindeer belonging to a shareholder will not be reduced, in which case equivalent reductions will be carried out among the other owners in proportion to their number of reindeer. According to section 22(3), if it becomes clear that reindeer numbers in the following herding year would exceed the maximum allowable number, the cooperative may decide that the number of reindeer must be reduced during the current herding year. The cooperative's decision can be enforced immediately, unless the Administrative Court decides otherwise as a result of a claim. According to section 22(4), if the owner does not reduce the number of his or her reindeer in accordance with the decision of the cooperative, the chair of the cooperative may decide that the cooperative will carry out the reduction on behalf of the owner.

2.7 At the time of the facts, the highest allowable number of reindeer for the Ivalo cooperative was 6,000. The authors contend that this number had not been exceeded during the four years before 2011. In fact, the number had only been exceeded once during the past decade (in 2004/05).

2.8 According to the authors, for several years the Cooperative's slaughtering plans have been formulated in a way that, in practice, has led to the number of the authors' reindeer decreasing dramatically, much more so than for the Ivalo group. The reason for this is the model used by the Cooperative for reducing reindeer numbers. The model fails to take into account the fact that—in contrast with the practices of the Ivalo herding group—the nature-based herding methods of the Nellim group, which rely on free-grazing in natural pastures, amount to an inbuilt control mechanism for the size of the herd. Calf losses are an integral part of traditional Sami herding methods.

2.9 Every year, a large proportion of the newborn calves belonging to the Nellim group disappear in the forest, owing to a range of different natural conditions and, in particular, their exposure to predators. At the time of the round-ups, which take place from October to January, between 30 and 50 per cent of the calves that have been born in spring go missing. In comparison, the calf losses of the Ivalo group are much smaller, because their reindeer are kept closer to human settlements, which reduces their exposure to predators. Furthermore, the herding area of the Nellim group is located in a wide and remote border area on Finnish, Norwegian and Russian territory. According to recent scientific studies, there is a dense population of bears in this area, which is the main reason for the heavy annual calf losses. Current legislation[1] forbids the killing or disturbing of bears and eagles, either entirely, or during the spring and summer, which is when most of the calf losses occur. The only lawful means of combating heavy calf losses would be to stop traditional free-grazing on natural pastures and to introduce artificial extra feeding, which would not be economically feasible in Nellim and would amount to a forced change to traditional herding practices.

2.10 The imbalance in predation pressure is not taken into account when the slaughtering plan is decided upon by a majority in the Cooperative. The plan lays down a slaughtering percentage (usually 70 per cent or more), which is based on the number of adult reindeer that the owners had at the end of the previous herding year in May. As a result, the number of animals to be slaughtered is determined without taking into account the losses that have occurred in the intervening months. Even if around 90 per cent of the female adult reindeer have

---

[1] The authors refer to the Nature Conservation Act and the Game Husbandry Act, which hinder control of the numbers of predators that prey on reindeer.

given birth to a calf, up to 50 per cent of the calves are no longer alive at the time of the round-up. In calculating the number of reindeer to be slaughtered, the newborn calves are not taken into account, but they can nevertheless be used to fulfil the slaughter obligation. The Nellim herders, unlike the Ivalo group in the Cooperative, do not have enough calves to fulfil their slaughter quota. As a result, they are forced to kill their adult female reindeer, which they need as a productive base for their herding economy.[2]

2.11 In 2005, one of the authors, Kalevi Paadar, complained to Rovaniemi Administrative Court about the Cooperative's decision to decrease the number of reindeer in a way that would threaten his occupation and lifestyle as a Sami reindeer herder. His complaint was dismissed on 13 December 2005, as the Court considered the Cooperative's decision to be legally valid. Kalevi Paadar appealed the dismissal to the Supreme Administrative Court, which, on 10 April 2007, upheld the judgment of the Rovaniemi court.

2.12 In its spring meeting on 31 May 2007, the Cooperative approved the slaughter plan for the 2007/08 herding year. The plan imposed slaughter obligations on all shareholders in the same percentage, on the basis of the number of live reindeer held in the previous herding year. The reindeer not slaughtered in the 2006/07 herding year (the so-called backlog reindeer) were to be slaughtered first.

2.13 At its autumn meeting on 7 October 2007, the Cooperative decided, with regard to the backlog reindeer, that it would carry out the reductions on behalf of the owners. For the authors, this meant that all of their animals taken to the round-up would be slaughtered until the Cooperative's decisions on reducing reindeer numbers that had been taken in the previous years had been implemented. In addition, the authors were requested to slaughter a share corresponding to the current year's slaughter percentage. According to the authors, the total slaughter numbers demanded by the Cooperative exceeded the number of adult reindeer that they had at the end of the previous herding year. Even counting the likely number of calves (equivalent to 50 or 60 per cent of the number of adult female reindeer), the slaughter demands exceeded the total number of reindeer that the authors estimated they would have at the time of the round-ups.[3] Almost no animals would be

---

[2] Reindeer herding in Finland is based mainly on calf slaughter, where only some of the young animals are left alive to compensate for the annual loss of adults.

[3] According to the figures provided by the authors, the total number of adult reindeer owned by the four families was 418 for the 2011/12 herding year; the predicted slaughter request for the 2011/12 herding year was estimated at 932. This is despite the fact that the authors' adult reindeer numbers had already decreased between 2003 and 2010.

left, and the authors would no longer be able to pursue reindeer husbandry since, according to the law, herders cannot buy new reindeer and continue herding once they have lost all their reindeer.

2.14 The Nellim case is not unique in the Sami areas of Lapland. There are other similar disputes between cooperatives and Sami groups belonging to them with regard to numbers of reindeer to be slaughtered. However, most of the Sami cooperatives in the State party apply slaughter systems that differ from the one used in Ivalo by the way in which they take calf loss into consideration. In those systems, different slaughter percentages apply to adult reindeer and to calves, and heavy calf loss is not punished by the additional killing of adult reindeer as it is under the Ivalo model. The fundamental problem with the Ivalo model is that the reindeer reduction is not carried out in proportion to the actual number of live reindeer found in the round-ups, but in proportion to a number which is severely distorted at the time of slaughter. The other models enable the owner to retain his or her proportionate share of the cooperative's total number of reindeer, regardless of the high number of missing calves.

2.15 The authors filed a complaint against the Cooperative's decision of 7 October 2007, with Rovaniemi Administrative Court, and requested interim protection measures. They claimed that setting the slaughter plan in the same way for all of the Cooperative's shareholders prevented the Sami from practising their livelihood and their culture and was therefore discriminatory against them. On 11 October 2007, the Court ordered the slaughter to be halted. By then, the Cooperative had already slaughtered part of the authors' herd. On 19 October 2007, the Administrative Court dismissed the case without examining the merits. The judgment made no reference to the authors' Sami origin or to the Covenant. On the same date, the authors filed an urgent request for interim measures with the Supreme Administrative Court, mentioning in their application that the slaughtering would continue the next day, which was a Saturday. As there was nobody who could look at the appeal during the weekend, the slaughter continued on 20 October 2007. However, on 23 October 2007, the Supreme Administrative Court ordered it to stop.

2.16 On 4 April 2008, the Supreme Administrative Court reversed the judgment of Rovaniemi Administrative Court and returned the case to it for retrial. In its judgment of 15 August 2008, Rovaniemi Administrative Court rejected the authors' claims. It considered that the shareholders were to be treated equally regardless of their ethnic background. Therefore, the Cooperative's decision of 7 October 2007 could not be considered discriminatory against the Sami people in the light of the Constitution and the international treaties binding upon the State party.

2.17 In September 2008, the authors appealed to the Supreme Administrative Court, arguing that implementation of the Cooperative's decision of 7 October 2007 would mean the end of their reindeer husbandry, as the forced slaughter would include their so-called capital reindeer, that is to say, the female reindeer. It would also mean the disappearance of the Nellim herd as an independent unit, as there would not be a sufficient number of herders or of reindeer left. The livelihood of the Sami in Nellim would therefore come to an end. These claims, uncontested by the Cooperative, were made with reference to, inter alia, article 27 of the Covenant.

2.18 The Court requested a statement from the Government concerning the implementation of section 22 of the Act and matters related to the position of the Sami as indigenous people. Statements were received from the Ministry of Agriculture and Forestry, the Ministry for Foreign Affairs, the Ministry of Justice, the Finnish Game and Fisheries Research Institute and the Reindeer Herders' Association.

2.19 On 2 February 2011, the Supreme Administrative Court upheld the judgment of Rovaniemi Administrative Court. The Court found that the effects of the Cooperative's decision "on the manner of implementation of reindeer slaughter for specific years are not such that they would constitute an infringement of operational conditions for livelihood and culture, even if the potential differences in the approaches to reindeer herding are taken into account. Further, in the matter, on the one hand general equality needs to be considered, i.e. equality among all reindeer owners, and on the other hand, the realization of equality among the Sami reindeer owners, in particular taking into account the premises for reindeer herding carried out in the traditional manner. In this respect, it has not been shown, taking into account the perspectives presented by both sides, that the reindeer herding cooperative would have superseded requirements concerning equality in deciding, inter alia, on the method of slaughter of the appellants' so-called backlog reindeer. On the above-mentioned grounds, the decision of the Ivalo Reindeer Herding Cooperative dated 7 October 2007 on the method of implementation for reduction of the number of reindeer is not contrary to ... the Constitution of Finland or basic rights and liberties and human rights."

2.20 The Court's judgment is final and cannot be appealed against. Domestic remedies have therefore been exhausted. On 18 September 2011, the board of the Cooperative decided that the authors must slaughter all of their reindeer starting on 26 September 2011.

2.21 The authors add that, in recent years, two issues have caused tension between them and the other members of the Cooperative. One concerns the way that pastures have been divided between the two herding groups by a fence, leading to difficulties for the Nellim group in carrying out traditional Sami reindeer herding and arguably being one reason for the group's higher calf losses. The fence makes it impossible for the Nellim herd to move along their natural migration routes and return to their winter grazing grounds once summer is over. The fact that the Ivalo herding group has a majority vote in the Cooperative keeps the fence closed at that time of the year. The other issue concerns the forestry operations of the Finnish Forest Service. Traditional Sami reindeer herding depends on the natural forest and is adversely affected by forestry, which is why the Nellim group is opposed to logging and other forestry measures in its area. The Ivalo group is the only herding group within the Sami Homeland in Finland that practises extensive reindeer feeding and herds reindeer using non-Sami methods. As a result, this herding group is less vulnerable to forestry activities. The Ivalo group and, hence, the Ivalo cooperative, has been actively against actions by the Nellim group and other Sami herding cooperatives aimed at bringing about a reduction in forestry operations by the Forest Service.

2.22 In 2010, a lawsuit initiated by the Paadars against the Forest Service resulted in a settlement between the two parties whereby most of the remaining forests around Nellim were saved for the purpose of reindeer herding. However, if the Paadars lose their reindeer, the agreement will become void, since, under the terms of the agreement, the forests are exempt from forestry operations only so long as the Paadars or their relatives are reindeer herders.

THE COMPLAINT

3.1 The authors allege that the State party violated article 14, paragraph 1, of the Covenant when the Supreme Administrative Court rejected the appeal without weighing the legal claims, arguments and facts of the case. Furthermore, by requesting a statement from the Government, the Court subordinated itself to the Executive, thus violating the authors' right to a fair trial.

3.2 The forced slaughtering of their reindeer entails violations of the authors' rights under article 27 of the Covenant to enjoy their own indigenous culture in community with other Sami. The authors and their families cannot continue their way of life after the slaughtering, because the families will no longer have any reindeer left. This will mean the end of the authors' and their families' Sami livelihood. When taking decisions, the Cooperative is obliged to take into consideration the preservation of the Sami culture, in accordance with section 17, subsection 3, of the Finnish Constitution, and article 27 of the Covenant.

3.3 The decision of the Ivalo Reindeer Herding Cooperative, a public law entity, to slaughter the authors' reindeer is discriminatory both in its purpose and its effects, in violation of article 26 of the Covenant. The authors have been targeted for disproportionate slaughtering of their reindeer because of their Sami way of herding, their Sami ethnicity and their fight against further logging by the Forestry Service on their traditional lands. Even if the discriminatory intent cannot be demonstrated through evidence admissible in court, the effect of the slaughtering would be discriminatory as it affects exclusively those members of the Cooperative who belong to the Sami indigenous people and use the traditional and culturally constitutive Sami herding methods.

3.4 The threat faced by the authors of having their reindeer slaughtered on account of a Reindeer Husbandry Act that does not recognize traditional Sami reindeer herding is the result of a lack of recognition of Sami land rights by the State party. In this respect, the authors recall the concluding observations on the fifth periodic report of Finland, in which the Committee indicated that "the State party should, in conjunction with the Sami people, swiftly take decisive action to arrive at an appropriate solution to the land dispute with due regard for the need to preserve the Sami identity in accordance with article 27 of the Covenant" (CCPR/CO/82/FIN, para. 17). The authors also refer to the report of the Special Rapporteur on the rights of indigenous peoples, in which it is indicated that "Finland should step up its effort to clarify and legally protect Sami rights to land and resources. In particular, Finland should ensure special protections for Sami reindeer husbandry, given the centrality of this means of livelihood to the culture and heritage of the Sami people" (A/HRC/18/35/Add.2, para. 84).

3.5 The authors add that the Anar Sami language is under acute threat, as there are only 300 people who speak it. The survival of the language depends on communities in which the language is used in collective practices. Nellim is one of the most important villages for the language, and the reindeer husbandry of the Nellim herding group is an essential collective practice for Anar Sami language speakers. If the planned slaughters are carried out, the Nellim herding group and reindeer herding as a traditional Sami livelihood in Nellim village will cease to exist, as the village depends on reindeer husbandry and small-scale tourism for its survival. Accordingly, the future of the group and of the village as a whole—and therefore of the Anar Sami language—is under threat.

THE STATE PARTY'S OBSERVATIONS ON ADMISSIBILITY AND THE MERITS

4.1 In its note verbale of 22 November 2011, the State party indicated that it had no objections concerning the admissibility of the present communication. On 23 March 2012, the State party submitted observations on the merits.

4.2 The State party refers to sections 21 and 22 of the Reindeer Husbandry Act. It also refers to the Government Bill for the Reindeer Husbandry Act (HE 244/1989), according to which circumstances and practices regarding reindeer herding differ from area to area. In mountain areas they are part of the Sami culture and have special local features. The Bill also indicates that reindeer herding as a whole involves so many features in common that it would not be appropriate to include different provisions for different areas in the Act, but rather only provisions that are applicable to all reindeer herding.

4.3 Under section 14 of the Game Animal Damages Act (105/2009), a new compensation system has been established whereby compensation should be paid for losses of reindeer calves, even if the remains are not found. The compensation is payable for the period between the calving and the last day of the next November. It is calculated for each cooperative on the basis of the producer price of reindeer meat, the estimated calving percentage in the herding area, the number of female reindeer in the territory of the cooperative and the estimated percentage of calf mortality caused by big wild animals in that territory. The compensation for other reindeer found killed is multiplied by 1.5. If the cooperative has suffered exceptionally severe losses, the amount of compensation is multiplied by 3.

4.4 Regarding the national proceedings in the present case, the Supreme Administrative Court, in its judgment of 11 February 2011, stated that the decision of the Cooperative to reduce the number of reindeer should be assessed from the standpoint of equality, among all reindeer owners on the one hand and among Sami owners on the other hand. Failure to respect the requirements of equality had not been substantiated. In the long term, compliance with section 21 of the Act should contribute to maintaining the opportunities for reindeer herding, which is part of Sami culture. Thus, the decision on forced slaughter taken by the Cooperative could not be considered to violate the Constitution or the Covenant.

4.5 Since the year 2000, the maximum permitted number of reindeer for the Ivalo cooperative has been 6,000 and the maximum permitted number for an individual owner has been 500. According to the State party, these numbers are sufficient for carrying on traditional Sami reindeer herding.

4.6 In the 2004/05 herding year, the Cooperative had a total of 6,080 live reindeer. As a result, on 30 July 2005, it decided to adopt a slaughter plan for the 2005/06 herding year. Through the appeals filed by Kalevi Paadar, the conformity of the slaughter plan for the 2005/06 herding year with the requirements of the Act was confirmed by the judgment of the Supreme Administrative Court. On 31 May 2006, the Cooperative adopted a new slaughter plan. On 31 May 2007, the Cooperative issued a slaughter list that indicated each shareholder's so-called arrears (i.e. the reindeer not slaughtered earlier, as well as the so-called extras—the reindeer slaughtered earlier in excess of the slaughtering obligation). No complaints were made against these decisions.

4.7 On 7 October 2007, the Cooperative decided to enforce the decisions. The authors complained to Rovaniemi Administrative Court in regard to this latest decision. On [11] October 2007, the Court stayed the enforcement. However, on 19 October 2007, the Court dismissed the case because the authors had not filed a complaint against the slaughter plan which was at the origin of the decision on forced slaughter and which had been approved in a meeting of the Cooperative.

4.8 It appears from both parties' pleadings to the Supreme Administrative Court that most herders in the Cooperative are Sami. Furthermore, according to the judgment of Rovaniemi Administrative Court, the Cooperative has calculated that at its meetings, native Sami people usually hold between 58 and 60 per cent of all voting rights, on average.

4.9 Following the authors' appeal, the Supreme Administrative Court issued, on 23 October 2007, an interim measure prohibiting the slaughtering. On [4] April 2008, it quashed the Rovaniemi court's judgment and referred the matter back to the Rovaniemi court for reconsideration. The Supreme Administrative Court held that the decision of 7 October 2007 could be complained against because it was the first decision on reindeer slaughter taken under section 22, subsection 4, of the Act.

4.10 Rovaniemi Administrative Court reconsidered the complaint but rejected it on 15 August 2008. It nevertheless upheld the prohibition on enforcement of the Cooperative's decision until a final decision was adopted on the case. The authors appealed this judgment to the Supreme Administrative Court, which rejected the appeal on [2] February 2011.

4.11 Reindeer herding cooperatives have been introduced as administrative units because they are needed for organizing the herding for different purposes, for example for agricultural aid and compensation for damage caused by big wild animals. The units are large because they are set up according to local reindeer herding needs. Most cooperatives have both Sami and non-Sami owners as shareholders. Due to the fact that under Finnish law it is prohibited to register ethnicity, it is not possible to provide official statistics on the number of Sami and non-Sami shareholders in different cooperatives.

4.12 The authors indicate that the Nellim herding group has aspired to separate from the Ivalo cooperative and set up its own. However, the State party indicates that the group has not managed to do so because no agreement has been reached within the Ivalo cooperative on how to delimit the territory of the Nellim group.

4.13 Essentially, the authors base their communication on the practice of traditional Sami reindeer herding. However, they do not indicate what they mean by this practice. It is not stated whether they are referring to a nomadic way of life, with herders moving from one place to another with the herd. Normally, the herders move in motorized vehicles and live in stationary buildings constructed for herding purposes.

4.14 Despite the various possible methods of reindeer herding—traditional, developing, mixed and modern—all reindeer herders share the same responsibility of keeping the number of their live reindeer within the prescribed maximum in order to ensure the sustainable production capacity of the cooperative's winter pasture. The reindeer population in Finland is dominated by female animals, in order to maximize the production of calves and the income of the herders. The high proportion of calves has made it possible to increase the number of reindeer. As a rule, the calves are slaughtered before the reindeer move on to winter pastures, which helps to avoid excessive consumption of these pastures. The purpose of these practices has been to improve the profitability of reindeer herding and thus to safeguard the livelihood of herders in the future.

4.15 According to the judgment of [2] February 2011, the Cooperative has Sami members who have fulfilled their slaughtering obligation.

It thus appears that the present case does not concern unequal treatment between Sami and non-Sami herders but rather differences between members of the Cooperative. The judgment shows that there are very different opinions concerning reindeer herding methods.

4.16 The Ministry of Agriculture and Forestry has investigated the damage caused to reindeer by wild animals in the territory of the Ivalo cooperative and has found that in essence it does not differ from the damage elsewhere in the herding area or in the Sami Homeland. An incident took place in 2004 when a bear caused exceptionally severe damage during the calving period. However, this incident did not occur in the territory of Nellim but in the southern part of the Cooperative's territory. Under section 41 of the Hunting Act, it is possible to apply for an exceptional licence to kill a big wild animal that causes damage. The authors have not applied for an exceptional licence. In autumn, they have the opportunity to hunt bears in the reindeer herding territory within an established quota. During the period covered by the communication, the quota was not filled so quickly that the authors could not benefit from it. The competent authorities are not aware of any applications for licences to kill wild animals causing damage to reindeer in the territory of Nellim specifically.

4.17 The authors indicate that they carry out reindeer herding by the traditional method. According to the State party, this method should enable the herders to monitor the extent of the damage caused to reindeer by big wild animals much more efficiently than by the method of completely free pasturing. The Regional Council of Lapland has specifically proposed shepherding as one means of reducing damage caused to reindeer by wild animals.

4.18 With respect to the authors' claims under article 14, paragraph 1, of the Covenant, the State party indicates that the national courts, including the Supreme Administrative Court, thoroughly assessed the authors' complaint—also from the standpoint of the special rights of the Sami—taking into account international human rights obligations, especially those deriving from the Covenant. They reasoned their judgments appropriately and extensively. A fair trial, as set out in article 14, is guaranteed when the court in question, such as the Supreme Administrative Court in the present case, obtains all the necessary information for a thorough examination of the case. Fair trial guarantees ensure that all parties to legal proceedings have had the right to be heard.

4.19 The State party concludes that the facts of this case do not reveal any breach of articles 14 and 26; nor of article 27 read alone and in the light of article 1.

AUTHORS' COMMENTS ON THE STATE PARTY'S OBSERVATIONS

5.1 On 18 June 2012, the authors submitted comments on the State party's observations. They reiterate that the judgment of the Supreme Administrative Court means the end of reindeer herding for the Nellim herding group, a fact that the State party does not dispute. The complete loss of a whole reindeer herding group has a substantial impact and, accordingly, amounts to a denial of the right to enjoy the Sami culture. The pastures and the circumstances of the Nellim herding group and the Ivalo herding group are different—a fact that should be taken into consideration in decisions concerning, for instance, forced slaughtering. The law and its application lead to different and unequal treatment of these two groups.

5.2 In its observations, the State party does not consider the role of predators in the issue at hand. The authors disagree with the State party's assessment that the compensation provided to cover losses is sufficient and constitutes an effective manner of tackling the problems caused by exceptionally harmful animals. First of all, the loss of calves in Nellim is highly significant and takes place on roughly the same scale every year. Second, most of the losses are caused by bears that are part of a sizeable group living in the Paatsjoki river valley. Between the years 2000 and 2008, the survival rate of calves in the Paatsjoki reindeer herding cooperative was 52 per cent; that is to say, almost half of the calves born disappeared in the forest before counting time in autumn. Over the same period, the survival rates for the four authors' calves were 53 per cent (Kari Alatorvinen), 56 per cent (Eero Paadar), 58 per cent (Kalevi Paadar) and 58 per cent (Veijo Paadar). In contrast to these rates, the survival rate for the Ivalo cooperative as a whole is 66 per cent.

5.3 Even though the difference in calf survival rates between the Nellim group and the Cooperative does not look significant at first glance, it is enough to make it impossible for the Nellim herders to fulfil slaughter quotas set by the Cooperative. The Cooperative's rate of 66 per cent includes the much lower rates of the Nellim group, which means that the difference is greater than it appears to be.

5.4 In 2011, the Regional Council of Lapland issued a report on predators and their impact on reindeer herding. According to the report, because of the current number of predators, economically profitable reindeer husbandry has collapsed in the area of Lapland most affected by predators. The bear population in that area increased from 170 in 1995 to between 370 and 420 in 2010 (i.e. by 120 to 150 per cent).

The real numbers may even be higher, as there are fewer people to record sightings of predators in northern Finland than in other parts of the country. The report also points out that damage occurring in summer, for example that caused by bears, is extremely difficult both to locate and to document, owing to a rapid utilization of carcasses by predators and scavengers, as well as processes of decomposition.

5.5 In relation to the new compensation system that is set up to cover losses of calves without any documentation being required, introduced pursuant to the Game Animal Damages Act 105/2009, the Regional Council points out that the operationalization of this instrument has proved to be inadequate and problematic. The authors contend that this statement contradicts the observation by the State party that the new system has clearly improved the position of reindeer owners because compensation sums have risen while damage has decreased. The Regional Council's report states that the slight decrease in damage that has taken place since the peak year of 2007 is the result of falls in reindeer numbers due to predators. According to a scientific study quoted by the Regional Council, slaughter volumes collapsed at the same time in parts of the southern and eastern reindeer husbandry areas that are subject to the most severe damage from predators. There are now 27 cooperatives that suffer from predator problems, which is nearly half of all the reindeer herding cooperatives in the State party.

5.6 The compensation system for calf losses introduced by the Game Animal Damages Act was not yet in force when the Ivalo cooperative's decisions on slaughter that are referred to in the present communication were taken. However, even if the compensation system worked properly, the problem raised by the authors would not be solved. The herders losing significantly more calves to predators than the majority in the Cooperative would still need to slaughter their productive base (i.e. their adult female reindeer) in order to fulfil their slaughter quota. Monetary compensation, even if substantial, could not replace the loss of livelihood. Furthermore, according to the report of the Regional Council, compensation for calf losses is in fact far from substantial and does not cover the real losses. For example, in 2011, in regard to the Paatsjoki cooperative, the compensated share of the total number of calves born was only 6 per cent, while the real annual loss of calves was close to 50 per cent.

5.7 The Ministry for Foreign Affairs requested the Sami Parliamentary Council to comment on the forced slaughter in the Nellim herding group. In its response, dated 23 March 2012, the Council states that the Reindeer Husbandry Act does not recognize Sami reindeer herding, despite the fact that, under section 17(3) of the Constitution of

Finland, the Sami people have a right to maintain and develop their own language and culture. Furthermore, the Government Bill on the Sami Parliament Act and the amendment to the Constitution state that reindeer herding, fishing and hunting are part of the Sami culture and traditional Sami livelihoods. The ruling of the Supreme Administrative Court focuses merely on the formal method of performing the reduction in the number of reindeer and fails to take a stand on the authors' main argument, namely that the Cooperative's decision on forced slaughtering violates article 27 of the Covenant. The authors have therefore been denied a fair trial, under article 14, paragraph 1, of the Covenant. The Sami Parliament is of the view that all Sami reindeer herders and members of their families must be able to practise reindeer husbandry in the Sami Homeland as part of their livelihood and culture and that inadequate national legislation obstructs or threatens this right. Through reindeer husbandry, Sami communities and the Sami language develop and remain viable. The authors' right to enjoy their own language is also violated by the Cooperative's decision on forced slaughter.

ISSUES AND PROCEEDINGS BEFORE THE COMMITTEE

Consideration of admissibility

6.1 Before considering any claim contained in a communication, the Human Rights Committee must decide, in accordance with rule 93 of its rules of procedure, whether or not the case is admissible under the Optional Protocol to the Covenant.

6.2 As required under article 5, paragraph 2(a), of the Optional Protocol, the Committee has ascertained that the same matter is not being examined under another procedure of international investigation or settlement.

6.3 The Committee observes that the State party has expressed no objections regarding admissibility and that domestic remedies have been exhausted. As all admissibility criteria have been met, the Committee declares the communication admissible and proceeds to its examination on the merits.

Consideration of the merits

7.1 The Human Rights Committee has considered the communication in the light of all the information made available to it by the parties, as provided under article 5, paragraph 1, of the Optional Protocol.

7.2 The Committee notes the authors' claim that their right to a fair trial under article 14, paragraph 1, of the Covenant has been violated because the Supreme Administrative Court rejected their appeal without weighing their legal claims, arguments and facts, and that by requesting a statement from the Government, the Court subordinated itself to the Executive. The Committee considers that the materials made available to it do not suggest that the courts acted arbitrarily in evaluating the facts and evidence in the authors' case or that the proceedings were flawed and amounted to a denial of justice. The Committee therefore does not find that the facts complained of constitute a violation of the authors' rights under article 14, paragraph 1, of the Covenant.

7.3 The authors claim to be victims of violations of articles 26 and 27 of the Covenant, in that the decisions on the forced slaughter of their reindeer taken in 2007 by the Ivalo Reindeer Herding Cooperative, in application of section 22 of the Reindeer Husbandry Act, had discriminatory effects on them. When deciding on the number of reindeer to be slaughtered in order to comply with the maximum permitted number of reindeer for the Cooperative and for each shareholder, the Cooperative did not take into consideration the authors' traditional Sami methods of herding or the fact that such methods involve the loss of greater numbers of calves. As a result, the reduction percentage imposed by the Cooperative on all stakeholders on the basis of their reindeer numbers at the beginning of the herding year had a negative impact on the authors, because at the time of slaughtering in autumn, their herds had been subjected to heavier losses than those of the other stakeholders, caused by predators.

7.4 The State party indicates that, according to the judgment of the Supreme Administrative Court, the Cooperative has Sami members who have fulfilled their slaughtering obligations. It thus appears that the present case does not concern unequal treatment between Sami and non-Sami herders, but rather differences between members of the Cooperative. The judgment shows that there are very different opinions concerning reindeer herding methods.

7.5 For the Committee, it is undisputed that the authors are members of a minority within the meaning of article 27 of the Covenant and, as such, have the right to enjoy their own culture. It is also undisputed that reindeer husbandry is an essential element of their culture. In this context, the Committee recalls its previous jurisprudence that economic activities may come within the ambit of article 27 if they are an essential element of the culture of an ethnic community. The Committee also recalls that, under article 27, members of minorities shall not be denied the right to enjoy their culture and that measures whose impact amounts to a denial of that right will not be compatible with the obligations under article 27.[4]

7.6 The Committee recalls paragraph 6.2 of general comment No 23 (1994), which states:

Although the rights protected under article 27 are individual rights, they depend in turn on the ability of the minority group to maintain its culture, language or religion. Accordingly, positive measures by States may also be necessary to protect the identity of a minority and the rights of its members to enjoy and develop their culture ... in community with the other members of the group. In this connection, it has to be observed that such positive measures must respect the provisions of articles 2(1) and 26 of the Covenant both as regards the treatment between different minorities and the treatment between the persons belonging to them and the remaining part of the population. However, as long as those measures are aimed at correcting conditions which prevent or impair the enjoyment of the rights guaranteed under article 27, they may constitute a legitimate differentiation under the Covenant, provided that they are based on reasonable and objective criteria.

7.7 In the present case, the authors claim that their calf losses are higher than those of the Ivalo group. However, the materials submitted to the Committee do not contain figures in that respect. The authors provide some figures on their reindeer numbers and the reduction imposed by the Cooperative with respect to 2010/11 but not with respect to 2007/08 and earlier years. It is also unclear what the progression was of the reductions imposed on their herds prior to 2007, how this compared to the reductions imposed on the other members of the Cooperative, and how, in concrete terms, they have come to a situation where all their reindeer have to be slaughtered. In the absence of information in that respect, the Committee is not in a position to conclude, given the limited evidence before it, that the impact of the Ivalo cooperative's reindeer reduction methods upon the authors was such as to amount to a denial of the authors' rights under articles 26 and 27. Despite this conclusion, the Committee deems it important to recall that the State party must bear in mind, when taking steps affecting rights under article 27, that although different activities in themselves may not constitute a violation of this article, such

---

[4] Communication No 511/1992, *Ilmari Länsman et al.* v. *Finland*, Views adopted on 26 October 1994, paras. 9.2 and 9.4; communication No 671/1995, *Jouni E. Länsman et al.* v. *Finland*, Views adopted on 30 October 1996, para. 10.2; and communication No 1023/2001, *Jouni Länsman et al.* v. *Finland*, Views adopted on 17 March 2005, para. 10.1.

activities, taken together, may erode the rights of Sami people to enjoy their own culture.[5]

8. The Human Rights Committee, acting under article 5, paragraph 4, of the Optional Protocol to the International Covenant on Civil and Political Rights, is of the view that the facts before it do not reveal a breach of articles 26 or 27 of the Covenant.

APPENDIX

INDIVIDUAL OPINION OF COMMITTEE MEMBERS WALTER KÄLIN, VÍCTOR MANUEL RODRÍGUEZ RESCIA, ANJA SEIBERT-FOHR AND YUVAL SHANY (DISSENTING)

[1] We are unable to agree with the view rendered by the Committee that the facts before it do not reveal a breach of article 27 of the Covenant. We regret that the decision of the majority fails to sufficiently take into account the facts of the case. According to undisputed facts submitted by the authors, the board of the Ivalo Reindeer Herding Cooperative decided that the authors—members of the Nellim herding group—must slaughter all of their reindeer starting on 26 September 2011. The decision to slaughter the authors' reindeer results from the cooperative system established by the State under the Reindeer Husbandry Act of 1990. Pursuant to section 21(1) of that Act, the Ministry of Agriculture and Forestry determines the maximum number of live reindeer that a reindeer herding cooperative may keep in its territory. Under section 22(1) of the Act, if the number of live reindeer of a cooperative or a reindeer owner exceeds a maximum number, the cooperative must decide on the reduction of the number of reindeer to the maximum allowable number. If the owner does not reduce the number of his or her reindeer in accordance with the decision of the cooperative, the chair of the cooperative may decide that the cooperative will carry out the reduction on behalf of the owner. In the present case, the authors' complaint against the Cooperative's decision to carry out the reduction on behalf of the owner on the basis of the slaughter plan adopted by the Cooperative for the 2007/08 herding year was dismissed by Rovaniemi Administrative Court and the Supreme Administrative Court. As a result, the authors now face the slaughter of all of their reindeer.

---

[5] Communication No 671/1995, op. cit., para. 10.7.

[2] Reindeer husbandry is an essential element of the authors' culture and is thus protected by article 27 of the Covenant, pursuant to which persons belonging to ethnic minorities shall not be denied the right, in community with the other members of their group, to enjoy their own culture. The Committee's approach in the past has been to inquire whether interference by the State party in that husbandry is so substantial that the State party has failed to properly protect the authors' right to enjoy their culture.[1]

[3] In the present case, the slaughter of all their reindeer constitutes a particularly grave interference with the authors' rights under the Covenant, since it would deprive them of their livelihood which is essential for their ability to continue to enjoy their traditional culture. We recognize that this interference does not result from a direct order by an organ of the State party to slaughter their herds but is a consequence of the decision taken by the Ivalo Reindeer Herding Cooperative. However, under article 27 of the Covenant, a State party is not only under an obligation to refrain from taking measures that amount to a denial of the right of members of a minority to enjoy their culture but is also obliged to take positive measures of protection "against the acts of other persons within the State party".[2] In this regard, we accept that it is reasonable and consistent with article 27 of the Covenant to allow herding cooperatives to impose slaughtering quotas on their members in order to achieve the purposes of the Reindeer Husbandry Act to restrict the number of reindeer for economic and ecological reasons and to secure the preservation and well-being of the Sami minority.[3] However, in cases of an apparent conflict between the legislation, which seems to protect the rights of the minority as a whole, and its application to a single member of that minority, the Committee has been guided by the consideration that restrictions upon the right of individual members of a minority must be shown not only to have a reasonable and objective justification in the particular circumstances of the case but also to be necessary for the continued viability and welfare of the minority as a whole.[4] The State party has not shown that slaughtering all of the authors' animals was necessary in order to achieve this goal, nor does the material in front of the Committee allow us to conclude that in the present case the objective

---

[1] [Paragraph numbers have been editorially inserted in this opinion.] Communication No 779/1997, *Äärelä and Näkkäläjärvi* v. *Finland*, Views adopted on 24 October 2001, para. 7.5.

[2] General comment No 23 (1994), para. 6.1.

[3] See communication No 197/1985, *Kitok* v. *Sweden*, Views adopted on 27 July 1988, para. 9.5.

[4] Ibid., para. 9.8; and communication No 24/1977, *Lovelace* v. *Canada*, Views adopted on 30 July 1981, para. 16.

of restricting the number of reindeer could not have been achieved otherwise, and that attaining this objective justifies the decision to slaughter all of the authors' reindeer despite its substantial impact on the right of the authors to enjoy their culture. For these reasons, we conclude that the Committee should have found the State party to be in violation of its obligations under article 27 of the Covenant.

[Report: UN Doc. CCPR/C/110/D/2102/2011]

Human rights — Prohibition of torture and cruel, inhuman or degrading treatment or punishment — Freedom from arbitrary arrest and detention — Persons deprived of liberty to be treated with humanity and respect for inherent dignity of the person — Freedom from arbitrary interference with privacy, family and home — No implied right of the State to engage in any activity aimed at destruction of rights and freedoms — Admissibility of author's communication to Human Rights Committee — Consideration of merits — Right to effective remedy — International Covenant on Civil and Political Rights, 1966, Articles 2, 7, 9, 10 and 17 — Remedy for violation — United Nations Human Rights Committee

HORVATH *v.* AUSTRALIA[1]

(Communication No 1885/2009)

United Nations Human Rights Committee.[2] 27 *March* 2014

SUMMARY:[3] *The facts:*—The author, Ms Horvath, an Australian citizen, was resident in the Australian State of Victoria. On 8 March 1996, Constables J and D of the Victorian Police issued the author with a certificate for her car declaring it to be unroadworthy. The following evening, they attended the author's property without a warrant to inspect her car for signs of recent use. The author, who was present with her partner CL and two friends, would not allow the constables to remain on her property, and she and CL attempted to make them leave by force. Eight further officers then arrived and arrested the author who was injured but arrested and taken to a police station where she was not given medical treatment. She was later discovered by a police doctor and was taken by ambulance to Frankston Hospital. She spent five days in hospital and required facial surgery. She was left with scarring on her nose, possible aggravation of hay fever, anxiety and depression. Proceedings against

---

[1] The author was represented by counsel, Ms Tamar Hopkins.
[2] The members of the Committee who participated in the examination of this communication were Mr Yadh Ben Achour (Tunisia), Mr Lazhari Bouzid (Algeria), Ms Christine Chanet (France), Mr Ahmad Amin Fathalla (Egypt), Mr Cornelis Flinterman (the Netherlands), Mr Yuji Iwasawa (Japan), Mr Walter Kälin (Switzerland), Ms Zonke Zanele Majodina (South Africa), Mr Gerald L. Neuman (United States of America), Sir Nigel Rodley (United Kingdom), Mr Víctor Manuel Rodríguez Rescia (Costa Rica), Mr Fabián Omar Salvioli (Argentina), Ms Anja Seibert-Fohr (Germany), Mr Yuval Shany (Israel), Ms Margo Waterval (Suriname) and Mr Andrei Paul Zlătescu (Romania).
[3] Prepared by Ms E. Fogarty.

the author for assaulting a police officer and traffic infringements were dismissed by the Frankston Magistrates' Court.

In June 1997, the author filed proceedings for damages against various police officers under the Crown Proceedings Act 1958 (Victoria) and the State of Victoria under Section 123 of the Police Regulation Act 1958 (Victoria).[4] On 23 January 2001, the County Court awarded her damages of $A 120,000 against one officer for assault and malicious prosecution; $A 120,000 against another officer for negligence, transferred to the State of Victoria; and $A 30,000 against four officers for trespass, wrongful arrest and false imprisonment, also transferred to the State of Victoria.

In November 2002, the State of Victoria successfully appealed its liability for damages before the Court of Appeal, which also reduced the total damages payable by the officers to the author to $A 143,525. The author's application for leave to appeal to the High Court was refused.

Despite consistent efforts by the author, she received no payments of damages from the officers. She also filed a complaint to the Ethical Standards Department of Victoria Police, which commenced and then dropped disciplinary proceedings for lack of evidence, despite the courts' factual findings, and without consulting the author or her companions.

On 19 August 2008, the author submitted her communication to the Human Rights Committee. She claimed that the State Party had violated her rights under Articles 2,[5] 7,[6] 9,[7] 10[8] and 17[9] of the International Covenant on

---

[4] For the text of Section 123 of the Police Regulation Act 1958, see footnote to para. 3.2 of the Views of the Committee.

[5] Article 2 of the Covenant provided: "... (2) Where not already provided for by existing legislative or other measures, each State Party to the present Covenant undertakes to take the necessary steps, in accordance with its constitutional processes and with the provisions of the present Covenant, to adopt such legislative or other measures as may be necessary to give effect to the rights recognized in the present Covenant. (3) Each State Party to the present Covenant undertakes: (a) To ensure that any person whose rights or freedoms as herein recognized are violated shall have an effective remedy, notwithstanding that the violation has been committed by persons acting in an official capacity; (b) To ensure that any person claiming such a remedy shall have his right thereto determined by competent judicial, administrative or legislative authorities, or by any other competent authority provided for by the legal system of the State, and to develop the possibilities of judicial remedy; (c) To ensure that the competent authorities shall enforce such remedies when granted."

[6] Article 7 of the Covenant provided: "No one shall be subjected to torture or to cruel, inhuman or degrading treatment or punishment. In particular, no one shall be subjected without his free consent to medical or scientific experimentation."

[7] Article 9 of the Covenant provided: "(1) Everyone has the right to liberty and security of person. No one shall be subjected to arbitrary arrest or detention. No one shall be deprived of his liberty except on such grounds and in accordance with such procedure as are established by law ... (5) Anyone who has been the victim of unlawful arrest or detention shall have an enforceable right to compensation."

[8] Article 10(1) of the Covenant provided: "(1) All persons deprived of their liberty shall be treated with humanity and with respect for the inherent dignity of the human person."

[9] Article 17 of the Covenant provided: "(1) No one shall be subjected to arbitrary or unlawful interference with his privacy, family, home or correspondence, nor to unlawful attacks on his honour and reputation. (2) Everyone has the right to the protection of the law against such interference or attacks."

Civil and Political Rights, 1966 ("the Covenant"). In particular, she submitted that the State had failed to provide her with an effective remedy, as no disciplinary action had been taken against the officers, and there was no statutory scheme to allow her to recover compensation for the abuse of her human rights. She further submitted that she had been subjected to cruel, inhuman and degrading treatment during the raid, which was neither authorized nor justified, and that she was subjected to arbitrary, unlawful arrest and detention. Finally, she submitted that the invasion of her home constituted arbitrary and unlawful interference with her home, family and privacy, as did Constable C's malicious prosecution.

Held:—The State Party had violated the author's rights under Article 2(3) in connection with Articles 7, 9(1) and (5), 10(1) and 17 of the Covenant.

(1) The author's claims were admissible. The same matter was not being examined under another procedure of international investigation or settlement, and domestic remedies had been exhausted. The State's claims that the author had failed to exhaust domestic remedies because she had not made an additional claim before the Victims of Crime Assistance Tribunal, which was limited to making minimal and effectively symbolic awards, and had not canvassed all possible avenues to enforce the domestic court judgments, were not accepted. The author's decision to pursue damages against the responsible officers under the Crown Proceedings Act was an appropriate form of redress, as indicated by the fact that the domestic courts had acknowledged that her rights had been violated, had established the officers' civil liability under that Act, and had awarded her damages. The fact that the decisions of the domestic courts had not been fully enforced, despite her efforts, was not attributable to the author. It could not be expected that, in addition to the proceedings she had commenced and succeeded in, the author had to seek compensation before the Victims of Crime Assistance Tribunal (paras. 7.1-7.6).

(2) Article 2(2) and (3) of the Covenant respectively required that States take necessary steps and make necessary changes to domestic laws and practices to give effect to Covenant rights; and that States make reparations to individuals whose rights were violated. Article 2(3) did not dictate what particular form of remedy States had to provide, nor did the Covenant provide for individuals to require that States criminally prosecute third parties. In determining whether an effective remedy existed, the Committee could take into account the availability and effectiveness of any and all remedies, including the cumulative effect of several remedies of various forms such as criminal, civil, administrative and disciplinary remedies (paras. 8.2 and 8.5).

(3) Article 2(3) also obliged States Parties to investigate allegations of violations promptly, thoroughly and effectively through independent and impartial bodies. The disciplinary proceedings undertaken in this case did not satisfy that obligation. The proceedings had been dismissed for a purported lack of evidence despite the clear factual conclusions drawn by the domestic courts; without obtaining the evidence of the author, her companion or friends; and without a public hearing. The author had also been denied

access to the file and had no capacity to reopen the proceedings in light of the factual findings of the domestic courts (paras. 8.2-8.3).

(4) Section 123 of the Police Regulation Act 1958 was ineffective as a remedy to persons who had suffered violations of their rights by police officers. That Section limited the responsibility of the State for the wrongful acts of its agents to an exceptionally narrow class of cases where officers were negligent, but were acting in good faith and "necessarily or reasonably" within the course of their duty. The Act failed to provide an alternative mechanism for full compensation for violations committed by agents of the State in other circumstances. Section 123 of the Act was incompatible with Article 2(2) and (3) of the Covenant (paras. 3.2 and 8.5).

(5) Actions for damages in domestic courts could provide an effective remedy in cases of alleged unlawfulness or negligence by State agents; to that end, Article 2(3) of the Covenant encompassed the obligation to ensure that competent authorities enforced such remedies when granted. State Parties were to use all appropriate means and to organize their legal systems to guarantee that remedies could be enforced in a manner consistent with the Covenant. In situations where the execution of a final judgment became impossible in light of the circumstances, other legal avenues had to be available to ensure victims received adequate redress. The author's success in her civil claim had been nullified by the impossibility of enforcing the judgment in her favour and the fact that no effective alternative existed. The Victims of Crime Assistance Scheme, of which the Tribunal was an element, with its low compensation awards and no-fault attributes, was not an adequate alternative course of redress for serious harm inflicted by State agents (paras. 8.6-8.7).

(6) The facts before the Committee revealed a violation of Article 2(3) in connection with Articles 7, 9(1) and 17, as well as Articles 9(5) and 10(1) of the Covenant. Under Article 2(3)(a), the State Party was obliged to provide the author with an effective remedy, including adequate compensation. The State Party was also under an obligation to take steps to prevent similar violations in the future, and was to review its legislation to ensure that it conformed with the Covenant's requirements. The State Party was to provide the Committee, within 180 days, with information about the measures taken to give effect to its Views, which it was requested to publish and disseminate widely (paras. 8.8-11).

Individual opinion of Ms Seibert-Fohr (joined by Messrs Iwasawa and Kälin and with whom Mr Neuman agreed) (partly dissenting): (1) The main issue of the present case was the State Party's failure to recognize its responsibility for the violent police misconduct, and not the remedies available to the author. Given the gravity of the ill-treatment and the State Party's denial of responsibility, the Committee had to find that the police officer's acts, which were clearly attributable to the State Party, amounted to a violation of Article 7 of the Covenant. That finding would have also provided the necessary precondition for the analysis of the author's compensation claim under Article 2(3) of the Covenant (para. 1).

(2) The violation of Article 7 of the Covenant was insufficiently remedied because the author's ill-treatment was neither compensated nor subject to an independent official investigation. It was the failure to provide for an effective remedy for the violation of Article 7 which led to a violation of Article 2. The obligation to provide the author with an effective remedy, including adequate compensation, was to be read on an understanding informed by an autonomous interpretation of Article 2 (para. 2).

(3) Section 123 of the Police Regulation Act 1958 (Victoria) was not incompatible with Article 2; the failure to provide for an effective remedy did not result from that provision (para. 3).

Individual opinion of Mr Neuman (partly dissenting): (1) It was wrong to suggest that the State Party had refused to "enforce" a judgment of its domestic courts (paras. 1-3).

(2) The majority's overgeneralization of issues had obscured significant distinctions among violations for which different remedial responses might be sufficient. Its discussions of obligations under Article 2(3) of the Covenant should be more nuanced in the future (para. 4).

(3) The word limit on Views should be abolished since it prevented the Committee from discharging its responsibilities (para. 5).

The following is the text of the Views of the Committee:

1. The author of the communication is Corinna Horvath, an Australian national. She claims that her rights under articles 2, 7, 9 (paras. 1 and 5), 10 and 17 were violated by Australia. The author is represented by counsel.

THE FACTS AS SUBMITTED BY THE AUTHOR

2.1 On 9 March 1996, around 9.40 p.m., two police officers, constables J and D, arrived at the author's house in Summerville, State of Victoria, to inspect the author's car for evidence that it had been recently driven. The constables had issued an unroadworthy certificate the previous day. The author, who was then aged 21, did not allow the police to remain on the premises as they had no warrant, and she and her companion, CL, used force to make them leave. The police officers called for reinforcements and, at about 10.30 p.m., eight officers arrived at the house stating that they intended to arrest the author and CL for having attacked constables J and D on their first visit and that they did not need a warrant for that.

2.2 Constable J kicked the front door open and in so doing, struck on the face DK, one of a group of friends who were also present, causing him injury. Then, Constable J brought DK to the floor, struck him on the right side of the head and hit him with a baton across his lower back. Constable J then pulled the author to the floor and punched her in the face. With the assistance of another policeman, Constable J rolled the author over and, despite her bleeding nose, handcuffed her, dragged her out to the police van and took her to the police station at Hastings.

2.3 The author suffered a fractured nose and other facial injuries, including bruising and a chipped tooth. She also had some bruising, scratches and abrasions to other parts of her body. The police officers handcuffed the author in a manner that prevented her from reducing the pain and blood flow from her nose or otherwise relieving her injuries. At the police station, she was not provided with immediate medical treatment. Instead, she was left screaming in pain in the cell. She was eventually discovered by a police doctor who contacted her parents, who arranged to have her taken by ambulance to Frankston Hospital. A week later, she was readmitted to hospital for five days in relation to her nose injury. After some months, she recovered from her physical injuries but was left with some scars on her nose and a possible aggravation of hay fever. She also suffered from anxiety and depression, for which she received treatment.

2.4 On 6 June 1997, the author and three other plaintiffs filed proceedings for damages against four police officers individually, and against the State of Victoria under section 123 of the Police Regulation Act 1958 (Victoria), before the County Court of Victoria. On 23 February 2001, Judge Williams of the County Court held that, with regard to the author, Constable J was liable for assault and malicious prosecution; Sergeant C was liable for negligence; and all four officers were jointly liable for trespass, wrongful arrest and false imprisonment. The officers were also held to be liable for various similar claims with regard to CL and the two remaining plaintiffs.

2.5 Judge Williams ordered the following damages awards: (a) $A 120,000 for negligence against Sergeant C, transferred to the State; (b) $A 90,000 for assault, against Constable J; (c) $A 30,000 for trespass, wrongful arrest and false imprisonment, against all the defendants, transferred to the State; and (d) $A 30,000 for malicious prosecution, against Constable J alone. The officers were also held liable for various similar claims in relation to CL and the two remaining plaintiffs.[1]

2.6 On 9 April 2001, the State of Victoria filed an appeal against Judge Williams' decision regarding its liability for damages. On

---

[1] See para. 4.8.

7 November 2002, the Court of Appeal overturned Judge Williams' decision that the State was liable to pay for damages arising from the intentional actions of Constable J and the negligence of Sergeant C. The Court found that the latter's negligence was not a cause of the injuries to the author, but rather that they were caused by intentional actions that in effect severed the causal chain of liability of Sergeant C. As a consequence, the liability of the officers remained, but the liability of the State to pay damages was overturned. The author was awarded damages totalling $A 143,525. With respect to the claim against the State of Victoria, the author sought leave to appeal against the judgment of the Court of Appeal in the High Court of Australia, which was refused on 18 June 2004.

2.7 The author filed a complaint to the Ethical Standards Department of Victoria Police. As a result, disciplinary proceedings were launched, but they were subsequently dropped for lack of evidence, despite the strong factual findings against the police officers recorded during the court proceedings outlined above. The author had no standing in the proceedings and was not called as a witness. On 4 August 2004, she made a complaint to the Police Ombudsman which was then transferred to the Office of Police Integrity.

2.8 At the time the author submitted the communication to the Committee, the situation in respect of compensation was as follows: (a) she had not received any damages from the individual police officers; (b) she had not received costs to pay her legal team; and (c) the State of Victoria continued to maintain a legal landscape that absolved its liability to compensate victims of intentional human rights abuses. The situation in respect of disciplinary matters was as follows: (a) all or most of the police involved in the incident remained employed by the State of Victoria, with no disciplinary or criminal action having been successfully taken against any of them, despite Judge Williams' findings of serious misconduct. None of the occupants of the house was consulted by police investigators from the Ethical Standards Department; and (b) the legal system of Victoria does not ensure effective discipline or prosecution of police engaged in human rights abuses.

2.9 Constable J brought charges against the author for assault against police and traffic infringements, which were dismissed by the Magistrates' Court in Frankston on 9 November 1996. In his judgment of 23 February 2001, Judge Williams found that Constable J had conducted a prosecution for assault against the author that was not based upon a proper motive, but arose from a mixture of ill-will and a desire to justify ex post facto the general conduct of the police throughout the whole affair. On that basis, Judge Williams found that the tort of malicious prosecution had been committed.

THE COMPLAINT

Article 2

3.1 The author claims that the State party violated article 2, paragraph 3, of the Covenant, as it did not provide her with an effective remedy. She received no compensation and no disciplinary action was taken against the perpetrators of the assault.

3.2 There is no statutory scheme in Victoria that provides adequate compensation for human rights abuses. Under common law, the State is not responsible for police conduct because when police act on the basis of a power under law, they act independently, not as agents of the State. Section 123 of the Police Regulation Act 1958 remedies that situation only partially by holding the State liable only where police act reasonably in good faith.[2] Moreover, the Act creates an exceptionally narrow class of State liability for actions or omissions of police officers. In order for the State to be liable, the actions of the police must be negligent, yet the police must also be acting in good faith, and the act or omission must be "necessarily or reasonably done" in the course of their duty. It is very difficult to imagine a case that satisfies those criteria. In the present case, the trial judge was satisfied that the negligent planning and supervision of the raid by Sergeant C was a reasonable yet negligent action done in good faith, and that the abuse suffered by the author flowed from that negligence. However, the Court of Appeal overturned that analysis, holding that the actions of the police during the raid effectively severed the causal chain. The Court of Appeal found that there was a "common design" agreed between the officers to commit intentional torts that outweighed any negligence of Sergeant C in planning the raid.

3.3 Four States in Australia ensure State compensation for victims of police tort even when police actions are intentional or in bad faith. In two of them, the State will pay punitive damages awarded against officers.

---

[2] Section 123 reads: "*Immunity of members*: (1) A member of the force ... is not personally liable for anything necessarily or reasonably done or omitted to be done in good faith in the course of his or her duty as a member of the force or police recruit. (2) Any liability resulting from an act or omission that, but for subsection (1), would attach to a member of the force or police recruit, attaches instead to the State. (3) This section applies to acts or omissions occurring before as well as after the commencement of this section."

3.4 The State party has failed to ensure that the perpetrators are tried before a criminal court. As a result of their status as police officers, they were not brought before a court as any other perpetrator of similar abuse would have been. Furthermore, the State permitted the officers involved to continue occupying positions in which their unacceptable behaviour could be repeated.

Article 7

3.5 The author claims that she was subjected to cruel, inhuman and degrading treatment during the raid. The degradation was enhanced by her being handcuffed, taken into custody and later charged. Her arrest was cruel and unjustified.

3.6 The level of force used against the author during the raid went far beyond the force required to detain her and was not necessary. The trial judge found that Constable J "pulled her to the floor and began 'brutally and unnecessarily' to punch her in the face, thereby fracturing her nose and rendering her senseless. In the result, Horvath had no recollection of J's assault on her. With the assistance of S, J then rolled Horvath over and, despite her bleeding nose, handcuffed her and then dragged her out to the van."[3]

3.7 Article 7 imposes two obligations on States parties: a substantive (or negative) obligation to prevent violations and a procedural (or positive) obligation to provide an effective investigation into allegations of substantive violations. In the present case, the investigation was carried out by the Ethical Standards Department, a unit within the Victoria Police. The Victoria Police disciplinary system was criticized in a 2007 report of the Office of Police Integrity entitled "A fair and effective Victoria Police disciplinary system". The author's case is mentioned in that report in a manner which makes it clear that the failure of the disciplinary process to hold police accountable is of concern.

3.8 The County Court of Victoria came to clear findings of fault against the police. Despite the fact that the standards of proof in civil and disciplinary proceedings are the same, the disciplinary process failed to achieve the same result. Owing to the failure to investigate the case effectively or use the findings in the civil proceedings as evidence to remove the police perpetrators from duty, the perpetrators remained employed and were not subjected to any form of discipline.

---

[3] Details concerning the author's injuries and psychological consequences are contained in the judgment of the County Court of Victoria.

That inaction condones a violation of article 7 and effectively authorizes further potential violation of article 7.

Article 9 (paras. 1 and 5)

3.9 The author was subjected to arbitrary arrest and detention, in violation of article 9, paragraph 1, of the Covenant. Without a warrant, the police had no right to enter the author's house and arrest her. The detention was not justified or lawful. Judge Williams found that she had been falsely arrested and imprisoned. Furthermore, the State party did not grant her an enforceable right to compensation, which entails a violation of article 9, paragraph 5.

Article 10

3.10 The assault, constraint by handcuffing, arrest, detention and delay in medical treatment suffered by the author were inhumane and a violation of article 10, in addition to article 7. Her detention in a situation in which medical attention was required added to the trauma she experienced.

Article 17

3.11 In the absence of a warrant or a reason to believe that the author had committed a serious indictable offence, the police invasion of the author's house constituted arbitrary and unlawful interference with her home, family and privacy. Furthermore, the malicious prosecution of the author for assaulting Constable J was an unlawful attack on her honour and reputation and a disproportionate action which could not be justified by any interpretation of a pressing social need.

Exhaustion of domestic remedies

3.12 The author claims that she exhausted domestic remedies in attempting to claim damages from the State of Victoria. She learned through her lawyer that the individual police officers against whom judgment was entered did not have the resources to pay the judgment amount and cost or any substantial portion thereof. Furthermore, the author cannot obtain compensation through the Victims of Crime Compensation Tribunal, since the acts to which she was subjected were non-criminal.

3.13 Section 123 of the Police Regulation Act 1958 provides no effective remedy for victims of police abuse, even when the abuse is the result of misconduct during police operations and procedures. Victims of police abuse in Victoria are reliant on damages being paid by the individual perpetrators. That is problematic because police officers organize their assets in ways that shield them from potential liability to civil actions. In cases where the individual police officer has no capacity to pay or has no assets in his/her name, the victim is not compensated. That is neither an effective compensation scheme, nor does it provide any incentive to the Victoria Police to prevent further abuses.

Remedies sought

3.14 The author seeks: (a) to be awarded compensation, assessed according to the standards applicable under Australian domestic law; (b) that the State party be directed to enact legislation allowing for compensation by the State party for the illegal activities of police officers; (c) that the State party be directed to ensure that people have genuine access to civil action alleging police abuse and receive assistance in that regard, in order to ensure that civil actions have a systemic impact on reform within police agencies; and (d) that the State party be directed to introduce reforms to the current disciplinary procedures applicable to police officers in the State of Victoria to ensure that: (i) all police who are found civilly liable for human rights abuses are disciplined and removed from the force; (ii) the State party prosecutes police who have committed criminal offences; and (iii) police not subject to civil proceedings are investigated and subject to proceedings that can result in their removal from duty where appropriate.

OBSERVATIONS OF THE STATE PARTY ON ADMISSIBILITY AND ON THE MERITS

4.1 The State party submitted its observations on 24 March 2010.

Claims under article 2

4.2 The State party contends that the author failed to substantiate her claim of a violation of article 2. In particular, she failed to substantiate her claim that the four members of the Victoria Police against whom judgment was made did not have the resources to pay the damages awarded and did not have any assets in their names.

Furthermore, domestic legal avenues are available to the author to determine whether her assertion is correct. The Rules of the Supreme Court of Victoria set out a process for discovery in aid of enforcement. The Court may, on application by a person entitled to enforce a judgment, order a person bound by the judgment to attend court, be orally examined on material questions, and produce any document or thing in the possession, custody or power of the person relating to the material questions. There is no evidence that the author sought such an order.

4.3 Even if the four members of the police do not have the resources to pay or assets in their names, domestic avenues remain available to the author to recover all or part of the judgment debt. A judgment for the payment of money made in the Supreme Court of Victoria, which includes the Court of Appeal, may be enforced by a number of means, including warrant of seizure and sale, attachment of debts, attachment of earnings, a charging order against the property of the debtor and, in certain circumstances, committal for trial and sequestration (seizure of property). In particular, the Supreme Court Rules provide that a judgment creditor may apply to the Court for an attachment of earnings order. The effect of such an order is that the judgment debtor's employer must pay a reasonable proportion of the debtor's earnings to the creditor. The author is also entitled to apply to the Court of Appeal for an order that the judgment debt be paid by instalments. The author has made no attempt to recover the judgment debt, whether by an order for an attachment of earnings or otherwise.

4.4 In 2003, about six months after the Court of Appeal judgment against Constable J was entered, he voluntarily chose to become bankrupt. The author has not provided information as to what contact, if any, she had with the trustee appointed to administer Constable J's estate in order to ensure that her interests were taken into account in the administration process. Constable J's bankruptcy was discharged at the expiry of three years. The author did not seek to enforce the judgment against him following the discharge of his bankruptcy in July 2006.

4.5 According to a document submitted by the author, she learned in 2007 that her lawyer had not taken any steps to recover the judgment debt. Although the author instructed her lawyers in 2008 to take bankruptcy proceedings against the remaining police officers, the bankruptcy register shows no record of any creditor's petition issued in relation to the individual police officers.

4.6 The author has not pursued compensation from the Victims of Crime Assistance Tribunal or its predecessor, the Crimes

Compensation Tribunal, despite being eligible to make an application for compensation up to $A 60,000. The absence of a criminal prosecution in respect of the acts of the individual police officers does not preclude application to the Tribunal. The author has therefore failed to exhaust domestic remedies on that basis as well.

4.7 The State party contends that the author's claims under article 2 are without merits. In Australia, the common law rule set out in *Enever* v. *The King* provides that a "police officer is himself responsible for unjustifiable acts done in the intended exercise of his lawful authority". The liability for such acts is not transferred to the State. Section 123(1) of the Police Regulation Act 1958 modifies the common law position, providing that a police officer "is not personally liable for anything necessarily or reasonably done or omitted to be done in good faith in the course of his or her duty". Under section 123(2), liability for such an act or omission attaches instead to the State of Victoria. The outcome is a compensatory scheme whereby, in the event of any unlawful act or omission by a police officer, either the State or the individual police officer will be held liable. That scheme balances an appropriate level of protection and the need to ensure that there is no encouragement to develop an attitude of irresponsibility among police officers. It ensures that there is no scope for impunity and that compensation will be awarded where appropriate. Individual liability has an important deterrent effect. The function of awards of exemplary, aggravated or punitive damages would be undermined if they were simply to be transferred to the State. Consequently, the State's refusal to indemnify acts or omissions of police officers that fall outside the scope of section 123 is consistent with article 2.

4.8 The outcome of the decision of the Court of Appeal of Victoria was that the individual police officers were personally liable to pay damages for assault, trespass, false imprisonment and malicious prosecution. The damages awarded to the author included compensatory damages, aggravated damages and exemplary damages totalling $A 143,525. Of that amount, she was awarded $A 93,525 for the assault against her by Constable J; $A 30,000 for trespass and false imprisonment by all the defendant officers; and $A 20,000 for malicious prosecution against her by Constable J. Hence, the author's right to adequate and effective reparation has been realized. The State party does not accept that the author has successfully proved that she faced difficulties in enforcing the judgment made in her favour, as judicial processes for enforcement are available to her. In any event, a breach of article 2 cannot depend on whether the individual police officers against whom judgment was made have the resources to pay or have assets in their names.

4.9 Regarding the author's claim that the State party breached article 2 by failing to criminally prosecute those allegedly responsible for violating her rights, the State party recalls the Committee's jurisprudence that the Covenant does not provide a right for an individual to require that the State party criminally prosecute another person. Further, the State party has effective legal processes in place to address any alleged violations of inhuman or degrading treatment or punishment by police officers, and those processes have been adequately invoked in the present case.

4.10 The Police Regulation Act 1958 establishes a disciplinary process which is overseen by the Chief Commissioner of Police and undertaken by the Ethical Standards Department of Victoria Police. The Department is responsible for investigating police misconduct and corruption and dealing with service delivery and disciplinary issues. It deals with claims in a prompt and impartial manner. Since November 2004, the Office of Police Integrity has been the independent body that detects, investigates and prevents police corruption and serious misconduct. Furthermore, criminal sanctions are available for conduct constituting serious violations of human rights. The statutory requirement that the Deputy Ombudsman (Police Complaints) be informed of disciplinary investigations provides an important independent check on the adequacy and appropriateness of the disciplinary process.

4.11 As a result of a complaint filed by the author on 21 March 1996, preliminary investigations were undertaken. The Ethical Standards Department informed the author about the status of the investigations on several occasions. When the file was opened, the Department also informed the author that she could make an additional complaint to the Deputy Ombudsman (Police Complaints). The Deputy Ombudsman responded on 30 April 1997 that the time taken to arrange medical treatment for the author was not unreasonable and that the proposal to charge Sergeant C and Constable J with disciplinary offences was appropriate in the circumstances. As a result of the preliminary investigation, Constable J was charged with disgraceful conduct and Sergeant C with being negligent in the discharge of his duty. An inquiry for Constable J was conducted on 25 August 1998 and for Sergeant C on 31 August 1998. As the hearing officer could not reasonably be satisfied on the evidence before him, all charges were dismissed. In respect of the inquiry for Constable J, the hearing officer also noted inconsistencies in the evidence provided by civilian witnesses. At the time the inquiries were concluded, the civil proceedings had not concluded and no findings of fact had been made by the trial judge which could have been considered by the hearing officer. That outcome does not undermine the adequacy of the process to respond to complaints of alleged police misconduct. It is the general practice of the Committee not to question the evaluation of the evidence made in domestic processes.

4.12 The disparity between the findings of the trial judge and the outcome of the disciplinary proceeding can be explained by reference to the different standards of proof which apply in each forum. In disciplinary proceedings involving allegations of serious misconduct, the usual civil standard requiring proof on the balance of probabilities applies, but is increased by an additional requirement that the degree of certainty required must be particularly high given the gravity of the consequences which flow from an adverse finding. That standard is consistent with the serious nature of such proceedings and the punishment, including dismissal, which can result.

Claims under article 7

4.13 Based on the author's failure to make use of all judicial and administrative avenues that offer her a reasonable prospect of redress, the State party submits that the author failed to exhaust domestic remedies. If the Committee finds that the claim under article 7 is admissible, the State party submits that the allegations are without merit.

4.14 The author's treatment did not amount to cruel, inhuman or degrading treatment or punishment. The State party accepts that a conclusion that the treatment was unacceptable or inappropriate is open on the facts, particularly in light of the Court of Appeal's decision to uphold the award of damages to the author for assault and false imprisonment. Nevertheless, her treatment during the incident did not amount to a breach of article 7. For treatment in the context of an arrest to be degrading, there must be an exacerbating factor beyond the usual incidents of arrest. Since arrest, like detention, contains an inherent aspect of humiliation, an element of reprehensibleness must also be present for it to qualify as a violation of article 7. Any exacerbating factor or element of reprehensibleness in the author's purported arrest or detention was insufficient to meet the threshold level of severity required for a breach of article 7. Furthermore, the author has not substantiated the claim that she suffered ongoing adverse physical or mental effects.

4.15 Failure to provide necessary medical attention can, in certain circumstances, amount to a breach of article 7. However, in the present case police records confirm that the author received appropriate and timely medical treatment while in custody. She was treated by a doctor within 20 minutes of arriving at the police station, at 11.00 p.m. on 9 March 1996. At midnight, an ambulance arrived and the author was administered further treatment. She was released from custody at 12.20 a.m. on 10 March 1996 and conveyed to hospital by ambulance. She was readmitted to hospital approximately one week later in relation to her nose injury. There is nothing to suggest that she received anything other than appropriate and timely medical treatment while in detention. On 30 April 1997, the Deputy Ombudsman observed that the time taken to arrange medical treatment for the author was not unreasonable.

4.16 The author claims that the failure to effectively investigate and discipline police involved in the raid condones violations of article 7 and effectively authorizes further potential violations. However, that claim overlaps with her claim under article 2 and should be considered in conjunction with it. States have an obligation to ensure that complaints made in relation to article 7 are investigated promptly and impartially by competent authorities. In the present case, the successful civil action against members of the police demonstrates that individuals remain liable for their acts and omissions. If, as the author proposes, civil liability for all acts and omissions of police officers were to be transferred to the State, it would effectively absolve individuals of their potential individual civil liability. That liability acts as an important deterrent to police officers.

Claim under article 9, paragraph 1

4.17 The State party argues that domestic remedies have not been exhausted and that the claim is without merit. The author's purported arrest and detention should not be characterized as unlawful or arbitrary in the context of article 9, paragraph 1. As was recognized by the Court of Appeal of Victoria, the members of Victoria Police involved in the raid were of the opinion that they had authority to enter the premises and arrest the author under section 459A of the Crimes Act 1958 (Victoria).

Claim under article 10

4.18 The State party argues that domestic remedies have not been exhausted and that the claim is without merit. Further, the author does not clearly identify which treatment is alleged to fall within the scope of article 10.

4.19 The principle that treatment prohibited by the Covenant under article 7 must entail elements beyond the mere fact of deprivation of liberty is also relevant to article 10. Any element of humiliation that may have accompanied the handcuffing and detention was insufficient to meet the threshold required to establish a breach of article 10. Following her arrest, the author was brought directly to the police station, where her handcuffs were removed. Handcuffing, in the context of what was considered to be a lawful arrest, and in the context of her clear non-cooperation with police, was not unreasonable in the circumstances. The author's alleged inability to reduce the pain and blood flow from her nose or otherwise relieve her injuries was insufficient to reach the level of humiliation or debasement prohibited by article 10. Consequently, the purported arrest, handcuffing and detention cannot in themselves amount to a breach of article 10.

4.20 As to the alleged delay in medical treatment, the State party submits that the author's treatment in detention did not breach article 10. Police records confirm that the author received prompt medical treatment while in custody. There was no medical advice to indicate that she should not be detained. The nature of her injuries and the short period of detention are relevant considerations in that regard. The author was briefly admitted to hospital within hours of her arrest and was subsequently discharged. She did not spend a significant period in hospital until almost a week after the incident, indicating that the treatment she required was not urgent.

Claim under article 17

4.21 The State party argues that domestic remedies have not been exhausted and that the claim is without merit. The State party reiterates its arguments in connection with article 9 of the Covenant and submits that the author has presented no evidence to suggest that her honour and reputation were maliciously attacked. To the extent that the charges against her may have been prosecuted without reasonable cause and maliciously, she was successful in her claim for malicious prosecution against Constable J.

AUTHOR'S COMMENTS ON THE STATE PARTY'S OBSERVATIONS

5.1 On 2 July 2010, the author submitted comments on the State party's observations. The author reiterates her allegations and states that she has exhausted all avenues in seeking to recover the judgment debt.

5.2 Once the judgments became enforceable against the individual police officers, letters of demand were forwarded to them seeking payment of the amounts owed to the author. In response, the police officers' counsel informed the author's counsel that Constable J had declared himself bankrupt and therefore the author was prevented, under the provisions of the Bankruptcy Act, from pursuing any further action against him. As for the remaining defendants, they had minimal assets, according to the research undertaken by the author's counsel. Under Australian law, superannuation is not accessible in a bankruptcy. Therefore, effectively, if any of the defendants were declared bankrupt, they would have no assets which would be distributable to the author and the other plaintiffs. A warrant of seizure and sale, or a charging order against a property of a debtor is only of benefit if there are assets which can be seized or property which can be charged. The author's counsel, having obtained information from the defendants and carried out his own searches, was of the view that any application to issue a warrant or a charging order would be futile and result in no monies being available. Accordingly, the author's counsel opted to attempt to negotiate a settlement. As a result, the non-bankrupt defendants offered a final settlement of $A 45,000, payable to the author and her three co-plaintiffs. That settlement was accepted. Constable J was obliged to notify the Trustee in Bankruptcy of the money owed to the author. As no communication was received from the Trustee, it was apparent that no funds were available for distribution to the creditors.

5.3 Regarding the State party's observation that the author could have pursued a claim for compensation in the Victims of Crime Assistance Tribunal, she states that the Tribunal does not provide compensation for pain and suffering and focuses on timely and practical measures to assist victims of crime. The Tribunal may award amounts as financial assistance and special financial assistance. Financial assistance is granted for medical and counselling expenses, loss of earnings and damage to clothes during an act of violence. Special financial assistance may be seen as compensatory in nature. The Tribunal awards modest amounts when an applicant suffers any significant adverse effect as a direct result of an act of violence. It uses categories of offences to determine the maximum level of special financial assistance to be awarded. It is possible that in the author's case, if she did not establish that she had suffered a very serious injury, she would be eligible for financial assistance of either $A 130-$A 650 or $A 650-$A 1,300, which are the amounts awarded for offences that result in serious injury and assault respectively. The awards are symbolic and are not intended to reflect the level of compensation to which victims of crime may be entitled under common law or otherwise. An extendable time limit of two years applies to claims before the Tribunal. The presumption is that an application concerning the present communication would be inadmissible, since the incident occurred in 1996.

5.4 Furthermore, the Tribunal does not make any findings of guilt. Its investigative powers are limited to establishing whether an act of violence occurred and whether the application for financial assistance should be granted to meet expenses related to that act. It does not have the capacity to remedy the breaches outlined in the present communication. Accordingly, an award from the Tribunal is not an effective remedy for the author. To comply with the requirement to exhaust domestic remedies an author must access those remedies which are available and effective in redressing the wrong. Such remedies must also provide the State with an opportunity to respond to and remedy the issue within its jurisdiction.

5.5 The author disagrees with the State party's arguments regarding the individual responsibility of perpetrators. It is the State's responsibility to ensure that its police do not violate human rights and to remedy violations when they occur. By directly compensating victims, the State ensures that its obligations in that respect are fulfilled. Such a position does not relieve the individual perpetrators of liability in civil proceedings. It is also possible for the State to pursue the individual perpetrators for reimbursement. Currently, the practical effect of section 123 of the Police Regulation Act is to absolve the State of responsibility for police who act in bad faith, unreasonably and outside the course of their duty. In the light of that, the State of Victoria is obliged to change its domestic laws, as other States have already done. Furthermore, police violence occurs in part owing to systemic failures in training, oversight and disciplinary measures. State liability for the actions of its agents ensures that such systemic failures are addressed.

5.6 Regarding the State party's observations on the effectiveness of the disciplinary system in Victoria, the author argues that the Ethical Standards Department lacks practical independence and that findings of criminal or torturous conduct against police are rare. She claims that she was not called to give evidence in the hearing of the disciplinary charge against Constable J and nor were any of the civilian witnesses. The hearing occurred two years after the incident and the investigation took 11 months. Such a delay is inexcusable.

5.7 The author requested a copy of the disciplinary file related to her case, but it was denied to her on the grounds that it would divert too much of the State's resources. The only publicly released information about the process was contained in a brief paragraph in the Office of Police Integrity report entitled "A fair and effective Victoria Police disciplinary system". There was no public scrutiny of the investigation, the hearing or the decision, and no appeal mechanism was open to the author. As for the role of the Deputy Ombudsman as a safeguard of the process, the author claims that mere notification was all that was required and that there is no supervision as such.

5.8 The State party's reference to the standard of proof to explain the difference in outcomes between the disciplinary and the civil proceedings is unjustified and unsupported. It does not address the fact that the disciplinary hearing failed to adduce viva voce evidence from civilian witnesses to the police misconduct, which reflects a systemic and serious failure of the process in circumstances where it was purported that there was insufficient evidence to make a finding of misconduct. The difference in outcomes between the two processes lies in the lack of adequacy, transparency, accountability and independence of the disciplinary hearing process.

5.9 Once the civil proceedings had concluded that the police had lied on matters of major significance, there was the opportunity to reopen or recommence disciplinary proceedings and refer a prosecution brief to the Office of Public Prosecutions. The State failed to pursue those avenues.

5.10 The author reiterates that the treatment to which she was subjected breached article 7 of the Covenant. She was 21 at the time and the treatment was premeditated and intended to punish and intimidate her. She was repeatedly punched, causing very serious and cruel suffering in the form of a broken nose, facial injuries, bruising to her face and other parts of her body, a chipped tooth, loss of consciousness, fear, anguish, distress, intimidation and ongoing psychological conditions. The assault continued while she was helpless and unconscious. The treatment was unnecessarily prolonged by the arrest and transport to the police station, where she continued to be handcuffed. According to Judge Williams, the police viewed the author with "extraordinary bigotry and bias", describing her as a "filthy, dirty, drug-affected female". That provides support for her claim that the intention was to debase, degrade and punish her.

5.11 Regarding the State party's observations with respect to article 9, the author reiterates that the police entry into the house was inappropriate, unjust and unreasonable. It was also unlawful, as stated by Judge Williams. The police could have utilized less invasive ways to effect an arrest if it was truly necessary, such as obtaining a warrant or conducting static observations of the premises. Even if the entry to the premises was believed to be lawful by individual police officers, it does not mean that what occurred after entry was lawful. The assault and transportation to the police station were not proportionate in the circumstances.

5.12 If the Committee considers that there was no breach of article 9, including paragraph 5, the author submits that those actions violated her freedom of movement under article 12 of the Covenant.

5.13 The author reiterates her claims under article 17. She states that a malicious prosecution by necessity breached her right to privacy and not to be subjected to unlawful attacks on her reputation.

ADDITIONAL OBSERVATIONS FROM THE STATE PARTY

6.1 In August 2011, the State party submitted further observations on admissibility and on the merits. With respect to compensation under the Victims of Crime Assistance Scheme, the State party argues that at the time of the incidents in question, the author would have been entitled to make a claim under the Criminal Injuries Compensation Act 1983 (Victoria) and to compensation of up to $A 50,000, including an award of compensation for pain and suffering of up to $A 20,000. The categories of special financial assistance relied upon by the author did not come into force until 2000. Awards made under the Scheme serve similar purposes to public law damages available in other jurisdictions, in terms of both compensation and vindication.

6.2 Compensation under the Victims of Crime Assistance Act 1996 is an effective remedy for the purposes of article 2. The author remains eligible to pursue such compensation. As she has not done so, she has failed to exhaust all available domestic remedies.

6.3 In jurisdictions that have a separate public law cause of action for breach of human rights, public law damages may serve the objectives of compensating the claimant for loss and suffering caused by the breach, vindicating the right in question by emphasizing its importance and the gravity of the breach and deterring State agents from committing future breaches. Damages are generally not awarded unless one or more of those objectives is served. Where damages are appropriate, the concern is to restore the claimant to the position in which she would have been had the breach not been committed.

6.4 The State party rejects the author's claim that only full payment of compensatory damages, aggravated damages, exemplary damages and full legal costs by the State of Victoria will constitute an "effective remedy". Section 123 of the Police Regulation Act means that the State of Victoria will be liable for breaches of human rights by individual police officers where those breaches occur in accordance with practices and procedures promulgated by Victoria Police or in circumstances in which the conduct is contributed to by systemic issues such as inadequate training, policies and procedures. It is only when a police officer acts well outside the authorized policies and procedures, such that Victoria Police and the State of Victoria cannot be said to have contributed in any way to the conduct, that the State of Victoria will not be liable for the breach.

6.5 Regarding the claims under article 12, the State party submits that the author has failed to exhaust domestic remedies for the reasons specified above, and that the claim is without merits. The right to liberty and freedom of movement are distinct concepts. While restrictions not amounting to a breach of the right to liberty may in some circumstances amount to a breach of freedom of movement, that will not always be the case. The facts of the current case do not give rise to issues regarding liberty of movement as contemplated in article 12. Even if that was the case, any restriction on the author's liberty of movement was within the scope of restrictions permitted under article 12, paragraph 3.

6.6 Section 459A of the Crimes Act 1958 (Victoria) provides that a police officer may enter and search premises for the purpose of arresting a person where the officer believes, on reasonable grounds, that the person has committed a serious indictable offence. Entry, search and arrest in those circumstances are actions provided for by law and necessary to protect national security, public order and the rights and freedoms of others.

6.7 As was recognized by the Court of Appeal, the police officers believed that they had the authority to enter the premises and arrest the author under section 459A. While the Court of Appeal ultimately found that the entry and arrest were unlawful, the belief of the police officers should be taken into consideration in assessing their actions.

ISSUES AND PROCEEDINGS BEFORE THE COMMITTEE

Consideration of admissibility

7.1 Before considering any claim contained in a communication, the Human Rights Committee must, in accordance with rule 93 of its rules of procedure, decide whether or not the case is admissible under the Optional Protocol to the Covenant.

7.2 The Committee has ascertained, as required under article 5, paragraph 2(a), of the Optional Protocol, that the same matter is not being examined under another procedure of international investigation or settlement.

7.3 The author claims that the treatment to which she was subjected in connection with the incidents that occurred on 9 March 1996 and subsequent events violated her rights under articles 7, 9 (paras. 1 and 5), 10 (para. 1) and 17 of the Covenant. The Committee notes that the essence of the claims made by the author before the Committee is based on the same grounds as those she brought before the national judicial authorities. In that regard, the County Court of Victoria established the liability of the police officers who raided her house for trespass, assault, wrongful arrest, false imprisonment, malicious prosecution and negligence. The Court of Appeal found that the individual police officers were liable to pay damages for assault, trespass, false imprisonment and malicious prosecution. The Committee considers that, in addressing the substance of the author's claims, the domestic courts acknowledged that the author's rights had been violated and established the perpetrators' civil responsibility for acts which fall under the scope of the above-mentioned provisions of the Covenant. In view of the acknowledgement by the domestic courts of the civil responsibility of State agents for domestic law violations which are covered by articles 7, 9 (para. 1) and 17 of the Covenant, and their liability to pay damages, the Committee considers that the real issue before it is whether the author obtained an effective remedy for the violations of her rights under the Covenant, after the final decision of the domestic courts became enforceable.

7.4 The Committee notes the author's claims under article 2 that she did not receive full compensation, as established by the national courts, and that no criminal and disciplinary actions were taken against the perpetrators of the assault. The Committee also notes the State party's challenge to the admissibility of the communication on the ground that domestic remedies were not exhausted, as the author did not seek the enforcement of the judgment in her favour, in application of the Rules of the Supreme Court of Victoria regarding the process for discovery in aid of enforcement, following the discharge of Constable J's bankruptcy. The State party also claims that the author did not pursue compensation from the Victims of Crime Assistance Tribunal. The Committee further notes the information provided by the author regarding the steps taken to seek the enforcement of the judgment and the final settlement that she and her co-plaintiffs felt obliged to accept. The Committee notes the author's argument that the awards provided by the Victims of Crime Assistance Tribunal are symbolic and are not intended to reflect the level of compensation to which victims of crime may be entitled under common law or otherwise.

7.5 The Committee considers that, in choosing to file proceedings for damages against the police officers under the Crown Proceedings Act, the author sought an appropriate avenue of redress, as demonstrated inter alia by the fact that she was successful in her judicial claims and that compensation was awarded to her under the Act. The fact that the judgment of the Court of Appeal was not fully enforced, despite the efforts she undertook subsequently in that respect, is not attributable to the author. Accordingly, for the purpose of admissibility, it cannot be expected that, in addition to those proceedings, the author would seek compensation from the Victims of Crime Assistance Tribunal. The Committee therefore concludes that domestic remedies have been exhausted.

7.6 As the Committee does not see any other obstacle to admissibility, it decides that the communication is admissible insofar as it appears to raise issues under articles 7, 9 (para. 1), 10 (para. 1) and 17 of the Covenant on their own and read together with article 2 (para. 3); and under article 9 (para. 5) on its own.

Consideration of the merits

8.1 The Human Rights Committee has considered the communication in the light of all the information made available to it by the parties, as provided for under article 5, paragraph 1, of the Optional Protocol.

8.2 The Committee notes the author's claims that the State party failed to ensure that the perpetrators be tried before a criminal court and that her complaints before the disciplinary bodies of the Victoria Police were unsuccessful. In that connection, the Committee considers that article 2, paragraph 3, of the Covenant does not impose on States parties any particular form of remedy and that the Covenant does not provide a right for individuals to require that the State criminally prosecute a third party.[4] However, article 2, paragraph 3, does impose on States parties the obligation to investigate allegations of violations promptly, thoroughly and effectively through independent and impartial bodies.[5]

---

[4] Communication No 563/1993, *Bautista de Arellana* v. *Colombia*, Views adopted on 27 October 1995, para. 8.6.
[5] General comment No 31 (2004) on the nature of the general legal obligation imposed on States parties to the Covenant, para. 15.

Furthermore, in deciding whether the victim of a violation of the Covenant has obtained adequate reparation, the Committee can take into consideration the availability and effectiveness not just of one particular remedy but the cumulative effect of several remedies of a different nature, such as criminal, civil, administrative or disciplinary remedies.

8.3 In the present case, the disciplinary claims before the Police Department were dismissed for lack of evidence. In that respect, the Committee notes the author's allegations, uncontested by the State party, that neither the author nor the other civilian witnesses were called to give evidence; that the author was refused access to the file; that there was no public hearing; and that once the finding was made in the civil proceeding, there was no opportunity to reopen or recommence disciplinary proceedings. In view of those shortcomings and given the nature of the deciding body, the Committee considers that the State party failed to show that the disciplinary proceedings met the requirements of an effective remedy under article 2, paragraph 3, of the Covenant.

8.4 The Committee further notes that the author was successful in her civil suit and that compensation was ordered by the national judicial bodies with reference to the police officers' liability in relation to trespass, assault, wrongful arrest, false imprisonment, malicious prosecution and negligence—unlawful acts of which she was found to be a victim. However, her efforts to seek the enforcement of the final judgment were unsuccessful. In the end, the author was left with no other option but to accept a final settlement involving a quantum which represented a small portion of the quantum granted to her in court.

8.5 With reference to section 123 of the Police Regulation Act (Victoria), the Committee notes that the provision limits the responsibility of the State for wrongful acts committed by its agents without providing for an alternative mechanism for full compensation for violations of the Covenant by State agents. Under those circumstances, the Committee considers that section 123 is incompatible with article 2, paragraph 2, and with article 2, paragraph 3, of the Covenant, as a State cannot elude its responsibility for violations of the Covenant committed by its own agents. In that respect, the Committee recalls that article 2, paragraph 2, requires States parties to take the necessary steps to give effect to the Covenant rights in the domestic order, and to make such changes to domestic laws and practices as are necessary to ensure their conformity with the Covenant.[6] The Committee also recalls that under article 2, paragraph 3, States parties are required to make reparation to individuals whose Covenant rights have been violated. Without such reparation the obligation to provide an effective remedy, which is central to the efficacy of article 2, paragraph 3, is not discharged. In addition to the explicit reparation required by articles 9, paragraph 5, and 14, paragraph 6, the Committee considers that the Covenant generally entails appropriate compensation.[7]

8.6 The Committee further considers that actions for damages in domestic courts may provide an effective remedy in cases of alleged unlawfulness or negligence by State agents. It recalls that the obligation of States under article 2, paragraph 3, encompasses not only the obligation to provide an effective remedy, but also the obligation to ensure that the competent authorities enforce such remedies when granted. That obligation, enshrined in article 2, paragraph 3(c), means that State authorities have the burden to enforce judgments of domestic courts which provide effective remedies to victims. In order to ensure that, States parties should use all appropriate means and organize their legal systems in such a way as to guarantee the enforcement of remedies in a manner that is consistent with their obligations under the Covenant.

8.7 In the present case, the success of the author in obtaining compensation in her civil claim has been nullified by the impossibility of having the judgment of the Court of Appeal adequately enforced, owing to factual and legal obstacles. The procedure established in the domestic law of the State party to remedy the violation of the author's rights under articles 7, 9, paragraph 1, and 17 of the Covenant proved to be ineffective and the compensatory award finally proposed to the author was inadequate, in view of the acts complained of, to satisfy the requirements of an effective reparation under article 2, paragraph 3, of the Covenant. The Committee considers that in situations where the execution of a final judgment becomes impossible in view of the circumstances of the case, other legal avenues should be available in order for the State to comply with its obligation to provide adequate redress to a victim. However, in the present case the State party has not shown that such alternative avenues existed or were effective. The State party refers to

---

[6] General comment No 31, para. 13.
[7] General comment No 31, para. 16.

compensation under the Victims of Crime Assistance Scheme, but the Committee is not convinced that, given the nature of the Scheme, including its no-fault attributes, the author could indeed obtain adequate redress through it for serious harm inflicted by State agents. The Committee notes in that respect that the State party has not provided information about cases in which persons with claims similar to those of the author obtained adequate redress through the Scheme.

8.8 In view of the foregoing, including the shortcomings regarding the disciplinary proceedings, the Committee considers that the facts before it reveal a violation of article 2, paragraph 3, in connection with articles 7, 9, paragraph 1, and 17 of the Covenant. In view of that finding, the Committee will not consider whether the circumstances of the case constitute a separate violation of articles 7, 9, paragraph 1, and 17. Neither will it consider whether there was a violation of article 10, paragraph 1, on its own and read together with article 2, paragraph 3; and of article 9, paragraph 5.

9. The Human Rights Committee, acting under article 5, paragraph 4, of the Optional Protocol to the International Covenant on Civil and Political Rights, is of the view that the State party has violated the author's rights under article 2, paragraph 3, in connection with articles 7, 9, paragraphs 1 and 5, 10, paragraph 1, and 17 of the Covenant.

10. In accordance with article 2, paragraph 3(a), of the Covenant, the State party is under an obligation to provide the author with an effective remedy, including adequate compensation. The State party is also under an obligation to take steps to prevent similar violations in the future. In that connection, the State party should review its legislation to ensure its conformity with the requirements of the Covenant.

11. Bearing in mind that, by becoming a party to the Optional Protocol, the State party has recognized the competence of the Committee to determine whether or not there has been a violation of the Covenant and that, pursuant to article 2 of the Covenant, the State party has undertaken to ensure for all individuals within its territory or subject to its jurisdiction the rights recognized in the Covenant and to provide an effective and enforceable remedy when a violation has been established, the Committee wishes to receive from the State party, within 180 days, information about the measures taken to give effect to the Committee's Views. The State party is also requested to publish the present Views and disseminate them widely in the State party.

APPENDIX I

INDIVIDUAL OPINION BY COMMITTEE MEMBER ANJA SEIBERT-FOHR, JOINED BY COMMITTEE MEMBERS YUJI IWASAWA AND WALTER KÄLIN (PARTLY DISSENTING)

1. The main issue of the present case is the State party's failure to recognize its responsibility for the violent police misconduct. On 9 March 1996, as established by the County Court of Victoria, the author was tackled by a police officer who pulled her to the floor and began to brutally punch her face rendering her senseless and leaving her with a badly beaten and broken nose. She was rolled over and handcuffed despite her bleeding nose and dragged to a van. Although the County Court established the individual police officer's civil liability on those grounds, the State party continues to deny responsibility for cruel, inhuman or degrading treatment. We regret that the majority of the Committee decided not to consider that important aspect of the case and instead characterized the remedies available to the author as the real issue. To our minds, given the gravity of the ill-treatment and the State party's denial of responsibility, it was indispensable for the Committee to find that the police officer's acts, which were clearly attributable to the State party, amounted to a violation of article 7. Such a finding also would have provided the necessary precondition for the Committee's analysis of the author's compensation claim under article 2, paragraph 3, which does not provide for an independent, free-standing right.

2. We concur that the violation of article 7 was insufficiently remedied because the author neither received any payment for the ill-treatment inflicted on her by Constable J, nor was her ill-treatment subject to an independent official investigation to which she had access. The procedure established under domestic law thus did not provide the author with an effective remedy as required under article 2, paragraph 3(a), of the Covenant. The Committee's reference to subparagraph (c), however, is misleading as it was not the failure to enforce a judicial remedy but the failure to provide for an effective remedy in the first place which led to a violation of article 2. We emphasize that aspect because without that clarification, the Committee's reasoning might be understood as granting a right to have domestic civil remedies effectuated even to the extent that they go beyond the requirements of article 2, paragraph 3(a), such as by providing for punitive damages. That is not what article 2 requires and therefore the Committee's conclusion that the State party is under an obligation to provide the author with an

effective remedy, including adequate compensation, should be read on the basis of an understanding which is informed by an autonomous interpretation of article 2.

3. We disagree with the Committee's finding that section 123 of the Police Regulation Act 1958 (Victoria), which provides that the State incurs responsibility for a specific category of police misconduct, is incompatible with article 2. In fact, the damage award ordered by the County Court initially had been transferred to the State on the basis of that Act. The failure to provide for an effective remedy did not result from that provision, but from the subsequent application of common law to the case by the Court of Appeal in combination with the State party's failure to establish the availability of an alternative remedy for cases in which individual officers lack the means to pay compensation. We emphasize that point in order to highlight the particularity of the present case and to avoid misunderstandings which could give rise to an overly broad interpretation of the Committee's views.

APPENDIX II

INDIVIDUAL OPINION BY COMMITTEE MEMBER GERALD L. NEUMAN (PARTLY DISSENTING)

1. I agree in substance with the dissenting opinion of my fellow Committee members. I write very briefly to note a few other aspects of the Committee's Views with which I cannot concur.

2. The majority View cuts too many corners in dealing with the issues that do not relate to the brutal attack by Constable J that violated article 7. It treats most of the claims as a unit, although they are different in their character and in their factual bases, and it does not give sufficient consideration to the author's settlement with the other three officers.

3. Moreover, it would be wrong to suggest that the State party has refused to "enforce" a judgment of its domestic courts. The tort judgment, granting damages in magnitudes that exceed the requirements of the Covenant, ran only against the individual officers by its own terms. The majority more appropriately shifts in paragraph 8.7 to the subject of "alternative avenues" by which the State party would provide the author adequate compensation from public funds, which was definitely not what the court's judgment entailed.

4. My concern about the majority's expression of its reasons extends beyond the present case. The overly generalized way in which the

majority discusses the issues obscures significant distinctions among violations for which different remedial responses may be sufficient and may have been sufficient in the present case. The Committee should engage in more nuanced discussion of obligations under article 2, paragraph 3, in the future.

5. Unfortunately, my ability to address those issues here is impaired by the fact that the United Nations has insisted upon imposing a word limit on the Committee's Views for budgetary reasons. That practice is antithetical to the Committee's carrying out of its responsibilities, and should be abolished.

[Report: UN Doc. CCPR/C/110/D/1885/2009]

Human rights — Liberty of movement — Equality before the law — Right to freedom from discrimination — Right to effective remedy — International Covenant on Civil and Political Rights, 1966, Articles 12 and 26 — Admissibility of author's communication to Human Rights Committee — Case previously submitted to European Court of Human Rights — Whether European Court had considered claim on the merits — Remedy for violation — United Nations Human Rights Committee

ORY v. FRANCE[1]

(Communication No 1960/2010)

United Nations Human Rights Committee.[2] 28 *March* 2014

SUMMARY:[3] *The facts*:—The author, Mr Ory, was a French citizen and a member of the Traveller community. He lived an itinerant lifestyle in a caravan in Le Mans, Sarthe, and had no regular income. He was consequently subject to Act No 69-3 of 1969 ("the 1969 Act") and associated Decree No 70-708 of 1970 ("the 1970 Decree"). The 1969 Act and 1970 Decree required persons with no fixed abode to register with a commune, which could not be changed, and required persons who lived in mobile shelters and had no regular income to be issued with a travel booklet which had to be stamped by the authorities every three months. Failure to comply attracted criminal sanctions.

On 29 February 2004, the author was stopped by gendarmes and found not to have vehicle insurance or a sufficiently recent stamp in his travel booklet. On 11 March 2006, the author was stopped again, and was advised that the La Flèche police court had entered a judgment in absentia in November 2005 with respect to the two offences of February 2004, fining him 300 euros and 150 euros respectively for each offence. Notification of the hearing had been sent to his commune of registration, but the author had not received it.

The author applied to have the judgment concerning the travel booklet set aside, submitting that the requirements of the 1969 Act and 1970 Decree

---

[1] The author was represented by counsel, Jérôme Weinhard.
[2] The members of the Committee who participated in the examination of this communication were Mr Yadh Ben Achour (Tunisia), Mr Cornelis Flinterman (the Netherlands), Mr Yuji Iwasawa (Japan), Mr Walter Kälin (Switzerland), Mr Gerald L. Neuman (United States of America), Sir Nigel Rodley (United Kingdom), Mr Fabián Omar Salvioli (Argentina), Ms Anja Seibert-Fohr (Germany), Mr Yuval Shany (Israel), Mr Konstantine Vardzelashvili (Georgia), Ms Margo Waterval (Suriname) and Mr Andrei Paul Zlătescu (Romania).
[3] Prepared by Ms E. Fogarty.

were contrary to the right to liberty of movement and freedom from discrimination enshrined in the European Convention on Human Rights, 1950. On 20 December 2006, the author was again found guilty with respect to his travel booklet, but his fine was reduced to 100 euros. His appeal to the Court of Appeal of Angers (Maine-et-Loire) was dismissed although his fine was again reduced to 50 euros. A further appeal to the Court of Cassation was also dismissed.

On 22 December 2008, the author filed a claim with the European Court of Human Rights. This was declared inadmissible on 1 September 2009 as it was filed over six months after domestic remedies were exhausted.

On 1 April 2010, the author submitted his communication to the Human Rights Committee. He claimed that the State Party had violated his rights under Articles 12[4] and 26[5] of the International Covenant on Civil and Political Rights, 1966 ("the Covenant"). He submitted that the requirement that he carry a regularly stamped travel booklet or face criminal sanctions made him subject to regular police checks, constituting a clear infringement on his right to liberty of movement within his country. He further submitted that the 1969 Act and 1970 Decree were focused on persons living Traveller lives, but were not applicable to other persons with no fixed abode, such as bargees or homeless persons, constituting external discrimination and unequal treatment before the law. He further claimed that the requirement that Travellers register at a commune, which could not be changed, constituted unequal treatment, noting that persons who lived in fixed abodes were free to change their domicile.

Held:—The State Party had violated the author's rights under Article 12 of the Covenant.

(1) Although a similar claim had been lodged with the European Court of Human Rights, the Court had not "examined" the claim on the merits, as it had been deemed inadmissible on procedural grounds for having been made more than six months after domestic remedies were exhausted. The Court's consideration therefore did not pose any obstacle to admissibility. The State's submission that the author had not asserted that the obligation for Travellers to register with a commune was contrary to Article 12 of the Covenant before the domestic courts was noted, as was the author's submission that he did not

---

[4] Article 12 of the Covenant provided: "(1) Everyone lawfully within the territory of a State shall, within that territory, have the right to liberty of movement and freedom to choose his residence ... (3) The above-mentioned rights shall not be subject to any restrictions except those which are provided by law, are necessary to protect national security, public order (*ordre public*), public health or morals or the rights and freedoms of others, and are consistent with the other rights recognized in the present Covenant ..."

[5] Article 26 of the Covenant provided: "All persons are equal before the law and are entitled without any discrimination to the equal protection of the law. In this respect, the law shall prohibit any discrimination and guarantee to all persons equal and effective protection against discrimination on any ground such as race, colour, sex, language, religion, political or other opinion, national or social origin, property, birth or other status."

in fact challenge this aspect of the 1969 Act and 1970 Decree, but instead was concerned with their impact on his liberty of movement. A separate consideration of the obligation to register with a commune was deemed inadmissible. However, the author's claims under Article 12 of the Covenant, with respect to liberty of movement, and Article 26 of the Covenant, with respect to equality before the law, were admissible (paras. 7.1-7.4).

(2) Any limitations a State imposed on the rights protected under Article 12 of the Covenant could not nullify the principle of liberty of movement and were governed by the requirement of necessity. The 1969 Act and the 1970 Decree clearly placed a restriction on the exercise of a right to liberty of movement for the persons to whom they applied. Although the need for State Parties to ensure that persons who regularly changed their place of residence remained identifiable and contactable as a matter of security and public order was recognized, the State Party had not demonstrated that the obligation to have a travel booklet issued and stamped every three months on pain of criminal sanctions was necessary and proportionate to that end. The restriction placed on the author's right to liberty of movement was not compatible with Article 12(3) and was therefore a violation of Article 12(1). In light of that finding, the Committee did not conduct a separate consideration of the author's Article 26 claim (paras. 8.2-9).

(3) Under Article 2(3)(a) of the Covenant, the State Party was obliged to provide the author with an effective remedy by expunging his criminal record and providing him with adequate compensation for the harm suffered. It was also to review the relevant legislation and its application in practice, taking into account the State Party's obligations under the Covenant, and was to take measures to prevent similar violations in the future. The State Party was to provide the Committee, within 180 days, with information about the measures taken to give effect to its Views, which it was requested to publish (paras. 10-11).

Individual opinion of Mr Salvioli (concurring): (1) The Committee should have explored the author's serious claims concerning violations of Article 26 of the Covenant. The Committee had remained silent on the two key human rights issues of equality before the law and non-discrimination, which lay at the heart of the communication (paras. 1-2).

(2) The claim of discrimination against a specific group of persons, namely Travellers, had been sufficiently substantiated. For the State's purpose of maintaining links between persons with no fixed abode and administrative authorities, requiring registration with a commune was sufficient. However, the State Party had failed to show or justify the additional need for Travellers to be issued with a travel booklet requiring regular stamping. No reasonable explanation was offered as to why regular "checks" of Travellers had to be undertaken (paras. 3-6).

(3) The requirement that Travellers have a travel booklet stamped regularly did not meet the tests of reasonableness, necessity and proportionality.

The Committee therefore should have concluded that Article 26 of the Covenant had also been violated (para. 8).

The following is the text of the Views of the Committee:

1.1 The author of the communication dated 1 April 2010 is Claude Ory, born on 1 December 1980 at Château-Gontier, France. He claims to be a victim of a violation by France of his rights under articles 12, paragraph 1, and 26 of the International Covenant on Civil and Political Rights. He is represented by counsel.

1.2 On 18 October 2010, the Special Rapporteur on new communications and interim measures decided that the admissibility of the communication should be considered jointly with the merits.

THE FACTS AS PRESENTED BY THE AUTHOR

2.1 The author is a member of the Traveller community.[1] He lives in a caravan, in Le Mans (department of Sarthe), and is thus subject to Act No 69-3 of 3 January 1969[2] and the associated Decree No 70-708 of 31 July 1970, which require him to have a travel permit (*titre de circulation*) that must be stamped regularly by the authorities,[3] failing which he is liable to criminal sanctions.[4] In 2004, as he did not have a regular income, the author held a travel card (*carnet de circulation*), issued on 2 February 1998, that needed to be stamped by the police every three months and had last been stamped on 27 August 2003.

2.2 On 29 February 2004, while he was driving his truck to work, the author was checked by gendarmes in the commune of Mézeray (department of Sarthe). He was found to have neither vehicle insurance

---

[1] Administrative term designating the Roma community in France. The term was used in Act No 69-3 of 1969 in place of the term "nomad", which had been used in the Act of 16 July 1912 concerning the exercise of itinerant trades and regulating the movement of nomads.

[2] Act No 69-3 of 3 January 1969 on the exercise of itinerant activities and the regime applicable to persons travelling in France without a fixed abode or residence.

[3] Pursuant to article 4 of the Act of 3 January 1969, persons who have no fixed abode or residence, who live in a mobile shelter and have a regular income receive a travel booklet (*livret de circulation*), which must be stamped "at intervals not less than three months in length". Persons who have no regular income, on the other hand, are issued a travel card (*carnet de circulation*), which must be stamped every three months (art. 5).

[4] Article 20 of Decree No 70-708 of 31 July 1970, implementing Title I and certain provisions of Title II of Act No 69-3 of 3 January 1969, on the exercise of itinerant activities and the regime applicable to persons travelling in France who have no fixed abode or residence, provides that: "Persons who do not have their travel permit stamped within the time limits laid down in article 5 of the Act of 3 January 1969 or article 18, paragraph 2, of the present Decree shall be liable to the fine provided for category 5 minor offences."

nor a stamp in his travel card. On 11 March 2006, when he was once again checked by gendarmes in Aubigné-Racan (Sarthe), he was informed of the consequences of the two offences committed on 29 February 2004. He was taken to the station and was questioned for four hours. He was informed that the La Flèche (Sarthe) police court had issued a judgment in absentia dated 23 November 2005, in which he had been ordered to pay a fine of 150 euros for not having a valid travel permit; he was also fined 300 euros and had his driving licence suspended for one month for not having insurance. The address on the court summons referred to his travel permit and his commune of registration. Thus, since the town hall of Arnage (Sarthe) was not his habitual residence and he did not receive his mail there, it had not been possible to inform him that the hearing was to be held, and he was therefore tried in absentia.

2.3 The author has no fixed abode or residence in France and lives in his vehicle on a permanent basis. He acknowledges that he had not had his travel booklet stamped by the administrative authority within the prescribed time limit. He filed an application to have the judgment in absentia of 23 November 2005 set aside, and the deputy prosecutor of Le Mans summoned him to a hearing at the La Flèche police court on 24 May 2006. He requested the assistance of counsel for his defence, which he was able to obtain through legal aid. After he requested a deferral, his case was finally heard on 27 September 2006. His defence lawyer asked for the case to be dismissed, citing Protocol 4 to the European Convention on Human Rights, which, in its article 2, provides that everyone who is lawfully within the territory of a State shall, within that territory, have the right to liberty of movement and freedom to choose his or her residence. On 20 December 2006, the court overruled the objection based on the assertion that the report noting the absence of a stamp was invalid, found the author guilty of that offence, and sentenced him to a fine of 100 euros (instead of the 150 euros initially set).

2.4 On 28 December 2006, the author filed an appeal against that judgment with the Court of Appeal of Angers (Maine-et-Loire). He once again requested legal assistance, which was granted. During the proceedings, his lawyer argued that the offence in question constituted discrimination under article 14 of the European Convention on Human Rights, which prohibits discrimination. The author asserts, firstly, that persons who exercise itinerant activities or trades are exempted from the obligation to have a stamped travel card and, secondly, that the provisions apply exclusively to persons who dwell permanently in a vehicle, trailer or any other mobile shelter while other persons who have no fixed abode or residence, such as homeless persons or bargees, are exempted. The President of the Court of Appeal considered referring the case to the Court of Justice of the European Union for a preliminary ruling.[5] In the end, however, on 19 April 2007, he refused the appeal on the grounds that the author's situation was of his own choosing and made him subject to specific obligations that served the national public interest, which therefore were in no way discriminatory; he reduced the fine to 50 euros. The author lodged an appeal in cassation on 19 April 2007. His request for legal aid was refused on the basis of a lack of serious grounds. He was thus not able to retain counsel and his appeal was dismissed by the court of cassation on 4 March 2008.

2.5 On 22 December 2008, the author filed an application in respect of the same case with the European Court of Human Rights. On 1 September 2009, the Court declared the application inadmissible under article 35, paragraph 1, of the Convention, since more than six months had elapsed between the final decision at the national level (of the court of cassation) and the submission of the application.

THE COMPLAINT

3.1 The author states, firstly, that he does not challenge the validity of the first charge (lack of vehicle insurance), but does contest the second, i.e., the failure to have a stamped travel card while having had no fixed abode or residence in France for more than six months, which falls within the scope of article 3 of the Act of 3 January 1969.

3.2 In respect of the infringement of the freedom of movement, the author notes that French law requires him to have a travel permit and to present it to law enforcement officials upon request, under penalty of criminal sanctions. He recalls that this is part of an old legal regime dating back to the nineteenth century; the modern travel permits are direct successors to the travelling performers' permits introduced pursuant to the circular of 6 January 1863 and then the "anthropomorphic nomad identity cards" introduced under the Act of 16 July 1912. Successive laws have maintained the principle of requiring travel cards. The author is thus subject to regular police checks, which, he asserts, are a clear infringement of his right to liberty of movement within his country, as provided for in article 12 of the Covenant. He rejects the

---

[5] There is a procedure under which national courts may request the Court of Justice of the European Union for its interpretation or view on the validity of European law in the context of a case before it.

conclusions of the Court of Appeal of Angers (see para. 2.4), observing that he has not chosen his way of life but is heir to a long family tradition, on both his father's and his mother's sides of the family, of living in a mobile shelter.[6] He adds that he was brought up in that way, that his brothers and sisters live the same way, that he has never lived in a house and that life on the road is the only way of life that he has ever known.

3.3 In respect of equality before the law, the author points out that, under French law, the domicile of any citizen, for the purpose of exercising his or her civil rights, is "the place of his or her main place of residence".[7] However, Travellers, who are subject to Act No 69-3 of 3 January 1969, do not have a domicile and reside habitually in a land-based mobile shelter. Rather than mentioning a domicile, the specific legal regime applicable in this case requires that persons register with a commune for administrative purposes; they are not free to choose or to change that commune, contrary to the rights provided for by articles 103 et seq. of the Civil Code, on change of domicile. The author submits that he does not have the same civil rights as citizens who have a fixed residence.

3.4 According to the author, the unfavourable treatment of persons subject to the stamp system constitutes legally sanctioned internal and external discrimination. It is legally sanctioned because it is laid down by the law. It is internal because, of those required to hold the travel permits provided for by Act No 69-3, persons who practise itinerant activities or trades are not subject to the stamp system. Other persons of no fixed abode, such as those living in houseboats (bargees) or on the street, are not subject to the administrative requirement to have a travel permit either. The author argues that the discrimination is also external because the vast majority of the population, who live in fixed residences as defined in article 2 of Decree 70-708 of 31 July 1970 and therefore have a domicile, have not been required to have these "passports" for the last century. The stamp system, and the travel permit system in general, thus, according to the author, infringe the freedom to come and go within a State only of those persons who are subject to them. This constitutes both internal and external discrimination against them and gives rise to inequality of rights in respect of the concept of a domicile. Accordingly, the author requests moral and material compensation, as well as to have his conviction expunged from his police record. He demands to be placed on an equal footing with all his

---

[6] The author encloses a copy of his family tree.
[7] Civil Code, art. 102.

fellow-citizens, i.e., to be able to maintain his way of life and have the right to have a domicile as provided for in the Civil Code, as well as the freedom to change and to choose that domicile, without being obliged to have and to present a travel permit on pain of being found guilty of an offence.

STATE PARTY'S OBSERVATIONS ON ADMISSIBILITY

4. On 29 September 2010, the State party submitted its observations on admissibility, arguing that the communication should be declared partially inadmissible for non-exhaustion of domestic remedies. According to the State party, the author has argued before the Committee that he does not have the freedom to choose or to change his place of residence. However, before the national courts, the contentious proceedings dealt only with the lack of a stamp in his travel card. This is the only offence for which domestic remedies have been exhausted. In this respect, the State party is of the view that the matters described in the communication concerning the choice of commune of registration are completely unrelated to the issue considered by the national courts and are thus inadmissible under article 5, paragraph 2(b), of the Optional Protocol.

STATE PARTY'S OBSERVATIONS ON THE MERITS

5.1 On 28 January 2011, the State party submitted its observations on the merits of the communication. It again argues that the author's allegations concerning the choice of his commune of residence were not raised in the national courts. Furthermore, according to the State party, the author cites only the provisions of the French Civil Code regarding the commune of registration, without specifying which provisions of the Covenant have allegedly been breached. Accordingly, this part of the communication should be considered inadmissible.

On the freedom to choose and to change the commune of registration

5.2 On the merits, the State party begins by addressing the question of freedom of choice and of a commune of registration. It recalls that the habitual residence of the persons covered by Act No 69-3 of 3 January 1969 is, by definition, a mobile residence: "a vehicle, trailer, or any other mobile shelter", according to article 3 of the Act. To ensure that persons who have such a residence can enjoy and exercise their civil and political rights and fulfil their duties, legislators developed the system of a commune of registration to allow such persons to maintain a link with the administrative authorities. According to the State party, this address is used purely for administrative purposes and does not constitute a residence within the meaning of article 12 of the Covenant. The permanent residence of such persons is their trailer or other mobile shelter, and their place of residence is where that mobile shelter is at any given time. The right to free choice of residence, protected under article 12 of the Covenant, therefore applies only to the author's permanent residence, which is by nature mobile.

5.3 The State party adds that, contrary to the author's claims, a person travelling in France who has no fixed abode or residence can choose the commune in which he or she wishes to be registered for administrative purposes, but must provide a valid reason for that choice (family ties, for example). The prefect may not overrule that choice except for serious reasons, related, in particular, to public order, and must issue an explicitly substantiated decision in such cases.[8] In consequence, according to the State party, the restrictions that are placed on the right to freely choose one's commune of registration are extremely limited and are in compliance with article 12, paragraph 3, of the Covenant, which provides that this right may be subject to restrictions when these are "provided by law, are necessary to protect national security, public order, public health or morals or the rights and freedoms of others, and are consistent with the other rights recognized in the present Covenant".

5.4 As regards article 26 of the Covenant, which the author invokes, the State party argues that article 7 of the Act of 3 January 1969 provides that "any person who requests the issuance of a travel permit ... is required to make known the commune in which he or she wishes to be registered". The choice of commune of registration thus applies to any person over the age of 16 who has not had a fixed residence for more than six months, if he or she dwells permanently in a vehicle, trailer or any other mobile shelter (art. 3). Referring to the Committee's general comment No 18 (1989), on non-discrimination,[9] the State party also adds that registration with a commune enables a person travelling in France who has no fixed abode or residence to effectively enjoy and exercise his or her civil and political

---

[8] Article 23 of Decree No 70-708 of 31 July 1970 (see note 4 above).
[9] *Official Records of the General Assembly, Forty-fifth Session, Supplement No 40*, vol. I (A/45/40 (Vol. I)), annex VI, sect. A, para. 7.

rights, including the right to vote. The Committee has indicated that the enjoyment of rights and freedoms on an equal footing does not mean identical treatment in every instance.[10] The establishment of a specific legal regime for persons travelling who have no fixed abode or residence does indeed take account of the specific characteristics of their situation. In any event, it cannot, according to the State party, be argued that the author and all other persons in his situation are, as he contends, deprived of their right to have a domicile, as guaranteed by French civil law. There is no legal obstacle that would prevent a person living in a mobile residence from changing his or her way of life and choosing a domicile within the meaning of article 102 of the Civil Code. However, in the context of an itinerant way of life, registration with a commune provides a means of exercising one's rights and does not entail any discrimination.

The travel card

5.5 As regards the matter of the travel permit and the obligation to have it stamped, which the author considers a clear infringement of his right to liberty of movement within the country, the State party recognizes that the constraints entailed by this requirement constitute a restriction within the meaning of article 12, paragraph 3, of the Covenant, but contends that the restriction is laid down by law and is justified for reasons of public order. According to the State party, the fact that persons of no fixed abode who do not show proof of a regular income have an obligation to have their travel card stamped at regular intervals is the counterpart of their recognized right to change their place of residence every day, if they so wish. This requirement allows the administrative authorities to maintain a link with them and makes it possible for the authorities to contact them, as well as, where necessary, to conduct checks under conditions that take account of their itinerant way of life.

5.6 Considering the travel permit requirement in the light of article 26 of the Covenant, the State party argues that the obligation to have the permit stamped is not restricted to a specific community, but applies to all persons over the age of 16 who have not had a fixed abode or residence for more than six months if they dwell permanently in a vehicle, trailer or any other mobile shelter (Act of 3 January 1969, art. 3). Thus, any person who chooses to adopt an itinerant

---

[10] Idem, para. 8.

way of life, as defined above, must have a travel permit, which must be stamped by the administrative authorities at regular intervals. Accordingly, fairground workers and caravaniers (employees working on large building sites) are also required to have travel permits. The State party adds that, contrary to the author's claims, the itinerant way of life is, from a legal point of view, indeed the choice of the person concerned, a choice which is respected by the public authorities.

5.7 In conclusion, the State party reiterates that the specific regime applicable to the author and to other people in the same situation is a consequence of their high level of mobility, as compared to persons who have adopted a sedentary lifestyle. The difference in treatment is therefore objectively justified by the difference between their situations. Finally, the State party adds that the author's claims concerning the travel permit do not reflect the unanimous position of all Travellers, because some members of that community felt that these documents were highly valuable as identity papers.

AUTHOR'S COMMENTS ON THE STATE PARTY'S OBSERVATIONS ON THE MERITS

6.1 The author responded to the State party's observations on the merits on 4 April 2011.

On the claim in relation to article 12

6.2 The author does not dispute the fact that the requirement to register with a commune does not contravene the principle of the freedom of choice of residence, guaranteed under article 12. He specifies that it is the principle of freedom of movement that he wishes to assert. The author notes that a French citizen who has a fixed residence is not obliged to possess an administrative document in order to move about the country. In addition, other persons of no fixed residence, such as bargees and homeless persons, are not obliged to have a special administrative document either. People considered to be "travelling" are the only ones who are invariably subject to this system, under the Act of 3 January 1969. According to the author, the simple possession of such a permit, which for some has become a symbol of their identity, would not be so serious if failure to have the permit did not make a person liable to criminal penalties, including fines and terms of imprisonment, if such a person is found to be travelling without a permit or without proof of the possession of the permit. In addition, the obligation to have the travel card stamped by the police at regular intervals, on pain of criminal penalties, constitutes a serious infringement of the freedom of movement.

6.3 The system also makes it possible, each time the permit holder requests a stamp, for the authorities to check the wanted-persons file, which includes those persons wanted on administrative and judicial grounds.[11] The author adds that the system of travel permits makes it possible for the police to maintain a special file on persons of no fixed abode or residence. That file currently comprises more than 200,000 records.[12] The National Commission for Information Technology and Civil Liberties, as well as other interested persons, has drawn attention to the existence of undeclared databases and messages linked to the file on persons of no fixed abode or residence. This case has also given an opportunity to disseminate a confidential internal gendarmerie document dating from 1992, entitled *La criminalité de certaines minorités ethniques non sédentarisées* (criminality among certain non-sedentary ethnic minorities). According to the author, this terminology clearly refers to Travellers. The document states that almost a third of the 120,000 individuals whose names figure in the administrative file of persons of no fixed abode or residence are known offenders. It also notes that "it is up to staff, in particular, to make a clear distinction between individuals classified as persons of no fixed abode or residence, who can be required to produce their administrative documents ... without following any particular procedure and persons who are settled, whose identity documents are checked within the legal framework defined by articles 78-1 to 78-5 of the Code of Criminal Procedure". According to the author, such guidelines provide clear evidence of the specific and discriminatory nature of travel permit checks. The checks involve the use of police intelligence related specifically to the Traveller population, described as a "non-settled ethnic minority", who are subject to specific, systematic and stigmatizing checks made possible by the travel permit system.

---

[11] Decree of 15 May 1996 concerning the wanted persons file, maintained by the Ministry of the Interior and the Ministry of Defence.

[12] The author explains that this file, which was created under the terms set out in a decree of 22 March 1994, is managed by the national gendarmerie. It is used for the computerized processing and monitoring of travel permits. Since 2005, it has included digital photographs of permit holders. The file may be consulted by law enforcement officials (police and gendarmerie), the prefectural services, and authorized third parties (treasury departments and health, judicial and military authorities).

On the claim in relation to article 26

6.4 The author again asserts that the Travellers' way of life should be analysed from a sociological standpoint that takes into account the cultural capital handed down from generation to generation and goes beyond a legal analysis of individual "choice". Although living in a fixed structure is the norm today, this mode of life should not be imposed on persons who have never experienced it. The author recalls that he has never known anything other than the Travellers' way of life and that his family—going back as far as his great-grandparents—has led an itinerant way of life and practised itinerant trades. He adds that, beyond the restriction that they place on the freedom of movement, travel permits are also just one of the ways in which Travellers are treated differently from the rest of the population. Although the justification given is the mobility of this population group, it appears that other mobile populations, such as bargees, travelling salespeople and homeless persons, are not subject to the same types of checks. Furthermore, the way that Travellers are defined is related not to their mobility, but to the fact that they have been dwelling in mobile shelters for at least six months.[13] However, the lack of a fixed residence, cited by the State party as justification for the specific treatment of Travellers, is also common to bargees, nomads and fairground workers. These people used to be considered to be on an equal footing, under Ordinance No 58-923 of 7 October 1958,[14] which gave these three categories of persons the possibility of freely choosing their domicile and which had modified the Civil Code in order to do so. Although the provision relating to domiciles was maintained in the case of bargees, it was abrogated in the case of nomads and fairground workers (terms replaced in recent legislation by the category of "Travellers") by the Act of 3 January 1969, which introduced the concept of the commune of registration for these two categories. The author adds that the bill relating to the aforementioned Act shows that the introduction, in article 8 of the Act, of a quota whereby Travellers registered with a municipality could account for no more than 3 per cent of the local population was intended to ensure that the electoral situation in the municipalities concerned would not be significantly changed by any influx of voters without actual ties to the commune. According to the author, the fact that an effort was made to decrease the effective

---

[13] Act of 3 January 1969, art. 3.
[14] The author adds that the 1958 Ordinance was never implemented for practical reasons.

electoral representation of this sector of the population demonstrates the inequality before the law of which Travellers are victim.

ISSUES AND PROCEEDINGS BEFORE THE COMMITTEE

Consideration of admissibility

7.1 Before considering any claim contained in a communication, the Human Rights Committee must, in accordance with rule 93 of its rules of procedure, decide whether the communication is admissible under the Optional Protocol to the Covenant.

7.2 In accordance with article 5, paragraph 2(a), of the Optional Protocol, the Committee has ascertained that a similar complaint filed by the author (complaint No 3257/09) was found inadmissible by the European Court of Human Rights on 1 September 2009 under article 35, paragraph 1, of the European Convention on Human Rights, since the period between the final decision at the national level (of the court of cassation) and the submission of the application was more than six months. The Committee also recalls that, upon its acceptance of the Optional Protocol, the State party entered a reservation to article 5, paragraph 2(a), of the Protocol specifying that the Committee "shall not have competence to consider a communication from an individual if the same matter is being examined or has already been considered under another procedure of international investigation or settlement". The Committee notes, however, that the European Court of Human Rights has not "examined" the case in the sense of article 5, paragraph 2(a), of the Optional Protocol, inasmuch as its decision pertained only to an issue of procedure.[15] Article 5, paragraph 2(a), of the Optional Protocol, as modified by the State party's reservation, therefore does not represent an impediment to the examination of the communication by the Committee.

7.3 The Committee has also noted the State party's argument that the author has not exhausted domestic remedies with regard to the issue of the choice and change of domicile under the system of registration introduced by the Act of 3 January 1969 (art. 7 et seq.). The Committee observes that the author does not contest this argument and that he has also specified that, of the safeguards set forth in

---

[15] See communications No 1505/2006, *Vincent* v. *France*, inadmissibility decision of 31 October 2007, para. 7.2; No 1389/2005, *Bertelli Gálvez* v. *Spain*, inadmissibility decision of 25 July 2005, para. 4.3; and No 1446/2006, *Wdowiak* v. *Poland*, inadmissibility decision of 31 October 2006, para. 6.2.

article 12, paragraph 1, he wishes to assert only the right to liberty of movement. Accordingly, the Committee declares the part of the communication relating to choice and change of domicile inadmissible under article 5, paragraph 2(b), of the Optional Protocol.

7.4 The Committee considers that all other criteria for admissibility have been met and declares the communication admissible in respect of the arguments put forward by the author under articles 12, paragraph 1 (in respect of liberty of movement), and 26 of the Covenant.

Consideration of the merits

8.1 The Human Rights Committee has considered the present communication in the light of all the information made available to it by the parties, as required under article 5, paragraph 1, of the Optional Protocol.

8.2 The Committee notes the author's claim that, by fining him 150 euros for the criminal offence (reduced by the Court of Appeal of Angers to a fine of 50 euros) of lacking a valid stamp on his travel permit, the State party allegedly acted in violation of its obligations to guarantee him: (1) the right, under article 12, paragraph 1, of the Covenant to move about freely within the territory of the State party; and (2) his right, under article 26 of the Covenant, to equality before the law and equal protection of the law, without discrimination. The Committee notes the State party's argument that the restrictions imposed on the application of article 12 by Act No 69-3 of 3 January 1969 are consistent with paragraph 3 of that article because they are justified by reasons of public order. In particular, it asserts that the requirement to have a stamped travel permit permits the maintenance of an administrative link with members of the itinerant population and to carry out checks as necessary.

8.3 The Committee recalls its general comment No 27 (1999) on freedom of movement, in which it states that the limitations that may be imposed on the rights protected under article 12 must not nullify the principle of liberty of movement, and are governed by the requirement of necessity provided for in article 12, paragraph 3, and by the need for consistency with the other rights recognized in the Covenant.[16] Article 5 of Act No 69-3 of 3 January 1969, which was applicable to the author at the time of the events in question, required persons who had had no fixed abode or residence for more than six

---

[16] See general comment No 27 (1999), *Official Records of the General Assembly, Fifty-fifth Session, Supplement No 40*, vol. I (A/55/40 (Vol. I)), annex VI, sect. A, para. 2.

months, who were living in a mobile shelter and had no regular income, to have a travel card which had to be stamped every three months in order for them to be able to travel in France. Article 20 of Decree No 70-708 of 31 July 1970 also provides that, in the event of failure to obtain such a stamp within the prescribed period, the person concerned will be liable to a fine corresponding to a category 5 minor offence.[17] This provision clearly places a restriction on the exercise of the right to liberty of movement by the persons in question (art. 12, para. 1). The Committee must therefore determine whether such a restriction is authorized by article 12, paragraph 3, of the Covenant.

8.4 It is not disputed that an obligation to have a travel permit and to have it stamped at regular intervals by the authorities is established under the Act. The Committee takes note of the State party's statement that the objective of these measures is to help to maintain public order. It is therefore incumbent upon the Committee to assess whether this restriction is necessary and proportionate to the aim pursued.[18] The Committee recognizes the State party's need to check, for the purposes of maintaining security and public order, that persons who regularly change their place of residence are and remain identifiable and contactable.

8.5 The Committee observes, however, that the State party has not demonstrated that the obligation to have the travel card stamped at frequent intervals or to make failure to fulfil that obligation subject to criminal charges (Decree No 70-708 of 31 July 1970, art. 20) are measures that are necessary and proportionate to the end that is sought. The Committee concludes that this restriction of the author's right to liberty of movement is not compatible with the conditions set forth in article 12, paragraph 3, and consequently constitutes a violation of article 12, paragraph 1, in his regard.

8.6 In the light of its finding in respect of article 12, paragraph 1, the Committee will not consider separately the claims based on the violation of article 26 of the Convention.

9. The Human Rights Committee, acting under article 5, paragraph 4, of the Optional Protocol to the International Covenant on Civil and Political Rights, is of the view that the facts before it disclose a violation of article 12, paragraph 1, of the Covenant.

---

[17] See note 4 above. Article 131-13 of the Criminal Code provides that category 5 minor offences are punishable by a fine of a maximum of 1,500 euros; this amount may be increased to 3,000 euros in the case of a repeat offence.

[18] General comment No 27, para. 14.

10. Pursuant to article 2, paragraph 3(a), of the Covenant, the State party is required to provide the author with an effective remedy by, inter alia, expunging his criminal record and providing him with adequate compensation for the harm suffered, and to review the relevant legislation and its application in practice, taking into account its obligations under the Covenant. The State party is also under an obligation to take measures to prevent similar violations in the future.

11. Bearing in mind that, by becoming a party to the Optional Protocol, the State party has recognized the competence of the Committee to determine whether or not there has been a violation of the Covenant and that, pursuant to article 2 of the Covenant, the State party has undertaken to ensure for all individuals within its territory or subject to its jurisdiction the rights recognized in the Covenant and to provide an effective and enforceable remedy when a violation has been established, the Committee wishes to receive information from the State party, within 180 days, concerning the measures taken to give effect to the Committee's Views. The State party is also invited to publish the present Views.

APPENDIX

INDIVIDUAL OPINION OF MR FABIÁN OMAR SALVIOLI (CONCURRING)

1. I agree with the Committee's decision in the case of *Ory* v. *France* (communication No 1960/2010), in which it found a violation by the State party of article 12 of the International Covenant on Civil and Political Rights with respect to the victim.

2. However, I regret that in its decision the Committee did not find it necessary to explore the author's serious claims[1] concerning the violation of article 26 of the Covenant.[2] The Committee has remained silent on two key human rights issues, namely equality before the law and non-discrimination, which lie at the heart of the communication.

3. In this case, it has been sufficiently substantiated that there is discrimination against a specific group of individuals (namely, members of the "Traveller communities"), many of whom—including the author—are of French nationality. For administrative and legal purposes, the "commune of registration" is sufficient for the State's

---

[1] As set out in the Committee's Views, paras. 3.3 and 3.4, and later in para. 6.4.
[2] The Committee's Views, para. 8.6.

purposes (namely, the need to maintain a link with the administrative authorities). However, the State has been unable to show or justify an additional need for members of the "Traveller communities" to have a travel card stamped on a regular basis.

4. In its response to the communication, the State cites as reasons for the travel permit requirement the need to maintain a link between the State and members of Traveller communities and to carry out "checks".[3]

5. Regarding the first of the State's reasons, such a link is perfectly well maintained by requiring members of the Traveller communities to register with a commune as provided for in article 7 of Act No 69-3.[4]

6. As for the need to make "checks", the State's arguments are far too general, and it gives no reasonable explanation as to why these persons must be subject to special checks.

7. The Committee has previously defined the parameters of the principles of equality and non-discrimination by stating that a rule or measure that is apparently neutral or lacking any intention to discriminate can have a discriminatory effect resulting in a violation of article 26 if the detrimental effects of the rule or decision exclusively or disproportionately affect persons of a particular race, colour, sex, language, religion, political or other opinion, national or social origin, financial status, birth or other status. However, rules or decisions with such an impact do not amount to discrimination if they are based on objective and reasonable grounds.[5]

8. In special situations States may adopt differentiated measures, but these must pursue a legitimate aim, be provided for by law and, above all, be reasonable and proportionate. In this case, the requirement for members of the "Traveller communities" to have their travel permits stamped regularly does not meet the tests of reasonableness, necessity and proportionality. Consequently, the Committee should have concluded that article 26 of the Covenant was also violated with respect to the author of the communication, and the State should take this into account when providing redress, including by abolishing the stamp requirement so as to ensure that such violations are not repeated.

[Report: UN Doc. CCPR/C/110/DR/1960/2010]

---

[3] See the Committee's Views, para. 5.5.
[4] No changes were made to the "commune of registration" system in the recent revision of the Act.
[5] General comment No 18 on article 26, HRI/GEN/1/Rev.9 (Vol. I), 10 November 1989; see also communication No 1474/2006, *Prince* v. *South Africa*, Views adopted on 31 October 2007, para. 7.5, and communication No 998/2001, *Althammer et al.* v. *Austria*, Views adopted on 8 August 2003, para. 10.2.

Governments — Separation of executive and courts — Independent prosecutors — Exercise of statutory powers and discretion — Independent decision-making — Taking relevant considerations into account — Effect of opinions and advice of others on independence of decisions — Shawcross exercises — Threats — Impact of threats on independent decision-making — The rule of law — Whether decision of Director of Serious Fraud Office to discontinue investigation lawful — Criminal Justice Act 1987

Relationship of international law and municipal law — Treaties — Interpretation and application — Convention on Combating Bribery of Foreign Public Officials in International Business Transactions, 1997 — Article 5 — Relevance — Organization for Economic Cooperation and Development — OECD Working Group on Bribery in International Business Transactions — Whether municipal courts to desist from interpretation of unincorporated international instruments — Value of uniform interpretation of international instruments — Whether municipal courts can consider unincorporated international instruments considered by decision-makers when assessing legality of decisions — Criminal Justice Act 1987 — Serious Fraud Office — Investigations and prosecutions — Anti-terrorism, Crime and Security Act 2001

Treaties — Interpretation — Convention on Combating Bribery of Foreign Public Officials in International Business Transactions, 1997 — Article 5 — Relevance — Investigation and prosecution of bribery of foreign public officials — Applicable rules and principles of Contracting Parties — Parties not to be influenced by considerations of national economic interest, potential effect on relations with other States or identity of natural or legal persons involved — National security — Intersection of national security and relations with other States — European Convention on Human Rights, 1950 — Article 2 — Right to life — Vienna Convention on the Law of Treaties, 1969 — Article 31 — Interpretation of treaties in good faith in light of object and purpose — The law of England

REGINA (CORNER HOUSE RESEARCH AND ANOTHER) v.
DIRECTOR OF THE SERIOUS FRAUD OFFICE
(JUSTICE INTERVENING)[1]

([2008] EWHC 714 (Admin))

England, High Court, Queen's Bench Division (Administrative Court)
10 *April* 2008

(Moses LJ and Sullivan J)

([2008] UKHL 60)

England, House of Lords. 30 *July* 2008

(Lord Bingham of Cornhill, Lord Hoffmann, Lord Rodger of Earlsferry, Baroness Hale of Richmond and Lord Brown of Eaton-under-Heywood)

SUMMARY:[2] *The facts*:—In February 2007, the claimants, Corner House Research and Campaign Against Arms Trade, two non-profit organizations, sought judicial review of the decision of the defendant, the Director of the Serious Fraud Office ("SFO"), to discontinue an investigation. The investigation, which commenced in July 2004, pursuant to Section 1(3)[3] of the Criminal Justice Act 1987 ("the 1987 Act"), concerned allegations that the British company BAE Systems plc ("BAE") had engaged in corruption contrary to the Anti-terrorism, Crime and Security Act 2001, in particular, in relation to the Al-Yamamah arms contract between the United Kingdom and Saudi Arabia.

In October 2005, BAE contacted the Attorney General,[4] seeking to stop the investigation on public interest grounds, arguing that it would adversely

---

[1] Before the High Court, the claimants were represented by Dinah Rose QC, Philippe Sands QC and Ben Jaffey, instructed by Leigh Day & Co. The defendant was represented by Philip Sales QC, Hugo Keith and Karen Steyn, instructed by the Treasury Solicitor. BAE Systems plc, an interested party, was represented by Clare Montgomery QC, instructed by Allen & Overy LLP.
Before the House of Lords, the claimants were represented by David Pannick QC, Dinah Rose QC, Philippe Sands QC and Ben Jaffey, instructed by Leigh Day & Co. The defendant was represented by Jonathan Sumption QC, Philip Sales QC, Vaughan Lowe QC, Hugo Keith, Karen Steyn and Rachel Kamm, instructed by the Treasury Solicitor. JUSTICE intervened before the House of Lords by written submission, represented by Nigel Pleming QC, Thomas de la Mare and Shaheed Fatima, instructed by Mayer Brown International LLP.
[2] Prepared by Ms E. Fogarty.
[3] Section 1(3) of the Criminal Justice Act 1987 provided: "The Director may investigate any suspected offence which appears to him on reasonable grounds to involve serious or complex fraud."
[4] Section 1(2) of the Criminal Justice Act 1987 provided: "The Attorney General shall appoint a person to be the Director of the Serious Fraud Office (referred to in this Part of this Act as 'the Director'), and he shall discharge his functions under the superintendence of the Attorney General."

affect UK–Saudi relations and jeopardize the contract. The Attorney General commenced a "Shawcross exercise"[5] to canvass Ministers' views, citing Article 5 of the Organization for Economic Cooperation and Development ("OECD") Convention on Combating Bribery of Foreign Public Officials in International Business Transactions, 1997 ("the Bribery Convention").[6] Although the Cabinet Secretary highlighted the strategic interest in ongoing cooperation with Saudi Arabia on counter-terrorism and Middle East policies, and high-value military projects, the Attorney General and Director both considered that it was in the public interest for the investigation to continue.

In autumn 2006, the SFO advised that it intended to investigate certain Swiss bank accounts for evidence of bribery of Saudi officials. Saudi Arabia subsequently threatened that, if the investigation continued, it would withdraw from existing bilateral agreements and end negotiations for Typhoon aircraft purchases. The Cabinet Secretary advised the Attorney General that, if carried out, the threat would have severe consequences contrary to the public interest. In December 2006, the Prime Minister asked the Attorney General to reconsider the public interest issues raised.

On 14 December 2006, the Director publicly announced his decision to discontinue the investigation on national security grounds, stating that he considered his decision was consistent with Article 5 of the Bribery Convention, but that, even if he had thought otherwise, the risk was such that he would still have discontinued the investigation.

In seeking judicial review of the Director's decision, the claimants asserted that the Director had unlawfully acceded to the threat, contrary to the rule of law; failed to take account of the risk that surrender to the threat posed to the UK's national security, criminal law system and the rule of law; misdirected himself and taken into account irrelevant considerations by misinterpreting Article 5; and failed to take account that Saudi Arabia would breach its international law obligations if it carried out its threat. They further submitted that the advice of Ministers was tainted with considerations contrary to Article 5; and that the Shawcross exercise was improperly conducted, as Ministers expressed their opinions on what the Director should do.

Judgment of the High Court (10 April 2008)

Held (unanimously):—The Director's decision was unlawful.

(1) Courts were traditionally reluctant to interfere with independent prosecutors' exercises of discretion; it took a wholly exceptional case on its legal merits to justify a judicial review. Under Section 1 of the 1987 Act, the

---

[5] See para. 6 of the judgment of the High Court. A Shawcross exercise is the process by which the Attorney General may seek the opinions of his ministerial colleagues in deciding whether or not it is in the public interest to prosecute in a case where there is sufficient evidence to do so. Under the exercise, the ultimate decision remains with the Attorney General alone, and he is not to be put under pressure by his colleagues.

[6] See para. 9 of the judgment of the High Court.

Director possessed a wide discretionary power to investigate and prosecute; in exercising his discretion, the Director was entitled to take into account and lawfully accord appropriate weight to the judgement of other experts as to the risk to life and national security, noting also that he and the UK Government were obliged to protect and safeguard the lives of UK citizens under Article 2 of the European Convention on Human Rights, 1950[7] (paras. 49-55).

(2) The executive branch of government was responsible for making decisions on the merits in cases concerning foreign relations and national security, and the law accorded the executive a very wide margin of discretion in such matters. The present application, however, concerned the nature and implications of the threat made in the context of the Director's investigation rather than foreign relations (paras. 56-9).

(3) Courts fulfilled their obligation to protect the rule of law by ensuring that decision-makers exercised their statutory powers independently and without surrender to third parties. In yielding to the threat, the Director had ceased to exercise his powers independently; while he may have independently assessed the consequences of the threat, the investigation would have continued but for that threat. The suggestion that the courts were powerless in resisting threats of foreign governments, due to the principle that the courts would not adjudicate on acts done abroad by virtue of sovereign authority, was misplaced. The courts had to protect the rule of law by upholding the principle that, when making a decision in exercise of a statutory power, an independent prosecutor was not entitled to surrender to threats. A resolute refusal to concede to such a threat was the only way the law could resist and discourage further threats in the future (paras. 60-80).

(4) Both domestic and international law recognized the defence of duress and the justification of necessity; while it was unnecessary to identify when necessity might justify surrender, it was for the courts to determine whether a particular threat was imminent, and whether the decision-maker was compelled to yield. In the present case, there had been no specific, direct threat against anyone's life. While there was a serious risk of unpredictable terrorist attacks in respect of which Saudi Arabian intelligence might be valuable, that did not support the Director's submission that he was under a sufficient degree of duress to surrender to the threat (paras. 81-5).

(5) Submission to a threat was lawful only where it was demonstrated that the decision-maker had no alternative; such necessity preserved the rule of law, and avoided the possibility of any suspicion that investigations or prosecutions

---

[7] Article 2 of the European Convention on Human Rights, 1950, provided: "*Right to life*: (1) Everyone's right to life shall be protected by law. No one shall be deprived of his life intentionally save in the execution of a sentence of a court following his conviction of a crime for which this penalty is provided by law. (2) Deprivation of life shall not be regarded as inflicted in contravention of this article when it results from the use of force which is no more than absolutely necessary: (a) in defence of any person from unlawful violence; (b) in order to effect a lawful arrest or to prevent the escape of a person lawfully detained; (c) in action lawfully taken for the purpose of quelling a riot or insurrection."

might be discontinued only on the pretext of threats, rather than some other basis (such as protection of diplomatic or economic interests). The Director accepted that he did not take into account the damage to national security, the integrity of the criminal justice system and the rule of law that discontinuing the investigation could cause, which was alleviated by other ongoing investigations. In the absence of those assurances and considerations, the Director's decision was unlawful (paras. 86-102).

(6) It was well established that municipal courts did not and could not have competence to adjudicate on or enforce rights arising out of transactions entered into by independent sovereign States at the level of international law. However, in cases where a decision-maker expressly took an international instrument into account in decision-making, a court might be compelled to consider the correctness of his interpretation to assess the lawfulness of his decision. Since the Director chose to justify his decision by invoking Article 5, the Court was not debarred from seeking to interpret the Bribery Convention in determining the legality of the exercise of his discretion (paras. 103-22).

(7) The mere fact that national security was not stated within the Bribery Convention as a permitted consideration did not mean it was prohibited. Article 5 expressly preserved the "applicable rules and principles of each party"; several Contracting Parties' domestic laws provided for non-disclosure or cessation of prosecutions on grounds of national security or overriding public interest, and it was, further, a fundamental obligation of governments to protect their citizens' lives. Nevertheless, according to Article 31(1) of the Vienna Convention on the Law of Treaties, 1969,[8] the Bribery Convention had to be interpreted in good faith, in the light of its ordinary meaning and purpose. That purpose was to ensure Contracting Parties resisted damaging reactions from States wishing to avoid investigations or prosecutions of their public officials. States' national security, however, frequently depended to some extent on relations with other States, deteriorations in which could have national security implications. If investigations could be halted wherever relations between States had national security implications, Article 5 would have little utility. Unless a uniform distinction could be drawn between relations with other States and national security implications arising from those relations, Contracting States could potentially escape the Bribery Convention's application by relying on a broad definition of national security (paras. 123-42).

(8) The purpose of Article 5 of the Bribery Convention could only be achieved if national security considerations could be taken into account only when falling within the customary international law doctrine of necessity. Adopting that standard would promote consistency, and ensure individual States could not be the sole judge of whether their own investigations and

---

[8] Article 31(1) of the Vienna Convention on the Law of Treaties, 1969, provided: "*General rule of interpretation*: (1) A treaty shall be interpreted in good faith in accordance with the ordinary meaning to be given to the terms of the treaty in their context and in the light of its object and purpose."

prosecutions had justifiably been halted. Noting that, the Contracting Parties had invested the OECD Working Group on Bribery in International Business Transactions ("WGB") with the authority to interpret the Bribery Convention; if the Court struck down the Director's decision by deciding where the line should be drawn, it would damage the uniformity upon which the Bribery Convention depended. Further, a definitive ruling on Article 5 was not necessary in the present case, as the Director's decision had already been found unlawful (paras. 143-8).

(9) The Director had failed to recognize that the rule of law required that his decisions be reached through an exercise of independent judgement and that he resist the pressure exerted by a specific threat, and failed to satisfy the Court that he had done all he reasonably could to resist it. His decision was quashed (paras. 159-71).

The Director appealed with permission from the High Court.

Judgment of the House of Lords (30 July 2008)

Held (unanimously):—The appeal was allowed.

Per Lord Bingham of Cornhill (with whom Lord Hoffmann agreed): (1) The Director was a public official entrusted with discretionary powers to investigate and prosecute suspected offences which he reasonably considered involved serious fraud. His decisions were not immune from judicial review, but only in exceptional circumstances would a court overturn the decisions of an independent prosecutor or investigator. The Director's powers were not unfettered, however; he was obliged to act lawfully; to direct himself correctly in law; and to seek to exercise his powers in good faith and to promote the statutory purpose for which they were conferred, uninfluenced by external factors (paras. 30-2).

(2) The Divisional Court's determination that the Director yielded to the threat too quickly and could have done more to resist it overlooked the fact that he had no diplomatic access to representatives of Saudi Arabia, and he was obliged and entitled to rely on others' expert assessments. That approach involved no affront to the rule of law. Referral of the matter to the United Nations, as suggested by the claimants, would probably not have achieved cooperation. While the Director accepted that he did not, at the time, consider whether ceasing the investigation would threaten national security by indicating that the UK would submit to threats, his firm view was that the circumstances were exceptional and unlikely to affect future cases. A discretionary decision was not, in any event, vitiated by failure to take into account considerations that the decision-maker was not legally obliged to take into account. The Director did not surrender his discretionary decision-making power to a third party, and took a decision he was lawfully entitled to make. It was doubtful whether any responsible decision-maker in his position could have decided otherwise (paras. 40-1).

(3) With respect to the application of Article 5 of the Bribery Convention, it was common ground that, had the Director ignored Article 5, an unincorporated treaty provision not applicable in domestic law, his decision could not have been impugned on grounds of inconsistency with it. He did, however, publicly state that he was acting in accordance with that Article. Whether domestic courts could or should interpret international instruments in the absence of a body of jurisprudence was questionable, but it would be unfortunate if decision-makers were deterred from seeking to give effect to the UK's international obligations on the basis that their decisions might be vitiated for a court's contrary understanding. Furthermore, as the Divisional Court had stated, the Contracting Parties to the Bribery Convention had established the WGB as a forum to discuss and resolve differences of approaches to the interpretation and application, in light of which national courts should hesitate before undertaking unilateral interpretation (paras. 43-5).

(4) Article 5 of the Bribery Convention permitted national prosecutors and investigators to act in accordance with their national rules and principles, but not to be influenced by national economic interests, the potential effects on relations with other States, and the identity of natural or legal persons involved. The first and third prohibitions were clear; however, the ambit of the second was more doubtful. A prosecutor or investigator was plainly not to be influenced by the prospect of cooling of relations between his State and another State, but it was not clear whether the Bribery Convention's drafters had intended to include multiple loss of life within the ambit of the second prohibition, or to deny Contracting Parties the right to rely on a severe threat to national security (paras. 46-7).

Per Lord Rodger of Earlsferry: The Director would have made the same decision even if he had believed that his decision was not compatible with Article 5 of the Bribery Convention. He received advice from several sources as to the national security threat posed by continuing the investigation, and clearly weighed that advice carefully before acting on it, as he was so entitled. Even supposing the House was competent, it was unnecessary to interpret Article 5 (paras. 50-1).

Per Baroness Hale of Richmond: It had been lawful for the Director to take account of the threat to lives in the United Kingdom if Saudi Arabian intelligence cooperation was withdrawn. The withdrawal of Saudi security cooperation would indeed have had a consequence of importance to the public as a whole, being a risk to public safety, and he had been entitled to rely on the judgement of others with expertise in that field. The House did not need to consider whether national security considerations were contrary to Article 5 of the Bribery Convention, noting the Director's statement that he would have made the same decision regardless (paras. 52-6).

Per Lord Brown of Eaton-under-Heywood: The Court would, on occasion, decide questions of State obligations under unincorporated treaty law;

however, it was right that it declined to construe Article 5 of the Bribery Convention in this case. Construing unincorporated treaties was generally undesirable, particularly where the Contracting Parties had provided for a mechanism to resolve disputes, such as the WGB. National courts should avoid assuming that role in the absence of compelling reasons. The Director clearly believed that his decision was consistent with Article 5, but was adamant that, regardless, he would have taken the same decision. His interpretation was a reasonable and tenable one (paras. 66-7).

The text of the speeches delivered in the House of Lords commences at p. 457. The following is the text of the judgment of the High Court, delivered by Moses LJ:

JUDGMENT OF THE HIGH COURT

LORD JUSTICE MOSES

Introduction

1. This is the judgment of the Court.
2. Between 30 July 2004 and 14 December 2006 a team of Serious Fraud Office lawyers, accountants, financial investigators and police officers carried out an investigation into allegations of bribery by BAE Systems plc (BAE) in relation to the Al-Yamamah military aircraft contracts with the Kingdom of Saudi Arabia. On 14 December 2006 the Director of the Serious Fraud Office announced that he was ending the SFO's investigation.
3. In October 2005 BAE sought to persuade the Attorney General and the SFO to stop the investigation on the grounds that its continued investigation would be contrary to the public interest: it would adversely affect relations between the United Kingdom and Saudi Arabia and prevent the United Kingdom securing what it described as the largest export contract in the last decade. Despite representations from Ministers, the Attorney General and the Director stood firm. The investigation continued throughout the first half of 2006.
4. In July 2006 the SFO was about to obtain access to Swiss bank accounts. The reaction of those described discreetly as "Saudi representatives" was to make a specific threat to the Prime Minister's Chief of Staff, Jonathan Powell: if the investigation was not stopped, there would be no contract for the export of Typhoon aircraft and the previous close intelligence and diplomatic relationship would cease.

5. Ministers advised the Attorney General and the Director that if the investigation continued those threats would be carried out; the consequences would be grave, both for the arms trade and for the safety of British citizens and service personnel. In the light of what he regarded as the grave risk to life, if the threat was carried out, the Director decided to stop the investigation.

6. The defendant in name, although in reality the Government, contends that the Director was entitled to surrender to the threat. The law is powerless to resist the specific and, as it turns out, successful attempt by a foreign government to pervert the course of justice in the United Kingdom, by causing the investigation to be halted. The court must, so it is argued, accept that whilst the threats and their consequences are "a matter of regret", they are a "part of life".

7. So bleak a picture of the impotence of the law invites at least dismay, if not outrage. The danger of so heated a reaction is that it generates steam; this obscures the search for legal principle. The challenge, triggered by this application, is to identify a legal principle which may be deployed in defence of so blatant a threat. However abject the surrender to that threat, if there is no identifiable legal principle by which the threat may be resisted, then the court must itself acquiesce in the capitulation.

Facts

8. Since this case has aroused public concern, we should stress that which is well-recognised in the field of public law. This court is not concerned to conduct an enquiry into the facts which led to the Director's decision, save to the extent necessary to reach a conclusion as to whether that decision was lawful. The defendant has disclosed facts which are sufficient for the purpose of reaching a conclusion but they are not comprehensive and it is no part of the court's function in these judicial review proceedings to achieve a more complete account of the events, unless omission inhibits a correct legal conclusion. We emphasise that, through the efforts of Treasury Counsel and those by whom he is assisted, there has been sufficient disclosure to enable us to reach a solution to the essential question whether the Director acted lawfully. We turn, then, to the facts on which the court needs to rely.

9. On 14 October 2005 the SFO issued a statutory notice to BAE requiring it to disclose details of payments to agents and consultants in respect of the Al-Yamamah contracts. On 7 November 2005, in response to that notice, BAE's solicitors wrote to the Attorney General in a memorandum described as "strictly private and confidential"

seeking to persuade him to halt the investigation on the grounds that it would be:

seriously contrary to the public interest on the grounds that it would adversely and seriously affect relations between the UK and Saudi Arabian Governments and would almost inevitably prevent the UK securing its largest export contract in the last decade.

The Group Legal Director told the Attorney General that he had discussed those issues with the Permanent Secretary at the Ministry of Defence. The Legal Secretary to the Law Officers replied that it was not appropriate for law officers to receive a memorandum cloaked with confidentiality. The representations were then sent to the Director of the SFO. The foundation for BAE's fears, described in its memorandum, was that compliance with the Statutory Notice would be regarded by the Saudi Arabian Government as a serious breach of confidentiality by BAE and by the UK Government.

10. On 15 November 2005 the SFO's Case Controller, Matthew Cowie, questioned BAE's solicitors as to:

... why the pursuance by the SFO *of its independent statutory powers of investigation* could properly be regarded as a breach of duty of confidentiality by the United Kingdom Government. (Our emphasis.)

He reminded the solicitors for BAE that it was a participant in the Organisation for Economic Co-operation and Development (OECD) process, committed to the principles of the OECD's Convention on Combating Bribery of Foreign Public Officials in International Business Transactions, 1997 (the Convention), and set out the terms of Article 5 of the Convention:

Investigation and prosecution of the bribery of a foreign public official shall be subject to the applicable rules and principles of each Party. They shall not be influenced by considerations of national economic interest, the potential effect upon relations with another State or the identity of the natural or legal persons involved.

11. On 6 December 2005 the Director and the Attorney General started what is known as a "Shawcross exercise". We shall consider later the claimants' challenge based on the conduct of that exercise. For the moment, it is sufficient to recall that a Shawcross exercise is the means by which facts including any consideration affecting public policy can be sought from Government ministers by the Attorney General in order to acquaint himself with all that is relevant to his decision

whether it is in the public interest to pursue a prosecution. The letter, inviting the views of the Government, drew specific attention to Article 5 of the Convention prohibiting parties to the Convention from being influenced by considerations of national economic interest or the potential effect upon relations with another state. It recorded that the Attorney had assured the OECD working group in 2004 that:

none of the considerations prohibited by Article 5 would be taken into account as public interest factors not to prosecute foreign bribery cases.

The letter reminded the Cabinet Secretary that he would have to have regard to the Convention in any comments made in response.

12. On 16 December 2005 the Cabinet Secretary, in response to the Shawcross exercise, commented that:

it is, of course, for the Attorney General and the prosecuting authorities to decide whether there should be a prosecution, and also to decide how Article 5 bears on the current circumstances. We have, however, assumed that it may be possible for considerations of the kind mentioned in Article 5 at least to be taken into account for the purpose of taking an early view on the viability of any investigation.

13. The note did, indeed, take into account those considerations prohibited by Article 5. It emphasised the importance of the relationship with Saudi Arabia and that the Al-Yamamah air defence programme, including the upgrade programme for Tornado aircraft, was a cornerstone of that relationship. It referred to the procurement by the Saudis of the next generation of attack aircraft, the Typhoon. After referring to such commercial considerations it turned to counter-terrorism work and the vital strategic interest of stability in the Middle East. It referred to the importance of Saudi Arabia in the fight against Islamic terrorism and the damage to British security interests should the investigation continue. It described Saudi Arabia as a key country in the Middle East in its advocacy of moderate foreign policy. Its stability was of vital strategic interest to the United Kingdom and to the west generally.

14. The response of the SFO is of considerable importance in this application. At this early stage it was, again, the Case Controller who understood the implications of the Cabinet Office's response. His advice, dated 19 December 2005, to the Director, deserves quotation. In answer to the question as to whether the public interest consequences should be considered by the SFO at the stage the investigation had reached he referred to the duty of the SFO to investigate crime and pursue reasonable lines of enquiry in the light of domestic and

international obligations. He referred to Article 5 of the OECD Convention and the likely ratification in the future of Article 35 of the UN Convention on corruption, and then continued:

those international instruments envisage an independent role for law enforcement outside of [*sic*] economic or political considerations. *To have any meaningful effect they must have application, regardless of the seriousness of the consequences stated.* There are always likely to be economic and political consequences of any major enquiry into defence contracts. That is why such considerations must ultimately be irrelevant to the independent conduct of such enquiries. It is impossible for the Director of the SFO to weigh up these competing public interest considerations. (Our emphasis.)

15. The brief then continued:

If it is conceded that public interest features of this importance have to be considered by the investigating authority or by the Attorney General, at this stage in the investigation, how should the public interest in the rule of law as opposed to economic and political consequences be balanced?

The SFO does not concede this point and believes identical considerations apply to the role of the Attorney General.

16. The brief summarises the effect of the note in response to the Shawcross exercise and continues:

The only challenge we can make, if it is conceded that this issue is not covered by Article 5 of the OECD Convention[,] is if we have grounds to believe that the Cabinet are not fully apprised of considerations that are capable of altering the balance of the public interest.

Have they given full consideration to the public interest in the rule of law, the independence of the SFO and MDP and the role of central government, all of which could suffer reputational damage if it emerged that an investigation by the SFO had been cut short, [the words which follow have been deleted from public scrutiny]. (Our emphasis.)

17. The Attorney General and the Director resisted the representations to halt the investigation on public interest grounds. Their view is recorded in a letter dated 25 January 2006:

Having weighed all the public interest considerations and having regard to the OECD Convention ... the Attorney General considers that it is in the public interest for the SFO investigation to proceed.

18. It is important to appreciate that the grounds upon which it was said that the public interest would be damaged by continuing the investigation at the end of 2005 are the same grounds as those resurrected later in 2006. But on this occasion, in early 2006, the Attorney

General and the Director were of the view that they were not such as to justify discontinuing the investigation. What changed later in 2006?

19. Investigations continued throughout 2006 until, as we have said, the SFO was about to obtain access to bank accounts in Switzerland. This provoked an explicit threat made with the specific intention of halting the investigation. We should pause in the narrative to record the evidence in relation to that threat. On 29 September 2006 the Cabinet Secretary wrote to the Attorney General's Legal Secretariat to report what he described as "some significant recent developments". He referred to the earlier commercial, diplomatic and counter-terrorism co-operation considerations which he said had become even more compelling:

... the severe damage to the public interest ... we feared was likely in December 2005 is now imminent. If the Saudis are already deciding to take such steps in relation to the Typhoon programme, then we must anticipate that they could follow though [*sic*] [redaction] in relation to counter-terrorism and the bi-lateral relationship ... the Saudis['] understanding of the manner and direction of the investigation affect the likelihood of this damage occurring at any given time, and the recent course of the investigation ... has taken us to the brink of such consequences. We accept entirely that these matters are for the Attorney General to decide, acting independently of Government. We would be grateful if he would, in light of these developments, consider reviewing the decision recorded in your letter to me of 25 January 2006.

20. The Government has contended that it is not in the public interest for the details of those "significant recent developments" to be disclosed. It issued Public Interest Immunity certificates to that effect. We should record that in order to allay concern that the omission might cause these proceedings to be resolved on the basis of a misapprehension as to the true facts, the court was shown unredacted versions of all the documents disclosed, including the letter of 29 September 2006. This is not the occasion to determine the propriety of such a procedure. We have not taken up time, either at an interlocutory stage or at the hearing, to reach any final conclusion as to the correct procedure to be adopted in judicial review proceedings where the Government takes the view that it is not in the public interest to lay all the cards on the table. But, fundamentally, it is the obligation of the defendant, in the instant case the Government, to ensure that its response to the challenge is not misleading.

21. However, the opportunity to see the unredacted version has ensured that the challenge can be advanced on a fair and accurate factual basis. We have proceeded on this basis because we take the view that we have sufficient information to do justice to the challenge

and to ensure, in the light of the information we have been given by the Government, that its resistance is not on a misleading factual basis.

22. The allegation made by the claimants is clear. It sets out a report from the *Sunday Times* dated 10 June 2007. The report states that:

Bandar (Prince Bandar bin Sultan bin Abdul Aziz of al-Saud) went into Number 10 and said "get it stopped" [words omitted]. Bandar suggested to Powell he knew the SFO were looking at the Swiss accounts ... if they didn't stop it, the Typhoon contract was going to be stopped and intelligence and diplomatic relations would be pulled.

23. There has never been a specific admission of those facts by the Government. On the contrary, in both the summary and the detailed grounds of resistance, the defendant merely stated that on 29 September 2006 the Attorney General's office had received further representations from the Cabinet Secretary regarding the public interest in the light of more recent developments (see § 7 of the summary and § 8 of the detailed grounds). It is true that those responses were to a challenge based on Article 5 of the Convention. Accordingly, Collins J, in refusing leave, was unaware that "the recent developments" were an explicit threat designed to interfere with the course of the investigation. It was only as a result of the efforts of Treasury Counsel and Treasury Solicitor that some redacted documents were disclosed. In response to that letter of 29 September 2006, the Legal Secretary to the Law Officers referred to representations made and consequences threatened by "Saudi representatives" (letter of 3 October 2006).

24. No admission of a specific threat was made in the Government's skeleton argument. In those circumstances the court asked Mr Sales QC, on behalf of the defendant, to explain the factual basis upon which the court should proceed. We were told that we should base our judgment on the facts alleged by the claimants. We shall do so: there is no other legitimate basis. Moreover, the facts alleged are of particular significance in the instant application. The significant event which was soon to lead to the investigation being halted was a threat made by an official of a foreign state, allegedly complicit in the criminal conduct under investigation, and, accordingly, with interests of his own in seeing that the investigation ceased.

25. The letter from the Legal Secretariat dated 3 October 2006 recorded that the Attorney General had noted the strength of the representations made by the Saudi representatives, but concluded:

The Attorney is of the firm view that, if the case is in fact soundly based, it would not be right to discontinue it on the basis that the consequences threatened by the Saudi representatives may result.

26. The history thereafter shows that the Director of the SFO was persuaded that the Government of Saudi Arabia intended to carry out the threat if the investigation was not halted. The Assistant Director appreciated the significance of the source of the threat. In her letter to the Legal Secretary dated 27 October 2006, Helen Garlick suggested that caution should be exercised when considering the views of the official who had made the threat. In addition, she exhibited a healthy scepticism as to the fears expressed by the Cabinet Secretary.

27. She pointed out that the arguments were the same as those pressed the previous year. She said:

This is an old issue and in our view nothing new emerges from this recent correspondence.

The feared consequences had not occurred despite the fact that the enquiry in October 2005 had provoked submissions on the public interest. Accordingly, she advised that caution should be exercised when considering the views of he who had uttered the threat (the rest of that part of her letter has been redacted) and continued:

The SFO and MDP [Ministry of Defence Police] would expect that, if our investigation directly impinges on wider operations, proper guidance and briefing on the substance of that threat and risk would be undertaken and furthermore, that we would have been alerted to this at the outset of the investigation and certainly during the [course] of the Shawcross representation in November last year.

28. In order to assess the likelihood that the threat would be carried out and the consequences of that threat the Director met the United Kingdom Ambassador to Saudi Arabia on three occasions in November and early December 2006. We have no note of those meetings but Mr Wardle recalls in his first statement that on 30 November 2006 the Ambassador directly confirmed to him that the threats to international security were very grave indeed and were as represented by the Cabinet Secretary in his letter dated 29 September 2006.

as he put it to me, British lives on British streets were at risk . . . (See § 28 of his first witness statement.)

29. The Director and his case team proposed to explore whether BAE might plead guilty to corruption on what the Director describes as a limited basis. On 5 December 2006, he discussed this possible approach with the Attorney, who had no objection. But on the evening of that day, 5 December 2006, the Legal Secretary suggested that the

Prime Minister be briefed. The Prime Minister's response was to make further representations to the Attorney General.

30. It is apparent that on the same day, 5 December 2006, Prince Bandar met Foreign Office officials (see Hansard 16 May 2007, Col. 781 W). He had shortly before spent the week in Paris negotiating the purchase of alternative fighter aircraft with President Chirac.

31. The representations made by the Prime Minister are recorded in a personal minute from the Prime Minister to the Attorney General dated 8 December 2006. In that minute the Prime Minister asked the Attorney if he would consider again the public interest issues raised by the ongoing investigation.

It is my judgment on the basis of recent evidence and the advice of colleagues that these developments have given rise to the real and immediate risk of a collapse in UK/Saudi security, intelligence and diplomatic cooperation. This is likely to have seriously negative consequences for the UK public interest in terms of both national security and our highest priority foreign policy objectives in the Middle East.
[redaction]
The issue, in Saudi eyes, is not so much about the specifics of any element of the investigation, [redaction] but one of cumulative damage to overall competence in their relationship with the UK. I am advised in strong terms that we are now at high risk of a serious collapse in that confidence.

Article 5 of the OECD Convention on Combating Bribery prohibits you from being influenced by considerations of the national economic interest or the potential effect upon relations with another state. As you know, I strongly support our commitment to the Convention and am proud of this Government's record on putting bribery issues onto the agenda and into law. While this letter is not primarily concerned with the serious damage being done to our bilateral relationship by the investigation, it is of course of concern to me, not least because of the critical difficulty presented to the negotiations over the Typhoon contract.

My primary duty is however to UK national security and it is on this basis that I must urge you to consider the public interest in relation to the pursuit of this investigation.

The damage being currently done to Saudi confidence in the UK as an international partner has these two important consequences for the public interest: our direct national security, through our exchanges with the Saudi authorities in countering international terrorism; and the Government's highest foreign policy priority of working towards peace and stability in the Middle East. As you will know, it is my strong belief that our Middle East work is fundamentally also a matter of our national security—directly in the threat to our soldiers in Iraq, and indirectly through the effects of Middle East stability more widely. In both of these objectives, I want to explain to you how the help and confidence of the Saudi authorities is critical to success, and how recent developments are throwing that cooperation into jeopardy.

. . .

In summary, it is in my judgement very clear that the continuation of the SFO investigation into Al Yamamah risks seriously damaging Saudi confidence in the UK as a partner. It is also my judgement that such damage risks endangering UK national security, both directly in protecting citizens and service people, and indirectly through impeding our search for peace and stability in this critical part of the world. This letter, and the attached papers, I hope help to explain those judgements. The Defence Secretary endorses what is said earlier in this letter about the impact on Defence interests and both he and the Foreign Secretary share my overall view, as expressed here, on the damaging impact of the SFO investigation. This assessment is formed on the basis of advice from the Government's most senior national security official advisors.

I understand and respect the constitutional position and the independent judgement you are required to make on extremely difficult and delicate issues of this nature, and I know any intervention you make in the conduct of this investigation must be your decision alone. For my part, after much careful thought I have come to the conclusion that the seriousness of these risks to the national interest is such that I would be failing in my duty if I did not bring them directly to your attention [and] ask you to consider them. That is why I am taking the exceptional step of writing to you myself.

32. The note from the Permanent Secretary, Intelligence, Security and Resilience dated 23 November 2006 stresses that the intelligence and security relationship with Saudi Arabia is fundamental to what he describes as the United Kingdom's global counter-terrorist strategy. Were the Saudis to withdraw co-operation, he says that the United Kingdom would be deprived of the support of a key partner in that strategy. He points out that the Saudi leadership has made counter-terrorism a top priority and that:

The Saudis undoubtedly view the US as their key foreign partner, including on security issues. But they continue to be receptive to assistance and advice on security and counter-terrorism from the UK.

33. The second attachment was a letter from the Permanent Under-Secretary to the Foreign Office, stressing the United Kingdom's dependence on Saudi Arabia's support for its policies in Israel and Palestine. The loss of Saudi co-operation would, he said, severely disable the United Kingdom's efforts to promote peace and security in the Middle East.

34. The Director was shown that minute at a meeting with the Legal Secretariat on 11 December 2006. The following day he had a third meeting with the Ambassador at which the Ambassador repeated that the risk that Saudi Arabia would carry out the threat to withdraw co-operation with the UK on counter-terrorism was "real and acute".

He repeated that there was a real threat to UK lives and expressed the view that the SFO could not pursue any attempt to prosecute without endangering UK national security. On 11 December 2006 the Prime Minister and the Attorney General met. A letter dated 12 December 2006 sent from the Prime Minister's Principal Private Secretary to the Legal Secretary records the highlights of that meeting:

The Attorney, opening the meeting, said that while he could see the force of the points in the Prime Minister's minute, he had to weigh these up against other considerations. In particular, he was concerned that halting the investigation would send a bad message about the credibility of the law in this area, and look like giving into threats. He was clear however that he felt justified in questioning whether the grounds of the investigation were soundly based and in exploring legal options for resolving the case as quickly as possible.

The Prime Minister responded that, as per his minute, he felt higher considerations were at stake. Proceeding with the case would result in the end of Saudi–UK cooperation. [Redaction] Losing the confidence Saudi Arabia placed in the UK risked very serious damage to the UK national interest in the fields of counter-terrorism and the search for peace and stability in the Middle East. [Redaction] While the Prime Minister understood that halting the investigation was not a step to be taken lightly, he was clear that in this case there was a supervening national interest at stake, and that the British people would regard these as higher interests.

In discussion, the following main points were made:

- [Redaction]
- Any proposal that the investigation be resolved by parties pleading guilty to certain charges would be unlikely to reduce the offence caused to the Saudi Royal Family, even if the deal were accepted, and the process would still drag out for a considerable period;
- [Redaction]
- It was important that the Government did not give people reason to believe that threatening the British system resulted in parties getting their way. But the Government also needed to consider the damage done to the credibility of the law in this area by a long and failed trial, and its good reputation on bribery and corruption issues compared with many of its international partners.

Summing up, the Prime Minister said that while he accepted that supervision of the investigation had to be a matter for the Attorney, the Prime Minister would be failing in his duty to national security and the public interest not to bring the potential damage to Britain's counter-terrorist effort, Middle East diplomacy and other important aspects of the relationship with Saudi Arabia to the Attorney's attention. This was the clearest case for intervention in the public interest he had seen. The Attorney said he would consider the Prime Minister's representations, with due regard to the need for separation between the law and public policy.

It is not clear whether Mr Wardle ever saw this letter before he made his decision to halt the investigation. He attended a meeting with the Law Officers on 13 December 2006. In a note prepared the following day by Helen Garlick, the Director is recorded as saying:

In the last few days the representations on public interest had been made with renewed and increasing force by HM Ambassador. If further investigation will cause such damage to national and international security he accepted that it would not be in the public interest.

He and the Attorney General differed as to the sufficiency of the evidence and he is recorded as asking for time to consider the Attorney General's reservations as to the evidence and to take leading counsel's advice.

35. At that meeting the Attorney General asked for Helen Garlick's views and she expressed the view that the SFO had not sought to place the interests of the investigation above those of national and international security. She said that although the Attorney General and the Director were qualified to make judgments on the law and the evidence, on questions of security they had to take the advice of others. She assumed that the Attorney General had better advice and expressed the view that if the investigation:

... caused another 7/7, how could we say that our investigation which at this stage might or might not result in a successful prosecution was more important?

36. The Attorney General expressed his views about the strength of the evidence and Helen Garlick continued:

If the investigation was ended on public interest grounds there were a number of implications. One [Redaction], two, the US might well take up the case into [Redaction], three, the Swiss might launch a money-laundering and corruption investigation, based on material we had asked them to get which we were not being allowed to acquire.
The AG asked us to enquire into the Swiss and US positions.
Throughout the meeting he made it clear that he, whilst he had wished to test the SFO case, was committed to supporting it provided it was viable, whatever the outcome might be. He was extremely unhappy at the implications of dropping it now.

37. That same day, 13 December 2006, the Director told the Attorney that he had concluded that to continue the investigation risked:

real and imminent damage to the UK's national and international security and would endanger the lives of UK citizens and service personnel.

He confirmed his decision the next morning, 14 December. The decision was announced in a press release that day:

This decision has been taken following representations that have been made both to the Attorney General and the Director of the SFO concerning the need to safeguard national and international security.

It has been necessary to balance the need to maintain the rule of law against the wider public interest.

No weight has been given to commercial interests or to the national economic interest.

38. On the same day, 14 December 2006, the Attorney General announced that decision in the House of Lords. He referred to the views of the Prime Minister and of the Foreign and Defence Secretaries that the investigation would cause serious damage to UK/Saudi security, intelligence and diplomatic co-operation, and the likelihood that this would have "seriously negative consequences for the United Kingdom public interest in terms of both national security and our highest priority foreign policy objectives in the Middle East . . .". He also said:

Article 5 of the OECD Convention . . . precludes me and the Serious Fraud Office from taking into account considerations of the national economic interest or the potential effect upon relations with another state, and we have not done so.

In response to Lord Thomas of Gresford, who suggested that the Attorney General's two statements were contradictory, the Attorney General spoke of:

. . . a very difficult balance to strike. The short statement from the SFO makes that clear by saying that it has been necessary to balance the need to maintain the rule of law against the wider public interest.

The Director's reasons for discontinuing the investigation

39. The Director, in his first witness statement, states that the reason why he discontinued the investigation was that to continue:

would risk an immediate cessation of co-operation in relation to national and international security which might have devastating effects on the UK's national security interest—both locally in the UK and in the wider international field in the Middle East . . . a compelling case had been made out that the UK's national security and innocent lives would be put in serious jeopardy if the SFO's investigation continued. (§ 48.)

He says:

It was this feature of the case which I felt left me with no choice but to halt the investigation.

40. In reaching that decision he says that he had well in mind that the United Kingdom is a signatory to the Convention and he had in mind Article 5. He took the view that to discontinue the investigation was compatible with Article 5 because he was not influenced by considerations of national, economic interest, nor what he describes as:

the potential effect upon relations with another state, *per se* ... (§ 48.)

41. He did not consider what his decision would have been had he taken the view that it was not compatible with Article 5 but he says that he is in no doubt whatever that he would have decided to discontinue the investigation even had he thought to do so was incompatible with that Article:

The threat which I considered existed to UK national and international security if the investigation continued was so great that I did not believe that there was any serious doubt about the decision I should make ... (§ 51.)

42. In his second statement, dated 31 January 2008, the Director was in a position to focus on amendments to the grounds of the application and in particular the issue which they raised as to the Director's role in protecting the rule of law. He draws attention to the references to the need for an independent decision by the Director under the superintendence of the Attorney General, rather than for Government. He refers to a letter from Detective Superintendent Allen of the Ministry of Defence Police dated 11 January 2006 to the Attorney General which we have not seen. In the letter the officer drew attention to the rule of law, the OECD Convention and the damage which would be done to the Government's reputation "for leadership and commitment to anti-corruption".

43. The Director states that before October 2006 it had not been suggested to him that the danger to Saudi Arabian co-operation with the UK in combating terrorism was imminent. But he says that in that month the position changed significantly, because of:

... actual representations made by Saudi representatives as to the consequences of continuing the investigation. (Paragraph 19.)

He says that he instinctively wanted to stand up to such threats but that following his first meeting with the Ambassador he began to entertain the thought that the national security public interest might be so compelling that he would have no real alternative to discontinuing the investigation. He explains the reference to balancing the need to maintain the rule of law against the wider public interest, as a reference to the need to balance the public interest in pursuing a criminal investigation against other public interests.

44. At the end of that second statement he emphasises that the subject of the criminal investigation was BAE and not any Saudi officials. He points out that further investigations were continuing in relation to BAE's conduct in other countries. We suspect that the Director felt the need to refer to those other investigations in an attempt to rebut any suggestion that the SFO's investigation of corruption and bribery was less than enthusiastic. That, of course, is not the ground upon which his decision is challenged.

The parties

45. The first claimant, Corner House Research (Corner House), is a non-profit-making organisation which conducts research, education and campaigns in relation to overseas corruption and the role of the United Kingdom in combating bribery. It emphasises the corrosive effect of bribery and corruption in its distortion of markets and its contribution to the spread of organised crime. Of particular relevance is the acknowledgement by leaders of all the G8 countries of the impact of bribery and corruption on national security: it encourages terrorism. (See the final communiqué from the 2006 G8 St Petersburg Summit "Fighting High Level Corruption", July 2006, p. 874.) Both the Home Office's strategy document on combating organised crime and the Foreign Office acknowledged the threat to national security caused by the instability which flows from corruption. The second claimant, Campaign Against Arms Trade, is an unincorporated association engaged in campaigning and lobbying against the arms trade.

46. It is important to stress the limits of this application for Judicial Review brought by the claimants. The reason given for discontinuing the investigation was not the fear that the evidence would not support the allegation of bribery. Accordingly, this court is not concerned with the issue which troubled the Attorney General, namely that after a lengthy investigation the prosecution would collapse because bribery could not be proved. We emphasise this feature in fairness to BAE. By s. 108 of the Anti-terrorism, Crime and Security Act 2001, domestic courts have jurisdiction over anything done abroad by a body incorporated under UK law which would constitute an offence at common law, or under the Prevention of Corruption Acts 1889-1916 if done within

the United Kingdom. The essence of any bribery offence in relation to payments to an agent is the absence of approval by the employer or principal. The need to rebut the defence of consent is a particular difficulty in relation to offences overseas, as the Attorney General pointed out in his evidence to the Constitutional Affairs Committee (Q335, 27 June 2007) and as is noted at § 4.93 in the Law Commission Consultation Paper (No 185) "Reforming Bribery".

47. According to the Attorney General's evidence, BAE has always contended that any payments it made were approved by the Kingdom of Saudi Arabia. In short they were lawful commissions and not secret payments made without the consent or approval of the principal. The cause of anti-corruption is not served by pursuing investigations which fail to distinguish between a commission and a bribe. It would be unfair to BAE to assume that there was a realistic possibility, let alone a probability, of proving that it was guilty of any criminal offence. It is unfortunate that no time was taken to adopt the suggestion (§ 34) to canvass with leading counsel the Attorney's reservations as to the adequacy of the evidence.

48. Equally, we should stress that Prince Bandar has had no opportunity in these proceedings to give his account of the circumstances which have led to the allegation that he threatened the United Kingdom as to the consequences if the investigation was continued. In order to determine the legality of the Director's decision we have, for the reasons we have given, been compelled to proceed on a factual basis which has not been disputed or denied. It is that factual base, namely that he issued a threat to force the end of the investigation, which gives rise to the first of the issues which found the claimants' challenge. We shall identify all the grounds in the order in which we shall deal with them.

The claimants' challenge

49. By a process of amendment and re-amendment the Director's decision is challenged on six grounds.

(i) It was unlawful for the Director to accede to the threat made by Prince Bandar or his agent; such conduct was contrary to the constitutional principle of the rule of law;
(ii) the Director failed to take into account the threat posed to the UK's national security, the integrity of its system of criminal justice and the rule of law caused by surrender to the type of threats made in the instant case;

(iii) the Director mis-directed himself and thus took into account irrelevant considerations by mis-interpreting Article 5 of the OECD Convention;
(iv) the Director failed to take into account as a relevant consideration that if the threats made by Saudi Arabia were carried out, it would commit an act in breach of its international law obligations;
(v) the advice on the public interest given by ministers was tainted by irrelevant considerations, in particular commercial interests of the United Kingdom and its diplomatic relations with Saudi Arabia;
(vi) the Shawcross exercise was conducted improperly in that ministers expressed their opinions as to what the Director's decision should be.

The Director's decision and the rule of law

50. The power of the Director of the Serious Fraud Office to investigate a suspected offence is conferred by statute (s. 1(2) Criminal Justice Act 1987). Although he is required to discharge his functions under the superintendence of the Attorney General, any decision he makes as to investigation or prosecution is for him to reach independently.

51. That the width of this prosecutorial discretion is wide cannot be doubted. Although the decision of a prosecutor is susceptible to judicial review, the courts have traditionally been most reluctant to interfere with the exercise of his discretion (see, e.g., the citation of domestic authority in *Sharma* v. *Brown-Antoine* [2007] 1 WLR 780 at 788B-C). Recently Laws LJ said that it would "take a wholly exceptional case on its legal merits to justify a judicial review" of the Director's decision to investigate or not (*R (Bermingham)* v. *Director of SFO* [2007] QB 727 §§ 63-4). He described the discretion whether to investigate as even more *open-ended* than the decision to prosecute.

52. Thus, in the instant application, to seek to impugn the Director's decision, taken on the grounds that to continue the investigation would be to imperil national security, seems to be a more than usually Quixotic task. The decision is subject to the Code for Crown Prosecutors, which, since the fourth edition (published in 2000), makes specific reference to national security. The process by which decisions to prosecute are taken is well known; there are two stages: the evidential stage and, if passed, the public interest stage. The Code lists a wide range of public interest factors in favour and against prosecution. Amongst the factors identified is the danger that:

details may be made public that could harm sources of information, international relations or national security ... (5.11.i.)

53. It is true that the question whether a prosecution is in the public interest will usually be decided after the prosecutor has collated all the information necessary to reach a conclusion as to whether the evidence is sufficient to found a successful prosecution. The Code (at 5.1) does not envisage any need to consider the public interest if the evidence is insufficient. But a prosecutor is entitled to conclude an investigation well before all potential evidence is gathered, for example when he foresees that the process will be so long and costly as not to be worth the candle. Moreover, there is a danger in placing the evidential and public interest issues in too confined a pair of compartments. An investigation which raises public interest issues may well be required to pass a more stringent evidential test than one in which no public interest issue arises. The instant case is an example of the overlap: once it is accepted that a prosecution would seriously damage commercial and diplomatic relations with Saudi Arabia, it would be folly to pursue a prosecution without a rigorous analysis of its prospect of success.

54. We must start, therefore, by accepting, at least as a generality, that the Director's discretion is of sufficient width to entitle him to take into account risk to life and to national security in deciding whether to continue an investigation. For example, the need to protect the safety, or even the life of an informant may lead to a decision to discontinue a prosecution. Article 2 of the ECHR requires the Director and a government in a democratic society to protect and safeguard the lives of its citizens. The obligation was described by Lord Hope as essential to the preservation of democracy:

It is the duty of the court to do all it can to respect and uphold that principle. (See *A* v. *SSHD* [2005] 2 AC 68 at § 99.)

55. The court, in an application for judicial review, is not in a position to assess the extent of the risk to life or to national security, asserted by those who advised the Attorney General and the Director. The Director, himself, was not in any position to exercise an independent judgment as to the gravity of the risk of which he had been informed in the last three months of 2006, as the Assistant Director acknowledged in the meeting on 13 December. He may lawfully accord appropriate weight to the judgment of those with responsibility for national security who have direct access to sources of intelligence unavailable to him (see *Huang* v. *Home Secretary* [2007] 2 AC 167 at § 16).

56. The separation of power between the executive and the courts requires the courts not to trespass on what Lord Phillips CJ described as one of *the forbidden areas*, a decision affecting foreign policy (*R on the application of Abbasi* v. *Secretary of State for Foreign and Commonwealth Affairs* [2002] EWCA 1598 § 106). In a case touching foreign relations and national security the duty of decision on the merits is assigned to the elected arm of government. Even when the court ensures that the Government complies with formal requirements and acts rationally, the law accords to the executive an especially wide margin of discretion (*R (Al Rawi)* v. *Foreign Secretary* [2007] 2 WLR 1219 § 148). The courts are under no less an obligation to respect and maintain the boundary between their role and the role of government than the executive.

57. But to describe the claimants' application as a challenge either to the relevance of national security to the decision of the Director, or to the Government's assessment of the risk to national security misses the essential point of this application. The essential point, as we see it, derives from the threat uttered, it is said, by Prince Bandar to the Prime Minister's Chief of Staff. The nature and implications of that explicit threat have a significant impact on this application. The challenge was originally resisted, in part, on the basis that the Director was entitled to discontinue the investigation as a result of the *very grave threats* to national and international security (see, e.g., Detailed Grounds of Resistance § 10). But there is an ambiguity in the use of the word *threat* in that context. *Threat* as used in response to the claimants' original challenge meant no more than risk. The Director's decision was taken after assessment of the risk to security. But the grounds of resistance did not mention the fact that representatives of a foreign state had issued a specific threat as to the consequences which would flow from a refusal to halt the investigation. It is one thing to assess the risk of damage which might flow from continuing an investigation, quite another to submit to a threat designed to compel the investigator to call a halt. When the threat involves the criminal jurisdiction of this country, then the issue is no longer a matter only for Government, the courts are bound to consider what steps they must take to preserve the integrity of the criminal justice system.

58. The constitutional principle of the separation of powers requires the courts to resist encroachment on the territory for which they are responsible. In the instant application, the Government's response has failed to recognise that the threat uttered was not simply directed at this country's commercial, diplomatic and security interests; it was aimed at its legal system. In written argument, the Director suggested that we

should attach significance to the fact that the threat was not directed against him. But it was. While he, personally, was not being threatened with any adverse consequences, the threat was effectively being made to him, in his capacity as Director, and in relation to his statutory functions. The Government acted merely as a conduit, passing the threat on to him with an assessment of the danger should it be carried out. That threat was made with the specific intention of interfering with the course of the investigation. The Saudis knew what was proposed: the SFO intended to inspect Swiss bank accounts. Those who uttered and adopted the threat intended to prevent the course which the SFO wished to pursue. It is unlikely that so blatant a threat would have been made had those responsible not believed that it might well succeed.

59. Had such a threat been made by one who was subject to the criminal law of this country, he would risk being charged with an attempt to pervert the course of justice. The course of justice includes the process of criminal investigation (*R* v. *Cotter* [2002] 2 Cr App R 29 at §§ 30 and 31). But whether or not a criminal offence might have been committed, the essential feature is that it was the administration of public justice which was traduced, it was the exercise of the Director's statutory powers which was halted.

60. Threats to the administration of public justice within the United Kingdom are the concern primarily of the courts, not the executive. It is the responsibility of the court to provide protection. To put it plainly:

> One thread runs consistently through all the case law: the recognition that public authorities must beware of surrendering to the dictates of unlawful pressure groups. The implications of such surrender for the rule of law can hardly be exaggerated. As suggested in certain of the authorities, there may be a lawful response. But it is one thing to respond to unlawful threats, quite another to submit to them—the difference, although perhaps difficult to define, will generally be easy to recognise. Tempting though it may sometimes be for public authorities to yield too readily to threats of disruption, they must expect the courts to review any such decision with particular rigour—this is not an area where they can be permitted a wide area of discretion. As when fundamental human rights are in play, the courts will adopt a more interventionist role.

These words of Simon Brown LJ (in *R* v. *Coventry Airport ex parte Phoenix Aviation* [1995] 3 All ER 37 at p. 62) concerned the surrender of the discretion of port authorities to pressure as to which legal trades they should choose to handle. The rationale for the court's intervention is its responsibility to protect the rule of law. Simon Brown LJ's words were obiter but the sources to which he referred establish a well-settled principle. The surrender of a public authority to threat or pressure undermines the rule of law (see Lawton LJ's emphatic response to those who sought to frustrate the exercise of statutory powers in *R* v. *Chief Constable of Devon and Cornwall Constabulary, ex p CEGB* [1982] QB 458, 472-3, cited by Simon Brown LJ at p. 61). That principle must apply with even greater force where the exercise of statutory powers in relation to the administration of justice has been halted by threats.

61. Mr Sales wisely counselled this court to exercise restraint. He warned that to invoke the rule of law adds nothing to the argument in this case. There continues to be debate about the meaning and scope of the rule of law: see Lord Bingham, "The Rule of Law" [2007] CLJ 67 at 68 and Professor Craig's paper on the Rule of Law (Appendix 5) in response to the request of the House of Lords Select Committee on the Constitution, "Relations between the executive, the judiciary and Parliament" HL Paper 151(2006-7) (§ 23).

62. He argued that, in the context of the Director's decision, the rule of law requires no more than he should act in a manner consistent with the well-recognised standards which the courts impose by way of judicial review. The Director must exercise the powers conferred on him by the 1987 Act reasonably, in good faith, for the purposes for which they were conferred and without exceeding the limits of such powers (see Lord Bingham's sixth sub-rule, p. 78). Thus, as Lord Hoffmann has observed, judicial review gives effect to the rule of law (*R (Alconbury Developments Ltd)* v. *Secretary of State for the Environment* [2003] 2 AC 295 § 73).

63. At the heart of the obligations of the courts and of the judges lies the duty to protect the rule of law:

the rule of law enforced by the courts is the ultimate controlling factor on which our constitution is based ... (Per Lord Hope in *R (Jackson)* v. *Attorney General* [2006] 1 AC 262 § 107.)

64. The legislature has sought to reinforce the separation of powers by statutory regulation of the relationship between the executive and the judiciary in the Constitutional Reform Act 2005. Section 1 recognises the rule of law as an existing constitutional principle. The Act acknowledges the relationship between the independence of the judiciary and the rule of law in s. 3.

65. The rule of law is nothing if it fails to constrain overweening power. The Honourable J. J. Spigelman AC, Chief Justice of New South Wales, has described judges and lawyers as:

boundary riders maintaining the integrity of the fences that divide legal constraint from the sphere of freedom of action ... (Address on Judicial Independence to the 7th Worldwide Common Law Judicial Conference, April 2007.)

So too must the courts patrol the boundary between the territory which they safeguard and that for which the executive is responsible.

66. It is beyond question that had the Director decided to halt the investigation in response to a threat made by those susceptible to domestic jurisdiction, the court would have regarded the issues which arose as peculiarly within their sphere of responsibility.

67. We turn then to how the courts discharge that responsibility. The courts fulfil their primary obligation to protect the rule of law, by ensuring that a decision-maker on whom statutory powers are conferred, exercises those powers independently and without surrendering them to a third party.

68. No revolutionary principle needs to be created. Mindful of Mr Sales' minatory words, we can deploy well-settled principles of public law. In yielding to the threat, the Director ceased to exercise the power to make the independent judgment conferred on him by Parliament. There are many authorities which illustrate the proposition that by the surrender of independent judgment to a third party, a public body abdicates its responsibility (see *Fordham Judicial Review Handbook, 4th Edn*, 50.2, pp. 861-2). But we need look no further than *Sharma*:

It is well established that a decision to prosecute is ordinarily susceptible to judicial review, and surrender of what should be an independent prosecutorial decision to political instruction (*or the Board would add, persuasion or pressure*) is a recognised ground of review. (Governing Principles at [5], p. 788A (our emphasis).)

69. That line of well-established authority demonstrates how the courts protect the rule of law by ensuring the independence of the decision-maker, free from pressure and threat.

70. Independence is fundamental to the proper exercise of the Director's powers. Those authorities on which the Director relied to establish the width of his discretion support that proposition. One of the very bases for affording a prosecutor so wide an ambit of judgment is the recognition of his independence (see the references by Lord Bingham CJ to the independence of the Director of Public Prosecutions, answerable to the Attorney General and to no one else, and to the independent judgment of Treasury Counsel in *R* v. *DPP ex p Manning* [2001] 1 QB 330 at § 23). The Director of the SFO is answerable to no one. By the 1987 Act, Parliament has conferred on

him alone the power to reach an independent, professional judgment, subject only to the superintendence of the Attorney General. Whatever superintendence may mean, it does not permit the Attorney General to exert pressure on the Director, let alone make a decision in relation to an investigation which the Director wishes to pursue.

71. The reason why the executive, the Attorney General and the Director himself stress that the decision was for the Director alone is instructive. All appreciate that to make a decision under the influence of pressure would be to abdicate the responsibility to reach an independent, professional judgment, imposed by statute. The essential purpose of s. 1(2) of the 1987 Act is undermined if the Director's decision is made in submission to threats.

72. Mr Sales responds that the Director did exercise an independent judgment, in the light of the advice he received as to the dangers to national security were the threat to be carried out. But that is no answer at all. We accept that, in assessing the *consequences* of the threat, the Director exercised what may be described as independent judgment, notwithstanding its total reliance on the advice of others. But that misses the point. In halting the investigation he surrendered to a threat made with the specific intention of achieving surrender. We know he would not have done so but for the threat. He had not stopped the investigation throughout 2005. He was about to pursue it in Switzerland.

73. The Government's answer is that the courts are powerless to assist in resisting when the explicit threat has been made by a foreign state. Saudi Arabia is not under our control; accordingly the court must accept that there was nothing the Director could do, still less that the court can do now. Mr Sales said, as we have already recalled, that whilst it is a matter of regret, what happened was *a part of life*. The court cannot intervene but should leave the Government to judge the best course to adopt in response to the threat.

74. This dispiriting submission derived from the uncontroversial proposition that the courts in England will not adjudicate upon acts done abroad by virtue of sovereign authority (see *Buttes Gas* v. *Hammer* [1982] AC 888 at 931G-932F and *R* v. *Bow Street Magistrate ex p Pinochet (No 3)* [2000] 1 AC 147 at 210).

75. The legal relationships of the different branches of government and the separation of powers depend on internal constitutional arrangements. They are of no concern to foreign states (see Lord Millett in *R* v. *Lyons* [2003] 1 AC 976 at § 105).

76. Those decisions were not concerned with threats to the administration of justice within the United Kingdom. Such threats, as we have

sought to demonstrate, are particularly within the scope of the courts' responsibility. It is difficult to identify any integrity in the role of the courts to uphold the rule of law, if the courts are to abdicate in response to a threat from a foreign power.

77. Mr Sales' submission appears to us not to be one of principle but rather one of practicality: resistance is useless, the judgment of the Government is that the Saudi Arabian Government will not listen and the authorities in the United Kingdom must surrender. That argument reveals the extent to which the Government has failed to appreciate the role of the courts in upholding and protecting the rule of law.

78. The courts protect the rule of law by upholding the principle that when making decisions in the exercise of his statutory power an independent prosecutor is not entitled to surrender to the threat of a third party, even when that third party is a foreign state. The courts are entitled to exercise their own judgment as to how best they may protect the rule of law, even in cases where it is threatened from abroad. In the exercise of that judgment we are of the view that a resolute refusal to buckle to such a threat is the only way the law can resist.

79. Surrender deprives the law of any power to resist for the future. In *Ex p Phoenix Aviation*, Simon Brown LJ criticised the public authorities who failed to consider what he described as *the awesome implications for the rule of law*, and the inevitable impact upon the *ever more enthusiastic* future conduct of the protesters [p. 62]. The context of the threat, in the present case, was the investigation of making bribes to foreign public officials, an offence introduced in 2001. If the Government is correct, there exists a powerful temptation for those who wish to halt an investigation to make sure that their threats are difficult to resist. Surrender merely encourages those with power, in a position of strategic and political importance, to repeat such threats, in the knowledge that the courts will not interfere with the decision of a prosecutor to surrender. After all, it was that appreciation which, no doubt, prompted the representatives of the Saudi Arabian Government to deliver the threat. Had they known, or been told, that the threat was futile because any decision to cave in would be struck down by the courts, it might never have been uttered or it might have been withdrawn.

80. Certainly, for the future, those who wish to deliver a threat designed to interfere with our internal, domestic system of law, need to be told that they cannot achieve their objective. Any attempt to force a decision on those responsible for the administration of justice will fail, just as any similar attempt by the executive within the United Kingdom would fail.

81. Mr Sales suggests that the law must recognise that there are cases when the prosecutor has no choice but to accede to the threat. He draws attention to the case of Leila Khalid in 1970 (described by Edwards, in *The Attorney General, Politics and the Public Interest* (1984) p. 324). Khalid was a member of the PLO, in custody following her attempt to hijack an aeroplane. The PLO threatened to kill Swiss and German hostages, unless she was released. Sir Peter Rawlinson, the Attorney General, accepted the advice that prosecution would increase the danger to the lives of those hostages and ordered her release. Edwards describes the decision as *clearly defensible*, since the Attorney General was faced with the *awful dilemma of measuring the freedom and, possibly, the lives of the hostages against non-enforcement of the criminal law* (p. 325).

82. The release of Khalid was not the subject of any review by the courts. But we acknowledge that there may be circumstances so extreme that the necessity to save lives compels a decision not to detain or to prosecute. But it is for the courts to decide whether the reaction to a threat was a lawful response or an unlawful submission. As Simon Brown LJ recognised (*Ex p Phoenix* at p. 62, cited [above at] § 60) although the difference is difficult to define, it will be generally easy to recognise. And it is for the courts in drawing the line between unavoidable submission and unlawful surrender to review *with particular rigour* a decision and rule whether the decision-maker yielded *too readily*.

83. In the case of Khalid, those who had made the threat had the power to carry it out immediately; the Attorney General's choice was to release Khalid or let the foreign nationals whose governments were in the process of negotiations be killed. Both in domestic and in customary international law (as to which see below at § 144), the law recognises the defence of duress and, in some circumstances, the justification of necessity (see, e.g., the conjoined twins case at *Re A (children)* [2002] 4 All ER 961 and the discussion in *Smith & Hogan Criminal Law 11th Edn*, 314-25).

84. It is unnecessary for this court to attempt to identify those circumstances in which necessity may justify submission to a threat, designed to prevent a prosecutor from exercising his power to continue an investigation. There is no reported case of so blatant a threat. To say that the threat must be imminent merely opens the discussion as to what that means and what standard is to be applied to test the imminence of the threat. Mr Wardle says that *he felt he had no choice* (paragraph 50 of his first statement). It is for the court to assess whether he and the Government yielded too readily.

85. It was not suggested either in evidence or in argument that the threat to the lives of citizens and servicemen was to be likened to that made against the Swiss and German hostages in *Khalid*. There was, it is true, ample reference to direct threats to UK citizens (e.g. Prime Minister's minute of 8 December 2006 and the references to the risk described by the Ambassador). But we must recall that, unlike the Khalid incident, there was no specific, direct threat made against the life of anyone. The threat made was to withdraw co-operation in relation to counter-terrorism. In order to assess the risk to life, it is necessary to hypothesise that a terrorist outrage was planned within the United Kingdom or elsewhere against British citizens or servicemen, of which Saudi Arabian intelligence had become aware and which it deliberately withheld. We readily accept that in 2006 and even now there is a serious risk of unpredictable terrorist attack, the greater the sources of intelligence the better that may be avoided and, as we are told, Saudi Arabia remains an irreplaceable source. But those factors do not, in our view, require us to accept that the Director was faced with the same degree of compulsion as the Attorney General in *Khalid* had to confront.

86. Apart from the absence of a specific, immediate threat there is another significant feature. In order properly to scrutinise the decision taken to submit, the courts are bound to question whether all the steps which could reasonably be taken to divert the threat had been pursued. Absent such an inquiry, the courts are in no position to assess whether the decision-maker has yielded too readily. In *Khalid* it was plain that the dilemma was *awful*. It is difficult, at least on the information now disclosed in relation to *Khalid*, to see what other steps could have been taken after prolonged negotiations, short of military intervention. The facts as described show how imminent was the risk to life and why it was the Attorney General had no choice if he was to save the lives of the hostages.

87. Contrast the instant case. There is no evidence whatever that any consideration was given as to how to persuade the Saudis to withdraw the threat, let alone any attempt made to resist the threat. The Director did not himself consider this issue. His assessment of the threat and its consequences relied on the advice of others. There is nothing to suggest that those advising him on this issue had made any attempt to resist the threat. They merely transmitted the threat to the Director, and explained the consequences if it was carried out. When this question was raised, in argument, Mr Sales responded that that issue was not one which the defendant had come to court to meet. Moreover, he suggested the court should assume that due consideration

had been given as to whether the Saudis might be persuaded to withdraw their threat and as to how its consequences might be avoided.

88. We are not prepared to make any such assumption. It is not implicit in Mr Wardle's statement. The defendant and Government were well aware that the accusation was that they had surrendered too readily; it was for them to show not only that the consequences of the threat were dire but that the threat itself could not be mitigated or withdrawn. It was explicitly argued by the claimants, in the context of state necessity, that it cannot be plausibly asserted that the decision was the only means of safeguarding the state's interest against a grave and imminent peril:

There is no indication of any assessment by the UK of whether there were other means available to safeguard the UK's essential interest... (Paragraph 47(vi)(e) claimants' written submissions.)

89. This challenge was not met by any additional evidence either before the proceedings started or when the point was raised during the first day of oral argument. We accept that Mr Sales has had to look after the interests of four other departments, besides those of the Director. But if it was to be argued that the Director had no alternative, then to focus merely on the consequences of the threat, if it was carried out, was insufficient. It was incumbent on the Director, once it was alleged that he ought not to have succumbed to the threat, to satisfy the court that he had not given way without the resistance necessary to protect the rule of law.

90. No one suggested to those uttering the threat that it was futile, that the United Kingdom's system of democracy forbad pressure being exerted on an independent prosecutor whether by the domestic executive or by anyone else; no one even hinted that the courts would strive to protect the rule of law and protect the independence of the prosecutor by striking down any decision he might be tempted to make in submission to the threat. If, as we are asked to accept, the Saudis would not be interested in our internal, domestic constitutional arrangements, it is plausible they would understand the enormity of the interference with the United Kingdom's sovereignty, when a foreign power seeks to interfere with the internal administration of the criminal law. It is not difficult to imagine what they would think if we attempted to interfere with their criminal justice system.

91. The reason no attempt appears to have been made to persuade the Saudis that the threat could not succeed is not difficult to find. The response of the Case Controller on 19 December 2005 and of the Ministry of Defence detective superintendent (§ 42) never seems to

have reached the higher reaches of Government: to submit would damage the rule of law and the independence of the SFO. Mr Cowie spoke of *reputational* damage; but as Lawton and Brown LJJ understood, the damage is not merely to the reputation of the SFO and the Government but to the reputation and very existence of the rule of law. The evidence laid before us shows no sufficient appreciation of the damage to the rule of law caused by submission to a threat directed at the administration of justice.

92. In response to the challenge on the second ground we have identified (§ 49(ii)), Mr Wardle accepts that he did not take into account the damage to national security, the integrity of the criminal justice system and to the rule of law by discontinuing the investigation in response to the threat (first statement paragraph 58). He is bound to acknowledge that omission. Before the House of Lords Constitutional Committee he was asked by Mr Tyrie (Q246):

> What was your reaction when you discovered that another government, effectively, was putting a gun to our heads and saying, "You are not to investigate further, otherwise we will withdraw co-operation arrangements and leave your country less well defended"?
>
> My reaction was, I suppose, I was resigned to it.
>
> Q269 David Howarth: Does that also apply to the obvious problem which would flow from Mr Tyrie's question, which is that if other countries get to know that Britain gives in to this sort of pressure, that in itself could be a threat to our national security? Was that risk taken into account in the decision?
>
> Robert Wardle: No, it was not expressed in the risk, and I am not sure how much of a risk it really is. I think this was an exceptional case. We are continuing other investigations, both into BAE Systems Plc and into other areas, where we are doing our best to pursue them. I think that the risk of people thinking we can get away with it, which is effectively, I think, what you are saying, will be lessened if we are able to pursue those investigations, which we are, indeed, doing [3/1564].

93. The Director now asserts that although he did not consider the issue, it was considered at the meeting between the Prime Minister and the Attorney General on 11 December 2006, an assertion also made in his Amended Summary Grounds (§ 68). This is not borne out by the note of the meeting on 11 December 2006, at which the Attorney General's concern is recorded:

halting the investigation would send a bad message about the credibility of the law in this area and look like giving in to threats[, and]

It was important that the Government did not give people reason to believe that threatening the British system resulted in parties getting their way. But the Government also needed to consider the damage done to the credibility of the law in this area by a long and failed trial, and its good reputation on bribery and corruption issues compared with many of its international partners.

94. These passages reveal that the issue of damage to the rule of law was never properly considered. It was indeed important that *the British system* did not give way to threats but the response recorded is no answer to that issue; the discussion appears to have been diverted onto a different path, the adequacy of the evidence on which the Director's view differed from that of the Attorney General, nor does the reference to the Government's good reputation on bribery and corruption issues compared with many of its international partners begin to meet the issue of damage to the rule of law.

95. The Director's response in Committee (cited [above] at § 93) again misses the point; the suggestion was that damage to the criminal justice system could be alleviated by pursuing other investigations. But there is no suggestion that those other investigations were being pursued despite threats. A failure to resist a threat cannot be excused by demonstrating a willingness to prosecute absent such a threat. The question was how to avoid threats in the future; to say that other investigations will be pursued provides no answer, without assurance that any threat to stop an investigation would be resisted.

96. The issue for the Government and for the Attorney General, in the exercise of the task he acknowledged of *making sure the Government upholds the Rule of Law* (evidence to Constitutional Affairs Committee Q363 27 June 2007), was how the rule of law might be protected. The point was missed as to the effect on national security and on the rule of law of submission to the threat.

97. There can be no dispute as to the need for the courts to safeguard the integrity of the judicial process and to avoid bringing British justice into disrepute (Lord Brown's description of *A* v. *SSHD (No 2)* [2006] 2 AC 221 in *SSHD* v. *MB(FC)* [2007] UKHL at § 91). The fulfilment of that need is demonstrated in the recognition by the House of Lords in *A (No 2)* of the rule which excludes evidence obtained by torture, and their refusal to allow so fundamental a rule to be compromised even to fight terrorism. *A (No 2)* is an illustration of how the law demands that the means used to resist terrorism must be lawful. The different approaches, the one permitted to the executive, the other demanded of the judiciary, were explained by Lord Nicholls

(§§ 70-1). The demands on the judiciary stem from their obligation to enforce the rule of law.

98. Lest it be thought that there is any true distinction between national security and the rule of law, we need only refer to the Attorney General's adoption of the principle that preserving the rule of law constitutes an important component in the means by which democracy is secured (speech to the Cour de Cassation June 2004). This was echoed by the G8 communiqué (referred to [above] at § 45).

99. The principle we have identified is that submission to a threat is lawful only when it is demonstrated to a court that there was no alternative course open to the decision-maker. This principle seems to us to have two particular virtues.

100. Firstly, by restricting the circumstances in which submission may be endorsed as lawful, the rule of law may be protected. If one on whom the duty of independent decision is imposed may invoke a wide range of circumstances in which he may surrender his will to the dictates of another, the rule of law is undermined.

101. Secondly, as this case demonstrates, too ready a submission may give rise to the suspicion that the threat was not the real ground for the decision at all; rather it was a useful pretext. It is obvious, in the present case, that the decision to halt the investigation suited the objectives of the executive. Stopping the investigation avoided uncomfortable consequences, both commercial and diplomatic. Whilst we have accepted the evidence as to the grounds of this decision, in future cases, absent a principle of necessity, it would be all too tempting to use a threat as a ground for a convenient conclusion. We fear for the reputation of the administration of justice if it can be perverted by a threat. Let it be accepted, as the defendant's grounds assert, that this was an exceptional case; how does it look if on the one occasion in recent memory, a threat is made to the administration of justice, the law buckles? The Government Legal Service has every reason to be proud of its reputation for giving independent and, on occasion, unpalatable advice; but can that be maintained if in exceptional cases, when a threat comes from a powerful and strategically important ally, it must yield to pressure? Our courts and lawyers have the luxury and privilege of common law and statutory protection against power which threatens the rule of law. All the more important, then, that they provide support and encouragement to those in a less happy position. How do they do so, if they endorse surrender, when in Uganda the courts are forced to resist when those whom they have released on bail are re-arrested on the courtroom steps by armed agents of the executive, or when the Chief Justices of Fiji and Pakistan are deposed by military rulers?

102. The Director failed to appreciate that protection of the rule of law demanded that he should not yield to the threat. Nor was adequate consideration given to the damage to national security and to the rule of law by submission to the threat. No one took any steps to explain that the attempt to halt the investigation by making threats could not, by law, succeed. The Saudi threat would have been an exercise in futility, had anyone acknowledged that principle. We are driven to the conclusion that the Director's submission to the threat was unlawful.

Article 5

103. Throughout the period of 2005-6, during which the Director considered whether to halt the investigation, both he and the Attorney General were determined that the decision should be consistent with the United Kingdom's obligations under Article 5 of the OECD Convention. For convenience we set it out again, with emphasis added:

Investigation and prosecution of the bribery of a foreign public official shall be subject to the applicable rules and principles of each Party. They shall not be influenced by considerations of national economic interest, *the potential effect upon relations with another State* or the identity of the natural or legal persons involved.

104. The Legal Secretary to the Law Officers had made it clear, on 6 December 2005, that his consideration of the responses received from other departments as a result of the Shawcross exercise would be governed by Article 5. He recorded the Attorney General's assurance to the OECD Working Group in 2004 that none of the considerations prohibited by Article 5 would be taken into account as public interest factors not to prosecute foreign bribery cases. Neither the Attorney General nor the Director ever indicated that they would resile from that approach. On the contrary, when the decision to discontinue the investigation was taken on 14 December 2006, the Attorney General made it clear to Parliament that:

Article 5 of the OECD Convention . . . precludes me and the Serious Fraud Office from taking into account considerations of the national economic interest or the potential effect upon relations with another state, and we have not done so. (Hansard 14 December 2006, Col. 1712.)

This assurance was repeated to the OECD on 12 January 2007.

105. The claimants' essential argument is that the decision was taken because of the potential effect of the investigation upon relations

with another state. For that reason, the grounds upon which the decision was taken were contrary to the prohibition contained within Article 5. In taking the view that his decision to discontinue was compatible with Article 5, the Director mis-directed himself and erred in law.

Justiciability

106. Despite the repeated assertions that his decision was compatible with Article 5, the defendant contended that the court should not rule on whether the decision was compatible with the Convention. To do so would require the court to give its own view as to the meaning of Article 5 of the Convention. That Convention is an international instrument which does not form part of English law; consequently the court has no jurisdiction either to interpret it or to apply it.

107. The starting point for this submission must be the principle that municipal courts do not and cannot have competence to adjudicate upon or to enforce rights arising out of transactions entered into by independent sovereign states between themselves at the level of international law (see *JH Rayner (Mincing Lane) Limited* v. *Department of Trade and Industry* [1992] AC 418 at 499F-500D and *R* v. *Lyons* [2003] 1 AC 976 at § 27 and *R (Campaign for Nuclear Disarmament)* v. *Prime Minister & Others* [2002] EWHC 2777 (Admin) at § 23).

108. *CND* provides a useful benchmark against which to test the claimants' invitation to rule on the compatibility of the Director's decision with Article 5. In that case, CND sought declaratory relief by way of an advisory declaration as to the true meaning of Resolution 1441 at a time when it feared that the UK Government would take military action against Iraq without a further Resolution. It is important to note that the Government had not itself publicly declared any definitive view of the position in international law. The court was being asked to interpret an international instrument, not incorporated into English domestic law, in circumstances where no right, interest or duty under domestic law required determination (see § 36).

109. Further, in circumstances in which the Government had not given any view as to the legal effect of Resolution 1441, to require the court to give its interpretation would damage the United Kingdom's interests in international relations, themselves a forbidden area (see §§ 41 and 42).

110. In the course of his judgment Simon Brown LJ contrasted that application with a case where it is necessary to examine an international convention for the purpose of reviewing the legality of the decision

under domestic law (see § 36). Richards J, in concurring, identified what he described as a further exception to the basic rule enunciated in *Lyons*:

Where a decision-maker has expressly taken into account an international treaty and the court thinks it appropriate to examine the correctness of the self-direction or advice on which the decision is based. (§ 61(iv).)

111. He contrasted that exception with CND's application in which the Government had avoided any direction on the interpretation of Resolution 1441.

112. Further, it is important not to overlook the context in which it is said that the court should depart from the basic rule that national courts have no jurisdiction to interpret or apply international treaties. Since there is no domestic legal obligation which expressly requires the Director to take into account Article 5 of the Convention, we are prepared to accept, for the purposes of these submissions, that it was for him to decide whether it was a relevant consideration for his decision, not for the court (see, e.g., *R (Al Rawi)* v. *Foreign Secretary* [2007] 2 WLR 1219 at 1269 §§ 131-2). But we add this caveat: in view of the Attorney General's assurance to the OECD Working Group in 2004, a failure to have regard to the Convention would probably have been flawed on the basis that it was an "obviously material" consideration: see *In re Findlay* [1985] AC 318 at 334.

113. The authorities which Richards J described as a further exception were *R* v. *Secretary of State for the Home Department ex p Launder* [1997] 1 WLR 839, 867C-F and *R* v. *Director of Public Prosecutions ex p Kebilene* [2002] AC 326, 341 and 367E-H. As Richards J pointed out, both of them were cases where the court had regard to the European Convention on Human Rights before the Human Rights Act 1998 came into force. These cases do no more, submits Mr Sales, than establish the limited grounds upon which the courts may derogate from the basic rule enunciated in *Lyons*.

114. In *Launder* the question relevant for the purposes of this application was the extent to which the court could review the Secretary of State's decision to extradite an accused if to do so would violate the accused's rights under the European Convention prior to the incorporation of that Convention into United Kingdom law. The accused had contended that the legal, penal and judicial system in Hong Kong, after 1 July 1997, would not protect his right to a fair trial and, if convicted, to appropriate punishment. The Secretary of State had asserted that he had taken account of the applicant's representations that extradition to Hong Kong would be a breach of the

Convention in reaching his decision that he should be extradited. The court took the view that the Secretary of State was entitled to reach the conclusion that there was no serious risk of injustice or oppression and had not overlooked what he described as the Human Rights context (p. 869A-B).

115. In reaching that conclusion Lord Hope pointed out that prior to incorporation, whilst the Convention might influence the common law, it did not bind the executive. He continued:

The whole context of the dialogue between the Secretary of State and the applicant in this case was the risk of an interference in the applicant's human rights. That in itself is a ground for subjecting the decisions to the most anxious scrutiny ... then there is the question whether judicial review proceedings can provide the applicant with an effective remedy, as Article 13 requires, where complaints are raised under the Convention in extradition and deportation cases ... If the applicant is to have an effective remedy against a decision which is flawed because the decision-maker has mis-directed himself on the Convention which he himself says he took into account, he must surely be right to examine the substance of the argument. The ordinary principles of judicial review permit this approach because it was to the rationality and legality of the decisions, and not to some independent remedy that Mr Vaughan directed his argument. (867C-F.)

116. Mr Sales contended that that passage, which provides the foundation for the claimants' arguments, also sets the boundaries to the circumstances in which the court is permitted to interpret an international instrument for the purposes of considering whether a domestic decision is compatible with the International Convention. It identifies four conditions which must be satisfied before it is appropriate for the court to do so. They are said, by Mr Sales, to be demonstrated in the passage of Lord Hope's speech which we have already cited:

(i) that the decision relates to an individual's human rights where domestic law requires anxious scrutiny of the grounds upon which the decision was taken;
(ii) that the Treaty obligation requires the domestic legal order to produce a remedy;
(iii) that there exists an authoritative legally developed jurisprudence as a source of interpretation. In *Launder* (and in *R* v. *Director of Public Prosecutions ex p Kebilene* [2002] AC 326) the court was able to draw upon the authority of the European Court of Human Rights. Absent such an authoritative source domestic courts would only be arrogating to themselves a power which rests only in an international authority;

(iv) even if those conditions were satisfied, the subject matter of the case, in the instant application foreign relations and national security, may be such as to require the courts to refrain from intervention.

117. *Ex p Kebilene* adopts the principles identified by Lord Hope in *Ex p Launder*. In *Kebilene* the question was whether the court could review the soundness of the advice on the basis of which the DPP consented to the prosecution of the applicants under the Prevention of Terrorism (Temporary Provisions) Act 1989. The Director had sought advice as to whether s. 16A was compatible with the European Convention on Human Rights. Lord Bingham CJ took the view that it was appropriate for the court to review the legal advice:

... on which the Director has made clear, publicly, that he relied; for if the legal advice he relied on was unsound he should, in the public interest, have the opportunity to reconsider the confirmation of his consent on a sound legal basis. (P. 341E.)

He considered that that approach was compatible with Lord Hope's observations and *Ex p Launder*. Lord Steyn endorsed that approach although he cited only a short portion of the speech of Lord Hope, referring to the need for an effective remedy (367E-G and Lord Hope at 375F-376A).

118. Under ordinary principles of public law a court may be required to determine the lawfulness of a self-direction or advice on which a decision is based. Where that self-direction or advice turns on a point of interpretation of an international instrument then the court may be compelled to consider the correctness of that interpretation. But in doing so, it is not purporting to do any more than assess the legality of the decision under domestic law. As Lord Hope put it, in doing so, the court is doing no more than reviewing the rationality and legality of the decision by testing that decision against the standard which the decision-maker has chosen to adopt. A court may only interpret an international instrument in the context of reviewing the legality of a decision under domestic law and only for that purpose (see Simon Brown LJ at paragraph 36 in *CND*).

119. In the instant application, the Director has chosen, publicly (to echo Lord Bingham's description of the decision of the Director in *Kebilene*), to justify his decision by reference to Article 5. The public justification for the decision depended upon the assertion that it was necessary to discontinue the investigation for reasons which were compatible with Article 5, that is, national security. In order to achieve

public acceptance of a controversial decision, he invoked compliance with the UK's international obligations under Article 5. If the Director mis-directed himself as to such compatibility then his public justification and reasons for the decision are flawed. The fact that the Attorney General and Director chose to justify the decision by invoking compatibility with the Convention entitles this court to review the legality of the decision under ordinary domestic law principles. For example, if it could be demonstrated that the true reason for the decision was commercial, contrary to the assertion of the Director, then that decision would be susceptible to review on the grounds that no reasonable decision-maker could have reached that view.

120. Nor do we think that the court should refrain from assessing compliance with Article 5, because of the reference to *the potential effect on relations with another* state. We accept that assessment of the potential effect of relations with another state is a matter for Government and not for the courts. Since the public justification for this decision was that it was not taken under the influence of the potential effect upon relations with another state, the court is entitled to assess the legality of the decision, because that requires consideration of the scope of the prohibition. By reason of the grounds upon which the Director and the Attorney General have publicly chosen to rely, the court is not debarred, on the grounds of trespass into a forbidden area, from seeking to interpret the Convention in determining the legality of the exercise of the Director's discretion under domestic law; we distinguish *CND* where no domestic law issue arose.

121. There is a further ground which affords justification for the court to venture upon an interpretation of the Convention. It is true, as Mr Sales points out, that the Convention, unlike the European Convention on Human Rights, does not require any effective domestic remedy. But Article 1 of the Convention requires the parties to create a criminal offence for the bribery of a foreign public official. Section 109 of the Anti-terrorism, Crime and Security Act 2001 was brought into force for the very purpose of complying with the UK's obligation under Article 1. In those circumstances the exercise of discretion, whether to continue to investigate or to prosecute in a manner which undermines the very purpose for which the criminal offence was created, seems to us a matter susceptible to the review of the courts. Parliament has chosen to honour the UK's international obligation under Article 1 and the decision of the Director ought to be considered in that context.

122. In the light of our view that we are doing no more than applying ordinary public law principles to the decision we turn then to the interpretation of Article 5.

The absence of any reference to national security in the Convention

123. The claimants adopt the position that absent any express reference to national security it was not open to the Director to discontinue the investigation on national security grounds.

124. It is true that a number of bilateral and multilateral treaties to which the United Kingdom is a party refer specifically to national security (e.g., the bilateral 1994 Treaty between the USA and the United Kingdom on Mutual Legal Assistance in Criminal Matters (Article 3(1)) and the multilateral 1966 International Covenant on Civil and Political Rights).

125. The flaw in this argument is that Article 5 preserves *the applicable rules and principles of each party* by which investigation and prosecution of the bribery of a foreign public official are to be pursued. In the case of three of the Contracting Parties, the United Kingdom, Canada and Germany, the OECD Working Group on Bribery in International Business Transactions (the WGB) has evaluated their applicable rules. We shall return later to the importance of the WGB in ensuring compliance under Article 12 of the Convention. In Canada, as in the United Kingdom, the prosecutorial code refers to disclosure which might harm international relations or security. We were informed that the WGB had raised no objection to either code. In German domestic law, proceedings may be discontinued in circumstances where there is a risk of a severe disadvantage for Germany or an overriding public interest against prosecution. The OECD Review of Implementation described those provisions as references mainly to offences involving national security interests (see p. 11 of the OECD Review). The WGB recorded that those provisions complied with the standards of the Convention (p. 19). Since the wide discretion of the prosecutor is preserved in the opening sentence of Article 5, there was, in our view, no need for specific reference to national security.

126. Further, the right of a State to protect its security in the sense of protecting the lives of its citizens against terrorism is fundamental. As the PCIJ put it in the case of the *SS Wimbledon* (PCIJ Reports Series A No 1 (1923) p. 37):

The right of a State to adopt the course which it considers best suited to the exigencies of its security and to the maintenance of its integrity, is so essential a right that in case of doubt, treaty stipulations cannot be interpreted as limiting it, even though those stipulations do not conflict with such an interpretation.

127. Associated with the right of a state to take those measures which it considers necessary to protect its citizens, is the importance of

those international norms which protect human rights and, in particular, the right to life. Some norms have a special or privileged status because of their content (see "Higgins, President of the International Court of Justice" [2006] ICLQ 800). Their special or privileged status is recognised by international law in the maxim that a general provision does not derogate from a special one. The right to life is expressed in Article 3 of the Universal Declaration of Human Rights, 1948, Article 6 of the International Covenant on Civil and Political Rights (1966) and, of course, Article 2 of the ECHR. The obligation of a government in a democratic society to protect and safeguard the lives of its citizens was, as we have already recalled, described by Lord Hope as essential to the preservation of democracy.

128. Accordingly, we reject the claimants' contention that because the Convention makes no specific reference to national security, in the sense of protecting and safeguarding the lives of UK citizens and soldiers, it was a prohibited consideration.

129. But that does not dispose of the issue. Article 31(1) of the Vienna Convention on the Law of Treaties requires that:

A treaty should be interpreted in good faith in accordance with the ordinary meaning to be given to the terms of the treaty in that context and in the light of its object and purpose.

130. In order to achieve the objective of the Convention, two features are essential. Firstly, that some distinction is drawn between national security, consideration of which is not excluded by Article 5, and *the potential effect upon relations with another state*. Unless a distinction is drawn, Article 5 is deprived of any sensible effect. Secondly, that distinction must be applied in a manner which is uniform throughout the Contracting Parties. Without uniformity of standards, the Convention cannot achieve its objective: uniformity of standards requires uniformity of interpretation.

The distinction between national security and relations with another state

131. We deal first with the distinction on which the efficacy of Article 5 depends. Reliance upon the commentary adopted by the negotiating conference on the same day as the OECD Convention is relevant, either pursuant to Article 31(3)(b) of the Vienna Convention as declarations constituting state practice, or as part of the context under Article 31(1), or as a supplementary means of interpretation under Article 32. Paragraph 6 of the Annex to the 1997 OECD Revised Recommendation, which the commentaries describe as

complementing Article 5, states that prosecutorial discretion should not be influenced by consideration of national economic interest and *fostering good political relations.*

132. That commentary does not seem to us to be of assistance in determining how to distinguish between being influenced by considerations of the potential effect upon relations with another state and being influenced by fears for national security. Yet, if the reference to the potential effect upon relations with another state in Article 5 is to have any effective content, a line must be drawn.

133. The very context of the Convention demonstrates how important it is to draw that line. The context is the intention of one state to investigate and prosecute bribery of a public official of another state. The purpose of the Convention is to ensure that the Contracting Parties resist a damaging reaction by a state which wishes to avoid the investigation and prosecution of its public official. The Convention foresees that the reaction of the other state may be to threaten to damage the investigating state's economic interests, and to impede co-operation. A foreign state whose public official is under investigation, is likely, if it wishes to escape investigation, to deploy threats to the relationship with the investigating state in the most effective way it can. If that foreign state is powerful and of strategic importance, it is all the more likely that one of the effects of a deterioration in relations will be damage to the national security of the investigating state by a diminution or withdrawal of co-operation in intelligence, nowadays an essential currency of the exchange between states which share a friendly relationship.

134. The defendant's submissions demonstrate the difficulty in making any distinction. He contends (at § 66 of the written argument) that it matters not if the cause of the damage to national security is a deterioration in relations with the foreign state. He contends that "it cannot plausibly be supposed" that the contracting states intended that that causal mechanism should be taken to govern the ability of the investigating state to base its decision on national security.

135. Moreover, the facts of this investigation in 2005 and 2006 demonstrate the difficulty in drawing the line between a consideration which may properly influence the prosecutor and that which is proscribed by Article 5. The reasons given, in the representations to the Attorney General of the Government, are replete with references to the effect on relations with Saudi Arabia. The letter dated 29 September 2006 referred back to the response of Government to the Shawcross exercise on 16 December 2005. That response in December 2005 referred not only to the Al-Yamamah Air Defence Programme but:

the importance of relations with Saudi Arabia, in terms of the UK national interest, range more widely. The central consideration is the potential impact on our national security and particularly as regards our counter-terrorism work, and the broader search for stability in the Middle East.

The letter of 29 September 2006 referred to:

very strong indications that the severe damage to the public interest (over and above that to the national economic interest covered by Article 5 ....) we feared was likely in December 2005 is now imminent. If the Saudis are already starting to take such steps in relation to the Typhoon programme, then we must anticipate that they could follow though [*sic*] then [redaction] in relation to counter-terrorism *and the bilateral relationship*. (Our emphasis.)

It is noteworthy that the Cabinet Secretary appears to have overlooked that not only the national economic interest but also what he calls the "bilateral relationship" was covered by Article 5.

136. The personal minute from the Prime Minister dated 8 December 2006 spoke of the real and immediate risk of collapse not only in security and intelligence but also in diplomatic co-operation. The minute acknowledged that Article 5 covered not only influence by consideration of national economic interest but also the potential effect upon relations with another state. It explained the damage to UK national security, consequential on:

... our exchanges with the Saudi authorities in countering international terrorism; and the Government's highest foreign policy priority of working towards peace and stability in the Middle East. As you will know, it is my strong belief that our Middle East work is fundamentally also a matter of our national security.

137. The attachments to the minute make clear that it is the breakdown in a joint approach with the Saudi authorities in relation to the Middle East which would cause consequential damage to national security. This is emphasised in the attachments to the minute, particularly from Sir Richard Mottram, who speaks of the danger if the Saudis withdrew co-operation that the United Kingdom would be denied the support of a "key partner in our Global counter-terrorist strategy". The second attachment, the letter from the Permanent Under-Secretary, speaks of the dramatic impact withdrawal of Saudi co-operation on Middle East issues would have on the UK's ability to pursue its objectives in the region. The UK depends on Saudi Arabian support in advancing its policies on Israel and Palestine. Saudi Arabia had potential to act as a moderating influence in what he described as a highly charged region.

138. The letter, dated 12 December 2006, records the Prime Minister's fear that if Saudi Arabia lost the confidence it placed in the UK, it would very seriously damage the UK's national interest in what he describes as the fields of counter-terrorism and the search for peace and stability in the Middle East. The Prime Minister's summary linked the UK counter-terrorist effort, Middle East diplomacy and what he describes as other important aspects of the relationship with Saudi Arabia.

139. The causal connection between damage to the relationship with Saudi Arabia and damage to national security was echoed in the Attorney General's references to the views of the Prime Minister and the Foreign and Defence Secretaries which he repeated in the House of Lords on 14 December 2006:

They have expressed the clear view that continuation of the investigation would cause serious damage to UK/Saudi security, intelligence and diplomatic co-operation, which is likely to have seriously negative consequences for the United Kingdom public interest in terms of both national security and our highest priority foreign policy objectives in the Middle East.

He then continued, in the passage we have already quoted, by assuring Parliament that those considerations precluded by Article 5 had not been taken into account.

140. This evidence again demonstrates the difficulty of distinguishing between consideration of the potential effect upon relations with another state and consideration of national security. National security is, to a significant extent, dependent upon co-operation with other states. That co-operation is dependent on fostering or maintaining good relations. If the investigating state depends upon good relations with the foreign state whose public official it seeks to investigate for its own national security, Article 5 seems to have little, if any, utility. It is all too easy for a state which wishes to maintain good relations with another state whose official is under investigation to identify some potential damage to national security should good relations deteriorate, all the more so where that other state is powerful and of strategic importance.

Uniformity of interpretation

141. Article 5 recognises how susceptible each of the contracting Parties may be to permitting self-interest to overcome the need to combat bribery. Only by multilateral co-operation and uniformity

can the object of the Convention to stamp out bribery in international business transactions be achieved:

> ... recognising that achieving equivalence among the measures to be taken by the Parties is an essential object and purpose of the Convention, which requires that the Convention should be ratified without derogations affecting this equivalence ... (See 8th preamble.)

142. Self-interest is bound to have the tendency to defeat the eradication of international bribery. The Convention is deprived of effect unless competitors are prepared to adopt the same discipline. The state which condones bribery in its economic or diplomatic self-interest will merely step into the commercial shoes of the states which honour their commitment. Unless a uniform distinction is drawn between the potential effect upon relations with another state and national security, some signatories of the Convention will be able to escape its discipline by relying upon a broad definition of national security, thus depriving the prohibited consideration of the effect upon relations with another state of any force.

State necessity

143. The solution offered by the claimants is more likely to achieve uniformity and the objective of the Convention by closely defining the circumstances in which considerations of the potential effect on relations with another state may be taken into account, notwithstanding Article 5, because of the potential impact on an investigating state's national security. It does so by invoking the doctrine of necessity in customary international law which is recognised as excusing a state from a breach of its international obligation or, as it is put in the *argot* of international law, as precluding the wrongfulness of an act not in conformity with an international obligation.

144. The source of this submission is Article 25 of the International Law Commission's Draft Articles on State Responsibility. Article 25 provides that:

> 1. Necessity may not be invoked by a State as a ground for precluding the wrongfulness of an act not in conformity with an international obligation of that State unless the act:
>
> (a) Is the only way for the State to safeguard an essential interest against a grave and imminent peril; and
> (b) Does not seriously impair an essential interest of the State or States towards which the obligation exists, or of the international community as a whole.

2. In any case, necessity may not be invoked by a State as a ground for precluding wrongfulness if:

(a) The international obligation in question excludes the possibility of invoking necessity; or
(b) The State has contributed to the situation of necessity.

145. It is important to appreciate that this doctrine of necessity only arises where a state has not acted in conformity with an international obligation. The doctrine does not provide that there has been no breach, but that the state is not responsible for that breach. Thus the conditions under which a state may escape the consequences of its breach of an international obligation are narrowly defined. It applies only to exceptional cases where:

The only way a state can safeguard an essential interest threatened by grave and imminent peril is, for the time being, not to perform some other international obligation of lesser weight or urgency. (See the commentary to the ILC articles, Report of the ILC 53rd Session 2001 at 80.)

146. In the case concerning the *Gabčíkovo–Nagymaros* project (International Court of Justice Judgment of 25 September 1997) the International Court of Justice confirmed that those strict conditions reflect customary international law.

147. The doctrine of necessity provides a clear basis for distinguishing between those decisions which are influenced by the potential effect upon relations with a foreign state and those decisions which, while they are influenced by those considerations, are nevertheless justified by national security. A prosecutor would only be able to discontinue an investigation or prosecution in circumstances where that was the only means of protecting the security of its citizens. Moreover, such an approach would achieve uniformity since each of the contracting states would be required to bring itself within the strict conditions identified in Article 25 before it could justify its action. That uniformity would be enhanced by the principle identified by the ICJ in *Gabčíkovo–Nagymaros* that the state in question cannot be the sole judge of whether the conditions of necessity had been met (see paragraph 51).

148. The only way, as we see it, of achieving the purpose of Article 5 is to permit consideration of national security only in circumstances which on an international plane would be regarded as justifying the defence of state necessity. We can see no other way of distinguishing national security and relations with another state.

149. Were such a distinction not to be drawn, in every case where an investigating state fears that the consequences of a deteriorating relationship will be a loss of intelligence co-operation and consequential damage to national security, the investigating state will be able to withdraw. The feared consequences to national security were caused by the fear of loss of Saudi co-operation in counter-intelligence. But that counter-intelligence was only a part, if an essential part, of the UK's relations with Saudi Arabia. There is no rational means of distinguishing between the counter-intelligence relationship and any other aspect of the relationship between the UK and Saudi Arabia. The sharing of intelligence information was integral, as all the advice and memoranda from Government emphasised, to the relationship between Saudi Arabia and the UK.

Conclusion on Article 5

150. Before we base any decision on that ground, we must recall that we are a national court exercising jurisdiction in relation to a domestic decision. If each of the Contracting Parties draws a line between that which is a permitted consideration and that which is forbidden, the objective of uniform discipline cannot be achieved. The Convention provides its own mechanism for uniform interpretation and compliance in Article 12:

The Parties shall co-operate in carrying out a programme of systematic followup to monitor and promote the full implementation of this Convention. Unless otherwise decided by consensus of the Parties, this shall be done in the framework of the OECD Working Group on Bribery in International Business Transactions and according to its terms of reference ...

151. A Foreign and Commonwealth official, Nigel Dickerson, has described the defence advanced by the Government to the WGB's investigation of the decision to discontinue and Phase 2(bis) of WBG's continuing assessment. Mr Dickerson is anxious to ensure that the UK's defence is not hampered by any decision of this court.

152. As Miss Rose QC points out, the considerations which inhibited this court's intervention in *CND* are not the same. In that case the UK had not purported to give any interpretation of the international instrument. In this case, the UK has invoked the Article in its public domestic defence of its decision. Moreover, it has informed the WGB of these proceedings, and told the WGB that the question whether the Director's decision "was compatible with Article 5 ... is therefore now likely to be determined by the English High Court". In

these circumstances, we would not regard the fact that the UK now has to defend itself at an international level as a ground for precluding this court from assessing the legality of the decision in accordance with domestic law.

153. But there are two considerations which seem to us to compel a cautious, perhaps pusillanimous approach. Firstly, we have emphasised the need for uniformity. That requires that the line between that which is permitted and that which is precluded be drawn in a manner which is authoritative and uniform. The Contracting Parties have invested the authority to draw that line not on the domestic courts of those Parties but on the WGB. If this court was to strike down the decision by deciding where the line should be drawn it would damage the uniformity on which the Convention depends. Miss Rose contended that there can only be one meaning to the Convention. We agree, but to the extent that it is a matter of interpretation, the words of demarcation must have an autonomous meaning, and that is for the WGB, through which the Contracting Parties achieve consensus.

154. Secondly, a ruling on Article 5 is not necessary for our decision. We have already concluded that under conventional domestic law principles, the Director's decision was unlawful. A decision as to Article 5 is not, therefore, necessary.

155. We must recall that the question we have to consider is whether Mr Wardle misdirected himself as to the meaning of Article 5. He has made no attempt to explain how he drew the distinction between being influenced by considerations of the potential effect on relations with Saudi Arabia and being influenced by fears for national security. He merely asserts that *he was not influenced by the potential effect upon relations with another state* (§ 48). His addition of the coda *per se* is not illuminating, nor are we enlightened by his statement in the next sentence:

I understood, of course, that continuing the investigation would damage the UK's relations with Saudi Arabia, but, in and of itself, that consideration did not concern me.

156. The Director appears to be making a distinction between fears of damage to the UK's relations and fears of the consequences of such damage. But that does not assist in identifying that which is permitted and that which is prohibited by Article 5. In every case an investigating state will be concerned as to the consequences of damage to its relations with the other state. Those consequences might deter an investigating state, absent the prohibition in Article 5. Although we have grave doubts as to whether Article 5 can achieve its objective if a distinction

is drawn between considerations of national security and consideration of the effect on relations with another state, we have also acknowledged that the Convention has not excluded considerations of national security. Thus we have accepted that there is a distinction; the difficulty lies in making it.

157. Faced with the WGB's apparent endorsement of the domestic rules and principles of prosecutions in the UK, Canada and Germany and absent any further ruling of the WGB, we express no concluded view as to whether it was open to the Director to take the view that his decision was in compliance with Article 5. The Government will have to defend itself before the court of the WGB. It will be for that body to determine whether it was open to the UK to yield to the explicit threat, which we note does not appear in Mr Dickerson's description given to the WGB in January and March 2007 (see § 6 of his statement).

158. Because we have deliberately drawn back from reaching a conclusion on this ground we are spared any comment on the unattractive alternative submission that, despite seeking public acceptance of the decision by invoking Article 5, the Director is entitled to pray in aid his subsequent evidence that he would have made the same decision, even if to do so would have involved acting in breach of the Convention. If the fight against international bribery and corruption is to succeed, there must surely be transparency in the standards which are to be applied in deciding whether to investigate and prosecute, and rigour in the way they are interpreted. But we must remind ourselves that neither an absence of transparency nor [one] of rigour, without more, is a ground for judicial review.

Other issues

159. The claimants focused on the three issues we have already covered. We shall follow its course and dispose briefly of two of the remaining submissions. They contended (issue iv) that the Director ought to have taken into account Saudi Arabia's threatened breach of its own international law obligations.

160. Our discussion of the principles relating to Article 5 provides the answer. Firstly, it was for the Director to determine those considerations relevant to his decision to discontinue, subject to his obligation to exercise the power conferred on him by the 1987 Act (see our previous reference to *Al Rawi* at § 56). Secondly, it is not for this court to determine whether the Saudi threat to withdraw co-operation breached Security Council Resolution 1373/2001 (see, e.g., *Buttes Gas* at 931G-932F). However, the fact that no consideration appears

to have been given by either the Attorney General or the Director as to whether it could properly be contended in response to the threat that carrying it out would be contrary to Resolution 1373/2001 is a further illustration of the lack of any resistance to the threat.

161. The submission (issue v) that the advice on public interest from ministers during the Shawcross exercise was tainted by reference to matters proscribed by Article 5 misses the target. Ministers could not and did not make the decision impugned. The WGB will decide whether the Director was influenced by considerations outwith Article 5.

162. But we are not surprised that the allegation is made. Since, as we have already indicated, the Director has failed to explain how he distinguished between the influence of a consideration of the potential effect on relations between Saudi Arabia and considerations of national security, no one can be confident that he maintained that distinction in reaching his conclusion. But that does not entitle us to reject his assurance that he was not influenced by considerations which were in his view prohibited by Article 5. The Director has escaped judgment on this issue because we have accepted that there is a distinction and that it is for the WGB to determine where the boundary is to be defined.

163. The final challenge (issue vi) complains that ministers breached the rules announced by the Attorney General, Sir Hartley Shawcross, on 29 January 1951. The Shawcross rules require ministers to limit their observations to informing the Attorney General of considerations which may affect his decision; they should not tell him what his decision should be. The Prime Minister, so it is alleged, broke the rules by forcefully expressing his opinion that the investigation should be halted.

164. A number of hotly contested issues arise in relation to the Shawcross exercise. It is disappointing to record that we do not need to resolve them. The starting point is a dispute as to the content of those rules. The claimants rely on the statement by Sir Hartley to the House of Commons (Hansard 29 January 1951, Vol. 483, Cols. 683-4):

I think the true doctrine is that it is the duty of an Attorney General, in deciding whether or not to authorise the prosecution, to acquaint himself with all the relevant facts, including, for instance, the effect which the prosecution, successful or unsuccessful as the case may be, would have upon public morale and order, and with any other considerations affecting public policy.

In order so to inform himself, he may, although I do not think he is obliged to, consult with any of his colleagues in the Government; and indeed, as Lord Simon once said, he would in some cases be a fool if he did not. On the other hand, the assistance of his colleagues is confined to informing him of particular considerations which might affect his own decision, and does not consist, and must not consist, in telling him what the decision ought to be. The responsibility for the eventual decision rests with the Attorney General, and he is not to be put, and is not put, under pressure by his colleagues in the matter.

165. The Government interpret this statement as meaning that ministers must not instruct the Attorney General to make a particular decision, must not direct him what his decision ought to be. But there is no objection to their giving an opinion as to where they think the public interest lies. Indeed, the head of the Legal Secretariat to the Attorney General recalls a number of previous occasions, as do his predecessors, when opinions as to where the public interest lay have been vigorously expressed.

166. Both interpretations may be respectably derived from the original statement (as both Edwards *op. cit.* 323-4 and Marshall in *Constitutional Conventions, The Rules and Forms of Political Accountability* (1993) pp. 113-14 acknowledge). There might, we venture to suggest, be some advantage in public clarification of what the Government, in submission, suggests is an ambiguity in the existing statement. But we take the view that it is not for this court to resolve for the following reasons.

167. In even the most forceful expression of views, the Prime Minister made it clear that the decision was for the Attorney General and the Director. The Director has stated that he formed his own judgment and we accept his assurance. In those circumstances, the interesting question whether, even if a breach of the rules could be established, such a breach is justiciable does not fall to be resolved.

168. The significant feature of this argument lies in the repeated assertion that, as the Prime Minister acknowledged, the decision was for the independent judgment of the Director. However the Shawcross rules are to be interpreted, the danger which flows from the Government's expression of too vigorous an opinion, is that it makes it all the more difficult for the independent decision-maker clearly to demonstrate that his decision was exercised independently and free from what Sir Hartley describes as *pressure by his colleagues*. The rationale behind the Shawcross rules is the need to preserve independence of judgment and the freedom from pressure which such independence requires.

169. How piquant it is, then, that the more the defendant stresses that he reached a conclusion free from pressure imposed by the UK Government, the more he demonstrates the inconsistency in submitting to pressure applied by the government of a foreign state. We have identified a principle of law which seeks to protect him from both.

Conclusion

170. The claimants succeed on the ground that the Director and Government failed to recognise that the rule of law required the decision to discontinue to be reached as an exercise of independent judgment, in pursuance of the power conferred by statute. To preserve the integrity and independence of that judgment demanded resistance to the pressure exerted by means of a specific threat. That threat was intended to prevent the Director from pursuing the course of investigation he had chosen to adopt. It achieved its purpose.

171. The court has a responsibility to secure the rule of law. The Director was required to satisfy the court that all that could reasonably be done had been done to resist the threat. He has failed to do so. He submitted too readily because he, like the executive, concentrated on the effects which were feared should the threat be carried out and not on how the threat might be resisted. No one, whether within this country or outside, is entitled to interfere with the course of our justice. It is the failure of Government and the defendant to bear that essential principle in mind that justifies the intervention of this court. We shall hear further argument as to the nature of such intervention. But we intervene in fulfilment of our responsibility to protect the independence of the Director and of our criminal justice system from threat. On 11 December 2006, the Prime Minister said that this was the clearest case for intervention in the public interest he had seen. We agree.

[Report: Transcript]

[The following is the text of the speeches delivered in the House of Lords:]

JUDGMENT OF THE HOUSE OF LORDS

LORD BINGHAM OF CORNHILL

1. The issue in this appeal is whether a decision made by the appellant, the Director of the Serious Fraud Office, on 14 December 2006, to discontinue a criminal investigation was unlawful. The Queen's Bench Divisional Court (Moses LJ and Sullivan J) held it to be so: [2008] EWHC 714 (Admin). That court accordingly quashed the Director's decision and remitted it to him for reconsideration. In this appeal to the House the Director contends, as he contended below, that the decision was not unlawful. Mr Robert Wardle, the Director

who made the decision under review, has now been succeeded in his office, but this change of office-holder does not affect the issue to be decided. The respondents are public interest organisations. The House has received written submissions on behalf of JUSTICE.

The facts

2. By sections 108-10 of the Anti-terrorism, Crime and Security Act 2001 it was made an offence triable here for a UK national or company to make a corrupt payment or pay a bribe to a public officer abroad. The payment or bribe must not be authorised or approved by the officer's principal. The enactment of these sections gave effect to the UK's obligation under the OECD Convention on Combating Bribery of Foreign Public Officials in International Business Transactions (1997).

3. Under section 1(3) and (5) of the Criminal Justice Act 1987 the Director "may investigate any suspected offence which appears to him on reasonable grounds to involve serious or complex fraud", and "may ... institute and have the conduct of any criminal proceedings which appear to him to relate to such fraud". In performing his functions the Director is subject to the superintendence of the Attorney General (section 1(2) of the Act). On 29 July 2004 the Director, as authorised by section 1(3), launched an investigation into allegations of corruption against BAE Systems Plc. That company has observed but not participated in these proceedings. No finding has been made against it. One aspect of the investigation concerned what is known as the Al-Yamamah contract, a valuable arms contract between Her Majesty's Government and the Kingdom of Saudi Arabia for which BAE was the main contractor. The contract contained a confidentiality clause binding on both Governments. A valuable extension to the contract, providing for the supply of Typhoon aircraft, was in course of negotiation in 2004-6. Between 30 July 2004 and 14 December 2006 a team of SFO lawyers, accountants, financial investigators and police officers investigated the allegations of corrupt payments allegedly made by BAE in connection with this contract. During the investigation the SFO issued a number of statutory notices to BAE seeking information and disclosure. The fifth of these notices, issued on 14 October 2005, required BAE to disclose details of payments to agents and consultants in connection with the Al-Yamamah contract.

4. In response to this notice BAE wrote an unsolicited letter dated 7 November 2005 to the Attorney General, Lord Goldsmith QC, enclosing a memorandum marked "Strictly Private and Confidential". The gist of the memorandum was that disclosure of the required

information would adversely affect relations between the UK and Saudi Arabia and jeopardise the Al-Yamamah contract because the Saudis would regard it as a serious breach of confidentiality by BAE and HMG. The letter said that the issues canvassed in the memorandum had been discussed with Sir Kevin Tebbit, Permanent Under-Secretary of State at the Ministry of Defence, who on the same date, 7 November, telephoned the Legal Secretary to the Law Officers (hereafter "the Legal Secretary") to express his view that this was a unique case in which the public interest should be considered at an early stage. The Legal Secretary replied to BAE. He said that the Law Officers were aware of BAE's letter but had not read the memorandum, that it was not appropriate for representations to be made privately to the Law Officers, that the proper recipient of such representations was the SFO and that the letter and memorandum had been forwarded to the Director.

5. Mr Cowie, the SFO's Case Controller, wrote to BAE's solicitors on 15 November 2005. In his letter he complained of BAE's failure to comply with the fifth notice and questioned why the pursuit by the SFO of its independent powers of investigation could properly be regarded as a breach of confidentiality on the part of HMG. He made reference to the OECD Convention on Bribery and quoted the terms of Article 5 of the Convention:

Investigation and prosecution of the bribery of a foreign public official shall be subject to the applicable rules and principles of each Party. They shall not be influenced by considerations of national economic interest, the potential effect upon relations with another State or the identity of the natural or legal persons involved.

Mr Cowie invited BAE's solicitors to supply any material there might be pertaining to the national interest.

6. On 15 November 2005 Sir Kevin Tebbit telephoned the Director to tell him that the investigation created a serious risk of damage to important aspects of the UK's relationship with Saudi Arabia. He suggested that the question of where the balance of the public interest lay should be considered at that stage. The Director considered that if he was to insist on compliance by BAE with the fifth notice he should be in a position to inform the company that its public interest representations had been fully considered with all the relevant authorities. He therefore sought the advice of the Attorney General. On 30 November 2005 the Secretary to the Cabinet asked the Attorney General whether it would be proper for the government to make any representations as to the public interest considerations raised by the SFO

investigation and, if so, whether such representations could be made at the investigation stage. The Attorney General said he would consider this and respond. On 2 December 2005 the Attorney General and the Director decided that it would be appropriate to invite the views of other Government ministers, in order to acquaint themselves with all the relevant considerations, so as to enable them to assess whether it was contrary to the public interest for the investigation to proceed. This practice is familiarly known as a "Shawcross exercise", since it is based on a statement made by Sir Hartley Shawcross QC, then the Attorney General, in the House of Commons on 29 January 1951. The effect of the statement was that when deciding whether or not it is in the public interest to prosecute in a case where there is sufficient evidence to do so the Attorney General may, if he chooses, sound opinion among his ministerial colleagues, but that the ultimate decision rests with him alone and he is not to be put under pressure in the matter by his colleagues.

7. On 6 December 2005 the Attorney General initiated a Shawcross exercise. The Legal Secretary, on his behalf, wrote to the Cabinet Secretary inviting ministers to provide any information which might be relevant to the decision whether it was in the public interest to continue the investigation. The letter quoted Article 5 of the OECD Convention, and referred to the Attorney General's assurance to an OECD working group evaluating the UK's compliance with the Convention in 2004 that "none of the considerations prohibited by Article 5 would be taken into account as public interest factors not to prosecute" foreign bribery cases. The letter made clear that the final decision would be one for the SFO and the Attorney General acting independently of government and having due regard to the OECD Convention. The letter was copied to a number of official recipients. On 7 December 2005 the Director spoke to BAE's Group Legal Director, who wished to make further representations as to the public interest. The Director told him that as BAE was the suspect in a criminal investigation it would be better if he made any representations in writing, by the following day. The Director indicated that since BAE was a suspect he did not think he would give much weight to the company's views on the public interest in continuing the investigation.

8. BAE sent a further memorandum to the Director on 8 December 2005. The Cabinet Secretary responded to the Attorney General's invitation on 16 December, attaching a note which had been seen by the Prime Minister, the Foreign Secretary and the Defence Secretary, and which had their support. The note was largely directed to the importance of the commercial relationship between the UK and Saudi

Arabia but also stressed the importance of the UK's relationship in the context of national security, counter-terrorism and the search for stability in the Middle East. Saudi Arabia was described as "a key partner in the fight against Islamic terrorism". The note accepted that the decision was one for the Attorney General and the Director acting independently of government but asked them to consider the points made in the note.

9. After receipt of the Cabinet Secretary's letter and note, Mr Cowie drafted a brief to the Director (copied to Helen Garlick, Assistant Director) dated 19 December. It pointed out that "The SFO must investigate crime. It has a reasonable belief that crime has been committed. It must investigate all reasonable lines of enquiry and do so in the light of our domestic and international obligations." He suggested that Article 5 of the OECD Convention (and another instrument yet to be ratified) envisaged an independent role for law enforcement "outside of economic or political considerations". He addressed the question how the public interest in the rule of law might be balanced against economic and political consequences. He went on to question whether the Cabinet had given full consideration to the public interest in the rule of law, the independence of the SFO and the Ministry of Defence Police, all of which could suffer reputational damage if it emerged that an investigation by the SFO had been cut short.

10. On 11 January 2006 the Director and other SFO officers attended a meeting with, among others, both Law Officers. He expressed his view that the Al-Yamamah investigation should continue. The Attorney General reached the same conclusion. By letter dated 25 January 2006 the Legal Secretary informed the Cabinet Secretary that the Attorney General, in consultation with the Director, had concluded that it was in the public interest for the investigation to continue.

11. The Al-Yamamah investigation did continue and in the autumn of 2006 the SFO intended to investigate certain bank accounts in Switzerland to ascertain whether payments had been made to an agent or public official of Saudi Arabia. The SFO had obtained the co-operation of the Swiss authorities. This attempt to gain access to Swiss bank information provoked an explicit threat by the Saudi authorities that if the Al-Yamamah investigation were continued Saudi Arabia would withdraw from the existing bilateral counter-terrorism co-operation arrangements with the UK, withdraw co-operation from the UK in relation to its strategic objectives in the Middle East and end the negotiations then in train for the procurement of Typhoon aircraft.

12. On 29 September 2006 the Cabinet Secretary wrote to the Legal Secretary to update him "on some significant recent

developments of which we think the Attorney General should be made aware". Reference was made to the public interest considerations canvassed in the Cabinet Secretary's earlier letter of 16 December 2005, which were said still to apply "and if anything the significance of UK/Saudi co-operation on counter-terrorism and the broader search for stability in the Middle East has become even more compelling". There were said to be strong indications that severe damage to the public interest, over and above the national economic interest, was now imminent in relation to counter-terrorism and the bilateral relationship. The Attorney General showed this letter to the Director at a meeting on 30 September. On 3 October the Legal Secretary replied to the Cabinet Secretary, expressing the Attorney General's firm view that if the case against BAE was soundly based, which the SFO were reviewing, "it would not be right to discontinue it on the basis that the consequences threatened by the Saudi representatives may result".

13. The Attorney General was concerned to ensure that the case against BAE was indeed soundly based and so, following the meeting on 30 September 2006, the SFO undertook further work. In particular, the Attorney General considered that evidence needed to be obtained to show who (under the Saudi constitutional arrangements) was the principal contracting party in relation to the Al-Yamamah contract and whether the financial arrangements at the centre of the investigation had been approved or authorised by that principal. In a letter to the Legal Secretary after the meeting, the Assistant Director dismissed the Saudis' reliance on the confidentiality clause in the Al-Yamamah contract and asserted that the SFO's duty was to continue to investigate alleged corruption despite the acknowledged importance to the company and the MOD of maintaining commercial relations with the Kingdom of Saudi Arabia. On 27 November 2006 the Director agreed to try to obtain evidence from Saudi Arabia to address the issue of the principal's consent.

14. To that end, the Director held the first of three meetings with HM Ambassador to Saudi Arabia (Sir Sherard Cowper-Coles) on 30 November 2006 to explore with him the possibility of obtaining evidence on this issue. At this meeting the Ambassador told the Director that the threats to national and international security were very grave indeed. He said that "British lives on British streets were at risk."

15. At the beginning of December 2006 the Director and his case team proposed to explore whether BAE might plead guilty to corruption on what was called a "limited basis". This proposal was discussed with the Attorney General, who had no objection, but on 5 December

it was suggested to the Director (and he agreed) that the Prime Minister should be informed of this changed approach. On the same day Prince Bandar, National Security Adviser to the Kingdom of Saudi Arabia, met officials of the Foreign and Commonwealth Office in Riyadh.

16. On 6 December 2006 the Director agreed with the Legal Secretary what the latter should say to the Prime Minister's Private Secretaries, and later that day the Legal Secretary telephoned the Director to say that he had approached the Prime Minister's Office and been told that the Prime Minister wished to make further representations before BAE was approached. This caused some delay and the Director put off a proposed visit by the SFO to BAE.

17. The further representations made by the Prime Minister were set out in a "personal minute" from the Prime Minister to the Attorney General dated 8 December 2006. The Prime Minister asked the Attorney General to consider again the public interest issues raised by the ongoing investigation. In his letter the Prime Minister expressed his judgment, based on evidence and the advice of colleagues, that recent developments had given rise to a real and immediate risk of a collapse in UK/Saudi security, intelligence and diplomatic co-operation, which was likely to have seriously negative consequences for the UK public interest in terms of both national security and the UK's highest priority foreign policy objectives in the Middle East. The Prime Minister expressed strong support for the OECD Convention, but considered that his primary duty was to UK national security, and on that basis urged the Attorney General to consider the public interest in relation to the pursuit of the investigation. The papers attached to the Prime Minister's minute were: (1) a note dated 23 November 2006 on the value of Saudi co-operation in the field of counter-terrorism by Sir Richard Mottram, Permanent Secretary for Security, Intelligence and Resilience in the Cabinet Office, which drew on material from the Secret Intelligence Service and the Security Service, and (2) a letter dated 24 November 2006 by Sir Peter Ricketts, Permanent Under-Secretary at the FCO, on the importance of Saudi Arabia to the UK's efforts to win peace and stability in the Middle East. It was arranged that the Director should attend at the Attorney General's office on Monday 11 December to read the Prime Minister's minute. Before that meeting, on 8 December, the Director had a second meeting with the Ambassador, who confirmed his view of the damage to national security which any continuation of the investigation would in his assessment inevitably cause. He said that lives were at risk.

18. On 11 December the Director met the Legal Secretary and read the Prime Minister's minute and its attachments. On the same day the

Prime Minister and the Attorney General met. The effect of the meeting was summarised in a letter dated 12 December from the Prime Minister's Principal Private Secretary to the Legal Secretary. The Attorney General pointed out that he had to weigh the points in the Prime Minister's minute against other considerations. He was concerned that halting the investigation would send a bad message about the credibility of the law in this area, and look like giving in to threats. He felt justified, however, in questioning whether the grounds for the investigation were soundly based and in exploring legal options for resolving the case as quickly as possible. The Prime Minister felt that higher considerations were at stake, as indicated in his minute. It was important that the Government did not give people reason to believe that threatening the British system resulted in parties getting their way. But the Government also needed to consider the damage done to the credibility of the law in this area by a long and failed trial, and its good reputation on bribery and corruption issues compared with many of its international partners. The Prime Minister recognised that supervision of the investigation was a matter for the Attorney General but considered this the clearest case for intervention in the public interest he had seen. The Attorney General said he would consider the Prime Minister's representations, with due regard to the need for separation between law and policy. The Director did not attend this meeting and did not see a copy of the letter until after he had made his decision on 14 December.

19. The Attorney General decided that in discharge of his function of superintending the SFO he should himself review the case in detail, with the benefit of full briefing from SFO investigators and lawyers, sight of the underlying material and advice from independent leading counsel. His review was carried out over the period 12-14 December 2006 and involved the consideration of many files.

20. On 12 December the Director attended a third meeting with the Ambassador. Also present were the Solicitor General and the Legal Secretary. The Ambassador repeated his view that the risk of Saudi Arabia withdrawing its co-operation with the UK in countering terrorism was real and acute. He expressed the view that there was a real threat to British lives.

21. On 13 December 2006 the Director attended a meeting with the Attorney General, the Solicitor General, the Legal Secretary and Helen Garlick (the Assistant Director). She made a record of the meeting the next day. In answer to a question from the Attorney General, the Director said that in the last few days representations on public interest had been made with renewed and increasing force by

HM Ambassador. If further investigation would cause such damage to national and international security he accepted that it would not be in the public interest. What he could not accept was the view that there was insufficient evidence to continue, although he would wish to consider that aspect and explore it with counsel. The Attorney General then asked Helen Garlick for her view. She replied that the SFO had never sought to place the interests of the investigation above those of national and international security. While the SFO was qualified to make judgments on the law and evidence, on questions of national security it had to take the advice of others. The SFO's only source was the Ambassador, but he had said that "British lives on British streets were at risk." If the Saudi action caused "another 7/7" how could the SFO say that its investigation, which might or might not result in a successful prosecution, was more important? The Attorney General expressed doubts (not shared by the Director) about the strength of the case, and was recorded by the Assistant Director as being "extremely unhappy at the implications of dropping it now". The Attorney General and the Director agreed that the latter should reflect on his decision overnight.

22. The Director discussed the matter further with his case team that evening. On the morning of 14 December he confirmed to the Legal Secretary that his conclusion remained the same: that in his view continuing the Al-Yamamah investigation would risk serious harm to the UK's national and international security. He accordingly decided that the Al-Yamamah investigation (but not other investigations pertaining to BAE) should be discontinued. His decision was announced in a press release the same day. It read:

The Director of the Serious Fraud Office has decided to discontinue the investigation into the affairs of BAE SYSTEMS Plc as far as they relate to the Al Yamamah defence contract with the government of Saudi Arabia.

This decision has been taken following representations that have been made both to the Attorney General and the Director of the SFO concerning the need to safeguard national and international security.

It has been necessary to balance the need to maintain the rule of law against the wider public interest.

No weight has been given to commercial interests or to the national economic interest.

The Attorney General made a statement in Parliament the same day. He referred to the strong public interest in upholding and enforcing the criminal law, in particular against international corruption, and also to the views of the Prime Minister and the Foreign and Defence

Secretaries as to the public interest considerations raised by the investigation. They had, he said,

> expressed the clear view that continuation of the investigation would cause serious damage to UK/Saudi security, intelligence and diplomatic co-operation, which is likely to have seriously negative consequences for the United Kingdom public interest in terms of both national security and our highest priority foreign policy objectives in the Middle East. The heads of our security and intelligence agencies and our ambassador to Saudi Arabia share this assessment.

The Attorney General pointed out that Article 5 of the OECD Convention precluded him and the SFO from taking into account considerations of the national economic interest or the potential effect upon relations with another state, and added that "we have not done so".

The judgment of the Divisional Court

23. The judgment of the Divisional Court, given by Moses LJ, does not lend itself to simple or succinct summary. The breadth of the Director's discretion in relation to prosecution and investigation was accepted, as was the reluctance of the courts to interfere with the exercise of the discretion (para. 51). Authority was cited. Reference was made (para. 52) to the Code for Crown Prosecutors, where the familiar two-stage test is explained and an illustrative list of factors which may be relevant to the public interest test is given. One common public interest factor telling against prosecution is that details may be made public that could harm national security. The court accepted, as a generality, that the Director's discretion was of sufficient breadth to entitle him to take into account a risk to life and national security in deciding whether to continue an investigation (para. 54). By Article 2 of the European Convention on Human Rights, the Director and the Government were required to protect and safeguard the lives of British citizens. On an application for judicial review the court could not assess the extent of the risk to life or to national security by those who advised the Attorney General and the Director, and the Director himself could not exercise an independent judgment on these matters (para. 55). He might lawfully accord appropriate weight to the judgment of those with responsibility for national security who had direct access to sources of intelligence unavailable to him. In cases touching on foreign relations and national security the duty of decision on the merits lay with the Government, and the courts were obliged to maintain the boundary between their role and that of the Government.

24. The essential point of the claimants' challenge did not, however, relate to the relevance of national security to the Director's decision or the Government's assessment of the risk to national security but to the threat uttered (as it was said) by Prince Bandar to the Prime Minister's Chief of Staff (para. 57). It was one thing to assess the risk of damage which might flow from continuing an investigation, quite another to submit to a threat designed to compel the investigation to call a halt. When the threat involved the criminal jurisdiction of this country, the issue was no longer a matter only for the Government, and the courts were bound to consider what steps they must take to preserve the integrity of the criminal justice system. The constitutional principle of the separation of powers required the courts to resist encroachment on the territory for which they were responsible (para. 58). Had the threat been made by a person subject to English criminal law he would risk being charged with an attempt to pervert the course of justice (para. 59) and threats to the administration of justice within the UK were the concern primarily of the courts, not the executive (para. 60). The decisions of the Court of Appeal in *R* v. *Coventry City Council, ex p Phoenix Aviation* [1995] 3 All ER 37 and *R* v. *Chief Constable of Devon and Cornwall, ex p Central Electricity Generating Board* [1982] QB 458 were cited. Reference was made to the existing constitutional principle of the rule of law, now recognised in section 1 of the Constitutional Reform Act 2005, but the rule of law amounted to nothing if it failed to constrain overweening power (paras. 61-5). It was beyond question that had the Director decided to halt the investigation in response to a threat made by those susceptible to domestic jurisdiction, the courts would have regarded the issues which arose as peculiarly within their sphere of responsibility (para. 66).

25. The court then considered how the courts discharge that responsibility, and held that the courts fulfil their primary obligation to protect the rule of law by ensuring that a statutory decision-maker exercises the powers conferred on him independently and without surrendering them to a third party (para. 67). In yielding to the threat, the Director ceased to exercise the power to make the independent judgment required of him by Parliament (para. 68). The court accepted (para. 72) that in assessing the consequences of the threat the Director exercised an independent judgment, despite his total reliance on the advice of others, but that was not the point: in halting the investigation he surrendered to a threat made with the specific intention of achieving surrender. The court could identify no integrity in the role of the courts to uphold the rule of law if they (the courts) were to abdicate in response to a threat from a foreign power (para. 76). Surrender deprived the law of any power to resist for the future, as recognised in

Phoenix Aviation (para. 79). Reference was made to the case of Leila Khalid, a PLO terrorist released by the Attorney General in face of a threat to kill Swiss and German hostages held by the PLO, and the court accepted that there might be circumstances so extreme that the necessity to save lives might compel a decision not to detain or prosecute (paras. 81-2). But it was for the courts to decide whether the reaction to a threat was a lawful response or an unlawful submission (para. 82), and in the present case the court had to assess whether the Director and the Government yielded too readily (para. 84). The present case was distinguishable on its facts from that of Leila Khalid (para. 85).

26. The court was also bound to question whether all the steps which could reasonably be taken to divert the threat had been pursued (para. 86). It did not accept that due consideration had been given to persuading the Saudis to withdraw their threat (paras. 87-8). No one had suggested to the Saudis that threats were futile since Britain's democracy forbade the exertion of pressure on an independent prosecutor (para. 90). There had been no sufficient appreciation of the damage to the rule of law caused by submission to a threat directed at the administration of justice (para. 91), which the Director had not specifically considered at the time (para. 92).

27. The court laid down the principle that submission to a threat is lawful only when it is demonstrated to a court that there was no alternative course open to the decision-maker (para. 99). That principle had two particular virtues: by restricting the circumstances in which submission might be endorsed as lawful, the rule of law might be protected (para. 100); and, as this case was said to demonstrate, too ready a submission might give rise to the suspicion that the threat was not the real ground for the decision at all, but was a pretext (para. 101). The court was driven to the conclusion that the Director's submission to the threat was unlawful (para. 102).

28. The court also addressed a separate ground on which the claimants sought to challenge the Director's decision: that the Director had taken account of the potential effect of the investigation upon relations between the UK and Saudi Arabia, a consideration which he was precluded from taking into account by Article 5 of the OECD Convention (para. 105). It was argued for the Director that since the Convention was an unincorporated treaty and had no effect in domestic law he was not bound by Article 5 and therefore this issue was not justiciable (para. 106). The court concluded that since the Director had publicly claimed to observe the prohibition in Article 5 his legal self-direction could be reviewed, particularly since section 109 of the 2001 Act had been enacted to give effect to the Convention (paras. 119, 121).

29. The claimants also attached significance to the absence of any reference to national security in Article 5 (para. 123), but the court did not accept that it was for that reason a prohibited consideration (para. 128). It did, however, find it difficult to distinguish between national security and relations with another state (paras. 131-40). It concluded that the doctrine of necessity as recognised in international law provided a clear basis for distinguishing the one from the other (para. 147). But the court drew back from giving a final ruling on interpretation. It had recognised (paras. 141-2) the virtue of uniformity in the interpretation of international treaties and acknowledged (para. 150) that the parties had, under the Convention, established a standing Working Group on Bribery as a mechanism for monitoring compliance with it. The court held that it was for the Working Group to achieve a consensus on the interpretation of the Convention (para. 153), and a ruling was not in any event necessary since the court had already held the Director's decision to be unlawful (para. 154). The court therefore expressed no concluded view whether it had been open to the Director to consider that his decision was in compliance with Article 5 (para. 157).

The main issue

30. It is common ground in these proceedings that the Director is a public official appointed by the Crown but independent of it. He is entrusted by Parliament with discretionary powers to investigate suspected offences which reasonably appear to him to involve serious or complex fraud and to prosecute in such cases. These are powers given to him by Parliament as head of an independent, professional service who is subject only to the superintendence of the Attorney General. There is an obvious analogy with the position of the Director of Public Prosecutions. It is accepted that the decisions of the Director are not immune from review by the courts, but authority makes plain that only in highly exceptional cases will the court disturb the decisions of an independent prosecutor and investigator: *R* v. *Director of Public Prosecutions, ex p C* [1995] 1 Cr App R 136, 141; *R* v. *Director of Public Prosecutions, ex p Manning* [2001] QB 330, para. 23; *R (Bermingham and others)* v. *Director of the Serious Fraud Office* [2006] EWHC 200 (Admin), [2007] QB 727, paras. 63-4; *Mohit* v. *Director of Public Prosecutions of Mauritius* [2006] UKPC 20, [2006] 1 WLR 3343, paras. 17 and 21 citing and endorsing a passage in the judgment of the Supreme Court of Fiji in *Matalulu* v. *Director of Public Prosecutions* [2003] 4 LRC 712, 735-6; *Sharma* v. *Brown-Antoine and others* [2006] UKPC 57, [2007] 1 WLR 780, para. 14(1)-(6). The House was not

referred to any case in which a challenge had been made to a decision not to prosecute or investigate on public interest grounds.

31. The reasons why the courts are very slow to interfere are well understood. They are, first, that the powers in question are entrusted to the officers identified, and to no one else. No other authority may exercise these powers or make the judgments on which such exercise must depend. Secondly, the courts have recognised (as it was described in the cited passage of *Matalulu*)

> the polycentric character of official decision-making in such matters including policy and public interest considerations which are not susceptible of judicial review because it is within neither the constitutional function nor the practical competence of the courts to assess their merits.

Thirdly, the powers are conferred in very broad and unprescriptive terms.

32. Of course, and this again is uncontroversial, the discretions conferred on the Director are not unfettered. He must seek to exercise his powers so as to promote the statutory purpose for which he is given them. He must direct himself correctly in law. He must act lawfully. He must do his best to exercise an objective judgment on the relevant material available to him. He must exercise his powers in good faith, uninfluenced by any ulterior motive, predilection or prejudice. In the present case, the claimants have not sought to impugn the Director's good faith and honesty in any way.

33. The first duty of the Director is, in appropriate cases, to investigate and prosecute. The Director and his colleagues performed that duty. They launched the investigation into BAE. They pursued it by serving a series of statutory notices to obtain the information they needed. They rejected strong representations made by the company and senior ministers including the Prime Minister at the end of 2005 that the investigation should be discontinued on public interest grounds. The duty to prosecute was spelled out in clear terms in the Case Controller's brief to the Director of 19 December 2005. They continued the investigation until the autumn of 2006, by which time they were on the point of obtaining access to potentially significant Swiss bank accounts. That provoked the threat or threats by Saudi representatives which gave rise to these proceedings. Even then the Attorney General (3 October 2006) was of the firm view that the investigation should be continued if it was soundly based and the Assistant Director (27 October) explicitly recognised the SFO's duty to continue to investigate. A month later the Director agreed to

try and obtain evidence from Saudi Arabia bearing on the issue of principal's consent.

34. In para. 18 of its judgment the Divisional Court recorded that in early 2006 the Attorney General and the Director were of the view that the public interest grounds relied on did not justify discontinuing the investigation and posed the question: "What changed later in 2006?" The Director gives the answer very clearly in para. 21 of his second witness statement:

It was only following my first meeting with the Ambassador on 30 November 2006 that I seriously began to entertain the thought that the national security public interest might be so compelling that I would have no real alternative. Ultimately, I was convinced by my discussions with the Ambassador and the Prime Minister's minute that there was a very real likelihood of serious damage to UK national security.

It will be recalled that at the first meeting the Ambassador had described the threats to national and international security as very grave indeed and had said that British lives on British streets were at risk. At the second meeting he had again said that lives would be at risk. At the third he had spoken of a real threat to British lives. The Assistant Director, in the light of those statements, envisaged that the withdrawal of co-operation might lead to "another 7/7". It is not suggested that the fears expressed by the Ambassador and senior ministers were fanciful or ill-founded, or that the Director should have discounted them as being so.

35. The evidence makes plain that the decision to discontinue the investigation was taken with extreme reluctance. As the Director put it in his second witness statement (para. 11):

The investigation and prosecution of serious crime is a major public interest that the SFO exists to promote. My job is to investigate and prosecute crime. The Al Yamamah investigation was a major investigation. The idea of discontinuing the investigation went against my every instinct as a prosecutor ...

The Attorney General on 13 December 2006 was said to be "extremely unhappy" at the implications of dropping the investigation at that stage. What determined the decision was the Director's judgment that the public interest in saving British lives outweighed the public interest in pursuing BAE to conviction. It was a courageous decision, since the Director could have avoided making it by disingenuously adopting the Attorney General's view (with which he did not agree) that the case was evidentially weak. Had he anticipated the same consequences and made the same decision in the absence of an explicit Saudi threat it would seem that the Divisional Court would have upheld the decision, since it regarded the threat as "the essential point" in the case.

36. The Divisional Court was right to hold that a person subject to the jurisdiction of the court who sought to impede an SFO investigation would be at risk of prosecution for attempting to pervert the course of justice, and also right to hold that the Saudis were not subject to the court's jurisdiction. But there is little assistance to be gained in resolving the present problem from the authority which the Divisional Court cited. The underlying dispute in *R v. Chief Constable of Devon and Cornwall, ex p Central Electricity Generating Board* [1982] QB 458 was between a public board seeking to exercise its statutory powers and perform its statutory obligations and a group of protesters unlawfully trying to stop it doing so. The effect of the decision was to remind the board of its right to exercise self-help and the police that they had the power to ensure that the board could perform its functions. In this context both Lord Denning MR and Lawton LJ (at pp. 471E and 473A) referred to the rule of law. But the case involved no choice between competing aspects of the public interest.

37. *R v. Coventry City Council, ex p Phoenix Aviation and others* [1995] 3 All ER 37 involved three applications for judicial review. The underlying dispute was between three sea and airport authorities and groups unlawfully seeking to prevent the authorities handling live animal cargoes. The Divisional Court held, first, that the authorities had no discretion to refuse to handle the cargoes. On that basis there was again no choice between competing aspects of the public interest: there were authorities subject to a public duty on one side and groups unlawfully seeking to prevent the authorities performing their duty on the other. But the court went on to consider what the position would be if the authorities had had a discretion, and in that context emphasised the importance of maintaining the rule of law. The court said (at p. 62e-h) that public authorities must beware of surrendering to the dictates of unlawful pressure groups, that it is one thing to respond to unlawful threats and quite another to submit to them, and that yielding to the threats would encourage the protesters to concentrate on an even smaller number of outlets. The Divisional Court in the present case relied strongly on these dicta. But even on the assumption which underlay this part of the judgment, there were on one side authorities with a discretion to perform their public duties and on the other protesters seeking unlawfully to prevent them doing so. The court pointed out, moreover, that the police had ample powers to control unlawful protest and ensure that the general public, including other

port users, were not intolerably affected by it (p. 63j). Thus there was no significant factor to weigh against the public interest in performance by the authorities of their public duty. In *R* v. *Chief Constable of Sussex, ex p International Trader's Ferry Ltd* [1999] 2 AC 418 the situation and the outcome were different, because the Chief Constable had a discretion how best to deploy the resources available to him and protection of the company's right to ship live animal cargoes had to be balanced against the other demands on and duties of the police.

38. The Divisional Court held (para. 68) that "No revolutionary principle needs to be created ... we can deploy well-settled principles of public law." But in para. 99 of its judgment the court did lay down a principle which, if not revolutionary, was novel and unsupported by authority:

The principle we have identified is that submission to a threat is lawful only when it is demonstrated to a court that there was no alternative course open to the decision-maker.

The virtues which the court saw in that principle have been summarised in para. 27 above, but the second of those (that, as this case was said to demonstrate, "too ready a submission may give rise to the suspicion that the threat was not the real ground of the decision at all; rather it was a useful pretext") should not be understood as reflecting on the good faith of the Director or the Attorney General which has never been in issue. The objection to the principle formulated by the Divisional Court is that it distracts attention from what, applying well-settled principles of public law, was the right question: whether, in deciding that the public interest in pursuing an important investigation into alleged bribery was outweighed by the public interest in protecting the lives of British citizens, the Director made a decision outside the lawful bounds of the discretion entrusted to him by Parliament.

39. The decision of the then Attorney General to release Leila Khalid to avert a threat by the PLO to execute Swiss and German hostages was described as "clearly defensible" in Edwards, *The Attorney General, Politics and the Public Interest* (1984), p. 325, and is not criticised by the Divisional Court. It is perhaps the only occasion on which a British public prosecutor has been deflected from what would otherwise have been his duty by a foreign threat. But the case is not easily distinguished. It is true that the threat to the hostages was more direct and immediate than that to the British public in the present case. But the Ambassador did not give the Director to understand that the contingency of which he warned was remote or improbable, the

potential loss of life in the present case was much greater and the threat here was to those whose safety it is the primary duty of the British authorities to protect.

40. The Divisional Court accepted that the Attorney General had no choice but to release Leila Khalid. Here, it was found, there were other things the Director could have done. It could have been explained to the Saudis that under the British constitution the Director is independent of the Government and any attempt to deflect him from his duty would be futile. Attempts should have been made to dissuade the Saudis from implementing their threat. It was submitted in argument that the Saudi threat to withdraw security co-operation put them in breach of Security Council Resolution 1373 (2001) on measures to counter terrorism and a complaint could have been lodged with the United Nations. These findings and contentions overlook the important fact that the Director was a prosecutor with no diplomatic access to representatives of the Government of Saudi Arabia. He was, as the Divisional Court rightly held, obliged and entitled to rely on the expert assessments of others. These findings and contentions are also untenable on the facts. Evidence before the House shows that the Saudis were repeatedly told of the separation, under our system, between the prosecuting authority and the executive but, according to the Ambassador, found it difficult to accept that the UK Government and the Prime Minister could not stop the investigation if they chose to do so. Considerable thought was given within the SFO to the possibility of persuading the Saudis to withdraw their threat, but this was not in the Ambassador's view a viable course of action. The notion of complaining to the United Nations, if put to the Divisional Court, did not receive its endorsement. As a means of achieving wholehearted co-operation such an initiative would seem unpromising. The Director has accepted that he did not at the time assess whether there would be a threat to British national security if other countries learned that Britain had given in to pressure but has also explained that his view at the time was, and remains, that the case was wholly exceptional and unlikely to have any appreciable effect on other corruption cases. A discretionary decision is not in any event vitiated by a failure to take into account a consideration which the decision-maker is not obliged by the law or the facts to take into account, even if he may properly do so: *CREEDNZ Inc. v. Governor General* [1981] 1 NZLR 172, 183.

41. The Director was confronted by an ugly and obviously unwelcome threat. He had to decide what, if anything, he should do. He did not surrender his discretionary power of decision to any third party, although he did consult the most expert source available to him in the

person of the Ambassador and he did, as he was entitled if not bound to do, consult the Attorney General who, however, properly left the decision to him. The issue in these proceedings is not whether his decision was right or wrong, nor whether the Divisional Court or the House agrees with it, but whether it was a decision which the Director was lawfully entitled to make. Such an approach involves no affront to the rule of law, to which the principles of judicial review give effect (see *R (Alconbury Developments Ltd)* v. *Secretary of State for the Environment, Transport and the Regions* [2001] UKHL 23, [2003] 2 AC 295, para. 73, per Lord Hoffmann).

42. In the opinion of the House the Director's decision was one he was lawfully entitled to make. It may indeed be doubted whether a responsible decision-maker could, on the facts before the Director, have decided otherwise.

Article 5 of the OECD Convention

43. It is common ground that had the Director ignored Article 5 of the OECD Convention, an unincorporated treaty provision not sounding in domestic law, his decision could not have been impugned on the ground of inconsistency with it. But the Director publicly claimed to be acting in accordance with Article 5. The claimants accordingly contend (1) that it is open to the domestic courts of this country to review the correctness in law of the Director's self-direction; (2) that our courts should themselves interpret Article 5; (3) that the Director's interpretation should be held to be incorrect; and (4) that the Director's decision should be quashed. Each of these steps in the argument is, in the judgment of the House, problematical.

44. In support of step (1) in this argument reliance was placed in particular on *R* v. *Secretary of State for the Home Department, ex p Launder* [1997] 1 WLR 839, 866-7 and *R* v. *Director of Public Prosecutions, ex p Kebilene* [2000] 2 AC 326, 341-2, 367, 375-6. Both cases concerned decision-makers claiming to act consistently with the European Convention at a time when it had not been given effect in domestic law. The courts accepted the propriety of reviewing the compatibility with the Convention of the decisions in question. But there was in the first case no issue between the parties about the interpretation of the relevant Articles of the Convention, and in the second there was a body of Convention jurisprudence on which the courts could draw in seeking to resolve the issue before it. Whether, in the event that there had been a live dispute on the meaning of an unincorporated provision on which there was no judicial authority, the

courts would or should have undertaken the task of interpretation from scratch must be at least questionable. It would moreover be unfortunate if decision-makers were to be deterred from seeking to give effect to what they understand to be the international obligations of the UK by fear that their decisions might be held to be vitiated by an incorrect understanding.

45. Step (2) in the claimants' argument calls for consideration of Article 12 of the Convention. This provides:

Monitoring and Follow-up
The Parties shall co-operate in carrying out a programme of systematic follow-up to monitor and promote the full implementation of this Convention. Unless otherwise decided by consensus of the Parties, this shall be done in the framework of the OECD Working Group on Bribery in International Business Transactions and according to its terms of reference, or within the framework and terms of reference of any successor to its functions, and Parties shall bear the costs of the programme in accordance with the rules applicable to that body.

It was pointed out, correctly, that this provision does not provide for a binding judicial interpretation of the Convention. It does, on the other hand, provide for a forum in which and a means by which differences of approach to the interpretation and application of the Convention can be discussed and either reconciled or resolved. As the Divisional Court rightly recognised, uniformity in these respects is highly desirable. For that reason, a national court should hesitate before undertaking a task of unilateral interpretation where the contracting parties have embraced an alternative means of resolving differences.

46. The clear effect of Article 5 is to permit national investigators and prosecutors to act in accordance with the rules and principles applicable in their respective states, save that they are not to be influenced by three specific considerations: (i) national economic interest, (ii) the potential effect upon the relations with another state, and (iii) the identity of the natural or legal persons involved. It is obvious why the parties wished to prohibit the paying of attention to (i): a bribery investigation or prosecution may very probably injure commercial, and thus economic, interests. The reason for excluding consideration of (iii) is also obvious: investigators and prosecutors should not be deterred from acting by the high ministerial office or royal connections of an allegedly corrupt person. The ambit of consideration (ii) is more doubtful. Clearly the investigator or prosecutor is not to be deterred by the prospect or occurrence of a cooling of relations between his state and that of the allegedly corrupt official, even if this escalates into a

diplomatic stand-off involving (for instance) the denial of visas, the cutting off of cultural and sporting exchanges, the obstruction of trading activities, the expulsion of diplomats and the blocking of bank accounts. But can the negotiators have intended to include multiple loss of life within the description "potential effect upon relations with another State"? And can they, if so, have intended to deny to member states the right to rely on a severe threat to national security? An affirmative answer is given by Rose-Ackerman and Billa, "Treaties and National Security Exceptions" (Yale Law School, 2007). A negative answer was given by the Attorney General in Parliament on 1 February 2007 (HL Debates, Hansard, col. 378):

> I do not believe that the Convention does, or was ever intended to, prevent national authorities from taking decisions on the basis of such fundamental considerations of national and international security. I do not believe that we would have signed up to it if we had thought that we were abandoning any ability to have regard to something as fundamental as national security, and I do not believe that any other country would have signed up either.

The extreme difficulty of resolving this problem on a principled basis underlines the desirability of resolving an issue such as this in the manner provided for in the Convention.

47. In my opinion, it is unnecessary and undesirable to resolve these problematical questions in this appeal, for two reasons. First, it is clear that the Director throughout based his adherence to Article 5 on a belief that it permitted him to take account of threats to human life as a public interest consideration. Secondly, the Director has given unequivocal evidence that he would undoubtedly have made the same decision even if he had believed, which he did not, that it was incompatible with Article 5 of the Convention. I cannot doubt, given its conclusion in para. 41 above, that he would indeed have done so.

48. I would allow the appeal and set aside the order of the Divisional Court save as to costs. The costs provision imposed by the Divisional Court on the Director as a condition of granting him leave to appeal will be given effect.

LORD HOFFMANN

49. I have had the advantage of reading in draft the speech of my noble and learned friend Lord Bingham of Cornhill. For the reasons he gives, with which I agree, I too would allow this appeal.

LORD RODGER OF EARLSFERRY

50. I have had the privilege of considering the speeches of my noble and learned friends, Lord Bingham of Cornhill and Lord Brown of Eaton-under-Heywood, in draft. For the reasons which they give, with which I am in entire agreement, I too would allow the appeal.

51. In particular, I am satisfied that, as he deposed in his affidavit, the Director would have made the same decision, even if he had believed that it was incompatible with Article 5 of the OECD Convention. That is consistent with the other evidence. The Director had received advice from a number of sources about the threat to national security if the investigation continued. It is plain that he weighed the advice carefully before acting on it, as he was fully entitled to do. In the light of the advice, the Director concluded that he had no option but to discontinue the investigation because of the potential threat to national and international security—British lives would be put at risk. In these circumstances, it is unnecessary, even supposing that it would be competent, for the House to interpret Article 5.

BARONESS HALE OF RICHMOND

52. I confess that I would have liked to be able to uphold the decision (if not every aspect of the reasoning) of the Divisional Court. It is extremely distasteful that an independent public official should feel himself obliged to give way to threats of any sort. The Director clearly felt the same for he resisted the extreme pressure under which he was put for as long as he could. The great British public may still believe that it was the risk to British commercial interests which caused him to give way, but the evidence is quite clear that this was not so. He only gave way when he was convinced that the threat of withdrawal of Saudi security co-operation was real and that the consequences would be an equally real risk to "British lives on British streets". The only question is whether it was lawful for him to take this into account.

53. Put like that, it is difficult to reach any other conclusion than that it was indeed lawful for him to take this into account. But it is not quite as simple as that. It is common ground that it would not have been lawful for him to take account of threats of harm to himself, threats of the "we know where you live" variety. That sort of threat would have been an irrelevant consideration. So what makes this sort of threat different? Why should the Director be obliged to ignore threats to his own personal safety (and presumably that of his family) but entitled to take into account threats to the safety of others? The answer

must lie in a distinction between the personal and the public interest. The "public interest" is often invoked but not susceptible of precise definition. But it must mean something of importance to the public as a whole rather than just to a private individual. The withdrawal of Saudi security co-operation would indeed have consequences of importance for the public as a whole. I am more impressed by the real threat to "British lives on British streets" than I am by unspecified references to national security or the national interest. "National security" in the sense of a threat to the safety of the nation as a nation state was not in issue here. Public safety was.

54. I also agree that the Director was entitled to rely upon the judgment of others as to the existence of such a risk. There are many other factors in a prosecutor's exercise of discretion upon which he may have to rely on the advice of others. Medical evidence of the effect of a prosecution upon a potential accused is an obvious example. Of course, he is entitled, even obliged, to probe that evidence or advice, to require to be convinced of its accuracy or weight. But in the end there are some things upon which others are more expert than he could ever be. In the end there are also some things which he cannot do. He is not in a position to try to dissuade the Saudis from carrying out their threat. Eventually, he has to rely on the assurances of others that despite their best endeavours the threats are real and the risks are real.

55. I am therefore driven to the conclusion that he was entitled to take these things into account. I do not however accept that this was the only decision he could have made. He had to weigh the seriousness of the risk, in every sense, against the other public interest considerations. These include the importance of upholding the rule of law and the principle that no one, including powerful British companies who do business for powerful foreign countries, is above the law. It is perhaps worth remembering that it was BAE Systems, or people in BAE Systems, who were the target of the investigation and of any eventual prosecution and not anyone in Saudi Arabia. The Director carried on with the investigation despite their earnest attempts to dissuade him. He clearly had the countervailing factors very much in mind throughout, as did the Attorney General. A lesser person might have taken the easy way out and agreed with the Attorney General that it would be difficult on the evidence to prove every element of the offence. But he did not.

56. As to whether the safety of British lives on British streets is a prohibited consideration under Article 5 of the OECD Convention, we do not need to express a view. Professor Susan Rose-Ackerman and Benjamin Billa of Yale Law School make a powerful case that there is

no implicit exception for "national security" under the OECD Convention ("Treaties and National Security Exceptions", Yale Law School, 2007). But the Director has made it clear that he would have reached the same conclusion in any event and as a matter of domestic law he was entitled to do so.

57. For these reasons, although I would wish that the world were a better place where honest and conscientious public servants were not put in impossible situations such as this, I agree that his decision was lawful and this appeal must be allowed.

LORD BROWN OF EATON-UNDER-HEYWOOD

58. I have had the advantage of reading in draft the opinion of my noble and learned friend Lord Bingham of Cornhill and agree with everything that he says. On the first part of the case—the question whether the Director acted lawfully in "surrender[ing] to a threat" as the first certified question puts it—there is almost nothing that I wish to add to my Lord's opinion. The Divisional Court appears to have founded its decision very largely on my judgment in the Divisional Court in the *Phoenix Aviation* case: *R* v. *Coventry City Council, ex parte Phoenix Aviation and others* [1995] 3 All ER 37. That was, however, a strikingly different case. As I pointed out (at p. 62), on the assumption that the port authorities there had a discretion whether or not to handle the export of live animals, they (or, in the case of Plymouth, the city council who were trying to stop their own port authority from continuing to permit this trade) "gave [not] the least thought" to the implications for the rule of law in barring this trade because of threats of disruption. The contrast with the position here could hardly be starker. As Lord Bingham has explained, the Director (and the Attorney General to whose superintendence he was subject) gave prolonged and profound thought to the implications for the rule of law in suspending this investigation in response to the Saudi Arabian threat. It is, indeed, some indication of the Director's recognition of the extreme undesirability of doing so that he stood out for so long. In the end, however, the reality and the gravity of the threat having become ever more apparent to him, he concluded that there was no alternative:

I considered the threat to the UK's national and international security to be of such compelling weight that it was imperative that I should halt the SFO investigation at this point, in the public interest. It was this feature of the case which I felt left me with no choice but to halt the investigation. This was not a conclusion which I arrived at lightly; far from it.

59. The second certified question goes to the true construction and application of Article 5 of the OECD Convention and the respondents' argument here, powerfully advanced by Ms Dinah Rose QC, is that the Director wrongly believed himself to be acting consistently with Article 5 and should now be required to exercise his discretion afresh. True it is that he has stated:

[E]ven had I thought that discontinuing the investigation was not compatible with article 5 of the Convention, I am in no doubt whatever that I would still have decided, by reason of the compelling public interest representations ... that the investigation should be discontinued. The threat which I considered existed to UK national and international security if the investigation continued was so great that I did not believe there was any serious doubt about the decision I should make.

Nevertheless, submit the respondents, there could be no certainty that he (or rather his successor) would reach the same decision once the Court had stated publicly that this would involve a breach of the Convention. He would then have to face up to the political consequences of such an act.

60. The position here is not, submit the respondents, as it was in *R* v. *Secretary of State for the Home Department ex parte Fininvest Spa* [1997] 1 WLR 743. There the Italian prosecuting authorities had requested the UK's assistance under the European Convention on Mutual Assistance in Criminal Matters, 1959 (which was incorporated into domestic law). Article 2 of the Convention imposed a duty on the Secretary of State to assist save in the case of a political offence where he had a discretion to refuse. The Secretary of State, rightly as the Divisional Court ultimately held, declined to regard the particular offences in question as political and accordingly gave no thought to the exercise of a discretion. I pointed out, however, that in any event the Secretary of State had no need to have reached a decision on whether the offences were political:

He could instead, had he wished, have decided that whether or not they were— whether or not in other words a discretion arose under article 2(a)—he would not in any event exercise it to refuse cooperation with the Italian authorities in the particular circumstances of this case. Had he followed that course or, indeed, had he deposed in the present proceedings that, even had he reached a contrary view on the political offence question, he would still have decided to comply with the request, his decision would in my judgment be proof against this particular ground of challenge, irrespective of whether or not he directed himself correctly on the substantive issue.

61. The respondents submit that it is one thing for a decision-maker to say, and for the Court to accept, that even had he understood the law correctly he would still have reached the same decision in circumstances where, as in *Fininvest*, the decision would have remained perfectly lawful; quite another where, as here, the same decision taken on a correct legal understanding would *ex hypothesi* have been unlawful.

62. I see the force of this (although, of course, in this case, unlike the position in *Fininvest*, any unlawfulness would be under international law, not domestic law), and I accept also the respondent's submissions, first, that there are indeed occasions when the Court will decide questions as to the state's obligations under unincorporated international law (two such cases being *R* v. *Secretary of State for the Home Department ex parte Launder* [1997] 1 WLR 839 and *R* v. *Director of Public Prosecutions ex parte Kebilene* [2000] 2 AC 326, both concerned with the European Convention on Human Rights before it took effect in domestic law) and, secondly, that nothing in either *R (Campaign for Nuclear Disarmament)* v. *Prime Minister* [2002] EWHC 2777 (Admin) or, more recently, in *R (Gentle)* v. *Prime Minister* [2008] 2 WLR 879 (both concerning essentially unreviewable decisions) would preclude the Court from doing so here.

63. Why, then, should the Court here not accede to the respondents' invitation to construe Article 5 and, if it accepts the respondents' contended for construction, quash the Director's decision and require it to be re-determined?

64. There is not to my mind any one simple answer to this question although I am perfectly clear that the invitation must be declined and that the Divisional Court was right to have done so.

65. Although, as I have acknowledged, there are occasions when the Court will decide questions as to the state's obligations under unincorporated international law, this, for obvious reasons, is generally undesirable. Particularly this is so where, as here, the Contracting Parties to the Convention have chosen not to provide for the resolution of disputed questions of construction by an international court but rather (by Article 12) to create a Working Group through whose continuing processes it is hoped a consensus view will emerge. Really this is no more than to echo para. 44 of Lord Bingham's opinion. For a national court itself to assume the role of determining such a question (with whatever damaging consequences that may have for the state in its own attempts to influence the emerging consensus) would be a remarkable thing, not to be countenanced save for compelling reasons.

66. Are there such compelling reasons here? In my judgment there are not. There seem to me to be very real differences between this case and both *Launder* and *Kebilene*. In the first place, as Lord Bingham

points out at para. 43, there is a marked distinction between seeking to apply established Convention jurisprudence to the particular case before the court (as there) and determining, in the absence of any jurisprudence whatever on the point, a deep and difficult question of construction of profound importance to the whole working of the Convention (as here). Secondly, it seems to me tolerably plain that the decision-makers in both *Launder* and *Kebilene*, deciding respectively on extradition and prosecution, would have taken different decisions had their understanding of the law been different. In each case the decision-maker clearly intended to act consistently with the UK's international obligations whatever decision that would have involved him in taking. That, however, was not the position here. Although both the Director (and the Attorney General) clearly believed—and may very well be right in believing—that the decision was consistent with Article 5, it is surely plain that the primary intention behind the decision was to save this country from the dire threat to its national and international security and that the same decision would have been taken even had the Director had doubts about the true meaning of Article 5 or even had he thought it bore the contrary meaning. All that he and the Attorney General were really saying was that they believed the decision to be consistent with Article 5. This clearly they were entitled to say: it was true and at the very least obviously a reasonable and tenable belief. Both the Director's and Attorney General's understanding of Article 5 was clearly apparent from their public statements: it was implicit in these that they understood Article 5 not to preclude regard being had to fundamental considerations of national and international security merely because these would be imperilled by worsening relations with a foreign state.

67. The critical question is not, as the respondents' arguments suggest, whether the Director's successor would make the same decision again once the courts had publicly stated that this would involve a breach of the Convention; rather it is whether the court should feel itself impelled to decide the true construction of Article 5 in the first place. It simply cannot be the law that, provided only a public officer asserts that his decision accords with the state's international obligations, the court will entertain a challenge to the decision based upon his arguable misunderstanding of that obligation and then itself decide the point of international law at issue. For the reasons I have sought to give it would certainly not be appropriate to do so in the present case.

68. Since writing the above I have chanced upon an article in the July 2008 Law Quarterly Review Vol. 124, p. 388, "International Law in Domestic Courts: The Developing Framework", by Philip Sales QC and Joanne Clement. This has strongly confirmed to me the view

I have already taken. The following passage in particular seems to me worth quoting (omitting the footnoted references) at pp. 405 and 406:

Part of the problem here is that the executive may not have any practical option but to direct itself by reference to international law, and if the rule in *Launder* is treated as unlimited it will lead to very extensive direct application of treaties and international law in the domestic courts, thereby for practical purposes undermining the basic constitutional principle about non-enforceability of unincorporated treaties. One solution might be for the domestic courts, in recognition of the limits of their competence to provide a fully authoritative ruling on the point, the limits of their competence under domestic constitutional arrangements to rule on the subject-matter in question and the dangers posed to the national interest by them ruling definitively on the point at all, either to decline to rule or to allow the executive a form of "margin of appreciation" on the legal question, and to examine only whether a tenable view has been adopted on the point of international law (rather than ruling on it themselves, as if it were a hard-edged point of domestic law). This is the approach which has been adopted by the ECtHR, when it has to examine questions of international law which it does not have jurisdiction to determine authoritatively itself. Adoption of a "tenable view" approach would be a way— under circumstances where the proper interpretation of international law is uncertain, the domestic courts have no authority under international law to resolve the issue and the executive has responsibility within the domestic legal order for management of the United Kingdom's international affairs (including the adoption of positions to promote particular outcomes on doubtful points of international law)—to allow space to the executive to seek to press for legal interpretations on the international plane to favour the United Kingdom's national interest, while also providing a degree of judicial control to ensure that the positions adopted are not beyond what is reasonable.

The article goes on to suggest that the *Launder* approach must indeed be subject to limitations, dependent perhaps upon "the intensity of judicial scrutiny judged appropriate in domestic law terms in the particular context". I have no doubt this is so and that the question will require further consideration on a future occasion. I have equally no doubt, however, that in this particular context the "tenable view" approach is the furthest the Court should go in examining the point of international law in question and, as I have already indicated, it is clear that the Director held at the very least a tenable view upon the meaning of Article 5.

69. It follows that the Divisional Court's order cannot be saved by reference to this second part of the case. I too would accordingly allow the Director's appeal and make the order proposed by Lord Bingham.

[Reports: [2009] 1 AC 756; [2008] 3 WLR 568; [2008] 4 All ER 927]

Human rights — Asylum — European Convention on Human Rights, 1950 — Article 8 — Right to respect for private and family life — "Flagrant breach" of Article 8 right being so fundamental as to amount to nullification or destruction of very essence of right — "Flagrant breach" not distinct from "complete denial" and "nullification" — Article 8 rights of all persons affected by decisions to be taken into account — Article 14 — Prohibition of discrimination — Discrimination on grounds of sex — Whether aliens can claim entitlement under Convention to remain in Contracting State to escape discriminatory or arbitrary system in country of origin in exceptional circumstances — Right of States to control entry, residence and expulsion of aliens — Best interests of the child

Relationship of international law and municipal law — Treaties — European Convention on Human Rights, 1950 — Article 8 — Sharia law — Family law — Custody of children — Lebanese automatic entitlement of father or male paternal relative to custody of children from age seven — The law of England

EM (LEBANON) v. SECRETARY OF STATE FOR THE HOME
DEPARTMENT
(AF (A CHILD) AND OTHERS INTERVENING)[1]

([2008] UKHL 64)

England, House of Lords. 22 *October* 2008

(Lord Hope of Craighead, Lord Bingham of Cornhill, Baroness Hale of Richmond, Lord Carswell and Lord Brown of Eaton-under-Heywood)

SUMMARY:[2] *The facts*:—The claimant, EM, was a Lebanese national who was refused asylum by the defendant, the Secretary of State for the Home Department. In the 1990s the claimant had married another Lebanese national and Muslim in Lebanon under Sharia law. During that marriage, the claimant's husband subjected her to serious violence. In 1996, the claimant gave birth to

---

[1] The claimant was represented by Frances Webber and Stephanie Harrison, instructed by JM Wilson, Birmingham. The defendant was represented by Monica Carss-Frisk QC and Nicola Greaney, instructed by the Treasury Solicitor. AF as intervener was represented by Henry Setright QC, Teertha Gupta and Margaret Phelan, instructed by Dawson Cornwell. JUSTICE and Liberty as interveners were represented by Rabinder Singh QC and Raza Husain, instructed by Freshfields Bruckhaus Deringer LLP.
[2] Prepared by Ms E. Fogarty.

their son, AF. After a failed attempt to remove AF from the hospital following his birth, to take him to Saudi Arabia, the claimant's husband had no further contact with AF. The claimant and her husband subsequently separated and divorced, and the husband spent time in prison for theft and failure to support AF. Although the prevailing Lebanese law provided for fathers to retain custody of children, the divorce court ruled that AF should remain with the claimant until the age of seven, after which, under Islamic law, physical custody compulsorily passed to the father or a male paternal relative.

After AF's seventh birthday, the claimant and AF went into hiding. In December 2004, they fled Lebanon with the help of an agent, arriving in the United Kingdom that month. Upon arrival, the claimant claimed asylum, asserting that if she were returned, she would face charges of kidnapping and possible mistreatment in prison. She also claimed that her removal would be contrary to the right to respect for family life under Article 8[3] of the European Convention on Human Rights, 1950 ("the Convention"), read in conjunction with Article 14,[4] on the basis that, because she was a woman, she would lose custody of her son.

The defendant refused the claimant's asylum and Article 8 claims, determining that she did not have a well-founded fear of persecution, and that removal would not amount to a "flagrant" disregard for her right to respect for family life. The claimant's appeals to the Asylum and Immigration Tribunal and Court of Appeal were dismissed, with the Court of Appeal holding that the potential for the claimant to have supervised visits with her son in Lebanon precluded a finding that her Article 8 right, alone or in conjunction with Article 14, would be completely denied. The claimant appealed to the House of Lords on her Article 8 claim.

Held (unanimously):—The appeal was allowed.

Per Lord Hope of Craighead: (1) The question to be decided was whether the claimant and AF would run a "real risk" of a "flagrant" denial of the right to respect for family life if they were removed to Lebanon (paras. 2-4).

(2) Under Lebanese law, while the claimant might be allowed supervised visits, under no circumstances would she retain custody of AF. In cases of separated parents, the close relationship which existed between a mother and child up to the age of seven could not survive under that system, creating a real

---

[3] Article 8 of the European Convention on Human Rights,1950, provided: "*Right to respect for private and family life*: (1) Everyone has the right to respect for his private and family life, his home and his correspondence. (2) There shall be no interference by a public authority with the exercise of this right except such as is in accordance with the law and is necessary in a democratic society in the interests of national security, public safety or the economic wellbeing of the country, for the prevention of disorder or crime, for the protection of health or morals, or for the protection of the rights and freedoms of others."

[4] Article 14 of the European Convention on Human Rights provided: "*Prohibition of discrimination*: The enjoyment of the rights and freedoms set forth in this Convention shall be secured without discrimination on any ground such as sex, race, colour, language, religion, political or other opinion, national or social origin, association with a national minority, property, birth or other status."

risk that the very essence of the family life between the mother and child would be nullified. Although that system was arbitrary and discriminatory when measured by the human rights standards outlined in the Convention, Strasbourg jurisprudence indicated that, in the absence of very exceptional circumstances, aliens could not claim any entitlement under the Convention to remain in a Contracting State to escape the discriminatory effects of the system of family law in their own States. To hold otherwise would place too great a burden on Contracting States (paras. 5-7 and 10).

(3) Contracting States were obliged to protect persons from States not party to the Convention who could show that they would suffer persecution or were at real risk of a violation of the rights protected by Articles 2, 3 and 6. However, limits had to be set on the extent to which Contracting States could be held responsible outside those areas, seen against the general principle of international law that States had the right to control the entry, residence and expulsion of aliens in their territories. Contracting States did not undertake to guarantee men and women throughout the world enjoyment of the rights set out in the Convention, nor to alleviate the religious and cultural differences between their own laws and that of an alien's country of origin. Except in wholly exceptional circumstances, the Strasbourg court would likely hold that an alien subject to expulsion could not claim the entitlement to remain in a Contracting State to benefit from the equality of treatment as to respect of family life that subsisted in that State. The return of a woman and child who had come to a Contracting State to escape the system of family law in their country of origin, however objectionable, would not violate Article 8 read in conjunction with Article 14 of the Convention. On a pragmatic basis, Contracting States could not be expected to return aliens only to countries whose family law was compatible with the principle of non-discrimination assumed by the Convention (paras. 13-15).

(4) The key to identifying those cases where the breach of Articles 8 and 14 of the Convention would be flagrant lay in an assessment of the effects on both the mother and child of destroying or nullifying their shared family life. Cases where such a violation was flagrant were very exceptional, but where humanitarian grounds against removal were compelling, it had to follow that a Contracting State was obliged not to remove. The case for allowing the claimant and AF to remain on humanitarian grounds was indeed compelling, particularly when the effects on AF were taken into account. The claimant had cared for AF since birth; they had a settled and happy relationship in the UK that comprised the only family life AF knew. He had never had any contact with his paternal family. Those circumstances rendered this an exceptional case in which removal did pose a real risk of a flagrant denial of the claimant's and AF's Article 8 rights (paras. 17-18).

Per Lord Bingham of Cornhill: (1) It was established that Articles other than Article 3 of the Convention could, in principle, be engaged in relation to removal of individuals from the UK, but that the threshold was very high. Only in cases where a qualified right would be completely denied or nullified in the destination country could it be said that removal would breach the Convention. The threshold was "flagrant" denial of the relevant right, which connoted to a breach so fundamental as to amount to a nullification or destruction of the very essence of the right (paras. 33-4).

(2) The importance of the right to respect for family life was recognized both in the Strasbourg jurisprudence and domestically, as was the particular bond that arose at birth between a mother and child. Two fundamental aspects of the Article 8 right were the mutual enjoyment by parent and child of each other's company, and the right to care for one's own children. The question to be determined in this appeal was subsequently whether, on the particular facts of the case, the removal of the claimant and AF would so flagrantly violate her, his and their mutual Article 8 rights as to completely deny or nullify them. Since AF's birth, AF's only family life was with the claimant, with whom he shared a bond of deep love and mutual dependence. That relationship could not be replaced by any new relationship between AF and his father. On the evidence, it was clear that both AF's and the claimant's Article 8 rights upon return would be flagrantly violated, completely denied and nullified. In no meaningful sense could the potential of supervised visits by the claimant to AF be described as family life (paras. 36-41 and 44).

Per Baroness Hale of Richmond: (1) The word "flagrant" was intended to convey a breach that was so fundamental as to amount to a nullification or destruction of the very essence of the right guaranteed (para. 45).

(2) The defendant, and the Asylum and Immigration Tribunal, were obliged to take into account the Article 8 rights of all persons affected by their decisions. The only family life AF had ever known was with the claimant. If he was obliged to return to a country where he would be removed from the claimant, with only the possibility of supervised contact with her, the very essence of his right to respect to family life would be destroyed, and for reasons which could not be justified under Article 8(2) due to their arbitrary nature, which paid no regard to his interests (paras 46-8 and 50).

Per Lord Carswell: (1) In deciding this case, the House was applying the domestic law of the UK by reference to the values enshrined in the Convention. It was not passing judgment on the law or institutions of any other State, nor making comparisons with Sharia law (para. 52).

(2) The Court of Appeal set the bar too high in considering that if the claimant retained any vestige of her right to family life, by way of the possibility of supervised contact, her claim would fail. The correct test was whether the very essence of the right would be destroyed. That did not require the absolute terms adopted by the Court of Appeal but remained a stringent test that would only be satisfied in very exceptional cases. The claimant's Article 8 rights would be flagrantly violated if she were returned to Lebanon. Her circumstances were exceptional, even if AF's rights were not also considered; however, once his rights were included, that conclusion was stronger still (paras. 53-5 and 57-9).

Per Lord Brown of Eaton-under-Heywood: It was not the arbitrary and discriminatory character of the rule of Sharia law that dictated the age at which a child's physical custody automatically passed to his father or another male paternal relative which qualified this case as one for protection under Article 8, notwithstanding that such a rule was wholly incompatible with the Convention. Rather it was the highly exceptional facts of the case, which, in combination, provided utterly compelling humanitarian grounds against removal (para. 60).

The following is the text of the speeches delivered in the House of Lords:

LORD HOPE OF CRAIGHEAD

1. After the conclusion of the hearing, and following deliberation, the parties were informed that the appeal would be allowed for reasons to be given later. The following are my reasons for inviting the House to allow the appeal, to set aside the orders below and to quash the Secretary of State's decision that the appellant and her son must be returned to Lebanon.

2. The case for allowing the appellant and her son to remain in this country on humanitarian grounds is compelling. That is shown by the facts that my noble and learned friend Lord Bingham of Cornhill has described. But the appellant does not wish to rely on the Secretary of State's discretion. She claims that she has a right to remain here under article 8 of the European Convention on Human Rights read in conjunction with article 14. So the question is whether she has established that she and her son would run a real risk of a flagrant denial of the right to respect for their family life guaranteed to her by those articles if they were to be removed from this country to Lebanon.

3. I take the wording of the test to be applied to determine whether there would be a flagrant denial of this right from what Judges Bratza, Bonello and Hedigan said in their joint partly dissenting opinion in *Mamatkulov and Askarov* v. *Turkey* (2005) 41 EHRR 494, 537-9. That was a case where political dissidents claimed that they would not receive a fair trial if they were extradited to Uzbekistan because, among other things, torture was routinely used to secure guilty verdicts and because suspects were frequently denied access to a lawyer. Their case was that they ran a real risk of a flagrant denial of justice. In para. O-III 14 the judges said:

In our view, what the word "flagrant" is intended to convey is a breach of the principles of fair trial guaranteed by article 6 which is so fundamental as to amount to a nullification, or destruction of the very essence, of the right guaranteed by that article.

In paras. O-III 17 and O-III 19 they used the expression "a real risk" to describe the standard which the evidence has to achieve in order to show that the expulsion or extradition of the individual would, if carried out, violate the article.

4. I have gone directly to what those judges said about the test in *Mamatkulov* rather than to what was said in *R (Ullah)* v. *Special Adjudicator, Do* v. *Immigration Appeal Tribunal* [2004] 2 AC 323 and *R (Razgar)* v. *Secretary of State for the Home Department* [2004] 2 AC 368 for several reasons. First, their description of it is the most up to date guidance that is available from Strasbourg. Second, it combines in a simple formula the approach described in *Devaseelan* v. *Secretary of State for the Home Department* [2003] Imm AR 1, para. 111, referred to with approval by Lord Bingham of Cornhill and Lord Carswell in paras. 24 and 69 of *Ullah* with Lord Steyn's use of the expression "the very essence of the right" in para. 50 of *Ullah*. And, third, it shows that Carnwath LJ in the Court of Appeal [2007] UKHRR 1, paras. 37-8, was, with great respect, wrong to regard words such as "complete denial" or "nullification" on the one hand and "flagrant breach" or "gross invasion" on the other as indicating different tests. Attempts to explain or analyse the formula should be resisted, in the absence of further guidance from Strasbourg. There is only one test, although I think that how it is to be applied in an article 8 read with article 14 case needs some explanation. The use by the partly dissenting judges of the expression "a real risk" is also significant. It shows that what was said about the standard of proof in the context of article 3 in *Soering* v. *United Kingdom* (1989) 11 EHRR 439, para. 91, applies to cases such as this where the rights in issue are among the qualified rights to be found elsewhere in the Convention.

5. There is however one aspect of this case which I have found particularly difficult. The appellant came to this country as a fugitive from Shari'a law. Her son had reached the age of seven when, under the system that regulates the custody of a child of that age under Shari'a law in Lebanon, his physical custody would pass by force of law to his father or another male member of his family. Any attempt by her to retain custody of him there would be bound to fail. This is simply because the law dictates that a mother has no right to the custody of her child after that age. She may or may not be allowed what has been described as visitation. That would give her access to her son during supervised visits to a place where she could see him. But under no

circumstances would his custody remain with her. The close relationship that exists between mother and child up to the age of custodial transfer cannot survive under that system of law where, as in this case, the parents of the child are no longer living together when the child reaches that age. There is a real risk in all these cases that the very essence of the family life that mother and child have shared together up to that date will be destroyed or nullified.

6. This system was described by counsel during the argument as arbitrary and discriminatory. So it is, if it is to be measured by the human rights standards that we are obliged to apply by the Convention. The mutual enjoyment by parent and child of each other's company is a fundamental element of family life. Under our law non-discrimination is a core principle for the protection of human rights. The fact is however that Shari'a law as it is applied in Lebanon was created by and for men in a male dominated society. The place of the mother in the life of a child under that system is quite different under that law from that which is guaranteed in the Contracting States by article 8 of the Convention read in conjunction with article 14. There is no place in it for equal rights between men and women. It is, as Lord Bingham points out, the product of a religious and cultural tradition that is respected and observed throughout much of the world. But by our standards the system is arbitrary because the law permits of no exceptions to its application, however strong the objections may be on the facts of any given case. It is discriminatory too because it denies women custody of their children after they have reached the age of custodial transfer simply because they are women. That is why the appellant removed her child from that system of law and sought protection against its effects in this country.

7. It seems to me that the Strasbourg court's jurisprudence indicates that, in the absence of very exceptional circumstances, aliens cannot claim any entitlement under the Convention to remain here to escape from the discriminatory effects of the system of family law in their country of origin. There is a close analogy between this case and *N v. United Kingdom* (Application No 26565/05) (unreported) 27 May 2008 which followed the decision of this House in *N v. Secretary of State for the Home Department (Terrence Higgins Trust intervening)* [2005] 2 AC 296.

8. In *N's* case the appellant was found after her arrival in this country from Uganda to have an AIDS-defining illness for which she was still receiving beneficial medical treatment when the appeal was heard. She claimed that the treatment that she needed would not be available to her in Uganda and she would die within a matter of months if she were to be

returned to that country, whereas she could expect to live for decades if she were to remain in this country. That being so, it was argued, the United Kingdom would be in breach of its obligations under article 3 of the Convention if she were to be returned to Uganda. As Lord Nicholls of Birkenhead said in para. 1, the appeal raised a question of profound importance about the obligations of the United Kingdom in respect of the expulsion of people with HIV/AIDS. The cruel reality was that if the appellant were to be returned to Uganda her ability to obtain the necessary medication was at best problematic. In para. 4 Lord Nicholls described her position as similar to having a life-support machine switched off. Yet the House, with considerable misgivings in what was plainly a very sad case, dismissed her appeal.

9. Following that decision the appellant lodged an application against the United Kingdom in Strasbourg. The Grand Chamber declared her application inadmissible. In para. 42 of the decision it said:

Aliens who are subject to expulsion cannot in principle claim any entitlement to remain in the territory of a Contracting State in order to continue to benefit from medical, social or other forms of assistance and services provided by the expelling State. The fact that the applicant's circumstances, including his life expectancy, would be significantly reduced if he were to be removed from the Contracting State is not sufficient in itself to give rise to breach of article 3. The decision to remove an alien who is suffering from a serious mental or physical illness to a country where the facilities for the treatment of that illness are inferior to those available in the Contracting State may raise an issue under article 3, but only in a very exceptional case, where the humanitarian grounds against the removal are compelling.

In para. 44 the Grand Chamber recalled that, although many of the rights it contains have implications of a social or economic nature, the Convention is essentially directed at the protection of civil and political rights.

Advances in medical science, together with social and economic differences between countries, entail that the level of treatment available in the Contracting State and the country of origin may vary considerably. While it is necessary, given the fundamental importance of article 3 in the Convention system, for the court to retain a degree of flexibility to prevent expulsion in very exceptional cases, article 3 does not place an obligation on the Contracting State to alleviate such disparities through the provision of free and unlimited health care to all aliens without a right to stay within its jurisdiction. A finding to the contrary would place too great a burden on the Contracting States.

10. That was a case about article 3, not one of the qualified Convention rights. Yet even in such a case, where there was a very real

risk that the harm that would result from the applicant's expulsion to the inferior system of health care in her country of origin would reach the severity of treatment prescribed by that article, the court held that, other than in very exceptional cases, there was no obligation under the Convention to allow her to remain here. This was because it was not the intention of the Convention to provide protection against disparities in social and economic rights. To hold otherwise, even in an article 3 case, would place too great a burden on the Contracting States. Similar observations about the limits that must be set on practical grounds to the qualified obligations that they have undertaken in the area of civil and political rights are to be found in *F* v. *United Kingdom* (Application No 17341/03) (unreported) 22 June 2004 and *Z and T* v. *United Kingdom* (Application No 27034/05) (unreported) 28 February 2006. These decisions were not available to the House when it was considering the cases of *Ullah* [2004] 2 AC 323 and *Razgar* [2004] 2 AC 368, the judgments in which were delivered on 17 June 2004.

11. In *F* v. *United Kingdom* the applicant was an Iranian citizen who had claimed asylum here on the basis that he feared persecution as a homosexual. His application for asylum was rejected. But he claimed that there would be a breach of article 8 if he were to be removed to Iran because a law in that country prohibited adult consensual homosexual activity. His application was declared inadmissible by the Strasbourg court. At p. 12 of its decision the court observed that its case law had found responsibility attaching to Contracting States in respect of expelling persons who were at risk of treatment contrary to articles 2 and 3 of the Convention. It said that this was based on the fundamental importance of these provisions, whose guarantees it was imperative to render effective in practice: *Soering* v. *United Kingdom* (1989) 11 EHRR 439, para. 88. But it went on to say this:

Such compelling considerations do not automatically apply under the other provisions of the Convention. On a purely pragmatic basis, it cannot be required that an expelling Contracting State only return an alien to a country which is in full and effective enforcement of all the rights and freedoms set out in the Convention.

12. In *Z and T* v. *United Kingdom* the applicants were citizens of Pakistan. They were also Christians. They feared that they would be subjected to attack by Muslim extremists if they were to be returned to Pakistan because they were Christians. The case raised a question as to the approach to be taken to article 9 rights that were allegedly at risk on expulsion. It was argued that the flagrant denial test should not be applied, as this would fail to respect the primacy of the applicants'

religious rights. The Strasbourg court rejected this argument. It found that, even assuming that article 9 was capable of being engaged in the case of the expulsion of an individual by a Contracting State, the applicants had not shown that they were personally at risk or were members of such a vulnerable or threatened group, or in such a precarious position as Christians, as might disclose a flagrant violation of article 9 of the Convention. But at p. 7 of its judgment the court said that it considered that very limited assistance, if any, could be obtained from article 9 by itself:

> Otherwise it would be imposing an obligation on Contracting States effectively to act as indirect guarantors of freedom of worship for the rest of the world. If, for example, a country outside the umbrella of the Convention were to ban a religion but not impose any measure of persecution, prosecution, deprivation of liberty or ill-treatment, the court doubts that the Convention could be interpreted as requiring a Contracting State to provide the adherents of that banned sect with the possibility of pursuing that religion freely and openly on their own territories. While the court would not rule out the possibility that the responsibility of the returning state might in exceptional circumstances be engaged under article 9 of the Convention where the person concerned ran a real risk of flagrant violation of that article in the receiving state, the court shares the view of the House of Lords in the *Ullah* case that it would be difficult to visualise a case in which a sufficiently flagrant violation of article 9 would not also involve treatment in violation of article 3 of the Convention.

The reference in the last sentence endorses Lord Carswell's observation in para. 67 of his opinion in *Ullah* [2004] 2 AC 323 that he found it difficult to envisage a case, bearing in mind the flagrancy principle, in which there could be a sufficient interference with the article 9 rights which did not also come within the article 3 exception.

13. Running through these three recent cases is a recognition by the Strasbourg court that, while the Contracting States are obliged to protect those from other jurisdictions who can show that for whatever reason they will suffer persecution or are at real risk of death or serious ill-treatment or will face arbitrary detention or a flagrant denial of a fair trial in the receiving country, limits must be set on the extent to which they can be held responsible outside the areas that are prescribed by articles 2 and 3 and by the fundamental right under article 6 to a fair trial. Those limits must be seen against the background of the general principle of international law that States have the right to control the entry, residence and expulsion of aliens. In *N* v. *United Kingdom* a distinction was drawn between civil and political rights on the one hand and rights of a social or economic nature on the other. Despite its

fundamental importance in the Convention system, article 3 does not have the effect of requiring a Contracting State to guarantee free and unlimited health care to all aliens who are without a right to stay within its jurisdiction. In *F* v. *United Kingdom*, an article 8 case, a distinction of a different kind was drawn. On the one hand there are those guarantees which, as they are of fundamental importance, must always be rendered effective in practice. On the other there are the qualified rights of a civil or political nature which, on a purely pragmatic basis, the Contracting States cannot be required to guarantee for the rest of the world outside the umbrella of the Convention.

14. As this case shows, the principle that men and women have equal rights is not universally recognised. Lebanon is by no means the only State which has declined to subscribe to article 16(d) of the United Nations Convention on the Elimination of All Forms of Discrimination against Women of 18 December 1979 which declares that States Parties shall ensure, on a basis of equality of men and women, the same rights and responsibilities as parents, irrespective of their marital status, in all matters relating to their children and that in all cases the interests of the children shall be paramount. For the time being that declaration remains in most, if not all, Islamic States at best an aspiration, not a reality. As the court said in *Soering*, para. 91, there is no question of adjudicating on or establishing the responsibility of the receiving State, whether under general international law, under the Convention or otherwise. Everything depends on the extent to which responsibility can be placed on the Contracting States. But they did not undertake to guarantee to men and women throughout the world the enjoyment without discrimination of the rights set out in the Convention or in any other international human rights instrument. Nor did they undertake to alleviate religious and cultural differences between their own laws and the family law of an alien's country of origin, however extreme their effects might seem to be on a family relationship.

15. The guidance that is to be found in these decisions indicates that the Strasbourg court would be likely to hold that, except in wholly exceptional circumstances, aliens who are subject to expulsion cannot claim an entitlement to remain in the territory of a Contracting State in order to benefit from the equality of treatment as to respect for their family life that they would receive there which would be denied to them in the receiving State. The return of a woman who arrives here with her child simply to escape from the system of family law of her own country, however objectionable that system may seem in comparison with our own, will not violate article 8 read with article 14. Domestic violence and family breakdown occur in Muslim countries

just as they do elsewhere. So the inevitable result under Shari'a law that the separated mother will lose custody of her child when he reaches the age of custodial transfer ought, in itself, to make no difference. On a purely pragmatic basis the Contracting States cannot be expected to return aliens only to a country whose family law is compatible with the principle of non-discrimination assumed by the Convention.

16. How then can one distinguish between those cases where a violation of articles 8 and 14 that results from applying Shari'a law will be flagrant [and] those where it will not? It is hard to envisage a case where the way the law deals with a child custody case will also violate article 3. The possibility of a violation of that article may have a part to play in the assessment in more extreme article 9 religious persecution cases, as Lord Carswell's observation in *Ullah*, para. 67, and its adoption by the Strasbourg court in *Z and T*, p. 7, indicate. That may be the case in some article 8 cases, as in *F*. But it is likely to be absent in article 8 plus article 14 cases where the complaint is about the effects of discriminatory family law on the relationship that exists between individuals. It has not been suggested in this case that there is a risk that the application of the Shari'a law would result in persecution of the appellant approaching the level prescribed by article 3. So that check as to whether a flagrant breach has been established cannot be relied on in the assessment.

17. There remains the observation that the Grand Chamber made in *N* v. *United Kingdom*, 27 May 2008, para. 42, that an issue under article 3 may be raised only in a very exceptional medical treatment case where the humanitarian grounds against the removal are compelling. *D* v. *United Kingdom* (1997) 24 EHRR 423, where the applicant was critically ill and close to death, was such a case. This suggests that the key to identifying those cases where the breach of articles 8 and 14 will be flagrant lies in an assessment of the effects on both mother and child of destroying or nullifying the family life that they have shared together. The cases where that assessment shows that the violation will be flagrant will be very exceptional. But where the humanitarian grounds against their removal are compelling, it must follow that there is an obligation not to remove. The risk of adding one test to another is obvious. But in the absence of further guidance from Strasbourg as to how the flagrancy test is to be applied in article 8 cases, I would adopt that approach in this case.

18. As I said at the outset of this opinion, the case for allowing the appellant and her son to remain in this country on humanitarian grounds is compelling. This is particularly so when the effects on the child are taken into account. His mother has cared from him since his

birth. He has a settled and happy relationship with her in this country. Life with his mother is the only family life he knows. Life with his father or any other member of his family in Lebanon, with whom he has never had any contact, would be totally alien to him. This enables me to conclude that this is a very exceptional case and that there is a real risk of a flagrant denial of their article 8 rights if the appellant and her child were to be returned to Lebanon. I would allow the appeal.

LORD BINGHAM OF CORNHILL

19. By article 8 of the European Convention on Human Rights, given domestic effect by the Human Rights Act 1998, everyone in this country has the right to respect for their family life, which may be the subject of interference by a public authority only if the interference is lawful, proportionate and directed to a legitimate end. The enjoyment of this right is, by article 14, to be secured without discrimination on any ground such as sex. The appellant claims that if she and her son AF are removed from this country to Lebanon on the direction of the respondent Secretary of State, her right to respect for her family life will be infringed and will be so on a discriminatory basis attributable to her being a woman. This claim rests not on any treatment she or AF will suffer in this country but on the consequences if she and her son are returned to Lebanon. Thus this is what has been described as a foreign case: the only conduct by a British authority of which the appellant complains is her removal to a place where she will suffer these consequences. Her challenge is directed to the decision to remove her. The burden lying on a claimant in a foreign case such as this is, the appellant acknowledges, a very exacting one. But she contends that, on the exceptional facts of her case, and recognising the interests of AF, she discharges it. The courts below held that she did not. The appellant submits that those courts did not correctly understand and apply the test laid down by the authorities, and that the interests of AF (who was first given leave to intervene in the House) should be taken into account. Her submissions are supported by AF, and also by JUSTICE and Liberty.

20. The appellant EM is a Lebanese national now aged 36. She came to this country on 30 December 2004 with her son AF, the second intervener, who was born on 16 July 1996 and is now aged 12. She claimed asylum.

21. The appellant is Muslim and married in Lebanon according to Muslim rites. Her evidence, accepted as true in these proceedings, is

that during her marriage her husband subjected her to violence, beating her, trying to throw her off a balcony and trying, on one occasion at least, to strangle her. She had a mental breakdown. Her husband was imprisoned for theft from her father's shop and, later, for failing to support AF. He ended her first pregnancy by hitting her on the stomach with a heavy vase, saying he did not want children. On the day AF was born he came to the hospital with his family to take the child away to Saudi Arabia, but was prevented from doing so. He has not seen AF since.

22. The appellant divorced her husband in Lebanon because of his violence. Under the prevailing law the father retained legal custody of AF, but the divorce court ruled that the child should remain in the appellant's care until he reached the age of seven. Thereafter, Islamic law as applied in Lebanon entitled the father to require that physical custody should be transferred to himself or to a male member of his family.

23. After the divorce the appellant supported herself and AF by running a hairdressing salon. When AF was approaching the age of seven she began trying to leave the country to avoid having the child taken from her. After AF's birthday, she moved out of her parents' house and lived in hiding to prevent his removal from her care. Her former husband issued proceedings in the Lebanese court. The police attended at her parents' house and her former husband harassed them. The appellant and her child left Lebanon with the assistance of an agent, leaving the country on 20 December 2004. It appears that, if she returned to Lebanon, she would be at risk of imprisonment on a charge of kidnapping AF.

24. There was unchallenged evidence before the lower courts of Islamic law as applied in Lebanon in custody cases where (as in this case) the husband or both parties are Muslim. Even during the seven-year period when a child is cared for by the mother, the father retains legal custody and may decide where the child lives and whether the child may travel with the mother. In the absence of consent by the father, the transfer to the father at the stipulated age is automatic: the court has no discretion in the matter and may not consider whether transfer is in the best interests of the child. As a result, women are often constrained to remain in abusive marriages for fear of losing their children. If the father were found to be unfit as a parent, the child would be passed to the paternal grandfather or some other member of the father's extended family, not to the mother. The evidence was that in this situation the mother might, or might not, have contact with the child. The parent with physical custody cannot be compelled to send

the child to the other parent's home on visits, but if ordered by the court must bring the child to a place where the mother could see him or her. A custody hearing, if held in Lebanon, would not consider whether custody should remain with the mother but only the appropriateness of allowing the appellant to have access to AF during supervised visits.

25. The appellant's application for asylum was refused by the Secretary of State in a letter of 21 February 2005, largely devoted to issues arising under the Refugee Convention. But the Secretary of State considered, and rejected, her claim under article 8 of the European Convention on Human Rights, ruling that she had not demonstrated a real risk of mistreatment such as to engage article 8. It was not accepted that she would be unable to obtain a reasonable, fair and impartial administration of her case in both the religious and civil courts.

26. The appellant exercised her right of appeal. In a decision dated 8 June 2005 the Immigration Judge (Mr C. J. Deavin) found that the appellant did not have a well-founded fear of persecution for a (Refugee) Convention reason, and so rejected her asylum claim. He also held (para. 94) that she could not choose where she wished to lead her life, and that her removal would not engage article 8. In para. 95 of his Decision he said:

It is likely, of course, that her child will be taken away from her, in accordance with the law of the land, but there is every likelihood that she will be allowed visitation rights. It is unrealistic on her part to expect to have the child entirely to herself.

27. On an application for reconsideration of this decision, a Senior Immigration Judge (Mr Andrew Jordan) thought it arguable that inadequate consideration had been given to whether removal would violate the appellant's human rights and (perhaps) those of AF, if those were justiciable. He was also troubled at the prospect that the case had to be considered on the basis of the appellant's rights, paying scant regard to those of AF and, in particular, his best interests. He acknowledged the difficulty of ruling on the best interests of AF in the absence of the father. He was also concerned about certain aspects of the asylum claim. He ordered reconsideration.

28. The matter then came before the Asylum and Immigration Tribunal (Mr C. M. G. Ockelton, Deputy President, Mr N. W. Renton, Senior Immigration Judge, and Mr D. R. Humphrey, Immigration Judge) which gave its Determination and Reasons on 22 November 2005. The AIT first considered, and rejected, the

appellant's asylum claim. With reference to her claim under article 8, the AIT referred to recent decisions of the House in *R (Ullah)* v. *Special Adjudicator* [2004] UKHL 26, [2004] 2 AC 323 and *R (Razgar)* v. *Secretary of State for the Home Department* [2004] UKHL 27, [2004] 2 AC 368, which (para. 15) established that "The appellant can only succeed if she can show that the country to which she returns has a flagrant disregard for the rights protected by article 8." The tribunal continued (para. 16):

On the material before us, that is clearly not so. There is a judicial system, to which the appellant has access. The system of family law to which she, by her religion, is subject, is one which in this respect she does not like: but that does not permit her to choose the law of another country, nor does it permit us to say that it is a system to which nobody should be subject. As a result, we cannot say that the removal of the appellant and her son to Lebanon would itself constitute a breach of the rights they have under article 8 while they remain in the jurisdiction of this country. After their removal, they simply have no such rights: they are subject to the law of their own country, which is not a party to the European Convention on Human Rights.

The tribunal refused leave to appeal against its decision but Buxton LJ granted it on one ground, later enlarged. The appellant's claim to asylum lapsed.

29. The appellant's appeal to the Court of Appeal came before Carnwath and Gage LJJ and Bodey J, each of whom gave judgments: [2007] UKHRR 1. In his leading judgment, Carnwath LJ made detailed reference to four authorities in particular: *Ullah* and *Razgar*, mentioned above, *In re J (A Child) (Custody Rights: Jurisdiction)* [2005] UKHL 40, [2006] 1 AC 80, and *Marckx* v. *Belgium* (1979) 2 EHRR 330. The critical divide between the parties was as to the appropriate test in a foreign case under article 8 and its application to the facts of the appellant's case. For the appellant Ms Webber contended that her right to have her claim to custody reviewed on a non-discriminatory basis would be completely denied or nullified if she and AF were returned to Lebanon. Ms Greaney, for the Secretary of State, criticised this as too narrow a formulation of the appellant's right. Article 8 protected the right to family life. Although the appellant would lose custody of her son, this did not establish that she would lose all contact with him. Thus her enjoyment of family life with her child, though severely restricted, would not be completely denied or nullified. Carnwath LJ said (paras. 36-40):

36. With considerable misgivings, I am forced to the conclusion that Miss Greaney is correct. My misgivings are due principally to the natural reluctance

of an English judge to send a child back to a legal system where a crucial custody issue will be decided without necessary reference to his welfare. That would be an overriding consideration in other jurisdictions, but it is not suggested that it can be determinative in the context of asylum law.

37. In addition I have not found it easy to give effect to the different expressions which have been used to define the test. If "complete denial" or "nullification" is the test, I agree with Miss Greaney's analysis. The right in question is the right protected by article 8, of which custody is but one important aspect. On the evidence her article 8 right would not be completely denied.

38. However, one finds many other formulations in the passages of high authority cited above: "flagrant denial", "gross violation", "flagrant violation of the very essence of the right", "flagrant, gross or fundamental breach", "gross invasion of [her] most fundamental human rights", "particularly flagrant breaches". To my mind there is a difference in ordinary language between "complete denial" of the rights guaranteed by article 8, and "flagrant breach" or "gross invasion" of those rights. In short, the former is quantitative; the latter qualitative.

39. If one or more of the latter expressions provided the test, I would find it difficult to think they are not satisfied in this case. This is not a case where the answer could realistically be affected by representations from the receiving state (a factor mentioned by Lord Bingham of Cornhill in *Ullah*, para. 24). The parent/child relationship is a fundamental aspect of the rights guaranteed by article 8, perhaps the most fundamental; in Lord Steyn's words, it goes to "the very essence" of the right to family life. The ability to participate in that relationship on an equal basis to the father is similarly fundamental to the rights guaranteed by article 14. Those rights are also recognised as fundamental by the wider international community. The facts disclose the almost certain prospect of an open "breach" or "violation" of those rights. A breach which is open, unmitigated, and in Convention terms indefensible can fairly be described as "flagrant" in the ordinary use of that word.

40. However, I am persuaded that that is not the right approach. The word "flagrant" was first used in *Soering* v. *United Kingdom* (1989) 11 EHRR 439 not, I think, as a definitive test, but to illustrate the extreme circumstances which would be needed to bring the Convention into play in a "foreign" case. As Lord Bingham of Cornhill pointed out in *Ullah*, the Strasbourg case-law reveals no examples of cases which have been held to meet that test. The different expressions used in the domestic cases have been used for a similar purpose. Linguistic analysis and comparison is unlikely to be helpful. Lord Bingham of Cornhill's adoption of the *Devaseelan* formula, with the agreement of the whole House, was clearly intended to provide a single authoritative approach. Applying that test, I conclude that the appeal on this central issue must fail.

The appellant's appeal under article 14 of the European Convention was also rejected.

30. Gage LJ reached the same conclusion, also with misgiving. He noted (para. 54) that the well-established principle of domestic law which requires the welfare of the child to be treated as paramount was agreed to be irrelevant, and continued:

55. For my part I have not found this an easy case. On the one hand to deny a mother the right to care for her child seems totally wrong. Judge Martens in a different context described the right to care for "your own children" as "a fundamental element of an elementary right" (see *Gül v. Switzerland* (1996) 22 EHRR 93). To deny this right offends against all principles of fairness to a party involved in litigation over the custody of her child or children. It will undoubtedly place a substantial obstacle in the way of this appellant maintaining and fostering her relationship with her son. It is an entirely arbitrary rule without any apparent justification.

56. On the other hand I see the force of the submission made on behalf of the respondent that not all the appellant's rights as a mother will be denied. She will have rights of visitation and will not lose contact with her son. In that sense her rights cannot be said to be completely nullified.

57. In my judgment this is a case, as envisaged by Lord Carswell in *Ullah*, where the concept of flagrant breach or violation is not easy to apply. Not without some hesitation, I have concluded that the risk of such breaches of her human rights as may occur in respect of the appellant's right to care for her son are not sufficient to be categorised as flagrant. In reaching this conclusion, in my view, the appellant's rights of visitation/contact must be taken into account and set against the denial of the right to custody/residence of her child. It is important to note that we are considering her rights and not those of her son. There is no reason to suppose that the Shari'a Court will prevent the appellant from seeing her son. The form and nature of visitation rights remain undefined but in my judgment it must be supposed that the appellant will continue to be permitted to see her son. In that way her ability to maintain her relationship with him will still exist, albeit on a less intense level than before. In the circumstances I would hold, as the AIT held, that the risk of breaches of her article 8 and 14 rights in all the circumstances are not such as can be said to be flagrant. For the avoidance of doubt I would also hold that the discrimination against her on grounds of gender in the Shari'a Court, whether considered as a breach of her article 8 rights or separately as a breach of article 14 rights, is not sufficient to tip the balance so as to cross the high threshold required.

58. For these reasons and the reasons given by Carnwath LJ, with which I agree, I would dismiss this appeal, and dispose of the applications as he proposes. This is not an outcome for which I have any enthusiasm.

31. Acknowledging the right to care for one's child as "a fundamental element of an elementary human right" (as quoted by Baroness Hale of Richmond, in *Razgar* [2004] 2 AC 368, para. 53), Bodey J regarded

the anticipated interference with the appellant's right to respect for her family life to be flagrant, both by virtue of article 8 read alone and especially when read with article 14 (paras. 66, 76). But applying what he understood to be the correct test, he concluded with express misgivings that the appellant could not cross the threshold to obtain relief (paras. 66, 71, 76, 80-2).

Ullah

32. In *R (Ullah)* v. *Special Adjudicator, Do* v. *Immigration Appeal Tribunal* [2004] 2 AC 323 the appellants sought to resist removal to Pakistan and Vietnam respectively on the ground that they would be unable to practise their religion in those countries as guaranteed by article 9 of the European Convention. Thus, as in the present case, the appellants' claims rested not on the conduct of the British authorities (save in removing her) but on the expected consequences in the foreign country. Theirs were foreign cases in the same sense as the appellant's. The question in the appeal was whether removal could be resisted in reliance on any article of the Convention other than article 3. That removal could be resisted in a foreign case engaging article 3 was clearly established by well-known authority, notably *Soering* v. *United Kingdom* (1989) 11 EHRR 439 and *Chahal* v. *United Kingdom* (1996) 23 EHRR 413. But could other articles of the Convention be relied on? The Court of Appeal [2002] EWCA Civ 1856, [2003] 1 WLR 770, para. 64, had held that where the Convention was invoked on the sole ground of the treatment to which an alien, refused the right to enter this country or remain here, was likely to be subjected by the receiving State, and that treatment was not sufficiently severe to engage article 3, the English court was not required to recognise that any other article of the Convention was or might be engaged. The decision of the Secretary of State in such cases was not subject to the constraints of the Convention.

33. Although separate opinions were delivered, the members of the House were at one in giving two answers to the question. First, they held that articles other than article 3, including article 8, could in principle be engaged in relation to the removal of an individual from this country: paras. 21, 35, 39-49, 52, 53, 62, 67. Secondly, they held that the threshold of success in such a case was a very high one. In para. 24 of my opinion, to which much argument was addressed in the present case, in the courts below and in argument before the House, I expressed myself as follows:

24. While the Strasbourg jurisprudence does not preclude reliance on articles other than article 3 as a ground for existing extradition or expulsion, it makes it quite clear that successful reliance demands presentation of a very strong case. In relation to article 3, it is necessary to show strong grounds for believing that the person, if returned, faces a real risk of being subjected to torture or to inhuman or degrading treatment or punishment: *Soering*, para. 91; *Cruz Varas*, para. 69; *Vilvarajah*, para. 103. In *Dehwari*, para. 61 (see para. 15 above), the Commission doubted whether a real risk was enough to resist removal under article 2, suggesting that the loss of life must be shown to be a "near certainty". Where reliance is placed on article 6 it must be shown that a person has suffered or risks suffering a flagrant denial of a fair trial in the receiving state: *Soering*, para. 113 (see para. 10 above); *Drodz*, para. 110; *Einhorn*, para. 32; *Razaghi* v. *Sweden*; *Tomic* v. *United Kingdom*. Successful reliance on article 5 would have to meet no less exacting a test. The lack of success of applicants relying on articles 2, 5 and 6 before the Strasbourg court highlights the difficulty of meeting the stringent test which that court imposes. This difficulty will not be less where reliance is placed on articles such as 8 or 9, which provide for the striking of a balance between the right of the individual and the wider interests of the community even in a case where a serious interference is shown. This is not a balance which the Strasbourg court ought ordinarily to strike in the first instance, nor is it a balance which that court is well placed to assess in the absence of representations by the receiving state whose laws, institutions or practices are the subject of criticism. On the other hand, the removing state will always have what will usually be strong grounds for justifying its own conduct: the great importance of operating firm and orderly immigration control in an expulsion case; the great desirability of honouring extradition treaties made with other states. The correct approach in cases involving qualified rights such as those under articles 8 and 9 is in my opinion that indicated by the Immigration Appeal Tribunal (Mr C. M. G. Ockelton, deputy president, Mr Allen and Mr Moulden) in *Devaseelan* v. *Secretary of State for the Home Department* [2003] Imm AR 1, para. 111:

> The reason why flagrant denial or gross violation is to be taken into account is that it is only in such a case—where the right will be completely denied or nullified in the destination country—that it can be said that removal will breach the treaty obligations of the signatory state however those obligations might be interpreted or whatever might be said by or on behalf of the destination state.

Lord Steyn (para. 50) said:

It will be apparent from the review of Strasbourg jurisprudence that, where other articles may become engaged, a high threshold test will always have to be satisfied. It will be necessary to establish at least a real risk of a flagrant violation of the very essence of the right before other articles could become engaged.

Lord Walker of Gestingthorpe agreed with my opinion (para. 52) and Baroness Hale of Richmond with those of myself, Lord Steyn and Lord Carswell, while deferring detailed analysis of article 8 to *R (Razgar)* v. *Secretary of State for the Home Department* [2004] 2 AC 368, which was heard by the same committee immediately following *Ullah*. Lord Carswell, in paras. 69-70 of his opinion, said:

69. The adjective "flagrant" has been repeated in many statements where the court has kept open the possibility of engagement of articles of the Convention other than article 3, a number of which are enumerated in para. 24 of the opinion of Lord Bingham of Cornhill in the present appeal. The concept of a flagrant breach or violation may not always be easy for domestic courts to apply—one is put in mind of the difficulties which they have had in applying that of gross negligence—but it seems to me that it was well expressed by the Immigration Appeal Tribunal in *Devaseelan* v. *Secretary of State for the Home Department* [2003] Imm AR 1, 34, para. 111, when it applied the criterion that the right in question would be completely denied or nullified in the destination country. This would harmonise with the concept of a fundamental breach, with which courts in this jurisdiction are familiar.

70. If it could be said that in principle article 9 is capable of engagement, it does not seem to me that the case of either appellant comes within the possible parameters of a flagrant, gross or fundamental breach of that article such as to amount to a denial or nullification of the rights conferred by it. I accordingly agree that both appeals should be dismissed.

The difficulty of resisting removal in reliance on article 9 was evidenced by the rejection of the appellants' claims on the facts. In *Razgar* the answers given in *Ullah* were treated as laying down the relevant principles (paras. 2, 26, 32, 37, 41-2, 66, 72) although opinion was divided on the application of those principles to the facts of that case.

The threshold test

34. It was not submitted in argument that the threshold test laid down in *Ullah* misrepresented or understated the effect of the Strasbourg authority as it stood then or stands now. It is true, as Carnwath LJ pointed out in the Court of Appeal (para. 38), that different expressions have at different times been used to describe the test, but these have been used to describe the same test, not to lay down a different test. Nor, as I would understand the joint partly dissenting opinion of Judges Bratza, Bonello and Hedigan in *Mamatkulov and Askarov* v. *Turkey* (2005) 41 EHRR 494, 537, para. OIII 14, did they envisage a different test when they said, with reference to article 6 (omitting footnotes):

While the court has not to date found that the expulsion or extradition of an individual violated, or would if carried out violate, article 6 of the Convention, it has on frequent occasions held that such a possibility cannot be excluded where the person being expelled has suffered or risks suffering a flagrant denial of a fair trial in the receiving country. What constitutes a "flagrant" denial of justice has not been fully explained in the court's jurisprudence but the use of the adjective is clearly intended to impose a stringent test of unfairness going beyond mere irregularities or lack of safeguards in the trial procedures such as might result in a breach of article 6 if occurring within the Contracting State itself. As the court has emphasised, article 1 cannot be read as justifying a general principle to the effect that a Contracting State may not surrender an individual unless satisfied that the conditions awaiting him in the country of destination are in full accord with each of the safeguards of the Convention. In our view, what the word "flagrant" is intended to convey is a breach of the principles of fair trial guaranteed by article 6 which is so fundamental as to amount to a nullification, or destruction of the very essence, of the right guaranteed by that article.

35. In adopting and endorsing the test formulated by the AIT in *Devaseelan* I did not in para. 24 of my opinion in *Ullah* [2004] 2 AC 323 understand that tribunal to be distinguishing a "flagrant denial or gross violation" of a right from a complete denial or nullification of it but rather to be assimilating those expressions. This was how the point had been put to the House by the Attorney General for the Secretary of State, as is evidenced from the report of his argument (p. 337D):

If other articles can be engaged the threshold test will require a flagrant breach of the relevant right, such as will completely deny or nullify the right in the destination country: see *Devaseelan* v. *Secretary of State for the Home Department* [2003] Imm AR 1. A serious or discriminatory interference with the right protected would be insufficient.

It is difficult, with respect, to see how the point could be put more clearly, and any attempt at paraphrase runs the risk of causing confusion.

The right to respect for family life

36. The importance of the right to respect for family life has been recognised in Strasbourg and domestic jurisprudence. The Strasbourg case law has recognised the bond which arises at birth between child and parent (*Ahmut* v. *Netherlands* (1996) 24 EHRR 62, para. 60) and reference has been repeatedly made to "the mutual enjoyment by parent and child of each other's company" as "a fundamental element of family life" (*McMichael* v. *United Kingdom* (1995) 20 EHRR 205, para. 86; *Johansen* v. *Norway* (1996) 23 EHRR 33, para. 52; *Bronda* v. *Italy*

(1998) 33 EHRR 81, para. 51; *P, C and S* v. *United Kingdom* (2002) 35 EHRR 1075, para. 113). Judge Martens, in a dissenting judgment, has described the right to care for one's own children as "a fundamental element of an elementary human right" (*Gül* v. *Switzerland* (1996) 22 EHRR 93, 120, para. 12). More general statements are found in the domestic case law. In *M* v. *Secretary of State for Work and Pensions* [2006] UKHL 11, [2006] 2 AC 91, para. 5, reference was made to "the love, trust, confidence, mutual dependence and unconstrained social intercourse which are the essence of family life". In *Huang* v. *Secretary of State for the Home Department* [2007] UKHL 11, [2007] 2 AC 167, para. 18, it was said:

Human beings are social animals. They depend on others. Their family, or extended family, is the group on which many people most heavily depend, socially, emotionally and often financially. There comes a point at which, for some, prolonged and unavoidable separation from this group seriously inhibits their ability to live full and fulfilling lives.

My noble and learned friend Baroness Hale has said (*In re B (Children) (Care Proceedings: Standard of Proof) (CAFCASS intervening)* [2008] UKHL 35, [2008] 3 WLR 1, para. 20) that "Taking a child away from her family is a momentous step, not only for her, but for her whole family . . ."

37. Families differ widely, in their composition and in the mutual relations which exist between the members, and marked changes are likely to occur over time within the same family. Thus there is no predetermined model of family or family life to which article 8 must be applied. The article requires respect to be shown for the right to such family life as is or may be enjoyed by the particular applicant or applicants before the court, always bearing in mind (since any family must have at least two members, and may have many more) the participation of other members who share in the life of that family. In this context, as in most Convention contexts, the facts of the particular case are crucial.

38. The question to be determined in this appeal is accordingly this: whether, on the particular facts of this case, the removal of the appellant and AF to Lebanon will so flagrantly violate her, his and their article 8 rights as to completely deny or nullify those rights there. This is, as Ms Carss-Frisk QC for the Secretary of State emphasised, a very hard test to satisfy, never found to be satisfied in respect of any of the qualified Convention rights in any reported Strasbourg decision.

The present case

39. It seems likely that, following her marriage, the appellant's immediate family consisted of herself and her husband. It would have been the life of that family which would have fallen within the purview of article 8 had the Convention applied in Lebanon, which it did (and does) not. But there has been no familial contact between the appellant and her husband since the birth of AF, and AF has never seen his father since the day he was born. Nor has he had any contact with any of his father's relatives. Thus, realistically, the only family which exists now or has existed for the last five years at least consists of the appellant and AF. It is the life of that family which is in issue: *Beoku-Betts* v. *Secretary of State for the Home Department* [2008] UKHL 39, [2008] 3 WLR 166.

40. It is no doubt a feature of their family life together that the appellant renders for AF the sort of services which a mother ordinarily does render for a growing adolescent. But it would be wrong to regard the relationship between the appellant and AF as simply one in which the mother renders services for the son. The evidence makes plain that the bond between the two is one of deep love and mutual dependence. It cannot be replaced by a new relationship between AF and a father who has inflicted physical violence and psychological injury on the mother, who has been sent to prison for failing to support him, whom he has never consciously seen and towards whom AF understandably feels strongly antagonistic. Nor can it be replaced by a new relationship with an unknown member or members of the father's family.

41. Two members of the Court of Appeal, although taking no account of AF's right, appear to have held that the appellant's article 8 right would be flagrantly violated if she were returned to Lebanon, but felt unable to conclude that her right would be completely denied or nullified. As indicated above, these expressions do not propound different tests. But it is in my opinion clear that on return to Lebanon both the appellant's and AF's right to respect for their family life would not only be flagrantly violated but would also be completely denied and nullified. In no meaningful sense could occasional supervised visits by the appellant to AF at a place other than her home, even if ordered (and there is no guarantee that they would be ordered), be described as family life. The effect of return would be to destroy the family life of the appellant and AF as it is now lived.

42. Considerable emphasis was laid in argument for the appellant and the second intervener on the arbitrary and discriminatory character of the family law applied in Lebanon, and it is plain that this would fall

foul of both article 8 and article 14. But Lebanon is not a party to the European Convention, and this court has no standing to enforce observance of other international instruments to which Lebanon is party. Its family law reflects a religious and cultural tradition which, in one form or another, is respected and observed throughout much of the world. This country has no general mandate to impose its own values on other countries who do not share them. I would therefore question whether it would avail the appellant to rely on the arbitrary and discriminatory character of the Lebanese custody regime had she not shown, as in my opinion she has, that return to Lebanon would flagrantly violate, or completely deny and nullify, her and AF's right to respect for their family life together.

43. The Court of Appeal and the courts below were disadvantaged by the absence of representations on behalf of AF. The hearing before the House has underscored the importance of ascertaining and communicating to the court the views of a child such as AF. In the great majority of cases the interests of the child, although calling for separate consideration, are unlikely to differ from those of an applicant parent. If there is a genuine conflict, separate representation may be called for, but advisers should not be astute to detect a conflict where the interests of parent and child are essentially congruent.

44. For these reasons I would allow the appeal, set aside the orders below and quash the Secretary of State's decision. The appellant and the Secretary of State are invited to make written submissions on costs within 14 days.

BARONESS HALE OF RICHMOND

45. As to the test to be applied in these cases, I have nothing to add to what is said by my noble and learned friend, Lord Bingham of Cornhill, in paragraph 34 of his opinion. In the words of Judges Bratza, Bonello and Hedigan in *Mamatkulov and Askarov* v. *Turkey* (2005) 41 EHRR 494, 537, para. OIII 14, "... what the word 'flagrant' is intended to convey is a breach ... which is so fundamental as to amount to a nullification, or destruction of the very essence, of the right guaranteed ...". So far as we are aware, Strasbourg has never yet found that test to be satisfied in a case where the breach of article 8 would take place in the foreign country to which a family is to be expelled, rather than as the result of the expulsion of one of its members (as in, e.g., *Al-Nashif* v. *Bulgaria* (2002) 36 EHRR 655). The possibility is, however, acknowledged, both in *Bensaid* v. *United Kingdom* (2001) 33 EHRR

205, 219-20, paras. 46-9, and in the dissenting opinion of Judges Tulkens, Bonello and Spielmann in *N* v. *United Kingdom* (Application No 16565/05) (unreported) 27 May 2008, p. 31, para. 26.

46. In this case, the only family life which this child has ever known is with his mother. If he were obliged to return to a country where he would inevitably be removed from her care, with only the possibility of supervised visits, then the very essence of his right to respect for his family life would be destroyed. And it would be destroyed for reasons which could never be justified under article 8(2) because they are purely arbitrary and pay no regard to his interests. The violation of his right is in my view of greater weight than the violation of his mother's right. Children need to be brought up in a stable and loving home, preferably by parents who are committed to their interests. Disrupting such a home risks causing lasting damage to their development, damage which is different in kind from the damage done to a parent by the removal of her child, terrible though that can be.

47. That is what makes this case so different from the general run of child abduction cases. In the general run of such cases, a family life of some sort has been established in the country of origin and it is the abduction rather than the return which has interfered with that family life. In this case there was no family life established in the Lebanon between this child and his father or his father's family. A family lawyer in this country might raise an eyebrow at the fact that the mother was able to keep her child entirely away from his father. But the evidence is that, not only was he extremely violent towards her, but also that he had little or no interest in his own child. Be that as it may, from the child's point of view, we have to deal with the situation as it now is. To deprive him of his mother's care and place him in the care of people who are complete strangers to him and who have shown so little concern for his welfare would be to deprive him of the only family life he has or has ever had. The discriminatory laws of Lebanon are the reason why that is a real risk in this case. They are also the reason why the interference cannot be justified. But it is the effect upon the essence of the child's right with which we have to be concerned.

48. It has been a great help to be able to consider this case from the child's point of view. In the oral hearing where we considered the child's application to intervene, the Secretary of State acknowledged that the child might have a separate article 8 claim of his own. Our recent decisions in *Beoku-Betts* v. *Secretary of State for the Home Department* [2008] UKHL 39, [2008] 3 WLR 166 and *Chikwamba* v. *Secretary of State for the Home Department* [2008] UKHL 40, [2008] 1 WLR 1420 have made it clear that, not only the Secretary of State,

but also the asylum and immigration appeal tribunal, must take account of the article 8 rights of all those who are affected by their decisions. This means, as Lord Bingham says in para. 43 of his opinion, that they call for separate consideration.

49. Separate consideration and separate representation are, however, two different things. Questions may have to be asked about the situation of other family members, especially children, and about their views. It cannot be assumed that the interests of all the family members are identical. In particular, a child is not to be held responsible for the moral failures of either of his parents. Sometimes, further information may be required. If the Child and Family Court Advisory and Support Service or, more probably, the local children's services authority can be persuaded to help in difficult cases, then so much the better. But in most immigration situations, unlike many ordinary abduction cases, the interests of different family members are unlikely to be in conflict with one another. Separate legal (or other) representation will rarely be called for.

50. For these reasons, which are merely a family lawyer's postscript to those given by Lord Bingham, I too would allow this appeal.

LORD CARSWELL

51. I have had the advantage of reading in draft the opinion prepared by my noble and learned friend Lord Bingham of Cornhill. I agree so entirely with his reasons and conclusions that it would be superfluous to do more than add a few observations of my own.

52. In deciding this appeal by the application of article 8 of the European Convention on Human Rights the House is applying the domestic law of this country, as it is bound to do. We have to do so by reference to the values enshrined in the Convention, the common values of the States who are members of the Council of Europe. We are not passing judgment on the law or institutions of any other State. Nor are we setting out to make comparisons, favourable or unfavourable, with Shari'a law, which prevails in many countries, reflecting, as Lord Bingham has said (para. 42), the religious and cultural tradition of those countries. For this reason I share the doubts expressed by Lord Bingham and by my noble and learned friend Lord Hope of Craighead about the appellant's right to rely on a claim of discrimination under article 14 of the Convention. I am satisfied, on the other hand, that she has established a good claim under article 8.

53. Where the Court of Appeal went wrong was in misinterpreting the expressions of opinion of the House in *R (Ullah)* v. *Special*

Adjudicator [2004] UKHL 26, [2004] 2 AC 323 and *R (Razgar)* v. *Secretary of State for the Home Department* [2004] UKHL 27, [2004] 2 AC 368. The test to be applied in this case, which belongs to the class described as "foreign cases", is whether the action of the United Kingdom authorities in removing the appellant to Lebanon would constitute a flagrant breach of her rights contained in article 8 of the Convention. The Court of Appeal concluded that for the test to be satisfied the appellant's article 8 rights had to be completely denied or nullified, with the consequence that if she retained any vestige of those rights her claim must fail. That formula is excessively restrictive and sets the bar too high.

54. I entirely agree with Lord Bingham (para. 35) that any attempt at paraphrase of the test runs the risk of causing confusion, and I do not propose to make any such attempt. It is instructive, however, to re-examine what the members of the Appellate Committee said in *Ullah* and *Razgar*, which will reaffirm that the correct test (as set out in *Mamatkulov and Askarov* v. *Turkey* (2005) 41 EHRR 494) is the destruction of the very essence of the right guaranteed by article 8.

55. The members of the Committee in *Ullah* were all in agreement in their approach to the test to be applied. Lord Bingham at para. 24 referred with approval to the formula of the Immigration Appeal Tribunal in *Devaseelan* v. *Secretary of State for the Home Department* [2002] UKIAT 702, [2003] Imm AR 1, para. 111:

> The reason why flagrant denial or gross violation is to be taken into account is that it is only in such a case—where the right will be completely denied or nullified in the destination country—that it can be said that removal will breach the treaty obligations of the signatory state however those obligations might be interpreted or whatever might be said by or on behalf of the destination state.

It may be noted, however, that he did so in the same paragraph as his consideration of the test applied under articles 2 and 3 of the Convention, defined by the European Court of Human Rights as a "near-certainty" or "real risk". Lord Steyn stated in para. 50, after a review of the Strasbourg case law:

> It will be apparent from the review of Strasbourg jurisprudence that, where other articles may become engaged, a high threshold test will always have to be satisfied. It will be necessary to establish at least a real risk of a flagrant violation of the very essence of the right before other articles could become engaged.

56. In para. 69 of my opinion in *Ullah* I also expressed approval of the IAT's formulation of the test in *Devaseelan*, but added significantly that this would harmonise with the concept of a fundamental breach. In *Razgar* (which was heard along with *Ullah*) at para. 72 I used the

phrase "a very grave state of affairs, amounting to a flagrant or fundamental breach of the article, which *in effect* constitutes a complete denial of his rights" (emphasis added). I returned to the topic in *Government of the United States of America* v. *Montgomery (No 2)* [2004] UKHL 37, [2004] 1 WLR 2241. In para. 26 of my opinion, with which the other members of the House agreed, I stated:

> In the *Ullah* case and the *Razgar* case the House accepted the validity of these propositions, but also underlined the extreme degree of unfairness which would have to be established for an applicant to make out a case of indirect effect. It was of opinion that it would have to amount to a virtually complete denial or nullification of his article 6 rights, which might be expressed in terms familiar to lawyers in this jurisdiction as a fundamental breach of the obligations contained in the article.

57. It may be seen from the expressions of opinion which I have quoted that it was not the intention of the House in either *Ullah* or *Razgar* to define the standard of flagrancy in the absolute terms adopted by the Court of Appeal in the present case. This accords with the views of Judges Bratza, Bonello and Hedigan in *Mamatkulov* (2005) 41 EHRR 494, para. OIII 14, quoted by Lord Bingham at para. 34 above, where they expressed the test in familiar Strasbourg terms of "destruction of the very essence" of the right guaranteed. The test therefore remains as set out in *Ullah* and *Razgar* and does not require redefinition or paraphrase, still less amendment. If correctly applied it forms a correct and workable means of determining "foreign cases", though it remains clear that it is a stringent test, which will only be satisfied in very exceptional cases.

58. When it comes to applying it in the present case, I have no hesitation in reaching the conclusion, for the reasons summarised by Lord Bingham in paras. 39 and 40, that the appellant's article 8 rights would be flagrantly violated if she were removed to Lebanon. The facts of the case are very exceptional and, as my noble and learned friend Lord Brown of Eaton-under-Heywood says, provide compelling humanitarian grounds against removal. I should be prepared so to hold even without taking into account the effect upon the child AF, but when that is added into the scale—as it is now clear that it should be taken into account—the conclusion is even more clear.

59. I would therefore allow the appeal.

LORD BROWN OF EATON-UNDER-HEYWOOD

60. I have had the advantage of reading in draft the opinions of my noble and learned friends, Lord Bingham of Cornhill and Lord Hope

of Craighead. I agree with them entirely and for the reasons they give I too would allow this appeal and make the order proposed. I agree not least with what Lord Bingham says in para. 42 of his opinion, a view echoed in paras. 14 and 15 of Lord Hope's opinion. It is certainly not the arbitrary and discriminatory character of the rule of Shari'a law dictating that at the age of seven a child's physical custody automatically passes from the mother to the father (or another male member of his family)—wholly incompatible though such a rule is with certain of the basic principles underlying the Convention—which, uniquely thus far in the jurisprudence both of Strasbourg and the UK courts, qualifies this particular "foreign" case as one for protection under article 8. Rather it is the highly exceptional facts of the case (as set out in my Lords' opinions) which in combination provide utterly compelling humanitarian grounds against removal.

[Reports: [2009] 1 AC 1198; [2008] 3 WLR 931; [2009] HRLR 6; [2009] Imm AR 189]

Territory — Overseas territories — Governance — Turks and Caicos Islands — Right to self-determination — Judicial review — Whether Orders for peace, order and good government generally beyond scrutiny by courts

Relationship of international law and municipal law — Treaties — European Convention on Human Rights, 1950 — Protocol No 1 to European Convention, 1952 — West Indies Act 1962 — Constitution of Turks and Caicos Islands 2006 — Orders in Council — Turks and Caicos Islands Constitution (Interim Amendment) Order 2009

Human rights — Right to self-determination — Whether right to self-determination a free-standing principle in Turks and Caicos Islands — Whether State's undertaking to hold free elections including commitment not to amend decisions of electorate unless compelling grounds for democratic order — Due process — Right to a fair hearing by an independent and impartial court established by law — Right to a fair trial — Trial by jury — Whether a fair hearing conditional on trial by jury

Treaties — European Convention on Human Rights, 1950 — Article 6 — Right to a fair trial — Protocol No 1 to European Convention, 1952 — Article 3 — Right to free elections — Article 4 — Withdrawal from Article 3 — The law of England

REGINA (MISICK) v. SECRETARY OF STATE FOR
FOREIGN AND COMMONWEALTH AFFAIRS[1]

([2009] EWHC 1039 (Admin))

England, High Court, Queen's Bench Division (Administrative Court). 1 May 2009

(Carnwath LJ and Mitting J)

---

[1] The claimant was represented before the High Court and the Court of Appeal by Mr Edward Fitzgerald QC, Ms Alison Gerry and Ms Ruth Brander, instructed by Simons Muirhead and Burton. The Secretary of State was represented before the High Court by Mr Jonathan Crow QC and Mr Jeremy Johnson, instructed by the Treasury Solicitor, and before the Court of Appeal by Mr Philip Havers QC and Mr Jerry Johnson, instructed by the Treasury Solicitor.
For related proceedings, see 165 ILR 544.

([2009] UKCA Civ 1549)

Court of Appeal. 12 *August* 2009

(Laws, Richards and Hughes LJJ)

SUMMARY:[2] *The facts*:—In 2003, Mr Misick ("the claimant") was elected Premier of the Turks and Caicos Islands ("the TCI"), a British overseas territory over which Her Majesty's Government in the United Kingdom exercised ultimate control under Section 26 of the 2006 TCI Constitution.[3] The TCI Constitution was itself enacted under Section 5(1) of the West Indies Act 1962 (UK)[4] ("the 1962 Act").

In June 2008, the House of Commons Foreign Affairs Committee published a report on the Overseas Territories, expressing grave concerns about allegations of corruption in the TCI. In July 2008, the Governor of the TCI appointed a Commissioner to conduct an inquiry into those allegations; the claimant provided oral evidence to the Commissioner's inquiry and vacated his position as Premier. On 28 February 2009, the Commissioner released his interim report, highlighting possible systemic corruption, political amorality, administrative incompetence and serious dishonesty on the part of serving and former members of the TCI legislature. The Commissioner advised that his final report would be likely to recommend suspending the legislature, and, in light of the risk of prejudice and jury tampering, suspending the Constitution's Section 6(2)(g)[5] right to trial by jury for persons tried as a result of the inquiry.

On 18 March 2009, acting under Section 5(1) of the 1962 Act, the Governor presented the Turks and Caicos Islands Constitution (Interim Amendment) Order 2009 ("the Order") to Her Majesty in Council. Under the Order, Section 6(2)(g) of the TCI Constitution was abolished for relevant persons and representative government was replaced with direct administration by the Governor for a period of two years. The Order was laid before Parliament on 25 March 2009, with its implementation stayed pending the Commissioner's final report.

The claimant, a potential subject of proceedings as a result of the inquiry, sought permission to apply for judicial review, challenging the legality of the Order for violating the right to trial by jury and the right to self-determination.

---

[2] Prepared by Ms E. Fogarty.
[3] Section 26 of the 2006 Constitution provided: "(1) The executive authority of the Turks and Caicos Islands is vested in Her Majesty. (2) Subject to this Constitution, the executive authority of the Turks and Caicos Islands shall be exercised on behalf of Her Majesty by the Governor, either directly or through officers subordinate to him or her. (3) Nothing in this section shall preclude persons or authorities other than the Governor from exercising such functions as are or may be conferred upon them by any law."
[4] See para. 17 of the High Court judgment.
[5] See para. 23 of the High Court judgment.

Judgment of the High Court (1 May 2009)

Held (unanimously):—Permission to apply for judicial review was refused.

(1) Section 6(1)[6] of the TCI Constitution provided that everyone charged with a criminal offence be afforded a fair hearing by an independent and impartial court established by law. The repeal of Section 6(2)(g) in no way displaced that right. Trial by jury, although a powerful tradition in the common law, was not seen as essential in many parts of the world, including other common law countries, nor under Article 6 of the European Convention on Human Rights, 1950 ("the European Convention")[7] (which applied both in the UK and in the TCI). The majority of criminal offences in the UK were tried without a jury (paras. 23-6).

(2) The international law principle of the right to self-determination was not incorporated into the domestic law of the TCI. Under Article 3 of Protocol No 1 to the European Convention, 1952,[8] States Parties undertook to hold free elections, which the European Court of Human Rights held included an obligation not to amend the decisions of the electorate except where there were compelling grounds for the protection of the democratic order. The Commissioner's report did, however, give compelling evidence of a failure in the democratic order. Further to that, the Secretary of State had advised that the UK would, in accordance with Article 4 of the Protocol,[9] withdraw the application of Article 3 to the TCI (paras. 27-30).

(3) Section 5 of the 1962 Act conferred on Her Majesty the power to make Orders in Council expedient for the "peace, order and good government" of the TCI. The courts would not inquire into whether legislation within the territorial scope of such a power was in fact for the "peace, order and good government" of a territory, leaving that determination to the relevant minister. Although in principle such determinations were open to judicial review, other

---

[6] See para. 23 of the High Court judgment.

[7] Article 6(1) of the European Convention on Human Rights, 1950, provided that: "*Right to a fair trial*: (1) In the determination of his civil rights and obligations or of any criminal charge against him, everyone is entitled to a fair and public hearing within a reasonable time by an independent and impartial tribunal established by law ..."

[8] Article 3 of Protocol No 1 to the European Convention, 1952, provided: "*Right to free elections*: The High Contracting Parties undertake to hold free elections at reasonable intervals by secret ballot, under conditions which will ensure the free expression of the opinion of the people in the choice of the legislature."

[9] Article 4 of Protocol No 1 to the European Convention provided: "*Territorial application*: Any High Contracting Party may at the time of signature or ratification or at any time thereafter communicate to the Secretary General of the Council of Europe a declaration stating the extent to which it undertakes that the provisions of the present Protocol shall apply to such of the territories for the international relations of which it is responsible as are named therein.

Any High Contracting Party which has communicated a declaration in virtue of the preceding paragraph may from time to time communicate a further declaration modifying the terms of any former declaration or terminating the application of the provisions of this Protocol in respect of any territory ..."

than in the most exceptional cases, the courts would not question them. The circumstances of the present case were not so exceptional (paras. 17 and 31-3).

(4) There was nothing objectionable in the Order being targeted at particular individuals and being retrospective. While those making the Order had no doubt contemplated that the claimant might be one of the persons affected by it, whether it would in fact apply to him depended on decisions yet to be taken. It was not open to the claimant to argue that the suspension of the legislature was "disproportionate" in the circumstances, nor that the validity of the Order was affected because of any alleged "flaw" in the inquiry itself (paras. 35, 37 and 40-1).

The claimant sought permission to appeal.

Judgment of the Court of Appeal (12 August 2009)

Held (unanimously):—The appeal was dismissed.

(1) It was a first principle of UK constitutional law that Parliament in enacting primary legislation was sovereign. In cases such as this, where neither the law of the European Union nor the Human Rights Act 1998 were engaged, Parliament's power to make laws was unconfined (para. 12).

(2) Determining the scope of the power granted under Section 5 of the 1962 Act was a matter of the provision's construction, dependent on its words and on the court's ascertainment of statutory purpose. Sections 5 and 7[10] conferred on the Crown authority to make and alter colonial constitutions to which they applied. In normal circumstances, the limitations the law ordinarily imposed on the scope of delegated legislation to interfere with constitutional or fundamental rights could not simply be read across. However, here, the powers conferred by Section 5 were plainly intended to be plenary in nature (paras. 12 and 17-18).

(3) Orders made under the 1962 Act were not inherently beyond the scope of judicial review. They were, and remained, subordinate legislation in the UK framework and were in principle subject to judicial review jurisdiction by way of claims of irrationality, illegality and unlawfulness. However, given the breadth of the powers under the 1962 Act, the suspension of jury trial and representative government under the Order did not engage any such claims (para. 18).

(4) There was no principle of law by which the suspension of jury trial promulgated for objective reasons could be said to be repugnant to the plenary powers given by Section 5 of the 1962 Act. The suspension of jury trial was not specifically directed at the claimant or other named individuals, and any questions concerning the merit in trying those individuals would be properly addressed during any criminal trials (paras. 21-3 and 31).

(5) The Crown was not obliged to make a constitution for the TCI that included an elected legislature, and was entitled to unmake any such provision that so provided (para. 24).

---

[10] Section 7 of the West Indies Act 1962 provided for supplementary provisions as to Orders in Council.

The text of the judgment of the Court of Appeal, delivered by Laws LJ, commences at p. 533. The following is the text of the judgment of the High Court, delivered by Carnwath LJ:

JUDGMENT OF THE HIGH COURT

LORD JUSTICE CARNWATH

1. The Claimant Mr Michael Misick is the former Premier of the Turks and Caicos Islands. He seeks permission to challenge the legality of "The Turks and Caicos Islands Constitution (Interim Amendment) Order 2009". The Order was expressed to be made under the West Indies Act 1962 on 18 March 2009, and laid before Parliament on 25 March 2009. The Order is a response to an interim report by Sir Robin Auld, as Commissioner appointed to investigate allegations of corruption and financial mismanagement. Its effect when brought into force, will be to suspend temporarily parts of the Turks and Caicos Islands' Constitution, by, among other things, removing the right to jury trial, and replacing representative government by the House of Assembly by a system of direct administration by the Governor.

2. The government's stated intention is not to bring the Order into force until Sir Robin's final report is received, time for which has been extended to 31 May 2009. But the Governor has not ruled out earlier implementation if—

circumstances arose in the Territory prior to that date which justified suspending relevant parts of the Constitution.

3. By order of Wyn Williams J the case was to be listed for a "rolled-up hearing", with full argument to follow immediately if permission were granted. However, the parties have since agreed that only permission should be determined at this stage, and the hearing before us proceeded on that basis. Accordingly, we are concerned only with whether any of the grounds discloses an arguable case which merits further investigation at a full oral hearing (see White Book para. 54.4.2).

4. In view of the importance of the case both for the parties and the public we have been assisted by fuller argument than would be normal on a permission application. For the same reason this judgment is rather longer than is typical.

Background

5. The present system of government of the Territory is derived from the 2006 Constitution. It is a Crown dependency. Her Majesty's government in the UK exercises ultimate control under section 26 of the Constitution. The Constitution provides for a Governor, a Cabinet and an elected House of Assembly. By section 33 the Governor is responsible for external affairs, defence, internal security and the regulation of international financial services and certain other matters, but he is otherwise required to act on the advice of the Cabinet, the majority of whom are elected members of the House of Assembly. The Claimant is a citizen of the territory and has been active in politics there for many years. He became the head of the Progressive National Party (PNP) in 2002. He became Premier following elections in 2003 and was re-elected in February 2007.

6. In June 2008 the House of Commons Foreign Affairs Committee published a report on Overseas Territories. It expressed grave concerns about allegations of corruption in the Territory. On 10 July 2008, the Governor appointed Sir Robin Auld as Commissioner to conduct an Inquiry under the Commissions of Inquiry Ordinance. Section 8 of the Ordinance provides that evidence given before a Commission is not admissible in civil or criminal proceedings against him, except for perjury or contempt.

7. The terms of reference required him—

To inquire into whether there is information that corruption or other serious dishonesty in relation to past and present elected members of the House of Assembly (previously known as the Legislative Council) may have taken place in recent years.

He was asked to report within sixteen weeks his preliminary findings and recommendations—

concerning:

(a) instigating criminal investigations by the police or otherwise
(b) any indications of systemic weaknesses in legislation, regulation and administration
(c) any other matters relating thereto.

In relation to (a), he was "directed to refer such information and/or evidence [as he] may obtain to the TCI prosecuting authorities".

8. In December 2008, following an attempt to pass a motion of no confidence, the Claimant advised the Governor to prorogue the Assembly

for 15 weeks. In February 2009 he announced that he would vacate his office at the end of March. Hon. Galmo Williams was elected as the new leader of PNP on 28 February and thereafter appointed as Premier by the Governor. We were told that the Assembly resumed sittings on 1 April.

9. Meanwhile, following a period of reviewing written evidence, the Commissioner held an oral hearing in the Territory in January and February 2009. The Claimant among others gave evidence. On 28 February the Commissioner delivered his Interim Report, including the recommendations which led to the Order in Council.

10. He said that his investigations prior to the oral proceedings had disclosed—

much information pointing to possible systemic corruption or of other serious dishonesty involving past and present elected Members of the Legislature in recent years. I had also found indications of systemic weaknesses in legislation, regulation and administration and in related matters calling for attention by way of recommendation.

The oral proceedings had provided—

further information in abundance pointing, not just to a possibility, but to a high probability of such systemic venality. Coupled also with clear signs of political amorality and immaturity and of general administrative incompetence, they have, in my view, demonstrated a need for urgent suspension in whole or in part of the Constitution and for other legislative and administrative reforms ... (Paras. 6-7.)

11. He was submitting the Interim Report "at this early stage" to identify "in more detail the broad concerns that [he had] expressed ... at the close of the Commission's oral proceedings". He continued:

(8) ... As I then indicated, government of the Territory is at a near standstill. The Cabinet is divided and unstable. The House of Assembly stands prorogued until 1 April 2009. The Territory's finances are in dire straits and poorly controlled. There is a settled pattern of recourse to disposals of Crown land to fund recurrent public expenditure, for want of governmental revenue from other more fiscally conventional sources. I should have added that the financial position is so bad that the Government cannot pay many of its bills as they fall due. Governmental and other audit recommendations lie ignored and unattended. In short, there are widespread fears on the part of the people of the Territory that they are leaderless and that their heritage is at risk of continuing to drain away.

(9) This Report—for the above reasons compiled in haste—consists of a list of recommendations under Parts (b) and (c) of the Commission's Terms of Reference, namely as to constitutional and other systemic reforms and related

matters. They will require considerable development and elaboration in my Final Report, so as to provide more comprehensively for the middle and the long term. Some are of great urgency to meet what I consider chronic ills collectively amounting to a national emergency. The others are for the middle and longer terms, but require early consideration with a view to making ready for their timely introduction in due course.

(10) As I have said, I am also satisfied on the information before me under Part (a) of the Commission's Terms of Reference of a high probability of systemic corruption and/or other serious dishonesty involving past and present elected Members of the House of Assembly and others in recent years.

However, I am not ready to formulate provisional findings or recommendations for institution of criminal investigation in relation to any individual or any such interests he or she may have. When I am ready to do so, I shall, as I have publicly indicated, give each individual concerned an opportunity to make representations. I shall then take any such representations into account before making findings and recommendations under Term of Reference (a) in my further Report.

Accordingly, I make no findings or recommendation in this Interim Report under that Term of Reference, save peripherally in recommendations (2), (16) and (17) below for preparation for the appointment of a Special Prosecutor to direct and conduct such investigations as I may recommend in my further Report, for additional Judges and trial by Judge alone."

12. Under the heading "Criminal Trial by Judge alone" (para. 16), he noted that his proposal would involve removal of the right to trial by jury under section 6(g) of the Constitution, and commented:

But trial by jury is not a pre-condition of the "fair trial" requirement of Article 6 of the ECHR, of which this provision is an elaboration. Trial without jury is also a feature of a number of jurisdictions throughout the World, including India and Holland. If, as is clearly the case, it is Article 6 compliant in the many jurisdictions that permit trial of even the most serious offence without jury, it is not such a big step to take where national and "cultural" conditions are such, as here, that no fair or effective trial of such matters considered in this Inquiry could take place with a jury.

13. He then noted seven reasons why that step should be taken in this case, the first being that:

the stance taken by all attorneys acting for Ministers and/or other Members of the House of Assembly and others in the Inquiry was that their respective clients could not possibly be given a fair hearing by a jury, given the wide adverse publicity to allegations against them before, during and as a result of the work of the Commission; all or most of the attorneys expressed with some cogency, in my view, the high likelihood that any trial judge, faced with an application for a stay of the prosecution on account of such prejudice, would stay it.

Other reasons included "the clear risk ... of jury-tampering" and the potential complexity of allegations of corruption or other serious dishonesty of the sort canvassed in the Inquiry—taxing for any jury panel, whether in the TCI or any jurisdiction ...

14. On 16 March the Governor issued a statement responding to the Interim Report. He said:

In light of the accumulation of evidence in relation to TCI in the last year or so, and fortified by the Commissioner's interim report, the UK Government has formed the view that parts of the Constitution will need to be suspended and has decided to take steps to enable it to do so.

On the same day he was making public a draft Order in Council which would suspend parts of the Constitution initially for two years "although this period could be extended or shortened". The draft Order would be submitted to Her Majesty in Council at a meeting on 18 March, and, if made, laid before Parliament on 25 March. He added:

Unless the Commissioner's final report significantly changes the current assessment of the situation, the Order will be brought into force after the final report is received. However, the Order could be brought into force sooner if circumstances arose in the Territory prior to that date which justified suspending relevant parts of the Constitution.

15. The Order has now been made and laid before Parliament, but implementation now awaits the delivery of the Commissioner's final report, unless a decision is made to bring it into effect earlier.

The Claimant's case

16. The Claimant submits that the making of the Order in Council is outside the powers conferred by the West Indies Act 1962. As helpfully summarised by Mr Fitzgerald QC, the case falls into two main parts:

(i) *Abolition of the constitutional right to jury trial*

  (a) The removal of the constitutional right to trial by jury by using secondary legislation and without consultation is not in accordance with the principle of legality;
  (b) It is specifically directed at the elected officials who were the subject of the Commission of Inquiry, and is thus objectionable as being both *in personam* and retrospective.

(c) It would also in the circumstances violate other provisions of the Constitution, in particular the right to a fair trial and the right not to be compelled to give evidence.

(ii) *Removal of representative government*

(a) The Order is inconsistent with the international law principle of self-determination;
(b) It is inconsistent with the right to stand for election and, once elected, to sit as a member of parliament, guaranteed by Article 3 of Protocol 1 of the European Convention on Human Rights;
(c) It is contrary to the principle of legality and is a disproportionate and irrational response to the alleged crimes of certain elected representatives; and
(d) It is based on the recommendations of a flawed Inquiry and on recommendations which are themselves *ultra vires* the Inquiry's terms of reference.

Consideration

17. Section 5 of the West Indies Act 1962 empowers Her Majesty to provide by Order in Council for the government of the territory. The 2006 Constitution was made under this section. Section 7 makes clear that the power to make an Order includes power to vary or revoke. The relevant part of section 5(1) provides:

Her Majesty may by Order in Council make such provision *as appears to Her expedient* for the government of any of the colonies to which this section applies, and for that purpose may provide for the establishment for the colony of such authorities as She thinks expedient and may empower such of them as may be specified in the Order to make laws either generally *for the peace, order and good government* of the colony or for such limited purposes as may be so specified subject, however, to the reservation to Herself of power to make laws for the colony for such (if any) purposes as may be so specified. (Emphasis added.)

18. At the heart of the debate on both issues is an attempt to limit the apparently wide scope of such a legislative power by reference to what are said to be fundamental principles of international or common law. We have the advantage that similar arguments have been the subject of recent consideration by the House of Lords in *R (Bancoult)* v. *Home Secretary (No 2)* [2008] 3 WLR 955 ("*Bancoult (No 2)*"), although it is not easy to extract from the sixty or so pages of the five speeches clear majority positions on some points.

19. In *Bancoult* the right in question (derived from the 29th chapter of Magna Carta) was that of a British citizen not to be removed from his country except by statutory authority. Although it was accepted that the principle could be regarded as important or even "fundamental" (see e.g. paras. 45, 89), the House decided by a majority that the Order (in that case made under prerogative powers) had validly nullified that right.

20. It may be necessary to bear in mind that that case related to a "ceded" territory, rather than a "settled" colony, as in this case. (For a full discussion of this "arcane", but still relevant distinction, see Lord Rodger's speech in *Bancoult (No 2)* at para. 80 ff). Mr Fitzgerald argued that the powers of the Crown are more limited in the case of a settled colony, citing Coke's report of *Calvin's case* 7 Rep. 17b, where it was said to be clear that:

If a King comes to a kingdom by conquest, he may change and alter the laws of that kingdom; but if he comes to it by title and descent, he cannot change the laws of himself without the consent of Parliament.

I am not convinced that this is of much assistance in the present context. The issue is not whether Parliament has consented, which is clear from the 1962 Act, but what it has consented to. That is a matter of construction of the Act.

21. It is convenient to consider first the status of the "rights" on which the Claimant relies, and secondly the principles by which they are said to qualify the apparently wide powers conferred by the Act; and then to draw the balance.

The rights

22. In this case, the right to a jury trial has been traced back to Magna Carta, and long-settled practice thereafter. The right to self-determination through an elected Parliament is said to be recognised generally by international law, and specifically by Article 3 of the First Protocol to the European Convention of Human Rights, which (as is common ground) applies in the Territory. I deal with some of the detail below. However, I conclude that while the rights on which the Claimant relies are undoubtedly of great importance, there is nothing in the authorities to support the argument that they have some special status going beyond that considered in *Bancoult (No 2)*.

Jury trial

23. Section 1 of the 2006 Constitution begins by asserting that "every person in the Islands is entitled to the fundamental rights and

freedoms of the individual", one of which is the protection of the law; and states that the subsequent provisions are to have effect "for the purpose of affording protection to the aforesaid rights". Section 6 is headed "Provisions to secure the protection of law". Sub-section (1) provides that everyone charged with a criminal offence shall be afforded "a fair hearing ... by an independent and impartial court established by law". Section 6(2) sets out particular rights of those charged with a criminal offence, the last of which is that such a person—

(g) shall, when charged on information in the Supreme Court, have the right to trial by jury.

The Order would simply repeal paragraph (g) while leaving the remainder of the section in place, including the general right to a "fair hearing".

24. Mr Fitzgerald relies not only on the central place of jury trial in the common law, but more specifically on section 1 of the Constitution, which, he says, shows that the right to jury trial is not simply a creation of the Constitution but part of the settled law of the territory.

25. There is no doubt that the right to jury trial for serious offences has a powerful tradition in the common law, at least in the UK and the USA. For example, Mr Fitzgerald might have referred to Lord Devlin's often quoted observation—

trial by jury is more than an instrument of justice and more than one wheel of the constitution: it is the lamp that shows that freedom lives. (*Trial by Jury* (1956) p. 164.)

This was recently cited by Lord Steyn in the House of Lords, to support the statement that:

The jury is an integral and indispensable part of the criminal justice system. The system of trial by judge and jury is of constitutional significance ... (*R* v. *Connor; R* v. *Mirza* [2004] UKHL 2, [2004] 1 AC 1118, para. 7.)

26. On the other hand, as the Commissioner's interim report pointed out, jury trial is not seen as essential in other parts of the world, nor under Article 6 of the Human Rights Convention. Mr Crow also fairly makes the points that the great majority of criminal offences are tried without a jury, and that it is hard to point to a principled basis for drawing a clear line. (For those interested, the Wikipedia entry on jury trial has a surprisingly full, comparative treatment of the issue. The "positive belief" about jury trial in the US is contrasted with sentiment in other countries in which it is considered "bizarre and risky" for issues of liberty to be entrusted to untrained laymen.)

Right to self-determination

27. In support of this right, Mr Fitzgerald relies on international treaty obligations. For example, Article 1 of both the United Nations International Covenants, 1966, provides:

1. All peoples have the right of self-determination. By virtue of that right they freely determine their political status and freely pursue their economic, social and cultural development.
2. ...
3. The States Parties to the present Covenant, including those having responsibility for the administration of Non-Self-Governing and Trust Territories, shall promote the realization of the right of self-determination, and shall respect that right, in conformity with the provisions of the Charter of the United Nations.

The "right of peoples to self-determination", as evolved from the UN Charter, has been described by the International Court of Justice as "one of the essential principles of contemporary international law" (*East Timor (Portugal* v. *Australia)* ICJ Reports 1995, p. 90, para. 29).

28. However, as Mr Crow points out, that principle has not been incorporated into domestic law. While of course the right is protected by specific statutes in this country and is in practice taken for granted, nothing in any of the cases relied on by Mr Fitzgerald would enable it to be treated as a free-standing principle in the Territory derived from international law.

29. He finds more specific assistance in the European Convention on Human Rights. Article 3 of Protocol 1 states:

The High Contracting Parties undertake to hold free elections at reasonable intervals by secret ballot, under conditions which will ensure the free expression of the opinion of the people in the choice of the legislature.

He points out that this has been held to include a right to respect for the decision of the electorate once made:

... once the wishes of the people have been freely and democratically expressed, no subsequent amendment to the organisation of the electoral system may call that choice into question, except in the presence of compelling grounds for the democratic order. (*Lykourezos* v. *Greece*, No 33554/03, para. 52.)

Mr Crow points to the concluding words of that quotation as particularly apt in the present context, where the Commissioner's report does indeed give compelling evidence of a failure of the democratic order.

30. However, this aspect of the argument has in my view been overtaken by events. Following the hearing we have been informed by

the Treasury Solicitor that, if a decision is taken to bring the Order into force, the UK will in effect withdraw Article 3. This can be done without Parliamentary sanction. It requires a declaration to the Council of Europe under Article 4 of the First Protocol modifying the application of the Protocol to the territory by withdrawing the application of Article 3. It will be made clear that this is a temporary measure, pending steps to restore the principles of good governance in the Territory.

The width of the Crown's powers

31. On the other side of the balance it is necessary to consider the potential limitations on the Crown's power. Provisions in the form of section 5 have a long history. The wording has been held to confer a very wide law-making power. On the other hand, in seeking limits to the scope of the power Mr Fitzgerald's arguments also have a long and respectable pedigree, extending over two centuries. It is enough to summarise the four main lines of argument which have been touched on before us:

(i) *Repugnancy*: Before the Colonial Laws Validity Act 1865 it was sometimes argued that colonial laws could be declared invalid as repugnant to "fundamental principles" of English law. As Lord Hoffmann explained in *Bancoult (No 2)*:

The background to the Act is the statement of Lord Mansfield in *Campbell* v. *Hall* (1774) 1 Cowp 204, 209 that although the King had power to introduce new laws into a conquered country, he could not make "any new change contrary to fundamental principles". If the King's power did not extend to making laws contrary to fundamental principles (presumably, of English law) in conquered colonies, it was regarded as arguable, in the first half of the nineteenth century, that the same limitation applied to the legislatures of settled colonies. It was never altogether clear what counted as fundamental principles and the Colonial Laws Validity Act was intended to put the question to rest by providing that no colonial laws should be invalid by reason of repugnancy to any rule of English law except a statute extending to the colony. (Para. 36.)

In this case, Mr Crow did not seek to rely on the 1865 Act (for reasons which were not entirely clear to me). However, like Lord Hoffmann in *Bancoult (No 2)* (para. 39) one may question whether this line of argument adds anything in a modern context to the doctrines of English public law.

(ii) *Principle of legality*: Recent House of Lords authority recognises the principle that certain rights are so important that they cannot be overridden by general words in a statute:

Parliamentary sovereignty means that Parliament can, if it chooses, legislate contrary to fundamental principles of human rights ... But the principle of legality means that Parliament must squarely confront what it is doing and accept the political cost. Fundamental rights cannot be overridden by general or ambiguous words. This is because there is too great a risk that the full implications of their unqualified meaning may have passed unnoticed in the democratic process. In the absence of express language or necessary implication to the contrary, the courts therefore presume that even the most general words were intended to be subject to the basic rights of the individual. (*R* v. *Home Secretary, ex p Simms* [2000] 115, per Lord Hoffmann at p. 131E-G; see also per Lord Steyn at p. 130E-G; and also *R* v. *Home Secretary, ex p Pierson* [1998] AC 539 at 589A, 573H-574B and 575D.)

In *Bancoult (No 2)* Lord Hoffmann treated this principle as relevant to the argument before him, but inapplicable because the words of the Order itself were quite clear; and while the importance of the individual was something to be taken into account by the Crown in exercising its legislative powers, there was—

no basis for saying the right of abode is in its nature so fundamental that the legislative powers of the Crown cannot touch it. (Para. 45.)

(iii) *Judicial review principles*: There is no dispute before us that the decision to make the Order is reviewable on "ordinary principles" of judicial review. In *Bancoult (No 2)* Lord Hoffmann referred to the "ordinary principles of legality, rationality and procedural impropriety" (following Lord Diplock's classic formulation in *CCSU*). Lord Carswell emphasised that, since the Human Rights Act 1998 did not apply, "*Wednesbury* unreasonableness", not "proportionality" was the test (para. 131).

(iv) *Human rights*: Even without the underpinning of a specific statute such as the 1998 Act, human rights have been given a special status in judicial review. In *Bancoult (No 2)* Lord Carswell (para. 131) accepted that in the context of human rights—

... the more substantial the interference with human rights, the more the court will require by way of justification before it is satisfied that the decision is reasonable ... (Following Sir Thomas Bingham MR in *R* v. *Ministry of Defence, ex p Smith* [1996] QB 517, 554.)

A related principle is that "domestic legislation should as far as possible be interpreted so as to conform to the state's obligation under a (human rights) treaty" *Lewis* v. *AG of Jamaica* [2001] 2 AC 50, 78F per Lord Slynn, at least where the language of the statute is uncertain or ambiguous (cf. *R* v. *Secretary of State for the Home Department, ex parte Brind* [1991] AC 696).

32. I am not convinced that in the modern law, there is any real distinction between these different ways of formulating the argument. In the end, short of arguments of irrationality, the issue must be one of construction of the statutory language conferring the power. As to that, the majority in *Bancoult (No 2)* left no doubt. Lord Hoffmann said:

... the words "peace, order and good government" have never been construed as words limiting the power of a legislature. Subject to the principle of territoriality implied in the words "of the Territory", they have always been treated as apt to confer plenary law-making authority. For this proposition there is ample authority in the Privy Council (*R* v. *Burah* (1878) 3 App Cas 889; *Riel* v. *The Queen* (1885) 10 App Cas 675; *Ibralebbe* v. *The Queen* [1964] AC 900) and the High Court of Australia (*Union Steamship Company of Australia Pty Ltd* v. *King* (1988) 166 CLR 1). The courts will not inquire into whether legislation within the territorial scope of the power was in fact for the "peace, order and good government" or otherwise for the benefit of the inhabitants of the Territory. (Para. 50.)

Relying on the same line of cases Lord Rodger (with whom Lord Carswell agreed on this point: para. 130) said:

... it is not open to the courts to hold that legislation enacted under a power described in those terms does not, in fact, conduce to the peace, order and good government of the Territory. Equally, it cannot be open to the courts to substitute their judgment for that of the Secretary of State advising Her Majesty as to what can properly be said to conduce to the peace, order and good government of BIOT. This is simply because such questions are not justifiable. The law cannot resolve them: they are for the determination of the responsible ministers rather than judges. In this respect, the legislation made for the colonies is in the same position as legislation made by Parliament for this country ... (Para. 109.)

33. Even allowing for the differences between the various speeches, those of the majority in my view provide a clear message that the Crown's power to legislate for the good government of a territory (whether under the prerogative or a statute such as the present), although in principle subject to judicial review, is in practice not open to question in the courts other than in the most exceptional circumstances, which did not include the abrogation of the basic right relied

on in that case. I see no reason to think the rights claimed in this case, important as they are, should be accorded greater weight.

Other points

34. I can deal much more shortly with the other points in Mr Fitzgerald's argument.

35. I fail with respect to understand the argument that the Order would violate other provisions in Constitutions, such as the right to a fair trial and the right not to be compelled to give evidence. Those safeguards remain in place, and can be enforced through the domestic courts. The Order simply removes the right to insist on a jury trial as such, but does nothing to diminish the responsibility of the court to ensure that whatever form of trial is adopted is "fair" in the broadest sense.

36. Mr Fitzgerald went as far as to suggest that the setting up of the Commission made it unfair to resort to criminal proceedings, or led to some form of legitimate expectation that there would be no prosecution, or that at least that any trial would be with a jury. Again, with respect I see nothing in these points. As has been seen, section 8 of the Commissions of Inquiry Ordinance clearly contemplates that there may be criminal proceedings and provides appropriate protection. The terms of reference for the inquiry made it clear that this was a possible outcome, and it is not suggested that any specific representation to the contrary was made by the Commissioner or anyone else.

37. Similarly, I see nothing in the arguments that the removal of jury trial is objectionable because it is targeted at particular individuals, or retrospective. On the latter point Mr Fitzgerald relied initially on general statements by the US Supreme Court in *Calder* v. *Hull* 3 US 386 (1798). However, I think he accepted ultimately that English authority is against him, as respects procedural matters such as rules of evidence (see *R* v. *Makanjuola* [1995] 3 All ER 730G-732F). He suggested that the issue of jury trial was not a normal procedural issue, but he provided no authority to support the distinction.

38. His argument that the legislation is "targeted" at particular individuals such as his client was supported by reference to *Liyanage* v. *The Queen* [1966] 2 WLR 682, in which the Privy Council declared invalid two Acts passed by the Parliament of Ceylon following an abortive coup d'état in 1962. The Acts purported to change the law, so as among other things to legalise the detention of the alleged conspirators retrospectively, widen the category of cases which could

be tried without a jury, and prescribe new minimum penalties. Lord Pearce said:

It goes without saying that the legislature may legislate, for the generality of its subjects, by the creation of crimes and penalties or by enacting rules relating to evidence. But the Acts of 1962 had no such general intention. They were clearly aimed at particular known individuals who had been named in a White Paper and were in prison awaiting their fate. The fact that the learned judges declined to convict some of the prisoners is not to the point. That the alterations in the law were not intended for the generality of the citizens or designed as any improvement of the general law is shown by the fact that the effect of those alterations was to be limited to the participants in the January coup and that, after these had been dealt with by the judges, the law should revert to its normal state. (P. 695B-E.)

Mr Fitzgerald points by analogy to the temporary nature of the changes to the law in this case.

39. However, he fairly acknowledges Lord Pearce's subsequent comment:

lack of generality in criminal legislation need not, of itself, involve the judicial function, and their Lordships are not prepared to hold that every enactment in this field which can be described as *ad hominem* and *ex post facto* must inevitably usurp or infringe the judicial power ... Each case must be decided in the light of its own facts and circumstances, including the true purpose of the legislation, the situation to which it was directed, the existence (where several enactments are impugned) of a common design, and the extent to which the legislation affects, by way of direction or restriction, the discretion or judgment of the judiciary in specific proceedings ... (P. 695E-G.)

40. I do not think it arguable that this much more extreme case provides any support for the Claimant's case before us. It is no doubt in the contemplation of those making the Order that the Claimant is one of those subject to risk of prosecution in the light of the Commissioner's final report. But that is the most that can be said. The Order is expressed to be of general effect. Whether it is applied to the Claimant is dependent on decisions yet to be made as to whether he will be prosecuted, and if so on what evidence, for what offences, and in what form.

41. Turning to the incidental points under the other main issue, it is not in my view open to the Claimant to argue in judicial review proceedings that the suspension of the legislature is a "disproportionate" response, short of irrationality which is not alleged. Nor in my view is it relevant to the validity of the Order itself to seek to show that the inquiry was "flawed" in some way or that it went beyond its terms

of reference, even if (which I do not accept) there were any serious grounds to support these allegations.

Conclusion

42. I conclude that there are no arguments which offer a realistic prospect of the Claimant's case succeeding at a full hearing, and that it would be wrong therefore to grant permission. Looking at the matter more generally, I remind myself of the gravity of the provisional conclusions drawn by the Commissioner. If they are substantiated in the final report, it is clearly vitally important that the UK government should be able to take urgent action to deal with the matter, and indeed would be open to serious criticism if it failed to do so. As made clear in *Bancoult (No 2)* the Court will not enter into discussion of the merits of the particular measures. In the end, the challenge comes down to one of statutory construction or rationality, and on that basis it is bound in my view to fail. I would dismiss the application.

[Report: [2009] ACD 62]

[The following is the text of the judgment of the Court of Appeal, delivered by Laws LJ:]

JUDGMENT OF THE COURT OF APPEAL

LORD JUSTICE LAWS

1. This is a renewed application for permission to appeal, with the substantial judicial review to follow if permission is granted, against the refusal of the Divisional Court (Carnwath LJ and Mitting J) on 1 May 2009 to grant permission to the applicant to bring judicial review proceedings in order to challenge the legality of the Turks and Caicos Islands Constitution (Interim Amendment) Order 2009 ("the order"). The order was expressed to be made under the West Indies Act 1962 on 18 March 2009 and laid before Parliament on 25 March. The order is not yet in force. If it comes into force it will, for a period of two years, abolish the right to jury trial in the Turks and Caicos Islands ("the TCI") and replace representative government by the national assembly with a system of direct administration by the Governor.

2. The order was a response to an interim report published on 16 March 2009 by the Governor of the TCI compiled by Sir Robin Auld, who had been appointed by the then Governor on 10 July 2008 to conduct a commission of enquiry into possible corruption or other serious dishonesty by members of the legislature in recent years. In the interim report summary, paragraph 6, the Commissioner stated his finding that:

... there is information of possible corruption and/or other serious dishonesty, including misfeasance in public office, in relation to five present elected Members of the House of Assembly ...

3. They included the Honourable Michael Misick, formerly Premier of the TCI. He is the applicant in these proceedings. The Commissioner recommended among other things (summary, paragraph 8) partial suspension of the 2006 Constitution and interim direct rule from Westminster and trial by judge alone and partial reversal of the burden of proof in relation to criminal process prompted by the interim report. The body of the report reveals deep concerns as to the financial and political state of the TCI. The Commissioner referred to "chronic ills collectively amounting to a national emergency". Detailed citations from the report are given in Carnwath LJ's judgment below at paragraphs 10-13.

4. On 16 March 2009, when the report was published, the Governor of the TCI issued a statement as follows:

In light of the accumulation of evidence in relation to TCI in the last year or so, and fortified by the Commissioner's interim report, the UK Government has formed the view that parts of the Constitution will need to be suspended and has decided to take steps to enable it to do so.

5. Although the Commissioner's final report has, as I understand it, been received since the judgment of the Divisional Court, the order, as I have said, has not yet been brought into force. The Treasury Solicitor on instructions gave an assurance subject to liberty to apply to the court that it would not be brought in before 11 August 2009. That of course is yesterday, but I assume the assurance is in effect until today.

6. The provisions of the order sought to be challenged are twofold. Both aspects amend the 2006 Constitution of the TCI. First, for a period of two years the order removes the office of Premier and all ministerial offices, provides that "the cabinet shall cease to exist", dissolves the house of assembly, calls all members of the house to vacate their seats and sets in place a system of administrative government by the Governor subject only to directions from the Secretary of State. Secondly, and again for a two-year period, the order suspends section 6(2)(g) of the Constitution, which declared and affirmed the

right to trial by jury. The *vires* or purported *vires* of the order was, as I have said, the West Indies Act 1962. Section 5(1) provides in part:

Her Majesty may by Order in Council make such provision as appears to Her expedient for the government of any of the colonies to which this section applies, and for that purpose may provide for the establishment for the colony of such authorities as She thinks expedient and may empower such of them as may be specified in the Order to make laws either generally for the peace, order and good government of the colony or for such limited purposes as may be so specified subject, however, to the reservation to Herself of power to make laws for the colony for such (if any) purposes as may be so specified.

7. The 2006 Constitution was itself made by order under this provision. Section 7 of the 1962 Act makes it clear that the power to make an order under section 5(1) includes power to vary or revoke an earlier order.

8. There is an ancillary matter which I shall briefly describe. The Secretary of State has determined that before the order is brought into force the application of Article 3 of the First Protocol to the European Convention on Human Rights will be withdrawn from the TCI. Article 3 of Protocol 1 (A3P1) provides:

The High Contracting Parties undertake to hold free elections at reasonable intervals by secret ballot, under conditions which will ensure the free expression of the opinion of the people in the choice of the legislature.

9. Article 4 of the First Protocol allows the United Kingdom to withdraw A3P1 from the TCI without any preconditions. It is to be noted that the Human Rights Act 1998 does not extend to the TCI. The withdrawal of A3P1 from the Turks and Caicos will be an act done in the course of the United Kingdom's treaty-making powers.

10. In his skeleton argument prepared for his leave application Mr Fitzgerald QC for the applicant sought to challenge the prospective withdrawal of A3P1, but he has not pursued his arguments to that end before us this morning. It seems to me he was right not to do so. Since the withdrawal of A3P1 will be an act done in the course of the United Kingdom's treaty-making powers, it is not justiciable in proceedings of this kind.

11. Mr Fitzgerald submits that the power conferred by sections 5 and 7 of the 1962 Act is subject to implied limitations, such that the provisions contained in the order to which the applicant objects are beyond the statute's scope and therefore *ultra vires*. In very broad terms, Mr Fitzgerald described these limitations as the principle of legality and fundamental rights, and in relation to the abrogation of

representative government the right to self-determination, which he submits is a norm of customary international law having effect *erga omnes*.

12. Evidently it is necessary to start with first principles. It remains a first principle of our constitutional law that Parliament in enacting primary legislation is sovereign. Parliamentary sovereignty has been qualified though not departed from in different ways by our adoption of the law of the European Union through the European Communities Act 1972 and by the Human Rights Act 1998. I ventured some observations about the law's development in this constitutional area in *Thoburn* v. *Sunderland City Council* [2003] QB 151. Where neither the EU nor the Human Rights Act touches the case in hand, which is the position here, Parliament's power to make any law of its choosing is unconfined. We have not yet reached the point where outside the two European spheres Parliament lacks the legal authority to legislate contrary to liberal political norms or so as to curtail hallowed personal rights such as trial by jury; though increasingly and quite independently of the two Europes the court will insist that such legislation must be crystal clear, leaving no room for doubt as to the actual intention of the legislature. These general considerations demonstrate to my mind what is in truth elementary: that the scope of the powers given by section 5 of the West Indies Act 1962 is a matter of that provision's correct construction and of nothing else, and its correct construction will depend not only on the provision's words but on the court's ascertainment of the statutory purpose—see for example (though in a very different context) the seminal authority of *Padfield* v. *Minister of Agriculture, Fisheries and Food* [1968] AC 997.

13. Mr Fitzgerald cites well-known learning to show that basic or fundamental rights can only be abrogated by the appearance of specific words in the enabling legislation—see for example *R (Simms)* v. *SSHD* [2000] AC 115 per Lord Hoffmann at 131 E-G. I have, with respect, already emphasised the same point. Section 5 of the West Indies Act 1962 is, submits Mr Fitzgerald, in general terms. He submits that that is insufficient to authorise the abrogation of jury trial and representative government. Moreover, he submits that the suspension of representative government not only violates the international norm of self-determination but also the United Kingdom's international obligations arising under the United Nations Charter and Article 25 of the International Covenant on Civil and Political Rights, 1966. He cites the *East Timor* case (International Court of Justice (ICJ) Reports 1995, p. 90, para. 29) for the proposition that the right of self-determination is an international law norm having effect *erga omnes*, and cases such as

Trendtex Trading Corporation Ltd v. *Central Bank of Nigeria* [1977] QB 529, 553-4 for the proposition that such norms form part of the common law.

14. Furthermore, Mr Fitzgerald would have us reject the original court's reliance on the recent decision of the House of Lords in *Bancoult (No 2)* [2009] 1 AC 453, which was the latest chapter in the saga of the Chagos Islanders' claims of homeland rights. The case was much concerned with the breadth of the term "peace, order and good government". This expression appeared in the Order in Council made under prerogative powers which was sought to be challenged in *Bancoult (No 2)* and of course also appears, as I have shown, in the text of section 5(1) of the Act of 1962. It was the subject of considerable discussion in *Bancoult (No 2)*. Lord Hoffmann said this at paragraph 50:

... the words "peace, order and good government" have never been construed as words limiting the power of a legislature. Subject to the principle of territoriality implied in the words "of the Territory", they have always been treated as apt to confer plenary law-making authority. For this proposition there is ample authority in the Privy Council (*R* v. *Burah* (1878) 3 App Cas 889; *Riel* v. *The Queen* (1885) 10 App Cas 675; *Ibralebbe* v. *The Queen* [1964] AC 900) and the High Court of Australia (*Union Steamship Company of Australia Pty Ltd* v. *King* (1988) 166 CLR 1). The courts will not inquire into whether legislation within the territorial scope of the power was in fact for the "peace, order and good government" or otherwise for the benefit of the inhabitants of the Territory.

Lord Rodger said at paragraph 109:

... it is not open to the courts to hold that legislation enacted under a power described in those terms does not, in fact, conduce to the peace, order and good government of the Territory. Equally, it cannot be open to the courts to substitute their judgment for that of the Secretary of State advising Her Majesty as to what can properly be said to conduce to the peace, order and good government of BIOT. This is simply because such questions are not justiciable. The law cannot resolve them: they are for the determination of the responsible ministers rather than judges. In this respect, the legislation made for the colonies is in the same position as legislation made by Parliament for this country ...

15. The Divisional Court concluded as follows (Carnwath LJ, paragraph 33):

Even allowing for the differences between the various speeches, those of the majority in my view provide a clear message that the Crown's power to legislate for the good government of a territory (whether under the prerogative or a statute such as the present), although in principle subject to judicial review, is in practice not open to question in the courts other than in the most exceptional circumstances, which did not include the abrogation of the basic right relied on in that case. I see no reason to think the rights claimed in this case, important as they are, should be accorded greater weight.

16. Notwithstanding Mr Fitzgerald's reliance this morning on certain differences between the opinions of their Lordships, not least as regards the part played in *Bancoult (No 2)* by the Colonial Laws Amendment Act, it seems to me that Carnwath LJ's reasoning at paragraph 33, put in the broad terms in which it is expressed, is correct. However, the matter goes further. In fact it is to be noted that the provisions of the order which are objected to in this case were not made by way of subordinate legislation for the peace, order and good government of the TCI. As is pointed out at paragraph 10 of the skeleton argument prepared by Mr Havers QC for the respondent, the power to legislate for the peace, order and good government of the TCI is by section 5(1) of the 1962 Act delegated to the authorities to be established under the sub-section. By contrast the order was made by the Crown itself under the opening words of the sub-section:

Her Majesty may by Order in Council make such provision as appears to Her expedient for the government of any of the colonies to which this section applies ...

And/or the closing words of the sub-section:

... subject, however, to the reservation to Herself of power to make laws for the colony for such (if any) purposes as may be so specified.

17. It is in my judgment clear that sections 5 and 7 of the Act of 1962 conferred on the Crown authority to make and alter constitutions for the colonies to which the provisions apply. In those circumstances the limitations which the law ordinarily imposes on the scope of delegated legislation to interfere with constitutional rights or what are sometimes called fundamental rights, as expressed in such authority as *Simms* and other cases, cannot simply be read across. The reason is that it is a premise of those limitations that the subordinate legislation in question is made within a constitutional order, which very emphatically includes the fundamental rights in question. That constitutional order has a higher legal source than the subordinate legislation and is logically and temporally prior to it. If, therefore, any part of the constitutional order is to be set aside by merely subordinate legislation, that must be so clearly authorised by the enabling primary legislation as to leave no room for doubt but that it was Parliament's plain intention that that

might be done. But there is no such constitutional order, legally or logically, prior to the instrument under challenge where that instrument is itself the Constitution or an amendment of it, and where the constitution-making power, here the Act of 1962, is plainly intended to be plenary in nature.

18. In the ordinary case, subordinate legislation is made within the constitutional framework. But the order challenged here was the constitutional framework, and the case is if anything *a fortiori* the position concerning provisions for a colony's peace, order and good government because, as I have said, the power to legislat[e] for the peace, order and good government of the TCI is in section 5 a delegated power, whereas the order is made by the primary decision-maker, the Crown. There is of course a higher law logically prior to the constitutional provisions contained in the order. That is the enabling statute, sections 5 and 7 of the 1962 Act, but as I have already stated, the powers thereby conferred are, properly construed, plenary in nature. This is not to say that orders made under the 1962 Act are altogether beyond the scope of judicial review. Such orders are and remain in the eye of English law subordinate legislation, and are in principle therefore subject to the judicial review jurisdiction even where the subordinate law-maker is the Crown itself. Claims of irrationality, illegality or unfairness might in principle run against such orders, although the circumstances in which they would properly do so must surely be very attenuated. But given the breadth of the powers of the 1962 Act, the suspension of jury trial and representative government done by the order of 2009 does not in my judgment engage any such judicial review claim.

19. Mr Fitzgerald's arguments contain, if I may say so, much learning. They are put in several ways. With respect, however, his case is in my view generally refuted by the considerations I have set out. I will deal with some individual points quite shortly.

Jury trial

20. Jury trial is of course a hallowed and historic institution within the traditions and practice of the criminal law in common law jurisdictions. However, as Carnwath LJ stated in paragraph 26:

> On the other hand, as the Commissioner's interim report pointed out, jury trial is not seen as essential in other parts of the world, nor under Article 6 of the Human Rights Convention. Mr Crowe also fairly makes the points that the great majority of criminal offences are tried without a jury, and that it is hard to point to a principled basis for drawing a clear line.

21. There is in my judgment no principle of law by which the suspension of jury trial promulgated for objective reasons can be said to be outwith or repugnant to the plenary powers given by section 5 of the 1962 Act.

22. Mr Fitzgerald in his latest skeleton argument, or what he has referred to as his speaking note, has a great deal to say (paragraph 4.13 and following) as to the historic nature of jury trial. In particular he emphasises that jury trial has been a feature of the law of the TCI since the territory was first settled, during the years when it was part of the colony of Jamaica, and since 1959 when the TCI became a separate colony, a period in which the TCI has had successive constitutions of 1962, 1965, 1969, 1976, 1988 and finally 2006. But all this, and the esteem in which jury trial is held, yields to the plenary powers of the 1962 Act. It is quite impossible to say that the provision concerning jury trial is irrational or to delve in these proceedings into the supposed merits or demerits of the proposal to put certain individuals including the applicant on trial, or to take issue with the supposed prejudicial effect of dealing with the facts of the case in the interim report and launching a prosecution afterwards. Such arguments as may properly be available will no doubt be run at any criminal trial which takes place.

23. In fact, as the applicant acknowledges, the applicant's evidence to the commission is not admissible in any relevant later criminal proceedings against him. Equally, nothing can be made of the suggestion that the suspension of jury trial is specifically directed at the applicant and other named individuals. Finally, on this part of the case it is with respect useful to set out paragraphs 5.26 and part of 5.27 of the Commissioner's report.

> 5.26 I confirm my Interim Recommendation 16 for *Criminal Trial by Judge alone,* and as provided by the *2009 Constitution Order,* yet to be brought into force. I have in mind a provision for the introduction of a special court or courts and/or special procedure of trial by judge alone for cases where trial with a jury would risk impairment of the administration of justice. This would cover, but not necessarily be confined to, cases of possible corruption and/or other serious dishonesty giving rise to this Inquiry. See, for example, the provisions in England & Wales under sections 43 and 44 of *Criminal Justice Act 2003* for trial by judge alone in cases respectively of serious and complex fraud and where there is a danger of jury tampering; also, in Northern Ireland under the *Justice and Security (Northern Ireland) Act 2007,* sections 1-9. See also the widespread use of *bench* trials (i.e. trial without jury at the option of the defendant) in common law jurisdictions, for example, in many of the States of the United States, the Commonwealth, including Canada, Australia and New Zealand, the Falkland Islands and St Helena.

5.27 Such a course would involve the removal of the present right to trial by jury contained in section 6(g) of the present TCI Constitution, for suspension of which the 2009 Constitution Order provides, but ideally leaving it for decision by the trial judge on a case by case basis. But trial by jury is not a precondition of the *fair trial* requirement of Article 6 of the *ECHR*, which section 6(g) reproduces in substance. Trial without jury is also a feature of a number of jurisdictions throughout the World, including India and Holland. If, as is clearly the case, it is Article 6 compliant in the many jurisdictions that permit trial of even the most serious offence without jury, it is not such a big step to take where national and *cultural* conditions are such, as here, that no fair or effective trial could take place with a jury. There are, in my view, at least seven reasons why such a step should be taken:

(1) the stance taken by all attorneys acting for Ministers and/or other Members of the House of Assembly and others in the Inquiry was that their respective clients could not possibly be given a fair hearing by a jury, given the wide adverse publicity to allegations against them before, during and as a result of the work of the Commission; all or most of the attorneys expressed with some cogency, in my view, the high likelihood that any trial judge, faced with an application for a stay of the prosecution on account of such prejudice, would stay it;
(2) the contrary consideration, if any prosecution were to survive such a stay application, is that, in this small community of close family political and commercial affiliations, it would, in the event, be well nigh impossible to secure convictions of politicians by jury trial, where the panel is of only seven jurors entitled to bring in majority verdicts by as few as five, and where, for so many potential jurors in this jurisdiction, much turns on commitment to party politics and local and family allegiances . . .

Self-determination and international obligations

24. I take the same view in relation to the suspension of representative government. The Crown was not obliged to make a constitution for the TCI that must have included an elected legislature. It was entitled to unmake such a provision. Moreover, I would draw attention to this passage in Mr Havers' skeleton, with which I agree.

19. Moreover, the Appellant's contention that the 2009 Order is inconsistent with "the right to self determination" is simply wrong. Article 1(3) of the International Covenant on Civil and Political Rights states:

The States Parties to the present Covenant, including those having responsibility for the administration of Non-Self-Governing and Trust Territories, shall promote the realization of the right of self-determination, and shall respect that right, in conformity with the provisions of the Charter of the United Nations.

20. Thus, there is no obligation to impose any particular system of government, but there is a responsibility for the administration of Non-Self-Governing and Trust Territories. The 2009 Order is made in compliance with that responsibility in order to respond to the UK's assessment of the situation in the TCI as fortified by the Interim Report from the Commission which identifies "clear signs of political amorality and immaturity and of general administrative incompetence". The United Kingdom is obliged to take responsibility for the administration of the TCI and, in response to the situation in the TCI as they saw it, which was confirmed by the Interim Report, was obliged to take appropriate action so as to fulfil its duty under Article 1(3) of the ICCPR. This obligation is more directly imposed by Article 73(a) and (b) of the Charter of the United Nations:

Chapter XI: Declaration regarding Non-Self-Governing Territories Article 73

Members of the United Nations which have or assume responsibilities for the administration of territories whose peoples have not yet attained a full measure of self-government recognize the principle that the interests of the inhabitants of these territories are paramount, and accept as a sacred trust the obligation to promote to the utmost, within the system of international peace and security established by the present Charter, the well-being of the inhabitants of these territories, and, to this end:

(a) to ensure, with due respect for the culture of the peoples concerned, their political, economic, social, and educational advancement, their just treatment, and their protection against abuses;
(b) to develop self-government, to take due account of the political aspirations of the peoples, and to assist them in the progressive development of their free political institutions, according to the particular circumstances of each territory and its peoples and their varying stages of advancement;

As is made clear in the Minister's Written Statement dated 16.3.09, the 2009 Order is calculated "to restore the principles of good governance".

25. Article 25 of the ICCPR does not advance Mr Fitzgerald's argument. It only guarantees rights to be exercised in the context of a form of constitution or government that is in place. If that constitution is itself compatible with Article 1, as in my judgment is the case here, there can be no separate violation of Article 25 if the state citizens anyway enjoy such rights as the Article 1 Constitution confers. Moreover, the measures on which Mr Fitzgerald relies have not been incorporated into domestic law, nor is there a free-standing principle of customary law which may be said to be incorporated into our domestic law. In *Bancoult (No 2)* Lord Hoffmann said this at paragraph 66:

As for international law, I do not understand how, consistently with the well-established doctrine that it does not form part of domestic law, it can support any argument for the invalidity of a purely domestic law such as the Constitution Order.

26. In his speaking note Mr Fitzgerald advances a number of strategic considerations in favour of the right to self-determination, matters which belong in my view not to the rights and wrongs of the law but rather to the unfolding tableau of political history and debate. Such an approach does not in the end assist. It is out of tune with the nature of hard-edged enforceable law.

27. For all these reasons, then, I would refuse permission to appeal.

28. I should add that the organisation JUSTICE intervened in the proceedings with my permission. They did so by written submissions only. I have considered those submissions carefully. With great respect, they contain nothing which persuades me to depart from the conclusions I have set out above.

29. Finally, I have already noted that Mr Fitzgerald does not pursue any argument concerning the withdrawal of A3P1 from the TCI.

LORD JUSTICE RICHARDS

30. I agree.

LORD JUSTICE HUGHES

31. I also agree. I do so as a committed admirer of jury trial. I would not myself want to be thought to endorse at any rate reasons numbers 3-7 of the Commissioner's suggested justifications for dispensing with it, although reasons 1 and 2 seem to me on the face of it at least to be soundly based on the applicant's own arguments. But justification is not the point. The power to dispense with jury trial is clearly present and the contrary is simply not arguable.

Order: Application refused

[Report: 8 ALR Int'l 745]

Human rights — Right to respect for private life — Participation in political activities — Whether applicant's removal from elected office affecting aspects of his private life — Whether Article 8 of European Convention on Human Rights, 1950 applicable — Territorial scope of application of Convention — Overseas territories — Admissibility of application

MISICK v. UNITED KINGDOM[1]

(Application No 10781/10)

European Court of Human Rights (Fourth Section)
16 *October* 2012

(Garlicki, *President*; Björgvinsson, Bratza, Hirvelä, Nicolaou, Kalaydjieva and De Gaetano, *Judges*)

SUMMARY:[2] *The facts*:—The applicant, Mr Misick, was a British Overseas Territories Citizen resident in and belonging to the Turks and Caicos Islands ("the TCI"), a British Overseas Territory in the West Indies. A former Premier of the TCI, he was at the relevant time an elected member of the TCI legislature, the House of Assembly. Following a report on corruption in the TCI, the United Kingdom Government suspended parts of the 2006 TCI Constitution and established direct rule by means of an Interim Order in Council. That Order dissolved the House of Assembly and removed all elected officials for a two-year period. The applicant sought leave to apply for judicial review to challenge the legality of the Order in the English courts. The High Court refused permission and the applicant's appeal was dismissed by the Court of Appeal on 12 August 2009 (165 ILR 515). On 14 August 2009, the United Kingdom Government removed the application to the TCI of Article 3 of Protocol No 1 to the European Convention on Human Rights. The Order entered into force on the same day and the Governor assumed responsibility for administering the TCI.

On 9 February 2010, the applicant lodged an application complaining that the United Kingdom had violated his right to respect for private life under Article 8 of the European Convention on Human Rights, 1950 ("the Convention")[3] by removing him as the elected representative of his constituency.

---

[1] The applicant was represented by Mr E. Fitzgerald QC. For related proceedings, see 165 ILR 515.
[2] Prepared by Ms Karen Lee, Co-Editor.
[3] For the text of Article 8 of the Convention, see para. 21 of the judgment.

Held (unanimously):—The application was inadmissible. Since Article 8 of the Convention was not applicable, the application was incompatible *ratione materiae* with the provisions of the Convention.

(1) The Convention had to be read as a whole and interpreted so as to promote internal consistency and harmony between its provisions. Article 8 of the Convention could not, however, fill a gap in human rights protection left by the Respondent State's decision to withdraw the application of Article 3 of Protocol No 1 to the TCI. Article 8 should not be interpreted so as to incorporate the requirements of Article 3 of Protocol No 1 (paras. 21-3).

(2) While the notion of private life in Article 8 of the Convention was a broad term, its application to professional or public activities was not open-ended. The Convention organs had had the opportunity to consider its applicability to participation in political activities (paras. 24-7).

(3) The Court's approach to the application of Article 8 of the Convention to politicians in freedom of expression cases suggested that participation in politics, in particular the exercise of parliamentary mandate, was a matter of public life, to which Article 8 had limited application. Article 8 considerations could arise when aspects strictly related to private life were at stake. The applicant had not, however, demonstrated how the dissolution of the House of Assembly encroached upon his privacy or private life guarantees, including his ability to develop relationships with the outside world. Article 8 had no role to play in his assertion of a right to take part in public life as an elected politician (paras. 28-30).

The following is the text of the decision of the Court:

THE FACTS

1. The applicant, Mr Michael Misick, is a British Overseas Territories Citizen and Turks and Caicos Islands Belonger, who was born in 1966 and lives on Providenciales, an island in the Turks and Caicos Islands. He was represented before the Court by Mr E. Fitzgerald QC, a barrister practising in London.

2. The facts of the case, as submitted by the applicant, may be summarised as follows.

3. The Turks and Caicos Islands ("the Territory") are a British Overseas Territory in the West Indies. At the relevant time, the 2006 Constitution set out the rules regarding government of the Territory. The Constitution was made pursuant to powers conferred by the West Indies Act 1962 which allowed Her Majesty to make Orders in Council for, *inter alia*, the peace, order and good government of the Territory. The Constitution provided for a Governor, a Cabinet and an elected House of Assembly.

4. The applicant is the former Premier of the Turks and Caicos Islands and was, at the relevant time, the elected representative of the North Caicos East constituency and so an elected member of the House of Assembly. He is a citizen of the Territory and has been active in politics there for many years. He became the head of the Progressive National Party in 2002. He became Premier following elections in 2003 and was re-elected in February 2007.

5. In June 2008 a committee of the United Kingdom Parliament published a report on Overseas Territories. It expressed grave concerns about allegations of corruption in the Territory.

6. On 10 July 2008 the Governor appointed Sir Robin Auld as Commissioner to conduct an Inquiry into the allegations.

7. On 28 February 2009 the Commissioner delivered his Interim Report. He was satisfied that there was a high probability of systemic corruption and/or other serious dishonesty involving past and present elected members of the House of Assembly and others in recent years.

8. On 16 March 2009 the Governor issued a statement responding to the Interim Report. He indicated that the United Kingdom Government had formed the view that parts of the 2006 Constitution would need to be suspended and had decided to take steps to enable it to do so. On the same day he made public a draft Order in Council which would suspend parts of the 2006 Constitution initially for two years.

9. The applicant resigned as Premier on 23 March 2009. He remained an elected member of the House of Assembly.

10. The Order in Council was subsequently made by Her Majesty in Council in the form of the Turks and Caicos Islands Constitution (Interim Amendment) Order 2009 ("the Order") and laid before Parliament. The Order provided that parts of the 2006 Constitution were suspended and direct rule was assumed over the people of the Territory. In particular, the Order dissolved the House of Assembly and removed all elected officials for a period of two years.

11. The applicant sought leave to apply for judicial review to challenge the legality of the Order. Regarding the removal of direct rule, the applicant argued that the Order was inconsistent with the international law principle of self-determination; that it was inconsistent with the right to stand for election and, once elected, to sit as a member of parliament, guaranteed by Article 3 of Protocol No 1 to the Convention; that it was contrary to the principle of legality and a disproportionate and irrational response to the alleged crimes of certain elected representatives; and that it was based on the recommendations of a flawed Inquiry and on recommendations which were themselves *ultra vires* the Inquiry's terms of reference.

12. A hearing took place in the Divisional Court on 29 April 2009. Following the hearing, and at the request of the court, the Government confirmed by letter that before bringing the Order into effect they would withdraw the application of Article 3 of Protocol No 1 from the Turks and Caicos Islands.

13. On 1 May 2009 the Divisional Court refused permission to seek judicial review. Regarding specifically the applicant's argument under Article 3 of Protocol No 1, Lord Justice Carnwath indicated:

> 30. ... [T]his aspect of the argument has in my view been overtaken by events. Following the hearing we have been informed by the Treasury Solicitor that, if a decision is taken to bring the Order into force, the UK will in effect withdraw Article 3. This can be done without Parliamentary sanction. It requires a declaration to the Council of Europe under Article 4 of the First Protocol modifying the application of the Protocol to the territory by withdrawing the application of Article 3. It will be made clear that this is a temporary measure, pending steps to restore the principles of good governance in the Territory.

14. As to potential limitations on the Crown's power to make laws for the peace, order and good government of the Territory, Carnwath LJ examined, *inter alia*, the special status of human rights in judicial review. He referred to the House of Lords judgment in *R (Bancoult)* v. *Home Secretary (No 2)* [2008] UKHL 61, where that court had examined the statutory language conferring the power, and continued:

> 33. Even allowing for the differences between the various speeches [in *Bancoult*], those of the majority in my view provide a clear message that the Crown's power to legislate for the good government of a territory ... although in principle subject to judicial review, is in practice not open to question in the courts other than in the most exceptional circumstances, which did not include the abrogation of the basic right relied on in that case. I see no reason to think the rights claimed in this case, important as they are, should be accorded greater weight.

15. The applicant appealed against the refusal of permission to the Court of Appeal arguing, *inter alia*, that the Divisional Court had erred in finding that the Crown's power to legislate was not limited by any requirement to comply with fundamental rights. The appeal was refused on 13 August 2009.

16. On 14 August 2009, by letter to the Secretariat of the Council of Europe, the Government removed the application of Article 3 of Protocol No 1 to the Turks and Caicos Islands.

17. The Order entered into force on 14 August 2009. Following its entry into force, the Governor was responsible for administering the Territory.

A. *Relevant domestic law*

18. Section 5 of the West Indies Act 1962 empowers Her Majesty to provide by Order in Council for the government of the Territory. The relevant part of section 5(1) provides:

Her Majesty may by Order in Council make such provision as appears to Her expedient for the government of any of the colonies to which this section applies, and for that purpose may provide for the establishment for the colony of such authorities as She thinks expedient and may empower such of them as may be specified in the Order to make laws either generally for the peace, order and good government of the colony or for such limited purposes as may be so specified subject, however, to the reservation to Herself of power to make laws for the colony for such (if any) purposes as may be so specified.

19. Section 7 makes clear that the power to make an Order includes power to vary or revoke the Order.

20. The Turks and Caicos Islands Constitution (Interim Amendment) Order 2009 entered into force on 14 August 2009. It dissolved the House of Assembly and removed all elected officials for a period of two years.

COMPLAINT

The applicant complained under Article 8 of the Convention that his removal from his position as the elected representative of the North Caicos East constituency violated his right to respect for private life.

THE LAW

21. The applicant argued that he had been in involved in public life for many years and had been an elected member of the House of Assembly for over five years. His desire and commitment to represent the people of the Turks and Caicos Islands and take part in public life was, he submitted, clearly part and parcel of his life and therefore fell within the aspects of a person's private life protected by Article 8, which provides:

1. Everyone has the right to respect for his private and family life, his home and his correspondence.
2. There shall be no interference by a public authority with the exercise of this right except such as is in accordance with the law and is necessary in a democratic society in the interests of national security, public safety or the economic well-being of the country, for the prevention of disorder or crime, for the protection of health or morals, or for the protection of the rights and freedoms of others.

22. The Court notes at the outset that the applicant's complaint concerns his participation in public life as a politician and, more specifically, a member of the legislature, namely the House of Assembly. He relied on Article 3 of Protocol No 1 to the Convention in the context of the domestic judicial review proceedings, but was prevented from doing so in the proceedings before this Court by the Government's withdrawal of the application of that Article to the Turks and Caicos Islands. The applicant does not seek to challenge the respondent State's decision to withdraw the application of Article 3 of Protocol No 1 to the Territory.

23. The Court reiterates that the Convention must be read as a whole, and interpreted in such a way as to promote internal consistency and harmony between its various provisions (see *Stec and Others* v. *United Kingdom* (dec.) [GC], Nos 65731/01 and 65900/01, § 48, ECHR 2005-X; and *Austin and Others* v. *United Kingdom* [GC], Nos 39692/09, 40713/09 and 41008/09, § 54, ECHR 2012). However, it is not for Article 8 to fill a gap in fundamental rights protection which results from the decision of the respondent State to exercise the possibility provided for in Protocol No 1 to withdraw the application of its Article 3 to the Territory. The Court therefore emphasises that Article 8 should not, in principle, be interpreted in such a way as to incorporate the requirements of Article 3 of Protocol No 1 in respect of territories to which the latter Article does not apply (see, *mutatis mutandis*, *Austin and Others*, cited above, § 55).

24. The notion of "private life" in Article 8 is a broad term not susceptible to exhaustive definition (see, among many other authorities, *Niemietz* v. *Germany*, 16 December 1992, § 29, Series A No 251-B; and *S and Marper* v. *United Kingdom* [GC], Nos 30562/04 and 30566/04, § 66, ECHR 2008). Among other aspects, it protects a right to identity and personal development and a right to establish and develop relationships with other human beings and the outside world. It may include activities of a professional or business nature. There is, therefore, a zone of interaction of a person with others, even in a public

context, which may fall within the scope of "private life" (see *PG and JH* v. *United Kingdom*, No 44787/98, § 56, ECHR 2001-IX; *Perry* v. *United Kingdom*, No 63737/00, § 36, ECHR 2003-IX (extracts); and *Gillan and Quinton* v. *United Kingdom*, No 4158/05, § 61, ECHR 2010 (extracts)).

25. However, the application of Article 8 to professional or public activities is not open-ended. Article 8 does not, for example, guarantee a right of recruitment to the civil service (see *Vogt* v. *Germany*, 26 September 1995, § 43, Series A No 323; and *Vilho Eskelinen and Others* v. *Finland* [GC], No 63235/00, § 57, ECHR 2007-II) or a right to freedom of profession (see *Thlimmenos* v. *Greece* [GC], No 34369/97, § 41, ECHR 2000-IV). In *Sidabras and Džiautas* v. *Lithuania*, Nos 55480/00 and 59330/00, §§ 46-7, ECHR 2004-VIII, the Court concluded that notwithstanding its approach in *Vogt* and *Thlimmenos*, the far-reaching ban on former KGB agents taking up private sector employment, at issue in the case, did affect "private life" such as to engage Article 8. It noted in this context that the ban had created serious difficulties for them in terms of earning their living, with obvious repercussions on the enjoyment of their private lives, and that the publicity caused by the ban and its application to them had caused them to suffer constant embarrassment and had impeded their establishment of contacts with the outside world (§§ 48-9. See also the Court's recent judgment in *DMT and DKI* v. *Bulgaria*, No 29476/06, § 103, 24 July 2012 (not yet final)). Similarly, in *Albanese* v. *Italy*, No 77924/01, § 54, 23 March 2006, the Court concluded that a number of limitations imposed on the activities of the applicant as a result of his bankruptcy influenced his ability to develop relationships with the outside world and that Article 8 was accordingly engaged. However, in the subsequent case of *Calmanovici* v. *Romania*, No 42250/02, §§ 137-9, 1 July 2008, the Court declared the applicant's complaint under Article 8 concerning his temporary suspension from his functions as a police officer to be incompatible *ratione materiae* with the provisions of the Convention. It observed, *inter alia*, that the applicant did not allege that he was prevented from finding employment in the private sector and thus distinguished its judgment in *Sidabras and Džiautas*, cited above.

26. The Convention organs have also had an opportunity to consider the applicability of Article 8 to participation in political activities. In *Baškauskaitė* v. *Lithuania*, No 41090/98, Commission decision of 21 October 1998, unreported, the Commission examined an application brought by an individual who had been refused registration as a

candidate in presidential elections. It rejected her complaint under Article 3 of Protocol No 1, finding the Article to be inapplicable to the election of a Head of State. As to her complaint that the decisions of the authorities depriving her of the possibility to stand as a candidate had an impact on her relations with other people and on her professional activities, therefore constituting an unjustified interference with her private life, the Commission found that there had been no interference with her private life under Article 8 of the Convention. In particular, it indicated that it was unable to detect what concrete restrictions were imposed on, or impediments were suffered by, the applicant in this respect, or what other obligations the Lithuanian authorities had failed to meet, in depriving her of the possibility to run in the presidential election, which could have encroached upon her private life.

27. In *Mółka* v. *Poland* (dec.), No 56550/00, ECHR 2006-IV, the Court raised of its own motion a complaint under Article 8 in the context of facilities at a polling station not adapted to suit those in wheelchairs which had prevented the applicant from exercising his right to vote in municipal elections (to which Article 3 of Protocol No 1 did not apply). It noted that the case related to the applicant's involvement in the life of his local community and the exercise of his civic duties. Although it ultimately considered it unnecessary to decide on the applicability of Article 8 given that the case was inadmissible for other reasons, it nonetheless indicated that it might be arguable that the situation at issue in the case touched on the applicant's possibility of developing social relations with other members of his community and the outside world, and was pertinent to his own personal development. It is, however, noteworthy that there was extensive reference in the decision to the applicant's disability, and the Court also referred to other international texts stressing the importance of full participation of people with disabilities in society, and in particular in political and public life.

28. Turning to the facts of the present case, the Court must determine whether the applicant's removal from elected office can be said to touch on aspects of his private life, such as to engage the guarantees of Article 8. In this respect, the Court considers it instructive to examine how Article 8 is applied to politicians and public figures in the context of the Court's case-law concerning the balance between the right to privacy and protection from defamation (matters which in principle tend to engage Article 8 of the Convention) and the right to freedom of expression (see, for a recent discussion of this area, *Von*

Hannover v. *Germany (No 2)* [GC], Nos 40660/08 and 60641/08, § 110, ECHR 2012). The Court has frequently explained that the protection of privacy enjoyed by public figures under Article 8 is reduced. Thus in *Von Hannover* v. *Germany*, No 59320/00, § 64, ECHR 2004-VI, the Court reiterated that in certain special circumstances the public's right to be informed could even extend to aspects of the private life of public figures, particularly where politicians were concerned (see also *Standard Verlags GmbH* v. *Austria (No 2)*, No 21277/05, § 48, 4 June 2009; *Von Hannover (No 2)*, cited above, § 110; and *Axel Springer AG* v. *Germany* [GC], No 39954/08, § 91, 7 February 2012). In *Karakó* v. *Hungary*, No 39311/05, § 28, 28 April 2009, the Court concluded that the applicant's allegation that his reputation as a politician had been harmed by the impugned publication was not a sustainable claim regarding the protection of his right to respect for personal integrity under Article 8 of the Convention, as he had failed to demonstrate that the allegations in the publication were of such a seriously offensive nature that their publication had an inevitable direct effect on the applicant's private life. In *Lahtonen* v. *Finland*, No 29576/09, § 66, 17 January 2012, it reiterated that the limits of permissible criticism in the context of defamation complaints were wider as regards a politician than as regards a private individual (see also *Lingens* v. *Austria*, 8 July 1986, § 42, Series A No 103; and *Saaristo and Others* v. *Finland*, No 184/06, § 59, 12 October 2010).

29. The Court is of the view that its approach to the application of Article 8 to politicians in freedom of expression cases lends weight to the idea that participation in politics, in particular the exercise of parliamentary mandate, is very much a matter of public life, to which Article 8 can have only limited application (compare and contrast *Mółka*, cited above). Where aspects strictly related to private or family life are at stake—such as a right to privacy when engaging in activities of a purely private nature—the Court has acknowledged that Article 8 considerations may arise notwithstanding the public nature of politics. However, in a case like the present one, where the applicant has not provided any concrete details of how the dissolution of the House of Assembly encroached upon his privacy or private life guarantees, including his ability to develop relationships with the outside world, but merely seeks to assert a right to take part in public life as an elected politician, the Court considers that Article 8 has no role to play.

30. The Court therefore concludes that Article 8 of the Convention is not applicable in the present case. The application is therefore

incompatible *ratione materiae* with the provisions of the Convention and must accordingly be declared inadmissible pursuant to Article 35 §§ 3(a) and 4.

For these reasons, the Court unanimously
Declares the application inadmissible.

[Report: (2013) 56 EHRR SE13]

Comity — Act of State doctrine — Judicial acts of foreign State acting within its territory — Whether lawful — Whether subject to adjudication by English courts — Relevance of cogent evidence and argument — Role of proper respect

Relationship of international law and municipal law — Act of State doctrine — Whether courts of one State barred from sitting in judgment on acts of a foreign State — Whether doctrine applicable to foreign court decisions

State immunity — Act of State doctrine — Limitations on act of State doctrine — Russian courts setting aside Russian arbitral awards — Whether due to interference by Russian State — Whether judicial acts of State for purposes of act of State doctrine — Judicial standards and duty of courts to adhere to rule of law — Issue estoppel — Dutch court setting aside Russian arbitral awards — Relevance — Differing meanings and standards of "public order" across States — Whether arbitral awards enforceable in England — The law of England

Yukos Capital SARL *v.* OJSC Rosneft Oil Company (No 2)[1]

([2012] EWCA Civ 855)

England, Court of Appeal. 27 *June* 2012

(Rix, Longmore and Davis LJJ)

Summary:[2] *The facts*:—While Yukos Capital SARL ("the respondent") was part of the Russian "Yukos Group" of companies involved in oil production and trading, it entered into a loan agreement with another member of the Group, OSJC Yuganskneftegaz ("YNG"). The Yukos Group was subsequently forcibly broken up and the majority of its assets and liabilities, including those of YNG, were acquired by the State-owned OJSC Rosneft Oil Company ("the appellant"). The respondent remained in private hands and was incorporated in Luxembourg.

In 2006, a Russian arbitration tribunal gave four awards in favour of the respondent against YNG in relation to the loan agreement, totalling

---

[1] The appellant was represented by Lord Grabiner QC, Mr Ciaran Keller and Mr Conall Patton, instructed by Travers Smith LLP. The respondent was represented by Mr Gordon Pollock QC, Mr Jonathan Nash QC and Mr James Willan, instructed by Byrne and Partners LLP.
[2] Prepared by Ms E. Fogarty.

approximately US $425 million. The liability was transferred to the appellant. The appellant successfully applied to the Russian Arbitrazh Court for the awards to be annulled, alleging that the loan agreement was part of an illegal tax evasion scheme.

The respondent was granted leave to enforce the awards in the Netherlands after the Amsterdam Court of Appeal held that it was plausible that the annulment decisions were the result of a partial and dependent system of administration of justice and that it would not be possible to recognize them in the Netherlands. The respondent recovered US $425 million.

On 11 March 2010, the respondent issued a claim in the United Kingdom for post-award interest in the amount of US $160 million. It submitted that the annulment decisions should not be recognized as a matter of English private international law on the ground that the Arbitrazh Court lacked independence, impartiality and substantive justice. It further alleged that there had been a campaign against it by the Russian State involving numerous unfounded tax penalties imposed by taxation tribunals; that the case had to be seen against the general background of the Russian State's efforts to renationalize strategic energy assets and destroy the political aspirations of Yukos Group's Chief Executive Officer, Mr Khordorkovsky; and that there were clear examples of interference by the Russian Government in the judicial process.

The commercial court agreed with the respondent's two submissions that the act of State doctrine and non-justiciability did not apply, and that issue estoppel arising out of the Amsterdam court's decision barred the appellant from asserting that the award annulment decisions were not partial and dependent. The appellant appealed both decisions.

Held (unanimously):—The appeal was allowed in part. The appellant's claim that the act of State doctrine prevented consideration of the respondent's claim was dismissed. Its claim that there was no issue estoppel was allowed.

(1) The act of State doctrine was a long-standing doctrine of Anglo-American jurisprudence under which the courts of England did not sit in judgment on the exercises of sovereign power by other sovereign States within their own territory. This reflected the principle that every State was bound to respect the independence of every other State, and that for one State's courts to sit in judgment on acts of another State might imperil amicable inter-State relations (paras. 40-4 and 56).

(2) There were, however, limitations to the act of State doctrine. First, the relevant act had to take place within the territory of the foreign State (although exceptional circumstances might occasionally require extraterritorial application). Secondly, the doctrine did not apply to acts which were in breach of clearly established rules of international law, were contrary to English principles of public policy, or involved grave infringements of human rights. Thirdly, judicial acts were not regarded as acts of State for the purposes of the doctrine, which in its classic statement referred to legislative and executive

(governmental or official) acts only. Where a foreign court acted in a way which was an abuse of its own responsibilities as a court of law, the courts of England were not obliged to give effect to its potential jurisdiction or past acts. Fourthly, immunity did not attach to a State's commercial activities. Finally, immunity did not apply to cases involving determinations of fact only. Only the third limitation was applicable to the present case (paras. 68-9, 73, 92 and 95).

(3) The act of State doctrine did not prevent the investigation of, or adjudication upon, the conduct of the judiciary of a foreign State, whether the conduct was in the past or future, and whether it was systemic or confined to a particular case. Whereas in a property case, comity would seem to require that the validity or lawfulness of the legislative or executive acts of a friendly foreign State acting within its territory should not be subject to the adjudication of the English courts, comity only cautioned that the judicial acts of a foreign State acting within its territory should not be challenged without cogent evidence (paras. 86-7, 90 and 125).

(4) Sovereigns acted on their own plane; they were responsible to their people, but were only responsible internationally in accordance with international law and internationally recognized norms. Courts, however, were always responsible for their acts both domestically and internationally, which were recognizable and enforceable internationally only to the extent that they observed substantive or natural justice, or the rule of law. Judicial acts were judged by judicial standards. Most countries subscribed to the doctrine that justice according to the law was expected of courts and judges; the process of judgment through the courts was universally recognized (even in its breach) as an activity that had to be carried out fairly and transparently, in accordance with law (paras. 87 and 90).

(5) When a party to litigation in England was asking an English court to recognize a decision of a foreign court, subject to any treaty or convention limitations, the English court had to be entitled to adjudicate on whether a foreign court decision should be recognized or enforced. Comity demanded, however, that such enquiries be conducted with proper respect for the courts of friendly foreign nations and that cogent grounds were required to support any allegation that a foreign court's decision should not be recognized for failure of substantial justice. That, however, was a matter of evidence and argument, not a question of immunity or non-justiciability (para. 125).

(6) The core question was whether, in the modern world, the English court could be asked to recognize a judicial decision which a party to that decision alleged was reached by judicial corruption. It should not in principle be open to another party to such decisions to claim immunity from adjudication on the grounds that an investigation into the allegations was protected by deference due to the legislative or executive acts of a foreign sovereign. The judiciary could not ignore the need for a concerted international response to such a threat to the rule of law. Although the respondent's allegation was yet to be proved, it had the right to ask the English courts to consider it (paras. 135-6).

(7) With respect to the second preliminary matter, the primary requirements for the application for a foreign issue estoppel were: that the earlier judgment relied upon was final and conclusive, made on the merits, and given by a court of a competent jurisdiction; that the parties to the earlier and later proceedings were the same; and that the issue to be decided was the same in both actions. In addition, the application of the estoppel had to work justice rather than injustice; the court had a discretion to refuse to give effect to a foreign judgment if there were special circumstances making recognition unjust. Although the first two requirements to establish an issue estoppel were satisfied, the third requirement was not (para. 147).

(8) The Dutch decision was to allow enforcement of the awards and refuse recognition of the annulment decisions as a matter of Dutch public order. The decision sought from the English courts was a decision that the Russian courts (whether particularly or generally) were partial and dependent on the executive, and that their decisions should not be recognized as a matter of English public order. Concepts of "public order" and standards adopted inevitably differed between countries. The cogent evidence required varied in degree in different countries. It was also a matter of high policy to determine the circumstances in which English courts should recognize a State's judgments where the interests of that State were at stake. The English courts were bound to refer to the concepts of English public order, not Dutch public order. The appellant was therefore not issue estopped from contradicting in England the respondent's assertion that the Russian courts' decisions were partial and dependent (paras. 149-51 and 156-7).

The following is the text of the judgment of the Court, delivered by Rix LJ:

LORD JUSTICE RIX

Introduction

1. This is the judgment of the court, to which each of its members has contributed.

2. We are concerned in this appeal with arbitration and litigation on an international scale, but also with allegations which go to the heart of questions of the rule of law in a friendly foreign state.

3. The problem is this. A claimant, incorporated in Luxembourg but originally part of a Russian group, obtains a Russian arbitration award under a Russian contract against a Russian company, part of a Russian resources group now within majority Russian state ownership and control. At the time when the contract between the original parties was entered into, both parties had been members of the same Russian

group, then in private hands. By the time the award is issued, however, the defendant company, to which the liability has passed by a process of universal company succession, is within Russian state control, while the claimant company has survived in private hands outside the state takeover. It is now said by the defendant company (but had not been said at the arbitration) that the contract under which the award had been made was part of an unlawful tax scheme operated by the original parties to the contract when they were associated companies within a single group.

4. Following the making of the arbitration award, there are proceedings in the Russian courts which lead to the setting aside of the award. The claimant contends that those judicial proceedings are a travesty of justice but typical of the campaign of state interference which has been waged by the Russian state.

5. The claimant seeks to enforce the award, despite its having been set aside by the courts of the country where it was made, in another foreign nation, namely the Netherlands, pursuant to the New York Convention.

6. The Dutch court at first instance refuses enforcement, on the ground that the award has been set aside in Russia; but on appeal in the Amsterdam Court of Appeal the award is recognised for enforcement, while the Russian court's decision setting aside the award is refused recognition. The refusal of recognition is on the ground that it can be inferred, from the general nature of the subservience of the Russian courts to state influence in matters of state importance, that the decision of the Russian court in setting aside the award was "partial and dependent", in other words was dictated by bias or intimidation. As a result the Russian award is enforced in the Netherlands. However, there remains an outstanding claim for post-award interest, albeit the award itself does not provide for post-award interest.

7. Meanwhile the claimant proceeds to England, where it also seeks to enforce the award and post-award interest, both pursuant to the New York Convention and at common law. Enforcement proceedings are therefore commenced in the commercial court in London.

8. The defendant says: the award has gone, it has been set aside by the Russian courts; and the allegations of bias which the claimant makes, or at any rate a large part of the claimant's case which is concerned to allege a conspiracy on the part of the Russian state to steal the assets of the private group to which the claimant company originally belonged, and ultimately to purloin the group itself, by forcing it into bankruptcy by unlawful tax demands and/or by buying its assets in rigged auctions, raises issues about the executive or

administrative acts of a foreign sovereign within its own territory upon which the courts of England cannot adjudicate. That is said in reliance on the act of state doctrine, and/or on the associated doctrine of judicial abstinence, the doctrine of non-justiciability. The defendant also says that the award should in any event not be enforced in England because it wrongly gives effect to an unlawful scheme of fraudulent tax evasion.

9. The claimant says: the award has not gone, for the Russian courts' setting aside of the award was partial and dependent, as the Dutch court has correctly found in proceedings which in any event bind and estop the defendant under the doctrine of issue estoppel. As for the doctrines of act of state and of non-justiciability, they do not apply. The act of state doctrine does not apply because there is no attempt here to challenge the validity of any act of state. The doctrine of non-justiciability does not apply because the case is concerned with judicial standards, which are justiciable. As for the new allegation of unlawful tax evasion, that allegation is itself said to be part of the Russian state's unlawful campaign, with the assistance of the tax and judicial authorities, to strip and acquire control of the assets of the private group to which the claimant originally belonged.

10. In the commercial court, Hamblen J agreed with the claimant on two preliminary issues which are concerned with issue estoppel and the act of state doctrines. He held that the defendant is estopped by the decision of the Amsterdam Court of Appeal from saying that the Russian court's decision setting aside the arbitration award is not partial and dependent. The claimant therefore sees its way open to argue in England that there is no impediment so far as that Russian court decision is concerned to enforcing the award in England. He also held that there is no room in this case for the application of the doctrines of act of state or non-justiciability. Hamblen J's judgment is reported at [2011] EWHC 1461 (Comm), [2012] All ER (Comm) 479. The judge treated the two issues entirely separately, and determined the estoppel issue first.

11. On this appeal the parties have renewed their submissions below. Those submissions raise complex and intriguing issues. Thus what is the rationale of the act of state doctrine? Is it a narrow doctrine which requires the *validity* (as distinct from the lawfulness, morality or motives) of the foreign sovereign's acts to be impugned, or else requires some positive remedy to be sought from the English court which is predicated on an attack on those sovereign acts? Or is it a broader doctrine which prevents the English court "sitting in judgment" on those acts? Does the doctrine apply to judicial acts at all? How is it that the English court does appear regularly to consider the quality of justice

in foreign states in cases concerned with the English long-arm statute and issues of *forum non conveniens*, or in cases concerned with extradition? How is it that the English court does regularly consider the persecutory acts of foreign sovereigns, both in the past and potentially in the future, in the context of cases concerned with claims to asylum? How do the act of state doctrines fit with the doctrine of estoppel, where there may be a conflict between rules of public policy? When, on a claim to enforce a foreign arbitration award, there is competing reliance on decisions of the state where the award was made and of another state where the award is taken for enforcement, and when issues of public policy may be said to be involved, should the English court be deciding any issue of public policy for itself, or should it be content to abide by the foreign courts' decisions, and if so, which one?

The awards

12. There are in fact four awards, made between Yukos Capital SARL ("Yukos Capital") as claimant and OJSC Yuganskneftegaz ("YNG") as respondent. They were issued by a tribunal acting under the rules of the International Commercial Court at the Chamber of Commerce of Trade and Industry of the Russian Federation. The defendant in these proceedings, in this court the appellant, OJSC Rosneft Oil Company ("Rosneft"), is the universal successor to the rights and liabilities of YNG, pursuant to an amalgamation that took place on 1 October 2006. The awards were made a little earlier, on 19 September 2006. The amount awarded by the four awards was about US $425 million, which has now been paid pursuant to Yukos Capital's enforcement proceedings in the Netherlands. However, Yukos Capital now seeks, in these further enforcement proceedings in England, to recover post-award interest, in the further sum of more than $160 million.

13. Yukos Capital was at one time a member of the Yukos Group, a well-known Russian group of companies involved in oil production and trading. I will refer to "Yukos" as the group, and to Yukos Capital as the claimant in the awards, the Dutch proceedings and these proceedings respectively.

14. After the forced break-up of Yukos in Russia, Rosneft acquired the majority of Yukos's assets. At that time Rosneft was wholly owned and controlled by the Russian state. It remains so owned and controlled, not wholly but by a majority. The break-up of Yukos and the acquisition of its assets by Rosneft has been referred to as the "re-nationalisation" of Yukos or its assets. However, Yukos Capital remained in private hands.

15. YNG was a former production subsidiary of Yukos, and was incorporated in Russia. However, by the time that the awards were made, YNG had been acquired by Rosneft. Thus the awards when made and when subsequently set aside by the Russian courts were against an award debtor effectively controlled by the Russian state.

16. The awards were in respect of loan agreements which Yukos Capital alleges but Rosneft denies YNG had accepted in the arbitrations to be valid. Rosneft now pleads that the loan agreements were part of an illegal scheme of tax evasion (see para. 23(2) of Rosneft's defence). In brief, Rosneft says that the scheme involved the manipulation of Yukos's oil trading in order to accumulate profits in Russia's low tax regions, thereby depriving YNG of revenues to which it should have been entitled. It is said that this scheme has been held to be illegal and fraudulent by the Russian courts. It is also said that a recent decision of the European Court of Human Rights in *OAO Neftyanaya Kompaniya Yukos* v. *Russia* (Application No 14902/04, 20 September 2011, and thus post Hamblen J's judgment) has found that the Russian courts properly found Yukos's tax arrangements to be unlawful based on well-founded findings and an application of the law that was neither arbitrary, unreasonable, nor unforeseeable, and that Russia's tax assessments pursued a legitimate and non-discriminatory aim.[3]

17. The awards were subsequently set aside by the Russian Arbitrazh Courts on Rosneft's applications. There were two first instance decisions dated 23 May 2007 by the Moscow Arbitrazh Court, which is the supervisory court with jurisdiction to consider annulment of awards under Russian law. The judge observed:

> 9. ... The challenge was entertained notwithstanding the expiry of the 3 month period in which challenge could be brought. The Awards were set aside on what Yukos Capital contends were the flimsiest of grounds including, for instance, that Yukos Capital had been permitted to amend its claim and that one of the arbitrators had spoken at a major conference of which Yukos' lawyers were co-sponsors.

The decisions to set aside were upheld on appeal on 13 August 2007 by the Federal Arbitrazh Court (Moscow District), and permission to

---

[3] See paras. 659-66 of the Strasbourg court's judgment. Thus the court rejected any violation of article 18 of the ECHR. However, it found a violation of article 6 in that Yukos was given insufficient time to prepare a response to a 2000 tax assessment, a violation of article 1 of Protocol No 1 in relation to the imposition and calculation of penalties pursuant to 2000-1 tax assessments, and a violation of article 1 of Protocol No 1 in the failure to strike a fair balance between the legitimate aim of enforcement proceedings and the measures employed.

appeal to the Supreme Arbitrazh Court was refused by that court on 10 December 2007.

18. Yukos Capital contends that these decisions (the "annulment decisions" as they have been called) should not be recognised by the English court because they were the product of a judicial process that was partial and dependent and therefore offend against English principles of substantial justice.

The Dutch enforcement proceedings

19. Yukos Capital applied in the Netherlands for "*exequatur*" (i.e. leave to enforce) under Dutch codes and the New York Convention. It started those proceedings on 9 March 2007, at which time the awards still stood in Russia. Following the decisions in the Moscow Arbitrazh Court of May 2007, Yukos Capital amended its application to complain that those decisions should be ignored as being neither impartial nor independent. Rosneft responded by relying on the annulment decisions and invoking public policy to resist enforcement. The Dutch court's judgment at first instance was rendered on 28 February 2008. Enforcement was refused on the ground that an annulment decision by the courts of the seat of the arbitration should only be disregarded in "extraordinary circumstances" and such circumstances had not been sufficiently asserted.

20. There was a complete re-hearing on appeal to the Amsterdam Court of Appeal. Yukos Capital undertook to prove that the annulment decisions were the result of partial and dependent proceedings and therefore should not be recognised. On this occasion Yukos Capital made a detailed statement of appeal, which ran to 100 pages, and submitted 124 exhibits. It also offered to prove further matters by live witnesses, including expert witnesses, if necessary. Rosneft also submitted a lengthy document by way of defence, but no documentary evidence. However, it too offered to produce live testimony. It took the view that only evidence (from Yukos Capital) directed at the particular judges and decisions concerned could be relevant, and that there was no such evidence. Yukos Capital's approach was rather to invite an inference to be drawn as to the annulment decisions from broader considerations of Russian justice in circumstances where Russian state interests were concerned.

21. The Amsterdam Court of Appeal agreed with the approach of Yukos Capital. Thus it rejected the need for direct evidence of the partiality and dependence of the individual judges concerned (for such "by their very nature take place behind the scenes" at para. 3.9.4). It found that Rosneft had insufficiently refuted or contested, but Yukos

Capital had properly substantiated, its submission and evidence that the Russian judiciary is "not impartial and independent but is guided by the interests of the Russian state and is instructed by the executive" (para. 3.9.3). It concluded that it was so likely (or "plausible") that the annulment decisions were the result of "an administration of justice which is to be qualified as partial and dependent, that it is not possible to recognize those judgments in the Netherlands" (at para. 3.10). Accordingly, Yukos Capital was given leave to enforce the awards. In coming to these conclusions the court considered itself to be applying "rules of general private international law" and "Dutch public order" (paras. 3.4-5). Its decision was made on 28 April 2009.

22. In coming to these conclusions the Amsterdam Court of Appeal relied on findings in the courts of various European countries that "the criminal prosecution of executives of Yukos Oil Company in Russia is politically inspired" (para. 3.8.8). It cited some expert testimony given in *Cherney* v. *Deripaska*[4] (3 July 2006, Commercial Court) to this effect:

Professor Stephan does not dispute that in the Yukos case serious irregularities occurred. The principal criticism concerns the criminal proceedings brought in the courts of general jurisdiction against the leading figures. But the arbitrazh court also failed to exercise a sufficient stringent review of the tax assessments. There are also grounds for concern as to whether the arbitrazh court overseeing the Yukos bankruptcy was sufficiently proactive in limiting the discretion of the receiver. But the Yukos case, in which the principal target, Mr Khordorkovsky, was a prominent oligarch, involved the renationalization of critical energy resources carried out by administrative agencies acting on behalf of the Russian State, that renationalization being a central policy of the Putin administration.

23. A further appeal by Rosneft to the Dutch Supreme Court did not bear fruit. It was rejected on jurisdictional grounds, on the basis that Dutch law does not permit a second appeal against the grant of an *exequatur*. There is currently an application to Strasbourg by Rosneft, to the effect that such a rule had never been previously imposed in an international arbitration enforcement case and amounted to an unfair denial of justice.

The English proceedings

24. On 11 March 2010 Yukos Capital issued two claims in England. One is an arbitration claim seeking permission to enforce the

---

[4] We will have to refer to the *Cherney* v. *Deripaska* jurisprudence below.

awards pursuant to section 101 of the Arbitration Act 1996 (the "1996 Act") (and thus pursuant to the New York Convention); the other is a Part 7 claim claiming the amount awarded as debt and/or damages plus post-award interest. Both claims were issued on the basis that no part of the awards had been paid. Now that the awards themselves have been paid, it would seem that only the Part 7 claim is in issue. Interest is claimed pursuant to article 395 of the Russian Civil Code and/or section 35A of the Senior Courts Act 1981. In due course particulars of claim in respect of both claims were served in a single document. Para. 10 of the particulars of claim asserts Yukos Capital's case that the annulment decisions "are not to be recognised as a matter of English private international law".

25. Rosneft's defence disputes any obligation to honour an award which has been set aside by the supervisory court, and relies both on common law and on section 103(2)(f) of the 1996 Act for this purpose. The awards "no longer exist in a legal sense", and in any event Yukos Capital is issue estopped by the annulment decisions from asserting that the awards are valid and binding on the parties. Further, it would be "contrary to the public policy of the United Kingdom" to recognise or enforce the awards either at common law, or pursuant to section 103(3) of the 1996 Act, "because the Loan Agreements were part of an illegal and fraudulent tax scheme and/or amounted to an abuse of right and/or were sham or otherwise void transactions under Russian law" (para. 23(2) of the defence).

26. Yukos Capital's reply is an important document, and has gone through various amendments. In its latest form (a re-re-amended reply plus Annex 1, dated March 2011, for which Hamblen J gave permission to amend in his order dated 14 June 2011 pursuant to his judgment under appeal) it sets out its latest case for explaining why the annulment decisions should not be recognised. First, it relies on the decision of the Amsterdam Court of Appeal for an issue estoppel that the annulment decisions were, or were likely to be, the result of a partial and dependent judicial process and were accordingly procured in circumstances contrary to natural justice, substantial justice, and article 6's guarantee of a fair trial. Alternatively it sets out anew its case why the annulment decisions were tainted by bias, with the same consequences. That case is particularised or expanded in paras. 6, 6A (referring to Annex 1) and 7 of the reply. The critical allegations to which objection is taken by Rosneft on act of state grounds are set out below.

27. Hamblen J's judgment, which in this respect reflects an element of common ground, refers to three allegations, the "first", "second" and

"third" allegations (see paras. 175ff, 191ff and 196ff of his judgment). We emphasise that Yukos Capital's allegations are yet to be proved in these courts.

28. The first allegation is labelled "the campaign against Yukos". The judge helpfully summarises it as follows (at para. 177):

(1) Entirely unsubstantiated tax demands were made, after Yukos had previously been given a clean audit by the tax authorities; and that those demands were pursued in such a manner as was intended to impede their discharge by Yukos. Thereafter, the tax demands were upheld by the Russian courts in proceedings which were grossly unfair and involved a manifestly improper application of Russian tax law; and any judge who found in favour of Yukos was summarily removed. Enforcement of the tax demands was then carried out in a manner intended not to maximise recovery, but to ensure that Yukos' assets were transferred at the lowest possible price to Rosneft. This process included enforcing against Yukos' critical production facilities first; the admission by the courts of manifestly unsubstantiated claims by Rosneft; and rigged auctions by the bankruptcy manager. All challenges by Yukos to these manifestly inappropriate acts were dismissed by the courts.

(2) This needs to be put in the political context of the Russian Federation's desire to re-nationalise strategic energy assets and to destroy Mr Khordorkovsky (who was a political opponent) so as to explain why these were not the ordinary application of Russian law and practice uninfluenced by executive interference, but that the Russian government procured each of the steps taken against Yukos Oil.

(3) Against that background and in the light of the clear examples of interference by the Russian state in the judicial process, it is unthinkable that the Russian government would have allowed the Russian courts (or that the Russian courts would have dared) to uphold awards worth over US $400 million against Rosneft (i.e. the recipient of Yukos' assets) in favour of, effectively, Yukos' former shareholders, including Mr Khordorkovsky. On that basis, the court will be invited to infer that the Annulment Decisions were the result of a partial and dependent judicial process.

29. This first allegation is alleged by Rosneft to be outlawed for adjudication by the act of state doctrine. In particular Rosneft objects to the following passages in Yukos Capital's pleadings:

(i) part of para. 6(1)(b) of the reply: "and having regard to the campaign against the Yukos group and its former CEO Mr Mikhail Khordorkovsky referred to hereafter and the fact that cases against Yukos are perceived in Russia as raising important issues of State policy, a fair minded and informed observer would

conclude that there was a real possibility or real danger that the Russian Courts were biased against the Claimant";
(ii) para. 6(4) of the reply: "formed part of a wider campaign waged by the Russian state for political reasons against the Yukos Group and its former CEO, Mikhail Khordorkovsky";
(iii) para. 7(6) of the reply: "Since at least December 2003 the Russian state has conducted a campaign intended to deprive Yukos of its assets and render it insolvent; to transfer Yukos' assets to enterprises under state control; and to detain its former owner Mr Khordorkovsky in prison. Full particulars of this campaign will be provided in expert evidence in due course, but its principal features include unwarranted tax assessments for enormous sums accompanied by demands for payment within days; dismissal with no or no adequate reasoning of all attempts to challenge the relevant assessments; refusals to engage in any negotiation to settle the alleged tax liabilities; preventing or impeding payment of the tax demands notwithstanding that Yukos had sufficient assets to do so; the conduct of rigged auctions where the only bidders were companies fronting for state owned enterprises; the imprisonment of Mr Khordorkovsky on trumped up charges and (as his sentence approached its conclusion in 2007) the laying of further charges against him inconsistent with the charges on which he had previously been convicted";
(iv) para. 10(2)(c) of the reply: "at all material times Yukos operated its businesses in accordance with all relevant tax laws and paid all sums properly due to the appropriate tax authorities. Insofar as it has been found liable in Russian Courts to pay enormous sums by way of additional tax and penalties the tax assessments and judicial decisions supporting them were procured by the Russian State as part of the campaign referred to at paragraph 7(5)[5] above and/or should not be recognised by the English Court for the reasons set out in paragraphs 6 and 7 above."

30. The second allegation has been labelled "Specific instances of unjust Yukos-related Proceedings". It charges that there are numerous other instances of unfair proceedings or perverse judicial decisions in Yukos-related proceedings being conducted at about the same time before the same courts to support an inference that the annulment

---

[5] *Sic*, but probably an error for para. 7(6).

decisions are similarly likely to be the product of partiality or bias. The relevant pleading for these purposes is para. 6A of the reply and Annex 1. Para. 6A reads:

More generally, the Russian Arbitrazh Courts have, when adjudicating proceedings involving Yukos or companies associated with it, acted in a manner which demonstrates that the cases have not been decided in accordance with the relevant law and/or in a fair manner, but involved bias and/or deliberate misapplication of the law. It is to be inferred that there was, or was a real risk of, a similar bias and/or deliberate misapplication of the law against Yukos Capital (which was also a Yukos interest) in the case at issue. Yukos Capital shall rely on the examples set out in Annex 1.

31. The first ten pages of Annex 1 are objected to (paras. 1-2 of Annex 1), but not the last eight pages. It is not clear what the difference is between them, but in the course of the appeal Lord Grabiner QC on behalf of Rosneft explained the objection as follows: Rosneft's case is that these allegations offend against the act of state doctrine because, by challenging as a "deliberate misapplication" of Russian law the Russian court decisions upholding the tax assessments, Yukos Capital necessarily requires the English court to hold that the tax assessments levied by the Russian state were unlawful under Russian law. On this basis, the judge's label probably needs reformulating, and this second allegation appears to be regarded as lying down very closely with the first allegation but as concentrating on unlawful tax assessments. So perhaps the label should be "Unlawful tax assessments".

32. As for these first two allegations, Rosneft's rejoinder pleads that "the English court should not adjudicate upon [the averments] or investigate or call into question such acts of a sovereign state within the limits of its own territory, by reason of the doctrines of Act of State and/or non-justiciability".

33. The third allegation ("Bias in cases involving matters of importance to the Russian Federation") is a more generalised case that Russian judges tend in matters of significant interest to the Russian state to act, or indeed to be instructed by the executive to act, in a biased manner in support of the state interest. In this connection objection is taken solely to para. 7(1) of the reply, which reads:

The Judges of Russian Courts are susceptible to improper influences where significant state interests are, or are perceived to be, in issue, whether by way of indications made out of court to Judges (known colloquially in Russia as "telephone justice" and decisions "to order") or the tendency of Judges assigned to such matters to act in accordance with the perceived interests of the Russian Federation irrespective of the merits of the case.

34. As for this third allegation, objection is made by Rosneft not in terms of the act of state doctrine itself, but in terms of the doctrine of judicial abstinence on the ground of non-justiciability (para. 6(1)(i) of Rosneft's rejoinder).

35. Rosneft has nevertheless accepted that it is open to the English courts to find that the individual decisions of the Russian supervisory courts (the "annulment decisions") were obtained by fraud, corruption, bias or lack of independence on the part of those courts. The concession has been put in the following way. In his judgment Hamblen J recorded that Rosneft "acknowledges that the court can determine whether the Annulment Decisions were partial and dependent" (at [185]). (The judge regarded that concession as being contradictory, for it did not extend to other decisions such as the tax assessments (*ibid.*).) No such acknowledgment is stated in Rosneft's skeleton argument to this court, but on the contrary the act of state doctrine is alleged to extend to the acts of a government "including through its courts" (citing *Philippine National Bank* v. *United States District Court* 397 F 3d 768 (9th Cir. 2005)). However, at the hearing of this appeal Lord Grabiner stated within minutes of opening as follows:

Yukos Capital's response is to assert that the Russian annulment decisions were reached by a partial and dependent process ... Now, it is open, we accept, to Yukos to try to prove that assertion by reference to evidence about the annulment proceedings themselves, for example by saying that they did not get a fair hearing or that the judge was biased or that his reasoning was perverse. In principle, we accept that that would not be objectionable. But Yukos wants to pray in aid a very much wider contention that there was a concerted political campaign by the Russian state ...

36. The distinction between what is objected to and what is not objected to is not entirely clear. But we suppose that it is essentially this: that the annulment decisions and the courts which made them can be attacked on the basis of any complaint which might be made in any dispute between private citizens; but they cannot be attacked on the basis either that Russian courts are generally not independent of the Russian state where state interests are concerned, or that in this particular case the annulment decisions were part of a campaign of expropriation and political enmity.

37. Thus, as to that campaign, the judge expressed Rosneft's case in outline in the following summary:

[112] Rosneft contended that the allegations made by Yukos Capital engage the Act of State principle. It submitted that the essence of the allegation requires the English court to adjudicate upon and call into question

the legitimacy and legality of the acts of a recognised (and friendly) foreign state or government within its own territory, including the legitimacy and legality of the decisions of its courts. The allegation made is that all the events relating to the Yukos matter (for example, the tax claims, their pursuit through the Russian courts, the resulting judgments of the Russian courts, the enforcement of those judgments under Russian law in Russia by the relevant arm of the executive, the decisions of the Russian courts upholding that enforcement process, the auction of the YNG shares effected by the Russian state, and even extending, so it is alleged, to the Russian decisions annulling the Awards in this case) are part of a governmental and political campaign involving, it is effectively alleged, the expropriation of assets from Yukos by illegitimate and illegal means, arranged and directed by the Russian state or government.

The two preliminary issues

38. By his order of 22 July 2010 Mr Justice David Steel ordered preliminary issues to determine:

(a) Whether the Defendant is issue estopped by the judgment of the Amsterdam Court of Appeal dated 28 April 2009 from denying that the judgments of the Russian civil courts annulling the arbitral awards which are the subject of these claims were the result, or likely to be the result, of a partial and dependent judicial process ...
(c) The issues relating to Act of State/non-justiciability pleaded in the Defendant's Rejoinder (on the assumption that the facts pleaded in the Claimant's Reply are true) and whether paragraph 7(1) of the Claimant's Reply should be struck out.

39. Hamblen J answered these issues as follows, in his order:

1. Rosneft is estopped, by the decision of the Amsterdam Court of Appeal dated 28 April 2009, from denying that the decisions referred to in paragraphs 11 to 14 of Rosneft's Amended Defence were the result of a partial and dependent judicial process.
2. Yukos Capital is not prohibited from alleging, and the Court is not prohibited from adjudicating, any of the issues raised by Yukos Capital's Re-Re-Amended Reply on the grounds of Act of state and/or non-justiciability and/or comity.

Act of state: the jurisprudence

40. The act of state doctrine is a long-standing doctrine of Anglo-American jurisprudence (Hamblen J commented that there is nothing

similar in the civil law). It can be traced back to decisions in our courts such as *Blad* v. *Bamfield* (1674) 3 Swans 605 and *Duke of Brunswick* v. *Hanover* (1848) 2 HL Cas 1, *per* Lord Cottenham at 17. In the former case Lord Nottingham said at 607 that it would be "monstrous and absurd" to pretend to judge the validity of the King of Denmark's patent in Denmark or to try whether the English have a right to trade in Iceland. In the latter case Lord Cottenham LC said at 17 that the courts of England "cannot sit in judgment upon the act of a Sovereign, effected by virtue of his Sovereign authority abroad".

41. Some 100 years ago the doctrine was given new impetus in a series of three cases in the United States Supreme Court. In *Underhill* v. *Hernandez* 168 US 250 (1897) at 254 Chief Justice Fuller said:

> Every sovereign State is bound to respect the independence of every other sovereign State, and the Courts of one country will not sit in judgment on the acts of the government of another done within its own territory. Redress of grievances by reason of such acts must be obtained through the means open to be availed of by sovereign powers as between themselves.

In *Oetjen* v. *Central Leather Co.* 246 US 297 (1918) Justice Clarke said this (at 245-6):

> The principle that the conduct of one independent government cannot be successfully questioned in the courts of another ... rests at last upon the highest considerations of international comity and expediency. To permit the validity of the acts of one sovereign state to be re-examined and perhaps condemned by the courts of another would very certainly "imperil the amicable relations between governments and vex the peace of nations".

And in *Ricaud* v. *American Metal Company Limited* 246 US 304 Justice Clarke observed (at 304):

> when it is made to appear that the foreign government has acted in a given way on the subject-matter of the litigation, the details of such action or the merit of the result cannot be questioned but must be accepted by our courts as a rule for their decision.

42. These Supreme Court authorities were applied in England by the Court of Appeal in *Luther* v. *Sagor & Co.* [1921] 3 KB 532 and *Princess Paley Olga* v. *Weisz* [1929] 1 KB 718 (see, for instance, at 724-5 and 728-9). In the latter case Russell LJ at 736 put the matter in this way:

> This Court will not inquire into the legality of acts done by a foreign government against its own subjects in respect of property situate in its own territory.

That limitation to "its own subjects" is controversial. These authorities may, however, have to be reassessed today, as matters concerned with private rights and private international law principles rather than sovereign authority: see *Kuwait Airways Corporation* v. *Iraqi Airways Co. (Nos 4 and 5)* [2002] 2 AC 883 at 972H-973C.

43. In *Buck* v. *Attorney General* [1965] 1 Ch 745 (CA) Diplock LJ emphasised the international aspects of the principle, and its analogy to the doctrine of sovereign immunity (at 770):

As a member of the family of nations, the Government of the United Kingdom (of which this court forms part of the judicial branch) observes the rules of comity, videlicet, the accepted rules of mutual conduct as between state and state which each state adopts in relation to other states and expects other states to adopt in relation to itself. One of those rules is that it does not purport to exercise jurisdiction over the internal affairs of any other independent state, or to apply measures of coercion to it or to its property, except in accordance with the rules of public international law. One of the commonest applications of this rule by the judicial branch of the United Kingdom Government is the well-known doctrine of sovereign immunity ... For the English court to pronounce upon the validity of a law of a foreign sovereign state within its own territory, so that the validity of that law became the res of the res judicata in the suit, would be to assert jurisdiction over the internal affairs of that state. That would be a breach of the rules of comity. In my view, this court has no jurisdiction so to do.

44. In *Attorney General* v. *Nissan* [1970] AC 179 at 237 Lord Pearson said this about acts of state, albeit the state he was there talking about was the Crown and not a foreign sovereign. In such a case it appears that the doctrine of act of state differs, in that it is a narrower class of act which falls within the doctrine. When, however, a relevant act of state is determined, a similar doctrine of non-justiciability prevails. Lord Pearson said:

As to the alleged act of state, it is necessary to consider what is meant by the expression "act of state", even if it is not expedient to attempt a definition. It is an exercise of sovereign power. Obvious examples are making war and peace, making treaties with foreign sovereigns, and annexations and cessations of territory. Apart from these obvious examples, an act of state must be something exceptional. Any ordinary governmental act is cognisable by an ordinary court of law (municipal not international): if a subject alleges that the governmental act was wrongful and claims damages or other relief in respect of it, his claim will be entertained and heard and determined by the court. An act of state is something not cognisable by the court: if a claim is made in respect of it, the court will have to ascertain the facts but if it then appears that the act complained of was an act of state the court must refuse to adjudicate upon the claim. In such a case the court does not come to any decision as to the legality or illegality, or the rightness or wrongness, of the act complained of; the decision is that because it was an act of state the court has no jurisdiction to entertain a claim in respect of it. This is a very unusual situation and strong evidence is required to prove that it exists in a particular case.

45. We come now to *Buttes Gas and Oil Co.* v. *Hammer (No 3)* [1982] AC 888, from which the modern law of foreign act of state may be said to take its impetus. Lord Wilberforce there also discerned a separate but analogous doctrine of non-justiciability, albeit he traced it back to old underpinnings in the same anthology of cases.

46. *Buttes Gas* concerned a defamation action, the issues in which embraced two conflicting oil concessions which neighbouring states in the Arabian Gulf had granted over their territorial and offshore waters. The foreign relations of the United Kingdom and of Iran were also involved. At the heart of the defamation dispute was a boundary issue which made it impossible to say what the territorial limits of the neighbouring states were. The defendants submitted that the action raised issues which were non-justiciable by the English courts and should therefore be stayed. It was for the purpose of that submission that the act of state doctrine and its jurisprudence were reviewed. Lord Wilberforce, with whose speech the other members of the judicial committee agreed, drew from the English and American authorities at least two principles: one specific, a territorial act of state principle, the other general, the principle of non-justiciability. The former did not apply, but the latter did.

47. Lord Wilberforce expressed each doctrine in the following terms. Of the former he said (at 931B):

A second version of "act of state" consists of those cases which are concerned with the applicability of foreign municipal legislation within its own territory, and with the examinability of such legislation—often, but not invariably, arising in cases of confiscation of property. Mr Littman gave us a valuable analysis of such cases ... suggesting that these are cases within the area of the conflict of laws, concerned essentially with the choice of the proper law to be applied ...

In that context issues might still arise as to whether effect would be given in England to the foreign law or act, if it was contrary to public policy or international law. It appears that Lord Wilberforce was here perhaps seeking to narrow the territorial principle, for instance by referring to "legislation". However, this version of the doctrine did not apply because what the *Buttes* case was concerned about was not so much a foreign municipal law as "an act or acts operating in the area of transactions between states" (at 931D-E).

48. Lord Wilberforce therefore turned to a wider and general principle, which on our current understanding is not so much a *separate* principle as a more *general and fundamental* principle, the principle of non-justiciability. Thus he said (at 931G):

> So I think that the essential question is whether, apart from such particular rules as I have discussed ... there exists in English law a more general principle that the courts will not adjudicate upon the transactions of foreign sovereign states. Though I would prefer to avoid argument on terminology, it seems desirable to consider this principle, if existing, not as a variety of "act of state" but one for judicial restraint or abstention.

49. Lord Wilberforce then derived that more general principle from the very cases which we have examined above. It is not entirely clear to us whether that more general principle is confined, as some of the expressions in those cases would seem to confine it, to what transpires territorially within a foreign sovereign state: but we are of the view, expressed in the judgment of this court in *Kuwait Airways Corporation v. Iraqi Airways Co. (Nos 4 and 5)* [2002] 2 AC 883 at [287] and [319], that the principle may even extend to extraterritorial (or perhaps one might speak of transnational) acts, as in *Buttes Gas* itself, with its international boundary disputes. However, in the present case, we are concerned only with what has occurred within Russia itself.

50. At 937 Lord Wilberforce considered some of the issues which would arise in that case, if it was allowed to proceed. He emphasised first, the question of the boundary dispute between four nations; and secondly, that the dispossession of any rights depended on a series of interstate transactions, an examination of the motives of sovereigns, and questions of unlawfulness under international law. He then concluded with this well-known passage (at 938A-C):

> It would not be difficult to elaborate on these considerations, or to perceive other important inter-state issues and/or issues of international law which would face the court. They have only to be stated to compel the conclusion that these are not issues upon which a municipal court can pass. Leaving aside all possibility of embarrassment in our foreign relations (which it can be said not to have been drawn to the attention of the court by the executive) there are—to follow the Fifth Circuit Court of Appeals—no judicial or manageable standards by which to judge these issues, or to adopt another phrase (from a passage not quoted), the court would be in a judicial no-man's land: the court would be asked to review transactions in which four sovereign states were involved, which they had brought to a precarious settlement, after diplomacy

and the use of force, and to say that at least part of these were "unlawful" under international law.

51. Earlier in his speech, Lord Wilberforce had also indicated some concepts which could be used to paint the contours of the doctrine or doctrines. Thus a question as to foreign land "may arise incidentally or collaterally to some other question, and may be decided" (at 926H). That is then contrasted with the questions which arose in *Buttes Gas* itself, which were said to be "at the heart of the case" (at 927B). Nor was the doctrine avoided simply because there was no allegation of unlawfulness under the local (Sharjah) law itself: on the contrary, it was all the more problematic that the issue arose "in a different, and international dimension" (at 927C). And then this:

This cannot be decided simply as a fact upon evidence: it calls, on the contrary, for adjudication upon the validity, meaning and effect of transactions of sovereign states.

52. In *Williams and Humbert Ltd* v. *W & H Trade Marks (Jersey) Ltd* [1986] 1 AC 368 the defendant's application to strike out the plaintiff's action by reason of the act of state doctrine failed. It was alleged that the plaintiff was seeking to rely indirectly on Spanish expropriatory decrees in order to prove its title: but it was held that the plaintiff's title did not depend on the decrees but on the general law anterior to those decrees. What was said about the act of state doctrine was therefore obiter. Nevertheless, Lord Templeman, with whose speech the other members of the House of Lords agreed, said this (after considering cases such as *Luther* v. *Sagor* and *Princess Paley Olga* v. *Weisz*) at 431D-E:

These authorities illustrate the principle that an English court will recognise the compulsory acquisition law of a foreign state and will recognise the change of title to property which has come under the control of the foreign state and will recognise the consequences of that change of title. The English court will decline to consider the merits of compulsory acquisition. In their pleadings the appellants seek to attack the motives of the Spanish government and to question the good faith of the Spanish administration in connection with the enactment, terms and implementation of the law of the 29 June 1983. No English judge could properly entertain such an attack launched on a friendly state which will shortly become a fellow member of the European Economic Union.

It was common ground before us that any implied limitation of those propositions to members or future members of the EU would not be sustainable. In our respectful view, it was not intended.

53. In *Regina* v. *Bow Street Metropolitan Stipendiary Magistrate, ex parte Pinochet Ugarte (No 3)* [2000] 1 AC 147 at 269 Lord Millett said this about the act of state doctrine and its closeness to an aspect of state immunity *ratione materiae*:

Immunity ratione materiae is very different. This is a subject matter immunity. It operates to prevent the official and governmental acts of one state from being called into question in proceedings before the courts of another, and only incidentally confers immunity on the individual. It is therefore a narrower immunity but it is more widely available. It is available to former heads of state and heads of diplomatic missions, and anyone whose conduct in the exercise of the authority of the state is afterwards called into question, whether he acted as head of government, government minister, military commander or chief of police, or subordinate public official. The immunity is the same whatever the rank of the office-holder. This too is common ground. It is an immunity from the civil and criminal jurisdiction of foreign national courts but only in respect of governmental or official acts. The exercise of authority by the military and security forces of the state is the paradigm example of such conduct. The immunity finds its rationale in the equality of sovereign states and the doctrine of non-interference in the internal affairs of other states: see *Duke of Brunswick* v. *King of Hanover* (1848) 2 HL Cas 1; *Hatch* v. *Baez*, 7 Hun 596; *Underhill* v. *Hernandez* (1897) 168 US 250. These hold that the courts of one state cannot sit in judgment on the sovereign acts of another . . .

Given its scope and rationale, it is closely similar to and may be indistinguishable from aspects of the Anglo-American act of state doctrine. As I understand the difference between them, state immunity is a creature of international law and operates as a bar to the jurisdiction of the national court, whereas the act of state doctrine is a rule of domestic law which holds the national court incompetent to adjudicate upon the lawfulness of the sovereign acts of a foreign state.

54. Lord Phillips of Worth Matravers also covered this ground, at 286 as follows:

There would seem to be two explanations for immunity ratione materiae. The first is that to sue an individual in respect of the conduct of the state's business is, indirectly, to sue the state. The state would be obliged to meet any award of damage made against the individual. This reasoning has no application to criminal proceedings. The second explanation for the immunity is the principle that it is contrary to international law for one state to adjudicate upon the internal affairs of another state. Where a state or state official is impleaded, this principle applies as part of the explanation for immunity. Where a state is not directly or indirectly impleaded in the litigation, so that no issue of state immunity as such arises, the English and American courts have none the less, as a matter of judicial restraint, held themselves not competent to entertain litigation that turns on the validity of the public acts of a foreign state, applying what has become known as the act of state doctrine. Two citations well illustrate the principle ...

and Lord Phillips proceeded to cite the classic statements of Chief Justice Fuller from *Underhill* v. *Hernandez* at 252 and of Diplock LJ from *Buck* v. *Attorney General* at 770.

55. The subject of the act of state doctrine played an important role in *Kuwait Airways Corporation* v. *Iraqi Airways Co. (Nos 4 and 5)* [2002] 2 AC 883, although there it was held that its application, as well as any reliance on Iraqi law as the *lex situs* or the *lex loci delicti*, was excluded by an exception founded in international law or English public policy. I will deal with the exceptions to the doctrine separately below. For the present it will suffice to cite the terms in which their Lordships described the act of state doctrine.

56. Thus Lord Nicholls of Birkenhead referred to the act of state principle through the submissions of IAC's counsel ("An English court will not sit in judgment on the sovereign acts of a foreign government or state. It will not adjudicate upon the legality, validity or acceptability of such acts, either under domestic law or international law. For a court to do so would offend against the principle that the courts will not adjudicate upon the transactions of foreign sovereign states" at [24]), but continued:

[25] My Lords, this submission seeks to press the non-justiciability principle too far. Undoubtedly there may be cases, of which the *Buttes* case is an illustration, where the issues are such that the court has, in the words of Lord Wilberforce, at p. 938, "no judicial or manageable standards by which to judge [the] issues" ...

[26] This is not to say an English court is disabled from ever taking cognisance of international law or from ever considering whether a violation of international law has occurred. In appropriate circumstances it is legitimate for an English court to have regard to the content of international law in deciding whether to recognise a foreign law ... Nor does the "non-justiciable" principle mean that the judiciary must shut their eyes to a breach of an established principle of international law committed by one state against another when the breach is plain and, indeed, acknowledged ...

Thus Lord Nicholls did not for himself formulate the doctrine other than in terms of Lord Wilberforce's more general principle.

57. Lord Steyn said (at [112]) that "it is well established that courts must not sit in judgment on the acts of a foreign government within its own territory".

58. Lord Hope of Craighead, under the heading of "Justiciability", said this:

[135] Important questions of principle are raised by the highly unusual facts of this case. There is no doubt as to the general effect of the rule which is known as the act of state rule. It applies to the legislative or other governmental acts of a recognised sovereign state or government within the limits of its own territory. The English courts will not adjudicate upon, or call into question, any such acts. They may be pleaded and relied upon by way of defence in this jurisdiction without being subjected to that kind of judicial scrutiny. The rule gives effect to a policy of "judicial restraint or abstention": see *Buttes Gas and Oil* v. *Hammer (No 3)* [1982] AC 888, 931F-934C per Lord Wilberforce ...

Lord Steyn and Lord Hoffmann agreed with Lord Nicholls (as well as giving reasons of their own); Lord Steyn also agreed with Lord Hope.

59. *AK Investment CJSC* v. *Kyrgyz Mobil Tel Ltd* [2011] UKPC 7, [2011] 4 All ER 1027 concerned an attempt by a claimant to enforce a Kyrgyz judgment against the defendants, and a counterclaim by the defendants, against the claimant and others, for a declaration that the judgment had been obtained by fraud, and for damages for that fraud. The question was whether the defendants should be given leave to serve their counterclaim out of the jurisdiction. The Privy Council held that leave should be granted, since it had been sufficiently shown that there was no prospect of justice being done in the courts of Kyrgyszstan.

60. In reliance on the act of state doctrine, the claimant and intended defendants to the counterclaim submitted that the court should abstain from sitting in judgment on the independence of the Kyrgyz judicial system. Lord Collins referred (at [90]) to two questions: the first was as to the standard of proof to be satisfied by a party which asserts that justice will not be done in the foreign jurisdiction: did that have to be proved, or did only the *risk* of it have to be proved? The second question was whether it was open to allege that "as a result, for example, of endemic corruption, justice cannot be obtained in the foreign legal system in general".

61. Lord Collins proceeded to demonstrate that the earliest cases of relevance had arisen during the period of Nazi control in Germany: it had been open to a Jewish refugee to sue his German employer in England by showing that he could not get justice in Germany: *Oppenheimer* v. *Louis Rosenthal & Co. AG* [1937] 1 All ER 23 (CA). In *The Abidin Daver* [1984] AC 398 at 411 Lord Diplock said that a stay of an English action on the ground of *forum non conveniens* could be resisted on the ground that justice could not be obtained in the otherwise more appropriate forum but that such a claimant "must assert this candidly and support his allegations with positive and cogent evidence". Lord Collins concluded, after citation of other authority, that, on the first question, it was only a real risk that had to be shown. He said:

[95] The better view is that, depending on the circumstances as a whole, the burden can be satisfied by showing that there is a real risk that justice will not be obtained in the foreign court by reason of incompetence or lack of independence or corruption. Of course, if it can be shown that justice "will not" be obtained that will weigh more heavily in the exercise of the discretion in the light of all other circumstances.

Lord Collins was there speaking in the context of the seeking and disputing of long-arm jurisdiction, where issues arise at an interlocutory stage and do not require to be judged by the standard of proof applicable at trial.

62. Lord Collins then turned to the second question, concerning the act of state doctrine. Despite two Australian cases in which a doctrine of judicial restraint in such circumstances was said to be applicable (*Voth* v. *Manildra Flour Mills Pty Ltd* (1990) 171 CLR 538, and *Mokbel* v. *A-G for the Commonwealth of Australia* [2007] FCA 1536, (2007) 244 ALR 517), Lord Collins relied inter alia on the decision in this court in *Al-Koronky* v. *Time-Life Entertainment Group Ltd* [2006] EWCA Civ 1123, [2007] 1 Costs LR 57 for his conclusion that the act of state doctrine did not apply. In *Al-Koronky* this court said that it was entitled to take into account evidence about the lack of independence of the judiciary in the Sudan for the purposes of requiring security for costs in English proceedings. Lord Collins also found support for his conclusion in "many cases in the United States courts in which the standard of justice in the foreign court has been examined in the context of forum non conveniens questions" (at [102]). Lord Collins expressed the relevant principles as follows:

[97] Comity requires that the court be extremely cautious before deciding that there is a risk that justice will not be done in the foreign country by the foreign court, and that is why cogent evidence is required. But, contrary to the appellants' submission, even in what they describe as endemic corruption cases (i.e. where the court system itself is criticised) there is no principle that the court may not rule ...

[101] The true position is that there is no rule that the English court (or Manx court) will not examine the question whether the foreign court or the foreign court system is corrupt or lacking in independence. The rule is that considerations of international comity will militate against any such finding in the absence of cogent evidence. That, and not the act of state doctrine or the principle of judicial restraint in *Buttes Gas and Oil* v. *Hammer (Nos 2 and 3)*, is the basis of Lord Diplock's dictum in *The Abidin Daver* and the decisions which follow it. Otherwise the paradoxical result would follow that, the worse the system of justice in the foreign country, the less would it be permissible to make adverse findings on it.

63. Most recently, in *Lucasfilm Ltd* v. *Ainsworth* [2011] UKSC 39, [2012] 1 All ER (Comm) 1011, the Supreme Court was concerned with the question whether a breach of foreign copyright was justiciable in England. The act of state doctrines in play in the present case were not directly invoked, but, in their judgment with which Lord Phillips and Lady Hale concurred, Lord Walker and Lord Collins SCJJ discussed them in the context of analogous jurisprudence regarding the justiciability of foreign intellectual property rights. The conclusion was that claims for breach of US copyright were justiciable. On the way to that conclusion Lord Walker and Lord Collins considered whether the grant of intellectual property rights was an act of state for the purposes of the act of state doctrine. They cited a decision (by a majority) of the US federal circuit court to the effect that it was: *Voda* v. *Cordis Corp.* (2007) 476 F 3d 887 where Gajarsa CJ (Prost CJ concurring) said (at 904):

In this case, none of the parties or amicus curiae have persuaded us that the grant of a patent by a sovereign is not an act of state ... Therefore, assuming arguendo that the act of state doctrine applies, the doctrine would prevent our courts from inquiring into the validity of a foreign patent grant and require our courts to adjudicate patent claims regardless of validity or enforceability.

However, Newman CJ, dissenting, was said by Lord Walker and Lord Collins (at [85]) to be right to point out (at 914) that not every governmental action and not every ministerial activity is an act of state; and they cited *Mannington Mills Inc.* v. *Congoleum Corp.* (1979) 595 F 2d 1287 at 1293-4 (3d Cir.) in support, rejecting the proposition that the mere issuance of patents by a foreign power constitutes an act of state.

64. Lord Walker and Lord Collins continued:

[86] It has been said that the grant of a national patent is "an exercise of national sovereignty" (Jenard Report on the Brussels Convention (OJ 1979 C59 pp. 1, 36)), and the European Court has emphasised that the issue of patents necessitates the involvement of the national administrative authorities (*Gesellschaft für Antriebstechnik mbH & Co. KG* v. *Lamellen und Kupplungsbau Beteiligungs KG*, Case C-4/03 [2006] ECR I-6509 (para. 23)). But in England the foreign act of state doctrine has not been applied to any acts other than foreign legislation or governmental acts of officials such as requisition, and it should not today be regarded as an impediment to an action for infringement of foreign intellectual property rights, even if validity of a grant is in issue, simply because the action calls into question the decision of a foreign official.

65. It is said that there is a third doctrine, closely allied to the doctrine of non-justiciability, to the effect that the courts will not

investigate acts of a foreign state where such an investigation would embarrass the government of our own country: but that this doctrine only arises as a result of a communication from our own Foreign Office. The judge referred to this doctrine as the "political embarrassment principle" (at [146]-[148]). It appears to be based on Lord Wilberforce's brief comment in *Buttes Gas* at 938A; and on equally brief comments in *Korea National Insurance Corporation* v. *Allianz Global Corporate & Speciality AG* [2008] EWCA Civ 1355 at [32] (a paragraph which begins with the words "These statements give no support for the view that . . ."), and in *Berezovsky* v. *Abramovich* [2011] EWCA Civ 153, [2011] 1 WLR 2290 at [100]. None of those cases concerned such a principle, and in none of them was a communication received from the Foreign Office. We would be cautious about giving weight to this third doctrine, which in any event it is common ground does not arise in this case. It is acknowledged that the potential for the disruption of international relations (or what is also described as the rule of comity) is one of the philosophical underpinnings of all act of state doctrines: see, for instance, the famous dictum of Justice Clarke in *Oetjen* v. *Central Leather*, cited at [41] above.

66. We have confined ourselves thus far to cases, concerning the act of state doctrines, which have occurred in the House of Lords or the Supreme Court or Privy Council since *Buttes Gas*. In sum, it seems to us that Lord Wilberforce's principle of "non-justiciability" has, on the whole, not come through as a doctrine separate from the act of state principle itself, but rather has to a large extent subsumed it as the paradigm restatement of that principle. It would seem that, generally speaking, the doctrine is confined to acts of state within the territory of the sovereign, but in special and perhaps exceptional circumstances, such as in *Buttes Gas* itself, may even go beyond territorial boundaries and for that very reason give rise to issues which have to be recognised as non-justiciable. The various formulations of the paradigm principle are apparently wide, and prevent adjudication on the validity, legality, lawfulness, acceptability or motives of state actors. It is a form of immunity *ratione materiae*, closely connected with analogous doctrines of sovereign immunity and, although a domestic doctrine of English (and American) law, is founded on analogous concepts of international law, both public and private, and of the comity of nations. It has been applied in a wide variety of situations, but often arises by way of defence or riposte: as where a dispossessed owner sues in respect of his property, the defendant relies on a foreign act of state as altering title to that property, and the claimant is prevented from calling into question the effectiveness of that act of state.

67. However, the doctrine, although frequently expressed in the wide terms exemplified in the citations set out above, has its limitations, founded in the very language of the doctrine and in its rationale. We will examine those limitations next, for they are relevant to the submissions of Yukos Capital to the effect that the doctrine does not apply to the disputed allegations in this case. For these purposes, however, it may be necessary to observe the extent to which those submissions both rely and do not rely on such limitations.

Limitations on the act of state doctrine

68. The first limitation is that, as stated above, the act of state must, generally speaking, take place within the territory of the foreign state itself. *Buttes Gas* is an example where, in the context of boundary disputes between states, the principle of non-justiciability was applied to acts which need not have been confined to territorial limits. Thus Lord Wilberforce appears to have contemplated that in at any rate such special circumstances the doctrine could extend beyond the territorial boundaries of the state. However, that is perhaps a unique example of such an extension. In the present case it is not suggested that any of the acts of state relied upon by Yukos Capital took place outside Russia.

69. A second limitation is that, again exceptionally, the doctrine will not apply to foreign acts of state which are in breach of clearly established rules of international law, or are contrary to English principles of public policy, as well as where there is a grave infringement of human rights. That limitation was discussed and applied in *Kuwait Airways* v. *Iraqi Airways*, where Lord Nicholls said this:

[28] The acceptability of a provision of foreign law must be judged by contemporary standards. Lord Wilberforce, in a different context, noted that conceptions of public policy should move with the times: see *Blathwayt* v. *Baron Cawley* [1976] AC 397, 426. In *Oppenheimer* v. *Cattermole* [1976] AC 249, 278, Lord Cross said that the courts of this country should give effect to clearly established rules of international law. This is increasingly true today. As nations become ever more interdependent, the need to recognise and adhere to standards of conduct set by international law becomes ever more important. RCC Resolution 369 was not simply a governmental expropriation of property within its territory. Having forcibly invaded Kuwait, seized its assets, and taken KAC's aircraft from Kuwait to its own territory, Iraq adopted this decree as part of its attempt to extinguish every vestige of Kuwait's existence as a separate state. An expropriatory decree made in those circumstances and for this purpose is simply not acceptable today.

[29] ... A breach of international law of this seriousness is a matter of deep concern to the worldwide community of nations ... Such a fundamental breach of international law can properly cause the courts of this country to say that, like the confiscatory decree of the Nazi government of Germany in 1941, a law depriving those whose property has been plundered of the ownership of their property in favour of the aggressor's own citizens will not be enforced or recognised in proceedings in this country. Enforcement or recognition of this law would be manifestly contrary to the public policy of English law ... International law, for its part, recognises that a national court may properly decline to give effect to legislative and other acts of foreign states which are in violation of international law: see the discussion in *Oppenheim's International Law*, 9th ed. (1992), vol. I (ed. Jennings and Watts), pp. 371-6, para. 113.

See also Lord Steyn at [115].

70. Lord Hope agreed, but was anxious to stress the narrowness of the exception. He reasoned the matter as follows:

[137] IAC accepts however that the normal rule is subject to an exception on grounds of public policy. The proposition which it accepts is that the exception applies if the foreign legislation constitutes so grave an infringement of human rights that the courts of this country ought to refuse to recognise the legislation as valid as a law at all: *Oppenheimer* v. *Cattermole* [1976] AC 249, 278, per Lord Cross of Chelsea. The proposition which it disputes is that the public policy exception extends to breaches of international law ...

[138] It is clear that very narrow limits must be placed on any exception to the act of state rule. As Lord Cross recognised in *Oppenheimer* v. *Cattermole* [1976] AC 249, 277-8, a judge should be slow to refuse to give effect to the legislation of a foreign state in any sphere in which, according to accepted principles of international law, the state has jurisdiction. Among these accepted principles is that which is founded on the comity of nations. The principle normally requires our courts to recognise the jurisdiction of the foreign state over all assets situated within its own territories: see Lord Salmon, at p. 282. A judge should be slow to depart from these principles. He may have an inadequate understanding of the circumstances in which the legislation was passed. His refusal to recognise it may be embarrassing to the executive, whose function is so far as possible to maintain friendly relations with foreign states.

[139] But it does not follow ... that the public policy exception can only be applied where there is a grave infringement of human rights. This was the conclusion which was reached on the facts which were before the House in the *Oppenheimer* case. But Lord Cross based that conclusion on a wider point of principle. This too is founded upon the public policy of this country. It is that our courts should give effect to clearly established principles of international law ...

[140] As I see it, the essence of the public policy exception is that it is not so constrained. The golden rule is that care must be taken not to expand its

application beyond the true limits of the principle. These limits demand that, where there is any room for doubt, judicial restraint must be exercised. But restraint is what is needed, not abstention, And there is no need for restraint on grounds of public policy where it is plain beyond dispute that a clearly established norm of international law has been violated.

71. And so Lord Hope agreed that, in the context of Iraq's flagrant breaches of international law, and the UN Security Council resolutions which marked them, judicial restraint was not called for:

Respect for the act of state doctrine and the care that must be taken not to undermine it do not preclude this approach. The facts are clear, and the declarations by the Security Council were universal and unequivocal ... (At [149].)

The rule of law required nothing else:

It is now clear, if it was not before, that the judiciary cannot close their eyes to the need for a concerted, international response to these threats to the rule of law in a democratic society. Their primary role must always be to uphold human rights and civil liberties. But the maintenance of the rule of law is also an important social interest ... (At [145].)

72. In this context, it should be said that the exception where English public policy is concerned embraces discrimination, at any rate where it amounts to a form of persecution as in the context of Nazi legislation or to what has been referred to as "flagrant" breaches of human rights; but it has not as yet recognised expropriation without compensation as having been outlawed by clearly established international norms. In this connection we would refer to this court's consideration of at least some of the relevant jurisprudence in *Kuwait Airways* v. *Iraqi Airways* at [269]-[283]. The *Kuwait Airways* case itself was exceptional in that the expropriation was achieved by a process of invasion condemned internationally through resolutions of the United Nations Security Council which have the force of law. Although Yukos Capital complains of a campaign of expropriation, aimed at Yukos and its principal, Mr Khordorkovsky, it has not alleged, either in its pleadings or, as far as we have been told, in argument below, that its case falls outside the limits of the act of state doctrines on such grounds of exception, if those doctrines would otherwise prima facie apply. The argument has not been addressed to us. The judge merely commented:

[204] In the light of my conclusion that the "pure" Act of State principle does not apply it is not necessary to decide whether, if it did, Yukos Capital's case arguably comes within the exception. It was accepted that for this purpose

all the allegations made by Yukos Capital must be assumed to be true and that the issue would be whether, on that basis, its claim should be struck out. I would only observe that whilst, as Rosneft submitted, the exception is a narrow one and the only example of its application,[6] the *Kuwait Airways* case, was a case of extreme facts, the principle does extend to "flagrant" breaches of human rights, and that whether a breach is sufficiently "flagrant" is very fact dependent.

That might suggest that the point remained to be taken. Mr Gordon Pollock QC, who appears on behalf of Yukos Capital, accepted that there had been no respondent's notice in respect of any such point, nor did he seek to argue it.

Judicial acts

73. A third limitation, we would suggest, is that judicial acts will not be regarded as acts of state for the purposes of the act of state doctrine. Of course in certain circumstances, judicial acts will be regarded as acts for which a state may be responsible in human rights law. That is the essence of human rights law: to render the state, including its organs such as its courts, liable for acts which may be in breach of that law. However, for the most part, the vindication of such rights is either for the domestic courts or for an international court such as the Strasbourg court. Where, however, a foreign court may act in a way which is an abuse of its own responsibilities as a court of law, the courts of this country are not obliged to give effect to the potential jurisdiction or past acts of such a court, provided that the failings of the foreign court are sufficiently cogently brought home to the English court. We consider that this is the teaching of the Privy Council in *AK Investment* v. *Kyrgyz Mobil* [2011] 4 All ER 1027 (see at paras. [59]-[62] above).

74. On behalf of Yukos Capital, Mr Pollock relies on *AK Investment* as undermining the whole of Rosneft's case on act of state. However, he nevertheless accepts, or is willing for the sake of argument to accept if not formally to concede, that court decisions are themselves acts of state. He takes his stand upon a separate footing, not that court decisions are not acts of state, but on the proposition that the act of state doctrine may be invoked only where the validity of an act of state is in dispute, or where a judicial remedy is sought in respect of such acts. We will revert to this submission below. For the present, however, we observe that in such circumstances it is not clear to us what the distinguishing principle is supposed to be which separates court

---

[6] We do not think this is correct.

decisions which have the effect, for instance, of altering the title to property, or grant to or remove from a litigating party a financial asset or claim, and other acts of state which have the same effect.

75. Lord Grabiner's submission on behalf of Rosneft is that the *AK Investment* case is only the latest in a line of cases which allows consideration of acts of state where a future risk of injustice has to be assessed, as where a jurisdictional issue of *forum conveniens* is under consideration, but not where past acts have to be adjudicated upon and findings made. Or, as the matter is put in Rosneft's skeleton: "the Act of State principle applies only to acts which have already occurred; it does *not* apply to potential conduct of a state in the future" (para. 38). The judge rejected this distinction, referring to it as unprincipled, and observing that a judgment as to the future may have to be grounded in an inquiry and findings as to the past (at [168]-[171]).

76. In this connection we have been referred to *Cherney* v. *Deripaska (No 2)* [2008] EWHC 1530 (Comm), [2009] 1 All ER (Comm) 333 (Christopher Clarke J) and *Berezovsky* v. *Abramovich* [2010] EWHC 647 (Comm) (Sir Anthony Colman), [2011] 1 WLR 2290 (CA).

77. In *Cherney* the issue was whether service out of the jurisdiction should be permitted to serve the defendant in Russia. It was held that although Russia was the natural forum for the litigation, there was a risk that substantial justice would or could not be done in the natural forum so that justice required the case to be tried in England. In coming to that conclusion, the judge considered expert evidence concerning the corruption and partiality of the Russian courts and of the interference of the executive in judicial proceedings where the state's strategic interests were in play, and also evidence about other cases, such as the dispute between Yukos and Rosneft itself. The decision was upheld on appeal: *Cherney* v. *Deripaska (No 2)* [2009] EWCA Civ 849, [2010] 2 All ER (Comm) 456. Mr Pollock is able to say that allegations very similar to some at least of the challenged allegations in this case were there considered.

78. In his judgment below, Hamblen J set out details of those wide-ranging allegations (at [163]) and commented as follows:

[164] In the light of this evidence [Christopher Clarke J] concluded that he was "satisfied that, in this particular case, there is a significant risk that Mr Cherney will not obtain in Russia a trial unaffected by improper interference by state actors and that substantial justice may not be done" (at [260]).

[165] A challenge to that conclusion was rejected on appeal. The Court of Appeal held that there was cogent evidence to support it. It referred to evidence of misuse of the criminal justice system as a tool of governmental policy (including ". . . the well-known proceedings against Mr Khordorkovsky

of Yukos ..."—at [62]), of manipulation of the judicial process ("... the proceedings against Yukos and Mr Khordorkovsky provide one obvious example ..."—at [64]) and of the government's willingness to interfere in the judicial process in circumstances where it considers that national interests are engaged ("... it can be said with some justification that the Yukos case involved both what might be described as the re-nationalisation of strategic assets and the damaging of a political opponent ..."—at [66]).

79. Lord Grabiner, however, relies on the following observations in the judgment of Waller LJ as supporting his analysis:

[29] I should make clear again, having regard to points made by Mr Malek, that the judge is not conducting a trial. It is not a situation in which he has to be satisfied on the balance of probabilities that facts have been established. He is in many instances seeking to assess risks of what might occur in the future. In so doing he must have evidence that the risk exists, but it is not and cannot be a requirement that he should find on the balance of probabilities that the risks will eventuate ...

80. In our judgment, however, those observations were in no way directed to making any distinction for the purposes of the act of state doctrine, which was not in issue at all in that case, but for the different purpose of commenting on what a court has to be satisfied about for the purposes of its ultimately discretionary decision as to where a case can best be heard in the interests of justice. In such circumstances, they throw no light on the present issue.

81. In *Berezovsky*, the question was whether Mr Berezovsky's claim could be struck out. On this occasion the act of state doctrine was in issue. Mr Berezovsky alleged that he had been intimidated by Mr Abramovich into disposing of an interest at an undervalue. He supported that claim by an allegation that he had been previously threatened by President Putin in relation to the same interest (and had therefore left Russia) and that it was on this ground that he believed Mr Abramovich when he repeated similar threats, saying that he was acting on the authority of the President himself. At first instance, Sir Anthony Colman explained the structure of the argument as follows:

[166] ... no allegation is pleaded against the sovereign state or its President as such. The substance of what is pleaded is the content of RA's threat. Whereas it is pleaded that it was said that President Putin would or could cause BB's interests to be expropriated, it is not alleged that RA was in truth the mouthpiece of President Putin, but merely that his known relationship with the Kremlin and with the President was such that BB believed that RA

was in a position to work jointly with President Putin to further a common enterprise to the mutual benefit of the President and RA ...

[167] There is no allegation against the State, either as a necessary part of the tort of intimidation or for the purpose of obtaining a remedy against the Russian State, that the President or the State has already acted unlawfully or is about to do so. The ambit of the allegation is BB's understanding of what RA was telling him and his interpretation of the risk involved if he ignored RA's suggestion for the transfer of his interests in Sibneft ...

[168] The facts alleged in this case therefore differ crucially from the facts before the court in *R (on the application of Yukos Oil Co.)* v. *FSA* [2006] EW [HC] 2044 (Admin) in which the underlying issue involved the allegation that the assets of the company seeking listing *had been* wrongly expropriated by Russia. This was alleged as an accomplished fact necessary for the relief claimed. Whether it was true would have to be determined by the FSA and subsequently the court.

[169] In the present case the allegations relating to the President and the Russian officials are simply deployed as part of the background against which RA's threat is said to have been understood by BB to be coercive. Not only are these allegations not at the heart of the cause of action, they are collateral to the conduct giving rise to the tort.

[170] The Act of State doctrine does not involve precluding the English courts from receiving evidence of this kind and evaluating its truth. In no sense can it be said that the English court is thereby trespassing on territory within the ambit of the exclusive sovereign jurisdiction of a foreign state. It is therefore unnecessary to consider the public policy submission in relation to this issue.

82. At an earlier stage of his judgment, when he was considering the submissions on act of state jurisprudence made by Mr Abramovich's counsel, Sir Anthony Colman made this observation:

[98] It is to be observed that these authorities are concerned with the issue whether past conduct of the government of a foreign state has been unlawful and not whether future conduct would be unlawful if ever it took place. Thus in the *Yukos Case* it was an essential part of the claimant's case that the corporate assets had in truth been wrongfully expropriated.

83. In this court, the first instance judge's conclusion was upheld, but on somewhat different reasoning: not on the ground that the disputed allegations were merely collateral (see [98]), but on the ground that all that Mr Berezovsky was seeking to show was that certain facts had occurred, not that they were invalid or wrongful (at [97]). It was in this context that Longmore LJ said this (at [87]):

On the basis of *Al-Koronky* v. *Times Life Entertainment* [2006] EWCA Civ 1123 para. 42, Mr Popplewell [counsel for Mr Abramovich] accepted, at this level of authority, that potential conduct of a state in the future could not fall within the first principle because the principle only applied to acts which have already occurred. The second principle could in an appropriate case, however, apply to future acts.

That, however, appears to be an obiter observation, since the essence of the ruling was that mere reliance on acts *which had occurred*, for their existence as facts, did not trespass against the act of state doctrine. Thus even though what was being referred to was past acts, they were still not within the act of state doctrine.

84. But is it the case that *Al-Koronky* is founded on the distinction between past conduct and future conduct? One would not discern this from Lord Collins' treatment of that case in *AK Investment*. What Sedley LJ (giving the judgment of this court) said in *Al-Koronky* was this:

> [41] ... He further submitted that the contents of the unidentified Sudanese lawyer's advice amounted to a general attack on a foreign country's judiciary which gave rise to an issue which, on grounds of comity, could not be entertained by the courts of this country.
>
> [42] For this last proposition Mr Shaw cited the otherwise unreported decision of *Jeyaretnam* v. *Mahmood* (1992) *The Times* May 21, in which, for the purpose of an application to discharge an order for service on a defendant out of the jurisdiction, Brooke J (as he then was) declined to evaluate allegations of lack of independence or impartiality in the defendant's home country of Singapore on the grounds that such allegations were not justiciable, in the same way as the allegations in *Buttes Oil and Gas* v. *Hammer* [1982] AC 888 were held to be not justiciable. While we accept that any court is always reluctant to pass judgment on the judiciary of a foreign country in the context of jurisdictional disputes, we doubt if there is any general principle that the courts of this country will never do so in any context. First, as noted by Morland J in *Skrine & Co.* v. *Euromoney Publications Ltd* [2001] EMLR 16, para. 18(1) the *Buttes Oil* case concerned past transactions of foreign states, not the likely behaviour of judges in the future. Secondly, in the context of dealing with asylum-seekers it is frequently relevant to consider whether the courts of a foreign state afford any remedy against persecution, the risk of which is said to be a reason against returning the applicant to his home state. Thirdly, any such principle would not sit happily with cases decided in relation to the law of repressive regimes such as Nazi Germany ...

85. That was said in relation to a case concerning security for costs. It rejected the application of the act of state doctrine to an allegation of state partiality of a foreign country's courts, and refused to follow *Jeyaretnam* v. *Mahmood* in this respect. Lord Collins in *AK Investment*

also declined to follow *Jeyaretnam* or *Skrine* (at [99]). As it is, we respectfully think that Sedley LJ misstates the decision in *Skrine*, which was another case, like *Jeyaretnam*, which applied the act of state doctrine so as to strike out pleading allegations which criticised the behaviour and impugned the integrity of a foreign judiciary, on this occasion the judiciary in Malaysia. All that Morland J said at para. 18(1) of *Skrine* was as follows:

It would not assist the parties nor is it necessary to set out in this judgment extensive citation of authority or quotations from judgments. I shall set out the principles on which my judgment is based.

1. An English court must exercise judicial restraint or abstention and not adjudicate upon in relation to a friendly foreign state the acts or transactions of its sovereign, its executive or its judiciary (see *Buttes Gas* v. *Hammer* [1982] AC 888—where a stay was ordered because the defendants in a slander action were unable to justify because of this principle) (see also the judgment of Brooke J in *Jeyaretnam* v. *Mahmood* (transcript 21 May 1992) a libel action).

There was plainly no attempt there to explain the act of state doctrine in terms of past as distinct from future acts of state, but simply a reliance on *Buttes Gas* (which binds us) and *Jeyaretnam* (which does not).

86. In our judgment the time has come, in accordance with the rationalisation and highly authoritative guidance of Lord Collins and the Privy Council in *AK Investment*, to hold that the act of state doctrine does not prevent an investigation of or adjudication upon the conduct of the judiciary of a foreign state, whether that conduct lies in the past, or in the future, and whether or not its conduct in the past is relied upon as the foundation for an assessment of the risk as to its conduct in the future. As Hamblen J stated in the present case, such a distinction is without principle: it is truly so, for such a distinction has never even been formulated. In our judgment the doctrinal basis of the decisions in *Jeyaretnam* and *Skrine* cannot be supported and should not be followed.

87. So the position is, to put the matter broadly, that whereas in a property case comity would seem to *require* (at any rate as a principle of restraint rather then abstention) that the validity or lawfulness of the legislative or executive acts of a foreign friendly state acting within its territory should not be the subject of adjudication in our courts, comity only *cautions* that the judicial acts of a foreign state acting within its territory should not be challenged without cogent evidence. If then the

question is asked—Well, why should acts of a foreign judiciary be treated differently from other acts of state, and what is the basis of that difference?—the answer, in our judgment, is that judicial acts are not acts of state for the purposes of the act of state doctrine. The doctrine in its classic statements has never referred to judicial acts of state, it has referred to legislative or executive (or governmental or official) acts of a foreign sovereign. Two examples will suffice for more: Lord Hope speaks of the "legislative or other governmental acts" of the foreign sovereign in *Kuwait Airways* v. *Iraqi Airways* at [135]; and Lord Collins speaks of "foreign legislation or governmental acts of officials such as requisition" in *Lucasfilm* v. *Ainsworth* at [86]. It is not hard to understand why there should be a distinction. Sovereigns act on their own plane: they are responsible to their own peoples, but internationally they are responsible only in accordance with international law and internationally recognised norms. Courts, however, are always responsible for their acts, both domestically and internationally. Domestically they are responsible up to the level of their Supreme Court, and internationally they are responsible in the sense that their judgments are recognisable and enforceable in other nations only to the extent that they have observed what we would call substantive or natural justice, what in the United States is called due process, and what internationally is more and more being referred to as the rule of law. In other words the judicial acts of a foreign state are judged by judicial standards, including international standards regarding jurisdiction, in accordance with doctrines separate from the act of state doctrine, even if the dictates of comity still have an important role to play. As Lord Lindley said in *Pemberton* v. *Hughes* [1899] 1 Ch 781 at 790:

If a judgment is pronounced by a foreign court over persons within its jurisdiction and in a manner with which it is competent to deal, English courts never investigate the propriety of the proceedings in the foreign court, *unless they offend against English views of substantial justice* ... (Emphasis added.)

Hamblen J rightly gave prominence to this famous passage as early as para. [11] of his judgment.

88. It is true that at least one American case can be cited in which the act of state doctrine has been applied to the judicial acts of a foreign court. Thus in *Philippine National Bank* v. *United States District Court for the District of Hawaii* 397 F 3d 768, to which Rosneft refers in its skeleton argument, the US Court of Appeals for the ninth circuit held that the act of state doctrine applied to prevent adjudication of a claim that a judgment of the Philippine Supreme Court was invalid, and did

so even though the judgment at least in part purported to dispose of property outside Philippine territory (see at 773). The judgment of Circuit Judge Canby states:

The class plaintiffs in the district court argue that the act of state doctrine is directed at the executive and legislative branches of foreign governments, and does not apply to judicial decisions. Although the act of state doctrine is normally inapplicable to court judgments arising from private litigation, there is no inflexible rule preventing a judgment sought by a foreign government from qualifying as an act of state. See *Liu* v. *Republic of China*, 892 F 2d 1419, 1433-4 & n. 2 (9th Cir. 1989) (citing *Restatement (Second) of Foreign Relations of the United States* § 41 cmt. D (1965) ("A judgment of a court may be an act of state"). There is no question that the judgment of the Philippine Supreme Court gave effect to the public interest of the Philippine government. The forfeiture action was not a mere dispute between private parties; it was an action initiated by the Philippine government pursuant to the "statutory mandate to recover property allegedly stolen from the treasury." *In the Estate of Ferdinand Marcos Human Rights Litig.* 94 F 3d at 546. We have earlier characterized the collection efforts of the Republic to be governmental. *Id.* The subject matter of the forfeiture action therefore qualifies for treatment as an act of state.

89. That statement, even if it acknowledges the exceptional nature of such an application of the act of state doctrine, clearly has resonance for what Rosneft complains about the allegations of Yukos Capital in this case. Nevertheless, and despite the fact that so much of the learning about the doctrine has crossed the Atlantic in both directions, we do not agree that that doctrine applies to prevent adjudication on an otherwise appropriate challenge to a foreign court decision. We refer to the fact that in *AK Investment* Lord Collins cites a number of US federal court decisions in which allegations of impropriety against foreign courts have been adjudicated in the context of *forum non conveniens* and enforcement of judgments (at [102]).

90. In our judgment, therefore, the act of state doctrine does not apply to allegations of impropriety against foreign court decisions, whether in the case of particular decisions or in the case of a systemic dependency on the dictates or interference of the domestic government. Nor is there an absence of justiciable standards by which to adjudicate such allegations. The courts have long been familiar with the standards by which to judge bias and other breaches of due process in the operation of courts and other tribunals. Moreover, even if there are countries in the world in which the courts are not free from interference by the state and are not independent of them in at any rate those cases in which the state takes an interest in the result, there is barely a

country in the world which does not subscribe to the doctrine that justice according to the law is what is expected of its courts and judges, or does not subscribe to what is more and more being expressed as a global deference to the rule of law. Thirdly, where a state may nevertheless depart from those doctrines by requiring or engineering a perverted or biased result, it does so in the main, not by a process of legislative, administrative or executive act, for which it takes responsibility, but in secrecy. Although it must be acknowledged that there are areas of state activity which are always more or less clothed in secrecy, such as its intelligence services, the process of judgment through the courts is universally recognised (even in its breach) as an activity which has to be carried out fairly and transparently and in accordance with law.

91. For these reasons we agree with the holding of Hamblen J at [201] below that "there is no rule against passing judgment on the judiciary of a foreign country: see the *Abidin Daver* [1984] AC 398 and the subsequent decisions reviewed in the *AK Invest[ment]* case".

The commercial exception

92. We turn to another exception to or limitation on the act of state doctrine, which is not in issue in this case, but which demonstrates the way in which caution needs to be maintained when considering how far broad statements of principle, made in another era when the doctrine of absolute sovereign immunity held sway, still apply or extend in the modern world in which it is now accepted, as a matter of general international law, that there is no immunity for the state's commercial activities.

93. Thus in *The Playa Larga* [1983] 2 Lloyd's Rep 171 (CA), where the defendant to a claim in conversion was the Cuban state's sugar trading company, and the goods in question were on the high seas at the relevant time and thus not within Cuban territory, this court held, first, that the territorial act of state doctrine did not apply, secondly that the doctrine of non-justiciability did not apply, for the court was not in a judicial no-man's land, and thirdly, obiter, that even if the act of state doctrine could have prima facie applied, then—

that conduct was not immune from the jurisdiction of the English Courts since its activity was a trading rather than a governmental activity. What the Cuban government did was to induce breaches of contract by Cubazucar.

That decision was made in the light of the House of Lords confirming at the highest level in this country that the absolute doctrine of sovereign immunity had made way in English law, because it had done so in international law, to the qualified or restricted doctrine which made an exception for the commercial activities of states: *I Congreso del Partido* [1983] 1 AC 244. The modern history of the change from an absolute theory to the modern doctrine, now enshrined in our State Immunity Act 1978, is briefly traced in this court in *Kuwait Airways* v. *Iraqi Airways*, as itself throwing light on the modern ramifications of the act of state doctrine: see at [312]-[313].

94. More recently still, in the *Korea National Insurance Corporation* case, Waller LJ, giving the judgment of this court, said:

These statements [from *Buttes Gas* and this court in *Kuwait Airways*] give no support to the view that, where in a commercial context allegations are made against a state, not in relation to some sovereign act carried out in its own jurisdiction, but in relation to acts which affect the rights of a party under a commercial contract, that the court should exercise restraint to the extent of not being prepared to decide the same, at least without some indication from the executive that a decision will embarrass the diplomatic relations between the United Kingdom and the State. If a foreign state were an insured under an insurance contract the insurers cannot be precluded from alleging a fraudulent claim simply because that might embarrass the state. It cannot be any different if a state entity makes the claim and it is asserted that both the entity and the state owner were involved in the fraud.

The Kirkpatrick *exception*

95. Yet another exception, however, has been relied upon, and is one of the cornerstones of Yukos Capital's opposition to this appeal. Thus, it is submitted by Mr Pollock that the act of state doctrine does not apply in cases where there is no "sitting in judgment on" the acts of state alleged but only a question or acknowledgment of whether certain facts have occurred. For these purposes he submits that it does not matter that the finding or acknowledgment of such facts involves some inherent impropriety, provided that there needs to be no investigation into the validity, lawfulness or motives of the state's acts.

96. For these purposes he relies on the following cases, beginning with the American decisions in *Sharon* v. *Time Inc.* 599 F Supp 538 (SDNY 1984) and *Kirkpatrick* v. *Environmental Tectonics Corporation International* 493 US 400 (1990).

97. In *Sharon* v. *Time* Mr Sharon brought defamation proceedings against Time Magazine for publishing an article about his activities during a time when he had been defence minister of Israel. Time relied

on the act of state doctrine as excluding the court's competency. It was not in dispute that the underlying facts concerning the massacre of civilians in refugee camps had occurred, and that such actions were "illegal and abhorrent". An Israeli enquiry (the Kahan Commission) had already taken place into the events. It was held that the act of state doctrine did not apply because (i) the defence allegation was not that Mr Sharon had acted pursuant to his ministerial authority but that he had done so outside that authority in a personal capacity (at 544); and (ii) the issue was not concerned with the propriety of those acts, but as to Mr Sharon's complicity. As Sofaer DJ put it (at 546):

By contrast, the litigation here involves no challenge to the validity of any act of state. With respect to Sharon's alleged acts, no one is suggesting that these acts—by which Time claims Sharon condoned the massacre of unarmed noncombatant civilians—have validity in the sense that they cannot be attacked. All agree—Israel, the United States and the world community— that such actions, if they occurred, would be illegal and abhorrent. The issue in this litigation is not whether such acts are valid, but whether they occurred.

98. In *Kirkpatrick* the claimant brought an anti-racketeering claim against a competitor on the ground that it had obtained a military procurement contract from the Nigerian government by bribery. It was common ground that Nigerian law prohibited both the payment and the receipt of bribes. The defendant relied on the act of state doctrine to exclude enquiry into the claim. The defence was rejected on the ground that the only issue was whether the alleged bribes had occurred. If they had, their legality and their consequences were a matter of US law, not Nigerian law. In any event it was common ground that any such bribes were illegal under Nigerian law. Justice Scalia delivered the judgment of the US Supreme Court. He said (at 405-6):

In every case in which we have held the act of state doctrine applicable, the relief sought or the defense interposed would have required a court in the United States to declare invalid the official act of a foreign sovereign performed within its own territory. In *Underhill* v. *Hernandez*, 168 US 250, 254 ... holding the defendant's detention of the plaintiff to be tortuous would have required denying legal effect to "acts of a military commander representing the authority of the revolutionary party as government, which afterwards succeeded and was recognized by the United States." In *Oetjen* v. *Central Leather Co.*, *supra*, and in *Ricaud* v. *American Metal Co.*, *supra*, denying title to the party who claimed through purchase from Mexico would have required declaring that government's prior seizure of the property, within its territory, legally ineffective. See *Oetjen*, *supra*, 246 US, at 304 ... *Ricaud*, *supra*, 246 US, at 310 ... In *Sabbatino*, upholding the defendant's claim to the funds would have required a holding that Cuba's expropriation of goods located in Havana was null and void. In the present case, by contrast, neither the claim nor any asserted defense requires a determination that Nigeria's contract with Kirkpatrick International was, or was not, ineffective.

Petitioners point out, however, that the facts necessary to establish the respondent's claim will also establish that the contract was unlawful. Specifically, they note that in order to prevail respondent must prove that petitioner Kirkpatrick made, and Nigerian officials received, payments that violate Nigerian law, which would, they assert, support a finding that the contract is invalid under Nigerian law. Assuming that to be true, it still does not suffice. The act of state doctrine is not some vague doctrine of abstention but a "*principle of decision* binding on federal and state courts alike." *Sabbatino, supra*, 376 US, at 427 ... (emphasis added). As we said in *Ricaud*, "the act within its own boundaries of one sovereign state ... becomes ... a rule of decision for the courts of this country". 246 US, at 310 ... Act of state issues only arise when a court *must decide*—that is, when the outcome of the case turns upon the effect of official action by a foreign sovereign. When that question is not in the case, neither is the act of state doctrine. That is the situation here. Regardless of what the court's factual findings may suggest as to the legality of the Nigerian contract, its legality is simply not a question to be decided in the present suit, and there is thus no occasion to apply the rule of decision that the act of state doctrine requires. Cf. *Sharon* v. *Time, Inc.*, 599 F Supp 538, 546 (SDNY 1984) ("The issue in this litigation is not whether [the alleged] acts are valid, but whether they occurred").

99. Justice Scalia concluded (at 409-10) as follows:

The short of the matter is this: Courts in the United States have the power, and ordinarily the obligation, to decide cases and controversies properly presented to them. The act of state doctrine does not establish an exception for cases and controversies that may embarrass foreign governments, but merely requires that, in the process of deciding, the acts of sovereigns taken within their own jurisdiction shall be deemed valid. That doctrine has no application to the present case because the validity of no foreign sovereign act is at issue.

100. These American authorities have been followed in two cases in the English courts, in *A Ltd* v. *B Bank* [1997] 1 L Pr 586 (CA) and in *Berezovsky* v. *Abramovich* [2011] EWCA Civ 153 (*supra*).

101. In *A* v. *B Bank* the plaintiff's claim was to restrain the use in this country by the defendant commercial bank of foreign banknotes, on the ground of infringement of the plaintiff's UK patent. The central bank of the foreign country intervened, but no allegation of infringement was made against the central bank or its state and the only complaint was of use of the defendant's banknotes in the UK, for the plaintiff's UK patent gave only territorial rights in this country. The trial judge had stayed the proceedings on the ground that the claim was

non-justiciable. This court reversed that decision on the twin grounds that the use of the banknotes in the UK was commercial, and that in any event the matters complained of occurred in this country and not in the territory of the foreign state. The judgments also referred to *Kirkpatrick*, as supporting, for instance, the following propositions (*per* Leggatt LJ at 592-3) that "the Court is not asked to adjudicate upon, or even to consider the lawfulness of the issue of currency, nor is any claim made that might interfere with sovereign functions of the State of X", and (*per* Morritt LJ at 596) that "the principle . . . is limited to the proposition that the courts . . . will not adjudicate upon the validity of acts done abroad by virtue of foreign sovereign authority". It seems to us that the claim to rely on the act of state doctrine was so far outwith the principles of that doctrine as to render its citation of no help in this.

102. We have already cited *Berezovsky* v. *Abramovich*. For the reasons stated above, it was pertinent for this court to cite *Kirkpatrick* in support of its own conclusion that the act of state doctrine was not involved where the only issue was whether certain acts had occurred, not whether they were invalid or wrongful.

103. In the present case, however, it is plain that Yukos's case goes well beyond the situation in *Sharon* v. *Time*, *Kirkpatrick*, *A* v. *B Bank* or *Berezovsky* v. *Abramovich*. In the present case, Yukos does not merely seek to show that certain events occurred (and did so in Russia and as a matter of state policy), but that such events are not to be regarded as valid or effective or lawful, but invalid, ineffective, wrongful, arbitrary, and directed by the hostile motive of a campaign of expropriation and wrongful imprisonment. The disputed allegations (set out more fully above) speak of a "campaign waged by the Russian state for political reasons", of "a deliberate misapplication of the law". That deliberate misapplication was set out at length in Annex 1 to the re-re-amended reply and started with "massive tax re-assessments in respect of Yukos, ultimately in excess of US $24 billion, which were arbitrary, manifestly not consistent with Russian law and practice, and usually based on doctrines applied uniquely to Yukos . . . ". It is therefore alleged that the annulment decisions themselves have to be regarded as ineffective to set aside and nullify the arbitration awards as they otherwise purport to do. The judge himself, in describing Yukos's case, does so in these terms (taken from [175]-[177]): "a campaign against Yukos with the aim (in particular) of re-nationalising Yukos' assets and destroying a political opponent" . . . "Entirely unsubstantiated tax demands . . . any judge who found in favour of Yukos was summarily removed . . . rigged auctions . . . All challenges to these manifestly inappropriate acts were dismissed by the courts . . . the political context of the Russian

Federation's desire to re-nationalise strategic energy assets and to destroy Mr Khordorkovsky (who was a political opponent) so as to explain why these were not the ordinary application of Russian law and practice uninfluenced by executive in[ter]ference, but that the Russian government procured each of the steps taken against Yukos Oil".

104. In our judgment, whatever might otherwise be the width or narrowness of the act of state doctrines, we cannot agree that these four authorities (or any others) support treating the allegations in this case as simply being concerned with proving what occurred and not with castigating what occurred as wrongful and therefore to be regarded as ineffective. Moreover, inasmuch as Yukos Capital submits, as it does, that "it is no part of Yukos Capital's case that any act of state was illegal or wrongful", or that "It is no part of Yukos' case in these proceedings, let alone a necessary part, that anything done by the Russian state was invalid and lacked any legal effect ... It simply does not follow ... that if a judgment is shown to be a manifest misapplication of Russian law then it is not 'valid'" (Yukos Capital's skeleton argument at paras. 79-80), those submissions are not understood and seem to us to fly in the face of Yukos Capital's pleading. That pleads that Russian law was deliberately misapplied as a matter of state policy, and inter alia on that ground the English court is asked to find that the tax assessments and decisions and the annulment decisions are to be regarded as ineffective and invalid. In this respect at least, it is like the position in *Kuwait Airways* v. *Iraqi Airways* where, but for the application of an exception based upon international law and English public policy, the act of state doctrine may have been applied to the acquisition pursuant to Iraqi decree of the stolen Kuwaiti aircraft. Or it is like *Luther* v. *Sagor*, where the act of state doctrine was applied to hold that the Russian decree declaring Russian sawmills to be the property of the Russian Soviet Republic "could not be impugned" (to cite the headnote).

Challenge to validity

105. We come finally, therefore, to Yukos Capital's most fundamental formulation as to the narrow limits of the act of state doctrines, and that is that they are engaged only where there is a challenge to the *validity* of an act of state or where the English court is requested to grant a *remedy* in respect of such acts. Before the judge, the submission was confined to the first half of that proposition, namely to the need for a challenge to the validity of an act of state. For this purpose, "validity" was contrasted with any wider formula which might speak, instead, of lawfulness or, on the other side, unlawfulness, wrongfulness or any

such concept. However, in this court Mr Pollock accepted that his formula before the judge, which the judge accepted, was too narrow, and amended it as set out above. In doing so, it remained unclear whether Mr Pollock was continuing to use "validity" in some narrow sense. However, he took the trouble to set out his reformulated submission in the following written terms:

4. The doctrine is only engaged where the English Court is required to adjudicate upon the actions of the foreign sovereign by determining that they are invalid or by granting a remedy in respect of those actions.

5. The reason why the doctrine is limited in this way is that it is founded upon a principle of jurisdiction. By adjudicating upon the foreign sovereign's actions in the way described, the English Court is arrogating to itself a jurisdiction over those actions: it is claiming to have authority to judge the foreign sovereign's actions within his own territory and to grant remedies in respect of them. This is impermissible.

6. By contrast, the English court is not *adjudicating upon* the foreign sovereign's actions (in the way described in 4 above) by receiving evidence as to what the sovereign in fact did and evidence that those actions were not justified by reference to the established law of the state, and making findings of fact to this effect (on the civil standard of proof). In doing this the English Court is not exercising any jurisdiction over the sovereign or his actions and the doctrine is not engaged.

106. Mr Pollock's ammunition for this submission, to the extent that it did not extend across the whole of the act of state jurisprudence, was again focused on *Kirkpatrick* in the United States and on *Berezovsky* v. *Abramovich* in England. In *Kirkpatrick* Mr Pollock emphasised the opening sentence of the passage from Justice Scalia's judgment which we have cited above at [98] ("In every case ... the relief sought or the defense interposed would have required the court to declare invalid the official act of a foreign sovereign performed within its own territory" at 405). In *Berezovsky* he emphasised the following passage from the judgment of this court, which begins (at [95]) with a reference to *A* v. *B Bank* as being based on a triple ratio, the third of which is that "on the authority of *Kirkpatrick*, there was no challenge to the validity of any act of the foreign state". (So there was not, neither in *Kirkpatrick*, nor in *A* v. *B Bank*, nor in *Berezovsky*, as explained above.) This court then continued:

[95] ... All three reasons were treated as having equal weight and Mr Rabinowitz correctly submitted that we are, therefore, now bound by authority to say that the act of state doctrine only applies to challenges to the validity of the act of state relied upon, unless there is subsequent higher authority to a different effect.

[96] Nevertheless some caution may be appropriate. Lord Hope has, subsequently to *A Ltd*, in *Kuwait Airways* reiterated the traditional English law formulation that the court will not "adjudicate upon or call into question" acts of a foreign state within its own territory. If it were an essential part of an English litigant's case that an act of state was "wrongful" whether by its own law or by international law, and if that was disputed by the other side, it could well be said that that argument (and any decision upon it) was indeed "adjudicating upon or calling into question" that act, even if it was not specifically alleged that the act was "invalid". It is worth remarking that *Dicey, Morris & Collins, Conflict of Laws*, 14th ed. (2006) para. 5-045 cites *Kirkpatrick* without any endorsement and does not even refer to it in the Table of Cases.

[97] This perhaps difficult question does not, however, need to be resolved in the present case because not only is it no part of Mr Berezovsky's case to say that the acts on which he relies were invalid; it is no part of his case either to say that they were wrongful. His concern is only to prove that they occurred as appears to have been the case in *Sharon* v. *Time Inc.* quoted in the above citation from *Kirkpatrick*. In these circumstances I cannot think that any question of act of state can arise ...

107. So ultimately, that issue raised in *Berezovsky*, which can perhaps be expressed as to whether it makes a critical difference to reliance on the act of state doctrine whether the challenge is to the act's *validity* or its general *wrongfulness*, was left unresolved.

108. The judge below, Hamblen J, sought to resolve it, albeit Mr Pollock no longer relies on his formulation. The judge said this:

[134] However, that comment [a reference to *Berezovsky* at [96]] does not alter the fact that the Court of Appeal held that it was bound to hold that "the act of state doctrine only applies to challenges to the validity of the act of state relied upon" and that I am equally so bound. In any event, I consider that it is important that the limits of the Act of State principle are defined with reasonable clarity. Limiting it to necessary challenges to the validity of an act does so. Extending it to cases where such validity is merely called into question, or to wider issues of legality or wrongfulness, makes it of a potentially broad and uncertain application. In this connection it is worth noting that the Act of State principle is a common law doctrine and does not exist in the civil law. Further, in a number of cases where it has been applied the same result can be reached through the application of ordinary rules of conflicts of laws—*Dicey, Morris & Collins* at para. 5-045.

[135] I accordingly hold that the "pure" Act of State principle only applies to challenges to the validity of the act of state relied upon. I further hold that guidance as to what this requires is to be found in the *Kirkpatrick* case, as the Court of Appeal has held. I further hold, in line with that guidance, that as a general rule "validity" in this context means determining that the act is of no

legal validity or effect and that "challenges" to such validity means that it is an issue which the court must decide in order to reach its decision in the case before it.

109. Now in our judgment we would agree that challenges to foreign acts of state, in order to invoke the act of state doctrine, must, as Lord Wilberforce put it, lie at "the heart" of a case, and not be a matter of merely ancillary or collateral aspersion: and that a test of necessity to a decision may therefore be a useful test. That is as long as it is remembered that the purpose of the doctrine is to prevent such challenge at the outset, as a matter of immunity *ratione materiae*. However, now that the matter has been fully argued in this case, we would not, with respect, agree that anything turns on the particular words in which the principle is expressed: as if the words "challenges" or "validity" were sacrosanct. This can be seen from the reasoning of Justice Scalia itself, as well as from the jurisprudence in general.

110. Thus we would again emphasise: the teaching of *Kirkpatrick* (and the cases which follow it) is *not* to do with any difference, were there to be any, between concepts of validity, legality, effectiveness, unlawfulness, wrongfulness and so on. Validity (or invalidity) is just a useful label with which to refer to a congeries of legal concepts, which can be found spread around the cases. Similarly, the word "challenge" is not sacrosanct: the cases refer to the prohibition on adjudication, sitting in judgment on, investigation, examination, and so on. What *Kirkpatrick* is ultimately about, however, is the distinction between referring to acts of state (or proving them if their occurrence is disputed) as an existential matter, and on the other hand asking the court to enquire into them for the purpose of adjudicating upon their legal effectiveness, including for these purposes their legal effectiveness as recognised in the country of the forum. It is the difference between citing a foreign statute (an act of state) for what it says (or even for what it is disputed as saying) on the one hand, something which of course happens all the time, and on the other hand challenging the effectiveness of that statute on the ground, for instance, that it was not properly enacted, or had been procured by corruption, or should not be recognised because it was unfair or expropriatory or discriminatory. As to the last possibilities, there can be a still further distinction to be made between the act of state which *cannot* be challenged for its effectiveness despite some alleged unfairness, and the act of state which is sufficiently outrageous or penal or discriminatory to set up the successful argument that it falls foul of clear international law standards or English public policy and therefore *can* be challenged.

111. In this respect the relevant paragraph of Justice Scalia's judgment in *Kirkpatrick* which begins with the sentence relied upon (see at [98] above) makes perfectly clear what he meant by that statement ("In every case ... the relief sought or the defence interposed required a court ... to declare invalid the official act of a foreign sovereign"). Thus he proceeded to illustrate that statement by referring to the four most famous previous act of state cases in the United States, namely *Underhill* v. *Hernandez, Oetjen* v. *Central Leather, Ricaud* v. *American Metal* and *Banco Nacional de Cuba* v. *Sabbatino* 376 US 398 (1964).

112. In *Underhill* the plaintiff claimed for false imprisonment and assault against the commander of a revolutionary Venezuelan army. The revolutionary forces had gone on to form a government recognised by the United States. The act of state doctrine was pleaded by the defendant and the action failed. It did so because the plaintiff's action could not succeed without "denying legal effect" (*per* Justice Scalia) to the defendant's actions. It is odd to think of the acts of Commander Hernandez as "valid" or "invalid": however the act of state doctrine meant that their legal effect could not be enquired into, or as Chief Justice Fuller said: "the courts of one country will not sit in judgment on the acts of the government of another done within its own territory". Clearly, by "to declare invalid" Justice Scalia meant the same as to find wrongful or unlawful and on that ground ineffective. In *Oetjen*, a military commander of the Mexican revolutionary government seized and sold hides belonging to a Mexican citizen. The hides were shipped to the United States, and their original owner or his assignees sued to recover them, but failed, since, as Justice Scalia said, to deny the title of the purchaser from the commander in Mexico would have required finding "the government's prior seizure ... legally ineffective". As Justice Clarke there said: the action of the Mexican government "is not subject to reexamination and modification by the courts of this country". To similar effect was *Ricaud*, where Justice Clarke said that "the details of such action and the merit of the result cannot be questioned but must be accepted by our courts as a rule for their decision". Finally, in *Sabbatino* the Cuban government sought to recover the price of expropriated sugar from the expropriated owner's US receiver, whom the purchaser of the sugar had been persuaded to pay. The claim succeeded, because the receiver could not, by reason of the act of state doctrine, show that the expropriation without (sufficient) compensation was unlawful under international law. The receiver was not seeking any remedy, but was resisting the Cuban government's claim, and to do so was asking the court to find that the transfer of title in Cuba was unlawful and ineffective. As Justice

Scalia said in *Kirkpatrick*: "the defendant's claims to the funds would have required a holding that Cuba's expropriation of goods located in Havana was null and void". Or as Justice Harlan put it in *Sabbatino* at 428:

rather than laying down or reaffirming an inflexible and all-encompassing rule in this case, we decide only that the judicial branch will not examine the validity of a taking of property within its territory by a foreign sovereign government, extant and recognised by this country at the time of suit, in the absence of treaty or other unambiguous agreement regarding controlling legal principles, even if the complaint alleges that the taking violates customary international law.

113. In our judgment, the act of state doctrines cannot be reduced to a single formula such as the judge adopted (distinguishing validity or invalidity from all other forms of lawful or wrongful conduct) or such as Mr Pollock has sought to reformulate on this appeal. Such formulae accord with neither the English nor the United States jurisprudence. On the contrary, we consider that the act of state doctrines ultimately reflect more complex considerations, and would refer to the analysis in this court in *Kuwait Airways* v. *Iraqi Airways* concluding in its [317]-[323]. This court there reasoned that—

[317] In our judgment, these authorities indicate that English law is seeking to balance (at least) three separate insights as to the appropriate role of national courts when faced with reliance on foreign legislative or executive acts by way of defence to what might otherwise be a wrong for which those courts are called upon to provide a remedy.

[318] First, there is the prima facie rule that a foreign sovereign is to be accorded that absolute authority which is vested in him to act within his own territory as a sovereign acts. This rule reflects concepts of both private and public international law as to territorial sovereignty. As such, we think that the rule is founded primarily on a view as to the comity of nations ... each sovereign says to the other: "We will respect your territorial sovereignty. But there can be no offence if we do not recognise your extraterritorial or exorbitant acts."

[319] The second insight, however, is that, whether the sovereign acts within his own territory or outside it, there is a certain class of sovereign act which calls for judicial restraint on the part of our municipal courts. This is the principle of non-justiciability. It is or leads to a form of immunity ratione materiae ... In essence the principle of non-justiciability seeks to distinguish disputes involving sovereign authority which can only be resolved on a state to state level from disputes which can be resolved by judicial means.

[320] The third insight is that the rule whereby there is a principle of judicial restraint in so far as a sovereign acts within his own territory is only a prima facie rule. It is subject to certain exceptions ...

[323] We think that behind these three competing insights, which between them strive to produce a balanced answer to the conflicting needs of private rights, sovereign immunities and international relations, there is the constant theme of the role of universal, or at least generally accepted, principles of private and public international law ...

114. In the House of Lords in *Kuwait Airways* v. *Iraqi Airways*, despite the large measure of agreement for the speeches of both Lord Nicholls and Lord Hope, a possible tension between the two can be observed. To recapitulate what we have set out above, Lord Nicholls did not seek so much to formulate the act of state doctrines, as to regard the question of Kuwait Airways' claim in conversion as being prima facie subject to the double actionability rule of private international law, and to treat Iraqi Airways' reliance on the principle of non-justiciability as being subject to established principles of international law. In these two respects, he considered that—

[28] The acceptability of a provision of foreign law must be judged by contemporary standards ... An expropriatory decree made in these circumstances and for this purpose is simply not acceptable today.

Lord Nicholls therefore stressed that these principles must move with the times. *Tempora mutantur et nos mutamur in illis*. Lord Hope, on the other hand, set out his understanding of the act of state doctrine in a paragraph which began with the sentence "Important questions of principle are raised ..." (at [135]) and went on (at [140]) to caution that "The golden rule is that care must be taken not to expand its application [that is, the application of the public policy exception] beyond the true limits of the principle ... These limits demand that, where there is any room for doubt, judicial restraint must be exercised." Lord Steyn, commending the "internationalism" of the Court of Appeal's judgment (at 1102G), developed that idea as follows:

[115] This conclusion on English public policy does not reflect an insular approach ... In recent years, particularly as a result of French scholarship, principles of international public policy (l'ordre public véritablement international) have been developed in relation to subjects such as traffic in drugs, traffic in weapons, terrorism, and so forth ... Similarly, there may be an international public policy requiring states to respect fundamental human rights ...

115. We recognise these differences of emphasis. Lord Hope's broad restatement as to the general effect of the act of state doctrine—that "It applies to the legislative or other governmental acts of a recognised foreign state or government within the limits of its own territory. The

English court will not adjudicate upon, or call into question, any such acts"—is the clearest modern formulation of the doctrine at the highest level, but it perhaps needs to be understood as qualified by Lord Wilberforce's two insights that his principle of non-justicability can also extend beyond international boundaries, and that the principle is one of restraint rather than abstinence (as Lord Hope himself commented). However, it is also proper to have regard to the various limitations on that broad doctrine, only one of which was in issue in that case. We think that on the whole we prefer to speak of "limitations" rather than "exceptions". The important thing is to recognise that increasingly in the modern world the doctrine is being defined, like a silhouette, by its limitations, rather than to regard it as occupying the whole ground save to the extent that an exception can be imposed. That after all would explain why it has become wholly commonplace to adjudicate or call into question the acts of a foreign state in relation to matters of international convention, whether it is the persecution of applicant asylum refugees, or the application of the Rome Statute with regard to international criminal responsibility or other matters mentioned by Lord Steyn. That is also perhaps an element in the naturalness with which our courts have been prepared, in the face of cogent evidence, to adjudicate upon allegations relating to the availability of substantive justice in foreign courts. It also has to be remembered that the doctrine was first developed in an era which predated the existence of modern international human rights law. The idea that the rights of a state might be curtailed by its obligations in the field of human rights would have seemed somewhat strange in that era. That is perhaps why our courts have sometimes struggled, albeit ultimately successfully, to give effective support to their abhorrence of the persecutions of the Nazi era: see the analysis of *Oppenheimer* v. *Cattermole* [1976] AC 249 in the *Kuwait Airways* case in this court at [273]ff (and compare the reasoning of this court in *Oppenheimer* v. *Cattermole* itself [1973] Ch 264).

The earlier Yukos FSA *case*

116. The allegations which have surfaced in this case have been the subject-matter of prior judicial attention in *R (on the application of Yukos Oil Company)* v. *Financial Services Authority* [2006] EWHC 2044 (Admin) (Charles J, the *Yukos FSA* case). OJSC Rosneft and OJSC Rosneftegaz were interested parties. Charles J concluded that the act of state doctrine applied and that therefore the FSA's decision could

not be judicially reviewed. He regarded the contrary argument as unarguable (at [90]-[91]).

117. The *Yukos FSA* case arose out of the decisions or proposed decisions of the FSA and the London Stock Exchange to approve the prospectus of Rosneft and its parent Rosneftegaz regarding the proposed listing and offering of shares in Rosneft GDRs. Yukos Oil Company and another Yukos company sought judicial review in an attempt to prevent such listing and offering. Their case was similar to the case made by Yukos Capital in this court as to how the Russian state had campaigned to expropriate the Yukos assets and pass them into the arms of Rosneft. They had earlier made similar representations to the FSA and the LSE, but the latter had rejected them on the ground of advice from Michael Brindle QC that the act of state doctrines prevented any account being taken of them. Charles J explained:

> 6. In the skeleton argument put in on behalf of Rosneft, the claimants' assertions of dishonest expropriation are described as a conspiracy theory. The three main elements of the expropriation allegation or conspiracy theory are, in my view, accurately summarised in a very truncated form in paragraph 9 of the skeleton argument of Rosneft which reads as follows, with some omissions:
>
>> There are three main elements. First, it is alleged that a series of arbitrary purported tax assessments were issued against Yukos by the Russian tax authorities and that Yukos's assets were then frozen by the Russian court preventing it from paying those tax assessments. Secondly, complaint is made about the conduct of the bailiff appointed by the Russian court and of the court itself in enforcing the tax liabilities. Thirdly, Yukos complains about the auction of its shares in YNG in respect of which it alleges that there are reasonable grounds to suspect, if not more, that there was a concerted plan to deprive Yukos of its interest in YNG by unlawful means.
>
> 7. On the claimants' case that plan involved the participation of officers of the Russian state and of the Russian courts.
>
> 8. The allegations are, therefore, extremely serious ones and at their heart are allegations against various parts or emanations of the Russian Federation including its courts.

118. Charles J went on to conclude that Mr Brindle's advice was correct. He rejected the submission that earlier authority might have been decided differently in modern times because of the existence and effect of the European Convention on Human Rights. He referred in particular to *Oetjen, Luther* v. *Sagor, Buttes Gas* and *Williams and Humbert.* He allowed that there might be room for development of the principles, but said that it was not for a first instance court to attempt to do so. There was no appeal.

119. On this appeal, Lord Grabiner submits that Charles J was right, and that in any event it would be an abuse of process to allow Yukos now to go behind that decision. He submits that although the Yukos company involved in this litigation is different from the Yukos company involved in that case, it should be regarded as a privy to that company; and that this case involves an abusive collateral attack on Charles J's decision. He acknowledges that there is no estoppel, on the ground that estoppel does not operate in judicial review, but he relies on the modern principles of abuse of process, such as are found described in *Johnson* v. *Gore Wood* [2002] 2 AC 1. Lord Bingham there said in an already classic passage at 31:

> I would not accept that it is necessary, before abuse may be found, to identify any additional element such as a collateral attack on a previous decision or some dishonesty, but where those elements are present the later proceedings will be much more obviously abusive, and there will rarely be a finding of abuse unless the later proceeding involves what the court regards as unjust harassment of a party.

120. Hamblen J rejected the submission on the basis that the issues in the two cases were different. He reasoned that Charles J applied the act of state doctrine in its "pure" form, in that the challenge there was as to the validity of the transfer of Yukos's assets to Rosneft: the relevant allegation by Yukos to the FSA and the LSE was that the listing should not be allowed to proceed in that it would involve the laundering of the proceeds of crime, contrary to the Proceeds of Crime Act 2002. Such an allegation was inconsistent with the idea that the assets had been validly transferred by the exercise of sovereign authority. In the present case, however, he accepted the submission of Yukos Capital that "the decision which is required to be made is whether the Annulment Decisions offend against English principles of substantial justice".

121. That distinction leads directly to the essential reasoning which determined the judge's decision in this case. We will revert to *Yukos FSA* below.

The judge's reasoning

122. The judge's essential reasoning is contained in the following passage of his judgment, dealing with Yukos's so-called first allegation, the allegation of a campaign against Yukos:

> [180] In order to reach its determination in the present case the court will not need to declare that the Annulment Decisions, or any other acts relied upon, were invalid or ineffective.

[181] As Yukos Capital submitted, its case involves inviting the court to find only that—as a matter of fact—there was a co-ordinated activity aimed at re-nationalising Yukos' assets which, in fact, involved the executive intervening in the judicial process. Whether such intervention was "valid" or "invalid", "lawful" or "unlawful", is not an issue which the court was required to decide. For the purpose of Yukos Capital's case in these proceedings what matters is whether it happened.

[182] Rosneft further submitted that even if the case does not "turn on" the issue of validity, nevertheless the allegations relied upon are in themselves non-justiciable. In this connection it stressed in particular the allegations made in relation to the "three main elements" of the campaign identified in the *Yukos FSA* case; namely, unwarranted tax assessments; the conduct of the bailiffs and the courts in enforcing those assessments which resulted in forced insolvency, and the rigged auctions. Even if no declaration of invalidity of these acts was sought, Yukos Capital's case nevertheless involved an inquiry into and at least inferential determination of the legality of those acts.

[183] This is very similar to the argument rejected by the Supreme Court in the *Kirkpatrick* case. There too it was said that findings would necessarily be made which bore on the legality of the acts of state. However, the Supreme Court made it clear that that was insufficient to engage the Act of State principle. The "factual predicate" was the need to rule upon that legality and to declare the act invalid or ineffective.

[184] The irrelevance of legality/illegality to Yukos Capital's case was well illustrated by the example that it would make no difference to its case if Russian law expressly permitted the executive to instruct the judiciary how to resolve cases of strategic importance. Despite that being the legal act of the executive, to do so would still offend against English principles of substantial justice.

[185] Rosneft's case is also contradictory. It acknowledges that the court can determine whether the Annulment Decisions were partial and dependent. If so, it must similarly have to acknowledge that Yukos Capital can support that case with examples of other partial and dependent decisions. However, inquiry into the subject matter of those other decisions (for example, the tax assessments) is apparently not permissible. So, Yukos Capital can seek to show that the court decisions relating to the tax assessments were partial and dependent, as borne out by the unwarranted nature of the tax assessments, but not invite the court to inquire into the tax assessments themselves.

[186] For all these reasons I find the allegations concerning the campaign against Yukos Capital do not engage the "pure" Act of State principle. In particular, I find that its case does not concern the validity of any Acts of State. I further find that even if the principle extends to wider issues of legality its case does not require the court to decide upon or determine such issues.

[187] I further find its case does not engage the judicial abstention principle. It does not involve allegations in respect of which "the court has no measurable standard of adjudication" or which puts it in a "judicial no-man's land".

[188] The case does not involve issues of acute political sensitivity, diplomacy or international law, which are beyond the English court's competence as a (domestic) judicial body. The court is well able to assess and determine what, in fact, took place between 2003 and 2006; to analyse (with the assistance of expert evidence) whether those events were consistent with ordinary taxation and judicial processes; and to draw appropriate inferences as to whether the acts were performed as part of a scheme controlled by the Russian government, as Yukos Capital alleges.

[189] Further, as Yukos Capital points out, the allegations now being made have already been subjected to judicial scrutiny applying manageable standards as borne out by:

(1) the Yukos-related extradition cases;
(2) the fact that the ECHR is considering very similar allegations under the aegis of the European Convention on Human Rights—see the admissibility of the complaint to the ECHR (*Yukos* v. *Russian Federation* [2009] ECHR 287).
(3) the award issued by a Tribunal (Prof. Böckstiegel, Lord Steyn and Sir Franklin Berman QC) in *Rosinvestco UK Ltd* v. *Russian Federation*. In *Rosinvestco*, the Tribunal considered each of the steps on which Yukos Capital now relies (e.g. the tax assessments, the bankruptcy auction, etc.). Whilst recognising that it was not an appellate court on Russian law, it considered whether there was a manifest misapplication of Russian law (e.g. paras. 446-55). It drew inferences from the primary facts, e.g. as to what occurred during the bankruptcy auctions. It was able to conclude that the tax assessments upheld by the Russian courts were not *bona fide* (paras. 489-97) and that the auction process (paras. 518-24) was set up under the control of the Russian Federation to bring Yukos' assets under Respondent's control. From its findings, the Tribunal was able to conclude that the acts of the Russian state were not *bona fide* (para. 567), were not justified by enforcement of tax laws (para. 574), were linked to the strategic objective of returning petroleum assets to the control of the Russian state and to an effort to suppress a political opponent (para. 617), were part of a scheme to deprive Yukos of its assets (para. 620) and (cumulatively) were structured and intended to remove Yukos' assets from its control (para. 621). These conclusions were reached by the application of proper judicial standards, and this is the sort of factual and legal enquiry which the Commercial Court is well able to perform.

123. In relation to the so-called second allegation (instances of unjust Yukos-related proceedings), the judge relied on essentially the

same considerations, while emphasising (i) that there was an inherent contradiction in Rosneft saying that the annulment decisions could themselves be investigated for manifest misapplications of Russian law from which an inference of partiality and dependence could be drawn, while preventing Yukos from investigating other decisions from which a wider conclusion of partiality and dependency could be drawn; and (ii) that Annex 1 is concerned solely with court bias, without allegations concerning an underlying political campaign as an explanation. In relation to the so-called third allegation (bias in cases involving matters of importance to the Russian Federation), as to which Rosneft relies solely on the principle of non-justiciability, the judge pointed out that *The Abidin Daver* and the *AK Investment* case show that allegations of even systemic corruption or partiality are not subject to act of state doctrines.

Discussion

124. As we hope will have become clear from our discussion of the jurisprudence concerning the act of state doctrines and their limitations, we agree with some but not all of this reasoning.

125. We agree, for the reasons stated above, that the act of state doctrines do not extend to prevent examination of the substantial justice available in the courts of foreign jurisdictions, whether in a particular case or on a systemic basis. If that can be done in order to secure jurisdiction in England, as the authorities demonstrate it can be done, it must follow that it can be done where there is established jurisdiction in England, as here to enforce a foreign award. Moreover, the right to examine the question of substantial justice in a foreign jurisdiction must we think be a fortiori the position when, as here, a party to litigation in England is asking the English court to recognise a decision of a foreign court. For Rosneft is asking the English court to recognise the annulment decisions in Russia as removing the basis of Yukos's claim to be entitled to enforce the arbitration awards. An English court, subject to the requirements of any treaty or convention, must, we think, always be entitled to ask and adjudicate on the issue whether a foreign court decision should or should not be recognised or enforced. Subject to treaty or convention, that is the proper business of the courts and they are armed and completely familiar with judicial standards by which to judge what are ultimately issues about judicial standards. Of course, comity demands that such enquiries are conducted with that proper respect which is owed in the international sphere to the courts of friendly foreign nations. That is why the English

courts will require cogent grounds for any allegation that a foreign court decision should not be recognised on the grounds of a failure of substantial justice. However, that is a matter of evidence and argument, not a matter of any immunity or doctrine of non-justiciability.

126. We think that to some extent these conclusions were anticipated in *Dallah Real Estate and Tourism Holding Co.* v. *Ministry of Religious Affairs of the Government of Pakistan* [2009] EWCA Civ 755, [2010] UKSC 46, [2011] 1 AC 763, albeit no act of state issues were raised in that case. Thus in this court at [91] Rix LJ said:

Finally, I bear in mind (see para. 76 above) the problem of an award perhaps improperly set aside in the country of origin. This is a delicate matter. However, it seems to me that it is not something which can be dealt with simply as a matter of an open discretion. The improper circumstances would, I think, have to be brought home to the court asked to enforce in such a way as either, in effect, to destroy the defence based on article V(1)(e) [of the New York Convention], or, which is effectively the same thing, to prevent an issue estoppel arising out of the judgment of the courts of the country of origin. In this connection see *Carl Zeiss Stiftung* v. *Rayner & Keeler Ltd (No 2)* [1967] 1 AC 853, 947 and *Dicey, Morris & Collins, The Conflict of Laws* 14th ed. (2006), vol. 1, rules 41 to 45.

127. In the Supreme Court in *Dallah*, Lord Collins referred to the decision of the Amsterdam Court of Appeal in the current litigation between Yukos Capital and Rosneft, at [129] of his judgment, in the context of his view that that and other like cases "rest rather on the power of the enforcing court, under article VII(1) of the New York Convention, to apply laws which are more generous to enforcement than the rules of the New York Convention".

128. In this context, so far at any rate as concerns the annulment decisions themselves, Rosneft concedes that the English court may investigate the question of substantial justice and issues of bias and lack of independence, and it does so apparently without making an exception for such issues which arise out of influence brought to bear by the Russian state itself. No particular reason is given for this concession, but we suppose that it is made under the pressure of the realisation that the English court cannot be expected to lend its support to a corrupt decision of a foreign court. Rosneft also concedes that even systemic dependency on the dictates of state demands can be investigated for the future, but not for the past. We have given our reasons for agreeing with the judge that this distinction is unprincipled. The principle which we would hold operates in this sphere is that act of state doctrines do not extend to judicial acts. A state may be regarded as

entitled (within the bounds of acknowledged international immunities) to a form of immunity or abstention from adjudication upon its legislative and executive acts, at any rate where it acts within its territory and exceptionally, perhaps, even extra-territorially. What, however, falls at any time within the proper province of the courts does not come within the rationality of such doctrines. Different principles apply with respect to judicial acts. Only the more normal restraints of judicial comity hold sway in that judicial context, as well of course as other principles, such as principles of estoppel, and all the rules which govern the recognition or enforcement of foreign judgments.

129. When, however, we pass from an investigation of the substantial justice of the annulment decisions themselves, or of Yukos Capital's contention of a systemic failure of the Russian courts to resist the influence of dependency on state pressure in matters of state interest, and we come instead to Yukos Capital's separate allegations of a more personally directed campaign of expropriation or political hostility (the "campaign"), the situation is more complicated. What is the function of these allegations? They all share in the same function of going to support the overarching contention that "where, as appears hereafter, the orders purporting to annul the Awards were tainted by bias and/or were obtained contrary to the principles of natural or substantial justice and/or in circumstances which deprived the Claimant of a fair trial, the purported annulments are of no effect" (re-re-amended reply, para. 2). That is a plea, in terms, that the annulment decisions are of no effect. We would accept that it is not a plea which says in terms that the campaign is of no effect, but it is all aimed at the goal of saying that the annulment decisions are of no effect. It is for this purpose that the reply refers to "unwarranted tax assessments", to "deliberation misapplication" of Russia's tax law in relation to those tax assessments, and to "rigged auctions", and to the imprisonment of Mr Khordorkovsky "on trumped up charges". If those tax assessments were lawful, if the tax decisions based on those assessments were lawful, if the recovery of tax was lawful and the auctions by which the transfer of assets were lawful, and if the charges against Mr Khordorkovsky were justified, then Yukos Capital would have nothing to complain about in these respects; and all these events would add nothing in support to the allegation that the annulment decisions were simply the last in a long line of events which amounted to a political campaign against Yukos Capital.

130. It follows that it is not accurate to say that all that Yukos Capital wants to demonstrate is that certain events occurred; or that the court need not decide (or "declare", which is not so much a reference to

a discretionary remedy, but to the nature of adjudication) that the annulment decisions or any other acts relied upon were invalid or ineffective (or wrongful). If the tax assessments, tax decisions, auctions and imprisonment occurred, but were lawful and not wrongful, then they would be of no use to Yukos Capital. What Yukos Capital wishes to show is that the whole campaign was unlawful. We do not think, therefore, that the *Kirkpatrick/Berezovsky* line of authority is of assistance to Yukos Capital.

131. Moreover, although the campaign allegation may not be necessary to the overarching contention if there is other independent material to support that contention, it is necessary to that contention as at least one, and perhaps the principal, support for it. It is therefore in no way collateral or ancillary. It lies at the heart of Yukos Capital's case, and is in that sense necessary to it.

132. In these circumstances, we consider that the question of whether the act of state doctrine applies to some at least of Yukos Capital's allegations is not an easy one. The difficulty is illustrated by the fact that those allegations have already been the subject of adjudication in a case like *Cherney* (where the doctrine was not in issue) but immune from adjudication in the *Yukos FSA* case itself (where it was in issue).

133. Ultimately, however, we have concluded that the doctrine does not bar any part of Yukos Capital's case. The essential issue is whether the annulment decisions should be recognised. That is a judicial question raised in respect of judicial acts. On the way to resolving that judicial question the court is asked to take into account, and resolve whether, other judicial decisions emanating from tax courts or tribunals are, or are not, to be recognised as in effect achieving the expropriation or destruction of Yukos. Those too are judicial acts which are said to be equally corrupt and therefore make it more likely that the annulment decisions are corrupt themselves. The tax decisions take their starting line from tax assessments. We would accept that such assessments are probably to be regarded as executive or administrative acts: but unlike legislation or decrees or the acts of commanders in the field, which are the familiar terrain of the act of state jurisprudence, such assessments function within a tax code which is designed to operate according to law and to be subject to legal and indeed judicial rulings. If the tax decisions may be the subject matter of examination for the purpose of an issue of substantial justice, we do not see how they can be divorced from the originating tax assessments. Indeed, it would probably not be possible to consider the tax decisions without inevitably considering the tax assessments as part and parcel of those decisions. It is

understandable that the motives of the executive may be of a political rather than a judicial nature, but we do not think that affects a critical alteration of the situation. Just as the commercial exception to the doctrine of sovereign immunity depends on the fact of the commercial activity, rather than the motives for which the activity may have been entered into or a contract subsequently breached: so it seems to us that the motives for or with which a state operates its judicial system do not alter the fundamental point that the state is operating under the colour of that system, rather than by reference to sovereign power. Those motives may throw light on the allegations of impropriety, but they are not in themselves a ground for wresting such activities out of the judicial sphere into that of the executive.

134. We are assisted to this conclusion by the understanding that similar allegations have been adjudicated in English courts in the past, even if not upon a similar rationalisation of the act of state principles. We consider that *Yukos FSA*, where the act of state doctrine was relied on for rejecting the claim for judicial review, does not bind us. We do not consider that there is any abuse of process involved in Yukos Capital presenting the allegations which it does in this case. We are not satisfied that there is true privity between Yukos Oil Company in that case and the claimant in this case. In any event the issues are different. Here Yukos Capital claims to enforce arbitration awards, which it is entitled to seek to do. It is met with the annulment decisions of the Russian courts. It must be entitled to seek to show that such decisions are not worthy of recognition by the English court. It is accepted that no issue of estoppel arises. There is no true collateral attack on the decision of Charles J who was considering whether as a matter of judicial review the listing of Rosneft could be objected to, an entirely different issue from the issue in this case, even if similar issues of act of state arose there also. There is no dishonesty, and no unjust harassment.

135. Ultimately, and looking at the arguments in this case more broadly, the question is whether in the modern world the English court can be asked to recognise judicial decisions which a party to those decisions alleges have been brought about by judicially corrupt means. In a world which increasingly speaks about the rule of law, it should not in principle be open to another party to those decisions to claim an immunity from adjudication on the ground that an investigation into those allegations is protected by deference due to the legislative or executive acts of a foreign sovereign. As Lord Nicholls said in *Kuwait Airways* (at [28]): "As nations become ever more interdependent, the need to recognise and adhere to standards of conduct set by

international law becomes ever more important." Replace "international law" by "international recognition of proper judicial standards mandated by the rule of law" and that observation fits this case. We also bear in mind Lord Hope's comments on the rule of law in the same case at [145]: "It is now clear, if it was not before, that the judiciary cannot close their eyes to the need for a concerted, international response to these threats to the rule of law in a democratic society." Their Lordships were of course speaking about Iraq's international delinquency in invading Kuwait and despoiling it of its assets: however, their observations are equally pertinent to judicial bias and dependency in the face of state interference in the judicial process.

136. Of course, Yukos Capital's allegations have yet to be proved. We are considering only the right to ask the English court to consider those allegations on the present hypothesis that they may be correct.

137. The question might have arisen, if our conclusion had been to the contrary, as to whether some limitation on or exception to the act of state doctrine based on fundamental human rights or discrimination could be supported. No such argument has been raised before this court, and there is scant reference to this topic in the judgment below (see at [72] above). It is not clear at all to us whether this is an issue which had to be taken at this stage, if at all, or which may be open at a later stage to the extent that the act of state doctrine has some prima facie bite upon at least some of the allegations in dispute. As it is, the problem does not arise.

Issue estoppel: background facts

138. The judge set out the course of the Dutch proceedings at paras. [17]-[41] of his judgment and they are summarised at the beginning of this judgment. The salient points are as follows.

139. The district court at first instance refused leave to enforce the awards holding that an annulment decision of the law of the seat could only be disregarded in extraordinary circumstances which had not been sufficiently asserted.

140. Yukos Capital then appealed filing a lengthy statement of appeal pursuant to Dutch procedures which permitted a complete rehearing of the case with the admission of new evidence. Paragraphs 5-157 set out the history of the relationship between the Russian state and Rosneft on the one hand and Yukos Capital on the other. Paragraphs 158-66 developed allegations relating to the "bias and

dependency of the Russian courts". Paragraphs 182-232 constituted a criticism of the annulment decisions. There were 124 exhibits filed in support of the statement of appeal.

141. Rosneft submitted a lengthy defence to the submissions and exhibits of Yukos Capital but did not themselves file any expert or factual evidence in response.

142. In its judgment of 28 April 2009 the Amsterdam Court of Appeal set out Yukos Capital's allegations and the main elements of its evidence and said that it had to assess

whether the decision of the Russian civil courts to set aside the arbitral awards can be recognised in the Netherlands, more in particular whether these judgments were rendered by a judicial instance that is impartial and independent.

143. The Court of Appeal then recorded its findings including—

(i) "Rosneft and the Russian state are closely intertwined" (para. 3.9.1);
(ii) "the case at issue also involves considerable interests that the Russian state considers to be its own" (para. 3.9.2);
(iii) Rosneft had insufficiently refuted or contested (there was a dispute over the better translation) that

... in cases pertaining to (parts of) the (former) Yukos Group or the (former) directors of this group, which involve state interests that the Russian state considers to be its own, the Russian judiciary is not impartial and independent but is guided by the interests of the Russian state and is instructed by the executive.

The court of appeal held that this was "properly substantiated" by Yukos Capital, and that Rosneft had failed to advance any concrete facts or to submit documents to shed a different light on that evidence (para. 3.9.2);

(iv) the rejection of Rosneft's argument that direct evidence of partiality and dependence of the individual judges concerned was required, pointing out that "partiality and dependency by their very nature take place behind the scenes" (para. 3.9.4).

144. The Court of Appeal then concluded as follows:

3.10 Based on the foregoing, the Court of Appeal concludes that it is [so plausible/likely] that the Russian civil court judgments setting aside the arbitral awards are the result of an administration of justice which is to be qualified as partial and dependent, that it is not possible to recognise those judgments in the Netherlands. This entails that in considering Yukos Capital's application for enforcement of the arbitral awards, the setting aside of that decision by the Russian court must be ignored.

145. Accordingly, the Court of Appeal, having also dismissed Rosneft's other New York Convention defences to enforcement, gave leave to enforce the awards.

146. Rosneft lodged an appeal with the Supreme Court which held that there was no right of appeal from a decision of the Court of Appeal which permitted enforcement.

147. It is the decision of the Amsterdam Court of Appeal on which Yukos Capital relies in order to assert that Rosneft is estopped from objecting to enforcement of the awards in England. The primary requirements for the application of a foreign issue estoppel are agreed to be those set out by Lord Brandon of Oakbrook in *The Sennar (No 2)* [1985] 1 WLR 490, 499 A-B:

... in order to create an estoppel of that kind, three requirements have to be satisfied. The first requirement is that the judgment in the earlier action relied on as creating an estoppel must be (a) of a court of competent jurisdiction, (b) final and conclusive and (c) on the merits. The second requirement is that the parties (or privies) in the earlier action relied on as creating an estoppel, and those in the later section in which that estoppel is raised as a bar, must be the same. The third requirement is that the issue in the later action, in which the estoppel is raised as a bar, must be the same issue as that decided by the judgment in the earlier action.

It was further agreed that, because the application of the estoppel must work justice rather than injustice, the court had a discretion to refuse to give effect to a foreign judgment if there were special circumstances making it unjust to recognise the decision, see *Henderson* v. *Henderson* (1843) 3 Hare 100 at 114-15, *Carl Zeiss Stiftung* v. *Rayner & Keeler* [1967] 1 AC 853, 947D *per* Lord Upjohn and *Arnold* v. *National Westminster Bank* [1991] 2 AC 93, 107C *per* Lord Keith of Kinkel.

148. The judge held that the requirements of *The Sennar* were satisfied and there was no room for the exercise of any residual discretion.

149. Lord Grabiner for Rosneft accepted that the first two of Lord Brandon's requirements were satisfied but had two submissions—

(i) The issue to be decided by the English court was not the same issue as that decided by the Dutch Court of Appeal inasmuch as the Dutch decision was a decision to allow enforcement of the awards and refuse recognition of the annulment decision as a matter of Dutch public order, whereas the decision sought from the English courts was a decision that the Russian courts (whether generally or in this particular case) were partial and dependent on the executive and that their decision should not be recognised as a matter of the public order of England.

(ii) The residual discretion should be exercised in Rosneft's favour because it would be unjust to permit enforcement of the awards in England when the Dutch court never had occasion to consider Rosneft's act of state defence. More widely he submitted that an allegation attacking the integrity of the judicial system of a foreign country was a most serious matter and should be the subject of a decision of the courts of the country where enforcement was sought.

Same issue?

150. The issue in the Dutch proceedings was whether the annulment decisions setting aside the arbitral awards were "partial and dependent"; if they were, then they were not to be recognised by the Dutch courts. Mr Pollock for Yukos Capital submitted that the issue in the English proceedings is exactly the same since, if the decisions were "partial and dependent", the English courts will not recognise them. It is true that the Dutch courts treat the decision as one of Dutch public order and the English courts will treat it as a matter of English public order. But the public policy, submitted Mr Pollock, is the same in each country and the issue to be decided in accordance with that public policy is identical.

151. The difficulty with Mr Pollock's submission is that "public order" or "public policy" is inevitably different in each country. The standards by which any particular country resolves the question whether the courts of another country are "partial and dependent" may vary considerably and it is also a matter of high policy to determine the circumstances in which this country should recognise the judgments of a state where the interests of that very state are at stake. Normally such recognition will be given and, if it is to be refused, cogent evidence of partiality and dependency will be required. Our own law is (or may be) that considerations of comity necessitate specific examples of partiality and dependency before any decision is made not to recognise the judgments of a foreign state. It is our own public order which defines the framework of any assessment of this difficult question; whether such decisions are truly to be regarded as dependent and partial as a matter of English law is not the same question as whether such decisions are to be regarded as dependent and partial in the view of some other court according to that court's notions of what is acceptable or otherwise according to its law.

152. Lord Collins addressed this issue in *AK Investment*, a case in which it was agreed that the claimants would be unlikely to obtain a fair hearing in Kyrgyzstan and it was held that that fact militated in favour of proceedings in the Isle of Man rather than in Kyrgyzstan which might have otherwise been regarded as a more natural forum for the dispute. In relation to an argument that a judgment of the Kyrgyz court would (or might) not be recognised in an English or an Isle of Man court because justice could not be obtained in Kyrgyzstan, Lord Collins cited a dictum of Lord Diplock in *The Abidin Daver* [1984] AC 398, 411—

the possibility cannot be excluded that there are still some countries in whose courts there is a risk that justice will not be obtained.

He then said (in a passage from which we have already partially cited but bears repetition)—

101. The true position is that there is no rule that the English court (or Manx court) will not examine the question whether the foreign court or the foreign court system is corrupt or lacking in independence. The rule is that considerations of international comity will militate against any such finding in the absence of cogent evidence. That, and not the act of state doctrine or the principle of judicial restraint in *Buttes Gas and Oil Co.* v. *Hammer (Nos 2 and 3)*, is the basis of Lord Diplock's dictum in *The Abidin Daver* and the decisions which follow it. Otherwise the paradoxical result would follow that, the worse the system of justice in the foreign country, the less it would be permissible to make adverse findings on it.

102. The conclusion is also supported by the many cases in the United States courts in which the standard of justice in the foreign court has been examined in the context of forum non conveniens questions. It was said in *Blanco* v. *Banco Industrial de Venezuela SA* (1993) 997 F 2d (para. 50), quoting earlier decisions, that it "is not the business of our courts to assume the responsibility for supervising the integrity of the judicial system of another sovereign nation". That is not the enunciation of the act of state doctrine (well known in the United States) or the doctrine of judicial restraint in foreign relations cases (which has its origin in the United States), but simply a reflection of the fact that comity considerations require the court not to pass judgment on the foreign court system without adequate evidence. Evidence of corruption in the foreign court system is admissible (as, e.g., in *Cariajano* v. *Occidental Petroleum Corp.* (2010) 626 F 3d 1137), but it must go beyond generalised, anecdotal material: see *Tuazon* v. *RJ Reynolds Tobacco Co.* (2006) 433 F 3d 1163 and 1179 and *Stroitelstvo Bulgaria Ltd* v. *Bulgarian-American Enterprise Fund* (2009) 589 F 3d 417. Cases in which justice in the foreign legal system has been found wanting have been rare but they are by no means unknown: *Rasoulzadeh* v. *Associated Press* (1983) 574 F Supp 854, affirmed

(1985) 767 F 2d 908 and *Osorio* v. *Dole Food Co.* (2009) 665 F Supp 2d 1307 are examples in the contexts of forum non conveniens and enforcement of foreign judgments respectively.

153. It is thus clear that cogent evidence is required before it is possible to call a foreign court decision partial and dependent. The relevant degree of cogency may well differ in different countries.

154. The English rules about foreign judgments procured by fraud provide a possible analogy with the present case. English law is that a foreign judgment may be impeached for fraud in an English court whether by original action or in defence to an action for enforcement of that judgment, see *Abouloff* v. *Oppenheimer & Co.* (1882) 10 QBD 295 approved by the House of Lords in *Owens Bank* v. *Bracco* [1992] 2 AC 443. English law could, of course, be different and say that a foreign judgment is to be recognised unless it is set aside for fraud in the country where it is given. (Lord Templeman thought that should indeed be the law in relation, at least, to those countries whose judgments the United Kingdom had agreed to register and enforce, see *Owens Bank* v. *Etoile Commerciale* [1995] 1 WLR 44, 50.) If the judgment creditor went first of all to a third country where the law was that a foreign judgment must be recognised even if arguably obtained by fraud, an English court would presumably neither recognise that judgment nor regard it as giving rise to an issue estoppel, simply because English public policy in this case is different from the third country's public policy. Lord Collins also touched on this point in *AK Investment* in relation to an argument that the English (and Isle of Man) law on this point should be changed to accord with Lord Templeman's view in the Privy Council precisely because (inter alia) the current law ignored the doctrine of issue estoppel. He said (para. 116) that, on any view, the question whether the law should be altered might require a nuanced approach depending on the "reliability of the foreign legal system" as well as the scope for challenge in the foreign court and the type of fraud alleged.

155. This can be further illuminated by supposing not merely that the Dutch courts have determined that the annulment decisions are partial and dependent (as they have) but that the courts of another state have determined that the decisions are in fact impartial and independent. By which judgment are the parties in England to be regarded as issue estopped? The answer can hardly be the judgment which happens to be the first in time but must be that the English court will make up its own mind according to its own concept of public order not that of some other state.

156. It was put to the judge that the issue decided in Holland was that the Russian judgments should not be recognised as a matter of Dutch public order and that that was not the same issue as had to be decided in England. The judge's response in para. 94 was:

the finding that the annulment decisions were the result of a partial and dependent legal decision was both necessary and fundamental to the decision. That the Amsterdam Court of Appeal determined that issue in the context of a different legal question (i.e. by reference to Dutch public order) makes no difference.

We cannot, with respect, agree because, for the reasons given, it makes a great deal of difference whether the issue is being determined by reference to Dutch public order or English public order which is (or may well be) different. The point is that English public order is as explained by Lord Collins in *AK Investment* and the English court must determine the matter by reference to those considerations not by whatever considerations make up Dutch public order.

157. We would therefore hold, differing in this respect from Hamblen J, that Rosneft are not issue estopped from contradicting in England Yukos Capital's assertion that the Russian courts' decisions, setting aside the awards in their favour, were partial and dependent. That is an issue which will have to be tried.

Discretion in special circumstances

158. Strictly speaking, there is in the light of our earlier conclusions no need to consider the question of discretion. But we will deal with it briefly.

159. The trouble with the "discretionary in special circumstances" exception is that it is so amorphous. In *Arnold* v. *National Westminster Bank* the exercise of discretion depended on further material becoming available since the original decision. That is not the position in this case.

160. Nevertheless, if we had decided that there was an issue estoppel in this case on the basis that in truth the issue in the Dutch proceedings was the same as the issue in these English proceedings, we would be inclined to invoke the exception for rather the same reasons as we have already decided that the issue for the English court is that of English public order. It must ultimately be for the English court to decide whether the recognition of a foreign judgment should be withheld on the grounds that that foreign judgment is a partial and dependent judgment in favour of the state where it was pronounced. That is a

question so central to the respect and comity normally due from one court to another that to accept the decision of a court of a third country on the matter would be an abdication of responsibility on the part of the English court. On matters of this kind, we should accept our own responsibilities just as we would expect courts of other countries to accept theirs.

161. We would therefore, if necessary, have accepted Lord Grabiner's wider submission under the head of the court's residual discretion and need not consider his narrower submission which, in the light of our earlier ruling on act of state, does not arise.

162. In the event, we have not had to consider what, if any, effect the doctrine of act of state might have had on the question of issue estoppel. If, however, we had considered that the act of state doctrine had applied to Yukos Capital's allegations, in whole or in part, this might have been a further reason supporting the view that no issue estoppel arose on matters of English public policy.

Conclusion

163. In sum, we have upheld the judge on the question of act of state, but upheld Rosneft's appeal on the question of issue estoppel.

[Reports: [2014] QB 458; [2013] 3 WLR 1329; [2012] 2 Lloyd's Rep 208; [2013] 1 All ER 223; [2012] 2 CLC 549]

Jurisdiction — Justiciability — Agency of United Kingdom providing locational intelligence to United States authorities for use in drone strikes — UK Agency under responsibility of Secretary of State — Claimant seeking declaration that UK Agency employees might be guilty of assisting or encouraging crime under English law or ancillary to war crime and/or crime against humanity — Whether claimant effectively seeking advisory opinion — Whether issues justiciable — Whether declaratory relief entailing condemnation of United States activities — Whether United Kingdom sitting in judgment on acts of a foreign State — Whether any exceptional circumstances

Governments — United Kingdom Government — United States Government — Conduct and responsibilities of United Kingdom Agency, General Communications Headquarters — United States Central Intelligence Agency — UK Agency under responsibility of Secretary of State — Claimant requesting clarification of UK policies and practices concerning provision of locational intelligence to US agents for potential use in drone attacks — UK policy to "neither confirm nor deny" matters where disclosure could compromise national interests — Claimant seeking permission to apply for judicial review of Secretary of State's "decision" to provide intelligence for use in drone strikes

International criminal law — Terrorism — Counter-terrorism measures — Drone strikes — Locational intelligence sharing — Defence of combatant immunity — Relevance — Principal and secondary criminal liability — Whether UK Agency employees might be guilty of assisting or encouraging crime under English law or ancillary to war crime and/or crime against humanity — Serious Crime Act 2007 — International Criminal Court Act 2001

War and armed conflict — Drone strikes in Pakistan killing civilians — United Kingdom providing locational intelligence to United States for potential use in drone strikes — Claimant seeking judicial review of decision to provide intelligence — National security concerns — The law of England

Regina (Khan) v. Secretary of State for
Foreign and Commonwealth Affairs[1]

([2012] EWHC 3728 (Admin))

England, High Court, Queen's Bench Division (Administrative Court)

21 *December* 2012

(Moses LJ and Simon J)

([2014] EWCA Civ 24)

Court of Appeal. 20 *January* 2014

(Lord Dyson MR; Laws and Elias LJJ)

Summary:[2] *The facts*:—In 2010, it was reported in several media outlets that the United Kingdom General Communications Headquarters ("GCHQ"), an agency under the responsibility of the defendant Secretary of State for Foreign and Commonwealth Affairs ("the Secretary of State"), was providing "locational intelligence" to United States authorities for use in missile strikes by unmanned aircraft, or "drones", in various places, including Pakistan.

Mr Noor Khan ("the claimant") lived in Miranshah, North Waziristan, in the Federally Administered Tribal Areas of Pakistan. On 17 March 2011, while presiding over a peaceful outdoor meeting of local elders in North Waziristan, the claimant's father, Mr Malik Daud Khan, was killed by a missile fired from a drone believed to have been operated by the US Central Intelligence Agency ("CIA"). Forty-nine other people were also killed in the attack.

On 16 December 2011, the claimant's solicitors wrote to the Secretary of State for clarification of the UK's policies and practices in relation to providing locational intelligence to US agents for potential use in drone attacks. In reply, on 6 February 2012, the claimant was advised that the Government would not depart from its policy to "neither confirm nor deny" assertions concerning matters where public disclosure could damage public interests, including national security and vital relations with international partners.

---

[1] The claimant was represented by Mr Martin Chamberlain QC, Mr Oliver Jones and Mr Robert McCorquodale, instructed by Leigh Day & Co. The Secretary of State was represented by Mr James Eadie QC, Mr Andrew Edis QC, Mr Malcolm Shaw QC and Miss Karen Steyn, instructed by the Treasury Solicitor.

[2] Prepared by Ms E. Fogarty.

The claimant sought permission to apply for judicial review of the Secretary of State's "decision" to provide "intelligence to the US authorities for use in drone strikes in Pakistan, amongst other places". He requested a declaration that GCHQ employees who passed locational intelligence to US agents foreseeing that it could be used to target or kill individuals were not entitled to the defence of combatant immunity, and could be criminally liable for assisting or encouraging the commission of a crime under Sections 44 to 46[3] (in conjunction with Section 52 and Schedule 4[4]) of the Serious Crime Act 2007 ("the 2007 Act"), or as an ancillary to a war crime and/or crime against humanity under Section 52 of the International Criminal Court Act 2001 ("the 2001 Act").[5] He further sought a declaration that the Secretary of State had no power to direct or authorize GCHQ or other Crown officers to pass on intelligence in the circumstances outlined above; and, prior to directing or authorizing the passing of locational information to US agents, had to formulate, publish and apply a policy setting out when such intelligence could be transferred.[6]

The Secretary of State argued that permission should be refused on the principal grounds that the claimant was effectively seeking an advisory opinion; that the issues raised were non-justiciable; and that the relief requested necessarily entailed a condemnation of US activities. In support, a witness statement was provided by the Head of the Counter Terrorism Department in the Foreign and Commonwealth Office, discussing the impact critical judicial comment on drone attacks was expected to have on UK interests and relations with the US and Pakistan.

Judgment of the High Court (21 December 2012)

Held (unanimously):—Permission was refused.

(1) The real purpose of the claimant's application was to persuade the Court to make a public pronouncement condemning the US's activities in North Waziristan, with a view to halting such activity. However, it was well established that the courts of one State would not sit in judgment on the legality, validity or acceptability of the acts of another sovereign State, whether under domestic or international law. The attitude and approach of one State to the acts and conduct of another were a matter of high policy, crucially connected to the conduct of inter-State relations. Sitting in judgment

---

[3] For the text of Sections 44 and 45, see para. 32 of the High Court judgment.
[4] For the text of Section 52 and Schedule 4 of the Serious Crime Act 2007, see para. 51 of the High Court judgment.
[5] Section 52 of the International Criminal Court Act 2001 provided: "*Conduct ancillary to genocide, etc. committed outside jurisdiction*: (1) It is an offence against the law of England and Wales for a person to engage in conduct ancillary to an act to which this section applies ..."
[6] See para. 6 of the High Court judgment for full details.

on the acts of another sovereign State imperilled those relations, as the judgment of a State's national court reflected that State's judgment (paras. 13-16 and 59).

(2) The Court did not give advisory opinions on whether proposed conduct was lawful, unless it served a cogent public or private interest, and particularly when applications were fact-dependent rather than concerning matters of pure law. The claimant was effectively seeking an advisory opinion on whether impugned conduct breached criminal law, which was particularly fact-sensitive. Any declaration that failed to identify with particularity the factual circumstances in which the 2007 Act (and/or the 2001 Act) would be infringed would be useless, inaccurate and misleading. If a declaration merely repeated applicable statutory provisions or was imprecise, it would offer no useful guidance on future conduct, while if it was too wide it could be misleading by including lawful activity within the scope of criminal conduct (paras. 28-31 and 33).

(3) The claimant's assumptions and allegations about the transfer and use of GCHQ intelligence were an insufficient factual basis for a declaration. Whether a GCHQ officer was guilty of an offence depended on the nature of his conduct and state of mind. Since employees were unlikely to know whether or how intelligence was disseminated, no sensible guidance could be given as to the circumstances in which it could be lawfully passed. It was not possible to produce a meaningful declaration that accurately identified the necessary *mens rea* without reference to specific facts (paras. 36, 39 and 41).

(4) Contrary to the claimant's assertions, a declaration was not the only way the legality of transferring locational intelligence could be monitored. GCHQ activities were subject to the scrutiny of the Intelligence and Security Committee and the Intelligence Services and Interception Commissioners. A declaration would not fill any void, and would be far less effective than oversight by the Parliamentary Committee tasked with ensuring that legality did not give way to expediency (paras. 47-9).

(5) Whether GCHQ employees could rely on the defence of combatant immunity (which turned on the status of the conflict in North Waziristan in international law) was irrelevant since there was no risk that GCHQ officers would ever be prosecuted and there were no concrete facts likely to found a criminal charge (para. 46).

(6) A declaration concerning the secondary criminal liability of GCHQ officers for encouraging or assisting crime would have been regarded by the principals, who were said to have been encouraged or assisted, as a direct accusation of criminal activity. As those principals were agents of the US, the court would be presumed to be judging the activities of the US. The claimant was unable to demonstrate that any hearing or judgment on his application could avoid giving the impression that US conduct in North Waziristan was on trial (paras. 55-7).

The claimant appealed.

Judgment of the Court of Appeal (20 January 2014)

Held (unanimously):—The appeal was dismissed.

(1) It was common ground that the Court would not decide whether drone strikes carried out by US officials were lawful. Each sovereign State was bound to respect the independence of every other sovereign State. The courts of one State would not sit in judgment on the legality, validity or acceptability of the sovereign acts of foreign States except in exceptional circumstances, such as breaches of established rules of international law, grave breaches of human rights, or where the acts were contrary to English principles of public policy. While it was arguable whether courts lacked jurisdiction to sit in judgment on the acts of foreign States, or whether they would not sit because those acts were non-justiciable, such distinctions had no present practical relevance (paras. 25-8).

(2) Accepting that the Court could not adjudicate on whether a CIA official who executed a drone strike was guilty of murder or any other offence, the claimant sought relief on the basis that, since the CIA official's acts would be unlawful under English law if they had been committed by UK nationals, a GCHQ officer who encouraged or assisted that act could be liable as a secondary party under Sections 44 to 46 of the 2007 Act. However, examining the secondary liability of the GCHQ officer for "encouraging and assisting crime" of the principal still ultimately hinged on an allegation or assumption that the principal had committed an offence. In reality, the Court would be asked to condemn the acts of the persons who operated the drone bombs, which would inevitably be understood by the US as a condemnation of its acts; as a finding that its policy on using drones was unlawful; and that its agents who operated drones were guilty of criminal offences, over which the Court had no jurisdiction (paras. 32, 34-7 and 44).

(3) The claimant's secondary case, that there was a significant risk that GCHQ officers might be guilty of conduct ancillary to war crimes and/or crimes against humanity, contrary to Section 52 of the 2001 Act, similarly foundered. The claimant was still ultimately inviting the Court to make a finding that the principal who executed the drone strike was guilty of a war crime and/or crime against humanity. Since that principal was, in reality, a CIA official implementing US policy, such a finding would still involve the UK courts sitting in judgment on the US (paras. 47 and 50-1).

(4) However the claims were presented, the claimant's arguments involved serious criticisms of the acts of a foreign State. It was only in certain established circumstances that the UK courts would exceptionally sit in judgment of such acts; no such exceptional circumstances existed here. Permission was refused (paras. 53-4).

The text of the judgment of the Court of Appeal, delivered by the Master of the Rolls, commences at p. 643. The text of the judgment of the High Court, delivered by Moses LJ, commences on the opposite page.

JUDGMENT OF THE HIGH COURT

LORD JUSTICE MOSES

1. The claimant seeks to challenge, by way of judicial review, what he calls 'a decision' of the Secretary of State for Foreign and Commonwealth Affairs in relation to the passing of intelligence by employees of GCHQ to forces of the United States. I deliberately describe the nature of these proceedings in vague terms; it will become necessary to examine the extent to which it is possible to be more precise. The Secretary of State's opposition to the grant of permission has led to the need to resolve certain preliminary issues.

2. The claimant seeks to impugn what the claim form describes as a decision to provide "intelligence to the US authorities for use in drone strikes in Pakistan, amongst other places". It is alleged that employees of GCHQ are assisting US agents by supplying what is described as "locational intelligence" for use in drone strikes in Pakistan. By assisting US agents to direct armed attacks in Pakistan, GCHQ employees are said to be at risk of committing offences under the criminal law of England and Wales, as secondary parties to murder. The claimant submits that there is no armed conflict in Pakistan, as it is recognised under international law, still less an international armed conflict, and thus GCHQ employees are not entitled to combatant immunity.

3. Even if GCHQ employees would not be guilty of murder, there is a significant risk that they are guilty of conduct ancillary to crimes against humanity or war crimes. It follows, says the claimant, that the Secretary of State must publish a policy identifying the circumstances in which intelligence may lawfully be passed on if it relates to the location of individuals who may be targeted in a drone strike.

4. The Secretary of State advances his objection to permission on four bases. But each has an impact on the other and resolution will depend upon their cumulative effect. The Secretary of State contends, first, that the court will be required to adjudicate upon the acts of foreign sovereign states, second, that the claimant is seeking a declaration as to whether future conduct is proscribed by domestic criminal law, third, that the court should not be lured into giving an advisory opinion and fourth, at the suggestion of Mitting J when ordering this hearing, that the case cannot be tried at all in the absence of a statutory closed material procedure.

5. The parties debated rival versions of what the court would have to resolve, should permission be granted. For example, the claimant disavows any intention, or need, to resolve the legality of United States' actions in Pakistan, whilst the Secretary of State warns that this court is being invited to rule on that very issue. In *R (Gentle)* v. *Prime Minister* [2008] 1 AC 1356, Lord Rodger sought to lift the cloak of a claim for a public inquiry in exercise of a right under Article 2 of the European Convention on Human Rights. He identified the real aim or target of the complaint: it was an attempt to investigate why—as the claimants in that case saw it—the Attorney General changed his mind and gave wrong advice as to the legality of the invasion of Iraq ([34] and [35]). Similarly, this Court must cast a critical eye on the claimant's own description of the issues and identify what he is "really after". It is necessary to analyse the nature of the claim, to see what, in reality, it entails.

6. I must set out in full the relief the claimant seeks. He seeks a declaration that:

(a) a person who passes to an agent of the United States Government intelligence on the location of an individual in Pakistan, foreseeing a serious risk that the information will be used by the Central Intelligence Agency to target or kill that individual:

   (i) is not entitled to the defence of combatant immunity; and
   (ii) accordingly may be liable under domestic criminal law for soliciting, encouraging, persuading or proposing a murder (contrary to s. 4 of the Offences Against the Person Act 1861), for conspiracy to commit murder (contrary to s. 1, or 1A, of the Criminal Law Act 1977) or for aiding, abetting, counselling or procuring murder (contrary to s. 8 of the Accessories and Abettors Act 1861);

(b) Accordingly the Secretary of State has no power to direct or authorise GCHQ officers or other Crown servants in the United Kingdom to pass intelligence in the circumstances set out in (a) above.

(c) Alternatively, where a GCHQ officer or other Crown servant has information relating to the location of an individual, whom it knows or suspects the United States Government intends to target or kill, the officer may not pass the intelligence to an agent of the United States Government if there is a significant risk that doing so would facilitate the commission of a war crime or crimes against humanity contrary to the International Criminal Court Act 2001.

(d) Accordingly, before directing or authorising the passing of intelligence relating to the location of such an individual to an agent of the United States Government, the Secretary of State must formulate, publish and apply a lawful policy setting out the circumstances in which such intelligence may be transferred.

I should mention, at this stage, that the references to the provisions of various criminal statutes require amendment. The claimant now rests his case as to potential criminality on sections 44-6, section 52(2) and Schedule 4 of the Serious Crime Act 2007, which give rise to a risk of committing offences under the International Criminal Court Act 2001.

7. The facts on which the claim is based start from the claimant's own description of tragic events in Datta Khel, North Waziristan Agency in the Federally Administered Tribal Areas of Pakistan. On 17 March 2011 his father Malik Daud Khan was presiding over an outdoor meeting of the local Jirga to settle, with other elders, a commercial dispute. A missile was fired from a drone and the claimant's father was killed with 49 others who were attending the Jirga.

8. The claimant asserts that the missile was fired from a drone operated by the CIA. He describes a community "plagued with fear" as drones hover over their skies day and night. The community are fearful of gathering together lest such a congregation arouse suspicion; and children do not dare attend school. He concludes: "my hope is that this brutal assassination will end. The people of NWA are against these strikes. I am against these drone strikes."

9. The allegation that the strikes are linked to agents of the US Government and to United Kingdom employees of GCHQ is based on a number of reports, the effect of which can be summarised in the report of *The Sunday Times*, dated 25 July 2010:

> GCHQ, the top-secret communications agency, has used telephone intercepts to provide the Americans with "locational intelligence" on leading militants in Afghanistan and Pakistan, an official briefed on its operations said. Insiders say GCHQ can provide more extensive and precise technical coverage in the region than its American sister organisation, the National Security Agency, because Britain has a better network of intercept stations in Asia ... GCHQ uses satellites and planes to collect and analyse the location of telephones used by militants. The Sunday Times have agreed not to disclose further details of these operations at the request of the agency ... Cheltenham-based GCHQ said it was proud of the work it did with America, which it said was in "strict accordance with the law".

10. The response of the Secretary of State has been to invoke the consistent and conventional policy of neither confirming nor denying the assertions; to do so would risk damaging the important public interest in preserving the confidentiality of national security and 'vital' relations with international partners. The claimant suggests that that policy has already been breached in the reported assertion of acting "in strict accordance" with the law. Such an assertion is said to be

inconsistent with the policy of saying nothing. The dispute led to a late attempt by the Secretary of State to introduce material which was said to cast doubt on the accuracy of the report of GCHQ's comment. It was far too late for the Secretary of State to introduce that material and I have ignored it.

11. I do not, however, think that the point is of any significance. GCHQ's reported assertion of the legality of its activities does not amount to a breach of the policy of 'no comment'. The real question is the impact of that policy on the issues which require resolution: does the fact that the claimant is compelled to rely on unconfirmed reports preclude the grant of permission? The extent to which it is possible to identify a firm factual foundation is an important question which I shall have to determine, but at this stage I shall merely note that, through no fault of the claimant, his case rests on a respectable but unconfirmed report.

12. It is relevant to the analysis of the nature of this claim to observe that the claimant has also launched proceedings, as a petitioner in the Court in Peshawar. In those proceedings he contends that the Government of Pakistan, and various Ministries, are under a constitutional obligation to take all necessary action to stop "illegal drone strikes" and "safeguard its citizens from target killing by an external force". He pleads that "the act of killing of innocent people on March 17 2011 was extra-judicial killing, more generally referred to as murder". The prayer refers to criminal offences by those inside and outside Pakistan in drone operations.

13. It is plain, from the nature of the claims, that the purpose of the proceedings in England and in Pakistan is to persuade a court to do what it can to stop further strikes by drones operated by the United States. That is, as Lord Rodger would have put it, the real aim of both sets of proceedings. In this country, however, that presents the claimant with a formidable difficulty. His legal advisers acknowledge, as they have to acknowledge, that they cannot seek from this court a declaration that the United States' drone strikes are unlawful. They recognise that a domestic court would refuse to make such a declaration.

Judgment on the acts of a foreign state

14. It is necessary to explain why the courts would not even consider, let alone resolve, the question of the legality of United States' drone strikes. The principle was expressed by Fuller CJ in the United States Supreme Court in *Underhill* v. *Hernandez* (1897) 168 US 25, 252:

Every sovereign state is bound to respect the independence of every other sovereign state, and the courts of one country will not sit in judgment on the acts of the government of another done within its own territory. Redress of grievances by reason of such acts must be obtained through the means open to be availed of by sovereign powers as between themselves ... (Cited with approval in *Buttes Gas and Oil Co.* v. *Hammer (No 3)* [1982] AC 888, 933, and *R* v. *Jones (Margaret)* [2007] 1 AC 136, 163.)

15. The principle that the courts will not sit in judgment on the sovereign acts of a foreign state includes a prohibition against adjudication upon the "legality, validity or acceptability of such acts, either under domestic law or international law" (*Kuwait Airways Corporation* v. *Iraqi Airways Co. (Nos 4 and 5)* [2002] 2 WLR 1353, 1362). The rationale for this principle is, in part, founded upon the proposition that the attitude and approach of one country to the acts and conduct of another is a matter of high policy, crucially connected to the conduct of the relations between the two sovereign powers. To examine and sit in judgment on the conduct of another state would imperil relations between the states (*Buttes Gas* 933).

16. The damage to relations with another sovereign state leads to a further well-settled proposition: that states do not distinguish between legal assertions made by a state and declarations of law by a national court. It does not ameliorate the damage to foreign relations for the state to protest that it is not responsible for the conduct of its courts. The judgment of the court will be regarded by other states as the judgment of the country; the country is bound, in any event, to comply with the decisions of the court in obedience to the rule of law (see *R (Campaign for Nuclear Disarmament)* v. *Prime Minister* [2002] EWHC 2777 (Admin), [2003] 3 LRC 335 [43] per Simon Brown LJ).

17. In *CND* evidence was adduced on behalf of the Foreign and Commonwealth Office as to the damage which would be caused to international relations were the court to give a definitive view as to the legal effect of United Nations Resolution 1441 in relation to the invasion of Iraq. Damage would have been caused by forcing the Government even to enter into a discussion as to the effect of that Resolution ([41] and [43]). Evidence from Mr Morrison of the FCO in the instant case echoes the evidence adduced in *CND*. He says that if the Secretary of State were required to make a substantive response to the claim, the likely consequence would be serious harm to national security and international relations. The United Kingdom Government would be compelled to express a definitive view on legal issues, complicating and damaging relations with our most important bilateral ally and, in consequence, damaging the United Kingdom's security.

18. All of these considerations are, as Simon Brown LJ said in *CND*, "self-evident" ([41]). They were not in dispute. But I have set them out again because a major part of the argument on behalf of the claimant concerned Mr Chamberlain's deft attempts to side-step the impediments which these principles present to the progress of the claim.

19. The course adopted by Mr Chamberlain was to guide the court through a sequence of authorities. They were designed to illustrate that there was no irrefragable principle of non-justiciability, that there was no absolute principle against making a declaration as to criminal offences, and no bar, in principle, to a declaration based on facts which were not admitted. I am prepared to follow Mr Chamberlain up his path but wish to make clear, at the outset of the journey, that questions of justiciability are rarely solved by distinguishing between issues of principle and issues of discretion. Lord Bingham described the approach of the courts in terms which avoided identification of absolute principle:

> It must ... have been obvious that an inquiry such as the claimant's claim would be drawn into consideration of issues which judicial tribunals have traditionally been very reluctant to entertain because they recognise their limitations as suitable bodies to resolve them ... (*Gentle* [8(2)].)

20. These are words which suggest discretion, not jurisdiction. But I propose to follow the course set by Simon Brown LJ in *CND* ([47(2)]). It does not matter whether the questions which go to the issue whether this court should hear this application for judicial review are to be regarded as questions of principle or questions of discretion.

Identification of a legal right in domestic law: deploying a legitimate defence in domestic criminal law

21. There are, undoubtedly, cases in which the courts have been prepared to resolve disputed issues of international law, if it is necessary for the purposes of resolving a private right or obligation, even if to do so would hamper international relations and cause embarrassment to the United Kingdom. In *R* v. *Home Secretary, ex parte Adan* [2001] 2 WLR 143, the court was compelled by the terms of the Asylum and Immigration Act 1996, and the United Kingdom's treaty obligations, to question whether France and Germany were misapplying the Refugee Convention. If a claimant has a legal right, it is justiciable in the courts (*R (Gentle)* v. *Prime Minister* [2008] 1 AC 1356 per Lord Bingham ([8(2)])). There are cases in which the courts are compelled to interpret and apply international law for the purposes of determining private rights and obligations under domestic law (*CND* ([61](iii))).

22. This is not the occasion for repetition of the review of such cases conducted in *R (Abbasi)* v. *Secretary of State for FCO* [2002] EWCA Civ 1598 [50]-[51], in *CND* [22]-[33], and in *R (Al-Haq)* v. *Secretary of State for Foreign and Commonwealth Affairs* [2009] EWHC 1910 (Admin). Those cases demonstrate that the mere fact that the issues are those which the courts "have traditionally been very reluctant to entertain" will not necessarily be dispositive of the issue of justiciability. If a domestic right or obligation can be identified and can only be vindicated by consideration of the actions of other states under international law, then the courts may be compelled to undertake that task to the extent that it is necessary for that purpose.

23. There is, however, an important caveat. Rights must be recognised before they can be vindicated. The process of identifying a right should involve consideration of:

what exercise of the right would entail. Thus the restraint traditionally shown by the courts in ruling on what has been called high policy—peace and war, the making of treaties, the conduct of foreign relations—does tend to militate against the existence of the right. (*Gentle* [8(2)].)

24. The necessary vindication of a legal right, once it has been recognised, includes the right to deploy a legitimate defence in a criminal case. In *Jones (Margaret)*, the defendants failed to establish that the United Kingdom's actions in Iraq afforded a defence to criminal charges. But Lord Hoffmann (at [67]) saw "much force" in the submission that it would be "contrary to the right to a fair trial under Article 6 of the Convention for a defendant to be told that he could not rely on a defence otherwise open to him" because it raised questions that were not justiciable.

25. The paradigm of a case in which the court is required to consider issues of high policy was *R* v. *Gul (Mohammed)* [2012] 1 Cr App R 37. The defendant sought to resist the accusation that his actions were acts of terrorism by contending that he was doing no more than encouraging self-defence against coalition forces who were invading Iraq. He contended that those forces were not entitled to combatant immunity because the conflict was a non-international armed conflict. The conclusion of the court, that there was nothing in international law which required the court to exempt those who attacked coalition forces from the scope of the Terrorism Act 2001, is not of significance in the instant case. But *Gul* does make good the proposition that it may be necessary to resolve questions of international law for the purposes of resolving a legitimate defence under domestic criminal law.

26. By a parity of reasoning, the claimant contends that it is necessary to decide on the nature of the United States' attacks in North Waziristan in order to determine whether employees of GCHQ would be entitled to combatant immunity, were they to be prosecuted for offences under the Serious Crime Act 2007. If they were immune from prosecution under the 2007 Act, they could only be prosecuted under the International Criminal Court Act 2001.

27. This case, submits Mr Chamberlain, concerns only the legality of the activities of employees of GCHQ. It is concerned with domestic criminal law and the compliance of GCHQ employees with the requirements of the criminal law. The need to consider how international law would classify the actions of the United States arises only for the purpose of determining issues of domestic criminal law. In contrast to *CND* this case is not concerned with questions of interpretation of an instrument operating purely on the plane of international law ([36]). It does not require the court to pass judgment on the legality of the United States' actions in North Waziristan.

An advisory opinion on the criminal law

28. By this means Mr Chamberlain attempts to secure a foothold in domestic law (*CND* [40]). But a survey of the domestic ground reveals further impediments. The court is being asked to give an advisory opinion; it is being asked to give an advisory opinion on a difficult point of criminal law, and the point of law depends upon sparse and unproven facts.

29. The courts will not give advisory opinions as to whether proposed conduct is lawful, save where it would serve a cogent public or private interest (*R (Rusbridger)* v. *Attorney General* [2004] 1 AC 357 [23]). The principle that the courts will not make declarations as to future conduct or in relation to a future decision is often qualified by a reference to "exceptional circumstances" (*Rusbridger* [16], *CND* [52]), leaving the courts to ponder the few examples where courts have granted such declarations (some are given in *Rusbridger* [23] and [24]) and the many examples where the courts have refused.

30. The *Guardian* failed to obtain a declaration as to whether its advocacy for abolition of the monarchy was prohibited by the Treason Felony Act 1848, when read with Article 10 of the Convention, on the grounds that such a declaration was unnecessary ([28]) and raised no live, practical question ([36]). The application in this case cannot be so lightly dismissed. But it does labour under the difficulty that it raises an issue as to whether the conduct impugned breaches the criminal law.

Questions as to whether conduct amounts to a criminal offence are peculiarly sensitive to the facts of the particular case. Applications for an advisory opinion are more likely to be accepted in relation to issues of pure law; they are most likely to be rejected where the answer will depend on the facts (*Rusbridger* [23]).

31. Usually an application for a declaration which raises questions as to the criminal law will fail because a declaration from a civil court will risk usurping the function of the criminal courts. That is not a risk, as both sides recognise, in this case. There is no realistic chance of any employee of GCHQ being prosecuted. In this case the problem is different: the efficacy of the declaration will depend on the facts. Absent a declaration which identifies with particularity the factual circumstances in which the Serious Crime Act 2007 would be infringed, a declaration would be useless, inaccurate or misleading. If it is imprecise, it affords no guidance as to future conduct and if it is too wide it may be misleading by including lawful activity within the scope of criminal conduct.

32. The provisions of the 2007 Act on which the claimant relies demonstrate the problem. Section 44 provides:

44 Intentionally encouraging or assisting an offence

(1) A person commits an offence if—

   (a) he does an act capable of encouraging or assisting the commission of an offence; and
   (b) he intends to encourage or assist its commission.

(2) But he is not to be taken to have intended to encourage or assist the commission of an offence merely because such encouragement or assistance was a foreseeable consequence of his act.

45 Encouraging or assisting an offence believing it will be committed

A person commits an offence if—

   (a) he does an act capable of encouraging or assisting the commission of an offence; and
   (b) he believes—
       (i) that the offence will be committed; and
       (ii) that his act will encourage or assist its commission.

33. Leaving aside, for a moment, the issues of jurisdiction, a declaration which merely replicates the wording of the statute is of no assistance whatever. Making a declaration which merely substitutes

references to employees of GCHQ for "a person" would be an exercise in futility. In what circumstances is it suggested that a GCHQ employee will infringe the 2007 Act? What must he avoid doing? What, since *mens rea* is essential, must he avoid thinking?

34. Any court, be it a civil or criminal court, seeking to answer these questions is hardly encouraged to read:

The offences are rendered complex because the sections (and the rest of that part of the Act) include extended definitions of (i) what suffices as relevant conduct by D; and (ii) the subdivision of the elements of the offence to be committed by P, into conduct, circumstances and consequences. Unfortunately, several of the fundamental terms in the offences are left undefined, including core elements of the *actus reus*: "encouraging" and "assisting". The Law Commission report No 300 will serve as an interpretative document, but given the degree of difference between what was proposed and what was enacted, considerable caution is warranted. In addition, caution must be exercised in reading the statute itself since the true scope of the offences in ss. 44 to 46 cannot be appreciated without reference to the ensuing 20 sections. (*Smith & Hogan: Criminal Law 13th Edition* p. 464.)

35. The alleged factual premise on which the claimant's application is based is that employees of GCHQ are passing on intelligence which may be used to find the location of those whom the US agents wish to target. The claimant says that the Secretary of State cannot escape merely by reliance on a policy of neither confirming nor denying the allegation. There is one example of a declaration granted in the face of the exercise of such a policy by the police. In *Re C's Application for Judicial Review* [2009] 1 AC 908 declarations as to the scope of the Regulation of Investigatory Powers Act 2000 in relation to surveillance and monitoring of legal consultations in prison were made and upheld, despite the fact that the police would neither confirm nor deny that such surveillance took place. It is of note that assurances were sought from the police that such surveillance would not take place and they were refused ([1]). But the declarations in that case were not concerned with the facts but with the pure legal issue of the impact of Article 8(2) of the ECHR on the authorisation of surveillance under section 28 of RIPA 2000. No one suggested (see the argument between pp. 913-14) that the facts alleged should not be accepted.

36. But in the instant case the utility of the declaration does depend on factual precision. The mere assumption that targets are identified with the aid of intelligence from GCHQ is not a sufficient factual basis for a declaration. Whether an employee of GCHQ is guilty of an offence will depend upon the nature of the employee's activities, the

effect of those activities in a particular case (encouragement or assistance) and that employee's state of mind (knowledge or belief). Since an employee is unlikely to be in a position to know whether or how intelligence is disseminated no sensible guidance could possibly be given as to the circumstances when intelligence may lawfully be passed on and when it may not. If GCHQ is run on anything like the system we have, over thirty years later, learnt was adopted in the huts of Bletchley Park, the notion that those obtaining the intelligence have anything other than an inkling of how it may be deployed is little more than fanciful.

37. It is hard to see the point of any declaration which merely says that those who pass on intelligence may be at risk of breaking the law, if their activities and their state of mind fall within the scope of sections 44 or 45 of the Serious Crime Act 2007.

38. The states of mind identified in sections 44 and 45 are crucial to criminal liability. That exposes this claim to difficulties similar to those faced by Woolf J in *Attorney General* v. *Able* [1984] 1 QB 357. The Attorney General sought a declaration as to whether the supply of a booklet relating to suicide was an offence contrary to the Suicide Act 1961. Woolf J contrasted the application for a direction to the civil court with an Attorney General's reference to the Court of Appeal (Criminal Division). On such a reference the Court of Appeal clarifies the law in relation to specific facts. Woolf J said:

If a civil court declares conduct criminal it performs the same task as a jury. If it declares that certain conduct is not criminal it performs the same task as a judge withdrawing a case from the jury.

The danger, as Woolf J saw it, was:

While of course recognising the advantages of the law being clear in relation to future conduct, it would only be proper to grant a declaration if it is clearly established that there is no risk of treating conduct as criminal which is not clearly in contravention of the criminal law ... (808A-B.)

39. That is the very danger in the declaration sought in this case. Merely passing on intelligence could not amount to an offence under the 2007 Act unless a particular state of mind could be proved against the provider at the time of provision. So how is the declaration to be drafted to have any meaningful utility? If cast too wide it would not only be useless but, as Woolf J explains, it would be misleading, since it would risk including conduct which did not clearly contravene the criminal law.

40. Woolf J, in *Able*, set out the intention which must be proved and the consequences of distribution which must be proved in any particular case (812D-F). Even if they were proved, he acknowledged that there might be some exceptional circumstance which meant that the offence was not established (812G). He therefore concluded that the different forms of declaration submitted all suffered from the fatal defect that they indicated that an offence had been committed, when, in fact, no offence would be committed (813B). Accordingly, he refused to grant any declaration.

41. The same difficulty is apparent in the instant application. It is not possible to produce a meaningful declaration which accurately identifies the necessary *mens rea* without reference to specific facts.

42. Mr Chamberlain sought to diminish the apparent difficulty of composing a meaningful declaration by reference to a policy document published by the Government in relation to intelligence officers' work with foreign security services implicated in improper treatment of detainees (*Consolidated Guidance to Intelligence Officers and Service Personnel on the Detention and Interviewing of Detainees Overseas and on the Passing and Receipt of Intelligence Relating to Detainees*).

43. The contents were challenged by the Commission in *R (Equality & Human Rights Commission)* v. *Prime Minister* [2012] 1 WLR 1389. The court did consider whether the policy accurately identified the *mens rea* necessary to establish secondary liability under s. 134 of the Criminal Justice Act 1988 (assisting torture), although it rejected the complaint that the guide was erroneous. Mr Chamberlain argued that if the Government was prepared to publish such guidance, then the Secretary of State ought equally to be prepared to publish guidance in relation to the dissemination of intelligence to be used in drone attacks.

44. The Consolidated Guidance does not assist Mr Chamberlain. In the main, it sets out a series of procedural steps which officers should follow. The primary obligation is to consult senior personnel (Paragraph 11 and Table). The only cases where this will be unnecessary is where the officer knows or believes torture will take place, or judges that it will not. The Table starts with a prohibition: "if you know or believe torture will take place ... 1. You must not proceed and Ministers will need to be informed." This reveals that the author has never had the difficulty of explaining to a jury the difference between knowledge, belief and suspicion. Clearly, the Guidance is of greater use in its requirement to consult senior personnel.

45. Merely repeating the provisions of ss. 44-6 of the 2007 Act in published guidance, and telling employees that if they intentionally

encourage or assist an offence or encourage or assist an offence believing it will be committed is, as I have explained, of no utility whatever. Examination of the Guidance, which Mr Chamberlain holds out as an exemplar, merely shows that the claimant cannot overcome the difficulties inherent in a vague, and possibly misleading, declaration by seeking to transpose those difficulties into a written policy.

46. Mr Chamberlain suggests, by way of riposte, that there is a point in determining whether employees would have a defence of combatant immunity, a point which turns on the status of the conflict in North Waziristan in international law. But I can see no point in identifying whether the employees have a defence to a criminal charge in circumstances where there is no risk they will ever be prosecuted and where the existence of facts likely to found a criminal charge is a matter of imaginative conjecture.

The only means of redress

47. Mr Chamberlain prayed in aid the fact that there was no likelihood of prosecution. He submitted that, absent any prospect of a criminal prosecution, a declaration is the only way the legality of passing information used for the location of drone strikes may be monitored. It is the only redress open to the claimant, at least in this jurisdiction. This was the key factor which persuaded Walker J in *R (Haynes)* v. *Stafford Borough Council* [2007] 1 WLR 1365 to make declarations as to whether the local authority's grant of a pet shop licence to the Parrot Society involved the commission of criminal offences contrary to the Pet Animals Act 1951. There was, so the judge concluded, a public interest in resolving the issue and no other means of redress for the claimant.

48. I do not dispute that oversight of the legality of the operations of the Security and Intelligence Agencies and GCHQ is an important matter of public interest. But it is not correct to assert that a declaration is the only means of testing the lawfulness of the activities of GCHQ. There was debate as to whether a complaint to the Investigatory Powers Tribunal would be effective, or could resolve the issues in this application. It would be concerned only with a specific complaint about a specific incident. If, for any reason, it rejected the complaint (for example, because GCHQ was not involved in the attack on 17 March 2011 or because the activities were lawful) it could do no more than state that no determination had been made in the complainant's favour (s. 68(4) Regulation of Investigatory Powers Act 2000). The complainant would never know why his complaint had been rejected.

49. GCHQ activities are, however, subject to the scrutiny of the Intelligence and Security Committee, by virtue of the Intelligence Services Act 1994 and of the Intelligence Services and Interception Commissioners, whose remit is to hold the Security Services and those responsible for intelligence accountable. There is no basis on which this court could or should conclude that a declaration would fill a void and impose the rule of law on a lawless territory. An abstract declaration would be far less effective than the oversight of the Parliamentary Committee charged with ensuring, amongst other things, that legality does not give way to expediency. As Simon Brown LJ remarked in *CND*, the Government has access to the best advice: "Why should it be thought that the advice obtained is likely to be wrong?" ([44]).

Adjudicating on United States activities

50. Faced with these obstacles, Mr Eadie QC suggests that the claimant is back where he started, facing the fundamental objection that he is asking the court to pass judgment on the activities of the United States. He suggested (recalling Simon Brown LJ in *R v. DPP ex p Camelot* (1997) 10 (Admin) L Rep 93, 104 [32]) that the court should be all the more wary of accepting an invitation to launch these proceedings and negotiating the obstacles when the claimant's case involves determining the lawfulness of the actions of the United States in North Waziristan. Mr Chamberlain sought to avoid this suggestion by reference to the jurisdiction provisions of the Serious Crime Act 2007.

51. The relevant provisions read:

52 Jurisdiction

(1) If a person (D) knows or believes that what he anticipates might take place wholly or partly in England or Wales, he may be guilty of an offence under section 44, 45 or 46 no matter where he was at any relevant time.
(2) If it is not proved that D knows or believes that what he anticipates might take place wholly or partly in England or Wales, he is not guilty of an offence under section 44, 45 or 46 unless paragraph 1, 2 or 3 of Schedule 4 applies.
(3) A reference in this section (and in any of those paragraphs) to what D anticipates is to be read as follows—

    (a) in relation to an offence under section 44 or 45, it refers to the act which would amount to the commission of an anticipated offence . . .

Schedule 4 Extra-Territoriality

1(1) This paragraph applies if—

(a) any relevant behaviour of D's takes place wholly or partly in England or Wales;
(b) D knows or believes that what he anticipates might take place wholly or partly in a place outside England and Wales; and
(c) either—

  (i) the anticipated offence is one that would be triable under the law of England and Wales if it were committed in that place; or
  (ii) if there are relevant conditions, it would be so triable if it were committed there by a person who satisfies the conditions.

(2) "Relevant condition" means a condition that—

(a) determines (wholly or in part) whether an offence committed outside England and Wales is nonetheless triable under the law of England and Wales; and
(b) relates to the citizenship, nationality or residence of the person who commits it.

52. The "relevant condition" to which the claimant draws attention is s. 9 of the Offences Against the Person Act 1861. By that section and s. 3 of the British Nationality Act 1948, a British citizen may be tried in England or Northern Ireland for murder or manslaughter committed on land anywhere outside that territory. So Mr Chamberlain contends that an employee, D, could be tried because there are relevant conditions which would permit P, the principal, to be tried if he were a British citizen.

53. Let it be assumed that none of the US agents involved in drone strikes, if they are involved, are British citizens. On the basis of these provisions, Mr Chamberlain argued that an employee of GCHQ could be guilty of an offence under sections 44 or 45, even though those carrying out a drone strike with the aid of information supplied could not be guilty of any offence under the criminal law of England and Wales, because they are not British citizens and, accordingly, are not caught by s. 9 of the 1861 Act.

54. It seems, as Mr Edis QC pointed out, curious that a defendant can be guilty of the offence of murder and subject to a mandatory life sentence when the principal is not guilty of any offence at all. I do not propose to resolve the difficulty. The very fact that there is enormous difficulty is significant in this case; it would be quite wrong to make a declaration in an area of law so fraught with difficulty that no

prosecution under these provisions, a prosecution with requires the Attorney General's fiat (section 53), has as yet been brought.

55. There is still less any incentive to consider a declaration when it is appreciated what it entails. Mr Chamberlain's proposition, even if it is right, that a person may be guilty of secondary liability for murder under ss. 44-6, although the principal could not, is no answer to the fundamental objection to the grant of a declaration: that it involves, and would be regarded "around the world" (see Simon Brown LJ in *CND* [37]) as "an exorbitant arrogation of adjudicative power" in relation to the legality and acceptability of the acts of another sovereign power. It is beyond question that any consideration as to whether a GCHQ employee is guilty of a crime under Part 2 of the Serious Crime Act 2007, headed "Encouraging or Assisting Crime", would be regarded by those who were said to have been encouraged or assisted as an accusation against them of criminal activity and, in the instant case, an accusation of murder. After all, that is the very nature of Mr Noor Khan's accusation in Pakistan. No amount of learned and complex analysis of the interstices of domestic criminal legislation would or could diminish that impression. For the reasons given by Mr Morrison and Simon Brown LJ in *CND*, that consequence is inevitable. Even if the argument focused on the status of the attacks in North Waziristan (international armed conflict, armed conflict not of an international nature, pre-emptive self-defence) for the purposes of considering whether the United Kingdom employee might have a defence of combatant immunity, it would give the impression that this court was presuming to judge the activities of the United States.

56. But, in any event, I reject the suggestion that the argument can be confined to an academic discussion as to the status of the conflict in North Waziristan. The topsy-turvy nature of the declaration sought merely provokes the question: of what crime is it said the GCHQ employee may be guilty? Since it is said to be a crime of secondary liability that inquiry leads, inexorably, to questions as to the criminal activity of the principals, employees of the United States. What is the crime, which GCHQ employees may be accused of assisting or encouraging?

57. These difficulties are, to my mind, insuperable. The claimant cannot demonstrate that his application will avoid, during the course of the hearing and in the judgment, giving a clear impression that it is the United States' conduct in North Waziristan which is also on trial. He has not found any foothold other than on the most precarious ground in domestic law. If, as I have concluded, any declaration could, at best, merely replicate the words of a congeries of criminal provisions which resist comprehension, save perhaps to the most sophisticated

interpreter (and even he suggests that they are baffling), then what is sought is shown to be damaging to the public interest without any countervailing justification or advantage. And all of this in circumstances where the conduct of GCHQ is subject to oversight and there is no prospect of prosecution. In short, there is no need or reason, even if led by so skilful and firm a guide as Mr Chamberlain, to "go there".

58. I reach this conclusion without any need to consider the issue raised by Mitting J as to whether, if permission were granted, it would be possible to try the application for judicial review. The issue was raised after Ouseley J held, in *AHK* v. *Home Secretary* [2012] EWHC 1117 (Admin), that, absent statutory provision, a closed material process is not available in judicial review proceedings, following the decision in *Al Rawi* v. *Security Service* [2012] 1 AC 531.

59. If I revert to Lord Rodger's approach, which I mentioned at the outset, the real aim and target of these proceedings is not to inform GCHQ employees that if they were prosecuted, no defence of combatant immunity would be available. The real aim is to persuade this court to make a public pronouncement designed to condemn the activities of the United States in North Waziristan, as a step in persuading them to halt such activity. Mr Chamberlain knows he could never obtain permission overtly for such a purpose. His stimulating arguments have been an attempt to shroud that purpose in a more acceptable veil. That he has, in my view, failed, is no reflection on his admirably clear and attractive efforts. I would refuse permission.

MR JUSTICE SIMON

60. I agree.

[Report: [2013] ACD 23]

[The following is the text of the judgment of the Court of Appeal, delivered by the Master of the Rolls:]

JUDGMENT OF THE COURT OF APPEAL

MASTER OF THE ROLLS

1. The claimant lives in Miranshah, North Waziristan Agency ("NWA"), in the Federally Administered Tribal Areas of Pakistan.

His father was a member of the local Jirga, a peaceful council of tribal elders whose functions included the settling of commercial disputes. On 17 March, the claimant's father presided over a meeting of the Jirga held outdoors at Datta Khel, NWA. During the course of the meeting, a missile was fired from an unmanned aircraft or "drone" believed to have been operated by the US Central Intelligence Agency ("CIA"). The claimant's father was one of more than 40 people who were killed.

2. In 2010, it was reported in several media outlets, including *The Sunday Times*, on the basis of a briefing said to emanate from official sources, that the General Communications Headquarters ("GCHQ"), an agency for which the defendant Secretary of State is responsible, provides "locational intelligence" to the US authorities for use in drone strikes in various places, including Pakistan.

3. On 16 December 2011, the claimant's solicitors wrote to the Secretary of State seeking clarification of the policies and practices of the UK Government in relation to the passing of information to US agents for use in drone attacks in Pakistan. On 6 February 2012, the Treasury Solicitor replied saying that it would not be possible to make an exception to the long-standing policy of successive governments to give a "neither confirm nor deny" response to questions about matters the public disclosure of which would risk damaging important public interests, including national security and vital relations with international partners.

4. The claimant then issued these proceedings claiming judicial review of "a decision by the Defendant to provide intelligence to the US authorities for use in drone strikes in Pakistan, among other places". The relief claimed was a declaration that:

(a) A person who passes to an agent of the United States Government intelligence on the location of an individual in Pakistan, foreseeing a serious risk that the information will be used by the Central Intelligence Agency to target or kill that individual:

  (i) is not entitled to the defence of combatant immunity; and
  (ii) accordingly may be liable under domestic criminal law for soliciting, encouraging, persuading or proposing a murder (contrary to s. 4 of the Offences Against the Person Act 1861), for conspiracy to commit murder (contrary to s. 1, or 1A, of the Criminal Law Act 1977) or for aiding, abetting, counselling or procuring murder (contrary to s. 8 of the Accessories and Abettors Act 1861);

(b) Accordingly the Secretary of State has no power to direct or authorise GCHQ officers or other Crown servants in the United Kingdom to pass intelligence in the circumstances set out in (a) above.

(c) Alternatively, where a GCHQ officer or other Crown servant has information relating to the location of an individual, whom it knows or suspects the United States Government intends to target or kill, the officer may not pass the intelligence to an agent of the United States Government if there is a significant risk that doing so would facilitate the commission of a war crime or crimes against humanity contrary to the International Criminal Court Act 2001.

(d) Accordingly, before directing or authorising the passing of intelligence relating to the location of such an individual to an agent of the United States Government, the Secretary of State must formulate, publish and apply a lawful policy setting out the circumstances in which such intelligence may be transferred.

5. The application for permission to apply for judicial review was dismissed by the Divisional Court (Moses LJ and Simon J) on 21 December 2012. The claimant sought leave to appeal and that application was directed to be considered by this court in a rolled up hearing by Pitchford LJ.

6. The reformulated relief now claimed is for:

(a) A declaration that a UK national who kills a person in a drone strike in Pakistan is not entitled to rely on the defence of combatant immunity. Accordingly a GCHQ officer or other Crown servant in the United Kingdom may commit an offence under ss. 44-6 of the Serious Crime Act 2007 (the "2007 Act") when passing locational intelligence to an agent of the US Government for use in drone strikes in Pakistan.

(b) In the alternative, the Appellant seeks a declaration that:

(i) In circumstances where a defence of combatant immunity applies, the passing of locational intelligence by a GCHQ officer or other Crown servant in the United Kingdom to an agent of the US Government for use in drone strikes in Pakistan may give rise to an offence under the International Criminal Court Act 2001 ("ICCA 2001").

(ii) Accordingly, before directing or authorising the passing of intelligence relating to the location of such an individual to an agent of the US Government, the Secretary of State must formulate, publish and apply a lawful policy setting out the circumstances in which such intelligence may be transferred.

7. In order to understand why the primary relief claimed is formulated in this way, it will be necessary to consider the 2007 Act and in particular the extra-territoriality provisions contained in Schedule 4. The purpose for which the claim is brought is in order to establish that the reported policy and practice of the UK Government is unlawful. In short, it is the claimant's case that the policy and practice involves requiring GCHQ officers to encourage and/or assist the commission of murder contrary to sections 44 to 46 of the 2007 Act.

8. About a week before the hearing before the Divisional Court, the Secretary of State served a public interest immunity ("PII") certificate in respect of the information contained in the sensitive annex to a witness statement by Paul Morrison dated 16 October 2012. Mr Morrison was then the Head of the Counter Terrorism Department in the Foreign and Commonwealth Office. The Divisional Court did not consider the PII certificate. Instead, they decided to adjudicate on the Secretary of State's threshold objections to the claim which were that the court should refuse permission on the principal ground that the issues raised were non-justiciable and/or that it would be a wrong exercise of discretion to grant relief which would necessarily entail a condemnation of the activities of the United States. The court upheld these objections and refused permission to apply for judicial review.

9. Mr Martin Chamberlain QC, who has argued this case with conspicuous skill, says that, if the claimant can overcome the threshold objections, then the question of how the claim can be tried will have to be considered separately. The court will then have to decide (i) whether to uphold the PII certificate; if so (ii) whether the claim can fairly be tried without the material denied to the court by operation of PII; and (iii) whether to make a closed material procedure declaration under section 6(1) of the Justice and Security Act 2013. Mr Chamberlain emphasises, therefore, that the court should not assume that the claim will be determined on the same exiguous facts as are currently known to the claimant. He says that this is important when considering the Secretary of State's objection that the relief sought by the claimant would be futile unless at this stage the claimant can identify specific offences that would necessarily be committed by giving effect to a policy or practice of sharing locational intelligence for use in drone strikes.

The Serious Crime Act 2007

10. The claimant's primary case is based on the proposition that a GCHQ officer who passes locational intelligence may commit an offence under sections 44 to 46 of the 2007 Act. Before I explain the argument, I need to refer to the relevant provisions of the Act.

11. Part 2 of the 2007 Act is entitled "Encouraging or Assisting Crime". Section 44 concerns "intentionally encouraging or assisting an offence"; section 45 "encouraging or assisting an offence believing it will be committed"; and section 46 "encouraging or assisting offences believing one or more will be committed". These provisions, which are

by no means straightforward, define the relevant *actus reus* and *mens rea* of the respective offences. Section 50 provides that a person is not guilty of an offence under Part 2 if he acts reasonably.

12. Section 52 provides:

(1) If a person (D) knows or believes that what he anticipates might take place wholly or partly in England or Wales, he may be guilty of an offence under section 44, 45 or 46 no matter where he was at any relevant time.

(2) If it is not proved that D knows or believes that what he anticipates might take place wholly or partly in England or Wales, he is not guilty of an offence under section 44, 45 or 46 unless paragraph 1, 2 or 3 of Schedule 4 applies.

Only subsection (2) is applicable here. Accordingly, the relevant provisions of Schedule 4 need to be considered.

13. So far as material, Schedule 4 provides:

1(1) This paragraph applies if—

(a) any relevant behaviour of D's takes place wholly or partly in England and Wales;
(b) D knows or believes that what he anticipates might take place wholly or partly in a place outside England and Wales; and
(c) either—

(i) the anticipated offence is one that would be triable under the law of England and Wales if it were committed in that place; or
(ii) if there are relevant conditions, it would be so triable if it were committed there by a person who satisfied the conditions.

(2) "Relevant condition" means a condition that—

(a) Determines (wholly or in part) whether an offence committed outside England and Wales is nonetheless triable under the law of England and Wales; and
(b) Relates to the citizenship, nationality or residence of the person who commits it.

2(1) This paragraph applies if—

(a) Paragraph 1 does not apply;
(b) Any relevant behaviour of D's takes place wholly or partly in England and Wales; and
(c) D knows or believes that what he anticipates might take place wholly or partly in a place outside England and Wales; and
(d) What D anticipates would amount to an offence under the law in force in that place.

The claimant's primary case

14. The following is a summary of Mr Chamberlain's submissions. A UK national who with the requisite intent kills a person outside England and Wales is guilty of murder in English domestic law unless he can rely on a defence available in English law and he may be tried here for the offence: see section 9 of the Offences Against the Person Act 1861. A UK national who kills a person in Pakistan by means of a drone strike is likely to be guilty of murder unless he can rely on the defence of combatant immunity. The defence of combatant immunity is derived from international law, but is recognised by English national law: see *R* v. *Gul (Mohammed)* [2012] EWCA Crim 280, [2012] Cr App R 37 para. 30.

15. It is clear that, on a plain reading of para. 1 of Schedule 4 to the 2007 Act, there are two alternative circumstances in which an offence of encouraging or assisting an act committed in a place wholly or partly outside England and Wales can be committed. These are either (i) that the anticipated offence is one that would be triable under the law of England and Wales if it were committed outside England and Wales, or (ii) if there are relevant conditions, it would be so triable if it were committed outside England and Wales by a person who satisfies the relevant conditions. The "relevant condition" is one which "relates to the citizenship, nationality or residence of the person who commits it". Mr Chamberlain submits, therefore, that it is not necessary for the English court to find that the notional "principal" has committed an offence triable in England and Wales. Rather, the question is whether any conduct which the UK national is assisting *would* be within the jurisdiction of the English court *if* the notional principal were a UK national. This construction is supported by the authors of *Simester and Sullivan's Criminal Law* (5th ed. 2013) at p. 368. The Secretary of State does not accept this construction, but he accepts that it is arguable. Mr Andrew Edis QC submits that the mere use of conditional language is insufficient to show that Parliament intended to depart from the general common law position that secondary liability can only arise in respect of an offence committed abroad if that offence is triable in England and Wales.

16. I find Mr Chamberlain's submissions persuasive, but I do not find it necessary to express a concluded view about them. He submits, on the basis of his construction, that the claimant's case does not require a finding that any official of the United States has committed an offence falling within the jurisdiction of the English court.

17. Mr Chamberlain advances a number of reasons why it is unlikely that a defence of combatant immunity would succeed in English law if it were advanced by a UK national who was charged as a principal with the offence of murder by drone strike (no other defence has been suggested as a realistic possibility). He submits that the defence would not be available for several reasons. First, CIA officials are not members of the US armed forces and GCHQ officials are not members of the UK's armed forces. They cannot, therefore, be combatants. Secondly, it has never been suggested that there is an armed conflict with Pakistan. In so far as it is suggested that there is an armed conflict with Al-Qaeda taking place in Afghanistan and elsewhere, that is wrong because (a) Al-Qaeda is not a sufficiently coherent grouping to be capable of being a party to an armed conflict; and (b) the acts of violence with which Al-Qaeda is associated are too sporadic to reach the threshold of violence required to establish the existence of an armed conflict. Thirdly, if there is an armed conflict in Pakistan between the US and those who are targeted by the drone strikes, it is of a non-international nature.

18. The US view is that the engagement with Al-Qaeda is an armed conflict and that the defence of combatant immunity is in principle available to US officers who execute drone strikes in Pakistan. That view would not, of course, be binding on our courts.

19. For reasons that will become apparent, I do not find it necessary to examine these arguments further. I accept that it is certainly not clear that the defence of combatant immunity would be available to a UK national who was tried in England and Wales with the offence of murder by drone strike.

20. To summarise, Mr Chamberlain submits that the practice and policy of the Secretary of State gives rise to a risk that GCHQ officials who provide locational intelligence to the US are committing offences contrary to sections 44 to 46 of the 2007 Act. He accepts that in any individual case an official would not be guilty of an offence unless he had the requisite *mens rea*. He also accepts that in any individual case the section 50 defence of reasonableness might be available. But he says that these issues which are likely to arise in individual cases are not material for present purposes because this claim concerns the lawfulness of the policy and not the guilt of individual officials in particular cases. Mr Chamberlain's fundamental point is that this case is not concerned with the lawfulness of drone strikes under US law.

21. That is the background against which the issues of justiciability and discretion fall to be considered.

Justiciability and discretion

22. In his witness statement Mr Morrison explains why in his opinion if the court were to grant permission to the claimant to apply for judicial review, "the likely consequence would be serious harm to the national security and the international relations of the United Kingdom". He says that the UK's bilateral relationships with the US and Pakistan are critical to the UK's national security as they are both key partners in efforts to combat the very real threat of terrorism faced by the citizens of all three countries. A key feature of international relations is that law, politics and diplomacy are bound together and the assertion of legal arguments by a state is often regarded as a political act. The UK's international alliances could be damaged by the assertion of arguments under international law which might affect the position of those states. This is particularly so since this case raises difficult legal issues "such as the scope of a state's right under international law to use force in self-defence against non-state actors, which are the subject of intense international legal scrutiny and debate". The risk of damage would be compounded

by the fact that the Court itself, would necessarily have to make a series of determinations regarding the conduct of the Governments of third States (both the United States and Pakistan). In particular, the Court would have to reach conclusions as to whether the conduct of the United States, and members of the US Administration, amounted to serious violations of international law and criminal law.

23. He also says:

Whatever the findings of the Court, an intervention by a judicial body into this complex and sensitive area of bilateral relations is liable to complicate the UK's bilateral relations with both the US and Pakistan, and there is a clear risk of damage to essential UK interests.

And:

There is a strong risk that any finding or assumptions by a UK court in this case would cause the US to revisit and perhaps substantially modify the historic intelligence sharing relationship and national security cooperation.

24. Mr James Eadie QC, in a careful and cogent series of submissions, argues that, even if Mr Chamberlain's construction of the 2007 Act is correct, there are powerful reasons why the court should refuse permission in this case. He says that the court should refuse to grant permission as a matter of discretion. But he also says that

permission should be refused on the ground that the claim is not justiciable.

25. I shall start with the question of justiciability. It is common ground that our court will not decide whether the drone strikes committed by US officials are lawful. Moses LJ stated the principle correctly in his judgment:

> 14. It is necessary to explain why the courts would not even consider, let alone resolve, the question of the legality of United States' drone strikes. The principle was expressed by Fuller CJ in the United States Supreme Court in *Underhill* v. *Hernandez* (1897) 168 US 25, 252:
>
>> Every sovereign state is bound to respect the independence of every other sovereign state, and the courts of one country will not sit in judgment on the acts of the government of another done within its own territory. Redress of grievances by reason of such acts must be obtained through the means open to be availed of by sovereign powers as between themselves (cited with approval in *Buttes Gas and Oil Co.* v. *Hammer (No 3)* [1982] AC 888, 933, and *R* v. *Jones (Margaret)* [2007] 1 AC 136, 163).
>
> 15. The principle that the courts will not sit in judgment on the sovereign acts of a foreign state includes a prohibition against adjudication upon the "legality, validity or acceptability of such acts, either under domestic law or international law" (*Kuwait Airways Corporation* v. *Iraqi Airways Co. (Nos 4 and 5)* [2002] 2 WLR 1353, 1362). The rationale for this principle is, in part, founded upon the proposition that the attitude and approach of one country to the acts and conduct of another is a matter of high policy, crucially connected to the conduct of the relations between the two sovereign powers. To examine and sit in judgment on the conduct of another state would imperil relations between the states (*Buttes Gas* 933).

26. In *Yukos Capital Sarl* v. *OJSC Rosneft Oil Co. (No 2)* [2012] EWCA Civ 855, [2013] 3 WLR 1329, the Court of Appeal considered many of the authorities in this area of the law. Neither party has sought to question the court's analysis of the case-law. There is scope for argument as to whether the courts have no jurisdiction to sit in judgment on the acts of the government of another country (i.e. cannot do so); or whether they *will* not do so because those acts are not justiciable. But in my view such distinctions are of no practical relevance here. I note that in *Buttes Gas* at p. 931F-G, Lord Wilberforce said:

> So I think that the essential question is whether, apart from such particular rules as I have discussed ... there exists in English law a more general principle that the courts will not adjudicate upon the transactions of foreign sovereign

states. Though I would prefer to avoid argument on terminology, it seems desirable to consider this principle, if existing, not as a variety of "act of state" but one for judicial restraint or abstention.

27. The rationale for the rule has been variously expressed. In *Oetjen* v. *Central Leather Co.* (1918) 246 US 297, 303-4, in a passage cited by Rix LJ in *Yukos*, Clarke J said:

The principle that the conduct of one independent government cannot be successfully questioned in the courts of another ... rests at last upon the highest considerations of international comity and expediency. To permit the validity of the acts of one sovereign state to be re-examined and perhaps condemned by the courts of another would very certainly "imperil the amicable relations between governments and vex the peace of nations".

28. None of this is in dispute in the present case. The principle is one which applies save in exceptional circumstances. One such exception is that it will not apply to foreign acts of state which are in breach of clearly established rules of international law or are contrary to English principles of public policy, as well as where there is a grave infringement of human rights.

29. But the court will also usually not sit in judgment on the acts of a sovereign state as a matter of discretion. In *R (Campaign for Nuclear Disarmament)* v. *Prime Minister of the United Kingdom* [2002] EWHC 2777 (Admin), 126 ILR 727, CND sought permission to apply for judicial review, seeking a declaration that it would be unlawful under international law for the United Kingdom to resort to force against Iraq without a fresh United Nations Security Council resolution authorising military action. The application was dismissed by the Divisional Court. The reasons for the decision included that the court would not embark on the determination of an issue which would be damaging to the public interest in the field of international relations, national security or defence. Simon Brown LJ said at para. 47(ii):

Whether as a matter of juridical theory such judicial abstinence is properly to be regarded as a matter of discretion or a matter of jurisdiction seems to me for present purposes immaterial. Either way, I regard the substantive question raised by the application to be non-justiciable.

30. Maurice Kay J said at para. 50 that the "international law" ground was more appropriately categorised as going to jurisdiction than justiciability. He did not consider that the reason why the application must fail was because of an exercise of judicial discretion. Richards J said at paras. 55 to 58 that he was satisfied that the claim should be rejected on discretionary grounds. Far from justifying the exceptional

exercise of the court's jurisdiction to grant an advisory declaration, the circumstances made such a course inappropriate and contrary to the public interest. But he also went on at paras. 59 to 61 to reject the claim on the ground that it was not justiciable. He reached that conclusion essentially for the same reasons as he had decided to reject the claim as a matter of discretion.

31. Moses LJ said at para. 20 of his judgment in the present case that it did not matter whether the questions which go to the issue whether the court should hear the application for judicial review were to be regarded as questions of principle or questions of discretion. I agree.

32. How do these principles apply in the present case? Mr Chamberlain accepts that our courts cannot adjudicate on the question of whether a CIA official who executes a drone strike is guilty of murder or indeed any other offence. His argument is that the principles have no application here. He is not asking the court to sit in judgment on the acts of CIA officials either by declaring that they are unlawful or by condemning them in any other way. He is not inviting the court to adjudicate on the legality or acceptability of the acts of the CIA officials either under our domestic law or under international law. He seeks relief on the basis that the acts of the CIA officials, *if committed by UK nationals*, would be unlawful in English law. The assumption that the operation of drone bombs by US nationals is treated as if executed by UK nationals is a necessary link in a chain of reasoning which comprises (i) a finding that the act of the principal who operates the bombs is murder in English law; (ii) a GCHQ employee who encourages or assists such an act is liable as a secondary party to murder under sections 44 to 46 of the 2007 Act; and (iii) the Secretary of State's practice and policy of providing locational guidance is unlawful.

33. In short, Mr Chamberlain says that what the court would have to determine in order to grant the primary relief he seeks is (i) the correct construction of the 2007 Act (a question of domestic statutory interpretation) and (ii) whether there is an armed conflict in Pakistan of a kind which gives rise to combatant immunity under international law and whether officials of GCHQ or the CIA are properly described as lawful combatants in such an armed conflict in English law.

34. Moses LJ explained why the court could or would not grant relief in this case in the following forthright terms:

55. There is still less any incentive to consider a declaration when it is appreciated what it entails. Mr Chamberlain's proposition, even if it is right, that a person may be guilty of secondary liability for murder under ss. 44-6,

although the principal could not, is no answer to the fundamental objection to the grant of a declaration: that it involves, and would be regarded "around the world" (see Simon Brown LJ in *CND* [37]) as "an exorbitant arrogation of adjudicative power" in relation to the legality and acceptability of the acts of another sovereign power. It is beyond question that any consideration as to whether a GCHQ employee is guilty of a crime under Part 2 of the Serious Crime Act 2007, headed "Encouraging or Assisting Crime", would be regarded by those who were said to have been encouraged or assisted as an accusation against them of criminal activity and, in the instant case, an accusation of murder. After all, that is the very nature of Mr Noor Khan's accusation in Pakistan. No amount of learned and complex analysis of the interstices of domestic criminal legislation would or could diminish that impression. For the reasons given by Mr Morrison and Simon Brown LJ in *CND*, that consequence is inevitable. Even if the argument focused on the status of the attacks in North Waziristan (international armed conflict, armed conflict not of an international nature, pre-emptive self-defence) for the purposes of considering whether the United Kingdom employee might have a defence of combatant immunity, it would give the impression that this court was presuming to judge the activities of the United States.

56. But, in any event, I reject the suggestion that the argument can be confined to an academic discussion as to the status of the conflict in North Waziristan. The topsy-turvy nature of the declaration sought merely provokes the question: of what crime is it said the GCHQ employee may be guilty? Since it is said to be a crime of secondary liability that inquiry leads, inexorably, to questions as to the criminal activity of the principals, employees of the United States. What is the crime, which GCHQ employees may be accused of assisting or encouraging?

57. These difficulties are, to my mind, insuperable. The claimant cannot demonstrate that his application will avoid, during the course of the hearing and in the judgment, giving a clear impression that it is the United States' conduct in North Waziristan which is also on trial. He has not found any foothold other than on the most precarious ground in domestic law . . .

35. I agree with these paragraphs. It is true that, if Mr Chamberlain's construction of section 52 and Schedule 4 of the 2007 Act is correct, the court will not be asked to make any finding that CIA officials are committing murder or acting unlawfully in some other way. Nor will the court be asked to say whether the US policy of drone bombing is unlawful as a matter of US law. As a matter of strict legal analysis, the court will be concerned with the hypothetical question of whether, subject to the defences available in English law, a UK national who kills a person in a drone strike in Pakistan is guilty of murder. The court is required to ask this hypothetical question because, if Mr Chamberlain is right, that is what the 2007 Act requires in order to

give our courts jurisdiction to try persons who satisfy the "relevant conditions" set out in para. 1 of Schedule 4.

36. But none of this can disguise the fact that in reality the court will be asked to condemn the acts of the persons who operate the drone bombs. Whilst for the purposes of the 2007 Act these persons are to be treated as if they are UK nationals, everyone knows that this is a legal fiction devised by Parliament in order to found secondary liability under sections 44 to 46. In reality, the persons who operate the drones are CIA officials and in doing so they are implementing the policy of the US Government. Mr Chamberlain says that the fact that a foreign state may misinterpret English domestic law and, as a result, feel that it is being accused of something that it is not being accused of, is no reason for the English court to refuse to decide the issue. He argues that the court could and, it is to be assumed, would make it clear in its judgment that a finding of breach of sections 44 to 46 of the 2007 Act did not involve a finding that the assisted party had committed an offence under English law. The fact that the judgment of the English court may be misunderstood by persons in a foreign state is not a good reason to refuse permission to apply for judicial review.

37. In my view, a finding by our court that the notional UK operator of a drone bomb which caused a death was guilty of murder would inevitably be understood (and rightly understood) by the US as a condemnation of the US. In reality, it would be understood as a finding that (i) the US official who operated the drone was guilty of murder and (ii) the US policy of using drone bombs in Pakistan and other countries was unlawful. The fact that our courts have no jurisdiction to make findings on either of these issues is beside the point. What matters is that the findings would be understood by the US authorities as critical of them. Although the findings would have no legal effect, they would be seen as a serious condemnation of the US by a court of this country.

38. I would reach this conclusion without the benefit of the evidence of Mr Morrison. His evidence fortifies my conclusion. I say this despite the fact that he did not focus precisely on the effect of Mr Chamberlain's argument that the court would not be making a finding about US officials or their guilt of criminal offences in US law. In my view, it is clear from the tenor of his statement that his opinion would not have been different if [he] had focused on that particular point.

39. Before I leave this topic, I need to refer to *Rahmatullah* v. *Secretary of State for Defence* [2012] UKSC 48, [2013] 1 AC 614. This is an authority on which Mr Chamberlain places considerable reliance. The applicant in that case was captured by British forces in Iraq and

handed over to US forces who detained him at a US airbase in Afghanistan. A memorandum of understanding between the Governments of the UK and the US provided that any prisoner of war transferred by one power to the other would be returned on request. The applicant sought a writ of habeas corpus directed to the Secretary of State on the grounds that his detention was unlawful and that, although he was detained by the US, the Secretary of State enjoyed a sufficient degree of control over him to bring about his release.

40. One of the arguments deployed in opposing the application was that the issuing of a writ of habeas corpus would amount to an impermissible interference within the forbidden territory of the executive's foreign relations since it would involve the court sitting in judgment on the acts of the US. Part of the argument was that the detention by the US was unlawful since it was in breach of international Conventions (the Geneva Conventions).

41. The Supreme Court held that the writ should issue. The basis of the decision was that the UK had control of the custody of the applicant. The detention of the applicant was, at least, prima facie unlawful as being in breach of the Geneva Conventions (paras. 36, 40 and 53). At para. 53 of his judgment, Lord Kerr said:

This court is not asked to "sit in judgment on the acts of the government of another, done within its own territory" as in *Underhill* v. *Hernandez* (1897) 168 US 250, 252. The illegality in this case centres on the UK's obligations under the Geneva Conventions. It does not require the court to examine whether the US is in breach of its international obligations ... Here there was evidence available to the UK that Mr Rahmatullah's detention was in apparent violation of GC4. The illegality rests not on whether the US was in breach of GC4, but on the proposition that, conscious of those apparent violations, the UK was bound to take the steps required by article 45 of GC4.

42. At para. 70, he repeated that the legality of the US's detention of the applicant was not under scrutiny. Rather, it was the lawfulness of the UK's inaction in seeking his return that was in issue.

43. Mr Chamberlain submits that the Supreme Court had little hesitation in enquiring into the legality of the applicant's detention by the US Government. However, the court was careful to say that, on the facts of that case, it was not being asked to sit in judgment on the acts of the US. There was clear prima facie evidence that the applicant was being unlawfully detained. But that conclusion depended on the effect of the Geneva Conventions, not on an examination of the legal basis on which the US might claim to justify the detention: see para. 53. The court applied well-established principles to an unusual situation. I do

not consider that this decision tells us anything as to how these principles should be applied in the very different circumstances that arise in the present case.

44. I would, therefore, refuse permission to appeal in relation to the claimant's primary case for the reasons given by Moses LJ at paras. 55 to 57 of his judgment: see para. 35 above: an application for judicial review would have no real prospects of success.

45. Mr Eadie submits that the court should in any event not grant a declaration in this case because this is not one of those very exceptional cases where a civil court will grant a declaration as to the criminality of conduct: see *R (Rusbridger)* v. *Attorney General* [2004] 1 AC 357 approving the observation by Viscount Dilhorne in *Imperial Tobacco Ltd* v. *Attorney General* [1981] AC 718 at p. 742C-D: the facts should be determined in, and in accordance with the procedures of, criminal proceedings. Mr Eadie submits in particular that the question whether the notional UK national who kills a person in a drone strike in Pakistan is entitled to rely on the defence of combatant immunity is fact-sensitive; and this feature of the case is "a factor of great importance" (per Lord Steyn in *Rusbridger* at para. 23) which alone is sufficient to take it outside the exceptional category.

46. In view of my conclusion on the non-justiciability/discretion issues which I have discussed above, it is unnecessary for me to express a concluded view on this issue (and others that were debated before us).

The claimant's secondary case

47. The secondary case is that, even if the applicable law was international humanitarian law (and not ordinary domestic criminal law), there is good (publicly available) evidence that drone strikes in Pakistan are being carried out in violation of international humanitarian law, because the individuals who are being targeted are not directly participating in hostilities and/or because the force used is neither necessary nor proportionate. Accordingly, even if they are not liable under sections 44 to 46 of the 2007 Act, there is a significant risk that GCHQ officers may be guilty of conduct ancillary to crimes against humanity and/or war crimes, both of which are statutory offences under section 52 of the International Criminal Court Act 2001 ("the 2001 Act"). In these circumstances, Mr Chamberlain submits that, before directing or authorising the passing of intelligence relating to the location of a targeted individual to an agent of the US Government, the Secretary of State should formulate, publish and apply a lawful policy

setting out the circumstances in which such intelligence may be lawfully transferred, which he has failed to do.

48. It can therefore be seen that an essential building block in the secondary claim for a declaration that the Secretary of State should formulate, publish and apply a lawful policy is that GCHQ officers may be committing offences under section 52 of the 2001 Act.

49. The elements of crimes against humanity and war crimes are identified in the 2001 Act as supplemented by the *International Criminal Court Act 2001 (Elements of Crimes) (No 2) Regulations 2004/3239*. Paras. 7(1)(a) and (b) of Article 7 of the Schedule to the Regulations specify the elements of the crime against humanity by murder or extermination: the attack must be part of a widespread or systematic attack against a civilian population or of a mass killing of members of a civilian population, and the perpetrator must know it. Paras. 8(2)(c)(i) and 8(2)(e)(i) of Article 8 of the Schedule specify the elements of war crimes: the attack must be against a person not taking a direct part in hostilities and the perpetrator must intend that this is so.

50. As Mr Edis says, there is some uncertainty as to the mental element required of a person being prosecuted for conduct which is "ancillary" to a war crime or a crime against humanity. I shall assume that, in order to render unlawful any conduct by a notional GCHQ official, he or she must know and intend that the recipient will use the information in order to commit an act which is part of a widespread or systematic attack against, or a mass killing of, a civilian population and/or to attack civilians who are not taking a direct part in hostilities in an ongoing armed conflict.

51. Whatever the precise mental element required for the offence under section 52 of the 2001 Act may be, I am satisfied that the secondary claim in this case founders on the same rock as the primary claim. The claimant is inviting the court to make a finding condemning the person who makes the drone strike as guilty of committing a crime against humanity and/or a war crime. Since that person is a CIA official implementing US policy, such a finding would involve our courts sitting in judgment of the US.

52. For these reasons, I would not grant permission to appeal in respect of the secondary case either.

Overall conclusion

53. In the end, despite the attractive way in which Mr Chamberlain has presented his argument, I consider that both the primary and secondary claims are fundamentally flawed for the same reason. There

is no escape from the conclusion that, however the claims are presented, they involve serious criticisms of the acts of a foreign state. It is only in certain established circumstances that our courts will exceptionally sit in judgment of such acts. There are no such exceptional circumstances here. I would refuse permission to appeal.

54. Although this is a refusal of permission to appeal, the judgment may be cited as a precedent.

[Report: [2014] 1 WLR 872]

Human rights — Right to liberty and security — Individuals detained by British troops in Iraq — British troops part of Multinational Force under United Nations Security Council Resolutions — Whether rights of individuals under European Convention on Human Rights, 1950 breached — Whether obligations under United Nations Security Council Resolutions overriding rights under European Convention — United Nations Charter, 1945, Article 103 — Human Rights Act 1998

Relationship of international law and municipal law — Treaties — United Nations Charter, 1945, Article 103 — European Convention on Human Rights, 1950, Article 5 — United Nations Security Council Resolution 1483 — United Nations Security Council Resolution 1511 — Coalition Provisional Authority — Coalition Provisional Authority Regulation 1 — Legal effect of Security Council Resolutions — Whether defendant having duty to detain individuals for security reasons — Whether any duty overriding defendant's obligations under Article 5 of European Convention — Human Rights Act 1998, Schedule 1

War and armed conflict — Occupation — Iraq — Detention of Iraqi civilians during occupation — Whether unlawful — Whether contrary to Article 5 of European Convention on Human Rights, 1950 — Whether duty to detain Iraqi civilians under United Nations Security Council Resolutions — Whether duty overriding obligation under Article 5 of European Convention

Claims — Jurisdiction — Law of the forum — Whether governing assessment of damages — Procedural and substantive law — State responsibility — Occupation of Iraq — Unlawful detention — Ill-treatment — Claims in tort — Human rights — Damages — Aggravated damages — Private International Law (Miscellaneous Provisions) Act 1995 — The law of England

IRAQI CIVILIANS v. MINISTRY OF DEFENCE[1]

([2014] EWHC 3686 (QB))[2]

---

[1] The claimants were represented by Richard Hermer QC, Maria Roche and Andrew Scott, instructed by Leigh Day. The defendant was represented by Derek Sweeting QC and James Purnell, instructed by the Treasury Solicitor.

[2] On 12 May 2016, the Supreme Court ([2016] UKSC 25) held that the Iraqi civilians' claims were time-barred.

England, High Court, Queen's Bench Division. 7 *November* 2014

(Leggatt J)

SUMMARY:[3] *The facts*:—The claimants, Iraqi civilians, sought damages from the defendant, the Ministry of Defence, for alleged unlawful detention and ill-treatment by British Armed Forces on various dates while those forces were present in Iraq. From 1 May 2003 to 28 June 2004, the Coalition forces, including the United States and United Kingdom, were occupying powers in Iraq. In this capacity, they established the Coalition Provisional Authority ("CPA"), issuing CPA Regulation 1 on 16 May 2003, which provided that the CPA assumed all executive, legislative and judicial authority necessary to achieve its objectives, to be exercised under relevant United Nations Security Council Resolutions and the laws of war. Resolution 1483, adopted on 22 May 2003, called upon the CPA to work towards the restoration of security and stability in Iraq. Resolution 1511, adopted on 16 October 2003, reaffirmed Iraq's sovereignty and territorial integrity and underscored the CPA's temporary authority and responsibilities, including under Resolution 1483.

The claimants' claims were made on two legal bases: first, the law of tort (in relation to which Iraqi law was applicable); and second, the Human Rights Act 1998 ("the 1998 Act") and, in particular, Articles 3[4] and 5[5] of the

---

[3] Prepared by Ms E. Fogarty.
[4] Article 3 of the European Convention provided: "*Prohibition of torture*: No one shall be subjected to torture or to inhuman or degrading treatment or punishment."
[5] Article 5 of the European Convention provided: "*Right to liberty and security*: (1) Everyone has the right to liberty and security of person. No one shall be deprived of his liberty save in the following cases and in accordance with a procedure prescribed by law: (a) the lawful detention of a person after conviction by a competent court; (b) the lawful arrest or detention of a person for noncompliance with the lawful order of a court or in order to secure the fulfilment of any obligation prescribed by law; (c) the lawful arrest or detention of a person effected for the purpose of bringing him before the competent legal authority on reasonable suspicion of having committed an offence or when it is reasonably considered necessary to prevent his committing an offence or fleeing after having done so; (d) the detention of a minor by lawful order for the purpose of educational supervision or his lawful detention for the purpose of bringing him before the competent legal authority; (e) the lawful detention of persons for the prevention of the spreading of infectious diseases, of persons of unsound mind, alcoholics or drug addicts or vagrants; (f) the lawful arrest or detention of a person to prevent his effecting an unauthorised entry into the country or of a person against whom action is being taken with a view to deportation or extradition. (2) Everyone who is arrested shall be informed promptly, in a language which he understands, of the reasons for his arrest and of any charge against him. (3) Everyone arrested or detained in accordance with the provisions of paragraph 1(c) of this Article shall be brought promptly before a judge or other officer authorised by law to exercise judicial power and shall be entitled to trial within a reasonable time or to release pending trial. Release may be conditioned by guarantees to appear for trial. (4) Everyone who is deprived of his liberty by arrest or detention shall be entitled to take proceedings by which the lawfulness of his detention shall be decided speedily by a court and his release ordered if the detention is not lawful. (5) Everyone who has been the victim of arrest or detention in contravention of the provisions of this Article shall have an enforceable right to compensation."

European Convention on Human Rights, 1950 ("the European Convention"), incorporated into the 1998 Act under Schedule 1. The claimants asserted that they had been unlawfully detained during the occupation, contrary to Article 5 of the European Convention. The defendant submitted that the detention was lawful pursuant to Resolutions 1483 and 1511.

Held:—(1) The defendant was under a duty under Resolutions 1483 and 1511 to detain individuals where considered necessary for imperative reasons of security, but that obligation did not override its obligations under Article 5 of the European Convention.

(a) The term "duty" had to be understood in the same sense as "obligation" in Article 103 of the UN Charter (para. 23).

(b) Resolution 1483 imposed a duty on the UK as an occupying power to detain individuals where necessary for imperative reasons of security. That reflected the duty of occupying powers to restore public order and safety as far as possible, as captured in the 1907 Hague Regulations and the Fourth Geneva Convention, 1949, which were specifically referenced in para. 5 of Resolution 1483. Resolution 1483 did not, however, require the UK to discharge those obligations in a manner inconsistent with its obligations under the European Convention. Neither did it suggest that the Hague Regulations and the Geneva Convention had primacy over any other international obligations. Para. 5 of Resolution 1483 required the UK, as far as possible, to comply with both its obligations under international humanitarian law and its other obligations, including under the European Convention. There was no inconsistency between detaining an individual considered to be a threat to security and applying the procedural safeguards in relation to such detention under Article 5 of the European Convention, which the European Court of Human Rights had held in *Hassan*[6] continued to apply in situations of armed conflict. There was no potential conflict of obligations requiring Article 103 of the UN Charter for resolution (paras. 24-9).

(c) Like Resolution 1483, Resolution 1511 imposed a duty on the occupying powers to detain individuals where necessary for imperative reasons of security. However, nothing in its language required it to be interpreted to authorize taking such a measure in so far as doing so would violate the UK's obligations under the European Convention (paras. 30-1).

(2) Whether mental distress caused by the defendant in the commission of a tort was a type of injury for which the defendant could be held liable was a question of substance governed by Iraqi law. If it was, assessing damages payable was a matter of procedure governed by English law.

(a) The relevant distinction between matters of procedure and substance was contained in Part III of the Private International Law (Miscellaneous) Provisions Act 1995, which established the applicable law for determining

---

[6] *Hassan* v. *United Kingdom*, 161 ILR 524.

issues arising in tort claims. Questions of procedure were governed by the law of the forum, while questions of substance were governed by the law of Iraq as the law of the place where the alleged tort was committed. In applying the distinction to actions in torts, consideration had to be given to: (i) whether there was an actionable injury for which the defendant was liable (a question of substance); and (ii) whether the claimant could be awarded damages or restitution for that wrong (a question of procedure) (paras. 33-5).

(b) With respect to "aggravated damages", that term was to be understood as denoting damages that were purely compensatory in purpose and which were awarded for a tort as compensation for mental distress caused by the defendant. The law governing the availability of aggravated damages was to be determined by: (i) whether the mental distress caused by the defendant was an actionable injury (a question of substance governed by the applicable law); and (ii) if such a liability existed under Iraqi law, whether English law, as the law of the forum, provided a suitable remedy (a procedural question). The second question was plainly to be answered in the affirmative. English law provided the remedy of damages, which had to be assessed as in a case involving liability under English law (paras. 37-9).

The following is the text of the judgment of the Court:

INTRODUCTION

1. Over 600 cases are currently pending in the High Court in which Iraqi civilians are claiming damages from the Ministry of Defence ("MOD") for their allegedly unlawful detention and alleged ill-treatment by British armed forces on various dates during the period when British forces were present in Iraq. The claims are made on two legal bases. The first is the law of tort. It is common ground that, pursuant to Part III of the Private International Law (Miscellaneous Provisions) Act 1995, the applicable law which is to be used for determining the issues arising in these claims is the law of Iraq. The second legal basis is the Human Rights Act 1998. The claimants allege violations of articles 3 and 5 of the European Convention on Human Rights (the "Convention") incorporated in Schedule 1 to the 1998 Act.

2. By an order dated 5 March 2014 (as varied on 24 June 2014), the court gave directions for a trial of preliminary issues in this litigation. Most of the issues were aimed at identifying the applicable period of limitation and whether the proceedings were begun before that period expired. These limitation issues affect almost all the claims. The limitation issues raise questions of Iraqi law which are the subject of expert

evidence. Regrettably, the claimants' expert witness, Mr Saleh Majid, has been ill and has also been affected by his wife's recent serious ill health. About two weeks before the hearing, it became clear that Mr Majid would not be able to give evidence and that, as there was insufficient time before the hearing for another expert to be instructed in his place, the trial of the limitation issues would have to be adjourned. I granted the claimants' application for an adjournment on 15 October 2014 and have since given directions for a new trial which will also encompass additional issues.

THE REMAINING ISSUES

3. This has left only two preliminary issues which can be decided now. These issues, which are raised in relation to a number of specified test cases, concern:

(a) the legal effect of two UN Security Council Resolutions (1483 and 1511); and
(b) whether the availability of aggravated damages is governed by Iraqi or English law.

4. These issues have been succinctly argued by counsel.

Issue 1: the effect of UNSCR 1483 and 1511

5. The first issue is:

Where detention occurred following the entry into force of UNSCR 1483 on 22 May 2003 and/or UNSCR 1511 on 16 October 2003:

(a) Was the defendant under a duty pursuant to those resolutions to detain individuals where necessary for imperative reasons of security?
(b) If so, did that duty override the defendant's obligations under Article 5, ECHR?

The resolutions

6. The two UN Security Council Resolutions in question were promulgated during the period when the UK was an occupying power in Iraq. The war-fighting phase of the conflict began on 20 March 2003, when a coalition of armed forces led by the United States and including a large force from the UK invaded Iraq. Major combat operations were formally declared complete on 1 May 2003. It is

common ground that from that date until 28 June 2004 the US and the UK were occupying powers within the meaning of article 42 of the Hague Regulations 1907.

7. On 8 May 2003 the Permanent Representatives of the UK and the US at the United Nations addressed a joint letter to the President of the Security Council. The letter explained that the US, the UK and their coalition partners had created the Coalition Provisional Authority ("CPA") in order to "exercise powers of government temporarily and, as necessary, especially to provide security, to allow the delivery of humanitarian aid, and to eliminate weapons of mass destruction". On 16 May 2003 the CPA issued CPA Regulation No 1 whereby the CPA assumed:

all executive, legislative and judicial authority necessary to achieve its objectives, to be exercised under relevant UN Security Council Resolutions, including Resolution 1483 (2003), and the laws and usages of war.

8. UNSCR 1483 was adopted by the Security Council on 22 May 2003. Amongst other recitals, the resolution noted the letter of 8 May 2003 from the Permanent Representatives of the US and the UK "recognising the specific authorities, responsibilities and obligations under applicable international law of the states as occupying powers under unified command (the 'Authority')". At paragraph 4, the resolution called upon the Authority:

consistent with the Charter of the United Nations and other relevant international law to promote the welfare of the Iraqi people through the effective administration of the territory, including in particular working towards the restoration of conditions of security and stability and the creation of conditions in which the Iraqi people can freely determine their own political future;

At paragraph 5, the resolution further called upon "all concerned to comply fully with their obligations under international law including in particular the Geneva Conventions of 1949 and the Hague Regulations of 1907".

9. UNSCR 1511 was adopted by the Security Council on 16 October 2003. It reaffirmed previous resolutions on Iraq, including UNSCR 1483, and (in paragraph 1) reaffirmed the sovereignty and territorial integrity of Iraq, underscoring in that context:

the temporary nature of the exercise by the [CPA] of the specific responsibilities, authorities and obligations under applicable international law recognised and set forth in Resolution 1483 (2003), which will cease when an internationally recognised, representative government established by the people of Iraq is sworn in and assumes the responsibilities of the [CPA] ...

The resolution set out steps to be taken to achieve this goal and (at paragraph 13) authorised a multinational force ("MNF") under unified command "to take all necessary measures to contribute to the maintenance of security and stability in Iraq . . .".

10. Thereafter steps were taken to prepare for the transfer of sovereignty from the CPA to an interim Iraqi government. In anticipation of this transfer of authority, the Security Council on 8 June 2004 adopted Resolution 1546.

UNSCR 1546

11. UNSCR 1546 was preceded by two letters dated 5 June 2004 written to the President of the Security Council by, respectively, the Prime Minister of the interim government of Iraq (Dr Allawi) and the US Secretary of State (Mr Powell). The letter from Dr Allawi sought a new resolution of the Security Council to authorise the MNF to contribute to maintaining security in Iraq, "including through the tasks and arrangements set out in the letter from [Mr Powell]". The letter from Mr Powell confirmed that the MNF was prepared to continue to contribute to the maintenance of security in Iraq and stated:

Under the agreed arrangement, the MNF stands ready to continue to undertake a broad range of tasks to contribute to the maintenance of security and to ensure force protection. These include activities necessary to counter ongoing security threats posed by forces seeking to influence Iraq's political future through violence. *This will include* combat operations against members of these groups, *internment where this is necessary for imperative reasons of security*, and the continued search for and securing of weapons that threaten Iraq's security . . . [Emphasis added.]

12. UNSCR 1546, in paragraph 9, reaffirmed the authorisation for the MNF established under UNSCR 1511 and, in paragraph 10, decided that the MNF "shall have the authority to take all necessary measures to contribute to the maintenance of security and stability in Iraq in accordance with the letters annexed to this resolution". The letters annexed to the resolution were the two letters written to the President of the Security Council, referred to above.

The Al-Jedda *case: decision of the House of Lords*

13. In *Al-Jedda* v. *Secretary of State for Defence* [2008] 1 AC 332 the claimant, who had been detained by UK forces at detention facilities in Iraq since October 2004, sought judicial review of his detention on the

ground that it was contrary to article 5 of the Convention. His claim failed on the basis that his rights under article 5 were overridden by an obligation on the UK to detain him pursuant to UNSCR 1546 (and later resolutions which extended its temporal effect).

14. The defendant's argument for that conclusion was based on article 103 of the UN Charter, which states:

In the event of a conflict between the obligations of the Members of the United Nations under the present Charter and their obligations under any other international agreement, their obligations under the present Charter shall prevail.

15. In summary, the House of Lords decided as follows:

(a) UNSCR 1546 authorised detention considered to be necessary for imperative reasons of security even where such detention was contrary to article 5 of the Convention.
(b) Detention carried out pursuant to that authorisation was a matter, not just of right, but of obligation under the UN Charter.
(c) By reason of article 103 of the UN Charter, that obligation prevailed over the UK's obligation to secure rights under article 5 of the Convention.

16. The purpose of the preliminary issue in this litigation is, essentially, to determine whether the reasoning of the House of Lords in relation to UNSCR 1546 also applies to the earlier resolutions, UNSCR 1483 and UNSCR 1511.

The Al-Jedda *case: decision of the European Court*

17. After losing his case in the English courts, Mr Al-Jedda sought just satisfaction in Strasbourg. The European Court of Human Rights held that his internment had violated article 5(1) of the Convention and rejected the argument which had succeeded in the English courts that article 5 was overridden by UNSCR 1546: see *Al-Jedda* v. *United Kingdom* (2011) 35 EHRR 23. The European Court approached the case by considering the purposes for which the United Nations was created. As well as maintaining international peace and security, these purposes include under article 1 of the UN Charter "promoting and encouraging respect for human rights and fundamental freedoms". In addition, article 24(2) of the Charter requires the Security Council, in discharging its responsibility for the maintenance of international peace and security, to "act in accordance with the Purposes and Principles of

the United Nations". Against this background, the Court held (at para. 102) that, in interpreting its resolutions, there must be a presumption that the Security Council does not intend to impose any obligation on Member States to breach fundamental principles of human rights.

18. Applying this presumption, the European Court concluded (at para. 109) that neither UNSCR 1546 nor any other resolution imposed an obligation on the UK to detain an individual considered to constitute a risk to the security of Iraq indefinitely without charge. In those circumstances the Court found no conflict between the UK's obligations under the UN Charter and its obligations under article 5(1) of the Convention.

Hassan *v.* UK

19. A further, recent judgment of the European Court of Human Rights delivered on 16 September 2014 in the case of *Hassan* v. *United Kingdom* (29750/09) has important implications for the preliminary issue (and for this litigation more generally). The case concerned an Iraqi national (Tarek Hassan) who, on the facts found by the Court, was arrested by UK forces on 23 April 2003 and detained until 2 May 2003, when he was released. The Court found that during the period of his detention Mr Hassan was within the jurisdiction of the UK for the purpose of article 1 of the Convention. The Court rejected an argument that in a situation of international armed conflict article 5 of the Convention ceased to apply, but held (at paras. 102-3) that, notwithstanding the absence of any formal derogation, article 5 was to be interpreted and applied in the light of the applicable rules of international humanitarian law ("IHL").

20. Adopting this approach, the European Court held (at para. 104) that, in a situation of international armed conflict, article 5 could be interpreted as permitting the taking of prisoners of war and the detention of civilians who pose a threat to security in accordance with the Third and Fourth Geneva Conventions, although such detention does not fall within any of the cases set out in sub-paragraphs (a)-(f) of article 5(1). With regard to procedural safeguards, the Court considered that article 5(2) and (4) "must also be interpreted in a manner which takes into account the context and applicable rules of [IHL]" (para. 106). Noting that articles 43 and 78 of the Fourth Geneva Convention provide that internment "shall be subject to periodical review, if possible every six months, by a competent body", the Court said (at para. 106):

Whilst it might not be practicable, in the course of an international armed conflict, for the legality of detention to be determined by an independent "court" in the sense generally required by Article 5(4) ... nonetheless, if the Contracting State is to comply with its obligations under Article 5(4) in this context, the "competent body" should provide sufficient guarantees of impartiality and fair procedure to protect against arbitrariness. Moreover, the first review should take place shortly after the person is taken into detention, with subsequent reviews at frequent intervals, to ensure that any person who does not fall into one of the categories subject to internment under international humanitarian law is released without undue delay.

The parties' arguments

21. In answer to the questions posed in the preliminary issue, Mr Sweeting QC on behalf of the defendant submitted that the effect of UNSCR 1546, as determined by the House of Lords in the *Al-Jedda* case, was to vest in the MNF after the establishment of the Iraqi interim government the same powers and obligations with regard to maintaining security which the CPA had possessed during the occupation phase both under IHL and pursuant to UNSCRs 1483 and 1511. Those powers and obligations included, again on the authority of the House of Lords in the *Al-Jedda* case, a duty to intern individuals where necessary for imperative reasons of security which overrode the UK's obligations under article 5 of the Convention by reason of article 103 of the UN Charter. Mr Sweeting submitted that this analysis must apply equally to UNSCRs 1483 and 1511, unless and until the Supreme Court departs from the decision of the House of Lords in the *Al-Jedda* case.

22. On behalf of the claimants, Mr Hermer QC submitted that the decision of the House of Lords in the *Al-Jedda* case does not assist the defendant as it was concerned with a different Security Council Resolution, which had materially different wording. Mr Hermer submitted that there is nothing in the text of UNSCR 1483 or 1511 which imposed a duty on the defendant to intern any individuals, still less was there anything in either resolution which required detention that violated article 5.

Findings on the effect of UNSCR 1483

23. Given the nature of the defendant's argument based on the decision of the House of Lords in the *Al-Jedda* case which the preliminary issue is intended to test, the term "duty" in the phrasing of the

preliminary issue must be understood in the same sense as the term "obligation" in article 103 of the UN Charter. I have in mind, therefore, the conclusion of the House of Lords in the *Al-Jedda* case that the term "obligation" in article 103 is not to be given a narrow meaning and that article 103 applies where conduct is authorised by the Security Council as where it is required.

24. In this sense, I think it clear that UNSCR 1483 did impose a duty on the UK in its role as an occupying power in Iraq to detain individuals where to do so was considered necessary for imperative reasons of security.

25. Article 43 of the Hague Regulations 1907 provides, with reference to occupying powers:

The authority of the legitimate power having in fact passed into the hands of the occupant, the latter shall take all the measures in his power to restore, and ensure, as far as possible, public order and safety, while respecting, unless absolutely prevented, the laws in force in the country.

This provision is supplemented by provisions of the Fourth Geneva Convention. Articles 41, 42 and 78 of that Convention provide:

41. Should the power, in whose hands protected persons may be, consider the measures of control mentioned in the present Convention to be inadequate, it may not have recourse to any other measure of control more severe than that of assigned residence or internment, in accordance with the provisions of articles 42 and 43 . . .

42. The internment or placing in assigned residence of protected persons may be ordered only if the security of the detaining power makes it absolutely necessary . . .

78. If the occupying power considers it necessary, for imperative reasons of security, to take safety measures concerning protected persons, it may, at the most, subject them to assigned residence or to internment.

26. In the *Al-Jedda* case (at para. 32) Lord Bingham drew from these provisions the conclusion that "if the occupying power considers it necessary to detain a person who is judged to be a serious threat to the safety of the public or the occupying power there must be an obligation to detain such person".

27. It seems to me that, by calling in paragraph 5 of UNSCR 1483 upon "all concerned to comply fully with their obligations under international law including in particular the Geneva Convention of 1949 and the Hague Regulations of 1907", the Security Council imposed an additional layer of obligation on the obligations which were already binding on the UK under international law as an occupying power. Those obligations were now also the subject of a decision

of the Security Council which the UK, as a member of the United Nations, was obliged by article 25 of the UN Charter to accept and carry out.

28. I see nothing in paragraph 5, however, which requires the UK to discharge its obligations under the Geneva Conventions and the Hague Regulations in a way which is inconsistent with the UK's obligations under international law to abide by the European Convention on Human Rights. Although paragraph 5 mentions, in particular, the Geneva Conventions and Hague Regulations, it does not purport to give obligations under those instruments primacy over any other international law obligations. I would therefore construe paragraph 5 as requiring the UK, so far as possible, to comply with its obligations under both IHL and the Convention. There is nothing in that paragraph, or anywhere else in UNSCR 1483, which can be interpreted as authorising or requiring the UK to take steps sanctioned by the Geneva Conventions and Hague Regulations which violate obligations under the Convention (or vice versa). Nor is there anything in the decision of the House of Lords in the *Al-Jedda* case which suggests, let alone dictates, any such result.

29. Furthermore, the difficulty which previously existed of reconciling the rules of IHL applicable during an international armed conflict with article 5 of the Convention has now been dissolved by the decision of the European Court of Human Rights in *Hassan* v. *UK*. As I have mentioned, the Court has held that article 5 is not to be interpreted as preventing the detention of individuals in accordance with powers conferred by IHL on the ground that such detention is considered necessary for imperative reasons of security. There is no inconsistency between detaining an individual who is considered to be a threat to security and applying the procedural safeguards in relation to such detention which, according to the European Court in *Hassan*, article 5 still potentially requires even in a situation of international armed conflict. No inconsistency, therefore, of the kind which the House of Lords perceived in the *Al-Jedda* case in relation to the post-occupation period between the UK's obligations to secure Convention rights and an obligation to intern for imperative reasons of security can arise. In short, there is no potential conflict of obligations which article 103 of the UN Charter need be invoked to resolve.

Findings on the effect of UNSCR 1511

30. A similar analysis applies to the position under UNSCR 1511. Paragraph 13 of that resolution authorised the UK forces which became part of the MNF "to take all necessary measures to the maintenance of

security and stability in Iraq". Given the background that the UK remained an occupying power, the measures available to be taken in accordance with IHL included internment where necessary for imperative reasons of security. In these circumstances I consider that UNSCR 1511 also imposed a duty (in the relevant sense) to detain individuals where necessary for such reasons.

31. There is, however, nothing in the language of UNSCR 1511 which requires it to be interpreted as authorising the taking of such a measure in so far as doing so would violate the UK's obligation to secure rights under the Convention. For the reasons that I gave in *Serdar Mohammed* v. *MOD* [2014] EWHC 1369 (QB) at paras. 208-17, I do not consider that I am prevented from reaching this conclusion by the decision of the House of Lords in the *Al-Jedda* case on the meaning of a later, differently worded resolution; nor that I am prevented in doing so from taking into account the presumption applied by the European Court in *Al-Jedda* v. *United Kingdom* (2011) 53 EHRR 23 that, unless it uses clear and unambiguous language to the contrary, the Security Council does not intend states to take measures which conflict with their obligations under international human rights law. In any event, in the light of the judgment of the European Court in *Hassan*, there is no potential inconsistency between detaining an individual who is considered to be a threat to security and complying with article 5.

Conclusion on the first issue

32. Accordingly, my answers to the two questions raised by the first preliminary issue are as follows:

(a) Pursuant to UNSCR 1483 and UNSCR 1511, the defendant was under a duty (in the sense of an "obligation" within the meaning of article 103 of the UN Charter) to detain individuals where considered necessary for imperative reasons [of] security.
(b) However, that duty did not override the defendants' obligations under article 5 of the Convention. Rather, the UNSCRs required the duty to be performed consistently with the UK's obligations under article 5 (as those obligations applied in a situation of international armed conflict).

Issue 2: aggravated damages

33. The second preliminary issue which can be decided now is:

Whether the availability of aggravated damages is a matter of procedure governed by English law or a substantive matter governed by Iraqi law.

A further limb of this issue which asks whether, if a substantive matter, aggravated damages are available under Iraqi law cannot be decided without expert evidence.

34. The relevant distinction between matters of procedure and substance is that drawn by Part III of the Private International Law (Miscellaneous) Provisions Act 1995 which, as mentioned earlier, establishes the applicable law to be used "for determining the issues arising in a claim" in tort: see section 9(4).[1] Section 10 of the Act abolished the common law rules for choosing the applicable law, replacing them with statutory rules set out in sections 11 and 12. The 1995 Act does not, however, affect any other common law rules: see section 14(2). In particular, section 14(3)(b) makes it clear that nothing in Part III "authorises questions of procedure in any proceedings to be determined otherwise than in accordance with the law of the forum".

35. Two decisions of the highest authority establish how the distinction between questions of procedure, which are governed by the law of the forum, and questions of substance concerning "the issues arising in a claim", which are governed by the applicable law, is to be applied. In *Harding* v. *Wealands* [2007] 2 AC 1, 13, Lord Hoffmann, with whose speech the rest of the House of Lords agreed, explained the test (at para. 24) as follows:

In applying this distinction to actions in tort, the courts have distinguished between the kind of damage which constitutes an actionable injury and the assessment of compensation (i.e. damages) for the injury which has been held to be actionable. The identification of actionable damage is an integral part of the rules which determine liability. As I have previously had occasion to say, it makes no sense simply to say that someone is liable in tort. He must be liable for something and the rules which determine what he is liable for are inseparable from the rules which determine the conduct which gives rise to liability. Thus the rules which exclude damage from the scope of liability on the grounds that it does not fall within the ambit of the liability rule or does not have the prescribed causal connection with the wrongful act, or which require that the damage should have been reasonably foreseeable, are all rules which determine whether there is liability for the damage in question. On the other hand, whether the claimant is awarded money damages (and, if so, how much) or, for example, restitution in kind, is a question of remedy.

36. The test has recently been further discussed by the Supreme Court in *Cox* v. *Ergo Versicherung AG* [2014] 2 WLR 948. The question in that case was whether the availability of damages for

---

[1] In each of the test cases all the relevant events occurred before the entry into force of the Rome II Regulation on 11 January 2011.

bereavement and loss of dependency in a claim arising out of a fatal accident in Germany was governed by German law (the applicable law pursuant to the 1995 Act) or English law (as the law of the forum). Lord Sumption, with whom three of the other four members of the Court agreed, considered that the relevant German damages rules were substantive because they determined the scope of the liability. In particular, a rule which required the victim of a tort to mitigate loss was substantive because it determined "the extent of the loss for which the defendant ought fairly, reasonably or justly to be held liable" (para. 17). So too was a rule of German law which made damages available for psychological distress in certain circumstances, and made damages for bereavement as such unavailable. Lord Sumption described these rules (at para. 17) as "paradigm examples of rules governing the recoverability of particular heads of loss, the avoidance of which lies within the scope of the defendant's duty".

37. Once the scope of the liability had been determined, the only question of procedure was whether English law, as the law of the forum, provided a remedy which harmonised or was "cognate" with the liability according to its nature and extent as fixed by German law (see paras. 19 and 21). As an example of a case where English law did not afford a suitable remedy, Lord Sumption cited *Phrantzes* v. *Argenti* [1960] 2 QB 19, where Parker LCJ declined to order a father to provide the dowry to which his daughter would have been entitled under the law of Greece because English law gave the court no power to grant relief which was consistent with the daughter's right under Greek law. No such difficulty arose in the *Cox* case itself because English law provided a remedy that harmonised with the defendant's substantive liability under German law to compensate the claimant for the loss of a financial benefit, namely the remedy of damages.

38. The formulation of the preliminary issue in this case begs the question of what is meant by "aggravated damages". The term has sometimes been used to refer to a monetary award which is intended to serve a punitive or partly punitive purpose. It is common ground, however, that the reference to "aggravated damages" is to be understood as denoting damages which are purely compensatory in purpose and which are awarded for a tort as compensation for mental distress caused by the manner in which the tort has been committed, or the motive with which it was committed, or by subsequent conduct of the defendant: see *Rookes* v. *Barnard (No 1)* [1964] AC 1129, 1221, per Lord Devlin; and see the report of the Law Commission on "Aggravated, Exemplary and Restitutionary Damages" (September 1997), pp. 10-11, paras. 1.1 and 1.4.

39. In order to determine what law governs the availability of aggravated damages in this sense, applying the distinction between questions of substance and procedure as drawn in the *Harding* and *Cox* cases, it is necessary to ask two questions. The first question is whether mental distress caused by the defendant's motive or conduct in the commission of the tort is a type of injury for which the defendant can be held liable. This is a question of substance governed by the applicable law which is agreed to be the law of Iraq. The second, procedural question is whether, if such a liability exists under Iraqi law, English law as the law of the forum provides a suitable remedy which "harmonises" with the liability. The answer to this second question is plainly 'yes', since English law provides the remedy of damages which is a suitable form of compensation for such mental distress. The assessment of damages would have to be carried out in the same way as the court would assess aggravated damages in a case where liability has been established under English law.

40. By the end of the oral argument it was unclear whether there was any real difference between the parties about the correct approach. It was not in dispute that whether injury to feelings is a type of harm for which the defendant can be liable is a question of substance governed by the law of Iraq. In so far as Mr Hermer QC sought to argue, however, that English law governs the question whether such harm can be increased by the defendant's motive or conduct in committing the tort, I reject that contention as inconsistent with the decisions of the House of Lords in *Harding* and of the Supreme Court in *Cox*.

Conclusion on the second issue

41. I would accordingly answer the question raised by the second preliminary issue as follows:

(a) It is a question of substance governed by the law of Iraq whether mental distress caused by the defendant's conduct or motive in the commission of a tort is a type of injury for which the defendant can be held liable.
(b) If it is, assessing any damages payable as compensation for such an injury is a matter of procedure governed by English law.

[Report: [2015] 2 All ER 714]

INDEX

Abbreviations used in the index
ABC/Anti-Bribery Convention (OECD Convention on Combating Bribery of Foreign Public Officials in International Business Transactions (2009))
ACHPR (African Charter on Human and Peoples' Rights (1981))
ACHR (American Convention on Human Rights (1969))
ADRDM (American Declaration of the Rights and Duties of Man (1948))
CEDAW (Convention on the Elimination of All Forms of Discrimination Against Women (1979))
CERD (Convention on the Elimination of Racial Discrimination (1965))
CJA (Criminal Justice Act)
CJEU (Court of Justice of the European Union)
CRC (UN Convention on the Rights of the Child (1989)/Child Rights Committee)
CRPD (Convention on the Rights of Persons with Disabilities (2006)/Committee on the Rights of Persons with Disabilities)
Disabilities Convention (1999) (Inter-American Convention for the Elimination of All Forms of Discrimination against Persons with Disabilities (1999))
EC (European Community)
EC–I (EC–Israel Association Agreement (1995))
EC–I Protocol (EC–Israel Association Agreement (1995), Protocol)
EC–PLO (EC–PLO Association Agreement (1995))
ECHR (European Convention on Human Rights)
ECtHR (European Court of Human Rights)
ED (Executive Decree)
GC (Geneva Convention)
HOC (House of Commons)
HR (Hague Regulation)
HRC (Human Rights Committee)
IAComHR (Inter-American Commission on Human Rights)
IACtHR (Inter-American Court of Human Rights)
ICCPR (International Covenant on Civil and Political Rights (1966))
ICESCR (International Covenant on Economic, Social and Cultural Rights (1966))
ILC (International Law Commission/ILC Draft Articles)
IVF (*in vitro* fertilization)
Maputo Protocol (2003) (ACHPR Protocol on Rights of Women in Africa (2003))
OP (Optional Protocol)
Oviedo Convention (Oviedo Convention for the Protection of Human Rights and Dignity of the Human Being with regard to the Application of Biology and Medicine)
PAHO (Pan-American Health Organization)
ROC (Rules of Court)
ROP (Rules of Procedure)
SFO (Serious Fraud Office)
TC (Torture Convention (1984))
TCI (Turks and Caicos Islands)

TEC (EEC Treaty (1957))
TFEU (Lisbon Treaty on the Functioning of the European Union (2007))
TRNC (Turkish Republic of Northern Cyprus)
UDHR (Universal Declaration of Human Rights (1948))
UNC (United Nations Charter (1945))
UNCESCR (United Nations Committee on Economic, Social and Cultural Rights)
UNGA (United Nations General Assembly)
UNSCR (United Nations Security Council Resolution)
VCDR (Vienna Convention on Diplomatic Relations (1961))
VCLT (Vienna Convention on the Law of Treaties (1969))
Venice Commission (European Commission for Democracy through Law)
WHO (World Health Organization/WHO Constitution)
WMA (World Medical Association)

abuse of process
    act of State doctrine, as limitation on 577-8, 584, 604-14
    jurisprudence
        Johnson v. Gore Wood 606
        Yukos 577-8, 584, 604-14
abuse of rights/destruction of Convention rights and freedoms (ECHR 17)
    jurisprudence
        Garaudy 282-3
        Lawless 282
        Lehideux 282-3
        Norwood 282-3
        Orban 282-3
        Paksas 280-1
        Pavel Ivanov 282-3
        WP v. Poland 282-3
ACHR (1969)
    applicability "over all persons subject to their jurisdiction" (ACHR 1(1))/extraterritorial jurisdiction
        Cantos 96
        Perozo 96
    derogation: *see* suspension of guarantees (ACHR 27)
    economic, social and cultural rights (San Salvador Protocol (1988)) 72, 127
    restrictions: *see* ACHR (1969), justified restrictions/interference (ACHR 30)
ACHR (1969), interpretation
    international humanitarian law/human rights law as aid (VCLT 31(3)(c)) 89
        ADRDM (1948) 90-1
        ICCPR 6 (right to life) 99-100
        UDHR (1948) 98-9
    intertemporal law/developments subsequent to conclusion of treaty as "relevant rule" (VCLT 31(3)(c)) ("living-tree" principle) 106-13
    jurisprudence (principles of interpretation)
        Anzualdo Castro 106-7
        Artavia Murillo 77-115
        Atala Riffo 106-7
        González (Cotton Field) 81-2, 89-90
        Heliodoro Portugal 106-7
        Ivcher Bronstein 81-2
        Kawas Fernández 106-7

INDEX 679

Kichwa Indigenous People of Sarayaku 106-7
Restrictions to the Death Penalty (ACHR 4(2) and 4(4)) 89-90
Right to Information on Consular Assistance in the Framework of the Guarantees of the Due Process of Law 89, 106-7
Street Children 89
Tiu Tojín 106-7
[natural and] ordinary meaning in context (VCLT 31(1)) 82-9
object and purpose/spirit and purpose (teleological approach) (VCLT 31(1)), interpretation most favourable to the weaker party 113-15
phrases
  "conception" 82-9
  "every person" (ACHR 4(1)) (applicability to embryo) 98
  "human being"/ "person" (ACHR 1(2)) 95-6
responsibility for, IACtHR 80-1
State practice as aid 110-13
systematic and historical interpretation (*Artavia Murillo*) 89-106
  relevant elements 89-90
travaux préparatoires 89-90
  "from the moment of conception" (ACHR 4(1)) 91
ACHR (1969), justified restrictions/interference (ACHR 30)
jurisprudence
  Artavia Murillo 116-37
  Atala Riffo 119-20
  Chaparro Álvarez and Lapo Íñiguez 119-20
  Kimel 119-20
  Meaning of "Laws" in ACHR 30 119-20
  Tristán Donoso 119-20
proportionality (restrictions on IVF treatment) 116-37
act of State doctrine
Note: There is considerable overlap between act of State doctrine, judicial review/justiciability of acts of forum State and judicial review/justiciability of acts of foreign State in and outside its own territory. Entries under the present heading are limited so far as possible to the principle as stated in *Underhill*: "Every sovereign State is bound to respect the independence of every other sovereign State, and the courts of one country will not sit in judgment on the acts of the government of another done within its own territory. Redress of grievances by reason of such acts must be obtained through the means open to be availed of by sovereign powers as between themselves."
definition/characteristics
  discretionary nature 650-7
  justiciability, interrelationship with, *Yukos* 569-614
  State immunity from jurisdiction and, *Yukos* 580
  State responsibility defence, exclusion 631
limitations/exceptions
  commercial activities exception 592-3
  factual enquiry vs finding on legality of action (*Kirkpatrick* limitation) 593-604
  international law/human rights violations including public policy considerations 581-4
    status of rule under consideration (*Sabbatino/Kuwait Airways*), relevance, developments in international law and 581-4
  judicial acts 584-92
    jurisprudence reviewed 584-92
  territorial limitation/act exclusively within own territory 581

act of State doctrine (*cont.*)
reasons for/justification
comity 578-80, 589-90, 609-11, 617-21
embarrassment to executive 579-80
international effects 650-7
national security 631
sovereign equality of States (UNC 2(1)) (*par in parem non habet jurisdictionem*) 630-1
admissibility (ECtHR) (six-month rule (ECHR 35(1)))
continuing violation 280-1, 301-2
interpretation by reference to specific circumstances 28
admissibility (HRC including OP 1:5)
"being examined under another procedure of international investigation or settlement" (OP 1:5(2)(a))
ECtHR decision relating to procedure 397
supervision of implementation of ECtHR decision (ECHR 46(2)) 323-4
Paksas 323-6
ratione materiae, "same matter", in absence of correlation between ECHR and ICCPR 324
substantiation of complaint requirement 324
admissibility/competence (ACHR 44-7)
new facts not included in the application 29-30
purpose of case considerations 62-4
Artavia Murillo 62-4
Five Pensioners 63
Mapiripán Massacre 63
Río Negro Massacres 63
Vélez Restrepo 63
subsidiarity of IAComHR/IACtHR system
Acevedo Jaramillo 64
Artavia Murillo 64
Cabrera García and Montiel Flores 64
advisory opinion (municipal courts), *Khan* 634-5
American Declaration of the Rights and Duties of Man (1948) (ADRDM)
scientific technology, right of access to (ADRDM XIII) 72
travaux préparatoires (ADRDM 1) 90-1
***amicus curiae* brief**, IACtHR 17-21
amparo as effective remedy
ACHR 25 24-6
in Costa Rica 24-6
Anti-Bribery Convention (2009) (OECD)
context (VCLT 31(1)) 447
enforcement "shall not be influenced by" (ABC 5) 475-7
necessity (ILC 25) 450-2
threat to national security 445-6, 476-80
threat to national security and relations with another State distinguished 446-55
travaux préparatoires (OECD Revised Recommendation (1997)) 446-7
uniformity of interpretation, importance 449-50, 452-3
implementing legislation (UK) 458
monitoring and follow-up (ABC 12) 452-3, 476
object and purpose (preamble 8) 449-50
arbitral award, review by municipal courts, jurisprudence, *Dallah* 610

INDEX 681

***Artavia Murillo* (IVF) (merits)**: *see also* reproductive rights
  ACHR 4(1) (right to life from the moment of conception), interpretation/relevance 77-115
    Constitutional Chamber's views 42-5
    Court's conclusions
      "conception" 87-8, 91, 97
      CRC provisions 102
      "every person" 98
      ICCPR 6 (right to life) 99-100
      non-absolute nature of right 115
      status of unborn child under ACHR 4, UDHR 3, ICCPR 6, CRC and ADRDM 106
    Court's considerations 80-115
      ACHPR 4/Maputo Protocol (2003) 106
      "born" (UDHR 1) 98-9
      CEDAW reports 100-1
      CRC 1 ("child") and 6(1) (inherent right to life) 101-2
      EC Directive 98/44/EC (legal protection of biotechnological inventions) 108-9
      ECHR 2(1) (everyone's right to life) 102-5
      "every person" (applicability to embryo) 98
      evolutionary/"living-tree" principle (VCLT 31(3)(c)) 106-13
      "human being"/"person" (ACHR 1(2)) 95-6
      ICCPR 6 (right to life) 99-100
      object and purpose/spirit and purpose (teleological approach) (VCLT 31(1)), interpretation most favourable to the weaker party 113-15
      Oviedo Convention (1997) 108
      travaux préparatoires (ACHR 4(1) ("moment of conception")) 91
      travaux préparatoires (ADRDM 1) 90-1
    dissenting opinion 162-87
    parties' arguments
      Commission/interveners 77-8
      State 78-80
    relevant principles: *see also* ACHR (1969), interpretation
      IACtHR's responsibility for interpretation of ACHR 80-1
      international humanitarian law/human rights law as aid (VCLT 31(3)(c)) 89
      ordinary meaning (VCLT 31(1)) 82-9
      right to life as fundamental right 81
      systematic and historical interpretation 89-106
      travaux préparatoires 89-90
    State practice 110-13
  ACHR 4(1) (right to life from the moment of conception), proportionality of restriction/interference (ACHR 30) 116-37
    Court's conclusions 129, 132, 136-7
    Court's considerations 119-36
      embryonic loss 133-6
      indirect discrimination 124-33
      indirect discrimination (disability) 126-9
      indirect discrimination (financial situation) 132-3
      indirect discrimination (gender) 129-32
      non-discrimination obligation (ACHR 1) and differential treatment distinguished 124-6
      severity of the interference 121-3, 137
      summary of requirements 119-21

***Artavia Murillo* (IVF) (merits)** (*cont.*)
    Court's final conclusion 137-8
    parties' arguments 117-19
        Commission and interveners 116-17
    alleged violation of rights to personal integrity (ACHR 5), personal liberty (ACHR 7), and private and family life (ACHR 11 and 17) (scope)
        Court's considerations 66-72
            ACHR 11 (privacy) and ACHR 17 (family life), interrelationship 68-9
            ACHR 17 (family life), non-derogability 68-9
            ACHR 17(2) (right to found a family) 68-9
            Constitutional Chamber's decision as absolute prohibition of IVF 74-7
            health care 69-72: *see also* health-care obligations and the right to private life/personal integrity; reproductive rights, health care and
            liberty and security of person (ACHR 7) 66
            private and family life (ACHR 11) 66
            private life/privacy, definitions 66-72
            private life/privacy and reproductive rights 67-72
            scientific technology, right of access to 72
        parties' arguments
            Commission/interveners 65, 73
            State 65-6, 73-4
    costs and expenses 152-4
        Court's considerations 152-4
        equitable basis 154
        evidence of, need for 152-4
        parties' claims (interveners) 152
        parties' claims (State) 152
    Court's decision 155-7
    compliance/implementation obligation (ACHR 68(1)) 154-5
    evidence 30-7
        admissibility (documentary evidence) 32-4
            challenge relating to evaluation/probative value distinguished 33-4
            effective electronic links 32-3
            litigation expenses vouchers 33
        admissibility (statements of presumed victims and of testimonial evidence) 34-7
            challenge relating to evaluation/probative value distinguished 36-7
            failure to provide timely translation, relevance 35
            failure to respond to questions posed by State, relevance 34-5
            relevance to purpose established by Court Order requirement 36
        ancillary nature 34
        Commission requests relating to 31-2
        evaluation principles 30
        municipal court practice distinguished 35-6
        summary of evidence received 31-2
    facts: *see also* Costa Rica, IVF (*in vitro* fertilization)
    facts (IVF in Costa Rica)
        assisted reproduction and IVF techniques 37-9
        Constitutional Chamber judgment of 15 March 2000 41-5
            right to life (ACHR 4) 42-5
        Executive Decree No 24029-S of 3 February 1995 40-1

IAComHR recommendations (2010)/IVF and Embryo Transfer Bill (2010) 14-15, 48-9
  incidence (1995-2000) 41
  proceedings in Costa Rica (Ileana Henchoz and Karen Espinoza) 45-8
facts (situation of presumed victims)
  Andrea Bianchi Bruna and Germán Moreno Valencia 59-60
  Carlos Eduardo de Jesús Vargas Solórzano and María del Socorro Calderón Porras 57-8
  Enrique Acuña Cartín and Ana Cristina Castillo León 58-9
  Giovanni Vega and Joaquinita Arroyo 55-6
  Grettel Artavia Murillo and Miguel Mejías Carballo 49-50
  Ileana Henchoz and Miguel Yamuni 50-2
  Karen Espinoza and Héctor Jiménez 56-7
  Oriéster Rojas and Julieta González 53
  Víctor Sanabria León and Claudia Carro Maklouf 54-5
opinion (concurring) (García-Sayán J) 157-61
opinion (dissenting) (Vio Grossi J) 161-87
procedural background
  amicus curiae briefs (ROP 44) 17-21
    time-limits (ROP 44(3)) 20-1
    working language of case requirement (ROP 44(1)) 21
  appointment of common interveners (ROP 24(2)) 16
  filing of briefs, time-limits (ROP 28) 21
  IACtHR proceedings 16-21
  IAComHR proceedings 14-15
  pleadings and motions brief (interveners) 16
    answering brief (State) 16
  public hearing 17
purpose of the case (Constitutional Chamber's judgment)
  Court's considerations 62-4
  parties' arguments
    Commission 60-1
    State 61-2
reparations (ACHR 63(1)) 138-55
  compensation for non-pecuniary damage 149-52
    Court's considerations 151-2
    equitable basis 151-2
    parties' arguments (Commission and interveners) 149-50
    parties' arguments (State) 150-1
  compensation for pecuniary damage 145-9
    Court's considerations 147-9
    equitable principle 148-9
    nexus/causal connection, need for 147-9
    parties' arguments (Commission/interveners) 145-6
    parties' arguments (State) 146
  compliance 154-5
  judgment as 144-5
  measures to ensure availability of IVF treatment 141-3
  measures of psychological reparation 140-1
  measures to raise awareness on reproductive health 143-4
  publication and dissemination of judgment 141
  summary of requirements 138-9
  "victim" 139-40

Artavia Murillo **(IVF) (preliminary objections)**
  exhaustion of domestic remedies (ACHR 46(1)(a))
    Court's considerations 23-6
      amparo as effective remedy (ACHR 25) 24-6
      timeliness of objection 23-4
    Court's decision 26
    parties' arguments
      Commission 22-3
      State 21-2, 24-5
  new facts not included in the application 29-30
    Court's considerations/joinder to the merits 29-30
    parties' arguments
      Commission 29
      State 29
  six-month rule (ACHR 46(1)(b)/ROP 39) 26-9
    Court's considerations 27-9
      interpretation by reference to specific circumstances 28
    Court's decision 29
    parties' arguments
      Commission 27
      State 26-7
Association Agreements: *see* EC Association Agreements, jurisprudence; EU treaties with third parties (TFEU 218 [EC 300])

British Indian Ocean Territory (BIOT)
  Bancoult 2 524-5, 528-31, 533, 537-8, 542-3

Cairo Conference on Population and Development (1994) Programme of Action 70-2
CEDAW (1979)
  General Recommendations
    24 (women and health) 69, 130-1
    25 (temporary special measures) 124-5
  health-care rights (ICCPR 12) including those relating to reproduction 100-1
  reproductive autonomy (CEDAW 16(e)) 69
child care in context of respect for family life (ECHR 8), jurisprudence
  Ahmut 506-7
  B (Children) 506-7
  Beoku-Betts 508, 510-11
  Bronda 506-7
  EM (Lebanon) 506-11: *see also EM (Lebanon)* (deportation to country where risk of flagrant breach of human rights/ECHR 8)
  Gül 506-7
  Johansen 506-7
  M 506-7
  McMichael 506-7
  P, C and S 506-7
child custody, inherent right to life (CRC 6(1)) 101-2
Child Rights Convention (1989) (CRC)
  "child" (CRC 1) 101-2
  travaux préparatoires, "before as well as after birth" (preamble) 101-2

combatant immunity
  combatant activities in time of war, limitation to 633-4, 639, 642-3, 649, 653-5
  jurisprudence
    Gul 633-4
    Khan 633-4, 639, 642-3, 649
compensation for breach of ICCPR (ICCPR 2(3)), *Ory* 400
***Corner House Research* (High Court) (Moses LJ)** 409-57
  analysis and conclusions
    conduct of Shawcross exercise 455-6
    Director's obligations to secure the rule of law 457
    enforcement "shall not be influenced by" (ABC 5)
      monitoring and follow-up (ABC 12) 452-3
      necessity (ILC 25) 450-2
      threat to national security 445-6
      threat to national security and relations with another State distinguished 446-55
      uniformity of interpretation, importance 449-50, 452-3
    judicial review of implementation of unincorporated treaty 439-44
    rule of law, obligation to uphold in face of threat to administration of public justice 425-39, 457
    separation of powers 427-31
  facts
    commission and bribe distinguished 423-4
    Director's reasons for discontinuing the investigation 421-3
    discontinuance of investigation
      AG/Director's decision against (25 January 2006) 413-14
      AG/Director's decision in favour of (13 December 2006) 420-1
    limited remit of Court/untested nature of evidence 410, 424
    parties
      Campaign Against Arms Trade 423
      Corner House 423
    SFO statutory notice to BAE requesting disclosure of payments/BAE's request to halt investigation on public interest grounds 410-11
    Shawcross exercise 411-14
    threat (Saudi Arabia) 414-20
      Prime Minister's representations relating to 417-20, 448-9
***Corner House Research* (House of Lords)**
  analysis and conclusions
    Anti-Bribery Convention (2009), monitoring and follow-up (ABC 12) 476
    criteria governing Director's exercise of discretion 470-1
    Director's reasons for discontinuing the investigation 471-5
    Director's right to rely on expert advice 474-7
    enforcement "shall not be influenced by" (ABC 5), threat to national security 476-80
    judicial review of decisions relating to investigation and prosecution 469-70
    judicial review of implementation of unincorporated treaty 475-6, 480-4
    public interest test 471-5
  facts
    AG's exercise of superintending function 464-6
    Anti-Bribery Convention (2009) (OECD)/implementing legislation 458
    CJA 1987 (Director's investigation and prosecution powers) 458

Corner House Research (**House of Lords**) (*cont.*)
    discontinuance of investigation
        AG/Director's decision against (25 January 2006) 461
        AG/Director's decision in favour of (13 December 2006) 464-6
        SFO statutory notice to BAE requesting disclosure of payments/BAE's request to halt investigation on public interest grounds 458-9
        Shawcross exercise 459-61
        threat (Saudi Arabia) 461-6
            Prime Minister's representations relating to 463-4
    High Court judgment (summary) 466-9
    opinions
        Bingham LJ 457-77
        Brown LJ 480-4
        Hale LJ 478-80
        Hoffmann LJ 477
        Rodger LJ 478

Costa Rica
    amparo as effective remedy 24-6
    Constitutional Jurisdiction Law 1989 by article
        2 (exclusive competence of Constitutional Chamber) 25-6
        4 (constitutional jurisdiction of Constitutional Chamber) 25
        11 (finality of judgments and rulings of Constitutional Chamber) 25
        75 (constitutionality action: requirements) 41-2
    IVF (*in vitro* fertilization): *see also Artavia Murillo* (IVF) (merits)
        Constitutional Chamber judgment of 15 March 2000 41-5
            as absolute prohibition of IVF 73-7
            annulment of Executive Decree No 24029-S, grounds 42
            right to life (ACHR 4) and 42-5
        Executive Decree No 24029-S of 3 February 1995 by article 40-1
            2 (definition) 40
            9-13 (techniques) 40-1
        IAComHR recommendations (2010)/IVF and Embryo Transfer Bill (2010) 14-15, 48-9
        incidence (1995-2000) 41
        proceedings brought by Ileana Henchoz and Karen Espinoza 45-8

costs (IACtHR) (ROC 55(1))
    equitable basis 154
    evidence of, need for 152-4

criminal proceedings, judicial review of decision to bring, jurisprudence
    Bermingham 425, 469-70
    Corner House: *see Corner House Research* (High Court) (Moses LJ); *Corner House Research* (House of Lords)
    Ex parte C 469-70
    Manning 469-70
    Matalulu 469-70
    Mohit 469-70
    Sharma v. *Browne-Antoine* 425, 430, 469-70

customary international law "as part of" municipal law
    jurisprudence, *Trendtex* 536-7
    jus cogens/peremptory norm and 536-9

Cyprus, Republic of, recognition of State/jurisdiction over area under control of TRNC, *Anastasiou* 215-16

democracy, Venice Commission's Guidelines on 272-3
Disabilities Convention (1999) (Inter-American) by article, III (obligation to take legislative and other measures to eliminate discrimination) 128
Disabilities Convention (2006) (CRPD)
disability as evolving concept (preamble) 127
reproductive rights and 126-7
UNGA Resolution 48/96 (standard rules on the equalization of opportunities for persons with disabilities) 128

EC Association Agreements, jurisprudence
Anastasiou 215-16
Demirel 203-4, 226
El-Yasini 226-7
Faroe Seafood 207
Firma Brita: see Firma Brita
Huygen 207
Ilumitrónica 207
Jany 226-7
Les Rapides Savoyards 206, 208, 230-1
Racke 203-4, 226-7
Sfakianakis 206-7, 230-1, 233
ECHR (1950), interpretation
context (VCLT 31(2)), treaty as a whole 549
jurisprudence
Austin 549
Stec 549
UDHR terminology, adoption of 102
ECtHR
judgments, binding force and execution (ECHR 46 [53 and 54])
Assanidze 296-7
Paksas 296-7
VGT 296-7
municipal courts, primacy in determining compliance with Convention/subsidiarity principle 249-51
Rules of Court (1998 *et seq.*)
24 (composition of Chamber) 258
28 (inability to sit, withdrawal or exemption) 258
29(1) (ad hoc judges) 258
52(1) (allocation of cases) 257
54(4)/ECHR 29(3) (joinder of merits and admissibility) 258
59(3) (individual applications: public hearing) 258
72 (relinquishment to Grand Chamber) 258
Rules of Court (2014)
60(2) (itemized claims with documentary evidence) 297-8
60(3) (rejection of claim in case of non-compliance with Rule 60(1) and (2)) 297-8
74(2) (separate opinions) 249-50
EC–Israel Association Agreement (1995)
Note: The Agreement entered into force on 1 June 2000
applicability of Chapter 2 provisions (EC–I 7) 195-6
Association Council (EC–I 67) 196
conclusion and entry into force 194-5, 219

EC–Israel Association Agreement (1995) (*cont.*)
  dispute settlement
    appropriate measures in case of failure to fulfil an obligation (EC–I 79(2)) 196
    reference to Association Council (EC–I 75(1)) 196, 210, 219, 232-3
  object and purpose (preamble) 195
  objective (reinforcement of free market) (EC–I 6(1)) 219, 227
  prohibition of customs duties on industrial products (EC–I 8) 195-6, 219
  Protocol 4: *see* EC–Israel Association Agreement (1995), Protocol 4 ("originating products" and methods of administrative cooperation)
  territorial scope (EC–I 83)/dispute relating to applicability to occupied territories 197-8, 208-9, 210-11, 219, 225-9
    Commission report on the implementation of the EC–Israel interim agreement on trade and trade-related matters 198
    Notice to importers—Importations from Israel into the Community (8 November 1997) 197
    Notice to importers—Importations from Israel into the Community (23 November 2001) 198
    reply to European Parliament written question P-2747/00 212
  terms of agreement 196
EC–Israel Association Agreement (1995), Protocol 4 ("originating products" and methods of administrative cooperation): *see also Firma Brita*
  administrative cooperation mechanism (EC–I Protocol 4:32), mutual trust as basis 206
  Customs Cooperation Committee (EC–I Protocol 39) 221
  origin criteria (EC–I Protocol 4:2)
    products obtained in Israel including materials sufficiently worked or processed there (EC–I Protocol 4:2(2)(b)) 196, 219
    products wholly obtained in Israel (EC–I Protocol 4:2(2)(a)) 196
    "sufficiently worked or processed" (EC–I Protocol 4:5)
      processing operations (EC–I Protocol 4:6) 205
      total value (EC–I Protocol 4:5(2)(a)) 205
  proof of origin (Title V)
    EC–Switzerland Association Agreement (1972) compared 206-7
    EUR.1 movement certificate (EC–I Protocol 4:17(1)(a)) as 196-7, 205, 219-20
    invoice declaration as (EC–I Protocol 4:17(1)(b)) 219-20
      conditions for making out (EC–I Protocol 4:22(1)(a)) 220, 228
      making out by approved exporter (EC–I Protocol 4:23) 220, 228
    issue of EUR.1 movement certificate (EC–I Protocol 4:18(1)(a)) 196-7, 205
  proof of origin (Title V), verification of EUR.1 movement certificate (EC–I Protocol 4:32)
    action in case of failure to meet requirements (EC–I Protocol 4:32(6)) 197, 205, 231-4
    binding effect of results on importing country 206-9, 230-2
    dispute settlement (Customs Cooperation Committee) (EC–I Protocol 4:33) 197, 209-10, 221, 232-3
    notification of results of verification (EC–I Protocol 4:32(5)) 205
    reasonable doubt of importing State as to authenticity (EC–I Protocol 4:32(1)) 197, 205
    request for (EC–I Protocol 4:32(2)) 197, 205
    text 220-1
    verification by exporting State (EC–I Protocol 4:32(3)) 197, 205

INDEX 689

EC–PLO Association Agreement (1995)
Note: The Agreement entered into force on 1 July 1997
conclusion and entry into force 198-9, 221
dispute settlement, reference to the Joint Committee (EC–PLO 67) 199
objective (reinforcement of free market) (EC–PLO 3) 221-2, 227
objectives (EC–PLO 1(2)) 199
prohibition of new customs duties (EC–PLO 5) 199, 222
purpose (preamble) 198-9
relief from customs duties for products originating in the West Bank and Gaza Strip (EC–PLO 6) 199, 222
territorial scope (EC–PLO 73) 199, 222, 225-9
EC–PLO Association Agreement (1995), Protocol 3 ("originating products" and methods of administrative cooperation)
issue of EUR.1 movement certificate (EC–PLO Protocol 3:16(1)) 223
  for products originating in the West Bank and Gaza Strip (EC–PLO Protocol 3:16(4)) 223
origin criteria (EC–PLO Protocol 3:2)
  products obtained in the West Bank and the Gaza Strip including materials sufficiently worked or processed there (EC–PLO Protocol 3: 2(2)(b)) 199, 222
  products wholly obtained in the West Bank and the Gaza Strip (EC–PLO Protocol 3:2(2)(a)) 199, 222
proof of origin (Title V)
  EUR.1 movement certificate (EC–PLO Protocol 3:15(1)(a)) as 222-3
  invoice declaration (EC–PLO Protocol 3:15(1)(b)) as 222-3
    conditions for making out (EC–PLO Protocol 3:20(1)(a)) 223, 228
    making out by approved exporter (EC–PLO Protocol 3:21(1)) 223, 228
    for products originating in the Community, West Bank or Gaza Strip (EC–PLO Protocol 3:20(2)) 223
EEC–Switzerland Association Agreement (1972), proof of origin of goods 206-7
EEC–Turkey Association Agreement (1963), proof of origin of goods 207
effective remedy before national authority, need for (ECHR 13)
"effective", *Paksas* 278-9
right to challenge decision of constitutional court 294-5
  Christine Goodwin 294-5
  James 294-5
  Paksas 294-5
  Roche 294-5
  Tsonyo Tsonev 294-5
effective remedy before national authority, need for/examples (ICCPR 2(3))
administrative or disciplinary remedies 378
cancellation of criminal record 400
cumulative remedies of a different nature 377-8
damages/compensation: *see* compensation for breach of ICCPR (ICCPR 2(3))
enforcement of tribunal/court decision, need for 375-80
legislative changes to ensure conformity with obligations 400
measures to ensure non-repetition (ICCPR 2(3)(a)) 328, 400
  revision of decision in breach of State's ICCPR obligations 328
prompt, thorough and effective investigation through independent and impartial bodies 377-8
State responsibility considerations and 378-9

effective remedy for human rights breaches, jurisprudence
  Artavia Murillo 21-6
  Furla 23-4
  Horvath 375-7, 380, 382
  Velásquez Rodríguez 23-4
EM (Lebanon) **(deportation to country where risk of flagrant breach of human rights/ECHR 8)**
  benchmark/threshold test
    "exceptional circumstances" test 489-97, 509-11, 513-14
    "flagrant denial or gross violation of a right" test 505-6, 509-13
  child care in context of respect for family life (ECHR 8) 506-11
  jurisprudence
    D v. *UK* 496
    Devaseelan 490, 506, 511-13
    F v. *UK* 492-5
    Mamatkulov 489-90, 505-6, 513
    N (House of Lords/ECtHR) 491-3, 496
    Razgar 490, 505, 511-13
    Soering 490
    Ullah 490, 494, 496-506, 511-13
    Z and T 492-6
  non-discrimination obligation (ECHR 14)/Sharia law 490-1, 511
  opinions
    Bingham LJ 497-509
    Brown LJ 513-14
    Carswell LJ 511-13
    Hale LJ 509-11
    Hope LJ 489-97
estoppel: *see* recognition/enforcement of foreign judgment (including State immunity considerations), as *res judicata*/issue estoppel
EU law, customary international law and 226-7
EU legal order, treaties with third parties as integral part of 203-4, 226
EU treaties with third parties (TFEU 218 [TEC 300]): *see also Firma Brita*
  preliminary ruling (TFEU 218(11)), *Firma Brita* 203-4
evidence (IACtHR)
  admissibility (documentary evidence)
    challenge relating to evaluation/probative value distinguished 33-4
    effective electronic links 32-3
    litigation expenses vouchers 33
    ROP provisions relating to 32
  admissibility (statements of presumed victims and of testimonial evidence)
    ancillary nature 34
    challenge relating to evaluation/probative value distinguished 36-7
    failure to provide timely translation, relevance 35
    failure to respond to questions posed by State, relevance 34-5
    relevance to purpose established by Court Order requirement 36
  evaluation, principles governing 30
  jurisprudence
    Artavia Murillo 30-7
    Claude Reyes 35-6

Díaz Peña 34
Escué Zapata 32-3
Kichwa Indigenous People 30, 32, 34
Loayza Tamayo 34
Miguel Castro Castro Prison 35-6
Servellón García 35-6
Velásquez Rodríguez 32
White Van 30
municipal court practice distinguished 35-6
timeliness 32
exhaustion of local remedies (ACHR 46(1)(a))
admissibility requirement, timeliness of objection 23-4
effective remedy, need for: *see also* judicial protection/effective remedy (ACHR 25)
finality of decision/exclusion of appeal and 25-6
jurisprudence
Artavia Murillo 21-6
Bozano 23-4
Reverón Trujillo 23-4
Velásquez Rodríguez 23-4
exhaustion of local remedies (ECHR 35(1)) (including effectiveness of remedy), *Paksas* 277-9
exhaustion of local remedies (ICCPR OP 1:5(2)(b)), "effective" remedy, need for 326
extradition, deportation or expulsion to country where risk of breach of human rights including torture/inhumane treatment (ECHR 3/ICCPR 7/TC 3) and "flagrant breach of justice" (including "foreign cases")
benchmark/threshold
"exceptional circumstances" test 489-97, 509-11, 513-14
"flagrant breach" 505-6, 509-13
jurisprudence
Bensaid (ECHR 8) 509-10
D v. UK 1657
Devaseelan 490, 506, 511-13
EM (Lebanon): *see EM (Lebanon)* (deportation to country where risk of flagrant breach of human rights/ECHR 8)
F v. UK 492-6
Mamatkulov 489-90, 505-6, 513
N (House of Lords/ECtHR) 491-3, 496
Razgar 490, 505, 511-13
Soering 490
Ullah 490, 494, 503-6, 511-13
Z and T 492-6

fair and public hearing, entitlement "[i]n the determination of civil rights and obligations or of any criminal charge by a court of law" (ECHR 6(1))
"civil rights and obligations"
impeachment proceedings 275-7
Paksas 275-7
"criminal charge"
impeachment proceedings 275-7
Paksas 275-7

fair and public hearing, entitlement "[i]n the determination of civil rights and obligations or of any criminal charge by a court of law" (ECHR 6(1)) (*cont.*)
    res judicata/*non bis in idem* principle (ECHR Protocol 7:4(1)), impeachment proceedings 275-7
fair and public hearing (ICCPR 14), "criminal charge", impeachment distinguished 325
fair trial (municipal law/general), jury trial, right to (*Misick*) 525-6, 539-41, 543
family life, respect for (ACHR 17)
    ECHR provisions distinguished 68-9
    jurisprudence
        Artavia Murillo: see Artavia Murillo (IVF) (merits)
        Atala Riffo 68-9
        Gelman 68-9
        Juridical Status and Human Rights of the Child 68-9
    non-derogability (ACHR 27(2)) 68-9
    right to found a family (ACHR 17(2)) 68-9
family/private life, respect for (ECHR 8)
    free elections, right to (ECHR Protocol 1:3) and 545-53
    health care, right to 69-70: *see also* health-care obligations and the right to private life/personal integrity
    "private life": *see Misick*, ECtHR proceedings; private life/privacy, definitions/scope, jurisprudence
Finland, Reindeer Husbandry Act 1990: *see Paadar* (Sami rights)
Firma Brita: *see also* EC–Israel Association Agreement (1995)
    AG Bot's opinion 193-217
        CJEU's jurisdiction to give preliminary ruling (TFEU 218(1)) 203-4
        conclusion 216-17
        jurisprudence reviewed 206-8
        Question 1 (binding effect of verification) 209
        Question 2 (obligation to refer the matter to the Customs Cooperation Committee (EC–I Protocol 4:33)) 209-10
            reference to Association Council (EC–I 75(1)) as appropriate procedure 210
        Questions 1 and 4 (elective determination as to classification of goods originating in the occupied territories) 210-16
        summary 193-4
        verification procedures (Protocol 4:32)
            binding effect of results on importing country 206-9
            mutual trust as basis of administrative cooperation mechanism 206
    costs 233
    Court's judgment (Fourth Chamber) 217-34
        CJEU's jurisdiction to give preliminary ruling (TFEU 218(1)) 226
        Court's ruling 233-4
        pacta tertiis nec nocent nec prosunt (VCLT 34) 218, 227-8
        Questions 1 and 2 (binding effect of verification/dispute settlement) 230-3
            Court's conclusion 233
            Customs Cooperation Committee (EC–I Protocol 4:33) vs Association Council (EC–I 75(1)) 232-3
            verification procedures (Protocol 4:32), binding effect 230-2
        Questions 1 and 4 (elective determination as to classification of goods originating in the occupied territories) 225-9, 234
            Court's conclusion 228-9
    factual background 201-2
        background to CJEU proceedings 193-4, 217-18, 223-5

INDEX 693

legal framework
  EC–Israel Association Agreement (1995) (summary of provisions) 195-8, 204-5, 219-21
  EC–PLO Agreement (1997) (summary of provisions) 198-9, 221-3
  Euro-Mediterranean partnership 194-5
  Israel–Palestine Interim Agreement (1995) (summary of provisions) 199-201
  VCLT 1 (applicability to treaties between States) 218
  VCLT 1 (international agreements not within the scope) 218
  VCLT 31 (general rules of interpretation) 218
  questions referred to CJEU 202-3, 224-5
forum [non] conveniens
  act of State/non-justiciability distinguished 585-6
  Cherney 585-6
France, travellers in: *see Ory* (travellers' right to freedom of movement (ICCPR 12))
free elections, right to (ECHR Protocol 1:3)
  European Parliament elections, applicability of Protocol 1:3 provisions/withdrawal 527-8
  family/private life, respect for (ECHR 8), applicability to 545-53
  as fundamental principle of a political democracy 287-8
  jurisprudence
    Ādamsons 287-8
    Hirst 287-8
    Mathieu-Mohin 287-8
    Misick 527-8, 535, 545-53
    Paksas: *see Paksas* (ECtHR), alleged violation of ECHR Protocol 1:3 (free elections) (admissibility); *Paksas* (ECtHR), alleged violation of ECHR Protocol 1:3 (free elections) (merits)
    Tănase 287-8
    Ždanoka 288-94
  justified restrictions/requirements
    lawfulness 288
    legitimate aim 289
    non-retroactivity 288
    "proportionate to the legitimate aim" 289-94
  margin of appreciation 287-8
freedom of movement (ICCPR 12)
  restrictions, requirements (ICCPR 12(3))
    HRC General Comment 27 (freedom of movement) 398-9
    national security/public order 398-9

General Assembly resolutions in number/date order
  181 (II) (future government of Palestine) 211
  3384 (XXX) (Declaration on the Use of Scientific and Technological Progress in the Interests of Peace and for the Benefit of Mankind) 72
  48/96 (standard rules on the equalization of opportunities for persons with disabilities) 128
General Comments (HRC)
  6 (ICCPR 6 (right to life)) 99-100
  17 (ICCPR 24 (rights of the child)) 99-100
  18 (ICCPR 26 et al. (non-discrimination)), differential treatment, requirements 124-5
  19 (ICCPR 23 (the family)), right to found a family/procreate (para. 5) 68-9
  23 (ICCPR 27 (minorities)) 350
  27 (ICCPR 12 (freedom of movement: derogations)) 398-9

General Comments (UNCESCR)
  14 (ICCPR 12: right to the highest standard of physical and mental health) 70-1
  20 (non-discrimination: "other status" grounds) 124-5

health
  definition (WHO Preamble) 70-1
  reproductive rights and: *see* reproductive rights
  UNCESCR General Comment No 14 (ICCPR 12: right to the highest standard of physical and mental health) 70-1
health-care obligations and the right to private life/personal integrity 69-72
  CEDAW 12 (non-discrimination)/General Recommendation No 24 (women and health) 69, 100-1
  jurisprudence
    Albán Cornejo 70-1
    Díaz Peña 69-70
    Furlan 69-70
    Glass 69-70
    McGinley and Egan 69-70
    P and S v. Poland 67, 69-70
    Vélez Loor 69-70
    Ximenes Lopes 70-1
    Yardımcı 69-70
    Yean and Bosico Girls 69-70
  scientific technology, right of access to
    ADRDM XIII 72
    ICESCR 15(b) 72
***Horvath* (HRC)**
  alleged violation of ICCPR 2(3) (effective remedy)
    Committee's conclusion 360
      individual opinions 382
    Committee's Views
      cumulative remedies of a different nature 377-8
      disciplinary proceedings 378
      enforcement of tribunal/court decision, need for 378-80
      prompt, thorough and effective investigation through independent and impartial bodies 377-8
      State responsibility for conduct of police (ILC 4), obligation to provide effective remedy 378-9
    parties' positions
      author 361-2
      State party 364-8
  alleged violation of ICCPR 7 (cruel or inhuman treatment)
    individual opinions 381-2
    parties' positions
      author 362-3, 373
      State party 368-9
  alleged violation of ICCPR 9 (arbitrary arrest)
    parties' positions
      author 363, 373-4
      State party 369

INDEX 695

alleged violation of ICCPR 10 (humane treatment of detained persons)
  parties' positions
    author 363
    State party 369-70
alleged violation of ICCPR 17 (respect for home, family and private life)
  parties' positions
    author 363, 374
    State party 370
author/claim 358
exhaustion of local remedies (OP 1:5(2)(b))
  Committee's views (absence of effective remedy) 375-7
  parties' arguments
    author 363-4
    author's comments on State party's observations 370-3
    State party 364-70, 374-5
facts as submitted by the author 358-61
individual opinions (partly dissenting)
  Neuman 382-3
  Seibert-Fohr joined by Iwasawa and Kälin 381-2
remedies
  author's requests 364
  legislative changes to ensure conformity with obligations 380
  request for information on measures taken to give effect to Committee's Views 380

HRC (UN Human Rights Committee)
  request for information on measures taken to give effect to Committee's Views 400
  victim, "actually affected" 324-5
  Views, budgetary limitations on length 383

human/fundamental rights and freedoms (municipal law/general), legality principle and 529

Hutchinson **(life/long-term imprisonment (ECHR 3)) (ECtHR)**
  admissibility 244
  Court's assessment
    primacy of municipal courts' role in determining compliance with Convention 249
    review mechanism in respect of whole life sentences (applicability to *Hutchinson*) 248-9
    Newell; McLoughlin, effect 248-9
    review mechanism in respect of whole life sentences (general principles) (*Vinter*) 245-8
  Court's decision 249-50
  dissenting opinion (Kalaydjieva J) (primacy of municipal courts) 250-1
  factual background 238-9
  parties' arguments, applicant 244
  relevant domestic law
    Criminal Justice Act 2003: The court directs the reader to discussion of the Criminal Justice Act 2003 in *Vinter* (156 ILR 128-31)
    Human Rights Act 1998 (HRA) 240
    Secretary of State's discretion to release (Crime (Sentences) Act 1997 and Prison Service Order 4700) 239-40
  relevant jurisprudence
    Newell; McLoughlin 240-3
    Vinter 240-3

IACtHR: *see also amicus curiae* brief, IACtHR; evidence (IACtHR)
 judgment, compliance/implementation obligation (ACHR 68(1)) 154-5
 Rules of Procedure (2001/2009)
  19(1) (judge: exclusion of national of respondent State) 2
  25(2) (designation of common intervener) 16
  28(1) (filing of briefs), time-limits 21
  44 (*amicus curiae* briefs) 17-21
  44(1) (*amicus curiae* briefs: in working language of the case) 21
  44(3) (*amicus curiae* briefs: time-limits) 20-1
  58 (procedure for taking evidence) 32
  65(2) (separate opinions) 161-2
 Statute by article, 24(3) 161-2
ICCPR (1966), interpretation, *travaux préparatoires* as supplementary means of interpretation (VCLT 32), right to life (ICCPR 6) 99-100
impeachment: *see* Lithuania (1990-) (Republic of), impeachment proceedings (Statute of the Seimas 1998/9) by article; *Paksas* (ECtHR)
independent and impartial tribunal (including ACHR 8(1), ECHR 6(1) and ICCPR 14(1)), *Paadar* 349
indirect discrimination: *see* non-discrimination obligation/indirect discrimination
intelligence services, means of supervising 639-40
international humanitarian law/human rights law (*jus in bello*), jurisprudence, *Hassan* 668-9
international law (including customary international law), applicability, private rights and obligations under municipal law 632-4
Iraq, post-conflict administration
 CPA (Coalition Provisional Authority)
  creation 665
  powers, obligation to exercise in conformity with international law including GC (1949) and HR (1907) 665, 669-71
 CPA regulations and other instruments, Regulation 1 (text) 665
 internment/assignment of place of residence (GC IV 78), legality, for imperative reasons of security 669-71
 liberty and security of person, right to (ECHR 5/ICCPR 9)
  effect of UNSCR 1483 (2003) 669-71: *see also Iraqi Civilians*, issue 1: relationship between UNC 103, UNSCR 1483 and 1511, and ECHR 5
 multinational force, authorization to "take all necessary measures [for] the maintenance of security and stability in Iraq", UNSCR 1511 666
 UNSCR 1483 (2003), text (extracts) 665
 UNSCR 1546 (2004) 666
Iraqi Civilians
 background (trial of limitation issues) 663-4
 issue 1: relationship between UNC 103, UNSCR 1483 and 1511, and ECHR 5 664-72
  Court's conclusion 672
  Court's findings on the effect of UNSCR 1483
   equivalence of "duty" (UNSCR 1483 and 1511) and "obligation" (UNC 102) 669-70
   obligation to detain for imperative reasons of security 669-71
  Court's findings on the effect of UNSCR 1511 671-2
  jurisprudence
   Al-Jedda (ECtHR) 667-8, 671-2
   Al-Jedda (House of Lords) 666-7
   Hassan 668-9, 671-2
   Serdar Mohammed 671-2

parties' arguments
    claimants 669
    defendant 669
points for determination 664
relevant legal instruments
    UNSCR 1483 665
    UNSCR 1511 665-6
    UNSCR 1546 666
issue 2: aggravated damages
    "aggravated" damages 674
applicable law 672-5
Court's conclusion 675

Israel, Declaration of the Establishment of State (14 May 1948) 211

Israel, occupied territory
annexation, condemnation (UNSCR 242 (1967)) 211
legal status
    EC–Israel Association Agreement (1995), applicability 210-16, 225-9
    part of the territory of Israel, whether 210-11
origin of goods, classification of goods for purpose of EC preferential treatment: *see Firma Brita*

Israel–Palestine Interim Agreement on the West Bank and the Gaza Strip (1995) 199-201
Annex V (economic relations) 214-15

issue estoppel: *see* recognition/enforcement of foreign judgment (including State immunity considerations), as *res judicata*/issue estoppel

IVF (*in vitro* fertilization): *see* reproductive rights

judicial protection/effective remedy (ACHR 25)
amparo as 24-6
non-appealability and 25-6
jurisprudence
    Artavia Murillo 24-6
    Herrera Ulloa 25-6

judicial review/justiciability (act of foreign State/foreign relations or prerogative power/recognition and enforcement of foreign law), jurisprudence: *see also Corner House Research* (High Court) (Moses LJ); *Corner House Research* (House of Lords); criminal proceedings, judicial review of decision to bring
I Congreso del Partido 592-3
A v. *B Bank* 595-6
AK Investment 577-8, 584-5, 589
Al-Koronky 578, 586-8
Al-Rawi 441
Berezovsky 579-80, 586-8, 598-600
Blad v. *Bamfield* 569-70
Buck 571
Buttes 572-4, 579-81
CND 440-1, 631-2
Duke of Brunswick v. *King of Hanover* 569-70
Jeyaretnam 588-9
Jones (Margaret) 630-1, 633
Khan 630-2, 650-7
Kirkpatrick 593-604
Korea National Insurance Corp. 579-80, 593

judicial review/justiciability (act of foreign State/foreign relations or prerogative power/recognition and enforcement of foreign law), jurisprudence (*cont.*)
  Kuwait Airways 592-3, 602-4
  Kuwait Airways (Nos 4 and 5) 570-1, 576-7, 631
  Lucasfilm 579
  Luther v. *Sagor* 570-1
  Nissan 571-2
  Oetjen 570, 579-80, 601-2
  Philippine National Bank v. *Hawaii District Court* 590-2
  Pinochet (No 3) 575-6
  Playa Larga 592-3
  Princess Paley Olga v. *Weisz* 570-1
  Rahmatullah 655-7
  Ricaud 570, 601-2
  Sabbatino 601-2
  Sharon 593-4
  Skrine 588-9
  Underhill 570, 601-2, 630-1
  Voth 578
  Williams v. *Humbert* 574
  Yukos 569-614, 651-2
  Yukos FSA 604-14
jury trial: *see* fair trial (municipal law/general), jury trial, right to; *Misick*, right to jury trial
***jus cogens*/peremptory norm**
  incorporation/"as part of" municipal law 536-9
  jurisprudence
    East Timor 536-7
    Misick 536-9
  self-determination, right of 536-9
just satisfaction obligation (ECHR 41 [50]), costs and expenses
  "actually, necessarily and reasonably incurred", evidence of, need for 297-8
  legal costs, in municipal courts, limitation to proceedings intended to prevent or redress ECHR violation 297-8

Khan
  act of State/non-justiciability
    combatant immunity considerations 633-4, 639, 642-3, 649
    discretionary nature 650-7
    reasons for 630-2, 650-7
      international effects 650-7
    State responsibility for conduct of judicial authorities (ILC 4(1)) and 631
  background 627-30, 643-6
    PII (public interest immunity certificate) 646
    Serious Crimes Act: *see* United Kingdom, aiding and abetting/complicity or association (Serious Crimes Act, Part 2) by section
  claimant's primary case (domestic law basis) 648-9
  claimant's secondary case (international law basis) 657-8
  declaration as requested remedy
    as advisory opinion on criminal law/objections to 634-6
    claimant's request for 628, 644-5
    futility in absence of possibility of prosecution 639

as inevitable judgment on legality of actions of foreign government 642-3
as supervision of intelligence services, alternatives to 639-40
international law, applicability to private rights and obligations under municipal law 632-4
judgment (Court of Appeal) 643-59
  conclusion 658-9
judgment (High Court) 627-43

legal certainty/legality principle
  Misick 529, 538-9
  Simms 538-9
legislative changes to ensure conformity with obligations 400
liberty and security of person, right to (ACHR 7)
  freedom of opinion and 66
  jurisprudence
    Artavia Murillo 66
    Atala Riffo 66
    Chaparro Álvarez and Lapo Íñiguez 66
life, right to (ACHPR 4)
  applicability to unborn child 106
    Maputo Protocol (2003) 106
life, right to (ACHR 4)
  "every person" (applicability to embryo) 98
  as fundamental right 81
  IVF (*in vitro* fertilization): see *Artavia Murillo* (IVF) (merits); reproductive rights
  jurisprudence (nature of State's obligations)
    Pueblo Bello Massacre 81
    Street Children 81
    Xákmok Kásek Indigenous Community 81
  restrictions on, conditions (ACHR 30), proportionality 116-37
  travaux préparatoires, "from the moment of conception" (ACHR 4(1)) 91
life, right to (ECHR 2), applicability to unborn child 102-5
life, right to (ICCPR 6)
  applicability to unborn child 99-100
  HRC General Comment 6 (right to life) 99-100
  HRC General Comment 17 (ICCPR 24 (rights of the child)) 99-100
  travaux préparatoires 99-100
life/long-term imprisonment (including ECHR 3/ICCPR 7 provisions), jurisprudence: see also *Hutchinson* (life/long-term imprisonment (ECHR 3)) (ECtHR)
  Newell; McLoughlin 240-3, 248-9
  Vinter 240-3, 245-8
Lithuania (1990-) (Republic of): see also *Paksas* (ECtHR); *Paksas* (UNHRC)
  Citizenship Act by article, 16(1) (grant of citizenship by way of exception) 271
  Constitution 1992 by section
    29 (equality before the law) 271
    56 (election as member of Seimas, eligibility) 269
    59 (taking of oath) 270
    68 (initiation of legislation) 271
    71 (signature and promulgation of laws by the President) 271
    74 (removal from office following impeachment) 267-9
    78 (election as President: eligibility) 270
    78 (election as President: registration as candidate for) 270

Lithuania (1990-) (Republic of) (*cont.*)
    82 (election as President: taking of oath) 270
    84(21) (President's powers: grant of citizenship) 271
    86 (immunity of President while in office) 267
    102 (Constitutional Court, role and status) 266-7
    104 (judicial independence) 267
    105 (determination of constitutionality of laws) 266-7
    105(3)(4) (responsibility of Seimas for determining effect of impeachment) 268-9
    106 (application for constitutional review of legislation) 266-7
    107 (declaration of unconstitutionality: effect) 266-7
    107(2) (finality of Constitutional Court decisions) 268-9
    107(3) (declaration of unconstitutionality: Seimas's decision following) 266-8
  Constitution, related legislation, Presidential Elections Act (2004 Amendment) 269
  Constitutional Court Act 1993 by article
    48 (judicial impartiality) 267
    72 (declaration of unconstitutionality: effect of adoption of subsequent legal act) 266-7
    83(2) (finality of Court's decisions) 266-7
  impeachment proceedings (Statute of the Seimas 1998/9) by article 267-9
    227 (concept of impeachment) 267
    228 (persons liable to) 267
    229 (grounds) 267
    230 (right to institute) 267
    239 (investigation committee sittings) 267-8
    239 (questioning of witnesses and experts) 267-8
    241 (investigating committee's report) 267-8
    245 (Seimas decisions following investigating committee's report) 267-8
    246 (Seimas impeachment proceedings) 267-8
    246(3) (criminal procedure law, applicability) 267
    247-58 (Seimas impeachment proceedings) 267-8
    259 (removal from post of impeached person) 269
    260 (Seimas impeachment proceedings: adoption of resolution) 267-8
  Presidential Office Act by article, 3 (form of oath) 270-1

marriage, right of (ICCPR 23(1)) 68-9
marriage, right of (UDHR 16(1)) 68-9
measure of damages/compensation including valuation of company/property/assets
  applicable law, procedure (*lex fori*) vs substance (*lex loci delicti*) 672-5
  jurisprudence
    Cox 673-5
    Harding 673, 675
    Iraqi Civilians 672-5
    Phrantzes 674
    Rookes 674
  punitive damages: *see* punitive damages
minority rights (ICCPR 27)
  enjoyment of own culture, jurisprudence, *Paadar* 349-51
  HRC General Comment 23 350
Misick
  background
    Bancoult 2 524-5, 528-31, 533, 537-8, 542-3
    Commission of Inquiry terms of reference 520

INDEX 701

Commissions of Inquiry Ordinance, s. 8 (admissibility of evidence given before the Commission in civil or criminal proceedings against the Commissioner) 520
HOC Report on Overseas Territories (2008) 520
Interim Report (February 2009) 521-3, 534
  proposed removal of the right to trial by jury (Constitution 6(6)) 522-3, 540-1
prorogation of TCI Assembly (December 2008) 520-1
status of claimant 520
TCI system of government 520
Court of Appeal proceedings 533-43
  Court's conclusion 543
  Hughes LJ (jury trial) 543
ECtHR proceedings (alleged breach of ECHR 8 as a result of denial of ECHR Protocol 1:3 rights) (admissibility) 545-53
  Court's decision 552-3
  ECHR interpretation, general principles 549
  factual background 545-8
  relevant domestic law (West Indies Act ss. 5(1) and 7/Order suspending the Constitution) 548
High Court proceedings 519-33
  Court's conclusion 533
Order suspending the Constitution (18/25 March 2009)
  as alleged breach of
    fair trial obligations 531
    non-retroactivity principle 531
    prohibition of criminal legislation directed at individuals 531-2
  status 523, 533-4
right to jury trial
  claimant's case 523-4, 534-5
  Court's assessment (Court of Appeal) 539-41
  Court's assessment (High Court) 525-6
right to self-determination/free elections (ECHR Protocol 1:3)
  claimant's case 524, 534-5
  Court's assessment (Court of Appeal) 541-3
  Court's assessment (High Court) 527-8
  as *jus cogens*/peremptory norm, relevance 536-9
  suspension of application to TCI 527-8, 535
  UNC 73(b) (obligation to promote self-government) 541-3
West Indies Act 1962, s. 5(1) (power to make Orders for the "peace, order and good government" of the TCI) 524-5, 548
  limits on 528-31
    human rights 529-30
    judicial review principles 529, 532-3
    legality principle/fundamental rights 529, 538-9
    repugnancy principle 528
  parliamentary sovereignty and 529, 536
  text 524

non-appealability and 25-6
non-discrimination obligation (ACHR 1)
  differential treatment distinguished 124-6
  indirect discrimination 124-33

non-discrimination obligation (ACHR 1) (*cont.*)
  jurisprudence
    Apitz Barbera 124
    Artavia Murillo 124-33
    Furlan 128
    Juridical Status and Rights of Undocumented Migrants 124-5
    Nadege Dorzema 124-5
    Xákmok Kásek Indigenous Community 124
    Yean and Bosico Girls 124-5
non-discrimination obligation (CEDAW 2(f)), indirect discrimination (CEDAW General Recommendation 25 (temporary special measures)) 124-5
non-discrimination obligation (ECHR 14), Sharia law and 490-1, 511
non-discrimination obligation/equality before the law (ICCPR 26), jurisprudence, *Paadar* 349-51
non-discrimination obligation/indirect discrimination
  CEDAW General Recommendation 25 (temporary special measures) 124-5
  CRPD 25 (health) 126-7
  disability and 126-9
  gender and 129-32
  HRC General Comment 18 (ICCPR 26 et al. (non-discrimination)) 124-5
    financial situation and 132-3
    jurisprudence
      Althammer 124-5
      Artavia Murillo 124-33
      DH v. *Czech Republic* 124-5
      Furlan 128
      HM v. *Sweden* 124-5
      Hoogendijk 124-5
      Hugh Jordan 124-5
      Juridical Status and Rights of Undocumented Migrants 124-5
      Kichwa Indigenous People of Sarayaku 128
      LR v. *Slovakia* 124-5
      Mapiripán Massacre 128
      Nadege Dorzema 124-5
      Ximenes Lopes 128
      Yean and Bosico Girls 124-5
  obligation to take positive measures to prevent 128
  UNCESCR General Comment 20 (non-discrimination: "other status" grounds) 124-5
non-self-governing territories (UNC 73-4), self-government, obligation of Administering Power to promote (UNC 73(b)) 541-3

***Ory* (travellers' right to freedom of movement (ICCPR 12))**
  admissibility (OP 1:5)
    Committee's Views
      "being examined under another procedure of international investigation or settlement" (OP 1:5(2)(a)) (ECtHR decision on procedure) 397
      exhaustion of local remedies (OP 1:5(2)(b)) 397-8
    State party's observations 391
  authors/joinder of admissibility and merits 387
  Committee's decision 399
  Committee's Views (ICCPR 2(3) (justified restrictions)) (including HRC General Comment 27) 398-9

INDEX 703

facts as presented by the authors 387-9
individual opinion (Salvioli) (concurring) (ICCPR 26) 400-1
parties' arguments (merits)
   authors 389-91
   authors' comments on State party's observations 394-7
   State party 391-4
      freedom to choose and to change the commune of registration 391-3
      travel card 393-4
remedies
   compensation for harm suffered 400
   measures to ensure non-repetition (ICCPR 2(3)(a)) 400
   request for information on measures taken to give effect to Committee's Views 400
Oviedo Convention (1997) 108

Paadar **(Sami rights)**
admissibility 348
complaint/alleged violation of
   ICCPR 14(1) (independent and impartial tribunal) 340
      Committee's Views 349
   ICCPR 26 (non-discrimination obligation/equality before the law) 341
      Committee's Views 349-51
   ICCPR 27 (minority rights) 340-2
      Committee's Views 349-51
   State party's observations on 342-5
   author's comments on 346-8
facts as submitted by the authors 334-40
individual opinion (Kälin, Seibert-Fohr, Shany) (dissenting) (ICCPR 27) 351-3
procedural background
   complaint/author 333-4
   suspension of challenged measures 334
Paksas **(ECtHR)**: *see also* Lithuania (1990-) (Republic of)
alleged violation of ECHR 6 (fair hearing)
   applicant's arguments 274-5
   Court's analysis (Constitutional Court proceedings as determination of civil rights and obligations or a criminal charge) 275-7
alleged violation of ECHR 7 (*nullum crimen nulla poena sine lege*/non-retroactivity),
   applicant's arguments 275
alleged violation of ECHR 13 (effective remedy) in conjunction with ECHR Protocol 1:3 (free elections) 294-5
alleged violation of ECHR Protocol 1:3 (free elections) (admissibility) 274-7
   applicability of ECHR 17 (abuse of rights) 280-1
      parties' arguments (applicant) 282
      parties' arguments (government) 281-2
   applicability *ratione materiae*/limitation to election of members of the Seimas 277
Court's conclusion 283
exhaustion of local remedies 277-9
   Court's analysis (absence of effective remedy) 278-9
   parties' arguments (applicant) 278
   parties' arguments (government) 277-8
six-month rule 279-81
   Court's analysis (continuing violation) 280-1
   parties' arguments (applicant) 280
   parties' arguments (government) 279-80

Paksas (ECtHR) (*cont.*)
  alleged violation of ECHR Protocol 1:3 (free elections) (merits) 284-94
    Court's assessment (general principles) 287-8
      application to *Paksas* 288-94
    Court's assessment (justified restrictions/requirements)
      lawfulness 288
      legitimate aim 289
      non-retroactivity 288
      "proportionate to the legitimate aim" 289-94
    Court's conclusion 294
    parties' submissions
      applicant 286
      government 284-5
  alleged violation of ECHR Protocol 7:4(1) (*res judicata/non bis in idem* principle) 275
  background
    applicant's status 258-9
    criminal proceedings against applicant 265-6
    criminal proceedings against JB 266
    disqualification of applicant from elected office 263-5
    impeachment proceedings 261-3
    issue of Decree No 40 259
    proceedings concerning the lawfulness of Decree No 40 259-61
  Court's decision 298
  dissenting (partly) opinion (Costa J joined by Tsotsoria and Baka JJ) 298-302
    admissibility *ratione materiae* 298-301
    admissibility (six-month rule/continuing violation) 301-2
  just satisfaction obligation (ECHR 41)
    costs and expenses
      documentary evidence, need for 297-8
      limitation to proceedings intended to prevent or redress ECHR violation 297-8
    damage/compensation 296-7
  object and purpose/exceptional nature 282
  procedure 257-8
    joinder of admissibility and merits 258
  relevant domestic law and practice, impeachment proceedings (Statute of the Seimas):
      see Lithuania (1990-) (Republic of), impeachment proceedings (Statute of the Seimas 1998/9) by article
  relevant law and practice (domestic)
    competence of the Constitutional Court 266-7
    election of President and members of the Seimas 269-71
    impeachment proceedings (Statute of the Seimas) 267-9
      Constitutional Court clarifications of Constitution 107(2) 268-9
  relevant law and practice (other than domestic)
    Member State practice regarding impeachment 273-4
    Venice Commission's Guidelines on Elections 272-3
Paksas (UNHRC)
  admissibility (OP 1:5) (Committee's Views)
    "actually affected" requirement 324-5
    alleged breach of ICCPR 14/impeachment and "criminal charge" distinguished 325
    "being examined under another procedure of international investigation or settlement" (OP 1:5(2)(a))
      "same matter" in absence of correlation between ECHR and ICCPR 324
      supervision of implementation of ECtHR decision (ECHR 46(2)) 323-4

exhaustion of local remedies (ICCPR OP 1:5(2)(b))/effective remedy for alleged
    breach of ICCPR 25 (public affairs) 326
  substantiation requirement 324
admissibility (OP 1:5) (parties' arguments)
  author 310-11
  Lithuania 313-14
Committee's finding (OP 1:5(4)) 328
complaint/author 307
facts as submitted by the author 308-10
individual opinion (Neuman) (partly dissenting) 328-9
  alleged breach of ICCPR 25 (public affairs) 329
merits (Committee's Views on alleged breach of ICCPR 25 (right to take part in public
    affairs)), lifelong disqualification, objectivity/reasonableness 326-8
merits (parties' arguments)
  author 311-13
  author's comments on State party's submissions 320-2
  State party 314-20
  State party's additional observations 320-2
remedies
  measures to ensure non-repetition (ICCPR 2(3)(a)) 328
  revision of decision in breach of State's ICCPR obligations 328
  request for information on measures taken to give effect to Committee's Views 328
Palestine Liberation Organization (PLO): *see* EC–PLO Association Agreement (1995)
Pan-American Health Organization (PAHO), reproductive rights (*Health in the Americas*
    (2007)) 71-2, 129-30
preliminary ruling (CJEU/ECJ/CJEC) (TFEU 267 [234] [177]), jurisprudence, *Firma
    Brita* 203-4
private life/privacy (ACHR 11), jurisprudence
  Artavia Murillo: *see Artavia Murillo* (IVF) (merits)
  Atala Riffo 66
  Ituango Massacres 66
private life/privacy, definitions/scope, jurisprudence: *see also* family/private life, respect
    for (ECHR 8); private life/privacy (ACHR 11); reproductive rights
  AH v. Austria 67
  Albanese 550
  Artavia Murillo 66-72
  Atala Riffo 67
  Axel Springer 551-2
  Baškauskaitė 550-1
  Calmanovici 550
  Dickson 67
  DMT and DKI 550
  Dudgeon 67
  Evans 67
  Gelman 67
  Gillan and Quinton 549-50
  Karakó 551-2
  Lahtonen 551-2
  Lingens 551-2
  Misick 545-53
  Mółka 551-2
  Niemietz 67, 549-50

private life/privacy, definitions/scope, jurisprudence (*cont.*)
  P and S v. *Poland* 67
  Peck 67
  Perry 549-50
  PG and JH 549-50
  Pretty 67
  Rosendo Cantú 67
  RR v. *Poland* 67
  S and Marper 549-50
  Saaristo 551-2
  Sidabras 550
  Standard 551-2
  Thlimmenos 550
  Vilho Eskelinen 550
  Vogt 550
  Von Hannover 551-2
  X and Y v. *Netherlands* 67
public affairs, right to take part in (ICCPR 25), *Paksas* 326-8
public interest/purpose, definition 478-9
public order/public policy/*ordre public*, as variable concept 617-20
punitive damages
  "aggravated" damages 674
  Iraqi Civilians 672-5

racial discrimination, prohibition/equality before the law (CERD 5), indirect discrimination 124-5
recognition/enforcement of foreign judgment (including State immunity considerations)
  as *res judicata*/issue estoppel
    discretion in special circumstances 620-1
    requirements
      final and conclusive judgment by competent court on the merits 616
      identity of issue 616-20
      identity of parties 616
  Sennar (No 2) 616
  Yukos 614-21
remedies, legislative changes to ensure conformity with obligations 380
reparation for breach of treaty (ACHR 63(1)) (compensation)
  compliance 154-5
  costs and expenses: *see* costs (IACtHR) (ROC 55(1))
  equitable basis 148-9, 151-2
  for moral injury, equity and 151-2
  nexus/causal connection, need for 147-9
reparation for breach of treaty (ACHR 63(1)) (entitlement) ("injured party"), persons declared victims of violation of Convention right 139-40
reparation for breach of treaty (ACHR 63(1)) (obligation), *Chorzów Factory* principle of reparation (*restitutio in integrum*) 138
reparation for breach of treaty (ACHR 63(1)) (other than compensation)
  judgment as 144-5
  measures to ensure availability of IVF treatment 141-3
  measures of psychological reparation 140-1
  measures to raise awareness on reproductive health 143-4
  publication and dissemination of judgment 141

reproductive rights: *see also Artavia Murillo* (IVF) (merits); Costa Rica, IVF (*in vitro* fertilization)
    ACHR 4(1) (right to life from the moment of conception) and 77-115
        "conception" 82-9
        "every person" (applicability to embryo) 98
        travaux préparatoires 91
    assisted reproduction and IVF techniques 37-9
    embryonic loss 133-6
    financial situation and 132-3
    health care and 69-72: *see also* health-care obligations and the right to private life/personal integrity
    infertility as disability 126-9
        gender stereotyping 129-32
        "infertility" (WHO definition) 37, 126
        WMA Statement on Assisted Reproductive Technologies (2006) 126
    international instruments relating to: *see also* ACHR 4(1) (right to life from the moment of conception) and *above*
        ACHPR 4 (right to life)/Maputo Protocol on the Rights of Women in Africa (2003) 106
        ADRDM (1948) 72, 90-1
        Beijing Conference (1995), Declaration and Programme of Action 70-2
        Cairo Conference on Population and Development (1994) Programme of Action 70-2
        CEDAW 12 (health care) 100-1
        CEDAW 16(3) (reproductive autonomy) 69
        CEDAW General Recommendation No 24 (women and health) 69, 130-1
        CRC (1989)
            CRC 1 ("child") and 6(1) (inherent right to life) 101-2
            CRC preamble ("before as well as after birth") 101-2
        CRPD (2006), 25 (health) 126-7
        EC Directive 98/44/EC (legal protection of biotechnological inventions) 108-9
        ECHR 2(1) (everyone's right to life) 102-5
        HRC General Comment 19: ICCPR 23, para. 5 (right to found a family/procreate) 68-9
        ICCPR 6 (right to life) 99-100
        Oviedo Convention (1997) 108
        PAHO (*Health in the Americas* (2007)) 71-2, 129-30
        San Salvador Protocol (1988)
            14(1)(b) (right to enjoy benefits of scientific progress) 72
            18 (disability) 127
        UDHR 1 ("born") 98-9
        UNCESCR General Comment No 14 (ICCPR 12: right to the highest standard of physical and mental health) 70-1
    jurisprudence (including abortion and related issues)
        A, B and C 104-5, 120
        Artavia Murillo: see *Artavia Murillo* (IVF) (merits)
        Baby Boy 97
        Brüstle 108-9
        Costa and Pavan 105, 110, 120
        Dickson 67
        Evans 67, 105
        Gelman 67
        Kimel 120

reproductive rights (*cont.*)
    KL v. *Peru* 99-100
    LC v. *Peru* 100-1, 129-30
    LMR v. *Argentina* 99-100
    Paton 103
    RR v. *Poland* 120
    SH v. *Austria* 105, 109-10
    Vo 103-4, 108, 120
    parenthood/procreation, right to 67-9
    private life/privacy, relationship with 67-72
    proportionality (restrictions on IVF treatment) (ACHR 30) 116-37
        severity of the interference 121-3, 137
    State practice 110-13
res judicata/non bis in idem **principle (including double jeopardy rule)**
    impeachment proceedings 275-7
    Paksas 275-7
rule of law: *see Corner House Research* (High Court) (Moses LJ); *Corner House Research* (House of Lords); legal certainty/legality principle

Sami rights (Finland), Reindeer Husbandry Act 1990, alleged discriminatory effects of implementation/compatibility with ICCPR: *see Paadar* (Sami rights)
scientific technology, right of access to
    ADRDM XIII 72
    ICESCR 15(b) 72
    San Salvador Protocol (1988) 72, 127
    UNGA resolution 3384 (XXX) (Declaration on the Use of Scientific and Technological Progress in the Interests of Peace and for the Benefit of Mankind) 72
Security Council (Chapter VII action), resolutions under, 1483 (2003): *see* Iraq, post-conflict administration, UNSCR 1483 (2003)
Security Council resolutions by number and year
    242 (1967) (situation in the Middle East) 211
    338 (1973) (ceasefire in the Middle East) 211
self-determination, right of
    doctrine and practice
        ICCPR 1 541-3
    jus cogens/peremptory norm of international law 536-9
    Misick 527-8, 541-3
separation of powers
    Corner House 427-31
    rule of law and 427-31, 457
State responsibility for conduct of police/armed forces/military authorities/security forces (ILC 4), obligation to provide effective remedy for human rights breaches (ICCPR 2(3)) 378-9
State responsibility, defences/preclusion of wrongfulness (ILC 20-7), necessity (including ILC 25), *Corner House* 450-2
suspension of guarantees (ACHR 27), family life (ACHR 17) 68-9

travaux préparatoires **as supplementary means of interpretation (VCLT 32)**, in respect of
    ACHR 4(1) ("from the moment of conception") 91
    ADRDM 1 (right to life, liberty and security) 90-1
    Anti-Bribery Convention (2009) 446-7
    CRC preamble ("before as well as after birth") 101-2

INDEX 709

traveller community: *see Ory* (travellers' right to freedom of movement (ICCPR 12))
treaties, judicial review/justiciability, implementation of unincorporated treaty 439-44, 475-6, 480-4
treaties, third parties and (VCLT 34-8)
  jurisprudence, *Firma Brita* 218, 227-8
  pacta tertiis nec nocent nec prosunt (VCLT 34) 218, 227-8
treaty interpretation
  "any relevant rules of international law applicable in the relations between the parties" (VCLT 31(3)(c)), international humanitarian/human rights law as 89
  most favourable/liberal interpretation (VCLT 31(1)) 113-15
  ordinary meaning (VCLT 31(1)), "conception" (ACHR 4(1)) 82-9
  parties' intention at time of conclusion (jurisprudence)
    Anzualdo Castro 106-7
    Artavia Murillo 106-13
    Atala Riffo 106-7
    Golder 106-7
    Heliodoro Portugal 106-7
    Inze 106-7
    Kawas Fernández 106-7
    Kichwa Indigenous People of Sarayaku 106-7
    Rasmussen 106-7
    Right to Information on Consular Assistance in the Framework of the Guarantees of the Due Process of Law 106-7
    Tiu Tojín 106-7
    Toth 106-7
    TV Vest AS 106-7
  uniformity, desirability, Anti-Bribery Convention (2009) (ABC 5) 449-50, 452-3
Turks and Caicos Islands (TCI), Constitution 2006 by article
  1 (fundamental rights and freedoms) 525-6
  6(6) (trial by jury) 525-6, 539-41
  26 (executive authority) 520
    text 516
  33 (Governor's powers) 520

UN Charter (1945), primacy (UNC 103)
  Al-Jedda 666-8, 671-2
  Hassan 668-9, 671
  Iraqi Civilians 664-72
United Kingdom
  act of State doctrine
    limitations/exceptions
      commercial activities 592-3
      international law/human rights obligations including public policy considerations 581-4
      territorial limitation/act exclusively within own territory 581
      Yukos 581-97
    reasons for/justification, comity 578-80, 589-90, 609-11, 617-21
  advisory opinion (municipal courts) on criminal law, limitations 634-5
  aiding and abetting/complicity or association (Serious Crime Act, Part 2) by section 646-7
    44 (intentionally encouraging or assisting an offence) 646-7
    45 (intentionally encouraging or assisting an offence believing it will be committed) 646-7

United Kingdom (*cont.*)
    46 (encouraging or assisting offences believing one or more will be committed) 646-7
    50 (reasonableness defence) 646-7
    52 (failure to prove knowledge or belief that crime might take place in England or Wales) 640-1, 647
    Schedule 4 (extraterritorial crime) 647
  anti-corruption laws: *see also Corner House Research* (High Court) (Moses LJ); *Corner House Research* (House of Lords)
    Anti-Terrorism, Crime and Security Act 2001, Part 12 (bribery and corruption) as implementation of OECD Anti-Bribery Convention (2009) 458
    s. 108 (bribery and corruption: foreign officers etc.) 423-4
    Criminal Justice Act 1987 (fraud) (CJA) by section, 1(2) (appointment of Director, SFO/superintendence by AG) 425, 458
  Crime (Sentences) Act 1997 by section
    30(1) (release from life sentence on compassionate grounds) 239-40
    criteria (Prison Service Order 4700, chapter 12) 239-40
  Criminal Justice Act 1987 (fraud) (CJA) by section: *see* anti-corruption laws, Criminal Justice Act 1987 (fraud) (CJA) by section *above*
  intelligence services, means of supervising 639-40
  international law, applicability of private rights and obligations under municipal law 632-4
  judicial review/justiciability (foreign relations decisions/prerogative power of forum State), acts considered for, decisions relating to criminal proceedings (investigation/prosecution) 425-6, 469-70
  life/long-term imprisonment (including ECHR 3/ICCPR 7 provisions): *see also Hutchinson* (life/long-term imprisonment (ECHR 3)) (ECtHR)
  non-justiciability of act of State of foreign government within its own territory, reasons for/justification (*Underhill* doctrine), embarrassment to the executive 579-80, 630-1
  parliamentary sovereignty, legislative 529, 536
  Private International Law (Miscellaneous Provisions) Act 1995 (PILA) by section
    10 (abolition of common law rules) 673
    11 (applicable law in tort: general rule) 673
    12 (applicable law: displacement of general rule) 673
    14(2) (limitation of impact on common law to rules abolished under s. 10) 673
    14(3)(b) (rules of evidence and procedure: law of the forum as applicable law) 673
  public interest/purpose
    definition 478-9
    judicial review of SFO Director's decision based on 471-5: *see also Corner House Research* (High Court) (Moses LJ); *Corner House Research* (House of Lords)
    Shawcross exercise 411-14, 455-6, 459-61
  separation of powers, rule of law and 427-31
  treaties and municipal law (including implementing legislation/incorporation), unincorporated treaty, judicial review of consistency with treaty 439-44, 475-6, 480-4
  treaty interpretation, uniformity, desirability, Anti-Bribery Convention (2009) (ABC 5) 449-50, 452-3

Universal Declaration of Human Rights (1948) (UDHR), applicability to unborn child 98-9

Venice Commission (European Commission for Democracy through Law), Guidelines on Elections (extracts) 272-3

Victoria, State responsibility in respect of human rights obligations: *see Horvath* (HRC)

INDEX 711

Vienna Convention on the Law of Treaties (1969) (VCLT) (procedural aspects)
applicability/scope
　international agreements not within the scope (VCLT 3) 218, 226
　States (VCLT 1) 218
customary international law and, applicability to treaties with international organizations not covered by VCLT 226

WHO, "health" (WHO Preamble) 70-1
women: *see also* CEDAW (1979); reproductive rights
　ACHPR 4 (right to life)/Maputo Protocol on the Rights of Women in Africa (2003) 106
　Beijing Conference (1995), Declaration and Programme of Action 70-2

Yukos
　act of State doctrine, review of the jurisprudence: *see* judicial review/justiciability (act of foreign State/foreign relations or prerogative power/recognition and enforcement of foreign law), jurisprudence
　act of State/non-justiciability 569-614
　　limitations/exceptions 581-97
　　　abuse of process (including *Yukos FSA* considerations) 577-8, 584, 604-14
　　　challenge to the validity of the act 597-604
　　　commercial activities exception 592-3
　　　factual enquiry vs finding on legality of action (*Kirkpatrick* limitation) 593-604
　　　international law/human rights violations (public policy exception) 581-4, 604-14
　　　judicial acts (including review of the jurisprudence) 584-92
　　　territorial limitation/act exclusively within own territory 581
　　reasons for/justification, comity 578-80, 589-90, 609-11, 617-21
　　review of the jurisprudence 569-81
　Court's conclusion 621
　issue estoppel 614-21
　　background facts 614-17
　　identity of issue in Netherlands and UK proceedings 617-20
　　public policy as variable issue 617-20
　　requirements
　　　final and conclusive judgment by competent court on the merits 616
　　　identity of issue 616
　　　identity of parties 616
　procedural history
　　enforcement proceedings in the Netherlands courts 558, 562-3
　　enforcement proceedings in the UK Commercial Court 558-9, 563-9
　　problem (change of status of parties) 557-8
　　setting aside of award by Russian courts 558
　　summary of issues for consideration 559-60
　　Yukos-YNG awards 560-2

CONSOLIDATED TABLES OF CASES
VOLUMES 126-165

CONSOLIDATED TABLE OF CASES VOLUMES 126-165
ARRANGED ALPHABETICALLY

(Cases which are reported only in a note are distinguished from cases which are reported in full by the insertion of the word "note" in parentheses after the page number of the report.)

A and Others v. HM Treasury (JUSTICE intervening) (Nos 1 and 2) **149**.641
A and Others v. Secretary of State for the Home Department (No 1) **137**.1
A and Others v. Secretary of State for the Home Department (No 2) **137**.116
A and Others v. United Kingdom (Application No 3455/05) (Merits) **137**.115 (note), **148**.350
A, X and Y and Others v. Home Secretary **126**.585
AB v. Registrar of Births, Deaths and Marriages **133**.248, **136**.266
Abbasi and Juma Case **126**.685
Abbott v. Abbott **154**.639
Abdelrazik v. Minister of Foreign Affairs and Attorney General of Canada **155**.377
Abu Hamza and Others v. Secretary of State for the Home Department **155**.312
Abu Qatada Cases **142**.411, **149**.454, **150**.359, 461 (note), **153**.651, **155**.754, 776 (note)
Abyei Arbitration (Government of Sudan/ Sudan People's Liberation Movement/ Army) (Final Award) **144**.348
Accordance with International Law of the Unilateral Declaration of Independence in Respect of Kosovo (Advisory Opinion) **150**.1
Achabal Puertas v. Spain (Communication No 1945/2010) **159**.272
Adalah (Legal Center for Arab Minority Rights in Israel) and Others v. GOC Central Command, IDF and Others (HCJ 3799/02) **145**.407
Adams v. Secretary of State for Justice **154**.533

ADM and Tate & Lyle Ingredients Americas Inc. v. United Mexican States (ICSID Case No ARB(AF)/04/5) (Award) **146**.439, 445
ADM and Tate & Lyle Ingredients Americas Inc. v. United Mexican States (ICSID Case No ARB(AF)/04/5) (Correction, Supplementary Decision and Interpretation) **146**.439, 563
Aerial Drone Deployment on 4 October 2010 in Mir Ali/Pakistan (Case No 3 BJs 7/12-4) **157**.722
Afghanistan Political Persecution Case (Case Nos 2 BvR 260 and 1353/98) **130**.687, 695 (note)
African Development Bank Case **138**.498
Aguirre and Others v. Peru (Barrios Altos Case) **136**.1
Ahmad and Others v. United Kingdom (Application Nos 24027/07, 11949/08, 36742/08, 66911/09 and 67354/09) (Merits) **155**.219
Ahmed and Others v. HM Treasury (JUSTICE intervening) (Nos 1 and 2) **149**.641
AIC Limited v. Federal Government of Nigeria and Others **129**.571
AIG Capital Partners Inc. and Another v. Republic of Kazakhstan (National Bank of Kazakhstan intervening) **129**.589
Aisalla Molina, Franklin Guillermo (Ecuador–Colombia, Inter-State Petition IP-02) (Report No 112/10) (Admissibility) **150**.462
The Akademik Fyodorov (Government of the Russian Federation and Another v. Marine Expeditions Inc.) **131**.460

715

Al Barakaat International Foundation *v.* Council of the European Union (Case C-415/05P) **149**.167, 309, 333, 341
Al Bashir (Situation in Darfur, Sudan) (International Criminal Court) **150**.228
Al Fayed *v.* France (Application No 38501/02) (Admissibility) **145**.686 (note)
Al Fayed *v.* Lord Advocate and Advocate General **145**.656
Al Hassan-Daniel and Another *v.* Revenue and Customs Commissioners (JUSTICE intervening) **164**.451
Al Odah and Others *v.* United States and Others **137**.377, 605
Al Rawi Case **136**.624, 688 (note)
Al-Bihani *v.* Obama, President of the United States and Others **140**.716
Al-Gertani *v.* Bosnia and Herzegovina (Communication No 1955/2010) **164**.261
Al-Ghabra *v.* HM Treasury (JUSTICE intervening) **149**.641
Al-Dahas *v.* Attorney General of Kenya and Others **143**.331
Al-Haq *v.* Secretary of State for Foreign and Commonwealth Affairs **154**.423, 442 (note)
Al-Jedda *v.* Secretary of State for Defence (No 1) **137**.202
Al-Jedda *v.* Secretary of State for Defence (No 2) **163**.622
Al-Jedda *v.* United Kingdom (Application No 27021/08) (Merits) **147**.107
Al-Jedda Case [United Kingdom] **137**.202, **163**.622
Al-Moayad *v.* Germany (Application No 35865/03) (Admissibility) **141**.507
Al-Saadoon and Mufdhi *v.* United Kingdom (Application No 61498/08) (Admissibility) **147**.1, 5
Al-Saadoon and Mufdhi *v.* United Kingdom (Application No 61498/08) (Merits) **147**.1, 24
Al-Saadoon and Mufdhi Case [United Kingdom] **147**.532
Al-Sirri *v.* Secretary of State for the Home Department (United Nations High Commissioner for Refugees intervening) **140**.689, **159**.616
Al-Skeini Case [United Kingdom] **133**.499

Al-Skeini and Others *v.* United Kingdom (Application No 55721/07) (Merits) **147**.181
Alagić (Case IT-01-47-AR72) (Appeals Chamber) **133**.54
Alamieyeseigha Case **145**.619
Alexkor Ltd and Government of the Republic of South Africa *v.* Richtersveld Community and Others **127**.501
Allbutt and Others *v.* Ministry of Defence **158**.612
Allianz Via Insurance *v.* United States of America **127**.148
Altmann Case **147**.681, 725 (note)
Alvarez-Machain and Others Case **127**.691
Ame Case **148**.503
Amin *v.* Brown **132**.656
Amnesty International Canada and British Columbia Civil Liberties Association *v.* Chief of Defence Staff for the Canadian Forces and Others **156**.311
Annandale and Eskdale District Council *v.* North West Water Authority **127**.652
Apostolides *v.* Orams and Another **154**.443, 450, 498
Application for Execution of Judgments Nos 2867 and 3003 Filed by SG (SG *v.* IFAD) (Judgment No 3152) **164**.134
Application for Revision of the Judgment of 11 September 1992 in the *Land, Island and Maritime Frontier Dispute (El Salvador/Honduras: Nicaragua intervening)* (El Salvador *v.* Honduras) (Judgment) **129**.1
Application for Revision of the Judgment of 11 July 1996 in *Application of the Convention on the Prevention and Punishment of the Crime of Genocide (Bosnia and Herzegovina* v. *Yugoslavia)* (Yugoslavia *v.* Bosnia and Herzegovina) (Judgment) **155**.1
Application for the Suspension of the Execution of Judgment No 2867 Filed by the International Fund for Agricultural Development (SG *v.* IFAD) (Judgment No 3003) **164**.18
Application of the Convention on the Prevention and Punishment of the Crime of Genocide (Bosnia and Herzegovina *v.* Serbia and Montenegro) **160**.1

Application of the Convention on the Prevention and Punishment of the Crime of Genocide (Bosnia and Herzegovina v. Yugoslavia), Application for Revision of the Judgment of 11 July 1996 (Yugoslavia v. Bosnia and Herzegovina) (Judgment) **155**.1
Application of the Interim Accord of 13 September 1995 (the former Yugoslav Republic of Macedonia v. Greece) **162**.476
Application of the International Convention on the Elimination of All Forms of Racial Discrimination (Georgia v. Russian Federation) (Provisional Measures) (Preliminary Objections) [ICJ] **161**.1
The ARA Libertad (Argentina v. Ghana) (Request for Provisional Measures) [ITLOS] **156**.186, 239 (note)
Arar v. Syrian Arab Republic and the Hashemite Kingdom of Jordan **155**.368
Archer Daniels Midland Company and Tate & Lyle Ingredients Americas Inc. v. United Mexican States (ICSID Case No ARB(AF)/04/5) (Award) **146**.439, 445
Archer Daniels Midland Company and Tate & Lyle Ingredients Americas Inc. v. United Mexican States (ICSID Case No ARB(AF)/04/5) (Correction, Supplementary Decision and Interpretation) **146**.439, 563
The Arctic Sunrise (Netherlands v. Russian Federation) (Provisional Measures) **159**.68
Argentina v. Ghana (*The ARA Libertad*) (Request for Provisional Measures) [ITLOS] **156**.186, 239 (note)
Argentina v. Uruguay (Pulp Mills on the River Uruguay) **152**.1
Argentina v. Uruguay (Pulp Mills on the River Uruguay) (First Request for Provisional Measures) **152**.1, 14
Argentina v. Uruguay (Pulp Mills on the River Uruguay) (Second Request for Provisional Measures) **152**.1, 55
Argentina v. Uruguay (Pulp Mills on the River Uruguay) (Merits) **152**.1, 95
Argentine Necessity Case (Case No 2 BvM 1-5/03, 1, 2/06) **138**.1
Arias v. Venezuela **128**.684

Armando dos Santos v. Prosecutor General (Timor-Leste) **138**.604
Armed Activities on the Territory of the Congo (Democratic Republic of the Congo v. Uganda) (Provisional Measures) **146**.1, 12
Armed Activities on the Territory of the Congo (Democratic Republic of the Congo v. Uganda) (Counterclaims) **146**.1, 34
Armed Activities on the Territory of the Congo (Democratic Republic of the Congo v. Uganda) (Merits) **146**.1, 57
Armed Activities on the Territory of the Congo (New Application: 2002) (Democratic Republic of the Congo v. Rwanda) (Provisional Measures) **146**.263, 272
Armed Activities on the Territory of the Congo (New Application: 2002) (Democratic Republic of the Congo v. Rwanda) (Jurisdiction and Admissibility) **146**.263, 345
Arrest Warrant of 11 April 2000 (Democratic Republic of the Congo v. Belgium) (Request for Provisional Measures) **128**.1, 12
Arrest Warrant of 11 April 2000 (Democratic Republic of the Congo v. Belgium) (Judgment) **128**.1, 16
Artavia Murillo and Others ("*In vitro* fertilization") v. Costa Rica **165**.1
AS and DD (Libya) v. Secretary of State for the Home Department and Liberty **140**.654
Assange v. Swedish Prosecution Authority (Nos 1 and 2) **164**.461, 568 (note)
Asylum Legislation (Accelerated Airport Procedure) Constitutionality Case (Case No 2 BvR 1516/93) **130**.606
Asylum Legislation (Safe Countries of Origin) Constitutionality Case (Case Nos 2 BvR 1507 and 1508/93) **130**.640, 661 (note)
Asylum Legislation (Safe Third Countries) Constitutionality Case (Case Nos 2 BvR 1938 and 2315/93) **130**.662, 686 (note)
Atasoy and Sarkut v. Turkey (Communication Nos 1853 and 1854/2008) **157**.653
Attorney General (Barbados) and Others v. Joseph and Boyce **134**.469

Attorney General (Canada) *v.* SD Myers Inc.; United Mexican States (Intervener) **126**.553

Attorney General (Canada, on behalf of the United States of America) *v.* Khadr **157**.700

Attorney General (Uganda) *v.* Kigula and Others **143**.667

Attorney General's (England) Reference No 69 of 2013, *Re* **158**.746

Auditing of Accounts between the Netherlands and France pursuant to the Additional Protocol of 25 September 1991 to the Convention on the Protection of the Rhine against Pollution by Chlorides of 3 December 1976 (Netherlands/France) (Award) **144**.259

Austria, Republic of and Others *v.* Altmann **147**.681, 725 (note)

Avena and Other Mexican Nationals (Mexico *v.* United States of America) (Provisional Measures) **134**.95, 104

Avena and Other Mexican Nationals (Mexico *v.* United States of America) (Judgment) **134**.95, 120

Avena and Other Mexican Nationals (Mexico *v.* United States of America), Request for Interpretation of Judgment of 31 March 2004 (Provisional Measures) **148**.1, 147

Avena and Other Mexican Nationals (Mexico *v.* United States of America), Request for Interpretation of Judgment of 31 March 2004 (Judgment) **148**.1, 187

AWAS 39423 Ireland Ltd and Others *v.* Director-General of Civil Aviation and Spicejet Ltd **163**.569

Awas Tingni Case **136**.73

AY Bank Ltd (in liquidation), *Re*; AY Bank Ltd (in liquidation) *v.* Bosnia and Herzegovina and Others **149**.614

Ayliffe and Others *v.* Director of Public Prosecutions **132**.632, 668

Azanian People's Organization (AZAPO) and Others *v.* President of the Republic of South Africa and Others **131**.492

Aziz *v.* Aziz and Others (HM the Sultan of Brunei intervening) **136**.587

B (a Child) (Care Proceedings: Diplomatic Immunity), *In re* **145**.516

B and Others *v.* Secretary of State for Foreign and Commonwealth Affairs **131**.616

Bah *v.* Libyan Embassy **142**.167

Baker *v.* Canada (Minister of Citizenship and Immigration) **148**.594

Balaj (Case No IT-04-84*bis*-T) **158**.142

Bancoult Case (No 2) **138**.628

Bancoult Case (No 3) **162**.348

Banda, *Re* **154**.410

Bank for International Settlements Arbitration (Partial Award) **140**.1, 6

Bank for International Settlements Arbitration (Final Award) **140**.1, 81

Baoanan *v.* Baja and Others **152**.596

Barak, *Re* **163**.619

Barbados/Trinidad and Tobago Arbitration (Award) **139**.449

Barnette Case **145**.602

Barrios Altos Case (Chumbipuma Aguirre and Others *v.* Peru) (Merits) **136**.1, 7

Barrios Altos Case (Chumbipuma Aguirre and Others *v.* Peru) (Interpretation) **136**.1, 42

Barrios Altos Case (Chumbipuma Aguirre and Others *v.* Peru) (Reparations) **136**.1, 48

Basson Case **133**.424

Bat *v.* Investigating Judge of the German Federal Court **147**.633

Beaty Case **160**.686

Behrami *v.* France (Application No 71412/01) (Admissibility) **133**.1

Beit Sourik Village Council *v.* Government of Israel and Commander of the IDF Forces in the West Bank (HCJ 2056/04) **129**.189

Belgium/Netherlands (Iron Rhine Arbitration) (Award) (Interpretation of Award) **140**.130, 139, 230

Belhaj and Boudchar *v.* Straw and Others **159**.649

Belmarsh Case **137**.1

Benin/Niger (Frontier Dispute) (Judgment) **151**.370

Bici and Bici *v.* Ministry of Defence **145**.529

Bieber Case **156**.402, 423 (note)

Bijelić v. Montenegro and Serbia (Application No 11890/05) (Merits) **142**.146
Bin Laden aka Mohamed Case **127**.676
Black Sea Case, Maritime Delimitation in the Black Sea (Romania v. Ukraine) (Judgment) **144**.179
Bo Xilai **128**.713
Bond v. United States **164**.624
Bosnia–Herzegovina Genocide Case (Case No 3 StR 244/01) **131**.274
Bosnia and Herzegovina v. Serbia and Montenegro (Application of the Convention on the Prevention and Punishment of the Crime of Genocide) **160**.1
Botswana/Namibia (Kasikili/Sedudu Island) (Judgment) **151**.1
Boudellaa and Others v. Bosnia and Herzegovina and the Federation of Bosnia and Herzegovina **136**.309
Boumediene and Others v. Bush, President of the United States and Others **137**.605
Bouzari and Others v. Islamic Republic of Iran **128**.586
Boyce and Another v. The Queen **134**.439
Boyce and Others v. Barbados **134**.614 (note)
Brahimaj (Case No IT-04-84*bis*-T) **158**.142
Brita GmbH v. Hauptzollamt Hamburg-Hafen (Case C-386/08) **165**.188
British Arab Commercial Bank Plc v. National Transitional Council of the State of Libya **147**.667
Brown v. Attorney General of Jamaica **134**.615
Brown (aka Bajinya) and Others v. Government of Rwanda and Another **142**.568
Brzak and Another v. United Nations and Others **162**.765
Bulgakov v. Ukraine (Communication No 1803/2008) **159**.132
Burundi v. Landau **127**.98
Bustillo v. Virginia **134**.719

C and Others v. Director of Immigration **138**.537
CAA v. Singapore Airlines Limited **133**.371
Cal and Others v. Attorney General of Belize and Minister of Natural Resources and Environment **135**.77
Cameroon v. Nigeria (Land and Maritime Boundary Case) **141**.1
Cameroon v. Nigeria (Land and Maritime Boundary between Cameroon and Nigeria) (Preliminary Objections) **141**.1, 32
Cameroon v. Nigeria (Land and Maritime Boundary between Cameroon and Nigeria) (Request for Interpretation of Judgment) **141**.1, 173
Cameroon v. Nigeria (Land and Maritime Boundary between Cameroon and Nigeria) (Application for Permission to Intervene) **141**.1, 200
Cameroon v. Nigeria (Land and Maritime Boundary between Cameroon and Nigeria) (Merits) **141**.1, 206
Campbell Case **138**.354, 385
Canada (Her Majesty the Queen in Right of) v. Edelson and Others (PLA 7092/94) **131**.279
Cargill Inc. v. United Mexican States (ICSID Case No ARB(AF)/05/2) (Award) **146**.642
Cargill Inc. Case [Canada] **146**.800, **150**.598, 622 (note)
Caribbean Sea Case, Territorial and Maritime Dispute (Nicaragua v. Honduras) (Judgment) **144**.1
Cedeño v. Bolivarian Republic of Venezuela (Communication No 1940/2010) **159**.143
Center for the Defense of the Individual and Others v. Israel Defence Force Commander in the West Bank (HCJ 3278/02) **133**.314
Centre for Minority Rights Development ("CEMIRIDE") (Kenya) and Minority Rights Group International on behalf of Endorois Welfare Council v. Kenya (Communication No 276/2003) (Merits) **142**.1
Certain Property (Liechtenstein v. Germany) (Preliminary Objections) **149**.89
Certain Questions of Mutual Assistance in Criminal Matters (Djibouti v. France) (Judgment) **148**.1
Chabad v. Russian Federation **164**.570

Chafin v. Chafin **164**.579
Chagos Islanders v. United Kingdom (Application No 35622/04) (Admissibility) **162**.318
Chagos Islands Cases **162**.1, 318, 348
Chagos Marine Protected Area (Republic of Mauritius v. United Kingdom) (Decision on Challenge to an Arbitrator) (Award) **162**.1
Channel Tunnel Group Limited and France-Manche SA v. Secretary of State for Transport of the Government of the United Kingdom of Great Britain and Northern Ireland and le Ministre de l'Équipement, des Transports, de l'Aménagement du Territoire, du Tourisme et de la Mer du Gouvernement de la République Française (Partial Award) **132**.1
Chevron Corporation v. Naranjo and Others **163**.702
Choudhary v. Canada (Communication No 1898/2009) **164**.234
Christian and Others v. The Queen **130**.696
Chumbipuma Aguirre and Others v. Peru (Barrios Altos Case) **136**.1
Cissé v. International Bank for Reconstruction and Development (Decision No 242) **133**.117
Civil Aeronautics Administration v. Singapore Airlines Limited **133**.371
Clarification of Paragraph 5 of Operative Part of Constitutional Court Resolution No 3-P of 2 February 1999 **142**.383
CND Case **126**.727
Commercial Farmers Union and Others v. Minister of Lands and Rural Resettlement and Others **152**.647
Commission of the European Communities v. Belgium (Case C-437/04) **164**.144
Commission of the European Communities v. Ireland (Case C-459/03) **153**.1
Compliance of Article 1(3) of Law of St Petersburg with Charter of St Petersburg, Re **138**.482
Congo, Democratic Republic of v. Belgium (Arrest Warrant of 11 April 2000) **128**.1

Congo, Democratic Republic of v. Belgium (Arrest Warrant of 11 April 2000) (Request for Provisional Measures) **128**.1, 12
Congo, Democratic Republic of v. Belgium (Arrest Warrant of 11 April 2000) (Judgment) **128**.1, 60
Congo, Democratic Republic of v. Rwanda (Armed Activities on the Territory of the Congo) (New Application: 2002) **146**.263
Congo, Democratic Republic of v. Rwanda (Armed Activities on the Territory of the Congo) (New Application: 2002) (Request for the Indication of Provisional Measures) **146**.263, 272
Congo, Democratic Republic of v. Rwanda (Armed Activities on the Territory of the Congo) (New Application: 2002) (Judgment on Jurisdiction of the Court and Admissibility of the Application) **146**.263, 345
Congo, Democratic Republic of v. Uganda (Armed Activities on the Territory of the Congo) **146**.1
Congo, Democratic Republic of v. Uganda (Armed Activities on the Territory of the Congo) (Request for the Indication of Provisional Measures) **146**.1, 12
Congo, Democratic Republic of v. Uganda (Armed Activities on the Territory of the Congo) (Counterclaims) **146**.1, 34
Congo, Democratic Republic of v. Uganda (Armed Activities on the Territory of the Congo) (Merits) **146**.1, 57
Congo, Democratic Republic of and Others v. FG Hemisphere Associates LLC (No 1) [China, HKSAR] **147**.376
Congo, Democratic Republic of and Others v. FG Hemisphere Associates LLC (No 2) [China, HKSAR] **150**.684
Construction of a Wall in the Occupied Palestinian Territory (Advisory Opinion) **129**.37
Consular Assistance in the Framework of the Guarantees of the Due Process of Law, Right to Information on (Advisory Opinion OC-16/99) **154**.248
Conthe v. International Bank for Reconstruction and Development (Decision No 271) **133**.149

Corn Products International Inc. *v.* United Mexican States (ICSID Case No ARB (AF)/04/1) (Decision on Responsibility) **146**.581

Corner House Research Case **165**.402

Costa Rica *v.* Nicaragua (Dispute regarding Navigational and Related Rights) (Judgment) **151**.615

Cotigny and French Parachuting Federation *v.* Suarez and United States of America **127**.168

Council of Canadians and Others *v.* The Queen in Right of Canada **132**.335

Coy and Others *v.* Attorney General of Belize and Minister of Natural Resources and Environment **135**.77

Creighton Ltd *v.* Minister of Finance of Qatar and Others **127**.154

Croatia (Republic of) *v.* Republic of Serbia **164**.429

Croatia (Republic of) *v.* Snedden **153**.335

The "Cygnus" Case (Somali Pirates) **145**.491

Cyprus *v.* Turkey (Application No 25781/94) (Just Satisfaction) **159**.1

D *v.* International Finance Corporation (Decision No 304) **133**.196

DD (Afghanistan) *v.* Secretary of State for the Home Department **159**.616

De Boucherville *v.* State of Mauritius **155**.466

Death Penalty Constitutionality Case [Russian Federation] **142**.383

Death Penalty Constitutionality Case [Uganda] **143**.667

Delimitation of the Border between the State of Eritrea and the Federal Democratic Republic of Ethiopia, Decision regarding **130**.1

Demarcation of the Border between the State of Eritrea and the Federal Democratic Republic of Ethiopia, Statement regarding **130**.147

Demopoulos and Others *v.* Turkey (Application Nos 46113/99, 3843/02, 13751/02, 13466/03, 14163/04, 10200/04, 19993/04, 21819/04) (Admissibility) **158**.88

Diplomatic Privileges and Immunities of a Visiting Prince Case **142**.186

Dire Case **154**.700, 738 (note)

Dispute Concerning Access to Information under Article 9 of the OSPAR Convention (Ireland *v.* United Kingdom) (Final Award) [Arbitral Tribunal] **126**.334

Dispute regarding Navigational and Related Rights (Costa Rica *v.* Nicaragua) (Judgment) **151**.615

Distomo Massacre Case (Federal Republic of Germany *v.* Prefecture of Voiotia) (Case No 11163/11) [Italy] **150**.706

Distomo Massacre Case (Greek Citizens *v.* Federal Republic of Germany) (Case No III ZR 245/98) [Federal Republic of Germany] **129**.556

Distomo Massacre Case (Greek Citizens *v.* Federal Republic of Germany) (Case No 2 BvR 1476/03) [Federal Republic of Germany] **135**.186

Distomo Massacre Case (Prefecture of Voiotia *v.* Federal Republic of Germany) (Case No 11/2000) [Greece] **129**.513, 524 (note)

District Public Prosecutor (Serbia) *v.* Nikolić (Case No Kž. I 1594/02) **128**.691

Divoy *v.* Secretary-General (Case No 50) **127**.37

Djibouti *v.* France (Certain Questions of Mutual Assistance in Criminal Matters) (Judgment) **148**.1

Do *v.* Immigration Appeal Tribunal **131**.577

Doherty and Doherty *v.* South Dublin County Council and Others (No 2) **148**.632

Dos Santos, Armando *v.* Prosecutor General (Timor-Leste) **138**.604

Dubsky *v.* Government of Ireland and Others **149**.529

Dumez *v.* Iraq and Others **127**.144

E *v.* International Bank for Reconstruction and Development (Decision No 325) **133**.224

Early Warning Procedure Case **145**.407

Ecuador *v.* Occidental Exploration and Production Company (No 1) **138**.92

Ecuador *v.* Occidental Exploration and Production Company (No 2) **138**.158, 218 (note)

Eemshaven Port Authority Case **127**.225

El Salvador v. Honduras (Application for Revision of the Judgment of 11 September 1992 in the *Land, Island and Maritime Frontier Dispute (El Salvador/Honduras: Nicaragua intervening)* (Judgment) **129**.1

Ellis v. Ministry of Defence **158**.612

EM (Lebanon) v. Secretary of State for the Home Department (AF (a Child) and Others intervening) **165**.485

Emin v. Yeldag (Attorney General and Secretary of State for Foreign and Commonwealth Affairs intervening) **148**.663

EnCana Corporation v. Republic of Ecuador (LCIA Case No UN 3481) (Interim Award on Provisional Measures) **138**.219, 227

EnCana Corporation v. Republic of Ecuador (LCIA Case No UN 3481) (Partial Award on Jurisdiction) **138**.219, 232

EnCana Corporation v. Republic of Ecuador (LCIA Case No UN 3481) (Award) **138**.219, 249

Endorois Case **142**.1

Entico Corporation Ltd v. United Nations Educational, Scientific and Cultural Organization **156**.382

Eritrea–Ethiopia Boundary Commission Decision on Delimitation **130**.1

Eritrea–Ethiopia Boundary Commission Statement on Demarcation **130**.147

Eritrea/Ethiopia (Eritrea's Claims) (Eritrea–Ethiopia Claims Commission) **135**.197 (note), 695 (additional materials)
 Central Front (Claims 2, 4, 6, 7, 8 & 22) (Eritrea/Ethiopia) (Partial Award) **135**.295
 Civilians Claims (Claims 15, 16, 23 & 27-32) (Eritrea/Ethiopia) (Partial Award) **135**.374
 Damages Claims (Eritrea/Ethiopia) (Final Award) **140**.235
 Diplomatic Claim (Claim 20) (Eritrea/Ethiopia) (Partial Award) **135**.519
 Loss of Property in Ethiopia Owned by Non-Residents (Claim 24) (Eritrea/Ethiopia) (Partial Award) **135**.657
 Pensions (Claims 15, 19 & 23) (Eritrea/Ethiopia) (Final Award) **135**.503
 Prisoners of War (Claim 17) (Eritrea/Ethiopia) (Partial Award) **135**.199
 Western Front, Aerial Bombardment and Related Claims (Claims 1, 3, 5, 9-13, 14, 21, 25 & 26) (Eritrea/Ethiopia) (Partial Award) **135**.565

Estate of the Late Kazemi and Hashemi v. Islamic Republic of Iran and Others **147**.318, **154**.351, **159**.299

Ethiopia/Eritrea (Ethiopia's Claims) (Eritrea–Ethiopia Claims Commission) **135**.197 (note), 695 (additional materials)
 Central Front (Claim 2) (Ethiopia/Eritrea) (Partial Award) **135**.334
 Civilians Claims (Claim 5) (Ethiopia/Eritrea) (Partial Award) **135**.427
 Damages Claims (Ethiopia/Eritrea) (Final Award) **140**.376
 Diplomatic Claim (Claim 8) (Ethiopia/Eritrea) (Partial Award) **135**.544
 Economic Loss Throughout Ethiopia (Claim 7) (Ethiopia/Eritrea) (Partial Award) **135**.470
 Jus Ad Bellum (Claims 1-8) (Ethiopia/Eritrea) (Partial Award) **135**.479
 Ports (Claim 6) (Ethiopia/Eritrea) (Final Award) **135**.490
 Prisoners of War (Claim 4) (Ethiopia/Eritrea) (Partial Award) **135**.251
 Western and Eastern Fronts (Claims 1 & 3) (Ethiopia/Eritrea) (Partial Award) **135**.627

Euratom Case **136**.429

Eureko BV v. Slovak Republic (PCA Case No 2008-13) (Award on Jurisdiction, Arbitrability and Suspension) **145**.1

European Roma Rights Centre and Others v. Immigration Officer at Prague Airport and Another (United Nations High Commissioner for Refugees intervening) **131**.652

Eurotunnel Arbitration **132**.1

Evans (Maya) Case **153**.508

Execution of Judgments Nos 2867 and 3003 Filed by SG (SG v. IFAD) (Judgment No 3152), Application for **164**.134

Fang and Others v. Jiang Zemin and Others **141**.702
Fedotova v. Russian Federation (Communication No 1932/2010) **159**.193
Feldman v. United Mexican States (ICSID Case No ARB(AF)/99/1) (Preliminary Jurisdictional Issues) **126**.1, 9
Feldman v. United Mexican States (ICSID Case No ARB(AF)/99/1) (Merits) **126**.1, 26
Feldman v. United Mexican States (ICSID Case No ARB(AF)/99/1) (Correction and Interpretation of Award) **126**.1, 123
Feldman Karpa Case [Canada] **126**.536, **128**.610
Ferrini v. Federal Republic of Germany (Decision No 5044/2004) **128**.658
FG Hemisphere Associates LLC v. Democratic Republic of the Congo and Another [United States of America] **150**.842
FG Hemisphere Associates LLC v. Democratic Republic of the Congo and Others [China, HKSAR] **142**.216, **147**.376, **150**.684
FILT-CGIL Trento and Others v. United States of America (Decision No 530/2000) **128**.644
Firma Brita GmbH v. Hauptzollamt Hamburg-Hafen (Case C-386/08) **165**.188
FKAG and Others v. Australia (Communication No 2094/2011) **163**.266
Foreign Secretary and Defence Secretary v. Rahmatullah **153**.607
Forsyth Case **158**.572
France/Netherlands (Rhine Chlorides Arbitration) (Award) **144**.259
Franklin Guillermo Aisalla Molina (Ecuador–Colombia, Inter-State Petition IP-02) (Report No 112/10) (Admissibility) **150**.462
Frontier Dispute (Benin/Niger) (Judgment) **151**.370
FTZK v. Minister for Immigration and Border Protection **158**.441

Fuel Retailers Association of Southern Africa v. Director-General Environmental Management, Department of Agriculture, Conservation and Environment, Mpumalanga Province and Others **143**.426
Funnekotter and Others v. Republic of Zimbabwe (ICSID Case No ARB/05/6) (Award) **138**.410

Ganić Case **160**.651
Garcia v. Texas **163**.693
Garuda (PT) Indonesia Ltd v. Australian Competition and Consumer Commission **152**.365, **153**.406
General Comment No 22 on the Right to Freedom of Thought, Conscience and Religion **157**.596
Genocide Convention, Yugoslavia v. Bosnia and Herzegovina (Application for Revision of the Judgment of 11 July 1996 in the Case Concerning *Application of the Convention on the Prevention and Punishment of the Crime of Genocide (Bosnia and Herzegovina* v. *Yugoslavia)*) (Judgment) **155**.1
Genocide Convention (Application of), Bosnia and Herzegovina v. Serbia and Montenegro **160**.1
Gentle and Clarke, R on the Application of v. Prime Minister, Secretary of State for Defence and Attorney General **132**.721, **140**.624
Georges and Others v. United Nations and Others **162**.775
Georgia v. Russia (No 1) (Application No 13255/07) (Admissibility) (Merits) [ECtHR] **161**.333
Georgia v. Russia (No 2) (Application No 38263/08) (Admissibility) [ECtHR] **161**.487, 523 (note)
Georgia v. Russian Federation (Application of the International Convention on the Elimination of All Forms of Racial Discrimination) (Provisional Measures) (Preliminary Objections) [ICJ] **161**.1
Germany v. Prefecture of Voiotia (Case No 11163/11) **150**.706
Germany v. United States of America (LaGrand Case) (Judgment) **134**.1

Geuking v. President of the Republic of South Africa and Others **132**.568
Ghana, Republic of v. High Court (Commercial Division) Accra, *ex parte* Attorney General (NML Capital Ltd and Republic of Argentina, interested parties) **156**.240, 270 (note)
Ghana Refugié Sur Place Case (Case No 2 BvR 1058/85) **130**.560
Glenister v. President of the Republic of South Africa and Others **155**.628
Gorbachev, *Re* **163**.689
Görgülü v. Germany (Application No 74969/01) (Merits) **145**.85
Greenpeace v. Euratom **136**.429
Grovit v. De Nederlandsche Bank NV and Others **142**.403
Guarantees for the European Financial Stability Facility Case (Case Nos 2 BvR 987/10, 2 BvR 1485/10, 2 BvR 1099/10) **150**.636
Gul Case **152**.568
Guyana/Suriname Arbitration (Award) **139**.566

Habib v. Commonwealth of Australia **149**.478
Habyarimana and Ntaryamira v. Kagame **154**.739, 750 (note)
Hadžihasanović, Alagić and Kubura (Case IT-01-47-AR72) (Appeals Chamber) **133**.54
Hamdan v. Rumsfeld, Secretary of Defense and Others **137**.480
Hamdan v. United States of America **154**.751
Hamdi and Others v. Rumsfeld, Secretary of Defense and Others **137**.407
Hamza and Others v. Secretary of State for the Home Department **155**.312
Hans-Adam II (Prince) v. Municipality of Cologne (Case No 22 U 215/95) **149**.1
Hans-Adam II of Liechtenstein (Prince), *In re* (Case No 2 BvR 1981/97) **149**.26
Hans-Adam II of Liechtenstein (Prince) v. Germany (Application No 42527/98) (Admissibility) **149**.32, 38
Hans-Adam II of Liechtenstein (Prince) v. Germany (Application No 42527/98) (Merits) **149**.32, 53
Hape v. The Queen (Attorney General of Ontario intervening) **143**.140

Haradinaj, Balaj and Brahimaj (Case No IT-04-84*bis*-T) **158**.142
Haraldsson Case **140**.559
Harb v. Canada (Minister of Citizenship and Immigration) **131**.206
Harb v. His Majesty King Fahd Bin Abdul Aziz **136**.574, 586 (note)
Harksen v. President of the Republic of South Africa and Others **132**.529
Hasan Case **154**.700
Hashemi and Estate of the Late Kazemi v. Islamic Republic of Iran and Others **147**.318, **154**.351, **159**.299
Hassan v. Secretary of State for Defence **164**.391
Hassan v. United Kingdom (Application No 29750/09) (Merits) **161**.524
Hilaire, Constantine and Benjamin and Others v. Trinidad and Tobago **134**.293
Hingitaq 53, Petersen and Others v. Office of the Prime Minister of Denmark **143**.277, 298 (note)
HJ (Iran) v. Secretary of State for the Home Department **159**.428
Horgan v. An Taoiseach and Others **132**.407
Horvath v. Australia (Communication No 1885/2009) **165**.354
The Hoshinmaru (Japan v. Russian Federation) (Application for Prompt Release) **143**.1
HT (Cameroon) v. Secretary of State for the Home Department **159**.428
Hua Tian Long (No 3) **153**.430
Hungary v. Slovak Republic (Case C-364/10) **153**.92
Hutchinson v. United Kingdom (Application No 57592/08) **165**.235

ILO Administrative Tribunal Judgment No 2867 **164**.1
ILO Administrative Tribunal Judgment No 2867 upon a Complaint Filed against the International Fund for Agricultural Development [ICJ] **164**.37
ILO Administrative Tribunal Judgment No 3003 **164**.18
ILO Administrative Tribunal Judgment No 3152 **164**.134
Indonesia/Malaysia (Sovereignty over Pulau Ligitan and Pulau Sipadan) **151**.197

Indonesia/Malaysia (Sovereignty over Pulau Ligitan and Pulau Sipadan) (Application by the Philippines for Permission to Intervene) **151**.197, 212

Indonesia/Malaysia (Sovereignty over Pulau Ligitan and Pulau Sipadan) (Merits) **151**.197, 290

Indus Waters Kishenganga Arbitration (Islamic Republic of Pakistan *v.* Republic of India) **150**.311, **154**.1, **157**.362, 417

Indus Waters Kishenganga Arbitration (Islamic Republic of Pakistan *v.* Republic of India) (Interim Measures) **150**.311

Indus Waters Kishenganga Arbitration (Islamic Republic of Pakistan *v.* Republic of India) (Partial Award) **154**.1

Indus Waters Kishenganga Arbitration (Islamic Republic of Pakistan *v.* Republic of India) (Decision on Request for Clarification or Interpretation of Partial Award) **157**.417

Indus Waters Kishenganga Arbitration (Islamic Republic of Pakistan *v.* Republic of India) (Final Award) **157**.362

Institute of Cetacean Research and Others *v.* Sea Shepherd Conservation Society and Others **156**.718

Interim Accord of 13 September 1995, Application of the (former Yugoslav Republic of Macedonia *v.* Greece) **162**.476

Interlocutory Decision on the Applicable Law: Terrorism, Conspiracy, Homicide, Perpetration, Cumulative Charging (Case No STL-11-01/I) (Appeals Chamber) **145**.232

International Association of Independent Tanker Owners Case **142**.89

International Committee of the Red Cross *v.* Sibanda and Ngangura **153**.689

International Fund for Agricultural Development (Advisory Opinion) **164**.37

Interpretation of Certain Agreements and Commonwealth of Independent States' Decisions (Case No 01-1/1-98) **127**.16

Intertanko (International Association of Independent Tanker Owners) Case **142**.89

Intraline Resources Sdn Bhd *v.* Owners of the Ship or Vessel *Hua Tian Long* (No 3) **153**.430

Iran, Islamic Republic of *v.* United States of America (Oil Platforms) **130**.174

Iran, Islamic Republic of *v.* United States of America (Oil Platforms) (Preliminary Objection) **130**.174, 186

Iran, Islamic Republic of *v.* United States of America (Oil Platforms) (Counterclaim) **130**.174, 280

Iran, Islamic Republic of *v.* United States of America (Oil Platforms) (Merits) **130**.174, 323

Iran, Islamic Republic of, and Others *v.* Hashemi and Estate of the Late Kazemi **147**.318, **154**.351, **159**.299

Iraq *v.* Vinci Constructions **127**.101

Iraq, Republic of *v.* Beaty and Others **160**.686

Iraq, Republic of, and Others *v.* Simon and Others **160**.686

Iraqi Civilians *v.* Ministry of Defence **165**.660

Iraqi Civilians Case **165**.660

Ireland *v.* United Kingdom (Dispute Concerning Access to Information under Article 9 of the OSPAR Convention) (Final Award) [Arbitral Tribunal] **126**.334

Ireland *v.* United Kingdom (the MOX Plant Case) (Order No 3) (Order No 4) [Arbitral Tribunal] **126**.310, 314, 332

Ireland *v.* United Kingdom (the MOX Plant Case) (Request for Provisional Measures) [ITLOS] **126**.259

Iron Rhine Arbitration (Belgium/Netherlands) **140**.130

Iron Rhine Arbitration (Belgium/Netherlands) (Award) **140**.130, 139

Iron Rhine Arbitration (Belgium/Netherlands) (Interpretation of Award) **140**.130, 230

Islamic Human Rights Commission, R on the Application of *v.* Civil Aviation Authority, Foreign and Commonwealth Office and Ministry of Defence **132**.707

Issa and Others *v.* Turkey (Application No 31821/96) (Merits) **156**.1

Jamaa and Others *v.* Italy (Application No 27765/09) **163**.132
Japan *v.* Russian Federation (*The Hoshinmaru*) (Application for Prompt Release) [ITLOS] **143**.1
Japan *v.* Russian Federation (*The Tomimaru*) (Application for Prompt Release) [ITLOS] **143**.36
Javor and Others **127**.126
Jeong and Others *v.* Republic of Korea (Communication Nos 1642-1741/2007) **157**.620
Jones *v.* Ministry of the Interior of the Kingdom of Saudi Arabia and Another (Secretary of State for Constitutional Affairs and Another intervening) **129**.629
Jones (Margaret) Case **132**.608, 668
Jorgic (Case No 2 BvR 1290/99) **135**.152, 167 (note)
Jorgic *v.* Germany (Application No 74613/01) (Merits) **148**.234
Joseph and Boyce Cases **134**.439, 469, 614 (note)
JS (Sri Lanka) Case **159**.366
The Juno Trader (Saint Vincent and the Grenadines *v.* Guinea-Bissau) (Application for Prompt Release) **128**.267
Judgment No 2867 [ILO Administrative Tribunal] **164**.1
Judgment No 2867 of the Administrative Tribunal of the International Labour Organization upon a Complaint Filed against the International Fund for Agricultural Development (Advisory Opinion) [ICJ] **164**.37
Judgment No 3003 [ILO Administrative Tribunal] **164**.18
Judgment No 3152 [ILO Administrative Tribunal] **164**.134
JuRI-Nepal (Justice and Rights Organization) and Others *v.* Government of Nepal and Others **158**.476

Kachingwe and Others *v.* Minister of Home Affairs and Another **142**.691
Kadi *v.* Commission of the European Communities (Case T-85/09) **149**.167, 406

Kadi *v.* Council of the European Union and Commission of the European Communities (Case T-315/01) **149**.167, 250
Kadi *v.* Council of the European Union; Al Barakaat International Foundation *v.* Council of the European Union (Joined Cases C-402/05P and C-415/05P) **149**.167, 309, 341
Kafantayeni and Others *v.* Attorney General of Malawi **134**.649
Kafkaris *v.* Cyprus (Application No 21906/04) (Merits) **155**.70
Kalogeropoulou and Others *v.* Greece and Germany (Application No 59021/00) (Admissibility) **129**.537
Karpa Case **126**.1, 536, **128**.610
Kasikili/Sedudu Island (Botswana/Namibia) (Judgment) **151**.1
Kaunda and Others *v.* President of the Republic of South Africa and Others **136**.452
Kavanagh *v.* Governor of Mountjoy Prison and Others **132**.380
Kayano and Others *v.* Hokkaido Expropriation Committee (the Nibutani Dam Decision) **127**.173
Kazemi Estate *v.* Islamic Republic of Iran and Others **147**.318, **154**.351, **159**.299
Kennedy *v.* Trinidad and Tobago (Communication No 845/1999) (Admissibility) **134**.415, 418
Kennedy *v.* Trinidad and Tobago (Communication No 845/1999) (Views under Article 5(4) of the Optional Protocol) **134**.415, 428
Kenya (Sitamze) *v.* Minister for Home Affairs and Others **143**.349
Kenyan Diplomatic Residence Case (Case No IXa ZB 19/03) **128**.632
Kerajaan Negeri Selangor and Others *v.* Sagong bin Tasi and Others **135**.126
Khadr *v.* Canada (No 1) **143**.212
Khadr *v.* Canada (No 2) **143**.225
Khan Case **165**.622
Khodorkovskiy (Case No KAS06-129) **133**.365
Khodorkovskiy *v.* Russia (Application No 5829/04) (Merits) **153**.253
Kholodova *v.* Russian Federation (Communication No 1548/2007) **159**.217

Khurts Bat v. Investigating Judge of the German Federal Court **147**.633
Kibris Türk Hava Yollari and CTA Holidays Case **148**.683
Kigula Case **143**.667
Kim and Others v. Republic of Korea (Communication No 1786/2008) **157**.682
Kiobel v. Royal Dutch Petroleum Co. **164**.596
Kiyutin v. Russia (Application No 2700/10) (Merits) **145**.201
KJ International and Others v. MV *Oscar Jupiter* (Compania de Navigatie Maritime "Romline" SA and Others intervening) **131**.529
KM (Zimbabwe) v. Secretary of State for the Home Department **159**.587
Korea National Insurance Corporation v. Allianz Global Corporate & Specialty AG **163**.605
Korneenko v. Belarus (Communication No 1226/2003) **156**.271
Kosovo Advisory Opinion **150**.1
Kovsh v. Belarus (Communication No 1787/2008) **159**.257
Kubura (Case IT-01-47-AR72) (Appeals Chamber) **133**.54
Kuwait Airways Corporation v. Iraqi Airways Company ("Perjury Action") **126**.758
Kuwait Airways Corporation v. Iraqi Airways Company and Republic of Iraq ("Costs Action") **147**.532
Kuwait Airways Corporation v. Republic of Iraq and Bombardier Aerospace [Canada] **147**.303
Kwoyelo v. Uganda **150**.802
Kwoyelo Case **150**.802

La Générale des Carrières et des Mines v. FG Hemisphere Associates LLC **164**.347
LaGrand Case (Germany v. United States of America) (Judgment) **134**.1
Land and Maritime Boundary between Cameroon and Nigeria (Cameroon v. Nigeria) (Preliminary Objections) **141**.1, 32

Land and Maritime Boundary between Cameroon and Nigeria (Cameroon v. Nigeria) (Request for Interpretation of Judgment) **141**.1, 173
Land and Maritime Boundary between Cameroon and Nigeria (Cameroon v. Nigeria) (Application for Permission to Intervene) **141**.1, 200
Land and Maritime Boundary between Cameroon and Nigeria (Cameroon v. Nigeria) (Merits) **141**.1, 206
Land, Island and Maritime Frontier Dispute (El Salvador/Honduras: Nicaragua intervening), Application for Revision of the Judgment of 11 September 1992 (El Salvador v. Honduras) (Judgment) **129**.1
Land Reclamation by Singapore in and around the Straits of Johor (Malaysia v. Singapore) (Request for Provisional Measures) **126**.487
Latoni Case **150**.802
Lautsi and Others v. Italy (Application No 30814/06) **164**.176
League of Arab States v. T **127**.94
Leal Garcia v. Texas **163**.693
Legal Consequences of the Construction of a Wall in the Occupied Palestinian Territory (Advisory Opinion) **129**.37
Legality of Use of Force (Yugoslavia/Serbia and Montenegro v. Belgium) (Provisional Measures) (Preliminary Objections) **157**.1
Legality of Use of Force (Yugoslavia/Serbia and Montenegro v. Canada (Provisional Measures) (Preliminary Objections) **157**.296 (note)
Legality of Use of Force (Yugoslavia/Serbia and Montenegro v. France) (Provisional Measures) (Preliminary Objections) **157**.299 (note)
Legality of Use of Force (Yugoslavia/Serbia and Montenegro v. Germany) (Provisional Measures) (Preliminary Objections) **157**.306 (note)
Legality of Use of Force (Yugoslavia/Serbia and Montenegro v. Italy) (Provisional Measures) (Preliminary Objections) **157**.309 (note)
Legality of Use of Force (Yugoslavia/Serbia and Montenegro v. Netherlands) (Provisional Measures) (Preliminary Objections) **157**.312 (note)

Legality of Use of Force (Yugoslavia/Serbia and Montenegro v. Portugal) (Provisional Measures) (Preliminary Objections) **157**.323 (note)
Legality of Use of Force (Yugoslavia/Serbia and Montenegro v. Spain) (Provisional Measures) **157**.326 (note)
Legality of Use of Force (Yugoslavia/Serbia and Montenegro v. United Kingdom) (Provisional Measures) (Preliminary Objections) **157**.344 (note)
Legality of Use of Force (Yugoslavia/Serbia and Montenegro v. United States of America) (Provisional Measures) **157**.351 (note)
Lemeiguran and Others v. Attorney General of Kenya and Others **142**.328
Lewis v. Attorney General of Jamaica **134**.615
Liechtenstein v. Germany (Certain Property) (Judgment on Preliminary Objections) **149**.89
Liechtenstein/Pieter van Laer Painting Cases **149**.1, 26, 32, 89
Ligitan and Sipadan (Indonesia/Malaysia) **151**.197
Lisbon Treaty Constitutionality Case (Case Nos 2 BvE 2/08, 2 BvE 5/08, 2 BvR 1010/08, 2 BvR 1022/08, 2 BvR 1259/08 and 2 BvR 182/09) **141**.554
LM v. Netherlands, Minister for Netherlands Antilles Affairs and Aruban Affairs and Others **128**.681
Loewen Case **128**.334, 716
Loewen Group Inc. and Raymond L. Loewen v. United States of America (ICSID Case No ARB(AF)/98/3) (Competence and Jurisdiction) **128**.334, 339
Loewen Group Inc. and Raymond L. Loewen v. United States of America (ICSID Case No ARB(AF)/98/3) (Award) **128**.334, 359
Loewen Group Inc. and Raymond L. Loewen v. United States of America (ICSID Case No ARB(AF)/98/3) (Supplementary Decision) **128**.334, 420
Loewen, Raymond L. v. United States of America **128**.716
Logicom Case **148**.629

Louisa, MV (Saint Vincent and the Grenadines v. Kingdom of Spain) **148**.459, **157**.432
Louisa, MV (Saint Vincent and the Grenadines v. Kingdom of Spain) (Provisional Measures) **148**.459
Louisa, MV (Saint Vincent and the Grenadines v. Kingdom of Spain) (Merits) **157**.432
Lyons (Isidore Jack) Case **131**.538
Lyons (Michael Peter) Case **162**.674

Mabey Case **158**.572
McCartney, *In re* **154**.533
McCaughey and Another, *In re* (Northern Ireland Human Rights Commission and Others intervening) **153**.192
MacDermott, *In re* **154**.533
Macedonia, former Yugoslav Republic of v. Greece (Application of the Interim Accord of 13 September 1995) **162**.476
McFarland, *In re* **145**.637
Mahamdia v. People's Democratic Republic of Algeria (Case C-154/11) **153**.58
Malaysia v. Singapore (Land Reclamation by Singapore in and around the Straits of Johor) (Request for Provisional Measures) [ITLOS] **126**.487
Malaysia/Indonesia (Sovereignty over Pulau Ligitan and Pulau Sipadan) **151**.197
Malaysia/Singapore (Railway Land Arbitration) **162**.588
Malaysia/Singapore (Sovereignty over Pedra Branca/Pulau Batu Puteh, Middle Rocks and South Ledge) (Judgment) **151**.453
Mamatkulov and Askarov v. Turkey (Application Nos 46827/99 and 46951/99) (Merits) **134**.230
Mann v. Republic of Equatorial Guinea **153**.697
Mann Singh (Shingara) v. France (Communication No 1928/2010) **163**.249
Mara'abe and Others v. Prime Minister and Others (HCJ 7957/04) **129**.241
Marab and Others v. Israel Defence Force Commander in the West Bank and Another (HCJ 3239/02) **133**.332
Marchiori v. Environment Agency **127**.574

Margellos and Others v. Federal Republic of Germany (Case No 6/2002) **129**.525, 536 (note)
Maritime Delimitation and Territorial Questions between Qatar and Bahrain (Qatar v. Bahrain) (Merits) **139**.1
Maritime Delimitation in the Black Sea (Romania v. Ukraine) (Judgment) **144**.179
Matthew v. Trinidad and Tobago **134**.687
Mauritius v. United Kingdom (Chagos Marine Protected Area) (Decision on Challenge to an Arbitrator) (Award) **162**.1
Maya Indigenous Communities of the Toledo District v. Belize (Case 12.053) **135**.1
Mayagna (Sumo) Awas Tingni Community v. Nicaragua **136**.73
Mayagna (Sumo) Awas Tingni Community v. Nicaragua (Preliminary Objections) **136**.73, 83
Mayagna (Sumo) Awas Tingni Community v. Nicaragua (Merits, Reparations and Costs) **136**.73, 99
Mayagna (Sumo) Awas Tingni Community v. Nicaragua (Provisional Measures Order I) **136**.73, 217
Mayagna (Sumo) Awas Tingni Community v. Nicaragua (Provisional Measures Order II) **136**.73, 224
Mayagna (Sumo) Awas Tingni Community v. Nicaragua (Compliance Order I) **136**.73, 232
Mayagna (Sumo) Awas Tingni Community v. Nicaragua (Compliance Order II) **136**.73, 239
Mechan v. Foreign and Commonwealth Office **141**.727
Medellín v. Texas **136**.689, 751 (note)
Mexico v. Cargill Inc. **146**.800, **150**.598
Mexico v. Feldman Karpa **126**.536, **128**.610
Mexico v. United States of America (Avena and Other Mexican Nationals) **134**.95, **148**.1
Mexico v. United States of America (Avena and Other Mexican Nationals) (Request for the Indication of Provisional Measures) **134**.95, 104

Mexico v. United States of America (Avena and Other Mexican Nationals) (Judgment) **134**.95, 120
Mexico v. United States of America (Request for Interpretation of the Judgment of 31 March 2004 in *Avena and Other Mexican Nationals (Mexico* v. *United States of America)*) (Request for the Indication of Provisional Measures) **148**.1, 147
Mexico v. United States of America (Request for Interpretation of the Judgment of 31 March 2004 in *Avena and Other Mexican Nationals (Mexico* v. *United States of America)*) (Judgment) **148**.1, 187
Mihoubi v. Algeria (Communication No 1874/2009) **163**.299
Mike Campbell (Pvt) Ltd and William Michael Campbell v. Minister of National Security Responsible for Land, Land Reform and Resettlement and Attorney General **138**.354
Mike Campbell (Pvt) Ltd, William Michael Campbell and Others v. Republic of Zimbabwe (SADCT Case No 2/2007) **138**.385, **149**.475
Minister for Home Affairs (Australia Cth) and Others v. Zentai and Others **153**.366
Minister for Immigration and Multicultural Affairs (Australia) v. Haji Ibrahim **131**.1
Minister for Immigration and Multicultural Affairs (Australia) v. Khawar and Others **131**.158
Minister for Immigration and Multicultural and Indigenous Affairs (Australia), *ex parte* Ame, *Re* **148**.503
Minister of Citizenship and Immigration (Canada) v. Mugesera and Others **132**.271
Minister of Finance (Bermuda) v. Braswell and Others **132**.237, 270 (note)
Ministry of Defence v. Iraqi Civilians **165**.660
Misick v. United Kingdom (Application No 10781/10) [ECtHR] **165**.544
Misick Case [United Kingdom] **165**.515, 519, 533
Mitchell and Others v. Al-Dali and Others **129**.629
Mofaz **128**.709

Mohamad (Individually and for the Estate of Rahim, Deceased) and Others v. Palestinian Authority and Others **159**.723
Mohamed and Another v. President of the Republic of South Africa and Others **127**.468
Molina, Franklin Guillermo Aisalla (Ecuador–Colombia, Inter-State Petition IP-02) (Report No 112/10) (Admissibility) **150**.462
Montgomery Case (No 2) **145**.602
Morgan and Baker v. Hinton Organics (Wessex) Ltd and Coalition for Access to Justice for the Environment ("CAJE") **142**.542
Morocco v. Stichting Revalidatiecentrum "De Trappenberg" **128**.676
Morrison v. Peacock and Another **136**.255
Morrison and Others v. National Australia Bank Ltd and Others **160**.703
Mothers of Srebrenica Association and Others v. Netherlands and United Nations [Netherlands] **160**.558
Mothers of Srebrenica Cases **160**.558, 573
MOX Plant Case (Ireland v. United Kingdom) **126**.257 (note), 259, 310, 334
MOX Plant Case (Ireland v. United Kingdom) (Orders Nos 3 and 4) [Arbitral Tribunal] **126**.310
MOX Plant Case (Ireland v. United Kingdom) (Request for Provisional Measures) [ITLOS] **126**.259
MSS v. Belgium and Greece (Application No 30696/09) **163**.1
Mugabe Arrest Warrant Case **136**.572
Mugesera v. Canada (Minister of Citizenship and Immigration) **132**.271
Mullen Case **145**.564
Munyeshyaka **127**.134
Mustafić and Others v. Netherlands **153**.506 (note), **160**.650 (note)
Mutua and Others v. Foreign and Commonwealth Office **156**.629, 717 (note)
Myers, SD Inc. v. Government of Canada (Procedural Order No 18) **126**.161, 252 (note)

Myers, SD Inc. v. Government of Canada (Second Partial Award on Damages) **126**.161, 167
Myers, SD Inc. v. Government of Canada (Final Award on Costs) **126**.161, 226

N v. Secretary of State for the Home Department (Terrence Higgins Trust intervening) **148**.273
N v. United Kingdom (Application No 26565/05) (Merits) **148**.315
Naidenova and Others v. Bulgaria (Communication No 2073/2011) **159**.170
Namibia/Botswana (Kasikili/Sedudu Island) (Judgment) **151**.1
Narrain and Others v. Mauritius (Communication No 1744/2007) **156**.293
NATO Strategic Concept (German Participation) Case (Case No 2 BvE 6/99) **135**.168, 185 (note)
Navigational and Related Rights (Costa Rica v. Nicaragua) **151**.615
Nemariam and Others v. Federal Democratic Republic of Ethiopia and the Commercial Bank of Ethiopia (No 1) **135**.671
Nemariam and Others v. Federal Democratic Republic of Ethiopia and the Commercial Bank of Ethiopia (No 2) **135**.679
Netherlands v. Azeta BV **128**.688
Netherlands v. Mustafić and Others **153**.506 (note), **160**.650 (note)
Netherlands v. Nuhanović **153**.467, **160**.629
Netherlands, Kingdom of the v. Russian Federation (*The Arctic Sunrise*) (Request for Provisional Measures) [ITLOS] **159**.68
Netherlands/Belgium (Iron Rhine Arbitration) (Award) (Interpretation of Award) **140**.130, 139, 230
Netherlands/France (Rhine Chlorides Arbitration) (Award) **144**.259
Newfoundland and Labrador/Nova Scotia Arbitration (First and Second Phases) **128**.425
Ngassam v. Republic of Cyprus (Director General of Ministry of Interior and Attorney General) (Case No 493/2010) **156**.371

Nguyen Tuong Van v. Public Prosecutor **134**.660
Nibutani Dam Decision **127**.173
Nicaragua v. Honduras (Territorial and Maritime Dispute between Nicaragua and Honduras in the Caribbean Sea) (Judgment) **144**.1
Nikolić Case (Case No Kž. I 1594/02) **128**.691
NML Capital Ltd v. Republic of Argentina **147**.575
Nova Scotia/Newfoundland and Labrador Arbitration (First and Second Phases) **128**.425
Nuhanović v. Netherlands **153**.467, **160**.629

Oakes Case **156**.423 (note)
Obbo Case **140**.566
Öcalan v. Turkey (Application No 46221/99) (Merits) **156**.30, 114 (note)
Occidental Case **138**.35, 92, 158, 218 (note)
Occidental Exploration and Production Company v. Republic of Ecuador (LCIA Case No UN 3467) (Final Award) **138**.35
O'Donnell (a minor suing by her mother and next friend) and Others v. South Dublin County Council **149**.579
Oil Platforms (Islamic Republic of Iran v. United States of America) (Preliminary Objection) **130**.174, 185
Oil Platforms (Islamic Republic of Iran v. United States of America) (Counterclaim) **130**.174, 280
Oil Platforms (Islamic Republic of Iran v. United States of America) (Merits) **130**.174, 323
Onyango-Obbo and Another v. Attorney General of Uganda **140**.566
OO (aka Abu Qatada) (Jordan) v. Secretary of State for the Home Department **142**.411
Opinion 2/13 (Accession of the European Union to the European Convention on Human Rights) **161**.600
Orams and Another v. Apostolides (Case C-420/07) **154**.443, 450
Ory v. France (Communication No 1960/2010) **165**.384

Oscar Jupiter (KJ International and Others v. MV Oscar Jupiter (Compania de Navigatie Maritime "Romline" SA and Others intervening)) **131**.529
OSPAR Case **126**.334
Othman v. European Council and Another (United Kingdom intervening) (Case T-318/01) **149**.454
Othman v. United Kingdom (Application No 8139/09) (Merits) **150**.359, 461 (note)
Othman (aka Abu Qatada) (Jordan) v. Secretary of State for the Home Department **142**.411, **153**.651, **155**.754, 776 (note)

Paadar and Others v. Finland (Communication No 2102/2011) **165**.330
Padilla Case **137**.347
Pahang (Sultan of) Case **152**.543
Pakistan, Islamic Republic of v. India (Indus Waters Kishenganga Arbitration) **150**.311, **154**.1, **157**.362, 417
Pakistan Religious Persecution Case (Case Nos 2 BvR 478 and 962/86) **130**.571
Pakistan, through Secretary, Ministry of Finance v. Société Générale de Surveillance SA [Pakistan] **129**.323
Paksas v. Lithuania (Application No 34932/04) [ECtHR] **165**.252
Paksas v. Lithuania (Communication No 2155/2012) [UNHRC] **165**.303
Pant and Others v. Nepal Government and Others **138**.500
Parent and Others v. Singapore Airlines Limited and the Civil Aeronautics Administration **133**.264
PCATI Cases **133**.283, **145**.429
PD and EB (Iraq Sanctions) Case **158**.584
Pedra Branca (Malaysia/Singapore) **151**.453
People's Mojahedin Organization of Iran, In re **163**.723
Percy v. Director of Public Prosecutions **132**.632
Peruvian Genocide Case (Decision No 712/2003) **141**.720
Pham v. Secretary of State for the Home Department **162**.719

Philippines, Republic of the *v.* Maler Foundation and Others (Civil Appeal No 7 of 2007) **150**.741

Plaintiffs M70/2011 and M106/2011 *v.* Minister for Immigration and Citizenship and Another **150**.506

Pocket Kings Limited *v.* Safenames Limited and the Commonwealth of Kentucky **152**.525

Pope and Talbot Inc. *v.* Government of Canada (Award on Damages) **126**.127, 131

Pope and Talbot Inc. *v.* Government of Canada (Final Award on Costs) **126**.127, 156

Portion 20 of Plot 15 Athol (Pty) Ltd *v.* Rodrigues **133**.389

Potgieter *v.* British Airways Plc **133**.471

Prabakar Case **155**.444

President of the Council of Ministers (Italy) *v.* Marković and Others (Decision No 8157/2002) **128**.652

Priddle *v.* Secretary-General (Case No 57) **130**.545

Prince Hans-Adam II *v.* Municipality of Cologne (Case No 22 U 215/95) **149**.1

Prince Hans-Adam II of Liechtenstein, *In re* (Case No 2 BvR 1981/97) **149**.26

Prince Hans-Adam II of Liechtenstein *v.* Germany (Application No 42527/98) (Admissibility) **149**.32, 38

Prince Hans-Adam II of Liechtenstein *v.* Germany (Application No 42527/98) (Merits) **149**.32, 53

Procurator Fiscal (Scotland) *v.* Slater Main and Wanderer Fishing Company Limited **127**.661

Prosecutor (ICC) *v.* Omar Hassan Ahmad Al Bashir (Situation in Darfur, Sudan) **150**.228

Prosecutor (ICTY) *v.* Hadžihasanović, Alagić and Kubura (Case IT-01-47-AR72) (Decision on Interlocutory Appeal) (Appeals Chamber) **133**.54

Prosecutor (ICTY) *v.* Haradinaj, Balaj and Brahimaj (Case No IT-04-84*bis*-T) **158**.142

Prosecutor (Special Court for Sierra Leone) *v.* Taylor (Case SCSL-2003-01-I) (Immunity from Jurisdiction) (Appeals Chamber) **128**.239

PT Garuda Indonesia Ltd *v.* Australian Competition and Consumer Commission **152**.365, **153**.406

Public Committee against Torture in Israel and Another *v.* Government of Israel and Others (HCJ 769/02) **145**.429

Public Committee against Torture in Israel and Another *v.* State of Israel, General Security Service and Others (HCJ 5100/94, 4054/95, 6536/95, 5188/96, 7563/97, 7628/97 and 1043/99) **133**.283

Public Prosecutor (Norway) *v.* Haraldsson and Others **140**.559

Public Prosecutor (Serbia) *v.* Magazine "Svedok" **127**.315

Pulau Ligitan and Pulau Sipadan (Indonesia/Malaysia) **151**.197

Pulp Mills on the River Uruguay (Argentina *v.* Uruguay) **152**.1

Pulp Mills on the River Uruguay (Argentina *v.* Uruguay) (First Request for Provisional Measures) **152**.1, 14

Pulp Mills on the River Uruguay (Argentina *v.* Uruguay) (Second Request for Provisional Measures) **152**.1, 55

Pulp Mills on the River Uruguay (Argentina *v.* Uruguay) (Merits) **152**.1, 95

Qatada Cases **142**.411, **149**.454, **150**.359, 461 (note), **153**.651, **155**.754, 776 (note)

Qatar *v.* Bahrain (Maritime Delimitation and Territorial Questions between Qatar and Bahrain) (Merits) **139**.1

Quark Cases **131**.712, 749

Quark Fishing Limited *v.* United Kingdom (Application No 15305/06) (Admissibility) **131**.749

R *v.* Bieber **156**.402, 423 (note)
R *v.* Council of Canadians **132**.335
R *v.* Forsyth **158**.572
R *v.* Gul **152**.568
R *v.* Hape **143**.140
R *v.* Jones (Margaret) and Others **132**.608, 668
R *v.* Lyons **162**.674
R *v.* Lyons and Others **131**.538
R *v.* Mabey **158**.572
R *v.* McLoughlin **158**.746
R *v.* Newell **158**.746

R v. Oakes **156**.423 (note)
R v. PD and EB (Iraq Sanctions) **158**.582
R v. Seven Named Accused **127**.232
R v. Tang **143**.76
R (Abbasi and Juma) v. Foreign and Commonwealth Secretary and Home Secretary **126**.685
R (Adams) v. Secretary of State for Justice **154**.533
R (Al Rawi and Others) v. Secretary of State for Foreign and Commonwealth Affairs and Another (United Nations High Commissioner for Refugees intervening) **136**.624, 688 (note)
R (Al-Haq) v. Secretary of State for Foreign and Commonwealth Affairs **154**.423, 442 (note)
R (Al-Jedda) v. Secretary of State for Defence **137**.202
R (Al-Saadoon and Another) v. Secretary of State for Defence **147**.532
R (Al-Skeini and Others) v. Secretary of State for Defence (the Redress Trust and Others intervening) **133**.499
R (Alamieyeseigha) v. Crown Prosecution Service **145**.619
R (B and Others) v. Secretary of State for Foreign and Commonwealth Affairs **131**.616
R (Bancoult) v. Secretary of State for Foreign and Commonwealth Affairs (No 2) **138**.628
R (Bancoult) v. Secretary of State for Foreign and Commonwealth Affairs (No 3) **162**.348
R (Campaign for Nuclear Disarmament) v. Prime Minister of the United Kingdom, Foreign and Commonwealth Secretary and Defence Secretary **126**.727
R (Corner House Research and Another) v. Director of the Serious Fraud Office (JUSTICE intervening) **165**.402
R (European Roma Rights Centre and Others) v. Immigration Officer at Prague Airport and Another (United Nations High Commissioner for Refugees intervening) **131**.652
R (Evans) v. Secretary of State for Defence **153**.508
R (Gentle and Clarke) v. Prime Minister, Secretary of State for Defence and Attorney General **132**.721, **140**.624

R (Hassan) v. Secretary of State for Defence **164**.391
R (International Association of Independent Tanker Owners (Intertanko) and Others) v. Secretary of State for Transport (Case C-308/06) **142**.89
R (Islamic Human Rights Commission) v. Civil Aviation Authority, Foreign and Commonwealth Office and Ministry of Defence **132**.707
R (JS (Sri Lanka)) v. Secretary of State for the Home Department **159**.366
R (Khan) v. Secretary of State for Foreign and Commonwealth Affairs **165**.622, 627, 643
R (Kibris Türk Hava Yollari and CTA Holidays Ltd) v. Secretary of State for Transport (Republic of Cyprus, interested party) **148**.683
R (Marchiori) v. Environment Agency **127**.574
R (Misick) v. Secretary of State for Foreign and Commonwealth Affairs [United Kingdom] **165**.515, 519, 533
R (Mullen) v. Secretary of State for the Home Department **145**.564
R (Quark Fishing Limited) v. Secretary of State for Foreign and Commonwealth Affairs **131**.712
R (Saadi and Others) v. Secretary of State for the Home Department **133**.482
R (Smith) v. Oxfordshire Assistant Deputy Coroner (Equality and Human Rights Commission intervening) **156**.424
R (ST (Eritrea)) v. Secretary of State for the Home Department **159**.489
R (Sultan of Pahang) v. Secretary of State for the Home Department **152**.543
R (Ullah) v. Special Adjudicator **131**.577
R (Wellington) v. Secretary of State for the Home Department **155**.713
R (Youssef) v. HM Treasury (JUSTICE intervening) **149**.641
Rahmatullah v. Secretary of State for Foreign and Commonwealth Affairs and Secretary of State for Defence (No 1) **150**.819
Rahmatullah v. Secretary of State for Foreign and Commonwealth Affairs and Secretary of State for Defence (No 2) **150**.836

Rahmatullah v. Secretary of State for Foreign and Commonwealth Affairs and Secretary of State for Defence (No 3) **153**.607
Rahmatullah Cases **150**.819, 836, **153**.607
Railway Land Arbitration (Malaysia/Singapore) **162**.588
Rantsev v. Cyprus and Russia (Application No 25965/04) (Merits) **145**.106
Rasul and Others v. Bush, President of the United States and Others **137**.377
RB (Algeria) v. Secretary of State for the Home Department **142**.411
Registered Trustees of National Association of Community Health Practitioners of Nigeria and Others v. Medical and Health Workers Union of Nigeria **152**.464
Reineccius and Others v. Bank for International Settlements (Arbitration Tribunal) **140**.1
Reineccius and Others v. Bank for International Settlements (Arbitration Tribunal) (Partial Award) **140**.1, 6
Reineccius and Others v. Bank for International Settlements (Arbitration Tribunal) (Final Award) **140**.1, 81
Request for Interpretation of the Judgment of 31 March 2004 in *Avena and Other Mexican Nationals (Mexico* v. *United States of America)* (Mexico v. United States of America) (Provisional Measures) **148**.1, 147
Request for Interpretation of the Judgment of 31 March 2004 in *Avena and Other Mexican Nationals (Mexico* v. *United States of America)* (Mexico v. United States of America) (Judgment) **148**.1, 187
Reservations to Certain Commonwealth of Independent States Agreements, Advisory Opinion **127**.1
Resolution No 5 on Application by Courts of General Jurisdiction of Commonly Recognized Principles and Norms of International Law and International Treaties of Russian Federation **150**.726
Responsibilities and Obligations of States sponsoring persons and entities with respect to activities in the Area (Advisory Opinion) **150**.244

Réunion Aérienne v. Socialist People's Libyan Arab Jamahiriya (Case No 0914743) **150**.630
Reyes and Another v. Al-Malki **162**.688
Rhine Chlorides Arbitration (Netherlands/France) (Award) **144**.259
Richtersveld Community Case **127**.501
Right to Information on Consular Assistance in the Framework of the Guarantees of the Due Process of Law (Advisory Opinion OC-16/99) **154**.248
RM (a minor, through next friend JK) v. Attorney General (Kenya) **143**.299
Rodríguez Castañeda v. Mexico (Communication No 2202/2012) **163**.223
Romania v. Ukraine (Maritime Delimitation in the Black Sea) (Judgment) **144**.179
RT (Zimbabwe) and Others v. Secretary of State for the Home Department **159**.587
Ruddock and Others v. Vadarlis and Others **131**.83
Ruddock and Others v. Victorian Council for Civil Liberties Inc. and Others **131**.83
Rumsfeld, Secretary of Defense v. Padilla and Another **137**.347
Ruperas v. EUTELSAT **127**.139
Russian Federation v. Australia (*The Volga*) (Application for Prompt Release) [ITLOS] **126**.433
Russian Federation v. Noga Import/Export Company **127**.156
RV v. Director of Immigration and Secretary for Justice **138**.582

S v. Basson **133**.424
S v. Makwanyane and Another **127**.321
S (a Child) (Abduction: Custody Rights), *Re* **136**.540
Saadi v. Italy (Application No 37201/06) (Merits) **155**.162
Saadi Cases **133**.482, **155**.162
Sagong Tasi Case **135**.126
Saint Vincent and the Grenadines v. Guinea-Bissau (*The Juno Trader*) (Application for Prompt Release) [ITLOS] **128**.267

Saint Vincent and the Grenadines v.
Kingdom of Spain (MV *Louisa*) (Order on Request for Provisional Measures) (Merits) [ITLOS] **148**.459, **157**.432
Samantar v. Yousuf and Others **147**.726
Sanchez-Llamas v. Oregon **134**.719
Saramati v. France, Germany and Norway (Application No 78166/01) (Admissibility) **133**.1
Sassetti v. Multinational Force and Observers (Decision No 3857/1994) **128**.640
Schlumberger Logelco Inc. v. Coflexip SA **133**.405
Schreiber v. Federal Republic of Germany and Attorney General of Canada **147**.276, 302 (note)
Scimet v. African Development Bank **128**.582
SD Myers Inc. v. Government of Canada (Procedural Order No 18) **126**.161, 252 (note)
SD Myers Inc. v. Government of Canada (Second Partial Award on Damages) **126**.161, 167
SD Myers Inc. v. Government of Canada (Final Award on Costs) **126**.161, 226
Secretary for Security (China, HKSAR) v. Prabakar **155**.444
Secretary of State for Foreign and Commonwealth Affairs and Secretary of State for Defence v. Rahmatullah (No 3) **153**.607
Sedudu/Kasikili Island (Botswana/Namibia) (Judgment) **151**.1
Selangor and Others v. Sagong bin Tasi and Others **135**.126
Sengamalay v. International Bank for Reconstruction and Development (Decision No 254) **133**.131
Serbia, Government of the Republic of v. Ganić **160**.651
Serbia, Republic of v. ImageSat International NV **142**.644
Serbia and Montenegro/Yugoslavia v. Belgium (Legality of Use of Force) (Provisional Measures) (Preliminary Objections) **157**.1
Serbia and Montenegro/Yugoslavia v. Canada (Legality of Use of Force) (Provisional Measures) (Preliminary Objections) **157**.296 (note)

Serbia and Montenegro/Yugoslavia v. France (Legality of Use of Force) (Provisional Measures) (Preliminary Objections) **157**.299 (note)
Serbia and Montenegro/Yugoslavia v. Germany (Legality of Use of Force) (Provisional Measures) (Preliminary Objections) **157**.306 (note)
Serbia and Montenegro/Yugoslavia v. Italy (Legality of Use of Force) (Provisional Measures) (Preliminary Objections) **157**.309 (note)
Serbia and Montenegro/Yugoslavia v. Netherlands (Legality of Use of Force) (Provisional Measures) (Preliminary Objections) **157**.312 (note)
Serbia and Montenegro/Yugoslavia v. Portugal (Legality of Use of Force) (Provisional Measures) (Preliminary Objections) **157**.323 (note)
Serbia and Montenegro/Yugoslavia v. Spain (Legality of Use of Force) (Provisional Measures) **157**.326 (note)
Serbia and Montenegro/Yugoslavia v. United Kingdom (Legality of Use of Force) (Provisional Measures) (Preliminary Objections) **157**.344 (note)
Serbia and Montenegro/Yugoslavia v. United States of America (Legality of Use of Force) (Provisional Measures) **157**.351 (note)
SerVaas Inc. v. Rafidain Bank and Others **160**.668
Seven Named Accused Case **127**.232
Seychelles (Republic of) v. Osman and Ten Others **152**.513
SG v. International Fund for Agricultural Development (Judgment No 2867) **164**.1
SGS Société Générale de Surveillance SA v. Islamic Republic of Pakistan (ICSID Case No ARB/01/13) (Procedural Order No 2) **129**.360, 365
SGS Société Générale de Surveillance SA v. Islamic Republic of Pakistan (ICSID Case No ARB/01/13) (Disqualification of Arbitrator) **129**.360, 377
SGS Société Générale de Surveillance SA v. Islamic Republic of Pakistan (ICSID Case No ARB/01/13) (Objections to Jurisdiction) **129**.360, 387, 442 (note)

SGS Société Générale de Surveillance SA *v.* Islamic Republic of Pakistan (ICSID Case No ARB/01/13) (Discontinuance Order) **129**.360, 442 (note)
SGS Société Générale de Surveillance SA *v.* Pakistan, through Secretary, Ministry of Finance [Pakistan] **129**.323
SGS Société Générale de Surveillance SA *v.* Republic of the Philippines (ICSID Case No ARB/02/6) (Objections to Jurisdiction) **129**.444
Sharon and Yaron, *Re* **127**.110
Sibanda and Ngangura Case **153**.689
Šilih *v.* Slovenia (Application No 71463/01) (Merits) **153**.122
Simon Case **160**.686
Singapore/Malaysia (Railway Land Arbitration) **162**.588
Singapore/Malaysia (Sovereignty over Pedra Branca/Pulau Batu Puteh, Middle Rocks and South Ledge) (Judgment) **151**.453
Singarasa *v.* Attorney General of Sri Lanka **138**.469
Singarasa *v.* Sri Lanka (Communication No 1033/2001) **138**.451
Singh (Bikramjit) *v.* France (Communication No 1852/2008) **159**.233
Singh (Shingara Mann) *v.* France (Communication No 1928/2010) **163**.249
Sitamze Case **143**.349
SK (Zimbabwe) *v.* Secretary of State for the Home Department **159**.548
Slater Main Case **127**.661
Smith (Catherine) Case **156**.424
Smith (Susan) and Others *v.* Ministry of Defence **158**.612
Société Logicom *v.* Société CTT Marketing Limited and Société Ducros Transports **148**.629
Somali Pirates Case **145**.491
Sosa *v.* Alvarez-Machain and Others **127**.691
South Africa, Government of the Republic of, and Others *v.* Von Abo (Case No 283/10) **150**.783
Sovereignty over Pedra Branca/Pulau Batu Puteh, Middle Rocks and South Ledge (Malaysia/Singapore) (Judgment) **151**.453

Sovereignty over Pulau Ligitan and Pulau Sipadan (Indonesia/Malaysia) (Application by the Philippines for Permission to Intervene) **151**.197, 212
Sovereignty over Pulau Ligitan and Pulau Sipadan (Indonesia/Malaysia) (Merits) **151**.197, 290
ST (Eritrea) Case **159**.489
State Immunity in Labour Law Matters Case **142**.206
State Marine Corporation and Currence *v.* United States of America **128**.701
Stichting Greenpeace Nederland *v.* Euratom **136**.429
Stichting Mothers of Srebrenica and Others *v.* Netherlands (Application No 6554212) (Admissibility) **160**.573
Stichting Revalidatiecentrum "De Trappenberg" *v.* Kingdom of Morocco **128**.676
Succession of States and Individuals Case **142**.175
Sudan, Government of/Sudan People's Liberation Movement/Army (Abyei Arbitration) (Final Award) **144**.348
Sultan of Pahang Case **152**.543
Suspension of the Execution of Judgment No 2867 Filed by the International Fund for Agricultural Development (SG *v.* IFAD) (Judgment No 3003), Application for **164**.18
Swain *v.* Director of Public Prosecutions **132**.632, 668
Swarna *v.* Al-Awadi, Al-Shaitan and State of Kuwait **152**.617
Swissborough Diamond Mines (Pty) Ltd and Others *v.* Government of the Republic of South Africa and Others **132**.454
Syrian National Immunity Case (Case 12 Os 3/98) **127**.88

Tamils' Political Persecution Case (Case Nos 2BvR 502, 961 and1000/86) **130**.587
Tang Case **143**.76
Targeted Killing in Pakistan Case [Germany] **157**.722
Targeted Killings Case [Israel] **145**.429
Tatchell *v.* Mugabe **136**.572
Taunoa and Others *v.* Attorney General **155**.479

Taylor (Case SCSL-2003-01-I) (Immunity from Jurisdiction) (Special Court for Sierra Leone Appeals Chamber) **128**.239
Taylor and Another *v.* Attorney General of Jamaica **134**.615
Teitiota *v.* Chief Executive of the Ministry of Business, Innovation and Employment **158**.541
Telkom SA Ltd *v.* Member of the Executive Council for Agricultural and Environmental Affairs, Kwazulu-Natal and Others **133**.412
Territorial and Maritime Dispute between Nicaragua and Honduras in the Caribbean Sea (Nicaragua *v.* Honduras) (Judgment) **144**.1
Thomas *v.* Mowbray and Others **163**.329
Thor Shipping A/S *v.* The Ship *Al-Duhail* **140**.530
Thule Tribe Case **143**.277
The Tomimaru (Japan *v.* Russian Federation) (Application for Prompt Release) **143**.36
Turkish Citizen G *v.* Naumburg Higher Regional Court (Case No 2 BvR 1481/04) **145**.384

U (Algeria) *v.* Secretary of State for the Home Department **142**.411
Ullah *v.* Special Adjudicator **131**.577
United Mexican States *v.* Cargill Inc. **146**.800, **150**.598, 622 (note)
United Mexican States *v.* Feldman Karpa **126**.536, **128**.610
United States of America *v.* Ali **154**.700, 738 (note)
United States of America *v.* Alvarez-Machain and Others **127**.691
United States of America *v.* Barnette and Another **145**.602
United States of America *v.* Bin Laden aka Mohamed **127**.676
United States of America *v.* Dire **154**.700, 738 (note)
United States of America *v.* Eemshaven Port Authority **127**.225
United States of America *v.* Gurewardher **154**.700, 738 (note)
United States of America *v.* Hasan **154**.700, 738 (note)

United States of America *v.* Montgomery (No 2) **145**.602
United States of America *v.* Umar **154**.700, 738 (note)
United States of America (Attorney General of Canada on behalf of) *v.* Khadr **157**.700
Ure *v.* Commonwealth of Australia **164**.304

Van Zyl and Others *v.* Government of Republic of South Africa and Others **143**.473
Västerås, Municipality of *v.* Iceland **128**.705
Vinter and Others *v.* United Kingdom (Application Nos 66069/09, 130/10 and 3896/10) (Merits) **156**.115
Voiotia, Prefecture of *v.* Federal Republic of Germany (Distomo Massacre Case) (Case No 11/2000) [Greece] **129**.513, 524 (note)
The Volga (Russian Federation *v.* Australia) (Application for Prompt Release) **126**.433
Von Abo *v.* Republic of South Africa and Others **143**.577, 666 (note), **150**.783
VP *v.* Republic of Austria (Case No 30 Cdo 2594/2009) **150**.623

Wakaba and Others *v.* Attorney General **152**.431
Wall Advisory Opinion **129**.37
Waste Management Inc. *v.* United Mexican States (No 2) (ICSID Case No ARB(AF)/00/3) (Decision on Venue of the Arbitration) **132**.145, 150
Waste Management Inc. *v.* United Mexican States (No 2) (ICSID Case No ARB(AF)/00/3) (Decision on Preliminary Objection) **132**.145, 159
Waste Management Inc. *v.* United Mexican States (No 2) (ICSID Case No ARB(AF)/00/3) (Award) **132**.145, 177
Waweru *v.* Republic of Kenya **142**.308
Welkom Municipality *v.* Masureik and Herman t/a Lotus Corporation and Another **131**.423
Wellington Case **155**.713

Wilhelm Finance Inc. v. Ente Administrador del Astillero Rio Santiago **164**.407
Wilmington Trust SP Services (Dublin) Ltd v. Director-General of Civil Aviation and Spicejet Ltd **163**.569
Wokuri v. Kassam **152**.557

X v. Denmark (Communication No 2007/2010) **164**.286
X v. Israel **127**.310
X v. Saudi School in Paris and Kingdom of Saudi Arabia **127**.163
X and Another v. Secretary of State for the Home Department **137**.1
Xenides-Arestis v. Turkey (Application No 46347/99) **158**.1
Xenides-Arestis v. Turkey (Application No 46347/99) (Admissibility) **158**.1, 7
Xenides-Arestis v. Turkey (Application No 46347/99) (Merits) **158**.1, 56
Xenides-Arestis v. Turkey (Application No 46347/99) (Just Satisfaction) **158**.1, 72

Yaung Chi Oo Trading Pte Ltd v. Government of the Union of Myanmar (ASEAN ID Case No ARB/01/1) **127**.42
Yaung Chi Oo Trading Pte Ltd v. Government of the Union of Myanmar (ASEAN ID Case No ARB/01/1) (Provisional Measures) **127**.42, 46
Yaung Chi Oo Trading Pte Ltd v. Government of the Union of Myanmar (ASEAN ID Case No ARB/01/1) (Award) **127**.42, 55
Yong Vui Kong v. Public Prosecutor (Singapore) **143**.374
Yoon and Choi v. Republic of Korea (Communication Nos 1321 and 1322/2004) **157**.602
Youssef Case **149**.641
Yugoslavia v. Bosnia and Herzegovina (Application for Revision of the Judgment of 11 July 1996 in *Application of the Convention on the Prevention and Punishment of the Crime of Genocide (Bosnia and Herzegovina* v. *Yugoslavia)*) **155**.1

Yugoslavia, Federal Republic and National Bank of v. Republics of Croatia, Slovenia, Macedonia and Bosnia–Herzegovina **128**.627
Yugoslavia/Serbia and Montenegro v. Belgium (Legality of Use of Force) **157**.1
Yugoslavia/Serbia and Montenegro v. Belgium (Legality of Use of Force) (Provisional Measures) **157**.18
Yugoslavia/Serbia and Montenegro v. Belgium (Legality of Use of Force) (Preliminary Objections) **157**.147
Yugoslavia/Serbia and Montenegro v. Canada (Legality of Use of Force) (Provisional Measures) (Preliminary Objections) **157**.296 (note)
Yugoslavia/Serbia and Montenegro v. France (Legality of Use of Force) (Provisional Measures) (Preliminary Objections) **157**.299 (note)
Yugoslavia/Serbia and Montenegro v. Germany (Legality of Use of Force) (Provisional Measures) (Preliminary Objections) **157**.306 (note)
Yugoslavia/Serbia and Montenegro v. Italy (Legality of Use of Force) (Provisional Measures) (Preliminary Objections) **157**.309 (note)
Yugoslavia/Serbia and Montenegro v. Netherlands (Legality of Use of Force) (Provisional Measures) (Preliminary Objections) **157**.312 (note)
Yugoslavia/Serbia and Montenegro v. Portugal (Legality of Use of Force) (Provisional Measures) (Preliminary Objections) **157**.323 (note)
Yugoslavia/Serbia and Montenegro v. Spain (Legality of Use of Force) (Provisional Measures) **157**.326 (note)
Yugoslavia/Serbia and Montenegro v. United Kingdom (Legality of Use of Force) (Provisional Measures) (Preliminary Objections) **157**.344 (note)
Yugoslavia/Serbia and Montenegro v. United States of America (Legality of Use of Force) (Provisional Measures) **157**.351 (note)

Yukos Capital SARL *v.* OJSC Rosneft Oil
  Company (No 2) **165**.554
Yusuf and Al Barakaat International
  Foundation *v.* Council of
  the European Union and
  Commission of the European
  Communities (Case T-306/01)
  149.167, 180

Zaoui *v.* Attorney General (No 2) **131**.308
Zentai and Others Case **153**.366
Zhang *v.* Jiang Zemin and Others **141**.542,
  148.555, 593 (note)
Zivotofsky *v.* Clinton, Secretary of State
  154.674
Zrig *v.* Canada (Minister of Citizenship and
  Immigration) **131**.215

CONSOLIDATED TABLE OF CASES VOLUMES 126-165
ARRANGED ACCORDING TO COURTS AND TRIBUNALS (INTERNATIONAL CASES) AND COUNTRIES (MUNICIPAL CASES)

(Cases which are reported only in a note are distinguished from cases which are reported in full by the insertion of the word "note" in parentheses after the page number of the report.)

I. DECISIONS OF INTERNATIONAL TRIBUNALS

Administrative Tribunals

International Labour Organization Administrative Tribunal

2010
SG *v.* International Fund for Agricultural Development (Judgment No 2867) **164**.1

2011
Application for the Suspension of the Execution of Judgment No 2867 Filed by the International Fund for Agricultural Development (Judgment No 3003) **164**.18

2013
Application for Execution of Judgments Nos 2867 and 3003 Filed by SG (Judgment No 3152) **164**.134

Organization for Economic Cooperation and Development (OECD) Administrative Tribunal

2001
Divoy *v.* Secretary-General (Case No 50) **127**.37

2004
Priddle *v.* Secretary-General (Case No 57) **130**.545

World Bank Administrative Tribunal

2001
Cissé *v.* International Bank for Reconstruction and Development (Decision No 242) **133**.117
Sengamalay *v.* International Bank for Reconstruction and Development (Decision No 254) **133**.131

2002
Conthe *v.* International Bank for Reconstruction and Development (Decision No 271) **133**.149

2003
D *v.* International Finance Corporation (Decision No 304) **133**.196

2004
E *v.* International Bank for Reconstruction and Development (Decision No 325) **133**.224

African Commission on Human and Peoples' Rights

2010
Centre for Minority Rights Development ("CEMIRIDE") (Kenya) and Minority Rights Group International on behalf of Endorois Welfare Council *v.* Kenya (Communication No 276/2003) (Merits) **142**.1

Arbitration Tribunals

Arbitration Tribunal constituted under Article X of the ASEAN Agreement for the Promotion and Protection of Investments

2002
Yaung Chi Oo Trading Pte Ltd v. Government of the Union of Myanmar (ASEAN ID Case No ARB/01/1) (Provisional Measures) **127**.42, 46

2003
Yaung Chi Oo Trading Pte Ltd v. Government of the Union of Myanmar (ASEAN ID Case No ARB/01/1) (Award) **127**.42, 55

Arbitration Tribunal constituted under the Convention for the Protection of the Marine Environment of the North-East Atlantic (OSPAR Convention) (1992)

2003
Dispute Concerning Access to Information under Article 9 of the OSPAR Convention (Ireland v. United Kingdom) (Final Award) **126**.334

Arbitration Tribunals constituted under Annex VII of the United Nations Convention on the Law of the Sea (UNCLOS) (1982)

2003
The MOX Plant Case (Ireland v. United Kingdom) (Order No 3) **126**.310, 314
The MOX Plant Case (Ireland v. United Kingdom) (Order No 4) **126**.310, 332

2006
Barbados/Trinidad and Tobago (Award) **139**.449

2007
Guyana/Suriname (Award) **139**.566

2011
Chagos Marine Protected Area (Republic of Mauritius v. United Kingdom) (Decision on Challenge to an Arbitrator) **162**.1, 11

2015
Chagos Marine Protected Area (Republic of Mauritius v. United Kingdom) (Award) **162**.1, 59

Arbitration Tribunals (Various)

2001
Arbitration between Newfoundland and Labrador/Nova Scotia concerning Portions of the Limits of their Offshore Areas as defined in the Canada–Nova Scotia Offshore Petroleum Resources Accord Implementation Act and the Canada–Newfoundland Atlantic Accord Implementation Act (First Phase) **128**.425, 435

2002
Arbitration between Newfoundland and Labrador/Nova Scotia concerning Portions of the Limits of their Offshore Areas as defined in the Canada–Nova Scotia Offshore Petroleum Resources Accord Implementation Act and the Canada–Newfoundland Atlantic Accord Implementation Act (Second Phase) **128**.425, 504
Reineccius (Claim No 1), First Eagle SoGen Funds Inc. (Claim No 2), Mathieu and la Société de Concours Hippique de La Châtre (Claim No 3) v. Bank for International Settlements (Partial Award) **140**.1, 6

2003
Reineccius (Claim No 1), First Eagle SoGen Funds Inc. (Claim No 2), Mathieu and la Société de Concours Hippique de La Châtre (Claim No 3) v. Bank for International Settlements (Partial Award) **140**.1, 81

2004
Auditing of Accounts between the Kingdom of the Netherlands and the French Republic Pursuant to the Additional Protocol of 25 September

1991 to the Convention on the Protection of the Rhine Against Pollution by Chlorides of 3 December 1976 (Netherlands/France) (Award) **144**.259

EnCana Corporation v. Republic of Ecuador (LCIA Case No UN 3481) (Interim Award on Provisional Measures) (Partial Award on Jurisdiction) **138**.219, 227, 232

Occidental Exploration and Production Company v. Republic of Ecuador (LCIA Case No UN 3467) (Final Award) **138**.35

2005

Arbitration regarding the Iron Rhine ("Ijzeren Rijn") Railway between the Kingdom of Belgium and the Kingdom of the Netherlands (Award) **140**.130, 139

Arbitration regarding the Iron Rhine ("Ijzeren Rijn") Railway between the Kingdom of Belgium and the Kingdom of the Netherlands (Interpretation of Award) **140**.130, 230

2006

EnCana Corporation v. Republic of Ecuador (LCIA Case No UN 3481) (Award) **138**.219, 249

2007

The Channel Tunnel Group Limited and France-Manche SA v. Secretary of State for Transport of the Government of the United Kingdom of Great Britain and Northern Ireland and le Ministre de l'Équipement, des Transports, de l'Aménagement du Territoire, du Tourisme et de la Mer du Gouvernement de la République Française (Partial Award) **132**.1

2009

Abyei Arbitration (Government of Sudan/ Sudan People's Liberation Movement/ Army) (Final Award) **144**.348

2010

Eureko BV v. Slovak Republic (PCA Case No 2008-13) (Award on Jurisdiction, Arbitrability and Suspension) **145**.1

2014

Railway Land Arbitration (Malaysia/ Singapore) **162**.588

Court of Arbitration

2011

Indus Waters Kishenganga Arbitration (Islamic Republic of Pakistan v. Republic of India) **150**.311

2013

Indus Waters Kishenganga Arbitration (Islamic Republic of Pakistan v. Republic of India) (Partial Award) **154**.1

Indus Waters Kishenganga Arbitration (Islamic Republic of Pakistan v. Republic of India) (Decision on Request for Clarification or Interpretation of Partial Award) **157**.417

Indus Waters Kishenganga Arbitration (Islamic Republic of Pakistan v. Republic of India) (Final Award) **157**.362

ICSID Arbitration Tribunals

2002

SGS Société Générale de Surveillance SA v. Islamic Republic of Pakistan (ICSID Case No ARB/01/13) (Procedural Order No 2) (Disqualification of Arbitrator) **129**.360, 365, 377

2003

SGS Société Générale de Surveillance SA v. Islamic Republic of Pakistan (ICSID Case No ARB/01/13) (Objections to Jurisdiction) **129**.360, 387

2004

SGS Société Générale de Surveillance SA v. Republic of the Philippines (ICSID Case No ARB/02/6) (Objections to Jurisdiction) **129**.444

2009

Funnekotter and Others v. Republic of Zimbabwe (ICSID Case No ARB/05/6) (Award) **138**.410

NAFTA Chapter 11 Arbitration Tribunals

2000
Feldman v. United Mexican States (ICSID Case No ARB(AF)/99/1) (Interim Decision on Preliminary Jurisdictional Issues) **126**.1, 9

2001
Loewen Group Inc. and Raymond L. Loewen v. United States of America (ICSID Case No ARB(AF)/98/3) (Decision on Respondent's Objections to Competence and Jurisdiction) **128**.334, 339
SD Myers Inc. v. Government of Canada (Procedural Order No 18) **126**.161, 252 (note)
Waste Management Inc. v. United Mexican States (No 2) (ICSID Case No ARB(AF)/00/3) (Decision on Venue of the Arbitration) **132**.145, 150

2002
Feldman v. United Mexican States (ICSID Case No ARB(AF)/99/1) (Award on the Merits) **126**.1, 26
Pope and Talbot Inc. v. Government of Canada (Award on Damages) **126**.127, 131
Pope and Talbot Inc. v. Government of Canada (Final Award on Costs) **126**.127, 156
SD Myers Inc. v. Government of Canada (Second Partial Award on Damages) **126**.161, 167
SD Myers Inc. v. Government of Canada (Final Award on Costs) **126**.161, 226
Waste Management Inc. v. United Mexican States (No 2) (ICSID Case No ARB(AF)/00/3) (Decision on Preliminary Objection) **132**.145, 159

2003
Feldman v. United Mexican States (ICSID Case No ARB(AF)/99/1) (Decision on the Correction and Interpretation of the Award) **126**.1, 123
Loewen Group Inc. and Raymond L. Loewen v. United States of America (ICSID Case No ARB(AF)/98/3) (Award) **128**.334, 359

2004
Loewen Group Inc. and Raymond L. Loewen v. United States of America (ICSID Case No ARB(AF)/98/3) (Decision on Respondent's Request for Supplementary Decision) **128**.334, 420
Waste Management Inc. v. United Mexican States (No 2) (ICSID Case No ARB(AF)/00/3) (Award) **132**.145, 177

2007
Archer Daniels Midland Company and Tate & Lyle Ingredients Americas Inc. v. United Mexican States (ICSID Case No ARB(AF)/04/5) (Award) **146**.439, 445

2008
Archer Daniels Midland Company and Tate & Lyle Ingredients Americas Inc. v. United Mexican States (ICSID Case No ARB(AF)/04/5) (Decision on the Requests for Correction, Supplementary Decision and Interpretation) **146**.439, 563
Corn Products International Inc. v. United Mexican States (ICSID Case No ARB (AF)/04/1) (Decision on Responsibility) **146**.581

2009
Cargill Inc. v. United Mexican States (ICSID Case No ARB(AF)/05/2) (Award) **146**.642

Commonwealth of Independent States, Economic Court

1996
Advisory Opinion on Reservations to Certain Commonwealth of Independent States Agreements **127**.1

1998
Interpretation of Certain Agreements and Commonwealth of Independent States' Decisions (Case No 01-1/1-98) **127**.16

Court of Justice of the European Union (formerly Court of Justice of the European Communities)

General Court (formerly Court of First Instance)

2005
Kadi *v.* Council of the European Union and Commission of the European Communities (Case T-315/01) **149**.167, 250

Yusuf and Al Barakaat International Foundation *v.* Council of the European Union and Commission of the European Communities (Case T-306/01) **149**.167, 180

2009
Othman *v.* European Council and Another (United Kingdom intervening) (Case T-318/01) **149**.454

2010
Kadi *v.* Commission of the European Communities (Case T-85/09) **149**.167, 406

Court of Justice

2006
Commission of the European Communities *v.* Ireland (Case C-459/03) **153**.1

2007
Commission of the European Communities *v.* Belgium (Case C-437/04) **164**.144

2008
Kadi *v.* Council of the European Union; Al Barakaat International Foundation *v.* Council of the European Union (Joined Cases C-402/05P and C-415/05P) **149**.167, 309, 341

The Queen (on the Application of the International Association of Independent Tanker Owners (Intertanko) and Others) *v.* Secretary of State for Transport (Case C-308/06) **142**.89

2009
Orams and Another *v.* Apostolides (Case C-420/07) **154**.443, 450

2010
Firma Brita GmbH *v.* Hauptzollamt Hamburg-Hafen (Case C-386/08) **165**.188

2012
Hungary *v.* Slovak Republic (Case C-364/10) **153**.92

Mahamdia *v.* People's Democratic Republic of Algeria (Case C-154/11) **153**.58

2014
Opinion 2/13 (Accession of the European Union to the European Convention on Human Rights) **161**.600

Eritrea–Ethiopia Boundary Commission

2002
Decision Regarding Delimitation of the Border between the State of Eritrea and the Federal Democratic Republic of Ethiopia **130**.1

2006
Statement Regarding Demarcation of the Border between the State of Eritrea and the Federal Democratic Republic of Ethiopia **130**.147

Eritrea–Ethiopia Claims Commission

2003
Prisoners of War, Eritrea's Claim 17 (State of Eritrea/Federal Democratic Republic of Ethiopia) (Partial Award) **135**.199

Prisoners of War, Ethiopia's Claim 4 (Federal Democratic Republic of Ethiopia/State of Eritrea) (Partial Award) **135**.251

2004
Central Front, Eritrea's Claims 2, 4, 6, 7, 8 & 22 (State of Eritrea/Federal Democratic Republic of Ethiopia) (Partial Award) **135**.295

Central Front, Ethiopia's Claim 2 (Federal Democratic Republic of Ethiopia/State of Eritrea) (Partial Award) **135**.334

Civilians Claims, Eritrea's Claims 15, 16, 23 & 27-32 (State of Eritrea/Federal Democratic Republic of Ethiopia) (Partial Award) **135**.374

Civilians Claims, Ethiopia's Claim 5 (Federal Democratic Republic of Ethiopia/State of Eritrea) (Partial Award) **135**.427

2005

Diplomatic Claim, Eritrea's Claim 20 (State of Eritrea/Federal Democratic Republic of Ethiopia) (Partial Award) **135**.519

Diplomatic Claim, Ethiopia's Claim 8 (Federal Democratic Republic of Ethiopia/State of Eritrea) (Partial Award) **135**.544

Economic Loss Throughout Ethiopia, Ethiopia's Claim 7 (Federal Democratic Republic of Ethiopia/State of Eritrea) (Partial Award) **135**.470

Jus Ad Bellum, Ethiopia's Claims 1-8 (Federal Democratic Republic of Ethiopia/State of Eritrea) (Partial Award) **135**.479

Loss of Property in Ethiopia Owned by Non-Residents, Eritrea's Claim 24 (State of Eritrea/Federal Democratic Republic of Ethiopia) (Partial Award) **135**.657

Pensions, Eritrea's Claims 15, 19 & 23 (State of Eritrea/Federal Democratic Republic of Ethiopia) (Final Award) **135**.503

Ports, Ethiopia's Claim 6 (Federal Democratic Republic of Ethiopia/State of Eritrea) (Final Award) **135**.490

Western and Eastern Fronts, Ethiopia's Claims 1 & 3 (Federal Democratic Republic of Ethiopia/State of Eritrea) (Partial Award) **135**.627

Western Front, Aerial Bombardment and Related Claims, Eritrea's Claims 1, 3, 5, 9-13, 14, 21, 25 & 26 (State of Eritrea/Federal Democratic Republic of Ethiopia) (Partial Award) **135**.565

2009

Eritrea's Damages Claims (State of Eritrea/Federal Democratic Republic of Ethiopia) (Final Award) **140**.235

Ethiopia's Damages Claims (Federal Democratic Republic of Ethiopia/State of Eritrea) (Final Award) **140**.376

European Court of Human Rights

2000

Prince Hans-Adam II of Liechtenstein *v.* Germany (Application No 42527/98) (Admissibility) **149**.32, 38

2001

Prince Hans-Adam II of Liechtenstein *v.* Germany (Application No 42527/98) (Merits) **149**.32, 53

2002

Kalogeropoulou and Others *v.* Greece and Germany (Application No 59021/00) (Admissibility) **129**.537

2004

Görgülü *v.* Germany (Application No 74969/01) (Merits) **145**.85

Issa and Others *v.* Turkey (Application No 31821/96) (Merits) **156**.1

2005

Mamatkulov and Askarov *v.* Turkey (Application Nos 46827/99 and 46951/99) (Merits) **134**.230

Öcalan *v.* Turkey (Application No 46221/99) (Merits) **156**.30, 114 (note)

Xenides-Arestis *v.* Turkey (Application No 46347/99) (Admissibility) **158**.1, 7

Xenides-Arestis *v.* Turkey (Application No 46347/99) (Merits) **158**.1, 56

2006

Quark Fishing Limited *v.* United Kingdom (Application No 15305/06) (Admissibility) **131**.749

Xenides-Arestis *v.* Turkey (Application No 46347/99) (Just Satisfaction) **158**.1, 72

2007

Al Fayed *v.* France (Application No 38501/02) (Admissibility) **145**.686 (note)

Al-Moayad *v.* Germany (Application No 35865/03) (Admissibility) **141**.507

Behrami v. France (Application No 71412/01) (Admissibility) **133**.1
Jorgic v. Germany (Application No 74613/01) (Merits) **148**.234
Saramati v. France, Germany and Norway (Application No 78166/01) (Admissibility) **133**.1

2008
Kafkaris v. Cyprus (Application No 21906/04) (Merits) **155**.70
N v. United Kingdom (Application No 26565/05) (Merits) **148**.315
Saadi v. Italy (Application No 37201/06) (Merits) **155**.162

2009
A and Others v. United Kingdom (Application No 3455/05) (Merits) **137**.115 (note), **148**.350
Al-Saadoon and Mufdhi v. United Kingdom (Application No 61498/08) (Admissibility) **147**.1, 5
Bijelić v. Montenegro and Serbia (Application No 11890/05) (Merits) **142**.146
Georgia v. Russia (No 1) (Application No 13255/07) (Admissibility) **161**.333, 337
Šilih v. Slovenia (Application No 71463/01) (Merits) **153**.122

2010
Al-Saadoon and Mufdhi v. United Kingdom (Application No 61498/08) (Merits) **147**.1, 24
Demopoulos and Others v. Turkey (Application Nos 46113/99, 3843/02, 13751/02, 13466/03, 14163/04, 10200/04, 19993/04, 21819/04) (Admissibility) **158**.88
Rantsev v. Cyprus and Russia (Application No 25965/04) (Merits) **145**.106

2011
Al-Jedda v. United Kingdom (Application No 27021/08) (Merits) **147**.107
Al-Skeini and Others v. United Kingdom (Application No 55721/07) (Merits) **147**.181
Georgia v. Russia (No 2) (Application No 38263/08) (Admissibility) **161**.487, 523 (note)

Khodorkovskiy v. Russia (Application No 5829/04) (Merits) **153**.253
Kiyutin v. Russia (Application No 2700/10) (Merits) **145**.201
Lautsi and Others v. Italy (Application No 30814/06) **164**.176
MSS v. Belgium and Greece (Application No 30696/09) **163**.1
Paksas v. Lithuania (Application No 34932/04) **165**.252

2012
Ahmad and Others v. United Kingdom (Application Nos 24027/07, 11949/08, 36742/08, 66911/09 and 67354/09) (Merits) **155**.219
Chagos Islanders v. United Kingdom (Application No 35622/04) (Admissibility) **162**.318
Jamaa and Others v. Italy (Application No 27765/09) **163**.132
Misick v. United Kingdom (Application No 10781/10) **165**.544
Othman v. United Kingdom (Application No 8139/09) (Merits) **150**.359, 461 (note)

2013
Stichting Mothers of Srebrenica and Others v. Netherlands (Application No 6554212) **160**.573
Vinter and Others v. United Kingdom (Application Nos 66069/09, 130/10 and 3896/10) (Merits) **156**.115

2014
Cyprus v. Turkey (Application No 25781/94) (Just Satisfaction) **159**.1
Georgia v. Russia (No 1) (Application No 13255/07) (Merits) **161**.333, 360
Hassan v. United Kingdom (Application No 29750/09) (Merits) **161**.524

2015
Hutchinson v. United Kingdom (Application No 57592/08) **165**.235

Inter-American Commission on Human Rights

2004
Maya Indigenous Communities of the Toledo District v. Belize (Case 12.053) **135**.1

2010
Franklin Guillermo Aisalla Molina (Ecuador–Colombia, Inter-State Petition IP-02) (Report No 112/10) (Admissibility) **150**.462

Inter-American Court of Human Rights

1999
The Right to Information on Consular Assistance in the Framework of the Guarantees of the Due Process of Law (Advisory Opinion OC-16/99) **154**.248

2000
Mayagna (Sumo) Awas Tingni Community v. Nicaragua (Preliminary Objections) **136**.73, 83

2001
Barrios Altos Case (Chumbipuma Aguirre and Others v. Peru) (Merits) **136**.1, 7
Barrios Altos Case (Chumbipuma Aguirre and Others v. Peru) (Interpretation) **136**.1, 42
Barrios Altos Case (Chumbipuma Aguirre and Others v. Peru) (Reparations) **136**.1, 48
Mayagna (Sumo) Awas Tingni Community v. Nicaragua (Merits, Reparations and Costs) **136**.73, 99

2002
Hilaire, Constantine and Benjamin and Others v. Trinidad and Tobago **134**.293
Mayagna (Sumo) Awas Tingni Community v. Nicaragua (Provisional Measures Order I) **136**.73, 217

2007
Case of Boyce and Others v. Barbados **134**.614 (note)
Mayagna (Sumo) Awas Tingni Community v. Nicaragua (Provisional Measures Order II) **136**.73, 224

2008
Mayagna (Sumo) Awas Tingni Community v. Nicaragua (Compliance Order I) **136**.73, 232
Mayagna (Sumo) Awas Tingni Community v. Nicaragua (Compliance Order II) **136**.73, 239

2012
Artavia Murillo and Others ("*In vitro* fertilization") v. Costa Rica **165**.1

International Court of Justice

1996
Oil Platforms (Islamic Republic of Iran v. United States of America) (Preliminary Objection) **130**.174, 186

1998
Land and Maritime Boundary between Cameroon and Nigeria (Cameroon v. Nigeria) (Preliminary Objections) **141**.1, 32
Oil Platforms (Islamic Republic of Iran v. United States of America) (Counterclaim) **130**.174, 280

1999
Kasikili/Sedudu Island (Botswana/Namibia) (Judgment) **151**.1
Land and Maritime Boundary between Cameroon and Nigeria (Cameroon v. Nigeria) (Request for Interpretation of Judgment) **141**.1, 173
Land and Maritime Boundary between Cameroon and Nigeria (Cameroon v. Nigeria) (Application for Permission to Intervene) **141**.1, 200
Legality of Use of Force (Yugoslavia/Serbia and Montenegro v. Belgium) (Provisional Measures) **157**.1, 18
Legality of Use of Force (Yugoslavia/Serbia and Montenegro v. Canada) (Provisional Measures) **157**.296, 298 (note)
Legality of Use of Force (Yugoslavia/Serbia and Montenegro v. France) (Provisional Measures) **157**.299, 301 (note)
Legality of Use of Force (Yugoslavia/Serbia and Montenegro v. Germany) (Provisional Measures) **157**.306, 308 (note)
Legality of Use of Force (Yugoslavia/Serbia and Montenegro v. Italy) (Provisional Measures) **157**.309, 311 (note)
Legality of Use of Force (Yugoslavia/Serbia and Montenegro v. Netherlands) (Provisional Measures) **157**.312, 315 (note)

Legality of Use of Force (Yugoslavia/Serbia and Montenegro v. Portugal) (Provisional Measures) **157**.323, 325 (note)

Legality of Use of Force (Yugoslavia/Serbia and Montenegro v. Spain) (Provisional Measures) **157**.326 (note)

Legality of Use of Force (Yugoslavia/Serbia and Montenegro v. United Kingdom) (Provisional Measures) **157**.344, 347 (note)

Legality of Use of Force (Yugoslavia/Serbia and Montenegro v. United States of America) (Provisional Measures) **157**.351 (note)

2000

Armed Activities on the Territory of the Congo (Democratic Republic of the Congo v. Uganda) (Request for the Indication of Provisional Measures) **146**.1, 12

Arrest Warrant of 11 April 2000 (Democratic Republic of the Congo v. Belgium) (Request for Provisional Measures) **128**.1, 12

2001

Armed Activities on the Territory of the Congo (Democratic Republic of the Congo v. Uganda) (Counterclaims) **146**.1, 34

Maritime Delimitation and Territorial Questions between Qatar and Bahrain (Qatar v. Bahrain) (Merits) **139**.1

LaGrand Case (Germany v. United States of America) (Judgment) **134**.1

Sovereignty over Pulau Ligitan and Pulau Sipadan (Indonesia/Malaysia) (Application by the Philippines for Permission to Intervene) **151**.197, 212

2002

Armed Activities on the Territory of the Congo (New Application: 2002) (Democratic Republic of the Congo v. Rwanda) (Request for the Indication of Provisional Measures) **146**.263, 272

Arrest Warrant of 11 April 2000 (Democratic Republic of the Congo v. Belgium) (Judgment) **128**.1, 60

Land and Maritime Boundary between Cameroon and Nigeria (Cameroon v. Nigeria) (Merits) **141**.1, 206

Sovereignty over Pulau Ligitan and Pulau Sipadan (Indonesia/Malaysia) (Merits) **151**.197, 290

2003

Application for Revision of the Judgment of 11 September 1992 in the *Land, Island and Maritime Frontier Dispute (El Salvador/Honduras: Nicaragua intervening)* (El Salvador v. Honduras) (Judgment) **129**.1

Application for Revision of the Judgment of 11 July 1996 in *Application of the Convention on the Prevention and Punishment of the Crime of Genocide (Bosnia and Herzegovina* v. *Yugoslavia)* (Yugoslavia v. Bosnia and Herzegovina) (Judgment) **155**.1

Avena and Other Mexican Nationals (Mexico v. United States of America) (Request for the Indication of Provisional Measures) **134**.95, 104

Oil Platforms (Islamic Republic of Iran v. United States of America) (Merits) **130**.174, 323

2004

Avena and Other Mexican Nationals (Mexico v. United States of America) (Judgment) **134**.95, 120

Legal Consequences of the Construction of a Wall in the Occupied Palestinian Territory (Advisory Opinion) **129**.37

Legality of Use of Force (Yugoslavia/Serbia and Montenegro v. Belgium) (Preliminary Objections) **157**.1, 147

Legality of Use of Force (Yugoslavia/Serbia and Montenegro v. Canada) (Preliminary Objections) **157**.296, 298 (note)

Legality of Use of Force (Yugoslavia/Serbia and Montenegro v. France) (Preliminary Objections) **157**.299, 301 (note)

Legality of Use of Force (Yugoslavia/Serbia and Montenegro v. Germany) (Preliminary Objections) **157**.306, 308 (note)

Legality of Use of Force (Yugoslavia/Serbia and Montenegro v. Italy) (Preliminary Objections) **157**.309, 311 (note)

Legality of Use of Force (Yugoslavia/Serbia and Montenegro v. Netherlands) (Preliminary Objections) **157**.312, 316 (note)

Legality of Use of Force (Yugoslavia/Serbia and Montenegro v. Portugal) (Preliminary Objections) **157**.323, 325 (note)

Legality of Use of Force (Yugoslavia/Serbia and Montenegro v. United Kingdom) (Preliminary Objections) **157**.344, 346 (note)

2005

Armed Activities on the Territory of the Congo (Democratic Republic of the Congo v. Uganda) (Merits) **146**.1, 57

Certain Property (Liechtenstein v. Germany) (Judgment on Preliminary Objections) **149**.89

Frontier Dispute (Benin/Niger) (Judgment) **151**.370

2006

Armed Activities on the Territory of the Congo (New Application: 2002) (Democratic Republic of the Congo v. Rwanda) (Judgment on Jurisdiction of the Court and Admissibility of the Application) **146**.263, 345

Pulp Mills on the River Uruguay (Argentina v. Uruguay) (First Request for Provisional Measures) **152**.1, 14

2007

Application of the Convention on the Prevention and Punishment of the Crime of Genocide (Bosnia and Herzegovina v. Serbia and Montenegro) **160**.1

Pulp Mills on the River Uruguay (Argentina v. Uruguay) (Second Request for Provisional Measures) **152**.1, 55

Territorial and Maritime Dispute between Nicaragua and Honduras in the Caribbean Sea (Nicaragua v. Honduras) (Judgment) **144**.1

2008

Certain Questions of Mutual Assistance in Criminal Matters (Djibouti v. France) (Judgment) **148**.1

Georgia v. Russian Federation (Application of the International Convention on the Elimination of All Forms of Racial Discrimination) (Provisional Measures) **161**.1, 12

Request for Interpretation of the Judgment of 31 March 2004 in the Case Concerning *Avena and Other Mexican Nationals (Mexico* v. *United States of America)* (Mexico v. United States of America) (Request for the Indication of Provisional Measures) **148**.1, 147

Sovereignty over Pedra Branca/Pulau Batu Puteh, Middle Rocks and South Ledge (Malaysia/Singapore) (Judgment) **151**.453

2009

Dispute regarding Navigational and Related Rights (Costa Rica v. Nicaragua) (Judgment) **151**.615

Maritime Delimitation in the Black Sea (Romania v. Ukraine) (Judgment) **144**.179

Request for Interpretation of the Judgment of 31 March 2004 in *Avena and Other Mexican Nationals (Mexico* v. *United States of America)* (Mexico v. United States of America) (Judgment) **148**.1, 187

2010

Accordance with International Law of the Unilateral Declaration of Independence in Respect of Kosovo (Advisory Opinion) **150**.1

Pulp Mills on the River Uruguay (Argentina v. Uruguay) (Merits) **152**.1, 95

2011

Application of the Interim Accord of 13 September 1995 (the former Yugoslav Republic of Macedonia v. Greece) **162**.476

Georgia v. Russian Federation (Application of the International Convention on the Elimination of All Forms of Racial Discrimination) (Preliminary Objections) **161**.1, 64

2012
Judgment No 2867 of the Administrative Tribunal of the International Labour Organization upon a Complaint Filed against the International Fund for Agricultural Development (Advisory Opinion) **164**.37

International Criminal Court

2011
Prosecutor v. Omar Hassan Ahmad Al Bashir (Situation in Darfur, Sudan) **150**.228

International Criminal Tribunal for the former Yugoslavia

2003
Prosecutor v. Hadžihasanović, Alagić and Kubura (Case IT-01-47-AR72) (Decision on Interlocutory Appeal) (Appeals Chamber) **133**.54

2012
Prosecutor v. Haradinaj, Balaj and Brahimaj (Case No IT-04-84*bis*-T) **158**.142

International Tribunal for the Law of the Sea

2001
The MOX Plant Case (Ireland v. United Kingdom) (Request for Provisional Measures) **126**.259

2002
The *Volga* (Russian Federation v. Australia) (Application for Prompt Release) **126**.433

2003
Land Reclamation by Singapore in and around the Straits of Johor (Malaysia v. Singapore) (Request for Provisional Measures) **126**.487

2004
The *Juno Trader* (Saint Vincent and the Grenadines v. Guinea-Bissau) (Application for Prompt Release) **128**.267

2007
The *Hoshinmaru* (Japan v. Russian Federation) (Application for Prompt Release) **143**.1
The *Tomimaru* (Japan v. Russian Federation) (Application for Prompt Release) **143**.36

2010
MV *Louisa* (Saint Vincent and the Grenadines v. Kingdom of Spain) (Order on Request for Provisional Measures) **148**.459

2011
Advisory Opinion on Responsibilities and Obligations of States sponsoring persons and entities with respect to activities in the Area **150**.244

2012
The *ARA Libertad* (Argentina v. Ghana) (Request for Provisional Measures) **156**.186, 239 (note)

2013
The *Arctic Sunrise* (Kingdom of the Netherlands v. Russian Federation) (Request for Provisional Measures) **159**.68
MV*Louisa* (Saint Vincent and the Grenadines v. Kingdom of Spain) (Merits) **157**.432

Southern African Development Community Tribunal

2008
Mike Campbell (Pvt) Ltd, William Michael Campbell and Others v. Republic of Zimbabwe (Case No 2/2007) **138**.385, **149**.475

Special Court for Sierra Leone

2004
Prosecutor v. Taylor (Case SCSL-2003-01-I) (Immunity from Jurisdiction) (Appeals Chamber) **128**.239

Special Tribunal for Lebanon

2011
Interlocutory Decision on the Applicable Law: Terrorism, Conspiracy, Homicide, Perpetration, Cumulative Charging (Case No STL-11-01/I) (Appeals Chamber) **145**.232

United Nations Human Rights Committee

1993
General Comment No 22 on the Right to Freedom of Thought, Conscience and Religion **157**.596

1999
Kennedy v. Trinidad and Tobago (Communication No 845/1999) (Admissibility) **134**.415, 418

2002
Kennedy v. Trinidad and Tobago (Communication No 845/1999) **134**.415, 428

2004
Singarasa v. Sri Lanka (Communication No 1033/2001) **138**.451

2006
Yoon and Choi v. Republic of Korea (Communication Nos 1321 and 1322/2004) **157**.602

2011
Jeong and Others v. Republic of Korea (Communication Nos 1642-1741/2007) **157**.620

2012
Atasoy and Sarkut v. Turkey (Communication Nos 1853 and 1854/2008) **157**.653
Bulgakov v. Ukraine (Communication No 1803/2008) **159**.132
Cedeño v. Bolivarian Republic of Venezuela (Communication No 1940/2010) **159**.143
Fedotova v. Russian Federation (Communication No 1932/2010) **159**.193

Kholodova v. Russian Federation (Communication No 1548/2007) **159**.217
Kim and Others v. Republic of Korea (Communication No 1786/2008) **157**.682
Korneenko v. Belarus (Communication No 1226/2003) **156**.271
Naidenova and Others v. Bulgaria (Communication No 2073/2011) **159**.170
Narrain and Others v. Mauritius (Communication No 1744/2007) **156**.293
Singh (Bikramjit) v. France (Communication No 1852/2008) **159**.233

2013
Achabal Puertas v. Spain (Communication No 1945/2010) **159**.272
Al-Gertani v. Bosnia and Herzegovina (Communication No 1955/2010) **164**.261
Choudhary v. Canada (Communication No 1898/2009) **164**.234
FKAG and Others v. Australia (Communication No 2094/2011) **163**.266
Kovsh v. Belarus (Communication No 1787/2008) **159**.257
Mann Singh (Shingara) v. France (Communication No 1928/2010) **163**.249
Mihoubi v. Algeria (Communication No 1874/2009) **163**.299
Rodríguez Castañeda v. Mexico (Communication No 2202/2012) **163**.223

2014
Horvath v. Australia (Communication No 1885/2009) **165**.354
Ory v. France (Communication No 1960/2010) **165**.384
Paadar and Others v. Finland (Communication No 2102/2011) **165**.330
Paksas v. Lithuania (Communication No 2155/2012) **165**.303
X v. Denmark (Communication No 2007/2010) **164**.286

II. DECISIONS OF MUNICIPAL COURTS

Australia

2000
Minister for Immigration and Multicultural Affairs v. Haji Ibrahim **131**.1

2001
Ruddock and Others v. Vadarlis and Others; Ruddock and Others v. Victorian Council for Civil Liberties Inc. and Others **131**.83

2002
Minister for Immigration and Multicultural Affairs v. Khawar and Others **131**.158
Morrison v. Peacock and Another **136**.255

2005
Re Minister for Immigration and Multicultural and Indigenous Affairs, *ex parte* Ame **148**.503

2006
AB v. Registrar of Births, Deaths and Marriages **133**.248

2007
AB v. Registrar of Births, Deaths and Marriages **136**.266
Thomas v. Mowbray and Others **163**.329

2008
R v. Tang **143**.76
Thor Shipping A/S v. The Ship *Al Duhail* **140**.530
Zhang v. Jiang Zemin and Others **141**.542

2010
Habib v. Commonwealth of Australia **149**.478
Republic of Croatia v. Snedden **153**.335
Zhang v. Jiang Zemin and Others **148**.555, 593 (note)

2011
Plaintiffs M70/2011 and M106/2011 v. Minister for Immigration and Citizenship and Another **150**.506

PT Garuda Indonesia Ltd and Another v. Australian Competition and Consumer Commission **152**.365

2012
Minister for Home Affairs (Cth) and Others v. Zentai and Others **153**.366
PT Garuda Indonesia Ltd v. Australian Competition and Consumer Commission **153**.406

2014
FTZK v. Minister for Immigration and Border Protection **158**.441

2015
Ure v. Commonwealth of Australia and Director of National Parks **164**.304

Austria

1998
Syrian National Immunity Case (Case 12 Os 3/98) **127**.88

Barbados

2004
Boyce and Another v. The Queen **134**.439

2006
Attorney General and Others v. Joseph and Boyce **134**.469

Belgium

1997
Scimet v. African Development Bank **128**.582

2001
League of Arab States v. T **127**.94

2002
Burundi v. Landau **127**.98
Iraq v. Vinci Constructions **127**.101
Re Sharon and Yaron **127**.110, 113

2003
Re Sharon and Yaron **127**.110, 121

Belize

2007
Cal and Others *v.* Attorney General of Belize and Minister of Natural Resources and Environment; Coy and Others *v.* Attorney General of Belize and Minister of Natural Resources and Environment **135**.77

Bermuda

2002
Minister of Finance *v.* Braswell and Others **132**.237, 270 (note)

Bosnia and Herzegovina

2002
Boudellaa and Others *v.* Bosnia and Herzegovina and the Federation of Bosnia and Herzegovina **136**.309

Botswana

2005
Bah *v.* Libyan Embassy **142**.167

Canada

1999
Baker *v.* Canada (Minister of Citizenship and Immigration) **148**.594

2002
Schreiber *v.* Federal Republic of Germany and Attorney General of Canada **147**.276, 302 (note)

2003
Harb *v.* Canada (Minister of Citizenship and Immigration) **131**.206
Parent and Others *v.* Singapore Airlines Limited and the Civil Aeronautics Administration **133**.264
United Mexican States *v.* Feldman Karpa **126**.536
Zrig *v.* Canada (Minister of Citizenship and Immigration) **131**.215

2004
Attorney General of Canada *v.* SD Myers Inc.; United Mexican States (Intervener) **126**.553
Bouzari and Others *v.* Islamic Republic of Iran **128**.586

2005
Arar *v.* Syrian Arab Republic and the Hashemite Kingdom of Jordan **155**.368
Council of Canadians and Others *v.* The Queen in Right of Canada **132**.335, 337
Minister of Citizenship and Immigration *v.* Mugesera and Others **132**.271
United Mexican States *v.* Feldman Karpa **128**.610

2006
Council of Canadians and Others *v.* The Queen in Right of Canada **132**.335, 368

2007
Hape *v.* Her Majesty the Queen (Attorney General of Ontario intervening) **143**.140

2008
Amnesty International Canada and British Columbia Civil Liberties Association *v.* Chief of Defence Staff for the Canadian Forces and Others **156**.311, 315, 363
Khadr *v.* Canada (No 1) **143**.212

2009
Abdelrazik *v.* Minister of Foreign Affairs and Attorney General of Canada **155**.377
Khadr *v.* Canada (No 2) **143**.225, 228

2010
Khadr *v.* Canada (No 2) **143**.225, 264
Kuwait Airways Corporation *v.* Republic of Iraq and Bombardier Aerospace **147**.303
United Mexican States *v.* Cargill Inc. **146**.800

2011
Attorney General of Canada on behalf of United States of America *v.* Khadr **157**.700
Estate of the Late Kazemi and Hashemi *v.* Islamic Republic of Iran and Others **147**.318

United Mexican States v. Cargill Inc. **150**.598, 622 (note)

2012
Islamic Republic of Iran and Others v. Hashemi and Estate of the Late Kazemi; Estate of the Late Kazemi v. Islamic Republic of Iran and Others **154**.351

2014
Estate of Kazemi v. Islamic Republic of Iran and Others **159**.299

China, Hong Kong Special Administrative Region

2004
Secretary for Security v. Prabakar **155**.444

2008
C and Others v. Director of Immigration **138**.537
RV v. Director of Immigration and Secretary for Justice **138**.582

2010
FG Hemisphere Associates LLC v. Democratic Republic of the Congo and Others **142**.216
Intraline Resources Sdn Bhd v. Owners of the Ship or Vessel *Hua Tian Long* (No 3) **153**.430

2011
Democratic Republic of the Congo and Others v. FG Hemisphere Associates LLC (No 1) **147**.376
Democratic Republic of the Congo and Others v. FG Hemisphere Associates LLC (No 2) **150**.684

Cyprus

2010
Ngassam v. Republic of Cyprus (Director General of Ministry of Interior and Attorney General) (Case No 493/2010) **156**.371

Czech Republic

2001
Succession of States and Individuals Case **142**.175

2002
Diplomatic Privileges and Immunities of a Visiting Prince Case **142**.186

2008
State Immunity in Labour Law Matters Case **142**.206

2011
VP v. Republic of Austria (Case No 30 Cdo 2594/2009) **150**.623

Denmark

2003
Hingitaq 53, Petersen and Others v. Office of the Prime Minister of Denmark **143**.277, 298 (note)

France

1994
Javor and Others **127**.126, 127

1996
Javor and Others **127**.126, 132

1998
Munyeshyaka **127**.134

1999
Allianz Via Insurance v. United States of America **127**.148
Dumez v. Iraq and Others **127**.144
Federal Republic and National Bank of Yugoslavia v. Republics of Croatia, Slovenia, Macedonia and Bosnia–Herzegovina **128**.627
Ruperas v. EUTELSAT **127**.139

2000
Creighton Ltd v. Minister of Finance of Qatar and Others **127**.154
Russian Federation v. Noga Import/Export Company **127**.156

2003
X v. Saudi School in Paris and Kingdom of Saudi Arabia **127**.163

2004
Cotigny and French Parachuting Federation v. Suarez and United States of America **127**.168

2005
African Development Bank Case **138**.498

2008
Société Logicom *v.* Société CTT Marketing Limited and Société Ducros Transports **148**.629

2011
Réunion Aérienne *v.* Socialist People's Libyan Arab Jamahiriya (Case No 0914743) **150**.630

Germany, Federal Republic of

1986
Ghana Refugié Sur Place Case (Case No 2 BvR 1058/85) **130**.560

1987
Pakistan Religious Persecution Case (Case Nos 2 BvR 478 and 962/86) **130**.571

1989
Tamils' Political Persecution Case (Case Nos 2 BvR 502, 961 and 1000/86) **130**.587

1996
Asylum Legislation (Accelerated Airport Procedure) Constitutionality Case (Case No 2 BvR 1516/93) **130**.606
Asylum Legislation (Safe Countries of Origin) Constitutionality Case (Case Nos 2 BvR 1507 and 1508/93) **130**.640, 661 (note)
Asylum Legislation (Safe Third Countries) Constitutionality Case (Case Nos 2 BvR 1938 and 2315/93) **130**.662, 686 (note)
Prince Hans-Adam II *v.* Municipality of Cologne (Case No 22 U 215/95) **149**.1

1998
In re Prince Hans-Adam II of Liechtenstein (Case No 2 BvR 1981/97) **149**.26

2000
Afghanistan Political Persecution Case (Case Nos 2 BvR 260 and 1353/98) **130**.687, 695 (note)
Jorgic (Case No 2 BvR 1290/99) **135**.152, 167 (note)

2001
Bosnia–Herzegovina Genocide Case (Case No 3 StR 244/01) **131**.274
NATO Strategic Concept (German Participation) Case (Case No 2 BvE 6/99) **135**.168, 185 (note)

2003
Distomo Massacre Case (Greek Citizens *v.* Federal Republic of Germany) (Case No III ZR 245/98) **129**.556
Kenyan Diplomatic Residence Case (Case No IXa ZB 19/03) **128**.632

2004
Turkish Citizen G *v.* Naumburg Higher Regional Court (Case No 2 BvR 1481/04) **145**.384

2006
Distomo Massacre Case (Greek Citizens *v.* Federal Republic of Germany) (Case No 2 BvR 1476/03) **135**.186

2007
Argentine Necessity Case (Case No 2 BvM 1-5/03, 1, 2/06) **138**.1

2009
Lisbon Treaty Constitutionality Case (Case Nos 2 BvE 2/08, 2 BvE 5/08, 2BvR 1010/08, 2 BvR 1022/08, 2 BvR 1259/08 and 2 BvR 182/09) **141**.554

2011
Guarantees for the European Financial Stability Facility Case (Case Nos 2 BvR 987/10, 2 BvR 1485/10, 2 BvR 1099/10) **150**.636

2013
Aerial Drone Deployment on 4 October 2010 in Mir Ali/Pakistan (Case No 3 BJs 7/12-4) **157**.722

Ghana

2013
Republic of Ghana *v.* High Court (Commercial Division) Accra, *ex parte* Attorney General (NML Capital Ltd and Republic of Argentina, interested parties) **156**.240, 270 (note)

Greece

2000
Prefecture of Voiotia v. Federal Republic of Germany (Distomo Massacre Case) (Case No 11/2000) **129**.513

2002
Margellos and Others v. Federal Republic of Germany (Case No 6/2002) **129**.525

India

2015
AWAS 39423 Ireland Ltd and Others v. Director-General of Civil Aviation and Spicejet Ltd **163**.569
Wilmington Trust SP Services (Dublin) Ltd v. Director-General of Civil Aviation and Spicejet Ltd **163**.569

Ireland

2001
Kavanagh v. Governor of Mountjoy Prison and Others **132**.380, 382

2002
Kavanagh v. Governor of Mountjoy Prison and Others **132**.380, 394

2003
Horgan v. An Taoiseach and Others **132**.407

2005
Dubsky v. Government of Ireland and Others **149**.529

2007
Doherty and Doherty v. South Dublin County Council and Others (No 2) **148**.632
O'Donnell (a minor suing by her mother and next friend) and Others v. South Dublin County Council **149**.579

Israel

1997
Her Majesty the Queen in Right of Canada v. Edelson and Others (PLA 7092/94) **131**.279

1999
Public Committee against Torture in Israel and Others v. State of Israel, General Security Service and Others (HCJ 5100/94, 4054/95, 6536/95, 5188/96, 7563/97, 7628/97 and 1043/99) **133**.283

2002
Center for the Defense of the Individual and Others v. Israel Defence Force Commander in the West Bank (HCJ 3278/02) **133**.314

2003
Marab and Others v. Israel Defence Force Commander in the West Bank and Another (HCJ 3239/02) **133**.332

2004
Beit Sourik Village Council v. Government of Israel and Commander of the IDF Forces in the West Bank (HCJ 2056/04) **129**.189

2005
Adalah (Legal Center for Arab Minority Rights in Israel) and Others v. GOC Central Command, IDF and Others (HCJ 3799/02) **145**.407
Mara'abe and Others v. Prime Minister and Others (HCJ 7957/04) **129**.241

2006
Public Committee against Torture in Israel and Another v. Government of Israel and Others (HCJ 769/02) **145**.429

Italy

1994
Sassetti v. Multinational Force and Observers (Decision No 3857/1994) **128**.640

2000
FILT-CGIL Trento and Others v. United States of America (Decision No 530/2000) **128**.644

2002
President of the Council of Ministers v. Marković and Others (Decision No 8157/2002) **128**.652

2004
Ferrini v. Federal Republic of Germany (Decision No 5044/2004) **128**.658

2011
Federal Republic of Germany v. Prefecture of Voiotia (Case No 11163/11) **150**.706

Jamaica

2000
Lewis v. Attorney General of Jamaica **134**.615

Japan

1997
Kayano and Others v. Hokkaido Expropriation Committee (the Nibutani Dam Decision) **127**.173

Jersey

2012
La Générale des Carrières et des Mines v. FG Hemisphere Associates LLC **164**.347

Kenya

2006
Lemeiguran and Others v. Attorney General and Others **142**.328
RM (a minor, through next friend JK) v. Attorney General **143**.299
Waweru v. Republic of Kenya **142**.308

2007
Al-Dahas v. Attorney General and Others **143**.331

2008
Republic of Kenya v. Minister for Home Affairs and Others, *ex parte* Sitamze **143**.349

2010
Wakaba and Others v. Attorney General **152**.431

Malawi

2007
Kafantayeni and Others v. Attorney General of Malawi **134**.649

2008
Re Banda **154**.410

Malaysia

2005
Kerajaan Negeri Selangor and Others v. Sagong bin Tasi and Others **135**.126

Mauritius

2008
De Boucherville v. State of Mauritius **155**.466

Nepal

2007
Pant and Others v. Nepal Government and Others **138**.500

2014
JuRI-Nepal (Justice and Rights Organization) and Others v. Government of Nepal and Others **158**.476

The Netherlands

1991
Stichting Revalidatiecentrum "De Trappenberg" v. Kingdom of Morocco **128**.676, 678

1994
Kingdom of Morocco v. Stichting Revalidatiecentrum "De Trappenberg" **128**.676, 679

1998
Arias v. Venezuela **128**.684
LM v. Netherlands, Minister for Netherlands Antilles Affairs and Aruban Affairs and Others **128**.681
Netherlands v. Azeta BV **128**.688

1999
United States of America v. Eemshaven Port Authority **127**.225

2007
Stichting Greenpeace Nederland v. Euratom **136**.429

2010
The "Cygnus" Case (Somali Pirates) **145**.491

2011
Mustafić and Others v. Netherlands **153**.506 (note)
Nuhanović v. Netherlands **153**.467

2012
Mothers of Srebrenica Association and Others v. Netherlands and United Nations **160**.558

2013
Netherlands v. Mustafić and Others **160**.650 (note)
Netherlands v. Nuhanović **160**.629

New Zealand

2004
Zaoui v. Attorney General (No 2) **131**.308, 312

2005
Zaoui v. Attorney General (No 2) **131**.308, 389

2006
Fang and Others v. Jiang Zemin and Others **141**.702

2007
Taunoa and Others v. Attorney General **155**.479

2013
Teitiota v. Chief Executive of the Ministry of Business, Innovation and Employment **158**.541, 544

2014
Teitiota v. Chief Executive of the Ministry of Business, Innovation and Employment **158**.541, 560

Nigeria

2008
Registered Trustees of National Association of Community Health Practitioners of Nigeria and Others v. Medical and Health Workers Union of Nigeria **152**.464

Norway

1996
Public Prosecutor v. Haraldsson and Others **140**.559

Pakistan

2002
Société Générale de Surveillance SA v. Pakistan, through Secretary, Ministry of Finance; Pakistan, through Secretary, Ministry of Finance v. Société Générale de Surveillance SA (Order) (Judgment) **129**.323, 325, 327

Pitcairn Island

2004
The Queen v. Seven Named Accused **127**.232, 234, 284

2006
Christian and Others v. The Queen **130**.696

Portugal

2002
X v. Israel **127**.310

Russian Federation

2003
Re Compliance of Article 1(3) of Law of St Petersburg with Charter of St Petersburg **138**.482
Resolution No 5 on Application by Courts of General Jurisdiction of Commonly Recognized Principles and Norms of International Law and International Treaties of Russian Federation **150**.726

2006
Re Khodorkovskiy (Case No KAS06-129) **133**.365

2009
Re Clarification of Paragraph 5 of Operative Part of Constitutional Court Resolution No 3-P of 2 February 1999 **142**.383

Serbia

2002
District Public Prosecutor v. Nikolić (Case No Kž. I 1594/02) **128**.691, 692

2003
District Public Prosecutor v. Nikolić (Case No Kž. I 1594/02) **128**.691, 697
Public Prosecutor v. Magazine "Svedok" **127**.315

Seychelles

2011
Republic of Seychelles v. Osman and Ten Others **152**.513

Singapore

2004
Civil Aeronautics Administration v. Singapore Airlines Limited **133**.371
Nguyen Tuong Van v. Public Prosecutor **134**.660

2008
Republic of the Philippines v. Maler Foundation and Others (Civil Appeal No 7 of 2007) **150**.741

2010
Yong Vui Kong v. Public Prosecutor **143**.374

South Africa

1995
S v. Makwanyane and Another **127**.321
Welkom Municipality v. Masureik and Herman t/a Lotus Corporation and Another **131**.423, 425

1996
The Akademik Fyodorov (Government of the Russian Federation and Another v. Marine Expeditions Inc.) **131**.460
Azanian People's Organization (AZAPO) and Others v. President of the Republic of South Africa and Others **131**.492

1997
KJ International and Others v. MV *Oscar Jupiter* (Compania de Navigatie Maritime "Romline" SA and Others intervening) **131**.529
Swissborough Diamond Mines (Pty) Ltd and Others v. Government of the Republic of South Africa and Others **132**.454
Welkom Municipality v. Masureik and Herman t/a Lotus Corporation and Another **131**.423, 451

1999
Harksen v. President of the Republic of South Africa and Others **132**.529, 532
Portion 20 of Plot 15 Athol (Pty) Ltd v. Rodrigues **133**.389

2000
Harksen v. President of the Republic of South Africa and Others **132**.529, 557
Schlumberger Logelco Inc. v. Coflexip SA **133**.405

2001
Geuking v. President of the Republic of South Africa and Others **132**.568, 573
Mohamed and Another v. President of the Republic of South Africa and Others **127**.468

2002
Geuking v. President of the Republic of South Africa and Others **132**.568, 590
Telkom SA Ltd v. Member of the Executive Council for Agricultural and Environmental Affairs, Kwazulu-Natal and Others **133**.412

2003
Alexkor Ltd and Government of the Republic of South Africa v. Richtersveld Community and Others **127**.501, 505, 542

2004
Kaunda and Others v. President of the Republic of South Africa and Others **136**.452
S v. Basson **133**.424

2005
Potgieter *v.* British Airways Plc **133**.471
Van Zyl and Others *v.* Government of the Republic of South Africa and Others **143**.473, 478

2007
Fuel Retailers Association of Southern Africa *v.* Director-General Environmental Management, Department of Agriculture, Conservation and Environment, Mpumalanga Province and Others **143**.426
Van Zyl and Others *v.* Government of the Republic of South Africa and Others **143**.473, 545

2008
Von Abo *v.* Republic of South Africa and Others **143**.577, 581

2009
Von Abo *v.* Republic of South Africa and Others **143**.577, 624

2010
Von Abo *v.* Republic of South Africa and Others **143**.577, 643

2011
Glenister *v.* President of the Republic of South Africa and Others **155**.628
Government of the Republic of South Africa and Others *v.* Von Abo (Case 283/10) **150**.783
Republic of South Africa and Others *v.* Von Abo **143**.577, 666 (note)

Spain

1999
State Marine Corporation and Currence *v.* United States of America **128**.701

2003
Peruvian Genocide Case (Decision No 712/2003) **141**.720

Sri Lanka

2006
Singarasa *v.* Attorney General **138**.469

Sweden

1999
Municipality of Västerås *v.* Iceland **128**.705

Timor-Leste

2003
Armando dos Santos *v.* Prosecutor General **138**.604

Trinidad and Tobago

2004
Matthew *v.* Trinidad and Tobago **134**.687

Uganda

2004
Onyango-Obbo and Another *v.* Attorney General **140**.566

2009
Attorney General *v.* Kigula and Others **143**.667

2011
Kwoyelo *v.* Uganda **150**.802

United Kingdom, England

2001
Emin *v.* Yeldag (Attorney General and Secretary of State for Foreign and Commonwealth Affairs intervening) **148**.663
R (Marchiori) *v.* Environment Agency **127**.574, 577

2002
A, X and Y and Others *v.* Secretary of State for the Home Department **126**.585, 589, 631
B (a Child) (Care Proceedings: Diplomatic Immunity), *In re* **145**.516
R *v.* Lyons and Others **131**.538
R (Abbasi and Juma) *v.* Secretary of State for Foreign and Commonwealth Affairs and Secretary of State for the Home Department **126**.685

R (Campaign for Nuclear Disarmament) v. Prime Minister of the United Kingdom, Secretary of State for Foreign and Commonwealth Affairs and Secretary of State for Defence (CND Case) **126**.727
R (Marchiori) v. Environment Agency **127**.574, 620
R (Saadi and Others) v. Secretary of State for the Home Department **133**.482
S (a Child) (Abduction: Custody Rights), Re **136**.540

2003
AIC Limited v. Federal Government of Nigeria and Others **129**.571
Jones v. Ministry of the Interior of the Kingdom of Saudi Arabia and Another (Secretary of State for Constitutional Affairs and Another intervening) **129**.629, 636
Kuwait Airways Corporation v. Iraqi Airways Company ("Perjury Action") **126**.758

2004
A and Others v. Secretary of State for the Home Department (No 1) **137**.1
Bici and Bici v. Ministry of Defence **145**.529
Government of the United States of America v. Barnette and Another **145**.602
Government of the United States of America v. Montgomery (No 2) **145**.602
Jones v. Ministry of the Interior of the Kingdom of Saudi Arabia and Another (Secretary of State for Constitutional Affairs and Another intervening) **129**.629, 649
Mitchell and Others v. Al-Dali and Others **129**.629, 649
Mofaz, Re **128**.709
R v. Jones (Margaret) and Others **132**.608
R (Al-Skeini and Others) v. Secretary of State for Defence (the Redress Trust and Others intervening) **133**.499, 507
R (B and Others) v. Secretary of State for Foreign and Commonwealth Affairs **131**.616
R (European Roma Rights Centre and Others) v. Immigration Officer at Prague Airport and Another (United Nations High Commissioner for Refugees intervening) **131**.652
R (Mullen) v. Secretary of State for the Home Department **145**.564
R (Ullah) v. Special Adjudicator; Do v. Immigration Appeal Tribunal **131**.577
Tatchell v. Mugabe **136**.572
X and Another v. Secretary of State for the Home Department **137**.1

2005
A and Others v. Secretary of State for the Home Department (No 2) **137**.116
AIG Capital Partners Inc. and Another v. Republic of Kazakhstan (National Bank of Kazakhstan intervening) **129**.589
Amin v. Brown **132**.656
Ayliffe and Others v. Director of Public Prosecutions **132**.632
Bo Xilai **128**.713
Harb v. His Majesty King Fahd Bin Abdul Aziz **136**.574, 586 (note)
N v. Secretary of State for the Home Department (Terrence Higgins Trust intervening) **148**.273
Percy v. Director of Public Prosecutions **132**.632
R (Al-Jedda) v. Secretary of State for Defence **137**.202, 209
R (Al-Skeini and Others) v. Secretary of State for Defence (the Redress Trust and Others intervening) **133**.499, 622
R (Alamieyeseigha) v. Crown Prosecution Service **145**.619
R (Quark Fishing Limited) v. Secretary of State for Foreign and Commonwealth Affairs **131**.712
Republic of Ecuador v. Occidental Exploration and Production Company (No 1) **138**.92, 95, 125
Swain v. Director of Public Prosecutions **132**.632

2006
Re AY Bank Ltd (in liquidation); AY Bank Ltd (in liquidation) v. Bosnia and Herzegovina and Others **149**.614
Ayliffe and Others v. Director of Public Prosecutions **132**.668
Jones v. Ministry of the Interior of the Kingdom of Saudi Arabia and Another

(Secretary of State for Constitutional Affairs and Another intervening) 129.629, 713
Mitchell and Others v. Al-Dali and Others 129.629, 713
R v. Jones (Margaret) and Others 132.668
R (Al Rawi and Others) v. Secretary of State for Foreign and Commonwealth Affairs and Another (United Nations High Commissioner for Refugees intervening) 136.624, 688 (note)
R (Al-Jedda) v. Secretary of State for Defence 137.202, 251
R (Gentle and Clarke) v. Prime Minister, Secretary of State for Defence and Attorney General 132.721
R (Islamic Human Rights Commission) v. Civil Aviation Authority, Foreign and Commonwealth Office and Ministry of Defence 132.707
Republic of Ecuador v. Occidental Exploration and Production Company (No 2) 138.158, 160
Swain v. Director of Public Prosecutions 132.668

2007

Aziz v. Aziz and Others (HM the Sultan of Brunei intervening) 136.587
Grovit v. De Nederlandsche Bank NV and Others 142.403
Mechan v. Foreign and Commonwealth Office 141.727
R (Al-Jedda) v. Secretary of State for Defence 137.202, 287
R (Al-Skeini and Others) v. Secretary of State for Defence (the Redress Trust and Others intervening) 133.499, 693
Republic of Ecuador v. Occidental Exploration and Production Company (No 2) 138.158, 203, 218 (note)

2008

AS and DD (Libya) v. Secretary of State for the Home Department and Liberty 140.654
EM (Lebanon) v. Secretary of State for the Home Department (AF (a Child) and Others intervening) 165.485
Entico Corporation Ltd v. United Nations Educational, Scientific and Cultural Organization 156.382

Korea National Insurance Corporation v. Allianz Global Corporate & Specialty AG 163.605
Kuwait Airways Corporation v. Iraqi Airways Company and Republic of Iraq ("Costs Action") 147.532
Othman (Jordan) v. Secretary of State for the Home Department 142.411, 420
R v. Bieber 156.402, 423 (note)
R (Bancoult) v. Secretary of State for Foreign and Commonwealth Affairs (No 2) 138.628
R (Corner House Research and Another) v. Director of the Serious Fraud Office (JUSTICE intervening) 165.402, 409, 457
R (Gentle and Clarke) v. Prime Minister, Secretary of State for Defence and Attorney General 140.624
R (Smith) v. Oxfordshire Assistant Deputy Coroner (Equality and Human Rights Commission intervening) 156.424, 436
R (Wellington) v. Secretary of State for the Home Department 155.713

2009

Al-Sirri v. Secretary of State for the Home Department (United Nations High Commissioner for Refugees intervening) 140.689
Re Barak 163.619
Brown (aka Bajinya) and Others v. Government of Rwanda and Another 142.568
Morgan and Baker v. Hinton Organics (Wessex) Ltd and Coalition for Access to Justice for the Environment ("CAJE") 142.542
Othman (Jordan) v. Secretary of State for the Home Department 142.411, 449
Pocket Kings Limited v. Safenames Limited and the Commonwealth of Kentucky 152.525
R (Al-Haq) v. Secretary of State for Foreign and Commonwealth Affairs 154.423, 442 (note)
R (Al-Saadoon and Another) v. Secretary of State for Defence 147.538
R (Hassan) v. Secretary of State for Defence 164.391
R (JS (Sri Lanka)) v. Secretary of State for the Home Department 159.366, 372

R (Kibris Türk Hava Yollari and CTA Holidays Ltd) *v.* Secretary of State for Transport (Republic of Cyprus, interested party) **148**.683, 687

R (Misick) *v.* Secretary of State for Foreign and Commonwealth Affairs **165**.515, 519, 533

R (Smith) *v.* Oxfordshire Assistant Deputy Coroner (Equality and Human Rights Commission intervening) **156**.424, 458

RB (Algeria) *v.* Secretary of State for the Home Department **142**.411, 449

Republic of Croatia *v.* Republic of Serbia **164**.429

Republic of Serbia *v.* ImageSat International NV **142**.644

U (Algeria) *v.* Secretary of State for the Home Department **142**.411, 449

Wilhelm Finance Inc. *v.* Ente Administrador del Astillero Rio Santiago **164**.407

2010

Ahmed and Others *v.* Her Majesty's Treasury (JUSTICE intervening) (Nos 1 and 2) **149**.641

Al Hassan-Daniel and Another *v.* Revenue and Customs Commissioners (JUSTICE intervening) **164**.451

Al-Ghabra *v.* Her Majesty's Treasury (JUSTICE intervening) **149**.641

Al-Jedda *v.* Secretary of State for Defence (No 2) **163**.622

Apostolides *v.* Orams and Another **154**.443, 498

Government of the Republic of Serbia *v.* Ganić **160**.651

HJ (Iran) *v.* Secretary of State for the Home Department **159**.428

HT (Cameroon) *v.* Secretary of State for the Home Department **159**.428

R (Evans) *v.* Secretary of State for Defence **153**.508

R (JS (Sri Lanka)) *v.* Secretary of State for the Home Department **159**.366, 404

R (Kibris Türk Hava Yollari and CTA Holidays Ltd) *v.* Secretary of State for Transport (Republic of Cyprus, interested party) **148**.683, 715

R (Smith) *v.* Oxfordshire Assistant Deputy Coroner (Equality and Human Rights Commission intervening) **156**.424, 499

R (ST (Eritrea)) *v.* Secretary of State for the Home Department **159**.489, 496

R (Youssef) *v.* Her Majesty's Treasury (JUSTICE intervening) **149**.641

2011

British Arab Commercial Bank Plc *v.* National Transitional Council of the State of Libya **147**.667

Re Gorbachev **163**.689

Khurts Bat *v.* Investigating Judge of the German Federal Court **147**.633

Mutua and Others *v.* Foreign and Commonwealth Office **156**.629, 635, 717 (note)

NML Capital Ltd *v.* Republic of Argentina **147**.575

R *v.* Forsyth; R *v.* Mabey **158**.572

R *v.* Lyons **162**.674

R *v.* PD and EB (Iraq Sanctions) **158**.584

R (Adams) *v.* Secretary of State for Justice **154**.533

R (Sultan of Pahang) *v.* Secretary of State for the Home Department **152**.543

Rahmatullah *v.* Secretary of State for Foreign and Commonwealth Affairs and Secretary of State for Defence (No 1) **150**.819

Smith and Others *v.* Ministry of Defence **158**.612, 623

2012

Al-Sirri *v.* Secretary of State for the Home Department; DD (Afghanistan) *v.* Secretary of State for the Home Department **159**.616

Assange *v.* Swedish Prosecution Authority (Nos 1 and 2) **164**.461, 568 (note)

Hamza and Others *v.* Secretary of State for the Home Department **155**.312

Mutua and Others *v.* Foreign and Commonwealth Office **156**.629, 697, 717 (note)

Othman (Abu Qatada) *v.* Secretary of State for the Home Department **153**.651

R *v.* Gul **152**.568

R *v.* Oakes **156**.423 (note)

R (Khan) *v.* Secretary of State for Foreign and Commonwealth Affairs **165**.622, 627

R (ST (Eritrea)) *v.* Secretary of State for the Home Department **159**.489, 519

Rahmatullah v. Secretary of State for Foreign and Commonwealth Affairs and Secretary of State for Defence (No 2) **150**.836

RT (Zimbabwe) and Others v. Secretary of State for the Home Department; KM (Zimbabwe) v. Secretary of State for the Home Department **159**.587

Secretary of State for Foreign and Commonwealth Affairs and Secretary of State for Defence v. Rahmatullah; Rahmatullah v. Secretary of State for Foreign and Commonwealth Affairs and Secretary of State for Defence **153**.607

SerVaas Inc. v. Rafidain Bank and Others **160**.668

SK (Zimbabwe) v. Secretary of State for the Home Department **159**.548

Smith and Others v. Ministry of Defence; Ministry of Defence v. Ellis; Ministry of Defence v. Allbutt and Others **158**.612, 658

Wokuri v. Kassam **152**.557

Yukos Capital SARL v. OJSC Rosneft Oil Company (No 2) **165**.554

2013

Othman (Abu Qatada) v. Secretary of State for the Home Department **155**.754, 776 (note)

R (Bancoult) v. Secretary of State for Foreign and Commonwealth Affairs (No 3) **162**.348, 351

Smith and Others v. Ministry of Defence; Ellis v. Ministry of Defence; Allbutt and Others v. Ministry of Defence **158**.612, 673

2014

Re Attorney General's Reference No 69 of 2013; R v. McLoughlin; R v. Newell **158**.746

Belhaj and Boudchar v. Straw and Others **159**.649

Iraqi Civilians v. Ministry of Defence **165**.660

R (Bancoult) v. Secretary of State for Foreign and Commonwealth Affairs (No 3) **162**.348, 424

R (Khan) v. Secretary of State for Foreign and Commonwealth Affairs **165**.622, 643

2015

Pham v. Secretary of State for the Home Department **162**.719

Reyes and Another v. Al-Malki **162**.688

United Kingdom, Northern Ireland

2004

In re McFarland **145**.637

2011

In re McCaughey and Another (Northern Ireland Human Rights Commission and Others intervening) **153**.192

In re MacDermott; In re McCartney **154**.533

United Kingdom, Scotland

1978

Annandale and Eskdale District Council v. North West Water Authority **127**.652

1998

Procurator Fiscal v. Slater Main and Wanderer Fishing Company Limited **127**.661

2004

Al Fayed v. Lord Advocate and Advocate General **145**.656

United States of America

2001

United States of America v. Bin Laden aka Mohamed **127**.676

2003

Nemariam and Others v. Federal Democratic Republic of Ethiopia and the Commercial Bank of Ethiopia (No 1) **135**.671

Sosa v. Alvarez-Machain and Others; United States of America v. Alvarez-Machain and Others **127**.691, 697

2004

Al Odah and Others v. United States and Others **137**.377

Hamdi and Others v. Rumsfeld, Secretary of Defense and Others **137**.407

Rasul and Others *v.* Bush, President of the United States and Others **137**.377

Republic of Austria and Others *v.* Altmann **147**.681, 725 (note)

Rumsfeld, Secretary of Defense *v.* Padilla and Another **137**.347

Sosa *v.* Alvarez-Machain and Others; United States of America *v.* Alvarez-Machain and Others **127**.691, 769

2005

Raymond L. Loewen *v.* United States of America **128**.716

2006

Bustillo *v.* Virginia **134**.719

Hamdan *v.* Rumsfeld, Secretary of Defense and Others **137**.480

Sanchez-Llamas *v.* Oregon **134**.719

2007

Al Odah and Others *v.* United States and Others **137**.605, 609

Boumediene and Others *v.* Bush, President of the United States and Others **137**.605, 609

Nemariam and Others *v.* Federal Democratic Republic of Ethiopia and the Commercial Bank of Ethiopia (No 2) **135**.679

2008

Al Odah and Others *v.* United States and Others **137**.605, 645

Boumediene and Others *v.* Bush, President of the United States and Others **137**.605, 645

Medellín *v.* Texas **136**.689, 751 (note)

2009

Baoanan *v.* Baja and Others **152**.596

Republic of Iraq *v.* Beaty and Others; Republic of Iraq and Others *v.* Simon and Others **160**.686

2010

Abbott *v.* Abbott **154**.639

Al-Bihani *v.* Obama, President of the United States and Others **140**.716

Brzak and Another *v.* United Nations and Others **162**.765

Morrison and Others *v.* National Australia Bank Ltd and Others **160**.703

Samantar *v.* Yousuf and Others **147**.726

Swarna *v.* Al-Awadi, Al-Shaitan and State of Kuwait **152**.617

2011

FG Hemisphere Associates LLC *v.* Democratic Republic of the Congo and Another **150**.842

Garcia *v.* Texas **163**.693

Habyarimana and Ntaryamira *v.* Kagame **154**.739, 740, 750 (note)

2012

Chevron Corporation *v.* Naranjo and Others **163**.702

Habyarimana and Ntaryamira *v.* Kagame **154**.739, 747, 750 (note)

Hamdan *v.* United States of America **154**.751

Institute of Cetacean Research and Others *v.* Sea Shepherd Conservation Society and Others **156**.718, 721

Mohamad (Individually and for the Estate of Rahim, Deceased) and Others *v.* Palestinian Authority and Others **159**.723

In re People's Mojahedin Organization of Iran **163**.723

United States of America *v.* Dire; United States of America *v.* Ali; United States of America *v.* Umar; United States of America *v.* Gurewardher; United States of America *v.* Hasan **154**.700, 738 (note)

Zivotofsky *v.* Clinton, Secretary of State **154**.674

2013

Chabad *v.* Russian Federation and Others **164**.570

Chafin *v.* Chafin **164**.579

Institute of Cetacean Research and Others *v.* Sea Shepherd Conservation Society and Others **156**.718, 755

Kiobel and Others *v.* Royal Dutch Petroleum Co. and Others **164**.596

2014

Bond *v.* United States **164**.624

2015
Georges and Others *v.* United Nations and Others **162**.775

Zimbabwe

2004
International Committee of the Red Cross *v.* Sibanda and Ngangura **153**.689

2005
Kachingwe and Others *v.* Minister of Home Affairs and Another **142**.691

2008
Mann *v.* Republic of Equatorial Guinea **153**.697

Mike Campbell (Pvt) Ltd and William Michael Campbell *v.* Minister of National Security Responsible for Land, Land Reform and Resettlement and Attorney General **138**.354

2010
Commercial Farmers Union and Others *v.* Minister of Lands and Rural Resettlement and Others **152**.647